FEDERAL TAXATION OF INCOME, ESTATES AND GIFTS

SECOND EDITION

Collaborators—First Edition

MICHAEL ASIMOW

LOUIS A. DEL COTTO

MEADE EMORY

JAMES S. EUSTICE

ALAN L. FELD

THOMAS J. GALLAGHER, JR.

NORMAN H. LANE

MICHAEL B. LANG

JOHN W. LEE

LAWRENCE LOKKEN

FEDERAL TAXATION OF INCOME, ESTATES AND GIFTS

SECOND EDITION

BORIS I. BITTKER
Sterling Professor of Law Emeritus, Yale University

LAWRENCE LOKKEN
Professor of Law, New York University

Volume 1

WARREN, GORHAM & LAMONT
Boston • New York

For

ANNE S. BITTKER

Nulla Opera Sine Pulvere

Foreword to the Second Edition

THE PROHIBITION on mandatory retirement imposed in 1986 by the Age Discrimination in Employment Act was heralded as a great blow for freedom and liberty. Authors know better, at least if their books require periodic revisions. Those of us who have a literary bear by the tail yearn for retirement; but Congress has evinced no solicitude for our plight; and evidently the constitutional prohibition on involuntary servitude does not embrace the self-employed.

Our only escape from the fate of Sisyphus, therefore, is to find a successor; and it is not easy for authors to persuade themselves that anyone else can possibly fill their shoes. I count myself fortunate, however, in having Lawrence Lokken join me as co-author of this treatise. In addition to his extensive knowledge of federal income taxation, Professor Lokken has been intimately involved with the treatise itself, first as collaborator in the preparation of the first edition, and later as author of the supplements. I pass the torch to him with pleasure and confidence.

Now that the second edition of Volume 1 has been published, it is our hope and expectation that revised versions of the remaining four volumes will appear at intervals over the next four years. In the interim, the periodic supplements will continue to keep these later volumes (as well as revised Volume 1) current for the reader.

BORIS I. BITTKER

September 1988

Preface to the Second Edition

A PREFACE is usually written on the completion of a work to introduce the reader to what the author has done. By that standard, the title "Preface to the Second Edition" is premature because, as I write, only the first of the five volumes of the treatise has been completed in a second edition. This preface is rather a report on a work in progress.

The objective of the first edition, as stated by Professor Bittker in the original preface, persists as the goal of my work on the second edition:

> to provide guidance and orientation by emphasizing the purpose, structure, and principal effects of the Internal Revenue Code, without bogging down in details; to explain, rather than paraphrase, the statute and regulations; to examine the ambiguities and gaps in the legislative scheme without implying that there are no usable rules or guideposts; and, above all, to be concise, lucid, and accurate.

The intended audience also remains the same—practitioners, judges, Treasury and IRS employees, teachers, and students. For the tax planner, the second edition, like the first, is not meant to be used as a cookbook with recipes to be followed step by step to produce the ultimate in tax minimization, but rather is intended to assist in developing the knowledge and understanding that are the foundations of all good tax planning.

The nature of the material discussed has changed some since the publication of the first edition. The period elapsing between the first and second editions (roughly, the decade of the 1980s) has been marked by an unprecedented flurry of legislative activity, which has sparked an avalanche of regulations and other IRS pronouncements on recent legislation. Much of the new material in the second edition thus is about statutes and regulations, rather than about cases construing statutes and regulations. A striking example is Chapter 28 (new in the second edition), a 75-page essay on a single Code section (§469) that has yet to receive its first judicial construction. Even these 75 pages will surely expand greatly in the supplements before judges get a whack at §469 because the Treasury has only begun issuing regulations under the provision.

Particularly in dealing with new statutes and regulations, I have not eschewed detail, but have attempted to remain faithful to Professor Bittker's goal of not "bogging down in details." A consequence of the ever increasing bulk of the statutes and regulations is that details have become both more numerous and more essential to the solution of routine problems. Professor Bittker's original objective "to provide guidance and orientation" cannot be attained by restricting the discussion to a level of generality that gives only a distant view of the terrain where most tax problems arise. At the same time, this objective would be defeated if details so predominated that only an expert could fathom the discussion; the goal is to guide and orient the novice as well as the expert. In my opinion, the key to keeping details in proper perspective for all readers is to (1) start with a clear understanding of congressional purposes and of the basic architecture of the devices used to carry out these policies and (2) relate each detail, as it arises in the discussion, to this understanding. I have tried to do this in the writing, and I believe it is important that what I have written be read with the same approach.

As I work on the second edition, the immensity of Professor Bittker's achievement in writing the first edition impresses me daily. One of his gifts is an extraordinary power of explanation. He writes so clearly that it all seems simple. Never content to merely paraphrase, his statements of the rules usually contain unique insights into their meaning. He is like the fine violinist who, while flawlessly executing the most fiendishly difficult passages, impresses the listener with his musicality, not his technique. Professor Bittker's example has set the highest possible standard for me as I add to and occasionally reshape his work. I can only hope that I have not fallen terribly short of this standard.

Of necessity, I have followed Professor Bittker's example in other ways as well. The story is told of the student who came to Professor Bittker's office to ask a question. The knock at the door was greeted with a loud "Come in" competing with the rapid-fire clack of a typewriter. The clack ceased as the student entered. Bittker warmly greeted the student, listened to the question, and patiently answered it, all the while holding his hands an inch or two above the typewriter keyboard. As the student expressed his thanks and turned to leave, the clack resumed—before the student took the first step toward the door. The point of the story, doubtlessly apocryphal, is not that Professor Bittker is a remote and unfeeling individual who tolerates interruptions begrudgingly; my experiences and those of thousands of other beneficiaries of his generous advice contradict this. The point, rather, is that he understands well that his ambitious projects, most notably this treatise, require a most efficient use of his time. I now understand this too; were I half as effective as he is in putting this understanding into practice, this volume would have reached your hands much sooner.

In writing the first edition, Professor Bittker had the assistance of 10 collaborators. Collaborators were not used in the preparation of the second edition. Professor Bittker's tribute to the "massed typewriters" of the collaborators must therefore be succeeded by an acknowledgement of this author's lonely personal computer. The work of the original collaborators, however, remains important to the second edition. Although their work has been supplemented and modified to bring it in line with current law, none of it has been scuttled.

PREFACE TO THE SECOND EDITION

In his original preface, Professor Bittker made the customary acceptance of "full responsibility for the work's shortcomings." In my years of intensive use of the first edition, I found no such shortcomings. I must, however, follow his example by accepting responsibility for any shortcomings introduced in the second edition. Beyond that, I doubt that I could in good conscience find anyone to blame.

LAWRENCE LOKKEN

Preface to the First Edition

ALMOST HALF A CENTURY has passed since Paul and Mertens published the first edition of their pioneering treatise on federal income taxation, and the continuous flood of legislation, judicial decisions, regulations, rulings, and critical commentary suggests the need for a fresh analysis and synthesis of this vast body of law. My objective in this work has been to provide guidance and orientation by emphasizing the purpose, structure, and principal effects of the Internal Revenue Code, without bogging down in details; to explain, rather than paraphrase, the statute and regulations; to examine the ambiguities and gaps in the legislative scheme without implying that there are no usable rules or guideposts; and, above all, to be concise, lucid, and accurate. If these hopes are realized, the work will enable readers to cope with many issues without further research, will call their attention to statutory refinements and uncertainties that fall outside the mainstream, and will lead them to the sources that must be examined when a troublesome matter is being studied in depth.

These are challenging objectives and some may think they are doomed to fail because the Internal Revenue Code is a quagmire of detail in which no structural principles or logic can be discerned. I do not minimize the difficulties—how could I, after teaching the subject for more than three decades? Nevertheless, I am convinced that the Code is more than a laundry list of discrete items, that almost all provisions can be understood in the light of their antecedents and relationships to the rest of the Code, and that routes through the bog can be picked out. Without these convictions, I would not have undertaken the writing of a comprehensive treatise; after all, who would want to devote five volumes to an analysis of the Tariff Act?

Only the reader, of course, can decide whether the goals animating this work have been attained. For myself, I can only say that after devoting five years to this project, I am more convinced than when I started that the proportion of senseless detail to pervasive structural principles is relatively low, and that the Code, while not the most majestic attainment of human thought,* is much less rickety than is commonly believed.

------

*In his autobiography, Leonard Woolf suggests that tax law occupied a similarly modest rung on the intellectual ladder in Britain at the turn of the century:

> When I took the Civil Service examination, I could read Greek and Latin fluently, as I still can, but I had forgotten all the paraphernalia of syntax and

A word about the audience to which this work is directed. Most authors of tax books, on their own initiative or at the publisher's instigation, seek primarily to help attorneys and accountants with the problems arising in their practice. I do not spurn that audience; most of my former students are practitioners, and so are many of my best friends. But I have tried sedulously to write for the *entire* profession—for judges, teachers, students and government employees, as well as for practitioners; and I hope that the opinions expressed in this work, whether they prove to be right or wrong, will be received and judged in this light. My purpose throughout has been to provide orientation and guidance by an objective analysis of the tax law, not to advise practitioners on tactics; and I will be disappointed if the result of this effort is less useful to judges, revenue agents, and scholars than to the practitioners. Indeed, the dichotomy is not wholly realistic, since in the long run practitioners are not well served by works that judges and revenue agents view as excessively "practical."

In scope, the treatise is comprehensive, but within this framework it is selective rather than exhaustive. In citing cases, for example, I confined myself to those that are authoritative or recent or that review the earlier decisions, even though this necessarily meant that only a relatively small fraction of the corpus juris—amounting to perhaps as many as 100,000 decisions on federal tax issues—could be listed. In addition to screening the judicial and administrative material, I have endeavored to cite the most useful articles in the scholarly and professional journals and the published proceedings of tax institutes. There is surely no other branch of the law to which practitioners—who are often teachers without classrooms—have contributed so much; but all too often, their articles are not cited in booklength works or, almost as bad, are listed in such indiscriminate profusion that the reader is overwhelmed. I do not claim familiarity with all of the articles—30,000 or more—that can be found in the law journals and proceedings of tax institutes; but I have sampled the menu extensively, and the footnotes cite those that seem to me most worthy of note.

The vexing problem of providing a reasonably complete survey of the federal income, estate, and gift taxes without drowning the reader in detail is illustrated by the fact that this work allots only seven pages to the indirect foreign tax credit, a subject to which Owens and Ball devote a two-volume work almost 800 pages in length. If this proportion were applied to the entire field, the result would be an exhaustive treatise of 400,000 pages, or about 450 volumes. The contrast between what I have written and what could be written

---

writing Greek and Latin compositions. The result was that I got poor marks in the classical papers in which I should have amassed most of my marks and so did extremely badly. The best I could hope for was a place in the Post Office or Inland Revenue.

To escape these dismal alternatives, Woolf took an appointment in the Ceylon Civil Service, a decision that ultimately enriched British literature, though not the British Treasury. See Leonard Woolf, *Sowing* (Hogarth Press, 1960), p. 194.

is not always this dramatic; but it was impossible to complete the job in less than a lifetime without severe compression—a practice that is painful to specialists. Before starting, however, I reconciled myself to the fact that you can't paint a billboard with brushes designed for Persian miniatures.

In his lengthy and authoritative *History of the Crusades,* Steven Runciman suggests that it "may seem unwise for a lone British pen to compete with the massed typewriters of the United States,"[†] a remark whose ostentatious modesty clearly implies that an inspired British author, at least if his name is Runciman, can outshine any number of American drudges. By contrast, I want to acknowledge without qualification that the "massed typewriters of the United States" were the indispensable foundation for this treatise.

First and foremost, I am immensely indebted to my collaborators, whose outstanding contributions covered almost 40 percent of the final work—especially for their willingness to participate on the understanding that the outcome would be an integrated work rather than an anthology of independently written chapters. When soliciting their participation, I described my expectations as follows:

> The end product is to be an integrated whole, not a series of chapters by independent authors working in isolation. Since it cannot be written or revised by a committee of the whole, I will have to take responsibility for weaving the separate manuscripts into a seamless web. I hope to confine my major revisions to introductory, historical, and contextual material, and to insuring adequate cross-references (which may require moving material from one place to another), but no doubt I will want to alter the emphasis and in some instances the conclusions in particular sections. To the extent time permits, I will want each collaborator to review and comment on my proposed changes; but in the interest of unity, I will have to reserve ultimate control over the whole.

As events fell out, the editorial process was far more protracted and extensive than originally projected, as I acknowledged in a report to my patient collaborators shortly before the work went to press:

> I know that my drastic revisions have generated some disappointments, and I would be surprised if there were not more misgivings than have been expressed. To achieve our joint objective, however, I found it necessary to rewrite far more than anticipated because the contributed manuscripts varied so widely in the amount of case analysis, the balance between description and criticism, the relative length of footnotes, the number and complexity of illustrative examples, the amount of how-to-do-it advice, and similar matters. There are also many differences of emphasis and interpreta-

---

[†]Steven Runciman, *A History of the Crusades* (Cambridge University Press, 1951), I, xii.

tion between your drafts and my revisions. As a result, I fear that very few sentences, and surely not a single paragraph, of your drafts survived intact. I assure you, however, that I reviewed with great care all of your comments on my revised manuscript. You saved me from numerous errors, large and small; and, though I decided to stick to my guns in many instances, it was always with the realization that I might ultimately regret the decision.

In addition to my collaborators, whose names are listed opposite the title page, numerous full-time and part-time research assistants aided me, and so did many outside consultants in academic life and practice. Their contributions are recorded in the Acknowledgments to the first edition.

If the result of this collaborative process is a worthy contribution to the legal literature, the credit must be widely shared; but I accept full responsibility for the work's shortcomings.

BORIS I. BITTKER

Summary of Contents

Volume 1

Part 1
HISTORY, CONSTITUTIONALITY, AND STRUCTURAL PRINCIPLES

Part 2
EXCLUSIONS FROM GROSS INCOME

Part 3
BUSINESS AND PROFIT-ORIENTED DEDUCTIONS AND CREDITS

FEDERAL TAXATION OF INCOME, ESTATES AND GIFTS

Table of Contents

Volume 1

Part 1
HISTORY, CONSTITUTIONALITY, AND STRUCTURAL PRINCIPLES

Chapter 1
HISTORY AND CONSTITUTIONAL LIMITATIONS

Chapter 2
THE BASIC STRUCTURE OF
THE FEDERAL INCOME TAX

Chapter 3
ECONOMIC ASPECTS OF
FEDERAL INCOME TAXATION

Chapter 4
INTERPRETING THE INTERNAL REVENUE CODE

Chapter 5
INCOME—BASIC DEFINITIONAL CONCEPTS

Chapter 6
INCOME—THE EFFECT OF OFFSETTING LIABILITIES

Part 2
EXCLUSIONS FROM GROSS INCOME

Chapter 10
PROPERTY ACQUIRED BY GIFT AND INHERITANCE

Chapter 11
PRIZES, AWARDS, AND SCHOLARSHIPS

TABLE OF CONTENTS

Chapter 12
LIFE INSURANCE, ANNUITY, AND ENDOWMENT
CONTRACTS AND EMPLOYEE DEATH BENEFITS

Page

Chapter 13
COMPENSATION FOR PERSONAL INJURIES AND SICKNESS

Chapter 14
MISCELLANEOUS EMPLOYEE BENEFITS

TABLE OF CONTENTS

Chapter 15
INTEREST ON FEDERAL, STATE, AND LOCAL OBLIGATIONS

Chapter 16
OTHER EXCLUSIONS FROM GROSS INCOME

Part 3
BUSINESS AND PROFIT-ORIENTED DEDUCTIONS AND CREDITS

Chapter 20
EXPENSES INCURRED IN BUSINESS AND PROFIT-ORIENTED ACTIVITIES

Chapter 21
TRAVEL, ENTERTAINMENT, AND BUSINESS GIFTS

Chapter 22
SPECIALLY TREATED BUSINESS AND PROFIT-ORIENTED EXPENSES

Chapter 23
DEPRECIATION AND AMORTIZATION

Chapter 24
DEPLETION

Chapter 25
LOSSES

Chapter 26
OTHER BUSINESS DEDUCTIONS

Chapter 27
BUSINESS CREDITS

Chapter 28
LIMITATION ON LOSSES AND
CREDITS FROM PASSIVE ACTIVITIES

FEDERAL
TAXATION OF
INCOME, ESTATES
AND GIFTS

PART
1

History, Constitutionality,
and Structural
Principles

CHAPTER

1

History and Constitutional Limitations

¶1.1 HISTORY

¶1.1.1 Introductory

The sixteenth amendment, empowering Congress "to lay and collect taxes on incomes, from whatever source derived, without apportionment among the several States, and without regard to any census or enumeration," became effective on February 25, 1913. In the fiscal year 1913, the federal income tax on individuals and corporations produced $35 million of revenue, less than 5 percent of total federal receipts—a modest amount when compared to the yield of about $320 million from the tariff. For the fiscal year 1986, however, the federal income tax produced $412 billion— about 15 percent from corporate and 85 percent from individual income taxes.[1] This constituted almost 54 percent of total federal receipts (and about 89 percent of general tax revenues, excluding social security and other employment taxes) and was much greater than the total taxes collected by all state and local governments ($350 billion).[2] Moreover, in 1987, there were 45 states with corporate income taxes, and 40 with some form of personal income tax, most of them modeled or based on the federal law. While income taxes accounted for only 19.7 percent of combined state and local tax revenues in 1985, they constituted almost a third of state tax revenues (31.3 percent).[3] Given the steady shift of tax-raising functions from the local to the state level, the income tax promises to become an even larger revenue source for state and local governments in the decades ahead.[4]

These increases in the overall importance of the income tax reflect dramatic changes in the exemptions and rates. In 1913, for example, a married couple with two children paid a federal income tax of $60 on a net income of $10,000, a tax of $260 on a net income of $25,000, and a tax of $25,010 on a net income of $500,000. For 1987, the comparable tax bills

---

[1] Pechman, Federal Tax Policy 369 Brookings (5th ed. 1987).

[2] Id. at 394–97 (figures for 1985).

[3] Another source reports that personal and corporation income taxes accounted for 39.6 percent of state revenues for the fiscal year 1987 and that this figure was much higher for several states (71.5 percent for Oregon, 61.1 percent for Massachussetts, 60.7 percent for New York, 55.8 percent for Delaware, and 52.6 percent for California, for example). Gold, Recent Changes in State-Local Tax Levels, 38 Tax Notes 1401 (1988).

[4] Property taxes, historically the staple of local governments, have declined in importance in recent years. Over the period 1978 through 1986, property tax revenue per $100 of personal income declined 22.9 percent nationwide, while state and local nonproperty tax revenue per $100 of personal income (consisting in large part of income taxes) declined by 5.7 percent. Gold, supra note 3, at 1411.

were zero, $1,860, and $140,000.[5]

These facts are of great significance to the lawyer, as they are to other citizens. But of even more professional interest to lawyers is the manner in which the federal income tax affects the entire corpus juris: wills, trusts, and deeds; employment contracts, collective bargaining agreements, and pension arrangements; corporate security issues, liquidations, and mergers— every one of these legal events is permeated with, if not dominated by, tax problems. The traditional comparison of the partnership and the corporation as alternative methods of carrying on a business enterprise (limited liability, perpetual existence, etc.) is hopelessly inadequate if the federal income tax is disregarded; an alimony agreement that is drafted without one eye on the Internal Revenue Code probably will be badly drafted; and a sale of anything more valuable than a lame horse requires at least brief attention to the tax angle.

Taxes were once almost exclusively the province of accountants,[6] but today even the general practitioner of law must know his way around this area. Nor is it only the practitioner who is affected by the Internal Revenue Code; the legal scholar who seeks to understand the rise of the sale-and-leaseback method of financing industrial and commercial property, the growth of family controlled charitable foundations, or the popularity of limited partnerships with numerous unrelated investors must give due weight to the federal income tax. In its impact on our law for good or for ill, the federal income tax must be set down as one of the creative forces in legal history, like the invention of the trust and the doctrine of respondeat superior.

No other tax has had such an effect on the practice or structure of the law, at least not in our time. Many attorneys encounter the real property tax only at real estate closings, where its importance is minor; they may be acquainted with state sales, use, and gross receipts taxes and with federal taxes on alcohol and tobacco only as consumers; and most lawyers begin and end their professional careers in total ignorance of customs duties. The federal income tax is something else again; the lawyer might better be ignorant of the rule against perpetuities or the requisites of negotiability.[7]

---

[5] The figures for 1913 and 1987 are not precisely comparable because of differences in exemptions, deductions, and the impact of inflation, but the direction and degree of change are indisputable. The comparison with 1913 was more dramatic before tax reductions made in 1981 and 1986. In 1979, for example, families of four faced federal income tax liabilities of $374 on an income of $10,000; $3,497 on $25,000; and $313,924 on $500,000.

[6] On the respective jurisdictions of attorneys and accountants, see infra ¶¶110.2.2, 110.2.4.

[7] See generally Sneed, Some Reflections About the Impact of Federal Taxation on American Private Law, 12 Buffalo L. Rev. 241 (1962).

The income tax also affects the allocation of resources in our economy and our way of life in its broadest sense. For example, the federal tax benefits granted to the oil industry as compared to mass transit systems have been important factors in the development of our cities and suburbs, and the tax allowances enjoyed by charitable donors and tax-exempt organizations have undoubtedly played a role in the growth of most educational, cultural, and religious institutions.

Indeed, many are so impressed with the power of income taxation to influence private behavior as to suggest its use to remedy almost every social and economic ailment. These proposals are often oversimplified and misguided in their belief in the efficacy of income tax incentives and in their failure to evaluate more efficient solutions. Moreover, the asserted objectives of tax allowances may mask essentially private financial interests. On the other hand, direct expenditures for worthy social and economic programs may be politically difficult, and the indirect tax route may be more feasible. The Tax Reform Act of 1986 made a major shift away from the use of the tax system to accomplish goals other than the raising of revenue. The shift, however, was far from complete, and it is clear that the effect of income taxation on the allocation of resources in our economy will not soon be eliminated.

Appendix B contains a list of major tax laws with citations to the relevant committee reports; Appendix A contains tables of income reported, tax liabilities, rates, exemptions, revenue collected, etc.

¶1.1.2 Federal Income Taxation Before 1913

Until the Civil War, customs receipts were the backbone of the federal tax system. Except for a miscellany of excise taxes that were imposed temporarily when customs receipts declined and expenditures increased during the War of 1812, the only other important source of federal income was the sale of public lands. During the Civil War, customs receipts were once again unable to carry the load, and Congress found it necessary to seek other sources of federal revenue. Among the war taxes that it levied was an income tax.[8] The measure was amended several times; the 1864 version imposed a tax of 5 percent on income from $600 to $5,000, 7.5 percent on income from $5,000 to $10,000, and 10 percent on income above $10,000. The Confederacy also employed an income tax; its rates were steeper than the Union's, but its yield was much lower.

After the Civil War the federal income tax was repealed, and customs receipts once again became the basic source of federal revenue. Never again,

---

[8] The Civil War income tax was held constitutional in Springer v. US, 102 US 586 (1880), discussed below in ¶1.2.2.

however, were they the only source. Federal excises on tobacco and liquor produced almost as much as, and sometimes even more than, the tariff during the years between the Civil War and World War I. Throughout the 1870s and 1880s, moreover, agrarian and labor groups called for reductions in the tariff and for a revival of the federal income tax. To eastern business interests, on the other hand, the income tax meant "confiscation," "spoliation," and "communism," and throughout this period the Republican party held the fort against its assaults. The task became harder as the Democratic party gradually emerged from its handicap as the party of secession, and it finally became impossible when the Populist movement gained strength from the panic of 1893.

In 1894, during Grover Cleveland's second administration, a federal income tax, based largely on the Civil War statute, was passed by Congress after a bitter struggle, a notable feature of which was the oratory of William Jennings Bryan. A tax of 2 percent was imposed on individual incomes over $4,000, and a flat 2 percent tax was imposed on the income of business corporations. Congress thus went far beyond Cleveland's modest recommendation, made in his 1893 message to Congress, of a "small tax upon incomes derived from certain corporate investments." The income tax was carried by Democratic and Populist votes; but it must be viewed primarily as a regional victory of the South and Middle West over the Northeast, part of the same sectional movement that produced the Interstate Commerce Act in 1887, the Sherman Antitrust Act in 1890, and the unsuccessful campaign for bimetallism. A Populist effort to impose a progressive rate schedule on individual income was defeated, however, although the $4,000 exemption introduced a measure of graduation.

The tax became law on August 28, 1894,[9] to take effect as of January 1, 1895. By January 29, 1895, the Supreme Court had agreed to hear *Pollock v. Farmers' Loan & Trust Co.* and a companion case, in which the circuit court for the Southern District of New York had refused to grant an injunction in an action that attacked the tax as unconstitutional.[10] Intense public interest was aroused by the five days of argument before the Supreme Court, in which notable attorney-orators were engaged on both sides.[11] The tax was

---

[9] This occurred without President Cleveland's approval. The tax was a rider to the Wilson tariff bill, and Cleveland opposed its imposition of a tariff on sugar and other commodities. But since a veto would have kept alive the McKinley tariff schedules, Cleveland allowed the act to become law without his approval.

[10] Pollock v. Farmers' Loan & Trust Co., 157 US 429, 158 US 601 (1895), discussed below in ¶1.2.2.

[11] *Pollock* was a suit by a stockholder to enjoin his corporation from paying the tax, a legal form that was much criticized and is no longer encountered. See infra ¶115.9. Consequently, the tax was defended not only by the Attorney General but also by counsel for the corporation.

held unconstitutional, primarily on the ground that it was a "direct" tax (requiring the burden to be apportioned among the states in proportion to their population) so far as dividends, interest, and other income from personal property were concerned; and because the invalid portions were not separable from the remaining provisions, the tax was held invalid in toto.[12]

¶1.1.3   The Sixteenth Amendment

After the *Pollock* decision, advocates of a federal income tax turned to an amendment to the Constitution as a means of reviving the tax, although there was also some agitation for confronting the Supreme Court with a new statute in the hope of securing a reversal of the judicial position. William McKinley's victories in 1896 and 1900 over William Jennings Bryan, the candidate of the Democrats and Populists, reflected the temper of the times, however, and not even the financial demands of the Spanish-American War could restore the federal income tax.

But within a few more years after the *Pollock* case, in which Mr. Justice Field had called the income tax an "assault upon capital" and "the stepping-stone to . . . a war of poor against the rich,"[13] the very same tax found eminent support within the Republican Party itself. Both Theodore Roosevelt and William Howard Taft announced that they favored a federal income tax. Taft, indeed, expressed at one time the view that a constitutional amendment might not be required because of the changed membership on the Supreme Court, though he later recanted on this point. Bryan, apparently having more faith in the rule of precedent than the future Chief Justice, insisted that a constitutional amendment was necessary and that Taft's expression of hope for a change in the Supreme Court's views was insincere. Whether Taft himself was engaged in a campaign maneuver or not, the insurgent Republicans who followed Roosevelt were unquestionably serious.

In 1909, a combination of Democrats and Roosevelt Republicans laid plans for an income tax amendment to the Payne-Aldrich Tariff bill, then pending in the Senate. The proposal was to tax both corporate and individual incomes, with a $5,000 exemption. It was a direct challenge to the *Pollock* decision, except that interest from state, county, and municipal bonds was to be excluded in recognition of the Supreme Court's unanimity on this point.

The conservative wing of the Republican Party was able to head off the threat by winning over President Taft, but the price of victory was high. To obtain Taft's assistance in beating down the income tax on individuals, its

---

[12] For a more extended discussion, see infra ¶1.2.2.
[13] Pollock v. Farmers' Loan & Trust Co., 158 US at 607.

opponents were forced to agree to the enactment of a corporate income tax[14] and to a joint resolution proposing a constitutional amendment to permit an individual income tax on all types of income. Taft favored the amendment partly as a sop to the insurgents and partly because he thought that an income tax might be useful in times of great national need. The backers of the income tax were dismayed by Taft's open opposition, especially since a constitutional amendment could be defeated if only twelve state legislatures were won over by the conservatives. Amending the Constitution seemed a graver and more formidable undertaking before World War I than it does now. The first 10 amendments were virtually part of the original Constitution; the eleventh and twelfth had been adopted in 1789 and 1804; and for more than a century the only other amendments were the thirteenth, fourteenth, and fifteenth, representing the political settlement of a civil war. Moreover, even with an amendment to the Constitution, the battle in Congress would have to be fought again, perhaps at a less auspicious time.

The joint resolution passed by Congress in 1909 on Taft's insistence then worked its way through the state legislatures. The most influential opposition to the proposed amendment was generated by a message from Governor Charles Evans Hughes to the New York State Legislature in 1910. Governor Hughes stated that he believed the federal government should have the power to impose an unapportioned income tax, but he recommended against ratification because the words "from whatever source derived" in the proposed amendment, "if taken in their natural sense," would permit income from state and municipal bonds to be taxed by the federal government, a power that would "afford the opportunity for federal action in violation of the fundamental conditions of State authority." This message led to the defeat of ratification in New York in 1910. Some supporters of the amendment rejected Hughes' construction, but others were willing to accept it, and his views were quoted throughout the nation.[15] The Democrats and insurgent Republicans were successful in the state elections of 1910 and 1912, however, and by early 1913 36 states (including New York) had ratified the amendment.[16]

----

[14] The 1909 corporate income tax was held constitutional in Flint v. Stone Tracy Co., 220 US 107 (1911), discussed below in ¶1.2.2.

[15] For later echoes of this disagreement about the effect of the sixteenth amendment on the tax status of state and local governments, see infra ¶1.2.8.

[16] For a later claim that the sixteenth amendment was not properly ratified, see US v. Thomas, 788 F2d 1250 (7th Cir. 1986), cert. denied, 107 S. Ct. 187 (1986) (sixteenth amendment validly ratified notwithstanding numerous minor discrepancies in punctuation and usage between the official text of the amendment and the texts contained in resolutions of ratification adopted by various state legislatures); US v. Sitka, 845 F2d 43 (2d Cir. 1988) (same); US v. Stahl, 792 F2d 1438 (9th Cir. 1986) (same). See also Baker v. CIR, 37 TCM (CCH) 307 (1978) (ingeniously zany

The sixteenth amendment thus became a part of the Constitution on February 25, 1913—less than four years after the advocates of the income tax thought they had been defrauded of victory by their opponents' maneuver. Within a few months, moreover, Congress passed the Revenue Act of 1913, imposing a "normal" tax of one percent (with an exemption of $3,000 for an individual and $1,000 additional for a married person) and a "surtax" ranging from one percent on net income from $20,000 to $50,000 up to 6 percent on that part of any net income exceeding $500,000.[17] This should be compared with the income tax proposal that was defeated in 1909: a flat 2 percent on net income in excess of $5,000.

¶1.1.4 World War I, Normalcy, and Prosperity

Congress relied heavily on federal income taxation to finance military expenditures before and during World War I. Exemptions were lowered, rates were raised, and progression was increased, and these changes were accompanied by enactment of a federal estate tax and an excess profits tax. Under the Revenue Act of 1918, individual income tax liability at almost every income level was 10 to 15 times the amount imposed by the Revenue Act of 1913.[18] The number of taxpayers filing personal income tax returns increased more than tenfold from 1913 to 1918, although the group continued to be only a small percentage of the nation's population—about 4.4 million returns were filed in 1918, when the adult population was about 59 million.[19]

During the decade of "normalcy" and prosperity following World War I, rates were drastically lowered in several stages. Any illusion that the federal income tax would fade away with the advent of peace, however, was gradually dispelled. For 1929, when the process of cutting the individual tax rates ended, the tax liabilities of married couples with two dependents were much lower at all income levels than in 1918, when the World War I rates

---

theory that Ohio's ratification was invalid because Ohio did not become a state until 1953).

[17] The distinction between the flat rate normal tax and the progressive surtax was based on the theory that the former was a permanent feature of the federal fiscal landscape but that the surtax was a temporary expedient, imposed only in times of special need on upper-income taxpayers. This theory proved to be illusory, but the normal tax and surtax continued as separate components of the federal income tax until 1954, when they were amalgamated except as to corporations. For corporations, the amalgamation occurred in 1978. For the relationship between the normal tax, surtax, and interest from partially tax-exempt federal obligations, see infra ¶15.1.

[18] U.S. Bureau of the Census, Historical Statistics of the United States, Colonial Times to 1970, pt. 2, at 1111 (1975).

[19] Id. at 1110. See also 1933 Statistical Abstract of the United States 174.

were at their highest. But 1929 taxes did not drop to 1913 levels except for the lowest income brackets, as Table 1-1 discloses:

Table 1-1

Individual Income Tax Liabilities—
Married Couple With Two Dependents

	$5,000	*$15,000*	*Taxable Income Before Exemptions* *$25,000*	*$50,000*	*$100,000*	*$1,000,000*
Year						
1913	$ 10	$ 110	$ 260	$ 760	$ 2,510	$ 60,010
1918	156	1,622	3,672	10,982	34,982	702,982
1929	3	201	838	4,166	14,846	230,846

Source: U.S. Bureau of the Census, Historical Statistics of the United States, Colonial Times to 1970, Pt. 2, at 1112 (1975).

During the decade after World War I, corporate rates remained substantially stable, ranging from a low of 10 percent to a high of 13.5 percent.

Aggregate receipts from individual and corporate income taxes, which were $2.85 billion for 1918, ranged from $1.7 to $3.95 billion during the period 1919–1929, as compared with $35 million for 1913.[20] They constituted almost 70 percent of aggregate federal revenues during 1919–1929, as compared with the 10 percent of the aggregate that they contributed in 1913. This marked increase in the relative importance of federal income taxes occurred without a comparable increase in the relative number of individual taxpayers. For a total population of 65 to 75 million, only about 5 million tax returns were filed annually during 1919–1929, of which about 50 percent were nontaxable returns.[21]

¶1.1.5 Depression, Recovery, and New Deal

Following the stock market crash of October 24, 1929, the nation experienced in rapid succession a devastating economic depression, a period of recovery, the New Deal, and World War II, all of which had dramatic effects on the federal income tax. The initial reaction to the 1929 crash and ensuing depression was a tax cut, whose results for 1929 were described above.[22] But a balance-the-budget philosophy then caught hold, and the Revenue Act of 1932 raised the individual rates to levels approximating

---

[20] U.S. Bureau of the Census, supra note 18, pt. 1, at 172.
[21] Id.
[22] Supra ¶1.1.4.

those in force during World War I. This action was felt only by taxpayers who continued to have income, however, and the aggregate amount raised by the increased rate schedule was less than half of the amount produced in 1929, reflecting a drop in national income from $86.8 billion (1929) to $42.8 billion (1932).[23]

With the inauguration of President Franklin D. Roosevelt in 1933, deficit financing gradually came into vogue, based initially on a distinction between a balanced regular budget and a special budget for emergency expenditures to be financed by borrowing. The income tax provisions of the Revenue Act of 1934, which produced about 20 percent less revenue than the Revenue Act of 1932, were aimed primarily at preventing tax avoidance and evasion;[24] progression, however, was stepped up by substituting a rate schedule ranging from 4 percent to 59 percent for the previous range of 8 to 55 percent.

In 1935, Roosevelt sent to Congress a bitterly controversial tax message that reflected the social and populist ferment of the depression, recommending steeper progression in income tax rates, higher gift and death taxes, a corporate rate structure graduated from 11 to 17 percent to replace the existing 14 percent flat rate, and a constitutional amendment authorizing federal taxation of state and municipal bond interest.[25] Congress responded to this appeal by enacting a more progressive personal rate schedule, imposing a marginal rate of 73 percent on income above $1 million and 75 percent on income above $5 million, as well as a corporate rate schedule graduated from 12.5 percent to 15 percent.

In 1936, the Supreme Court's invalidation of special taxes on the processing of agricultural products[26] resulted in the loss of $500 million of anticipated taxes and the passage over a presidential veto of a soldiers' bonus. Congress also enacted a tax on undistributed corporate profits, graduated from 7 to 27 percent. This action elicited a storm of denunciation from the business community, and the tax was watered down in 1938 and repealed in 1939.[27] In the meantime, however, extensive legislative hearings on tax-avoidance schemes[28] led Congress to enact a series of countermeasures in the Revenue Act of 1937, including restrictions on personal holding

---

[23] U.S. Bureau of the Census, supra note 18, pt. 1, at 235.

[24] See Blakey, The Federal Income Tax, 348 n.5 (Longman's, Green and Co. 1940); Lowndes, The 1934 Edition of the Federal Revenue Act, 19 Minn. L. Rev. 62 (1934).

[25] Public Papers and Addresses of Franklin D. Roosevelt 270 (Random House 1938).

[26] US v. Butler, 297 US 1 (1986).

[27] Lent, The Impact of the Undistributed Profits Tax, 1936–1937 (1948).

[28] Hearings Before the Joint Comm. on Tax Evasion and Avoidance, 75th Cong., 1st Sess. (1937).

companies, disallowance of losses on intrafamily sales, and higher taxes on unreasonable accumulations of corporate earnings and profits.[29] In 1939, the Public Salary Tax Act eliminated a number of anomalies in federal and state income taxation by subjecting state officials, employees, and certain previously immune federal judges to the federal income tax and by consenting to the imposition of state income taxes on federal employees.[30]

A major technical achievement of the pre-World War II era was the enactment of the Internal Revenue Code of 1939, which consolidated and codified an accumulation of internal revenue laws scattered through numerous volumes of the Statutes at Large. Except to the extent that particular provisions were amended, the 1939 Code remained in force from year to year until 1954, when it was supplanted by the Internal Revenue Code of 1954.

¶1.1.6 World War II

The Revenue Act of 1940 began the process of putting the federal taxing system on a wartime footing, with a corporate excess profits tax ranging from 25 to 50 percent, provisions for the rapid amortization of defense facilities, and various defense taxes. Supplemental tax bills were enacted in rapid succession as war expenditures skyrocketed. Between 1939 and 1945, the federal income and excess profits taxes on individuals and corporations rose from about $2.2 billion to $25 billion.

Even more dramatic was the conversion of the personal income tax from a levy on a modest fraction of the populace to a mass tax, a metamorphosis attributable to lower exemptions, higher rates, improved economic conditions, and inflation. The number of taxable returns rose from less than 4 million in 1939 to almost 43 million in 1945, although the population increased during the same period by only about 10 percent.[31] Table 1-2 illustrates the increase between 1939 and 1945 in the tax liabilities of married couples with two dependents.

Although there have been innumerable changes in specific tax provisions since World War II, the mass character of the tax has not changed; all subsequent tax laws have carried forward the pay-as-you-go withholding system instituted in 1942.[32] Under pre-1942 law, down payments were not required, and the tax liability for an entire year fell due when taxpayers filed their returns early in the following year. Without a withholding system,

---

[29] See Paul, Background of the Revenue Act of 1937, 5 U. Chi. L. Rev. 41 (1937).
[30] Infra ¶¶1.2.7, 1.2.8.
[31] U.S. Bureau of the Census, supra note 18, pt. 1, at 10.
[32] Infra ¶111.4.2.

millions of taxpayers would undoubtedly be perpetually in debt to the Treasury for unpaid taxes.

Table 1-2

Individual Income Tax Liabilities—
Married Couple With Two Dependents

	Taxable Income Before Exemptions					
Year	*$5,000*	*$15,000*	*$25,000*	*$50,000*	*$100,000*	*$1,000,000*
1939	$ 48	$ 831	$ 2,327	$ 8,621	$ 31,997	$ 678,436
1945	589	3,639	8,522	24,111	62,301	838,850

Source: U.S. Bureau of the Census, Historical Statistics of the United States, Colonial Times to 1970, Pt. 2, at 1112 (1975).

¶1.1.7 The Period Since World War II

Since the end of World War II, income tax rates have frequently been altered in response to such objective conditions as cold and hot wars, unemployment, prosperity, and inflation, as well as to changing economic theories about the relationship of taxation to consumption, investment, and employment. Although theorists have displayed some interest in value-added taxation and, more recently, in expenditure taxes,[33] the individual and corporate income taxes have continued to be the workhorses of the federal tax system.

At a more technical level, the major innovations since the end of World War II, discussed in detail in later parts of this work, include the joint return authorized by the Revenue Act of 1948 and the related separate rate schedules for heads of households, unmarried persons, and married persons filing separate returns; taxation of the unrelated business income of charitable organizations and other tax-exempt groups; the investment credit (repealed in 1986); an explosion of other business incentives, including accelerated depreciation and rapid amortization of many outlays that under normal accounting principles would be deductible only if and when the project was sold or written off as a failure; complete revision of the tax treatment of foreign income and foreign taxpayers; limitations on the ability of domestic taxpayers to shelter foreign income from U.S. tax by accumulating it in foreign corporations; general averaging of income exceeding the amount received during a five-year base period (repealed in 1986); the recapture of excess depreciation and some other deductions; a succession of

---

[33] Infra ¶3.7.

minimum and alternative minimum taxes; a plethora of provisions aimed primarily at tax shelter investors (including at-risk limitations on losses and credits from some investments and a limitation on deductions for passive activity losses); and a battery of new penalty provisions.

The post-World War II era has also seen a major downward shift in marginal rates. The highest marginal rate for individuals, which was 90 percent at the end of the war and for nearly two decades thereafter, was lowered to 70 percent in 1964, to 50 percent for earned income in 1969, to 50 percent for all income in 1981, and, finally, to 28 percent by the Tax Reform Act of 1986. The highest corporate rate, in turn, was 52 percent in the immediate post-War period, and fell to 48 percent in 1964, 46 percent in 1981, and 34 percent for 1987 and succeeding years.

¶1.2 CONSTITUTIONAL STATUS OF THE FEDERAL INCOME TAX

¶1.2.1 Introductory

The Constitution vests Congress with the power "to lay and collect Taxes, Duties, Imposts and Excises, to pay the Debts and provide for the common Defence and general Welfare of the United States; but all Duties, Imposts and Excises shall be uniform throughout the United States"; and "to make all Laws which shall be necessary and proper for carrying into Execution the foregoing Powers."[1] Like all other federal powers, the right of Congress to levy and collect taxes is subject to a wide range of constitutional limits, including the due process clause, the right to trial by jury in criminal cases, and the prohibition of unreasonable searches and seizures. In addition, the taxing power is singled out by the Constitution for a special restriction—the "direct tax" clause—that led the Supreme Court to hold the 1894 income tax law unconstitutional,[2] an event providing the impetus for the sixteenth amendment. Once this great constitutional battle was terminated by ratification of the amendment, the direct tax clause sank into relative obscurity, but echoes of the old conflict account for the unwarranted inference that there are no other constitutional restraints on the taxing power. A review of the direct tax question, therefore, is in order before other, less dramatic constitutional issues are canvassed.

The taxing power is also subject to article I, section 9, clause 5, providing that "No Tax or Duty shall be laid on Articles exported from any State."

---

[1] U.S. Const. art. I, §8, cls. 1, 18. For a discussion of the terms "duties" and "taxes," see Michelin Tire Corp. v. Wages, 423 US 276, 287–301 (1976).

[2] Pollock v. Farmers' Loan & Trust Co., 158 US 601 (1895). This was the "second" (and final) *Pollock* case; for the first installment, see infra note 9.

It was held in *W.E. Peck & Co. v. Lowe* that this restriction does not apply to a nondiscriminatory federal tax on an exporter's income.[3] This rationale made it unnecessary to decide whether the power conferred by the sixteenth amendment to tax income "from whatever source derived" authorized a tax on exports, but the Court went on to observe that the amendment "has no real bearing and may be put out of view" because it does not extend the federal taxing power to new subjects but merely eliminates the requirement of apportioning a direct tax on income.[4]

¶1.2.2 The Direct Tax Clause of the Constitution

The power to tax conferred on Congress by article I, section 8, is subject to the procedural requirement that all revenue bills must originate in the House of Representatives[5] and to the substantive requirement of article I, section 9 that "No Capitation, or other direct, Tax shall be laid, unless in Proportion to the Census or Enumeration herein before directed to be taken."[6] The apportionment requirement is repeated and amplified by article I, section 2:

> Representatives and direct Taxes shall be apportioned among the several States which may be included within this Union, according to their respective Numbers, which shall be determined by adding to the whole Number of free Persons, including those bound to Service for a Term of Years, and excluding Indians not taxed, three fifths of all other Persons.[7]

Congress could readily apportion a poll tax among the states in proportion to population, save for difficulties caused by the constitutional requirement that untaxed Indians be excluded from the count and, until the Civil War, that three fifths of the number of slaves be included. But apportionment of a real property tax requires a different rate for every state in order to insure that the aggregate amount paid by each state is proportional to its

---

[3] W.E. Peck & Co. v. Lowe, 247 US 165 (1918).

[4] Id. at 172–73; see also infra note 31.

[5] U.S. Const. art. I, §7, cl. 1; see Flint v. Stone Tracy Co., 220 US 107 (1911) (revenue bill originating in House may be amended by the Senate). The Senate, however, appears not to be meaningfully restrained by this limitation. Armstrong v. US, 759 F2d 1378 (9th Cir. 1985) (origination clause not violated when Senate amended House bill by sutituting everything after enactment clause; neither is it objectionable that Senate substitution increased revenues, whereas House bill would have reduced them); Texas Ass'n of Concerned Taxpayers, Inc. v. US, 772 F2d 163 (5th Cir. 1985), cert. denied, 106 S. Ct. 2265 (1986) (following *Armstrong*).

[6] U.S. Const. art. I, §9, cl. 4.

[7] U.S. Const. art. I, §2, cl. 3.

population rather than to the value of the property within its borders. Diverse rates were contemplated by the framers of the Constitution in this situation, as is shown by the exemption of direct taxes from the requirement of article I, section 8, clause 1, that duties, imposts, and excises "shall be uniform throughout the United States."

The operation of the apportionment system is illustrated by a federal tax on land, imposed in 1861 as "a direct tax of twenty millions of dollars" which were apportioned among the states, territories, and District of Columbia by statute (e.g., "To the State of Maine, four hundred and twenty thousand eight hundred and twenty-six dollars").[8] The President was authorized to assign the states, territories, and District of Columbia to collection districts, to apportion "to each county and State district its proper quota of direct tax," and to establish the amount payable by the taxpayers in each district.

Both the purpose and the scope of the apportionment requirement are veiled in obscurity. In *Pollock v. Farmers' Loan & Trust Co.*, Chief Justice Fuller asserted: "Nothing can be clearer than that what the Constitution intended to guard against was the exercise by the general government of the power of directly taxing persons and property within any State through a majority made up from the other States."[9] Charles Beard buttressed this explanation by concluding that the apportionment provision was designed to prevent the legislative representatives of the populous manufacturing states from shifting the burdens of taxation to rural regions and that it "obviously implied" that direct taxes were to be a last resort.[10] Thus, since the mainstay of national finance would be taxes on consumption, wealthy citizens would not be called upon to support the national government by payments proportioned to their wealth. Beard also noted the ironic twist by which a provision intended to protect rural areas was used by the Supreme Court in the *Pollock* case to prevent agrarian and populist interests from shifting the burden of taxation to the urban population.

A competing theory is that the apportionment principle was concerned only with the slavery question, designed to induce the slave states to accept representation in the House of Representatives based on the number of free persons in the state plus only three fifths of the slaves by promising that direct taxes would be similarly apportioned. This link between the composition of the House of Representatives, direct taxation, and slavery is also evidenced by the provision of article V, prohibiting until 1808 any amendment of the Constitution to change either the direct tax clause or the clause

---

[8] 12 Stat. 292 (1861). Other examples of direct taxes are cited in Springer v. US, 102 US 586, 598–99 (1880).

[9] Pollock v. Farmers' Loan & Trust Co., 157 US 429, 582 (1895).

[10] Beard, An Economic Interpretation of the Constitution of the United States 169–71 (Macmillan 1925).

permitting free migration into the country of such persons as any existing state might permit. It has been suggested that the abolition of slavery by the post-Civil War amendments to the Constitution eliminated the direct tax clause's sole reason for existence.[11]

The scope of the apportionment rule is as murky as its purpose. The constitutional term "capitation tax" meant a per capita or poll tax, and there was general agreement that a periodic tax on the ownership of real estate—the kind of tax that produces the bulk of municipal revenue today—was also a "direct tax" as that term was used in the Constitution. Beyond this, there was no consensus. Chief Justice Fuller was surely mistaken when he said in the *Pollock* case, more than a century after the Constitution was adopted, that "the distinction between direct and indirect taxation was well understood by the framers of the Constitution and those who adopted it."[12] More evocative of the prevailing uncertainty is this extract from Madison's *Notes on the Constitutional Convention of 1789*: "Mr. King asked what was the precise meaning of direct taxation. No one answered."[13]

The term "direct tax" caused difficulty at the very outset of the Republic's existence. When Congress levied a tax on carriages in 1794, Madison argued that it was a direct tax, while Fisher Ames, drawing on Massachusetts experience, asserted that it was indirect. The Supreme Court, in a case in which ex-Secretary of the Treasury Hamilton participated in the argument, found the tax constitutional.[14] Mr. Justice Chase was "inclined to think" that poll taxes and taxes on land were the only "direct" taxes within the meaning of the Constitution. Expressing doubt that a tax on personal property was "direct," he found that it was not necessary to decide because "a tax on expense is an indirect tax; and I think, an annual tax on a carriage for the conveyance of persons, is of that kind."[15] Mr. Justice Paterson and Mr. Justice Iredell, who wrote separate opinions, were equally unable to suggest any examples of a direct tax except poll taxes and taxes on land.

As far as federal income taxation was concerned, the Supreme Court's most important foray into the morass before the *Pollock* case was *Springer v. United States*, decided in 1880.[16] In this case the Court unanimously upheld the Civil War income tax, which embraced "the annual gains, profits, and income of every person . . . whether derived from any kind of property, rents, interests, dividends, or salaries, or from any profession, trade, em-

---

[11] Seligman, The Income Tax 559 (Macmillan 1911).

[12] Pollock v. Farmers' Loan & Trust Co., supra note 9, at 573.

[13] 5 Elliot, Debates on the Adoption of the Federal Constitution 451 (J.P. Lippincott 1845).

[14] Hylton v. US, 3 US (3 Dall.) 171 (1796).

[15] Id. at 175.

[16] Springer v. US, 102 US 586 (1880).

ployment, or vocation . . . or from any other source whatever."[17] Citing the carriage tax case and other cases holding that taxes on the receipts of insurance companies, state bank notes, and inheritances were all indirect taxes, the Court ruled that the income tax was also indirect, saying: "Our conclusions are, that direct taxes, within the meaning of the Constitution, are only capitation taxes, as expressed in that instrument, and taxes on real estate; and that the tax of which the plaintiff in error complains is within the category of an excise or duty."[18]

Although these precedents were persuasive to the leading text writers of the day,[19] the Supreme Court in the *Pollock* case held by a vote of six to two (one Justice not sitting) that the 1894 federal income tax was unconstitutional insofar as it taxed income from real estate:

> [I]t is admitted that a tax on real estate is a direct tax. Unless, therefore, a tax upon rents or income issuing out of lands is intrinsically so different from a tax on the land itself that it belongs to a wholly different class of taxes, such taxes must be regarded as falling within the same category as a tax on real estate *eo nomine* . . . . An annual tax upon the annual value or annual user of real estate appears to us the same in substance as an annual tax on the real estate, which would be paid out of the rent or income. . . . If, by calling a tax indirect when it is essentially direct, the rule of protection could be frittered away, one of the great landmarks defining the boundary between the Nation and the States of which it is composed, would have disappeared, and with it one of the bulwarks of private rights and private property.[20]

The *Springer* case was distinguished because none of the income of the taxpayer in *Springer* was derived from real estate—a factual distinction that probably would have seemed immaterial to the *Springer* court.

In addition to holding that the inclusion of rents in the income tax base was unconstitutional, the Court in the *Pollock* case decided, all eight Jus-

---

[17] 13 Stat. 469, 479 (1865).

[18] Springer v. US, supra note 16, at 602.

[19] See references in Pollock v. Farmers' Loan & Trust Co., 157 US 429, 620–25 (1895).

[20] Id. at 580, 581, 583. Charles F. Southmayd, in whose name was established a Yale professorship formerly held by one of the authors of this work, was credited by Joseph H. Choate, who argued the *Pollock* case, with working out the theory that a tax on rent was necessarily a tax on the property from which the rent was derived, thus providing "the keystone of the whole argument, and indeed, of the decision." Choate, Memorial of Charles F. Southmayd, in Arguments and Addresses of Joseph Hodges Choate 139, 148 (Hicks, ed.; West 1926). See, however, 26 Cong. Rec. 6826–27 (1894), which shows that this argument was made during the debate preceding enactment of the 1894 tax, when an amendment to exempt rents from real estate on the ground that their inclusion would be unconstitutional was rejected.

tices agreeing, that the inclusion of municipal bond interest in the tax base constituted "a tax on the power of the States and their instrumentalities to borrow money" and that, so viewed, it was an unconstitutional violation of the federal system of government. This determination was not of fundamental importance because an income tax exemption for interest from state and municipal bonds was entirely feasible; indeed, all later income tax statutes have explicitly exempted such income.[21] It might even have been politically possible to reenact a federal income tax with an exemption for income derived from real property.

Two other questions were left unanswered because the Court was equally divided, and while these questions remained in doubt, reenactment of an income tax law was not likely. The first question was whether a tax on income from personal property was an improper direct tax. This was a fundamental issue because if investment income had to be excluded from the tax base, a federal income tax would fall almost entirely on earned income—wages, salaries, professional fees, etc.—and business profits, and a tax with so restricted a base was not likely to whet the political appetite. Second, the Court failed to decide whether the granting of a minimum exemption of $4,000 to individuals violated the uniformity clause of article I, section 8, clause 1, of the Constitution: "[A]ll Duties, Imposts and Excises shall be uniform throughout the United States." A third question, which was of great but transitory importance, was also left unanswered: whether the invalid provisions taxing income from real estate and municipal bond interest were separable from the rest of the statute or rendered it invalid in toto.

One week after the first *Pollock* decision, counsel for the appellants applied for a rehearing on the undecided questions, and in response the Attorney General suggested that the whole case be reargued. The Court set both applications for rehearing for argument in May 1895, and this time all nine Justices were on the bench. In a second opinion, the previous holding as to income from real estate was reaffirmed by a vote of five to four.[22] The same five Justices agreed that a tax on income from personal property (e.g., dividends and interest) was an invalid direct tax and that the invalid provisions were not separable from the rest of the tax, so that the statute was invalid in toto.

Mr. Justice Jackson, who did not sit on the first argument, voted to uphold the tax on all three counts. Since he was part of a minority of four, it was immediately assumed that one of the four Justices who at the first argument thought the tax on income from personal property was proper and that the provision taxing rents was separable from the rest of the statute

---

[21] Infra ¶15.2.1.
[22] Pollock v. Farmers' Loan & Trust Co., supra note 19.

must have switched sides. This in itself would not have been of earthshaking importance; but it was dramatic evidence of the power of a single judge, and the fact that the reports did not reveal the name of the "vacillating" judge lent an air of mystery to the event. Mr. Justice Shiras was long identified, on what now seems to be slim evidence, as the judge who switched, although some scholars have more recently awarded the blame—or credit—to others. It is also possible that the assumption of a switch is incorrect.[23]

The Court did not find it necessary in the second *Pollock* opinion to pass on the other question that was left undecided by the first opinion: Did the $4,000 exemption violate the uniformity clause of Article I? A few years later, however, when the Supreme Court sustained a federal inheritance tax despite certain exemptions, it held the term "uniform throughout the United States" required geographical uniformity, so that persons and property would be taxed in the same manner without regard to geographical location, rather than "intrinsic" uniformity (i.e., without exemptions).[24]

The *Pollock* case is often described as a "judicial veto" preventing Congress from taxing income until the sixteenth amendment was adopted in 1913. In point of fact, however, the decision intimated that a tax on salaries, wages, and business profits would not be a direct tax and hence would not have to be apportioned,[25] thus leaving Congress free to tax income from these sources if it was willing to exempt unearned income. While unearned income is only a small fraction of total national income,[26] it becomes an increasingly important component of individual income as income rises, and this meant that taxing earned income but not income from investments was not politically acceptable. Congress also was free after *Pollock* to enact an apportioned income tax, although such a contraption would have required different rate schedules for each state.[27] For these reasons, foes of the income tax hailed the *Pollock* case for sounding its death knell, while its friends turned their major attention to the arduous task of amending the Constitution to permit all types of income to be taxed without apportionment.

In 1909, however, a combination of Democrats and insurgent Republicans, hoping for a change in the Supreme Court's attitude, made a final

---

[23] There is a full account of the puzzle and a review of earlier comments in Shiras, Justice George Shiras, Jr., of Pittsburgh 168–83 (U. of Pittsburgh Press 1953).

[24] Knowlton v. Moore, 178 US 41 (1900). See infra ¶1.2.5 (due process, uniformity, and differential treatment).

[25] Pollock v. Farmers' Loan & Trust Co., 157 US 635 (1895).

[26] See U.S. Bureau of the Census, Historical Statistics of the United States, Colonial Times to 1970, pt. 2, at 236 (1975).

[27] See supra note 12.

effort to enact a tax on both earned and unearned income without waiting for a constitutional amendment. The proposal was to tax both corporate and individual incomes, with a $5,000 exemption. With the assistance of President Taft, congressional opponents were able to head off an income tax on individuals but were forced by Taft to agree to the enactment of a corporate income tax and to a joint resolution proposing a constitutional amendment to validate an individual income tax on all types of income.[28]

The 1909 corporate income tax was promptly attacked as a direct tax that, not being apportioned among the states in proportion to their population, was unconstitutional. But the Court adhered to its suggestion in the *Pollock* case that a tax on the conduct of business was an excise or indirect tax, not subject to the apportionment rule,[29] and it upheld the 1909 tax as an excise tax on the privilege of doing business in a corporate capacity:

> Within the category of indirect taxation . . . is embraced a tax upon business done in a corporate capacity, which is the subject-matter of the tax imposed in the act under consideration. The *Pollock Case* construed the tax there levied as direct, because it was imposed upon property simply because of its ownership. In the present case the tax is not payable unless there be a carrying on or doing of business in the designated capacity, and this is made the occasion for the tax, measured by the standard prescribed. The difference between the acts is not merely nominal, but rests upon substantial differences between the mere ownership of property and the actual doing of business in a certain way.[30]

The Court went on to hold that (1) the tax could be properly characterized as an indirect tax on the conduct of corporate business even though it reached income from all sources, including property not actively used in the business, (2) the tax did not infringe improperly on the allegedly exclusive power of the states to grant corporate franchises, and (3) corporate income from investments and other nonbusiness assets could be included in the tax base.

While this litigation concerning the constitutionality of the 1909 corporate income tax was on its way to the Supreme Court, the proposed amendment to the Constitution that had also been launched by Congress in 1909 was being ratified in one state after another. This process continued until February of 1913, when the Secretary of State certified that the sixteenth amendment had been duly ratified. Henceforth, any discussion of the direct tax clause of article I would have to take account of the new amendment:

---

[28] Supra ¶1.1.3.
[29] Pollock v. Farmers' Loan & Trust Co., 157 US 635 (1895).
[30] Flint v. Stone Tracy Co., 220 US 107, 150 (1911).

"The Congress shall have power to lay and collect taxes on incomes, from whatever source derived, without apportionment among the several States, and without regard to any census or enumeration."

¶1.2.3 The Effect of the Sixteenth Amendment

Ratification of the sixteenth amendment was quickly followed by enactment of the Revenue Act of 1913, which imposed an income tax on both individuals and corporations. Despite the constitutional change, litigation over the validity of income taxation continued. It was argued that (1) the sixteenth amendment only authorizes a tax reaching every species of income ("from whatever source derived") and all potential taxpayers, with no exceptions, (2) the Revenue Act of 1913, having exempted some taxpayers and types of income, could not claim the protection of the amendment, and hence (3) the 1913 tax was a direct tax, invalid under the *Pollock* decision for want of apportionment. The Supreme Court rejected this theory in *Brushaber v. Union Pacific Railroad*, decided in 1916:

> It is clear on the face of [the Sixteenth Amendment] that it does not purport to confer power to levy income taxes in a generic sense—an authority already possessed and never questioned—or to limit and distinguish between one kind of income taxes and another, but that the whole purpose of the Amendment was to relieve all income taxes when imposed from apportionment from a consideration of the source whence the income was derived. Indeed in the light of the history which we have given and of the decision in the *Pollock Case* and the ground upon which the ruling in that case was based, there is no escape from the conclusion that the amendment was drawn for the purpose of doing away for the future with the principle upon which the *Pollock Case* was decided, that is, of determining whether a tax on income was direct not by a consideration of the burden placed on the taxed income upon which it directly operated, but by taking into view the burden which resulted on the property from which the income was derived, since in express terms the amendment provides that income taxes, from whatever source the income may be derived, shall not be subject to the regulation of apportionment.[31]

In *Stanton v. Baltic Mining Co.*, decided a month later, the Court came close to saying that the *Pollock* case was erroneously decided:

> [B]y the previous ruling [in *Brushaber*] it was settled that the provisions of the Sixteenth Amendment conferred no new power of

---

[31] Brushaber v. Union Pac. R.R., 240 US 1, 17–18 (1916).

taxation, but simply prohibited the previous complete and plenary power of income taxation possessed by Congress from the beginning from being taken out of the category of indirect taxation to which it inherently belonged and being placed in the category of direct taxation subject to apportionment by a consideration of the sources from which the income was derived, that is, by testing the tax not by what it was— a tax on income, but by a mistaken theory deduced from the origin or source of the income taxed.[32]

The "mistaken theory," if we correctly interpret Mr. Chief Justice White's ponderous and labyrinthine prose, was the conclusion in *Pollock* that a tax on the income from property was the constitutional equivalent of a direct tax on the property itself. This interpretation of the Chief Justice's words is borne out by the fact that, as a dissenter in *Pollock*, he had rejected the "mistaken theory" at great length.[33]

As construed by the Supreme Court in the *Brushaber* and *Baltic Mining Co.* cases, the power of Congress to tax income derives from article I, section 8, clause 1, of the original Constitution rather than from the sixteenth amendment, which simply eliminated the requirement that an income tax, to the extent that it is a direct tax, must be apportioned among the states.[34] A corollary of this conclusion is that any direct tax that is not imposed on "income" remains subject to the rule of apportionment. Since the sixteenth amendment does not purport to define the term "direct tax," the scope of that constitutional phrase remains as debatable as it was before 1913; but the practical significance of the issue was greatly reduced once income taxes, even if direct, were relieved of the requirement of apportionment.

¶1.2.4 *Eisner v. Macomber*

In 1920 the Supreme Court decided *Eisner v. Macomber*,[35] the last of the early formative decisions on the constitutional status of federal income taxation. In this famous case, the taxpayer assailed the constitutionality of a provision of the Revenue Act of 1916, which included the value of a stock

---

[32] Stanton v. Baltic Mining Co., 240 US 103, 112–13 (1916).

[33] Pollock v. Farmers' Loan & Trust Co., supra note 29, at 608. Mr. Chief Justice White was the sole survivor of the *Pollock* Court when *Baltic Mining* was decided.

[34] The theory that the sixteenth amendment creates no new power to tax creates difficulty in at least one peripheral area: Whether, if Congress lacked the power to tax state and municipal bond interest before the sixteenth amendment (as *Pollock* held), its ratification remedied this gap by permitting Congress to tax income "from whatever source derived." See infra note 73.

[35] Eisner v. Macomber, 252 US 189 (1920).

dividend in the shareholder's income. The taxpayer, who owned 2,200 shares of the common stock of a corporation with only one class of common outstanding, received an additional 1,100 shares of the same class as a stock dividend. Because all other shareholders received similar stock dividends, her proportional interest in the corporation was not altered by the distribution. She argued, therefore, that she received no "income" but only a larger number of stock certificates to evidence her continued ownership of the same fractional interest in the corporation.

Because the taxpayer's investment, along with the corporate profits attributable to her investment, "still remains the property of the company . . . subject to business risks which may result in wiping out the entire investment," the Court held the taxpayer "received nothing that answers the definition of income within the meaning of the Sixteenth Amendment."[36] Having held that a stock dividend does not increase the shareholder's income, the Court moved directly to the conclusion that the tax was unconstitutional for want of apportionment. It failed, despite the length of the opinion, to explain why a tax on the receipt of a stock dividend is a "direct" tax requiring apportionment rather than an excise or indirect tax that is not subject to apportionment. The only sustained discussion of the direct tax issue appears in response to the government's second argument that "the tax is imposed, not upon the stock dividend, but rather upon the stockholder's share of the undivided profits previously accumulated by the corporation; the tax being levied as a matter of convenience at the time such profits become manifest through the stock dividend." The Court responded that, so viewed, the tax entailed "taxation of property because of ownership," permissible only if apportioned, unless the sixteenth amendment was applicable, a question it had just resolved against the government.[37]

---

[36] Id. at 211.

[37] Id. at 217. No other income tax case has been as extensively and acutely discussed as *Eisner v. Macomber*. A classic article by Thomas Reed Powell is Stock Dividends, Direct Taxes, and the Sixteenth Amendment, 20 Colum. L. Rev. 536 (1920). He concluded that the majority justices were better economists than the minority, but found a "stalemate" in the legal battle. E.R.A. Seligman, the distinguished economist, supported the majority (Studies in Public Finance, ch. 5 (1925)), while his son, an attorney, preferred the dissents (Implications and Effects of the Stock Dividend Decision, 21 Colum. L. Rev. 313 (1921)). Henry Simons agreed with the elder Seligman in approving the result of the decision, though he could not accept the Court's reasoning:

The decision that stock dividends should be ignored in calculating taxable income (except for the appropriate changes in the basis from which capital gains and losses are measured) was eminently sound, as a judgment about a question of legislative policy. It is most unfortunate, however, that a constitutional issue was ever raised; for brief experience with the legislation in question would almost certainly have led to general disapproval and early repeal. . . . Actually, an utterly trivial issue was made the occasion for injecting into our

In *Pollock*, to be sure, the Court held that the income from property is so essential an element of ownership that a tax on the income is tantamount to a direct tax on ownership of the property itself. A shareholder's opportunity to receive stock dividends, however, is a peripheral component of stock ownership, hardly comparable to the right to receive cash dividends. If taxes on long distance telephone calls, the manufacture of tobacco products, the transfer of firearms, the sale of adulterated butter, and a host of other events and transactions are excise or indirect taxes, it is difficult to understand why a tax on the receipt of a stock dividend does not belong in the same classification. If the Court had held that a tax on stock dividends was an excise, however, it would then have had to decide whether the taxing of stock dividends by including them in an income tax base was a constitutionally objectionable misjoinder of diverse elements.[38]

The decision in *Eisner v. Macomber* was avidly awaited by the financial world, especially since many corporations had announced that stock dividends would be declared if held nontaxable. When Mr. Justice Pitney began to read his opinion, its import was misunderstood by a representative of Dow, Jones & Company, and a report that the Court had held the dividend taxable was sent out on the ticker. A collapse of stock prices, especially of those corporations that had previously been expected to declare stock dividends, resulted. After the false report was corrected, there was a rebound, sending prices up more than they had dropped. One observer blamed the incident on the fact that Supreme Court opinions are read "in a low or mumbling tone."[39]

---

fundamental law a mass of rhetorical confusion which no orderly mind can contemplate respectfully, and for giving constitutional status to naive and ridiculous notions about the nature of income and the rationale of income taxes.

Simons, Personal Income Taxation 198-99 (U. of Chicago Press 1938). See also Sneed, The Configurations of Gross Income 125 (Ohio State U. Press 1967) (suggesting that whatever "rusty remnant" of *Eisner v. Macomber* remains "be consigned to the junk yard of judicial history"); Lowndes, Current Conceptions of Taxable Income, 25 Ohio St. LJ 151 (1964); Surrey, The Supreme Court and the Federal Income Tax: Some Implications of the Recent Decisions, 35 Ill. L. Rev. 779, 782 (1941).

[38] For this issue, see Penn Mut. Indem. Co. v. CIR, 277 F2d 16 (3d Cir. 1960), stating that a tax on the gross receipts of a mutual insurance company could be properly regarded as an "excise" even though the relevant provisions "occur in the middle of an income tax statute and are labeled by Congress as 'income tax' provisions". See also Simmons v. US, 308 F2d 160 (4th Cir. 1962); Powell, Constitutional Aspects of Federal Income Taxation, in The Federal Income Tax 89 (Haig, ed.; Columbia U. Press 1921) (re "confusion from commingling"); Surrey, supra note 37, at 793 ("the income tax is an aggregation of various indirect taxes, the most important being the tax on income itself").

[39] N.Y. Times, March 9, 1920, at 1, col. 3.

If the Supreme Court had upheld the constitutionality of the tax in *Eisner v. Macomber*, its practical results would almost certainly have been minor. The tax imposed on the taxpayer in *Eisner v. Macomber* would have been one of the last to be received by the Treasury because corporations could simply have refrained thereafter from issuing stock dividends—an abstention that would have entailed little inconvenience to the world of finance.[40] The real significance of the decision lies less in its impact on the taxability of stock dividends than in its implications for three more fundamental issues of income taxation.

First, the Court pointed out that "no part of the assets of the company is separated [by a stock dividend] from the common fund," a fact that, in its view, was inconsistent with the concept of "income." In this connection the Court quoted with approval the judicial definition of "income" employed in cases under the 1909 corporate tax: "Income may be defined as the gain derived from capital, from labor, or from both combined." By stressing the importance of a "severance" of gain from capital, the Court implied that it would not have approved of taxing, without apportionment, unrealized appreciation in property, although the definition of income most in vogue among economists takes account of the net increase or decrease in the value of a taxpayer's assets during the taxable year or other accounting period.[41] The decision in *Eisner v. Macomber* did not necessarily involve the constitutionality of taxing unrealized appreciation, however, since the applicable statutory provision taxed the stock dividend whether the post-dividend value of the taxpayer's stock exceeded or was less than its original cost.

Second, pointing to the fact that corporate profits belong to the corporation until distributed to the shareholders as dividends, the Court said that until then, "what is called the stockholder's share in the accumulated profits of the company is capital, not income." This view of the shareholder's relationship to corporate profits suggests that if Congress desired to tax shareholders on the undistributed profits of their corporations, it would have to apportion the tax among the states in proportion to population. The Court's remarks arose in a legislative context involving a separate corporate tax and might have been modified if corporate profits were not taxed to the corporation but only to its shareholders. The language chosen by the Court, however, was so broad that doubts about the constitutionality of taxing shareholders as though they were partners in the corporate enterprise, though less weighty than they once were, have not yet wholly disappeared.[42]

---

[40] See infra ¶92.6.1.

[41] Infra ¶3.1.1. See Shakow, Taxation Without Realization: A Proposal for Accrual Taxation, 134 U. Pa. L. Rev. 1111 (1986) (exploring practical issues arising in a system taxing unrealized gains).

[42] Congress has never experimented comprehensively with the idea known as complete integration, that is, the technique of taxing shareholders directly on corpo-

Finally, the statement that income is "the gain derived from capital, from labor, or from both combined" seems to exclude windfalls and other items that are received by a taxpayer without using either capital or labor. The Court, however, has drawn back from this statement.[43] Indeed, even before *Eisner v. Macomber*, the Court found it necessary to amplify it by including the profits from the sale of capital assets—a modification that was explicitly approved in *Eisner*.[44]

All three of the foregoing implications of *Eisner v. Macomber* have had a significant effect on the structure of the Internal Revenue Code and are discussed at greater length elsewhere in this work.[45] *Eisner v. Macomber* was the high-water mark in the Supreme Court's attempt to provide an all-purpose definition of income.[46] In later cases, the judiciary has bowed to legislative decisions regarding the term "income," and the direct tax clause of the Constitution has never again had the power that was attributed to it by *Pollock v. Farmers' Loan & Trust Co.* and *Eisner v. Macomber*.[47]

---

rate income, whether distributed or not, in lieu of taxing corporations. See infra ¶3.5.6. Two more limited integration schemes, however, have been adopted, and both have been found constitutional. In 1937, Congress adopted rules, now found in §§551–557, taxing U.S. shareholders of foreign personal holding companies on the undistributed incomes of these corporations. See infra ¶95.2.7. The provisions known as subpart F (§§951–964) were enacted in 1962 to tax U.S. shareholders of controlled foreign corporations on undistributed earnings of the corporations from investments and transactions deemed susceptible to tax haven abuse. See infra ¶68.3.3. The constitutionality of the foreign personal holding company rules and subpart F were both attacked shortly after their enactments, but no constitutional impediment to their implementation was found. *Eisner v. Macomber* is hardly mentioned in the opinions. Whitlock v. CIR, 494 F2d 1297 (10th Cir.), cert. denied, 419 US 839 (1974) (subpart F is constitutional); Garlock v. CIR, 489 F2d 197 (2d Cir.), cert. denied, 417 US 911 (1974) (attack on constitutionality of subpart F "borders on the frivolous in the light of this court's decision in Eder v. Commissioner"); Eder v. CIR, 138 F2d 27 (2d Cir. 1943) (constitutional objections to foreign personal holding company rules dismissed summarily).

[43] Infra ¶5.1.

[44] Doyle v. Mitchell Bros. Co., 247 US 179, 185 (1918), approved in Eisner v. Macomber, 252 US 207 (1920).

[45] See especially infra ¶5.1.

[46] See Magill, Taxable Income 67 (Ronald Press 1936):

Viewed against the cases that succeeded it, *Eisner v. Macomber* loses greatly in magnitude. Restricted on all sides to its facts, its bold definition of income partly discarded in result and subsequently regarded as a futile attempt to confine a term that must remain elastic, the decision has not actually resulted in the feared limitations on the taxing power.

[47] In Bromley v. McCaughn, 280 US 124 (1929), the Court discussed at some length the direct tax clause in upholding the constitutionality of the federal gift tax. See also Helvering v. Independent Life Ins. Co., 292 US 371 (1934) (rental value of property not taxable as income); Edwards v. Cuba R.R., 268 US 628 (1925) (governmental subsidy not taxable to recipient); Wyly v. US, 662 F2d 397 (5th Cir. 1981)

¶1.2.5 Due Process, Uniformity, and Differential Treatment of Taxpayers

Many of the most familiar structural features of today's income tax—including the personal exemptions, allowances for family status, progression in the rate structure, and the exclusion of the rental value of owner-occupied residences—were once attacked as violating both the due process clause and the constitutional provision requiring that "all Duties, Imposts and Excises shall be uniform throughout the United States." They were held in *Brushaber v. Union Pacific Railroad* to be consistent with the uniformity standard because only "geographical uniformity" is required and all taxpayers having the characteristics in question are taxed the same regardless of their residences.[48]

The due process claim was rejected in *Brushaber* almost as summarily:

> So far as the due process clause of the Fifth Amendment is relied upon, it suffices to say that there is no basis for such reliance since it is equally well settled that such clause is not a limitation upon the taxing power conferred upon Congress by the Constitution; in other words, that the Constitution does not conflict with itself by conferring upon the one hand a taxing power and taking the same power away on the other by the limitations of the due process clause.[49]

Evidently recognizing that this breathtaking exemption of the federal taxing power could hardly be defended when virtually all other legislative powers, including those explicitly granted by the Constitution, are tamed by the due process clause, the Court moved on to a theory that is easier to defend though harder to apply, that the courts can intervene if

> the act complained of was so arbitrary as to constrain to the conclusion that it was not the exertion of taxation but a confiscation of property, that is, a taking of the same in violation of the Fifth Amendment, or, what is equivalent thereto, was so wanting in basis for classification as to produce such a gross and patent inequality as to inevitably lead to

---

(minimum tax on tax preference items enacted in 1969 (eventually replaced by alternative minimum tax discussed below in ¶111.3) was an income tax covered by the sixteenth amendment).

[48] Brushaber v. Union Pac. R.R., 240 US 1 (1916), citing a number of earlier cases. See also US v. Ptasynski, 462 US 74 (1983) (uniformity clause not violated by §4994(e), which exempts from windfall profits tax oil produced, roughly speaking, north of Artic Circle or on northerly side of Alaska-Aleutian Range; although geographic terms used to define exemption, congressional decision to exempt "based on neutral factors").

[49] Brushaber v. Union Pac. R.R., supra note 48, at 24.

the same conclusion.[50]

A commentator has generalized this point:

> [T]here is no more incongruity in having the federal taxing power limited by the fifth amendment than in having state taxing power limited by the fourteenth amendment. The existence of power on the one hand and of constitutional restrictions on its exercise on the other is of the essence of our constitutional system. To borrow the simile of [a prior author], a train is not self-destructive because it has both motive power and brakes.[51]

In this spirit, the courts have applied to the distinctions drawn by Congress in imposing the federal income tax the familiar rule now used in reviewing regulatory and other economic legislation: "Normally, a legislative classification will not be set aside if any state of facts rationally justifying it is demonstrated to or perceived by the courts."[52] Among the legislative classifications assailed by taxpayers that have been sustained as reasonable by the courts are distinctions between corporations organized before a specified date and those organized thereafter, between single and married taxpayers, between domestic and foreign corporations, between corporations and partnerships, between securities held for two years or more and those held for less than two years, and between taxpayers employing relatives as baby-sitters and those employing unrelated persons.[53]

Even during the heyday of substantive due process in the economic area, when legislative decisions to regulate some businesses or persons but not others were subjected to intense constitutional scrutiny, the courts never used the due process clause to police the federal income tax. It is conceivable that the numerous legislative distinctions among taxpayers have invariably been so reasonable as to refute any allegation of arbitrary conduct. A more plausible hypothesis is that the tax laws have drawn so many distinc-

---

[50] Id. at 24–25.

[51] Powell, supra note 38, at 59.

[52] US v. Maryland Savings-Share Ins. Corp., 400 US 4, 6 (1970).

[53] Id.; Barclay & Co. v. Edwards, 267 US 442 (1924) (grandfather clause re exempt corporations); Flint v. Stone Tracy Co., 220 US 107 (1911) (corporations vs. unincorporated enterprises); Okin v. CIR, 808 F2d 1338 (9th Cir.), cert. denied, 108 S. Ct. 45 (1987) (alternative minimum tax imposed by §55); Whitlock v. CIR, 494 F2d 1297 (10th Cir.), cert. denied, 419 US 839 (1974) (taxing shareholders of controlled foreign corporations on undistributed corporate income); Mapes v. US, 576 F2d 896 (Ct. Cl. 1978) ("marriage penalty"); Davis v. US, 87 F2d 323 (2d Cir.), cert. denied, 301 US 704 (1937) (time limit on securities); Bryant v. CIR, 72 TC 757 (1979) (employment of relatives for care of dependents); Kellems v. CIR, 58 TC 556 (1972), aff'd per curiam, 474 F2d 1393 (2d Cir.), cert. denied, 414 US 831 (1973) ("singles penalty").

tions that even a Supreme Court confident of its power to distinguish between reasonable and arbitrary behavior in other statutory areas has hesitated to act as a referee of tax legislation.

With the waning of substantive due process doctrines in the economic area, judicial oversight of tax legislation in the name of the due process clause is even less likely, save in a few areas where civil liberties or "suspect classifications" are involved[54] or where traditional issues of procedural due process arise, as in administrative hearings and appeals, fraud investigations, criminal prosecutions, and summary enforcement devices.[55]

In an avalanche of recent litigation, some of it stimulated by organized tax protest movements, taxpayers have attacked the federal income tax as unconstitutional on such theories as: Federal Reserve notes are invalid because they are not convertible into gold; CIA expenditures are not properly reported by the Treasury Department; the Commissioner of Internal Revenue is holding an unlawful job and should be jailed as a criminal; requiring taxpayers to keep tax records and prepare returns constitutes involuntary servitude; and compulsion to file tax returns violates the privilege against self-incrimination. These imaginative attacks have uniformly been rejected by the courts, along with allegations that the Internal Revenue Code conflicts with the Bible, the Magna Carta, the Mayflower Compact, and the Northwest Ordinance. Persistent litigators have been enjoined, subjected to penalties for frivolous litigation, and prosecuted for failure to file returns.[56]

---

[54] See Black v. US, 534 F2d 524 (2d Cir. 1976) (racial discrimination alleged; injunction denied because other remedies available); McGlotten v. Connally, 338 F. Supp. 448 (DDC 1972), discussed infra ¶100.1.2.

[55] For a requirement of consistency in administrative action, see infra ¶110.1; see also infra ¶112.1.1 (selection of tax returns for audit), ¶114.4.1 (selection of fraud cases for prosecution).

[56] See US v. Stout, 601 F2d 325 (7th Cir. 1979) (Forms 1040 filed with name and address and identifying taxpayer but otherwise blank save for objections based on first, fourth, seventh, eighth, ninth, tenth, thirteenth, fourteenth, and sixteenth amendments; conviction for failure to file returns affirmed); Gardiner v. US, 531 F2d 953 (9th Cir. 1976); Baker v. CIR, 149 F2d 342 (4th Cir.), cert. denied, 326 US 746 (1975); Quimby v. Semerick, 42 AFTR2d 6146 (ED Tex. 1978) (not officially reported) (injunction against further litigation); Richardson v. CIR, 72 TC 818 (1979); Wilkinson v. CIR, 71 TC 633 (1979) (penalty for frivolous litigation); Cupp v. CIR, 65 TC 68 (1975).

The variety of unsuccessful constitutional challenges to tax legislation is indicated by the following cases: Regan v. Taxation With Representation, 461 US 540 (1983) (first amendment not violated by lobbying restriction imposed on charities claiming exemption under §501(c)(3); lack of similar restriction on veterans organizations exempt under §501(c)(19) not offensive to equal protection); US v. Lee, 455 US 252 (1982) (no first amendment violation in imposition of social security tax on Amish employer with Amish employees, even though tax violates Amish religious beliefs); Helvering v. National Grocery Co., 304 US 282 (1938) (accumulated earn-

¶1.2.6 Due Process and Retroactivity

Changes in rate schedules and substantive provisions are sometimes applicable to all income for the year in which the amendments are enacted, including amounts received or accrued before enactment. In a few instances, entire revenue acts were enacted after the close of the year to which they applied.[57] Since 1916, it has been settled that "current year retroactivity" (i.e., the application of the amended statute to all transactions during the year of the change, whether they occurred before or after its enactment)

---

ings tax does not violate tenth or sixteenth amendment); Barter v. US, 550 F2d 1239 (7th Cir. 1977) ("marriage penalty" constitutional); Nash Miami Motors, Inc. v. CIR, 358 F2d 636 (5th Cir.), cert. denied, 385 US 918 (1966) (Tax Court constitutional, does not violate Article III); Walker v. US, 240 F2d 601 (5th Cir. 1957) (separation of powers); Porth v. Broderick, 214 F2d 925 (10th Cir. 1954) (sixteenth amendment does not violate thirteenth amendment prohibition against involuntary servitude); Abney v. Campbell, 206 F2d 836 (5th Cir. 1953) (tax not arbitrary and discriminatory under fifth amendment; not involuntary servitude under thirteenth amendment); Keogh v. Neely, 50 F2d 685 (7th Cir. 1931) (guaranty of republican form of government); Farmer v. Rountree, 149 F. Supp. 327 (D. Tenn. 1956), aff'd, 252 F2d 490 (6th Cir. 1958) (refusal to pay portion of taxes because of alleged illegal foreign and military policies of United States not justified); Publishers New Press, Inc. v. Moysey, 141 F. Supp. 340 (SDNY 1956) (levy on newspaper's property pursuant to jeopardy assessment not invasion of freedom of press); Communist Party v. Moysey, 141 F. Supp. 332 (SDNY 1956) (freedom of speech and assembly not violated); N.A. Woodworth Co. v. Kavanagh, 102 F. Supp. 9 (ED Mich. 1952), aff'd per curiam, 202 F2d 154 (6th Cir. 1953) (not excessive fine or cruel and unusual punishment under eighth amendment); Sjoroos v. CIR, 81 TC 971 (1983) (equal protection not offended by exemption of cost-of-living allowances received by federal employees stationed in Alaska, even though no comparable exemption provided persons employed in private sector; exemption chosen as alternative to increasing allowances); Tingle v. CIR, 73 TC 816 (1980) (tax not violative of ninth amendment's reservation of powers to the people); Bryant v. CIR, 72 TC 757 (1979) (not unconstitutional to disallow deductions for child care payments to relatives; extensive discussion); Hecht v. CIR, 34 TCM (CCH) 115 (1975) (use of taxes to pay for Vietnam War does not violate Charter of Nuremburg Tribunal).

[57] The Revenue Act of 1918, 40 Stat. 1057, was enacted on February 24, 1919, applicable to the calendar year 1918; the Life Insurance Company Income Tax Act of 1959, Pub. L. No. 86-69, 73 Stat. 112, enacted on June 25, 1959, was effective for taxable years beginning after December 31, 1957.

In Untermyer v. Anderson, 276 US 440 (1928), the gift tax was held unconstitutional as applied to gifts made before the tax's enactment, but the precedential value of the decision is much in doubt. See US v. Hemme, 476 US 558 (1986) (*Untermyer*'s "authority is of limited value in assessing the constitutionality of subsequent amendments that bring about certain changes in operation of the tax laws, rather than the creation of a wholly new tax"); Ceppi's Est. v. CIR, 698 F2d 17 (1st Cir.), cert. denied, 462 US 1120 (1983) (questioning current validity and scope of *Untermeyer*); Sidney v. CIR, 273 F2d 928 (2d Cir. 1960) (more such doubt). See infra ¶120.1.2 for a more complete discussion of the retroactivity issue in the estate and gift tax context.

is not an unconstitutional deprivation of property without due process of law, even though the taxpayer cannot alter or rescind preenactment transactions in the light of the new rules and might have acted differently if the changes had been foreseen.[58] Application of the new law to the income of the prior year is also sanctioned by practice, although explicit judicial authority is scanty.[59] Generally, a retroactive change offends due process only if "the nature of the tax and the circumstances in which it is laid [are] so harsh and oppressive as to transgress the constitutional limitation."[60]

---

[58] US v. Darusmont, 449 US 292 (1981) (amendments increasing effective rate of minimum tax on tax preference items enacted October 4, 1976 to apply to all of 1976); Brushaber v. Union Pac. R.R., 240 US 1, 20 (1916) (citing Stockdale v. Insurance Cos., 87 US (20 Wall.) 323 (1873), a confusing opinion that was directly concerned only with retroactivity to the beginning of the calendar year of the legislation under attack, but that also said that Congress could tax income of a prior year if it so decided).

See generally Williams, Retroactivity in the Federal Tax Field, 1960 So. Cal. Tax Inst. 79 (extensively documenting legislative practice in this area); Committee on Tax Policy, Tax Section, New York State Bar Ass'n, Retroactivity of Tax Legislation, 29 Tax Lawyer 21 (1975); Hochman, The Supreme Court and the Constitutionality of Retroactive Legislation, 73 Harv. L. Rev. 692 (1960); Novick & Petersberger, Retroactivity in Federal Taxation, 37 Taxes 407, 499 (1959); Read, MacDonald, Fordham & Pierce, Materials on Legislation 536–42 (Foundation Press, 4th ed. 1982).

Retroactivity does not violate the constitutional prohibition on ex post facto laws (art. I, §9, cl. 3) because that limitation is concerned with criminal laws. See Mathes v. CIR, 63 TC 642 (1975) (citing Johannessen v. US, 225 US 227 (1912)).

[59] See Wilgard Realty Co. v. CIR, 127 F2d 514 (2d Cir.), cert. denied, 317 US 655 (1942) (1939 law changing method of determining basis of property received during period 1924–1938 upheld in absence of damage to reasonable expectations); Fife v. CIR, 82 TC 1, 13 (1984) (1976 amendment requiring that motion picture film be new to qualify for investment credit, retroactively applicable to all open years, valid as applied to purchase made in 1973 because, among other things, "Congress's intention . . . was to not to change the law but to clarify existing law"). See also DeMartino v. CIR, 88 TC 583 (1987) (statutory "clarification" of provision increasing interest rate on deficiencies in tax motivated transactions given retroactive effect for all open years, even though clarification contrary to Tax Court construction of original statute). But see People ex rel. Beck v. Graves, 280 NY 405, 21 NE2d 371 (1939) (16 years excessive as to state income tax law).

[60] Welch v. Henry, 305 US 134, 147 (1938). See US v. Hemme, supra note 57 (affirming "harsh and oppressive" standard). See also Corry, Retroactive Penalties Raise Constititional Issues, 36 Tax Notes 723 (1987) (arguing that amendment of penalty provision cannot constitutionally raise penalty rate for penalties that are assessed after date of enactment but are based on preenactment conduct). See DeMartino v. CIR, 88 TC 583 (1987) (statutory "clarification" of provision increasing interest rate on deficiencies in tax motivated transactions given retroactive effect, even though clarification contrary to Tax Court construction of original statute).

Rejection of the due process argument has usually been bottomed on custom, sometimes buttressed by the theory that midyear statutory changes are so common that taxpayers cannot reasonably expect the status quo to continue and should therefore take the likelihood of change into account when entering into business transactions.[61] As Mr. Justice Holmes observed, "We all know that we shall get a tax bill every year."[62] Moreover, a systematic avoidance of change disturbing the status quo would require the preservation for every taxpayer's lifetime of the statutory rules in force whenever he took a step that might have been encouraged by its contemporaneous tax consequences and that could not be reversed without a sacrifice, whether it was accepting or quitting a job, buying or selling an asset, or any of a myriad of other transactions.

As Judge Learned Hand has written:

> It is notoriously impossible nicely to adjust the weight of taxes, and it is no objection that upon occasion the result may disappoint reasonable anticipations. The injustice is no greater than if a man chance to make a profitable sale in the months before the general rates are retroactively changed. Such a one may indeed complain that, could he have foreseen the increase, he would have kept the transaction unliquidated, but it will not avail him; he must be prepared for such possibilities, the system being already in operation. His is a different case from that of one who, when he takes action, has no reason to suppose that any transactions of the sort will be taxed at all.
>
> No doubt the difference is one of degree, but constitutional matters are generally that; limitations like the Fifth Amendment are not like sailing rules, or traffic ordinances; they do not circumscribe the action of Congress by metes and bounds. Rather they are admonitions of fair dealing, whose disregard the courts will correct, if extreme and glaring. Custom counts for much in such matters, and consistency for little; men cannot hope to fit their doings in advance to a pattern which will be sure to endure. The most they can expect is that courts will

---

[61] See Welch v. Henry, supra note 60 (sustaining state income tax enacted in 1935 but taxing dividends received in 1933); Sidney v. CIR, supra note 57; Fife v. CIR, supra note 59 (Congress entitled to special deference with respect to retroactive provisions of investment credit rules because these rules underwent some statutory change nearly every year). In People ex rel. Beck v. Graves, supra note 59, a state income tax enacted in 1935 but applicable to income received as early as 1919 was held unconstitutional; one judge dissented on the ground that the income in question (royalties from out-of-state mining properties) had been thought taxable when received and was exempted only by a later judicial decision that was itself unexpected.

[62] Untermyer v. Anderson, 276 US 446 (1928) (dissent). See also infra ¶1.2.7 (income tax on federal judges taking office after income tax became a permanent policy).

intervene when the defeat of their expectations passes any measure that reasonable persons could think tolerable, and even then their grievance must be fairly outside the zone of possible debate.[63]

Power is one thing, its wise exercise another. Congress frequently exempts transactions from changes in the tax law by preserving the status quo ante in the interest of fairness. Sometimes an indulgence is granted to transactions completed before legislation is proposed by one of the tax-writing committees of Congress or is signed by the President. Exemptions also sometimes embrace transactions that were not consummated by the effective date of the legislation but were then in an advanced state of preparation, and occasionally taxpayers are allowed to elect to be governed by either the old or the new rules.[64] By using delayed effective dates, grandfather clauses, and transitional adjustments to temper the wind for taxpayers who are about to be shorn, Congress has minimized attacks on the constitutionality of retroactive legislation. The due process weapon remains available to the courts in "extreme and glaring" cases, to use Judge Learned Hand's verbal formula, but no federal income tax provision has actually been held unconstitutional on this ground.[65]

---

[63] Cohan v. CIR, 39 F2d 540, 545 (2d Cir. 1930). The Supreme Court has offered an even broader defense of retroactivity:

> Taxation is neither a penalty imposed on the taxpayer nor a liability which he assumes by contract. It is but a way of apportioning the cost of government among those who in some measure are privileged to enjoy its benefits and must bear its burdens. Since no citizen enjoys immunity from that burden, its retroactive imposition does not necessarily infringe due process.

Welch v. Henry, supra note 60, at 146–47.

[64] Numerous substantive provisions distinguish between transactions before and after a specified date; §1014(b), for example, contains six such distinctions. For an unusually long transitional period, see Tax Reform Act of 1969, Pub. L. No. 91-172, §421(b)(2), 83 Stat. 614, providing that §305(b)(2) shall not apply to certain distributions of stock until 1991 (infra ¶92.6.5).

A special effective date figured prominently in President Nixon's downfall. See Reg. §1.170A-4(b)(1); Staff of Joint Comm. on Internal Revenue Tax'n, Examination of President Nixon's Tax Returns 1969 Through 1972, H.R. Rep. No. 93-966 (1974).

[65] See also James v. US, 366 US 213 (1961) (nonretroactive application of changed judicial doctrine to defendant in criminal case), discussed infra ¶6.5; US v. Rexach, 558 F2d 37 (1st Cir. 1977) (principles governing retroactive application of judicial decisions); Central Ill. Pub. Serv. Co. v. US, 435 US 21 (1978) (same); Howell v. CIR, 77 TC 916 (1981) (Fay, J., concurring, suggesting that the second tier tax imposed by §4941(b)(1) (infra ¶101.2) amounts to a civil penalty and that its retroactive imposition would offend due process); Graetz, Legal Transitions: The Case of Retroactivity in Income Tax Revision, 126 U. Pa. L. Rev. 47 (1977); Feldstein, Compensation in Tax Reform, 29 Nat'l Tax J. 123 (1976) (compensation for defeated expectations); infra ¶3.3.4 (re capitalization of tax burdens and benefits); infra ¶¶110.4.3, 110.5.4 (retroactivity in application of regulations and rulings).

¶1.2.7 Salaries of Federal Judges

The Constitution provides that federal judges "shall, at stated Times, receive for their Services, a Compensation, which shall not be diminished during their Continuance in Office."[66] In 1863, Chief Justice Taney wrote to the Secretary of the Treasury to protest the application of the Civil War federal income tax to federal judges, stating that the levy was unconstitutional but that the question could not be decided in a judicial proceeding because of the judges' personal interest in the outcome.[67] Despite this confession of judicial impotence, the Supreme Court held in 1920 that Congress could not tax the salaries of federal judges. The sixteenth amendment, the Court held, "does not extend the [federal] taxing power to new or excepted subjects, but merely removes all occasion [necessity] otherwise existing for an apportionment among the states of taxes laid on income, whether derived from one source or another."[68] The decision evoked these observations from Judge Learned Hand:

> Again I have pondered on what it is to be a Bolshevik, and once I learned. There was a time when Congress thought it could reach the salaries of my brothers and myself by an income tax, until the Supreme Court manfully came to our rescue. A judge of much experience was talking with me one day about it; I was wrong enough in my law, as it afterwards turned out, and disloyal enough in temper to my class, to say that I thought the tax valid. "Do you know anything about it?" he asked with some asperity. "No," said I, "not a thing." "Have you ever read Taney's letter?" "No," said I again, for I was innocent of any learning. "Why, they can't do that," said he; "they can't do that, that's Bolshevism." And so it turned out, to my personal gratification, since when, freed from that Red Peril, I have enjoyed an immunity which the rest of you, alas, cannot share. [This was written in 1930.] Far be it from me to suggest that there are graver thrusts at the structure of society than to tax a Federal judge. Properly instructed, I have recanted

---

[66] U.S. Const. art III, §1.

[67] Opinion of the Justices, 157 US 701 (1863).

[68] Evans v. Gore, 253 US 245, 261–62 (1920). See Holmes, 1 Holmes-Laski Letters 335–36 (Harvard U. Press 1953):

> This morning brings a surprise—I was notified some time ago that prepayment of tax by companies issuing bonds counted as part of my income and that a small additional tax was due from me for two past years. I wrote back that I should pay as soon as I received my bill and that I didn't know it made any difference that by the decision of our court (I dissenting) I had overpaid by some thousands, as my salary was taxed. Answer comes that if I apply for a refund of it I shall receive prompt attention—I don't quite know whether to or not.

my heresy, and yet there hangs about "Bolshevism" a residual vagueness, a lack of clear outline, as of a mountain against the setting sun; which only goes to show, I suppose, that a fundamentally corrupt nature can never be wholly reformed.[69]

The taxpayer in *Evans v. Gore* was appointed to the federal bench in 1899. Although the Court did not limit its decision to judges appointed before the sixteenth amendment was ratified or before income taxation became a permanent feature of the federal fiscal system, later cases seized upon this distinction, holding that federal judges appointed after 1918, when the first revenue act explicitly taxing federal judicial salaries was enacted, were entitled only to the salary prescribed by statute, less applicable taxes. Thus, their salaries were not "diminished during their continuance in office" within the meaning of the Constitution by rate increases or other changes or by the restoration of a tax after a temporary suspension.[70] In so holding, the courts did not rest on the sixteenth amendment but on the broader rationale that the constitutional protection of judicial salaries was intended to insure judicial independence, a virtue that is not threatened by a nondiscriminatory tax imposed on judges along with all other citizens. By 1954, this principle had become so well entrenched that the statutory provision specifically taxing judicial salaries was eliminated as surplusage.[71]

¶1.2.8 The Income of State and Municipal Governments, Employees, and Bondholders

The Supreme Court held in *South Carolina v. Baker* that the Congress can, if it wishes, tax interest on state and local obligations.[72] This decision finally put to rest the holding in *Pollock v. Farmers' Loan & Trust Co.* that the 1894 federal income tax was unconstitutional in taxing the interest received by holders of state and municipal bonds.[73] It also marks the closing chapter in a long saga involving the federal government's power to tax

---

[69] Hand, The Spirit of Liberty 77–78 (Dillard, Ed.; Knopf 1953).

[70] O'Malley v. Woodrough, 307 US 277 (1939); Baker v. CIR, 149 F2d 342 (4th Cir.), cert. denied, 326 US 746 (1945).

The issue has never been litigated, but presumably the principles applicable to judicial salaries also apply to the constitutional prohibition (art. II, §1, cl. 7) of any diminution of the President's compensation during his term in office.

[71] See S. Rep. No. 1622, 83d Cong., 2d Sess. 168 (1954).

[72] South Carolina v. Baker, 108 S. Ct. 1355 (1988).

[73] Pollock v. Farmers' Loan & Trust Co., 158 US 601, 630 (1985). Because this part of *Pollock* rested on the doctrine of implied intergovernmental tax immunities rather than on the apportionment clause, it was supported by the Justices who dissented from the decision as respects other sources of income.

income received by private persons in their dealings with state and local governments.

The holding in *Pollock* on bond interest relied not upon the apportionment clause, requiring direct taxes to be apportioned among the states according to population, but on the broader theory that the tax was a burden on the power of the states and their instrumentalities to borrow money, impairing the independence of the states contemplated by the federal system of government established by the Constitution. On this theory, state and municipal bond interest would be immune even from a tax that was apportioned according to population.

During the debates in Congress and in the states preceding ratification of the sixteenth amendment, many of its opponents, most notably Charles Evans Hughes, then governor of New York, asserted that, by empowering Congress to tax incomes "from whatever source derived," the amendment would authorize a tax on state and municipal bond interest and possibly even a tax on the income of the states themselves.[74] Quoting Mr. Chief Justice Marshall's dictum that "the power to tax involves the power to destroy,"[75] they conjured up a future in which the states and cities would exist solely at the sufferance of Congress. For their part, the protagonists of the proposed amendment responded to this attack by asserting the sixteenth amendment would do no more than eliminate the apportionment requirement as to a federal income tax, without jeopardizing the existing doctrine of intergovernmental tax immunity.

After ratification, however, some of the amendment's supporters exchanged forensic roles with their opponents, claiming that, having been ratified despite claims by critics that it would permit Congress to levy taxes that were previously barred whether apportioned or not, the amendment should be so construed. Conversely, some of the amendment's opponents argued that it should be construed to embody the disclaimers that were put forth by its supporters during the preratification debates. Though hotly debated at one time, these opposing theories of the sixteenth amendment's impact on the doctrine of intergovernmental immunity were not resolved until *South Carolina v. Baker*. In the light of hindsight, we can see that the

---

[74] For a detailed review of the amendment's history (including the statutory precursors of the phrase "from whatever source derived"), see Dep't of Justice (Morris et al.), Taxation of Government Bondholders and Employees: The Immunity Rule and the Sixteenth Amendment 120–90 (1939), with an appendix reprinting many of the relevant documents. See also Ketcham, The Sixteenth Amendment (Ph.D. dissertation, Univ. of Illinois, 1924).

[75] McCulloch v. Maryland, 17 US (4 Wheat.) 316, 431 (1819). But see Mr. Justice Holmes, in Panhandle Oil Co. v. Mississippi ex rel. Knox, 277 US 218, 223 (1928) ("The power to tax is not the power to destroy while this Court sits"); Mr. Justice Frankfurter, in Graves v. New York ex rel. O'Keefe, 306 US 466, 489 (1939) (characterizing the Marshall statement as a "seductive cliche").

debaters were divided by what has become a false premise. Since 1913, the doctrine of intergovernmental immunity as it concerns nondiscriminatory taxes has had such rough going in the federal courts that an additional blow from the sixteenth amendment would have been barely perceptible.[76]

In 1938, for example, the Supreme Court held in *Helvering v. Gerhardt* that employees of the Port of New York Authority (created by an interstate compact between New York and New Jersey) could be taxed by the federal government on their salaries:

> A nondiscriminatory tax laid on their net income, in common with that of all other members of the Community, could by no reasonable probability be considered to preclude the performance of the function which New York and New Jersey have undertaken, or to obstruct it more than like private enterprises are obstructed by our taxing system. Even though, to some unascertainable extent, the tax deprives the states of the advantage of paying less than the standard rate for the services which they engage, it does not curtail any of those functions which have been thought hitherto to be essential to their continued existence as states. At most it may be said to increase somewhat the cost of the state governments because, in an interdependent economic society, the taxation of income tends to raise (to some extent which economists are not able to measure . . .) the price of labor and materials. The effect of the immunity if allowed would be to relieve respondents of their duty of financial support to the national government, in order to secure to the state a theoretical advantage so speculative in its character and measurement as to be unsubstantial. A tax immunity devised for protection of the states as governmental entities cannot be pressed so far.[77]

The *Gerhardt* case involved a governmental agency performing what were termed "proprietary" rather than "essential governmental" functions, and it was argued as though it would not affect policemen, firemen, teachers, and elected officials. The Court's broad reasoning, however, left little room for exempting any state salaries. In *Graves v. New York ex rel. O'Keefe*, decided less than a year later, the Court confirmed this by overruling *Collector v. Day*, which held the salaries of state judges were constitutionally immune from the Civil War income tax, and thereby ending any

---

[76] See generally Massachusetts v. US, 435 US 444 (1978); McCormack, Intergovernmental Immunity and the Eleventh Amendment, 51 NCL Rev. 485 (1973); Powell, The Waning of Intergovernmental Tax Immunities, 58 Harv. L. Rev. 633 (1945).

[77] Helvering v. Gerhardt, 304 US 405, 420–21 (1938). The sixteenth amendment is not even mentioned in the opinion.

hope of confining the *Gerhardt* decision to state and local governmental employees engaged in "proprietary" functions.[78]

Recognizing that *Gerhardt* exposed state officers and employees to federal tax liability for past years in which they had believed themselves exempt, Congress enacted the Public Salary Tax Act of 1939, eliminating liability for past years but making clear that they were to be taxed for the future. The Act simultaneously consented to nondiscriminatory state income taxation of federal officers and employees for the future, but similarly relieved them of retroactive liability to the states for past years.[79]

It took nearly 50 additional years to establish Congress' power to tax interest paid by states and municipalities to bondholders. Every income tax since 1913 has explicitly exempted such interest from tax, except in limited circumstances.[80] Secure behind this statutory shield, the owners of state and municipal bonds have not needed constitutional protection. A decision on the issue was provoked, however, when Congress enacted a provision denying the exemption to bonds issued in bearer form.[81] Although the purpose of the provision was to force state and local governments to issue their bonds in registered form, not to collect tax from bondholders, the State of South Carolina challenged the provision in *South Carolina v. Baker*, arguing, among other things, that a tax on interest on an unregistered bond of a state or local government would violate the constitutional doctrine of intergovernmental immunity.[82]

The Court acknowledged that the challenged provision was inconsistent with that doctrine as expressed in *Pollock*. The Court rejected the argument that *Pollock* could be distinguished on the ground that it involved a law meant to tax interest on state and local obligations, whereas the provision challenged in *South Carolina v. Baker* would only apply if an issuer ignored Congress' wish that the bonds be registered: "The United

---

[78] Graves v. New York ex rel. O'Keefe, supra note 75, overruling Collector v. Day, 78 US (11 Wall.) 113 (1871). See also Beer v. CIR, 64 TC 879 (1975), appeal dismissed, 77-2 USTC ¶9491 (6th Cir. 1976), cert. denied, 431 US 938 (1977) (state judicial salaries subject to federal income tax).

[79] Ch. 59, §4, 58 Stat. 574 (codified at 4 USC §111 (1939)). See Shaw, The Public Salary Tax Act of 1939, 27 Calif. L. Rev. 705 (1939). In holding in *Gerhardt*, supra note 77, that state employees are not constitutionally immune to federal income taxation, the Court suggested that Congress could immunize federal employees from state taxation if it so desired. The Court later held in the *O'Keefe* case, supra note 78, that such immunity was not to be implied from congressional silence. See also US v. County of Fresno, 429 US 452 (1977) (California tax on possessory interests of federal employees in housing located in national forests upheld).

[80] Infra ¶15.2.

[81] The provision was enacted in 1982 as §103(j)(1), but became §149(a) when the statutes on state and local bonds were reshuffled in 1986.

[82] South Carolina v. Baker, 108 S. Ct. 1355 (1988).

States cannot convert an unconsititutional tax into a constitutional one simply by making the tax conditional."[83] After reviewing the decisions allowing Congress to tax salaries paid by state and local governments and a line of decisions allowing the states to tax income received by private parties under contracts with the federal government (including a decision that the immunity of interest on federal obligations from state taxation is statutory rather than constitutional), the Court held:

> [T]he rationale underlying *Pollock* and the general immunity for government contract income has been thoroughly repudiated by modern intergovernmental immunity caselaw. . . . We thus confirm that subsequent caselaw has overruled the holding in *Pollock* that state bond interest is immune from a nondiscriminatory federal tax. We see no constitutional reason for treating persons who receive interest on government bonds differently than persons who receive income from other types of contracts with the government, and no tenable rationale for distinguishing the costs imposed on States by a tax on state bond interest from the costs imposed by a tax on the income from any other state contract. . . . [T]he owners of state bonds have no constitutional entitlement not to pay taxes on income they earn from state bonds, and States have no constitutional entitlement to issue bonds paying lower interest rates than other issuers.[84]

In *Gerhardt*, the Court reserved judgment on the power of Congress to tax the Port of New York Authority itself, and the opinion in *South Carolina v. Baker* makes no reference to the possibility of federal taxation of the states themselves or their political subdivisions or agencies. From its inception in 1913, the federal income tax has exempted income accruing to states and their political subdivisions "from any public utility or the exercise of any essential governmental function."[85] Although this language by negative

---

[83] Id.

[84] Id.

[85] IRC §115(a), carrying forward without change §116(d) of the 1939 Code.

When recommending the bill that became the Revenue Act of 1913, the Senate Finance Committee said that the reference to public utilities was

> inserted to meet the cases of States, cities, towns, and other political subdivisions which are in receipt of income from sources other than that of taxation and about which question was raised that such incomes might be held subject to the tax. One State enjoys a revenue from the gross earnings of a railway company to which a land grant was made by the State years ago. A city under its contracts with the street railway companies is entitled to a certain per cent of the net earnings per annum. While it was regarded improbable under the provisions of the bill that these revenues to States and municipalities would be construed as taxable income, to foreclose all doubt the amendment is inserted expressly exempting such revenues from the operation of the act.

inference suggests that proprietary or "nonessential" functions and the activities of state-owned corporations may give rise to taxable income, the IRS evidently does not attempt to tax income of this type, perhaps because the once-popular distinction between "essential" and "proprietary" functions has been discredited for many years.[86] The IRS may also recognize that the concept of "income" is not easily applied to organizations that do not operate for profit,[87] especially to governmental agencies deriving most of their revenue from compulsory levies rather than from voluntary transactions with willing buyers.

Congress has, however, imposed tax on state and local governments in one area: Section 511(a)(2)(B) taxes the "unrelated business income" of state colleges and universities. The Court of Claims has rejected the claim that this provision imposes an unconstitutional burden on a governmental function, citing Supreme Court cases upholding a federal admissions tax on tickets to a state university's football games and a federal excise tax on mineral waters produced by a state-owned spa.[88] In the two latter cases, the Supreme Court held that receipts can be taxed if derived from activities that can be conducted by private persons and hence are not "uniquely capable of being earned only by a state." Despite these decisions, Congress has exhibited no desire to expand the coverage of the federal income tax to reach a

---

S. Rep. No. 80, 63d Cong., 1st Sess. (1913), reprinted in 1939-1 (Part 2) CB 3, 4–5.

In several rulings, the IRS has held income of government-owned utilities exempt from federal tax, without referring to §115(a). See Rev. Rul. 59-41, 1959-1 CB 13 (income of nonprofit corporation operating water system for city "not . . . gross income within the meaning of section 61"); Rev. Rul. 57-151, 1957-1 CB 64 (water supply, fire protection, and sewage disposal). For the status of a government-owned business corporation operating an electric system, see Omaha Pub. Power Dist. v. O'Malley, 232 F2d 805 (8th Cir.), cert. denied, 352 US 837 (1956).

[86] Massachusetts v. US, 435 US 444, 457–58 (1978); New York v. US, 326 US 572, 583, 586 (1946). But see Alfred Dunhill of London, Inc. v. Cuba, 425 US 682, 703 (1976) (continued use of distinction in applying sovereign immunity and act of state doctrines); National League of Cities v. Usery, 426 US 833 (1976) (references to "governmental functions" of states). See generally Wells & Hellerstein, The Governmental-Proprietary Distinction in Constitutional Law, 66 Va. L. Rev. 1073 (1980). The IRS attempted to delineate the essential-proprietary distinction with respect to state employees during the brief period when their salaries seemed to be exempted from federal taxation only if they were engaged in essential governmental functions. See Mim. 3838, 1938-1 CB 181, declared obsolete by Rev. Rul. 67-406, 1967-2 CB 420.

[87] See Bittker & Rahdert, The Exemption of Nonprofit Organizations From Federal Income Taxation, 85 Yale LJ 299, 307–16 (1976).

[88] Iowa State Univ. of Science & Technology v. US, 500 F2d 508 (Ct. Cl. 1974), relying on Allen v. Regents of the Univ. Sys. of Ga., 304 US 439 (1938), and New York v. US, 326 US 572 (1946).

wider range of state and local governmental activities.[89]

¶1.2.9 Taxation of American Indians and Indian Tribes

As quasi-sovereign bodies, Indian tribes are not taxable entities.[90] Section 7871, added in 1982, requires that an Indian tribal government be treated for several purposes as though it were a state.[91] For example, interest on bonds issued by a tribal government to finance essential government functions is exempt from tax under §103(a)—the provision exempting interest on obligations of state and local governments.[92] Expenses incurred in lobbying a tribal government are deductible subject to the same limitations as expenses of lobbying state government.[93] Taxes levied by tribal governments are deductible under §164 as though they were state taxes.[94] Gifts and bequests to tribal governments qualify for the income, estate, and gift tax charitable deductions under the rules for gifts and bequests to states.[95]

Individual Indians, however, "are citizens and . . . in ordinary affairs of life, not governed by treaties or remedial legislation, they are subject to the payment of income taxes as are other citizens."[96] Thus, Indians must

---

[89] See also City of Woodway v. US, 681 F2d 975 (5th Cir. 1982) (city liable as transferee for tax on gain recognized by business corporation on making liquidating distribution to city; §115(a)(1) inapplicable because income "accrued" to the corporation, not the city); Troy State Univ. v. CIR, 62 TC 493 (1974) (same where state university received such a liquidating distribution); City of Bethel v. US, 594 F2d 1301 (9th Cir. 1979).

[90] Rev. Rul. 67-284, 1967-2 CB 55. See also Rev. Rul. 81-295, 1981-2 CB 15 (chartered Indian tribal corporation has same tax status as Indian tribe and is not taxable on income from activities on reservation). Section 115, which exempts state and local governments from tax, does not apply to Indian tribes, however, because §115 is not among the provisions as to which a tribe is treated as a state under §7871, which is described below in the text accompanying notes 91–96. See generally Cohen, Handbook of Federal Indian Law 265–67 (U. of New Mexico Press, rev. ed. 1971); Price, Law and the American Indian (Bobbs-Merrill 1973); Fiske & Wilson, Federal Taxation of Indian Income From Restricted Indian Lands, 10 Land & Water L. Rev. 63 (1975).

[91] Also, a subdivision of a tribal government is treated as a political subdivision of a state if it "has been delegated the right to exercise one or more of the substantial governmental functions of the Indian tribal government." IRC §7871(d).

[92] IRC §§7871(a)(4), (c). See infra ¶15.2 for §103(a).

[93] IRC §§162(e), 7871(a)(6)(B). See infra ¶20.3.7 for §162(e).

[94] IRC §7871(a)(3). See infra ¶32.1 for §164.

[95] IRC §7871(a)(1). For the charitable deductions, see infra ¶35.1 (income tax), ¶130.1 (estate tax).

[96] Squire v. Capoeman, 351 US 1, 6 (1956). See generally Washoe Tribe v. US, 1979-2 USTC ¶9718 (D. Nev. 1979) (not officially reported) (seizure of Indian tribe's funds to pay federal unemployment taxes on wages paid to member-employees upheld).

include in gross income their pro rata shares of tribal income when it is distributed to or constructively received by them, as well as other types of income, unless an exemption is granted by a treaty or agreement with their tribe or by an act of Congress dealing with Indian affairs. Income derived by individual Indians from restricted allotted land, held in trust by the United States, is subject to numerous exemptions from taxation based on statute or treaty. Some exemptions are general in application;[97] others are limited to particular tribes or types of income;[98] and the tax status of some receipts is governed by a combination of treaties, statutes, and executive orders.[99]

In general, Indian lands are held in three basic forms: (1) restricted lands allotted to individual Indians, subject to trust supervision by the United States; (2) tribal lands to which tribal members have rights of possession or use, also subject to federal restrictions and supervision; and (3) allocated lands held in fee by the allottee or his successor that are no longer subject to restrictions. Restricted Indian lands owned by individual allottees or held by or for particular tribes cannot be sold, leased, or otherwise disposed of without the approval of the United States. While these restrictions are in force, the individual Indian is considered a "noncompetent" ward of the United States—a term referring to restrictions on the Indian's legal power to manage his property, not to mental capacity. Upon termination of the trust, however, Indian lands can usually be freely conveyed or encumbered.

In the seminal case of *Squire v. Capoeman*, involving income earned from land restricted by the General Allotment Act, the Supreme Court held that a noncompetent Indian's income from his restricted allotment was not taxable, on the theory that preservation of the income derived from the trust property was inherent in the allotment system, which was designed to protect the Indian's interest until termination of the trust restrictions.[100]

---

[97] See Act of Feb. 8, 1887, Ch. 119, 24 Stat. 388 (General Allotment Act); Act of June 18, 1934, Ch. 576, 48 Stat. 984 (Indian Reorganization Act).

[98] See, e.g., Act of June 28, 1906, Pub. L. No. 321, 34 Stat. 539 (Osage Allotment Act); Act of Sept. 21, 1959, Pub. L. No. 86-322, 73 Stat. 592 (Catawba Indians of South Carolina).

[99] See, e.g., Squire v. Capoeman, supra note 96 ("we cannot agree that taxability . . . is unaffected by the treaty, the trust patent or the Allotment Act"); Stevens v. CIR, 452 F2d 741 (9th Cir. 1971) (all applicable legislation must be construed in pari materia). Cf. US v. Hallam, 304 F2d 620 (10th Cir. 1962) (construing General Allotment Act and certain other legislation); Jourdain v. CIR, 71 TC 980 (1979) (treaty exempting Indians from "molestation from the United States" does not create tax immunity).

[100] Squire v. Capoeman, supra note 96 (income from timber produced by restricted land). In so holding, the Court distinguished Superintendent of Five Civilized Tribes v. CIR, 295 US 418 (1935), which ruled that restraints on the alienation

Applying the *Capoeman* rationale, later courts have exempted income derived from the exploitation of Indian lands as well as tribal income held in trust, where the terms of the applicable statute or treaty could reasonably be construed to confer an exemption. The *Capoeman* shield has provided immunity, for example, for income attributable to mining, farming, rental of property, proceeds from the sale of crops or livestock raised on restricted land, and income from the sale of restricted land while title is held by the government.[101]

On the other hand, on the theory that preservation of the trust status of Indian land does not require sheltering tangential receipts from taxation, income derived from the reinvestment of exempt income, from the exploitation of restricted land leased from other Indians, or from activities conducted on tribal land under a license or permit is not exempt.[102] Moreover, wages, salaries, and other income from personal services, although performed on restricted tribal lands, are taxable, as is investment income from assets other than restricted Indian lands.[103] The outer limits of the *Capoeman* rationale are difficult to define, however, and the extent to

---

of Indian land did not imply tax exemption, on the ground that it involved income from investing surplus income from restricted land ("reinvestment income") rather than income derived directly from the restricted property.

[101] Squire v. Capoeman, 351 US 1, 6 (1956) (sale of timber); Stevens v. CIR, supra note 99 (farming and ranching); US v. Daney, 370 F2d 791 (10th Cir. 1966) (bonuses for execution of oil and gas leases); US v. Hallam, supra note 99 (land rentals and mineral royalties); Big Eagle v. US, 300 F2d 765 (Ct. Cl. 1962) (noncompetent Indian's share of tribal royalty income from mineral deposits); Rev. Rul. 74-13, 1974-1 CB 14 (income from restricted land purchased by Secretary of Interior and held in trust); Rev. Rul. 70-116, 1970-1 CB 11, clarified by Rev. Rul. 77-78, 1977-1 CB 12 (headright income derived from tribal mineral interests and held in trust by United States); Rev. Rul. 67-284, 1967-2 CB 55 (proceeds of sale of allotted land while fee title held by the government).

[102] Superintendent of Five Civilized Tribes v. CIR, supra note 100 (reinvestment income); Anderson v. US, 845 F2d 206 (9th Cir. 1988) (distribution to individual Indians of rents received by tribe under lease of unallotted land held in trust for tribe); US v. Anderson, 625 F2d 910 (9th Cir. 1980) (income from cattle ranching on tribal land); Critzer v. US, 597 F2d 708 (Ct. Cl. 1979) (income from motel and restaurant operated on restricted land); Holt v. US, 364 F2d 38 (8th Cir. 1966), cert. denied, 386 US 931 (1967) (income from grazing on leased tribal lands); Hoptowit v. CIR, 78 TC 137 (1982), aff'd without consideration of this issue, 709 F2d 564 (9th Cir. 1983) (income on sales in shop on reservation); Strom v. CIR, 6 TC 621 (1946), aff'd per curiam, 158 F2d 520 (9th Cir. 1947) (income from commercial fishing business conducted on unassigned tribal lands).

[103] Hoptowit v. CIR, 709 F2d 564 (9th Cir. 1983) (per diem payments to noncompetent Indian for service on Tribal Council); Fry v. US, 557 F2d 646 (9th Cir. 1977) (logging subcontractor taxable on income earned on tribal lands); CIR v. Walker, 326 F2d 261 (9th Cir. 1964) (employee of tribe taxable on his salary); Lafontaine v. CIR, 34 TCM (CCH) 742 (1975), aff'd per curiam, 553 F2d 382 (8th Cir. 1976) (wages earned on tribal lands taxable).

which income from improvements on exempt land is exempt as "directly derived" from the land thus is far from clear.[104]

Finally, the income tax status of an Indian with a certificate of competency is indistinguishable from that of any other citizen, and income attributable to formerly restricted Indian lands as well as to other sources is taxable under principles applicable to the populace generally.[105]

---

[104] See Stevens v. CIR, 452 F2d 741 (9th Cir. 1971) (relaxation of allotment system by Indian Reorganization Act of 1934 was not intended to reduce benefits of tax exemption).

[105] Choteau v. Burnet, 283 US 691 (1931); Rev. Rul. 67-284, 1967-2 CB 55.

CHAPTER

2

The Basic Structure of the Federal Income Tax

¶2.1. THE INCOME TAX BASE

¶2.1.1 Introductory

The definition of "income" enunciated by the Supreme Court in the early cases on the constitutionality of the federal income tax—"Income may be defined as the gain derived from capital, from labor, or from both combined"[1]—influenced the development of today's tax law in important ways,[2] but the base on which the tax is imposed is much more elaborately defined by the Internal Revenue Code. The statutory base is "taxable income," a term whose content not only reflects accounting principles and economic concepts[3] but also embodies numerous legislative judgments about fairness, administrative convenience, and the desirability of encouraging or not impeding a host of social, personal, and business activities.

For individuals, the major steps in computing taxable income are:

1. Gross income
2. Minus: Deductions allowed by §62 (most business deductions)
3. Equals: Adjusted gross income (AGI)
4. Minus: Itemized deductions (personal, investment, and business deductions not listed in §62) or standard deduction
5. Minus: Personal and dependency exemptions
7. Equals: Taxable income[4]

The statutory scheme is simpler for corporations:

1. Gross income
2. Minus: Deductions
3. Equals: Taxable income[5]

Although partnerships are not taxed as entities, they are required to compute taxable income (or loss) under rules set out in §703 and to report this amount on an information return that allocates to each partner his distributive share of the firm's income and loss. Each partner's distributive share is carried over to his return, where it is aggregated with other income in computing the partner's taxable income.[6]

¶2.1.2 Gross Income

Section 61(a) defines "gross income" as follows:

> Except as otherwise provided in this subtitle, gross income means all income from whatever source derived, including (but not limited to) the following items:

---

[1] Supra ¶1.2.4.
[2] See, e.g., infra ¶5.2 (realization concept), ¶5.4 ("gain").
[3] For definitions of economic income, see infra ¶3.1.1.
[4] The principal relevant statutory provisions are §61 (gross income), §62 (adjusted gross income), and §63 (taxable income).
[5] IRC §§61, 63(a).
[6] Infra ¶86.2.1.

(1) Compensations for services, including fees, commissions, fringe benefits, and similar items;
(2) Gross income derived from business;
(3) Gains derived from dealings in property;
(4) Interest;
(5) Rents;
(6) Royalties;
(7) Dividends;
(8) Alimony and separate maintenance payments;
(9) Annuities;
(10) Income from life insurance and endowment contracts;
(11) Pensions;
(12) Income from discharge of indebtedness;
(13) Distributive share of partnership gross income;
(14) Income in respect of a decedent; and
(15) Income from an interest in an estate or trust.

The present §61(a) has remained substantially unchanged since 1954.[7] The corresponding provision of the Internal Revenue Code of 1939 was somewhat more detailed. The Senate Finance Committee explained the 1954 change in phraseology as follows:

[Section 61(a) of the 1954 Code] corresponds to section 22(a) of the 1939 Code. While the language in existing section 22(a) has been simplified, the all-inclusive nature of statutory gross income has not been affected thereby. Section 61(a) [1954 Code] is as broad in scope as section 22(a).

Section 61(a) provides that gross income includes "all income from whatever source derived." This definition is based upon the sixteenth amendment and the word "income" is used as in section 22(a) in its constitutional sense. It is not intended to change the concept of income that obtains under section 22(a). Therefore, although the section 22(a) phrase "in whatever form paid" has been eliminated, statutory gross income will continue to include income realized in any form. . . .

After the general definition there has been included, for purposes of illustration, an enumeration of fifteen of the more common items constituting gross income. It is made clear, however, that gross income is not limited to those items enumerated. Thus, an item not named specifically in paragraphs (1) through (15) of section 61(a) will nevertheless constitute gross income if it falls within the general definition in

---

[7] The only change has been the addition in 1984 of the words "fringe benefits" in §61(a)(1).

section 61(a).[8]

The sparse language of §61(a) is slightly augmented by §§71–89, providing that a curiously mixed group of items (alimony, annuities, and some social security benefits, for example) is includable in gross income.

For many taxpayers, the determination of gross income is simple. Wage earners and salaried employees, for example, often have no gross income apart from their wages and salaries. For other taxpayers, however, the language of §61(a) is a deceptively simple starting point because it fails to mention a large number of preliminary decisions that determine whether particular transactions create gross income.[9] Thus, a taxpayer who borrows money has to determine whether the funds are embraced by the reference in §61(a) to "income from whatever source derived"; for reasons explained later,[10] they are not, but §61(a) sheds no light on this threshold question. Similarly, a merchant or manufacturer who sells $100,000 worth of merchandise in a given year does not have $100,000 of "gross income from business" within the meaning of §61(a)(2), but a lesser amount determined by subtracting the cost of goods sold from the gross receipts. Calculation of the company's cost of goods sold is, in turn, a complex process because it requires a determination of the volume and value of the goods on hand at the beginning and end of the taxable year and embraces not merely the amount paid for the merchandise or raw materials but also (in the case of a manufacturer) an appropriate fraction of overhead and other expenses.[11]

Section 61(a) is similarly silent on the subject of the rental value of owner-occupied dwellings. Although taxpayers who own their own homes are not taxed on the rent that they would have to pay if they were tenants, the exclusion of this economic value from the owner-occupant's gross income is sanctioned by long-standing practice rather than explicit statutory provision.[12]

Many other preliminary computations and adjustments are foreshadowed by §61(a)'s introductory clause—"except as otherwise provided in this subtitle." The principal statutory exclusions from gross income are described in §§101–134, which exclude such familiar receipts as gifts, bequests, life insurance proceeds, interest on state and municipal bonds, and

---

[8] S. Rep. No. 1622, 83d Cong., 2d Sess. 168 (1954); see also H.R. Rep. No. 1337, 83d Cong., 2d Sess. A18 (1954).

[9] See also §6501(e)(1)(A)(i) (gross income specially defined for purposes of extended statute of limitations).

[10] As explained below in ¶6.4.1, the borrowing of funds does not create income, but if the debt is subsequently cancelled, the debtor may have to report the resulting gain at that time.

[11] Infra ¶105.4.

[12] Infra ¶5.3.3.

scholarships.[13] In some instances, these items are excluded in their entirety; in others, only a portion is excluded and the balance is subject to tax; in still others, the exclusion is temporary and will be counterbalanced by inclusion of the amount (or some other adjustment) in a later year, probably resulting in an increased tax bill at that time.

Aside from the complexities entailed by these preliminary decisions about the composition of gross income, the exclusion of so many receipts of economic value means that gross income (and hence taxable income) may convey a wholly inaccurate impression of the taxpayer's financial status. Taxpayers with large fortunes invested in state and municipal bonds, for example, have no gross income, unless they engage in transactions other than their bond investments. Many taxpayers, however, seldom if ever receive excluded items; for them, gross income as defined by §61(a) may correspond very closely to what the layman, accountant, or economist would regard as their total income.

¶2.1.3 Adjusted Gross Income

AGI is an individual taxpayer's gross income, less the deductions specified by §62(a). Section 62(a) does not create any deductions, but simply determines whether deductions allowed by other provisions are to be deducted from gross income in computing AGI, or from AGI in computing taxable income. The principal §62(a) deductions are the following:

1. Deductions attributable to a trade or business of the taxpayer,[14] unless the business consists of the performance of services as an employee.
2. Deductions related to property held for the production of rents and royalties, such as taxes, repairs, and depreciation.
3. Contributions by self-employed individuals and owner-employees to qualified pension plans, and deductible contributions to individual retirement accounts (IRAs).[15]
4. Alimony payments, which are deductible under §62(a)(10) because the other spouse is taxed on receiving them. The payments are, in effect, treated as though they belonged to the payee rather than to the payor.[16]

---

[13] Infra Chs. 10–16.

[14] See Reg. §1.62-1(d) (expenses "must be those directly, and not those merely remotely, connected with the conduct of a trade or business").

[15] IRC §62(a)(6), (7). See infra ¶62.2 for plans for self employed persons and ¶62.5 for IRAs.

[16] Before 1977, alimony payments were classified as itemized deductions; for the change, see infra ¶77.3.

Items listed in §62(a) are sometimes described as "above the line" deductions because they are subtracted from gross income in reaching AGI; all other deductions are taken "below the line" because they are subtracted from AGI in computing taxable income.

Adjusted gross income is intended, roughly speaking, to reflect the amount available to an individual taxpayer to pay for food, lodging, shelter, and other elements of the cost of living.[17] This measure of the taxpayer's capacity to defray the cost of living serves two major purposes.

First, under §63 taxpayers are entitled to a standard deduction if they forgo so-called itemized deductions—the deductions not described in §62(a) (principally, interest, taxes, medical expenses, and charitable contributions).[18] The standard deduction serves to simplify the tax return when a taxpayer's itemized deductions are only a modest fraction of the amount available for the taxpayer's living expenses; conversely, taxpayers with above-normal amounts of such items take the itemized deductions in lieu of the standard deduction. The deductions taken in computing AGI, however, are unaffected by this choice; they are allowed whether the taxpayer takes the standard deduction or itemized deductions.

Second, a few deductions are linked to the taxpayer's adjusted gross income. In authorizing the deduction for medical expenses, for example, Congress wished to permit unusually heavy expenses to be deducted but not those that are about average (or less than average) for the taxpayer's income class.[19] This objective is accomplished by providing that medical expenses may be deducted only if, and to the extent that, they exceed a specified percentage of the taxpayer's income. Similarly, a floor on miscellaneous itemized deductions (primarily, employee business expenses and investment expenses) is imposed to limit these deductions to taxpayers that incur substantially more than the normal amounts of these items.[20] On the other hand, in authorizing charitable contributions to be deducted, Congress imposed a ceiling, related to the taxpayer's disposable income, so that contributions are deductible only up to that limit.[21] Also, a tax credit for child care expenses incurred in connection with a parent's job is calculated by a

---

[17] When computing the "effective rate" of tax, as distinguished from the statutory or nominal rate, tax analysts usually use AGI, although they often expand it to take account of items that are omitted from gross income. See infra ¶3.4.1; see also Joint Comm. on Tax'n, 94th Cong., 2d Sess., General Explanation of Tax Reform Act of 1976, reprinted in 1976-3 CB (Vol. 2) 653. The use of AGI as the starting point implies that while AGI is not an entirely satisfactory measure of tax-paying capacity, it is better than the major statutory alternatives, gross income and taxable income.

[18] See infra ¶30.5 for the standard deduction.

[19] Infra ¶36.1.1.

[20] See infra ¶30.4.

[21] Infra ¶35.3.1.

formula that reduces the credit when income exceeds a specified amount.[22] These provisions presuppose a yardstick for measuring the amount of income at the taxpayer's disposal for normal living expenses. Adjusted gross income is that yardstick.

Gross income is an inadequate measure of disposable income for these purposes because it must be used to meet the taxpayer's ordinary business expenses as well as the personal expenses of daily life. A physician whose gross income from fees is $200,000 and who has to pay out $80,000 for rent, salaries to a nurse and receptionist, medical supplies, accounting fees, and similar office expenses, for example, has only $120,000 left for personal expenses. For this reason, §62(a)(1) allows business expenses to be deducted in determining AGI. Similarly, because a landlord's disposable income from rents is diminished by maintenance expenses, interest, and taxes, expenses attributable to property held for rent are also allowed in computing AGI.[23]

Contributions by self-employed individuals and owner-employees to qualified pension plans are deductible above-the-line under §62(a)(6) in order to put these persons on a plane of relative equality with ordinary employees, who exclude from gross income (and hence from AGI) amounts contributed by their employers to qualified pension plans. The deduction allowed by §62(a)(7) for some contributions to IRAs serves a similar purpose. Finally, §62(a) permits deductible losses on sales and exchanges of property and several miscellaneous items to be deducted from gross income, again for the purpose of causing AGI to more accurately reflect taxpayers' disposable income.

As a general rule, §62(a)(1) permits all deductions attributable to the taxpayer's trade or business to be subtracted out in computing AGI, but employees are singled out by §62(a)(2) for more restrictive treatment. Business expenses paid or incurred by a taxpayer "in connection with the performance . . . of services as an employee" are usually deductible in determining AGI only if the expenses are covered by a reimbursement arrangement with the employer.[24] Expenses of actors and other performing

---

[22] Infra ¶37.1.

[23] IRC §62(a)(4).

[24] For the requirement of a reimbursement arrangement, see Rev. Rul. 55-288, 1955-1 CB 257 (arrangement must be specific); Moorman v. CIR, 26 TC 666 (1956) ("reimbursed expenses" deducted from salesman's commissions not qualified); infra ¶¶20.2.14, 21.2.4, and 21.4.3. See also Butchko v. CIR, 37 TCM (CCH) 894 (1978) (shortages paid by racetrack teller to employer are employee business expenses deductible only as itemized deductions). Prior to 1986, §62 deductions were also allowed for employee business expenses incurred for travel (including meals and lodging) while away from home, transportation expenses, and expenses incurred by an "outside salesman" engaged in soliciting business for the employer away from his place of business. IRC §62(2) (before amendment in 1986). For the "away from home" principle, see infra ¶21.1.2. For the "outside salesman" concept, see Lovern

artists are sometimes treated more liberally, but this liberalization only applies when several restrictive criteria are met.[25] Employee business expenses not meeting these tests can be deducted as itemized deductions to the extent they exceed the floor on miscellaneous itemized deductions (2 percent of AGI); even this is only permitted for taxpayers electing to itemize deductions—an election that is worthwhile only if itemized deductions exceed the standard deduction.[26]

Why are most employee business expenses disregarded in converting gross income into AGI? The answer lies in the simplifying function meant to be served by the standard deduction and the floor on miscellaneous itemized deductions. The standard deduction is intended to replace substantially all deductions for the vast majority of taxpayers whose expenditures are sufficiently close to the norm that a standardized allowance can reasonably be substituted for an itemization of particular expenses. The floor on miscellaneous itemized deductions, similarly, is intended to eliminate itemization for employee business expenses and a few other items, except where these expenses are out of the ordinary. Millions of taxpayers have small amounts of employee business expense, but few have enough of these expenses to warrant the costs of itemization. If employee business expenses were fully deductible above the line, these millions would find it advantageous to take the deduction, regardless of how small the expenses were or how difficult they were for the IRS to audit. Because this would vitiate the policy to eliminate the recordkeeping and audit costs of deductions for the vast generality of taxpayers, Congress subjected employee business expenses to the limitations for itemized deductions.[27] This decision, however, has placed great strain on the boundary between employees and independent contractors, since taxpayers fitting into the latter category can deduct all business expenses in computing AGI.[28]

---

v. CIR, 37 TCM (CCH) 1849-41 (1978) (dock representative of stevedoring firm not a salesman); Novak v. CIR, 51 TC 7 (1968) (securities salesman not an *outside* salesman); Rev. Rul. 58-175, 1958-1 CB 28 (industrial insurance agents who collect premiums not salesmen).

[25] An individual qualifies for this treatment if (1) he was employed as a performing artist by at least two employers during the taxable year, (2) deductible expenses incurred in this employment exceed 10 percent of pay, and (3) AGI (determined without unreimbursed employee business expenses) does not exceed $16,000. IRC §62(a)(2)(B), (b). In applying the two employer rule, an employer is counted only if at least $200 is received from the employer for performing arts services during the year. IRC §62(b)(2). If the taxpayer is married, this rule applies only if a joint return is filed and the return shows AGI of $16,000 or less. IRC §62(b)(3).

[26] See infra ¶30.5.1.

[27] Staff of Joint Comm. on Tax'n, 99th Cong., 2d Sess., General Explanation of the Tax Reform Act of 1986, at 78–79 (1987).

[28] For the distinction between common-law employees and independent contractors, see infra ¶111.4.2. (re wage withholding).

¶2.1.4 Taxable Income

Taxable income is the base to which the statutory rates are applied.[29] It is defined by §63(a) as the excess of gross income over all allowable deductions. For individuals, it is gross income reduced by the deductions described in §62(a), further reduced by either the standard deduction or the taxpayer's itemized deductions, and reduced still further by the personal and dependency exemptions. A taxpayer's tax liability is computed by applying the rates to taxable income, and reducing the resulting amounts by any allowable credits.

Because taxable income is the bottom line (or, nearly so, if the taxpayer has credits), it is the ultimate focus of both the computations under present law and proposals for reform. Because it is a residual figure, however, nearly all of the talk is about getting there, and little needs to be said about the concept itself.

¶2.2 PROGRESSION IN THE RATE SCHEDULES

Progression in personal income tax rates is a long-established, although persistently controversial,[1] feature of the federal income tax. The nominal rates of progression, which ran as high as 90 percent during the 1940s and 1950s and as high as 70 percent as recently as 1981, have been greatly reduced, however, most markedly by the Tax Reform Act of 1986.[2] For 1988 and succeeding years, there are two rates, 15 and 28 percent. For married individuals filing jointly, for example, the lower rate applies to the first $29,750 of taxable income, and the remainder is taxed at the higher rate.[3] The higher rate applies to taxable income in excess of $17,850 for unmarried individuals and $23,900 for unmarried heads of households.

The flattening of the rates is accentuated by a phasing out of the benefit of the 15 percent rate for higher income taxpayers.[4] The phase-out begins when taxable income reaches $71,900 on a joint return, $43,150 for an unmarried person, or $61,650 for an unmarried head of household. The phase-out works by increasing tax liability by 5 percent of the amount by which taxable income exceeds the starting point for the phase-out. If taxable income on a joint return is $100,000, for example, the added tax is $1,405 (5 percent of the excess of $100,000 over $71,900). The phase-out of the 15

---

[29] IRC §1 (individuals, estates, and trusts), §11 (corporations). See supra ¶2.1.1.
[1] For discussion of the policy underpinnings of progression, see infra ¶3.5.3.
[2] For a short history of progression in federal income tax rates, see supra ¶1.1.7.
[3] IRC §1(a). The rate brackets will be adjusted for inflation for 1989 and succeeding years. IRC §1(f). A special rate schedule is provided for 1987 with rates ranging from 11 to 38.5 percent. IRC §1(h).
[4] IRC §1(g).

percent rate stops when the added tax equals 13 percent of the amount initially taxed at 15 percent (that is, on a joint return, when the added tax is 13 percent of $29,750). On a joint return, the phase-out ends when taxable income equals $149,250 (5 percent of the excess of $149,250 over $71,900 is $3,867.50, which is also 13 percent of $29,750). For taxpayers whose income is within the phase-out range, the rule operates like a third rate bracket of 33 percent because each additional dollar of taxable income increases tax liability by 33 cents (28 cents of tax at the 28 percent rate plus a 5 cent giveback of the benefit of the 15 percent rate). When the stopping point is reached, however, tax liability (including the added tax under the phase-out rule) is a flat 28 percent of taxable income.[5]

Since the statutory rates are marginal rates, applicable to each additional increment to the taxpayer's taxable income, the average rate for a taxpayer whose income does not reach the top of the phase-out range is always lower than the marginal rate. Computations of so-called effective rates—based on economic income rather than taxable income—invariably show that progression's bark is worse than its bite.[6]

The stated purpose of the lowering of the rates in 1986 was not to greatly limit progressivity but rather to conform effective rates more closely to the statutory rates by broadening the base to which the statutory rates are applied.[7] A distribution of the tax burden among income classes similar to that of prior law, in other words, was meant to be achieved by eliminating exclusions, deductions, and other allowances utilized primarily by more affluent taxpayers, and subjecting this expanded taxable income to lower rates. Even the architects of the 1986 legislation would not contend that taxable income is now so nearly equated with economic income that the nominal progression shown in the rate schedules will precisely match the progression in effective rates. The gap, however, has surely been narrowed.

A hoped for consequence of the lowering of the highest marginal rate is a lessening of the incentives for taxpayers to shift income from high brackets to low ones by a variety of self-help strategies. Under prior law, possibilities for income shifting elicited the ingenuity and imagination of countless

---

[5] When the benefit of the 15 percent rate has been phased out, the rule goes on to phase out the benefit of the personal exemptions. This is accomplished by providing that the cap on the added tax under the phase-out rule is the sum of (1) 13 percent of the amount initially taxed at 15 percent and (2) 28 percent of the personal exemptions claimed on the return. IRC §1(g). For a married couple filing jointly with two dependent children, for example, the cap in 1988 is $6,052, and the benefits of the 15 percent rate and personal exemptions are fully recaptured if income equals or exceeds $192,930. When this limit is reached, tax liability (including the phase-out tax) is 28 percent of taxable income computed without the personal exemptions.

[6] Infra ¶3.4.1.

[7] Staff of Joint Comm. on Tax'n, 99th Cong., 2d Sess., General Explanation of the Tax Reform Act of 1986, at 6–11 (1987).

taxpayers, aided and abetted by regiments of lay and professional advisers. For its part, the IRS has done what it could to frustrate the resulting tax-avoidance devices and to contain the damage when it could not defeat them. The intensity of this struggle has probably been lessened by the 1986 changes, but the struggle will surely go on as long as the law provides more than one marginal rate.

Shifting devices are numerous and diverse, but, historically, most have fit into four categories: (1) the deferral of income from high-income years to years in which the taxpayer expects to have less income and, hence, to be subject to lower marginal tax rates on the transferred income, (2) the conduct of closely held enterprises by corporations rather than by proprietorships or partnerships, (3) the conversion of amounts that would be taxed as ordinary income if received in due course into long-term capital gains, and (4) the transfer of income from high-income individuals to children or other members of the same family or to related entities such as trusts.

The third of these techniques—conversion of ordinary income into capital gains—was neutralized by the repeal in 1986 of the lower rates previously applied to long-term capital gains.[8] The effectiveness of the others has been reduced but not eliminated. These efforts to escape the full impact of progression, which are examined in detail throughout this treatise, are discussed briefly below:

1. *Transfer of income from high- to low-income years.* Taxpayers whose income is currently higher than it is expected to be in later years (e.g., business executives and physicians during their peak years) are often able to shift income from years when it is earned until their retirement years, when income will be lower. For employees and self-employed persons, the most common devices accomplishing this result are qualified pension and profit-sharing plans. Under these, they are not taxed on the employer's contributions when made, even if their rights are vested and nonforfeitable, or on the investment income generated by these contributions. They are taxed, instead, only when the cash or other benefits are paid to them, ordinarily many years later.[9]

These deferred compensation plans must comply with elaborate statutory rules, but less formal arrangements are also feasible. An employment contract, for example, may provide for a stipulated current salary plus additional amounts to be paid by the employer for an extended period after the employee's retirement. Employees using the cash receipts and disbursements method of accounting, which is virtually universal for individual taxpayers, are not required to report the value of the employer's promise to

---

[8] See infra ¶50.1.
[9] See infra ¶61.1.1.

pay the deferred compensation until it comes due under the contract.[10] An author, actor, or other taxpayer who expects to earn an unusually large amount if a book, play, motion picture, or other venture is a smashing success can often arrange in advance with the publisher or producer to receive the earnings in installments over a period of years rather than in a lump sum, thus pushing into lower tax brackets an amount that would otherwise be taxed at the top rate.[11] A similar device is the arrangement often employed by state lotteries to pay the winner an annual sum for many years or life rather than the equivalent amount in a single year.

On the other hand, taxpayers sometimes employ devices to shift income from high- to low-income years even if they will thereby speed up, rather than defer, the tax liability. A taxpayer with a large current loss, for example, may take steps to accelerate income that would otherwise not be received until later years (e.g., by pressing customers to pay in advance), so that the income can be reported immediately and be partly or wholly offset by the loss.

The flattening of the rate structure in 1986 lessened incentives to shift income from year to year. The incentive is still powerful for a taxpayer who can shift income from a year in which income is taxed at the top rate to a loss year when the rate is effectively zero. In other situations, however, the lowering of the income level at which the top rate takes effect makes it unlikely that a shift from a high-income year to a low-income year will save much tax. For a married executive who expects an annual retirement income of at least $29,750, for example, compensation income will be taxed at 28 percent whether it is taken in cash as earned or deferred until retirement.[12]

This is not to say that tax incentives to defer income have been eliminated. If a taxpayer's financial position is otherwise unaffected, a delay in the imposition of a tax reduces the present value of the tax. (An obligation

---

[10] See infra ¶60.2.

[11] See infra ¶60.2.1.

[12] A tax savings of five percentage points can be realized if income is shifted from a salaried year in which taxable income is in the range in which the benefits of the 15 percent rate and personal exemptions are phased out ($71,900 to something in excess of $149,250 for a married couple) to a retirement year in which taxable income (including the shifted income) is below that range. This is so because each dollar less of taxable income in the phase-out range saves 33 cents (the normal 28 percent plus 5 cents of give back), whereas an added dollar of taxable income when income is below the phase-out range only costs 28 cents in tax. See supra text accompanying notes 4–5. Conversely, a five percentage point increase in tax results if income is shifted from a year when taxable income is above the phase-out range to a year in which it is within that range. Furthermore, a person contemplating a shifting of income to a later year must contemplate the possibility that Congress might raise the rates by the time that year arrives. But see infra note 13.

to pay a dollar tomorrow is less burdensome than an obligation to pay a dollar today because in the former case the obligor can invest the dollar for a day and keep the investment earnings.) A delay in a tax thus increases the present value of what the taxpayer keeps after taxes.[13] The effect of the flattening of the rates, in other words, is that the question of income today versus income tomorrow now depends more on the timing of the tax obligation than the marginal rates at which the income will be taxed.

2. *Use of corporation to conduct closely held business.* The transfer of family businesses to closely held corporations, which may or may not pay salaries to their shareholder-employees, is a common income-splitting device, which is examined later in this chapter.[14]

3. *Transfer of income from high- to low-income members of the same family or to related entities.* One of the earliest, most frequently litigated, and most elaborately regulated ways to escape the impact of progression is "income splitting,"i.e., the shifting of income from high-income taxpayers to low-income members of the same family or to related corporations or trusts that are taxed at lower rates. The classic case is a gift of marketable securities, rental real estate, or other income-producing property in trust for the taxpayer's children or grandchildren. If the donor retains no right to get the property back, no control over beneficial enjoyment of the income, and no administrative controls over the trust corpus, the income will be taxable to the beneficiaries or the fiduciary rather than to the donor.[15]

---

[13] Assume an employer contributes $1,000 for employee *A* to a pension plan and pays $1,000 of salary to employee *B*, who pays $280 of tax on the income and sets aside the remaining $720 for retirement. Assume further that the pension plan and *B* each invest in bonds yielding 10 percent and that *A* and *B* both withdraw their retirement savings after 20 years. The $1,000 held for *A* in the pension plan will grow to $6,727 because neither the $1,000 nor the earnings on it is diminished by taxes. *A*, however, pays a tax on his pension distribution of $1,884 (28 percent of $6,727), and is left with $4,843 after taxes. *B*, in contrast, loses in tax $280 of the original $1,000 and 28 percent of the annual return on his investment. As a consequence, his nest egg builds up to only $2,892.

If *B* took his pay in cash believing that Congress will surely raise tax rates by the time he retires, he likely made a bad choice even if his political judgment is perfect. Assume *A* has the misfortune of withdrawing his pension in a year in which Congress decides to hike the highest rate to 50 percent. After taxes, he still has nearly $500 more than *B* ($3,364 versus $2,892). Neither should *B* take great comfort in his ability to chose winning investments. If *B* makes 10 percent on his investments, for example, *A* will come out ahead so long as the pension trust earns at least 7.2 percent on its investments.

[14] Infra ¶2.5.

[15] These results may follow even if the donor does not relinquish all incidents of ownership, provided the retained rights satisfy the intricate rules laid down by §§671–77. See infra ¶80.1.1.

Under deeply entrenched principles, wage earners and salaried employees cannot escape tax liability on their earned income by transferring to children or other donees the right to collect the fruits of their labor.[16] If personal services are mingled with capital in the production of income, however, as in the case of proprietorships, partnerships, and family corporations, it is often feasible to shift income from high-income members of the family to their low-income children or other donees by transferring interests in the family enterprise, subject to limitations discussed elsewhere.[17]

Congress, in drafting the Tax Reform Act of 1986, chose not to rely on the dulling of income-splitting incentives that naturally flowed from the lowering of the rates; it also included a battery of provisions designed to squeeze nearly all benefit out of many common splitting devices. A trust, for example, is taxed at the highest rate of 28 percent on income in excess of $5,000, and the benefit of the 15 percent rate is phased out so fast that a trust with $26,000 or more of taxable income is taxed at a flat 28 percent. Income flowing from a direct gift to a child or grandchild may fare no better; unearned income of a child under the age of 14 is taxed at a flat rate equal to the highest marginal rate applied to his parents, which is 28 percent unless the parents' income is very modest. Incorporations of closely held businesses are impacted by the fact that the maximum rate on corporate income is 34 percent, six percentage points higher than the maximum rate for individuals.

¶2.3 THE INDIVIDUAL AS THE BASIC TAXABLE UNIT

Tax theorists often argue that the basic economic unit in our society is the family, consisting of husband, wife, and children (at least if they live at home or are below the age of legal independence), and that amalgamation of the income of all members of the group on a single family tax return should be mandatory.[1] From its inception, however, the federal income tax has been based on the contrary view that every individual should be permitted to file a personal income tax return embracing his or her own income but not the income of the taxpayer's spouse, children, or other relatives. In keeping with this basic legislative decision, bona fide business transactions between members of a family (e.g., salaries paid in a family business or a sale of property at a profit) ordinarily have the same tax effects as similar

---

[16] See infra ¶75.2.1.

[17] See infra ¶85.2 (family partnerships), ¶75.2.7 (corporations).

[1] See generally Bittker, Federal Income Taxation and the Family, 27 Stan. L. Rev. 1389 (1975), and authorities therein cited; Oldman & McIntyre, Taxation of the Family in a Comprehensive and Simplified Income Tax, 90 Harv. L. Rev. 1573 (1977).

arrangements between unrelated parties, although there are statutory exceptions specially treating some intrafamily transactions.

Husband and wife may—but have never been required to—file a joint tax return amalgamating their income and deductions. Until 1948, joint returns were rarely employed; the same rate schedule applied to both individual and joint returns, and the amalgamation of spouses' income on a joint return thus pushed them into higher rate brackets if both had income. The enactment of more favorable joint-return rules in 1948, however, changed this situation drastically.[2] Since then, joint returns have saved tax for almost all married couples, and separate returns have usually been filed by couples having nonfinancial reasons for doing so (e.g., hostility between spouses who live separately but remain married). As for children, Congress has never required their income and deductions to be reported on their parents' tax return; indeed, in 1944 it went to the opposite extreme of providing that children are taxable on their own earnings, even if under local law the parents are entitled to receive and spend them.[3]

Despite its bias in favor of individual treatment, the Code contains a host of provisions that take account of family relationships and responsibilities. Among the most important of these provisions are the following:

1. A different rate schedule for each of four marital and family categories (unmarried individuals, married couples filing joint returns and certain surviving spouses, married persons filing separate returns, and unmarried heads of households).[4]
2. Deductions for dependents, who with minor exceptions must be related to the taxpayer by marriage, blood, or adoption, within degrees specified by §152(a).[5]
3. A rule denying deductions for losses on sales between family members, and a rule insuring that a salary or other payment to a family member is not deductible before the recipient must report it as income.[6]
4. A rule that gain or loss is not recognized on sales and other transfers of property between spouses.[7]
5. "Constructive ownership" rules, under which stock and other property owned by one person may be attributed to a family member in

---

[2] See infra ¶111.3.2.
[3] IRC §73, discussed infra ¶75.4.3.
[4] See infra ¶¶111.3.2–111.3.5.
[5] See infra ¶30.3.
[6] See infra ¶78.1.
[7] See infra ¶44.8.

determining the tax consequences of a transaction of the latter person.[8]

By virtue of these (and many more specialized) statutory provisions, intrafamily transactions, even if negotiated on the same terms as an arm's-length arrangement, are often treated with greater severity than comparable transactions among unrelated persons. When these provisions do not apply, family transactions ordinarily qualify for normal tax treatment. Because family transactions have often been used as devices for shifting income from high-income taxpayers to low-income members of their families, however, the government's defensive arsenal against income splitting is placed on alert by any such transaction.[9] The reasonableness of the terms of an intrafamily transaction, further, may have to be established affirmatively, whereas bargains among unrelated persons are usually accorded a presumption of regularity if they have been negotiated at arm's length.

¶2.4 PARTNERSHIPS AS CONDUITS

Partnerships are not subject to tax but are instead treated as conduits whose income passes through to the partners, who in turn report their respective distributive shares of the firm's income or loss on their individual tax returns, whether these amounts are distributed or not. In keeping with the conduit principle, each partner takes into account an appropriate share of the firm's charitable contributions, tax-exempt interest, and other specially treated items, and these items retain their character when reported by the individual partner.[1] Since each partner's share of these items is amalgamated on his tax return with all of his other income and deductions, partners in an enterprise may pay quite different amounts of tax even if they share equally in the firm's profits and losses.

Although basic to the treatment of partnerships, the conduit principle is not pursued to its logical extreme. The partnership, for example, elects its own taxable year as though it were an independent taxpayer, although it may not adopt or change to a taxable year other than the calendar year or a fiscal year used by the principal partners unless there is a business purpose for doing so. Most, but not all, elections affecting the computation of taxable income are made at the partnership level and thus are binding on the partners in computing their distributive shares of partnership income.[2]

---

[8] See, e.g., infra ¶¶78.1, 93.1.7.

[9] See supra ¶2.2.

[1] IRC §702. Very generally, a partner's distributive share of partnership income and loss (and of particular items) is the portion of the item that is added to or subtracted from the partner's economic entitlements as a partner. See infra ¶86.2.

[2] See infra ¶¶86.1.3, 86.1.4.

Moreover, if a partner deals with his partnership as a supplier of services, lender of funds, landlord, or in any way other "than in his capacity as a member of such partnership," the transaction is treated as though it were between the partnership and an outsider.[3]

On the other hand, the conduit principle is paramount in the treatment of other major events in the life of a partnership. For example, partners do not recognize gain or loss on transferring property to the partnership in exchange for their partnership interests; instead, a partner's adjusted basis for property transferred to a partnership carries over to the firm, and is used in computing gain or loss on a subsequent sale.[4] Conversely, a partnership does not recognize gain or loss when it distributes property to the partners (whether in liquidation or otherwise). Similarly, partners usually do not recognize gain or loss on receiving such a distribution, but a carryover of basis preserves the possibility of recognizing gain or loss on a later sale or other disposition of the distributed property.[5]

¶2.5 CORPORATIONS AS SEPARATE TAXABLE ENTITIES

¶2.5.1 "Double Taxation" of Corporate Income

Since 1909, corporations have been subject to a federal income tax. For 1988, the rates are 15 percent on the first $50,000 of taxable income, 25 percent on the next $25,000, and 34 percent of taxable income in excess of $75,000.[1] The benefit of the lower rates, however, is phased out for corporations whose taxable income is greater than $100,000, however, so that the tax is a flat 34 percent of taxable income for corporations with taxable income exceeding $335,000.[2]

Because shareholders are taxed on a corporation's after-tax income when it is distributed to them as dividends, without an offsetting deduction to the corporation, existing law gives rise to the so-called double taxation of corporate income—a phenomenon that for many years has been a subject

---

[3] See infra ¶86.5.
[4] See infra ¶85.3.
[5] See infra ¶87.2.3.
[1] IRC §11(b).
[2] Id. Mechanically, the phase-out rule increases the tax by 5 percent of taxable income in excess of $100,000, but caps the increase at $11,750, an amount that equals the tax saved by the lower rates on the first $75,000 of taxable income. Id. For a corporation whose income is in the range in which the phase-out occurs ($100,000 to $335,000), the phase-out has the effect of a fourth rate bracket of 39 percent because each dollar of additional taxable income increases tax by 39 cents (34 cents under the normal rate of 34 percent and 5 cents of additional tax under the phase-out rule).

of controversy among economists, tax theorists, and financial analysts.[3] For both the tax planner and the tax theorist, however, the problems created by the separate taxation of corporations and their shareholders are more complex than the "double taxation" label implies.

First, when realized by a corporation, business income may be taxed either more heavily or more leniently than it would have been if the shareholders had conducted the same enterprise as a proprietorship or partnership. Thus, if $1,000 of business income is taxed at the top corporate rate (34 percent for 1988) and the after-tax earnings ($660) are paid as dividends to a shareholder taxed at the top marginal rate for individuals (28 percent), the after-tax residue is $475 ($660 less 28 percent thereof).[4] If the same shareholder had received $1,000 of business income from a proprietorship or partnership, the after-tax residue would be $720 ($1,000 less 28 percent thereof). This might be called the classic case of double taxation since it is the paradigm that critics of existing law usually employ. Indeed, a similar disparity between corporate and proprietorship income arises even if the corporate tax is the only tax on corporate income. If, for example, the dividend of $60 is paid to a shareholder whose tax rate is zero because of personal exemptions and deductions, the after-tax residue is $660, as compared with the $1,000 the taxpayer would have enjoyed if the income had been derived from a proprietorship.

At the other end of the spectrum from these instances of overtaxation of corporate income, however, are cases of undertaxation. Assume a married couple with $250,000 of taxable income enter into a new venture that produces $25,000 of additional income. If the venture is organized as a partnership, they are left with after-tax income of $18,000 ($25,000 less 28 percent thereof). If the business is incorporated and the retained earnings are retained, the only immediate tax is a corporate tax of 15 percent, which leaves $21,250. Although additional tax might be incurred in the latter situation when the earnings are distributed or realized indirectly by the

---

[3] See infra ¶3.5.6.

[4] The tax bite is somewhat more severe if the corporation, the shareholder, or both are in the range within which the benefits of the lower rate brackets are phased out. See supra ¶2.2 for the phase-out rule for individuals. If both are within the phase-out range, for example, the incremental corporate tax on the $1,000 is $390, the shareholder's dividends are $610, and the shareholder is left after taxes with $409 ($610 less 33 percent thereof).

The bite was markedly more severe before the 1986 rate reductions took effect. In 1986, for example, $1,000 of corporate income taxed at the highest corporate rate of 46 percent left $540 for distribution to shareholders, and if the distribution was made to a shareholder taxed at the highest individual rate of 50 percent, the after-tax amount left to the shareholder was $270 ($540 less 50 percent thereof). Under the even higher rates applied in earlier years, these computations made high-income shareholders appear as veritable paupers.

shareholders on a sale of their stock, this additional tax might be long delayed, and could be avoided altogether if the stock is held until the shareholders die.[5] If the 15 percent corporate tax is the only tax ever imposed on the income, the savings is obvious. A delay in the shareholder-level tax can also compensate fully for the second tier of tax if the delay is long enough.

Example 2-1

**Comparisons of Accumulations by
Incorporated and Unincorporated Businesses—
Single Accumulation From Operating Profits**

1. Accumulation possible through corporate form:

   Earnings accumulated in year 1 ($1,000 less tax of 15 percent ... $ 850

   Earnings accumulation after 10 years (future value of $850 in 10 years determined at the corporation's after-tax rate of return of 8.5 percent $1,922

   Shareholders' dividends after taxes (line 2 less 28 percent thereof) $1,384

   Value in year 1 of entitlement to dividends (present value of line 3, determined with a discount rate equal to the shareholders' after-tax rate of return of 7.2 percent) .... $ 690

2. Accumulation possible through partnership form:

   Value of accumulation in year 1 if business conducted as partnership ($1,000 less 28% thereof) .... $ 720

3. Advantage of partnership form (in present value) .... $ 30

Example 2-1 illustrates how the economic impact of the second tax can be evaluated where corporate earnings are initially accumulated but are expected to be ultimately taxed to the shareholders. It is assumed in the example that (1) a corporation has taxable income in year 1 of $1,000, which is taxed at 15 percent; (2) the corporation accumulates the $850 remaining after taxes, and invests it in securities yielding 10 percent before taxes; (3) the income on the securities is subject to a corporate tax of 15 percent, leaving the corporation with an after-tax return of 8.5 percent; (4)

---

[5] Under pre-1986 law, tax could often be saved by accumulating corporate earnings and having the shareholders realize these earnings indirectly as long-term capital gain by selling their stock. The sum of the lowest corporate rate (15 percent) and the highest individual capital gains rate (20 percent of 85 percent, or 17 percent) added up to only 32 percent of the corporate earnings, as compared with the highest individual ordinary income rate of 50 percent. The repeal of the capital gains preference in 1986 eliminated this opportunity.

the after-tax income on the securities is also accumulated; (5) the original accumulation and the accumulations of earnings on it are distributed to the shareholders after 10 years; and (6) the shareholders are taxed at 28 percent throughout the accumulation period. This last assumption has several implications: First, if the business were not incorporated the $1,000 earned in year 1 would then bear a tax of $280, leaving $720 after taxes. Second, when the shareholders make investments yielding 10 percent, their after-tax rate of return is 7.2 percent. Third, when the shareholders cash out corporate accumulations either through dividend distributions or stock sales, 28 percent is taken in tax.

On the assumptions made in Example 2-1, the ultimate tax burden is slightly less if the business is organized as a partnership. The edge would go to incorporation, however, if a longer accumulation period or a higher pretax rate of return were assumed or if the assumptions were varied in any one of many other ways. Other changes in the assumptions would tip the balance even further toward the partnership form.

These disparate consequences of conducting business in corporate form could be avoided by treating the corporation as a conduit (as is done with partnerships) and taxing its income, whether distributed or accumulated, directly to the shareholders.[6] The practical and political obstacles to the implementation of such a scheme, however, have kept it from being seriously considered by Congress, which has imposed conduit treatment only on some U.S.-owned foreign corporations and has allowed it on an elective basis only for closely held corporations.[7]

¶2.5.2 Corporate-Shareholder Relationships

Because the aggregate tax burden on shareholders and their corporations can be either heavier or lighter than the tax cost of doing business as a proprietorship or partnership, taxpayers who can arrange to realize income in a particular form, or in the most economical combination of forms, are handsomely rewarded. Tax planning is especially feasible for the owners of closely held businesses, where the nontax consequences of using one form of organization rather than another are often minor or easily neutralized by insurance or other devices.

The opportunities to reduce taxes by engaging in business through a closely held corporation, despite the double taxation of corporate income,

---

[6] This idea, known as corporate tax integration, is discussed elsewhere. Infra ¶3.5.6.

[7] See infra ¶68.3 (mandatory conduit treatment of some income of foreign controlled corporations); ¶95.2.7 (mandatory conduit treatment for all income of foreign personal holding companies; ¶95.6 (elective conduit treatment for closely held corporations qualifying as S corporations).

are enlarged by the fact that a shareholder can become an employee of his corporation and thereby qualify for such employee tax benefits as tax-free medical and group-term life insurance and participation in qualified pension and profit sharing plans, some of which are either denied to partners and self-employed persons (group-term life insurance) or granted to them on more restrictive terms (accident and health insurance).[8] These tax-saving devices have, not surprisingly, evoked a variety of countermeasures by the IRS to defend the revenue. The principal battlefields are:

1. *Problems in classifying and recognizing certain entities.* If a corporation is created solely to avoid taxes, the corporation may be disregarded as a dummy and the income taxed to the individual under §61(a).[9] Incentives for creating corporations to avoid taxes are sharply reduced by the 1986 changes in the rates, which peg the highest corporate rate at a level (34 percent) that is higher than the highest individual rate (28 percent). When the highest individual rate was significantly higher than the highest corporate rate, it was profitable to incorporate, for example, to employ the sole shareholder and then contract out his services at a higher price to third parties in order to shield the markup from taxation at the shareholder-employee's personal tax rate. Seldom would taxpayers now find this arrangement desirable. The doctrines developed under prior law, however, are available to frustrate creative taxpayers who find tax reasons to form dummy corporations.

Present law would more likely tempt a corporation actively engaged in business to make a contract under which income earned by the corporation is to be paid directly to its shareholders in hopes of avoiding corporate tax. The claim that the corporation is merely a nominee or agent of its shareholder is often not persuasive, and the income may be subject to the corporate tax even though not in fact received by the corporation.[10]

Still another problem in this area is the proper treatment of unincorporated organizations that possess, under contract and local law, the major indicia of corporate status: centralized management, transferable interests, limited liability, and an existence that survives the death, bankruptcy, or other misfortune of its investors. Under §7701(a)(3), which defines the word "corporation" to include "associations" and "joint-stock companies,"

---

[8] Infra ¶14.2 (group term life insurance), ¶13.2 (accident and health plans), ¶62.2 (pension and profit sharing plans).

[9] See generally Jones v. CIR, 64 TC 1066 (1975) (corporation not sham, but income allocated to sole shareholder); CIR v. Laughton, 113 F2d 103 (9th Cir. 1940) (remanded for determination of corporation's status); Alexandre, The Corporate Counterpart of the Family Partnership, 2 Tax L. Rev. 493 (1947); Johnson, Taxing Dividends of Family Corporations—A Dissent, 2 Tax L. Rev. 566 (1947).

[10] See infra ¶90.1.8.

unincorporated enterprises are sometimes taxed as though they had a corporate charter.[11]

2. *Unreasonable accumulations of surplus.* Double taxation of corporate earnings is often avoided by accumulating corporate income rather than paying it out as dividends to shareholders. Accumulation frees shareholders willing to forgo a current return of the burden of the second tax and leaves less patient shareholders with the remedy of selling portions of their stock in order to cash out their interests in the increase in corporate net worth resulting from the accumulated surplus.

The principal threat to plans of this type is §531, which imposes an "accumulated earnings tax" on the accumulated taxable income (roughly speaking, business income less corporate taxes and dividends) of any corporation "formed or availed of for the purpose of avoiding the income tax with respect to its shareholders . . . by permitting earnings and profits to accumulate instead of being divided or distributed."[12] Corporations accumulating their earnings beyond the reasonable needs of the business or in excess of a $250,000 minimum credit (whichever is greater) become subject to a tax of 27.5 percent of the first $100,000 of accumulated taxable income and 38.5 percent of amounts above $100,000. This tax is in addition to the corporation's regular income tax.

The statutory test of taxability is the existence of a tax-avoidance purpose for the accumulation, but in practice the critical issue is whether corporate earnings and profits have been permitted to accumulate "beyond the reasonable needs of the business." For this reason, corporations using their accumulated earnings to rehabilitate or replace plant and equipment, to expand product lines, to finance credit sales, or to develop the business in other ways have little to fear from §531, even though the decision to reinvest their profits rather than pay dividends also serves to eliminate the second tax on distributed profits. On the other hand, self-serving corporate resolutions or vague plans for expansion at an indefinite future date are not a sufficient shield against §531, especially if the corporation lends its profits to shareholders in the interim or invests them in marketable securities rather than plant, equipment, and inventory.

3. *Salaries to shareholder-employees.* Many closely held corporations whose dominant shareholders are employed in their businesses depend on shareholder's salaries to mitigate double taxation. If the amounts paid to shareholder-employees do not exceed the reasonable value of their services, the corporation can deduct them as business expenses under §162(a)(1).[13] Unlike accumulated earnings, which are subject to the 34 percent rate on

---

[11] See infra ¶90.1.2.

[12] For discussion of §531, see infra ¶95.1.

[13] See infra ¶22.2.

corporate income and usually cannot be made available for shareholder's living expenses without incurring the second tax, amounts paid as deductible salaries to shareholders are forever freed from corporate taxation, and are only burdened by tax at the shareholder level, where the maximum rate is 28 percent.

For this reason, it is tempting for closely held corporations to fix the salaries of shareholder-employees at the highest level that does not strip the corporation of working capital.[14] Because business profits and cash flow vary from year to year, this practice requires compensating changes in the salaries as the corporation's ability to pay them ebbs and flows. Variable salaries, though, invite a counterattack by the IRS, since amounts exceeding the reasonable value of the shareholder-employee's services can be treated as nondeductible constructive dividends even though paid in the guise of salary.[15] If successful, this attack frustrates the plan to avoid double taxation of the business profits.

4. *Other deductible payments to shareholders.* The constructive dividend doctrine, which is most frequently invoked against closely held corporations, is not limited to amounts purporting to be payments for the shareholder-employee's personal services. Excessive rent for the use of shareholder-owned property, interest on alleged loans by the corporation to the shareholder that are not intended to be repaid, the rent-free use of corporate property by a shareholder, below-market loans to shareholders, corporate reimbursement of personal expenditures, and many other payments and transactions that cannot be justified by arm's-length criteria may be treated as constructive dividends by the corporation to the favored shareholder.[16]

¶2.5.3 Multiple Corporations

Like individuals, corporations are ordinarily treated as discrete taxable units, each being taxed on its own income without regard to the income of its parents, subsidiaries, or affiliates. The analogy to individuals also holds for transactions between related corporations, which ordinarily have the

---

[14] If a corporation's taxable income after all allowable deductions (including shareholder's salaries) is less than $75,000, it is taxed under §11(b) at the rates of 15 and 25 percent, rates that are lower than the maximum individual rate of 28 percent. Some corporations might keep shareholder's salaries low enough to allow accumulations of income taxed at the lower corporate rates. Before this is done, however, thought should be given to what will be done with the accumulated earnings. If shareholders intend to cash them in soon either through dividends or stock sales, the accumulation could be penny wise and pound foolish, as is illustrated by Example 2-1, supra ¶2.5.1.

[15] See infra ¶92.2.

[16] Id.

same tax effect as transactions between unrelated persons, provided the terms resemble those that would be negotiated in arm's-length bargaining.

Unlike a family, however, related corporations may elect to file a single consolidated tax return instead of separate returns, in which event intra-group profits and losses are, in general, disregarded, and the group is taxed on the net income generated by its transactions with outsiders. This privilege is granted to members of an "affiliated group," a statutory term embracing corporations connected to each other through a common parent, provided 80 percent or more of the stock of each is owned by the parent or other members of the same group.[17]

If two related corporations that do not join in a consolidated return are both taxed at the top corporate rate of 34 percent, a transaction that shifts income from one to the other does not reduce tax because the transferred income is taxed at the same rate regardless of which corporation receives and reports it. Because, until 1986, the highest corporate rate was lower than the highest individual rate and was reached at a lower level of income, income shifting between related corporations has not generated as much spectacular litigation as income splitting among individuals, where, as recently as 1981, a successful shift of income from parent to child or grandchild could avoid a tax as high as 70 percent. The principal analogue in the corporate world to this dramatic result is the shifting of income from a profitable corporation to an affiliated corporation with offsetting losses or from a domestic corporation to a foreign subsidiary whose profits are not subject to U.S. taxation until repatriated by dividend payments to the parent.[18]

These possibilities, and other income-reducing opportunities of a more complex character, have led to countermeasures by the IRS and Congress, of which the most important are:

1. Section 1561, which, in effect, amalgamates the taxable income of related corporations in applying the rate schedule so that their aggregate tax burden is the same regardless of how their income is divided among them.[19]
2. Section 482, authorizing the IRS to allocate gross income, deductions, credits, and allowances between two or more organizations or businesses that are owned or controlled, directly or indirectly, by the same interests. This provision applies whether the enterprises are incorporated or not, but it is most often invoked by the IRS when two affiliated corporations have dealt with each other on terms that

---

[17] See infra ¶90.4.
[18] See infra ¶66.3.
[19] See infra ¶111.3.9.

cannot be justified by arm's-length standards.[20]

¶2.6 TRUSTS AND THEIR BENEFICIARIES

The tax status of trusts is governed by an uneasy compromise between competing theories of the proper taxable unit. In general, distributed income is taxed to beneficiaries rather than to the trust itself, while accumulated income is taxed to the trust. When accumulations are ultimately distributed to the beneficiaries, they are ordinarily taxed on these amounts, but are credited with the taxes previously paid by the trust. This division of tax responsibility between the trust and its beneficiaries, however, is sometimes displaced by rules, commonly known as grantor trust rules, that tax the grantor on the trust income as though he had retained the property instead of creating the trust.

The grantor trust rules, which when applicable take precedence over the rules governing ordinary trusts, originally taxed the grantor only if he could revoke the trust or reclaim the income for himself. In a series of cases culminating in the 1940 landmark decision in *Helvering v. Clifford*,[1] however, the courts went beyond the early statutory rules to hold that grantors could be taxed, even in the absence of a power to revoke, if they retained significant control over beneficial enjoyment of the trust income or corpus. A right to determine the proportion in which income should be distributed among the beneficiaries, for example, was held to be a sufficient basis for taxing the grantor, especially if the trust was to last for only a few years. These "Clifford trust" principles, which required an evaluation in each case of all relevant facts, were supplanted in 1945 by Treasury regulations that enunciated relatively precise rules to replace the vague judicial tests. The regulations, in turn, were replaced in 1954 by the elaborate statutory rules of §§671-677.

Under these provisions, grantors are taxed on trust income if they retain or vest in a nonadverse party (1) a reversionary interest that will take effect within ten years of the trust's creation, (2) specified rights to control beneficial enjoyment of the corpus or income, or (3) unusual administrative powers of a nonfiduciary character.[2] Although the grantor of a trust em-

---

[20] See infra ¶79.3.

[1] Helvering v. Clifford, 309 US 331 (1940), discussed infra ¶80.1.1.

[2] The grantor trust rules are described in more detail in Chapter 80. In addition to the rules described in the text, the 1954 codification includes a provision, §678, that treats a person other than a grantor as owner of trust property if the person has power to vest corpus or income in himself. These trusts, known as *Mallinckrodt* trusts, are described below in ¶80.8. Also, §679, added in 1976, treats a grantor as owner of a trust in which he has no interest or power if the trust has a foreign situs and one or more U.S. beneficiaries. See infra ¶80.1.7.

braced by these rules is "treated as the owner" of the trust property for tax purposes, he is not the owner under state law, which allocates ownership in accordance with the terms of the trust instrument. For tax purposes, however, the income is ordinarily treated as though it had been received by the grantor and then paid by him, as a nontaxable gift, to the recipient. If the latter person reports the amount as taxable income on the mistaken assumption that the trust is not a grantor trust, he is entitled to a refund of his tax when it becomes clear that the grantor is the proper taxpayer.[3]

Trusts that escape the grantor trust rules deflect tax liability away from the grantor, the income being taxed either to the beneficiaries or to the trust, depending on whether it is distributed or accumulated by the fiduciary.[4] This result is accomplished by including all of the income on the trust's return, with a deduction for amounts taxable to the beneficiaries, who then pick up these amounts for inclusion on their own returns. Since the trust is viewed as a conduit pro tanto, distributed income usually retains its original character (e.g., as tax-exempt interest, capital gain, or foreign-source income) in the hands of the beneficiaries, who must report their pro rata shares of specially treated items unless the governing instrument allocates them in a different ratio.

When trust income is received by the beneficiaries, it does not ordinarily qualify for the exclusion granted by §102(a) to "property acquired by gift, bequest, devise, or inheritance," but rather is usually within the rule of §102(b)(1), which denies the exclusion "where the gift, bequest, devise, or inheritance if of income from property." This is so even though the trust was intended as a gift by the grantor or was created by his will, and even if the distribution is charged by the fiduciary against corpus. For tax purposes, with a few exceptions, distributions are deemed to come from the trust's distributable net income, and only payments in excess of that amount qualify as tax-free gifts to the beneficiaries.[5]

Until 1986, when the rate schedules were set to tax trusts at the highest individual rate on income in excess of $5,000, income accumulated in a trust was often taxed to the trust at a much lower rate than would have been paid by the beneficiaries on distributed income, and trusts were a fertile ground for tax avoidance. An early device entailed the accumulation of income in years when the trust's tax rate was lower than the beneficiary's, with a subsequent distribution of the accumulated income along with the current year's income. Under the earlier taxing statutes, the beneficiary was taxed in the year of distribution on the current income but not on the

---

[3] For problems arising if inconsistent positions are taken and the statute of limitations has run, see infra ¶113.9.

[4] The rules for nongrantor trusts are described below in Chapter 81.

[5] Infra ¶81.1.1.

accumulation, since it had already been taxed to the trust. By a series of increasingly severe throwback rules, however, Congress has gradually closed the net on this device, as well as on its more sophisticated progeny. Although the original reason for the rules largely disappeared with the 1986 changes, they remain in the law.

Under the current throwback rules, distributions of accumulated income are taxed to the beneficiaries, roughly speaking, as though they had been paid out in the accumulation years. To prevent double taxation of these amounts, the beneficiary is given a credit for the taxes previously paid by the trust on them, as though the trust had made down payments of tax on his behalf. In keeping with this theory, the beneficiary is regarded as having received not only the income of the earlier years but also the taxes paid by the trust thereon, since, had the amounts been distributed in the earlier years, the trust would not have been taxed on them and, consequently, could have distributed a larger amount.[6]

---

[6] See infra ¶81.5.

CHAPTER

3

Economic Aspects of
Federal Income Taxation

¶3.1 ECONOMIC INCOME VS. STATUTORY INCOME

¶3.1.1 The Haig-Simons Definition of Income

Many economists have sought to define income,[1] and a few have concluded that the problem is insoluble.[2] Following Adam Smith's lead, some view income as the amount that can be spent without impairing the taxpayer's capital,[3] others prefer to limit the term to periodic receipts from continuing sources, and a few have restricted it still further to actual consumption.[4] Among contemporary American economists, however, the so-called Haig-Simons definition of income is the most widely accepted: "Personal income may be defined as the algebraic sum of (1) the market value of rights exercised in consumption and (2) the change in the value of the store of property rights between the beginning and end of the period in question."[5] An expanded version of the Haig-Simons definition is:

> [A] person's income during the period, in an economic sense, consists of the algebraic sum of:

---

[1] See Goode, The Economic Definition of Income, in Comprehensive Income Taxation 1 (Pechman, ed.; Brookings 1977); Wueller, Concepts of Taxable Income, 53 Pol. Sci. Q. 83, 557 (1938), 54 Pol. Sci. Q. 555 (1939).

[2] See Kaldor, An Expenditure Tax 70 (Allen and Unwin 1955) ("the problem of *defining* individual income, quite apart from any problem of practical measurement, appears in principle insoluble").

[3] J.R. Hicks, for example, defined an individual's income as "the maximum value which he can consume during a week, and still expect to be as well off at the end of the week as he was at the beginning." Hicks, Value and Capital 172 (1939). A similar definition: "[N]et individual income is the flow of commodities and services accruing to an individual through a period of time and available for disposition after deducting the necessary costs of acquisition." Hewett, The Definition of Income and Its Application in Federal Taxation 22 (1925).

[4] German and other continental economists are primarily responsible for the periodic-flow theory; Irving Fisher is the principal exemplar of the consumption theory. For citations, see Goode, supra note 1; Wueller, supra note 1.

[5] Simons, Personal Income Taxation 50, 61–62, 206 (U. of Chicago Press 1938).

1. The value of consumption during the period financed from factor income or transfer income (e.g., gifts) flowing to the person during the period or from accumulated wealth, plus (a) goods produced by the person for his or her own use, and (b) the value of the use of durable consumer goods possessed, such as homes.

2. Net increase in personal wealth during the period, whether from accumulation of net savings during the period or increases in the value of property held. This sum may of course be negative, so that income is less than consumption.[6]

Computationally, the Haig-Simons definition approaches the matter from a different perspective than the federal income tax laws and most other accounting systems. The Haig-Simons definition looks exclusively to the uses of income (consumption and savings), whereas taxable income consists of receipts and entitlements to future receipts. This difference, however, is only one of technique, not substance. In terms more familiar to tax lawyers and accountants, income, according to the Haig-Simons definition, consists of all receipts and other value accruing to the taxpayer, excluding amounts that do not add to the taxpayer's power to consume or save. A lawyer's fee is income to the lawyer under the definition because it is available to be spent on consumption or to be saved, but the lawyer's income is reduced by salary paid to an associate because the associate's pay reduces the lawyer's ability to consume and accumulate. For the same reasons, the prices received by a merchant on sales of goods are income, but reductions are made for the costs of goods sold and other expenses of the business. Borrowed money is not income; because the receipt of the money is matched by the obligation to repay, the loan does not increase the borrower's net resources.

The Haig-Simons concept, however, differs fundamentally from taxable income in many respects. As Mr. Justice Holmes once observed, "the income tax laws do not profess to embody perfect economic theory."[7] Gains and losses are only taxed on realization, rather than as they accrue; the value of goods and services created by the taxpayer's own efforts is ordinarily disregarded; and the rental value of owner-occupied residences and other assets is not taxed.[8] Economists loyal to the Haig-Simons definition ordinarily object to the third of these departures, but they usually accept, albeit reluctantly, the first two, primarily because of perceived administrative difficulties in measuring the value of the taxpayer's personal services and in

---

[6] Due & Friedlaender, Government Finance: Economics of the Public Sector 224 (Richard D. Irwin, 6th ed. 1977).

[7] Weiss v. Wiener, 279 US 333, 335 (1929).

[8] Infra ¶5.2 (realization), ¶5.3.2 (value of taxpayer's do-it-yourself activities), ¶5.3.3 (imputed value of owner-occupied residences and other consumer durables).

determining annual changes in the value of real estate and other assets whose market values are not readily ascertainable. A similar ambivalence marks the attitude of economists toward numerous other differences between Haig-Simons and statutory income.[9]

Also, some important issues in the computation of income are unresolved by the Haig-Simons definition, such as the appropriate chronological period (year, decade, or lifetime) and the appropriate tax-paying unit (individuals, married couples, families, households, or communes). Because opinions differ widely on these issues, application of the Haig-Simons definition to the facts of real life can produce many competing answers.

Despite these difficulties, economists customarily use the Haig-Simons definition as a standard in judging the merits of statutory definitions of income, and usually disapprove of departures from it unless justified by administrative or equity considerations. Moreover, tax theorists ordinarily use the definition as the model of a pure income tax when discussing such issues as the extent to which income taxes can be shifted by the nominal taxpayer to other persons, and it is either the starting point or a major influence in identifying tax preferences, in computing effective tax rates, and in compiling the tax expenditure budget.[10]

Unfortunately, economists have devoted little systematic attention to whether the departures from the Haig-Simons definition that are usually accepted as unavoidable undermine the validity of practical judgments based on an admittedly unattainable ideal. Even less have they addressed the effect of departures from the Haig-Simons definition in computing business income, such as the inability in practice to allocate expenditures for research and development, advertising, and goodwill between deductible current expenses and depreciable capital outlays.[11] When these seemingly unavoidable gaps between theory and practice are taken into account, along with other features of current law that seem too deeply entrenched to be eradicated (e.g., failure to compute depreciation on a sinking-fund basis), it is not clear whether changing isolated statutory provisions moves the tax base closer to the Haig-Simons definition or instead has the perverse effect

---

[9] See Bittker, A "Comprehensive Tax Base" as a Goal of Income Tax Reform, 80 Harv. L. Rev. 925 (1967); Galvin, More on Boris Bittker and the Comprehensive Tax Base: The Practicalities of Tax Reform and the ABA's CSTR, 81 Harv. L. Rev. 1016 (1968); Musgrave, In Defense of an Income Concept, 81 Harv. L. Rev. 44 (1967); Pechman, Comprehensive Income Taxation: A Comment, 81 Harv. L. Rev. 63 (1967); additional comments by the same authors, 81 Harv. L. Rev. 1032–43 (1968), reprinted with additional replies in Bittker, Galvin, Musgrave & Pechman, A Comprehensive Income Tax Base? A Debate (Federal Tax Press 1968). See also Goode, supra note 1.

[10] Infra ¶3.3 (shifting), ¶3.4.1 (effective tax rates), ¶3.6 (tax expenditure budget).

[11] See infra ¶26.4 (research and experimental expenditures), ¶20.4.5 (advertising expenses).

of increasing the distance between income as defined by the Code and the Haig Simons concept of income.[12]

¶3.1.2 Aggregate Personal Income vs. Taxable Income

In the absence of an authoritative computation of income based on Haig-Simons principles,[13] a detailed comparison between economic income and taxable income is not possible. It is possible, however, to trace the relationship of aggregate personal income, as estimated by the Department of Commerce, to adjusted gross income (AGI) and taxable income, as defined by the Code. As indicated by Table 3-1, taxable income was about 55 percent of personal income for 1984; the largest sources of difference were tax-exempt transfer payments (e.g., social security benefits) and the personal deductions and exemptions allowed in determining taxable income.

Table 3-1

Derivation of Adjusted Gross Income and
Taxable Income From Personal Income, 1984

(in Billions of Dollars)

1. Personal income.. $3,110.2
2. Less: Adjustments for conceptual differences (personal income items not included in AGI)
   a. Transfer payments (except taxable military retirement pay and government pensions)........ $375.5
   b. Untaxed employer contributions to qualified pension plans, group health and life insurance, unemployment benefit funds, and workmen's compensation $182.5
   c. Imputed income 51.5
   d. Investment income of nonprofit institutions and retained income of fiduciaries.................... 31.4
   e. Investment income retained by life insurers and pension funds 95.4
   f. Differences in accounting treatment................. 79.8

---

[12] See Goode, supra note 1, at 29–30; Zelinsky, Efficiency and Income Taxes: The Rehabilitation of Tax Incentives, 64 Tex. L. Rev. 973 (1986).

[13] For a computation of "comprehensive income," reaching a total of about $1.5 billion for 1977, see Minarik, The Yield of a Comprehensive Income Tax, in Pechman, supra note 1, at 277 et seq. The Minarik computation follows the Haig-Simons definition in many respects; but it excludes gifts, bequests, and unrealized gains and losses, among other items.

g. Other excluded or exempt income	122.7	938.9
3. Plus: Adjustments for conceptual differences (AGI items not included in personal income)		
a. Personal contributions for social insurance	$133.5	
b. Net gain from sale of assets	54.3	
c. Taxable private pensions	58.4	
d. Small business corporation income	8.2	
e. Other	1.3	255.8
4. Estimated adjusted gross income of taxable and nontaxable individuals		$2,427.1
5. Less: Nonreported adjusted gross income		287.2
6. Adjusted gross income reported on returns		$2,139.9
7. Less: Adjusted gross income reported on nontaxable returns		42.9
8. Adjusted gross income on taxable returns		$2,097.0
9. Less:		
a. Deductions on taxable returns	$227.3	
b. Exemptions on taxable returns	201.0	428.3
10. Taxable income on taxable returns[1]		$1,671.2
11. Plus: Taxable income on nontaxable returns		30.1
12. Total taxable income of individuals		$1,701.4

---

[1]Line 10 is greater than the excess of line 8 over line 9 because it includes returns of taxpayers subject only to the minimum tax, some of whom have deductions and exemptions in excess of adjusted gross income.

Source: Pechman, Federal Tax Policy, Tables B-1, B-3, and B4 (Brookings, 5th ed. 1987). Similar figures for selected years during the period 1970 through 1985 can be found in Selected Statistical Series, 1970–1988, 7 SOI Bulletin 77, 85–88 (1988).

¶**3.1.3 Comprehensive Tax Base Concept**

The disparities between taxable income and aggregate personal income as an economic concept have elicited numerous proposals for the enactment of a comprehensive tax base (CTB) to include many items that are now excluded or deducted from statutory gross income.[14] Although the Haig-Simons definition often serves as a guide in formulating proposals for a CTB, the proposals do not follow its dictates rigorously, but instead embody

---

[14]See Pechman, supra note 1; Commission to Revise the Tax Structure, Reforming the Federal Tax Structure (Fund for Public Policy Research 1973); Treasury Department, Blueprints for Basic Tax Reform (1977); Bittker, Galvin, Musgrave & Pechman, supra note 9; Special Committee on Simplification, ABA Tax Section, Evaluation of the Proposed Comprehensive Income Tax, 32 Tax Lawyer 563 (1979). See also infra ¶¶3.4.1 and 3.4.2 for the use of enlarged income concepts in computing effective tax rates.

judgments about equity, administrative convenience, and political feasibility—all of which are debatable rather than ineluctable. Moreover, some
CTB advocates are imbued primarily with the desire to eliminate distinctions among taxpayers that do not reflect differences in their ability to pay,
others want to reduce the misallocation of resources that they attribute to
tax incentives and other allowances interfering with free-market forces, and
some favor a broader tax base because it would permit the same amount of
revenue to be raised with a less progressive rate schedule. Given these
divergent objectives, it is not surprising that CTB proposals differ widely in
their structural details.

One specimen of the CTB movement, published in 1977, defines income to include substantially all items included in adjusted gross income, as
defined by §62, plus (1) the portion of realized capital gains that escaped tax
under the capital gains preference allowed for years prior to 1986, (2)
dividends excluded by §116 (repealed in 1986), (3) interest from state and
municipal bonds, (4) accrued interest on life insurance policies, (5) capital
gains on personal residences, (6) capital gains on the transfer of appreciated
property by gift or at death, (7) the rental value of owner-occupied homes,
(8) employee fringe benefits, (9) contributions to social insurance programs,
(10) veterans' benefits, (11) workmen's compensation payments, and (12)
transfer payments, such as social security or food stamps.[15] When these
changes in the tax base were applied to adjusted gross income as estimated
for 1977 ($1,186 billion), they resulted in comprehensive income of $1,506
billion (before personal and dependency exemptions), distributed among
adjusted gross income classes as indicated by Table 3-2. When these taxpayers are reassembled into "comprehensive income" (rather than AGI) classes,
the relative importance for each class of its AGI and its share of the additional items included in comprehensive income is indicated by Table 3-3.

Just as CTB models vary in the exclusions and deductions that they
would reduce or eliminate, so they vary in their proposals for using the new
tax base. At one extreme, it could be used to generate more governmental
revenue by preserving the existing rate structure; at the other extreme, the
rates could be cut to keep revenue constant. Most advocates of a CTB favor,
at a minimum, a sufficient increase in revenue to finance increases in
governmental programs like social security and aid to cities and states in
order to offset the adverse effects of the new tax provisions. Beyond this,
however, there is obviously room for an infinitude of middle grounds. As
for tax cuts, opinions vary as to the beneficiaries, depending on the degree
of progression favored by the theorist advocating the particular CTB pro-

---

[15] Minarik, supra note 13.

Table 3-2

**Distribution of AGI and
Comprehensive Income, by AGI Class, 1977**

Adjusted Gross Income ($Thousands)	Adjusted Gross Income		Comprehensive Income		Ratio of Comprehensive Income to Adjusted Gross Income
	Amount ($Billions)	Percentage of Total	Amount ($Billions)	Percentage of Total	
0–2.5	18.75	1.58	87.91	5.84	4.69
2.5–5	40.78	3.44	60.84	4.04	1.49
5–7.5	59.15	4.99	78.40	5.21	1.33
7.5–10	81.59	6.88	102.92	6.84	1.26
10–15	207.10	17.46	253.41	16.83	1.22
15–20	226.34	19.08	272.57	18.10	1.20
20–25	167.73	14.14	199.11	13.23	1.19
25–30	110.19	9.29	129.49	8.60	1.18
30–50	149.30	12.59	174.64	11.60	1.17
50–100	64.12	5.41	74.33	4.94	1.16
100–200	32.05	2.70	37.11	2.46	1.16
200–500	17.33	1.46	20.54	1.36	1.19
500–1,000	3.85	0.32	4.93	0.33	1.28
1,000 and over	7.71	0.65	9.33	0.62	1.21
All classes	1,185.99	100.00	1,505.54	100.00	1.27

Source: Pechman (ed.), Comprehensive Income Taxation, Table A-1 (Brookings 1977).

posal. The plan just described, for example, proffers five alternative ways of taxing the proposed CTB, embodying varying degrees of progression.[16]

Since the publication of this 1977 study, the law has moved nearer to a comprehensive tax base. In a series of revenue acts over the last decade, especially the Tax Reform Act of 1986, Congress has expanded the tax base and sharply lowered marginal rates; it might be seen as having thereby implemented the comprehensive tax base concept. Among the items included in Table 3-3, for example, the former exclusion of all social security benefits has been replaced by a provision taxing more affluent recipients on up to one half of their benefits, and the preference for capital gains has been repealed. Most of the items in Table 3-3, however, remain unaffected by

---

[16] Id. at 287.

Table 3-3

Components of Comprehensive Income Expressed as Percentage of the Total, by Comprehensive Income Class, 1977

Comprehensive Adjusted Income Class ($Thousands)	Gross Income	Imputed Rent[1]	Transfers[2]	Social Security Benefits	Employer Social Security Contribution	Employee Benefits[3]	Capital Gains[4]	Other[5]
0–2.5	61.8	2.8	11.1	16.4	3.1	− 3.9	0.6	0.3
2.5–5	53.0	2.3	17.0	22.3	2.0	− 2.3	1.1	− 0.1
5–7.5	60.0	1.7	15.5	17.0	2.3	− 2.7	1.1	− 0.3
7.5–10	70.8	1.4	11.3	9.2	2.9	− 3.4	1.3	− 0.3
10–15	78.0	1.2	6.4	4.1	3.6	4.7	− 1.4	0.7
15–20	80.6	1.0	4.0	2.1	3.9	5.7	− 1.3	1.5
20–25	81.5	0.9	2.7	1.3	3.8	6.7	− 1.5	1.7
25–30	82.4	0.8	1.9	1.0	3.4	7.1	− 1.8	1.6
30–50	82.7	0.7	1.3	0.8	2.7	8.0	− 2.1	1.7
50–100	83.9	0.5	1.0	0.6	1.3	− 6.8	3.8	2.1
100–200	84.8	0.6	0.2	0.2	0.5	− 3.7	5.5	4.5
200–500	81.4	0.6	0.3	0.1	0.2	− 2.4	8.5	6.6
500–1,000	74.0	0.5	0.0	0.0	0.1	− 1.3	17.5	6.5
1,000 and over	77.7	0.1	0.0	0.0	0.0	0.5	− 17.9	3.8
All classes	78.7	1.0	4.4	3.6	3.0	5.8	− 2.1	1.5

[1]Imputed rental value of owner-occupied homes net of property taxes, mortgage interest, and operating expenses.

[2]Aid to families with dependent children, supplemental security income, general assistance, unemployment compensation, workers' compensation, bonus value of food stamps, and insurance value of Medicaid.

[3]Employer-paid premiums for life, health, and disability insurance and employer contribution to pension funds.

[4]Excluded portion of long-term capital gains and the dividend exclusion.

[5]Negative numbers are adjustments for the excess of life expectancy recovery of employee contributions to pension plans over nontaxable pension benefits.

Source: Pechman (ed.), Comprehensive Income Taxation, Table A-3 (Brookings 1977).

these legislative developments, and few adherents of the comprehensive tax base model consider their goal as having been reached.

¶3.1.4 Horizontal and Vertical Equity

The traditional test of fairness in the distribution of tax burdens consists of two principles: Persons who are similarly situated should be treated equally ("horizontal equity"), and there should be appropriate differentiations between persons on each income level and those on the levels above and below ("vertical equity").[17] These principles are obviously too abstract to be useful unless content is given to the concept of equality. Moreover, a quantitative measure is essential; it is not feasible to define equity in terms of the taxpayer's intrinsic merits, contributions to society, or other intangible qualities.

As applied to income taxation, the horizontal equity principle is usually said to require that persons with equal incomes pay the same amount of taxes.[18] This would be an innocuous and trivial goal, however, if "equal income" meant equal *taxable* income, since persons with equal taxable incomes are automatically subject to the same tax liability (save for distinctions based on marital and family status).[19] When commentators refer to horizontal equity, therefore, they almost always have economic income rather than taxable income in mind. Because there are many meanings of "economic income,"[20] however, horizontal equity is an imprecise standard of fairness.

For example, if two taxpayers are identical in all respects except that one is an employee while the second's income is derived from investments, is horizontal equity satisfied, or violated, by imposing the same tax on them and disregarding the first taxpayer's commuting expenses, lunches bought during working hours, and increased domestic expenses because of work-induced fatigue? In the same vein, in deciding whether two taxpayers are equals, should above-average medical expenses, casualty losses, or family responsibilities be taken into account?

Another problem in applying the horizontal equity concept is that many tax allowances have been enacted to encourage or discourage investments and activities thought to be good or bad for the country as a whole. If, in order to preserve tangible evidence of our historic heritage, Congress provides a tax benefit to encourage rehabilitations of historic structures, is it inequitable that an individual who invests in a historical rehabilitation project pays less taxes than other individuals with the same income? Just as our sense of equity is not offended when a federal employee receives a government salary while persons employed in the private sector do not, it should not be considered unfair that a person's tax bill is reduced when that

---

[17] Graetz, Legal Transitions: The Case of Retroactivity in Income Tax Revision, 126 U. Pa. L. Rev. 47, 79–83 (1977), and articles therein cited; Musgrave, ET, OT and SBT, 6 J. Pub. Econ. 3 (1976).

[18] But see Feldstein, Compensation in Tax Reform, 29 Nat'l Tax J. 123 (1976) (horizontal equity means that individuals who are equally well off in the absence of a tax should remain equally well off after the tax is imposed).

[19] There are five rate schedules for, respectively, married couples filing joint returns and certain surviving spouses, heads of households, unmarried individuals, married individuals filing separate returns, and estates and trusts. See infra ¶¶111.3.2–111.3.8.

[20] Supra ¶3.1.3.

is the reward chosen by Congress for those who do things deemed to be in the national interest.

Many tax allowances provided for reasons foreign to the revenue raising function, further, are wholly or partially competed away, so that the nominal taxpayers are conduits through whom the benefits of the allowance pass to other persons.[21] Assume *A* receives $10,000 of taxable interest from $100,000 of corporate bonds, *B* receives $10,000 of tax-exempt interest from $200,000 of municipal bonds, and *C* receives $5,000 of tax-exempt interest from $100,000 of municipal bonds. Is horizontal equity violated because *A* pays a tax while *B*, who has the same economic income, pays nothing? Or, is this a false comparison, given that *B* has twice as much invested as *A*? If so, should *A* and *C* be viewed as equals because their investments are equal in amount? If so, is horizontal equity satisfied since *A*'s after-tax income is the same as *C*'s?[22]

Tax preferences intended as incentives, in fact, usually are efficient tools of congressional policy only if they are fully competed away. If a rehabilitation of a historical structure is as profitable as constructing a new building, for example, no tax preference for the rehabilitation is warranted; the arena for good is too vast for Congress to undertake to reward good that people do in their own self-interest. A preference for historic rehabilitations might rationally be considered if market forces cause people to tear down historic structures to make way for new construction and if the preference might alter the economic balance to make rehabilitations as profitable as new buildings. If the preference equalizes returns on rehabilitations and new construction, the taxes forgone by the preference go entirely to supporting the policy of increasing rehabilitations, and no investor in a rehabilitation is better off, after taxes, than an investor in new construction.

The concept of horizontal equity, however, is an important factor in people's perception of the fairness of the tax system. When taxpayers with apparently equal economic incomes pay vastly different taxes—when some taxpayers with high incomes pay less than many with much smaller incomes—the system is widely perceived as unfair. That many tax preferences are stimulants serving carefully considered congressional goals is often not reflected in public perceptions about taxes. People frequently have difficulty distinguishing between taxpayers who take advantage of tax preferences and taxpayers who cheat. When the former get a congressional stamp of approval, the perception arises that the latter cannot be all bad, and voluntary compliance, the keystone of our tax system, is threatened.

---

[21] Infra ¶3.3.2.

[22] For a more extended analysis of the horizontal equity concept in this context, see Bittker, Equity, Efficiency, and Income Tax Theory: Do Misallocations Drive Out Inequities? 16 San Diego L. Rev. 735 (1979).

Vertical equity as a principle of fairness is also problematical because it presupposes that equals are subject to the same tax liability as a prelude to determining whether each group of equals is properly differentiated from the next higher and lower groups of equals. Vertical equity also suffers from another ailment: The absence of an objective standard determining the proper differentiation between adjacent income categories. Thus, even if a consensus could be reached on the composition of each income group, vertical equity as a principle mandates only that there be some differentiation between each group and the next higher and lower groups, and does not specify the amount of the differentiation. The vertical equity principle does not prescribe whether tax rates should be proportional, progressive, or regressive; nor, if progression or regression is the chosen mode, does it indicate how steep the slope should be.

In an effort to liberate the principle of vertical equity from personal judgments about fairness, tax theorists sometimes treat the rate schedules of existing law as a "revealed social preference," i.e., as embodying a judgment by the people's political representatives of the proper differentiation between income brackets. The usual purpose of this exercise (which implies that what is, is fair or, at least, has been legitimated by the democratic process) is to establish that vertical equity is undermined by tax preferences and other allowances.

It is true that exemptions, deductions, and credits result in lower effective tax rates than the statutory rate schedules would produce if applied to a broader tax base.[23] After calling attention to the gap, which is portrayed as a violation of vertical equity, critics of existing law sometimes assert, explicitly or implicitly, that the American public has been misinformed or even betrayed. It is obviously tempting for the analyst to say: "I have no personal preference but am only performing the neutral analytical function of demonstrating that Congress has failed to deliver what it promised." The trouble with this forensic posture is that the statutory rates and the less-than-comprehensive tax base are interrelated parts of a single whole. If the rate schedule is a revealed social preference, so is the statutory tax base. Both come from Capitol Hill, which, although less lofty than Mount Sinai, is the only nonsectarian source of revelation in our society. This does not mean that whatever is, is right, but it does mean that there is no neutral proof that the political system worked correctly in fixing tax rates but erred in defining the tax base.[24] The approach taken in the Tax Reform Act of 1986, to lower rates as a trade-off for a broadening of the tax base, implicitly recognizes

---

[23] Infra ¶3.4.1.
[24] For further discussion, see Bittker, Effective Tax Rates: Fact or Fancy? 122 U. Pa. L. Rev. 780, 793–97 (1974).

that vertical equity is a function of both the nominal rates and the rules defining taxable income.

¶3.2 EFFECTS ON LABOR, CONSUMPTION, SAVINGS, AND INVESTMENT

¶3.2.1 Introductory

Imposing a new tax or increasing an existing tax changes the prior relationship between the cost of engaging in the taxed activities and the rewards accruing to them.[1] (Head taxes and taxes on the rental value of raw land do not alter behavior, but can be disregarded for practical purposes because they are not serious alternatives to more broad-based taxes.) A tax on income from personal services, for example, reduces the taxpayer's take-home pay without making the labor any less arduous; a tax on dividends and interest reduces the return from investments without reducing the risk of loss. The pretax market equilibrium can also be altered by taxes favoring a particular industry or form of business organization. If investments in oil and gas can be written off more rapidly than railroad equipment, for example, the former is favored over the latter; similarly, a tax regime that burdens corporate income more heavily than income earned through partnerships and proprietorships favors the latter forms of organization. These tax-induced changes in the returns from particular activities are not accompanied by equal changes in the prices buyers are willing to pay for the goods and services produced in these activities. The resulting difference between the values put on the activity by buyers and sellers may result in less-than-optimal uses of economic resources. When this happens, the tax imposes a burden on taxpayers in excess of its yield to the government.

Economists disagree about the extent of the distortion in taxpayer choices that is induced by the federal income tax; with respect to some tax provisions, there is disagreement about the direction of the change in behavior, not merely about its extent. Difficulties in measuring the excess burden of taxation can be attributed to three main causes. First, we do not have a purely competitive market but rather one that contains monopolistic elements and is affected by numerous governmental regulations. Second, income taxes have two opposing effects: By reducing the net remuneration from income-producing activities, they encourage taxpayers to engage in untaxed activities like leisure (the "substitution effect"); but by reducing the taxpayer's available funds, they induce taxpayers who wish to preserve or attain a particular standard of living to work more (the "income effect").

---

[1] See Polinsky, Economic Analysis as a Potentially Defective Product: A Buyer's Guide to Posner's Economic Analysis, 87 Harv. L. Rev. 1655, 1677–78 (1974).

Third, when taxation makes particular activities less remunerative, changes in behavior depend on the elasticity of the demand for goods and the supply of labor or capital, and these demand and supply curves are not easily plotted.

Even if the distortions caused by alternative taxing systems could be measured with precision, however, the public would not necessarily choose the tax imposing the smallest excess burden because its distributive effect might be viewed as inequitable. Moreover, interferences with the market are endemic in our society, and the public may prefer taxation over direct regulation as a method of changing some market outcomes. On the other hand, nothing can be said in favor of making decisions on these matters in ignorance. The principal areas that tax economists have sought to illuminate are briefly reviewed below, with citations to the relevant economic literature for those wishing to pursue the issues more fully than is warranted in a legal treatise.[2]

¶3.2.2 Work vs. Leisure

As stated above, taxing compensation from personal services decreases the economic reward for labor. Other things being equal, this alters the labor-leisure balance in favor of leisure, thus encouraging the laborer to work less and relax more. For most people, a law of diminishing marginal utility probably applies to both income and leisure. As income increases, the enjoyment from each additional dollar of income decreases; a $1,000 raise, for example, probably means more to a person earning $10,000 than a person earning $100,000. Similarly, as the number of leisure hours increases, the value of an additional hour of leisure probably declines; a quiet Sunday afternoon with the *New York Times* probably means more to a busy professional person, for example, than to a retiree. A person who views work solely as a source of money might therefore adjust the number of working hours so that the income from an additional hour of work equals the value to him of an additional hour of leisure. An income tax alters this balance because it takes away part of the income from work but does not subtract from the value of leisure. The tax thus causes additional hours of leisure to be substituted for work until the value to the individual of the last hour of leisure equals the after-tax income from his last hour of work.

This "substitution effect," however, is probably offset to some extent by an "income effect." To maintain a targeted standard of living after a tax

---

[2] See generally Goode, The Individual Income Tax (Brookings, rev. ed. 1976); Pechman, Federal Tax Policy (Brookings, 5th ed. 1987) (extensive annotated bibliography at 400–20); How Taxes Affect Economic Behavior (Aaron & Pechman, eds.; Brookings 1981).

is imposed or raised, it is necessary to work harder, longer, or both. If taxes go up, therefore, an individual is torn between a desire to play golf more often (the substitution effect) and the pressure to give up golf entirely and work longer hours so he will not have to buy a cheaper car or curtail other personal expenditures (the income effect). Whether the substitution effect or the income effect is stronger depends on an individual's relative preferences for income and leisure. The trade-off varies from one taxpayer to another and cannot be resolved by a priori reasoning.

Also, the work-leisure balance is importantly affected by noneconomic factors. Work can be a source of enjoyment, satisfaction, and status. For people with adequate incomes who derive substantial benefits beyond money from their work, neither the substitution nor the income effect of a tax is likely to be significant because leisure is so intertwined with work that income is not a material determinant of the quantity of work.

In a pioneering study published in 1934, Professor (later Senator) Paul Douglas concluded that a reduction in wages would, on the whole, induce people to enter the labor force and cause wage earners to work longer hours.[3] The income effect was strongest for the youngest and oldest age groups of both sexes, weakest for middle-aged workers, and stronger for females than for males. These results comport with a commonsense analysis: Since most middle-aged men already work full-time, they could not readily increase their earnings to offset higher taxes. On the other hand, when the primary breadwinner's take-home pay is reduced by taxation, one would expect high school students, retired persons, and housewives to give up their unpaid activities and seek gainful employment in order to restore the status quo ante.

Later studies have confirmed and refined the Douglas conclusions. It has been found that a reduction in the wages of middle-aged women induces them to leave the work force, that reduction of their husbands' wages generates greater participation by women, and that married women are more sensitive to wage rates than adult males.[4] These conclusions reflect the sociocultural patterns that prevailed when the studies were made; as the husband's role as primary breadwinner declines and more women embark on long-term careers, differences between men and women in their re-

---

[3] Douglas, The Theory of Wages 313 (Kelley & Millman 1934); see Break, The Incidence and Economic Effects of Taxation, in the Economics of Public Finance 187 et seq. (Blinder & Solow, eds.; Brookings 1974).

[4] See Boskin, The Economics of Labor Supply, in Income Maintenance and Labor Supply 163–81 (Cain & Watts, eds.; Academic Press 1973); Bosworth, Tax Incentives and Economic Growth (Brookings, 1984); Kosters, Effects of an Income Tax on Labor Supply, in The Taxation of Income From Capital (Harberger & Bailey, eds.; Brookings 1969) (citing earlier studies); How Taxes Affect Economic Behavior, supra note 2.

sponses to the competing tugs of the income and substitution effects of taxation will probably diminish or evaporate.

Efforts have been made to measure the impact of income taxes on the choice between work and leisure not only by statistical studies but also by questionnaires. When asked about the effect of taxes on their work habits, an overwhelming majority of wage earners, salaried employees, and self-employed professionals deny that the impact is substantial.[5]

Perhaps, these studies reflect the work-leisure choice of people addicted to work by training, experience, and social psychology.[6] It may be, for example, that the income and substitution effects will balance out differently for the children of affluence.

¶3.2.3 Savings vs. Consumption

A perennial objection to income taxation is that it discriminates against savings by taxing it twice — once when the invested funds are earned and a second time when the investment yield is realized.[7] Assume a taxpayer earns $100, which, in the absence of an income tax, can be either spent immediately or saved. If the taxpayer saves the $100 and invests it at an

---

[5] See Barlow, Brazer & Morgan, Economic Behavior of the Affluent 129–50 (Brookings 1966) (12 percent of individuals earning over $10,000 per year asserted they worked less because of taxes; half of these responses deemed suspect by authors); Brown & Levin, The Effects of Income Taxation on Overtime: The Results of a National Survey, 84 Econ. J. 833 (1974) (British study; 74 percent of men and 93 percent of women asserted that taxes did not affect decision to work overtime; of those acknowledging an effect, men divided 11 to 15 and women 6 to 2 on whether they worked less rather than more); Fields & Stanbury, Income Taxes and Incentives to Work, 61 Am. Econ. Rev. 435 (1971) (study of English solicitors and barristers; 19 percent reported taxes as a disincentive); Holland, The Effect of Taxation on Effort: Some Results for Business Executives, 62 Proc. Nat'l Tax A. 428 (1969).

The issue of the impact of taxes on incentives has a parallel in the welfare area, where the loss of governmental benefits when recipients find employment is tantamount to a tax on the earnings. For an effort to test the extent of the impact under experimental conditions, see Work Incentives and Income Guarantees: The New Jersey Negative Income Tax Experiment (Pechman & Timpane, eds.; Brookings 1975); Welfare in Rural Areas 109–48 (Palmer & Pechman, eds.; Brookings 1978). Although far from conclusive or unambiguous, these surveys suggest that high taxes are not a substantial deterrent to labor and that they produce only a negligible decline in annual output.

[6] See Bellow, Humboldt's Gift 3 (Viking Press 1975) ("Minds formed by five millennia of scarcity are distorted").

[7] See Fisher, The Double Taxation of Savings, 29 Am. Econ. Rev. 16 (1939); Ture, The Tax Bias Against Saving, 69 Proc. Nat'l Tax A. 18 (1976). For an estimate of the effects of existing law on particular types of saving, see Russek, The Tax Treatment of Individual Saving: A Look at Some Incentives, 69 Proc. Nat'l Tax A. 37 (1976).

annual yield of 10 percent, he will have $259 to spend after 10 years in the absence of an income tax. If an income tax of 28 percent is imposed, however, the choice is between spending $72 now ($100 less tax of 28 percent) and spending $144 at the end of 10 years ($72 plus after-tax interest of 7.2 percent, compounded annually).[8] By virtue of the tax, the relative value of savings as compared with consumption drops from 259 percent (259/100) to 200 percent (144/72). Thus, the thrifty taxpayer can spend 2.6 times as much as the spendthrift in the absense of a tax, but only 2 times as much if they are both subject to a tax of 28 percent.

The same phenomenon is illustrated in another way by Professor Marvin Chirelstein:

> Assume C and S, individuals, live in a country which at present imposes no income tax whatever. Each earns $1,000. C, a consumer, chooses to expend his $1,000 on a vacation. S, a saver, expends his $1,000 on a 6 percent bond with a view to receiving annual interest of $60 to use in future periods. Since they live in a tax-free world, both individuals get what they want for the same dollar expenditure.
>
> Now assume that their country adopts an income tax of 50 percent. How much must C and S earn in order to acquire, respectively, a $1,000 vacation and a $60-a-year income-stream? As to C, the answer is obviously $2,000. Since the vacation is not a deductible expense, it has to be purchased out of after-tax income. With the new 50 percent income tax in force, C will have to earn $2,000 in order to have $1,000 left for his annual trip to Florida. But what about S? The bond purchase *also* is not deductible—taxpayers are no more allowed to deduct amounts expended on "savings" than they are amounts expended on "consumption." At the same time, however, the interest on S's bond will *itself* be subject to the 50 percent income tax. In effect, earnings devoted to the purchase of an income-stream, *and* the income-stream itself, are both included in income. This means that S will actually have to earn $4,000 in order to be in the same position that he occupied before the new tax was enacted. Thus, the $4,000 would be reduced by the 50 percent tax to $2,000. The $2,000 that remained would then be used to buy a 6 percent bond yielding interest of $120 a year. The $120 of annual interest would *also* be taxed at the 50 percent rate, leaving a net after-tax income-stream of $60. In this sense, therefore, while C the consumer is required to earn only $2,000 because he pays the 50 percent income tax just once, S the saver is required to earn

---

[8] This assumes that the tax does not affect the interest rate. For discussion, see Warren, Fairness and a Consumption-Type or Cash Flow Personal Income Tax, 88 Harv. L. Rev. 931, 934–38 (1975).

$4,000 because his savings are subjected to a double imposition.[9]

The policy implications of these mathematical demonstrations largely depend on socioeconomic judgments about whether the tax base should be limited to consumption or should also take account of the command over goods and services that is inherent in the invested portion of a taxpayer's income. The latter is espoused on fairness grounds by many contemporary theorists, but an influential minority finds the double taxation complaint persuasive.[10] Double taxation of savings can be avoided by taxing consumption or personal expenditures, instead of income.[11]

Turning from theory to practice, economists do not agree on the extent to which the inclusion of savings in the income tax base actually causes taxpayers to favor current consumption over savings. Some believe that the substitution effect is of secondary importance in determining the volume of level of savings, others that it is rather substantial.[12]

Whatever may be its substitution effect, an income tax reduces the amount of private funds available for savings, and a progressive rate schedule bears more heavily on upper-income taxpayers, the traditional source of investment funds, especially for risky enterprises. Estimates of the decrease in private savings attributable to a progressive income tax (as compared with a proportional income tax or a tax on expenditures or retail sales) range from 5 to 13 percent.[13] These adverse effects may be diluted for more recent years, however, by a wider dispersion of funds available for investment, which increases the relative importance of savings by middle-income

---

[9] Chirelstein, Federal Income Taxation 290–91 (Foundation Press, 5th ed. 1988).

[10] Andrews, A Consumption-Type or Cash Flow Personal Income Tax, 87 Harv. L. Rev. 1113 (1974); Warren, supra note 8; Andrews, Fairness and the Choice Between a Consumption-Type and an Accretion-Type Personal Income Tax: A Reply to Professor Warren, 88 Harv. L. Rev. 947 (1975). See also Ture, supra note 7, and the authorities cited in note 2.

[11] See Kaldor, An Expenditure Tax (Allen and Unwin 1955); Broad-Based Taxes: New Options and Sources 133 et seq. (Musgrave, ed.; Johns Hopkins U. Press 1973); What Should Be Taxed: Income or Expenditure? (Pechman, ed.; Brookings 1980); Treasury Dep't, Blueprints for Basic Tax Reform 21–47 (Bradford, ed. 1984); Andrews, supra note 10; Mieszkowski, The Cash Flow Version of an Expenditure Tax (Treasury Dep't, OTA Paper No. 26, 1977); Warren, supra note 8.

[12] Break, The Incidence and Economic Effects of Taxation, in The Economics of Public Finance 192 et seq. (Blinder & Solow, eds.; Brookings 1974) (empirical estimates of substitution effect are small); Boskin, On Some Recent Econometric Research in Public Finance, 66 Am. Econ. Rev. 102, 107 (1976) (much larger effect). See generally The Role of Federal Tax Policy in Stimulating Capital Formation and Economic Growth, Hearings Before Subcomm. on Economic Growth and Stabilization, Joint Economic Comm., 95th Cong., 1st Sess. (1977).

[13] Break, supra note 12, at 195; Goode, supra note 2, at 67; Musgrave & Musgrave, Public Finance in Theory and Practice 478 (McGraw-Hill, 4th Ed. 1984).

individuals and employee pension trusts as compared with top-bracket tax-payers.

In addition to affecting the volume of savings by altering the choice between present and deferred consumption, an income tax influences the extent to which savings are divided between safe and risky investments. A rational investor with a given sum to invest analyzes the alternatives, comparing expected yields with risks in order to choose assets with a risk-return combination that accords with his preference. By reducing yields, the income tax has both an income effect (inducing the investor to take a greater risk to achieve the desired rate of return) and a substitution effect (prompting the investor to assume less risk because the rewards promised by higher risks are diminished).

It has been argued that the substitution effect would disappear if the deduction of a loss produced tax savings equal to the tax on an equal amount of gain because the tax would then reduce potential gains and potential losses by the same percentage, leaving investment risk unaffected.[14] With its substitution effect neutralized, the income effect would induce taxpayers to shift to riskier investments to obtain their targeted rates of return, thus increasing the level of risk taking in the economy.

Assuming the theoretical validity of this reasoning,[15] it could not easily be put into practice. Presently, the deductibility of capital losses is subject to time limits, dollar ceilings, and other restrictions that do not apply to the taxability of gains; if a taxpayer has gains in some years and losses in others, the gains can push the taxpayer into higher tax brackets, whereas losses are more likely to offset income that would otherwise be taxed at lower brackets; and taxpayers can be sure that their gains will be taxed, but not that they will have income against which losses can be offset. Because capital gains and losses are recognized for tax purposes only when realized by sale or exchange, it is generally believed that unlimited deductibility of capital losses would erode the tax base by encouraging taxpayers to realize losses promptly and defer realization of gains. Even if this objection were swallowed, complete parity of the treatments of gains and losses could be achieved only under a flat rate tax that allowed a taxpayer with a net loss for a year a payment from the government equal to the amount of the losses multiplied by the tax rate.

The aggregate effect of taxes on savings requires an estimate of the extent to which tax revenues are invested by the government in public projects. See Thurow, The Impact of Taxes on the American Economy 27–41 (Praeger 1971).

[14] See Domar & Musgrave, Proportional Income Taxation and Risk-Taking, 58 QJ Econ. 388 (1944).

[15] Feldstein, The Effect of Taxation on Risk Taking, 77 J. Pol. Econ. 755 (1969) (questioning the assumptions underlying Domar-Musgrave theory).

¶3.2.4 Business Investment

In addition to their effect on personal savings, taxes affect capital outlays by businesses for plant, equipment, and other productive facilities. A 1967 economic model devised to measure the magnitude of this effect divided business investment into two components: the replacement of used capital, assumed to be a constant proportion of existing capital; and increases in the aggregate amount of capital, assumed to be a constant fraction of the difference between the optimal level of capital in the economy and the actual level.[16] The optimal level for any investing firm, according to the model, is determined by the overall level of output and the net rate of return; if either increases, the desired level of capital increases correspondingly, widening the gap between the actual and optimal levels and thereby stimulating expansion. The model, therefore, predicts that increases in the net rate of return attributable to lower taxes will increase the optimal level of capital; in the short run, this will stimulate new investment, which in the long run will increase the level of replacement investment.

Applying the model to business behavior in the period from 1954 to 1963, its authors concluded that the introduction of accelerated depreciation, shorter useful lives for depreciable assets, and the investment credit resulted in dramatic increases in business investment.[17] Both the model and the conclusions based on its application to the 1954–1963 data have been challenged, however, by critics who argue that it overstates the effect of tax reductions; and the area remains rife with controversy.[18]

---

[16] Hall & Jorgensen, Tax Policy and Investment Behavior, 57 Am. Econ. Rev. 391 (1967).

[17] Id. For the depreciation rules in effect during this period, see infra ¶23.1; for the investment credit, see infra ¶27.2.

[18] See Coen, Tax Policy and Investment Behavior: Comment, 59 Am. Econ. Rev. 370 (1969); Eisner, Tax Policy and Investment Behavior: Comment, 59 Am. Econ. Rev. 378 (1969); Hall & Jorgensen, Tax Policy and Investment Behavior: Reply and Further Results, 59 Am. Econ. Rev. 388 (1969). See also Eisner, Components of Capital Expenditures: Replacement and Modernization Versus Expansion, 54 Rev. Econ. & Stat. 292 (1971); Feldstein & Foot, The Other Half of Gross Investment: Replacement and Modernization Expenditures, 53 Rev. Econ. & Statistics 49 (1971); Fellingham & Wolfson, The Effects of Alternative Income Tax Structures on Risk Taking in Capital Markets, 31 Nat'l Tax J. 339 (1978).

For efforts to rank the predictive success of alternative investment models by reference to actual changes in the level of investment, see Tax Incentives and Capital Spending (Fromm, ed.; Brookings 1971); Jorgensen & Hunter, A Comparison of Alternative Econometric Models of Quarterly Investment Behavior, 38 Econometrica 187 (1970); Nadiri, The Productive Performance of Econometric Models of Quarterly Investment Behavior, 38 Econometrica 291 (1970). For the use of questionnaires to measure the impact of taxes, see Eisner & Lawler, Tax Policy and Investment: An Analysis of Survey Responses, 65 Am. Econ. Rev. 206 (1975) (taxes have minimal effect). For comments on the *type* of investment induced by the law

¶3.3 SHIFTING AND INCIDENCE OF INCOME TAXES

¶3.3.1 The No-Shifting Hypothesis

Most popular discussions of federal income taxes—especially comparisons of the tax rates to which taxpayers at different income levels are subject—presuppose that those who pay the tax cannot shift it to their employers, suppliers, employees, or customers and hence bear the economic burden of the tax. In one sense, the no-shifting supposition is obviously false. The ultimate burden of every tax falls on human beings, but some taxes are imposed on corporations and other artificial entities. Taxes on entities are necessarily shifted to someone, but to whom? Taxes paid by individuals are also shifted in some circumstances.[1]

Neoclassical economists argue that if a uniform tax on economic income is imposed in an environment characterized by an inelastic supply of labor and capital and by perfect competition, a tax on income from capital (including corporate income) is borne by the suppliers of capital (the shareholders in the case of a corporation). The argument runs as follows: Each producer is assumed to face an upward sloping cost curve; that is, as a producer increases the quantity produced, more costly factors of production must eventually be utilized, and marginal cost is thus highest for the last good produced. A producer maximizes its profits by increasing production to the point where the cost of producing the last unit equals the market price for that unit; so long as it produces less, it could increase profits by increasing production, but when it reaches this point, a further increase in production results in a loss. The market price, which is the same for all units, is the price at which all buyers find sellers and all sellers find buyers. Because each supplier increases production to the point where its marginal cost equals the price, the market price equals marginal cost at equilibrium. When the price is higher, suppliers produce more, which either creates excess supply that brings the price down or runs marginal cost up to the price; when the price is lower than marginal cost, suppliers produce less until price and marginal cost are brought together. Because price is determined by marginal cost and because there is no profit on the marginal good, a tax on profits is not a factor in determining price. A producer, in other words, has no opportunity to raise its prices to cover the tax.

---

then existing, see Thurow, The Impact of Taxes on the American Economy 34–40 (Praeger 1971).

[1] See generally Bradford, Untangling the Income Tax 133–47 (Harvard 1986); Pechman, The Rich, the Poor, and the Taxes They Pay 31–40 (Westview 1986); Thurow, The Impact of Taxes on the American Economy 58–82 (Praeger 1971); Break, The Incidence and Economic Effects of Taxation, in The Economics of Public Finance 119 et seq. (Blinder & Solow, eds.; Brookings 1974).

Buried in the foregoing simplified description of the theory is a confusion in terminology. To an economist, a market return on the owner's investment is a cost. The theory thus is that a producer increases production until the cost of the last unit of production (including a market return on the additional capital required to produce the unit) equals the price. The market return on the owner's investment is taxable income. An income tax thus applies on the sale of the marginal good and is not wholly irrelevant at the marginal.

As long as savings rates are not affected, however, the tax on the marginal sale cannot be passed on through higher prices. Assume the rate of return on investments is 10 percent without taxes. If a 28 percent tax is imposed, the tax reduces every investor's return to 7.2 percent. Suppose one producer raises its price to yield a return on capital utilized in producing the marginal good to 13.89 percent before taxes, so that, after taxes, it is left with a 10 percent return. Other producers, seeing no other investment yielding more than 7.2 percent after taxes, rush in at the old price, the higher-priced producer promptly loses its customers, and the price returns to its pretax level.

The assumptions underlying the no-shifting hypothesis — perfect competition and inelastic supplies of capital and labor — are not a good reflection of reality, however. Even under an ideal income tax imposed in an environment of perfect competition, the tax on income from capital is probably shifted to consumers to some extent because of the way the tax affects savings.[2] Given a 10 percent rate of return and no income tax, a person with $100 has the choice between consuming $100 now or $10 annually forever. If a 28 percent income tax is imposed, the alternatives are $72 of immediate consumption or future annual spending of $5.184 per year (7.2 percent of $72). Because the after-tax return to savers is reduced by nearly one half, while the opportunity to consume immediately is reduced by only 28 percent, the tax makes the latter alternative more attractive, and reduces the propensity to save. Consumption demand, however, calls out the capital needed to produce consumer goods. The tax reduces aggregate consumption little, if at all, because the tax revenues allow the government to enter the market as consumer. Since the demand for capital remains high, a higher pretax return on investments is needed to keep the savings rate near where it was before the tax. This higher rate of return becomes part of each producer's economic cost and the theory described above holds that the market price equals economic cost when the market is in equilibrium. Under this theory, in other words, prices go up to cover at least part of any tax imposed on income from capital. Additional factors

---

[2] See supra ¶3.2.3.

bearing on the consumption-savings ratio of individuals, however, complicate the analysis still further.

The assumption of an inelastic supply of labor probably is also inaccurate, but the effect of the inaccuracy is less clear, even in theory. We do not know with precision whether the rival income and substitution effects of an income tax induce taxpayers to work longer or shorter hours, but it is inconceivable that there are no resulting behavioral changes. As explained elsewhere,[3] econometricians do not agree on the direction or extent of these changes.

Also, the no-shifting hypothesis does not take account of deviations from perfect competition, such as monopoly power, labor unions, governmental regulations, and other conditions that in real life undermine its basic premise. Imperfections in competition, however, do not necessarily cause an income tax to be shifted. If monopolistic firms are already charging all the traffic will bear, they cannot increase prices to recoup a new tax or an increase in an old tax without losing customers; in this respect, they resemble profit-maximizing firms in a competitive market. If they are not already maximizing their profits (because, for example, of public conceptions of a fair return, fear of stimulating antitrust suits, uncertainty about the reactions of consumers and competitors, or cost-plus pricing policies), the intrusion of a tax may prompt monopolistic firms to review their business practices, and they may conclude that a price increase will not evoke the adverse reactions that previously restrained them from exercising their economic power. In the absence of a consensus on the relative importance of competitive and administered prices in the economy,[4] the validity of the no-shifting conclusion cannot be conclusively established or rebutted.

¶3.3.2 Incidence of the Corporate Income Tax

Because the corporate income tax is imposed on corporations but not on proprietorships and partnerships, economists have been especially interested in whether its burden rests on shareholders as the beneficial owners of the corporation or is shifted to employees, suppliers, or customers.

When corporations operate in competitive markets with inelastic supplies of capital and labor and the tax base is economic income, the neoclassical economic theory previously described[5] teaches that they cannot shift the tax by changing the prices paid or charged by them for goods and services. If, apart from taxes, the corporate and proprietorship or partner-

---

[3] See supra ¶3.2.2.
[4] See Frankel, Discretionary Pricing and Tax Shifting, 6 Pub. Fin. Q. 3 (1978), and articles therein cited.
[5] Supra ¶3.3.1.

ship forms of organization were interchangeable, a corporate tax would thus cause the corporate form to disappear. The corporate form, however, has nontax advantages (e.g., limitation of owner liability and greater facility for handling large numbers of owners) that offset the added tax for some investments but not others. The imposition of a corporate tax causes disincorporations of enterprises for which noncorporate forms are feasible, and also causes funds to flow out of investments for which the corporate form is uniquely suited and into investments for which noncorporate forms are satisfactory. The relative abundance of funds for noncorporate projects is absorbed by investments whose pretax yields are lower than those on the divested corporate investments, and the remaining funds in the corporate sector are only invested in the most profitable projects. This flow of funds continues until after-tax returns on investments in the two sectors are equalized at a level that is lower for both sectors than before the corporate tax was imposed. To the extent that capital bears the corporate tax, in sum, the burden falls on all investors, not merely corporate investors.

To complete the analysis, however, it is necessary to determine whether the reduced rate of return reduces aggregate investment. If investment is insensitive to the decline in the rate of return, total output remains the same. Because laborers work with the same amount of capital as before, their productivity, and hence their wages, do not decline. On the other hand, if investment is sensitive to the after-tax rate of return, invested capital declines, dragging down the productivity of labor and lowering wages. If this is the outcome, the burden of the corporate tax is shared by labor.

On the basis of empirical studies of the relationship between the use of capital and the use of labor in the productive process, the economist who is primarily responsible for the foregoing analysis concluded that capital bears almost the full burden of the corporate tax.[6] But, another study published in 1963 reached the opposite conclusion for the period 1935 to 1959 (excluding 1943–1947). This study found a correlation between high rates of return on corporate investments and high taxes during the period under study, indicating that the tax burden was shifted by price adjustments and did not result in the previously predicted long-term reallocation of capital between

---

[6] Harberger, The Incidence of the Corporation Income Tax, 70 J. Pol. Econ. 215 (1962). See also Harberger, The State of the Corporate Tax: Who Pays It? in New Directions in Federal Tax Policy for the 1980s (Walker & Bloomfield, eds.; Ballinger 1983); McLure & Thirsk, A Simplified Exposition of the Harberger Model: Tax Incidence, 28 Nat'l Tax J. 1, 195 (1975); McLure, General Equilibrium Incidence Analysis: The Harberger Model After Ten Years, 4 J. Pub. Econ. 125 (1975); Shovin, The Incidence and Efficiency Effects of Taxes on Income From Capital, 84 J. Pol. Econ. 1261 (1976); Stiglitz, The Corporation Tax, 5 J. Pub. Econ. 303 (1976).

the corporate and noncorporate sectors.[7] The methodology of the 1963 study, however, was found wanting by critics who pointed out that the general state of the economy (a variable that was not tested in the 1963 econometric model) may have caused both the high tax rates and the high rates of return during the period under examination, so that a correlation between the latter two factors did not establish a cause-and-effect relationship between them.[8]

For the time being, therefore, the incidence of the corporate tax is veiled in obscurity. Acknowledging this melancholy fact, economists portraying the real-life impact of federal taxation usually offer the reader a choice of versions, based on alternative assumptions about the burden of the corporate tax. In a typical example, the corporate tax is allocated to families at different income levels in varying proportions, depending on whether the burden falls on dividends, income from all investments, or wages.[9]

¶3.3.3 Who Benefits From Tax Allowances?

Economists acknowledge that the benefits of many exclusions, deductions, credits, and other tax allowances can be competed away, so that the taxpayer who claims the allowance is a conduit through whom its benefits pass to others. Very little is known about the extent of this phenomenon.

The problem can be illustrated by assuming that a corporation subject to tax at 34 percent (the highest marginal rate under 1988 law) is about to invest $1,000 in an industrial bond paying 10 percent interest annually. Since the after-tax yield from the industrial bond is 6.6 percent, the taxpay-

---

[7] Krzyzaniak & Musgrave, The Shifting of the Corporate Income Tax (Johns Hopkins U. Press 1963).

[8] Break, supra note 1, at 138; Cragg, Harberger & Mieszkowski, Empirical Evidence on the Incidence of the Corporation Income Tax, 75 J. Pol. Econ. 811 (1967); Goode, Rates of Return, Income Shares, and Corporate Tax Incidence, in Effects of the Corporation Income Tax (Krzyzaniak, ed.; Wayne St. U. Press 1966); Gordon, The Incidence of the Corporation Income Tax in U.S. Manufacturing, 1925–1962, 57 Am. Econ. Rev. 731 (1967); Kotlikoff & Summers, Tax Incidence (National Bureau of Economic Research Working Paper 1986); Slitor, Corporate Tax Incidence: Economic Adjustments to Differentials Under a Two-Tier Tax Structure, id. at 136. See also Krzyzaniak & Musgrave, Incidence of the Corporation Income Tax in U.S. Manufacturing: Comment, 58 Am. Econ. Rev. 1358 (1968); Gordon, Incidence of the Corporation Tax in U.S. Manufacturing: Reply, 58 Am. Econ. Rev. 1360 (1968).

[9] See, e.g., Congressional Budget Office, The Changing Distribution of Federal Taxes: 1975–1990 (1987); Pechman, Who Paid the Taxes, 1966–85? (Brookings 1985). But see Feldstein, Imputing Corporate Tax Liabilities to Individual Taxpayers, 41 Nat'l Tax J. 37 (1988) (eschewing alternative assumptions and venturing a single allocation of corporate tax among income classes).

er should be equally willing to purchase a tax-exempt bond of the same investment quality with a 6.6 percent coupon; either investment would yield a net return of 6.6 percent. Since the market for both types of bonds is competitive, after-tax yields should equalize if all tax-exempt bonds are held by taxpayers subject to the same marginal rate. When this is so, the tax exemption confers no benefit on the investors but passes through to the tax-exempt borrowers in the form of lower interest costs.

On the other hand, if more exempt bonds are offered than top-bracket taxpayers are willing to buy, the issuers must pay more in order to attract less heavily taxed investors. If there are insufficient corporate purchasers, for example, exempt bonds must be priced to attract individuals, for whom the highest marginal rate for 1988 is 28 percent. To be equivalent to a 10 percent taxable bond for an individual in the 28 percent bracket, an exempt bond must pay 7.2 percent (the 10 percent taxable yield reduced by a 28 percent tax on that yield). If the market comes into equilibrium at an exempt yield of 7.2 percent, individuals taxed at the 28 percent marginal rate get no benefit from the tax allowance, but corporate buyers, who would have been willing to buy exempt bonds with a 6.6 percent coupon, get a windfall of six tenths of a percentage point. The Treasury's loss (the revenue it would have received if the funds had been invested in taxable bonds) is divided between the tax-exempt issuers, who can borrow at 7.2 percent when taxable issuers are paying 10 percent to finance projects of equal risk, and the corporate holders, who get a net return of 7.2 percent when they could realize only 6.6 percent after taxes on taxable bonds.

This example shows both the intended consequences and the inefficiencies of many tax incentives. The exemption for interest on state and local bonds is provided to subsidize borrowing by state and local governments, not to reward investors. If corporate investors taxed at the highest corporate rate purchase all exempt bonds, the subsidy mechanism works perfectly; the after-tax yields on exempt and taxable bonds equalize at a level where the Treasury's loss from the exemption equals the issuers' savings in interest costs. Part of the benefit of the exemption stays in private hands, in contrast, when this benefit is not fully competed away for all holders; when, that is, exempt bonds must be priced to attract individuals taxed at a lower rate.

Other tax preferences work similarly, but not as simply. The exempt bond case is special because the tax law imposes a unique restraint on competition in an otherwise competitive market: Only state and local governments can issue exempt bonds; other issuers are not allowed to compete for funds in this market. The effects of a tax incentive are not as easily traced when the tax law does not restrain competition. Nontax restraints on competition exaggerate the complexity.

Assume that Congress, in order to stimulate investment in equipment, provides a tax treatment for equipment costs that effectively exempts income from such property from tax.[10] If the pretax rate of return is 10 percent, a differential in after-tax returns apparently arises—10 percent for investments in equipment and 6.6 percent (10 percent less a tax of 34 percent of 10 percent) for other investments. In a perfectly competitive market, however, this differential attracts new investment in equipment, driving down the rate of return, while the flight of capital from other investments pushes up the rate of return on these investments. The after-tax return on all investments stabilizes at some point between 6.6 and 10 percent, and the benefit of the tax preference is shared by all investors. The increase in the after-tax rate of return on investments, further, might induce individuals to save more and consume less, which would tend to spread the benefit of the tax incentive among new as well as old investors. The congressional intention to stimulate investment in equipment is thereby achieved.[11]

If, in contrast, there are rigidities in the market that impede capital flows from one investment type to another, investment in equipment is not sufficient to equalize the returns on all investments. In this case, investors in equipment (mainly those who would have bought equipment without the

---

[10] This might be accomplished by allowing these costs to be written off fully when incurred. See infra ¶23.1.5.

[11] A phenomenon similar to the one observed in the exempt bond example is also present in this case if investors fall into different tax brackets. Assume some investors are taxed at 34 percent and others at 28 percent. If the rate of return on equipment settles at, say, 7 percent, taxpayers taxed at 34 percent buy only those nonequipment investments whose pretax yields are at least 10.61 percent. (The latter yield, reduced by a 34 percent tax, equals the tax-free 7 percent yield on equipment.) Taxpayers subject to the 28 percent rate, in contrast, prefer any nonequipment investment yielding more than 9.7 percent to an equipment investment (9.7 percent less 28 percent thereof is 7 percent).

Without the preference for equipment investments, all investors probably insist on the same pretax returns (assumed to be 10 percent), and the effect of the differing tax rates is that those taxed at the lower rate enjoy a higher after-tax return (assumed to be 7.2 percent for 28 percent taxpayers). With the introduction of the tax preference, 28 percent taxpayers might respond by (1) turning away from equipment investments, investing only in other investments that yield at least 10 percent before taxes or (2) reducing their after-tax yield to 7 percent (9.7 percent before taxes on nonequipment investments). Inevitably, the latter would occur because there would be nothing in the market to anchor these investors' expectations at the original 7.2 percent after-tax return.

The rate of return on the tax-free investment, in other words, becomes the after-tax rate of return for all investors. The 28 percent taxpayer might gain or lose by the introduction of the preference (depending on whether the rate of return on equipment is more or less than 7.2 percent), but the 34 percent taxpayer always gains. If the after-tax rate of return falls for 28 percent taxpayers, their propensity to save might also fall.

tax incentive) reap a windfall, and the congressional policy to stimulate investment is at least partially frustrated. In the short run, such rigidities inevitably arise from the fact that investors hold long-lived assets. Introduction of the tax preference induces existing holders of other investments to sell them and buy equipment. An investment switch can be made, however, only if there is a buyer for the old investment and a seller for the new one. The preference affects the prices buyers and sellers are willing to agree to. As a consequence, given perfect competition, the prices of equipment immediately rise, and the prices of other investments immediately fall, bringing after-tax returns on the two types of investment into equality. With respect to existing investments, in sum, the effect of the preference is to produce windfall gains to holders of equipment and windfall losses to holders of other investments, not to induce investment changes. The congressional policy to stimulate investment in equipment can only be played out with new investment (including reinvestment of economic depreciation on existing investment).

Even in the absence of such rigidities, the investment incentive is not necessarily good policy. When the tax break for equipment causes investors to shift from other assets to equipment, investors abandon investments that have higher pretax yields than the equipment they buy. The pretax rate of return on all investments is assumed to be 10 percent if all investments are taxed alike. Without tax preferences, that is, investors pass up any investment that cannot produce 10 percent before taxes. Assume that with the special break for equipment, after-tax rates of return equilibrate at 7 percent; before taxes, the tax-exempt return on equipment is 7 percent, and the taxable return on other investments is 10.61 percent (10.61 percent less 34 percent thereof is 7 percent). This means that with the tax incentive, any equipment investment that promises 7 percent before taxes is made, but other investments go begging unless they can yield at least 10.61 percent. The incentive, in other words, causes investors to move from other investments whose yields range from 10 to 10.61 percent to equipment investments yielding from 7 to 10 percent. The switch from more to less profitable investments decreases gross national product (GNP), at least in the short-run. By increasing the after-tax rate of return on all investments, the tax preference might induce additional savings; these savings would affect GNP in the long run, but the size of this effect is uncertain.

Also, the analysis given here does not show how much added investment in equipment is induced by the tax preference. Because the preference goes to those who would have invested in equipment in any event, as well as to those brought into equipment investments by the incentive, it is possible that the taxes lost by the preference could be greater than the incremental investment traceable to the preference. Further, the foregoing analysis examines the effects of a single tax preference in a law that otherwise applies uniformly to all economic income. In real life, tax preferences are allowed in many contexts, and they interact in ways difficult to identify and may even negate each other. Nontax imperfections in the market mechanism also affect the way in which a tax preference works through the economy. The point here is only that tax preferences enacted for the purpose of altering taxpayer behavior can have their intended effects. Whether these effects are desirable and come at a reasonable cost is another matter.

The foregoing discussion applies only to tax allowances relating to investments and activities taxpayers can control. The additional standard deduction for blind taxpayers,[12] for example, does not confront taxpayers with a choice; a person either is or is not blind, and it is inconceivable that anyone would deliberately blind himself in order to qualify for the deduction. Thus, this tax allowance is not competed away but remains with the taxpayer who claims it. In other contexts, the purposes of tax allowances are not carried out through competitive effects, but such effects nevertheless occur. The exclusion from gross income for employer-paid premiums for medical insurance, for example, probably is a powerful stimulant for the demand for medical services, a consequence surely intended by Congress. Economic theory tells us, however, that an increase in the demand for a good or service raises its price; high prices for medical services probably has never been congressional policy.

The fact that income and taxes are interdependent variables was once described in a discouragingly cosmic metaphor:

> The stone thrown into the ocean makes ripples which, as they diminish in height with the widening of the circles, may extend—could we but measure their infinitesimal magnitude—to shores thousands of miles away. And the light rays which their movement deflects from the course these rays would otherwise follow, may pursue their new way through the stellar universe far past the remotest stars of which the telescope informs us. Similarly, the effects, could we consider all of them in their (possibly) increasing variety though (probably) diminishing intensity, of any given tax, may extend through the future to and beyond the time when human beings shall have ceased to tenant the earth.[13]

This was written in 1924, and it might be thought that the same computer that now plots the travels of aerospace satellites could follow the ripples of an income tax to the farthest reaches of the national economy. Technological advances in the processing of numbers, however, have not been accompanied by comparably improved ways to measure human im-

---

[12] IRC §63(f)(2), discussed infra ¶30.5.1.
[13] Brown, The Economics of Taxation 12–13 (Henry Holt & Co. 1924).

pulses. As a result, the calculations disgorged by the computer are no better than the imprecise guesses that it feeds on, although the precision of the output can easily blind the layman to the deficiencies of the input.

Even if a tax exemption is not subjected to the corrosion of competition, it may nevertheless confer a smaller benefit on the taxpayer than meets the eye. The tax immunities accorded to military allowances and various other governmental benefits, for example, are undoubtedly taken into account by Congress in fixing the payment levels; if the exemptions were repealed, Congress would probably make compensating increases in benefits. If so, the tax exemption is a matter of form rather than substance for most beneficiaries of these payments. Repeal of the exemption would primarily hurt upper-bracket taxpayers, whose tax liabilities would likely rise by more than the increase in benefit payments.

¶3.3.4   Capitalization of Tax Benefits and Burdens

When a tax allowance is shifted from the nominal taxpayer to other persons, the tax-favored property or activity may increase in value to reflect its inherent tax benefit. A municipal bond with a 7.2 percent coupon can sell for the same price as a 10 percent taxable bond with similar investment characteristics, for example, because the interest on the municipal bond is tax-exempt; the municipal bond's market value includes the capitalized value of the tax exemption, which declines as maturity approaches and would abruptly disappear if the exemption were repealed.

Because the unexpected repeal of capitalized tax allowances can impose a burden analogous to a capital levy, tax theorists occasionally propose that taxpayers be compensated for the unanticipated repeal of a tax benefit,[14] and tax reform legislation frequently contains delayed effective dates, gradual phase-in provisions, and grandfather clauses to preserve existing private commitments or cushion taxpayers against the shock of repeal.[15]

A comprehensive system of compensating taxpayers for (or shielding against) loss from unanticipated changes in tax allowances, however, is inconceivable. In many cases, it is impossible to distinguish unanticipated changes from those that have already been capitalized or discounted by the market. Moreover, compensation entails insuperable valuation problems. It would be exceedingly difficult, for example, to measure the tax-induced increase in the value of houses that is attributable to an owner-occupant's right under existing law to exclude the rental value from income and to

---

[14] Feldstein, On the Theory of Tax Reform (Harvard Institute of Economic Research, Discussion Paper Series No. 408, 1975). But see Graetz, Legal Transitions: The Case of Retroactivity in Income Tax Revision, 126 U. Pa. L. Rev. 47 (1977); Graetz, Retroactivity Revisited, 98 Harv. L. Rev. 1820 (1985).

[15] See supra ¶1.2.6.

deduct mortgage interest and local real property taxes, or to determine the decline in value that would result from repeal of these allowances. It would be even more difficult to ascertain the loss attributable to repeal of a tax provision that induced taxpayers to train for entry into a tax-favored occupation, to accept employment under a tax-sheltered contract,[16] or to make other commitments that cannot be readily reversed when the activity's tax appeal is tarnished or destroyed. Prospects for a comprehensive shield become even dimmer when one recognizes that the repeal of tax allowances can blight settled expectations of nontaxpayers as well as taxpayers, that expectations can be upset by judicial decisions and administrative rulings as well as by legislative action, and that unanticipated increases and decreases in tax rates can also generate unexpected changes in the value of property and commitments.

The other face of the compensation coin—requiring taxpayers to disgorge windfalls attributable to unexpected relief from a tax burden—is rarely even mentioned, except for an occasional suggestion that a change in existing law is unwarranted because it will shower an undeserving group of taxpayers with gold. Outside the tax field, however, there are examples of symmetrical treatment of the burdens and benefits of governmental action. When New York City built its elevated railroad system, for example, adjacent landowners were compensated for the loss of light and air; but many years later, when the system was demolished, they were assessed to reflect the increased value of their property.[17] In the same vein, it could be argued that the repeal of an entrenched tax disadvantage (e.g., denial of amortization for purchased goodwill)[18] would increase the value of the taxpayer's property and warrant recognition of income equal to the value of the windfall. Computing the windfall's value, however, would be as difficult as computing the loss resulting from repeal of favorable tax provisions.

These considerations suggest that a truly comprehensive system of compensating or charging taxpayers for the burdens and benefits of tax changes would not be feasible. On the other hand, abrupt changes do impose sacrifices, and it is not surprising that Congress has responded to the problem with delayed effective dates, grandfather clauses, and other cushioning devices. These responses are crude expedients, exhibiting no consistent principles, but the underlying problem may be too intractable for a more systematic solution.

---

[16] For examples of this problem, see supra ¶1.2.7 (salaries of federal judges) and infra ¶13.1.3 (military pensions).

[17] See In re Third Ave. R.R. Bridge, 21 NY2d 293, 234 NE2d 445 (1967). For more general discussion, see Windfalls for Wipeouts: Land Value Capture and Compensation (Hagman & Misczynski, eds.; American Society of Planning Officials 1978).

[18] Infra ¶23.2.4.

¶3.4   DISTRIBUTIVE EFFECTS OF INCOME TAXATION

¶3.4.1   Marginal, Average, and Effective Rates

In assessing the distributive effects of federal income taxation, including variations in its burden among taxpayers in the same income class and between one income class and another, tax theorists customarily convert the statutory rates imposed on taxable income into "effective rates" based on the taxpayer's economic income.[1] The statutory schedules set out marginal rates; i.e., the rates rise in steps corresponding to specified tax brackets. For example, under 1988 law, married couples filing joint returns are taxed at 15 percent on the first $29,750 of taxable income and 28 percent on any excess.[2] The benefits of the 15 percent bracket and the personal exemptions are phased out for joint returns reporting taxable income in excess of $71,900. The phase-out effectively raises the marginal rate to 33 percent until the tax is a flat 28 percent of taxable income determined without personal exemptions. For a family of four, the flat 28 percent tax is reached in 1988 when this expanded taxable income is $192,930. At any lesser income level, the average rate of tax is less than 28 percent of this tax base. For a family of four in 1988, for example, the average rates are 9.15 percent of expanded taxable income of $20,000, 11.1 percent of $30,000, 15.9 percent of $50,000, 22.96 percent of $100,000, and 26.3 percent of $150,000.

These average rates, however, are not the same as the effective rates used by tax theorists. Assume a married couple with two minor children file a joint return reporting taxable income of $50,000 for 1988, resulting in a tax liability of $10,133, which is 17.53 percent of the sum of taxable income and the personal exemptions. It is unlikely that the effective rate of tax is also 17.53 percent because the couple's taxable income, even when expanded by adding back the personal exemptions, probably does not equal their economic income. Assume the couple owns municipal bonds on which interest of $5,000 is received during the year. The interest is excluded from taxable income but is economic income. If this is the only difference between taxable and economic income, the effective rate is 16.13 percent (the tax of $10,133 divided by the sum of taxable income of $50,000, personal exemptions of $7,800, and exempt interest of $5,000).

In actuality, the conversion of taxable income into economic income is often more complicated. Assume the couple (1) owns their home, which has a rental value of $10,000 for the taxable year, (2) consumes fruits and

---

[1] See generally Bittker, Effective Tax Rates: Fact or Fancy? 122 U. Pa. L. Rev. 780 (1974).

[2] See supra ¶2.2.

vegetables raised in a home garden, with a retail value of $1,000, (3) inherits $30,000, (4) owns marketable securities that increase in value during the year by $25,000, of which $10,000 is attributable to inflation, and (5) spends $900 getting to and from work. These items are not reflected in taxable income. If they are taken into account in determining economic income, the effective tax rate is only 8.59 percent, as shown by Table 3-4. Tax theorists, however, differ on the extent to which these additional items affect economic income, and the determination of effective rates thus is as open to argument as the definition of "economic income."[3]

Table 3-4

Effective Tax Rate on Economic Income

1. Taxable income			$ 50,000
2. Plus:			
a. Personal exemptions	$ 7,800		
b. Tax-exempt interest	5,000		
c. Rental value of home	10,000		
d. Home garden produce	1,000		
e. Inherited property	30,000		
f. Real increase in value of securities	15,000	68,800	
4. Less: Transportation to and from work		900	
5. Economic income			$117,900
6. Tax liability			$ 10,133
7. Effective rate (line 6 divided by line 5)			8.59%

    The usual starting point in computing effective tax rates is adjusted gross income as defined by §62 because *Statistics of Income*, the compilation of tax data published annually by the Treasury, classifies taxpayers by adjusted gross income class. Although AGI is better than taxable income as an approximation of economic income, it fails to take account of many items that most theorists would either include in economic income (e.g., pension and profit sharing contributions, excess of tax over economic depreciation, rental value of owner-occupied housing, and tax-exempt interest) or deduct from it (e.g., union dues paid by employees who do not itemize their personal deductions).[4] For this reason, an economic income base is usually obtained by making appropriate adjustments to AGI to take

---

[3] For citations, see Bittker, supra note 1, at 785.

[4] For the meaning of AGI, see supra ¶2.1.3; for its deficiencies as an "analytical measure of total income for purposes of determining a person's ability to pay income

account of these otherwise omitted items. If the item in question is reported on tax returns (e.g., tax-exempt interest), an econometrician can be reasonably confident of the amount to be added to AGI before determining the effective rate. Items not so reported must be estimated and imputed to taxpayers in various AGI classes by a tedious process that is fraught with uncertainties.[5]

A 1987 study by the Congressional Budget Office estimated effective federal tax rates by population deciles, the first decile consisting of the poorest 10 percent of all families and the tenth consisting of the most affluent 10 percent. Separate estimates were made for the richest 5 and one percent. Estimates were prepared for several years, and for each year, alter-

Table 3-5

Effective Federal Tax Rates (1988)
Assuming Corporate Tax Borne by Capital

Decile	Individual Income Tax	Social Insurance Taxes	Corporate Income Tax	Excise Taxes	All Taxes
First	− 0.8	5.0	1.1	4.5	9.7
Second	− 0.4	5.9	1.0	2.1	8.6
Third	1.7	8.6	1.3	1.6	13.3
Fourth	4.1	9.4	1.6	1.4	16.5
Fifth	5.9	9.8	1.6	1.1	18.5
Sixth	7.2	10.4	1.6	1.0	20.2
Seventh	8.3	10.5	1.7	0.9	21.4
Eighth	9.0	10.9	1.6	0.8	22.3
Ninth	10.4	10.6	1.7	0.8	23.4
Tenth	15.5	6.0	4.7	0.4	26.6
Top 5%	16.9	4.4	5.7	0.4	27.4
Top 1%	19.7	1.8	7.7	0.2	29.3
All	10.4	8.7	2.7	0.9	22.7

Source: Congressional Budget Office, The Changing Distribution of Federal Taxes: 1975–1990 (1987).

---

tax," see Staff of Joint Comm. on Tax'n, 94th Cong., 2d Sess., General Explanation of the Tax Reform Act of 1976, reprinted in 1976-3 CB (Vol. 2) 652–54.

    [5] See Pechman & Okner, Who Bears the Tax Burden? (Brookings 1974); Okner, Effective Individual Income Tax Rates, 32 Nat'l Tax J. 368 (1979). Other studies are cited in Bittker, supra note 1, at 785.

native estimates were made assuming that the corporate income tax is borne by capital income or by labor income.[6] The estimates for 1988 are shown in Table 3-5 (assuming the corporate tax is borne by capital income) and Table 3-6 (assuming the corporate tax is borne by labor income).

Table 3-6

Effective Federal Tax Rates (1988)
Assuming Corporate Tax Borne by Labor Income

Decile	Individual Income Tax	Social Insurance Taxes	Corporate Income Tax	Excise Taxes	All Taxes
First	−0.8	4.7	1.2	4.5	9.6
Second	−0.5	5.3	1.4	2.1	8.3
Third	1.5	8.0	2.1	1.6	13.3
Fourth	4.0	9.0	2.4	1.4	16.8
Fifth	5.8	9.6	2.6	1.1	19.2
Sixth	7.1	10.0	2.8	1.0	20.9
Seventh	8.2	10.3	2.9	0.9	22.3
Eighth	8.9	10.8	3.1	0.8	23.6
Ninth	10.3	10.5	3.1	0.8	24.7
Tenth	15.8	6.3	2.5	0.5	25.0
Top 5%	17.5	4.8	2.3	0.4	24.9
Top 1%	20.9	1.9	1.9	0.3	24.9
All	10.4	8.7	2.7	0.9	22.7

Source: Congressional Budget Office, The Changing Distribution of Federal Taxes: 1975–1990 (1987).

The estimates show the individual income tax as steadily progressive through all income ranges, although the effective rate for even the most affluent one percent of families is considerably below the 28 percent suggested by the rate tables. The effect of the corporate income tax is sharply progressive at the highest reaches of the income scale if it is assumed to be borne by shareholders and other owners of income-producing property; if it is assumed to be borne by labor, the corporate tax is mildly progressive through all income ranges except the highest, where its effect is regressive. The progressivity of the income taxes is offset to a large extent by social insurance and excise taxes.

---

[6] See supra ¶3.3.2.

¶3.4.2 High-Income, Low-Tax Taxpayers

In 1976, Congress directed the Treasury to make an annual report on the taxes paid by individual taxpayers "with high total incomes."[7] The term "high" is not defined, but at a minimum the report must cover individuals with "total income" over $200,000 who owe no income tax and must disclose the deductions, exclusions, and credits they used to avoid liability. Congress observed that "adjusted gross income," on which prior studies of the taxes paid by high-income taxpayers were based, "is not a very good analytical measure of total income for purposes of determining a person's ability to pay income tax"; it directed the Treasury to employ a better measure of total income, but required the Treasury to confine itself to information currently reported on tax returns.[8] Further confirming the latent definitional difficulties in measuring income, Congress suggested three alternative methods of calculating total income.[9]

The Treasury's most recent studies of nontaxable returns uses four measures of income: (1) adjusted gross income; (2) expanded income, consisting of adjusted gross income, plus preference items omitted from adjusted gross income, and minus investment interest expense not allowable in determining adjusted gross income; (3) adjusted gross income plus preference items; and (4) adjusted gross income less investment interest.[10] The preference items included in the second and third of these measures are limited to items reported on returns (including minimum tax returns). Thus, none of the income measures includes economic income not reported

---

[7] Tax Reform Act of 1976, Pub. L. No. 94-455, §2123, 90 Stat. 1915.

[8] Joint Comm. on Tax'n, supra note 4. In 1986, Congress departed from this policy by requiring that amounts received as tax-exempt interest be reported on returns filed for 1987 and subsequent years. IRC §6012(d).

[9] The legislative concern with high-income, low-tax taxpayers, along with the $200,000 bench mark, can be traced to a 1968 Treasury study that analyzed 1,100 individual tax returns for 1964, each with AGI of more than $200,000 but reporting tax at an effective rate of 22 percent or less. Effective rates were calculated based on "amended taxable income," defined by the study as AGI, plus the excluded portion of long-term capital gains, percentage depletion, and an adjustment for the excess of farm losses over farm gains. House Ways and Means Comm. & Senate Finance Comm., 91st Cong., 1st Sess., Treasury Dep't, Tax Reform Studies and Proposals, Pt. 1, at 79 (Comm. Print 1969). A similar Treasury study for 1970, which subjected the raw data to a more detailed analysis, indicates that reality may be either less or more dramatic than appearances because of deficiencies in "amended adjusted gross income" as a measure of economic income. Tax Subsidies and Tax Reform, Hearings Before the Joint Economic Comm., 92d Cong., 2d Sess. 152 (1972). The 1970 study also demonstrates that a one-year snapshot can be misleading, since a low effective rate for a particular year can result from a cash-basis taxpayer's belated payment and deduction of legitimate expenses attributable to income received, and heavily taxed, in an earlier year.

[10] Lerman, High-Income Returns, 1984, 6 Statistics of Income Bulletin 1 (1987).

on returns, including tax-exempt interest (for years before 1987), unrealized capital gains, imputed income on owner-occupied housing, and employee fringe benefits. Since the limitations on the deduction of investment interest expense are intended to match this interest with the eventual recognition of unrealized capital gains, the nearest approximation of economic income may be adjusted gross income plus preference items, but unreduced by investment interest.

Figures from a recent Treasury study for selected taxable years in the period 1977 through 1984 are given in Table 3-7 (number of nontaxable returns with more than $200,000 of income) and Table 3-8 (these returns as a percentage of all returns with more than $200,000 of income). In numbers, the nontaxable returns have steadily increased over the years, in part because the $200,000 benchmark has been eroded by inflation. The percentage figures have gone up in some years and down in others, probably largely in response to legislative changes. The lower percentage figures for 1979, for example, likely resulted from the Tax Reform Acts of 1976 and 1978, while the higher percentages for 1981 and 1983 reflect the proliferation of tax preferences in the Economic Recovery Tax Act of 1981. The probable causes of the lower percentage for 1984, in turn, are the Tax Equity and Fiscal Responsibility Act of 1982 and the Tax Reform Act of 1984. Studies for years affected by the Tax Reform Act of 1986 might show a further decline in the percentage of nontaxable returns in the $200,000-and-above class.

¶3.4.3 Effective Corporate Tax Rates

Although studies of effective tax rates have focused primarily on individuals, the effective rate of the federal corporate income tax has also received attention,[11] and corporations required to report to the SEC must include their effective tax rates among the information disclosed.[12]

---

[11] See Kaplan, Disparity in Corporate Rates Raises Questions About Underlying Tax Policy, Tax Notes, Nov. 17, 1975, at 13–36; Kaplan, Effective Corporate Tax Rates, 2 J. Corp. Tax'n 187 (1975); Weiss, Effective Corporation Income Tax Rates, 32 Nat'l Tax J. 380 (1979). But see Treasury Dep't, Effective Income Tax Rates Paid by U.S. Corporations in 1972 (1978) (computations, accompanied by a lavish sprinkling of skeptical salt); Fiekowsky, Pitfalls in the Computation of "Effective Tax Rates" Paid by Corporations (Treasury Dep't, OTA Paper No. 23, 1977).

[12] SEC Reg. S-X, Rule 3.16(o), 17 CFR §210.3-16(o) (1978).

Table 3-7

Number of Returns With Income Exceeding $200,000 Reporting No Taxable Income

Income Measure	Year				
	1977	1979	1981	1983	1984
Adjusted gross income (AGI)	60	70	226	447	532
Expanded income	85	114	304	579	325
AGI plus excluded preferences	95	127	363	810	673
AGI less investment interest	52	56	188	229	205

Source: Lerman, High-Income Returns, 1984, 6 Statistics of Income Bulletin 1, 3 (1987).

Table 3-8

Returns With Income Exceeding $200,000 Reporting No Taxable Income as Percentage of All Returns With Income Exceeding $200,000

Income Measure	Year				
	1977	1979	1981	1983	1984
Adjusted gross income (AGI)	.112%	.075%	.164%	.225%	.218%
Expanded income	.126	.093	.174	.232	.105
AGI plus excluded preferences	.134	.098	.194	.309	.207
AGI less investment interest	.104	.064	.147	.122	.089

Source: Lerman, High-Income Returns, 1984, 6 Statistics of Income Bulletin 1, 3 (1987).

The taxable income of businesses is a poor measure of economic income, both because of the tax allowances granted to all businesses (e.g., accelerated depreciation and the deferral of taxes on the income of foreign subsidiaries) and because of the numerous tax allowances for particular industries (e.g., preferences for oil and gas income, income from export sales, and Puerto Rican income). Adjusting for tax allowances, tax analysts have computed effective corporate rates that are substantially below the statutory rates as applied to taxable income. Moreover, there are wide variations from one industry to another and among companies within the same industry, depending on their opportunities to use particular tax allowances.[13] It is far from clear, however, that the net profits of companies or

---

[13] Kaplan, supra note 11, Tax Notes, Nov. 17, 1975, at 26–33. See also Congressman Vanik, Annual Corporate Tax Study, Tax Year 1976, Cong. Rec., Jan. 26,

industries subject to low effective rates are higher, measured by reference to invested capital, sales, or other relevant standards, than the profits of high-rate enterprises. As shown elsewhere,[14] in a perfectly competitive market, tax allowances reverberate throughout the economy, and raise the rates of return of all investors, not just those who invest in favored activities. An allowance disproportionately benefits investors in tax-favored activities only if rigidities in the market restrain new investment in these activities. Indeed, some economists are troubled by variations in effective corporate rates not on equity grounds but because they induce misallocations of resources—resulting, for example, in utility services that are "too cheap" and cigarettes that are "too expensive."[15] Laymen might view this state of affairs with equanimity rather than disapproval, although the corporate tax rate is not a very supple or predictable tool for allocating resources.

As is endemic in effective tax rate computations, the rate depends on the economic base chosen by the analyst. It is customary, for example, to treat the excess of accelerated depreciation over straight-line depreciation as a tax allowance that must be restored to economic income in computing effective corporate tax rates,[16] but it is arguable that even straight-line depreciation is excessive and that a sinking-fund method would produce a more accurate measure of income.[17] Sinking-fund depreciation would depress effective rates still further, as would a capitalization of portions of the costs of advertising, research, and created goodwill to reflect the future benefits expected to flow from these expenditures.[18] Conversely, the lack of adjustment for inflation tends to inflate taxable income for many corporations, and corrections for this would increase their effective rates.[19]

Finally, the adjustments used in computing the effective rate of the corporate income tax are, by and large, not concerned with special features of corporate income, but are equally applicable to the business income of individual proprietors and partners. For this reason, they could be used in computing the effective rates of the individual income tax; indeed, unless consistent adjustments are used for both categories of effective rates, they are not wholly comparable.

1978, at E168 et seq., which offers a rather different set of numbers—additional proof of the dependence of effective rate computations on their underlying assumptions.

[14] Supra ¶3.3.3.

[15] See Pechman, Federal Tax Policy 162–64 (Brookings 5th ed. 1987).

[16] Kaplan, supra note 11, 2 J. Corp. Tax'n at 189–90.

[17] See infra ¶23.1.4.

[18] See infra ¶20.4.5.

[19] See Bernard & Hayn, Inflation and the Distribution of the Corporate Income Tax Burden, 39 Nat'l Tax J. 171 (1986).

¶3.4.4 · Effect of Taxes on Distribution of Income

Since the distributive effect of the federal personal income tax can be reinforced or counterbalanced by state, local, and other federal taxes, tax economists have sought to measure the aggregate effective rate of all taxes, using the taxpayer's income as the base. To bring taxes based on the taxpayer's real property, retail purchases, and other events and transactions into the consolidated formula, however, they must be allocated among taxpayers by reference to income rather than according to the taxpayer's participation in the activity generating the tax liability in question. For example, the retail sales tax, which is paid on purchases of goods and services for consumption and thus is proportional to expenditures for taxable items, must be expressed as a fraction of income, not purchases. Similar conversions are required for corporate income taxes,[20] real property taxes, gift and inheritance taxes, excise taxes, and other levies.

A comprehensive and painstaking study published in 1985 employed eight sets of assumptions about the incidence of taxes.[21] The principal difference between these eight variants was in the assumptions made about the incidence of the corporate income tax. The two variants that figured most prominently in the author's conclusions assumed that the corporate tax is borne one half by shareholders and one half by property owners generally (variant 1c) or is borne one half by property income and one half by consumers (variant 3b). The study's conclusions for 1980 are summarized as follows:

> Under the most progressive assumptions (variant 1c) effective tax rates in 1980 ran from about 20 per cent at the lowest end of the income scale to 27 per cent at the top. Under the least progressive assumptions (variant 3b) effective tax rates declined from over 30 per cent at the lowest end of the distribution to about 25 per cent in the second decile and remained at that level until they declined to 22 per cent in the top percentile. For the distribution as a whole, the tax system was either moderately progressive (variant 1c) or slightly regressive (variant 3b). The differences in effective rates between the two variants were relatively small except at the bottom of the income scale, where the tax burden was much higher under variant 3b than it was under 1c, and at the top, where the tax burden was higher under variant 1c.

---

[20] For divergent assumptions regarding the incidence of the federal corporate income tax, see supra ¶3.3.2.

[21] Pechman, Who Paid the Taxes, 1966–85? (Brookings 1985). The results of the study are summarized in Pechman, The Rich, the Poor, and the Taxes They Pay 31–40 (Westview 1986).

Because the degree of progressivity or regressivity is relatively small under any of the incidence assumptions, it is clear that the tax system has very little effect on the distribution of income.[22]

A major objective of the study was to ascertain how effective rates changed during the period 1966 through 1985. The conclusions on this issue are summarized as follows:

The major influences on the distribution of tax burdens between 1966 and 1985 were a decline in the relative importance of the corporation income tax and the property tax [and] a rise in payroll taxes. Since the former two are progressive tax sources and the latter is regressive, the effect of these changes was to reduce the progressivity of the tax system. The federal tax cuts in 1981 also contributed to the reduction in progressivity. Between 1966 and 1985 tax burdens increased in the lower part of the income scale, declined sharply at the top, and remained roughly the same or rose slighty in between. The effective tax rate in the highest population decile fell from 1.79 times the burden in the lowest decile in 1966 to 1.16 in 1985 under variant 1c, and from 0.94 to 0.83 under variant 3b. . . .

The decline in the progressivity of the tax system during this period was caused by a decline in the progressivity of federal taxes. State and local taxes became somewhat more progressive or retained the same degree of progressivity, depending on the incidence assumptions. Individual income taxes remained progressive throughout the period, but less so at the end of the period than at the beginning because of the effect of bracket creep resulting from the growth of real incomes as well as inflation and the federal tax cuts enacted in 1981.

In 1966 the tax burden on capital income was substantially higher than the burden on the labour income. This pattern was reversed by 1985 as a result of the reduced roles of the corporation income tax and the property tax and the greater role of the payroll tax.[23]

¶3.4.5 Tax Impact vs. Fiscal Impact

The fairness of a tax system cannot be judged without taking account of the governmental benefits it makes possible. Ethically, a tax levied to finance welfare payments is not the same as a tax imposed to build a municipal marina for oceangoing yachts. In isolation, a computation of effective tax rates is ethically neutral; what ultimately counts is fiscal, rather than tax, fairness. Recognizing this, economists and other social analysts have en-

---

[22] Id. at 33–34.
[23] Id. at 36–39.

deavored to allocate the benefits of public expenditures to the citizenry, classified by income class.[24] The objective is a distribution of both benefits and burdens, permitting each income group's benefits to be compared with its taxes in a display of the consolidated incidence of the nation's fiscal system.

Any such allocation of governmental benefits, however, encounters a familiar problem in political economy: the absence of a free market to establish the citizen's evaluation of the benefits of governmental expenditures. Without a tollgate to exclude freeloaders from public education, highways, and other social goods and services, we do not know what any citizen or group of citizens would have been willing to pay for these benefits, or how much they would have consumed if they had been required to pay the market value of their shares. If it were possible to deaden the freeloader instinct with a truth serum, we could ascertain what particular public goods are worth to each user. Pending this improvement in medical technology, analysts who allocate governmental expenditures by income class must choose from a range of plausible assumptions that is even broader than the spectrum used to allocate the tax burden.

¶3.5 STRUCTURAL FEATURES OF FEDERAL INCOME TAXATION

¶3.5.1 Introductory

This section summarizes the views of tax economists on the principal features of federal income taxation. Since virtually all substantive tax provisions are of interest to economists, the review is confined to major issues that have stimulated substantial bodies of economic theory or empirical research. Citations to economic studies also appear elsewhere in this work in discussions of particular areas, such as accelerated depreciation, loss carryovers, the investment credit, percentage depletion, personal exemptions, charitable contributions, and medical expenses.

---

[24] See Burkhead & Miner, Public Expenditure 324–30 (Aldine 1971); Reynolds & Smolensky, Public Expenditures, Taxes, and the Distribution of Income (Academic Press 1977); Tax Foundation, Tax Burdens and Benefits of Government Expenditures by Income Class, 1961 and 1965, at 20 (1967); Gillespie, Effect of Public Expenditures on the Distribution of Income, in Essays in Fiscal Federalism 122, 125–28, 135–36 (Tables 3, 4) (Musgrave, ed. 1965); Herriot & Miller, Changes in the Distribution of Taxes among Income Groups: 1962 to 1968, 1971 Proc. Am. Statistical Ass'n (Bus. & Econ. Stat. Sec.) 106, 108 (1972); Musgrave, Case & Leonard, The Distribution of Fiscal Burdens and Benefits, 2 Pub. Fin. Q. 263 (1974).

¶3.5.2 Accretion vs. Realization of Gains and Losses

The Haig-Simons definition of income calls for periodic valuations of the taxpayer's assets and liabilities so that increases and decreases in net worth can be taken into account as they accrue.[1] With minor exceptions, however, gains and losses are taken into account under present law only when realized by sale, exchange, abandonment, or other disposition.[2] The realization approach defers tax on accrued but unrealized gains and losses. Because the present value of a deferred tax is less than that of an immediate tax, a realization system effectively taxes property gains at lesser rates than income that is taxed as earned even if the nominal rates of tax are the same for all income.[3] This differential disturbs the fairness of the tax and skews investment choices. Also, the deferral sometimes causes gain to be taxed at different marginal rates than those that would have applied when the gain accrued. The most dramatic example of this is where an individual dies holding appreciated property; the individual's estate and heirs take a basis for the property equal to its fair market value, which assures that the marginal rate of tax on predeath appreciation will be zero. If gain is realized before death, in contrast, the bunching of gain accruing over several years into the return for the year of realization might cause the gain to be taxed at rates higher than those that would have applied in the years of accrual.

Several practical problems stand in the way of implementation of an accrual approach. First, it would require annual valuations of all assets. This would be costly for taxpayers, and would lead to countless disputes between taxpayers and the IRS. Second, even if asset valuations were readily available, the accrual approach would burden taxpayers with the task of collecting and reporting data on the costs and prior valuations of all assets, and would generally be administratively complex. Third, because this approach would require taxpayers to pay tax on gains that have not been reduced to cash, taxpayers whose unrealized gains are high in relation to their money incomes would face a cash squeeze, particularly if the unrealized gains were in assets that were difficult to sell or could not be sold

---

[1] Supra ¶3.1.1.

[2] Infra ¶¶5.2, 40.2; see also infra ¶105.4.4 (write-down of inventory).

[3] This is not to say that property gains are presently undertaxed. Gains and losses are computed under current law without regard to inflation. In periods of inflation, gains are overstated and losses are understated. Thus, while the realization principle causes real gains to be undertaxed, present law also taxes amounts that are mere inflation illusion. Whether the present value of the deferred tax on realized gain, unadjusted for inflation, is more or less than would be a tax on real gain, imposed as the gain accrues, depends on the rate of inflation and the length of time the taxpayer holds the property. The problem of inflation is separately considered in ¶3.5.4.

without disrupting the taxpayer's business.[4] For these reasons and perhaps others, substitution of the accretion concept for the realization approach has not been high on the agenda of tax reformers, who have been content to let this sleeping dog lie, save for proposals to take appreciation and depreciation into account when assets are transferred by lifetime gifts or at death.[5]

A practical equivalent of the accrual system could perhaps be had by deferring recognition until realization, as under present law, but charging interest on the tax as compensation for the deferral.[6] The interest charge would give the deferred tax the same present value as a tax imposed as gains accrue. It would therefore compensate the government for its loss of the use of money during the deferral period, put the taxation of property gains on rough parity with the treatment of other income, and make the income tax a more neutral presence in the economy.

The interest alternative, however, is not without its problems.[7] Unless the taxpayer is taxed at the same rate for all years in which the asset is held, the tax imposed in the year of realization probably does not equal the sum of the taxes that would have been paid under an accrual system. A precise equivalence could be obtained only by throwing the gain back to the returns for the years in which it accrued, and this would require the same annual valuations of the property and complex computations that lead most scholars to believe that an accrual system is not practical.[8] Neither can the interest charge be computed accurately without relating the gain back to particular years. The value of the deferral is much different, for example, for a taxpayer cashing in gains accrued in a bull market of years ago than for

---

[4] See Treasury Department, Blueprints for Basic Tax Reform 73–74 (Bradford, ed. 1984) [hereinafter Blueprints]; Slawson, Taxing as Ordinary Income the Appreciation of Publicly Held Stock, 76 Yale LJ 623 (1967); Wetzler, Capital Gains and Losses, in Comprehensive Income Taxation 115–62 (Pechman, ed.; Brookings 1977), and articles therein cited.

[5] For constructive realization by gift or at death, see infra ¶10.5.2. This form of constructive realization is far less drastic than full-scale annual accretion; for a comparison, see Bittker, A "Comprehensive Tax Base" as a Goal of Tax Income Reform, 80 Harv. L. Rev. 925, 967–71 (1967).

[6] This is done in a few limited contexts. See IRC §453A (interest charge when gain on large real property sales reported on installment method), discussed infra ¶106.2; §1291 (interest charge on gains and large distributions with respect to stock of passive foreign investment companies), discussed infra ¶68.4.

[7] See Blueprints, supra note 4, at 74.

[8] In the throwback, further, gains and losses other than the now-realized gain would have to be taken into account because, under an accrual system, accrued losses would be offset against accrued gains and the net gain would be added to other income. Moreover, to determine the tax that would have been imposed on the gain accruing to a particular asset, the tax for each accrual year, increased to reflect the net accrued gain, would have to be apportioned among various segments of the income for the year, including accrued gain on each asset.

a taxpayer selling a long-held farm whose value recently blossomed in a development boom.[9]

To be practical, an interest alternative would have to (1) accept the tax computed in the normal way for the year of realization as a surrogate for the taxes that would have been imposed in the years of accrual, (2) allocate gain ratably over the years the taxpayer held the property, ignoring the actual pattern of accrual of the gain, and (3) determine the interest charge at statutorily prescribed rates.[10] The desirability of such a system depends on whether its enactment would enhance fairness and neutrality to an extent that would outweigh both the arbitrariness of its application in some cases and the substantial administrative burden it would thrust on taxpayers and the IRS. The Treasury has considered and rejected it on at least two occasions.[11]

Present law contains several counter-measures limiting the freedom that an unfettered realization concept would create. Most importantly, §1211 limits deductions for capital losses to the amount of the taxpayer's capital gains plus (for individuals) up to $3,000 of ordinary income.[12] This restriction might once have been explained as the price to be paid for reduced tax rates for capital gains, but, since the repeal of the capital gains preference in 1986, can only be justified as a curb on the discretion allowed taxpayers by the realization rule. Under a realization system, particularly one that forgives tax on gain inherent in property held at death, an unlimited deduction for capital losses would encourage taxpayers to promptly realize losses while deferring the realization of gains. The capital loss limitation thus seems to be a necessary adjunct of a realization system.[13]

---

[9] Also, it is argued that the interest charge should be at a rate equal to the rate of return on the taxpayer's investments, not a standard rate for all taxpayers. Because the benefit of the deferral is the taxpayer's investment return on the amount that would have been paid to the government in tax under an accrual system, an interest charge is neutral (i.e., economically efficient) only if it deprives the taxpayer of the amount of this benefit and no more or less. Blueprints, supra note 4, at 74.

[10] The system for passive foreign investment companies (supra note 6) follows the second and third of these steps, but computes the tax on the gain allocated to prior years at the highest marginal rates applicable to those years.

[11] Blueprints, supra note 4, at 74.

[12] See infra ¶50.2.4 (for noncorporate taxpayers); ¶50.3.2 (for corporations). See also IRC §267(a)(1) (disallowing losses on sales between related taxpayers), discussed infra ¶78.1. See generally Warren, The Deductibility by Individuals of Capital Losses Under the Federal Income Tax, 40 U. Chi. L. Rev. 291 (1973).

[13] In a major tax reform study completed in 1977, the Treasury asserted that if capital gains were taxed as ordinary income and if gains and losses were appropriately indexed for inflation, the reason for the capital loss limitation would disappear. Blueprints, supra note 4, at 72. Given a few years to reflect on the matter, however, the principal author of the study decided that "deductibility of net capital losses must be sharply limited" so long as the realization rule persists. Id. at xviii–xix.

Proponents of the accretion concept ordinarily focus on the appreciation and depreciation of physical and financial assets to the exclusion of human capital. A taxpayer who completes a course of vocational training or qualifies for an occupational license enjoys an accretion to net worth equal to the present value of the increased potential income stream; so do taxpayers whose experience, skill, and reputation are enhanced from year to year. Conversely, human capital depreciates in value as an individual progresses toward retirement age, physical or mental disability sets in, occupations are threatened by competition, or skills become obsolete. Tax theorists often toy with fanciful econometric models, but they have not manifested any enthusiasm for extending the accretion concept to human capital. A specialized aspect of this issue arose in a 1978 Tax Court case, in which the IRS contended that a taxpayer realized income on emerging from bankruptcy with his debts discharged since his expertise and business relationships in the retail grocery field constituted an asset that he could now put to economic use. The court rejected this ingenious but wholly novel theory: "We know of no case which taxes a taxpayer's expertise or skill, nor has respondent cited any authority. The difficulties involved in placing a value on such an ethereal asset are insurmountable and would involve only conjecture."[14]

Apart from these practical difficulties, the exclusion of human capital from the accretion concept might be defended in theory. Human capital, unlike other appreciated property, usually cannot be sold, except through daily use in employment or a professional practice. Human capital, in other words, is valuable, but has no fair market value. The tax law generally deals only with marketable quantities.

¶3.5.3 Progressive Tax Rates

Progression in the individual tax rate schedules, which entails taxing each increment to the taxpayer's income at a higher rate than the previous increment, has been a feature of the federal income tax since the Civil War, when income between $600 and $10,000 was taxed at 3 percent and amounts above $10,000 at 5 percent.[15] The 1894 federal income tax abandoned progression in favor of a flat rate of 2 percent on amounts in excess of $4,000, but even this concession to conservative opinion did not save it

---

[14] Davis v. CIR, 69 TC 814, 833–34 (1978). See also Andrews, A Consumption-Type or Cash Flow Personal Income Tax, 87 Harv. L. Rev. 1113, 1145–46 (1974), for the relationship between human and material wealth.

[15] 12 Stat. 473 (1862). For a 1798 antecedent, see Soltow, America's First Progressive Tax, 30 Nat'l Tax J. 53 (1977). See generally Shehab, Progressive Taxation: A Study in the Development of the Progressive Principle in the British Income Tax (Oxford U. Press 1953).

from a judicial veto.[16] When the individual income tax was revived in 1913, after ratification of the Sixteenth Amendment, Congress returned to the Civil War precedent of progression, but with a steeper slope (from one percent on the first $20,000 of net income to 7 percent on amounts above $500,000).[17] To meet the cost of World War I and the immediate postwar period, Congress made the rate schedules still steeper. It receded to less progressive rates in the mid-twenties as these financial pressures receded, but World War II brought a reversal in this trend. The all-time high was reached by the Revenue Act of 1944, which taxed income above $200,000 at 94 percent.[18] In the last 25 years, progression in the nominal rates has been steadily reduced. The top rate, for example, was reduced to 70 percent in 1964, to 50 percent on earned income in 1969, to 50 percent on all income in 1981, and to 28 percent in 1986.

In practice, progression's bark is worse than its bite, although some taxpayers at every income level get bitten. As indicated by Table 3-9, the aggregate amount of tax revenue contributed by the upper reaches of the progressive rate structure in 1976, when the highest marginal rate was 70 percent, was relatively trivial. Similar figures are given in Table 3-10 for 1984, after the elimination of the rates above 50 percent; they show that the upper brackets then raised significant amounts of revenue, but were still overshadowed by the revenues collected under rates near the bottom of the scale. For 1984, for example, 42.5 percent of all individual income taxes were imposed at rates in the range of 11 through 20 percent, whereas the rates in the range of 41 through 50 percent raised only 18.7 percent of the total. This pyramid-like effect of the rates is accounted for by several factors. Everyone who pays tax, for example, gets hit by the lower rates, while only those with large incomes are subject to the higher rates. Also, high income taxpayers are far less numerous than those with modest incomes. Moreover, for most taxpayers, but especially for the most affluent, taxable income is usually less than economic income.

---

[16] Pollock v. Farmers Loan & Trust Co., 157 US 429 and 158 US 601 (1895), discussed supra ¶1.2.2.

[17] Revenue Act of 1913, Pub. L. No. 16, §II, 38 Stat. 166.

[18] Individual Income Tax Act of 1944, Pub. L. No. 315, 58 Stat. 231. See also id. at §12(g), providing that the effective rate could not exceed 90 percent. Comparisons with earlier years are complicated by differences in the personal exemptions and other nontaxable amounts, as well as by the use until 1954 of a dual rate system, consisting of a normal tax on one base and a surtax on a somewhat different base. See supra ¶1.1.

Table 3-9

Distribution of Taxable Income and Individual Income Tax (1976), by Rate Bracket

Rate (%)	Amount (in Millions) by Rate Bracket		Percentage Distribution by Rate Bracket	
	Taxable Income	Tax	Taxable Income	Tax
14–20	354,610	60,267	52.87	39.27
21–25	184,669	42,587	27.53	27.75
26–30	41,017	11,458	6.12	7.47
31–35	22,755	7,291	3.39	4.75
36–40	22,501	8,394	3.36	5.47
41–50	20,337	9,365	3.03	6.10
51–60	7,155	3,969	1.07	2.59
61–70	7,564	5,096	1.13	3.32
50[1]	1,097	548	.16	.36
50[2]	8,974	4,487	1.34	2.92

[1]Alternative capital gain tax rate.
[2]Maximum tax on earned income.

Source: Treasury Department, Statistics of Income—1976, Individual Income Tax Returns, Table 3.12.

Table 3-10

Distribution of Taxable Income and Individual Income Tax (1984), by Rate Bracket

Rate (%)	Amount (in Millions) by Rate Bracket		Percentage Distribution by Rate Bracket	
	Taxable Income	Tax	Taxable Income	Tax
0	254,373	–0–	15.0%	0.0%
11–15	527,277	67,543	31.1	22.1
15–20	362,658	62,333	21.4	20.4
21–25	212,556	49,693	12.5	16.3
26–30	101,586	28,184	6.0	9.2
31–35	73,094	24,206	4.3	7.9
36–40	43,046	16,357	2.5	5.4
41–45	47,990	20,561	2.8	6.7
46–50	73,818	36,667	4.3	12.0

Source: Holik & Kalish, Individual Income Tax Rates (1984), 6 Statistics of Income Bulletin 37, 42 (1987).

Progression has always been a controversial aspect of income taxation.[19] Proponents have argued that as income increases, each additional
dollar provides less satisfaction to the taxpayer than its predecessor, with
the result that it becomes less and less painful to pay a fixed portion to
satisfy the government's tax claim. From this psychological assumption (the
so-called declining marginal utility of money), it is argued that if a millionaire and a poor taxpayer each get $100 of additional income, it is no more
of a sacrifice for the millionaire to pay a large fraction of it to the government than for the poor taxpayer to pay a smaller fraction.

Critics of progression reply that even if money has a declining marginal
utility to most individuals, it is impossible to know whether a particular
rich person places a lower value on his last $100 than a particular poor
person places on his; the world contains both miserly millionaires and
generous paupers. Moreover, even if millionaires feel less pain than paupers
when forced to contribute to the fisc, Congress can only guess at the extent
of the difference and, therefore, has no reliable guide for fixing the amount
of progression: "The moment you abandon . . . the cardinal principle of
exacting from all individuals the same proportion of their income or their
property, you are at sea without rudder or compass, and there is no amount
of injustice or folly you may not commit."[20] Given the deficiencies in the
interpersonal comparisons that underlie the justification for progressive
rates, its opponents assert that the only safe and fair standard is proportionality; taxing every dollar equally, whether it is received by a millionaire or
by a pauper.

Defenders of progression often respond by noting that even proportionality does not escape interpersonal comparisons. A proportional tax
must rest on the conclusion that either (1) all persons, rich and poor, place
approximately the same value on every dollar of income or (2) the utility of
money is irrelevant. The former is no more provable than the declining
utility thesis. If the utility of money is irrelevant, some other principle must
be articulated for preferring proportionality to progressivity or regressivity.
To say that proportionality is fairest unless progressivity is proven to be
fairer is an assumption, not an argument or proof. If equality, pure and
simple, were equity, a regressive tax—a per capita tax under which every
taxpayer paid the same amount—would be the ultimate in fairness. There

---

[19] The classic analysis of progression is Blum & Kalven, The Uneasy Case for
Progressive Taxation (U. of Chicago Press 1953), reprinted from 19 U. Chi. L. Rev.
417 (1952); see also Galvin & Bittker, The Income Tax: How Progressive Should It
Be? (American Enterprise Inst. 1969); Smith, High Progressive Tax Rates: Inequity
and Immorality? 20 U. Fla. L. Rev. 451 (1968); Hayek, Progressive Taxation Recon-
sidered, in On Freedom and Free Enterprise 265 (Sennholz, ed.; Van Nostrand
1956).
[20] McCullock, Taxation and the Funding System 142 (1845).

is, in short, no escape from human judgment. On balance, the legislative determination that the tax rate should rise with income accords with the electorate's sense of fairness.

¶3.5.4 Inflation

The high rates of inflation during the 1970s and early 1980s "elevated the question of whether and how the tax system should be adjusted to cope with rising prices from a matter of academic curiosity to a live political issue."[21] Inflation affects income tax computations in two principal ways:

1. *Statutory provisions using dollar amounts.* Many provisions are stated in terms of dollar amounts. Without adjustment for inflation, the effects of these provisions change as the value of the dollar changes. Each rate bracket, for example, applies to income within a specified dollar range, and, without adjustment, the real width of that range narrows as inflation erodes the purchasing power of the dollar, with the consequence that a taxpayer whose nominal income merely keeps up with inflation creeps into ever higher rate brackets. Even taxpayers who have reached the highest rate bracket are affected by bracket creep because, as the real value of the lower rate brackets decreases, the portions of these taxpayers' incomes that are taxed at the highest rate increase. Similarly, the personal exemption, which is meant to immunize a basic subsistence amount from taxation, performs

---

[21] Inflation and the Income Tax 1 (Aaron, ed.; Brookings 1976). See Hearings Before House Budget Comm., Task Force on Inflation, 96th Cong., 1st Sess. (July 24, 1979) (statement of Emil M. Sunley, Deputy Assistant Secretary of the Treasury (Tax Analysis)); Joint Comm. on Tax'n, 95th Cong., 2d Sess., Description of S. 2738, Relating to Adjusting the Income, Estate and Gift Taxes for Inflation (Comm. Print 1978); Treasury Dep't, Blueprints for Basic Tax Reform 40–42, 75–76 (Bradford, ed. 1984); Fellner, Clarkson & Moore, Correcting Taxes for Inflation (American Enterprise Inst. 1975); Bucovetsky, Inflation and the Personal Income Tax Base: The Capital Gains Issue, 25 Can. Tax J. 77 (1977); Committee Report, Price-Level Basis Adjustment — A Modest Proposal, 26 Tax Lawyer 189 (1972); Feldstein & Slemrod, Inflation and the Excess Taxation of Capital Gains on Corporate Stock, 31 Nat'l Tax J. 107 (1978); Feldstein & Summers, Inflation and the Taxation of Capital Income in the Corporate Sector (National Bureau of Economic Research, Working Paper No. 312, 1979); Halperin & Steurele, Indexing the Tax System for Inflation, in Uneasy Compromise: Problems of a Hybrid Income-Consumption Tax (Aaron, Galper, & Pechman, eds.; Brookings 1988); Note, Inflation and the Federal Income Tax, 82 Yale LJ 716 (1973); Rose, Inflation, Tax Rules, and the Price of Land Relative to Capital, 39 Nat. Tax J. 59 (1986); von Furstenberg, Individual Income Taxation and Inflation, 28 Nat'l Tax J. 117 (1975). See also Haig, The Concept of Income — Economic and Legal Aspects, in The Income Tax 16–17 (Haig, ed.; Columbia U. Press 1921) (early discussion of indexing). See generally Bradford, Untangling the Income Tax 32–58 (Harvard U. Press 1986).

that task less and less well over time if the cost of basic subsistence rises with inflation but the personal exemption does not.

Over the years, Congress has made many ad hoc adjustments to various statutory dollar amounts to reflect inflation.[22] Its first broad, systematic response to this problem came in 1981 with the enactment of provisions indexing for inflation the dollar amounts stated in the rate brackets, the personal exemption, and a few other provisions.[23] The movement to indexation of fixed dollar amounts progressed further in 1986,[24] but many provisions still contain unindexed dollar amounts.[25]

The change in congressional approach from ad hoc adjustments to indexing has great political significance. The ad hoc approach allowed each adjustment to be advertised as a tax cut, a politically attractive but disingenuous characterization of adjustments meant to keep the real value of tax liabilities roughly constant over time. Less obvious, but probably more important, the ad hoc approach allowed the tax burden to be shifted among income classes without direct discussion of the shift. For nearly everyone, inflation increased the percentage of nominal income taken in taxes, and the periodic adjustments reduced this percentage. Because the adjustments were not closely examined as inflation adjustments, however, there was little check on whether, for particular income groups, the adjustments accurately compensated for inflation. As a consequence, the real value of tax liabilities could increase for some income classes and fall for others, even while aggregate taxes remained roughly constant as a percentage of national

---

[22] Some economists expressed contentment with this system. See Sunley & Pechman, Inflation Adjustment for the Individual Income Tax, in Aaron, supra note 21, at 153.

[23] The transition to the indexed system has been fitful. The 1981 legislation made what was intended to be the last of the ad hoc adjustments, and provided that the rate brackets, personal exemption, and zero bracket amount were to be indexed for 1985 and subsequent years. The indexing device enacted in 1981 only applied for 1985 and 1986, however, because the Tax Reform Act of 1986 made what amounted to another ad hoc adjustment and provided that the dollar amounts adopted in 1986 are not to be indexed until 1989. See, e.g., IRC §1(f) (before and after amendment in 1986).

[24] See, e.g., IRC §1(f) (rate brackets), §32(i) (dollar ceilings used in computing earned income credit), §63(c)(4) (standard deduction), §151(d) (personal exemptions), §415(d) (dollar limits on benefits and contributions under pension, profit sharing, and stock bonus plans).

[25] E.g., IRC §21 (credit for child care expenses qualified by rules containing several unindexed dollar amounts); §22(d) (credit for elderly phased out for taxpayers whose income exceeds unindexed ceilings); §86(c) (social security benefits taxable to persons whose incomes exceed unindexed amounts); §§179(b)(1), (2) (election to expense costs of depreciable business assets subject to unindexed dollar limitations).

income.[26] Indexing adjusts more systematically for inflation, and assures that a shift in burden can be accomplished only by the politically difficult steps of explicitly increasing the taxes on some taxpayers to finance a reduction for others.

2. *Computation of taxable income.* More perplexing are the problems of computing taxable income with due allowance for inflation. These problems are of two kinds.

First, whenever costs incurred in one period are matched on a tax return against revenues of another period, taxable income is not stated accurately unless adjustment is made for any change in the value of the dollar between these two periods. Assume land purchased for $1,000 is sold years later for $1,200. Under present law, which ignores inflation in this context, the seller has gain of $200. Real gain or loss is $200 only if the value of the dollar remained constant while the land was held. If inflation occurred during this period, real gain can only be determined by restating the purchase price in dollars of the period of sale.[27] This is done by multiplying the purchase price by an index representing the change in the dollar's value due to inflation while the asset was held. If goods costing $1 when the land was purchased cost $1.30 when the land is sold, the factor is 1.3, and there is economic loss of $100 on the sale computed as shown in Example 3-1.

Example 3-1

Inflation Adjusted Gain or Loss on Sale of Property

1. Amount realized on sale... $1,200
2. Less: Inflation adjusted cost ($1,000 multiplied by 1.3)............. 1,300
3. Equals: Loss on sale... ($100)

---

[26] But see Cohen, Reflections on the U.S. Progressive Income Tax: Its Past and Present, 62 Va. L. Rev. 1317, 1326 (1976), concluding that as a result of statutory changes during the period 1946–1976, the 1976 federal income tax burden expressed as a percentage of a person's 1976 adjusted gross income is not substantially different from the 1946 federal income tax burden expressed as a percentage of his 1946 adjusted gross income, if he has adjusted gross income in 1976 that has purchasing power equivalent to his 1946 adjusted gross income.

[27] Real gain or loss could also be computed by translating the selling price into dollars of the period in which the property was purchased. The gain or loss is recognized for tax purposes, however, when the property is sold. Because tax is computed by applying a rate schedule to taxable income, income should be stated in the same dollars as the dollars in which the tax must be paid—the dollars of the period of sale, not purchase.

Similarly, if depreciable property is held during a period of inflation, each depreciation allowance should consist of a portion of the historical cost of the property, restated in dollars of the year for which the deduction is allowed. Assume a taxpayer purchases equipment for $1,000, and is allowed depreciation for the equipment equal to 20 percent of cost for the year the property is placed in service and 32 percent, 19.2 percent, 11.52 percent, 11.52 percent, and 5.76 percent of cost for the next five years. Assume inflation occurs at an annual rate of 5 percent throughout the recovery period for the property. Example 3-2 shows the depreciation allowances for this period, computed both under present law without regard to inflation (the column "unadjusted depreciation") and under a system of full indexation for inflation (the column "inflation adjusted depreciation"). If the equipment were sold, say, at the end of the fifth year for $100, gain would be computed as in Example 3-3.

Example 3-2

Inflation Adjustments for Depreciation

Year	Unadjusted Depreciation	Inflation Factor	Inflation Adjusted Depreciation
1	$200	1.00	$200
2	320	1.05	336
3	192	1.10	212
4	115	1.16	133
5	115	1.22	140
6	58	1.28	74

Example 3-3

Inflation Adjustment of Gain or Loss on Disposition of Depreciable Property

1. Amount realized on sale at end of year five.................................... $100
2. Less: Adjusted basis
   Cost less unadjusted depreciation for years one
   through five ($1,000 minus $942)................................. $ 58
   Multiplied by inflation factor for year of sale 1.22   70
3. Equals: Gain on sale.. $ 30

The foregoing relates to issues that are strictly internal to the tax laws; the taxpayer has income, loss, or deduction that exists apart from inflation, and the problem is to reckon it up in a way that takes account of the reality of inflation. Beyond this problem, however, is the fact that inflation creates income and losses for some taxpayers, and a tax law that ignores inflation overlooks these gains and losses completely.

Assume an individual stuffs a $100 bill into his mattress and leaves it there for a year while inflation of 5 percent occurs. Present law, which holds that a dollar is a dollar is a dollar, says the individual has no income, gain, or loss on his savings. The goods and services purchased by the $100 when it comes out of the mattress, however, could have been purchased for $95 a year earlier. The individual has a real loss of $5, which the tax law ignores.

In other fixed-dollar transactions, inflation causes gain as well as loss. Assume S deposits $100 in a bank at 7 percent interest, and the bank relends the $100 to B as a mortgage loan bearing interest at 9 percent. If inflation of 5 percent occurs during the ensuing year, the economics of the situation are as follows: S's real earnings on the account are $2. Although she earns interest of $7, the value of the original $100 balance (like the $100 in the mattress) has fallen by $5. Because the tax law overlooks the inflation-caused loss, S's after-tax return with a 28 percent tax rate is 4 cents ($2 of real profit less 28 percent of the $7 of interest), which amounts to an investment return of four tenths of one percent. Similarly, before taxes, the real cost of the mortgage loan to B is $4; inflation has diminished the real value of his mortgage obligation by $5, and this real gain offsets pro tanto the $9 of interest on the loan. Because B's inflation-caused gain also escapes the tax collector's attention, the real after-tax cost of the mortgage to B (assuming a 28 percent tax rate) is $2.48 ($5 less 28 percent of $9). That is, the tax law reduces the real rate of interest on B's mortgage from 4 percent to 2.48 percent. These problems arise whenever a taxpayer is the obligor or obligee of an instrument whose principal is a fixed dollar amount; S represents all holders of savings accounts, certificates of deposit, bonds, mortgages, and other fixed-principal instruments, and B represents the issuers of these instruments.

It is sometimes argued that the tax law can appropriately ignore the inflationary gains and losses of S and B because the holders and issuers of debt instruments factor their expectations about inflation and the relevant tax rules into the interest rates on the instruments.[28] Assume the real rate of interest is 3 percent and inflation is expected to be 5 percent. In a tax-free world, the interest rate would be 8 percent, an amount sufficient to compensate S for the expected 5 percent erosion of principal and also provide a real return of 3 percent. With a 28 percent tax imposed under a law that ignores inflation, the interest rate is 9.94 percent—the sum of the real return of 3

---

[28] Blueprints, supra note 4, at 75. The principal author of Blueprints recanted on this issue, however, after further reflection. Id. at xvii–xviii.

percent and an additional amount, which when reduced by a 28 percent tax leaves S with 5 percent to compensate for principal loss. The latter amount is 5 percent divided by .72, or 6.94 percent (6.94 percent less 28 percent thereof is 5 percent).[29] Under present law, in other words, the tax the borrower saves by deducting the compensation for principal loss (1.94 percent of principal in this example) is passed to the lender as additional interest, and is used by the lender to pay tax on the same amount. Both parties are left in the same after-tax position as they would be under a system of full indexation, and accomplish this without any of the complexities involved in indexing the tax treatment of debt instruments.

Things do not work out so neatly in real life, however. First, the additional interest reflecting the lack of indexation cannot precisely compensate all holders and issuers because there is more than one tax rate. Assume S in the example is taxed at 34 percent, and B at 28 percent. As shown above, B's real interest cost is 3 percent with an interest rate of 9.94 percent. S, in contrast, must have interest of 10.6 percent to realize a real return of 3 percent. (That is, to compensate for principal erosion, S must receive 7.6 percent; 7.6 percent less 34 percent thereof is 5 percent.) S and B cannot make a deal; more generally, present law discourages high bracket taxpayers from being creditors under fixed-principal instruments.

Conversely, if S is tax exempt and B is taxed at 34 percent, S demands only 8 percent (the sum of the 5 percent principal loss and real interest of 3 percent), but this interest rate diminishes the real cost of the borrowing to B to 0.28 percent after taxes (8 percent, less 28 percent thereof, less 5 percent reduction in real value of principal obligation), which is the equivalent of a pretax rate of 0.42 percent in an inflation-free world. In this case, S and B make a deal, probably at a rate that splits the windfall between them; more generally, present law encourages low bracket taxpayers to be lenders and higher bracket taxpayers to be borrowers.

Also, present law exaggerates the swings in interest rates that naturally occur to reflect inflationary expectations. With a fully indexed tax system,

---

[29] That this interest rate fully compensates for inflation is shown as follows: With inflation, S's economic return after taxes is:

Interest received		9.94%
Less: Tax at 28 percent	2.78%	
Less: Principal erosion	5.00	7.78
Net return		2.16%

In the absence of inflation, in contrast, S's return would be:

Interest received	3.00%
Less: Tax at 28 percent	0.84
Net return	2.16%

for example, S and B agree to a 3 percent interest rate if they expect no inflation and an 8 percent rate if they expect inflation of 5 percent. If they are both taxed at 28 percent, the lack of indexation causes their expectation of 5 percent inflation to push the interest rate from 3 percent to 9.94 percent.

Third, the lack of indexation accentuates the real gains and losses that occur when people guess wrong about inflation. Assume S lends to B at 9.94 percent on the expectation of 5 percent inflation, but inflation turns out to be 8 percent. If both parties are taxed at 28 percent, S sustains a real after-tax loss of 0.84 percent (9.94 percent, less 28 percent thereof, less 8 percent), and B has a real after-tax gain in equal amount. If the tax law were fully indexed for inflation, they would have agreed to an interest rate of 8 percent, and their mistake would have wiped out S's income and B's interest cost, but would not have effected a real transfer of wealth from S to B.

One of the disputed issues in the literature on indexation is the choice of an appropriate index for measuring inflation.[30] Because the prices of goods and services do not rise and fall in unison, a price index must consist of an average of the price variations in a prescribed basket of goods, and the fluctuation of a particular index depends on the makeup of the basket underlying it. Since a personal income tax is meant to vary with ability to pay, as reflected by the command over goods and services accruing to the taxpayer during the year, a broadly based consumer price index is generally appropriate for individuals. The selection of an appropriate index for the corporate tax is complicated by the absence of a well articulated rationale for the tax.[31]

Discussions of indexation usually cause wage and salary earners to cry, "Me too." Assume a union makes a three-year contract with an employer providing for no adjustments for purchasing-power loss during the contract's life. If inflation occurs during these three years, would a fully indexed tax system make allowances for the effects of inflation on the employees' wages? Yes, but in precisely the same way as present law does. When an employee's nominal wages remain constant during a period of inflation, real wages decline. The employee's tax liabilities, however, follow the same pattern; nominally, the tax remains constant, but in real terms the tax liability falls parallel to the fall in real wages. Without any explicit adjustment for inflation, the employee and the government share the employee's

---

[30] For problems in selecting the appropriate index, see Waggoner, Eliminating the Capital Gains Preference, Part I: The Problem of Inflation, Bunching, and Lock-In, 48 U. Colo. L. Rev. 313, 354–56 (1977); for foreign experience with indexing, see articles by Lent & Tanzi, in Aaron, supra note 21; Rosenn, Adjusting Taxation of Business Income for Inflation: Lessons From Brazil and Chile, 13 Tex. Int'l LJ 165 (1978).

[31] See infra ¶3.5.6.

loss of purchasing power in the proportion indicated by the tax rate. No inflation adjustment is needed because the tax on a particular year's wages is paid in dollars of that year.

The wage earner's case, however, highlights one of the strongest arguments for indexing income computations. Because the effects of no indexing differ greatly from one type of income to another and because the mix of income types varies from taxpayer to taxpayer, the distribution of the tax burden among taxpayer groups shifts with the rise and fall of inflation. Some have opposed inflation adjustments because they like the redistributive effects of inflation, which benefits borrowers at the expense of lenders and improves the relative status of earned income as compared with investment income.[32] If no indexation makes the law fairer, however, the law is only fair in times of high inflation. While fair some of the time is better than fair none of the time, one must take a cynical view of the political system to be content with "some of the time" as a goal.

To some extent, the Code already takes account of inflation. The preferential rate for capital gains under pre-1986 law was, in part, a response to assertions that capital gains are often illusory because of inflation;[33] provisions authorizing accelerated depreciation and other rapid write-offs of capital outlays are frequently defended as partial correctives for the fact that taxpayers can deduct only the historic cost, rather than the replacement value, of business assets;[34] and LIFO accounting also mitigates the effect of inflation by matching the taxpayer's most recent costs with current sales.[35]

As inflation adjustments, however, these provisions are crude tools. If a particular schedule provides the right amount of depreciation at a given level of inflation, depreciation is either excessive or insufficient at every other level of inflation. LIFO usually ensures that current income from inventory sales includes only real gains and losses, but illusory inflation gains are left buried in the books to be recognized on a liquidation or sale of the business.

Indexation of all aspects of the taxable income computation, in sum, is the only fair and efficient compensation for inflation. Full indexation, however, is complex. So far, Congress has been of the view that the administrative burdens of this complexity outweigh the gains in fairness and efficiency from indexation.

---

[32] See Beer & Walther, Inflation and the Progressivity of the Federal Individual Income Tax, 10 Cal. WL Rev. 537 (1974) (inflation enhances vertical equity).

[33] Infra ¶3.5.7.

[34] Infra ¶23.1 (accelerated depreciation). The effects of inflation and deflation are eliminated if capital outlays can be deducted in full when made, as is permitted by §174 (research and experimental expenditures).

[35] Infra ¶105.4.3.

¶3.5.5 Fluctuating Income

Taxable income and tax liabilities are computed on the basis of taxable years; subject to certain qualifications, each year's income and tax liability are determined independently of the results of other years. Because of the progressive individual rate structure, annual accounting can result in heavier burdens for taxpayers with fluctuating income than for those receiving the same amount of income in equal annual installments. Business and investment losses can be carried over from one year to another.[36] Excess personal exemptions and deductions, however, do not qualify for this privilege, and this imposes an additional burden on taxpayers whose income fluctuates widely from year to year.

These by-products of the annual accounting system were mitigated to some extent by a statutory averaging device, which was enacted in 1964, liberalized in 1969, restricted in 1984, and repealed in 1986. The version in effect prior to the 1984 amendments applied if a taxpayer's current income exceeded 120 percent of his taxable income over the preceding four years. This excess was referred to as "averageable income." The tax for a year in which the averaging rules applied was the sum of (1) the tax, regularly computed, on taxable income exclusive of averageable income and (2) five times the additional tax resulting from including one fifth of averageable income in current taxable income.[37] The intention was to approximate the results that would have occurred if averageable income had been recognized ratably over the taxable year and the preceding four years.

These intricate rules produced a substantial tax benefit only if the income bulge in a particular year was very great. They did not permit unused personal exemptions and deductions to be carried over from one year to another. More comprehensive averaging proposals have been devised by tax theorists, including plans for lifetime income averaging,[38] but they have had little support on Capitol Hill.

Congress repealed the income averaging rules in the belief that "in light of the significantly flatter rate structure" enacted in 1986, "there is no longer a need for income averaging."[39] The point was not that the rules had become superfluous; Congress decided on the repeal knowing that it would

---

[36] Infra ¶25.12 (net operating losses); infra ¶¶50.2.4, 50.3.2 (capital losses).

[37] IRC §§1301–1305, discussed infra ¶111.3. See David et al., Optimal Choices for an Averaging System — A Simulation Analysis of the Federal Averaging Formula of 1964, 23 Nat'l Tax J. 275 (1970).

[38] See generally Goode, The Individual Income Tax 234–38 (Brookings, rev. ed. 1976); Vickrey, Agenda for Progressive Taxation (Ronald Press 1947); Deutsch, On the Taxation of Life Income, 3 Pub. Fin. Q. 299 (1975); Krager & Adler, Taxation of Individuals With Fluctuating Incomes, 48 Calif. L. Rev. 31 (1960); Note, Income Averaging: A Canadian Suggestion, 77 Yale LJ 1223 (1968).

[39] S. Rep. No. 313, 99th Cong., 2d Sess. 45 (1987).

increase tax liabilities by approximately $2 billion per year.[40] Apparently, the belief was that no taxpayer can reasonably complain about a 28 percent tax even if, given a more even distribution of income among years, the average rate would be less. In the absence of income averaging rules, however, taxpayers with widely fluctuating income streams often utilize self-help expedients discussed elsewhere in this work, especially the deferral of income to their retirement years, in order to level off the bulges that would otherwise be subjected to abnormally high marginal rates.[41]

¶3.5.6 The Corporate Income Tax

The role of the corporate income tax in the federal income tax system has been a lively topic of debate among tax theorists for decades. Because the corporate tax is in addition to the personal income tax on dividends, it must be viewed as an independent tax, not a surrogate for a tax on shareholders. Some tax theorists approve of the corporate income tax, arguing that it is a reasonable charge for the privileges conferred by a corporate charter (limited liability, centralized management, etc.) and that publicly held corporations have a tax-paying capacity unrelated to their shareholders' personal circumstances because they are managed by directors and officers who are not responsive to shareholder control.[42]

Most economists, however, regard the corporate income tax as an anomaly.[43] The argument that the tax is a reasonable charge for the corporate charter is a dubious rationale for a federal tax because corporate charters are granted by state governments, who bear most of the costs of issuing

---

[40] Id.; Staff of Joint Comm. on Tax'n, 99th Cong., 2d Sess., General Explanation of the Tax Reform Act of 1986, at 26 (Comm. Print 1987).

[41] See infra ¶60.1.

[42] For a comparison of the tax burdens resulting from operating an enterprise in corporate and unincorporated form, see supra ¶2.5.1.

[43] See generally McClure, Must Corporations Be Taxed Twice? (Brookings 1979); McLure, Integration of the Personal and Corporate Income Taxes: The Missing Element in Recent Tax Reform Proposals, 88 Harv. L. Rev. 532 (1975). See also Bradford, Untangling the Income Tax 100–32 (Harvard U. Press 1982); Goode, The Corporation Income Tax 24–43, 203–17 (John Wiley & Sons 1951); Pechman, Federal Tax Policy 135–89 (Brookings, 5th ed. 1987); Auerbach, Tax Integration and the New View of the Corporate Tax: A 1980 Perspective, in Proceedings of the Seventy-Fourth Annual Conference on Taxation (Nat'l Tax Inst. 1981); Ault, International Issues in Corporate Tax Integration, 10 Law & Pol'y Int'l Bus. 461 (1978); Feldstein & Frisch, Corporate Tax Integration: The Estimated Effects on Captial Accumulation and Tax Distribution of Two Integration Proposals, 30 Nat'l Tax J. 37 (1977); New York State Bar Association, Tax Section, Report on the Integration of Corporate and Individual Income Taxes, 31 Tax Lawyer 37 (1977); Nolan, Integration of Corporate and Individual Income Taxes, 1978 S. Cal. Tax Inst. 899; Stiglitz, The Corporation Tax, 5 J. Pub. Econ. 303 (1976).

them and adjudicating disputes over corporate law issues. The argument that the independence of management from ownership gives corporations a separate ability to pay tax is also unpersuasive because managers bear little if any of the burden of the tax.[44] If the tax burden falls on the corporation's beneficial owners, critics charge, the tax is inequitable and economically inefficient; inequitable because it is the same whether shareholders are high- or low-bracket taxpayers, pension trusts, charitable organizations, or non-resident aliens, and inefficient because it taxes one form of investment more heavily than others and thereby interferes with the market's ability to direct investment into the most productive investments. If the burden is shifted in whole or in part to consumers, suppliers, or employees, it functions as a concealed excise tax, bearing no rational relationship to the economic status of those who indirectly pay it.

In the early days of the century, when the foundations of modern federal income taxation were laid, Congress might have addressed these arguments quite rationally, had anyone thought of them then. Today, considerations of the role of the corporate income tax must proceed under the shadow of an imposing political reality: The tax is a major source of federal revenue. If it were repealed, it would have to be supplanted by some other, equally productive revenue source—i.e., by a substantial new or increased tax. Many voters would be unhappy at the thought of paying taxes formerly paid by corporations.

The appropriateness of a corporate income tax nevertheless is a topic of lively interest among scholars if not among policy makers. The principal alternatives to the present system are discussed below.

1. *Complete integration.* The most comprehensive response to the criticisms of the corporate tax is known as complete integration, which entails repeal of the corporate income tax, coupled with a mechanism for taxing corporate income directly to shareholders when earned, whether distributed or not. Complete integration, in other words, would tax shareholders on corporate income in the same way that partners are now taxed on partnership income. This model has been accepted in a limited context since the enactment in 1958 of subchapter S, which permits certain closely held corporations and their shareholders to elect quasi-partnership status, under which they report their pro rata shares of corporate income, whether distributed or not, and the corporation is exempted from the corporate income tax.[45] The complete integration model can also be elected by mutual funds, and is mandatory for foreign personal holding companies.[46] Mandatory

---

[44] For the incidence of the corporate income tax, see supra ¶3.3.2.

[45] For subchapter S, see infra ¶95.6.

[46] IRC §551(a).

complete integration, however, has not been adopted as a broadly applicable regime in the United States or any other industrialized country.

Complete integration for widely held corporations is problematical for several reasons. First, it multiplies by thousands the number of persons taxed on corporate income and thus complicates tax collections. This problem could be met by imposing a corporate-level tax equal to the highest rate applicable to individual income (28 percent in 1988), and allowing shareholders a refundable credit for their ratable shares of the tax paid by the corporation. If a corporation's income were $1,000, for example, the corporation would pay $280 in tax; a holder of, say, 10 percent of the stock would include $100 in gross income, and take a credit against his tax equal to $28. If the shareholder skipped reporting the income, he would get no credit (a shareholder who took the credit without reporting the income would start bells ringing in IRS computers), and the government would be none the worse off.

The corporate-level withholding tax also solves another problem with complete integration. If the corporation pays no tax, the benefits of integration automatically go to all shareholders. It is usually thought desirable to withhold these benefits from some shareholders. Since 1950, for example, the unrelated business incomes of charities, pension trusts, and other exempt organizations have been taxed. A repeal of the corporate income tax, without more, would be inconsistent with the unrelated business income tax; when business income earned directly by an exempt organization is taxed, business income earned indirectly through share ownership cannot rationally be exempted. Similarly, it is usually thought appropriate that when a resident of one country owns stock in a corporation of another country, the latter country is entitled to a tax on corporate income allocable to the shareholder, and an elimination of all corporate-level tax would leave that country with the difficult task of collecting tax from a foreigner. Under the withholding system, the benefits of integration can be restricted by simply denying the credit to any shareholder who should not have these benefits.

Even with the withholding device, however, complete integration is complex. Corporate income would have to be allocated among all persons who own stock during the year, including those who buy and sell during the year, and each such person would have to be notified of their share of the income. A speculator who buys and sells with great rapidity would accumulate a stack of such notices inches deep. If the corportion has multiple classes of stock, income would have to be allocated among classes before it could be allocated among shareholders. Any change in corporate taxable income on audit would cause a change in the tax liability of each shareholder; a single audit could require millions of notices of deficiencies. The task of issuing these notices would be considerable; the job of collecting the deficiencies would be daunting.

The conventional wisdom is that these complexities make complete integration impractical. Advances in the computerization of taxpayer data, however, might challenge the conventional wisdom. Payments of dividends and interest are reported to the IRS, which systematically matches these reports with the recipients' returns; the tax on stockholders under complete integration could be administered and enforced similarly. With all returns entered into computers, audit changes in corporate income could be followed through with computer generated notices of deficiency to shareholders. A relatively small number of levies on wages would probably be sufficient to spread the word that these notices are not to be ignored.

A recent development in the financial community, further, gives evidence that complete integration can work for widely held entities. A form of business organization known as the master limited partnership has become popular.[47] A master limited partnership is a partnership that differs from traditional partnerships only in that it has hundreds, perhaps thousands, of partners, whose interests were issued in public securities offerings and are often traded on securities markets. A master limited partnership, in other words, is a publicly held entity that has been organized as a partnership rather than as a corporation. If the financial and business communities and the IRS can accommodate significant numbers of master limited partnerships, complete integration is feasible.[48]

2. *Dividend relief.* Most integration proposals offered as alternatives to complete integration apply only to corporate earnings distributed as dividends, and thus are usually called dividend relief or partial integration. Two types of dividend relief—a dividends paid deduction and a shareholder credit for corporate taxes—have been used by various countries.

A corporate deduction for dividends paid is perhaps the simplest form of integration. The simplicity, however, lies more in appearance than reality. Without further adjustment, for example, the deduction would wholly free from tax corporate income distributed to shareholders who are exempt from tax. Congress might consider this inconsistent with the tax on unrelated business income of exempt organizations; if so, it might expand the definition of unrelated business taxable income to include all dividends.

---

[47] See Canellos, Corporate Tax Integration: By Design or by Default, 35 Tax Notes 999, 1003–07 (1987).

[48] Rules enacted in 1987 treat many master limited partnerships as corporations. See infra ¶90.1.4. The concern underlying enactment of these rules, however, was seemingly revenue loss, not administrative difficulties. Most master limited partnerships organized before the rules were enacted are exempted from the rules for 10 years, for example, even though they raise the same administrative difficulties as newly organized entities.

Also, Congress might not want to allow dividend relief with respect to income distributed to foreign shareholders; if so, a special tax surcharge on foreigners' dividend receipts would have to be imposed to offset the effects of the corporate deduction. It would not be feasible to deny a corporation's deduction for dividends paid to exempt organizations and foreigners because shares are often held by nominees and corporations thus do not know the identity, let alone the tax status or nationality, of many of their shareholders.

Alternatively, shareholders can be allowed credits for the corporate tax. Under a credit scheme (often called an imputation system), a shareholder is treated as though he had paid the corporate tax imposed on earnings distributed to him as dividends. This imputed tax payment, which is computed as a percentage of the dividends, is both included in the shareholder's gross income and allowed as a credit against the shareholder's tax. That is, the shareholder must report a share of the corporation's pretax income (the dividend plus the imputed tax payment), but subtracts the imputed tax payment from his tax bill.

Assume a corportion earns $100, pays a tax of $34, and distributes its after-tax income of $66 to its sole shareholder. Assume the shareholder has other income of $900, and is taxed at a flat rate of 28 percent. The shareholder's tax under an imputation system is as shown in Example 3-4. As the example shows, given a 34 percent corporate rate, the credit is 51.52 percent (34 divided by 66) of the dividend.

Example 3-4

Shareholder's Tax Under Imputation System

1. Taxable income:
   From other sources .... $ 900
   From corporation (sum of dividend of $66 and $34 of
   corporate tax).. 100
   Total $1,000
2. Tax before credit at 28% .... $ 280
3. Less: Credit of $34 34
4. Final tax .... $ 246

Because the credit of $34 (51.52 percent of $66) is greater than 28 percent of the gross income attributable to the dividend (the sum of $66 and $34, or $100), the credit eliminates all tax on the dividend and also reduces the shareholder's tax on other income by $6. (Twenty-eight percent of the other income of $900 is $252, as compared with the final tax of $246.) By this $6, the final tax on the $100 of corporate earnings is reduced from the

$34 initially paid by the corporation to the $28 implied by the shareholder's 28 percent rate. The result is the same as with the deduction for dividends paid; with the deduction, the corporate-level tax is never collected, and the shareholder's 28 percent tax is the first and only tax on the earnings.

The imputation system is more complex than the deduction for dividends paid. An advantage of the system, however, is that the credit can simply be denied to any taxpayer Congress might find unworthy of dividend relief.

A third form of dividend relief is an exemption of dividend income from tax. This form is cruder than a dividends paid deduction or imputation system because it leaves the corporate tax as the final tax, whereas the other forms of dividend relief substitute a tax at the shareholder's rate. Under current law, where rates are relatively compressed, the difference is not great. A dividends received exclusion, further, can be targeted by denying the exclusion to shareholders who should not have dividend relief.

A feature common to all forms of dividend relief is that they can be allowed in large doses or small. If Congress, for example, decided that dividend relief was a good thing, but that it could afford only 30 percent of the cost of full dividend relief, it could allow corporations to deduct 30 percent of their dividend payments, provide an imputation credit equal to 15 percent of dividends received, or exclude 30 percent of dividends received from gross income.

¶3.5.7   Capital Gains and Losses

From 1921 through 1987, capital gains were taxed more leniently than ordinary income. The details have varied, but the statutory scheme usually embodied a reduced tax rate, an exclusion or deduction of part of the gain, or both.[49] Just before the repeal of the capital gains preferences in 1986, noncorporate taxpayers were allowed a deduction equal to 60 percent of net capital gain, and an alternative tax was provided for corporations under which the tax on net capital gain was capped at 28 percent.[50] Capital losses, even after repeal of the capital gains preferences, are deductible only against capital gains plus, in the case of individuals, a limited amount of ordinary income.[51]

Some early theorists, who defined income as periodic returns from recurring sources, opposed taxing capital gains, but the acceptance by most contemporary economists of the Haig-Simons definition, which includes

---

[49] See Appendix D.

[50] IRC §§1201, 1202 (before amendment and repeal in 1986).

[51] Infra ¶¶50.2.4, 50.3.2. See also Warren, The Deductibility by Individuals of Capital Losses Under the Federal Income Tax, 40 U. Chi. L. Rev. 291 (1973).

changes of net worth in income, predisposes them to disapprove of the special treatment of capital gains and losses.[52] The periodic-return school of thought is largely based on the view that recipients of capital gains view them as part of the original investment, which should not be invaded for current living expenses. Adherents of the Haig-Simons definition either reject this view of taxpayer psychology—it is possible, after all, that unexpected gains are spent more freely than periodic receipts—or consider it irrelevant.

The periodic-return rationale for distinguishing between ordinary income and capital gains has been supplanted in recent years by several other theories,[53] to which we now turn.

1. *Bunching of income.* The most common argument for special tax treatment for capital gains is that they would otherwise be unfairly subjected to the progressive rates in the year of realization. This rationale is concerned with two phenomena, which, because they sometimes overlap, are often confused in popular discussion.

One type of bunching is created by the sale of an asset that has appreciated in value gradually over a period of many years. Taxing the gain at the marginal rate applicable to the year of sale can produce a tax burden in excess of the liability that would have been incurred if fluctuations in the asset's value had been taxed in the years in which they actually occurred. The special status accorded to capital gains before 1988 moderated the impact of the progressive rates, but the relief was granted whether the property increased in value gradually, fluctuated wildly from year to year,

---

[52] See supra ¶3.1.1.
[53] See generally Bailey, Capital Gains and Income Taxation, in The Taxation of Income From Capital 11 (Harberger & Bailey, eds.; Brookings 1969); Bhatia, Accrued Capital Gains, Personal Income and Savings in the United States, 1948–1964, at 374 (Review of Income and Wealth, Series 16, No. 4, Dec. 1970) (also published as Brookings Reprint No. 200, 1971); Blum, A Handy Summary of the Capital Gains Arguments, 35 Taxes 247 (1957); David, Alternative Approaches to Capital Gains Taxation (Brookings 1968); Gravelle & Lindsey, Capital Gains, 38 Tax Notes 397 (1988); Nilson, Neutral Capital Gains Taxation Under Inflation and Tax Deferral, 31 Nat'l Tax J. 401 (1978); Feldstein & Yitzhaki, The Effect of the Capital Gains Tax on the Selling and Switching of Common Stock (Harvard Institute of Economic Research, Discussion Paper No. 532, 1977); Richman, Reconsideration of the Capital Gains Tax—A Comment, 14 Nat'l Tax J. 402 (1961); Somers, Reconsideration of the Capital Gains Tax, 13 Nat'l Tax J. 289 (1960); Waggoner, supra note 30; Waggoner, Eliminating the Capital Gains Preference, Part II: The Problem of Corporate Taxation, 49 U. Colo. L. Rev. 9 (1977); Wallich, Taxation of Capital Gains in the Light of Recent Economic Developments, 18 Nat'l Tax J. 133 (1964); House Ways and Means Comm., 86th Cong., 1st Sess., Tax Revision Compendium 1193–1299 (1959); Joint Comm. on the Economic Report, 84th Cong., 1st Sess., Federal Tax Policy for Economic Growth and Stability 367–404 (1955).

or jumped in value in one sudden burst. It was pure accident if the reduced tax corresponded to the taxes that would have been payable if the gain had been reported on an annual accrual basis. Moreover, the relief was granted whether or not the taxpayer's income in the year of sale was bunched as compared with earlier years.

The second type of bunching arises from once-in-a-lifetime or other unusual sales of highly appreciated assets, such as family farms, stock in closely held corporations, or fortunate investments, producing gain that greatly exceeds the taxpayer's average income. Here, the focus is not on whether the asset appreciated in value gradually but on the fact that the taxpayer's income in the year of sale is extraordinarily high. The capital gains rules gave relief in this situation, but the remedy bore no necessary relationship to the underlying problem since it was available whether the taxpayer's income in the year of sale is abnormally large or not. Moreover, during the years 1964 through 1986, general averaging rules applied to all types of bunched income[54] so that capital gains qualified for both types of relief.

In repealing the capital gains preferences, Congress stated that with the 1986 rate reductions, "the need to provide a reduced rate for net capital gain is eliminated."[55] This explanation suggests Congress may have viewed bunching problems as a rationale for the former preferences. With lower rates, the added tax (from being pushed into a higher bracket) is less, and because the highest rate is reached at a relatively low level of income, the possibility of a bunching changing the taxpayer's top marginal bracket at all is reduced.

2. *Lock-in effect.* Since gains and losses are taken into account only when realized by sale or exchange, investors can avoid paying taxes on appreciated assets by simply retaining them. Any tax on capital gains thus has a lock-in effect, reducing the liquidity of assets and discouraging taxpayers from switching from one investment to another. Since the taxpayer can reinvest only the after-tax proceeds received for the old asset, the new asset must promise a higher rate of return to justify the switch. Table 3-11 sets out the percentage of gain on the old asset, the applicable tax rate, and the return on the new investment that is required to make up for the tax on the old asset.

The lock-in rationale was accepted by Congress in 1938, when it reduced the holding period for full capital gain benefits from 10 years to 18 months:

---

[54] For IRC §§1301–1305, see infra ¶111.3.
[55] S. Rep. No. 313, 99th Cong., 2d Sess. 169 (1987).

Table 3-11

Multiple of Rate of Return on Old Investment Required for Advantageous Switch from Appreciated Old Asset[1]

Marginal Tax Rate on Capital Gains (%)	Gain on Old Asset as Fraction of Its Market Value[2]				
	1/10	*3/10*	*5/10*	*7/10*	*9/10*
10	1.010	1.031	1.053	1.075	1.099
25	1.026	1.081	1.143	1.212	1.290
35	1.036	1.117	1.212	1.324	1.460
50	1.053	1.176	1.333	1.538	1.818
60	1.064	1.220	1.429	1.724	2.174
70	1.075	1.266	1.538	1.961	2.703

[1]Returns computed in relation to current market values.

[2]When the gain on the old asset is the indicated fraction of its market value, the ratio of the rate of return on the new asset to that on the old must exceed the figure given below. The ratio is

$$\frac{M}{M - tc(M - C)}$$

where M is the current market value of the old asset, C is its cost or other basis, and tc is the marginal rate of tax on relized capital gain.

Source: Goode, The Individual Income Tax, Table 8-2 (Brookings rev. ed. 1976).

There is an essential difference between income derived from salaries, wages, interest, and rents and income derived from capital gains. It is always to the advantage of the taxpayer to receive the first class of income, no matter what the rate of tax as long as it is less than 100 per cent. On the other hand, the tax in respect of capital gains is optional— the taxpayer is not obliged to pay any tax unless he realizes a gain by the sale of the asset. There is no tax under existing law if a taxpayer transfers his money from one bank to another, but there may be a very heavy tax if he wishes to transfer his investment from a bond in one company to a bond in another company. Thus, an excessive tax on capital gains freezes transactions and prevents the free flow of capital into productive investments.[56]

The extent of the lock-in effect at particular levels of capital gains taxes, however, is unknown. It did not impress the 1986 Congress. The maximum rate on net capital gain was raised by the 1986 Act from 20 to 28 percent for individuals and from 28 to 34 percent for corporations. According to the formula used in constructing Table 3-11, for an asset 30 percent of whose value is gain, a rise in the capital gains rate from 20 to 28 percent increases from 1.062 to 1.092 the multiple of old rate of return to new rate of return needed to justify a sale. That is, whereas under prior law an asset yielding 10 percent could be exchanged without after-tax loss for an asset yielding 10.62 percent, the exchange is unwise under new law unless the new asset yields at least 10.92 percent. If, as Congress said in 1986, the reductions in ordinary income rates "eliminated" the need for a capital gains preference, it was not the lock-in effect that formerly required the preference.

Debate on the issue, however, has continued. The post-1986 debate has focused on the allegation of some that capital gains taxes as high as those of the 1986 Act produce a lock-in effect of such magnitude that a reduction of the capital gains rates would increase rather than decrease tax revenues. The allegation has been the subject of extensive econometrical research, whose results have been inconclusive. A Treasury study concludes that a reduction of the rate on capital gains to 15 percent would increase tax revenues.[57] A study done by the Congressional Budget Office, in contrast, asserts that although the Treasury's conclusion "cannot be ruled out with certainty, . . . the probability attached to this result is very low."[58]

Because, under §1014, assets take a new basis on the owner's death equal to their fair market values,[59] the lock-in effect is especially strong for older investors. Assume an individual owns an asset that is worth $100, has a basis of $70, and produces an annual yield of $10. The individual is offered another investment of comparable risk for $91.60 that pays $11 per year. If the individual is taxed at 28 percent and the proffered investment

---

[56] S. Rep. No. 1567, 75th Cong., 3d Sess. (1938), reprinted in 1939-1 (Part 2) CB 779, 783.

[57] Darby, Gillingham & Greenlees, The Direct Revenue Effects of Capital Gains Taxation: A Reconsideration of Time-Series Evidence (Treasury Dep't Research Paper No. 8801, 1988). For a critique, see Minarik, The New Treasury Capital Gains Study: What Is in the Black Box? 39 Tax Notes 1465 (1988).

[58] Toder & Ozanne, CBO Works on Capital Gains, 39 Tax Notes 1441, 1442 (1988) (by authors of CBO study; summarizing prior research as well as their own). See also Kiefer, Capital Gains Response to Tax Rate Changes, 39 Tax Notes 1455 (1988) (study by Congressional Research Service of Library of Congress indicating that over long run, reduction in capital gains rate would lose revenue).

[59] Infra ¶41.4.

will not be available later, the old investment should be sold and the proceeds invested in the new one, regardless of how long the individual expects to live. From the sale, the individual will have $91.60 after taxes (the $100 selling price less a tax of 28 percent of $30), just enough to cover the cost of the new investment, and the new investment will yield another dollar each year in income. But, assume the individual knows that he will die next week and that the $91.60 asset will still be available next week. The individual should hold the old asset and instruct his executor to sell it and buy the new one; from the sale, the executor will realize $100 after taxes, leaving him with the money for the new investment and $8.40 to spare.

More generally, if the values and availability of the old and new assets will remain constant forever, the old asset should be held until death unless the present value of the additional income (after taxes) from the new investment over the remainder of the investor's life exceeds the tax liability that would be incurred on a sale of the old investment. In this example, given the after-tax rate of return implicit in the new investment ($11 divided by $91.60, less 28 percent thereof, or 8.65 percent), a switch in investments is unwise unless the individual's life expectancy is at least 8.44 years.

This can be generalized by the following formula: A sale is warranted if

$$(1 + r)^e < (1 - tg) / (1 + s)^e$$

where r is the after-tax rate of return on the old investment, e is the individual's life expectancy, t is the tax rate, g is the percentage of the old investment's value that would be recognized as gain on a sale, and s is the after-tax rate of return on the new investment.

In real life, such a formula can only be a helpful tool because the projection of future rates of return from various investments is highly subjective. If one could learn authoritatively from the *Wall Street Journal* that over the next 10 years investment X will yield 12 percent, while another investment of equivalent quality (Y) will yield only 10 percent, investors would stampede out of Y and into X, and this would quickly equalize the rates of return on the two investments. When an investor makes the judgment that X will yield 12 percent while Y will yield only 10 percent, he is betting that he is smarter than the market, and many investors fare as well on such bets as they do at the crap tables.

In 1976, Congress replaced the date-of-death basis rule with a carryover basis principle, which required the heirs to use the decedent's basis for most inherited assets, but it repealed the change in 1980 before it took effect in any meaningful way.[60] Had the carryover principle remained in force, it would have alleviated the lock-in effect to some extent, but not as complete-

_____

[60] See infra ¶5.2.

ly as a Treasury proposal, advanced in 1963 and again in 1969 but never enacted, to treat the transfer of assets at death as a constructive realization of the decedent's gains and losses.[61]

3. *Inflation.* Because capital gains may result from reductions in the purchasing power of the dollar, they are often described as spurious. This is not an inaccurate label for the inflation-induced portion of capital gains, but capital gains can also be genuine; and even investors with spurious gains are better off than taxpayers holding debased fixed-dollar assets, such as bonds and annuities. Viewed as a remedy for inflation, therefore, the reduced rate of tax on capital gains is woefully inadequate and one-sided.[62]

4. *Incentive effects.* Tax concessions to capital gains are favored by some theorists as devices to increase savings and investment, to counteract the double taxation of corporate income, or to correct the income tax law's bias against savings. To advance closer to these objectives, a tax-free rollover privilege is sometimes advocated, under which capital gains would be exempted from tax if the taxpayer reinvests the proceeds of sale.[63] Under such an arrangement (which could be enacted as either a supplement or an alternative to a reduced rate on realized gains), the taxpayer's basis in the old asset would be carried forward, so that the gain on a sale would be taxed if and when the proceeds were withdrawn from the rollover account. The corporate reorganization provisions of existing law are a rudimentary rollover device, enabling the taxpayer to switch investments without realizing gains, but they are available only if the shift from one security to another is effected by a corporate merger or similar acquisition.[64]

All of the foregoing arguments in favor of tax concessions to capital gains presuppose that assets qualifying for these allowances can be distinguished from "ordinary" assets. From macroeconomic heights, the boundary may seem clear, but the troops on the ground find it veiled in obscurity. The classic capital asset is a share of stock or a bond issued by a publicly held corporation and owned by a casual investor. In real life, however, one must decide whether to accord the same treatment to the same security when held by a dealer, to stock in closely held corporations, to partnership interests, to real estate, and to assets owned and used by business firms.

---

[61] See id.

[62] See supra ¶3.5.4. For an estimate of the extent to which the statutory treatment of capital gains offsets (1) the inclusion of spurious gains and (2) the advantages of deferral, see Brinner, Inflation, Deferral, and the Neutral Taxation of Capital Gains, 26 Nat'l Tax J. 565 (1973).

[63] Smith, Federal Tax Reform 151–55 (McGraw-Hill 1961); Blum, Rollover: An Alternative Treatment of Capital Gains, 41 Tax L. Rev. 383 (1986); Clark, An Alternative to Capital Gains Taxation: A "Roll-Over" Account for Investment Assets, 4 How. LJ 157 (1958).

[64] See infra ¶94.1.

These definitional problems have generated an immense body of statutory, administrative, and decisional law, discussed elsewhere in this work,[65] which is a major source of complexity. It is tempting to blame these interpretative problems on a perverse legislative penchant for using the capital gain concept as a convenient dumping ground for miscellaneous tax relief and to suggest that the definitional issues could be easily solved if relief were confined to "real" capital gains. This is an illusion, which is quickly dispelled by immersion in the facts of life. Even if purged of its alleged impurities, the capital gain area would be riddled with definitional problems and would require a host of statutory provisions to forestall maneuvers to transmute ordinary income into capital gains and capital losses into ordinary losses.

¶3.6 THE TAX EXPENDITURE BUDGET

For many years tax theorists have asserted that federal income tax exemptions, credits, deductions, and other allowances can be the functional equivalents of federal expenditures and that the failure to acknowledge this parallelism enables "tax expenditures" to escape the congressional and public scrutiny to which the appropriation of governmental funds is subject. Professor Surrey, the leading proponent of a systematic "tax expenditure budget," describes the concept as follows:

> The federal income tax system . . . consists of two parts: one part comprises the structural provisions necessary to implement the income tax; the second part comprises a system of tax expenditures under which governmental financial assistance programs are carried out through special tax provisions rather than through direct government expenditures. This second system bears no basic relation to the structure of the income tax and is not necessary to its operation; it is simply grafted on to that structure. The system of tax expenditures provides a vast subsidy apparatus that uses the mechanics of the income tax as the method of paying the subsidies.
>
> Tax expenditure analysis treats tax expenditure provisions as involving two payments: the imputed tax payment that would have been made in the absence of the special provision (all else remaining the same) and the simultaneous expenditure of that payment as a direct grant to the person benefitted by the special provision. Since the hypo-

---

[65] Infra Part 6. For discussion and criticism of the scope of the capital gain and loss concept, see Surrey, Definitional Problems in Capital Gains Taxation, 69 Harv. L. Rev. 985 (1956); Miller, The "Capital Asset" Concept: A Critique of Capital Gains Taxation: I and II, 59 Yale LJ 837, 1057 (1950); American Law Institute, Definitional Problems in Capital Gains Taxation (Discussion Draft 1960).

thetical direct grant . . . may itself constitute income, the tax on this income could also be viewed as part of the tax expenditure.

Tax expenditures take a variety of forms, including exclusions from income, deductions, credits against tax, preferential rates of tax, and deferral of tax. The exclusion technique is employed, for example, for interest on state and local bonds. The deduction for charitable contributions is a tax expenditure in the form of a deduction from income. Tax expenditures taking the form of a tax credit include the investment tax credit [largely repealed in 1986] and the credit for certain research expenses [expiring at end of 1988]. Other tax expenditures, such as the preferential treatment of capital gains [repealed for taxable years after 1987], in effect provide a special rate of tax. Still other tax expenditures accelerate the timing of deductions or defer the inclusion of income. Items such as the Accelerated Cost Recovery System and the deduction for intangible drilling and development costs are examples of accelerated deductions while the treatment of qualified pension and profit sharing plans illustrates the deferral of income.[1]

Responding to these arguments, Congress institutionalized the tax expenditure concept in 1974, incorporating it into the congressional budget process by legislation that defines "tax expenditures" and "tax expenditures budget" as follows:

> The term "tax expenditures" means those revenue losses attributable to provisions of the Federal tax laws which allow a special exclusion, exemption, or deduction from gross income or which provide a special credit, a preferential rate of tax, or a deferral of tax liability; and the term "tax expenditures budget" means an enumeration of such tax expenditures.[2]

---

[1] Surrey, McDaniel, Ault & Koppelman, Federal Income Taxation 232–33 (Foundation Press 1986). See also Bradford, Untangling the Income Tax 239–65 (Harvard Univ. Press 1986); Surrey & McDaniel, Tax Expenditures (Harvard University Press 1985); Bittker, Accounting for Federal "Tax Subsidies" in the National Budget, 22 Nat'l Tax J. 244 (1969); Surrey & Hellmuth, The Tax Expenditure Budget —Response to Professor Bittker, 22 Nat'l Tax J. 528 (1969); Bittker, The Tax Expenditure Budget—A Reply to Professors Surrey and Hellmuth, 22 Nat'l Tax J. 538 (1969); Surrey & McDaniel, The Tax Expenditure Concept and the Budget Reform Act of 1974, 17 BC Indus. & Com. L. Rev. 679 (1976); Feldstein, The Theory of Tax Expenditures (Harvard Institute of Economic Research, Discussion Paper Series No. 435, 1975); Brannon, Brannon Cuts Tax Expenditures by $14 Billion! Tax Notes, Feb. 12, 1979, at 171 ("best that can be said for the official tax expenditures estimating procedure is that the arithmetic is neat"); Tax Foundation, The Tax Expenditure Budget: An Exercise in Fiscal Impressionism (Government Finance Brief No. 29, 1979).

[2] Congressional Budget Act of 1974, 31 USC §1302.

An analysis of tax expenditures has also become a regular part of the executive budget.[3]

The tax expenditure concept presupposes that "the structural provisions necessary to implement the income tax on individual and corporate net income" can be identified and distinguished from "special tax provisions" (or "tax subsidies") embodying "governmental financial assistance programs." The line between these two classes is not easily drawn, however. In recent years, the administration has presented two alternative tax expenditure budgets, one determined by comparing existing law to a "reference tax law" and the other based on a comparison to a "normal tax."[4] The former is preferred by the administration, and the latter is presented because it is the method by which the tax expenditure budget was prepared before 1983 and continues to be the method used by the Congressional Budget Office and the Joint Committee on Taxation.

Under the normal-tax method, a tax expenditure is the cost of any provision that diverges from a normative model of an income tax. The normative model is based on the Haig-Simons definition of income as the sum of the taxpayer's consumption and wealth accumulation during the year.[5] This definition, however, is modified in several respects. For example, the normative model, like present law, excludes unrealized gains and losses in a taxpayer's assets and imputed income of all forms, probably because these items, although included in Haig-Simons income, are generally thought to be beyond the reach of a practical income tax system. The normative structure also follows present law in making no allowance for inflation in the computation of income. When an asset is held during a period of inflation, for example, gain on sale of the asset is overstated because the sales price is stated in the cheaper dollars of the time of sale while the property's cost basis is stated in the dearer dollars of the time of purchase, but the tax expenditure budget makes no allowance for this overstatement.[6] Further, the normative structure takes as a given the present system of taxing most corporations on their income separately from the taxation of shareholders.

Under the administration's reference-tax-law approach, a provision is deemed to effect a tax expenditure only if it is an exception from some general rule stated in the law. Accelerated depreciation, for example, is a tax expenditure under the normative approach because depreciation is not ac-

---

[3] Office of Management and Budget, Special Analyses, Budget of the United States Government, Fiscal Year 1989, Special Analysis G, The Fiscal 1989 Tax Expenditure Budget (1988), reprinted in 38 Tax Notes 979 (1988) [hereinafter Special Analysis G]. For an estimate of tax expenditures, see Appendix A.

[4] Special Analysis G, supra note 3.

[5] See supra ¶3.1.1 for the Haig-Simons definition.

[6] See supra ¶3.5.4 for the effects of inflation on income measurements.

celerated under the Haig-Simons definition, but the reference-tax-law approach omits depreciation from the tax expenditure budget because, since 1981, the most accelerated allowable methods of depreciation have been the general rule, not an exception. Also, the reference-tax-law approach, unlike the normative approach, does not treat the expensing of research and development costs as a tax expenditure because expensing of these costs is considered the general rule, not an exception from a general capitalization requirement.

The reference-tax-law approach is intended to avoid many of the debatable judgments that must be made under the normative approach. The need for difficult judgments, however, is inherent in the tax expenditure mechanism. The lower rates on the first dollars of corporate income, for example, are considered a tax expenditure under the normative approach, but not under the reference-tax-law approach. The inclusion of this item under the normative approach is debatable because the Haig-Simons definition says nothing about rates; the reference-tax-law proponents, in contrast, make an equally debatable judgment in concluding that these rates are part of the general rules, not an exception from the top corporate rate. Also, the normative approach includes all governmental transfer payments (including, for example, welfare payments), whereas the reference-tax-law approach includes only those transfer payments (most importantly, social security and unemployment benefits) that derive from the transferee's employment. The broad inclusion of transfer payments under the normative approach follows quite directly from the Haig-Simons definition; the narrower inclusion under the reference-tax-law approach is based on a supposed general rule of present law excluding gifts and other receipts for which the recipient provides no consideration. The same distinction leads to the treatment of the exclusion for scholarships as a tax expenditure under the normative approach, but not under the reference-tax-law approach.

The administration's tax expenditure budget also presents alternative figures computed by two different methods. One set of figures is simply the tax revenues lost by each provision included in the tax expenditure list. The other set consists of estimates of the direct expenditures that would be required to duplicate the tax expenditures. The difference between these two approaches is most easily seen with respect to a tax credit. Since a credit is a dollar-for-dollar reduction of tax, the tax expenditure for a credit under the lost-revenues approach is the amount allowed as credit. The direct outlay equivalent of a credit, in contrast, is larger than the amount of the credit. Because a direct expenditure would be taxable to the recipient, it would provide an after-tax benefit equal to the credit only if it consisted of the sum of (1) the tax on the direct expenditure and (2) the credit amount. The direct outlay equivalent of a $100 credit for a taxpayer subject to a marginal tax rate of 28 percent, for example, is $139 (28 percent of $139 plus $100).

Under the lost-revenues approach, the amount shown in the tax expenditure budget for each tax expenditure provision is an estimate of the additional tax that would be collected if this provision were repealed but everything else in the world remained unchanged. Similarly, the amount shown under the outlay-equivalent approach is the direct expenditure that would be required to replicate the tax expenditure if nothing else changes. As a consequence, the figures shown for various items usually cannot be added together. The revenue gain from repealing two tax expenditure provisions, for example, might be greater than the sum of the tax expenditures for the two provisions because repeal of them both might push taxpayers into higher tax brackets than would the repeal of either of them alone. Many other interactions between tax expenditures are also assumed away by the all-other-things-being-the-same approach used in the estimates.

The ultimate effect of repealing a single tax expenditure, further, is likely to differ from the figure given for the item in the tax expenditure budget because the figure is computed assuming taxpayers will not alter their behavior in response to the repeal. In reality, some reaction is inevitable, and any reaction is certain to affect tax revenues. For example, if a person believes that a tax incentive for investment increases economic activity to such an extent that tax revenues are enhanced rather than diminished by the incentive, the person necessarily believes that repeal of the incentive would not increase tax collections.

The failure to reflect interactions or the lack of any prediction of ultimate effects, however, is not necessarily a deficiency in the tax expenditure budget. The principal object of the budget is to state tax expenditures on a basis comparable to the direct expenditure budget. The direct expenditure budget includes the amounts budgeted to be disbursed under all expenditure programs, unreduced by any collateral benefits expected from the expenditures. The budget is a statement of expected cash flows, not of ultimate costs and benefits.

That the budget is done on a cash flow basis has another important effect. Many tax expenditure provisions are deferral rules, not exemptions. The exclusion from employees' gross income of employer contributions to pension plans, for example, is a tax expenditure under both the normative and reference-tax-law approaches. The calculation of the tax expenditure for a particular year, however, does not take into account that the employees will be taxed on these contributions in subsequent years when pension benefits are distributed to them. A rule that defers tax has the effect of a loan from the government to the taxpayer. When the government makes a direct loan, the direct expenditure budget includes the full amount lent, unreduced by the repayment expected in a subsequent year. Tax expenditure loans effected through tax deferral rules thus are treated the same as direct loans.

¶3.7 INCOME TAXATION VS. CONSUMPTION TAXATION

For years, tax theorists have debated the relative merits of income and consumption taxes.[1] This debate, however, is carried on in somewhat different terms than the lay person might imagine. Generalizing from the federal income tax, on the one hand, and state retail sales taxes, on the other, people often think of an income tax as an annual levy at progressive rates and of a consumption tax as being imposed transaction by transaction at a flat rate. An income tax, however, can be a flat impost that is levied and collected transaction by transaction. Nonbusiness investment income of a nonresident alien individual or foreign corporation, for example, is subject to a flat 30 percent tax that is collected by requiring the payor of the income to withhold 30 percent of each item as tax.[2]

Conversely, a consumption tax can be an annual tax at progressive rates. Economic income is usually defined as the sum of the taxpayer's consumption for the year and the change in the value of his wealth over the year.[3] A consumption tax hits the first of these two elements, but not the second. Practically, taxable income is computed by including various receipts and accruals and subtracting out various disbursements and liabilities. Similarly, annual consumption can be computed as the sum of all receipts available to be spent on consumption (including, for example, borrowed funds as well as salaries, dividends, and interest income), reduced by all disbursements that are not consumption expenditures (most importantly, savings). Annual consumption, so defined, could be taxed at progressive rates, just as annual income now is.

Although theorists think of income and consumption taxes as opposites, Congress has not, and over the years has introduced many elements of an annual consumption tax into the tax we know as the federal income tax.[4] The most obvious example is the treatment of retirement savings. An employer is allowed deductions for its contributions to qualified pension or profit sharing trusts, and the trusts are tax exempt; employees, in contrast, are taxed on neither the contributions nor the trusts' income accumulations

---

[1] See generally Bradford, Untangling the Income Tax 59–99 (Harvard 1986); Goode, The Individual Income Tax 11–36 (Brookings, rev. ed. 1976); Pechman, Federal Tax Policy 207–12 (Brookings, 5th ed. 1987); What Should Be Taxed; Income or Expenditure (Pechman, ed.; Brookings 1980).

[2] See infra ¶66.2.

[3] See supra ¶3.1.1.

[4] See generally Uneasy Compromise: Problems of a Hybrid Income-Consumption Tax (Aaron, Galper & Pechman, eds.; Brookings 1988).

until distributions are received from the trusts. When distributions are spent on current consumption, this regime conforms to the consumption tax model; savings are excluded from the tax base, while consumption expenditures are taxed even when made from savings. Deductible contributions to individual retirement accounts (IRAs) are a similar example.

The exemption of interest on municipal bonds is a less obvious, but equally clear example of consumption tax treatment. If a person is taxed on income set aside for savings, but is exempted from tax on investment income and pays no additional tax when the investment is liquidated for consumption, the present value of his tax liability is the same as it would be if he were allowed a deduction for the amount saved, but were taxed on that amount and all income when spent on consumption. Assume two individuals, *A* and *B* each set aside $100 from current income to finance a consumption expenditure to be made two years later. *A* uses his $100 to make a deductible contribution to an IRA, and the IRA invests the $100 at 10 percent interest. After two years, the IRA contains $121. If the tax rate is 28 percent, the tax on the distribution from the IRA is $34, and *A* has $87 to spend after taxes. *B*, in contrast, pays tax immediately on her $100, leaving $72 after taxes; she invests the $72 in a municipal bond yielding 10 percent, and income on the bonds is reinvested in additional municipal bonds with an identical yield. After two years, *B* has $87 in municipal bonds, and can sell the bonds and spend the proceeds without further tax. *A* and *B* thus each accumulate $87 after taxes from the diversion of $100 of income into savings for two years.[5]

The treatment of municipal bonds is not unique. When a taxpayer buys a house for his personal use, no deduction is allowed for the amount invested in the house, but the taxpayer's investment return is exempt. The house produces housing services for the taxpayer as long as he lives there, and these services are economic income usually called imputed income.[6] Imputed income, however, is not taxed. Owner-occupied housing and other consumer durables are therefore treated the same as municipal bonds.

The retirement savings model (exclude savings from the tax base, but include consumption) is sometimes referred to as the qualified account

---

[5] The example is unrealistic in assuming that *A* and *B* both invest at the same 10 percent pre-tax return; in reality, the rate of return on tax-exempt bonds is lower than the rate on normally taxable investments. This difference, however, is caused by the hybrid nature of the present tax, which subjects many investors to income tax treatment on nonexempt investments and hence leads them to bid up the price for exempt bonds. If unlimited deductible contributions to IRAs were allowed (thereby making consumption tax treatment available for all investments), exempt bonds would hold no special attraction for investors, and the divergence between exempt and nonexempt rates of return would disappear.

[6] See infra ¶5.3.

approach, and the muncipal bond model (tax savings from earned income, but exempt investment income and dissavings for consumption) is known as the prepayment approach. In theory, both the government and taxpayers are indifferent as between the two approaches because the present value of all tax obligations are the same. Cash flows, however, are importantly affected; the government gets its take at the outset under the prepayment model, but only when the taxpayer liquidates savings to buy consumption under the qualified account approach. Also, the equivalence between the two approaches is broken if the tax rate changes over time. Taxpayers who prepay come out better than those using qualified accounts if the rates go up, whereas the latter group fares better if rates decline. A rate change could result from a revision of the statutory rates or from a change in the taxpayer's marginal rate under a constant rate schedule.

Consumption taxes take a variety of forms. At one extreme is the retail sales tax and its close relative, the value added tax (VAT).[7] A VAT is payable by all business units, regardless of whether they sell at retail. Under a variant of the VAT imposed by many European countries, the tax rate is applied to business gross receipts, with no deductions, but a credit is allowed for the taxes paid by the firm's vendors. Assume a farmer grows wheat and sells it to a miller who makes flour from it; the miller sells the flour to a baker who makes bread from it; the baker sells the bread to a consumer. Assume that in the absence of tax, the prices would be 50 cents for the wheat, 70 cents for the flour, and $1 for the bread. With a 10 percent VAT, the farmer pays 5 cents in tax (10 percent of 50 cents), but charges the miller 55 cents to reimburse himself for the tax. The miller pays 2 cents in tax (10 percent of 70 cents, less the 5 cents paid by the farmer on the wheat sale), but charges the baker 77 cents (the sum of the 55 cents paid to the farmer, 2 cents paid in tax, and 20 cents profit). The baker pays an additional 3 cents in tax (10 percent of $1 less the taxes paid by the farmer and miller), but charges the customer $1.10 (the sum of 77 cents paid to the miller, plus 3 cents of tax, plus 30 cents profit). In total, the government gets 10 cents and the consumer pays the pretax price for the bread plus 10 cents in tax.

The final result under a VAT thus is the same as under a retail sales tax. The VAT perhaps appears more complicated than a retail sales tax in this description, but is not fundamentally complex. Each firm reports only its sales revenues and the taxes paid by vendors on sales to the firm. The latter amounts are required to be shown on invoices provided by the vendors. The invoice requirement provides a paper trail that facilitates enforce-

---

[7] See generally McClure, The Value-Added Tax: Key to Deficit Reduction? (American Enterprise Institute 1987); Schenk, Value Added Tax: Does This Consumption Tax Have a Place in the Federal Tax System? 7 Va. Tax Rev. 207 (1987).

ment of the tax. Suppose the farmer gives the miller an invoice showing tax paid on the wheat sale, but the farmer never files a VAT return or pays the tax reported to the miller. When the miller is audited by the tax authorities, a check will be made of vendors shown on the invoices in the miller's records, and the farmer's fraud will be exposed. If the farmer provides an invoice showing no tax paid, in contrast, the miller will get no credit for the farmer's tax, and will thus have to pay tax on the full selling price to the baker. The same check exists for any intermediate seller, including the miller. It does not exist for the retailer (the baker in the example), but only a fraction of the total tax is paid by the retailer.

At the other extreme from a VAT or retail sales tax is a personal cash-flow tax.[8] A cash-flow tax would be imposed on individuals rather than firms, and would be computed annually on a basis bearing much resemblance to the present income tax. The tax base would consist of taxable receipts less deductible expenditures. Taxable receipts would include borrowed funds as well as salaries and investment returns; generally, any receipt that could be spent on consumption would be included. Deductions, in contrast, would be allowed for all expenditures other than consumption costs. Amounts invested in stocks, bonds, and other investments would be deductible, for example, as would debt repayments. The net taxable amount could be taxed at a single flat rate or at progressive rates. Since a flat-rate cash-flow tax would have the same effect as the much simpler VAT, however, the principal reason for resorting to a cash-flow tax would likely be to have a progressive consumption tax. Such a tax would operate like a progressive income tax, except that savings would be excluded from the tax base and net negative savings (i.e., an excess of consumption over income) would be included.

A pure cash-flow tax is probably not feasible because the tax base would have to include imputed income from taxpayer's homes and other property held for personal use. Most proposals for progressive consumption taxes thus embody aspects of the prepayment approach described earlier under which an investment is not deductible but both income on the investment and any amount received on liquidation of the investment are exempt. The imputed income problem, for example, can be solved by allowing no deduction for amounts paid for a home or other personal-use asset and then excluding from the tax base both the imputed income from the property and the price received on its eventual sale. This solution, however, presents another problem. If rates are progressive, the prepayment approach would often push taxpayers into higher tax brackets when they

---

[8] The classic works on personal consumption taxes are Kaldor, An Expenditure Tax (George Allen & Unwin 1955), and Andrews, A Consumption-Type or Cash Flow Personal Income Tax, 87 Harv. L. Rev. 1113 (1974).

purchase houses and other large consumer items because the tax base for the year of purchase would include both savings liquidated to finance the purchase and the principal amount of any mortgage loan; the inclusion of the mortgage loan proceeds, further, would often create a cash flow crunch for home buyers.

Although solutions for these problems are available,[9] the bunching problem illustrated by the home purchase example would be solved more generally by allowing the prepayment approach to be used for any asset. Under one proposal for a modified cash-flow tax, the cash flow technique illustrated above would only apply to investments deposited in qualified accounts and investments in closely held businesses.[10] Additions to these accounts and transfers of funds to such businesses would be deductible, and income accumulated in the accounts and businesses would not be taxed as earned. Any amount withdrawn from the account or business, however, would be taxed. The prepayment approach would be used for all other investments; no deduction would be allowed when the investments are made, but neither investment income nor amounts withdrawn for consumption would be taxed. Because the qualified account technique would be available for all investments and the prepayment approach could be used for any investment other than a closely held business, the modified cash-flow tax would be quite flexible in the timing of tax liabilities. This would allow a taxpayer to keep his taxable amount relatively level over his lifetime and thereby minimize his tax liability.

The substitution of a consumption tax for an income tax could raise troublesome transition problems, particularly for older taxpayers with substantial savings. Assume a person accumulates savings for retirement.[11] If the savings are accumulated while an income tax is in effect, but a consumption tax is substituted for the income tax shortly before he retires, the person is doubly taxed; the income tax hits the original savings and income on it, and the consumption tax applies to the spending of the accumulation. People who both save and spend either before or after the switchover, in contrast, are taxed just once.

Transition problems would be less severe, however, if the change were effected by adding additional consumption-tax features to the present hy-

---

[9] A home buyer's tax liability could be spread over the period he accumulates the funds used to pay for the home by (1) allowing the prepayment approach to be used for investment accounts set aside for subsequent home purchases and (2) excluding the mortgage loan proceeds from the tax base for the year of purchase and instead allowing no deduction for principal or interest payments on the loan.

[10] Dep't of Treasury, Blueprints for Basic Tax Reform 101–28 (Bradford ed. 1984)

[11] See generally Graetz, Implementing a Progressive Consumption Tax, 92 Harv L. Rev. 1575 (1979).

brid tax. For example, the present tax could be converted into something closely resembling the modified cash-flow tax described above by (1) lifting all limitations on deductions for contributions to IRAs, (2) exempting individuals from tax on interest and dividend income on portfolio investments, and (3) repealing the tax on corporations.

CHAPTER

4

Interpreting the Internal Revenue Code

¶4.1 THE FEDERAL INCOME TAX AND STATE LAW

¶4.1.1 Introductory

The Internal Revenue Code is a national law, but it taxes transactions whose legal effects are almost always prescribed by state rather than federal law.[1] Without the body of state law prescribing the rights and liabilities arising from taxpayers' daily activities, the federal tax collector would be a fish out of water. For example, so simple a matter as the deduction of a worthless debt under §166(a)(1) on the ground that the taxpayer's claim against the debtor is barred by the statute of limitations depends on state law rules, and these rules vary from one state to another.[2] Before the federal tax effect of a transaction can be determined, a host of threshold determinations of this type is usually required. The answers to these preliminary questions are often so clear as to be taken for granted. This does not mean that the Code is independent of state law but only that its reliance on state law is so pervasive that it rarely rises to the conscious level.

The notion that state law plays a secondary role, however, is widespread. This misapprehension is traceable to cases like *Lucas v. Earl*, in which the Supreme Court held that an individual was taxable on all his earnings from personal services, even though he had assigned one half to his wife under a contract that was valid under state law.[3] Salaries are taxable "to those who earned them," not to their assignees, the Court held. Because the contract transferred to the taxpayer's wife the right to collect and retain one half of his salary as a matter of state law, but failed to relieve him of the obligation to pay federal income taxes on that amount, the decision may seem to reject state law in favor of an overriding federal legal structure—an impression that is strengthened by the Court's statement that "this case is

---

[1] See generally Paul, The Effect on Federal Taxation of Local Rules of Property, in Paul, Selected Studies in Federal Taxation 1 (Callaghan, 2d ser. 1938); Cahn, Federal Taxation and Private Law, 44 Colum. L. Rev. 669 (1944); Cahn, Local Law in Federal Taxation, 52 Yale LJ 799 (1943); Teschner, Property Concepts and Nonproperty Taxes, 44 U. Colo. L. Rev. 323 (1973).

For articles discussing the conclusiveness of state court litigation in determining the federal tax effect of transactions, see infra note 44.

[2] Infra ¶33.3.

[3] Lucas v. Earl, 281 US 111 (1930), discussed infra ¶75.2.1. The taxable years before the Court were 1920 and 1921, long before the enactment of the joint return option that now allows essentially the same tax effect as was claimed in *Lucas v. Earl*.

not to be decided by attenuated subtleties." State law, however, supplied the foundation of the decision by establishing that (1) the amounts divided between the taxpayer and his wife were compensation for his services (rather than, for example, moneys coming to him as a gift or loan), (2) they were "earned" by him rather than by his wife or someone else, and (3) in the absence of the agreement, he would have been entitled to collect and retain everything paid by the employer.

Another case that might seem to discard state law in favor of a uniform federal rule is *Helvering v. Clifford*, which taxed a grantor of a trust on trust income.[4] The taxpayer in *Clifford* created a trust to last for five years, at which time the accumulated income was payable to his wife and the corpus was to revert to him. The grantor designated himself as trustee, retaining unusually broad powers to manage the trust corpus and the right, in his sole discretion, to pay the trust income over to his wife prior to termination. Despite the wife's undisputed legal right under state law to receive and retain the income, it was taxed to the grantor. *Clifford* is not inconsistent with applicable state rules. Despite its dismissal of the "niceties of the law of trusts or conveyances, or the legal paraphernalia which inventive genius may construct as a refuge from surtaxes,"[5] the factors listed by the Court as requiring the grantor to report the income—the fact that it was payable to a member of his immediate family, the breadth of his powers as trustee, the relative insignificance of the restraints on his ability to use the corpus for his personal benefit—all had their origin in the trust indenture, whose legal effect in turn depended on state law.

Only two years after *Clifford*, the Supreme Court acknowledged the importance of state law in another grantor trust case:

> Grantees under deeds, wills and trusts, alike, take according to the rule of the state law. The power to transfer or distribute assets of a trust is essentially a matter of local law. . . . Congress has selected an event, that is the receipt or distributions of trust funds by or to a grantor, normally brought about by local law, and has directed a tax to be levied if that event may occur. Whether that event may or may not occur depends upon the interpretation placed upon the terms of the instrument by state law. Once rights are obtained by local law, whatever they may be called, these rights are subject to the federal definition of taxability.[6]

Lucas v. Earl and *Clifford* are examples of a common phenomenon in federal tax law. Each is a decision attaching more weight to one set of

---

[4] Helvering v. Clifford, 309 US 331 (1940), discussed infra ¶80.1.1.

[5] Id. at 334.

[6] Helvering v. Stuart, 317 US 154, 161–62 (1942).

substantive rights created by state law than to another set, also arising under state law, in deciding which of several persons should be taxed on a particular item of income. In *Lucas v. Earl*, the fact that the income was compensation for the taxpayer's services was regarded as more significant for federal tax purposes than his contract with his wife. In *Clifford*, the grantor's control over the trust income and corpus and his legal relationship to the beneficiary were held to be more important than the latter's right to receive the income. Choosing among competing sets of state-created substantive rights is often unavoidable. In *Clifford*, for example, a decision in favor of the taxpayer would have elevated the wife's right to receive the income on the trust's termination to a position of greater importance for federal tax purposes than the husband's virtually unfettered right in the interim to manage the corpus and accumulated income and to advance income to his wife in such amounts and at such times as his fancy dictated. In a similar context, Judge John R. Brown spoke of "ignoring the flyspeck of legal title under state law" in favor of the taxpayer's other rights, stemming from the same body of state law, in deciding that a taxpayer could not deduct as rent under §162 payments to a trust for the use of business property previously transferred by him to a trustee for the benefit of his children.[7]

In these cases, the Court found little guidance in statutory language. In *Lucas v. Earl*, the controlling provisions were §§211(a) and 213(a) of the Revenue Act of 1918, imposing a tax on "the net income of every individual" and defining income in the broad terms that are now found, with minor variations, in IRC §61(a).[8] Given the husband-wife agreement to divide their earnings equally, the Court had to decide whether the wife's share of the husband's salary was income "of" the husband, who had performed the personal services, or "of" the wife, who was entitled to receive it under the marital agreement. As suggested above, state law was indispensable to the result reached by the Court, but this was not because state law shed any light on the meaning of the naked term "of" as used in the Revenue Act of 1918.

The same can be said of the landmark case of *Poe v. Seaborn*, holding that one half of the community income of a couple living in a community

---

[7] Mathews v. CIR, 520 F2d 323, 325 (5th Cir. 1975), cert. denied, 424 US 967 (1976). For more on this much-litigated area, see infra ¶75.3.5; see also Doll v. CIR, 149 F2d 239, 244 n.10 (8th Cir.), cert. denied, 326 US 725 (1945) ("[W]here the issue is the existence of a legal status left by the taxing statute to the determination of State law, the decision of a State court is controlling. Here, the real issue is whether a contract which has created such a legal status has effected 'any substantial change in . . . economic position'"; husband-wife partnership disregarded for federal tax purposes).

[8] Infra ¶75.2.1.

property state was taxable to each spouse.[9] Even though the income was attributable to the husband's personal services and was subject to his management, the Court held that the wife's rights under local law were so weighty that one half of the earnings constituted income "of" the wife.

Elsewhere in the Code, however, there is a profusion of terms taken from state law (e.g., "trust," "marriage," "corporation," "contract," "debenture," "lease," and "real property").[10] Since terms like these can have one meaning in New York and another in Hawaii, how should they be interpreted when used in a national law taxing transactions whose substantive legal results are almost always prescribed by state law?

In *Burnet v. Harmel*, a leading case on this issue, the Supreme Court said:

> The exertion of [Congress' power to tax income] is not subject to state control. It is the will of Congress which controls, and the expression of its will in legislation, in the absence of language evidencing a different purpose, is to be interpreted so as to give a uniform application to a nationwide scheme of taxation. . . . State law may control only when the federal taxing act, by express language or necessary implication, makes its own operation dependent upon state law. . . . The state law creates legal interests, but the federal statute determines when and how they shall be taxed.[11]

The issue in *Harmel* was whether a transfer of oil and gas rights was a "sale or exchange" of "capital assets" under what is now §1222. Local law characterized the arrangement as a "sale" of the oil and gas in place although it had substantially the same economic effect as a lease. Since mineral leases

---

[9] Poe v. Seaborn, 282 US 101 (1930).

[10] The Code also uses terms of its own invention that are akin to, but not identical with, state-law terms. Thus, although "earnings and profits" as used in §316(a) is not a state-law term, it bears a resemblance to the state-law concept of "earned surplus" (see infra ¶92.1.3); and there is a similar relationship between the "complete liquidation" of a corporation (IRC §331) and its "dissolution" under state law (see infra ¶93.6).

[11] Burnet v. Harmel, 287 US 103, 110 (1932). Later decisions quoting or paraphrasing *Harmel* include Helvering v. Stuart, 317 US 154 (1942) (Congress intended to adopt state law); Morgan v. CIR, 309 US 78 (1940) ("general power of appointment" as used in Section 302(f) of the Revenue Act of 1926); Lyeth v. Hoey, 305 US 188 (1938) ("inheritance" as used in §102(a) includes an amount received in the compromise of a will contest, even though not so defined by state law); and Heiner v. Mellon, 304 US 271 (1938) (use of term "trustee" by state law not conclusive). See also Blair v. CIR, 300 US 5 (1937) (validity of certain assignments dependent on state law); Isaacson, Rosenbaum, Speigleman & Friedman, P.C. v. US, 44 AFTR2d 5832 (Ct. Cl. 1979) (not officially reported) (compensation-dividend issue cannot be settled by certifying to state court issue of whether payments were "dividends" under state law).

were not treated as "sales" under several earlier revenue acts, the Court concluded that the preceding revenue act used the term in this established sense, thus disqualifying a mineral lease even though classified as a "sale" by local law.

If a transaction or event has identical legal consequences in substantially all states but is given a peculiar label by the law of a particular locality, it is easy for the courts to conclude that local usage is not controlling and that the federal tax treatment of the transaction should be uniform across the nation. But where legal rights and liabilities differ significantly from state to state, it is less clear whether Congress intended to adopt or disregard local usage. The *Harmel* case establishes a presumption in favor of "uniform application."

There are, unfortunately, at least two types of uniformity in many situations. The competing possibilities are illustrated by the earnings of minor children, which in some states can be retained by the children for themselves but in other states must be paid over to their parents. Before the enactment of the statutory predecessor of §73(a) in 1944,[12] the Code did not state explicitly whether the child or the parent was required to report such income, and the controlling provision was §1, imposing a tax on the income "of" every individual. If this vague term were interpreted to require children to report their wages and other earnings whether or not they were entitled to retain them under local law, national uniformity would be achieved in the sense that the service income of minors would be taxed everywhere to the person performing the services. On the other hand, if the earnings were taxed to whichever person was entitled by local law to receive and spend them, another type of national uniformity would be achieved; the governing factor—nationwide—would be legal control over the funds.[13] The *Harmel* presumption in favor of "uniform application" does not resolve the conflict between these two types of uniformity.

The *Harmel* formulation is also ambiguous in stating that "state law may control only when the federal taxing act, by express language or necessary implication, makes its own operation dependent upon state law."[14] In an ultimate sense, state law never controls; even when the Code expressly adopts state law for some purpose, this is done by Congress, which may revoke its acceptance of the state rules whenever it chooses. Occasional complaints that disregarding state law violates the Tenth Amendment (reserving to the states or "the people" any powers not delegated to the United States by the Constitution) miss the basic point—that the issue is the taxpayer's liability for federal income tax, the imposition of which is a

---

[12] Infra ¶75.4.3.

[13] See also infra note 27.

[14] Burnet v. Harmel, supra note 11, at 110.

federal responsibility.[15] Indeed, any attempt by a state to prescribe or alter the scope of the federal income tax or to exempt transactions from its reach would violate the supremacy clause of the Constitution, which provides that "the Laws of the United States which shall be made in Pursuance [of the Constitution] shall be the supreme Law of the Land."[16] In these cases, state law is treated no more cavalierly than the federally prescribed private law of the District of Columbia, and the same process is also employed in deciding tax cases involving rights created by the federal patent and copyright laws.[17]

Moreover, although the reference in *Harmel* to state law adopted by "express language or necessary implication" might seem to suggest that most legal terms used by the Code have an independent national meaning and that only a few are used in their local sense, precisely the opposite is true. The Code attaches tax significance to state-created legal rights, and most legal terms are used as abbreviated references to these substantive rights. Randolph Paul wrote 50 years ago that "much of our federal tax law is not federal tax law at all, but non-tax state law."[18] In the same vein, Dean Griswold said of tax practice that "it seems difficult to find a field which leads practitioners more widely through the whole fabric of the law."[19]

Paul's observation is illustrated by the Supreme Court's 1965 decision in *CIR v. Clay Brown*, holding that the term "sale" in §1222(3), referring to "the sale or exchange of a capital asset," is used in its customary sense rather than in a special tax sense:

> The transaction was a sale under local law. . . . "Capital gain" and "capital asset" are creatures of the tax law and the Court has been inclined to give these terms a narrow, rather than a broad, construction. . . . A "sale," however, is a common event in the non-tax world; and since it is used in the Code without limiting definition and without legislative history indicating a contrary result, its common and ordinary meaning should at least be persuasive of its meaning as used in the

---

[15] See Phillips v. CIR, 283 US 589 (1931) (transferee liability held constitutional); Kieferdorf v. CIR, 142 F2d 723 (7th Cir.), cert. denied, 323 US 733 (1944) (federal tax lien superior to rights created by state exemption statute).

[16] U.S. Const. art. VI, §2.

[17] See, e.g., Herwig v. US, 105 F. Supp. 384 (Ct. Cl. 1952) (transfer of motion picture rights in a novel held to be a "sale" for federal tax purposes although characterized as a "license" by federal copyright law); the case is especially noteworthy because the taxpayer, rather than the government, was endeavoring to escape from the private-law classification of the transaction.

[18] Paul, supra note 1, at 5.

[19] Griswold, The Need for a Federal Court of Tax Appeals, 57 Harv. L. Rev. 1153, 1183 (1944).

Internal Revenue Code.[20]

Although not in direct conflict, *Harmel* and *Clay Brown* manifest divergent approaches to the meaning of common legal terms. Both opinions interpret the same word ("sale") as used in the same provision: *Harmel* suggests that a uniform national "tax" definition should be adopted unless "express language or necessary implication" assigns a dominant role to the state definition, while *Clay Brown* implies that the term's nontax meaning, which necessarily comes from state law, should ordinarily control. Against this background, it is useful to examine the two possible extremes and then the middle ground: (1) provisions of the Code explicitly imposing a uniform national definition on a familiar state-law term; (2) provisions that explicitly subordinate national uniformity to state law; and (3) the broad intermediate area, illustrated by both *Harmel* and *Clay Brown*, where the Code uses legal terms without explicitly indicating whether they are to retain their customary local sense or be given a uniform national interpretation.

¶4.1.2 Federal Definitions Superseding State Law

The Code contains a few provisions that supersede the usual local meaning of familiar legal terms by substituting a uniform federal definition. An example is §704(e),[21] which attaches certain tax consequences to partnership interests created by "gift" and then goes on to provide that "for purposes of this section, an interest purchased by one member of a family [as defined] from another shall be considered to be created by gift from the seller."[22] Another example is §6013(d)(2), which provides that a person "legally separated from his spouse under a decree . . . of separate maintenance shall not be considered as married," thereby preventing the filing of a joint return[23] even though the couple are "married" under the law of the

---

[20] CIR v. Brown, 380 US 563, 569–71 (1965). See also Crane v. CIR, 331 US 1, 6 (1947) ("the words of statutes—including revenue acts—should be interpreted where possible in their ordinary, everyday senses"). These references to common usage do not explicitly defer to the meaning of the particular term under the governing state law, but when the term is a legal one, state law is the usual source of its meaning.

[21] Section 7701 also defines a few terms, but the definitions are often incomplete. Thus, §7701(a)(3) provides that if not "manifestly incompatible with the intent" of the Code, "the term 'corporation' includes associations, joint-stock companies, and insurance companies", but it does not state whether the term embraces all entities that are called "corporations" by the state by which they are chartered, or only those having a particular set of corporate indicia. See infra ¶90.1.6 (re professional corporations). See also the definitions in 1 USC §§1–5 of "person," "company," and other terms.

[22] IRC §704(e)(3), discussed infra ¶85.2.

[23] See infra ¶111.3.6.

marital domicile. A third example is §318, which provides that a taxpayer shall be "considered as owning" stock owned, directly or indirectly, by his spouse, children, and certain related entities, although he is not the owner under state law.

These federal definitions do not purport to alter substantive legal rights created by state law. A "purchase" under state law is a purchase for local purposes, even if it is treated as a gift by §704(e)(3); a couple separated under a legal decree remain married for local purposes if the law of their marital domicile so provides, even though they are not allowed to file a joint federal tax return; and a taxpayer does not become the "owner" of his children's stock under local law, even though he is treated as the owner by §318 for federal tax purposes. The federal definition does not violate or even disregard state law. Rather, it treats some of the substantive legal rights created by state law as irrelevant to a particular issue of federal tax liability.

In doing so, it puts two groups of taxpayers in the same boat although their rights under state law differ, and this may raise a due process issue, especially if the juxtaposition simultaneously separates either group from a third group of taxpayers with whom they have much in common under local law. Thus, §6013(d)(2) denies the right to file joint tax returns to married persons subject to a decree of separate maintenance, putting them in the same position for filing purposes as unmarried taxpayers and denying them a right allowed to other married couples. Similarly, §704(e)(3) imposes identical treatment on persons acquiring partnership interests by gift and those acquiring such interests by purchase from family members, but it does not impose this treatment on persons acquiring partnership interests by purchase from more distant relatives or by bequest from immediate family members. Whether these legislative classifications violate due process depends on whether the classification is reasonable. As pointed out elsewhere,[24] the courts have almost always bowed to the judgment of Congress when passing on the reasonableness of decisions of this type.

Another point about these provisions is their reliance on state law in the very process of substituting a federal definition for a term's meaning under state law. Section 6013(d)(2), for example, refers to "an individual who is legally separated from his spouse under a decree of . . . separate maintenance," thereby looking to state judicial decrees to identify the persons not to be "considered as married." Also, §704(e)(3) applies only to "purchases" and not to other forms of acquisition, without any suggestion that this distinction is to be administered by creating a uniform federal definition of the term "purchase" rather than by reference to its state-law meaning. The same inescapable link to state law is found in §318, which

---

[24] Supra ¶1.2.5.

attributes to the taxpayer property that is in fact "owned" by specified members of his family or related entities. Before stock can be attributed to the taxpayer under this provision, a determination must be made that it is "owned" by the related person, and this threshold issue can only be resolved by looking to state property law. Nothing demonstrates so clearly the pervasive presence of state law than its continued importance even when the Code substitutes a uniform national rule for terms with divergent local meanings.

¶4.1.3 Explicit Federal Adoption of State Law

At the other end of the spectrum from the relatively scarce federal definitions superseding local meanings of legal terms are Code provisions, also rather uncommon, explicitly providing that a state usage or determination is controlling. Thus, if a married couple is not divorced, legally separated, or subject to a written separation agreement, payments by one spouse to support the other are deductible by the payor and taxable to the recipient only if there is "a decree entered after March 1, 1954, requiring the husband to make the payments for [the wife's] support or maintenance."[25] Section 368(a)(1)(A) defines the term "reorganization" to include "statutory" mergers and consolidations, thus embracing transactions effected under state statutes but excluding mergers effected under the laws of foreign countries, as well as "practical" mergers.[26] Under §164(d)(2)(A), the deductibility of real property taxes explicitly depends on the local rules fixing the time when the taxes become a lien on the property.[27]

A more unusual example of explicit federal deference to state law is found in §162(c)(2), providing that a bribe, kickback, or other payment may not be deducted as a business expense if it violates a state criminal or occupational licensing law, "but only if such State law is generally enforced."[28]

While this list of Code provisions explicitly bowing to state common law, statutes, or agency determinations could be extended,[29] even the most

---

[25] IRC §71(a)(3), discussed infra ¶77.1.5.

[26] Infra ¶94.3.1.

[27] Infra ¶32.2.1.

[28] This provision is another example of the ambiguity inherent in the concept of a uniform national application of the revenue laws. It treats alike all taxpayers who violate state laws that are generally enforced by the particular state where the activity occurs, but this uniformity is achieved at the cost of treating differently taxpayers who engage in identical illegal activities in states that are lax in enforcing their laws. See infra ¶20.3.5.

[29] See, for example, §3121(d)(2), adopting "the usual common law rules applicable in determining the employer-employee relationship" in imposing social security taxes on "employees."

complete catalogue would be a thin pamphlet. In the overwhelming majority of cases, when the Code uses a familiar legal term, it neither explicitly adopts its local meaning nor explicitly supersedes it with a uniform national definition. The effect of this practice is discussed in the next section.

¶4.1.4 State Meaning Neither Supplanted nor Endorsed

The Code often uses a legal term without either adopting its state law meaning or explicitly supplanting the local meaning with a uniform federal definition. When the Code uses familiar legal terms, it rarely infuses them with a national meaning but, instead, ordinarily defers to state law by employing the terms as abbreviated ways of designating events and relationships that create taxable income, deductions, and other tax consequences. Indeed, the only alternative to these shorthand expressions would be detailed descriptions of the underlying facts triggering federal tax consequences, a practice that might increase the clarity of the Code but would require a far wordier statute than Congress has ever seen fit to enact. Thus, a Code provision referring to "contracts" conveys in a single word a meaning that would otherwise require paragraphs of black letter law describing the concepts of offer, acceptance, consideration, capacity to contract, and many others. Moreover, the use of such terms ordinarily points to the state law applicable to a particular set of facts, rather than to a more generalized national standard.

Common legal terms may be employed by Congress, not only to incorporate by reference a complex set of facts but also as a way of attaching tax consequences to facts that have a particular legal effect under state law. In these instances, the term refers to the legal result, as well as implying the existence of the underlying facts. For example, the references in §642(c)(2) to "mental disability" to change a will or trust refer to a want of legal power under the applicable state law, by reason of mental deficiency, to perform the specified acts. Thus, a person would be embraced by the statutory phrase if an attempt by him to change a will or trust would be ineffective in his own state, even if his emotional or cognitive disorientation would be considered mere eccentricity in a more tolerant state. Conversely, a person whose behavior did not fall below the legal standard in his own state would presumably not suffer from "mental disability" within the meaning of §642(c)(2) even if he would be stigmatized as non compos mentis in a more finicky state.[30]

---

[30] The conclusions in the text are qualified by the word "presumably," since §642(c)(2) is used here solely to illustrate a general principle, divorced from the provision's legislative history.

The local meaning of a common legal term may not control in such situations, however, if it is out of the mainstream. If used as an idiosyncratic label[31] for a transaction, event, or status that is outside the intended reach of the tax provision in question, the local term may be rejected in favor of a more conventional, nationally uniform definition. Conversely, if the taxpayer's rights, liabilities, or status are within the intended scope of a tax provision, the provision applies even if they are denoted by an unconventional local label that differs from the term used by the Code. What is important in these circumstances is not that the state attaches different legal consequences to an activity or set of facts than do other states, but that its label clashes with the term employed by the Code, either because the Code's term is used locally to denote legal results that the Code provision was not intended to comprehend or because a different label is used locally for results within the Code's intended scope.

A leading illustration of this point is *Morgan v. CIR*, in which the Supreme Court interpreted the term "general power of appointment," as used in the estate tax provisions of the Revenue Act of 1932.[32] At her death, a decedent possessed the power to appoint by will the property of two trusts created by her father. The terms of the trusts permitted her to appoint to anyone, including her own estate and creditors, but the powers were exercisable only by will. Because she could not have exercised the powers during her life, the executor contended that they were "special" rather than "general" powers of appointment under the law of Wisconsin, where both the decedent and her father were domiciled. This version of Wisconsin law was disputed by the government, but the Court found it unnecessary to resolve this issue:

> [W]e hold that the powers are general within the intent of the Revenue Act [of 1932], notwithstanding they may be classified as special by the law of Wisconsin.
>
> State law creates legal interests and rights. The federal revenue acts designate what interests or rights, so created, shall be taxed. Our duty is to ascertain the meaning of the words used to specify the thing taxed. If it is found in a given case that an interest or right created by local law was the object intended to be taxed, the federal law must

---

[31] Names, however, can be more than mere labels. As pointed out by Cahn, supra note 1, at 803: "Names in law are heavily encrusted with real distinctions and implications. Where nomenclature ends and substantial difference begins—that is the question." To some tax theorists, for example, "community property" is a mere label for rights that are virtually identical with the rights of married couples in common law states; to others, there is a world, or at least a continent, of difference. See infra ¶76.1.

[32] Morgan v. CIR, 309 US 78 (1940).

prevail no matter what name is given to the interest or right by state law.[33]

Although it refused to be bound by the state's label, the Court in *Morgan* affirmed the central importance of state law in applying the Code. First, the Court's reference to "an interest or right created by local law" acknowledges that the subject matter of federal taxation is almost always a right, liability, status, or other legal interest created by state law. Second, after holding that Wisconsin's label was not controlling, the Court went on to say:

> None of the revenue acts has defined the phrase "general power of appointment." The distinction usually made between a general and a special power lies in the circumstance that, under the former, the donee may appoint to anyone, including his own estate or his creditors, thus having as full dominion over the property as if he owned it; whereas, under the latter, the donee may appoint only amongst a restricted or designated class of persons other than himself.
>
> We should expect, therefore, that Congress had this distinction in mind when it used the adjective "general."[34]

The only source of the "distinction usually made between a general and a special power" is state law. Thus, in interpreting the phrase as used by Congress, the Court turned from its meaning in a particular state to its typical meaning in the states. Finally, the Court distinguished two other cases relied on by the taxpayer, saying, with evident approval:

> We think it clear that, in both cases, the courts examined the local law to ascertain whether a power would be construed by the state court to permit the appointment of the donee, his estate or his creditors, and on the basis of the answer to that question determined whether the power was general within the intent of the federal act.[35]

Most federal tax cases that seem to dismiss state law in favor of a federal rule turn out, on analysis, to be less dramatic. They ordinarily resemble the *Morgan* case in looking to the law of the taxpayer's own state to determine the legal consequences of his activities, while rejecting that state's label in order to give the federal statutory phrase a more general or

---

[33] Id. at 80–81.

[34] The Court also cited the legislative history of the Revenue Act of 1918 and the Treasury regulations as independent authorities for this interpretation of the disputed statutory phrase.

[35] Morgan v. CIR, supra note 32, at 82.

familiar definition.[36] But even this appeal from the particular to the general usually relies on state law, albeit the majority rule or other evidence of widespread custom.

Since the labels employed by a particular state's common or statutory law are not controlling, it should occasion no surprise that the federal courts are not bound by the labels that taxpayers bestow on a contract or transaction. A transaction may be treated as a mortgage for federal tax purposes, for example, even though the documents consistently describe it as a sale of the property coupled with a leaseback by the buyer to the seller.[37] When a label used by the parties does not accurately denote the transaction's legal consequences under state law, a different characterization for federal tax purposes may actually conform to, rather than depart from, the characterization that would be adopted for local purposes by the state courts.

Finally, a few legal terms used in the Code have been the subject of extensive interpretation in federal tax litigation in which nationally applicable principles have been developed with minimal reliance on state law. This is most likely to occur with broad, amorphous terms whose local meanings evolved in contexts far removed from the federal tax issues created by their use in the Code. For example, the Supreme Court has held that §102(a), which excludes "the value of property acquired by gift" from the donee's gross income, does not use the term "gift" "in the common-law sense."[38] This conclusion is quite understandable. Federal income tax problems involving the meaning of "gift" arise most frequently in transactions that have a compensatory flavor, leading the IRS to assert that the transfer was not a tax-free gift but a receipt of taxable compensation. For private-law purposes, however, the principal situation invoking the term "gift" is a transfer of property that the purported donor (or, more frequently, his executor) seeks to recover. In deciding whether the transferee is entitled to retain the property under state law, it is not necessary to distinguish between gifts and payments of compensation, since in either case the transfer is legally effective. For this reason, there is little reason to delineate a distinction between gifts and compensation for private law purposes. By contrast, in applying §102(a), this distinction is all-important. It is, therefore, not surprising that the federal tax cases interpreting the term "gift" as used in §102(a) give little attention to local law.

---

[36] For example, in a series of cases involving the federal tax status of state-chartered professional "corporations," the entity's local label was sometimes mentioned, but the courts went on to examine the legal rights created by local law and to compare them with conventional corporate characteristics. See infra ¶90.1.6.

[37] Infra ¶40.6.2.

[38] CIR v. Duberstein, 363 US 278, 285 (1960), discussed infra ¶10.2.1.

¶4.1.5 The Effect of State Adjudications

When a legal issue arising under state law must be decided in the course of a federal tax case, the federal court performs substantially the same function as when it decides a similar state issue in a diversity-of-citizenship case, and hence it "may be said to be, in effect, sitting as a state court."[39] In the absence of an authoritative decision by the highest state court, the federal court must give "proper regard"—but not conclusive force—to decisions of the state's trial and intermediate appellate courts when determining, as best it can, how the local issue would be decided by the highest state court.[40] State law issues are occasionally certified by federal courts to state courts for authoritative rulings.[41]

What if the local issue that is being disputed in the federal tax proceeding has already been decided by a state court in litigation by which the taxpayer is bound? Assume a taxpayer seeking to deduct a debt as worthless under §166(a)(1) offers as evidence of worthlessness a state court judgment in a suit he brought against the debtor, holding that collection is barred by the statute of limitations. If the IRS asserts that the debt is not yet worthless because the state court applied the wrong statute of limitations,[42] much can be said for treating the issue as foreclosed by the state judgment since it is binding on the taxpayer, whether it correctly interprets state law or not.[43] If

---

[39] CIR v. Bosch's Est., 387 US 456, 465 (1967); see also 382 F2d 295 (2d Cir. 1967) (decision on remand). But the "state court" analogy does not hold for the Supreme Court, which will ordinarily not reexamine a federal appellate court's determination of local law. 387 US at 462 (Point II).

[40] CIR v. Bosch's Est., supra note 39; Newman v. CIR, 68 TC 494 (1977) (effect of retroactive state court rulings); Linder v. CIR, 68 TC 292, 298–99 (1977) (Tax Court effort to determine whether New Jersey Supreme Court would follow an earlier, outmoded decision). See also Wright, Handbook of the Law of Federal Courts §58 at 267 (West, 3d ed. 1976); Friendly, In Praise of *Erie* —and of the New Federal Common Law, 39 NYU L. Rev. 383 (1964).

[41] See US v. Baldwin, 586 F2d 324 (4th Cir. 1978); Imel v. US, 523 F2d 853 (10th Cir. 1975). See also Isaacson, Rosenbaum, Speigleman & Friedman, P.C. v. US, 44 AFTR2d 5832 (Ct. Cl. 1979) (not officially reported) (refusal to certify issue); infra ¶40.5.2.

[42] Since the Commissioner cannot be a party to the private lawsuit, the judgment is not res judicata as to the government, nor does the principle of collateral estoppel apply. See Stephens & Freeland, The Role of Local Law and Local Adjudications in Federal Tax Controversies, 46 Minn. L. Rev. 223, 250–51 (1961). For the possibility of a certification of the state issue by the federal court to the local courts, see Wolfman, *Bosch*, Its Implications and Aftermath: The Effect of State Court Adjudications on Federal Tax Litigation, 3 U. Miami Inst. on Est. Plan. ¶69.205.4 (1969).

[43] See Rev. Rul. 73-142, 1973-1 CB 405 (state decree holding that decedent did not have power to appoint successor trustees binding in applying federal estate tax because, whether correct or not, it effectively terminated decedent's power). But see

the debtor happens to be the taxpayer's child, however, the taxpayer might not have prosecuted the case as vigorously as possible, and might even have preferred to lose than to win. In such a nonadversary situation, the local judgment may be tantamount to a consent decree, entered without much attention to the issues by a busy judge eager to clear his docket.

The tension between the state judgment's conclusive determination of the taxpayer's private law rights and federal fear of perfunctory decisions, collusion, and even fraud in nonadversary local proceedings has generated a series of dramatic cases in the Supreme Court. In *CIR v. Bosch's Estate*, the most recent, the Court apparently disregarded both of these factors by announcing that the federal court must follow the same procedure in ascertaining state law when the taxpayer's rights have already been determined by a state court as it would in the absence of such a determination. The result, evidently, is that a decision of the highest state court is controlling even if the lawsuit was of a nonadversary nature, whereas decisions of the state trial and intermediate appellate courts are to receive "proper regard" but are not conclusive even if rendered in an adversary proceeding.[44]

¶4.2 STATUTORY CONSTRUCTION

¶4.2.1 Introductory

In a typical recent year, taxpayers took about 52,000 administrative appeals to the IRS' appeals division, and about 49,000 petitions were filed in the U.S. Tax Court.[1] In many of these cases, the only disputed issue was a question of fact or of local law, but many turned on conflicting interpretations of the Code. If it was ever hoped that these interpretative issues would

---

American Nurseryman Publishing Co. v. CIR, 75 TC 271 (1980) (in determining qualification for S corporation election, court order voiding transfer of stock to ineligible holder ineffective because judicial reformation could not change tax effect of completed transaction).

[44] CIR v. Bosch's Est., supra note 39. Although the Court cited the legislative history of the tax provision in dispute (the marital deduction authorized by §2056 of the estate tax law), the opinion seemingly stakes out a much wider application; and the three dissenting opinions so construe it, as do the principal commentators. See Martin, *Bosch* and the Binding Effect of State Court Adjudications Upon Subsequent Federal Tax Litigation, 21 Vand. L. Rev. 825 (1968); Sobeloff, Tax Effect of State Court Decisions—The Impact of *Bosch*, 21 Tax Lawyer 507 (1968); Wolfman, supra note 42, ¶69.200. For earlier discussions, see Cardozo, Federal Taxes and the Radiating Potencies of State Court Decisions, 51 Yale LJ 783 (1942); Stephens & Freeland, supra note 42; articles cited supra note 1.

[1] Commissioner of Internal Revenue, 1986 Annual Report 35, 58.

diminish in number or difficulty as the Code became more detailed,[2] that dream has not been realized. The classic verdict on this point is by Judge Learned Hand:

> In my own case the words of such an act as the Income Tax, for example, merely dance before my eyes in a meaningless procession: cross-reference to cross-reference, exception upon exception—couched in abstract terms that offer no handle to seize hold of—leave in my mind only a confused sense of some vitally important, but successfully concealed, purport, which it is my duty to extract, but which is within my power, if at all, only after the most inordinate expenditure of time.[3]

It is not only the Code's "fantastic labyrinths" (Judge Hand's phrase) that bewilder taxpayers, their advisers, revenue agents, and federal judges. Unfortunately, the Code's simple phrases are often as troublesome as its complex verbiage. Thus, a flood of litigation stems from such disarmingly simple terms as "interest," "debt," and "gift," while another terse statutory phrase (imposing a tax on the income of "every individual") gave birth to many of the most momentous decisions in the entire income tax field.[4]

The sheer volume of interpretative issues spawned by the Code often leads tax experts to imagine that statutory construction is an occupational hazard peculiar to their calling, an illusion that is fostered by the aphorisms used by the courts in tax cases. Viewed in the perspective of history or even from the bench of a contemporary court of general jurisdiction, however, the Code is just another statute, which suffers from the same ailments that have afflicted legislative enactments since Parliament first tampered with the common law. Statutes are written in the English language, whose imprecision is both its curse and its glory[5] and whose inescapable ambiguities are compounded by the inability of even the most foresighted legislative drafts-

---

[2] Perhaps Cardozo had the tax law in mind when he observed, in Cardozo, The Nature of the Judicial Process 143 (Yale Univ. Press 1921):

> No doubt the ideal system, if it were attainable, would be a code at once so flexible and so minute, as to supply in advance for every conceivable situation the just and fitting rule. But life is too complex to bring the attainment of this ideal within the compass of human powers.

[3] Hand, Thomas Walter Swan, 57 Yale LJ 167, 169 (1947).

[4] These are the cases developing the assignment of income doctrine. See infra Ch. 75.

[5] English is not the only language of human speech to be riddled with ambiguities. "When the Almighty himself condescends to address mankind in their own language, his meaning, luminous as it must be, is rendered dim and doubtful by the cloudy medium through which it is communicated." Federalist No. 37, at 270 (B. Wright, ed.; Belknap Press of Harvard U. 1961) (Alexander Hamilton).

men to anticipate all of the variations that their handwork will encounter in the disorder of real life.

As Mr. Justice Frankfurter observed: "The imagination which can draw an income tax statute to cover the myriad transactions of a society like ours, capable of producing the necessary revenue without producing a flood of litigation, has not yet revealed itself."[6] Moreover, draftsmen are often unable to clarify all of the issues they do foresee, for want of time or because the legislature wants to evade rather than confront the problem. But these characteristics of the legislative process are not unique to the Code; they can be illustrated as readily by the statute of frauds, the Uniform Commercial Code, the Taft-Hartley Act, or any other statute of sufficient importance to generate a sizable body of litigated cases.

Since all statutes are sisters under the skin, the courts employ the usual tools of statutory construction to interpret the Code.[7] If a term is defined by the Code itself, that definition, like the internal definitions of any other statute, is entitled to priority. The Code contains numerous definitions, some of which are applicable only when the defined term is used in specified provisions,[8] while others apply throughout the Code unless "manifestly incompatible with the intent" of the provision where the term is used.[9] But

---

[6] Frankfurter, Some Reflections on the Reading of Statutes, 47 Colum. L. Rev. 527, 528 (1947).

[7] For general discussions of these tools, see Nutting & Dickerson, Cases and Materials on Legislation, ch. 5 (West, 5th ed. 1978); Read, MacDonald, Fordham & Pierce, Materials on Legislation 750–1030 (Foundation Press, 3d ed. 1973); 2A Sands, Statutes and Statutory Construction (Callaghan, 4th ed. 1973); Sanders & Wade, Legal Writings on Statutory Construction, 3 Vand. L. Rev. 569 (1950). For the application of these and other tools in tax cases, see Westin, Dubious Interpretative Rules for Construing Federal Taxing Statutes, 17 Wake Forest L. Rev. 1 (1981); Yorio, Federal Income Tax Rulemaking: An Economic Approach, 51 Fordham L. Rev. 1 (1982) (applying economic analysis and criteria of economic efficiency to selected problems of income taxation). For the relationship between the 1939 and 1954 Codes and the revenue acts they codified, see Fulman v. US, 434 US 528 (1978) (failure to include unrepealed provision in codification does not imply abandonment); Royter's Inc. v. US, 265 F2d 615 (3d Cir. 1959) (Statutes at Large control).

See also the more specialized judicial doctrines applicable to tax matters that are discussed in ¶4.3.

[8] See, e.g., IRC §§316(a) (defining "dividend" as used in Subtitle A of Code); 317(a) (defining "property" as used in Part I, Subchapter C, Chapter 1, Subtitle A); 213(d)(1) (defining "medical care" for purposes of §213).

[9] IRC §7701(a) (defining 46 words and phrases). See IRC §7701(c) ("includes" and "including"), §7701(d) (references to U.S. possessions include Puerto Rico); §7806 (cross-references, table of contents, arrangement of sections, etc., have no legal effect); 1 USC §1 (singular includes plural, and vice versa; masculine includes feminine). See also Prudential Ins. Co. of Am. v. US, 319 F2d 161, 166 (Ct. Cl. 1963) (taxpayer cannot use section heading to limit plain meaning of statutory language);

the list of internally defined terms is short, so that it is frequently necessary to follow the procedure employed in construing other statutes by looking to common understanding,[10] dictionaries,[11] technical works,[12] or cases construing the same term when used in a comparable setting in another statute. Thus, the holding period specified by §1222(3) for long-term capital gains ("held for more than one year") is construed to exclude the day of acquisition but to include the day of disposition. This is in accordance with "the general current of the modern authorities on the interpretation of contracts, and also of statutes, where time is to be computed from a particular day or a particular event [which] is to exclude the day thus designated, and to include the last day of the specified period."[13] Similarly, general principles of statutory construction apply in settling such perennial disputes as whether the words "shall" and "may" are mandatory or permissive or are interchangeable and whether "and" and "or" are used in the disjunctive or conjunctive sense.[14]

Webb v. CIR, 67 TC 293, 305 n.11 (1976) ("headings used in a statute are aids in ascertaining its meaning"); Carter v. Liquid Carbonic Pac. Corp., 97 F2d 1 (9th Cir. 1938) (title of act used as guide where statutory language was unclear).

As to the effect of reenacting a statutory provision after a debatable judicial or administrative construction, see CIR v. Glenshaw Glass Co., 348 US 426, 431 (1955) (reenactment did not imply approval of earlier decisions; reenactment doctrine is "unreliable indicium at best"); Helvering v. Reynolds, 313 US 428, 432 (1941) (reenactment principle "is no more than an aid in statutory construction"); CIR v. Bilder, 289 F2d 291 (3d Cir. 1961) (prior construction deemed binding because of statute's reenactment), rev'd, 369 US 499 (1962) (concluding that a different construction was appropriate).

[10] See, e.g., Rosenspan v. US, 438 F2d 905 (2d Cir.), cert. denied, 404 US 864 (1971):

> When Congress uses such a non-technical word [away from "home"] in a tax statute, presumably it wants administrators and courts to read it in the way that ordinary people would understand, and not "to draw on some unexpressed spirit outside the bounds of the normal meaning of words."

[11] See Crane v. CIR, 331 US 1 (1947) (meaning of "property"); South Jersey Sand Co. v. CIR, 267 F2d 591 (3d Cir. 1959) ("sand"); Rev. Rul. 76-339, 1976-2 CB 251 ("disposition" and "disposed of").

[12] South Jersey Sand Co. v. CIR, supra note 11 ("sand" as defined by works on mining).

[13] Hooper v. CIR, 26 BTA 758 (1932), appeal dismissed, (2d Cir., 1933), adopting rule stated in Sheets v. Selden's Lessee, 69 US (2 Wall.) 177, 190 (1865). See also 13 ULA, Uniform Statutory Construction Act §8(a) (West 1975).

For the importance of local law in construing legal terms used throughout the Code, see supra ¶4.1.

[14] See Seeley v. Helvering, 77 F2d 323 (2d Cir. 1935) ("and" in regulations construed); Indian Rolling Mills Co. v. CIR, 13 BTA 1141, 1144 (1928) ("shall" construed); Reg. §1.368-2(h) ("if the context so requires [throughout the Code], the conjunction 'or' denotes both the conjunctive and the disjunctive").

In deciding federal tax cases, the courts also employ the same generalized maxims of statutory construction—usually couched in Latin—that are regularly encountered in other areas of the law, such as *noscitur a sociis* (words in a list are to be construed harmoniously, taking color from each other), *expressio unius est exclusio alterius* (an explicit reference to one thing impliedly excludes others), and *ejusdem generis* (phrases like "and so on," "etc.," and "others" refer to items similar in nature to those explicitly mentioned).

But just as many proverbs have an equally popular opposite (for example, "look before you leap," but "he who hesitates is lost"), so canons of statutory construction often come in conflicting pairs (for example, "plain and unambiguous language must be given effect," but "a literal interpretation should be rejected if it is inconsistent with the manifest purpose of the statute or would produce an absurd result.").[15] Since the judicial tool kit contains a wide choice of rival maxims, it is rarely clear whether one that is quoted in an opinion aided the judge in reaching his conclusion or is only a makeweight or decoration. But this uncertainty about the weight of Janus-faced canons of statutory construction is equally characteristic of tax and nontax cases.

¶4.2.2 Extrinsic Aids to Construction

The courts and commentators once vigorously debated the propriety of resorting to such "extrinsic" aids to statutory construction as legislative debates, committee hearings and reports, prior laws, and administrative interpretations. The practice is now so common that it is difficult to recapture the intensity of that ancient war of words. Its principal contemporary legacy is an occasional assertion that the statute must be "ambiguous" on its face before resort to extrinsic aids is permissible, and its corollary—that a "plain meaning" must be enforced, however much it may conflict with the legislative history, since the latter may be used only to resolve, and not to create, ambiguity. The opposite view is that judges should not "make a fortress out of the dictionary" by rejecting any source of enlightenment,[16] even if the statutory language is clear. This approach is sometimes caricatured by the maxim, "Look at the Code only if the committee reports are ambiguous"[17] —or, as students of Roman law used to say, *quid non agnoscit*

---

[15] Opposing pairs of canons of statutory construction are set out in Llewellyn, Remarks on the Theory of Appellate Decision and the Rules or Canons About How Statutes Are to Be Construed, 3 Vand. L. Rev. 395, 401–06 (1950).

[16] Judge Learned Hand, in Cabell v. Markham, 148 F2d 737, 739 (2d Cir.), aff'd, 326 US 404 (1945).

[17] See Focht v. CIR, 68 TC 223, 244 (1977), acq. (dissenting opinion) ("It has been said, with more than a grain of truth, that judges in tax cases these days tend to

glossa, id non agnoscit curia.[18]

Judicial readiness to go outside the four corners of the statute even when the language is unambiguous is sometimes thought to be a recent innovation, but it has ancient and honorable precedents. As long ago as *Heydon's Case* (1584), it was held that

> the office of all the Judges is always to make such . . . construction [of statutes] as shall suppress the mischief [which the statute was intended to remedy] and advance the remedy, and to suppress subtle inventions and evasions for continuance of the mischief . . . and to add force and life to the remedy, according to the true intent of the makers of the Act, *pro bono publico.*[19]

This early groping for something more than the literal meaning of a statute was superseded in England in the early nineteenth century by the more explicit "Golden Rule" of statutory construction:

> The rule by which we are to be guided in construing acts of Parliament is to look at the precise words, and to construe them in their ordinary sense, unless it would lead to any absurdity or manifest injustice; and if it should, so to vary and modify them as to avoid that which it certainly could not have been the intention of the legislature should be done.[20]

The current American rule, as enunciated by the Supreme Court in 1940, sanctions the use of extrinsic aids in an even broader spectrum of cases than was contemplated by the English Golden Rule:

> There is, of course, no more persuasive evidence of the purpose of a statute than the words by which the legislature undertook to give expression to its wishes. Often these words are sufficient in and of

---

consult the statute only when the legislative history is ambiguous.") See also Tilford v. CIR, 705 F2d 828, 832 (6th Cir. 1983) (dissenting opinion) (discussing "Committee commands" and objecting to deference shown them by majority; such commands "are of dubious legal authority"); Hart v. US, 585 F2d 1025 (Ct. Cl. 1978) (effect of congressional "staff system" on reliability of committee reports; "legislation by committee report" extensively discussed in majority and dissenting opinions).

[18] Roughly translated: "If it can't be found in the commentaries, judges won't believe it." See Babeaux v. CIR, 601 F2d 730, 732 (4th Cir. 1979) (Judge Dumbauld, dissenting, in his role as Yankee interloper on the Fourth Circuit, Latinist, and legal historian).

[19] Heydon's Case, 76 Eng. Rep. 637, 638 (Ex. 1584). See Thorne, The Equity of a Statute, 31 Ill. L. Rev. 202, 214–15 (1936).

[20] Perry v. Skinner, 150 Eng. Rep. 843, 845 (Ex. 1837). For other versions of the Golden Rule and its subsequent English history, see Hopkins, The Literal Canon and the Golden Rule, 15 Can. B. Rev. 689 (1937).

themselves to determine the purpose of the legislation. In such cases we have followed their plain meaning. When that meaning has led to absurd or futile results, however, this Court has looked beyond the words to the purpose of the act. Frequently, however, even when the plain meaning did not produce absurd results but merely an unreasonable one "plainly at variance with the policy of the legislation as a whole" this Court has followed that purpose, rather than the literal words.[21]

On concluding that the "plain meaning" of the statutory language warranted looking "beyond the words to the purpose of the act," the Court embarked on an extensive examination of the law's legislative history, including prior drafts of the bill as enacted, committee reports and hearings, legislative debate, and other pending legislation.

Given this approach to statutory language with a troublesome "plain meaning," the threshold decision for a court is whether to simply enforce the statutory language as written, leaving correction of its deficiencies to Congress, or to resort to extrinsic aids to interpretation and then to decide, with the aid of this outside light, whether the plain meaning or something less obvious was intended by Congress. Such an inquiry does not require courts to delude themselves or others into believing that the Congress had an intent comparable to the intent of individuals. Judge Learned Hand's comment on this point cannot be improved upon:

> The issue involves the baffling question which comes up so often in the interpretation of all kinds of writings: how far is it proper to read the words out of their literal meaning in order to realize their overriding purpose?. . . . When we ask what Congress "intended," usually there can be no answer, if what we mean is what any person or group of persons actually had in mind. Flinch as we may, what we do, and must do, is to project ourselves, as best we can, into the position of those who uttered the words, and to impute to them how they would have dealt with the concrete occasion. He who supposes that he can be certain of the result is the least fitted for the attempt.[22]

---

[21] US v. American Trucking Ass'n, 310 US 534, 543 (1940).

[22] US v. Klinger, 199 F2d 645, 648 (2d Cir. 1952), aff'd per curiam, 345 US 979 (1953). See also Bishin & Stone, Law, Language, and Ethics 473–528 (Foundation Press 1972); Cox, Judge Learned Hand and the Interpretation of Statutes 370, 372–73 (1947); Hart & Wechsler, The Federal Courts and the Federal System (Foundation Press, 2d ed. 1973) ("statutory interpretation shades into judicial lawmaking on a spectrum, as specific evidence of legislative advertence to the issue at hand attenuates"); Frankfurter, supra note 6; Nutting, Ambiguity of Unambiguous Statutes, 24 Minn. L. Rev. 509 (1942).

Courts seldom if ever refuse to consider extrinsic aids, no matter how plain the statutory language. It is easy enough to adhere to the statute's plain meaning if the legislative history is ambiguous; conversely, if the extrinsic evidence is persuasive, a court may conclude that the meaning of the statutory language is less clear than it initially appeared to be.[23] In the latter case, it is common to quote Mr. Justice Holmes: "A word is not a crystal, transparent and unchanged, it is the skin of a living thought and may vary greatly in color and content according to the circumstances and the time in which it is used."[24] This excursion into semantic theory encourages the view that statutes never have a "plain meaning," as does Judge Learned Hand's famous observation in *Helvering v. Gregory*:

> [T]he meaning of a sentence may be more than that of the separate words, as a melody is more than the notes, and no degree of particularity [of the statutory language] can ever obviate recourse to the setting in which all appear, and which all collectively create.[25]

Knowing that a statute's "plain meaning," as originally perceived, may be altered by a blinding flash of extrinsic light, tax lawyers routinely refer to committee reports and similar sources in arguments before the IRS and the courts.

Once a court decides to look beyond the four corners of the statute, there are no formal restrictions on the material that may be taken into account in interpreting the statutory language. Just as a trial judge, when sitting without a jury, will often let in almost any evidence "for what it is worth" even if it is incompetent or immaterial under the normal rules of evidence, so the basic test for a proffered extrinsic aid to statutory construction is whether it can reasonably be thought to shed light on the issue to be decided. Thus, courts in federal tax cases look not only to such formal sources of legislative history as committee reports and legislative debates but also to less formal sources such as hearings, memoranda by trade groups, and commentators.[26] Prior judicial decisions and administrative

---

[23] See generally Jones, The Plain Meaning Rule and Extrinsic Aids in the Interpretation of Federal Statutes, 25 Wash. ULQ 2 (1939); Lyman, The Absurdity and Repugnancy of the Plain Meaning Rule of Interpretation, 3 Manitoba LJ (Pt. 2) 53 (1969); Nutting, supra note 22.

[24] Towne v. Eisner, 245 US 418, 425 (1918).

[25] Helvering v. Gregory, 69 F2d 809, 810–11 (2d Cir. 1934), aff'd, 293 US 465 (1935). See also Paul, Motive and Intent in Federal Tax Law, in Paul, Selected Studies in Federal Taxation 272 (Callaghan, 2d ser. 1938) ("a short training in tax law will convince the most stubborn of intellects that there is no such thing as words so plain that they do not have to be interpreted").

[26] Section 15 of the Uniform Statutory Construction Act, supra note 13, is conservative in sanctioning extrinsic aids only if the statute is "ambiguous." It is inapplicable to federal statutes, but nevertheless contains a useful compilation of

interpretations and regulations are also frequently examined because, whether endorsed, qualified, or rejected by legislation, they can illuminate its purpose.[27] The weight of any particular bit of evidence is, of course, a different matter from its relevance.

¶4.3 PERVASIVE JUDICIAL DOCTRINES

¶4.3.1 Introductory

During the nineteenth century, the practice of construing taxing statutes strictly against the government was said to be "founded so firmly upon principles of equity and natural justice as not to admit reasonable doubt."[1] As explained by Mr. Justice Story in 1842:

> In every case . . . of doubt, [taxing] statutes are construed most strongly against the government, and in favor of the subjects or citizens, because burdens are not to be imposed, nor presumed to be imposed, beyond what the statutes expressly and clearly import. Revenue statutes are in no just sense either remedial laws or laws founded upon any permanent public policy, and therefore are not to be liberally

---

sources that may be considered in determining legislative intent: the (1) object sought to be attained; (2) circumstances under which the statute was enacted; (3) legislative history; (4) common law or former statutory provisions, including laws upon the same or similar subjects; (5) consequences of a particular construction; (6) administrative construction of the statute; and (7) preamble.

See Flora v. US, 357 US 63 (1958), aff'd on rehearing, 362 US 145 (1960) (committee reports, hearings, floor debate, and contemporaneous views of Treasury officials and commentators); Claridge Apartments Co. v. CIR, 323 US 141 (1944) (letter written by bill's sponsor after enactment of the law); Helvering v. Griffiths, 318 US 371 (1943) (wide range of legislative materials); Keeler v. CIR, 70 TC 279 (1978) (prior committee report described as erroneous in later report). But see Mars, Inc. v. CIR, 88 TC 428 (1987) (declining to follow statement in committee reports on later statute stating that Tax Court construction of earlier statute was "incorrect"; "the views of one Congress as to the construction of a statute adopted many years before by another Congress have very little, if any, significance"); Graff v. CIR, 74 TC 743 (1980) (statement by member of Congress on floor not conclusive); Aparacor, Inc. v. US, 571 F2d 552 (Ct. Cl. 1978) (limited weight attached to comments by legislators after enactment of legislation). See also Newman & Surrey, Legislation: Cases and Materials 648–53 (Prentice-Hall 1955) (extensive list of sources of legislative history); Sands, supra note 7, ch. 48.

[27] See, e.g., S. Rep. No. 1622, 83d Cong., 2d Sess. 52 (1954) (§381 enacted to replace "uncertain and frequently contradictory" court decisions); id. at 48 ("the principle of *Kimbell-Diamond Milling Co.* . . . was effectuated" by §334(b)(2)); id. at 86 (§§671–678 "generally adopt the approach of the [Clifford] regulations").

[1] Cahoon v. Coe, 57 NH 556, 570 (1876).

construed.[2]

This approach, which bracketed taxing statutes with laws imposing criminal penalties or forfeitures, was not without challenge even in its heyday[3] and by now has been largely abandoned.[4]

Contemporary courts apply tax laws with greater tolerance—some would say enthusiasm. If strict construction is still a watchword, it is more likely to be used against the taxpayer in cases deciding the scope of statutory exceptions, deductions, and similar allowances.[5]

---

[2] US v. Wigglesworth, 28 F. Cas. 595, 597 (CCD Mass. 1842).

[3] For an extended nineteenth-century discussion of this subject, see Cooley, A Treatise on the Law of Taxation 265–75 (Callaghan, 2d ed. 1886), who favored a middle road:

> Construction is not to assume either that the taxpayer, who raises the legal question of his liability under the laws, is necessarily seeking to avoid a duty to the state which protects him, nor, on the other hand, that the government, in demanding its dues, is a tyrant, which, while too powerful to be resisted, may justifiably be obstructed and defeated by any subtle device or ingenious sophism whatsoever. . . . All construction . . . which assumes either the one or the other, is likely to be mischievous, and to take one-sided views, not only of the laws, but of personal and official conduct.

The trend away from strict construction has been strengthened by frequent inclusion in state laws of a directive to interpret the law with a view to accomplishing its objectives. 2A Sands, Statutes and Statutory Construction §58.03 n.14 (Callaghan, 4th ed. 1973).

[4] But see Ivan Allen Co. v. US, 422 US 617, 627 (1975) (penalty taxes to be strictly construed against government); Fullman, Inc. v. US, 434 US 528, 533 n.8 (1978) (strict construction principle not applicable to penalties that can be easily avoided by following statutory guidelines).

[5] See, e.g., Corn Prods. Ref. Co. v. CIR, 350 US 46 (1955) (strict construction of term "capital assets" in order to limit "preferential treatment" for capital gains); Interstate Transit Lines v. CIR, 319 US 590, 593 (1943) (income tax deductions are a "matter of legislative grace and . . . the burden of clearly showing the right to the claimed deduction is on the taxpayer"); Stiles v. CIR, 69 TC 558, 563 (1978) (as exceptions to the general rule, relief provisions are to be strictly construed).

Despite the popularity of the theory that many tax allowances are the equivalent of subsidies and constitute a program of "welfare for the rich"—see Bittker, Income Tax "Loopholes" and Political Rhetoric, 71 Mich. L. Rev. 1099, 1100 (1973)—it has evidently not been suggested that these provisions should be liberally construed in favor of the taxpayer, in the spirit of Cox v. Roth, 348 US 207 (1955) (welfare legislation is to be liberally construed in favor of its intended beneficiaries).

In litigated cases, the taxpayer has the burden of proof on factual issues, as explained infra ¶115.4; the discussion in the text is concerned with the resolution of legal questions.

It is far from clear, however, why the Code should be construed strictly against either the taxpayer or the government.[6] A more salutary attitude was advocated by Mr. Justice Holmes, responding to the once-popular adage that statutes in derogation of the common law should be strictly construed:

> The Legislature has the power to decide what the policy of the law shall be, and if it has intimated its will, however indirectly, that will should be recognized and obeyed. The major premise of the conclusion expressed in a statute, the change of policy that induces the enactment, may not be set out in terms, but it is not an adequate discharge of duty for courts to say: We see what you are driving at, but you have not said it, and therefore we shall go on as before.[7]

In applying the Code to particular transactions, the courts frequently distinguish between "tax avoidance" and "tax evasion" and between "form" and "substance," assert that transactions are to be taken at face value for tax purposes only if they are imbued with a "business purpose or reflect economic reality," and integrate all steps in a prearranged plan rather than give effect to each step as though it were an isolated transaction. These presuppositions or criteria are so pervasive that they resemble a preamble to the Code, describing the framework within which all statutory provisions are to function. But these judicial presuppositions, like the canons of statutory construction, are more successful in establishing attitudes and moods than in supplying crisp answers to specific questions.[8]

They are, however, extremely important despite their vagueness. Indeed, in some areas they are influential primarily because they are vague; when the meaning of a provision is veiled by fog, taxpayers usually tread

---

[6] See generally Griswold, An Argument Against the Doctrine That Deductions Should Be Narrowly Construed as a Matter of Legislative Grace, 56 Harv. L. Rev. 1142 (1943).

[7] Johnson v. US, 163 F 30, 32 (1st Cir. 1908) (Mr. Justice Holmes on circuit). For a similar comment by Mr. Justice Stone in a tax case, see White v. US, 305 US 281, 292 (1938) (duty of courts, in tax cases as in other litigation, is to decide "what [the] construction fairly should be"), quoted with approval by Griswold, supra note 6, at 1144–45; see also Cooley's earlier support for evenhandedness, supra note 3.

[8] Thus, Paul's monumental effort to provide a "restatement" of the law of tax avoidance contains few generalizations and demonstrates that the subject is "exquisitely uncertain," as Judge Jerome Frank points out in his introduction to Paul, Restatement of the Law of Tax Avoidance, in Paul, Studies in Federal Taxation. (Callaghan 1937); See generally Rice, Judicial Techniques in Combating Tax Avoidance, 51 Mich. L. Rev. 1021 (1953).

See also the Australian and Canadian statutory catchall prohibitions on tax-avoidance transactions, described by Blum, Motive, Intent, and Purpose in Federal Income Taxation, 34 U. Chi. L. Rev. 485, 524–25 n.107 (1967).

more warily than when the landmarks are clearly visible. As Mr. Justice Brandeis observed in a similar context:

> If you are walking along a precipice no human being can tell you how near you can go to that precipice without falling over, because you may stumble on a loose stone, you may slip, and go over; but anybody can tell you where you can walk perfectly safely within convenient distance of that precipice.[9]

Mr. Justice Holmes did not object to the in terrorem effect of uncertainty even in criminal law:

> Whenever the law draws a line there will be cases very near each other on opposite sides. The precise course of the line may be uncertain, but no one can come near it without knowing that he does so . . . and if he does so it is familiar to the criminal law to make him take the risk.[10]

Laymen are typically more inclined than the expert to trust paper work as a shield against tax liability. Tax lawyers are bombarded at cocktail parties with tax schemes that would not convince the most inexperienced revenue agent or that teeter on the brink of fraud. Randolph Paul's comments on this subject cannot be improved:

> Above all things, a tax attorney must be an indefatigable skeptic; he must discount everything he hears and reads. The market-place abounds with unsound avoidance schemes which will not stand the test of objective analysis and litigation. The escaped tax, a favorite topic of conversation at the best clubs and the most sumptuous pleasure resorts, expands with repetition into fantastic legends. But clients want opinions with happy endings, and he smiles best who smiles last. It is wiser to state misgivings at the beginning than to have to acknowledge them ungracefully at the end. The tax adviser has, therefore, to spend a large part of his time advising against schemes of this character. I sometimes think that the most important word in his vocabulary is "No. . . . "[11]

---

[9] Quoted in Mason, Brandeis: A Free Man's Life 352 (Viking Press 1946).

[10] US v. Wurzbach, 280 US 396, 399 (1930). Although judicial tolerance toward vagueness in criminal statutes has dwindled (US v. Harriss, 347 US 612 (1954)), the in terrorem effect of vagueness on would-be tax dodgers is usually approved by the commentators. See Blum, A Pronouncement on Tax Avoidance, 1961 Sup. Ct. Rev. 135, 158.

[11] Paul, The Lawyer as a Tax Adviser, 25 Rocky Mtn. L. Rev. 412, 416 (1953); infra ¶110.2.4.

¶4.3.2 Tax Avoidance vs. Tax Evasion

Although the terms are occasionally used interchangeably,[12] "tax avoidance" and "tax evasion" are usually differentiated—the former phrase denoting noncriminal modes of minimizing or avoiding tax liability; the latter, fraudulent behavior. The line between noncriminal conduct (which may or may not achieve its tax reduction objective) and fraudulent misconduct is discussed elsewhere in this work.[13] For present purposes, the term "tax evasion" is reserved for conduct that entails deception, concealment, destruction of records, and the like, while "tax avoidance" refers to behavior that the taxpayer hopes will serve to reduce his tax liability but that he is prepared to disclose fully to the IRS.[14]

Used in this sense, tax avoidance embraces a virtually unlimited spectrum of personal, financial, and business transactions. Taxpayers often organize corporations, establish trusts, make gifts, sell property, and borrow money—to mention only a few obvious areas—in ways or at times selected to reduce tax liabilities. In many cases, tax savings are so clearly allowed by statute that even the most severe moralist would direct any criticism at Congress rather than the taxpayer. When the Code requires the taxpayer to pick one of several options (for example, cash or accrual accounting, straight-line or accelerated depreciation), it would be quixotic to gladden the heart of the Commissioner of Internal Revenue by electing the most costly. Citizens who want to make a voluntary contribution to the Treasury can do so by sending in their checks at any time; there is no reason to use the tax return as a vehicle for such generosity. Similarly, it is hard to fault a taxpayer who engages in a transaction with significant nontax results (for example, operating a business as a proprietorship rather than in corporate form, or selling property rather than continuing to hold it), even though his decision is motivated more by the tax savings to be achieved than by the transaction's other consequences. Even Mr. Justice Holmes, who allegedly said that "I like to pay taxes; with them I buy civilization," did not give his money to the Treasury until his death.[15]

The Code bristles with elections, options, and statutory incentives. Congress expects, and often hopes, that they will be used. It may, indeed, be

---

[12] See Paul, supra note 8, at 9, 12. Justice Holmes' observation in Bullen v. Wisconsin, quoted infra note 16; IRC §482, which uses the term "evasion" but is applicable to a broad spectrum of transactions having no fraudulent overtones (infra ¶79.1).

[13] Infra ¶114.4.

[14] See, however, recent prosecutions of tax protesters for willful violations of law that entail no concealment, discussed infra ¶114.4.

[15] The original location of this widely quoted comment eludes us. In Compania General de Tabacos de Filipinas v. Collector, 275 US 87, 100 (1927), Holmes, dissenting, said, "taxes are what we pay for civilized society."

confusing to apply the tax-avoidance label to behavior so clearly sanctioned by Congress as the use of these statutory opportunities. In common parlance, that term often conjures up a transaction whose success depends on a debatable interpretation of an ambiguous statutory provision or on an inadvertent loophole in the law that will probably be closed if and when it comes to public attention. Used in this sense, "tax avoidance" implies risk, and this in turn raises the question: If the taxpayer is trying to take advantage of an ambiguous provision, should it be construed against him in order to discourage tax avoidance, at least if that was his sole or principal motive?

It is clear that the courts do not regard themselves as invested with a roving commission to extirpate tax avoidance. There are three classic statements justifying judicial disregard of the taxpayer's motive if, though close to the dividing line, he stays on the nontaxable side. One is a 1930 observation by Mr. Justice Holmes: "The fact that [the taxpayer] desired to evade the law, as it is called, is immaterial, because the very meaning of a line in the law is that you may intentionally go as close to it as you can if you do not pass it."[16] The second statement is by Judge Learned Hand:

> [A] transaction, otherwise within an exception of the tax law, does not lose its immunity, because it is actuated by a desire to avoid, or, if one choose, to evade, taxation. Any one may so arrange his affairs that his taxes shall be as low as possible; he is not bound to choose that pattern which will best pay the Treasury; there is not even a patriotic duty to increase one's taxes.[17]

The third, described as "the most eloquent short defense ever to appear of the state of being tax-conscious and, by implication, of the art of tax plan-

---

[16] Superior Oil Co. v. Mississippi, 280 US 390, 395–96 (1930). See also Mr. Justice Holmes' earlier statement to the same effect in Bullen v. Wisconsin, 240 US 625, 630–31 (1916):

> We do not speak of evasion, because, when the law draws a line, a case is on one side of it or the other, and if on the safe side is none the worse legally that a party has availed himself to the full of what the law permits. When an act is condemned as an evasion what is meant is that it is on the wrong side of the line indicated by the policy if not by the mere letter of the law.

The term "evade" is here used by Mr. Justice Holmes to denote an unsuccessful attempt to avoid taxation, not as synonymous with fraud. See supra note 12.

[17] Helvering v. Gregory, 69 F2d 809, 810 (2d Cir. 1934), aff'd sub nom. Gregory v. Helvering, 293 US 465 (1935), discussed at greater length in ¶¶4.3.4 and 94.5.1. Judge Hand's assurance that there is no "patriotic duty to increase one's taxes" was curiously echoed by the claim made by some taxpayers during the Vietnam War that paying their taxes would make them war criminals under the principles applied at the Nuremberg Trial. See supra ¶1.2.5, note 56.

ning,"[18] is also by Judge Learned Hand:

> Over and over again courts have said that there is nothing sinister in so arranging one's affairs as to keep taxes as low as possible. Everybody does so, rich or poor; and all do right, for nobody owes any public duty to pay more than the law demands: taxes are enforced exactions, not voluntary contributions. To demand more in the name of morals is mere cant.[19]

The statement that tax avoidance is practiced by rich and poor alike is exaggeration since wage earners have few opportunities to "arrange [their] affairs" so as to reduce their taxes; and it is not clear why Judge Hand felt impelled to commend persons engaged in tax avoidance for "do[ing] right," rather than merely to uphold their privilege to do so. These reservations aside, his central message—"the doctrine that a man's motive to avoid taxation will not establish his liability if the transaction does not do so without it"[20] —is widely accepted.

Judicial reluctance to decide tax cases on the basis of the taxpayer's state of mind is understandable. Tax planning is as American as apple pie. If doubts were routinely resolved against persons harboring a motive, purpose, or intent[21] to reduce tax liability, scrupulous taxpayers would pay a heavy price for candor in responding to the IRS' questions about their state of mind. At the same time, disingenuous taxpayers and persuasive liars would go scot-free, unless revenue agents, judges, and juries came to reject their disavowals of a tax-avoidance intent as too bizarre to be believed. In that event, however, taxpayers who were in fact too ignorant, naive, or openhanded to inquire into the tax effect of their transactions would be penalized along with the others. An intermediate approach, under which a tainted purpose would not automatically count against the taxpayer but would be fatal if it met a specified standard (e.g., "principal," "major factor," "proximate cause"), would be at least as difficult to apply in practice as a blanket rule, and would probably be as erratic in its results as the now-buried estate tax concept of "transfers in contemplation of death."[22]

---

[18] Chirelstein, Learned Hand's Contribution to the Law of Tax Avoidance, 77 Yale LJ 440, 456 (1968).

[19] CIR v. Newman, 159 F2d 848, 850–51 (2d Cir.) (dissenting opinion), cert. denied, 331 US 859 (1947).

[20] Chisholm v. CIR, 79 F2d 14, 15 (2d Cir. 1935), cert. denied, 296 US 641 (1936).

[21] For distinctions among these terms, see Blum, supra note 8, at 485; Paul, Motive and Intent in Federal Tax Law, in Paul, Selected Studies in Federal Taxation 255, 271–304 (Callaghan, 2d ser. 1938).

[22] See infra ¶126.4.4.

It would be a mistake, however, to conclude that the flavor of a stew is never impaired by a lavish infusion of tax avoidance motive. After asserting that the taxpayer's purpose was a neutral circumstance, both Holmes and Hand in the first two opinions quoted above went on to resolve the tax question in favor of the government, and it is hard to escape the conclusion that the aroma of tax avoidance contributed to the outcome.[23] Even if the taxpayer's purpose was wholly irrelevant in these cases, however, there are other circumstances in which it cannot be disregarded.

First, the Code contains many statutory provisions that explicitly make tax avoidance an operative factor in determining tax liability. Thus, §532 imposes a special tax on "every corporation . . . formed or availed of for the purpose of avoiding the income tax with respect to its shareholders"; §357(b)(1), involving assumptions of debt in certain transfers to controlled corporations, requires a determination of whether "the principal purpose of the taxpayer . . . was a purpose to avoid Federal income tax"; and §306(b)(4) exempts certain stock sales and redemptions from unfavorable tax treatment "if it is established to the satisfaction of the [IRS that the transactions were] not in pursuance of a plan having as one of its principal purposes the avoidance of Federal income tax."[24] Difficulties in administering statutory distinctions between transactions that are, and those that are not, dominated by tax-avoidance objectives have more than once led Congress to impose a disability on all transactions in a suspect category, whether guilty or not.[25]

Second, in deciding whether to accept at face value the form in which a transaction was cast by the taxpayer or to probe for its substance or net

---

[23] In Superior Oil Co. v. Mississippi, supra note 16, at 394, the Court said that a crucial document (relied on by the taxpayer to establish that a transaction was in interstate commerce and immune to a state sales tax) "seems to have had no other use than . . . to try to convert a domestic transaction into one of interstate commerce;" in Helvering v. Gregory, supra note 17, the taxpayer created a transitory corporation that was promptly, and pursuant to plan, liquidated. On the significance of tax avoidance in *Gregory*, see Chirelstein, supra note 18, at 464, concluding that Judge Hand favored "an interpretative rule of general application . . . that ambiguous transactions were to be characterized in the Commissioner's favor, unless the taxpayer could dispel the ambiguity by showing that the form which he had chosen carried with it, or was expected to carry with it, some appreciable economic effect beyond tax savings."

[24] See infra ¶95.1 (accumulated earnings tax), ¶91.4.3 (assumption of liabilities), ¶95.3.4 (Section 306 stock). For other instances and general discussion, see Blum, How the Courts, Congress and the IRS Try to Limit Legal Tax Avoidance, 10 J. Tax'n 300 (1959); Cohen, Tax Avoidance Purpose as a Statutory Text in Tax Legislation, 9 Tul. Tax Inst. 229 (1960); Fischer, Intent and Taxes, 32 Taxes 303 (1954).

[25] E.g., IRC §267(a)(1) (infra ¶78.1.1) (deduction denied for losses on sales between related taxpayers, whether at fair market prices or not), §166(d)(1) (infra ¶33.6) (nonbusiness bad debts are capital rather than ordinary losses).

effect, revenue agents and courts sometimes respond to the aroma of tax avoidance like hounds to the scent of foxes. They are likely to suspect that the form adopted by the taxpayer is a self-serving declaration—"motive is a persuasive interpreter of equivocal conduct"[26] —if tax considerations seem to be more influential than nontax results in shaping a transaction. Used as a divining rod, however, a tax-avoidance purpose serves only the preliminary purpose of advising the IRS and courts where to dig; it does not help in deciding whether what is actually found belongs on the taxable or the nontaxable side of the statutory line. In the words of Randolph Paul:

> In deciding a fact issue the courts will analyze and scrutinize with special zeal where tax avoidance appears as a motive. But that motive will be immaterial except as an eye-opening mechanism or interpreter of equivocal conduct; it will not negative the effect of a transaction which has really occurred.[27]

The Court of Appeals for the Eighth Circuit, however, has gone a bit further:

> When a taxpayer . . . boldly proclaims that his intent, at least in part, in attempting to create a trust is to evade taxes, the courts should examine the forms used by him for the accomplishment of his purpose with particular care; and, if his ingenuity fails at any point, the court should not lend him its aid by resolving doubts in his favor.[28]

Beyond those cases where a tax-avoidance intent is "boldly proclaimed," such a purpose may be inferred as frequently from the nature of the transaction. Whatever his state of mind, if he travels into a territory that is much frequented by tax-conscious citizens, revenue agents and courts are likely to subject his papers to searching scrutiny.

Finally, when construing ambiguous statutory language, the courts often reject interpretations that would sanctify legal formalities and thereby foster tax avoidance. Since a statutory construction affects all taxpayers, however, the state of mind of the litigant who happens to come before the court is less important in such cases than the objectives of taxpayers as a group. If a court concludes that taxpayers are likely to engage in a particular transaction primarily to reduce taxes rather than to achieve nontax business or personal objectives, the statutes affecting the transaction are often construed strictly in favor of the government, and this meaning is visited upon all taxpayers, even those wholly devoid of tax-avoidance purpose. The following comments in *Helvering v. Clifford*, taxing to the husband-grantor the

---

[26] Texas & N.O.R.R. v. Brotherhood of Ry. Clerks, 281 US 548, 559 (1930).
[27] Paul, supra note 8, at 152.
[28] Morsman v. CIR, 90 F2d 18, 22 (8th Cir.), cert. denied, 302 US 701 (1937).

income of a short-term trust established for the benefit of his wife, for example, refer to the state of mind of the "average" taxpayer and would probably not yield to proof that the litigant's outlook on life was different:

> We have at best a temporary reallocation of income within an intimate family group. Since the income remains in the family and since the husband retains control over the investment, he has rather complete assurance that the trust will not effect any substantial change in his economic position. It is hard to imagine that respondent felt himself the poorer after this trust had been executed or, if he did, that it had any rational foundation in fact.[29]

¶4.3.3 Form vs. Substance

In 1921, when today's federal income tax was still in its swaddling clothes, the Supreme Court recognized "the importance of regarding matters of substance and disregarding forms in applying the . . . income tax laws. . . . "[30] More recently, the substance-over-form principle has been called "the cornerstone of sound taxation."[31]

There are times, however, when form alone determines the tax consequences of a transaction. The numerous accounting elections, for example, drastically affect tax liabilities without altering taxpayers' relations with the outside world;[32] a taxpayer's right to report income on the cash rather than the accrual method, to elect accelerated rather than straight-line depreciation, and to use a fiscal or calendar year is not in any way impaired by the fact that these are matters of form rather than substance. Similarly, a taxpayer with several blocks of stock of the same company, purchased over a period of time at different prices, can sell either high-cost or low-cost shares merely by delivering one certificate rather than another or even, when a particular lot of shares cannot be traced to a separate certificate, by designating which shares he intends to sell.[33] Whichever form is employed to separate the shares sold from those retained, it has no nontax ramifications.

There are also a few statutory provisions that, the courts have held, deliberately elevate form above substance. An example is §71(c), which provides that a payment under a decree of divorce or separate maintenance is not taxable to the recipient if the decree fixes the amount "as a sum which

---

[29] Helvering v. Clifford, 309 US 331, 335–36 (1940), discussed infra ¶80.1.1.

[30] US v. Phellis, 257 US 156, 168 (1921).

[31] Weinert's Est. v. CIR, 294 F2d 750, 755 (5th Cir. 1961).

[32] Provisions like §472(c), which permits LIFO accounting for inventories to be used for tax purposes only if the same method is used in reporting to investors and lenders, are exceptions to this general principle. See infra ¶105.4.3 for §472(c).

[33] Infra ¶¶41.8.2, 41.8.3.

is payable for the support of minor children of the husband," a condition that usually requires "specific earmarking" and cannot be satisfied by evidence that in substance, though not in form, the payment was made for the support of the children.[34] Randolph Paul once said that "lawyers who do not know that form sometimes controls, should not be practicing law."[35]

Despite these examples of the occasional preeminence of form, the courts are ordinarily willing if not eager to take account of the substance behind the veil of form.[36] The appeal from form to substance is frequently deplored as more confusing than helpful, and the words themselves have been castigated by Judge Learned Hand as "vague . . . anodynes for the pains of reasoning."[37] A mature jurisprudence, however, could not consistently adhere to all formalities. To reach no further back than the Europe of the Middle Ages and Renaissance, for example, the Catholic Church's prohibition of usury set into motion a never ceasing inquiry into the form of transactions designed to evade the restriction, including sales of property with an option in the seller to repurchase for a higher price at a later date — a device that is still sometimes used in the hope of avoiding the tax results of a mortgage.[38]

Unfortunately, it is almost impossible to distill useful generalizations from the welter of substance-over-form cases. First, the facts of particular cases are usually complicated, and it is rarely clear which facts are crucial to the decision and which are irrelevant. This uncertainty about the precedential value of decisions is often compounded by the failure of courts to say whether their conclusions rest on findings of fact that might have gone the other way if a witness had been more credible or additional evidence had been offered on a particular point.

In *Knetsch v. United States*, for example, the Supreme Court held that a transaction (the purchase of 10, 30-year deferred annuity savings bonds, financed by a down payment and funds borrowed from the issuer against their cash surrender value) was "a sham," devoid of appreciable economic

---

[34] CIR v. Lester, 366 US 299 (1960), discussed infra ¶77.2.5. See also IRC §152(e)(2) (agreement between divorced parents regarding the dependency exemption for their children, discussed infra ¶30.3.5); Foxman v. CIR, 41 TC 535, 551 (1964) (partnership provisions permitting "partners themselves to determine their tax burdens inter sese to a certain extent").

[35] Paul, supra note 8, at 89, n.304. See also Blum, The Importance of Form in the Taxation of Corporate Transactions, 54 Taxes 613 (1976); Kingson, The Deep Structure of Taxation: Dividend Distributions, 85 Yale LJ 861, 863–66 (1976).

[36] Tax cases are not unique in searching for substance; a common analogue is the piercing of the corporate veil in private lawsuits. See Ballantine, Ballantine on Corporations §122 (Callaghan, rev. ed. 1946); Paul, supra note 12, at 66–73.

[37] CIR v. Sansome, 60 F2d 931, 933 (2d Cir.), cert. denied, 287 US 667 (1932).

[38] Noonan, The Scholastic Analysis of Usury 95–98 (Harvard U. Press 1957). For current parallels, see infra ¶¶31.1.4, 40.6.

results, because "there was nothing of substance to be realized by [the taxpayer] beyond a tax deduction."[39] The factual basis for this conclusion was that the taxpayer was paying interest to the issuer of the bonds at the rate of 3.5 percent on its financing loan to him, while the investment was growing in value by only 2.5 percent annually; the net annual cash loss of 1 percent of the borrowed funds was incurred only to achieve a tax deduction for the interest paid, and the transaction held out no promise of economic profit. Although the taxpayer had the right to refinance the loan if funds became available from other lenders at a lower rate, he either offered no evidence on the prospect of such a reduction in interest rates or failed to convince the trial judge that refinancing was a viable option, and the Supreme Court implicitly assumed that it was not.

A drastic, albeit unlikely, decline in interest rates could have converted the investment into a profitable venture, and another taxpayer, with faith in such a change, might have believed that an economic profit could be made from the very transaction that the Court characterized as a "sham." The Court incorporated the trial judge's findings of fact, thereby implying a limited scope for the decision, but other parts of the opinion suggest that any taxpayer purchasing a similar contract would be denied a deduction, regardless of his economic expectations, at least if he embarked on the investment when money market conditions were similar to those prevailing during 1953 and 1954, the years before the Court.

Another barrier to generalizing from the decided cases is uncertainty whether the courts, in particular cases, are interpreting the statutory provision on which the taxpayer relies or enunciating a principle to be applied throughout the Code. In his famous opinion in the *Gregory* case, for example, Judge Learned Hand said of certain transactions: "[T]heir only defect was that they were not what [the statutory predecessor of §368(a)(1)] means by a 'reorganization', because the transactions were no part of the conduct of the business of either or both companies; so viewed they were a sham."[40] Despite this reference to the meaning of a particular statutory provision, Judge Hand's language is regularly quoted as having much broader significance.[41] A related source of difficulty is the common judicial practice of citing the substance-over-form doctrine in combination with other broad

---

[39] Knetsch v. US, 364 US 361, 366 (1960). See Blum, *Knetsch v. US*: A Pronouncement on Tax Avoidance, 40 Taxes 296 (1962).

[40] Helvering v. Gregory, 69 F2d 810, 811 (2d Cir. 1934), aff'd sub nom. Gregory v. Helvering, 293 US 465 (1935). For more extensive discussion, see infra ¶94.5.1.

[41] See also Blum's comment (supra note 39, at 305) that the Supreme Court in *Knetsch* "was either saying a great deal about many and various tax-avoidance schemes not before the Court, or it was omitting to indicate why the interest deduction should be interpreted as [limited to transactions that appreciably affect the taxpayer's beneficial interests]."

concepts (most commonly, the business purpose and step transaction doctrines and the requirement of an accurate accounting method), thus obscuring the independent force of each of these grounds of decision.

Moreover, in practice, form usually has some substantive consequences, so that if two transactions differ in form, they probably are not identical in substance. This inconvenient fact of life may require distinguishing between "superficial formalities" and substantial formalities.[42]

Finally, for the reasons just canvassed, when a case holding that the form chosen by a particular taxpayer does not accurately reflect the substance of his transaction is compared with a decision supporting another taxpayer's version of a similar transaction, it is difficult, if not impossible, to ascertain whether the decisions are in conflict. Occasionally the Supreme Court grants certiorari because of a conflict among the circuit courts in cases of this type, but if each case rests on the "genuineness" of the particular taxpayer's transaction, the nature of the conflict is unclear. In *Knetsch*, for example, the conflict was with a case in which the trial judge did not find the transaction to be a sham.[43]

The substance-over-form doctrine is invoked by the government with greatest success with respect to transactions between related persons, since in these circumstances the form used often has minimal, if any, nontax consequences and is often chosen solely to reduce taxes. For example, a purported installment sale of property by parents to their children may, on analysis, be akin to a gift of the property because the alleged debt is more likely to be forgiven (or paid off with funds received as gifts from the parents) than to be enforced. Recognizing that "sales" within the family may not be what they purport to be and that evidence of their true nature is peculiarly within the control of the taxpayer, Congress has laid down several statutory rules that treat intrafamily sales differently from sales to third parties. An example is §267(a)(1), forbidding taxpayers to deduct losses on such sales, even if effected at the property's fair market value.[44]

Even if a transaction is not explicitly condemned by statute, its form may be disregarded by the courts in appropriate circumstances. For example, a sale and leaseback of real estate may be denied sales status,[45] and the

---

[42] Blueberry Land Co. v. CIR, 361 F2d 93, 101 (5th Cir. 1966) ("courts will . . . look beyond the superficial formalities").

[43] US v. Bond, 258 F2d 577 (5th Cir. 1958); see Blum, supra note 39, at 300–01.

[44] Section 267(a)(1) is discussed in ¶78.1. See also IRC §704(e)(3) (sale of partnership interest within family treated as gift; discussed infra ¶85.2), §166(d) (nonbusiness bad debt deductible only as capital loss, not as ordinary loss; discussed infra ¶33.6).

[45] Century Elec. Co. v. CIR, 192 F2d 155 (8th Cir. 1951), cert. denied, 342 US 954 (1952); contra Jordan Marsh Co. v. CIR, 269 F2d 453 (2d Cir. 1959). See infra ¶¶4.4.2, 40.6.2.

ostensible date of a sale may be ignored in favor of the time when payment could have been made.[46] Loans to members of the lender's family are also grist for the substance-over-form mill, since it is often a reasonable guess that the borrower will not be pressed for repayment as vigorously as an outsider.[47] The same can be said of loans by controlling shareholders to their own corporations and, conversely, of loans by their corporations to them, especially if the advances are proportionate to stock ownership.[48]

Transactions between parent and subsidiary corporations and among other members of an affiliated corporate group provide another set of tempting targets for legislative, administrative, and judicial marksmen armed with the substance-over-form weapon. Also, §482 permits the IRS to "distribute, apportion, or allocate gross income, deductions, credits, or allowances" among two or more organizations that are "owned or controlled directly or indirectly by the same interests . . . in order to prevent evasion of taxes or clearly to reflect the income of any of such organizations." Pursuant to this capacious charter of authority, the Treasury has promulgated extensive regulations that test all transactions among affiliated corporations by the standard of "an uncontrolled taxpayer dealing at arm's length with another uncontrolled taxpayer."[49] Many transactions that are vulnerable to attack under the substance-over-form doctrine are equally vulnerable under §482, and the two are often invoked in tandem by government briefs.

Mention should also be made of a diametrically opposite approach to transactions between related persons, exemplified by the statutory permission granted to affiliated corporations to file consolidated returns, under which intragroup transactions are disregarded and the income or loss of the group as a consolidated unit is based on its dealings with the outside world.[50] A similar, but more limited provision is made for married couples; gain or loss is never recognized on a sale, exchange, or other transfer of property between spouses, and the transferee-spouse takes the transferor's adjusted basis for the property, with the consequence that appreciation or depreciation accruing while the transferor held the property can be recognized on a subsequent sale by the transferee.[51]

---

[46] Hineman v. Brodrick, 99 F. Supp. 582, 583 (D. Kan. 1951) (receipt by farmer of money for sale of grain delayed two years "to effect a possible saving of federal taxes"); see infra ¶105.2.1.

[47] See infra ¶33.2.

[48] See ¶91.1 for the problem of characterizing advances by shareholders to their corporations as bona fide loans or as equity contributions; see ¶92.2 for the problem of determining whether a transfer of funds by a corporation to its shareholders is a dividend or a loan.

[49] Reg. §1.482-1(b); see infra ¶79.3.

[50] See infra ¶90.4.

[51] IRC §1041, discussed below in ¶44.8.

Transactions at arm's length with outsiders are far less vulnerable to substance-over-form attacks by the government than self-dealing transactions. For nontax reasons, the parties usually fully express their understanding in the documents, so that the chosen form ordinarily embodies the substance of their transaction. This fusion of form and substance is especially likely if they have divergent tax interests. Thus, when a business pays an employee for services, the desire to deduct the payment as a business expense usually leads the employer to resist any suggestion by the recipient that the payment be disguised as a tax-free gift rather than reported as taxable wages.[52]

This frequent opposition of interests does not mean that the characterization adopted by the parties to an arm's-length bargain is invariably conclusive. If an employer is a tax-exempt organization or a persistently unsuccessful enterprise with more deductions than it can use, for example, it may be willing to cooperate with an employee in characterizing compensation as a gift, either as a costless gesture of benevolence or in return for a concession by the employee. A similar bargain may be struck when two parties expect to be taxed at very different rates; if they can devise a legal form that assigns the tax advantages to the party who can best use them, the tax savings thus achieved can be divided between them. Thus, the amount to be paid under an alimony agreement is often affected by the fact that the husband's right to deduct the payment will reduce his taxes more than receiving the same amount will increase the wife's taxes.[53] Railroads and airlines with a long history of business losses often lease equipment rather than buy it, thereby enabling the lessor to derive a tax advantage from depreciation deductions or investment credits that would be useless to the lessee;[54] and many tax shelters similarly serve to shift tax allowances to investors who can deduct them from top-bracket income.

If a transaction is consummated in a form that fairly reflects its substance, it ordinarily passes muster despite the conscious pursuit of tax benefits; in this case, the choice of form resembles an election provided by statute. On the other hand, if the form does not coincide with the transaction's substance, the fact that it was negotiated at arm's length by unrelated taxpayers does not protect it against attack because the assumption of opposing tax interests is inapplicable. The substance-over-form doctrine can be successfully invoked, for example, in order to treat a purported lease of business equipment with an option in the lessee to purchase the property as a sale on credit if the option price is nominal in amount or the term of

---

[52] See infra ¶21.3.
[53] See infra ¶77.1.
[54] See infra ¶4.4.3.

the lease is coextensive with the anticipated useful life of the property.[55]

The presence of a third party with whom the taxpayer has bargained at arm's length also fails to protect a tax-avoidance plan if the formalities employed by the taxpayer have no significant impact on the other contracting party and are tolerated or accepted by him as an accommodation rather than as an integral part of the basic transaction. This phenomenon is characteristic of cases in which the taxpayer engages in preliminary mumbo jumbo to prepare assets for an impending sale or effects the transfer indirectly through a conduit. An acerbic comment by Chief Judge John R. Brown of the Court of Appeals for the Fifth Circuit can stand as a summary of this attitude. Refusing to allow the taxpayers in a complex transaction to hide behind a facade entailing the use of an intermediary named, by an appropriate fortuity, W.R. Deal, he said: "The Deal deal was not the real deal. That ends it."[56]

The Tax Court has struggled in recent years to develop the form-over-substance doctrine as a more objective and useful tool for tax shelter cases, most of which involve dealings with unrelated third parties. In one frequently cited case, the court held that an elaborate transaction in which the taxpayer purportedly purchased cattle was a sham, and that the taxpayer thus acquired nothing in the transaction.[57] The court enumerated eight factors relevant to whether a bona fide sale occurred—including whether the putative purchaser took possession, who bore the risk of loss to the property, who paid property taxes, and who received profits from the operation and sale of the property. The ultimate issue, the court said, is whether the burdens and benefits of ownership passed to the purchaser.

The court has also established a subcategory of the sham doctrine, called sham in substance, which the court defines as "the expedient of drawing up papers to characterize transactions contrary to objective economic realities and which have no economic significance beyond expected tax benefits."[58] A transaction is apparently a sham in substance if, in sub-

---

[55] See infra ¶¶4.4.2, 40.6.2.

[56] Blueberry Land Co. v. CIR, 361 F2d 93, 102 (5th Cir. 1966). See also Waterman S.S. Corp. v. CIR, 430 F2d 1185 (5th Cir. 1970) ("another attempt to ward off tax blows with paper armor").

[57] Grodt & McKay Realty, Inc. v. CIR, 77 TC 1221 (1981).

[58] Falsetti v. CIR, 85 TC 332 (1985) (no purchase occurred where (1) U.S. person sold property to Cayman Islands corporation, (2) corporation resold property at much higher price to U.S. partnership, (3) original U.S. seller later reimbursed partners of U.S. partnership for their investments in partnership, with interest, and (4) purchasers took no steps to search title, record deeds, or take control of property). See also Helba v. CIR, 87 TC 983 (1986) (partnerships' purported purchase of videotapes held to be sham in substance because (1) transactions made on terms unilaterally established by sellers, suggesting a lack of arms length bargaining, (2) notes given in payment of price effectively bore interest at 52 percent annually, (3)

stance, it effects no significant change in the parties' economic positions. A purported sale, for example, is a sham in substance if it does not transfer beneficial ownership of the property and putative payments of purchase price circulate among the parties in ways that cancel themselves out.

The Tax Court has also developed a standard based on objective criteria rather than subjective intention for testing tax shelters that are not shams in substance. For these transactions:

> Key indicators of presence or a lack of economic substance include presence or absence of arm's-length price negotiations, the relationship between the sales price and fair market value, the structure of financing of the transaction, whether there was a shifting of the benefits and burdens of ownership, and the degree of adherence to contractual terms. [Other indications of a lack of substance are:] (1) Tax benefits were the focus of promotional materials; (2) the investors accepted the terms of purchase without price negotiation; (3) the assets in question consist of packages of purported rights, difficult to value in the abstract and substantially overvalued in relation to tangible property included as part of the package; (4) the tangible assets were acquired or created at a relatively small cost shortly prior to the transactions in question; and (5) the bulk of the consideration was deferred by promissory notes, nonrecourse in form or in substance.[59]

When a transaction is found to be a sham, the taxpayer often loses not only the tax benefits sought by the transaction, but also the deduction for expenses incurred in effecting the transaction. Such expenses, the Tax Court has held, are "neither a cost of doing business nor an expense incurred with

---

the face amounts of the notes were so inflated as to cast doubt on whether the notes, though purportedly recourse notes, would ever be enforced, and (4) offering memoranda contained detailed information on expected tax benefits, but were largely silent on economic aspects of transactions). See Steele, Sham in Substance: The Tax Court's Emerging Standard for Testing Sale-Leasebacks, 14 J. Real Est. Tax'n 3 (1986).

Without using the words "sham in substance," the Court of Appeals for the Fourth Circuit has given a similar definition of sham:

> To treat a transaction as a sham, the court must find that the taxpayer was motivated by no business purpose other than obtaining tax benefits in entering the transaction, and that the transaction has no economic substance because no reasonable possibility of a profit exists.

Rice's Toyota World, Inc. v. CIR, 752 F2d 89, 91 (4th Cir. 1985).

[59] Rose v. CIR, 88 TC 386, 410–11, 412 (1987) (art tax shelter held to be sham where (1) taxpayers invested "primarily, if not exclusively" to obtain tax benefits, (2) price fixed at $550,000, but value negligible, and (3) price financed with nonrecourse debt not likely to be paid).

an intent to make a profit independent of tax consequences."[60]

A rogue offshoot of the substance-over-form doctrine suggests that when a taxpayer selects one of several forms that have identical practical consequences in the real world, the government can disregard the chosen form and tax the transaction as though the most costly of the alternatives had been employed. The implications of this theory are mind-boggling for even the most routine of business transactions. Thus, a $10,000 salary paid to the sole shareholder of a corporation could be analogized to a contribution by the shareholder-employee of his labor without charge, coupled with a distribution to him of a $10,000 dividend. If the services are worth $10,000, the hypothetical contribution-plus-dividend increases the value of the shareholder's stock by $10,000, while the dividend decreases it by the same amount. Judged by an arm's-length standard, the salary that was in fact paid for the shareholder's services is a reasonable business expense; yet nothing but its form distinguishes this transaction from its hypothetical alternative, and this form may have been chosen solely to reduce the corporation's federal income tax.[61]

The same mode of analyzing transactions between related taxpayers could be applied to virtually all contracts between shareholders and their corporations or between one affiliated corporation and another; in each instance, the same practical and economic results could ordinarily be achieved, although at greater tax cost, by combining a taxable dividend with a gratuitous transfer of the property or services.

Indeed, pushed to a drily logical extreme, the recasting of transactions to accord with the most costly practical equivalent would not have to await an actual transaction. Thus, a corporation's earnings could be treated as distributed when earned to its shareholders (who, after all, have complete control over the corporation's dividend policy) and then returned by them to the corporation as capital contributions. For some purposes, it would be entirely appropriate to describe the accumulation of earnings by the corporation as an abbreviated way of achieving the distribution and reinvestment of the funds, just as an economist, when computing opportunity costs, treats an investor's decision to hold an asset as the practical equivalent of selling it and immediately reinvesting the proceeds in the same asset. Whether this brutally realistic mode of analysis should be used to fix tax consequences is another matter.

---

[60] Price v. CIR, 88 TC 860, 886 (1987).

[61] The hypothetical dividend might have to be repaid at the suit of a creditor if the payment violated the applicable state dividend law, while the salary might not be vulnerable to this attack; but this nontax distinction might be too trivial to be taken into account, and would, in any event, arise only if state law distinguished between the two transactions, despite their practical equivalence.

On close inspection, the most-costly-alternative theory turns out to be a drastic extension, rather than a mere restatement, of the substance-over-form doctrine. Although a salary paid by a one-man corporation to its shareholder-employee is virtually identical in practical results to a dividend coupled with unpaid services, it does not follow that the salary is mere form and that the hypothetical combination of unpaid services and a dividend is the substance of the relationship. In actuality, both are formal ways by which the corporation receives services and the shareholder receives money. The legal issue is whether the shareholder-employee received the money as employee or as shareholder, and the substance-over-form doctrine sheds no light on this problem of characterization.

Since the practice of paying salaries to shareholder-employees antedates the federal income tax and is customary quite without regard to tax consequences, shareholder-employee salaries are routinely accepted at face value so far as the substance-over-form doctrine is concerned, provided only that the salary does not exceed the fair value of the services. While the most-costly-alternative theory would permit virtually all such cases to be recast as a combination of unpaid services and a dividend, the government has rarely even attempted to exploit this mode of increasing the tax bite.[62] Indeed, the Code imposes tax liability on the basis of so many fictions (e.g., the separate identity of corporations, the independence of family members from each other) that it virtually authorizes taxpayers to act on the same fictions.[63] As Holmes said in rejecting a taxpayer's request that the courts pierce a corporation's veil in a state tax case: "[I]t leads nowhere to call a corporation a fiction. If it is a fiction it is a fiction created by law with intent that it should be acted on as if true."[64]

---

[62] See especially Judge L. Hand, dissenting in Gilbert v. CIR, 248 F2d 399, 410–12 (2d Cir. 1957) (shareholders' right to deduct, as bad debts, their pro rata advances to their corporation when it became insolvent), discussed by Chirelstein, supra note 18, at 460–72. But see Charles McCandless Tile Serv. v. US, 422 F2d 1336 (Ct. Cl. 1970) (payments to shareholder-employees treated as dividends in part, although reasonable relative to services performed, discussed infra ¶22.2.2).

[63] Chirelstein (supra note 18, at 471) attributes to Judge L. Hand

a perception that the Internal Revenue Code is in part a clumsy system of implied elections, of which some, such as the choice to do business in corporate form, are freely exercisable by the taxpayer and binding on the Commissioner, while others, notably those involving self-dealing transactions, are within the Commissioner's discretion to approve or reject.

Viewed in the large, the Code's "clumsy system of implied elections" is even more favorable to the taxpayer because it is less restricted by the most-costly-alternative theory than Judge Hand evidently wished.

[64] Klein v. Board of Supervisors, 282 US 19, 24 (1930).

¶4.3.4 Business Purpose

As applied to tax matters, the business purpose doctrine originated with the *Gregory* case, involving the sole shareholder of a corporation that owned marketable securities, which she wanted to obtain in her personal capacity for sale to a third party. A straightforward distribution of the securities to her would have been taxable as a dividend. To avoid this result, the securities were transferred to a newly created second corporation, whose stock was issued to the taxpayer; she then dissolved the new corporation, receiving the securities as a liquidating distribution. Under the statutory predecessor of §368(a)(1), taken literally, this transaction was a tax-free corporate reorganization. The trial court held that "a statute so meticulously drafted must be interpreted as a literal expression of the taxing policy" and that the second corporation was entitled to recognition, despite its transitory life as a vehicle to transfer the securities from the first corporation to its sole shareholder.[65] The Court of Appeals for the Second Circuit reversed, holding that the transaction did not qualify as a "reorganization" when the purpose of the statutory definition of that term was taken into account:

> The purpose of the section is plain enough; men engaged in enterprises—industrial, commercial, financial, or any other—might wish to consolidate, or divide, to add to, or subtract from, their holdings. Such transactions were not to be considered as "realizing" any profit, because the collective interests still remained in solution. But the underlying presupposition is plain that the readjustment shall be undertaken for reasons germane to the conduct of the venture in hand, not as an ephemeral incident, egregious to its prosecution. To dodge the shareholder's taxes is not one of the transactions contemplated as corporate "reorganizations."[66]

The Supreme Court explicitly endorsed this reasoning, observing:

> Putting aside . . . the question of motive in respect of taxation altogether, and fixing the character of the proceeding by what actually occurred, what do we find? Simply an operation having no business or corporate purpose—a mere device which put on the form of a corporate reorganization as a disguise for concealing its real character, and the sole object and accomplishment of which was the consummation of a preconceived plan, not to reorganize a business or any part of a business, but to transfer a parcel of corporate shares to the petitioner.[67]

---

[65] Gregory v. CIR, 27 BTA 223, 225 (1932).
[66] Helvering v. Gregory, 69 F2d 809, 811 (2d Cir. 1934).
[67] Gregory v. Helvering, 293 US 465, 469 (1935).

Though its career was launched in a reorganization context,[68] the business purpose standard rapidly proliferated as an implied requirement of other statutory provisions. In 1949 Judge Learned Hand summarized its jurisdiction as follows:

> The doctrine of *Gregory v. Helvering* . . . means that in construing words of a tax statute which describes commercial or industrial transactions we are to understand them to refer to transactions entered upon for commercial or industrial purposes and not to include transactions entered upon for no other motive but to escape taxation.[69]

Judge Hand's reference to statutory provisions that describe "commercial or industrial transactions" seemingly excludes application of the business purpose doctrine to the so-called itemized deductions,[70] and indeed the concept of a business purpose is ill suited to allowances for payments that are not profit oriented, like alimony, medical expenses, and charitable contributions. Taxpayers routinely deduct these payments even though they serve personal rather than business purposes, and the Code obviously contemplates this practice.

More troublesome, however, is the status of interest paid on loans incurred in tax-avoidance transactions that promise no economic gain but will be worthwhile if the interest can be deducted. Section 163 allows interest to be deducted even though the funds are borrowed in a wholly personal context, but does it also allow a deduction for interest paid to finance a transaction serving only a tax-avoidance purpose? The leading case on this subject—*Knetsch v. United States*, discussed earlier[71]—denied an interest deduction for loans of this type on the ground that the transaction was a sham, without explicitly employing the business purpose doctrine. Some decisions on identical transactions, however, relied primarily on *Gregory* in reaching the same result, and these opinions were cited with apparent approval by the Supreme Court in *Knetsch*.[72] Another formulation is that such a transaction lacks economic reality; in effect, it is all form and no substance.

---

[68] For its ramifications in its original area of application, see infra ¶94.5.1. See also IRC §357(b)(1)(B) (statutory adoption of term "bona fide business purpose"; discussed infra ¶91.4.3).

[69] CIR v. Transport Trading & Terminal Corp., 176 F2d 570, 572 (2d Cir. 1949), cert. denied, 338 US 955 (1950).

[70] See infra ¶30.4.

[71] Supra ¶4.3.3.

[72] Knetsch v. US, 364 US 361, 366 n.4 (1960), citing Diggs v. CIR, 281 F2d 326 (2d Cir.), cert. denied, 364 US 908 (1960); Weller v. CIR, 270 F2d 294 (3d Cir.), cert. denied, 364 US 908 (1959), aff'g Emmons v. CIR, 31 TC 26 (1958), Weller v. CIR, 31 TC 33 (1958).

In another case of this type, the court was unwilling to characterize the transaction as a sham, but it denied the deduction because the loan did not have "purpose, substance, or utility apart from [its] anticipated tax consequences."[73] Recognizing that §163 is not limited to interest paid on profit-oriented borrowings, the court nevertheless held that some purpose other than tax avoidance was required. Conscious that taxpayers who can afford to pay cash often buy automobiles and residences on credit because the interest will be deductible, the court limited its decision to "pure" tax-avoidance transactions:

> Section 163(a) should be construed to permit the deductibility of interest when a taxpayer has borrowed funds and incurred an obligation to pay interest in order to engage in what with reason can be termed purposive activity, even though he decided to borrow in order to gain an interest deduction rather than to finance the activity in some other way. In other words, the interest deduction should be permitted whenever it can be said that the taxpayer's desire to secure an interest deduction is only one of mixed motives that prompts the taxpayer to borrow funds; or, put a third way, the deduction is proper if there is some substance to the loan arrangement beyond the taxpayer's desire to secure the deduction. . . . On the other hand, and notwithstanding Section 163(a)'s broad scope, this provision should not be construed to permit an interest deduction when it objectively appears that a taxpayer has borrowed funds in order to engage in a transaction that has no substance or purpose aside from the taxpayer's desire to obtain the tax benefit of an interest deduction; and a good example of such purposeless activity is the borrowing of funds at 4% in order to purchase property that returns less than 2% and holds out no prospect of appreciation sufficient to counter the unfavorable interest rate differential.[74]

By rephrasing the business purpose doctrine so that any "purposive activity" (other than the mere reduction of taxes) qualifies under provisions that embrace nonbusiness transactions, the court secured a deduction for the paradigmatic taxpayer who borrows to finance the American way of life, "spend now, pay later."

¶4.3.5 Step Transactions

The step transaction doctrine requires that the interrelated steps of an integrated transaction be analyzed as a whole rather than treated separately.

---

[73] Goldstein v. CIR, 364 F2d 734, 740 (2d Cir. 1966), cert. denied, 385 US 1005 (1967).

[74] Id. at 741–42.

Like the business purpose doctrine, it began as an interpretation of a detailed statutory provision,[75] but has been a successful cultural imperialist, on which the sun never sets. Its control is especially pronounced in the corporate-shareholder area.[76]

Because business transactions often have no sharp beginning or clearly defined end and because income must be computed annually, it is often necessary to divide a transaction into its constituent elements for tax purposes. If a thin segment is taken in isolation, however, it may be too artificial a base for tax computations. As a consequence, two or more formally separate steps may be amalgamated and treated as a single transaction if they are in substance integrated, interdependent, and focused on a particular end result. Under §351, for example, the tax treatment of a transfer of property to a corporation in exchange for its stock depends on whether the transferors have control of the corporation "immediately after the exchange,"[77] a phrase that seems to concentrate on an instantaneous point of time and thus to exclude cases where the requisite control is acquired in a series of nonsimultaneous exchanges. But the Treasury regulations, in conformity with case law, state that the statutory condition "does not necessarily require simultaneous exchanges . . . but comprehends a situation where the rights of the parties have been previously defined and the execution of the agreement proceeds with an expedition consistent with orderly procedure."[78] Another consequence of taking all integrated steps together in determining whether control exists "immediately after the exchange" is that momentary compliance with this statutory condition is insufficient if control is dissipated by a transfer of stock that, though some-

---

[75] It is dangerous to be dogmatic in pinpointing the source of this protean doctrine, particularly because in its earlier days it was sometimes regarded as an aspect of the pervasive injunction to look at substance rather than form. The earliest explicit statement of the step transaction doctrine, however, seems to be Warner Co. v. CIR, 26 BTA 1225, 1228 (1932) (acq.), which held that §204(a)(7) of the Revenue Act of 1926, relating to corporate reorganizations, "permits, if it does not require, an examination of the several steps taken which culminated in the taxpayer's acquisition of the . . . assets." See also Tulsa Tribune Co. v. CIR, 58 F2d 937, 940 (10th Cir. 1932) (rejecting, a few months before *Warner Co.* was decided, an "attempt [by the government] to break this transaction up into two elements by saying that Jones bought the property and then transferred it to the corporation in exchange for its capital stock"); Carter Publications, Inc. v. CIR, 28 BTA 160, 164 (1933) (acq.) ("the whole series of acts, corporate and otherwise, constituted only a single transaction").

[76] See generally Paul, Step Transactions, in Paul, Selected Studies in Federal Taxation 200 (Callaghan, 2d ser. 1938); Mintz & Plumb, Step Transactions in Corporate Reorganizations, 12 NYU Inst. on Fed. Tax'n 247 (1954); Murray, Step Transactions, 24 U. Miami L. Rev. 60 (1969).

[77] IRC §351(a), discussed infra ¶91.5.3.

[78] Reg. §1.351-1(a)(1). See also Rev. Rul. 79-250, 1979-2 CB 156, discussed infra ¶91.5.3.

what delayed, was contemplated from the outset as an essential part of the transaction.[79]

A similar example of the scope of the step transaction doctrine is the "creeping control" concept applied in determining whether an acquisition of stock of a target corporation by an acquiring corporation is "in exchange solely for . . . voting stock" within the meaning of §368(a)(1)(B). If, for example, the acquiring corporation buys 25 percent of the target corporation's stock for cash in 1989 and then acquires 75 percent in 1990 solely in exchange for its voting stock, does the 1990 transaction meet the requirement of §368(a)(1)(B) that "the acquisition" be solely for stock? Taken by itself, it does, but if the 1989 and 1990 acquisitions are viewed as interrelated steps in a single transaction, the statutory standard is not met because both cash and stock are used. Whether there is only a single nonqualified acquisition for cash plus stock or one acquisition for cash and a later, separable qualified acquisition for voting stock depends on the facts and circumstances. The latter conclusion is only appropriate if the 1989 purchase is consummated for its own sake, not as part of an integrated plan that includes the 1990 exchange.[80]

Although the foregoing illustrations all involve corporate-shareholder relations, the step transaction doctrine is also encountered frequently in other areas of tax law.[81]

While it is comparatively simple to foresee the results that flow from the application of the step transaction doctrine, it is more difficult to predict when the doctrine will be applied. At one extreme, if the parties have agreed to a series of steps, no one of which will be legally effective unless all are consummated, application of the doctrine is ordinarily assured. In the absence of such an all-or-nothing plan, however, predictions are more perilous. Sometimes a series of steps, although independent, may occur simultaneously or in rapid succession; the taxpayer may simply seize upon the fact that he is engaged in negotiations or has a lawyer at hand to achieve several independent objectives, each of which would be pursued on its own even if the others had to be abandoned. Recognizing this possibility, the Tax Court has said: "The test is, were the steps taken so interdependent that the legal relations created by one transaction would have been fruitless without a

---

[79] Reg. §1.351-1(a)(1).

[80] See generally Reeves v. CIR, 71 TC 727 (1979); infra ¶94.5.1.

[81] See, e.g., Redwing Carriers, Inc. v. Tomlinson, 399 F2d 652 (5th Cir. 1968) (sale of old equipment and purchase of new; although purportedly separate, events treated as a single transaction, subject to §1031); Century Elec. Co. v. CIR, 192 F2d 155 (8th Cir. 1951), cert. denied, 342 US 954 (1952) (re §1031, relating to like-kind exchanges); Coupe v. CIR, 52 TC 394 (1969) (acq. in result, 1970-1 CB xv) (three-party exchange); Magnolia Dev. Corp. v. CIR, 19 TCM (CCH) 934 (1960) (transaction with charity).

completion of the series?"[82]

Despite intimations to the contrary in the early cases, the step transaction doctrine does not require a prior agreement committing the parties to the entire series of steps once the first is taken; there is ample authority for linking several prearranged or contemplated steps, even in the absence of a contractual obligation or financial compulsion to follow through.[83] Moreover, while simultaneity is often the best evidence of interdependence, the step transaction doctrine has been applied to events separated by as much as 5 years and, on other facts, held inapplicable to events occurring within a period of 30 minutes.[84]

The step transaction doctrine is usually enunciated as a general principle, but the courts may be more ready to apply it to some provisions than to others, implicitly assuming that Congress would have intended this difference in approach. In applying a provision that involves only a single taxpayer, for example, it would be fruitless to ask whether several steps are linked together by contract, prearrangement, or expectations; the statutory focus may be wholly on the taxpayer's intent. Much can be said for declining to link commercial transactions (e.g., the incorporation of a proprietorship) with noncommercial events (e.g., gifts by the taxpayer to members of his family), even if they occur simultaneously.[85] But if the courts have been significantly influenced by considerations of this type, they have not explicitly said so.[86]

Although step transaction cases often are concerned with whether a particular step with significant legal or business consequences should be treated as part of a larger single transaction, there are also many cases where particular steps in an integrated transaction are disregarded as transitory events or empty formalities. These rather different results of the step transaction doctrine can be illustrated by two contrasting cases.

---

[82] Manhattan Bldg. Co. v. CIR, 27 TC 1032, 1042 (1957) (acq.), citing American Bantam Car Co. v. CIR, 11 TC 397 (1948), aff'd per curiam, 177 F2d 513 (3d Cir. 1949), cert. denied, 339 US 920 (1950). The interdependency test was proposed and extensively discussed by Paul, supra note 21. See also Mintz & Plumb, supra note 75, at 285, concluding that in reorganization cases the test "seems to be whether the step was intended, or even contemplated as an alternative" rather than the interdependency test proposed by Paul.

[83] See King Enters., Inc. v. US, 418 F2d 511 (Ct. Cl. 1969).

[84] Compare Douglas v. CIR, 37 BTA 1122 (1938) (acq.) (five-year delay in consummating corporate reorganization resulting from nonassignability of contracts and disputed claims) with Henricksen v. Braicks, 137 F2d 632 (9th Cir. 1943) (liquidation treated as independent of transfer of assets to new corporation 30 minutes later).

[85] See infra ¶95.5.3.

[86] For classification of step transaction cases by type of business transaction, see Mintz & Plumb, supra note 76; Murray, supra note 76.

First, assume a taxpayer transfers property to a corporation in exchange for its stock, intending to sell half of the stock to a third party as soon as the first step is completed. If the two steps are found to be interrelated and mutually dependent, the taxpayer does not have control of the transferee corporation "immediately after the exchange" within the meaning of §351(a), with the result that gain or loss is recognized on the exchange of property for stock.[87] The sale of the stock in this case is a serious, indeed a fateful, step in the integrated transaction.

Suppose, in contrast, that an individual proprietor has an opportunity to sell his entire merchandise inventory but would like to report the impending profit as capital gain rather than as ordinary income. Knowing that merchandise does not qualify for capital gain treatment[88] but that corporate stock usually does, he transfers the merchandise to a newly created corporation in exchange for its stock, which he promptly sells to a prospective buyer, who in turn liquidates the corporation in order to get the assets. On these facts, the sale of the stock would almost certainly be regarded as a step in an integrated transaction by which the merchandise was sold;[89] but, rather than being treated as a significant step (as was the sale of stock in the prior example), it would be disregarded, and the transaction would be taxed as though this unnecessary step had not occurred.

The classic formulation of this variation of the step transaction doctrine, in *Minnesota Tea Co. v. Helvering*, is: "A given result at the end of a straight path is not made a different result because reached by following a devious path."[90] The unnecessary step in this case was a distribution of cash by a bankrupt corporation to its shareholders, who were required to pay the funds over to the company's creditors. In holding that this was only a "devious path" by which corporate funds were routed to the creditors (rather than a true distribution to the shareholders), the Court said:

> The preliminary distribution to the stockholders was a meaningless and unnecessary incident in the transmission of the fund to the creditors . . . so transparently artificial that further discussion would be a needless waste of time. The relation of the stockholders to the matter was that of a mere conduit.[91]

When the step transaction doctrine is thus employed to eliminate transitory or unnecessary steps, it overlaps and becomes almost indistinguishable from the business purpose doctrine (under which the unnecessary step

---

[87] IRC §351(a), discussed infra ¶91.5.3.
[88] See infra ¶51.2.1.
[89] See infra ¶95.4.1.
[90] Minnesota Tea Co. v. Helvering, 302 US 609, 613 (1938).
[91] Id. at 613–14.

is disregarded because lacking in business purpose) and the substance-over-form principle (nullifying the unnecessary step as a formality that merely obscures the substance of the transaction). The *Gregory* case, for example, is often cited in support of the business purpose and substance-over-form doctrines, but it could be equally validly viewed as a step transaction case; indeed, it is cited in the *Minnesota Tea* case in support of the "devious path" formula.[92] A typical amalgamation of all three ideas is the following statement in a revenue ruling:

> The two steps of the transaction . . . were part of a prearranged integrated plan and may not be considered independently of each other for Federal income tax purposes. The receipt by A of the additional stock of X in exchange for the sole proprietorship assets is transitory and without substance for tax purpose since it is apparent that the assets of the sole proprietorship were transferred to X for the purpose of enabling Y to acquire such assets without the recognition of gain to A.[93]

The principal practical difference between the "critical step" and "unnecessary step" variations of the step transaction doctrine seems to lie in the taxpayer's greater ability to invoke the former than the latter. The reason for linking together all interdependent steps with legal or business significance, rather than taking them in isolation, is to base tax liabilities on a realistic view of the entire transaction. For this reason, and because the steps themselves are not ordinarily intended to obscure the transaction's substance, the taxpayer is usually as free as the Commissioner to insist that it be viewed as a whole.[94] When unnecessary or transitory steps are deliberately employed by the taxpayer, however, the courts are less disposed to

---

[92] Id. at 614.

[93] Rev. Rul. 70-140, 1970-1 CB 73. See also Perry v. US, 520 F2d 235 (4th Cir. 1975), cert. denied, 423 US 1052 (1976) (business purpose for isolated step in multistep integrated transaction insufficient; business purpose must be shown for transaction as a whole); J.M. Turner & Co. v. CIR, 247 F2d 370, 376 (4th Cir. 1957) ("it is the substance, not the form, of the transaction, which must control our conclusion, and a transaction accomplished in two mutually dependent steps should be viewed as a whole").

[94] See Helvering v. New Haven & S.S.L.R.R., 121 F2d 985, 988 (2d Cir. 1941), cert. denied, 315 US 803 (1942) (rejecting "the effort of the CIR to atomize the plan, as it were; i.e., to separate into its separate steps and treat the last as though it stood alone"); CIR v. Ashland Oil & Ref. Co., 99 F2d 588, 591 (6th Cir. 1938), cert. denied, 306 US 661 (1939) (taxpayer wanted to acquire assets of another corporation but was compelled to acquire its stock, which was promptly surrendered in complete liquidation; held, transaction was in effect an acquisition of assets; "closely related steps will not be separated either at the instance of the taxpayer or the taxing authority").

permit the taxpayer to retrace his steps in order to leave his devious path and get back on the straight and narrow.[95]

¶4.3.6 Disavowal of Form by Taxpayers

When taxpayers invoke the substance-over-form, business purpose, or step transaction doctrine in order to escape the normal tax consequences of a transaction to which they are parties, the judicial reaction gravitates between two extremes.[96]

At one end of the spectrum, taxpayers are told that the government can cut through their red tape if it wishes, but that it is equally free to leave them entangled in the form they selected. The classic statement of this principle is in *Higgins v. Smith*, a 1940 opinion of the Supreme Court holding that a taxpayer did not incur a deductible loss on selling depreciated securities to a wholly owned corporation.[97] Referring to *Burnet v. Commonwealth Improvement Co.*,[98] an earlier case taxing the gain on a similar sale despite the taxpayer's argument that the transaction resulted in a paper profit but no economic gain, the Court said:

> In the *Commonwealth Improvement Company* case, the taxpayer, for reasons satisfactory to itself, voluntarily had chosen to employ the corporation in its operations. A taxpayer is free to adopt such organization for his affairs as he may choose, and having elected to do some business as a corporation, he must accept the tax disadvantages.
>
> On the other hand, the Government may not be required to acquiesce in the taxpayer's election of that form for doing business which is most advantageous to him. The Government may look at actualities and upon determination that the form employed for doing business or carrying out the challenged tax event is unreal or a sham may sustain or disregard the effect of the fiction as best serves the purposes of the tax statute. To hold otherwise would permit the schemes of taxpayers to supersede legislation in the determination of the time and manner of

---

[95] Infra note 96.

[96] See generally Donaldson, When Substance-Over-Form Argument Is Available to the Taxpayer, 48 Marq. L. Rev. 41, 48–50 (1964); Rosen, Substance Over Form—A Taxpayer's Weapon, 1970 So. Cal. Tax Inst. 689.

[97] Higgins v. Smith, 308 US 473 (1940). Between the taxable year before the Court and the time of the Court's decision, Congress enacted the predecessor of §267(a)(1), which explicitly denies a deduction for such losses (infra ¶78.1.1). The Court held this statutory provision did not imply the law was otherwise in prior years.

[98] Burnet v. Commonwealth Improvement Co., 287 US 415 (1932). In this case the securities were sold by the corporation to its sole shareholder, but the Court in Higgins v. Smith did not regard this factual difference as relevant.

taxation.[99]

Another frequently quoted formulation of the same point is by Judge Learned Hand:

> It is true that the Treasury may take a taxpayer at his word, so to say; when that serves its purpose, it may treat his corporation as a different person from himself; but that is a rule which works only in the Treasury's own favor; it cannot be used to deplete the revenue.[100]

This judicial refusal to permit taxpayers to repudiate their own handi-work is occasionally supported by the traditional elements of estoppel. The form, as characterized by the taxpayer on the tax return, may be accepted at face value by the IRS. If the taxpayer later attempts to discard the form and portray events in a more realistic light, it may be administratively difficult or even impossible to correct all related prior returns of the taxpayer and other parties to the same transaction because memories have faded or the statute of limitations has run.[101]

Even when no irreversible waves have been set in motion, taxpayers have sometimes been denied the right to invoke the substance-over-form doctrine: "It would be quite intolerable to pyramid the existing complexities of tax law by a rule that the tax shall be that resulting from the form of transaction taxpayers have chosen or from any other form they might have chosen, whichever is less."[102] This attitude may be buttressed by a belief that a taxpayer's repudiation of a form deliberately chosen by him is unappeal-ing conduct even when prejudice to the government's interest cannot be proved.

At the opposite extreme, many cases hold that the substance-over-form doctrine is a two-way street, open to taxpayers as well as to the government. As early as 1929, for example, the Court of Appeals for the Fourth Circuit

---

[99] Higgins v. Smith, supra note 97, at 477–78.

[100] US v. Morris & Essex R.R., 135 F2d 711, 713 (2d Cir.), cert. denied, 320 US 754 (1943). See also Matthews v. US, 36 AFTR2d 5974 (DSC 1975) (not officially reported).

[101] See Unvert v. CIR, 72 TC 807 (1979), aff'd, 656 F2d 483 (9th Cir. 1981), cert. denied, 456 US 961 (1982) (review of cases on quasi-estoppel). For mitigation of the statute of limitations in the case of inconsistency by either the taxpayer or the IRS, see infra ¶113.9.

[102] Television Indus., Inc. v. CIR, 284 F2d 322, 325 (2d Cir. 1960). The taxpayer was not necessarily asking for the benefit of the cheapest alternative to the form used; the "substance" of a particular transaction may generate a lesser tax than would be owing if the form were taken at face value, but the former amount may be greater than would have resulted from an alternative way of reaching a similar business result. See in this connection the discussion of the most-costly-alternative theory in ¶4.3.3.

cited the "settled principle" that "courts will not permit themselves to be blinded or deceived by mere forms of law" and then observed:

> The rule just stated is of peculiar importance in tax cases; for, unless the courts are very careful to regard substance and not form in matters of taxation, there is grave danger on the one hand that the provisions of the tax laws will be evaded through technicalities and on the other that they will work unreasonable and unnecessary hardship on the taxpayer. It is instructive to note the many tax cases decided in recent years in which the courts have not hesitated to ignore corporate forms, and to decide the questions involved in the light of what the parties have actually done, rather than on the basis of the forms in which they have clothed their transactions.[103]

In a more graphic expression of the same sentiment, the Court of Appeals for the Ninth Circuit said, "One should not be garroted by the tax collector for calling one's agreement by the wrong name."[104]

In a similar vein, the Supreme Court has permitted taxpayers to disavow a tax-oriented contract on showing that its form conflicted with economic reality, despite the government's willingness to accept the contract as written.[105] The case involved an effort to shift liability for social security taxes on the wages of musicians from bandleaders to ballroom operators by vesting the latter with rights under a standard union contract that were not intended to be enforced. Despite this barefaced denial of the employment realities, the IRS was willing to accept the agreement, perhaps because the ballroom operators were more responsible taxpayers than the bandleaders. The operators, however, were allowed to repudiate the fictitious employer-employee relationship. In reaching this result, the Court hinted, without explicitly holding, that *Higgins v. Smith* and its other one-way-street cases should be confined to "the problem of corporate or assocation entity."[106] There are many lower court decisions that similarly allow the taxpayer to invoke the substance-over-form doctrine, and some important IRS rulings

---

[103] Western Maryland Ry. v. CIR, 33 F2d 695, 698 (4th Cir. 1929). Other early cases to the same effect are Weiss v. Stearn, 265 US 242 (1924) (looking to substance of transaction at taxpayer's behest) and Prairie Oil & Gas Co. v. Motter, 66 F2d 309 (10th Cir. 1933) (same).

[104] Pacific Rock & Gravel Co. v. US, 297 F2d 122, 125 (9th Cir. 1961). Despite this auspicious comment, the taxpayer lost; since the court found the agreement murky, perhaps it was a case of suicide rather than garroting. See also Clark v. US, 341 F2d 691, 695 (9th Cir. 1965) (quoting "garrote" metaphor but finding transaction correctly labeled).

[105] Bartels v. Birmingham, 332 US 126 (1947) (three Justices dissenting).

[106] Id. at 131.

appear to follow suit.[107]

Between these two extremes are cases that allow taxpayers to escape from the forms selected by them but impose a more stringent burden of proof than is ordinarily applicable in tax cases. Describing this middle ground, the Tax Court has observed that "the so-called 'two-way street' seems to run downhill for the Commissioner and uphill for the taxpayer."[108] When the sales price of a going business is allocated by the parties among the items purchased, for example, some courts permit the buyer or seller to repudiate the agreed on allocation only on "strong proof" of its failure to reflect economic reality; and in the Court of Appeals for the Third Circuit, the taxpayer can disavow the allocation only on showing that it was induced by mistake, fraud, or the like.[109] This intermediate approach has been applied primarily to taxpayers attempting to escape allocations in contracts for the sale of a going business or the stock of an incorporated enterprise with a concomitant covenant not to compete, and it is discussed elsewhere in that connection.[110]

¶4.4 RESTRUCTURED BUSINESS TRANSACTIONS

¶4.4.1 Introductory

A common phenomenon in federal income taxation is the "restructured transaction"—a business arrangement that is classified differently by the IRS and the courts than by the private parties who entered into it. Assume an owner of business equipment leases it for an extended period, with an option to purchase that is virtually certain to be exercised because the option price is nominal and the present value of the rents equals the value of the property. If the transaction is treated as the documents provide, the owner reports gain or loss when the option is exercised and can deduct

---

[107] See, e.g., Shaw v. CIR, 59 TC 375, 383–84 (1972) ("preference for substance over form in tax matters extends to claims of petitioner and respondent alike"); Weinert's Est. v. CIR, 294 F2d 750 (5th Cir. 1961) (taxpayer "has a right to assert the priority of substance").

The basic IRS ruling requiring certain purported leases of equipment to be treated as sales does not suggest that its principles are applicable only at the government's initiative, and its neutral language implies that taxpayers can invoke its standards as freely as revenue agents. Rev. Rul. 55-540, 1955-2 CB 39; see infra ¶4.4 for other rulings of similar import.

[108] Rogers v. CIR, 29 TCM (CCH) 869 (1970), aff'd, 445 F2d 1020 (2d Cir. 1971).

[109] See, e.g., Ullman v. CIR, 264 F2d 305 (2d Cir. 1959) ("strong proof"); CIR v. Danielson, 378 F2d 771 (3d Cir. 1967) (evidence sufficient to vary the terms of a written contract under common law, such as mistake or fraud); infra ¶4.4.6.

[110] Infra ¶4.4.6.

depreciation on the property in the interim. Conversely, the lessee can deduct the rent as a business expense as paid or accrued and can depreciate the property only on becoming its owner by exercising the option.

If it is determined that the lease should be treated as a sale of the property, the results are quite different. Viewed as a vendor of the equipment, the "lessor" must compute gain or loss when the "lease" is executed, and the "rent" must be divided between nontaxable principal payments and taxable interest.[1] The "lessee" is the owner of the property for tax purposes from the date of the lease, can depreciate the property, and must divide the "rent" between nondeductible capital outlays and deductible interest.[2]

Questions of this type can arise in connection with almost any tax allowance, but they may lie dormant for years and spring to life only when an alert taxpayer or revenue agent perceives that the events, if reclassified, would have a different set of tax consequences. Whenever the issue arises, however, the ingredients determining whether a transaction should be accepted at face value or restructured are usually the same. For this reason, some of the principal candidates for restructured treatment are examined here, and reference to this discussion is made in subsequent discussions of the tax allowances that turn on whether a transaction fits into one classification or another.

The restructuring of a transaction usually raises important threshold issues of procedure. Can the IRS hold the parties to the label they've selected if it so desires, or can taxpayers take the initiative in repudiating their own formal representations? Does the parol evidence rule prohibit the IRS or a party from introducing evidence of negotiations or prior understandings between the parties that are not reflected in the agreement as finally executed? If the IRS is successful in restructuring a transaction as to one taxpayer, must it act consistently vis-a-vis the other party or parties to the same arrangement? If consistency is desirable or mandatory, how can it be assured, given the decentralized judicial review that results from the concurrent existence of a single U.S. Tax Court, the Court of Claims, hundreds of federal district courts, and 12 courts of appeals? What is the standard of review applicable to an appeal from a lower court's decision in a

---

[1] For a summary of the principal tax consequences to the "lessor" and "lessee" if a purported lease is determined to be a sale, see Rev. Rul. 72-408, 1972-2 CB 86. For the imputation of interest when deferred payments do not bear sufficient explicit interest, see §§483 and 1274, discussed in Lokken, The Time Value of Money Rules, 42 Tax L. Rev. 1, 81–158 (1986).

[2] See IRC §162(a)(3) (rental or other payments for continued use of property deductible only if taxpayer is not taking title and has no equity; discussed infra ¶22.3).

restructuring case?[3] To avoid repetition, these procedural issues are discussed below,[4] and references to this unified discussion are made at appropriate points elsewhere.

When a transaction is restructured, the legal relationships between the parties to the transaction are not changed by its altered tax aspects. The parties continue to be bound by the contract as written, which determines where legal ownership resides, what payments must be made and when, and other nontax rights and duties—unless, as sometimes occurs, a parallel restructuring occurs under local law in determining, for example, the applicability of usury, recordation, or regulatory laws.[5] For these reasons, the term "reclassification" is sometimes used to indicate that a transaction's tax consequences are different from those ordinarily suggested by its label. If "restructuring" is too grandiose a term, "reclassification" may be too modest, since it may be understood as implying no more than a change of labels. As pointed out, whether a transaction is "restructured," "reclassified," "recast," or "realigned," the result is a different set of tax results from those that the parties bargained for.

The concepts applied in these cases have much in common with the pervasive judicial doctrines discussed in the preceding sections. In deciding whether the parties' characterization of a transaction should control for tax purposes, the courts commonly use language reminiscent of the form-over-substance and business purpose cases. Whether a purported lease is in substance a sale on credit, for example, can be seen as a subcategory of the form-over-substance inquiry, and whether the buyer-lessor in a sale-lease-back transaction becomes owner of the property that is the subject of the transaction is often approached as a question of sham.

¶4.4.2 Sale vs. Lease

Although most leases contemplate that the lessee will use the property for a limited period and then surrender possession to the owner, taxpayers sometimes enter into leases expecting that the lessee will probably retain the property for its entire economic life. For example, (1) the lessee might have

---

[3] Although the issue of "the general characterization of a transaction for tax purposes" commonly turns on the facts and circumstances of the particular case, it is "a question of law subject to [appellate] review" free of the restraints on review of questions of fact. Frank Lyon Co. v. US, 435 US 561, 581 n.16 (1978). If the reclassification question turns on whether a transaction is a sham, however, the issue of sham is a question of fact, on which a lower court's decision is only reversed if clearly erroneous. Rice's Toyota World, Inc. v. CIR, 752 F2d 89 (4th Cir. 1985).

[4] Infra ¶¶4.4.5–4.4.7.

[5] See generally Equipment Leasing—Leveraged Leasing (Fritch & Reisman, eds.; Practising Law Inst. 1977) for discussion of the numerous nontax ramifications of a restructured leveraged lease.

an option to purchase the property under circumstances that virtually compel exercise of the option, (2) the lease might vest ownership in the lessee when the periodic payments reach a specified dollar amount, (3) the lease term might extend for all of the property's expected economic life, or (4) some other circumstance might suggest little likelihood that the lessor will ever retake possession of the property. Any such circumstance suggests that the lessor is effectively parting with ownership—suggests the possibility, that is, that the transaction might most realistically be characterized as a sale on credit rather than a lease.[6]

In *Starr's Estate v. CIR*, the Court of Appeals for the Ninth Circuit attributed the popularity of borderline arrangements bearing the label "lease" to tax considerations:

> Yesterday's equities in personal property seem to have become today's leases. This has been generated not a little by the circumstance that one who leases as a lessee usually has less trouble with the federal tax collector. At least taxpayers think so.
>
> But the lease still can go too far and get one into tax trouble. While according to state law the instrument will probably be taken (with the consequent legal incidents) by the name the parties give it, the Internal Revenue Service is not always bound and can often recast it according to what the service may consider the practical realities.[7]

---

[6] See Kitchin v. CIR, 353 F2d 13 (4th Cir. 1965) (rejecting the alternative of holding the transaction open until lessee either exercises option to purchase the property or allows it to expire). See also Kronovet, Characterization of Real Estate Leases: An Analysis and Proposal, 32 Tax Lawyer 757, 759 (1979):

> [T]he test of traditional status, when applied to real estate leases, is a test which has no meaning in today's world of complex real estate lease financing. The . . . decision of the parties concerning their . . . status . . . as landlord, tenant or mortgagee is not an economic or real estate decision but is a tax decision, pure and simple. The parties bargain for and adopt such status labels solely to achieve a tax result without reference to economics, traditional roles, or other supposedly relevant matters.
>
> The only significant item is the tax agreement of the parties. With such agreement, there are sufficient technical devices available to the practitioner to enable him to fashion the transaction in order to achieve the expected result.

For a review of the early cases, see Blumenthal & Harrison, The Tax Treatment of the Lease With an Option to Purchase, 32 Texas L. Rev. 839 (1954).

[7] Starr's Est. v. CIR, 274 F2d 294, 294–95 (9th Cir. 1959). On occasion, however, taxpayers prefer to have a borderline transaction treated as a sale. See, e.g., Meiselman v. CIR, 300 F2d 666 (4th Cir. 1962); Robertson v. CIR, 19 BTA 534 (1930) (nonacq.) (lease-option restructured as sale at taxpayer's instance, although lease-option form was chosen to avoid state redemption laws in favor of buyers in possession).

In the words of an early ruling: "Whether an agreement, which in form is a lease, is in substance a conditional sales contract depends upon the intent of the parties as evidenced by the provisions of the agreement, read in the light of the facts and circumstances existing at the time the agreement was executed."[8] Although the IRS could identify "no single test, or any special combination of tests, [that] is absolutely determinative" of the issue,[9] the overriding factor is probably the way in which the parties have allocated among themselves the benefits and burdens of the ownership of the property. An owner reaps the profits and bears the losses that flow from the property. The benefits and risks of the unpredictability of the market rest with the owner; the owner of a cargo ship profits greatly if a bulge in international trade creates a demand for shipping beyond that available in existing ships, and loses his shirt (and probably the ship, too) if trade collapses. A seller on credit, in contrast, is a secured creditor who assumes a limited risk and profits by his continuing interest in the property only through the limited return of interest.

A lease shifts some of the benefits and burdens of ownership to the lessee, and gives the position of the owner-lessor characteristics that resemble some of those of a credit seller. For the duration of the lease term, unanticipated changes in the value of the use of the property usually fall on the lessee, and the lessor's return (rent) is typically fixed, like that of a creditor. The common law view of a lease as a transfer of an interest in the property, in other words, usually reflects economic reality.

In the typical situation, however, a lessor-owner has a residual interest in the property that differs in kind from that of a credit seller. The latter's

---

[8] Rev. Rul. 55-540, 1955-2 CB 39, 41. Revenue Ruling 55-540 sets out an extensive series of guidelines on the sale versus lease issue. The ruling is somewhat obsolete because it does not address the treatment of forms of leasing transactions developed over the last 30 years. It nevertheless retains usefulness as a statement of what continue to be the IRS'views on the transactions it does address. See Universal Drilling Co. v. US, 412 F. Supp. 1231 (ED La. 1976) (guidelines of Rev. Rul. 55-540 "are consistent with the jurisprudence"; after review of cases, court concluded that ship charter was lease rather than sale); Cubic Corp. v. US, 74-2 USTC ¶9667 (SD Cal. 1974) (not officially reported), aff'd per curiam, 541 F2d 829 (9th Cir. 1976) (taxpayer tried unsuccessfully to invoke Rev. Rul. 55-540, described by the court as entailing "a hindsight attempt to distill the intent of the parties by means of a narrow and restrictive test"). See also Meiselman v. CIR, supra note 7, at 668 (if facts show that a sale was "the real intent of the parties . . . then transaction should be so categorized for tax purposes"); Benton v. CIR, 197 F2d 745, 752 (5th Cir. 1952) ("good faith intent" controlling, rather than objective economic test; case predates Rev. Rul. 55-540); Transamerica Corp. v. US, 7 Cl. Ct. 441, 85-1 USTC ¶9210 (1985) (rejecting argument that *Frank Lyon Co. v. US* (discussed infra ¶4.4.3) requires that the form of a leasing transaction be respected unless there are no nontax motives for leasing format).

[9] Id.

security interest is only insurance against the possibility of the buyer not paying. A lessor's right to possession at end of the lease term, in contrast, usually means that the lease effects, at most, a temporary shift to the lessee of the vicissitudes of the market; whether the lessor profits or loses after the conclusion of the lease term depends on the value of the property.

Because it is a lessor-owner's residual interest in the profitability of the property that distinguishes him from a credit seller, in a particular case, the nature and extent of this interest determine whether a transaction cast as a lease is in substance a credit sale. In other words, a lease is a real lease, not a sale, unless it contains provisions that reduce the lessor's residual interest in the property to little more than security for payment.

An option to purchase the leased property can be an example of such a provision. If the lessee is required to pay more than the fair rental value of the property and is compensated for this burden by a low option price, the excess rent builds up an equity in the property that the lessee will lose if he fails to exercise the option and that therefore provides an irresistible incentive for the lessee to exercise in the absence of a market decline that destroys the equity.[10] As a result, the lessee's economic position resembles that of a purchaser who finances the purchase price with a nonrecourse mortgage payable in level installments (equal to the periodic rents) with a balloon at the end (equal to the option price). The lessor's interest is only a right to the periodic rents and the option price, and thus is like that of a nonrecourse lender. Like the purchaser's freedom to default on the mortgage, the lessee's freedom to let the option expire unexercised is likely to be illusory in view of the resulting loss of accumulated equity. If the market value of the property drops below the option price, the lessee will not exercise the option, but, similarly, a purchaser-mortgagor will not pay off a nonrecourse mortgage if the value of the property falls below the balance due.[11]

Not all options to purchase are inconsistent with true lease classification. If the rent reserved in a lease does not exceed the fair rental value of

---

[10] See IRC §162(a)(3) (rents not deductible if taxpayer has "equity" in rented property; discussed infra ¶22.3).

[11] The IRS has said:

> In the absence of compelling factors indicating a different intent it will be presumed that a conditional sales contract was intended if the total of the rental payments and any option price payable in addition thereto approximates the price at which the equipment could have been acquired by purchase at the time of entering into the agreement, plus interest and/or carrying charges.

Rev. Rul. 55-540, supra note 8, at §4.05. See also Transamerica Corp. v. US, supra note 8 (lease of airplanes with option to purchase recharacterized as immediate sale); M&W Gear Co. v. CIR, 446 F2d 841 (7th Cir. 1971) (combination of high "rent" and low option price, compared with value of property, supports Tax Court conclusion that purported lease with option to purchase was a sale).

the property, any option to purchase usually requires payment of the anticipated value of the property at exercise. In this situation, the rent paid by the lessee does not build up an equity, and, when the lease is executed, there is no reason to expect the lessee to exercise the option rather than to let it expire. Conversely, the lessor cannot expect to be better off if the lease option expires, permitting him to offer the property on the market, than if the lessee decides to exercise it. For these reasons a lease of this type should be treated as such; the lessee becomes a purchaser only if and when the option is exercised.

On the other hand, lease provisions other than purchase options sometimes point in the direction of sale treatment. Assume a lease provides rents over an initial lease term in amounts equal to the principal and interest payments that would be required in an installment sale, and allows the lessee to renew at nominal rents for an additional term that runs through the remainder of the property's expected economic life. The renewal option in this case is like a purchase option; it is the means for the lessee to hold on to an equity built up by high rents during the initial lease term, and because the lessee is unlikely to let this equity go, the option effectively limits the lessor's interest to a right to a series of payments. The lease is properly classified as a credit sale.[12] Similarly, sale treatment might be appropriate if a lease runs for a single term at a level rent but the lease term extends throughout the property's economic life.[13]

---

[12] See Rev. Rul. 55-540, supra note 8, at §4.06:

> If the sum of the specified "rentals" over a relatively short part of the expected useful life of the equipment approximates the price at which the equipment could have been acquired by purchase at the time of entering into the agreement, plus interest and/or carrying charges on such amount, and the lessee may continue to use the equipment for an additional period or periods approximating its remaining estimated useful life for relatively nominal or token payments, it may be assumed that the parties have entered into a sale contract, even though a passage of title is not expressly provided in the agreement.

See also Starr's Est. v. CIR, 274 F2d 294 (9th Cir. 1959) (purported lease of sprinkler system treated as sale; although even nominal rents ceased before end of economic useful life, lessor would get nothing but junk if it exercised right to remove system at end of lease term); Rev. Rul. 57-371, 1957-2 CB 214 (same); Rev. Rul. 55-541, 1955-2 CB 19 (lease of office equipment requiring very high rental payments during first 3 years and low payments during subsequent 10 years for use of equipment with estimated useful life of 10 to 15 years; treated as sale); Rev. Rul. 55-542, 1955-2 CB 59 (similar arrangement, under which title will pass to lessee at end of rental period upon payment of then depreciated value of equipment; treated as sale).
[13] See Rev. Rul. 60-122, 1960-1 CB 56 (contrasting two "leases" of business equipment by reference to the relationship between term of contract and anticipated useful life of property).

The slightly different twist on the issue is seen in *Swift Dodge v. CIR*.[14] The taxpayer, a car dealer, leased automobiles under 36-month leases containing a so-called terminal adjustment clause. Under this clause, the lessee was required to make a final payment on the expiration of the lease equal to the excess of a depreciated value stated in the lease over the actual wholesale value of the car at that time. Conversely, the taxpayer was required to pay the lessee an amount equal to any excess of the actual value over the stated depreciated value.[15] The leases were net leases that placed on the lessees all maintenance and insurance costs. The court found that leases shifted to the lessees all substantial benefits and burdens of ownership, including (by reason of the terminal adjustment clause) the risk of depreciation "at a rate greater than expected."[16] The only risk the taxpayer retained was "the risk of default," which is the "risk that would be assumed by the holder of a security interest in a conditional sale."[17] The court denied the investment credit, which the taxpayer had claimed as owner of the cars.[18]

¶4.4.3 Leveraged Leases and Other Multiple Party Transactions Involving Leases

In recent years, leasing transactions heavily financed with borrowed money have frequently come before the courts. Many of these leveraged leases are made in sale-leaseback transactions. In some of the transactions, the putative owner-lessor has concededly made an investment of some sort, and the issue is whether the investment is as true owner of the property or as a provider of financing to the lessee, who is the owner in substance. In other cases, the IRS takes the position that the investment is nothing more than an attempted purchase of tax benefits. The issue in these cases should probably be the same as that mooted in the sale vs. lease cases: Does the putative owner-lessor possess the benefits and burdens of ownership to any meaningful extent? The fact of there being multiple parties to the transactions, however, has cast these cases in a different and perhaps confusing light.

The relevance of the presence of multiple parties was first suggested by the Supreme Court in *Frank Lyon Co. v. US*, which involved the construc-

---

[14] Swift Dodge v. CIR, 692 F2d 651 (9th Cir. 1982).

[15] It was the taxpayer's practice to sell the car to the lessee in lieu of making the terminal adjustment whenever the lessee so requested.

[16] Swift Dodge v. CIR, supra note 14, at 654.

[17] Id.

[18] See also Leslie Leasing Co. v. CIR, 80 TC 411, 425 (1983) (following *Swift Dodge* in case appealable to same circuit, and leaving "to another day consideration of [Tax Court's own] position" on issue).

tion and financing of a bank building.[19] The bank constructed the building and sold it to the taxpayer, which leased it back to the bank. The taxpayer financed the price with a mortgage from a third party that accounted for all but $500,000 of the $7.6 million purchase price. The lease was initially for 25 years, a period equal to the term of the mortgage, and the rents coincided in time and amount with the mortgage payments. The lessee had a series of options to repurchase the building, each exercisable at a price equal to the outstanding balance on the mortgage plus a sum sufficient to return to the taxpayer its $500,000 investment with interest compounded at 6 percent. If none of the options to repurchase was exercised, the lessee had a series of options to renew the lease for 8 successive 5-year terms at rents sharply reduced from the initial 25-year term; the renewal rents, like the repurchase option prices, were calculated to return the taxpayer's $500,000 investment plus interest compounded at 6 percent. The lease was a net lease obligating the bank to bear real property taxes and the costs of maintaining and insuring the building.

The government contended that the taxpayer merely provided financing for the building, and had no ownership interest. During the primary 25-year term of the lease, the taxpayer was little more than a conduit between the bank and the mortgagee; apart from taxes, its cash flow was zero. The lessee's options to purchase the building or extend the lease term assured the bank of possession of the building for at least 65 years and effectively limited the taxpayer's financial interest to a recovery of its outlay with 6 percent interest.[20] The taxpayer's position, the government argued, most nearly resembled that of the holder of a second mortgage.[21]

The Court disagreed. It reaffirmed its historical refusal "to permit the transfer of formal legal title to shift the incidence of taxation attributable to ownership of property where the transferor continues to retain significant

---

[19] Frank Lyon Co. v. US, 435 US 561 (1978).

[20] The likelihood of exercise of the purchase or renewal options was increased by two facts. First, the bank constructed the property immediately before the sale to the taxpayer at a cost exceeding $10 million. The bank's costs thus exceeded the $7.6 million price received from the taxpayer by about $2.4 million, and the options were the means by which the bank reserved its $2.4 million equity in the building. Also, the building was specially constructed for use as the bank's headquarters.

[21] Other factors supporting this argument: (1) In the event of a destruction or condemnation of the building, the bank was entitled to all insurance or condemnation proceeds, exclusive of the amounts needed to repay the mortgage and allow the taxpayer recovery of its $500,000 with 6 percent interest; (2) the taxpayer's president was a member of the bank's board of directors; and (3) the structure of the transaction provided the taxpayer with substantial tax benefits that it could not have enjoyed as a second mortgagor.

control over the property transferred."[22] The taxpayer's legal title to the building, however, was found to have substance. The Court found significance in the fact that the transaction involved three parties: the taxpayer-lessor, the lessee, and the mortgage lenders who financed the taxpayer's purchase of the building.[23] Because the taxpayer was liable on the mortgage, its risk of loss was not limited to the loss of its investment, as would have been the case if the taxpayer had been a second mortgage lender. Also, the transaction was structured as a sale and leaseback because banking regulations precluded the bank from making a large investment in a building; tax considerations seemed not to be at the heart of the business plan.[24] Finally, the transaction was negotiated at arm's length, and the taxpayer competed in the transaction against other bidders. In sum:

> [W]here, as here, there is a genuine multiple-party transaction with economic substance which is compelled or encouraged by business or regulatory realities, is imbued with tax-independent considerations, and is not shaped solely by tax avoidance features that have meaningless labels attached, the Government should honor the allocation of rights and duties effectuated by the parties.[25]

---

[22] Id. at 572–73. Also, "we are not condoning manipulation by a taxpayer through arbitrary labels and dealings that have no economic significance." Id. at 583.

[23] On this ground, the Court distinguished its earlier opinion in Helvering v. Lazarus & Co., 308 US 252 (1939), where a taxpayer was held to have retained tax ownership of three buildings, notwithstanding its sale of the property to a trust that leased the buildings back to the taxpayer for 99 years. Lazarus "is to be distinguished" from Lyon, the court held, because the "transaction was one involving only two (and not multiple) parties." Frank Lyon Co. v. US, supra note 19, at 575.

See Bussing v. CIR, 88 TC 449, 458 (1987) (although under Frank Lyon "a genuine multiple-party transaction" is not a sham, this rule does not apply if one of the parties is not a real participant in the deal but is inserted to take advantage of the rule).

[24] The Court refers to "the absence of any differential in tax rates and of special tax circumstances for one of the parties," and distinguishes the case from situations "in which the form of the transaction actually created tax advantages that, for one reason or another, could not have been enjoyed had the transaction taken another form." Frank Lyon Co. v. US, supra note 19, at 583 n.18. This apparently means that so far as the evidence showed, the taxpayer realized no greater tax benefits from its ownership of the building than the bank would have realized if the transaction had been structured to make it the owner. That tax benefits might have been an important incentive for the taxpayer to enter into the transaction is not important, the Court seems to say, if the fisc would have yielded as much tax revenue to another party had the transaction taken a different form. See id. at 580 n.15.

[25] Id. at 583–84. But see Illinois Power Co. v. CIR, 87 TC 1417, 1442 (1986) (sale-leaseback of nuclear fuel treated as financing arrangement where (1) taxpayer (seller-lessee) consistently followed this treatment in tax returns and other financial reports, (2) taxpayer's use rights under the lease extended throughout useful life of the fuel and, during this time, taxpayer "bore significant burdens, risks, and respon-

In *Rice's Toyota World, Inc. v. CIR*, the *Frank Lyon* decision was read to require a threshold determination of whether a leveraged lease transaction is a sham and to establish this test: "To treat a transaction as a sham, the court must find that the taxpayer was motivated by no business purpose other than obtaining tax benefits in entering the transaction, and that the transaction has no economic substance because no reasonable possibility of a profit exists."[26] The taxpayer in *Rice's Toyota World* was an automobile dealer that entered into a sale-leaseback transaction involving a computer. The taxpayer bought the computer from a leasing company for about $1.5 million; $250,000 was paid in cash and by a three-year recourse note, and the remainder was payable under an eight-year nonrecourse note. The computer was immediately leased back to the leasing company for eight years, and a sublease was immediately made to a computer user. The rents receivable by the taxpayer exceeded the debt service on the nonrecourse note to the leasing company by only $10,000 each year. The taxpayer thus had to look primarily to the residual value of the computer at the end of the eight-year lease period for a recovery of its $250,000 out-of-pocket cost and for its economic profit.

The court held the taxpayer failed the first prong of the sham test — the business purpose inquiry — because (1) no serious investigation was made of whether the computer's value after eight years could be expected to be large enough to yield the taxpayer a profit and (2) the price paid by the taxpayer was inflated (approximately 160 percent of what the leasing company paid shortly before the transaction with the taxpayer) and was financed largely with nonrecourse debt. The second prong of the test — whether, objectively, there was a reasonable possibility of profit — was also failed, the court decided.

The court concluded that the taxpayer "did not purchase or lease a computer, but rather, paid a fee . . . for tax benefits."[27] The taxpayer was denied deductions for depreciation on the computer and for interest on the nonrecourse note that purportedly financed the taxpayer's purchase. The taxpayer was, however, allowed to deduct interest on deferred payments of its $250,000 cash investment in the property. Because the taxpayer's obligation to make these payments was with recourse, it could not "walk away

---

sibilities for the . . . fuel," (3) lease payments merely covered buyer-lessor's payments on debt incurred to finance its purchase, and (4) taxpayer had right to purchase fuel for amount determined with reference to buyer-lessor's cost rather than current market value).

[26] Rice's Toyota World, Inc. v. CIR, 752 F2d 89, 91 (4th Cir. 1985). See also Torres v. CIR, 88 TC 702, 718 (1987) ("a finding of lack of economic substance is inappropriate if either a business purpose or a reasonable possibility of profit apart from expected tax benefits is found to have been present").

[27] Rice's Toyota World, Inc. v. CIR, supra note 26, at 95.

without liability," and the obligation was real. "Under *Frank Lyon*, the court may not ignore transactions that have economic substance even if the motive for the transaction is to avoid taxes."[28] Because no purchase occurred in substance, however, no depreciable basis was acquired by taking on this obligation.[29]

The sham test is only a threshold inquiry; even if a leveraged lease transaction has economic substance, it is effective to provide the buyer-lessor with the tax benefits of ownership (primarily depreciation and interest deductions) only if it conveys the substance of ownership of the property. A person is owner for tax purposes if he possesses the benefits and burdens of ownership. Some of the factors relevant in applying this test to a sale-leaseback are:

> (1) The existence of useful life of the property in excess of the leaseback term; (2) the existence of a purchase option at less than fair market value; (3) renewal rental at the end of the leaseback term set at fair market rent; and (4) the reasonable possibility that the purported owner of the property can recoup his investment in the property from

---

[28] Id. at 96.

[29] See also Gefen v. CIR, 87 TC 1471, 1490 (1986) (partnership that made leveraged purchase and lease of computers held to be owner of computers because residual value of computers offered "a reasonable opportunity for economic profit, that is, profit exclusive of tax benefits"; "that a transaction generates tax benefits for investors does not necessarily mean that the transaction lacks economic substance"); Durkin v. CIR, 87 TC 1329, 1369 (1986) (partnerships purported to purchase motion pictures in heavily leveraged deals and licensed them back to the producer; held, partnerships did not acquire ownership of motion pictures because the "rights and liabilities commonly associated with ownership" stayed with producer; partnerships, however, acquired contractual rights to cash flows from the films, and these rights are depreciable property); Mukerji v. CIR, 87 TC 926, 967 (1986) (buyer-lessor in sale-leaseback of computers held to be owner in substance because (1) price paid did not exceed fair market value, (2) taxpayer's decision to invest based on realistic projections of economic profit, and (3) taxpayers "retained the significant benefits and burdens of ownership"); James v. CIR, 87 TC 905 (1986) (taxpayers had no interest in property they purportedly purchased where (1) purported seller to taxpayers had purchased the property, arranged financing, and leased the property, (2) taxpayers purchased subject to financing and leases arranged by seller, (3) seller acted as taxpayers' agent in collecting rents, making payments on debt, managing property, and selling it on the conclusion of leases, and (4) possibility of taxpayers realizing a profit from their investments was remote); Coleman v. CIR, 87 TC 178 (1986) (that buyer-lessor in heavily leveraged transaction did not have legal title established prima facie that it was not owner for tax purposes; taxpayers could overcome this prima facie case only with strong proof of ownership in substance; strong proof found lacking because (1) lease was net lease that placed maintenance responsibilities on lessee, (2) rents were assigned without recourse to lender that financed transaction, and (3) buyer-lessor generally did not have normal burdens and benefits of ownership).

the income producing potential and residual value of the property.[30]

If the taxpayer purchases property from one person and leases it to another, the purchase and lease might both be scrutinized, asking the questions, "Did the taxpayer become the owner in substance by the purported purchase, and, if so, did the taxpayer divest himself of ownership by the lease?"[31]

In 1975, the IRS announced a set of special guidelines applicable to taxpayers requesting an advance ruling on the tax status of leveraged lease transactions. To qualify for a favorable ruling, (1) the lessor must make and maintain a minimum unconditional "at risk" investment in the property of 20 percent of its cost; (2) the lessee may not furnish any of the cost of the property; (3) the lessee may not have a contractual right to purchase the property from the lessor for less than its fair market value when the right is exercised; and (4) the lessor must establish that it expects to realize a profit from the transaction, aside from the value of its tax benefits.[32] On meeting these requirements and certain other conditions, taxpayers will ordinarily receive favorable rulings; but a failure to satisfy the guidelines will not preclude a favorable ruling "in appropriate cases on the basis of all the facts and circumstances," nor are the standards intended to describe the legal principles governing whether a transaction is or is not a lease or to be used for audit purposes.[33]

¶4.4.4 "Tax Polarity" — Reallocation of Lump-Sum Sales Prices

A lump-sum sales price for a bundle of assets must usually be allocated among the assets.[34] The seller needs the allocation because gain or loss must be computed separately for each item. Also, the buyer must determine the cost of each item in order to compute depreciation and gain or loss on subsequent sales of the individual items. If the buyer and seller bargain separately for each item,[35] so that the aggregate amount paid is merely the sum of the separate prices — like the total on a supermarket cash register

---

[30] Torres v. CIR, 88 TC 702, 721 (1987).

[31] See Cooper v. CIR, 88 TC 84 (1987).

[32] Rev. Proc. 75-21, 1975-1 CB 715; Rev. Proc. 75-28, 1975-1 CB 752; see also Rev. Proc. 76-30, 1976-2 CB 647 (no ruling if property is not expected to be useful at end of lease's term except to the lessee); Javaras & Nelson, The New Leveraged Lease Guidelines, 53 Taxes 388 (1975).

[33] Rev. Proc. 75-21, 1975-1 CB 715, §3.

[34] See infra ¶¶41.8.1, 51.9.

[35] For the use of sealed bids to establish separate arm's-length prices for assets that would normally be sold in tandem by simulating an auction market, see Marx v. CIR, 29 TC 88 (1957) (acq.) (sealed bids required by Groucho Marx to distinguish compensation for personal services from payment for literary properties).

tape—the aggregate can be accurately allocated back to its separate components. Even if the parties deal on an all-or-nothing basis, an equally accurate allocation is possible if the items have readily ascertainable market values. The process however, of allocating a lump sum among its components turns from an exact science to a vague art, or even to guesswork, if the property consists of a going business, some of whose constituent items are difficult to value and would not have been sold in isolation, such as real estate, specialized equipment, goodwill, covenants not to compete, patents, industrial know-how, and franchises.

Knowing that they both must allocate the aggregate amount paid among the separate assets for tax purposes, the buyer and seller may seek to avoid future arguments with the IRS by agreeing on an allocation at the time of the sale.[36] Such an allocation may have some nontax consequences; for example, it may affect the damages to be paid if a particular asset is misrepresented or if the seller breaches a covenant not to compete. Nontax consequences of this type help to establish the validity of the allocation, unless they are too speculative to deserve attention. But an allocation of a lump-sum sales price does not become sacrosanct simply because it may affect nontax rights of the parties.

It is sometimes asserted that because buyer and seller often have opposing tax interests in allocating a lump-sum payment, self-interest frequently evokes an accurate breakdown of a sales price among constituent items. A typical expression of this theory is: "The tax avoidance desires of the buyer and seller in such a situation are ordinarily antithetical, forcing them, in most cases, to agree upon a treatment which reflects the parties' true intent with reference to the covenants, and the true value of them in money."[37]

This tax polarity theory can be illustrated as follows: Assume a sale is made for $100 of a going business consisting of depreciable equipment (value, $60; basis, $10) and goodwill (value, $40; basis, zero); the selling price is payable in installments over 10 years. If the original cost of the equipment substantially exceeds its current value, the parties' tax interests are adverse.[38]

---

[36] For the principles to be applied in the absence of an allocation by the parties in their agreement, see infra ¶41.7.

[37] Ullman v. CIR, 264 F2d 305, 308 (2d Cir. 1959) (allocation of lump-sum amount between stock and covenant not to compete). See also Balthrope v. CIR, 356 F2d 28, 32 (5th Cir. 1966) (tax polarity is "a solid barrier to unrealistic allocations"); Reg. §1.1245-1(a)(5) ("in general, if a buyer and seller have adverse interests as to the allocation of the amount realized [on a sale of two or more assets] between the section 1245 property and the non-section 1245 property, any arm's length agreement between the buyer and the seller will establish the allocation").

[38] The interests of buyer and seller in the allocation were more widely adverse before the elimination in 1986 of the preferential rate for long-term capital gains. For

The seller can generally report the sale on the installment method, a method that defers the tax on gain allocated to deferred payments and thereby reduces the present value of the tax.[39] Depreciation recapture, however, must be reported in the year of sale, regardless of when the selling price of depreciable assets is payable,[40] and all of the seller's gain on the equipment is recapture income.[41] The present value of the seller's tax on the gain on the sale is thus minimized by allocating the largest possible portion of the lump-sum selling price to goodwill since each dollar allocated to goodwill rather than equipment is gain taxable in the future, whereas the incremental allocation to equipment is taxed in the year of sale.

If the buyer intends to operate the business indefinitely, in contrast, it prefers to tilt the allocation toward the equipment. The buyer's cost for the equipment is recovered through depreciation deductions, probably over a period not in excess of seven years.[42] Goodwill, in contrast, is not depreciable, and no tax allowance for its cost is permitted until the goodwill is sold or lost. Because depreciation on the equipment produces a tax benefit over a relatively brief period, beginning immediately, whereas no tax benefit flows in the foreseeable future from the cost of goodwill, the present value of the buyer's tax liabilities are reduced by maximizing the allocation of purchase price to equipment.

It does not follow, however, that this opposition of interests must necessarily be resolved by the parties agreeing to allocate the price according to their best estimates of fair market value. The advantage to the seller

---

years in which a capital gains rate preference is allowed, the parties' positions are as follows: Sellers want to tilt the allocation in favor of capital assets and away from assets on which the gain is ordinary income. Buyers want the allocation to favor assets whose costs can be written off quickly (inventory and depreciable equipment, for example), rather than assets whose costs stay on the books indefinitely (goodwill and land, for example). Most often, however, assets of the latter sort yield capital gain for the seller, and many of the assets whose costs are quickly expensed produce ordinary income for the seller. Similarly, an amount allocated to a covenant not to compete is deductible by the buyer over the period of the restraint on competition, but is ordinary income to the seller. For the distinction between capital gains and ordinary income, see infra Chapters 51-55. See generally Beghe, Income Tax Treatment of Covenants Not to Compete, Consulting Agreements and Transfers of Goodwill, 30 Tax Lawyer 587 (1977); Stansbury, Advising Clients on Tax Treatment of Goodwill v. Covenant-Not-to-Compete Issue, 45 J. Tax'n 208 (1976).

[39] See infra ¶106.2.

[40] IRC §453(i).

[41] Generally, the recapture gain is (1) the lesser of the original cost or selling price of depreciable property, reduced by (2) the property's adjusted basis. See infra ¶55.1. In the example, it is assumed that the original cost of the depreciable property is far in excess of the property's current value, and the recapture gain is thus the excess of the selling price for the equipment over its adjusted basis, which is to say that all of the gain on the depreciable property is recapture income.

[42] See infra ¶23.1.

from an allocation in favor of goodwill (gain reported as payments received, rather than in year of sale) may be less than the disadvantage of such an allocation to the seller (indefinite deferral of cost write-off). If this is so, the parties might both gain by favoring equipment in the allocation and increasing the price to compensate the seller for the resulting acceleration of the taxation of a larger portion of its gain. That is, an increased allocation to equipment might decrease the present value of the aggregate of the parties' tax liabilities; although the present value of the seller's taxes would increase, the present value of the buyer's taxes would decline even more, making it possible for the buyer to make up the seller's loss through an increase in purchase price and still be ahead. The parties' gain comes completely at the Treasury's expense, but it is possible only if they are assured that their allocation will control for tax purposes. Without this assurance, the buyer should be reluctant to pay for the seller's agreement to an increased allocation to equipment because the parties cannot be sure this agreement is worth anything.

The potential tax savings through tax motivated allocations is increased if the parties are taxed at different rates. In the example, it is assumed that seller and buyer are both taxed at a single rate on all income and that the opportunity for maneuvering is only with respect to the timing of tax liabilities. If one of the parties is taxed at a lesser rate, a propitious allocation can reduce the absolute dollar amount of the parties' aggregate tax burden. If the seller is tax exempt,[43] for example, it suffers no tax cost in agreeing to any allocation the buyer might propose; although it might demand an increased price as a means of sharing the buyer's gains from a favorable allocation, the buyer can afford to acquiesce if the parties are assured the agreement will be given tax effect because only the fisc loses.

Occasionally, an allocation is fictitious to the point of fraud, as illustrated by the following anecdote by Randolph Paul:

> It is easy to give illustrations of prevailing techniques of misrepresentation. One favorite device is to put a transaction into two contracts, one of which is to be shown to the government's representatives, and the other of which is to be kept secret. This happened once in my experience in connection with a sale of stock to a buyer for about $5 million. Since the buyer had an option on the stock of about $3 million, it was obvious that $2 million was being paid for an agreement not to compete. A payment for this covenant would have been ordinary income and not capital gain. The seller insisted that this transaction be put in two documents, one which would recite the sale of stock for $5

---

[43] The seller might be an organization that is explicitly exempt from tax (a charity, for example) or it might be effectively exempted by the availability of net operating loss deductions that would otherwise go unused.

million, and the other of which would provide against competition without mentioning any consideration. I felt obliged to refuse to be an adviser in this transaction. As a result, my client, who had reluctantly agreed because of anxiety to procure the stock, went to another attorney who was willing to let the client do what the seller wished. The client never came to me with his subsequent problems.[44]

For these reasons, it should occasion no surprise that agreed on allocations of a lump-sum payment are often subjected to administrative and judicial scrutiny rather than accepted at face value. If the allocation has nontax consequences of significance, they should, of course, count in its favor; and, within limits, so should the opposing tax interests of the parties if they have not ganged up on the IRS. On the other hand, the courts are as willing to revise an egregious allocation in order to bring it into harmony with economic reality as they are, in appropriate circumstances, to restructure any of the other transactions herein discussed.

¶4.4.5　Role of the Parol Evidence Rule

The parol evidence rule is only a shadow of its former self in the contemporary law of contracts,[45] but it is frequently imported into the tax area by taxpayers hoping to bar the restructuring of a transaction or by the IRS as a defense against a taxpayer's effort to escape from the language of a written agreement. Although these attempts are almost invariably unsuccessful, they recur with such regularity as to justify a more fundamental examination of the parol evidence rule's function than is ordinarily found in tax decisions. Corbin summarizes the rule as follows:

> When two parties have made a contract and have expressed it in a writing to which they have both assented as the complete and accurate integration of that contract, evidence, whether parol or otherwise, of antecedent understandings and negotiations will not be admitted for the purpose of varying or contradicting the writing.[46]

---

[44] Paul, The Lawyer as a Tax Adviser, 25 Rocky Mtn. L. Rev. 412, 421 (1953); infra ¶51.9.

[45] See Sweet, Contract Making and Parol Evidence: Diagnosis and Treatment of a Sick Rule, 53 Cornell LQ 1036 (1968); see also Calamari & Perillo, The Law of Contracts 97–131 (West, 2d ed. 1977); Murray, Murray on Contracts 225–30 (Bobbs-Merrill, 2d rev. ed. 1974).

[46] Corbin on Contracts §573 (West 1960). See also Restatement (Second) of Contracts §239 (1979); 4 Williston on Contracts §631 (Jaeger, ed.; Voorhis, 3d ed. 1961).

The parol evidence rule has been described as a legal concept "whose mysteries are familiar to many but fathomed by few,"[47] but it is quite obvious that written agreements are rarely, if ever, restructured for federal tax purposes in order to reinstate a prior, inconsistent understanding between the parties. The issue of whether a purported lease should be treated for tax purposes as a sale, for example, is determined from the terms of the parties' agreement as written rather than from prior negotiations or understandings.[48]

This is not to suggest that prior discussions are irrelevant in determining whether an agreement should be restructured. On the contrary, if a purported lease with an option to purchase was preceded by an oral offer to purchase or sell the property, for example, the bid or asked price can help to establish whether "the total of the rental payments and any option price payable in addition thereto approximates the price at which the equipment could have been acquired by purchase at the time of entering the agreement, plus interest and/or carrying charges," which generally denotes a sale.[49] The unaccepted offer to purchase or sell the property is evidence—indeed, it may be the best evidence—of the equipment's normal sale price; but since the evidence is not used to vary or contradict the obligations of the parties under any subsequent written agreement, the parol evidence rule is not contravened.[50]

Misdirected efforts at using the parol evidence rule to avoid restructurings should be distinguished from other situations in which the rule is more pertinent. When the federal income tax consequences of a transaction turn on a taxpayer's rights and duties under a written contract whose meaning is disputed, the taxpayer or the IRS may offer evidence of prior negotiations or understandings between the parties in order to clarify or alter the meaning of the contract or to establish that it was not intended to be enforced. Since what is ordinarily at stake in these cases is the legal effect of the agreement under state law,[51] the proffered evidence is relevant only if it affects the rights and duties of the parties. Thus, it is necessary to determine whether the parol evidence rule (which, despite its label, is a rule of substantive law rather than a rule of evidence) would, under the law of the appropriate state, permit or bar this use of the preagreement discussions.[52]

---

[47] Murray, supra note 45, at 226.

[48] See supra ¶4.4.2.

[49] Rev. Rul. 55-540, 1955-2 CB 39, at §4.05.

[50] See Taft v. CIR, 27 BTA 808 (1933) (unequivocal offer to purchase property used to determine substance of transaction; purported lease treated as sale).

[51] See generally supra ¶4.1.

[52] For an excellent discussion, see Craft's Est. v. CIR, 68 TC 249 (1977), aff'd per curiam, 608 F2d 240 (5th Cir. 1979) (concurring Tax Court opinion appropriately distinguishes situations in which a tax provision turns on actual behavior rather

It is sometimes suggested that the IRS, being "a stranger to the contract,"[53] is not bound by, and cannot invoke, the parol evidence rule. Neither of these notions is well founded if the issue is the legal effect of the written agreement on the private parties who executed it. In this situation, the IRS should have the same power that the parties have to resort to their prior understandings to clarify the scope or meaning of the agreement as executed. In this connection, the contemporary trend in the law of contracts, which may or may not prevail in a particular state, is to enlarge these sources of enlightenment rather than restrict them.[54]

¶4.4.6   Attempts by Taxpayers to Restructure Transactions

If the IRS is content to accept a transaction at face value, can one of the parties take the initiative and demand that it be restructured to conform to economic reality? As pointed out earlier in this work, the courts have vacillated between (1) allowing taxpayers to invoke the substance-over-form, business purpose, and step transaction doctrines as freely as the IRS and (2) letting them stew in their own juice if that appeals to the government's appetite.[55] On the whole, however, the courts tend to apply the two-way-street approach when taxpayers endeavor to restructure a transaction to conform to its substance.

This tolerance may reflect a judicial feeling that the issue in most restructuring cases is the legal category to which the transaction belongs; that its classification should not depend on the labels used by the parties, even if they were deliberately chosen for their emotive effect; and that the words of the contract are not a representation of facts, giving rise to an estoppel, but only a statement of opinion about the transaction's legal status, which should not induce reliance by the IRS. In at least one area— attempts by a taxpayer to establish that a sale-leaseback or similar transaction was tantamount to a mortgage—there is a long commonlaw tradition, rooted in prohibitions on usury, allowing borrowers to disavow the form of an agreement, even if deliberately chosen.[56] Although it might be argued that revenue agents should be allowed to rely on the labels chosen by taxpayers

---

than on the extent of the taxpayer's rights under state law). See also Clark v. US, 341 F2d 691 (9th Cir. 1965) (taxpayer not allowed to introduce parol evidence to contradict integrated contract, where tax results depended on its legal effect). For other illustrations of the problem, which are less thoroughly analyzed, see Sullivan v. US, 363 F2d 724 (8th Cir. 1966), cert. denied, 387 US 905 (1967) (effect of stock purchase agreement) and cases there cited.

[53] See, e.g., Sullivan v. US, supra note 52.

[54] See supra note 45.

[55] See supra ¶4.3.6.

[56] See Helvering v. F. & R. Lazarus & Co., 308 US 252 (1939).

in order to expedite tax administration, the principal IRS ruling on the sale versus lease issue establishes standards that can evidently be invoked by taxpayers to establish that a purported lease is a sale.[57] While delay and inefficiency may result from allowing taxpayers to repudiate the form in which they chose to cloak a transaction, this ruling implies that the administrative cost is not excessive.

A burgeoning exception to these principles, however, has developed with respect to agreed on allocations of the sales price in contracts for the sale of a going business or the stock of an incorporated enterprise, when accompanied by a covenant not to compete. If the IRS chooses to hold the parties to the allocation, it is ordinarily allowed to do so unless the taxpayer establishes that the allocation is fictitious by greater proof than is required in run-of-the-mine tax cases. As usually formulated, this heavier burden requires "strong proof" by the taxpayer.[58] The Court of Appeals for the Third Circuit has escalated the standard to the level required to vary the terms of a written contract under common law—proof that the allocation was induced by mistake, fraud, duress, or undue influence,[59] and several other courts have followed suit.[60]

These decisions have given several reasons for imposing an abnormal burden of proof on taxpayers seeking to disavow an allocation: the tax polarity of the parties; the possibility of denying a bargained-for tax advantage to the taxpayer's opposite number; the administrative burden imposed on the IRS, which may have to litigate with both taxpayers and may be

---

[57] See, e.g., Rev. Rul. 55-540, 1955-2 CB 39.

[58] Montesi v. CIR, 340 F2d 97 (6th Cir. 1965); Ullman v. CIR, 264 F2d 305 (2d Cir. 1959). See Peterson Mach. Tool, Inc. v. CIR, 79 TC 72 (1982) (strong proof rule not applicable when parties to contract seek not to vary its terms but to construe ambiguous term favorably to their respective causes).

[59] CIR v. Danielson, 378 F2d 771 (3d Cir.) (4 to 3 decision), cert. denied, 389 US 858 (1967). See Koff, Judicial Treatment of Covenants Not to Compete: The Third Circuit Takes a Giant Step, 24 Tax L. Rev. 513 (1969).

[60] Schatten v. US, 746 F2d 319 (6th Cir. 1984) (applying *Danielson* to divorce settlement); Spector v. CIR, 641 F2d 376 (5th Cir. 1981) (applying *Danielson* to agreement for liquidation of partnership interest claimed by departing partner to be in substance a sale); Forward Communications Corp. v. US, 608 F2d 485 (Ct. Cl. 1979); Proulx v. US, 594 F2d 832 (Ct. Cl. 1979) (covenant not to compete found to lack "significant economic reality" but amount allocated thereto by parties controlling under *Danielson* rule); Dakan v. US, 492 F2d 1192 (Ct. Cl. 1974). But see Campbell v. US, 661 F2d 209 (Ct. Cl. 1981) (*Danielson* inapplicable where agreement contained no provision for question involved).

In Freeport Transp., Inc. v. CIR, 63 TC 107, 115 (1974) (acq.), the court refused to apply *Danielson* to a case appealable to the Court of Appeals for the Third Circuit, where both parties were before the Tax Court, because "to do so would produce a wholly incompatible result in two related cases, consolidated on motion by the respondent, for the sole purpose of protecting the revenues."

whipsawed by inconsistent decisions; and the difficulty of placing separate values on items that would not have been sold in isolation.[61] All these factors deserve some weight; except for the last point, however, they are not unique to allocation cases and can be encountered whenever a taxpayer seeks to restructure a two-party transaction. But in ordinary restructuring cases the customary burden of proof that taxpayers must bear when suing to set aside a deficiency or get a refund has evidently been adequate.

The context of the allocation cases is considerably changed by the elimination of the preferential rate for long-term capital gains. For years in which such a preference was allowed (generally, years before 1988), the tax interests of sellers and buyers in the allocations between goodwill and covenants not to compete were opposed. Sellers preferred allocations to goodwill because gain on a sale of goodwill is capital gain, while amounts received for

---

[61] See CIR v. Danielson, supra note 59, at 775 (unjust enrichment to taxpayer because sales price may take into account anticipated tax results of allocation; administrative burden and possible whipsaw of IRS); Ullman v. CIR, supra note 58 ("antithetical" tax interests of buyer and seller tend to induce allocations based on "true value"). In UMCO Corp. v. CIR, 32 TCM (CCH) 1009 (1973), the Tax Court treated the strong proof rule as a corollary of the tax polarity (supra ¶4.4.4) thought to be typical of transactions involving goodwill and covenants not to compete, observing: "Whether such a rule would be applied in situations other than the covenant not to compete-goodwill allocation cases where conflicting tax interests exist need not be decided here, for in this case there is no showing of any such tax conflict."

On the extent to which taxpayers' efforts to control the tax results of a transaction should be controlling, see Bennett v. CIR, 58 TC 381, 389 (1972) (acq.):

> Respondent [the IRS] also urges that Jones [the other contracting party] would not have assented to the transaction if [the taxpayer] had not agreed to allow it to take the form of a purchase of the stock from him and, on this ground, insists that we are precluded from holding that the arrangement was a redemption from Jones. However, in any transaction where the form differs from the substance, such difference is presumably dictated by someone who has the power to change the natural form of the transaction. The fact that the one causing such a change has the power to prevent the transaction from occurring in any other way is not sufficient, in itself, to show that the form chosen reflects the substance of the transaction.

See also Bartels v. Birmingham, 332 US 126 (1947); Robinson v. Elliot, 262 F2d 383, 385 (9th Cir. 1958) (lease with option to purchase held to be a sale, as contended by seller; as to impact of this decision on the lessee-purchaser, when such a party hopes to save taxes, he "will just have to take a gamble that his legal format will stick").

For concern with the administrative burden on the IRS, see Leisure Dynamics, Inc. v. CIR, 494 F2d 1340, 1348 (8th Cir. 1974) (dissenting opinion). For stress on valuation difficulties, see Amerada Hess Corp. v. CIR, 517 F2d 75, 85 (3d Cir.), cert. denied, 423 US 1037 (1975) (*only* the parties to [a covenant not to compete] could value it; there exists no outside valuation index"); Schulz v. CIR, 294 F2d 52, 55 (9th Cir. 1961) ("impossible task of assigning fair values to good will and to covenants").

a covenant not to compete are ordinary income. Buyers, in contrast, prefer allocations to covenants not to compete because amounts so allocated can be written off over the period covered by the covenant, whereas the cost of goodwill is not depreciable and produces no tax benefit until the goodwill is sold or lost. For years in which capital gains and ordinary income are taxed at the same rate, many sellers are indifferent about capital gains or ordinary income, and hence have no tax stake in the allocation between goodwill and covenants not to compete;[62] the preference of buyers for allocations to covenants not to compete continues because it is unrelated to the tax treatment of capital gains.

The absence in many of these cases of a tax incentive for arm's-length bargaining over an allocation changes their complexion and might lead some courts to take a more lenient attitude toward parties renouncing allocation agreements. The tax polarity justification for an elevated standard of proof is inapplicable in such cases. The most common case might become that of a buyer seeking to escape an allocation agreement made without appreciation of its great impact on him and unimportance to the other party.

Sometimes the parties to an agreed allocation buttress it with an explicit agreement to use the same figures in reporting the transaction to the IRS. On violating an implicit commitment to this effect, a buyer was held liable for the legal fees incurred by the seller in successfully defending itself in a resulting tax case.[63] If the allocation had been set aside in the tax case, however, holding the buyer liable for the seller's legal expenses would have smacked of a penalty for properly reporting the transaction. Moreover, a contract designed to discourage a taxpayer from reporting a transaction in accordance with his best judgment when the return is filed, even if it turns out to be wrong, might be viewed as contrary to public policy.

¶4.4.7 Consistency in Restructuring Two-Party Transactions

In theory, when a two-party transaction is restructured or an agreed upon amount is reallocated in accordance with the principles discussed

---

[62] Some sellers continue to want the capital gain produced by allocations to goodwill. A seller with capital losses, for example, prefers capital gain because capital losses generally can only be deducted against capital gains. See infra ¶¶50.2.4, 50.3.2.

[63] Stern & Co. v. State Loan & Fin. Corp., 238 F. Supp. 901 (D. Del. 1965) (applying Pennsylvania law). See also Penn-Ohio Steel Corp. v. Allis-Chalmers Mfg. Co., 28 AD2d 659, 280 NYS2d 679 (1967), aff'd per curiam, 21 NY2d 916, 289 NYS2d 753 (1968) (damage award for giving misleading information to IRS reversed for insufficient evidence); LeFevre, Lentz, Markhus & Price, Problems in Acquiring a Business: A Panel Discussion, 26 NYU Inst. on Fed. Tax'n 815, 821–22 (1968); Note, Tax Consequences of Asset Valuations in Arm's Length Agreements Between Unrelated Parties, 27 Tax L. Rev. 145, 146–47 (1971).

above, the new characterization should apply to all parties. The IRS ordinarily presses for consistency. If a seller disputes an agreed on allocation, for
example, the IRS usually assesses deficiencies against both the parties,[64]
while acknowledging that only one deficiency should be ultimately sustained.[65] This tactic resembles an interpleader action, except that the IRS is
not an indifferent stakeholder of a fixed amount, since the opposing tax
burdens of the private parties are almost never identical. Moreover, unless
the dispute is purely factual, the potential precedential weight of the cases
ordinarily leads the IRS to argue for one outcome rather than the other.

The IRS has no formal administrative tools to compel consistency of
treatment, however, since the two cases, if litigated, may be decided by
different trial and appellate courts. For this reason, the IRS may win, or
lose, both cases. If it wins the first to be litigated, inconsistency can be
avoided by a government concession in the other case. The prospect of
consistency is enhanced if the cases are consolidated in the Tax Court, since
any issues of fact are then likely to be resolved in the same way for both
parties.[66] Unfortunately, harmony is not guaranteed even in this situation;
since each taxpayer has the burden of proof in his own case, one might fail
to convince the judge that a witness is telling the truth, while the other
might simultaneously fail to prove by the requisite standard that the same
witness is mistaken.[67] The prospect of inconsistent findings at the trial level

---

[64] If the IRS neglects to move promptly, and the first taxpayer eventually wins,
the statute of limitations may bar an action against the second contracting party.
Sections 1311–1314, mitigating the effect of the statute of limitations, do not treat
buyers and sellers as "related taxpayers." These provisions do apply, however, with
respect to all tax years of each party separately; thus, if the seller is able to escape
from an agreed allocation, deficiencies if appropriate can be assessed for all of his
earlier years, not merely for open years, in order to insure consistency. See infra
¶113.9.

[65] See Dixie Fin. Co. v. US, 474 F2d 501 (5th Cir. 1973), where the government
won both cases at the trial level (one in the Tax Court and the other in a federal
district court) but announced that if one decision was affirmed, it would accept a
reversal of the other. See also Goodall v. CIR, 391 F2d 775, 782–83 (8th Cir.), cert.
denied, 393 US 829 (1968) (inconsistent deficiencies not improper where ultimate
consistent treatment of alternate taxpayers is intended and determination is not
frivolous); CIR v. Wilshire Holding Corp., 244 F2d 904 (9th Cir. 1956); Goldstein v.
US, 227 F2d 1, 5 (8th Cir. 1955) (quoting IRS commitment to treat other parties
consistently with result in litigated case); Oesterreich v. CIR, 226 F2d 798 (9th Cir.
1955); Fedders Corp. v. CIR, 39 TCM (CCH) 1 (1979), aff'd in unpublished opinion
(3d Cir. 1981), cert. denied, 454 US 862 (1981) (IRS "takes the position of a
stakeholder, leaving it to the Court to resolve the differences between the parties").

[66] See, e.g., Schulz v. CIR, 294 F2d 52, 55 (9th Cir. 1961) (consolidated cases
tried in Tax Court and appealed to same appellate court).

[67] See Drummond v. CIR, 35 TCM (CCH) 243 (1976), aff'd by unpublished
opinion (3d Cir. 1977) ("both parties have the burden of proving that respondent's
determination is erroneous, and respondent's position as stakeholder does not alter

is increased if one case is tried in the Tax Court and the other in a federal district court.[68] Because of the current lack of enforceable safeguards against inconsistent treatment of either the IRS or related parties, legislative measures against "whipsaw" have been actively discussed in recent years.[69]

---

this rule"). For discussion of the burden of proof in consolidated cases, see Freeport Transp., Inc. v. CIR, 63 TC 107 (1974) (acq.).

[68] See Dixie Fin. Co. v. US, supra note 65.

[69] See ABA Tax Section, Final Report of Special Committee on Whipsaw, 30 Tax Lawyer 127 (1976); Lake, The Whipsaw Problem in Federal Tax Controversies, 34 NYU Inst. on Fed. Tax'n 867 (1976). For a general survey, see Plumb, The Problem of Related Taxpayers: A Procedural Study, 66 Harv. L. Rev. 225 (1952).

CHAPTER

5

Income—Basic Definitional Concepts

¶5.1 INTRODUCTORY

Nowhere does the Code define the term "income." Section 61(a), the Code's basic definitional provision, undertakes only the more limited task of defining "gross income," which it describes as "all income from whatever source derived, including (but not limited to)" compensation for services, interest, dividends, gains on sales of property, and several other enumerated items.[1] Thus, §61(a) puts all items that are "income" (and no others) into gross income, but it does not purport to answer the threshold question whether a particular item is income. The House Ways and Means Committee report on the 1954 Code points out that the statutory phrase "all income from whatever source derived" is taken from the Sixteenth Amendment, and states that "the word 'income' is used [by §61(a)] in its constitutional sense."[2] The Senate Finance Committee's report makes a similar reference to the Sixteenth Amendment, and both reports state that the concept of income employed by the 1939 Code is carried forward without change into the 1954 Code.[3] Like the 1954 Code, however, the 1939 Code defined "gross income" but not "income" itself. The same is true of its statutory predecessors as far back as the Revenue Act of 1913, which simply mentioned a few specific items (wages, interest, rent, dividends, and some others), and then added the catchall phrase "and income derived from any

---

[1] See also IRC §6501(e)(1)(A) (special definition of gross income for purposes of extended statute of limitations; discussed infra ¶113.4).

[2] H.R. Rep. No. 1337, 83d Cong., 2d Sess. A18 (1954).

For the origin of the Sixteenth Amendment's term "from whatever source derived," see Department of Justice (Morris et al.), Taxation of Government Bondholders and Employees: The Immunity Rule and the Sixteenth Amendment 120–90 (1939); see also Ketcham, The Sixteenth Amendment (Ph.D. dissertation, U. of Ill. 1924).

[3] S. Rep. No. 1622, 83d Cong., 2d Sess. 68–169 (1954): "Section 61(a) provides that gross income includes 'all income from whatever source derived.' This definition is based upon section 22(a) [of the 1939 Code] in its constitutional sense. It is not intended to change the concept of income that obtains under section 22(a)."

source whatever."[4]

There is no hope, further, of finding an authoritative definition of income in the legislative and public debates that preceded and accompanied ratification of the Sixteenth Amendment; any inferences from these debates "would be as much the produce of judicial creation as the record of a discovered fact."[5] The Sixteenth Amendment did not confer the power to tax income on Congress; that power had existed from the founding of the Republic. Rather, the Sixteenth Amendment served the more limited (although critical) function of permitting Congress to tax individuals on certain types of income (primarily rents, interest, and dividends) without apportioning the tax among the states in proportion to population.[6]

Given this limited mission, the Sixteenth Amendment did not elicit an outpouring of popular or professional views about the meaning of the term income. The only interpretative issue that attracted much attention was whether the amendment would permit Congress to tax interest from state and municipal bonds, a question turning not on the term income but on the phrase "from whatever source derived."[7]

It was obvious enough to everyone that ratification of the Sixteenth Amendment would result in an individual income tax on such major sources as interest, rents, dividends, business profits, wages, salaries, and other compensation for personal services. If an inquisitive legislator, journalist, or man in the street had wondered about the peripheral items that had to be dealt with in later years—stock dividends, cancellation of indebtedness, unlawful receipts, windfalls, compensation for personal injuries, or loss of life—few answers would have been found in the few places where help might have been sought. Dictionary definitions of income were too terse to be helpful, accounting principles were relatively undeveloped in the early years of this century, and there was no consensus among economists.[8]

---

[4] IRC §22(a) (1939); Revenue Act of 1913, §II(B), 38 Stat. 167. The pre-1913 history of federal income taxation is described by Seligman, The Income Tax 430 et seq. (Macmillan, 2d ed. 1914). See also Department of Justice, supra note 2, app.

[5] Rottschaefer, The Concept of Income in Federal Taxation, 13 Minn. L. Rev. 637 (1929). See also Cairns, A Note on Legal Definitions, 36 Colum. L. Rev. 1099, 1100–02 (1936).

[6] See supra ¶1.2.3.

[7] See supra ¶1.2.8.

[8] The Haig-Simons definition of income (see supra ¶3.1.1) now commands widespread allegiance among economists, but it was enunciated by Haig in 1921 and refined by Simons in 1938, long after the Sixteenth Amendment was proposed and ratified. For surveys of economic thought about the concept of income in the nineteenth and early twentieth centuries, see Seligman, supra note 4; Wueller, Concepts of Taxable Income, 53 Pol. Sci. Q. 83, 557 (1938), 54 Pol. Sci. Q. 555 (1939). Seligman was more interested than most economists in the details of income taxation, but the discussion of current issues in his book (at 677–85) is limited to the

Nor was much to be learned from the administrative and judicial history of the prior income tax laws. The Civil War income tax was an avowedly temporary measure that did not give rise to a comprehensive body of experience, the 1894 income tax was aborted by the Supreme Court's decision in the *Pollock* case, and the 1909 corporation income tax had only begun to generate a few justiciable issues when Congress enacted the Revenue Act of 1913. The congressional debate on the Revenue Act of 1913, further, proceeded in important part on the mistaken premises that the power to tax income was derived from the Sixteenth Amendment and that the scope of the term income was a constitutional issue that could not be influenced by congressional action.[9]

It is perhaps just as well that Congress did not essay a comprehensive definition. The rudimentary level of legislative familiarity with the concept of income in 1913 is illustrated by an extended argument in the Senate about the computation of profit on the sale of a horse, which included this illuminating colloquy:

> *Mr. Cummins.* [S]uppose ten years ago I had bought a horse for $900, and this year I had sold him for $1,000, what would I do in the way of making a [tax] return? . . .
>
> *Mr. Williams* [a member of the Senate Finance Committee]. That thousand dollars is a part of the Senator's receipts for this year, and being a part of his receipts, that much will go in as part of his receipts, and from it would be deducted his disbursements and his exemptions and various other things.
>
> *Mr. Cummins.* Would the price I paid for the horse originally be deducted?
>
> *Mr. Williams.* No, because it was not a part of the transactions in that year; but if the Senator turned around and bought another horse that year, it would be deducted . . .

---

treatment of savings, irregular receipts, sales of property, life insurance companies, and a few deductions.

[9] See, e.g., 50 Cong. Rec. 3775 (1913). As pointed out in ¶1.2.3, Congress is vested with broad taxing power by Article I, §8 of the Constitution. The only subjects of taxation that were arguably added by the Sixteenth Amendment (as distinguished from those that were freed of the apportionment obligation) were interest on state and municipal bonds, the salaries of state officials and employees, and the salaries of federal judges. See supra ¶¶1.2.7, 1.2.8. Even if the power to tax income had arisen from the Sixteenth Amendment, Congress would not have been impotent in defining income because it could have chosen to exercise less than all of its power under the amendment by adopting a definition narrower than the constitutional meaning of the term, and even an expansive statutory definition, particularly one enacted contemporaneously with the adoption of the Amendment, probably would have had great influence with courts attempting to divine the constitutional meaning.

Mr. Bristow. Mr. President, I desire to ask a question, and see if I have this matter clear in my mind. As I understood the question of the Senator from Iowa, it was, if he bought a horse ten years ago for $100—

Mr. Cummins. Nine hundred dollars.

Mr. Bristow. And sold it this year for a thousand dollars, whether or not that thousand dollars would be counted as a part of his income for this year, regardless of what he paid for the horse ten years ago. Is that correct?

Mr. Williams. No; I did not say that. It would be a part of his gross receipts for the year, of course, but it may not necessarily be a part of his net receipts, and therefore not a part of his income that is taxable.

Mr. Cummins. But I asked the Senator from Mississippi specifically whether, in the case I put, the price that was originally paid for the horse could be deducted from the price received.

Mr. Williams. The price paid ten years ago? No; of course not. How could it? When a man puts in his return for his income of the previous year in order to be taxed he puts down everything he has received and everything he has paid out, subject to the exemptions and limitations otherwise provided in the bill. Necessarily that is so. To answer the Senator, I want to read the precise language of the provision.[10]

A deliberative assembly so confused about the treatment of a sale of a horse could hardly be expected to devote much attention to the more arcane aspects of the term "income." Indeed, Senator Cummins tried, without success, to strike out even the few items that were specifically named in the act ("salaries, wages, or compensation for personal service of whatever kind and in whatever form paid . . . interest, rent, dividend") on the ground that "the words 'net income' are as comprehensive and as complete as any words that can be found in the English language, and therefore . . . we ought not to imperil or hazard the bill by attempting to emphasize them or to explain them or to enlarge them."[11]

The most important of the early cases on the meaning of income, *Eisner v. Macomber*, concerned the power of Congress to tax a shareholder

---

[10] 50 Cong. Rec. 3775–76 (1913). By contemporary standards, Senator Williams' naivete about the basics of income determination were considerable. Some might argue, however, that he was simply ahead of his time. A system in which a taxpayer "puts down everything he has received and everything he has paid out" (i.e., reports all proceeds from sales and deducts the costs of investments when made) is a consumption tax, not an income tax, but finds favor these days among many in academe and politics. See supra ¶3.7.

[11] Id. at 3846.

on the value of a dividend of common stock paid to her by a corporation whose share capital consisted solely of one class of common stock. The Court held the tax unconstitutional:

> [The stock dividend] does not alter the preexisting proportionate interest of any stockholder or increase the intrinsic value of his holding or of the aggregate holdings of the other stockholders as they stood before. The new certificates simply increase the number of the shares, with consequent dilution of the value of each share. . . .
>
> The essential and controlling fact is that the stockholder has received nothing out of the company's assets for his separate use and benefit; on the contrary, every dollar of his original investment, together with whatever accretions and accumulations have resulted from employment of his money and that of the other stockholders in the business of the company, still remains the property of the company, and subject to business risks which may result in wiping out the entire investment. Having regard to the very truth of the matter, to substance and not to form, he has received nothing that answers the definition of income within the meaning of the Sixteenth Amendment.[12]

In reaching this conclusion, the Supreme Court reaffirmed a definition of income it had previously enunciated in construing the 1909 corporation income tax, but now elevated the definition from the status of statutory construction to constitutional dogma:

> After examining dictionaries in common use . . . we find little to add to the succinct definition adopted in two cases arising under the Corporation Tax Act of 1909 (*Stratton's Independence v. Howbert*, 231 US 399, 415; *Doyle v. Mitchell Bros. Co.*, 247 US 179, 185)—"Income may be defined as the gain derived from capital, from labor, or from both combined," provided it be understood to include profit gained through a sale or conversion of capital assets, to which it was applied in the *Doyle* case (at 183, 185).
>
> Brief as it is, it indicates the characteristic and distinguishing attribute of income essential for a correct solution of the present controversy. The Government, although basing its argument upon the definition as quoted, placed chief emphasis upon the word "gain," which was extended to include a variety of meanings; while the significance of the next three words was either overlooked or misconceived. "*Derived-from-capital*"; the "*gain-derived-from capital*," etc. Here we have the essential matter: *not* a gain *accruing* to capital, not a *growth or increment* of value in the investment; but a gain, a profit, something of

---

[12] Eisner v. Macomber, 252 US 189, 211 (1920), discussed further supra ¶1.2.4.

exchangeable value *proceeding from* the property, *severed from* the capital however invested or employed, and *coming in*, being *"derived,"* —that is, *received* or *drawn by* the recipient (the taxpayer) for his *separate* use, benefit and disposal; *that* is income derived from property. Nothing else answers the description.

The same fundamental conception is clearly set forth in the Sixteenth Amendment—"incomes, *from* whatever *source derived*"—the essential thought being expressed with a conciseness and lucidity entirely in harmony with the form and style of the Constitution.[13]

Once the Court concluded that a stock dividend was not income, it returned to the theory of *Pollock v. Farmers' Loan & Trust Co.*,[14] and held that a tax on "what is called the stockholder's share in the accumulated profits" is a tax on capital and hence is a direct tax that must be apportioned among the states according to population; not being a tax on income, it was not relieved of that constitutional mandate by the Sixteenth Amendment.[15] The Court warned that the Sixteenth Amendment should "not be extended by loose construction, so as to repeal or modify, except as applied to income, those provisions of the Constitution that require an apportionment according to population for direct taxes upon property, real and personal."[16] No attention was devoted to the counter-theory that the receipt of a stock dividend is not an essential feature of property and that a tax on this event should therefore be regarded as an indirect or excise tax to which the rule of apportionment does not apply.[17]

The pedagogic device of italicizing many of the words in the *Eisner v. Macomber* definition of income, coupled with the portentous warning that "nothing else answers the description," imbued this definition with a gravity that caused it to dominate legal thought in this area for decades. Aside from its direct impact on the taxability of stock dividends, a minor issue when viewed in proper perspective,[18] the most important implications of the definition are:

1. That Congress cannot tax as income the increase in net worth enjoyed by a taxpayer as a result of appreciation in the value of assets between the beginning and end of the taxable year because this gain has not yet been "severed" from the taxpayer's capital.[19]

---

[13] Id. at 207–08.

[14] Pollock v. Farmers' Loan & Trust Co., 158 US 601 (1895), discussed supra ¶1.2.1.

[15] Eisner v. Macomber, supra note 12, at 219.

[16] Id. at 206.

[17] See supra ¶1.2.4 note 40.

[18] See infra ¶92.6.1.

[19] See infra ¶5.2.

2. That undistributed corporate earnings cannot be taxed to shareholders because, although they increase the value of each shareholder's stock, they have not been "received . . . for his separate use".[20]
3. That windfalls, payments for personal injuries, gifts, bequests, and similar amounts cannot be taxed as income, because they are not "derived from capital, from labor, or from both combined."[21]

These three corollaries of *Eisner v. Macomber* have not been directly challenged by Congress. As pointed out subsequently in this work, Congress has nibbled around the edges of each one, and judicial decisions subsequent to *Eisner v. Macomber* have undermined it as a foundation for all three.

The decision itself was not unanimous. Mr. Justice Holmes (with Mr. Justice Day's concurrence) responded briefly, but decisively, to the lengthy majority opinion:

I think the word "incomes" in the Sixteenth Amendment should be read in "a sense most obvious to the common understanding at the time of its adoption" . . . For it was for public adoption that it was proposed. . . . The known purpose of this Amendment was to get rid of nice questions as to what might be direct taxes, and I cannot doubt that most people not lawyers would suppose when they voted for it that they put a question like the present to rest.[22]

Mr. Justice Brandeis (with whom Mr. Justice Clarke concurred) dissented at length, describing the financial practices of business corporations to support his conclusion that stock dividends can be the practical equivalent of cash dividends. He also pointed out that partnership income is taxed to the partners in proportion to their interests, even though not distributed to them or otherwise segregated for their individual use. Rejecting the majority's conclusion that undistributed corporate profits cannot be taxed to the shareholders, he noted that "the law finds no difficulty in disregarding the corporate fiction whenever that is deemed necessary to attain a just result."[23] Finally, like Holmes, Brandeis invoked the conception of income held by the man in the street in construing the Sixteenth Amendment:

[20] See supra ¶3.5.6. In a case involving the Civil War income tax, however, the Court had held that corporate profits could be taxed to the shareholders whether distributed or not. Collector v. Hubbard, 79 US (12 Wall.) 1 (1870).

[21] See infra ¶5.5.

[22] Eisner v. Macomber, 252 US 219–20 (1920). Three years earlier, however, in Towne v. Eisner, 245 US 418 (1918), Holmes had been equally positive that stock dividends are not income but merely a division of an existing investment. The case arose under a revenue act that did not explicitly mention stock dividends, but the act contained the familiar phrase "income from any source whatever;" and the decision necessarily held that the stock dividends were not embraced by this language.

[23] Eisner v. Macomber, supra note 22, at 231.

In terse, comprehensive language befitting the Constitution, [the people of the United States] empowered Congress "to lay and collect taxes on incomes from whatever source derived." They intended to include thereby everything which by reasonable understanding can fairly be regarded as income. That stock dividends representing profits are so regarded, not only by the plain people, but by investors and financiers, and by most of the courts of the country, is shown, beyond peradventure, by their acts and by their utterances.[24]

In the long run, the relaxed if not populist conception of income espoused by Holmes and Brandeis prevailed over the "awesome finality" of the majority's definition.[25] In *United States v. Kirby Lumber Co.*, the Supreme Court held that income was realized by a corporation on purchasing some of its own bonds for less than the price at which they had been issued.[26] Arguing that the transaction improved its balance sheet but did not produce any gain that was "severed" from its capital, the taxpayer relied on the definition in *Eisner v. Macomber*, and the court below, in harmony with the conclusion of other courts, agreed with this claim. But a unanimous Court, speaking through Mr. Justice Holmes, denigrated the weight of *Eisner v. Macomber*'s definition: "We see nothing to be gained by the discussion of judicial definitions. The [taxpayer] has realized within the year an accession to income, if we take words in their plain popular meaning, as they should be taken here."[27]

The next step in reducing the authority of *Eisner v. Macomber* was taken in 1940, when the Court held in *Helvering v. Bruun* that a landlord realized gain on the forfeiture of a leasehold for nonpayment of rent because the tenant had erected a building that added about $50,000 to the value of the property.[28] The taxpayer argued that this increase in value was not "severed" from his investment or received "for his separate use, benefit, and disposal." Despite the universality ascribed in *Eisner v. Macomber* to its definition of income—"nothing else answers the description"—the Court said in *Bruun*:

These expressions . . . were used to clarify the distinction between an ordinary dividend and a stock dividend. They were meant to show that in the case of a stock dividend, the stockholder's interest in the corporate assets after receipt of the dividend was the same as and

---

[24] Id. at 237.

[25] See Surrey, The Supreme Court and the Federal Income Tax: Some Implications of the Recent Decisions, 35 Ill. L. Rev. 779, 782 (1941).

[26] US v. Kirby Lumber Co., 284 US 1 (1931), discussed infra ¶6.4.1.

[27] Id. at 3. Holmes' reference to the "plain popular meaning" of the term "income" is reminiscent of his dissent in *Eisner v. Macomber*.

[28] Helvering v. Bruun, 309 US 461 (1940).

inseverable from that which he owned before the dividend was declared. We think they are not controlling here.

While it is true that economic gain is not always taxable as income, it is settled that the realization of gain need not be in cash derived from the sale of an asset. Gain may occur as a result of exchange of property, payment of the taxpayer's indebtedness, relief from a liability, or other profit realized from the completion of a transaction. The fact that the gain is a portion of the value of property received by the taxpayer in the transaction does not negative its realization.

Here, as a result of a business transaction, the respondent received back his land with a new building on it, which added an ascertainable amount to its value. It is not necessary to recognition of taxable gain that he should be able to sever the improvement begetting the gain from his original capital. If that were necessary, no income could arise from the exchange of property; whereas such gain has always been recognized as realized taxable gain.[29]

Although the *Bruun* opinion did not reject the famous definition promulgated by *Eisner v. Macomber*, it watered down the requirement of a realization by suggesting that any definite event — here the forfeiture of a leasehold — could properly be employed as the occasion for taking account of the taxpayer's gain.

After several smaller steps in the erosion of *Eisner v. Macomber*'s definition,[30] the coup de grace was delivered by the Supreme Court in 1955, when it decided in *CIR v. Glenshaw Glass Co.* that punitive damages awarded in private antitrust actions were taxable.[31] Rather than attempt even a verbal reconciliation of these windfalls with the concept of "gain

---

[29] Id. at 468–69. The opinion is confusing, partly because of a muddled stipulation of facts, which left open the possibility that the building was a portable structure, in which event the "severance" aspect of the *Eisner v. Macomber* definition would have been satisfied. (Mr. Chief Justice Hughes concurred in the result on the basis of the stipulation.) See Surrey, supra note 25, at 782–84 (*Bruun* "a complete denial of the doctrine that is the heart of *Eisner v.Macomber* [and marks] the end of one era in our tax history"); see also Lowndes, Current Conceptions of Taxable Income, 25 Ohio St. LJ 151, 173 (1964) (under *Bruun*, concept of realization requires "merely some event that freezes or fixes the gain with sufficient certainty so that it is proper to tax it"); Wright, The Effect of the Source of Realized Benefits Upon the Supreme Court's Concept of Taxable Receipts, 8 Stan. L. Rev. 164, 183 (1956).

On its facts, *Bruun* has been overruled by statute. IRC §§109, 1019 (discussed infra ¶16.1).

[30] See Magill, Taxable Income 65–80 (Ronald Press, rev. ed. 1945); Lowndes, supra note 29; Surrey, supra note 25; Note, The Supreme Court's Apparent Abandonment of a Definitive Concept of Taxable Income, 45 Harv. L. Rev. 1072 (1932).

[31] CIR v. Glenshaw Glass Co., 348 US 426 (1955).

derived from capital, from labor, or from both combined," the Court consigned the *Eisner v. Macomber* definition to an insignificant role, flatly denying that "nothing else answers the description":

> The Court was there endeavoring to determine whether the distribution of a corporate stock dividend constituted a realized gain to the shareholder, or changed "only the form, not the essence," of his capital investment . . . It was held that the taxpayer had "received nothing out of the company's assets for his separate use and benefit." . . . The distribution, therefore, was held not a taxable event. In that context— distinguishing gain from capital—the definition served a useful purpose. But it was not meant to provide a touchstone to all future gross income questions. . . .
>
> Here we have instances of undeniable accessions to wealth, clearly realized, and over which the taxpayers have complete dominion. The mere fact that the payments were extracted from the wrongdoers as punishment for unlawful conduct cannot detract from their character as taxable income to the recipients. . . . [W]e find no . . . evidence of intent to exempt these payments.[32]

The decline and fall of *Eisner v. Macomber* are less surprising than the tenacious grip it maintained on the bench and bar. The case was decided by a five-to-four vote, and it relied heavily on *Pollock v. Farmers' Loan and Trust Co.*, a decision that commanded almost no critical support and was repudiated politically by ratification of the Sixteenth Amendment. Yet, as late as 1953, Treasury regulations defined income as "the gain derived from capital, from labor, or from both combined,"[33] confirming Mr. Justice Douglas' comment in 1943 that "*Eisner v. Macomber* dies a slow death."[34]

---

[32] Id. at 430–31. See Bailey v. CIR, 88 TC 1293 (1987) (where urban renewal agency restored facade on taxpayer's building under agreement in which taxpayer agreed to restore interior and maintain facade, value of facade work not gross income because, by the agreement, taxpayer relinquished complete dominion over facade).

Although the constitutionality of taxing the amounts in question was conceded by the taxpayers, the opinion is as significant for constitutional purposes as it is in construing the Code, given the repeated statements by the courts that the term "income . . . from whatever source derived" is used in the same sense by the Sixteenth Amendment as by Congress. See supra notes 3, 4. The suggestion to the contrary by Mr. Justice Holmes in Towne v. Eisner, 245 US 425 (1918) ("it is not necessarily true that income means the same thing in the Constitution and the [Revenue] Act"), was not pursued in later cases. Indeed, Holmes himself employed the same "plain language" standard of interpretation for both purposes. See supra notes 22, 27.

[33] Reg. 118, §39.22(a)-1(a) (1953).

[34] Helvering v. Griffiths, 318 US 371, 404 (1943) (Douglas, J., dissenting).

When the *Eisner v. Macomber* definition lost its claim to exclusivity, income as a constitutional concept was relegated to a minor role, which can be summarized as follows:

1. If Congress explicitly directs that a particular item is to be included in the tax base, there is no need to decide whether it is income unless a tax on the item is a direct tax.[35] In this rare situation (which approaches the vanishing point if the *Pollock* case is no longer good law), the tax can be sustained only if (1) it is apportioned among the states according to population or (2) it is relieved of that requirement by the Sixteenth Amendment because the item is income in the constitutional sense.

2. If an item is not explicitly mentioned by the Code and gets into the tax base because it is gross income within the meaning of §61(a), that determination simultaneously establishes that it is income under the Sixteenth Amendment, which uses the term income in at least as broad a sense as §61(a). Any doubt about the item's status under the direct tax clause is thus dispelled.[36]

While *Glenshaw Glass* completed the process, begun by *Kirby Lumber*, of limiting the *Eisner v. Macomber* definition, it did little to resolve the continuing problems of statutory interpretation inherent in §61(a)'s use of the term income. To be sure, the Court announced that the statutory phrase "gains or profits and income derived from any source whatever" is "used by Congress to exert in this field 'the full measure of its taxing power' " by including "all gains except those specifically exempted."[37] This generalization, however, is clearly too broad; it is obvious that Congress did not intend to tax several major types of "gains" that are not specifically exempted. The rental value of owner-occupied residences and unrealized appreciation in taxpayers' property are examples.[38] Further, the Court in *Glenshaw*

---

[35] As to whether a nonapportioned, progressive tax can constitutionally be imposed on a tax base including both income and nonincome items, see supra ¶1.2.4 note 38.

[36] Department of Justice, supra note 2; Ketcham, supra note 2.

[37] CIR v. Glenshaw Glass Co., 348 US 426, 429–30 (1955). The "full measure" theory is old, as is indicated by the Court's citations, to which *Eisner v. Macomber* might have been added. Eisner v. Macomber, 252 US 203 (1920) ("Congress intended . . . to exert its power to the extent permitted by the Amendment"). See CIR v. Kowalski, 434 US 77, 82 (1977) ("cardinal principle" that Congress intended "to use the full measure of its taxing power").

[38] See infra ¶¶5.2, 5.3.3. The Court in *Glenshaw Glass* did not refer to a definition contained in the regulations in effect for the years at issue, which was slightly less broad than the Court's over-inclusive formula: "Income (in the broad sense) [means] all wealth which flows in to the taxpayer other than as a mere return of capital," and "gross income" includes all such income unless exempted "by statutory

Glass described the punitive damages received by the taxpayers as "clearly realized," although without indicating whether it regarded realization as indispensable.

Another source of uncertainty in the *Glenshaw Glass* opinion is its use of the ambiguous term "gain."[39] Does it embrace, for example, an employee's receipt of a bonus that was erroneously computed and will have to be repaid on demand, the collection of a debt that was written off in an earlier year as uncollectible, compensation for injury to the taxpayer's reputation caused by slander, or funds obtained by false pretenses with no intent to repay? As will be seen,[40] these questions have all been presented to the IRS or the courts for adjudication, and *Glenshaw Glass* provides little help in resolving them. To expect more would be to misapprehend *Glenshaw Glass*, whose principal lesson is: "Put not your faith in definitions."

In a refreshingly frank statement, the government's brief in a later case acknowledged that *Glenshaw Glass* should not be pushed to a dryly logical extreme:

> Notwithstanding its broad language, . . . we acknowledge that, just as this Court in *Glenshaw Glass* said of *Eisner v. Macomber* that it was never "meant to provide a touchstone to all future gross income questions" (348 US at 431), so also was *Glenshaw Glass* itself not

---

provision or otherwise." Reg. 118, §39.21-1 (1953). The regulations did not explain the term "otherwise."

[39] In arguing *Glenshaw Glass*, the government relied heavily on the term "gain" in §22(a) of the 1939 Code, evidently on the theory that some items not qualifying as income under the Sixteenth Amendment are nevertheless taxable. See Rapp, Some Recent Developments in the Concept of Taxable Income, 11 Tax L. Rev. 329, 360 et seq. (1956); Wright, supra note 29. It is curious that when §22(a) of the 1939 Code was replaced in 1954 by §61(a), the word "gain" was dropped. See supra note 3.

In the final sentence of *Glenshaw Glass*, the Court refers to "a clear legislative attempt [in the enactment of the predecessor of §61(a)] to bring the taxing power to bear upon all *receipts* constitutionally taxable" (emphasis added). This shift from the Court's earlier references to "gains" is probably inadvertent; in General Am. Investors Co. v. CIR, 348 US 434 (1955), a companion case to *Glenshaw Glass*, the Court referred (at 436) to "the legislative design to reach all *gain* constitutionally taxable unless specifically excluded" (emphasis added). Taken at face value, the phrase "constitutionally taxable receipts" would embrace even the "compensatory" items referred to in note 8 of the *Glenshaw Glass* opinion, as well as recoveries for wrongful death, which have long been accepted as excludable (infra ¶5.6), despite the absence of a specific statutory exclusion. See CIR v. Glenshaw Glass Co., supra note 37, at 432 n.8. Also see the government's concession that the statutory exclusions from gross income are not exhaustive, which was mentioned by Mr. Justice Harlan in Rudolph v. US, 370 US 269, 274 (1962).

[40] For erroneously computed amounts, see infra ¶6.3; for collection of previously charged-off debts, see infra ¶5.7.1; for compensation for slander, see infra ¶5.6; for unlawful receipts, see infra ¶6.5.

meant as the final answer to "all future gross income questions." It is too simple a syllogism to say that there was a "gain" of some "nature" or "form;" it is not within a specific statutory exclusion; therefore it is income. Just as it would be unworkable on the deduction side to try to account for every kind of expenditure having a relationship to the business, so also on the income side it is quite impossible to try to account for every kind of receipt.[41]

This message was even more bleakly stated in another Supreme Court decision on the scope of §61(a): "[N]o single, conclusive criterion has yet been found to determine in all situations what is a sufficient gain to support the imposition of an income tax. No more can be said in general than that all relevant facts and circumstances must be considered."[42]

Reporting in 1954 on its effort to improve the federal income tax by a critical examination and revision of its technical provisions, an Income Tax Project sponsored by the American Law Institute proposed no change in the then familiar phrase "all gains, profits, and income derived from any source whatever, excepting items specifically excluded . . . "[43] This ancient terminology was retained in the proposed tax statute, even though its authors felt free in other contexts to go "considerably beyond mere codification of the present law and mere restatement of present income tax rules,"[44] because no useful alternative was available:

> Attempts to define "income" have been unsatisfactory. Thus, . . . the *Eisner v. Macomber* . . . definition . . . is vulnerable on the ground of incompleteness: Does it, for example, cover income from cancellation of indebtedness? The economists' definitions (e.g., Henry Simons: "Personal income may be defined as the algebraic sum of (1) the market value of rights exercised in consumption and (2) the change in the value of the store of property rights between the beginning and end of the period in question." Simons, Personal Income Taxation 50 (1938)), apart from the fact that there is no unanimity in this area, are

---

[41] Brief for US at 43, Rudolph v. US, supra note 39.

[42] CIR v. Wilcox, 327 US 404, 407 (1946) (holding embezzled funds not taxable). Although *Wilcox* was limited to its facts by Rutkin v. US, 343 US 130, rehearing denied, 343 US 952 (1952), and was later overruled by James v. US, 366 US 213 (1961), the quoted language was not at issue or disapproved in either case. See infra ¶6.5.

[43] ALI Fed. Income Tax Stat., §X105A(a), at 25 (Feb. 1954 Draft). The accompanying nonexclusive enumeration of included items also conformed, in the main, to existing law. See Surrey & Warren, The Income Tax Project of the American Law Institute: Gross Income, Deductions, Accounting, Gains and Losses, Cancellation of Indebtedness, 66 Harv. L. Rev. 761 (1953).

[44] ALI Fed. Income Tax Stat., supra note 43, at xvi.

not here desirable. From a standpoint of income tax administration they initially cover too much ground and hence put too great a strain on the exclusion sections: for example, all forms of imputed income would be included.

The courts have not evolved a definition. Instead in the *Kirby Lumber Co.* case, 284 US 1 (1931), the Supreme Court abandoned the search for a definition. The judicial approach has given wide scope to [the predecessor of §61(a)], but has recognized that the content of "income" will be determined case by case. Essentially, it is a fluid content, determined by the interplay in particular cases of common usage, accounting concepts, administrative goals, and finally, judicial reaction to these forces. Each force and the judicial reaction reflect an underlying judgment as to what types of receipts should be taxed under an "income tax," such judgment being in turn derived from the connotations drawn from a tax of this type.

It is believed that this combination of wide inclusiveness and elasticity should be retained, and that a simple reference to "all gains, profits, and income" is sufficient. It is also believed that familiar wording should be continued to avoid generating new nebulous problems of definition.[45]

The principal commentators have independently advocated a similarly open-ended and, hence, necessarily unpredictable process of defining income.[46] Congress, by failing to substitute a detailed enumeration or definition for the catchall reference in §61(a) to "all income from whatever source derived," has in effect accepted the American Law Institute's approach.

¶5.2 REALIZATION

Under the definition of income most widely accepted by economists, an increase in the taxpayer's net worth during the relevant accounting

---

[45] Id. at 193–94. See also Surrey & Warren, supra note 43, at 769–75.

[46] See, e.g., Sneed, The Configurations of Gross Income 123 (Ohio State U. Press 1967) (§61(a) "should be regarded as presumptively embracing all items which reasonably may be described as 'clearly realized' gain" unless excluded by several broad policy objectives); Lowndes, supra note 29, at 182 ("a fitting approach to taxable income is to think of it as an occasion on which it is just and socially sensible to impose liability for an income tax"); Surrey, supra note 25. With the Lowndes view, compare Mullock, Current Conceptions of Taxable Income—A Comment, 26 Ohio St. LJ 43, 52 (1965) ("With justice and social desirability as criteria, we could throw away the Code, regulations, rulings, and decisions. The tax court would be transformed into a Lyceum wherein Plato and Aristotle would rule supreme") For the comprehensive tax base concept, see supra ¶3.1.3.

period is income, and a decline in net worth is an offset against income.[1] The economist's reason for taking increases and decreases in the value of the taxpayer's assets into account periodically, without waiting for a sale or similar event to terminate the taxpayer's investment, is that unrealized appreciation and depreciation alter the taxpayer's economic wellbeing and can be voluntarily realized by a sale. A decision to retain the assets is the functional equivalent (save for brokerage commissions and other transaction costs) of selling them and promptly reinvesting the proceeds in the same assets. The rationale is analogous to the investment adviser's admonition: Don't hold anything you would not purchase if you had idle cash. The argument for taxing unrealized appreciation is sometimes supported by the assertion that "equity requires that taxpayers be put on an inventory basis with respect to all their assets."[2] To this may be added an early pithy comment by Thomas Reed Powell: "Nothing in the nature of things makes separation from capital one of the requisites of income from capital. From a practical common-sense point of view there is something strange in the idea that a man may indefinitely grow richer without ever being subject to an income tax."[3]

The customary response to these arguments is a practical one; taxing unrealized appreciation would require annual valuations of everyone's assets, and valuing closely held enterprises, real estate, intangibles like patents and franchises, and other property that is not regularly traded in a public market would be a cumbersome, abrasive, and unpredictable administrative task. On the other hand, publicly traded securities, which can be readily valued, constitute a major segment of personal wealth.[4] With respect to other property, once the giant step of valuing the property was taken for the first taxable year, subsequent adjustments to keep pace with economic conditions might not be as difficult as usually assumed.[5]

---

[1] See supra ¶¶3.1.1, 3.5.2. For use of the realization concept by accountants, see Arnett, Recognition as a Function of Measurement in the Realization Concept, 38 Acct. Rev. 733 (1963). A few tax theorists oppose taxing capital gains whether realized or not. See generally supra ¶3.5.7; Wallich, Taxation of Capital Gains in the Light of Recent Economic Developments, 18 Nat'l Tax J. 133 (1965); Blum, Taxation of Capital Gains in the Light of Recent Economic Developments—Some Observations, 18 Nat'l Tax J. 430 (1965).

[2] Sneed, The Configurations of Gross Income 71 (Ohio St. U. Press 1967).

[3] Powell, Income From Corporate Dividends, 35 Harv. L. Rev. 362, 376 (1922). Conversely, Professor Powell probably found it strange that a person can be subject to income taxes although growing continually poorer.

[4] See Slawson, Taxing as Ordinary Income the Appreciation of Publicly Held Stock, 76 Yale LJ 623 (1967).

[5] For a fully worked out scheme for bringing unrealized appreciation and depreciation into the tax base, see Shakow, Taxation Without Realization: A Proposal for Accrual Taxation, 134 U. Pa. L. Rev. 1111 (1986). See also Stepek, The Tax Reform

In addition to the asset valuation problem, however, taxing unrealized appreciation would compel many taxpayers to sell or mortgage their assets in order to pay the tax (unless Uncle Sam was prepared to extend credit to them). The resulting involuntary and distress sales would be especially resented in the case of assets that are highly prized as a source of occupational opportunities or emotional satisfaction, such as farms, family businesses, heirlooms, and personal residences.

Another powerful deterrent to taxing unrealized appreciation is a deep-seated distrust of paper profits. The economic theorist may be entirely correct in asserting that a taxpayer who thinks his unrealized appreciation is illusory should sell out while he can and that the failure to do so is tantamount to an expression of faith in the property's current market price, but this analysis is not widely accepted by the public.[6]

Whatever may be said for or against taxing unrealized appreciation, the federal income tax has never applied to gains until they have been "realized" in some way. The realization principle is found in the Code only by implication,[7] but, despite occasional judicial statements that all gains are embraced by §61(a) unless specifically excluded by statute,[8] realization is so basic to the structure of the law that the principle is not challenged. Like other fundamental concepts, however, it is a bit vague around the edges, giving rise to some troublesome peripheral issues.

The concept of realization entered the law in a curiously unobtrusive fashion. Asked during the debate on the Revenue Act of 1913 if a $10,000 decline in the value of investment property could be used to offset $10,000 of dividends and personal service income, a leading member of the Senate Finance Committee responded, "I never thought about that," but went on to express the view that "depreciation in the value of [securities] is not like a depreciation by reason of the wear and tear arising out of the use of proper-

---

Act of 1986: Simplification and the Future Viability of Accrual Taxation, 62 Notre Dame L. Rev. 779 (1987) (critique of Shakow proposal).

[6] Also, recognition of unrealized losses in a temporarily depressed stock market could have a drastic and unforeseeable effect on federal revenues. For more on the policy underpinnings of the concept of realization, see Sneed, A Defense of the Tax Court's Result in *Prunier* and *Casale*, 43 Cornell LQ 339, 350–53 (1958).

[7] Section 1001(a) defines gain on a "sale or other disposition of property" as the excess of the amount realized in the disposition over the property's adjusted basis. Adjusted basis is cost, adjusted in numerous ways, but not by the inclusion of unrealized appreciation. IRC §§1012, 1016. If unrealized appreciation were taxed prior to disposition, the §1001(a) gain on disposition would, to this extent, duplicate previously taxed amounts. From §61(a)(3), which includes "gains derived from dealings in property," it can be implied that (1) such a gain is not taxed more than once and (2) the time for the single tax is when the "dealings" are completed by a disposition.

[8] See discussion of the *Glenshaw Glass Co.* case, supra ¶5.1.

ty."⁹ The senator's instinctive reaction against taxing unrealized changes in the value of assets was soon adopted by the Treasury as administrative practice.¹⁰ Then, in *Eisner v. Macomber*, the Supreme Court held that if the *"growth* or *increment* of value" in a taxpayer's investment were taxed before the gain was *severed from* the capital," the levy would be a direct tax that, despite the Sixteenth Amendment, would have to be apportioned among the states according to population.¹¹

Later cases, however, have been less strict. If, for example, an art collector trades an oil painting that cost $1,000, but is worth $10,000, for a $10,000 racehorse, the collector's $9,000 gain is realized, even though some might argue over whether his gain has been "severed" from his capital. The swap terminates the collector's investment in the painting, and it can be said that he realized the gain even if it is reinvested along with his original principal because he is no longer affected by fluctuations in the value of the work of art. But a sole proprietor who exchanges his business for all of the stock of a newly organized corporation also realizes gain or loss, even though the future value of the stock depends directly on the fluctuations in the value of the transferred assets.¹²

Another situation in which gain can be taxed even though it has only been realized in a loose sense is seen in *Helvering v. Bruun*, involving a landlord whose tenant defaulted in the payment of rent under a long-term lease after erecting a building on the leased premises. On regaining possession of the property, the landlord was held to realize income equal to the

---

⁹ 50 Cong. Rec. 3849 (1913) (remarks of Sen. Williams).

¹⁰ The first regulations under the 1913 statute (Reg. 33, Pt. 3, Art. 107) state that gross income includes "appreciation in value of assets, if taken up on the books of account as gain," but a 1918 revision (Reg. 33, Pt. II, Art. 106) provides that "gain realized . . . upon the sale or disposition of capital assets shall be returned as gross income." See also the 1918–1921 concept of a "readily realizable market value" in computing gain or loss on the exchange of property for other property (infra ¶43.2, note 1); Adams, When Is Income Realized? in The Income Tax 29 (Haig, ed.; Columbia U. Press 1921).

¹¹ Eisner v. Macomber, 252 US 189, 207 (1920) (discussed supra ¶¶1.2.4, 5.1). For prior uses of the realization concept, see Lynch v. Hornby, 247 US 339, 344 (1918) (dividends received after ratification of the Sixteenth Amendment are taxable as income, even though receipt was "a mere realization in possession of an inchoate and contingent interest that the stockholder had in a surplus of corporate assets previously existing"); Towne v. Eisner, 245 US 418 (1918) (realization required by Revenue Act of 1913). See also Magill, Taxable Income, Pt. I ("The Requirement of Realization") (Ronald Press, rev. ed. 1945) (extended historical review).

¹² See Insurance & Title Guar. Co. v. CIR, 36 F2d 842 (2d Cir. 1929), cert. denied, 281 US 748 (1930); Livingston v. CIR, 18 BTA 1184 (1930) (acq.). Under §351, gain or loss realized on such an exchange is ordinarily not recognized, but because it is realized, relief from taxation extends only so far as §351 allows. See infra ¶91.1.

value of the building, even though he could not "sever the improvement begetting the gain from his original capital."[13] The *Bruun* opinion is confusing, but it seems to imply that the value of the building could be taxed to the landlord even if, when the tenant vacated the premises, the land (or possibly the land and the building together) had a value below the taxpayer's cost basis for the land. More important, if an increase in the value of the property attributable to the building erected by the tenant can be taxed to the landlord as income, it is hard to see why he cannot also be taxed, if Congress so desires, on an increase in value resulting from trees and shrubs planted by the tenant, an adjacent highway built by the state, or an improvement in the national economy.[14]

A few months after deciding *Bruun*, the Supreme Court denigrated the concept of realization still further, describing it as a rule "founded on administrative convenience"—quite a demotion from the constitutional status it enjoyed under *Eisner v. Macomber*.[15] This slighting reference to "the rule that income is not taxable until realized" appears in *Helvering v. Horst*, which was concerned with whether the income from certain negotiable interest coupons was taxable to their original owner or to his son, to whom the coupons had been given and who cashed them at maturity shortly after the gift. Since the income in *Horst*, having been collected in cash, had been realized in the strictest sense, the Court could have avoided tampering with the concept of realization by focusing on whether income realized by the donee could properly be attributed to the donor. But the rationale adopted for taxing the donor was that Congress could have taxed the donor on the interest as it accrued during his ownership of the coupons and that, having refrained as a matter of administrative convenience from taxing him at this early stage, Congress implicitly indicated that he should be taxed if he gave the coupons away before they matured.[16] Thus, without mentioning *Eisner*

---

[13] Helvering v. Bruun, 309 US 461, 469 (1940) (discussed supra ¶5.1). See Surrey, The Supreme Court and the Federal Income Tax: Some Implications of the Recent Decisions, 35 Ill. L. Rev. 779, 783 (1941).

[14] Because Judge Learned Hand could see no basis for distinguishing events of this type from the tenant's construction of a building, he concluded in Hewitt Realty Co. v. CIR, 76 F2d 880, 884 (2d Cir. 1935), that the landlord could not be taxed in circumstances similar to the *Bruun* case until he sold the property. As he interpreted *Eisner v. Macomber*, "the question . . . is whether the value received is embodied in something separately disposable, or whether it is so merged in the land as to become financially a part of it, something which, though it increases its value, has no value of its own when torn away." The *Bruun* case rejected this construction of *Eisner v. Macomber*.

[15] Helvering v. Horst, 311 US 112 (1940) (discussed infra ¶75.3.4).

[16] As pointed out in ¶75.3.4, the Court's theory does not explain why the donor was taxed on the entire amount collected by his son rather than on the smaller amount that had accrued when the gift was made.

v. Macomber, the Court came close to approving a tax on increases in the taxpayer's net worth.

Although badly eroded, if not wholly undermined, as a constitutional principle,[17] realization as a rule of administrative convenience (or legislative generosity) remains largely intact. Merchants and manufacturers, for example, are not required to write up their inventories to fair market value.[18] As will be seen at many points hereafter,[19] however, any action that significantly alters the taxpayer's relationship to an asset may constitute a realization of gain or loss even though the event does not "sever" the gain or loss[20] from the taxpayer's original capital in the manner contemplated by *Eisner v. Macomber*.

In recent decades, the principal issue implicating the constitutionality of taxing appreciation in the absence of a sale or other transfer for value was a Treasury proposal, made in 1963 and renewed in 1969, to treat the transfer of property at death or by gift as a "constructive realization" of gain or loss.[21] The target of this proposal was §1014, under which a person acquiring property from a decedent, whether by will or by intestate succession, is allowed to use its value on the date of the decedent's death as his basis in computing gain or loss on a subsequent sale.[22] Because an increase or decrease in value during the decedent's lifetime is not taken into account on the decedent's final income tax return or on the executor's returns, the effect of §1014 is to forgive tax on the increase or permanently bar deduc-

---

[17] For a contrary view, virtually unique among recent commentators, see Roehner & Roehner, Realization: Administrative Convenience or Constitutional Requirement? 8 Tax L. Rev. 173 (1953).

[18] A lower of cost or market rule, however, allows inventory to be written down to fair market value. See infra ¶105.4.4. See also IRC §1256(a) (requiring regulated futures contracts to be "marked to market" as of the end of each taxable year; discussed infra ¶25.4.6); Reg. §1.471-5 (permitting, but not requiring, dealers in securities to value them at market, whether above or below cost).

[19] See especially infra ¶40.2.

[20] *Eisner v. Macomber* was concerned only with the realization of gain; indeed, the notion of "severing" a loss is bizarre. Congress can permit losses to be deducted whether realized or not, as it sees fit. Under present law, however, events that trigger the realization of gain ordinarily have the same effect as to losses, although the rules determining whether a realized gain or loss must be recognized sometimes distinguish between the two. See infra ¶40.1.

[21] See Hearings on President's 1963 Tax Message Before the House Ways and Means Comm., 88th Cong., 1st Sess. 24, 54–55, 128–40, 596 (1963) (including opinion of General Counsel of Treasury on constitutionality of taxing appreciation upon death); Hearings on Tax Reform Before House Ways and Means Comm., 91st Cong., 1st Sess., Pt. 2, at 3969–4185 (1969); Graetz, Taxation of Unrealized Gains at Death—An Evaluation of Current Proposals, 59 Va. L. Rev. 830 (1973); Kurtz & Surrey, Reform of Death and Gift Taxes: The 1969 Treasury Proposals, the Criticisms, and a Rebuttal, 70 Colum. L. Rev. 1365 (1970).

[22] See generally infra ¶41.4.

tion of the decrease. It was estimated that $11.5 billion of unrealized appreciation escaped taxation under §1014 in 1966,[23] a phenomenon described by two proponents of the Treasury proposals as "the most serious defect in our federal tax structure today."[24] Like transfers at death, transfers of property by gift during the owner's lifetime do not generate gain or loss, but the property ordinarily retains its original basis so that the donee's gain or loss on a sale is usually the difference between the sales price and the donor's cost.[25]

Congress was unwilling to enact the Treasury's constructive realization legislation proposal, but in 1976 it adopted a compromise—a carryover basis for inherited property, similar to the carryover basis that had long been applicable to inter vivos gifts.[26] This halfway house satisfied virtually no one. Proponents of a full-scale constructive realization approach thought it too mild; others objected to any departure from pre-1976 law; still others concentrated on technical difficulties in applying the new rules and favored modifications to make them easier for fiduciaries and the IRS to administer.[27] Faced by this welter of controversy, Congress postponed the effective date of the legislation and then, in 1980, repealed it entirely and restored prior law.[28] The experience with carryover basis seems to have stifled serious consideration of change in §1014.[29]

---

[23] Eilbott, The Revenue Gain From Taxation of Decedents' Unrealized Capital Gains, 22 Nat'l Tax J. 506 (1970).

[24] Kurtz & Surrey, supra note 21, at 1381.

[25] See generally infra ¶41.3.

[26] IRC §1023 (before repeal in 1980). See generally Joint Comm. on Tax'n, 94th Cong., 2d Sess., General Explanation of the Tax Reform Act of 1976, reprinted in 1976-3 CB (Vol. 2) 551-63; McGrath & Blattmachr, Estate Planning for Tax Shelters in View of the Impact of the Carryover Basis Rules, 47 J. Tax'n 130 (1977); see also Joint Comm. on Tax'n, 95th Cong., 2d Sess., General Explanation of the Revenue Act of 1978, at 405-20 (1979) (technical amendments of carryover basis rules).

[27] For extended analysis of the technical problems, see Statement of Donald C. Lubick, Assistant Secretary of the Treasury for Tax Policy, before House Ways and Means Comm., 95th Cong., 2d Sess. (Nov. 11, 1979) (Treasury proposals for simplification of carryover basis); Hearings on Technical Corrections Act of 1977 Before Subcomm. on Tax'n and Debt Management, Senate Finance Comm., 95th Cong., 1st Sess. (1977); Covey & Hastings, Cleaning Up Carryover Basis, 31 Tax Lawyer 615 (1978); see also Lewis, Taxing Unrealized Gains: The Nettle and the Flower, 4 Rev. Tax Individuals 3 (1980).

[28] See Crude Oil Windfall Profit Tax Act of 1980, Pub. L. No. 96-223, §401(d), 94 Stat. 229; Conf. Rep. No. 817, 96th Cong., 2d Sess. 156 (1980).

[29] In the development of the massive reform of 1986, for example, realization at death was not considered. In the Treasury report generally believed to be the first major step toward that reform, the only mention of the issue is in a list of items not covered in the proposal. U.S. Treasury Dep't, Tax Reform for Fairness, Simplicity, and Economic Growth, vol. I at 147 (1984). Even this mention disappeared thereaf-

¶5.3 IMPUTED INCOME

¶5.3.1 Introductory

Under existing law, two major sources of untaxed income are goods and services that people produce for their personal consumption and taxpayers' use of their own residences and other durable goods.[1]

The first of these categories of so-called imputed income is exemplified by a house painter whose home needs repainting at an estimated cost of $600 for the labor. If he is paid $10 per hour for overtime work and his marginal tax rate is 20 percent, he can earn enough in 75 hours of overtime to hire someone to paint his house—$750 (75 × $10), less income tax of $150, leaves $600. If he does the job himself, he is not taxed on the value of his labor, and if he can complete the work in 60 hours, he can either read a couple of good books during the remaining 15 hours or work for pay and earn $150 ($120 net after taxes).

The second category of imputed income is illustrated by comparing individuals A and B, each with $50,000 to invest. A buys securities with an 8 percent yield, using the annual income of $4,000 to rent a home. B buys a similar home for $40,000, invests the remaining $10,000 in securities and uses the annual income of $800 for repairs and real property taxes on the home. A and B are in substantially identical economic positions (assuming that depreciation on B's home is offset by increases in its market value), but A must report $4,000 of gross income each year, while B's gross income is only $800 and is partly offset by a deduction for property taxes.

A more detailed comparison is set out in Example 5-1, which contrasts the tax liabilities of a renter and an owner, each of whom has wages of $25,000 per year, occupies housing with a market rental value of $6,250 per year, and has $37,500 in assets, which yield 6 percent.[2] The yield on the renter's assets is all taxable income. The homeowner holds $15,000 as equity in his home, on which he receives no cash income; he could, however, have earned $900 by investing this $15,000 in other assets, or he could have rented the house for $6,250, netting $900 after $5,350 in expenses.

---

ter. See, e.g., H.R. Rep. No. 426, 99th Cong., 1st Sess. (1985); President's Tax Proposals to the Congress for Fairness, Growth, and Simplicity (1985).

[1] Imputed income is not exempted from tax by a specific statutory provision, but congressional silence on the subject is clearly tantamount to an affirmative grant of immunity. See generally Simons, Personal Income Taxation 110–24 (U. of Chicago Press 1938); Sneed, The Configurations of Gross Income 88–97 (Ohio St. U. Press 1967); Vickrey, Agenda for Progressive Taxation 17–52 (Ronald Press 1947); Marsh, The Taxation of Imputed Income, 58 Pol. Sci. Q. 514 (1943); see also infra note 17.

[2] Example 5-1 is based on Table 4-1 of Aaron, Shelter and Subsidies: Who Benefits From Federal Housing Policies? (Brookings 1972), and is reproduced with permission, revised to show tax liabilities under 1989 rates.

Example 5-1

Tax Liabilities of Renter and Homeowner
With Equivalent Earnings, Assets, and Expenses

Item	Renter	Homeowner
1. Economic income		
a. Wages	$25,000	$25,000
b. From assets of $37,500		
Savings account interest (at 6 percent)	2,250	1,350
Imputed net rent on $15,000 equity in house (at 6 percent)	–0–	900
c. Total	$27,250	$27,250
2. Housing cost*		
a. Money expenditure	$6,250	$5,350
b. Imputed net rent	–0–	900
c. Total	$6,250	$6,250
4. Taxable income**		
a. Economic income less imputed net rent	$27,250	$26,350
b. Less: Personal exemptions	8,000	8,000
c. Less: Itemized or standard deductions	5,000	5,450
d. Total	$14,250	$12,900
5. Tax liability	$2,138	$1,935

*Housing costs are 25 percent of wages for both renter and owner. Costs of homeownership include $900 net imputed rent, $2,250 in mortgage interest (10 percent on a $22,500 mortgage), $1,200 in property taxes, and $1,900 for maintenance and depreciation. The imputed net rent is both income (because it is produced by the homeowner's investment in the house) and a housing cost (because the homeowner consumes it).

**Renter claims personal exemptions of $8,000, and a standard deduction of $5,000; homeowner claims as deductions $3,450 in mortgage interest and property taxes, $2,000 in other deductions, and personal exemptions of $8,000. Tax liability computed under rates for 1988 and subsequent years.

¶5.3.2 Self-Help

The house painter illustration is just one of many examples of imputed income from services. A comprehensive list of comparable activity would be as diverse as life itself—lawyers who write their own wills, parents who tutor their own children, housekeepers who perform domestic services, tinkerers who repair their own appliances, homeowners who mow their own lawns and raise their own vegetables, entertainers who perform for their families instead of taking them to the movies, and infants who suck their own thumbs.[3] The list would also include taxpayers who help relatives, friends, and nonprofit organizations with unpaid services, instead of working for pay and donating the compensation to these beneficiaries.

In a few situations, the exclusion of imputed income is temporary rather than permanent; if a do-it-yourself project increases the value of the family residence, for example, the taxpayer may ultimately sell it at a profit that is attributable in part to his labor. In most cases, however, the value of the taxpayer's labor is permanently excluded from income. Ranked by the number of persons involved and the economic significance of the work, domestic services performed in the home by family members almost certainly dwarf any other type of imputed income. It has been estimated that inclusion of the value of unpaid household services in the gross national product would increase the GNP by at least 26 percent.[4]

Despite the importance of imputed income from services performed by taxpayers for themselves and their families, Congress has never sought to tax this source of economic gain. Most tax theorists have acquiesced, though sometimes grumblingly. For one thing, an attempt to reach all imputed income would require that taxpayers keep records of time spent on a wide range of activities in the home, and a serious effort by the IRS to verify the time sheets or the values placed by taxpayers on the services would be intolerably abrasive. Moreover, in theory, there is no reason to distinguish homeowners who mow their own lawns from their neighbors for whom an hour of leisure is worth more than a neatly trimmed lawn and who therefore lie in hammocks sipping lemonade while their grass grows tall. Rigorous consistency in the treatment of imputed income, in other words, requires taxing leisure as well as unpaid services rendered by taxpayers to themselves. If this were done, the tax would resemble a tax on the earnings the taxpayer could realize by bestirring himself; and while such a tax on vagrancy might be momentarily seductive to the theorist, it is not likely to command much support on Capitol Hill or among voters.[5]

---

[3] The thumb-sucking example comes from McIntrye & Oldman, Taxation of the Family in a Comprehensive and Simplified Income Tax, 90 Harv. L. Rev. 1572, 1611 (1977).

[4] Other estimates of the value of nonmarket services (of which unpaid household labor is a major component) are as high as 48 percent of GNP. See Brody, Economic Value of a Housewife, Research and Statistics Note (Dept. of Health, Education, and Welfare, Social Security Admin., Office of Research and Statistics, DHEW Pub. No. 75-11701, 1975); Bruch, Property Rights of De Facto Spouses Including Thoughts on the Value of Homemakers' Services, 10 Fam. LQ 101, 110–14 (1976).

[5] But see Hickland v. Hickland, 39 NY2d 1, 346 NE2d 243 (1976) (alimony based on husband's earning capacity, although he preferred to live life of subsistence farmer).

The argument has been made, further, that a tax on imputed income from a taxpayer's own services would be inconsistent with our conception of personal liberty.[6] Taxes can be paid only in cash. Even if the IRS were to relax this stricture, tax payments would have to be in the form of marketable goods and services. Taxes are a means of taking from private goods and services to make public goods and services. When an individual earns a dollar at his job, the government's taking of 28 cents in taxes, for example, represents a collective decision that each dollar of gain from market transactions is to be allocated 72 cents to private consumption and savings and 28 percent for public goods and services. If the tax base included imputed income from leisure and services performed for oneself, however, individuals would be forced into the market to raise funds for the tax because the tax could not sensibly consist of a requirement that 28 percent of a person's leisure time be spent in a box totally isolating him from outside stimuli or of a requirement that 28 percent of the lawn be left unmowed. Our sense of liberty, the argument goes, distinguishes between a person's freedom to do what he wishes with his time, on the one hand, and a person's freedom to do what he wishes with his possessions. A requirement that a person give over 28 percent of his purchasing power to the public fisc is not considered an invasion of personal liberty; as applied to income from wages, it is not forced labor because the taxpayer makes the decision to become employed for cash wages. A requirement that a person enter the market for goods and services to raise funds to pay a tax on imputed income from nonmarket transactions, in contrast, would be a form of forced labor; rather than merely taking a portion of his product for public use, it would make him a forced participant in the market.

Although there has never been any serious effort to alter the exemption of imputed income, its economic significance is slightly reduced by several provisions of current law. First, taxpayers get a tax credit for the cost of hiring someone to look after their children while at work, subject to restrictions described in a later chapter.[7] The credit effectively exempts a working parent from tax on income used for child care, and thus parallels the tax immunity of imputed income enjoyed by taxpayers who prefer to stay at home and care for their own children. Another statutory provision serving to equalize the tax treatment of imputed income and paid employment is the earned income credit granted by §32, which reduces the tax disparity between taxpayers who live on investment income and are therefore able to devote as much time as they want to keeping house and similar pursuits and

---

[6] Kelman, Personal Deductions Revisted: Why They Fit Poorly in an "Ideal" Income Tax and Why They Fit Worse in a Far From Ideal World, 31 Stan. L. Rev. 831, 838–44 (1979); Warren, Would a Consumption Tax Be Fairer Than an Income Tax, 89 Yale LJ 1081, 1113–17 (1980).

[7] IRC §21, discussed infra ¶37.1.

taxpayers who must work for a living and have less time to satisfy their own needs.[8] The rationale for both of these credits would be weakened if imputed income and leisure were taxable, since staying at home would then no longer create a tax advantage as compared with paid employment outside the home.[9]

In practice, the exemption of imputed income generates some troublesome peripheral issues, primarily for farmers, restaurateurs, and other taxpayers who produce goods for the public but also consume some of their own output. If a farmer who raises $1,000 worth of crops at an aggregate cost of $600 uses 10 percent of his output for home consumption, the proper way to separate his taxable business income from his exempt imputed income is to report the $900 received for the products sold to customers and deduct $540 of expenses (the portion of his expenses attributable to the crops sold to others), so that taxable income is $360. If instead he includes in gross income both the cash received from others ($900) and the value of the home-consumed produce ($100) and deducts all his agricultural expenses, the resulting income of $400 includes $40 of imputed income generated by raising produce for personal consumption.

To avoid being taxed on home-consumed produce, the Treasury instructs farmers to exclude both the value of home-consumed produce and the expenses of raising these crops.[10] This is most easily done if the farmer cultivates a garden patch exclusively for home use and raises a different crop for the market, although even in this situation the allocation of some expenses (for example, depreciation and repairs on all-purpose machinery) between business and personal activities might be too intricate for the ordinary farmer to compute. It would not be surprising if those farmers who make an effort to comply with the applicable rules rely more on guesswork than on cost accounting principles.[11]

Imputed income can also arise when a salesman working on a commission basis makes a sale to himself. When the issue was first litigated, the Tax

---

[8] For IRC §32, see infra ¶37.3.

[9] See Bittker, Federal Income Taxation and the Family, 27 Stan. L. Rev. 1389, 1425–26, 1433–37 (1975). If imputed income were taxable, however, an earned income allowance might be supported on a secondary ground—to offset the special costs incurred by taxpayers who work outside the home (e.g., for lunches, transportation, and more formal clothing); see infra ¶¶20.2.1–20.2.3.

[10] IRS Pub. No. 225, Farmer's Tax Guide 16 (1979 ed.). See Nowland v. CIR, 244 F2d 450 (4th Cir. 1957) (farm expenses incurred to produce food for personal consumption not deductible); Morris v. CIR, 9 BTA 1273 (1928) (acq.) (farmer's consumption of garden products not income); Sneed, supra note 1, at 96; Wright, The Effect of the Source of Realized Benefits Upon the Supreme Court's Concept of Taxable Receipts, 8 Stan. L. Rev. 164, 204 (1956).

[11] For litigated cases, see Nowland v. CIR, supra note 10; Calamaras v. CIR, 19 TCM 1045 (1960) (taxpayer's estimate accepted).

Court held that an insurance broker did not realize income when a company he represented allowed him to purchase a policy on his own life for the regular premium less the customary commission. But the decision was reversed by the Court of Appeals for the Fifth Circuit, and the Tax Court bowed to its judgment in a later case.[12] Since it does not require the usual arduous pursuit of a reluctant customer, the economic benefit accruing to an insurance salesman from purchasing a policy for less than its regular price is not exactly compensation for personal services, but it is a perquisite of his business status and may even be one of the attractions of representing the company whose policies he sells. This suggests that the spread ought to be taxed, whether it takes the form of a reduction in the premium or a rebate of his commission.

On the other hand, courtesy discounts allowed by employers on merchandise purchased by employees are not ordinarily taxable,[13] and self-employed businessmen are not taxed when they buy merchandise for personal consumption at a wholesale price, even if they get this advantage only because they do business with the supplier. Transactions between a taxpayer and a partnership of which he is a member can create similar problems. It has been held, for example, that a partner of a brokerage firm is not taxable on his aliquot share of the commissions he paid to the firm on securities purchased for his own account.[14]

Imputed income arises not only from services performed by taxpayers for themselves but also from working without pay for relatives, friends, or nonprofit organizations. Common examples are parents who manage a child's property or work without salary for a family corporation owned by their children. Unpaid services for charitable, religious, political, and other voluntary agencies also bulk large in the nation's economy but do not appear in the income tax base.

An exception to this immunity is the occasional entertainer or lecturer who is about to receive a fee for a performance and who arranges, at the last minute, for payment to an organization whose work he or she wishes to support; in these circumstances, the fee ordinarily is includable in gross income. With a little foresight and attention to the paper work, however, the

---

[12] CIR v. Minzer, 279 F2d 338 (5th Cir. 1960), rev'g Minzer v. CIR, 31 TC 1130 (1959); Bailey v. CIR, 41 TC 663 (1964). See also Alex v. CIR, 628 F2d 1222 (9th Cir. 1980) (insurance agent taxed on commissions on premiums that agent rebated to policy purchasers or paid himself; payments not deductible because unlawful under local law); CIR v. Daehler, 281 F2d 823 (9th Cir. 1960) (real estate salesman taxed on commission earned on his own purchase of lots); Haskell & Kauffman, Taxation of Imputed Income, 17 Nat'l Tax J. 232 (1964); infra ¶5.8.4 (bargain purchases), ¶60.4 (transfer of property for services), ¶75.2.3 (services performed for charity or members of taxpayer's family).

[13] See infra ¶14.1.

[14] Benjamin v. Hoey, 139 F2d 945 (2d Cir. 1944).

benefactor can usually avoid being taxed on the income from benefit nights or similar events.[15] There is no significant economic difference between addressing envelopes for a political party, lending one's name and prestige to its appeals for funds, and singing at a benefit performance for which tickets are sold. In each case, the organization gets valuable services without charge, and in each case the volunteers could provide assistance of equal value by working at their regular occupations and endorsing their paychecks to the organization. But the direct services enjoy the immunity accorded to imputed income; the alternative of working for pay and turning over the proceeds to the organization, though functionally equivalent, is a taxable event.

The popularity of communes among young people a generation ago raised a long latent aspect of the immunity of imputed income—the taxability of reciprocal back scratching. If a lawyer writes a will for a plumber in exchange for repair of a leaky faucet in his home, both should report income from the transaction even though no money changes hands.[16] If a group of parents organize a car pool or cooperative nursery school and take turns in providing the necessary services, even the most relentless Commissioner of Internal Revenue would hesitate to assert that taxable income is generated by their activities. This prudence might be rationalized on the theory that each participant generates tax-free imputed income by his own services, and receives the benefits provided by other parents as a tax-free gift. This theory collides with reality, however, if the parents do not help each other in the spirit of "disinterested generosity" that is the hallmark of a tax-free gift, but, rather, on a quid pro quo basis (in the same way that the lawyer and plumber agree to exchange services in the earlier example).[17]

As long as nonmarket transactions of this type are restricted to the arena of personal life and remain of minor economic significance, the IRS is not likely to mount an effort to treat them as exchanges of services rather than as tax-free imputed income. The IRS has, however, taken a vigorous stance against organized barter arrangements, ruling that members of a barter club, each entitled to call upon the services of other members having a value equal to the services provided by the member to fellow members, have income equal to the credits generated by their services.[18]

---

[15] See infra ¶¶75.2.3, 75.2.4.

[16] See Reg. §1.61-2(d) (services for services).

[17] CIR v. Duberstein, 363 US 278 (1960), discussed infra ¶10.2.1.

[18] Rev. Rul. 79-24, 1979-1 CB 565. See also Rev. Rul. 83-163, 1983-2 CB 26 (value of services received in services-for-services barter club is income in year received, even if services given in return are received in later year); Rev. Rul. 80-52, 1980-1 CB 100 (cash basis members of barter club realize income when amounts credited to their accounts can be used to purchase goods or services or be transferred for value to other members). See Baker v. CIR, 88 TC 1282 (1987) (taxability of

¶5.3.3 Owner-Occupied Residences

As pointed out earlier,[19] taxpayers who own their own homes enjoy the economic benefit of occupancy without being taxed on the rental value of the property; in effect, their investments are treated as nonproductive.[20] For 1970, the failure to tax imputed income from nonfarm home ownership resulted in the exclusion of an estimated $43.4 billion from income, an amount that would have increased tax collections by about $8.9 billion.[21] At one time, it was thought that including imputed rent in taxable income would be unconstitutional, but today few believe there is any constitutional impediment.[22]

To eliminate the existing immunity of this type of imputed income, which has been a consistent feature of the federal income tax since 1913, the homeowner could be treated as a landlord, required to include the fair rental value of the property in gross income and permitted to deduct prop-

---

owner of barter exchange). See generally Keller, The Taxation of Barter Transactions, 67 Minn. L. Rev. 441 (1982). Enforcement of the barter club rulings has proven to be a challenge for the IRS, but now is assisted by a requirement that barter exchanges report their transactions to the IRS. See infra ¶¶111.1.9, 112.2.3.

[19] Supra ¶5.3.1.

[20] Just as two house painters can paint their own homes without reporting any income but will gain the privilege of paying an income tax if each paints the other's house, so neighbors who realize no income from occupying their own homes will become taxable if each lives rent-free in the other's home.

[21] Goode, The Individual Income Tax 119 (Brookings, rev. ed. 1976). For general discussion of imputed income from owner-occupied residences and other assets, see Aaron, Shelter and Subsidies: Who Benefits From Federal Housing Policies? 53–55 (Brookings 1972); Congressional Budget Office, The Tax Treatment of Home Ownership: Issues and Options (1981); Goode, Imputed Rent of Owner-Occupied Dwellings Under the Income Tax, 15 J. Fin. 504 (1960). See also supra note 1.

[22] In Helvering v. Independent Life Ins. Co., 292 US 371 (1934), the Court said that a tax on the rental value of a building owned and occupied by the taxpayer would be a direct tax, which was not saved from the requirement of apportionment by the Sixteenth Amendment; it went on to find that the statute before it, properly construed, did not have this effect. The theory that such a tax would be direct assumes that owner occupancy is so crucial a feature of ownership that taxing rental value is tantamount to taxing the property itself, and the theory that the Sixteenth Amendment did not relieve the tax, even if direct, from the requirement of apportionment presupposes that the rental value of property is not income as that term is used in the Sixteenth Amendment. In US v. Atlas Life Ins. Co., 381 US 233, 246–47 (1965), the Court pointedly refrained from endorsing the *Independent Life* dictum, noting only that the earlier opinion "assumed that the rental value was not income, and could not constitutionally be taxed." For discussion of the direct tax problem, see supra ¶1.2.2. A curious footnote to this issue is the unsuccessful contention by the taxpayer in Brushaber v. Union Pac. R.R., 240 US 1 (1916), that the Revenue Act of 1913 was unconstitutional because it did *not* tax the rental value of owner-occupied residences.

erty taxes, mortgage interest, repairs, depreciation, and other expenses. If the result was a negative amount, consistency would suggest allowing the hypothetical landlord to deduct his loss, just as he could deduct the identical amount if he rented the premises to an outsider at the hypothetical rent. If there are not enough market transactions to compute fair rental values for particular types of residences or to determine when the hypothetical landlord's alleged repairs are required by market conditions rather than dictated by his personal wishes, it would be possible to promulgate a schedule of net rental values (based, for example, on local assessments) to be used instead of individual computations. Taxing income of this type has long been supported by economists; some, however, have reservations about the administrative feasibility of computing net rental values, and others are concerned about the impact of a change in the tax rules on taxpayers who bought residences expecting the current law to continue indefinitely.[23] In any event, proposals by tax theorists for change have had few responsive echoes on Capitol Hill.[24]

Owner-occupied residences are not the only source of imputed income of this type. Similar income is generated by automobiles, household furnishings, clothing, pleasure boats, and other consumer durable goods. The yield on a taxpayer's investment in such property is permanently exempted from tax, and the taxpayer is thus better off than a neighbor who invests the same amount in securities and uses the taxable interest or dividends to rent similar property for personal use.

¶5.4 "GAIN"—TAX-FREE RECOVERY OF CAPITAL

On selling property for more than its cost, a taxpayer's gain is not the entire sales price but the difference between the sales price and his cost; and if he sells the asset for less than cost, he realizes loss equal to the shortfall.[1] This elementary principle is now embodied in §1001(a),[2] but it was accepted by the Treasury and the courts even before it was explicitly prescribed by

---

[23] See supra ¶3.3.4 (re "tax capitalization").

[24] In a 1977 study proposing comprehensive revision of the income tax, the Treasury favored continued exclusion of the rental value of owner-occupied residences, primarily for the sake of simplicity, but proposed repeal of the existing deduction for local real property taxes. Blueprints for Basic Tax Reform 77–80 (Bradford ed. 1984).

[1] The term "cost" is used here as shorthand for "adjusted basis," which generally equals cost less depreciation or other cost recovery allowed prior to sale. IRC §§1012, 1016.

[2] See infra ¶40.1. The statutory offset for the taxpayer's investment is limited to the number of dollars invested by the taxpayer, without adjustment for inflation. For discussion of the effect of inflation, see supra ¶3.5.4.

Congress.[3] Some of the early cases concerned with the meaning of income implied (or were understood to imply) that the taxpayer has a constitutional right to deduct the cost of property from the sales price in computing taxable gain,[4] but the Supreme Court has never had to meet the issue head on.

The Court came close to grappling with the issue in *Stanton v. Baltic Mining Co.*,[5] and it seemed to hold that an allowance for the cost of property sold was a matter of legislative grace rather than constitutional right, at least for mining corporations and perhaps for any sales in the ordinary course of business. Under the Revenue Act of 1913, the income of the taxpayer, a mining company, was computed by deducting its business expenses plus an arbitrary depletion allowance from its gross receipts. Alleging that the depletion allowed by the statute (5 percent of gross receipts) was less than the actual cost of the minerals sold during the taxable year, the taxpayer argued that the tax was pro tanto a direct tax subject to the constitutional requirement of apportionment among the states according to population and that because the amount taxed was not income, the tax was not relieved of the apportionment requirement by the Sixteenth Amendment. In a murky opinion, the Court upheld the tax as an excise that did not need the support of the Sixteenth Amendment, but it is not clear whether the decision was intended to be confined to mining corporations (which encounter particular difficulty in allocating the cost of mineral deposits to the output of particular years)[6] or to embrace all businesses.

---

[3] See infra ¶40.1 note 2.

[4] See Magill, Taxable Income 344 et seq. (Ronald Press, rev. ed. 1945); Powell, Constitutional Aspects of Federal Income Taxation, in The Income Tax 63 et seq. (Haig, ed.; Columbia U. Press 1921). The reasoning was that (1) a tax on the sales price of property (unreduced by cost) would be a direct tax and (2) since the sales price is not income, a tax thereon is not relieved by the Sixteenth Amendment from the constitutional rule that direct taxes must be apportioned among the states according to their population. See supra ¶1.2.2. Doyle v. Mitchell Bros. Co., 247 US 179, 184–85 (1918), although concerned only with the meaning of the 1909 tax on corporate income, it has similar overtones:

> Whatever difficulty there may be about a precise and scientific definition of "income," it imports, as used here, something entirely distinct from principal or capital either as a subject of taxation or as a measure of the tax; conveying rather the idea of gain or increase arising from corporate activities. . . . In order to determine whether there has been gain or loss, and the amount of the gain, if any, we must withdraw from the gross proceeds an amount sufficient to restore the capital value that existed at the commencement of the period under consideration.

[5] Stanton v. Baltic Mining Co., 240 US 103 (1916).

[6] See supra ¶1.2.4. The Court might have given an even narrower answer to the taxpayer's complaint—that any inadequacy in the depletion allowance in the years of active mining operations would be redressed by a deduction on abandoning the

The courts have not been called upon to choose between these competing interpretations because Congress has permitted tax-free recovery of taxpayers' capital in the overwhelming bulk of situations in which the issue arises. On selling property, for example, a taxpayer can offset its cost (or other basis) either under §1001(a) or, if inventory property is involved, as part of the cost of goods sold.[7] Business expenses and such other costs as depreciation, interest, and taxes are also deductible, except in usual circumstances.[8]

Moreover, tax-free recovery of capital is so basic a presupposition of the federal income tax law that it has been permitted by administrative practice or judicial decision in a variety of situations in the absence of explicit statutory authorization. Thus, a taxpayer who was reimbursed by a tax adviser for an error resulting in an overpayment in a prior year was permitted to exclude the amount from gross income,[9] and a similar exclusion was granted for an amount appropriated by a state legislative body to reimburse an employee for his legal expenses in successfully defending an unjustified charge of official misconduct;[10] in both cases, the courts noted that the payment served only to restore the taxpayer's impaired capital. In the same vein, the courts have recognized that a taxpayer whose business goodwill is tortiously destroyed by a competitor is taxable on damages paid

---

mine when it was exhausted, thus allowing the entire cost of the mine to be deducted, either as depletion in the active years or as an abandonment loss in the year operations ceased.

[7] For IRC §1001(a), see infra ¶40.1; for inventory property, see infra ¶105.4.

Sullenger v. CIR, 11 TC 1076 (1948) (nonacq.), holds that a merchant's cost of goods sold includes payments for merchandise in excess of the legal prices set by the Office of Price Administration during World War II, and states that this result is required by the Constitution. Since the court seemed to conclude that the deduction was in any event authorized by Congress and sanctioned by administrative practice, the constitutional reference might be regarded as dictum, although it obviously was important, and possibly even essential, to the result. In 1976, the IRS withdrew its 1952 acquiescence in *Sullenger* and substituted a nonacquiescence, probably because the case might have to be attacked when disallowing questionable payments to foreign officials for business favors. 1976-1 CB 1. See infra ¶20.3.5. For cases rejecting the *Sullenger* constitutional theory, see CIR v. Weisman, 197 F2d 221 (1st Cir. 1952) (unlawful portion of wages paid to employees not deductible because not a "reasonable" allowance); Pedone v. US, 151 F. Supp. 288 (Ct. Cl.), cert. denied, 355 US 829 (1957).

[8] See infra ¶20.1.1.

[9] Clark v. CIR, 40 BTA 333 (1939); Rev. Rul. 57-47, 1957-1 CB 23 (acquiescence in *Clark* except as to interest or amount deducted under §212(3) with tax benefit).

[10] Cox v. Kraemer, 88 F. Supp. 835 (D. Conn. 1948). The taxpayer was allowed to exclude the grant, although the legal expenses for which he was reimbursed were deducted when incurred. This aspect of the decision is of doubtful validity, unless based on the court's alternative theory that the payment was a tax-free gift.

by the wrongdoer only to the extent the recovery exceeds the cost or other basis of the lost goodwill.[11]

The working hypothesis that capital must be recovered tax-free before a taxpayer has income or gain also underlies several cases in which taxpayers receiving damages for injury to property or for easements were allowed to exclude these amounts from income because they were less than the basis of the property and there was no practical way to allocate an appropriate fraction of the basis to the portion of the property that was affected.[12]

Although tax-free recovery of the taxpayer's capital is ordinarily a prerequisite to income or gain, taxpayers sometimes realize income although their receipts are less than their business outlays. One instance is familiar to every reader of this volume—the computation of income from professional practice without allowing the cost of professional training to be deducted as paid, to be amortized during the years of active practice, or to be deducted as a loss on retirement or death.[13] Income is also computed without an adequate allowance for diminution in investment or working capital if the taxpayer runs afoul of any of several provisions disallowing deductions that Congress considers to be dubious, even though the transaction may be above suspicion in a particular case.[14]

Finally, tax-free recovery of capital is sometimes allowed at a time when it may be useless. For example, an investment in purchased goodwill cannot be deducted until it becomes wholly worthless; since this event often follows a long series of loss years, there may be no income to be offset by the

---

[11] Raytheon Prod. Corp. v. CIR, 144 F2d 110 (1st Cir.), cert. denied, 323 US 779 (1944), states that a basis offset is permitted against the recovery if the taxpayer proves that the goodwill had been purchased or had otherwise acquired a basis. The court does not cite §1001(a) as authority for offsetting basis, perhaps because the statutory phrase ("the sale or other disposition of property") requires a little stretching to embrace a recovery of damages for tortious destruction.

[12] Strother v. CIR, 55 F2d 626 (4th Cir.), aff'd on other issues, 287 US 314 (1932) (damages for removing unknown amount of coal from taxpayer's mine); Inaja Land Co. v. CIR, 9 TC 727 (1947) (acq.) (payment for diverting polluted waters into taxpayer's fishing area and for an easement to continue the practice). See also Rev. Rul 81-277, 1981-2 CB 14 (payment by contractor to buyer to settle buyer's claim that building was not completed in accordance with specifications not includable in buyer's gross income, but reduces basis of building).

For the problem of determining whether the taxpayer's receipts are a tax-free recovery for lost capital or taxable compensation for lost profits, see Sager Glove Corp. v. CIR, 311 F2d 210 (7th Cir. 1962), cert. denied, 373 US 910 (1963) (lost profits); State Fish Corp. v. CIR, 48 TC 465 (acq.), supplemental opinion, 49 TC 13 (1967) (injury to goodwill); infra ¶41.8.

[13] See infra ¶22.1.3.

[14] See, e.g., IRC §267(a)(1) (losses on sales of property between related persons; discussed infra ¶78.1).

deduction.[15] Because income is computed on an annual basis rather than averaged over the taxpayer's lifetime, deductions often prove to be useless (both in the year of allowance and in any earlier and later years to which they are carried under the net operating loss carryover rules of §172),[16] with the result that the taxpayer must report income over the long haul without an adequate allowance for the impairment or exhaustion of capital. But these situations are limited in number, and they qualify rather than undermine the basic principle of tax-free recovery of capital.

¶5.5 WINDFALL RECEIPTS—GAIN WITHOUT PAIN

¶5.5.1 Punitive Damages

In *CIR v. Glenshaw Glass Co.*, decided in 1955, the Supreme Court held that exemplary damages for fraud and the punitive two thirds of a treble-damage antitrust recovery, received by a business corporation in settlement of a lawsuit against a competitor, were includable in the successful litigant's gross income.[1] In a companion case, the Court came to the same conclusion regarding a corporation's recovery of insider profits from a director who traded in its securities in violation of the Securities Exchange Act of 1934.[2] In both cases, the taxpayers argued that the receipts were not income within the definition enunciated in *Eisner v. Macomber*—"income may be defined as the gain derived from capital, from labor, or from both combined"[3]—because neither the taxpayer's capital nor the taxpayer's labor had generated the recovery. The Court held that the *Eisner v. Macomber* definition "was not meant to provide a touchstone to all future gross in-

---

[15] See infra ¶23.2.6.

[16] For IRC §172, see infra ¶25.11.

[1] CIR v. Glenshaw Glass co., 348 US 426 (1955), discussed supra ¶5.1 The taxpayer conceded that one third of the recovery was taxable, and the government conceded that the taxpayer's legal fees in obtaining the recovery were deductible. See Park & Tilford Distillers Corp. v. US, 107 F. Supp. 941, 942 (Ct. Cl.), cert. denied, 345 US 917 (1952): "If Congress were to select one kind of receipt of money which, above all others, would be a fair mark for taxation, it might well be 'windfalls.' " But see Wright, A Tax Formula to Restore the Historical Effects of the Antitrust Treble Damage Provision, 65 Mich. L. Rev. 245, 255–56 (1966) (favoring a tax exemption for part of the recovery in private antitrust actions). See also Koenig, Federal Taxation of Private Antitrust Recovery, 13 Stan. L. Rev. 264 (1961).

For IRS practice regarding punitive damages and similar receipts, see Supplemental Memorandum for the Petitioner, submitted by the solicitor General at the request of the Supreme Court, in CIR v. Glenshaw Glass Co., supra.

[2] General Am. Investors Co. v. CIR, 348 US 434 (1955).

[3] Eisner v. Macomber, 252 US 189, 207 (1920), discussed supra ¶1.2.4.

come questions," and that Congress intended "to tax all gains except those specifically exempted." It continued:

> Here we have instances of undeniable accessions to wealth, clearly realized, and over which the taxpayers have complete dominion. The mere fact that the payments were extracted from the wrongdoers as punishment for unlawful conduct cannot detract from their character as taxable income to the recipients. Respondents concede, as they must, that the recoveries are taxable to the extent that they compensate for damages actually incurred. It wouls be an anomaly that could not be justified in the absence of clear congressional intent to say that a recovery for actual damages is taxable but not the additional amount extracted as punishment for the same conduct which caused the injury. And we find no such evidence of intent to exempt these payments.[4]

Glenshaw Glass overturned two earlier lower court cases the had relied on *Eisner v. Macomber* to exclude punitive damages from income; one excluded exemplary damages imposed on a creditor for conspiring to damage the taxpayer's business by making false statements to its customers, and the other involved profits recovered from an employee whose surreptitious activities breached his fiduciary obligation to the taxpayer, making him a trustee ex maleficio.[5]

Sometimes punitive damages, taxable under *Glenshaw Glass*, are claimed along with compensatory damages that are exempt from tax (because, for example, they reimburse the taxpayer for an impairment of damaged capital). If the claim results in a lump-sum judgment or settlement, it must be allocated between the taxable and tax-free components by reference to the parties' own characterization, the relative amounts demanded in the complaint, or some other suitable yardstick.[6]

---

[4] General Am. Investors co. v. CIR, supra note 2, at 430–31. The Court also held that Highland Farms Corp. v. CIR, 42 BTA 1314 (1940) (nonacq.), holding that punitive damages were not income, had not been implicitly approved by the reenactment without change of §22(a) of the 1939 Code (the statutory predecessor of §61(a)), in the absence of evidence that the issue had been brought to the attention of Congress and in view of the IRS' prompt nonacquiescence in the decision.

For the broader implications of *Glenshaw Glass*, see supra ¶5.1.

[5] Central R.R. of N.J. v. CIR, 79 F2d 697 (3d Cir. 1935); Highland Farms Corp. v. CIR, supra note 4.

[6] Compare Thomson v. CIR, 406 F2d 1006 (9th Cir. 1969) (in absence of evidence for a different allocation, recovery in private antitrust action allocated one third to compensation, two thirds to punitive damages) and Rev. Rul. 58-418, 1958-2 CB 18 (in absence of other evidence, recovery in libel action divided between tax-free compensatory damages and taxable exemplary damages in same proportion as amounts demanded in complaint; similar allocation of legal expenses) with Parker v. US, 573 F2d 42 (Ct. Cl. 1978) (settlement allocated first to exempt bequest claim,

¶5.5.2 Found Property, Free Samples, Etc.

The regulations provide that treasure trove (property found by the taxpayer) is gross income in an amount equal to its value when reduced to "undisputed possession."[7] In a case involving a taxpayer who found about $4,500 in old currency in a piano seven years after purchasing it at an auction for $15, the court held that the currency was taxable in the year of discovery rather than when the piano was purchased.[8] A later year might have been appropriate if the taxpayer had advertised for the true owner and refrained from exerting dominion over the property until the search was abandoned, at least if state law imposed such an obligation on the finder. If the piano itself had proved to be more valuable than anticipated at the time of acquisition, in contrast, the taxpayer's bargain purchase would not have generated income until the property was sold, at which time the gain would be the difference between its cost and the amount realized on the sale.

Free samples are as American as apple pie and almost as prevalent as junk mail, but the taxability of the recipient is a murky issue that has generated surprisingly little litigation. Since the transferor's purpose is to advertise its products rather than to demonstrate affection for the recipient, a sample is not a tax-free gift under §102.[9] A sample thus would be taxed under a rigorous application of the *Glenshaw Glass* theory that Congress intended to tax all accessions to wealth over which the taxpayer has "complete dominion." This would be so even if the taxpayer took the unusual step of returning the unsolicited merchandise if state law imposed no legal obligation to do so, since the taxpayer is vested with undisputed ownership when the package is deposited on the doorstep. Despite the breadth of the language of *Glenshaw Glass*, it is hard to believe that it was meant to impose so extreme a rule of taxability or to tax the more ambiguous taxpayer who retains the free samples as a kind of involuntary warehouser. Moreover, in many cases, the samples are worth so little as to invoke the maxim *de minimis non curat lex*; sometimes indeed, they may be worth just what the recipient paid for them.

On the other hand, a taxpayer who sells the merchandise should be taxed. But it is not clear whether the income is realized when the property is

---

then to taxable income claim), Rev. Rul. 75-230, 1975-1 CB 93 (recovery for personal injury; amount of medical expenses treated as evidence of amount allocable to actual damages), and Rev. Proc. 67-33, 1967-2 CB 659 (presumption that antitrust damages were compensatory when actual damages exceeded settlement).

[7] Reg. §1.61-14(a). See generally Comment, Taxation of Found Property and Other Windfalls, 20 U. Chi. L. Rev. 748 (1953) (written before *Glenshaw Glass* decided by Supreme Court).

[8] Cesarini v. US, 296 F. Supp. 3 (ND Ohio 1969), aff'd per curiam, 428 F2d 812 (6th Cir. 1970).

[9] See infra ¶10.1

received, on the theory that the subsequent action demonstrates an intent ab initio to exercise dominion, or only when the property is sold, an approach that would presumably create capital gain rather than ordinary income. As a test of taxability, the unequivocal act of selling the merchandise is more easily applied than the taxpayer's intent at the time of receipt since the latter is not usually publicly disclosed. In its first published attempt to grapple with the issue, the IRS ruled that a reviewer of books for a newspaper was taxable on the value of unsolicited books sent to him by a publisher if he accepted them. A few months later this ruling was superseded by a milder substitute, holding that the receipt of such books is taxable to a reviewer who donates them to a charitable organization and claims a deduction for his generosity.[10] Given its context, the second ruling implies that a reviewer is not taxable if he retains the books or gives them away without claiming a charitable contribution deduction. In some circumstances, however, the retention of property may be unequivocal evidence of an exercise of dominion and a receipt of benefit.[11]

¶5.5.3 Unclaimed Deposits and Uncashed Checks

Trustees, brokers, and agents sometimes receive money or other property that the true owners abandon or fail to claim for so long that their rights are barred by the statute of limitations. This situation can also arise when the taxpayer is a debtor (e.g., a bank or public utility holding deposits or refunds for customers who cannot be located). If not claimed by the state under an escheat statute, assets of this type were taxed to the custodian even

---

[10] Rev. Rul. 70-498, 1970-2 CB 6, superseding Rev. Rul. 70-330, 1970-1 CB 14. See Haverly v. US, 513 F2d 224 (7th Cir.), cert. denied, 423 US 912 (1975) (sample textbooks sent by publishers to principal of public shool and donated by him to school library; held, "intent to exercise complete dominion over unsolicited samples is demonstrated by donating those samples to a charitable institution and taking a tax deduction therefore," and value constitutes gross income); Holcombe v. CIR, 73 TC 104 (1979) (taxpayer who collected old eye glasses and donated them to charity realized income equal to fair market value of glasses, but allowed charitable deduction in equal amount).

[11] See Gresen v. US, 831 F2d 916 (9th Cir. 1987), cert. denied, 108 S. Ct. 1469 (1988) (payments to Alaska residents from state's oil and gas royalties are gross income to recipients); Hornung v. CIR, 47 TC 428 (1967) (acq.) (professional football player taxed (1) on value of automobile received from sports magazine as most valuable player in championship game because it did not qualify as tax-free gift under §102 or as award for noteworthy service under §74 (infra ¶11.1.2) and (2) on rental value of two other automobiles made available by manufacturer; use of cars was accession to wealth under *Glenshaw Glass* and was not tax-free gift since manufacturer had commercial motive); Wills v. CIR, 411 F2d 537 (9th Cir. 1969) (same as to automobile and valuable ornamental belt).

before *Glenshaw Glass*.[12] The validity of these early cases might have been challenged on the ground that accessions to wealth resulting from the lethargy, amnesia, or disappearance of the taxpayer's customers are not gains "derived from capital, from labor, or from both combined," as required by *Eisner v. Macomber*, but any doubt on the issue is dispelled by *Glenshaw Glass*.

The proper taxable year, however, is less obvious. When the property itself is not segregated and the taxpayer's only mode of acknowledging liability to the true owner is a reserve account or other book entry, the concept of "dominon" is not easily applied. Cash received from a customer, for example, may have been deposited in the taxpayer's regular bank account when received, so that in a sense dominion has been exercised from the outset. Since the taxpayer simultaneousy admits the offsetting liability, the transaction might be analogized to a borrowing of funds, which does not generate tax liability unless, and until, the debt is discharged by less than full payment.[13]

Once the offsetting liability is eliminated by the statute of limitations, however, taxing the custodian is reasonable even if refunds might be made thereafter as a matter of good business judgment. Earlier taxability is appropriate if the taxpayer's own behavior (e.g., a book entry eliminating the liability) evinces a judgment that the chance of repayment is minimal or if repayment was unlikely from the outset (e.g., an overcharge paid by an unknown customer). Moreover, if unclaimed assets are a recurrent phenomenon in the taxpayer's business, an accounting method that does not sys-

---

[12] Universal, Inc. v. CIR, 109 F2d 616 (7th Cir. 1940) (refund of excise taxes collected from customers, whose claims against taxpayer were barred by statute of limitations); Boston Consol. Gas Co. v. CIR, 128 F2d 473 (1st Cir. 1942) (unclaimed deposits held by utility and transferred to surplus); Chicago, Rock Island & Pac. Ry. v. CIR, 47 F2d 990 (7th Cir.), cert. denied, 284 US 618 (1931) (excess fares collected by railroad from unknown passengers); Roxy Custom Clothes Corp. v. US, 171 F. Supp. 851 (Ct. Cl. 1959) (income when payables account was credited to eliminate liability); Fidelity-Philadelphia Trust Co. v. CIR, 23 TC 527 (1954) (bank deposits); Lime Cola Co. v. CIR, 22 TC 593, 601 (1954) (acq.) (income when amount credited to surplus); G.M. Standifer Constr. Corp. v. CIR, 30 BTA 184 (1934) (acq.), appeal dismissed, 78 F2d 285 (9th Cir. 1935) (income in year of dissolution); Lehman v. CIR, ¶42,540 P-H Memo BTA (1942) (dividends held for unknown transferees of customers held taxable to firm on expiration of statute of limitations); Rev. Rul. 75-300, 1975-2 CB 23 (utility taxed on unclaimed refunds when ordered by state commission to use them in construction program). But see Astor Holding Co. v. CIR, 135 F2d 47 (5th Cir. 1943) (tenannt's security deposit not includable in landlord's gross income "until something happens to make [it] the property of the lessor"); Rev. Rul. 71-189, 1971-1 CB 32 (bank not taxed on balances in inactive accounts because prohibited by state law from crediting amounts to earned surplus and required to continue FDIC insurance thereon).

[13] See infra ¶6.4.1.

tematically credit these amounts to income may not clearly reflect income as required by §446(b).[14] Finally, if checks issued by an accrual-basis taxpayer to pay wages, interest, refunds, and other deductible expenses are not presented to the taxpayer's bank for payment or are returned because the addressee cannot be found, the taxpayer is required to include these amounts in income to correct for the previous deductions, even if the liability remains outstanding.[15]

¶5.6 REIMBURSEMENT FOR WRONGFUL DEATH OR INJURY

In a series of early rulings and cases, the IRS and the courts held that damages for wrongful death, defamation, alienation of affections, breach of contract to marry, and similar invasions of "personal" or "family" rights were not includable in the recipient's gross income.[1] The exclusion was based partly on the theory that they were not "derived from capital, from labor, or from both combined" and hence were not income under *Eisner v.*

---

[14] See infra ¶105.1.6. See also National Ry. Time Serv. Co. v. CIR, 88 F2d 904 (7th Cir. 1937) (taxpayer's consistent method of accounting for unclaimed deposits approved).

[15] Chicago, Rock Island & Pac. Ry. v. CIR, supra note 12 (compensation for services, damage claims, etc.); infra ¶5.7.1.

[1] McDonald v. CIR, 9 BTA 1340 (1928) (acq.) (damages for breach of contract to marry); Hawkins v. CIR, 6 BTA 1023 (1927) (libel and slander); infra note 12 (effect of §104(a)(2), excluding damages received on account of personal injuries or sickness from gross income); IT 2422, VII-2 CB 186 (1928) (declared obsolete by Rev. Rul. 67-466, 1967-2 CB 427); IT 2420, VII-2 CB 123 (1928) (compensation for death of taxpayer's husband in sinking of Lusitania), declared obsolete by Rev. Rul. 69-43, 1969-1 CB 310, after being reaffirmed by Rev. Rul. 54-19, 1954-1 CB 179 (recovery under state wrongful-death statute); Sol. Op. 132, I-1 CB 92 (1922) (superseded but reiterated in part by Rev. Rul. 74-77, 1974-1 CB 33) (alienation of affections; slander and libel of "personal character," not affecting "business reputation or property rights"; payment received by parent for surrendering custody of a minor child); see US v. Kaiser, 363 US 299 (1960) (appendix listing IRS rulings on nontaxable recoveries).

If the recovery includes punitive damages, interest, or compensation for lost earnings, an appropriate portion must be included in gross income. Riddle v. CIR, 27 BTA 1339 (1933) (interest); Rev. Rul. 58-418, 1958-2 CB 18 (punitive damages); cases and rulings cited supra ¶5.5.1 note 6. See also Rev. Rul. 72-341, 1972-2 CB 32 (recovery under Title VII of Civil Rights Act of 1964 for discriminatory employment practices held taxable as substitute for wages); Burlington N., Inc. v. Boxberger, 529 F2d 284 (9th Cir. 1975) (in FELA case, evidence of damages for loss of future income should include proof of potential income tax liability).

See Knickerbocker, The Income Tax Treatment of Damages: A Study in the Difficulties of the Income Concept, 47 Cornell LQ 429 (1962); Note, Tax Consequences of Transfers of Bodily Parts, 73 Colum. L. Rev. 842, 849–58 (1973).

Macomber,[2] and partly on the absence of a statutory provision specifically requiring their inclusion in gross income. In *United States v. Supplee-Biddle Hardware Co.*, the Supreme Court held that the proceeds of insurance on the life of a shareholder-officer were not taxable to the employer corporation because life insurance proceeds "are not usually classed as income" and because "assuming, without deciding, that Congress could call the proceeds of such indemnity income, and validly tax it as such . . . such a purpose on its part should be express, as it certainly is not [in the Revenue Act of 1918]."[3] Building on this comment, the Tax Court later held: "If compensation for the loss of a life is not taxable as income unless expressly provided, compensation for injury to personal reputation should similarly require an express provision."[4]

The "personal right" and "explicit statutory provision" rationales for these exclusions were both undermined by the Supreme Court's 1955 decision in *CIR v. Glenshaw Glass Co.*, holding that the *Eisner v. Macomber* definition is not exhaustive, that windfall receipts are taxable even though not derived from capital or labor, and that Congress intended to tax all "accessions to wealth" unless specifically exempted.[5]

These early exclusions also rested on a more fundamental ground— that compensatory recoveries for personal wrongs are not gain or income:

> If an individual is possessed of a personal right that is not assignable and not susceptible of any appraisal in relation to market values, and thereafter receives either damages or payment in compromise for an invasion of that right, it can not be held that he thereby derives any gain or profit. It is clear, therefore, that the Government cannot tax him on any portion of the sum received.[6]

And:

> Even to the economist, character or reputation or other strictly personal attributes are not capital or otherwise measureable in terms of wealth, notwithstanding that all will recognize them as important factors of economic success. They are not property or goods. Such compensation as general damages adds nothing to the individual, for the very concept which sanctions it prohibits that it shall include a profit.[7]

---

[2] Eisner v. Macomber, 252 US 189 (1920), discussed supra ¶1.2.4.
[3] US v. Supplee-Biddle Hardware Co., 265 US 189, 195 (1924).
[4] Hawkins v. CIR, supra note 1, at 1025.
[5] CIR v. Glenshaw Glass Co., 348 US 426 (1955), discussed supra ¶5.5.1.
[6] Sol. Op. 132, I-1 CB 92 (1922), at 93.
[7] Hawkins v. CIR, 6 BTA 1023 (1927), at 1025.

This "no income" rationale was cited by the Supreme Court in *Glenshaw Glass* to distinguish the punitive damages involved in that case from the personal injury recoveries in the early rulings: "The long history of departmental rulings holding personal injury recoveries nontaxable on the theory that they roughly correspond to a return of capital cannot support exemption of punitive damages following injury to property."[8]

This observation was probably intended only to distinguish the rulings, not to endorse them. Many compensatory receipts have been held to be gross income to the extent that they exceed the cost or other basis of property transferred, relinquished, or lost by the taxpayer in the event giving rise to the recovery.[9] Recoveries for defamation of the taxpayer's business reputation, for example, are taxable even though the payment is purely compensatory, intended to restore the *status quo ante* without enriching the taxpayer.[10]

Taxing a recovery for personal injury or deprivation might be a harsh response to the taxpayer's misfortune, but it is not significantly different from taxing wages and salaries without allowing an offsetting deduction for the exhaustion of the taxpayer's physical prowess and mental agility during this working life. Taxpayers claiming deductions for "human depreciation" have been summarily told by the courts that Congress has not granted such an allowance.[11] Thus, if the courts were writing on a clean slate, the personal injury issue could be analogized to the human depreciation issue. Since defamation or alienation of affections does not entail the loss of something for which the taxpayer paid cold cash, this analogy implies that compensation for such a wrong is an accession to the taxpayer's wealth that must be included in gross income unless Congress chooses to grant an explicit exemption.[12]

---

[8] CIR v. Glenshaw Glass Co., supra note 5, at 432 n.8. The Court's reference to the personal injury rulings may have been based on a supplemental memorandum submitted by the Solicitor General in response to a request by the Court during oral argument of the case. See Supplemental Memorandum for Petitioner at 4-7, in Record, CIR v. Glenshaw Glass Co., supra.

[9] See Raytheon Prods. Corp. v. CIR, 144 F2d 110 (1st Cir.), cert. denied, 323 US 779 (1944) (recovery for destruction of goodwill).

[10] See Agar v. CIR, 19 TCM (CCH) 116 (1960), aff'd per curiam on other grounds, 290 F2d 283 (2d Cir. 1961) (settlement of libel claim taxable in absence of evidence that anything was paid for damage to taxpayer's personal, rather than business, reputation).

[11] See Bourne v. CIR, 23 BTA 1288, 1292 (1931), aff'd, 62 F2d 648 (4th Cir.), cert. denied, 290 US 650 (1933).

[12] In 1920, the IRS ruled that the statutory predecessor of §104(a)(2), excluding damages received on account of personal injuries or sickness from gross income, applied only to "physical injuries," and not to damages for alienation of affections. SM 1384, 2 CB 71 (1920). Two years later the IRS ruled that damages for alienation of affections, defamation of personal character, or surrender of a child's custody did

Even if the Supreme Court's reference in *Glenshaw Glass* to "the long history of departmental rulings holding personal injury recoveries nontaxable" was not intended to endorse their validity ab initio, it suggests the possibility that they were subsequently sanctified by congressional acquiescence. A case for conscious congressional acquiescence in the exclusion of such esoteric items as damages for alienation of affections could hardly be documented, but it is not fanciful to suggest that the basic theory of these cases and rulings has been approved by silence. Indeed, it is probable that most of the lawyers in Congress know that wrongful-death recoveries are regularly excluded from gross income by the decedent's executor and heirs. The theory that long-standing administrative rulings can acquire the force of law if the statute is repeatedly reenacted without change is often criticized[13] and rarely applied, but the rulings cited in *Glenshaw Glass* may qualify for this unusual legislative blessing.

In any event, the IRS seems content to let sleeping dogs lie; despite the breadth of the Supreme Court's language in *Glenshaw Glass*, the IRS subsequently issued several additional personal-right rulings. It has ruled, for example, that damages received by a prisoner of war as compensation for an enemy government's violation of its obligations under the Geneva Convention are not includable in gross income; and similar treatment has been accorded to amounts paid victims of Nazi persecution for damages to health, liberty, and occupational advancement, on the ground that these receipts constitute reimbursement for the loss of "personal rights."[14]

So far, we have looked only at recoveries for tortious invasions of the taxpayer's rights. If, before any misconduct occurs, a taxpayer is paid for a release of claims that might otherwise arise in the future, the courts have held the payment taxable.[15] The cases involved payments by motion picture

---

not constitute income. See Sol. Op. 132, I-1 CB 92 (1922). Moreover, subsequent interpretations of §104(a)(2) suggest a broader reach for the statutory exclusion than contemplated by SM 1384. See infra ¶13.1.

[13] For discussion of the reenactment doctrine, see infra ¶110.4.2.

[14] Rev. Rul. 56-518, 1956-2 CB 25, as clarified by Rev. Rul. 57-505, 1957-2 CB 50 (West Germany's payments to victims of Nazi persecution); Rev. Ruls. 58-370, 1958-2 CB 14 and 69-212, 1969-1 CB 34 (similar payments by Austria); Rev. Rul. 55-132, 1955-1 CB 213 (prisoners of war); but see Stanford v. CIR, 297 F2d 298 (9th Cir. 1961) (private pension paid by German company not covered by Revenue Ruling 56-518). See also Revenue Act of 1962, Pub. L. No. 87-834, §27(a), 76 Stat. 960, 1067 (exempting awards by Attorney General to persons of Japanese ancestry evacuated from their homes during World War II).

For the possibility of excluding governmental reparation payments as tax-free gifts under §102, see infra ¶10.5.2.

[15] Starrels v. CIR, 304 F2d 574 (9th Cir. 1962); Ehrlich v. Higgins, 52 F. Supp. 805 (SDNY 1943); Roosevelt v. CIR, 43 TC 77 (1964); Fanelli v. CIR, 20 TCM (CCH) 1617 (1961); see also US v. Garber, 607 F2d 92 (5th Cir. 1979) (professional blood donor convicted of willful failure to report income from sale of blood). Tax-

companies wishing to use a person's name or biography without interference by him or his family. The issue has not always been faced head on, however, either because the recipient has been unable to segregate the amount paid for a release of future claims from undeniably taxable amounts paid for advice, documents, or similar assistance or because, when the payment is made to heirs, it is not clear that they have any legally protected rights to release.

There are intimations in several of these cases that an amount paid for a release might be nontaxable if the payor's conduct, but for the release, would have invaded the taxpayer's right to privacy or other protected interests.[16] If pursued, however, this notion would prove extremely troublesome. Even if somehow restricted to payments for invasions of privacy, it could be invoked as plausibly by professional actors and other performers as by amateurs. If extended to physical injuries, as logic would require, the theory would be available not only to lion tamers and boxers but also to mundane taxpayers like truck drivers, butchers, and electricians, all of whose regular salaries compensate, at least to some extent, for injuries inherent to their occupations. For this reason, it seems more reasonable to tax amounts paid in advance for a release of claims, even if a payment to settle a lawsuit brought after the fact by a nonconsenting taxpayer might qualify for an exclusion.

A theory has been suggested to reconcile these seemingly conflicting currents.[17] Under this theory, a tort recovery is excludable from gross income if it compensates for loss of a right that would otherwise have been enjoyed tax free. The satisfactions that come from respect and admiration within one's community, for example, are not taxed; if this respect and admiration is wrongfully harmed and money in the form of a defamation recovery is received as a substitute, the substitute should also be exempt from tax. Similarly, because marital bliss is not taxable, exemption should also be allowed for a monetary substitute in the form of a recovery for breach of promise to marry or alienation of affections. Because a person is not taxed on love, affection, or financial support provided by a family

---

payers' consistent failure to persuade the courts that amounts like these should be excluded from gross income has led some to concede their taxability and to try, so far, unsuccessfully, to salvage capital gain treatment. See Miller v. CIR, 299 F2d 706 (2d Cir.), cert. denied, 370 US 923 (1962), discussed infra ¶51.10.2; Gordon, Recoveries for Violation of the Right of Privacy in Quasi-Contract and the Federal Income Tax: An Illustration of Law's Response to Changes in Attitudes About the Personality, 10 Wayne L. Rev. 368 (1964).

[16] Ehrlich v. Higgins, supra note 15; Fanelli v. CIR, supra note 15.

[17] Sneed, Configurations of Gross Income 229–41 (Ohio State U. Press (1967). See also US v. Kaiser, 363 U.S. 299, 311 (1960) (Frankfurter concurring) ("payment which compensates for a loss of something which would not itself have been an item of gross income is not a taxable payment").

member, a wrongful death recovery compensating for loss of these benefits should not be taxed.

Compensation for loss of a right whose exercise would have produced gross income, in contrast, is itself gross income under this theory. Business reputation and goodwill, for example, are normally used to produce business profits, and a recovery for tortious injury to business reputation or goodwill should therefore be taxed just as the lost profits would have been.

Further, parallel treatment of the enjoyment of a tax-exempt right and a monetary substitute is only appropriate when the right is taken from the taxpayer without his consent. If a taxpayer sells a personal right, the selling price ought to be taxed. A monetary recovery for tortious invasion of privacy is appropriately accorded the same tax exemption as would have been recognized for the enjoyment of the lost privacy, for example, because the nonmonetary alternative—no tort—was not available to the taxpayer; because, that is, a nonmarketable tax-exempt right has been replaced with money in a nonmarket transaction. If a person receives a payment for his consent to a film that might be considered an invasion of privacy, in contrast, the payment should be taxed because taxation of gain from voluntary market transactions is the general rule. The proper analogy in the latter case is wages; a person who relinquishes leisure for wages is taxed on the wages even though he could have enjoyed the leisure tax free.

¶5.7 RECOVERIES OF DEDUCTED ITEMS—TAX BENEFIT PRINCIPLES

¶5.7.1 Introductory

A taxpayer who recovers an item deducted in an earlier year is ordinarily taxed on the recovery unless the deduction provided no tax benefit because it did not reduce the taxpayer's tax liability.[1] Because each year's income tax return must be based on the facts as known during that year,[2] the rule taxes the recovery in the year received rather than requiring an amendment of the return claiming the deduction. Recoveries of amounts deducted in prior years are a familiar phenomenon. Creditors, for example, often

---

[1] See generally Corlew, The Tax Benefit Rule, Claim of Right Restorations, and Annual Accounting: A Cure for the Inconsistencies, 21 Vand. L. Rev. 995 (1968); Del Cotto & Joyce, Double Benefits and Transactional Consistency Under the Tax Benefit Rule, 39 Tax L. Rev. 473 (1984); Plumb, The Tax Benefit Rule Today, 57 Harv. L. Rev. 129 (1943); Plumb, The Tax Benefit Rule Tomorrow, 57 Harv. L. Rev. 675 (1944); Tye, The Tax Benefit Doctrine Reexamined, 3 Tax L. Rev. 329 (1948); White, An Essay on the Conceptual Foundations of the Tax Benefit Rule, 82 Mich. L. Rev. 486 (1983).

[2] See infra ¶105.1.4.

deduct seemingly worthless claims but subsequently collect part or all of the debt when the debtor's financial state unexpectedly improves. Another example is a local property tax that is deducted when paid but is partially refunded in a later year because it turns out that the taxpayer paid more than was owing.

In the early days of the federal income tax, it was not clear that taxpayers were taxable on recovering these previously deducted amounts. It was once thought anomalous to require income to be reported when taxpayers merely collected amounts that were owing to them or received refunds of amounts that had been paid by mistake, especially since *Eisner v. Macomber* defined income as "gain derived from capital, from labor, or from both combined."[3] As late as 1929, for example, the Board of Tax Appeals seemed uncertain about the validity of a Treasury regulation providing that income was realized on collecting a debt previously charged off as worthless.[4] Within a few months, however, the Board of Tax Appeals accepted the so-called tax benefit rule enunciated by this regulation,[5] and by 1931 it was described as a principle that "seems to be taken for granted, as indeed it must be,"[6] and it has been a basic part of the federal income tax structure ever since.

Although the taxability of recoveries of previously deducted amounts rests primarily on judge-made rather than statutory law, the courts have had difficulty in explaining its rationale. In *National Bank of Commerce of Seattle v. CIR*, involving a bank's collection of loans that had been deducted as bad debts, the court said that the deductions converted the claims from capital investments to potential income, to be taxed if collected:

> When . . . a loan becomes worthless, the amount thereof is loss of capital, but the income tax laws permit the bank to recoup its capital by deducting from the profits or income the amount of the loss. Thus the bank does not pay a tax on all its income, but on the amount of income less the loss on the worthless debt. The debt itself then loses its nature as capital, but represents that portion of the income which was not taxed, and the capital is the money taken from the profits or

---

[3] Eisner v. Macomber, 252 US 189 (1920), discussed supra ¶1.2.4.

[4] Reg. 62, Art. 151 (issued pursuant to Revenue Act of 1921, carrying forward principle enunciated by Reg. 33, Art. 125, under Revenue Act of 1913); Liberty Ins. Bank v. CIR, 14 BTA 1428, 1434 (1929) (nonacq.) (validity of regulation not decided because earlier deductions were erroneous when taken and, hence, subject to correction only by deficiency assessment, which was barred by statute of limitations), rev'd, 59 F2d 320 (6th Cir. 1932) (estoppel theory).

[5] Excelsior Printing Co. v. CIR, 16 BTA 886 (1929). Given the reservation expressed by the Board of Tax Appeals in *Liberty Insurance Bank* (supra note 4), it is surprising that the taxability of the recovery was accepted without discussion in *Excelsior Printing Co.*

[6] Putnam Nat'l Bank v. CIR, 50 F2d 158 (5th Cir. 1931).

income. If the loan, after being deducted from income, is paid, then the lender is receiving profit or income—otherwise the lender would double its capital on one transaction. In other words, the profits or income used to pay back the capital when the debt is charged off is represented by the worthless loan, so that when such loan is paid the profits are replaced.[7]

Less elaborate than this transubstantiation of capital into income is the "balancing entry" theory, whose premise is that the taxpayer's income over the long haul can be correctly computed only by requiring recoveries of previously deducted amounts to be included in gross income. In a case involving a recovery of embezzled funds that had been deducted in a prior year, for example, the Board of Tax Appeals said: "The Commissioner has added no more to income [in the year of recovery] than has been deducted previously, thus bringing the amount of income reported over the period in balance with the actual income of the taxpayer for this period."[8] Acknowledging that the recovery of stolen funds is "compensation for loss" rather than income in the usual sense, the Board pointed out:

> [L]osses will sometimes be deducted where the future will eventually disclose compensation, and there will be reported as income that which is in fact only compensation for loss. But the deductions are practical necessities due to our inability to read the future, and the inclusion of the recovery in income is necessary to offset the deduction.[9]

In a later opinion, the Board of Tax Appeals observed that, in order to reflect income accurately for the entire period, taxpayers have often been required to make an adjustment "during the taxable year in which actually no income was received" because of the discovery in that year that the earlier deduction, though reasonable when taken, was unnecessary.[10]

Still another rationale is based on a theory of waiver or estoppel:

> [T]he repayment of a debt is a return of capital. . . . [I]t does not become income merely because it is not returned as agreed or when expected, or even if the owner concludes in his own mind that he will

---

[7] National Bank of Commerce of Seattle v. CIR, 115 F2d 875, 876–77 (9th Cir. 1940). The recoveries were not received by the lending banks but by a successor in interest, which was held to occupy their status for this purpose.

[8] South Dakota Concrete Prods. Co. v. CIR, 26 BTA 1429, 1431 (1932).

[9] Id. at 1432.

[10] Barnett v. CIR, 39 BTA 864, 867 (1939) (restoration of depletion deducted on receipt of advance royalty on lease, where no production occurred). See also infra ¶24.1.3 note 34.

never get it again. To justify a tax upon the repayment of a debt by referring it to the statutory definition of gross income would undoubtedly extend the statute beyond the constitutional powers of Congress.

But a taxpayer may voluntarily submit to an otherwise illegal or unconstitutional imposition, and, if it is a condition of some benefit which is tendered to him, his acquiescence will be assumed or implied from his acceptance of the benefit. Deductions allowed by law from gross income are not matters of right but of grace. When a taxpayer claims and is allowed a bad debt against his taxable income there is no difficulty in finding an implied consent to be taxed in respect of future recovery of the bad debt, whether or not it is actually income. Whether this be called an implied agreement of waiver for valid consideration or an estoppel, is not of great importance.[11]

While divergent, these theories share the view that the recoveries are not economic gain in the ordinary sense and that their inclusion in income is an anomaly requiring explanation. A creditor's collection of a just debt does not increase his net worth, even if he previously concluded that the debtor would never pay, and a homeowner would not ordinarily think that partial refund of his local property tax, following recomputation of his liability, is an income-producing event. Thus, the taxpayers in these cases are treated as realizing income only because they deducted amounts that were later established to be in excess of their actual loss or cost.

Viewing the tax benefit rule "in its true character—as a necessary counterweight to the consequences of the annual accounting principle," one judge of the Tax Court observed:

> The need to assess and collect taxes at fixed and relatively short intervals underpins the principle of taxation that transactions which may possibly be subject to further developments substantially altering their character for tax purposes should nevertheless be treated as final and closed so that their tax consequences can be determined. . . . On the other hand, a taxpayer should not be permitted to take advantage of this governmental exigency to establish a distorted picture of his income for tax purposes. It is this countervailing consideration which spawned the tax benefit rule. . . . The most common, and most nearly accurate, explanation of the rule is that it recognizes the "recovery" in the current year of taxable income earned in an earlier year but offset by the item deducted.[12]

---

[11] Philadelphia Nat'l Bank v. Rothensies, 43 F. Supp. 923, 925 (ED Pa. 1942).
[12] Munter's Est. v. CIR, 63 TC 663, 678 (1975) (concurring opinion).

The Supreme Court later echoed this thought: "The basic purpose of the tax benefit rule is to achieve rough transactional parity . . . and to protect the Government . . . from the adverse effects of reporting a transaction on the basis of assumptions that an event in a subsequent year proves to have been erroneous."[13]

Even though the tax benefit rule is a counterweight to the consequences of the annual accounting principle, the tax on the recovery need not equal the tax savings generated by the prior deduction. Since marginal tax rates vary from year to year, particularly for individuals, the increased tax in the year of recovery is often more or less than the tax reduction enjoyed in the earlier year. With one short-lived exception,[14] however, the courts have been satisfied with the rough-and-ready adjustment that results from taxing the recovery at whatever rate prevails in the year of recovery, and have not insisted on exacting a tax equal to the amount saved by the taxpayer in the earlier year.

Once the courts concluded that recovered amounts are taxable not because they increase the taxpayer's net worth but because they are linked to a prior tax deduction, the door was opened to taxpayer claims that recoveries should be taxed only if the deduction actually reduced the taxpayer's tax liability for the earlier year and not if there were enough other deductions to eliminate any tax liability. This idea had a checkered career in the courts for more than a decade, and the IRS also wavered between accepting and rejecting it.[15] In 1942, however, Congress gave it formal

---

[13] Hillsboro Nat'l Bank v. CIR, 460 US 370, 383 (1983).

[14] In Perry v. US, 160 F. Supp. 270 (Ct. Cl. 1958), the Court of Claims adopted an "exact tax benefit" rule, under which the recovery was taxed at the rate that applied to the deduction. The court later overruled this decision and accepted the prevailing judicial view that the recovery is to be taxed at whatever rate is in effect for the year of receipt. Alice Phelan Sullivan Corp. v. US, 381 F2d 399 (Ct. Cl. 1967).

From 1954 to 1976, §1342 applied an exact tax benefit approach for certain recoveries of amounts paid as a result of a judicial decision in a patent infringement suit. Section 1346 (in force from 1941 to 1976) also utilized this principle in permitting a taxpayer receiving repayment of an unconstitutional federal tax to choose between (1) excluding the receipt and amending the earlier year's return (despite the running of the statute of limitations) to eliminate the deduction and (2) reporting the recovery when received. Sections 1342 and 1346 were repealed as "deadwood" by the Tax Reform Act of 1976. Pub. L. No. 94-455, 90 Stat. 1520, 1764-1846.

[15] For the twists and turns in the judicial doctrines and administrative rulings, see Tye, supra note 1, at 329. A model income tax statute drafted by an American Law Institute group proposed inclusion of all recoveries of deductible items in gross income, whether the deduction was taken or not, and, if a deduction was taken, whether or not it resulted in a reduction of the taxpayer's tax, subject to an option in the taxpayer to reopen the earlier year if the statute of limitations had not expired or if the amount exceeded specified dollar or percentage limits. ALI Fed. Income Tax Stat., Vol. 1, at 157-58 (Feb. 1954 Draft).

endorsement by enacting the statutory predecessor of §111, which excluded from gross income the recovery of certain previously deducted items if the deduction "did not result in a reduction of the taxpayer's tax" in prior years. Until 1984, §111 accorded this treatment explicitly only to recoveries of previously deducted bad debts, taxes, and "delinquency amounts" (primarily interest on past-due taxes). The regulations, however, applied the tax benefit principle to a much wider assortment of items, and in 1984 the statute was amended to reach all such recoveries.[16]

The tax benefit rule is therefore "both a rule of inclusion and exclusion: Recovery of an item previously deducted must be *included* in income; that portion of the recovery not resulting in a prior tax benefit is *excluded*."[17] Section 111 states only the exclusionary aspect of the rule, but by necessary implication it ratifies the judge-made inclusionary component, without which there would be no raw material on which §111 could operate. In the discussion that follows, the threshold issue of inclusion is examined first, and the exclusionary rule is discussed thereafter.

¶5.7.2 Inclusion of Recovered Items

As traditionally formulated, the inclusionary component of the tax benefit rule comes into play when the taxpayer recovers an item that would not be includable in income except for the fact that it was deducted or

---

[16] See infra ¶5.7.3.

[17] Putoma Corp. v. Cir, 66 TC 652, 664 n.10 (1976), aff'd, 601 F2d 734 (5th Cir. 1979).

Sometimes both features of the rule are merged into a single formulation, as in Nash v. US, 398 US 1, 3 (1970) ("the so-called tax benefit rule, *viz.* that a recovery of an item that has produced an income tax benefit in a prior year is to be added to income in the year of recovery"). On other occasions, the exclusionary qualification alone is described as the tax benefit rule, as in Alice Phelan Sullivan Corp. v. US, supra note 14 (describing tax benefit rule as "limitation" on principle that recovery of deducted items generates income). But see Rev. Rul. 77-67, 1977-1 CB 33 (referring to inclusionary aspect as "the" tax benefit rule). See also Continental Ill. Nat'l Bank & Trust Co. v. CIR, 69 TC 357, 370 (1977) (acq.) ("The exclusionary aspect of the rule has no real existence apart from the inclusionary aspect, but merely acts as a limitation on the amount included. So integrated are these aspects of the tax benefit rule, in fact, that the statutory articulation of the rule in section 111 recited only its exclusionary aspect, and assumes the inclusion").

credited[18] in computing tax liability for a prior year.[19] The Supreme Court held in *Hillsboro National Bank v. CIR*, however, that the rule is not limited to actual recoveries of money or property.[20]*Hillsboro* involved the liquidation of a corporation that had engaged in a dairy farming business. Among the assets distributed to shareholders in the liquidation was cattle feed, the cost of which had been deducted when incurred under the cash method accounting rules allowed for farmers.[21] Although the statutes then in effect provided that a corporation generally recognized no gain or loss on a distribution of property to shareholders in liquidation,[22] the Court required that the taxpayer recognize income under the tax benefit rule equal to the previously deducted cost of the feed. The purpose of the rule is not to tax recoveries, the Court said, but "to approximate the results produced by a tax system based on transactional rather than annual accounting."[23] A mon-

---

[18] Because the recovery of an amount that was taken as a credit is unusual, the tax benefit rule is usually described in terms of deductions. The exclusionary rule, however, applies to recoveries of credited items (IRC §111(b)), and this implies that the inclusionary rule applies too.

Other tax allowances may also serve as a foundation for the inclusionary rule. Thus, in Keystone Nat'l Bank in Pittsburgh v. US, 52 AFTR 1511 (WD Pa. 1957) (not officially reported), the taxpayer recovered funds that had been omitted from gross income when initially received because they were secretly misappropriated by an employee. The court held that the tax benefit resulting from this inadvertent omission warranted inclusion of the recovery. This conclusion could be explained by treating the omission as the equivalent of including the embezzled funds in gross income and deducting the same amount as a loss from theft, and treating the later recovery as a recoupment of the constructive deduction. See also Alsop v. CIR, 290 F2d 726 (2d Cir. 1961) (for cash basis taxpayer, unreported embezzled funds are income when received under cash method rules, without assistance of tax benefit rule).

For a case involving receipts in a year following an inventory write-down that did not produce a full tax benefit, see Union Trust Co. of Indianapolis v. US, 173 F2d 54 (7th Cir.), cert. denied, 337 US 940 (1949).

[19] For the recovery of items that could have been, but were not, deducted in earlier years, see infra note 50.

[20] Hillsboro Nat'l Bank v. CIR, 460 US 370 (1983). See also Weyher v. CIR, 66 TC 825 (1976) (on sale of mortgaged property, seller recovered prepaid interest).

[21] See infra ¶105.5.

[22] IRC §336(a) (before amendment in 1986). The Court said:

> When the later event takes place in the context of a nonrecognition provision of the Code, there will be an inherent tension between the tax benefit rule and the nonrecognition provision. . . . We cannot resolve that tension with a blanket rule that the tax benefit rule will always prevail. Instead, we must focus on the particular provisions of the Code at issue in any case.

Hillsboro Nat'l Bank v. CIR, supra note 20, at 385–86. The Court found that the policies of §336(a) were not upset by the application of the tax benefit rule on a liquidating distribution.

[23] Id. at 381.

etary recovery frequently signals the need for a transactional adjustment, but the common case should not be taken as the boundary of the doctrine. Rather, the Court held, a prior deduction must be recouped by reporting an equal amount of income under the tax benefit rule whenever a "later event [occurs that is] fundamentally inconsistent with the premise on which the deduction was initially based."[24] The taxpayer's deduction for cattle feed was premised on an assumption that the taxpayer's cattle would consume the feed. The taxpayer's use of the feed—distributing it to shareholders—was fundamentally inconsistent with that premise, and the deducted cost was thus required to be recovered by a tax benefit inclusion.

The Court reasoned as follows: Assume a taxpayer pays rent on business property for a period extending into the following taxable year, but is allowed to deduct the rent when paid. During the next year, prior to the end of the period covered by the rental payment, the taxpayer converts the property to a personal use. "This would be an event fundamentally inconsistent with the business use on which the deduction was based," and thus would require the inclusion in income of an amount equal to the rent for the period of personal use.[25] Similarly, if the taxpayer is allowed to write off the cost of property purchased for use in business and "the taxpayer converts the expensed asset to some other, non-business use, that action is inconsistent with his earlier deduction, and the tax benefit rule would require inclusion in income of the amount of the unwarranted deduction."[26] The same result must obtain "if a corporation turns expensed assets to the analog of personal consumption, as [the taxpayer] did here—distribution to shareholders."[27]

This principle embraces a wide range of receipts, of which the most important are the following:

1. *Recoveries on bad debts.* Probably, the most common example of a tax benefit recovery is the collection of a debt previously deducted as worthless. The rule applies to such a recovery whether the prior deduction was based on complete or partial worthlessness. The rule does not apply to debts charged off against a bad debt reserve, but an analogous treatment obtains; because the debt, when determined to be bad, was subtracted from the reserve, the recovery is added to the reserve to restore the subtraction.[28]

---

[24] Id. at 383. The Court continues: "That is, if that event had occurred within the same taxable year, it would have foreclosed the deduction." Id. This comment, however, is not helpful because there is no body of law indicating when an otherwise deductible expense becomes nondeductible because of a subsequent event within the same year.

[25] Id. at 385.

[26] Id. at 395.

[27] Id. at 396.

[28] Reg. §1.111-1(a)(1) (second sentence).

The reserve method for accounting for bad debts has generally been eliminated for taxable years after 1986.[29]

2. *Tax refunds.* Refunds of taxes (including interest or other payments
for delays or failures in filing returns or paying taxes) that were previously
deducted or credited were also listed by the original §111 as items to which
the exclusionary rule applies,[30] and this carries the clear implication that the
inclusionary rule also applies to these items. Thus, they must be included in
income except to the extent the prior deduction or credit produced no tax
benefit.[31]

3. *Casualty losses.* Casualty losses are deductible only to the extent
they are not compensated for by insurance or otherwise.[32] If the right to
compensation is unknown, contested, or otherwise doubtful during the taxable year of the loss, however, the taxpayer is entitled to deduct the loss
then, but must include in income any subsequent recoveries.[33]

4. *Other losses.* If a taxpayer deducts a loss on selling property, he must
report as income any subsequent recoupment of the loss, or any part of it,
whether received from the person from whom he bought the property (for
example, because of a misrepresentation of value or breach of warranty) or
from a third party for misconduct injuring the property.[34]

5. *Accrued liabilities abandoned by the creditor.* Taxpayer's using the
accrual method of accounting sometimes accrue business expenses that are
never paid, and cash method taxpayers sometimes pay expenses by checks

---

[29] See infra ¶33.5. If a debt charged against a bad debt reserve is recovered when
the taxpayer no longer uses the reserve method, the recovery is gross income under
the tax benefit rule. When a taxpayer goes off the reserve method, the balance in the
reserve is included in gross income. See infra ¶105.6.3. A prior charge-off reduces the
amount of this gross income, and thus represents an amount that was once deducted
as an addition to the reserve and that was not restored to gross income when the
reserve was terminated. If a recovery of the debt later undercuts the premise for the
charge off, matters can be squared only by including the recovery in gross income.

[30] IRC §§111(b)(2), (3) (before amendment in 1984). See also Schulz v. US, 43
AFTR2d 676 (ED Wis. 1979) (not officially reported) (credit of overpayment against
following year's tax liability constituted recovery, triggering application of tax benefit rule).

[31] But see Hillsboro Nat'l Bank v. US, 460 US 370 (1983) (where corporation
receives refund of personal property tax that, in earlier year, had been imposed on
shareholders' stock but had been paid by corporation, refund not gross income;
§164(e), which allows corporation to deduct its payment of shareholders' tax, construed to exempt corporation from tax benefit rule on refund; whacky decision).

[32] See infra ¶34.4.3.

[33] See Rev. Rul. 71-160, 1971-1 CB 75, and Rev. Rul. 71-161, 1971-1 CB 76
(where reimbursement provided by disaster relief statutes for previously deducted
casualty losses, reimbursements included in gross income, subject to exclusionary
rule); cf. Rev. Rul. 73-408, 1973-2 CB 15 (tax benefit rule not applicable in absence
of prior deduction).

[34] Reg. §1.111-1(a)(1) (last sentence).

that are never cashed or are returned because the addressee cannot be found. Unless subject to a local escheat law, these unclaimed or abandoned items cannot remain outstanding for tax purposes forever. The inclusionary aspect of the tax benefit rule requires them to be taken into income, but the date when this must happen is unclear.[35]

6. *Accrued liabilities assumed by transferees.* When an accrual basis taxpayer transfers property subject to liabilities encumbering the property, the liabilities taken over by the buyer or other transferee might include amounts the taxpayer has deducted. Deductions might have been taken for unpaid interest that was added to the principal of a mortgage and assumed by the buyer, or the assumed liabilities might include accrued but unpaid taxes on the property. The IRS contends that income must be recognized by such a transferor under the tax benefit rule in an amount equal to the previously taken deduction. The Tax Court rejects this theory, holding that the liability for the deducted item, like all other liabilities assumed or taken subject to by the transferee, is included in the amount realized on the transfer, and thus enters into the gain or loss on the sale or exchange, but that no tax benefit recovery occurs.[36]

Assume *T* holds Blackacre subject to a mortgage of $100. Interest of $5 accrues on the mortgage, but is not paid before *T* sells the property to *B* for $25 down and *B*'s agreement to take the property subject to the mortgage, including the accrued but unpaid interest. *T*'s amount realized on the sale is $130 (the sum of the $25 down payment, the $100 principal amount of the mortgage, and the $5 liability for interest), and if *T*'s basis for the property is, say, $80, he has gain on the sale of $50. The IRS argues *T* also has income of $5 under the tax benefit rule, but the Tax Court says the $50 gain is the only income on the transaction.

The Tax Court has the better side of the argument. One of the premises underlying an accrual method taxpayer's deduction is that the deducted item will eventually be paid; any event that causes the liability to disappear without payment is fundamentally inconsistent with the premises of the deduction, and triggers a tax benefit recovery. Payment in cash, however, is not a predicate of the deduction. If the watchdog is transferred to the watchman in payment of his salary, gain is recognized on the transfer of the watchdog, but there is no tax benefit recovery of the deduction for the salary. Similarly, if *T* transferred Blackacre to the mortgagee in satisfaction

---

[35] See Roxy Custom Clothes Corp. v. US, 171 F. Supp. 851 (Ct. Cl. 1959) (income when accounts payable credited to eliminate liability); Lime Cola Co. v. CIR, 22 TC 593, 601 (1954) (income when amount credited to surplus); G.M. Standifer Constr. Corp. v. CIR, 30 BTA 184 (1934), appeal dismissed, 78 F2d 285 (9th Cir. 1935) (income in year of settlement).

[36] Allan v. CIR, 86 TC 655 (1986). See Cunningham, Characterization of Income Recovered Under the Tax Benefit Doctrine, 7 Va. Tax Rev. 121 (1987).

of the mortgage, including the accrued but unpaid interest, the debt should be considered paid, not eliminated without payment.[37] In the example, the payment is less direct — Blackacre is transferred to a third party in exchange for his agreement to pay the liability, but payment should nevertheless be considered made, not avoided.

7. *Unnecessary bad debt reserves.* Prior to the elimination in 1986 of the reserve method for bad debts, taxpayers using this method made periodic additions to their reserves, which were deducted from income. As specific debts became worthless, they were charged to the reserve,[38] and any subsequent recoveries were credited to the reserve; subsequent additions to the reserve were calculated by methods reflecting these charges and credits and other factors affecting expectations as to future bad debts.[39] If the reserve becomes unnecessary (because, for example, the taxpayer sells its receivables or changes from the reserve method to a direct charge-off method), the balance in the reserve must be taken into income, since it was built up by prior deductions.[40]

8. *Cancellation of taxpayer's indebtedness.* When a debt is discharged for less than its face amount, the debtor ordinarily realizes income under *United States v. Kirby Lumber Co.* and later cases.[41] If the discharged debt gave rise to a tax deduction when it was incurred (e.g., an accrual basis taxpayer's liability for wages or business supplies), the *Kirby Lumber* principle overlaps the tax benefit doctrine in certain respects, creating problems that are discussed elsewhere in this work.[42]

A recovery is not gross income under the tax benefit rule, in contrast, if the payment of the recovered item gave rise to no tax allowance, such as a refund of an amount paid for an item of personal consumption or a nonde-

---

[37] The transfer in *Allan* was a transfer to the mortgagee in lieu of foreclosure.

[38] See supra text accompanying notes 28–29.

[39] See infra ¶33.5.

[40] See Arcadia Sav. & Loan Ass'n v. CIR, 300 F2d 247 (9th Cir. 1962) (sale of business); S. Rossin & Sons v. CIR, 113 F2d 652 (2d Cir. 1940) (shift to direct charge-off method); Geyer, Cornell & Newell, Inc. v. CIR, 6 TC 96 (1946) (acq.) (need for reserve terminated in prior year, not before the court, when taxpayer abandoned line of business). Although §111 does not apply to the recovery of specific debts charged to a bad-debt reserve (supra text accompanying notes 28–29), it is applicable if the reserve itself is includable in income because the need therefor has ceased. See M&E Corp. v. CIR, 7 TC 1276 (1946); Rev. Rul. 78-278, 1978-2 CB 134. The rules governing changes in accounting method also apply when a taxpayer abandons the reserve method in favor of the specific charge-off method. See ¶105.6. The principal difference between the tax benefit and change of accounting rules is that the latter frequently allow the income to be spread over a period of years.

See also Haynsworth v. CIR, 68 TC 703 (1977) (closing of subdivider's reserve for development expenses generates income).

[41] US v. Kirby Lumber Co., 284 US 1 (1931), discussed infra ¶6.4.1.

[42] See infra ¶6.4.5.

ductible tax (e.g., the federal income tax or a local real property tax paid by a taxpayer who did not itemize his personal deductions) or the recovery of long-lost property (e.g., forgotten bank accounts or misplaced jewelry). These events generate no income even if the taxpayer never expected to see the items again and views the recovery as a windfall. The same principle has been applied to the recovery of an amount that was not deductible when paid because the taxpayer was then an exempt organization.[43]

It is not clear whether the tax benefit rule applies if the taxpayer claims a tax allowance based on a status for which he would not have qualified if his right to the recovery had been known when the status was determined. Assume a grandparent pays a grandchild's college tuition bill; the tuition accounts for more than one half of the grandchild's support, and the payment thus qualifies the grandparent to take the personal exemption for the grandchild. In a later year, a substantial portion of the tuition is refunded to the grandparent, with the consequence that the grandparent's support for the grandchild for the year of payment falls below the one half necessary to qualify for the personal exemption. Is the grandparent required to report gross income for the year of the refund equal to the personal exemption taken in the earlier year? Probably, yes. The recovery is fundamentally inconsistent with the premise for the allowance of the exemption—the grandparent's furnishing of more than one half of the grandchild's support for the year.[44]

The status of a recovered amount that was improperly deducted is also problematical. The earliest cases held that the government's sole remedy for an erroneous deduction is to assess a deficiency for the deduction year; the IRS cannot indirectly extend the statute of limitations, these cases held, by seizing on a subsequent recovery as an occasion for rectifying an error in a return for a closed year.[45] Later cases softened this position by holding that the taxpayer cannot rely on the impropriety of the deduction if the earlier return was either deliberately or inadvertently misleading and that the recovery can be excluded only if the IRS should have known that the deduction was erroneous.[46]

---

[43] California & Hawaiian Sugar Ref. Corp. v. US, 311 F2d 235 (Ct. Cl. 1962). Cf. IRC §1016(a)(3) (basis of property reduced by depreciation for periods when taxpayer not subject to federal income taxation).

[44] Similar questions can arise with respect to the right to file as a surviving spouse or head of household—privileges that are restricted by §§2(a) and (b) to taxpayers with dependents within the meaning of §152.

[45] Canelo v. CIR, 53 TC 217, 226–27 (1969) (nonacq.), aff'd per curiam, 447 F2d 484 (9th Cir. 1971); Streckfus Steamers, Inc. v. CIR, 19 TC 1 (1952) (nonacq.). In Canelo, the Tax Court relied in part on the inapplicability of §§1311–1314, mitigating the statute of limitations in certain circumstances. See infra ¶113.9.

[46] Unvert v. CIR, 72 TC 807 (1979), aff'd, 656 F2d 483 (9th Cir. 1981); Mayfair Minerals, Inc. v. CIR, 56 TC 82, 89–91 (1971), aff'd per curiam, 456 F2d 622 (5th

The Court of Appeals for the Ninth Circuit, however, took the matter a step further, deciding in *Unvert v. CIR* that the application of the tax benefit rule does not depend on whether the prior deduction was proper or not:

> The erroneous deduction exception is . . . poor public policy. A taxpayer who properly claims a deduction for an expenditure that is recovered in a later year must treat the recovery as income, while [under the erroneous deduction exception] one who claims an improper deduction may not be required to include the recovery as income only because of the impropriety of the deduction. . . . [I]mproperly taken tax deductions should not be rewarded.[47]

The *Unvert* decision raises more questions than it answers. In that case, the statute of limitations ran on the year of the erroneous deduction before the IRS began its audit of the year of the recovery.[48] Does the rule apply only in that context? If the statute for the deduction year is still open, must the IRS make the adjustment for that year? Or, is it given a choice of denying the deduction or taxing the recovery? Or, must it allow the deduction and tax the recovery? It would be a strange doctrine that would bar the disallowance of a plainly erroneous deduction once the deducted expenditure was recovered.[49] If the deduction can be denied notwithstanding the recovery, however, are there occasions where the IRS' failure to pursue this remedy bars it from taxing the recovery? Suppose the statute of limitations on the deduction year is open when the IRS discovers the recovery, but runs before the IRS hits upon the idea of denying the deduction. Does it make any difference in this situation whether the deduction is clearly not allowable or is arguable, whether the deduction's weakness is apparent on the face of the return, or whether the IRS is diligent or dilatory in formulating its position in the case?

Boehm v. CIR involved the converse situation, where a recovered amount could have been deducted in an earlier year, but was not. The Court of Appeals for the Second Circuit held that an amount received in settle-

---

Cir. 1972). See generally Bishop, The Tax Benefit Rule After *Unvert*: Does It Compromise the Statute of Limitations? 51 J. Tax'n 272 (1979).

[47] Unvert v. CIR, 656 F2d 483, 486 (9th Cir. 1981).

[48] The deduction was taken in 1969, and the recovery occurred in 1972. If no extension of the time for filing was granted for either year and the taxpayer had not consented to an extension of the limitations period for the deduction year, that period expired soon after the return was filed for the year of recovery. See infra ¶113.2.

[49] All other things being equal, the IRS would prefer to assess the deficiency for the year of the deduction rather than the year of recovery because it could then collect interest for the period between the times when the deduction was taken and the recovery was received.

ment of a derivative stockholder's action by a taxpayer whose stock could have been—but was not—deducted as worthless in an earlier year was not includable in gross income when received.[50] The taxpayer claimed a loss in the earlier year, but abandoned the claim when it was disallowed by the IRS. The opinion, however, is not based on an estoppel rationale, and is broad enough to exclude recoveries where the taxpayer, although entitled to a deduction in the earlier year, never claims it. A contrary rule would open the door, whenever a debt or other item is collected after a long delay, to an assertion by the IRS that it could have been deducted in an earlier year and that the current receipt is a taxable recovery unless the hypothetical deduction would have produced no tax benefit. To be sure, *Boehm* enables the unusually prescient taxpayer to refrain from taking a deduction in a low tax year in order to prepare the way for a subsequent tax-free recovery in a high tax year. The likelihood of this abuse is slim, however, and it could be minimized by an exception for taxpayers who deliberately forgo a clearly proper deduction.

When the inclusionary branch of the tax benefit rule is applicable, it is sometimes necessary to determine whether the taxable recovery constitutes ordinary income or capital gain. The courts often impress the character of the original transaction on the recovery.[51] When employed, this relation-back doctrine taxes the recovery as ordinary income if the earlier loss or expense was deducted from ordinary income; conversely, the recovery is usually capital gain if the earlier deduction was a capital loss.

¶5.7.3 Exclusion of Items Deducted Without Tax Benefit

As applied to recoveries of deducted items, the exclusionary aspect of the tax benefit rule, now stated in §111(a), excludes a tax benefit recovery from income "to the extent such amount did not reduce income subject to tax."[52] For each year in which a recovery occurs, §111(a) is applied as follows: A test recomputation is made of taxable income for the deduction year. In the recomputation, the recovered portion of the deducted item is excluded from the taxpayer's deductions, and an exclusion is also made for any portion of the deduction that was recovered in a prior year. If a net operating loss is shown on the original return, it is recomputed, and the effect of the recomputation is followed through all years to which the loss can be carried. Recomputed income for the deduction year and other affected years is compared with the income originally reported. Any difference

---

[50] Boehm v. CIR, 146 F2d 553 (2d Cir.), aff'd on other issues, 326 US 287 (1945), rehearing denied, 326 US 811 (1946).

[51] See infra ¶51.10.6.

[52] Staff of Joint Comm. on Tax'n, 98th Cong., 2d Sess., General Explanation of the Revenue Provisions of the Deficit Reduction Act of 1984 at 521–22 (1984).

between the original and recomputed amounts represents the amount of the recovered deduction that yielded tax benefit, and to this extent, the recovery is gross income. If the recovery exceeds this amount, the excess is excluded from gross income by §111(a). If the deduction was partially recovered in a prior year, the exclusion for the current year is the amount just described, reduced by the exclusion for the prior year.[53]

Example 5-2 illustrates the rule. For 1989, the taxpayer is allowed $6,300 of deductions for bad debts. In 1990 and 1991, the taxpayer collects $1,800 and $3,000, respectively, on the debts written off in 1989.

Under §111(c), if a deduction increased a carryover, it is deemed usable with tax benefit unless the carryover expired unused prior to the year of the recovery. In Example 5-2, the §111 deductions of $6,300 increase a net operating loss carryover. If these deductions had not been allowed, the $1,300 of net operating loss (line 5) would not have existed; the deductions thus increase the carryover for the loss from zero to $1,300. In the example, the carryover is used with tax benefit by carrying it back to an earlier year. If the taxpayer had waived the right to carry the NOL back and had used the NOL as a carryforward,[54] the result would be the same, regardless of when, if ever, the carryforward actually produces tax benefit. The NOL would be carried first to 1990, the first year in which a partial recovery of the §111 items occurs. Because the carryover does not expire prior to the beginning of 1990, §111(c) requires that §111(a) be applied in 1990 by treating the deductions included in the carryover as though they had produced tax benefit, and this would be so even if the taxpayer has no net income to absorb any of the carryover in that year. Similarly, for 1991, the second year in the carryover period and the second year in which a tax benefit recovery occurs, the carryover has either produced tax benefit by having been used as a deduction in 1990 or is conclusively presumed productive of tax benefit because it is carried to the current year.

The regulations contain a similar example, shown below as Examples 5-3 and 5-4, that illustrates the application of the pre-1984 version of §111.[55] Under pre-1984 law, the amount that could be excluded on a full recovery of a previously deducted item is referred to as the "recovery exclusion."[56] The regulations construed the pre-1984 statute to treat the first dollars

---

[53] If the taxpayer has credits against tax, the effects of these credits must also be taken into account. If the income offset by the recovered deduction would otherwise have been rendered nontaxable by a credit that went unused, the deduction was taken without tax benefit, and §111(a) is available to exclude the recovery.

[54] The election to waive the carryback is provided by §172(b)(3)(C). See ¶25.11.3.

[55] Reg. §1.111-1(b)(3) Ex.

[56] IRC §111(b)(4) (before amendment in 1984).

Example 5-2

Determination of §111
Exclusion Under Present Law

	1989 Income as Reported	Recomputation of 1989 Income in Applying Test For: 1990	Recomputation of 1989 Income in Applying Test For: 1991
1. Gross income	$25,000	$25,000	$25,000
2. Less Deductions:			
a. Depreciation	$20,000	$20,000	$20,000
b. Section 111 items ($6,300 less cumulative amount recovered).........	6,300	4,500	1,500
c. Personal exemption	2,000	2,000	2,000
d. Total deductions...............................	$28,300	$26,500	$23,500
3. Taxable income (loss)..............................	($3,300)	($1,500)	$1,500
4. Adjustment under §172(d)(3) to eliminate personal exemption................	2,000	2,000	2,000
5. Net operating loss (used in 1987)...........	($1,300)	–0–	–0–
6. Deductions originally taken with tax benefit that are lost in recomputation:			
a. Increase in 1989 taxable income.......		–0–	$1,500
b. Decrease in NOL carryback..............		$1,300	1,300
7. Portion of recovered amount that produced tax benefit (sum of 6a and 6b)		$1,300	$2,800
8. Excludable amount:			
a. Cumulative recoveries		$1,800	$4,800
b. Less: Portion that produced tax benefit (line 7)................................		1,300	2,000
c. Exclusion		$500	$2,000
d. Exclusion for current year (line 8c, less exclusion for prior year).............		$500	$1,500
9. Gross income (recovery for year less current exclusion).................................		$1,300	$1,500

recovered as an excludable recovery of the recovery exclusion.[57] The comparison in Example 5-3 shows the portion of the deductions that yielded tax benefit. In this example, §111 deductions for 1981 are $6,300 (line 2b), and the portion producing tax benefit is $4,300, consisting of the sum of $3,000 (taxable income for the deduction year determined without the §111 items, line 3) and $1,300 (the net operating loss carryback to 1987, line 5). The recovery exclusion (the portion of the §111 items that produces no tax benefit) is $1,000—the excess of the §111 items ($6,300) over the amount of deduction that produces tax benefit ($5,300).

Under the pre-1984 ordering rule, recoveries of §111 deductions are excludable up to the amount of the recovery exclusion. If the taxpayer recovers $400 in 1982 in respect of the §111 items, the recovery is fully excluded because it is less than the recovery exclusion of $1,000. If $750 more is recovered in 1983, the taxpayer is allowed an exclusion of $600 (the excess of the $1,000 recovery exclusion over the $400 recovered in the preceding year), and $150 of the recovery is gross income. This rule is frequently more favorable to taxpayers than the rule enacted in 1984 because it always allows the excludable amount to be recovered first.

Example 5-3

Determination of Tax Benefit
Attributable to §111 Items

	1981 Return as Filed With Deduction of §111 Items	Recomputation of 1981 Income Without Deduction of §111 Items
1. Gross income	$25,000	$25,000
2. Less: Deductions		
a. Depreciation	$20,000	$20,000
b. §111 items (business bad debts and taxes)	6,300	
c. Personal exemption	1,000	1,000
d. Total deductions	$27,300	$21,000
3. Taxable income (loss)	($2,300)	$4,000
4. Adjustment under §172(d)(3) to eliminate personal exemption	1,000	
5. Net operating loss (used in 1978)	($1,300)	

---

[57] Reg. §1.111-1(b)(3) Ex.

Example 5-4

Computation of Recovery Exclusion
Under Pre-1984 Rules

6. Section 111 items (from line 2b of Example 5-2)..................... $6,300
7. Portion of §111 items used to reduce 1981 taxable income
   (line 3, as recomputed)... $4,000
8. Portion of §111 items carried back to reduce 1975
   taxable income (line 5)... 1,300
9. Total of §111 items deducted with tax benefit
   (line 7 plus line 8)... $5,300
10. Recovery exclusion (line 6 minus line 9) $1,000

Under current law, as well as under the pre-1984 statute, if the statute of limitations has run, all other deductions taken in the deduction year are left intact in the §111 recomputation.[58] Thus, in Example 5-2, the IRS cannot reduce or eliminate the recovery exclusion by showing that the 1989 deduction for depreciation (line 2a) was excessive, even though this possibility might have been disregarded on audit of the 1989 return because the auditing agent believed the deduction for the §111 items was sufficient to offset any adjustment to the depreciation allowance. On the other hand, the taxpayer cannot introduce deductions, however valid, that were not claimed on the 1989 return to establish that deducting the recovered item produced no tax benefit.[59] If the deduction year has not been barred by the statute of limitations, in contrast, adjustments can be made by the IRS assessing a deficiency for that year or the taxpayer filing an amended return for the year, and §111(a) will then be applied as though the adjustments had been included in the return as first filed.

The regulations provide that recoveries of deductions for depreciation, depletion, amortization, and amortizable bond premiums are not subject to the "rule of exclusion."[60] The Code explicitly requires the basis of property generating these deductions to be reduced by the "allowable" deductions

---

[58] Query, however, whether a deduction that was improper on its face (e.g., a personal exemption of $1,000 in 1977, when the amount was $750) must be left intact.

[59] First Nat'l Bank v. CIR, 22 TC 209 (1954), aff'd per curiam, 221 F2d 959 (2d Cir.), cert. denied, 350 US 887 (1955) (exclusion allowable only if deduction of recovered item "did not result" in a tax reduction; exclusion not allowed merely because deduction "would not have resulted" in a tax reduction had *other* deductions been claimed); US v. Rexach, 482 F2d 10 (1st Cir.), cert. denied, 414 US 1039 (1973), on remand, 411 F. Supp. 1288 (DPR 1976) (same; contrary rule would require auditing old returns on stale evidence).

[60] Reg. §1.111-1(a).

(whether deducted or not), so that gain or loss on a disposition of the property will be determined by reference to the reduced basis.[61] This leaves little room for an exclusionary principle that would reduce the taxpayer's gain to take account of deductions that were of no tax benefit. Thus, the sole statutory remedy for a taxpayer incurring deductions for depreciation, amortization, and depletion in a loss year is the net operating loss carryover authorized by §172, which permits excess business deductions to be used in profitable years within a specified carryover period.[62]

The taxpayer must look to the net operating loss carryover rather than to §111 for a remedy in another important category of cases, which can be illustrated by a business venture with expenditures for wages, supplies, and other deductible items that exceed income in one year, followed by substantial receipts in a later year. The receipts flow from and in a sense serve to recoup the expenditures, but it has been held that they cannot be excluded under §111 even if the prior deductions were of no tax benefit.[63] In reaching this conclusion, the court relied on the annual accounting rationale of *Burnet v. Sanford & Brooks Co.*, which held that taxable income is realized when payment is received under a long-term contract, even if the taxpayer incurred a loss over the life of the project.[64]

The Supreme Court's statement in *Hillsboro National Bank v. CIR*[65] of the inclusionary rule is a helpful guide for defining the boundaries of the exclusionary rule: The inclusionary rule applies on the occurrence of a later event that is fundamentally inconsistent with the premise of an earlier deduction; similarly, the exclusionary rule should apply to an item that would otherwise be gross income only if the gross income is recognized to

---

[61] IRC §1016(a)(2) (depreciation, amortization, and depletion); §1016(a)(5) (amortization of bond premium); §1011(a) (basis for gain or loss). See also infra ¶42.3.

Deductions for other items (e.g., losses) reduce the taxpayer's basis only to the extent of a "proper adjustment" under IRC §1016(a); to the effect that a basis adjustment is not required if the deduction is of no tax benefit to the taxpayer, see Ridge Realization Corp. v. CIR, 45 TC 508, 519–22 (1966) (nonacq.); see also Merchants Nat'l Bank v. US, 57-1 USTC ¶9380 (D. Kan. 1956) (not officially reported) (earlier improper write-down of bonds without tax benefit not chargeable to capital account; hence, unimpaired basis can be offset against sales proceeds in later year; but proper charge-off of a different debt reduced basis despite lack of tax benefit, so recovery is excludable under §111).

[62] For IRC §172, see infra ¶25.11.

[63] US v. Rexach, 482 F2d 10 (1st Cir.), cert. denied, 414 US 1039 (1973); see also Capitol Coal Corp. v. CIR, 250 F2d 361 (2d Cir. 1957), cert. denied, 356 US 936 (1958); Union Trust Co. of Indianapolis v. US, 173 F2d 54 (7th Cir.), cert. denied, 337 US 940 (1949) (similar result, but perhaps resting on inapplicability of IRC §111 to gain computed under IRC §1001).

[64] Burnet v. Sanford & Brooks Co., 282 US 359 (1931), discussed infra¶105.1.4.

[65] See infra text accompanying notes 20–27.

reflect an event fundamentally inconsistent with the premise of an earlier deduction. Receipts for goods and services in the ordinary course of business are outside the scope of §111, even if the expenses making these receipts possible were deducted without tax benefit in earlier years, because the receipts are not inconsistent with the earlier deductions; to the contrary, the expectation of these receipts was the factual premise for the deductions. On the other hand, refunds and abatements of amounts paid or accrued for wages or supplies qualify for exclusion if they were deducted without tax benefit, since these amounts were allowed as deductions on the supposition that they would not be refunded.

Because §111 is concerned with recoveries of items that were previously deducted or credited, a receipt must be closely associated with the prior allowance to qualify for exclusion. Assume a taxpayer accepts property worth $3,000 in settlement of a $5,000 claim and deducts the remaining $2,000 as a bad debt. A gain on a subsequent sale of the property is not a recovery of the bad debt deduction because neither the sale nor the realization of gain on the sale is inconsistent with the premise of the deduction; the loss on the debt is deemed closed out when the property is taken in payment, and appreciation or depreciation in the property's value is considered independent of the debt and the deduction.[66] On the other hand, if the taxpayer collects an additional $1,000 from the debtor (because, for example, the settlement was induced by fraud), this receipt is a partial recovery of the bad debt deduction.

Also, §111 presupposes that the recovery is received by the taxpayer who took the deduction. This principle ordinarily bars relief under §111 when otherwise qualified items are recovered by the original taxpayer's successor in interest (by liquidation, merger, etc.), but this barrier is lifted by §381(c)(12) for certain corporate liquidations and reorganizations.[67]

---

[66] Rev. Rul. 66-320, 1966-2 CB 37, relying on Allen v. Trust Co. of Ga., 180 F2d 527 (5th Cir.), cert. denied, 340 US 814 (1950). See also Sloane v. CIR, 188 F2d 254 (6th Cir. 1951) (insufficient relationship between bad debt deductions and later receipts from debtor for personal services to qualify latter for exclusion under §111); Brutsche v. CIR, 65 TC 1034, 1066 (1976), rev'd on other grounds, 585 F2d 436 (10th Cir. 1978) (§111 inapplicable; and even if it were, no showing of a recovery of item deducted in prior years); Waynesboro Knitting Co. v. CIR, 225 F2d 477 (3d Cir. 1955) (taxpayer received insurance policies on life of embezzler in partial settlement of claim against him and deducted remaining loss without tax benefit; held, insurance proceeds are taxable under §101(a)(2), despite tax benefit rule, because receipt of policies terminated original transaction and initiated new one); Continental Ill. Nat'l Bank & Trust Co. v. CIR, 69 TC 357, 370 (1977) (acq.) (charitable contribution of stock received in earlier transaction not a "recovery").

[67] Infra ¶95.5.1; but see Ridge Realization Corp. v. CIR, 45 TC 508, 523–26 (1966) (nonacq.) (successor entitled to use §111); see also Brutsche v. CIR, supra note 66, expressing doubt that recoveries by an S corporation qualify under §111 if the deductions were passed through to the shareholders.

Moreover, since a partnership is treated for most income tax purposes as a conduit, each partner takes into account his distributive share of the firm's recoveries.[68]

¶5.7.4 Application of Tax Benefit Principles to Credits

Section 111(b) states both an inclusionary rule and an exclusionary rule for credits. If a credit is allowed in one year and, in a subsequent year, "there is a downward price adjustment or similar adjustment," tax for the latter year is "increased by the amount of the credit attributable to the adjustment."[69] Assume an individual pays $1,000 for the care of his dependent children under circumstances entitling the individual to credit under §21 equal to 20 percent of the amount paid;[70] in a later year, $200 of the amount so paid is refunded. Unless the exclusionary rule described below applies, the individual's tax for the year of the recovery is increased by $40 (the credit rate of 20 percent applied to the amount of the recovery).

The foregoing rule does not apply, however, to the extent that the credit with respect to the recovered amount did not reduce the taxpayer's tax for any year.[71] Assume in this example the individual's tax liability, before the credit, was $150 for the year in which the child care expenses were paid. Because the child care credit is not refundable and cannot be carried to any other year, the $50 excess of the credit ($200) over the precredit tax ($150) does not reduce any tax. This unusable $50 includes the $40 attributable to the recovered amount. If the child care expenses had been $800 (the $1,000 originally paid less the $200 refund), the credit would have been only $160 (20 percent of $800), but the after-credit tax liability would have been the same (zero). The $40 of credit with respect to the recovered $200 therefore produced no tax benefit, and it need not be recaptured in the year of the refund.

Neither the inclusionary rule nor the exclusionary rule applies to the foreign tax credit or the investment credit. Under §905(c), when a taxpayer receives a refund of a foreign tax with respect to which the foreign tax was claimed, the credit is readjusted for the year in which it was claimed.[72] Assume a corporation pays a foreign income tax of $200 for 1988 and claims credit for the tax; in 1991, $40 of the foreign tax is refunded to the taxpayer. The corporation's 1988 return is amended to reduce the $200 credit to $160. Since the return for the year of the refund is not affected, §111(b), which pertains to tax liability for the year of recovery, is made

---

[68] Reg. §1.702-1(a)(8); see infra ¶86.2.1.
[69] IRC §111(b)(1).
[70] See infra ¶37.1 for the credit for expenses of dependent care.
[71] IRC §111(b)(2).
[72] See infra ¶69.1.1.

inapplicable. Similarly, if a taxpayer recovers a portion of the purchase price of property with respect to which the investment credit was claimed, the price adjustment is taken into account in applying a recapture rule within the investment credit rules, and §111 is inapplicable.[73]

¶5.7.5 Tax Detriment and Reverse Tax Benefit

There are a few examples other than the tax benefit doctrine of judicial and legislative departures from the annual accounting principle that seek to harmonize a transaction's tax consequences when it is finally closed with its tax treatment in an earlier year.

Among these analogues to the tax benefit rule, the most important is probably §1341, applicable when a taxpayer must refund an amount in excess of $3,000 that was included in income in an earlier year because he apparently had an unrestricted right to receive and retain it. In the year of repayment, the taxpayer is permitted by §1341 to pay the lesser of (1) a tax computed in the usual fashion with a deduction for the refunded amount or (2) a tax computed in the usual fashion on his other income (without deducting the refunded amount) minus the tax detriment suffered in the year when the refunded amount was received and included in income.[74] This approach guarantees that the tax saved in the year of the refund is at least as great as the tax paid when the item was received.[75]

If, however, the taxpayer takes the deduction in the usual way in the year of repayment (the first of the alternatives just described), the deduction allowable under §1341 is limited by what might be termed a reverse tax benefit rule, which serves to protect the government against a deduction that is excessive when compared with the amount included in income in the earlier year. This limitation was applied by the Supreme Court in *United States v. Skelly Oil Co.*, involving deductions claimed when the taxpayer refunded overcharges collected from its customers in earlier years on sales of natural gas.[76] Because the sales gave rise to percentage depletion deductions equal to 27.5 percent of the amounts received, so that the taxpayer's taxable income was increased by only 72.5 percent of the receipts,[77] the Court held that it could deduct only 72.5 percent of the amount refunded.

---

[73] See infra ¶27.4.

[74] For IRC §1341, see infra ¶6.3.

[75] As pointed out in ¶5.7.1 note 14, at one time the Court of Claims interpreted the inclusionary aspect of the tax benefit rule to require a comparable result, in that the tax attributable to a recovery was not to exceed the tax saved in the earlier year when the recovered item was deducted.

[76] US v. Skelly Oil Co., 394 US 678, 685–86 (1969) (divided court).

[77] For percentage depletion, see infra ¶24.1.1.

In so holding, the Court suggested that the decision would "affect only a few cases" because percentage depletion is "quite unusual [in allowing] a fixed portion of gross income to go untaxed," and it cited, with seeming approval, a Tax Court case allowing the taxpayer to deduct a similar refund (after adjusting for percentage depletion) even though the earlier receipts were included in income in a loss year for which no tax was payable.[78] On the other hand, the Court said in *Skelly Oil* that it could not believe "that Congress intended to give taxpayers a deduction for refunding money that was not taxed when received," which implies a broader scope for this reverse tax benefit principle than the Court was prepared to acknowledge.[79]

¶5.7.6 Foreign Expropriation Losses

Under §1351, enacted in 1966, a domestic corporation receiving money or property in respect of a foreign expropriation loss can elect to exclude the recovery from gross income, up to the amount allowed as deductions for the loss in prior taxable years.[80] In return for excluding the recovery, an electing corporation must pay an additional tax equal to the increased taxes that would have been payable for the loss years if the deductions were reduced by the amount of the recovery. Section 1351 thus results in a tax liability comparable to the amount that would have been due if the recovery had been predicted when the expropriation occurred and had been applied to reduce or eliminate the deductible loss.[81] If the recovery exceeds the prior

---

[78] O'Meara v. CIR, 8 TC 622, 632–35 (1947) (acq.). The IRS asserted that inclusion of the income in the year of receipt "brought the Government no tax benefit," but this may mean only that no tax was paid in that year. Since inclusion of the receipts in that year's gross income reduced the taxpayer's net operating loss, thereby reducing the amount carried over to other years, the government may in fact have realized a tax benefit in those other years.

For a painstaking analysis of *Skelly Oil* and its implications, see Rabinovitz, Effect of Prior Year's Transactions on Federal Income Tax Consequences of Current Receipts or Payments, 28 Tax L. Rev. 85 (1972).

[79] See Hintz v. CIR, 712 F2d 281 (7th Cir. 1983) (taxpayer repaid unemployment and sick pay benefits upon receiving back pay from employer pursuant to reinstatement order; held, no deduction for repayment because benefits tax free when received; *Skelly Oil* followed).

[80] For an extended explanation of §1351, see S. Rep. No. 1091, 89th Cong., 2d Sess., reprinted in 1966-1 CB 521. Sections 1331–1337 (formerly §127 of the 1939 Code), dealing with recovery of World War II losses, were repealed in 1976 as "deadwood." Pub. L. No. 94-455, 90 Stat. 1764, 1788. See also IT 4086, 1952-1 CB 29 (losses incurred in Korean War not covered by §127 of 1939 Code but may be deductible as losses incurred in business or transaction entered into for profit or as casualty losses).

[81] If the corporate rate schedule for the year of the recovery is different from the schedule for the year of the deduction, however, a test recalculation is made of the tax for the deduction year using the rates for the year of recovery, and the tax on the

deductions, the excess is treated as gain from an involuntary conversion of property, which can qualify for nonrecognition under §1033, relating to the replacement of converted property.[82]

Since it is elective, §1351 offers the taxpayer a choice between the normal tax benefit rules, under which prior deductions remain in force but recoveries are taxable if the deductions produced tax benefits, and a special rule, under which the recovery is excluded but the prior deductions must be disgorged.

Domestic corporations that do not avail themselves of §1351 are subject to §80, under which securities deducted as worthless because of a foreign expropriation (as defined) must be included in gross income if their value is restored in whole or in part, up to the amount of prior deductions resulting in a tax benefit. Amounts includable under §80 are taxed as ordinary income unless the correlative loss was taken into account as a loss from the sale or exchange of a capital asset.[83]

¶5.7.7 Damages for Antitrust Violations, Patent Infringements, and Breach of Contract or Fiduciary Obligations

Inspired by tax benefit principles, §186 provides a special rule for damages recovered for antitrust violations, patent infringements, and breach of contract or fiduciary obligations.[84] To the extent of the taxpayer's "unrecovered losses" (defined by §186(d) as the net operating losses attributable to the injury that could not be deducted in any carryover year), the damages (if included in gross income) are allowed as a deduction.

The regulations prescribe in some detail the method of determining whether a particular year's net operating loss is attributable to an injury subject to §186.[85] Since the exclusionary aspect of the normal tax benefit doctrine would permit damages to be excluded from gross income on proof that they constituted a recovery of prior deductions that produced no tax benefit, the principal contribution of §186 lies in its simplified method of

---

recovery is the amount that this recomputed tax is increased by the elimination of the recovered deduction. IRC §1351(d)(4).

[82] For IRC §1033, see infra ¶44.3.1.

[83] For a more detailed explanation of §80, see S. Rep. No. 1091, supra note 80. See also Rev. Rul. 76-41, 1976-1 CB 52 (no worthless-security loss of securities pledged to and seized by foreign government if domestic parent can regain expropriated securities through judicial proceedings in the United States); Rev. Rul. 75-501, 1975-2 CB 69 (expropriation of operating assets of domestic corporation's wholly owned domestic subsidiary, which owns a U.S. bank account and whose certificates are located here, does not render securities worthless).

[84] See S. Rep. No. 552, 91st Cong., 1st Sess., reprinted in 1969-3 CB 423, 599–600.

[85] Reg. §§1.186-1(d)(3), (4).

determining whether the taxpayer received tax benefits in prior years for the subsequently compensated injury. By concentrating on the taxpayer's net operating loss, §186 makes it unnecessary to associate the damages with any specific deductions.

¶5.8 INDIRECT RECEIPTS: PAYMENT OF TAXPAYER'S EXPENSES, BARGAIN PURCHASES, ETC.

¶5.8.1 Introductory

In *Old Colony Trust Co. v. CIR*, decided in 1929, the Supreme Court held that a corporate officer was required to include in gross income amounts paid by his employer to defray his state and federal income taxes.[1] In *United States v. Boston & Maine Railroad*, a companion case, the Court held that the taxpayer realized income when its federal income taxes were paid by the lessee of all its properties, under a 99-year lease requiring the lessee to pay "all taxes of every description, Federal, State, and municipal, upon the lessor's property, business, indebtedness, income, franchises, or capital stock, or said rental."[2]

Acknowledging that they would be taxable on earnings paid at their direction to creditors, the taxpayers in these cases sought to distinguish their situation on several grounds. Because the amounts to be reimbursed each year depended on the applicable tax laws, they contended there was no

---

[1] Old Colony Trust Co. v. CIR, 279 US 716, 719–20 (1929). These amounts were paid under a resolution of the employer's directors providing:

> [T]his company [shall] pay any and all income taxes, State and Federal, that may hereafter become due and payable upon the salaries of all the officers of the company . . . to the end that said . . . officers shall receive their salaries or other compensation in full without deduction on account of income taxes, State or Federal, which taxes are to be paid out of the treasury of this corporation.

The resolution was later amended to require the company to pay "the difference between what the total amount of [the officer's] tax would be, including his income from all sources, and the amount of his tax when computed upon his income excluding such compensation or salaries paid by this company." Id. at 720. For problems in drafting and interpreting tax reimbursement resolutions and agreements, see infra ¶5.8.2.

Employers of domestic servants often absorb the employee's share of federal social security taxes rather than withholding it from wages. The employer's payment constitutes additional compensation to the employee under *Old Colony*, but this principle is probably ignored as often as it is honored. See Rev. Rul. 74-75, 1974-1 CB 19; see also IRC §3121(a)(6) (employer's payment of employee's FICA tax does not constitute "wages" subject to withholding).

[2] US v. Boston & Me. R.R., 279 US 732, 733 (1929).

clearly defined amount otherwise owing to them that was discharged by the payments in question. They went on to argue that payment of their income taxes was not "income" within the common understanding of that term (despite the old maxim that "a penny saved is a penny earned"), that the tax payments were not received by them but were paid (or payable) directly to the government, and that the rejection by Congress of a 1917 proposal to prohibit agreements to pay another person's income tax impliedly sanctioned the exclusion of such payments from the obligee's gross income.[3] They also raised the specter of complex computations under the government's theory. Since each taxpayer was evidently entitled under its agreement to be reimbursed for the disputed taxes if they were found to be owing, these reimbursements would become includable in income; this would produce another round of taxes and reimbursements; and this process would continue for as many rounds as the agreement required.[4]

The Court rejected the taxpayer's claim in *Old Colony* in short order:

> [T]he question presented is whether a taxpayer, having induced a third person to pay his income tax or having acquiesced in such payment as made in discharge of an obligation to him, may avoid the making of a return thereof and the payment of a corresponding tax. We think he may not do so. The payment of the tax by the employers was in consideration of the services rendered by the employee and was a gain derived by the employee from his labor. The form of the payment is expressly declared [by the statute] to make no difference. . . . It is therefore immaterial that the taxes were directly paid over to the Government. The discharge by a third person of an obligation to him is equivalent to receipt by the person taxed. The . . . employee entered upon his duties in the years in question under the express agreement that his income taxes would be paid by his employer. . . . The taxes were paid upon a valuable consideration, namely, the services rendered by the employee and as part of the compensation therefor. We think therefore that the payment constituted income to the employee.[5]

The Court reached the same result in the *Boston & Maine* case, saying that the lessee's payment of the lessor's taxes under the lease "is merely a short cut whereby that which the lessee specifically agreed to pay as part of the rental [is paid] by discharging the obligation of the lessor to pay the tax to the Government."[6] The Court thereby rejected two possible grounds for

---

[3] S. Rep. No. 1039, 64th Cong., 2d Sess. (1917), reprinted in 1939-1 (Part 2) CB 47.

[4] For this problem, see infra ¶5.8.2.

[5] Old Colony Trust Co. v. CIR, supra note 1, at 729.

[6] US v. Boston & Me. R.R., supra note 2, at 734.

distinguishing the *Boston & Maine* case from *Old Colony*: (1) The controlling statute taxed compensation for personal services "in whatever form paid,"[7] but did not apply this term to rent, the type of income involved in *Boston & Maine*; (2) the *Boston & Maine* agreement predated the federal income tax, and hence could not be characterized as an attempt to avoid the tax.[8]

The *Old Colony* principle has been applied to tax reimbursement arrangements in several other areas. The most common illustration is the taxability of employees on gross compensation, including amounts withheld by the employer to pay the employee's social security taxes, even though participation is compulsory and does not entitle employees to name their own beneficiaries.[9] Another common example is the payment by a closely held corporation of its principal shareholder's personal expenses, an event that is treated as a constructive distribution to him of the amounts paid on his behalf.[10] Other examples are a divorced spouse's agreement to pay a specified amount of alimony net of taxes[11] and a lessee's agreement to pay a net annual dividend to the shareholders of a lessor corporation.[12] The principle that "income is not any the less taxable income of the taxpayer because by his command it is paid directly to another in performance of the

---

[7] Revenue Act of 1918, Pub. L. No. 254, §213(a), 40 Stat. 1057, 1065 (1919). The phrase "in whatever form paid" was dropped in 1954, when §22(a) of the 1939 Code was replaced by §61(a), but this change, like other simplifying changes in this provision, was not intended to have any substantive effect. See supra ¶2.1.1.

[8] See generally Brown, Shifting the Burden of Income Taxes by Contract, 96 U. Pa. L. Rev. 822 (1948) (written before IRS' change of policy in 1952, discussed infra note 25; Fishman, Income Tax Aspects of Third Party Payments of Taxpayer Obligations, 19 NYU Inst. on Fed. Tax'n 31 (1961).

[9] See Rev. Rul. 74-75, 1974-1 CB 19; see also Escofil v. CIR, 464 F2d 358 (3d Cir. 1972) (social security taxes withheld from employee's wages not deductible, which necessarily implies that they are includable in gross income); infra ¶5.9 (re constructive receipt of amounts withheld for civil service retirement programs, etc.).

[10] See, e.g., Sachs v. CIR, 277 F2d 879 (8th Cir.), cert. denied, 364 US 833 (1960) (corporate payment of fine imposed on dominant shareholder for filing fraudulent corporate tax returns); see also infra ¶92.2.

[11] Mahana v. US, 88 F. Supp. 285 (Ct. Cl.), cert. denied, 339 US 978 (1950), discussed infra ¶77.2.4.

[12] US v. Joliet & C.R.R., 315 US 44 (1942). In this case, involving a lease in perpetuity, the Court rejected the taxpayer's theory that for all practical purposes the property had been transferred outright to the lessee.

For tax-free covenant bonds, see IRC §32(2) (before amendment in 1984), §1451 (before repeal in 1984); Duffy v. Pitney, 2 F2d 230 (3d Cir.), cert. denied, 267 US 595 (1924); Rev. Rul. 71-82, 1971-1 CB 266; Magill, Taxable Income 239–41 (Ronald Press, rev. ed. 1945).

taxpayer's obligation to that other"[13] is also applied to tax the creator of a trust on trust income the trustee is directed to use to defray the transferor's living expenses or to support his legal dependents.[14]

The *Old Colony* principle, however, requires the drawing of troublesome lines to distinguish items that are properly attributable to the taxpayer, even though paid to someone else, from items that are not attributable to the taxpayer, especially in the following situations:

1. *Gifts and renunciations.* If a married couple directs a corporation in which they own stock to pay their next quarterly dividend to their children, *Old Colony* attributes the dividend to the shareholders, just as though they had received the dividend check and endorsed it over to their children. If they make a no-strings-attached gift of the stock to the children, dividends declared thereafter are paid to the children, not because of parental instructions, but because the children own the stock; hence, the dividends are taxed to the children rather than to the parents. This often difficult distinction between an effective gift of an income producing "tree" and an ineffective gift of the "fruit" is discussed in detail elsewhere in this work.[15]

A similarly troubled area is the renunciation of income to be produced by a taxpayer's personal services. An example is the case of an entertainer who performs for the benefit of a charity, where it is necessary to determine whether he directed that amounts otherwise owing to him be paid to the charity (taxable under *Old Colony*) or agreed to contribute his services to the charity, an act that is free of income tax consequences to the donor on the theory that profits from the use of the services are income of the charity, not the services performer.[16]

2. *Payments benefiting payor.* In *Old Colony*, the employee was the beneficiary of the employer's payments since he would have been required

---

[13] Raybestos-Manhattan, Inc. v. US, 296 US 60, 64 (1935), citing several other cases, including *Old Colony*. See also the Court's summary of *Old Colony* in Douglas v. Willcuts, 296 US 1, 9 (1935):

> We have held that income was received by a taxpayer when, pursuant to a contract, a debt or other obligation was discharged by another for his benefit. The transaction was regarded as being the same in substance as if the money had been paid to the taxpayer and he had transmitted it to his creditor. . . . The creation of a trust by the taxpayer as the channel for the application of the income to the discharge of his obligation leaves the nature of the transaction unaltered.

[14] This area, however, is now elaborately regulated by statute. See infra ¶80.4. See also Bergan v. CIR, 31 BTA 526 (1934), rev'd on other grounds, 80 F2d 89 (2d Cir. 1935) (where trust instrument required trustee to pay beneficiaries' taxes on amounts distributed to them, beneficiaries taxed on distribution plus taxes).

[15] See infra ¶75.3.3.
[16] See infra ¶75.2.3.

to pay the taxes from his own resources had the employer not paid them. From the employer's perspective the payments served to compensate the employee and, thus, to elicit his services; but the same result could have been achieved by making the payments directly to him. When the employer pays its own taxes, however, the employee, not being liable, derives no advantage from the payment, except to the extent that his job is made more secure by the employer's compliance with the law. For this reason, *Old Colony* does not apply to payments satisfying obligations of the payor (e.g., an employer's payment of its share of federal social security taxes),[17] even though the employee derives a benefit as a by-product of the payments. Thus, it has been held that a shareholder bringing a derivative action against his corporation is not taxable when the corporation pays his legal fees pursuant to a state law imposing primary obligation for these fees on the corporation.[18] A more routine example is an employer's payment of business expenses that an employee charged to his own account with the understanding that the employer would either pay the bill directly or reimburse him.[19] Similarly, a guarantor or surety is not taxed on payments by the principal obligor discharging the latter's obligation, even though they simultaneously reduce or eliminate the surety's secondary liability.

3. *Payments by liability insurers.* When damages resulting from a taxpayer's tortious behavior are paid by his insurance company, as in the case of an automobile accident caused by his negligence, he is not required to include the payment in income, even though his liability to the victim is thereby discharged. This exemption is universally recognized in practice, but has never been explained. If the liability arises in business, the exemption is usually not of great consequence because the insured would have to be allowed an offsetting deduction for the loss if the insurer's payment were treated as income. When the liability is personal, the exemption might derive from the treatment of premium payments on the policy as nonde-

---

[17] For amounts withheld from wages and contributed to federal or state retirement plans, see Cohen v. CIR, 63 TC 267 (1974), aff'd per curiam, 543 F2d 725 (9th Cir. 1976) (federal employee taxed on contributions); Sibla v. CIR, 68 TC 422 (1977) (state system; same result).

[18] Ingalls v. Patterson, 158 F. Supp. 627 (D. Ala. 1958). Primary liability for the legal fees was placed on the corporation, on the theory that the action benefited all shareholders equally. If state law required employers to pay their employees' rent, however, *Old Colony* would apply even though the payments satisfied the employer's own obligation, just as payment of the minimum wage rate or back pay under an NLRB order satisfies an obligation of the employer but is taxable to the employee. See also Ruben v. CIR, 97 F2d 926 (8th Cir. 1938) (shareholder not taxed on payment by corporation of judgment against him for fraud in transaction that benefited the corporation); but see Sachs v. CIR, 277 F2d 879 (8th Cir.), cert. denied, 364 US 833 (1960); Rev. Rul. 60-14, 1960-1 CB 16 (individual taxed on payment of his legal expenses by organization of which he was an official even though organization made payment to protect its reputaion).

[19] See infra ¶21.4.4.

ductible consumption expenditures. A premium payment is a purchase of protection from liability. Whether he has an accident or not, the insured gets what he pays for. The benefits of a consumption expenditure are not taxed; the tax rests on the income used to pay the expenditure, not on the benefits flowing from it. A purchaser of personal liability insurance is like a purchaser of an old car; there is no income if the car unexpectedly has 100,000 trouble-free miles in it, and no loss deduction is allowed if the car breaks down irretrievably on the way home from dealer's lot. Similarly, an insured's exemption from tax on the insurer's payment of a liability is a corollary of the denial of a loss deduction for premiums paid by an insured who sustains no reimbursable loss.

4. *Payments on assumed mortgages.* If a mortgagor of property sells the property to a buyer who assumes the mortgage as part of the price or takes the property subject to the mortgage, the mortgagor is not taxed on the buyer's payments on the mortgage. Often, this can be explained as a consequence of the buyer becoming primarily liable on the debt. There is, however, a broader justification that exempts the seller from tax on the buyer's mortgage payments even if, after the sale, the buyer's liability is not primary. Whether the buyer assumes the mortgage or merely takes subject to it, the debt is included in the seller's amount realized in the sale.[20] This inclusion is an application of the *Old Colony* principle, and an application of the principle to the buyer's payments on the debt would therefore cause the seller to be taxed twice on the same item. In effect, the seller's liability is deemed satisfied by the buyer's assumption or agreement to take subject to it, not by the buyer's payment of it.

¶5.8.2 Pyramiding Effect of Reimbursement Agreements ("Tax on a Tax")

In the *Old Colony* and *Boston & Maine* cases, the taxpayers argued vehemently that the government was seeking to pyramid their tax liabilities:

> It is . . . argued . . . that if these payments by the employer constitute income to the employee, the employer will be called upon to pay the tax imposed upon this additional income, and that the payment of the additional tax will create further income which will in turn be subject to tax, with the result that there would be a tax upon a tax. This it is urged is the result of the Government's theory, when carried to its logical conclusion, and results in an absurdity which Congress could not have contemplated.[21]

---

[20] See infra ¶43.5.
[21] Old Colony Trust Co. v. CIR, 279 US 716, 730–31 (1929).

The taxpayer's brief in *Boston & Maine* asserted that the government's theory required a choice among five different methods of computing income, each with a formidable label: Vertical Completed Pyramid Method, Vertical Truncated Pyramid Method, Hybrid Method, Horizontal Completed Pyramid Method, and Horizontal Truncated Pyramid Method.

Whether a tax reimbursement agreement has a pyramiding effect depends on the terms of the agreement. First, assume an employer agrees to pay an employee a bonus of $1,000 in 1989 and to reimburse him in 1990 for the amount of federal income tax payable on the 1989 bonus. The reimbursement is part of the employee's 1990 income under *Old Colony*, but the employee bears the 1990 tax on the reimbursement since the employer does not guarantee that he would receive $1,000 net of all taxes.

At the opposite extreme is a full-reimbursement agreement, under which the employee is guaranteed a bonus of $1,000 net after income taxes. Such an arrangement can take either of two forms. One is a lagged full-reimbursement agreement, under which the employer promises to reimburse the employee in 1990 for the 1989 tax on his 1989 bonus, in 1991 for the 1990 tax on the reimbursement received in 1990, in 1992 for any tax that may be imposed on the reimbursement received in 1991, and so on until the amount falls to the level where it can be rounded off to zero. Since the highest marginal income tax rate is less than 100 percent, the amounts to be reimbursed gradually diminish, but effectively reach zero only after many years. Example 5-5 shows the progression with an original payment of $1,000 and a constant tax rate of 28 percent.

Example 5-5

Lagged Full Reimbursement

Year	Reimbursement Received	Tax on Reimbursement
1	$1,000.00	$280.00
2	280.00	78.40
3	78.40	21.95
4	21.95	6.15
5	6.15	1.72
6	1.72	.48
7	.48	.13
8	.13	.04
9	.04	.01
10	.01	.00
Total	$1,388.89	$388.89

Instead of lagging the reimbursements, the parties can accomplish the same objective (a bonus, after taxes, of $1,000) by a single-sum full-reimbursement agreement, under which the employer agrees to pay the employee, in the year the services are performed, an amount that will, after taxes, yield a net amount of $1,000. The amount to be paid under such an agreement can be determined either by trial and error or, if a single tax rate applies to all of the income,[22] by the following algebraic formula:

$$\text{Gross amount} = (a)/(1 - r)$$

where a = net amount and r = tax rate. A more complicated formula is required if more than one rate applies to the income. Under the formula given, if the net amount is $1,000 and the tax rate is 28 percent, the gross amount is:

$$(\$1,000)/(1 - .28) = \$1,388.89$$

Apart from rounding differences and the consequences of changes in tax rates, the gross amount is the same under both methods; only the timing differs.

In the *Old Colony and Boston & Maine* cases, the taxpayers argued that the pyramiding of tax under a full-reimbursement agreement was "an absurdity which Congress could not have contemplated." Because the government disclaimed any intent to pursue the taxpayer beyond the first round of reimbursements,[23] the Court reserved judgment on the propriety of pyramiding until "an attempt to impose a tax upon a tax is undertaken."[24]

Although a catchy slogan, the phrase "tax on a tax" merely describes the fact that because the federal income tax is not deductible in determining

---

[22] Whether the income is taxed at more than one rate often depends on how the tax attributable to the income is determined. Assume the tax on the income is defined as the excess of (1) the taxpayer's entire tax liability for the year on all income, including the gross amount of this item, over (2) the tax liability for the year computed without this item. In this case, the item is subject to a single rate, the highest marginal rate applicable to the taxpayer, if it is no larger than the amount taxed at this rate. Assume, in contrast, the tax on the item is computed as the taxpayer's tax for the year multiplied by a fraction whose numerator is the amount of this item and whose denominator is adjusted gross income. In this case, the item is treated as taxed at the average rate, that is, some portion of the item is deemed taxed at each of the marginal rates applied to the taxpayer.

[23] The tax in *Boston & Maine* was pyramided, although perhaps by inadvertence. The lessee paid $61,422 to defray the lessor's 1918 federal income tax, and the IRS assessed tax of $3,921 on the theory that lessor's income was $65,343, an amount that after taxes of $3,921 is $61,422. This evidently assumed that the agreement provided for a single sum rather than for lagged reimbursement, although it is not clear that the parties so construed it.

[24] Old Colony Trust Co., supra note 21, at 731; US v. Boston & Me. R.R., 279 US 732, 736 (1929).

taxable income, the tax is a tax on pretax income, not after-tax income. Assume an employee receives a salary of $1,389. If the salary is taxed at 28 percent, the employee is left with $1,000 after taxes; the tax is 28 percent of the gross salary of $1,389, not 28 percent of the excess of $1,389 over the tax on that amount. The $389 the government takes in tax is itself subject to the tax. Similarly, if the employee is paid $1,000 under an agreement obligating the employer to pay the employee's tax on this amount, the tax should be $389, an amount equal to 28 percent of the sum of the tax and the employee's after-tax earnings. That the parties agree to a complex method of determining the employee's compensation should not deflect attention from the fact that everything the employer pays is compensation for the employee's services, and must be taxed to the employee as such. Further, the Court was wrong in assuming that the second and succeeding rounds of reimbursement differ in any meaningful way from the first round; in Example 5-5, the payment in year 2—the payment directly covered by the *Old Colony* holding—is a payment of tax on the year 1 amount, and the tax on this payment is thus a tax on a tax as much as any tax imposed in a later year.

Following *Old Colony*, however, the unsettled issue of pyramiding was not raised again by the IRS until 1952. During this period the obligor under a lagged reimbursement agreement was apparently permitted to deduct the full amount paid by it, although only part of this amount was taxed to the payee. Thus, in years 1 and 2 of Example 5-5, the employee would have been taxed on the amounts received ($1,000 and $280, respectively), but the amount paid in year 3 was not taxed to him, although deductible by the employer. Under this truncated pyramiding practice, there is no occasion for further reimbursements. The government lost (and the payor gained) the tax saved by the payor's deduction in year 3; the payee was unaffected because he nets $1,000 under either full or truncated pyramiding.

In 1952, the Treasury announced a change of policy, under which all federal income taxes reimbursed by a tax reimbursement agreement are taxed, regardless of the number of rounds involved. Under this policy, however, the IRS accepts the construction placed on the contract by the parties; when the reimbursements stop, so do the tax assessments.[25] The Treasury's right to make this change in policy, at least prospectively, has

---

[25] IR-Mim. 6779, 1952-1 CB 8 (agreements between lessors and lessees); IR-Mim. 51, 1952-2 CB 65 (all types of agreements). These rulings were listed as obsolete by Revenue Ruling 71-498, 1971-2 CB 434, but the principles announced therein are still followed. See Temp. Reg. §34.3402-1(d) Ex. 4 (state lottery prize that includes payment of withheld taxes). The rulings were assumed to state the law correctly when Congress enacted §110 (infra ¶5.8.3) and when it provided certain special relief for pre-1954 years in §92 of the Technical Amendments Act of 1958 (Pub. L. No. 85-866, 72 Stat. 1606, 1677). See S. Rep. No. 1622, 83d Cong., 2d Sess.

been upheld.[26]

Since the income tax on the payee under a tax reimbursement agreement depends not on the amount of salary, rent, or other item paid to him but on his taxable income, the parties must either include in the contract a method of computing the amount of tax to be reimbursed or resolve troublesome interpretative questions after the fact. Moreover, the method to be used affects, sometimes drastically, the cost of the agreement to the payor.

At one extreme, the agreement may provide that the amount to be reimbursed is the tax actually payable by the recipient on his taxable income for the year, less the amount of tax that would have been payable if the salary, rent, or other payment (or, in each subsequent year, the reimbursement received in that year) had not been received. An agreement of this type reimburses the payee for the incremental tax cost of receiving the underlying payment. The obligor under an agreement of this type is affected by such extraneous and unpredictable factors as the payee's marital status, personal exemptions and deductions, and participation in tax shelters.[27]

At the opposite extreme, the amount to be paid can be computed on the assumption that the amounts payable under the agreement are the only gross income received by a hypothetical taxpayer with specified characteristics (e.g., unmarried without dependents or itemized deductions, or a corporation with no other receipts or deductions). By gearing the amount to such a hypothetical taxpayer, the agreement relieves the payor of involvement with the payee's personal characteristics, but the amount due is either more or less than the tax actually allocable to the underlying payment.

Between these two extremes is an agreement to reimburse the payee at the payee's average rate for the year.[28] Under such an agreement, the reimbursement is the tax on all of the taxpayer's income for the year, including the amounts paid under the agreement, multiplied by a fraction whose numerator consists of these amounts and whose denominator is the taxpayer's adjusted gross income or taxable income.

---

16 (1954); S. Rep. No. 1983, 85th Cong., 2d Sess., reprinted in 1958-3 CB 922, 928–29.

[26] Safe Harbor Water Power Corp. v. US, 303 F2d 928 (Ct. Cl. 1962). This case also discusses the status of prior years under the 1952 rulings, for which also see Connecticut Ry. & Lighting Co. v. US, 142 F. Supp. 907 (Ct. Cl. 1956).

[27] On this point, see Rogan v. Mertens, 153 F2d 937 (9th Cir. 1946) (amount due in future under tax reimbursement agreement not includable in income).

[28] For an intermediate situation involving an employer's agreement with the IRS to pay the taxes that should have been paid by its employees on reimbursed moving expenses, involving computations based on the tax status of the average employee, see McGraw-Hill, Inc. v. US, 44 AFTR2d 5463 (Ct. Cl. Trial Judge's Report 1979).

¶5.8.3 Exemption From Pyramiding for Pre-1954 Corporate Leases

Under §110, enacted in 1954, a lessor under a pre-1954 lease is entitled to exclude from gross income any payment or reimbursement of its federal income taxes by the lessee, but the lessee is denied a deduction for the amount it pays. Applicable only if both taxpayers are corporations, this provision was enacted to give relief where the lessee's deduction for the payment would increase losses that produce no tax benefit.[29] If the lessee can use the deduction and lessor and lessee are both taxed at the top corporate rate, the Treasury's receipts are identical, whether the parties are subject to the *Old Colony* principle (as applied after 1952)[30] or to §110.

¶5.8.4 Bargain Purchases

When a taxpayer purchases property at arm's length for less than it is worth, he is ordinarily not taxed on the fruits of his astute negotiations when the purchase takes place.[31] Since the property's basis in his hands is its cost, however, his profit on the advantageous purchase will enter into his gain when he later sells the property. If he uses the property in his business, this profit will show up indirectly as higher taxable income from the business because depreciation deductions will be that much less than they would be if the property had been bought at fair market value.

The bargain element is usually taxed immediately, in contrast, if a purchase for less than fair market value is not an independent, arm's length transaction, but reflects an extraneous objective, such as the seller's desire to confer an economic advantage on the buyer. In *CIR v. Smith*, involving a sale of stock by an employer to an employee for less than fair market value pursuant to a stock option granted to him as additional compensation, the Supreme Court held that the taxpayer realized gain equal to the spread between the value of the stock and the lower amount paid on exercising the option. The Court found the statutory predecessor of §61(a) "broad enough to include in taxable income any economic or financial benefit conferred on the employee as compensation, whatever the form or mode by which it is effected."[32]

---

[29] See S. Rep. No. 1622, supra note 25, at 16–17.

[30] Supra note 25.

[31] See Hunley v. CIR, 25 TCM (CCH) 355 (1966) (bargain purchase not taxed despite broad reference to "accessions to wealth" in *Glenshaw Glass*). See Kohl, The Identification Theory of Basis, 40 Tax L. Rev. 623 (1985).

[32] CIR v. Smith, 324 US 177, 181, rehearing denied, 324 US 695 (1945) (citing *Old Colony*). For computation of the seller's gain or loss on a bargain sale, see infra ¶40.7.5.

In effect, the bargain purchase was treated in *CIR v. Smith* as a shortcut method by which the employer transferred the amount of the spread to the employee as compensation. Following the *Smith* case, there were numerous judicial, administrative, and legislative developments affecting the status of employees and others who receive stock options or are allowed to purchase property below market value as compensation for their services. These developments are discussed elsewhere in this work.[33]

In the *Smith* case, the purpose of the transaction was to compensate the taxpayer for his services. In other situations, the sale of property for less than its fair market value may be a way of paying rent, distributing a dividend to shareholders, making an intrafamily gift, or accomplishing some other objective. A discussion of these alternative characterizations follows.

¶5.8.5 Characterization of Indirect Receipts and Bargain Purchases

When someone pays the taxpayer's expenses or permits him to benefit from a bargain purchase, the transaction is tantamount to paying an equivalent amount directly to the taxpayer. This parallelism, however, does not serve by itself to characterize the transaction. In *Old Colony*, the payment of the taxpayer's income taxes was part of his compensation for services rendered,[34] and he was therefore taxed on the payment. In other circumstances, payment of an individual's taxes might be an indirect way of making a gift, in which event the beneficiary would be entitled to exclude the payment from gross income as a gift.[35] Similarly, a bargain purchase may be a device to pay compensation, rent, alimony, interest, or a corporate dividend; to make or repay a loan;[36] or to achieve some other objective.

Old Colony holds that indirect receipts have the same tax effect as amounts received directly, but the transaction's characterization depends on all the surrounding facts and circumstances. In some instances, this analysis may produce both income and an offsetting deduction,[37] or capital

---

[33] See infra ¶¶60.4.1, 60.5.1.

[34] The taxpayer's claim that the payment was a tax-free gift was rejected. See supra ¶5.8.4.

[35] See infra ¶10.2.1.

[36] Northern Ohio R.R. v. CIR, 6 TCM (CCH) 1230 (1947) (payment of lessor's taxes intended as loan).

[37] See IT 3382, 1940-1 CB 12, declared obsolete by Rev. Rul. 73-209, 1973-1 CB 614 (employer's payment of employee's city income tax includable in gross income but deductible by employee as a tax under predecessor to §164(a)(3) if taxpayer itemizes deductions); see also Reg. §1.162-11(a) (lessee's payment of lessor's real property taxes).

gain rather than ordinary income.[38]

¶5.9 EFFECT OF TAXPAYER'S ACCOUNTING METHOD — CONSTRUCTIVE RECEIPT

The taxable year in which income is realized is often affected by the taxpayer's accounting method. Under principles examined later,[1] a taxpayer can elect any method that clearly reflects income, but most use either the cash receipts and disbursements method or an accrual method. Under the cash method, which is almost universally employed for wages, salaries, and professional fees, taxpayers report income when they are paid (either in cash or in property) rather than when the services are rendered or the customer or client is billed, and deductions are taken when the taxpayer pays deductible expenses rather than when the liability arises.[2] By contrast, accrual accounting (ordinarily used by merchants, manufacturers, and other businesses) takes sales and other transactions into account when they occur, even though the taxpayer must wait for payment, while expenses are deductible when the obligation to pay arises rather than when payment is made.[3]

Taxpayers engaged in two or more trades or businesses may use a different method for each one.[4] Thus, an individual who operates a grocery store can use accrual accounting for that enterprise while reporting investment income, outside earnings, nonbusiness transactions, and personal deductions on the cash method.

Although a taxpayer's accounting method ordinarily affects only the taxable year in which income is reported and does not determine whether a transaction produces income, there are some exceptions to this principle. If, for example, a physician performs services, bills the patient, but is never paid, the transaction produces no gross income if the cash method is used; if the taxpayer uses accrual accounting, in contrast, the fee is gross income when earned, but a bad debt deduction is allowed if it is subsequently shown that the debt is uncollectible. In the latter case, the income and deduction may not cancel each other out because the tax cost of including the fee in gross income may be greater (or less) than the value of the later deduction. The fact that the transaction produces gross income for an accru-

---

[38] A buyer's payment of the seller's taxes enters into the computation of the seller's gain or loss on the sale of a capital asset if the buyer makes the payment as additional consideration. See, e.g., infra ¶32.2.1 (real property taxes defrayed by buyer as part of amount realized in certain situations).

[1] See IRC §446, discussed infra ¶105.1.5.

[2] See IRC §446(c)(1), discussed infra ¶105.2.1.

[3] See IRC §446(c)(2), discussed infra ¶105.3.1.

[4] See IRC §446(d), discussed infra ¶105.1.5.

al taxpayer but not for a cash taxpayer also creates differences between them for such diverse purposes as the obligation to file a tax return, the right to take certain deductions, and the running of the statute of limitations, all of which hinge in part on the amount of the taxpayer's gross income.[5]

Use of the cash method is so widespread that two of its basic aspects, sometimes overlooked or misunderstood, are worthy of note here.

1. *Receipt of property other than cash.* The term "cash" in the phrase "cash receipts and disbursements method" is not used in a literal sense. It is not limited to money but includes property or services when they are the medium of payment. Thus, if a lawyer prepares a will for a plumber who repairs the lawyer's bathtub as compensation for the legal services, the lawyer and plumber each realize income equal to the value of the services received. This is true even though neither receives a transferable asset that could be converted into cash. The principle that an economic benefit can be income to a cash method taxpayer is also exemplified by the common situation of taxpayers whose employers supply them with food, lodging, the use of an automobile, or other benefits as compensation; the value of these perquisites ordinarily is income, even though the taxpayer can rarely sell them to a third party.[6]

The regulations state that property and services are income to taxpayers using the cash method of accounting,[7] but other benefits—such as economic opportunities—are also ordinarily treated as the equivalent of cash to the extent of their fair market value. Thus, if a corporate employer sells its stock to an employee for less than its current value, the spread between market value and the price paid by the employee is ordinarily taxable to him, even if he uses cash accounting.[8]

2. *Constructive receipt.* Just as the term "cash" is used in a broad sense in the phrase "cash receipts and disbursements method," so the term "receipts" has a broader reach than its literal meaning suggests. It is not confined to actual receipts but also includes amounts readily available to the taxpayer, such as interest credited to a savings account and matured but uncashed bond coupons. Of administrative and judicial rather than statuto-

---

[5] See, e.g., IRC §151(e)(1)(A) (dependency exemption related to dependent's gross income; discussed infra ¶30.3.6); §6012(a)(1)(A) (reporting requirements as related to gross income; discussed infra ¶111.1.1); §6501(e)(1)(A) (effect of omission in excess of 25 percent of gross income on statute of limitations; discussed infra ¶113.4).

[6] There are numerous exceptions, which are discussed in Chapter 14.

[7] Reg. §§1.61-2(d), 1.446-1(c)(1)(i).

[8] See IRC §83, discussed infra ¶60.4.

ry origin, the doctrine of constructive receipt is summarized in the regulations as follows:

> Income although not actually reduced to a taxpayer's possession is constructively received by him in the taxable year during which it is credited to his account, set apart for him, or otherwise made available so that he may draw upon it at any time, or so that he could have drawn upon it during the taxable year if notice of intention to withdraw had been given. However, income is not constructively received if the taxpayer's control of its receipt is subject to substantial limitations or restrictions.[9]

A much quoted aphorism by Mr. Justice Holmes, although uttered in an opinion upholding the constitutionality of taxing a grantor on the income of a revocable trust, aptly summarizes the constructive receipt doctrine: "The income that is subject to a man's unfettered command and that he is free to enjoy at his own option may be taxed to him as his income, whether he sees fit to enjoy it or not."[10]

In general, taxpayers are free when entering into a contract to specify the dates of payment, but the constructive receipt doctrine may triumph over a paper thin escrow or similar self imposed restriction postponing formal receipt if the taxpayer gets substantially all of the benefits of ownership in the interim. Moreover, once payment is due, a taxpayer may be held to in constructive receipt if the debtor is ready, willing, and able to pay, but payment is postponed at the taxpayer's urging. These and other aspects of the cash method are discussed further elsewhere in this work.[11]

---

[9] Reg. §1.451-2(a). The regulations go on to illustrate at some length the types of requirements that in the view of the Treasury, are not "substantial limitations or restrictions" on the taxpayer's control. For further discussion, see infra ¶¶60.2.3, 105.2.3.

[10] Corliss v. Bowers, 281 US 376, 378 (1930), discussed infra ¶80.3.1.

[11] See infra ¶105.2.

CHAPTER

6

Income—The Effect of Offsetting Liabilities

¶6.1 OFFSETTING LIABILITIES AND OBLIGATIONS: IN GENERAL

If a taxpayer receives money or other property burdened with an obligation to return or repay it, he is not ordinarily enriched by the transaction and therefore does not realize income within the meaning of §61(a). This is obvious enough if the taxpayer is a trustee or bailee, who is entrusted with property but holds it for the benefit of the true owner.[1] It is equally fundamental that borrowed funds are not income to the debtor since the increase in his assets is offset by an equal increase in his liabilities.[2] If, however, the offsetting liability is terminated (e.g., by the statute of limitations or abandonment by the beneficial owner), the resulting increase in wealth must then be reported as income.[3]

The exclusion of funds received as fiduciary or borrower is most clearly justified when the obligation to return or repay is consensual, unconditional, and intended to be honored. When property or money is received subject to a contingent or disputed offsetting obligation, a different tax result may be warranted because the taxpayer's liability does not fully counterbalance the economic advantage of receiving or holding the property. The major categories of transactions producing income, even though the taxpayer does not get a clear title to the property or is burdened with a legal obligation, are:

1. *Claim of right.* Property may be received under a "claim of right," where the offsetting obligation to return the property is either unknown to the taxpayer or disputed by him. In this situation, the taxpayer is usually required to report the property when received, despite the cloud on his title, but is allowed a deduction when and if he returns the property.[4]

2. *Unlawful conduct.* If property is obtained unlawfully, the taxpayer is usually obligated to return the property, but his conduct evidences an intention not to honor this obligation. In this case, the offsetting obligation is not a defense against reporting illegal receipts. If the taxpayer disgorges the ill-gotten gains, however, a deduction is permitted.[5]

3. *Conditional obligations.* Funds may be received subject to an obligation that might or might not mature, such as a manufacturer's money back guarantee or an obligation to repair or replace property for a specified

---

[1] See infra ¶6.2.

[2] See Matarese v. CIR, 34 TCM (CCH) 791 (1975); Kohl, The Identification Theory of Basis, 40 Tax L. Rev. 623 (1985); Popkin, The Taxation of Borrowing, 56 Ind. LJ 43 (1980). For the status of funds that are ostensibly borrowed, but with no intent to repay, see infra ¶6.5 note 20.

[3] See infra ¶6.4.

[4] See infra ¶6.3.

[5] See infra ¶6.5.

period of time.[6] In general, the sale is treated as complete when made, and the sales price must be taken into income at that time. The obligation to make refunds, repairs, or other adjustments is considered too contingent to justify a tax deduction until the triggering event actually occurs.[7]

4. *Attenuated obligations.* Obligations, such as the liability of a bank or a utility company to refund deposits to customers who cannot be found, may lose their potency because of the passage of time or other factors. In general, the taxpayer must report unclaimed deposits and similar amounts as income when the likelihood of repayment becomes very slim, even though an obligation to refund the funds on demand continues to exist in theory, especially if the amounts are transferred from a reserve account to surplus on the taxpayer's books.[8]

¶6.2 NOMINAL VS. BENEFICIAL OWNERSHIP—AMOUNTS RECEIVED BY TRUSTEES, NOMINEES, AGENTS, AND OTHER CONDUITS

In circumstances so diverse as to defy useful generalization, funds are received by persons acting for the benefit of others. Often, it is obvious that the initial recipient is not required to include the funds in gross income. The receipts passing through the hands of cash register operators at a supermarket, for example, are clearly taxed to the employer, not to the employees. In other situations, the proper result is a bit more obscure. If an office messenger is given 50 cents with instructions to buy a container of coffee for the boss (costing 35 cents) and to keep the change, should the messenger's income tax return report only 15 cents, or should it report 50 cents of gross income, a deduction of 35 cents, and taxable income of 15 cents? If the messenger's customers pay by the month for their daily coffee to avoid having to search for coins when it is delivered, must the receipts be reflected on the messenger's tax return, or are they trust funds to be reported on a fiduciary return or to be disregarded unless and until any unexpended balance is abandoned by the customers?

In some situations, the tax liability of the recipient of funds is the same whether the amount received is disregarded or reflected on the tax return since, if included, it is offset by a deduction of an equal amount. For example, if an employee defrays the expenses of a business trip with person-

---

[6] See also Kinzy v. US, 87-2 USTC ¶9520 (ND Ga. 1987) (not officially reported) (newly hired life insurance agent required to report training advances even though advances repayable, at least in part, if employment terminated within 60 months of end of training period).

[7] See infra ¶¶105.3.4–105.3.6.

[8] See supra ¶5.5.3.

al funds, under a reimbursement arrangement with the employer, the employee's tax liability may be the same whether the transaction is treated as a loan to the employer that is subsequently repaid[1] or as a deductible business expense coupled with a later receipt of income. But an inclusion and offsetting deduction are not necessarily identical with disregarding the transaction entirely. The former treatment increases the taxpayer's gross income, and hence affects such procedural matters as the obligation to file a tax return and the statute of limitations on assessments.[2] Moreover, if the outlay and receipt occur in different years, the employee's tax liability for both years is affected by which treatment is proper.[3]

Although it is perilous to generalize in an area that embraces a myriad of diverse factual situations, the courts and the IRS generally permit recipients of funds to exclude them from gross income if restrictions severely limiting their right to deal with the funds effectively deprive them of any beneficial interest. If the receipts are income items (royalties received by an author's agent, for example), they must be included in the income of the real party in interest, even if not received from the agent until a later year.

The principal situations in which recipients of funds or property are viewed as conduits, nominees, agents, or constructive trustees are summarized further on. There are similarities in administrative and judicial treatment between these situations and two types of transactions discussed in other sections of this chapter—transactions in which funds or property are received by persons who have no claim of right to the assets[4] or who are subject to an offsetting obligation to make repayment.[5]

1. *Nominees to receive and expend funds for principals.* In a series of cases, it has been held that organizations created by members of an industry or trade group to receive and expend funds for the common benefit of the contributing members (to advertise a franchised product, for example) are not taxable entities. In a typical case of this type, the Tax Court said:

---

[1] See Flower v. CIR, 61 TC 140, 156 (1973), aff'd by unpublished opinion (5th Cir. 1974) (expenditures under reimbursement agreement treated as loans). See generally infra ¶21.4.

[2] See infra ¶111.1.1 (gross income bench mark for filing returns), ¶113.4 (extended statute of limitations when more than 25 percent is omitted from gross income).

[3] See Burnett v. CIR, 356 F2d 755 (5th Cir. 1966) (funds advanced by attorney to clients, subject to repayment on successful completion of litigation, not deductible when made); Rev. Rul. 78-388, 1978-2 CB 110 (moving expenses not deductible by accrual-basis business with right to be reimbursed by public agency).

[4] See infra ¶6.3.

[5] See supra ¶6.1.

While it is true that strictly speaking the funneling of funds to [the association] is not the equivalent of the flow of water through a conduit, the utilization of this analogy shows that an intermediary may be employed as a depository for funds in trust which are destined for an ultimate use that is specified within defined limits. The benefit, profit, or gain is not to accrue to the intermediary but rather to some other entity. The fact that no benefit, profit, or gain accrues to [the association] as an entity, along with the fact that a trust relationship does exist, is the primary reason for exclusion of the funds from gross income. . . . Thus, even though the money is not required to be spent in one year, nevertheless, the sums remaining unspent are still restricted to future use for advertising.[6]

The IRS evidently accepts these principles if the funds are received pursuant to an agreement explicitly requiring their use in programs controlled by the contributing members, but it seeks to tax the recipient organization if it has substantial discretion over the use to which the funds are put and it is not required to refund unexpended balances to the contributors upon termination of the advertising program.[7] Without such an obligation to refund, the association resembles a farmers' cooperative, which an early case held was a taxable entity rather than an agent or bailee for its members.[8]

---

[6] Ford Dealers Advertising Fund, Inc. v. CIR, 55 TC 761, 773–74 (1971) (nonacq.), aff'd per curiam, 456 F2d 255 (5th Cir. 1972). See also Florists' Transworld Delivery Ass'n v. CIR, 67 TC 333 (1976) (nonacq.) (same as to organization of retail florists operating as a clearinghouse between florists taking orders and receiving payment for flowers and members located in other cities who filled and delivered the orders); Schochet v. CIR, 44 TCM (CCH) 556 (1982) (payments received by taxpayer organization from franchisee photocopy stores to be expended on advertisement of franchised photocopy service were not income to organization, but interest on accumulated payments was income; deduction denied for advertising expenditures, even to extent of interest income, because taxpayer did not show that interest was so expended). But see Rev. Rul. 74-318, 1974-2 CB 14 (corporation organized by automobile dealers held taxable because it had substantial discretion in use of funds even though its charter required that all funds be expended for the stated purpose; IRS will not follow Ford Dealers Advertising Fund).

[7] Rev. Rul. 74-319, 1974-2 CB 15. See also the nonacquiescences in Dri-Powr Distribs. Ass'n Trust v. CIR, 54 TC 460 (1970) (nonacq.) (conduit treatment for trust fund to advertise and promote products), New York State Ass'n of Real Estate Bds. Group Ins. Fund v. CIR, 54 TC 1325 (1970) (nonacq.) (fund to purchase group insurance for members of trade association treated as conduit), and the acquiescence limited to "the facts and circumstances of the case" in Angelus Funeral Home v. CIR, 47 TC 391 (1967) (acq.), aff'd, 407 F2d 210 (9th Cir. 1969) (funds collected by funeral home from prospective customers under trust arrangement not taxable).

[8] Farmers Union Coop. v. CIR, 90 F2d 488 (8th Cir. 1937) (taxable income in absence of duty to distribute all profits to patrons). For current tax status of cooperative organizations, see infra ¶104.1.

The rejection of the trust fund theory where the recipient has a large measure of discretion over expenditures is illustrated by Revenue Ruling 76-276, holding that a congressman must include in gross income funds contributed to a trust to defray travel expenses incurred by him and his staff in the performance of their official duties but can deduct expenditures from the fund as business expenses.[9] On the other hand, the IRS has ruled that a scientist is not required to report funds received under a grant to pay research expenses if he cannot receive any part for himself and if any unexpended balance must be returned to the grantor. The theory of the ruling is that "where a taxpayer receives funds burdened with an obligation to be expended for a specific purpose and earmarked for such purpose, the funds so held do not constitute gain or income" to him.[10]

The trust fund theory can embrace funds received for an illegal purpose, as in the case of a bagman for a corrupt public official.[11] The IRS often

---

[9] Rev. Rul. 76-276, 1976-2 CB 14 (refunds to contributors on termination of trust deductible as losses). See also IRC §527(d) (certain uses of political funds not treated as income to candidate; discussed infra ¶102.5); Rev. Rul. 74-21, 1974-1 CB 14 (campaign contributions not includable in income of organizations formed exclusively to influence nomination and election of public officials).

Revenue Procedure 68-19, 1968-1 CB 810, states that while contributions used for expenses of political campaigns are not taxable to the candidates, political contributions diverted to personal use are gross income if the contributions are "not intended for the unrestricted personal use of the recipient." The procedure states further that political contributions are presumed not intended for unrestricted personal use, but that given a showing that they were so intended, the additional issue arises of whether they were received as a gift excludable from gross income by §102(a). The Court of Appeals for the Second Circuit has followed the procedure in holding that it was error for a trial court in a criminal evasion case to instruct the jury, without qualification, that political contributions diverted to personal use are gross income because this instruction removed from the jury the issue of whether the contributions were gifts. US v. Pisani, 773 F2d 397 (2d Cir. 1985).

[10] Rev. Rul. 59-92, 1959-1 CB 11. See also Illinois Power Co. v. CIR, 792 F2d 683 (7th Cir. 1986) (state regulator ordered taxpayer to increase its rates to certain customers in order to encourage conservation and further ordered increased amounts to be held as "special fund" for use to be determined later by regulator; several years later, taxpayer ordered to apply these amounts, plus interest at the rate of return allowed taxpayer, as credits on bills of all customers; held, increased amounts not gross income because taxpayer was "custodian" of funds with no "beneficial interest"; situation analogous to that of business that collects sales tax and remits it to government). But see Iowa S. Util. Co. v. US, 88-1 USTC ¶9228 (Fed. Cir. 1988) (rate surcharge collected during period of construction of power plant includable in gross income, notwithstanding requirement that compensating negative surcharge be allowed against customers' bills for 30 years after plant completed; Illinois Power distinguished).

[11] See, e.g., Mill v. CIR, 5 TC 691 (1945) (acq.) (operator of unlawful slot machines not taxed on portion of take paid over to association of fraternal lodges in whose clubrooms machines were installed); Roloff v. CIR, 41 TCM (CCH) 721

seeks to tax the intermediary in these cases, also denying deductions for amounts paid over to the official on the ground that bribes are not ordinary and necessary business expenses or that a deduction would frustrate public policy. This tactic is usually rejected by the courts on the theory that the intermediary has no claim of right to the funds.[12] In effect, judicial notice is taken of honor among thieves. The courts are realistic enough, however, to recognize that some thieves are not to be trusted, and assertions by self-styled intermediaries that they paid the illicit funds over to third parties are sometimes received with skepticism and rejected if not proved to the hilt.[13] On the other hand, if the intermediary is really only an agent, but deliberately reports as his own amounts received for the benefit of another taxpayer, the attempt to launder the funds may be a criminal offense, fraudulently designed to enable the ultimate recipient to ward off an audit or take advantage of the intermediary's lower income tax rate.[14]

A related issue has arisen in a series of rulings involving annuity and life insurance arrangements where the savings element of the premium payments is held by the insurer in a segregated fund. The question in these rulings is whether the segregated fund should be treated as held by the insurer as part of the asset pool backing up its contractual obligations (in which event income on investments of the fund belongs to the insurer) or as nominee for the owner of the policy (in which case the policy owner is taxed on the income).[15]

(1981) (taxpayer receiving payoffs from real estate developers taxable on retained amounts but not on portion shared with mayor and aldermen); Shaara v. CIR, 40 TCM (CCH) 643 (1980) (taxpayer acted as conduit in making kickback payments to public official on behalf of construction company; funds not includable in his gross income); Gorin v. CIR, 27 TCM (CCH) 315 (1968) (corrupt tax lawyer not taxed on amounts received from client for payment as bribe to IRS official).

[12] Pierson v. CIR, 35 TCM (CCH) 1256 (1976).

[13] See Pendola v. CIR, 50 TC 509, 519 (1968) (corrupt IRS employee who recruited co-workers in large scale fraudulent activities taxed on amounts received from tax preparer on failure to prove how much was paid over to others, even though it appeared that he paid "whatever was needed to get the job done"); Horwitz v. CIR, 5 TCM (CCH) 375 (1952) (black marketeer's claim that amounts taxed to him were proceeds of checks cashed as an accommodation for others rejected for failure of proof).

[14] See US v. Snyder, 549 F2d 171 (10th Cir. 1977) ("ten-percenter" prosecuted criminally for collecting racetrack winnings for others and reporting amounts as personal receipts on information returns).

[15] Rev. Rul. 82-54, 1982-1 CB 11 (insurance company considered owner of mutual fund shares purchased in connection with wraparound annuity contracts where shares cannot be purchased by general public, even though policyholder can choose among three mutual funds; ability to choose among general investment strategies is not sufficient control over investment decisions to cause ownership of mutual fund shares to be attributed to policyholders); Rev. Rul. 81-225, 1981-2 CB 12, clarified by Rev. Rul. 82-55, 1982-1 CB 12 (policyholder rather than insurance

2. *Cost companies.* A formal device for the sharing of expenses is a "cost company" created by members of an industry to conduct mining or other operations under an agreement to share expenses and output. Since they actively conduct business operations, these captive companies differ from purely passive corporations used to hold title to property or for similar nominee functions, which are ordinarily but not always treated as conduits.[16] Despite their business functions, cost companies were long treated by the IRS as nontaxable nominees for the real parties in interest. In 1977, however, the IRS withdrew its earlier rulings and ruled that cost companies are separate taxable entities, required to compute their own income, deductions, credits, and tax liabilities.[17]

Within a few months after cracking down on cost companies, the IRS demonstrated its ability to draw nice distinctions—without acknowledging or, perhaps, recognizing its own virtuosity—by issuing two rulings holding that in various situations, funds paid to foster parents by social welfare agencies for the care of children placed in their homes are not taxable because expended for the benefit of the children.[18]

3. *Employees hired out by employer.* Employees obligated to turn over their outside earnings to their employer are ordinarily viewed as mere agents, so that the fees or wages are taxable to the employer rather than to the employee.[19] If, however, the employer is the employee's alter ego (a wholly owned corporation created to avoid taxes, for example), the wheel may come full circle, and the amounts may be taxed to the employee even though they are paid directly to the purported employer.[20]

---

company considered owner of mutual fund shares purchased by insurance company in connection with deferred variable wraparound annuity contracts, unless mutual fund controlled by insurance company and mutual fund shares cannot be purchased separately); Christoffersen v. US, 749 F2d 513 (8th Cir. 1984) (following Revenue Ruling 81-225); Rev. Rul. 80-274, 1980-2 CB 27 (policyholders rather than insurer taxed where annuity contract required deposit of premiums in accounts with savings and loan association). Such contracts are also subject to several statutory requirements that are described in ¶12.1.

[16] See infra ¶90.1.8.

[17] Rev. Rul. 77-1, 1977-1 CB 161.

[18] Rev. Rul. 77-280, 1977-2 CB 14; Rev. Rul. 77-279, 1977-2 CB 12. Also, §131 excludes from gross income, under specified conditions and limitations, funds paid to foster parents as reimbursement for the expenses of caring for a foster child or as compensation for the additional care of a foster child with a physical, mental, or emotional handicap.

[19] See Rev. Rul. 65-282, 1965-2 CB 21 (employees of legal aid society not taxed on court awarded fees for representing indigent defendants). See generally infra ¶75.2.5.

[20] See CIR v. Laughton, 113 F2d 103 (9th Cir. 1940). For the treatment of compensation of this type as personal holding company income, see infra ¶95.2.2.

A related subject, discussed elsewhere,[21] is the taxability of persons who renounce, disclaim, or otherwise decline to accept compensation for their services, thus shunting benefits to charitable organizations, members of their families, or friends.

4. *Gift or sale of property subject to income charge.* When property is acquired by gift or purchase under an arrangement requiring the transferee to pay the income from the property to the transferor or some other person for a period of time or until a specified sum has been paid, it is necessary to determine whether the transferee is only a conduit through which the income passes to the original owner or is himself the beneficial owner of the income. If the transferor retains an income interest, the transferee is not taxed on income that passes through his hands to the transferor.[22] In contrast, if the transfer includes the income interest but income is diverted to the transferor as part of the unpaid purchase price or to meet some other obligation, the transferee must report the diverted income.[23]

5. *Statutory conduits.* As explained elsewhere, the Code treats partnerships, estates and trusts, S corporations, real estate investment trusts, and mutual funds as conduits, in whole or in part, by mandating a pass through of their income, deductions, credits, and other tax characteristics to their beneficiaries, members, or shareholders.[24]

6. *Tax-avoidance transactions.* In many tax-avoidance transactions, intermediaries are used as camouflage. When unmasked, they are described, and sometimes castigated, as nominees, agents, dummies, conduits, and the like. The details vary from one imaginative scheme to another, but a typical case is *CIR v. Court Holding Co.*, involving a corporation that was about to sell an appreciated building but called off the sale at the last minute in order to distribute the property to its shareholders in complete liquidation, thus enabling them to consummate the previously planned sale in the hope of

---

[21] See infra ¶¶75.2.4, 75.2.5.

[22] See Heminway v. CIR, 44 TC 96 (1965) (stock purchase subject to retained life interest in dividends; buyer "derived no income therefrom because he was obliged to pay over . . . the amount received"); Collins v. CIR, 14 TC 301 (1950) (5 percent profit share retained on transfer of interest by retiring partner); Malloy v. CIR, 5 TC 1112 (1945) (receipt of partnership interest subject to obligation to pay widow of transferor a fixed sum out of profits).

[23] See Ellison v. CIR, 80 TC 378 (1983) (where real property sold for cash plus stated sum payable out of first rents after sale, these rents are ordinary income to buyer and part of purchase price paid to seller); Hibler v. CIR, 46 TC 663 (1966) (business acquired for cash plus percentage of income until $70,000 received; held, payments part of purchase price and not excludable by transferee); Alstores Realty Corp. v. CIR, 46 TC 363 (1966) (building acquired for cash plus rent-free leaseback; held, transferee realized rental income equal to value of the leaseback).

[24] See infra ¶85.1.1 (partnerships); infra Chs. 80 and 81 (estates and trusts); infra ¶95.6 (S corporations), ¶95.7.1 (mutual funds).

avoiding a corporate tax on the transaction.[25] The Supreme Court held, however, that the gain was taxable to the corporation because the sale was in substance made by the corporation, and the shareholders were used by the corporation "as a conduit through which to pass title" to the property to the buyers.[26]

¶6.3 AMOUNTS RECEIVED UNDER CLAIM OF RIGHT

¶6.3.1 Introductory

Taxpayers frequently receive funds they claim as their own, but then are subsequently required to repay part or all of the amount received because, for example, the amount was paid by mistake or erroneously computed or because a controversy regarding the payment is decided against the taxpayer. Amounts of this type are ordinarily includable in gross income when received under the claim of right doctrine enunciated by the Supreme Court in *North American Oil Consolidated v. Burnet.* This case, decided in 1932, grew out of litigation between the taxpayer and the government over the right to income generated in 1916 by certain oil lands.[1] Early in 1916, the government secured the appointment of a receiver to operate the property and hold the income. In 1917, the receivership was terminated by court order, and the 1916 income was paid to the taxpayer. The Court's decree was affirmed by the Court of Appeals in 1920, and in 1922 an appeal to the Supreme Court was dismissed by stipulation. The IRS asserted that the 1916 income was taxable to the taxpayer when received in 1917, while the taxpayer argued that the proper year was either 1916 (when the income was earned) or 1922 (when the cloud on the taxpayer's claim to it was eliminated). In holding for the government, the Supreme Court pointed out that at no time during 1916 could the taxpayer have compelled the receiver to pay over the amount in dispute. Regardless of its method of accounting, the Court ruled, the taxpayer was not taxable in 1916 "on account of income which it had not yet received and which it might never receive."[2] Neither

---

[25] CIR v. Court Holding Co., 324 US 331 (1945), discussed infra ¶93.9.3.

[26] Id. at 334.

[1] North Am. Oil Consol. v. Burnet, 286 US 417 (1932). See generally Lister, The Use and Abuse of Pragmatism: The Judicial Doctrine of Claim of Right, 21 Tax L. Rev. 263 (1966); Rabinovitz, Effect of Prior Year's Transactions on Federal Income Tax Consequences of Current Receipts or Payments, 28 Tax L. Rev. 85 (1972); Wooton, The Claim of Right Doctrine and Section 1341, 34 Tax Lawyer 297 (1981).

[2] North Am. Oil Consol. v. Burnet, supra note 1, at 424. The Court also held that the receiver, being in control of only part of the taxpayer's business, was not taxable on the 1916 income. For the status of a receiver of all of a taxpayer's property, see infra ¶82.4.6.

could it hold the 1916 profits in abeyance until 1922, when the litigation was finally terminated:

> They became income of the company in 1917, when it first became entitled to them and when it actually received them. If a taxpayer receives earnings under a claim of right and without restriction as to its disposition, he has received income which he is required to return [i.e., to report], even though it may still be claimed that he is not entitled to retain the money, and even though he may still be adjudged liable to restore its equivalent. . . . If in 1922 the Government had prevailed and the company had been obliged to refund the profits received in 1917, it would have been entitled to a deduction from the profits of 1922, not from those of any earlier year.[3]

As the last sentence of this extract indicates, the Court's decision did not turn on the taxpayer's ultimate success in establishing its legal right to the funds collected in 1917; the funds would have been 1917 income even if the taxpayer had been forced in 1922 to disgorge them. The crucial fact was that the taxpayer received the funds in 1917 under a claim of right—a phrase taken from the law of adverse possession of real property[4]—even though the validity of its claim was disputed.

In a logical extension of *North American Oil Consolidated*, the Court of Appeals for the Second Circuit held a year later that the claim of right doctrine encompasses disputed amounts a taxpayer obtains by posting a bond for repayment, since the bond neither restricts the use of the funds nor adds to the taxpayer's existing contingent liability to repay. The Court of Appeals also applied the doctrine to disputed amounts that could have been obtained by posting a bond, but were not, since the taxpayer cannot "alter at will the accrual of income by failing to exercise an option to receive it."[5]

Although the *North American Oil Consolidated* opinion does not refer to the dichotomy between annual and transactional accounting, the claim of right doctrine harmonizes with the basic principle requiring income to be computed on the basis of annual accounting periods, and necessarily rejects the theory that the taxation of disputed amounts can be held in abeyance until the final results of the entire transaction are known. This point was made by the Supreme Court in *United States v. Lewis*, decided in 1951, which held that an employee who received a bonus in 1944 and repaid

---

[3] North Am. Oil Consol. v. Burnet, supra note 1, at 424.
[4] See Healy v. CIR, 345 US 278, 282 (1953) (title to real property can be acquired by adverse possession only if occupant asserts possession under claim of right; analogous use of term in income taxation); see generally 3 American Law of Property ¶15.4 (Casner, ed.; Little, Brown & Co. 1952).
[5] CIR v. Brooklyn Union Gas Co., 62 F2d 505, 507 (2d Cir. 1933).

about half of it in 1946, when a state court decided that it had been erroneously computed, could not reopen his 1944 return and get a refund based on a recalculation of that year's tax liability: "Income taxes must be paid on income received (or accrued) during an annual accounting period. . . . The 'claim of right' interpretation of the tax laws has long been used to give finality to that period, and is now deeply rooted in the federal income tax system."[6]

Because of this link between the claim of right doctrine and the annual accounting requirement, *North American Oil Consolidated* is sometimes said to be a decision concerning the time when income must be reported and only applies to amounts that otherwise constitute income. This is only a half-truth. By holding that the amount had to be reported in 1917, when it was received under a claim of right, the Court necessarily held that the amount was income—not only in the sense that it constituted profits from operating the disputed properties, but also in the sense that it was taxable to the taxpayer regardless of the outcome of the litigation. Had the Court permitted the disputed amount to be held in abeyance until 1922, when the litigation terminated, the taxpayer would not have been required to report anything if the private litigation had gone the other way and the amount was repaid. For taxpayers who ultimately repay an amount received under a claim of right, therefore, *North American Oil Consolidated* is not confined to timing, since it does not point to the proper year for reporting income that the taxpayer will have to report in one year or another over the long haul, but instead determines that the receipt is income.

A disputed receipt is income under the claim of right doctrine, however, only if it would be income in the absence of the dispute. Assume a lender receives repayment of a loan under circumstances raising a possibility that the repayment might have to be shared with other creditors of the borrower. Because the repayment would not be income if the taxpayer were clearly entitled to keep it, the cloud on the taxpayer's entitlement does not make it income, notwithstanding the claim of right doctrine.

¶6.3.2 Scope of Claim of Right Doctrine

An exhaustive catalog of the circumstances triggering application of the claim of right doctrine is not feasible because almost any business or profit oriented transaction, and even some personal activities, can result in the receipt of funds that the taxpayer may have to repay in a later year but can

---

[6] US v. Lewis, 340 US 590 (1951). See also US v. Skelly Oil Co., 394 US 678, 681 (1969) (claim of right doctrine "dictated by Congress' adoption of an annual accounting system as an integral part of the tax code"). For the distinction between annual and transactional accounting, see generally infra ¶105.1.4.

use freely in the interim. In addition to the disputed profits in *North American Oil Consolidated* and the erroneously computed employee bonus in *United States v. Lewis,* the courts have applied the doctrine to such receipts, later repaid in whole or in part, as salaries paid to shareholder-employees by an insolvent family corporation, executive compensation attacked as excessive by a minority shareholder's suit, profits from a sale of stock not owned by the seller, prepaid insurance premiums, short-swing profits on stock transactions violating §16(b) of the Securities Exchange Act, and profits derived by corporate executives from usurping a corporate opportunity.[7]

The principal areas of uncertainty or dispute in applying the claim of right doctrine are:

1. *Disclaimers.* Since the tax liability on receiving a disputed amount can exceed the tax reduction that will occur if the amount is actually repaid in a later year,[8] a taxpayer may seek to avoid the claim of right doctrine by rejecting a payment when it is proffered, depositing it into a special account, or otherwise acknowledging that its status is subject to controversy. A prompt repayment should establish that the amount was not received under a claim of right, unless the taxpayer's action is merely a ploy for tax avoidance purposes or the repayment is rejected by the original payor.[9]

---

[7] Healy v. CIR, supra note 4 (salaries paid by insolvent corporation); Bramlette Bldg. Corp. v. CIR, 424 F2d 751 (5th Cir. 1970) (rents from property belonging to taxpayer's president but confused with taxpayer's property and operated by it for 10 years); Van Wagoner v. US, 368 F2d 95 (5th Cir. 1966) (commissions on prepaid insurance premiums); Phillips v. CIR, 262 F2d 668 (9th Cir. 1959) (stock claimed by taxpayer but later held to belong to another person); Griffin v. Smith, 101 F2d 348 (7th Cir. 1938) (excessive salaries subsequently repaid in settlement of shareholders' suit); Board v. CIR, 51 F2d 73 (6th Cir.), cert. denied, 284 US 658 (1931) (usurpation of corporate opportunity; litigation settled by waiver of compensation for services); Etoll's Est. v. CIR, 79 TC 676 (1982) (partner taxed on amounts collected on accounts receivable of dissolved partnership because he claimed them as his own, even though other partners subsequently obtained judgment for portion of amount collected); Nordberg v. CIR, 79 TC 655 (1982) (gain on receipt of part payment of subordinated loan included in gross income even though subject to obligation to repay if necessary to meet superior creditors' claims against payor); Walet v. CIR, 31 TC 461 (1958) (short-swing profits repaid under §16(b) of Securities Exchange Act), aff'd without discussion of this point, 272 F2d 694 (5th Cir. 1959); Reeves v. CIR, 36 TCM (CCH) 500 (1977) (funds obtained by embezzlement or false pretenses); Marco S. Marinello Assocs. v. CIR, 34 TCM (CCH) 392 (1975), aff'd per curiam, 535 F2d 147 (1st Cir. 1976) (interim condemnation award taxable under claim of right doctrine even though subject to repayment on conclusion of condemnation proceeding).

[8] But see §1341, discussed infra ¶6.3.4.

[9] See Crellin's Est. v. CIR, 203 F2d 812 (9th Cir.), cert. denied, 346 US 873 (1953) (disregarding repayment of dividends paid in mistaken belief that retained earnings would otherwise be subject to personal holding company tax); Miller v. CIR, 22 TCM (CCH) 1790 (1963), aff'd by order, 65-1 USTC ¶9288 (9th Cir.) (not

A 1954 case held that a taxpayer's prompt book entry acknowledging an obligation to return an erroneously computed executor's fee, coupled with repayment of the amount in a later year, precluded taxing the amount under the claim of right doctrine in the year of receipt. Later cases, however, have required cash basis taxpayers to make actual repayment in the year of receipt, not merely to disclaim the right to retain the amount.[10] On the other hand, if acknowledgment of an obligation to repay is contemporaneous with receipt of payment, this may establish that the payment is a loan, rather than an amount received under a claim of right.[11]

2. *Special accounts, escrows.* A taxpayer who is not prepared to refund a disputed amount may seek to avoid the claim of right doctrine by establishing an escrow or custodial account. In general, actions that can be rescinded by the taxpayer, such as depositing the amount in a special bank account under the taxpayer's sole control, are ineffective.[12] Formal escrows, joint accounts in the names of the taxpayer and the other claimant, and special accounts subject to withdrawal limitations are effective, at least if the arrangement is made before the taxpayer receives the amount and probably even if it is established after receipt but in the same year, because the deposited amount is not, in the words of *North American Oil Consolidated*, received "under a claim of right and without restriction as to its

---

officially reported), cert. denied, 382 US 888 (1965) (wages taxed to discharged employee, although out of religious conviction employee attempted to repay them by deposit to employer's credit in bank account; bank, on employer's instructions, held amount in trust for taxpayer). See also Hope v. CIR, 471 F2d 738 (3d Cir.), cert. denied, 414 US 824 (1973) (proceeds of sale of stock taxable when received, despite rescission action in year of sale, resulting in partial rescission in following year).

[10] Quinn v. CIR, 524 F2d 617, 624 (7th Cir. 1975); US v. Merrill, 211 F2d 297 (9th Cir. 1954); Bates Motor Transp. Lines, Inc. v. CIR, 200 F2d 20 (7th Cir. 1952); Bishop v. CIR, 25 TC 969, 974 (1956). Generally, actual payment, not a mere promise to repay, is needed, but at least one court has evidenced some laxity on this point. Compare Quinn v. CIR, supra (only actual repayment suffices; promise to repay or delivery of promissory note not sufficient) and Bates Motor Transp. Lines, Inc. v. CIR, supra (mere acknowledgment of obligation to refund, coupled with reserve on taxpayer's books, insufficient where amounts due could only be estimated), with US v. Merrill, supra (promise to repay sufficient).

[11] Gilbert v. CIR, 552 F2d 478 (2d Cir. 1977) (despite conviction for embezzlement, taxpayer did not realize taxable income on making unauthorized withdrawals of corporate funds where he did not intend to retain amounts, used them for corporate purposes, accounted for them to corporate directors, and signed secured promissory notes for full amount taken).

[12] CIR v. Alamitos Land Co., 112 F2d 648 (9th Cir.), cert. denied, 311 US 679 (1940) (bank account under taxpayer's control); Rev Rul. 55-137, 1955-1 CB 215 (same as to bank account under joint control of taxpayer and bonding company responsible for repayment if subsequently ordered by court).

disposition."[13]

3.*Conduits, trustees.* Amounts paid to trustees, messengers, and other intermediaries are not received under a claim of right within the meaning of *North American Oil Consolidated* and hence are not taxed to them. This is true even if the custodian has discretionary powers over the funds because the control is exercisable only on behalf of the real parties in interest.[14] The claim of right doctrine, however, does reach putative trustees and agents who, properly or improperly, exercise control over the funds for their own benefit.[15] As the Tax Court has observed, "If one claims to be a trustee then he should act like one, but if he acts as the true owner then we see no reason not to treat him as such for tax purposes."[16] A genuine conduit is not taxed on the funds passing through his hands, however, even if he obtains speculative or remote benefits from the arrangement, such as prestige in the case of a person raising funds for a political campaign.[17]

4. *Prepaid income.* In an early decision holding that an accrual basis automobile club was taxable on prepaid membership fees, despite its obligation to provide services on demand to the members, the IRS relied on *North American Oil Consolidated*, and the Supreme Court seemed to endorse this rationale.[18] In later cases reaching the same result, however, the Supreme Court refrained from relying on *North American Oil Consolidated*, stressing

---

[13] See Mutual Tel. Co. v. US, 204 F2d 160 (9th Cir. 1953) (utility company's receipts under disputed rate increase not taxable where deposited into account subject to withdrawal only with utility commission's consent); Preston v. CIR, 35 BTA 312 (1937) (joint account with other claimant); Rev. Rul. 70-66, 1970-1 CB 115 (escrowed funds). See also Miele v. CIR, 72 TC 284 (1979) (prepaid legal fees deposited in segregated bank account pursuant to state code of professional responsibility).

[14] See, e.g., Lashells' Est. v. CIR, 208 F2d 430 (6th Cir. 1953) (commissions or commercial bribes not taxable to go-between). See generally supra ¶6.2 (nominal vs. beneficial ownership).

[15] See, e.g., Diamond v. CIR, 56 TC 530 (1971) (taxpayer failed to prove status as conduit); Angelus Funeral Home v. CIR, 47 TC 391 (1967), aff'd, 407 F2d 210 (9th Cir.), cert. denied, 396 US 824 (1969) (prepayments for funeral expenses not taxable when received by taxpayer as custodian or trustee, although tied to use of taxpayer's facilities; amounts received under another contract taxable for want of restraints on taxpayer's use of funds).

[16] Latimer v. CIR, 55 TC 515, 520 (1970) (fire insurance proceeds received by lessor under lease requiring use of funds to replace damaged building, but actually applied to other purposes).

[17] Pierson v. CIR, 35 TCM (CCH) 1256 (1976) (political bag man); see also Cosman v. US, 440 F2d 1017 (Ct. Cl. 1971) (ex-wife not taxed on amounts received from ex-husband to pay premiums on insurance on his life, where benefits would go to their children or, in conjectural circumstances, to her); Escobar v. CIR, 45 TCM (CCH) 1326 (1983) ("unwilling pawn" not taxed on gain on sale of stock held in his name because he never had control of sale proceeds).

[18] Automobile Club of Mich. v. CIR, 353 US 180 (1957).

instead the IRS' authority to require a taxpayer to use an accounting method that clearly reflects income, as well as Congress' repeal of certain statutory provisions, discussed elsewhere in this work, that explicitly authorized the deferral of prepaid income.[19] In this important area, therefore, the claim of right doctrine has receded into the shadows.[20]

5. *Illegal receipts.* The tax status of illegal receipts is another area in which the claim of right doctrine has played a leading role. In *CIR v. Wilcox*, decided in 1946, the Supreme Court held that embezzled funds were not income, citing *North American Oil Consolidated* for the proposition that "without some bona fide legal or equitable claim, even though it be contingent or contested in nature, the taxpayer cannot be said to have received any gain or profit within the reach of [the predecessor of §61(a)]."[21]

This theory, which elevated the claim of right doctrine from a basis for taxing the recipient of disputed income to a prerequisite to taxing anyone on anything, was abandoned in 1961 when *Wilcox* was overruled by *James v. United States.*[22] In *James*, examined further later in this chapter, the Supreme Court held that "when a taxpayer acquires earnings, lawfully or unlawfully, without the consensual recognition, expressed or implied, of an obligation to repay and without restriction as to their disposition," the receipts are gross income.[23] The decision might be read to make the words "claim of right" a term of art largely disconnected from the usual meaning of the words; the essence of the claim of right doctrine, according to this reading of *James*, is not that the taxpayer has a legal claim or even a semblance of a right, but that the taxpayer possesses funds without restriction and without "a consensual recognition . . . of an obligation to repay."[24] Alternatively, if the claim of right doctrine is given a more conventional and literal meaning, *James* must be taken as a repudiation of the application of the doctrine to illegal income.

6. *Ambiguous receipts.* The claim of right doctrine is sometimes mentioned in decisions on whether payments are nontaxable deposits or prepaid income. For example, if a payment by lessee to lessor on signing a lease is to serve as security for the lessee's compliance with the terms of the lease and

---

[19] American Auto. Ass'n v. US, 367 US 687 (1961). See generally infra ¶105.3.4.

[20] But see George Blood Enter., Inc. v. CIR, 35 TCM (CCH) 436 (1976) (prepaid insurance commissions taxed under claim of right doctrine despite contingent obligation to refund unearned amounts); Rev. Rul. 83-12, 1983-1 CB 99 (*George Blood* followed without mention of claim of right doctrine).

[21] CIR v. Wilcox, 327 US 404, 408 (1946).

[22] James v. US, 366 US 213 (1961).

[23] Id. at 219; see generally infra ¶6.5.

[24] See Peters v. CIR, 51 TC 226, 231 (1968) (consensual recognition rationale of *James* implicit in *North American Oil Consolidated*); Reeves v. CIR, 36 TCM (CCH) 500 (1977) (doctrine of *North American Oil Consolidated* was "reaffirmed and expanded" by *James*).

is to be applied against the final month's rent if all prior payments are made as they fall due, it is necessary to determine whether the amount is a nontaxable deposit or a taxable prepayment of rent; the annual accounting concept precludes holding the issue in abeyance until the end of the lease. The courts are likely to treat the amount as a deposit if it must be held in a segregated account or if interest is credited to the lessee, but otherwise as prepaid rent.[25] This distinction is substantially the same as the boundary between disputed amounts held as custodian or trustee and similar amounts held under a claim of right.

¶6.3.3 Deduction of Repaid Amounts

In *North American Oil Consolidated*, the Supreme Court required the taxpayer to report the amount it received in 1917 as income for that year, although its right to retain the amount was not finally settled until 1922.[26] Since the taxpayer ultimately prevailed in its claim to the disputed amount, the Court did not have to pass on the effect of a repayment, but it observed that a deduction would have been allowed in 1922 if the taxpayer had then been required to refund the receipts.[27] No statutory authority was cited for this dictum, but it is clear that the relevant provisions of current law in the case of corporate taxpayers are §162, relating to business expenses, and §165, relating to losses.[28] If deductions allowed to a corporation under §162 or §165 cannot be fully used when allowed, they enter into the computation of a net operating loss, which can be carried to prior and later years under §172.[29]

---

[25] See, e.g., New Capital Hotel, Inc. v. CIR, 261 F2d 437 (6th Cir. 1958); J. & E. Enter., Inc. v. CIR, 26 TCM (CCH) 944 (1967); but see Rev. Rul. 82-28, 1982-1 CB 11 (coupon clearinghouse not taxed on security deposits received from retailers to cover losses from invalid coupons submitted by retailers, even though not segregated and no interest paid, because deposits could not be applied as compensation for services or other taxable item). For the issue of whether an amount received by a seller of goods or services is prepaid income or a deposit, see infra ¶105.3.4.

[26] North Am. Oil Consol. v. Burnet, 286 US 417 (1932).

[27] See supra text accompanying note 3.

[28] For §§162 and 165, see generally infra ¶¶20.1 and 25.1. For the possibility that §1341 supplies an independent statutory foundation for deducting repayments, see infra ¶6.3.4. For the effect of shareholder-employee agreements to refund compensation to the extent held unreasonable under §162(a), see infra note 49; infra ¶22.2.4 note §§55–56. See also US v. Simon, 281 F2d 520 (6th Cir. 1960) (deduction disallowed where taxpayer under no legal or moral obligation to make repayment, payee and payor were commonly controlled, and repayment made solely to produce tax benefit). For circumstances in which repayments create capital losses rather than deductions from ordinary income, see infra ¶51.10.6

[29] For §172, see infra ¶25.11.

If the taxpayer is an individual rather than a corporation, the status of a repayment is more complicated. Repayments qualifying under §162 or §165(c)(1) as expenses and losses incurred in the taxpayer's trade or business are subject to the same rules as repayments by corporations; they are deductible when paid or accrued, and excess deductions are taken into account in computing net operating losses. If an individual must rely on §165(c)(2), relating to losses incurred in transactions entered into for profit but are not connected with a trade or business, or on §212, relating to expenses incurred for the production of income, the refund can be deducted, but an excess deduction can be taken into account only to a limited extent in computing a net operating loss.[30]

Finally, if an individual receives a claim of right item incident to activity that is not a trade or business or a transaction entered into for profit, the right to deduct a repayment is open to question. For example, if an individual sells a personal residence at a profit and must later repay part of the sales price because the amount was miscalculated or the condition of the property was misrepresented to the buyer, the IRS could argue that the repayment cannot be deducted because the loss was not incurred in a transaction entered into for profit.[31] It is obviously unfair, however, to disregard the taxpayer's contingent obligation to repay in applying the claim of right doctrine to include a disputed receipt in gross income, and then to disallow a deduction if the contingency is resolved against the taxpayer. For this reason, the Treasury apparently concedes the propriety of a deduction in this situation, perhaps on the theory that a deduction in the event of repayment is an appropriate corollary of the claim of right doctrine itself.[32]

Another unlitigated issue in this area is the effect of a repayment of a disputed amount within the same taxable year as the amount is received. Taxable income is the same whether (1) the disputed amount is included in gross income because received under a claim of right and then deducted from gross income in computing taxable income for the same year or (2) the receipt and repayment are treated as a wash and disregarded. But gross income, and, in the case of an individual taxpayer, adjusted gross income, have ancillary consequences, since they affect the obligation to file a return, the amounts that can be deducted for charitable contributions and medical expenses, and some other matters. For these purposes, a wash is different

---

[30] For §§165(c)(2) and 212, see infra ¶¶25.3 and 20.5. For the effect of nonbusiness deductions on net operating losses, see infra ¶25.11.2.

[31] See generally infra ¶25.3.

[32] See Reg. §1.1341-1(h) Ex. (deduction allowed under §1341 for repayment following sale of personal residence at gain; no indication that amount repaid less than gain); but see National Life & Accident Ins. Co. v. US, 244 F. Supp. 135 (MD Tenn. 1965) (no deduction for interest refunded on early redemption of U.S. bonds in absence of explicit statutory authorization).

from an inclusion of the disputed amount in gross income coupled with an offsetting deduction. Since the purpose of the claim of right doctrine and the related deduction rule is to provide within an annual accounting system for transactions spread over more than one year, not to either favor or disfavor taxpayers subject to the rules, the policy of the rule is best served by treating a receipt and repayment in a way that is as neutral on tax obligations over the long run as is possible within the confines of an annual accounting system. Where receipt and repayment occur within a single year, this can be accomplished by excluding the receipt and payment from the taxpayer's gross income and deductions.

¶6.3.4 Effect of Repayment on Tax Liability

In *United States v. Lewis*, the Supreme Court held that an employee who repaid in 1946 part of an erroneously computed bonus received in 1944 could not reopen his 1944 return in order to recalculate that tax liability; a deduction in 1946 for the repayment was the taxpayer's only remedy. The claim of right doctrine, the Court said, could not be cast off "merely because it results in an advantage or disadvantage to a taxpayer."[33] The taxpayer in *Lewis* preferred a refund for the earlier year, either because his marginal tax rate was higher in that year than in the year of repayment, or because a refund would bear interest, or both. For other taxpayers, the Court noted, a deduction in the year of repayment could be more valuable than a refund, even with interest. In a later case, the Court observed that "these discrepancies were accepted as an unavoidable consequence of the annual accounting system."[34]

Under §1341, enacted in 1954 in response to the *Lewis* case, however, qualified taxpayers effectively get the better of these alternatives.[35] Technically, the provision does not alter the *Lewis* holding; it pertains only to the computation of tax for the year in which a deduction for a repayment is allowed, and does not allow a refund of tax paid for the year of the earlier inclusion. The tax liability for the year of repayment, however, is computed in a way that gives the taxpayer the equivalent of a refund (without interest) for the earlier year if the taxpayer is advantaged thereby. Specifically, under §1341, the tax for the year of repayment is the lesser of two amounts. The first is a tax computed in the normal fashion with a deduction for the repayment. The second is the excess of (1) a tax for the repayment year

---

[33] US v. Lewis, 340 US 590, 592 (1951).

[34] US v. Skelly Oil Co., 394 US 678, 681 (1969).

[35] See S. Rep. No. 1983, 85th Cong., 2d Sess., reprinted in 1958-3 CB 922, 1003–05 (1958); S. Rep. No. 1622, 83d Cong., 2d Sess. 118, 451–52 (1954). See generally Emanuel, The Scope of Section 1341, 53 Taxes 644 (1975); Rabinovitz, supra note 1.

computed without the deduction, over (2) the decrease in tax that would have resulted for the earlier year if the repaid amount had been excluded from that year's gross income. Since the tax is the lesser of these amounts, "the taxpayer always wins and the Government always loses"[36] under §1341. Because the remedial mechanism does not entail a refund for the earlier year,[37] the taxpayer is not credited with interest.

Under §1341, the decrease in the prior year's tax that would have resulted from excluding the repaid amount is determined by recomputing all items affected by the exclusion, including, for example, percentage limitations on the deductions for charitable contributions and medical expenses. If the statute of limitations has run for that year, however, errors pertaining to other income and deductions are not corrected.[38]

The effect of §1341(a) is illustrated by Example 6-1, which assumes that (1) a married couple files joint returns for 1988 and 1991; (2) income for 1988 consists of professional fees of $80,000, including a disputed fee of $30,000 received under a claim of right; (3) the taxpayers make a charitable contribution of $25,000 the deduction for which is limited to 30 percent of adjusted gross income;[39] and (4) in 1991, professional fees of $30,000 are received, and $10,000 of the disputed receipt from 1988 is repaid to settle the dispute. For simplicity, Example 6-1 disregards the taxpayer's personal exemptions and, for 1991, the standard deduction.

On these assumptions, the tax liability for 1991 is $3,000 (column C, line 6) when computed in the usual manner by deducting the $10,000 repayment, but only $2,853 (column D, line 8) when computed under §1341(a)(5) by disregarding the repayment but taking into account the decrease in tax ($1,680—column D, line 7) that would have resulted for 1988 had the refunded $10,000 not been included in gross income for that year.

Section 1341 comes into play if (1) an item was included in gross income for a prior taxable year because it appeared that the taxpayer had an unrestricted right to such item,[40] (2) a deduction is allowable for the current taxable year because it has been established that the taxpayer did not have

---

[36] US v. Skelly Oil Co., supra note 34, at 692 (Mr. Justice Stewart, dissenting). For a limited restriction on this one-way-street explanation of §1341, see supra ¶5.7.4.

[37] See Shipley v. US, 608 F2d 770 (9th Cir. 1979), for the procedural problem created for the taxpayer if the statute of limitations is about to run on refunds for the repayment year and tax liability for the inclusion year is still being litigated.

[38] See Reg. §1.1341-1(d)(4)(ii). For computation of the decrease in tax if two or more inclusion years are involved, see Reg. §1.1341-1(d)(3) (pro rata allocation of deduction to amounts included in prior years).

[39] For this percentage limitation, see infra ¶35.3.2.

[40] See Shipley v. US, supra note 37 (§1341 covers amounts that taxpayer failed to report as gross income but were picked up in audit of prior year's return).

an unrestricted right to the item or a portion thereof, and (3) the deduction exceeds $3,000.

Example 6-1

Tax Liability on Repayment of Amount Received
Under Claim of Right—Determined Under §1341

	1988		1991	
	A As Reported	B Under §1341(a)(5)	C Under §1341(a)(4)	D Under §1341(a)(5)
1. Undisputed fees...........	$50,000	$50,000	$ 30,000	$30,000
2. Disputed fee................				
a. Amount included in income...............	$30,000	$20,000	—	—
b. Amount repaid and deducted.................	—	—	($10,000)	—
3. Adjusted gross income.	$80,000	$70,000	$ 20,000	$30,000
4. Charitable contribution ($25,000 donated—30 percent of AGI deductible).......	$25,000	$21,000	—	—
5. Taxable income	$55,000	$49,000	$ 20,000	$30,000
6. Tax liability	$11,533	$ 9,853	$ 3,000	$ 4,533
7. Decrease in 1988 tax liability on recomputation (col. A, line 6 minus col. B, line 6)...				$ 1,680
8. Tax liability for 1991 determined under §1341 (a)(5) (col. D, line 6 minus col. A, line 7)				$ 2,853
9. Tax liability for 1991 (lesser of col. C, line 6 and col. D, line 8)...				$ 2,853

The first of these conditions deserves close attention. Section 1341 was enacted primarily to deal with the repayment of amounts received under a claim of right, and this phrase is used both in its statutory label ("Computation of Tax Where Taxpayer Restores Substantial Amount Held Under Claim of Right") and in the regulations.[41] The operative language of §1341(a)(1), however, refers to items included in gross income "because it appeared that the taxpayer had an unrestricted right to such item," and this

---

[41] Reg. §§1.1341-1(a)(1), (2) ("claim of right" defined for purposes of §1341 by reference to statutory language); but see IRC §7806(b) (no interpretative inferences to be drawn from descriptive matter).

phrase is narrower than the claim of right doctrine.[42] It seems to deny relief for amounts that are in dispute when received, even if they must be included in income because received under a claim of right. This creates the astonishing possibility that §1341 is inapplicable to the granddaddy of all claim of right cases, *North American Oil Consolidated*, because, given the continuing litigation, it could hardly have been said that it "appeared" in 1917 that the taxpayer had an "unrestricted right" to the disputed amount.

By construing the statutory term "unrestricted right" to mean "unrestricted use" — an interpretation for which the 1954 legislative history offers some support[43] — §1341(a)(1) can be stretched to cover disputed amounts received under a claim of right. This construction, however, creates a difficulty under §1341(a)(2), which refers to deductions allowed "because it was established after the close of [the taxable year of inclusion] that the taxpayer did not have an unrestricted right to such item," a phrase that is more appropriate for the taxpayer's legal right than for his freedom to use the funds. Moreover, as applied to uncollected amounts included in an accrual taxpayer's gross income, "unrestricted right" also refers to legal rights, rather than to the taxpayer's ability to use the item.

Without resolving this problem, the regulations provide that an item is covered by §1341(a)(1) if "it appeared from all the facts available in the year of inclusion that the taxpayer had an unrestricted right to such item."[44] In applying this standard, a 1968 ruling looks to the facts that were available to the taxpayer and distinguishes between three types of appearances: (1) a "semblance" of an unrestricted right; (2) an unchallengeable right, which is more than an apparent right; and (3) no right at all, which is less than an apparent right.[45] If the taxpayer's right to the item was unchallengeable in the year of inclusion (type 2 in the foregoing summary) but was undermined by facts arising subsequently, §1341 does not apply because the taxpayer's right to the item in the year of inclusion is never denied. As examples, the ruling cites a repayment of prepaid interest when a debt is paid in advance and a payment of liquidated damages under a contract; in these cases, the

---

[42] It is also broader in that it encompasses amounts included in an accrual basis taxpayer's gross income, such as billed but uncollected fees, even if the inclusion was required by normal principles of accrual accounting without any reference to the claim of right doctrine. This overreach, however, is harmless because the second requirement of §1341 — that a deduction be allowable to reflect a determination that the taxpayer does not have an unrestricted right to the item — is not satisfied unless the item is disputed.

[43] See S. Rep. No. 1622, supra note 35, at 451 (provision applies if taxpayer "becomes entitled to a deduction because the item or a portion thereof is no longer subject to his unrestricted use").

[44] Reg. §1.1341-1(a)(2).

[45] Rev. Rul. 68-153, 1968-1 CB 371.

taxpayer is entitled to a deduction, but not to §1341 relief.[46] At the other end of the spectrum are amounts to which the taxpayer had no right at all (type 3), such as embezzled funds, which are also outside the scope of §1341, although here too the taxpayer is entitled to a deduction for amounts repaid.[47]

This leaves type 1 items—the golden mean, as it were—to which the taxpayer has a right that "appears" unrestricted in the year of inclusion, but that turns out to be fatally defective. Typical items meeting this standard are commissions received or accrued by a salesman subject to a condition requiring a refund or credit in a later year if the customer fails to pay for the goods.[48] Another possible example is a shareholder-employee's repayment of a salary pursuant to an agreement, in force when the salary was received, to refund any amount that cannot be deducted by the employer because the IRS finds it to be excessive in amount.[49]

The IRS' denial of §1341 treatment for all type 2 and 3 items represents an exceedingly ungenerous reading of §1341. The rule on prepaid interest, which seemingly extends to all prepaid items, illustrates the point. In *North American Oil Consolidated* and *Lewis*, the facts that were the basis of the taxpayers' claims to the disputed items all existed when the items

---

[46] Id. See also Rev. Rul. 67-48, 1967-1 CB 50 (liquidated damages for breach of employment contract); Rev. Rul. 58-226, 1958-1 CB 318 (refund of prepaid interest).

[47] See McKinney v. US, 574 F2d 1240 (5th Cir. 1978), cert. denied, 439 US 1072 (1979); Zadoff v. US, 86-2 USTC ¶9567 (SDNY 1986) (not officialy reported) (benefit of §1341 denied to purchasing agent required to pay to employer (1) kickbacks received from vendors to the employer and (2) salary for the period he was receiving these kickbacks); Perez v. US, 553 F. Supp. 558 (MD Fla. 1982) (§1341 inapplicable when taxpayer restores kickbacks; *McKinney* not limited to embezzlements); Yerkie v. CIR, 67 TC 388 (1976); Rev. Rul. 82-74, 1982-1 CB 110 (taxpayer who refunds insurance proceeds when arson discovered is entitled to deduction, but not §1341 treatment).

[48] Rev. Rul. 72-78, 1972-1 CB 45. See also Rev. Rul. 68-153, 1968-1 CB 371 (refunds by utility company to customers on retroactive reduction of rates by state utility commission).

[49] The IRS contends that such a repayment is a type 2 item as to which §1341 relief is unavailable. Rev. Rul. 69-115, 1969-1 CB 50; see also Rev. Rul. 67-437, 1967-2 CB 296 (same as to shareholder-employee's agreement to reimburse family corporation for travel expenses disallowed as deductions). The IRS' argument is that the employee's right to the salary is absolute when received and that the reimbursement obligation arises from a subsequent event, the disallowance of the deduction. The true source of this obligation, however, is the infirmity in the employer's claim for deduction. The disallowance of the deduction merely establishes the existence of the infirmity and does not create it. The IRS' action in disallowing the refund is like a court decision that an employee's bonus was erroneously computed and must be refunded in part. The IRS' theory has not found favor in the courts, which have usually applied §1341 in this situation. Van Cleave v. US, 718 F2d 193 (6th Cir. 1983); Pahl v. CIR, 67 TC 286 (1976).

were received, and only the legal effect of those facts remained to be determined in the future. In a prepayment situation, the obligation to refund arises from two facts, one of which exists when the amount is received (the agreement to refund if the prepaid item is not fully earned) and one of which arises later (the principal payment or other event establishing that the item will never be fully earned). The prepayment situation thus differs factually from the classic claim of right cases. The statutory language, however, does not require that this difference be determinative of the application of §1341. The inclusion of a prepayment is premised on an assumption that the item will eventually be fully earned; the inclusion is required, in the words of §1341, because "it appeared that the taxpayer had an unrestricted right to the item." A refund of a prepayment is deductible because it contradicts the assumption that was the basis for taxing the prepayment—because, that is, "it was establshed after the close of such prior taxable year . . . that the taxpayer did not have an unrestricted right to such item.".

Notwithstanding an occasional loose reference to amounts that are "deductible under the provisions of section 1341,"[50] it is clear that the taxpayer must look elsewhere, primarily to §§162 and 165, to establish that a deduction is allowable.[51] Section 1341 merely provides a method for computing tax liability if "a deduction is allowable" under the circumstances described in §1341(a).[52]

The principal requirement with respect to the deduction is that it must have arisen because it was established that the taxpayer did not have an unrestricted right to the item. This denies §1341 treatment for voluntary refunds, even if they are deductible because they serve a bona fide business purpose like preserving the taxpayer's reputation. On the other hand, the taxpayer does not have to be dragged through the courts before it can be said that the absence of an unrestricted right was adequately established.[53]

Legal fees and other expenses incurred in contesting the restoration of an amount previously included in income do not qualify for §1341 relief[54] because they are not amounts previously included in income and hence

---

[50] Blanton v. CIR, 46 TC 527, 529 (1966).

[51] See supra ¶6.3.3.

[52] See US v. Skelly Oil Co., 394 US 678, 683 (1969) ("it is necessary to refer to other portions of the Code to discover how much of a deduction is allowable").

[53] Compare Pike v. CIR, 44 TC 787, 799 (1965) (lawyer's repayment of stock profits deductible under §162(a) because related to professional reputation, but §1341(a) not applicable in absence of evidence of at least "probable validity" of adverse claim to amount repaid) with Rev. Rul. 58-456, 1958-2 CB 415 (litigation not essential; §1341 applies if amount paid pursuant to demand by government agency in circumstances entitling it to enforce demand by legal action). See also Rev. Rul. 72-78, 1972-1 CB 45 Rev. Rul. 68-153, 1968-1 CB 371, which applied §1341 to amounts repaid without litigation.

[54] Reg. §1.1341-1(h).

cannot be the subject of a later determination that the taxpayer did not have an unrestricted right to the amounts paid out. Bad debt deductions are also excluded,[55] probably for a similar reason—a debtor's failure to repay does not establish that the taxpayer did not have an unrestricted right to these funds when they were originally earned or otherwise acquired.

Section 1341 is subject to the following additional qualifications and special rules:

1. *Inventory and stock in trade.* Section 1341(b)(2) excludes deductions allowable for items included in gross income on sales of inventory or other property held primarily for sale to customers in the ordinary course of the taxpayer's trade or business.[56] A deduction for an amount paid as damages for breach of a warranty made on a sale of an inventory item, for example, does not qualify for §1341 relief. This disqualification reflects a legislative expectation in 1954, when §1341 was enacted, that refunds by merchants and manufacturers could be charged against reserves for estimated expenses authorized by §462 of the 1954 Code, but it was not changed when §462 was repealed.[57] The disqualification does not apply, however, to refunds by regulated public utilities, if paid under an order of a court or public agency or to settle an existing or threatened lawsuit.

2. *Negative tax liability.* When the recomputation of tax for the year of inclusion results in a decrease exceeding the tax for the repayment year (determined without the deduction for the repayment), the excess is treated by §1341(b)(1) as an overpayment of tax on the last day of the repayment year, and is refunded or credited accordingly. If in Example 6-1 the decrease in 1988 tax liability (line 7) were $6,533 instead of $1,680, the tax liability for 1991 (line 9) would be minus $2,000 ($4,533, less $6,533). This amount would be refunded or credited as though it were an overpayment made by the taxpayer on December 31, 1991.

3. *Net operating and capital losses.* In determining which of the alternative computations—§1341(a)(4) (deduction) or §1341(a)(5) (decrease in prior year's tax liability)—produces the lower tax liability, a deduction for

---

[55] Reg. §1.1341-1(g).

[56] See Reg. §1.1341-1(f); Rev. Rul. 68-153, 1968-1 CB 371 (disqualification does not cover railroad freight charges). For an analogous exclusion, see §1221(1) (definition of capital asset; discussed infra ¶51.2).

A provision exempting repayments under price redetermination clauses of certain pre-1958 subcontracts was repealed as obsolete in 1976. See Joint Comm. on Tax'n, 94th Cong., 2d Sess., General Explanation of Tax Reform Act of 1976, reprinted in 1976-3 CB (Vol. 2) 494. For the current status of repayments under contracts of this type and under government contracts subject to renegotiation, see infra ¶106.4.6.

[57] See S. Rep. No. 1622, 83d Cong., 2d Sess. 452 (1954). For the repeal of §462 and the current status of reserves for estimated expenses, see infra ¶105.3.6.

the repayment that produces a net operating loss for the repayment year is treated by §1341(b)(4)(A) as a net operating loss carryback; if the exclusion of the repaid amount from the prior year's income produces either a net operating loss or a net capital loss, §1341(b)(4)(B) requires that the loss be carried to earlier or later years under §172 or §1212, as the case may be, but not to years after the repayment year. Once this determination has been made, these losses can be carried over to post-repayment years in the manner provided by §1341(b)(5).[58]

¶6.4 INCOME FROM DISCHARGE OF DEBT FOR LESS THAN FACE AMOUNT

¶6.4.1 Introductory

As pointed out earlier in this work,[1] borrowed funds are excluded from gross income, even though they increase the taxpayer's assets and can be used as he sees fit, because the obligation to repay increases his liabilities by the same amount, and the loan therefore produces no gain. Usually, the debt is fully paid at maturity, thus validating the assumption on which the funds were excluded. The prediction of full repayment, however, sometimes proves erroneous because the taxpayer is able to discharge the debt for less than the amount received. Although this means that the taxpayer has received and excluded from income more than he pays out, the federal income tax was almost 20 years old before the courts unequivocally accepted the government's theory that the discharge of a debt for less than its face amount could generate income.

An obstacle to government success in this early period was *Eisner v. Macomber*, which defined income as "the gain derived from capital, from labor, or from both combined."[2] An improvement in the debtor's financial position resulting from settling a debt for less than its full amount did not seem to be a gain derived from either capital or labor.[3] Moreover, if the

---

[58] For explanation and illustrations of these complex rules, see Reg. §1.1341-1(b), (d)(4) Ex. 5. See also Hendershott, Restoration — Claim of Right — One Aspect of Section 1341, 48 Taxes 585 (1970).

[1] Supra ¶6.1.

[2] Eisner v. Macomber, 252 US 189, 207 (1920), discussed supra ¶1.2.4.

[3] See, for example, Meyer Jewelry Co. v. CIR, 3 BTA 1319 (1926), which also cited as controlling the statement in *Eisner v. Macomber* that "enrichment through increase in value of capital investment is not income in any proper meaning of the term." The court nevertheless suggested that there might be other circumstances in which the cancellation of a debt would constitute income, and it also hinted that the taxpayer could be required to reduce the basis of the property purchased with the borrowed funds. For this procedure, see infra ¶6.4.7.

creditor accepts less than the amount due because the debtor is in financial distress, taxing the debtor might have seemed anomalous, even heartless, especially since the closer the debtor approaches to the abyss of bankruptcy, the greater the discount on his obligations and, therefore, the heavier the tax burden if the discount is taxed. This reluctance to kick someone when he is down, however, should not have impeded the imposition of tax on gain realized by a corporate debtor on open market purchases of its own bonds at less than their face amount, where the decline in value is attributable to an increase in interest rates rather than doubts about collectibility.[4]

The government's early efforts to tax gain from below-face debt cancellations encountered still another obstacle in 1926, when the Supreme Court decided *Bowers v. Kerbaugh-Empire Co.*[5] In this case, its first pronouncement on the subject, the Court held that no income was realized by a taxpayer who borrowed German marks before World War I, converted the borrowed funds into dollars that were advanced to a subsidiary (which lost them in unsuccessful business activities), and then repaid the loans after the war with devalued marks costing about $685,000 less in dollars than the borrowed marks were worth when received. Observing that "the whole transaction was a loss," the Court said: "The loss was less than it would have been if [German] marks had not declined in value; but the mere diminution of loss is not gain, profit, or income."[6]

Despite this inauspicious beginning, the government persisted and finally succeeded in *United States v. Kirby Lumber Co.*,[7] decided by the

---

[4] Another explanation for a debtor's ability to settle a debt for less than the face amount should be acknowledged. If the debtor has a talent for fraud, he may be able to conceal his assets successfully, outwit his creditors, and settle his debts for a song. Profits from this gambit should perhaps be classed as income from unlawful activities rather than as income from the discharge of a debt for less than its face amount. See infra ¶6.5 note 20.

The reason for a less-than-face cancellation of a debt may be relevant in determining its tax effect. For example, a cancellation may be a gift. If *A* loans his friend *B* $10,000 for five years without interest, *A* will probably be willing to accept less than $10,000 in repayment of the debt before maturity because of the time value of money. The economic benefit of using the funds for the five-year period is an indirect gift from *A* to *B*, which the latter is entitled to exclude from income. A below face cancellation of the debt should be treated as a method of conferring the tax-free gift on *B* in one fell swoop rather than in installments over the original life of the debt. See Forrester v. CIR, 4 TC 907, 921 (1945) (acq.). See also infra Chapter 46 for the imputation of interest on gift loans.

For the effect of the statute of limitations and a state no-claims statute, see Bankhead's Est. v. CIR, 60 TC 535 (1973).

[5] Bowers v. Kerbaugh-Empire Co., 271 US 170 (1926).

[6] Id. at 175. Gains and losses from dealings in foreign currencies are now governed by a detailed set of rules described in ¶65.7.

[7] US v. Kirby Lumber Co., 284 US 1 (1931).

Supreme Court in 1931. The taxpayer, a corporation, issued about $12 million of bonds in July 1923 and purchased some of the bonds on the open market later in the same year for about $138,000 less than their issue price. The government asserted that the difference was taxable income, arguing that *Kerbaugh-Empire* was not controlling in the absence of an overall loss. In a suprisingly terse opinion, the Court upheld the government's contention. The constitutional doubts that had clouded the area were dismissed without even citing *Eisner v. Macomber*.

> In Bowers v. Kerbaugh-Empire Co . . . [the taxpayer] owned the stock of another company that had borrowed money repayable in marks or their equivalent for an enterprise that failed. At the time of payment the marks had fallen in value, which so far as it went was a gain for the [taxpayer], and it was contended by the [government] that the gain was taxable income. But the transaction as a whole was a loss, and the contention was denied. Here [in *Kirby Lumber*] there was no shrinkage of assets and the taxpayer made a clear gain. As a result of its dealings it made available $137,521.30 [of] assets previously offset by the obligation of bonds now extinct. We see nothing to be gained by the discussion of judicial definitions. The defendant in error has realized within the year an accession to income, if we take words in their plain popular meaning, as they should be taken here.[8]

The result is entirely justifiable, but the opinion's cryptic explanation set afloat several erroneous ideas leading to a confusing patchwork of rules and exceptions that dominates the area to this day.

First, the Court carried forward the *Kerbaugh-Empire* theory that the taxability of a debt discharge depends on "the transaction as a whole"—not merely whether the taxpayer borrowed more than it paid back, but also the fate of the borrowed funds. Such an analysis is usually impossible, however, since borrowed funds are ordinarily absorbed into the business so completely that tracing the travels of interchangeable dollars lacks even the surface plausibility that it could claim in *Kerbaugh-Empire*.[9]

---

[8] Id. at 3. Although the opinion refers to "extinct" bonds, later cases hold that it is immaterial whether the bonds are retired or held for reissue. Montana, Wyo. & S.R.R. v. CIR, 31 BTA 62 (1934), aff'd per curiam, 77 F2d 1007 (3d Cir.), cert. denied, 296 US 604 (1935).

[9] For cases in which the taxpayer was unable to trace borrowed funds into business losses, see Church's English Shoes, Ltd. v. CIR, 229 F2d 957 (2d Cir. 1956); Capitol Coal Corp. v. CIR, 26 TC 1183 (1956), aff'd, 250 F2d 351 (2d Cir. 1957). For other situations where borrowed funds are linked to particular investments, see infra ¶15.4.1 (interest to carry tax-exempt securities), ¶31.4 (interest expense allocated among passive, investment, business, and personal uses).

Kirby Lumber itself demonstrates the difficulty of tracing borrowed funds. Although the Court said the taxpayer suffered "no shrinkage of assets" but "made a clear gain," there was nothing in the record to support this suggestion. Contrary to a common assumption, the taxpayer in *Kirby Lumber* issued the bonds not for cash but in exchange for its own preferred stock with dividend arrearages,[10] and it is not clear how one should determine whether such a transaction, followed by a below face purchase, resulted in a "clear gain." Is it necessary to ascertain the fate of the funds or assets received by the taxpayer when the preferred stock was issued? Even where funds can be traced to a particular project, as in *Kerbaugh-Empire*, the attribution is artificial because the borrowed funds usually free up funds that can be used to finance other projects.[11] It is unclear, therefore, how an examination of "the transaction as a whole" can be limited to the projects directly financed by the borrowed funds.

More important, the tax consequences of activities and investments financed with borrowed money are usually analyzed without reference to the source of the funds. If a corporation borrows funds that it advances to a subsidiary and the subsidiary becomes bankrupt, for example, the corporation has a loss on the advance to the subsidiary that is deductible when the subsidiary's obligation becomes uncollectible. This deduction is unaffected, either in its timing or its amount, by the tax consequences of the parent corporation's borrowing. If the tax consequences of the borrowing are tied into the transactions in which the borrowed funds are used, confusion is the very best that can be expected. Assume the parent corporation in the example is able to pay off its debt at less than face. If the corporation is allowed to offset against this gain its loss on the advance to the subsidiary, the offset is a second allowance for a single loss unless the rules for losses are modified to take the offset into account.[12] Given the infinite range of uses to which

---

[10] See Bittker, Income From the Cancellation of Indebtedness: A Historical Footnote to the *Kirby Lumber Co.* Case, 4 J. Corp. Tax'n 124 (1977).

[11] See Reg. §1.861-8(e)(2)(i) ("money is fungible. . . . All activities and property require funds and . . . management has a great deal of flexibility as to the source and use of funds").

[12] It is not clear whether there was a doubling or a compensating adjustment in *Kerbaugh-Empire*, where the taxpayer borrowed funds from a bank in order to lend them to its subsidiary and then repaid less than the amount it borrowed. The opinions say the subsidiary suffered business losses, but do not indicate whether the taxpayer wrote off its loans to the subsidiary as bad debts. If these loans were still outstanding after the parent settled its bank loans and were subsequently written off as uncollectible, it is possible that the taxpayer would not be allowed to deduct the full amount that it loaned to the subsidiary but only the cost incurred to repay the borrowed German marks. Conversely, a repayment in full by the subsidiary would have generated gain to the parent equal to the amount excluded by the latter from income in the year of its settlement with the bank because the exclusion would have required a reduction in its basis for its loans to the subsidiary.

borrowed funds can be put, any such modification would have far reaching and complex applications. Income can be computed fairly and much more simply by analyzing the consequences of a borrowing transaction independently of the gains and losses flowing from the taxpayer's uses of the borrowed funds.

Further, taken to its logical conclusion, the holistic approach of *Kerbough-Empire* could swallow the holding in *Kirby Lumber*. Several kinds of changes in circumstance can make it possible for a debtor to repurchase its bonds for less than their issue price, but all of them are suggestive of a decline in the value of the debtor's assets. Its creditors might have come to doubt its ability to pay the debt when due, or the market rate of interest on bonds of comparable risk might have risen, making the taxpayer's bonds less attractive than new issues bearing interest at current rates.[13] Other possibilities are a general increase in the riskless rate of return on investments and a shift by the borrower into riskier activities. Creditor doubts about a debtor's financial stability are usually sparked by a decline in the value of the debtor's business as a going concern that is larger than the consequential fall in the value of the bonds. A similar loss of going concern value results from an increase in the market rate of interest; one of the few reliable stock market phenomena is that an increase in interest rates ordinarily causes stock prices to drop, reflecting a lower present value for the stream of income expected from corporate assets. Whichever of these events accounted for the taxpayer's discount repurchase of its bonds in *Kirby Lumber*, the transaction as a whole probably was no more profitable than the *Kerbaugh-Empire* transaction.[14]

The *Kirby Lumber* Court, however, assumed the contrary. The lower courts have not directly attacked this unrealistic aspect of *Kirby Lumber*, but because the Court invited examination of "the transaction as a whole," they have grafted exceptions onto the *Kirby Lumber* principle when it is glaringly obvious that the taxpayer's ability to settle its debt for less than the amount owing is evidence of financial distress. Courts have, however, per-

---

The trial court's opinion states that the subsidiary deducted its losses, but if the subsidiary later defaulted on its debts to its parent or settled them for less than face amount, its earlier deductions might have disqualified it from relying on the *Kerbaugh-Empire* rationale, thus requiring it to report debt discharge income. See 300 F. 938, 939–40 (SDNY 1924).

[13] See supra note 4.

[14] For this reason, the analogy in CIR v. Jacobson, 336 US 28, 39 (1949), between a repurchase of the taxpayer's own bonds at a discount and a profitable transaction in the bonds of another company is unpersuasive. If the taxpayer buys another company's bonds at a discount and later sells them at face value (or sells them short at face and later buys bonds at a discount to settle the short sale), the spread is pure profit; fluctuations in the value of the taxpayer's own bonds, by contrast, are ordinarily offset by changes in the value of its assets.

ceived the difficulties of the *Kerbaugh-Empire* approach, and have recognized that *Kirby Lumber* must be read to restrict *Kerbaugh-Empire*; at least one court has found *Kerbaugh-Empire* entirely moribund.[15]

The second theme in the *Kirby Lumber* opinion focuses not on the long-term results of the borrowing transaction but on the immediate impact of repayment. According to the Court, the taxpayer "realized within the year an accession to income," citing *Burnet v. Sanford & Brooks Co.*[16] In that case, the leading exemplar of the annual accounting concept, the Court held that a taxpayer realized income in the taxable year in which it recovered damages for breach of contract, even though the recovery was compensation for losses sustained in earlier years in performing its part of the agreement.

This focus on the current taxable year not only collides with the Court's concern with "the transaction as a whole," but is troublesome even in isolation. All that happened in the year before the Court was a purchase of the bonds for less than their face amount. Because this reduced the company's liabilities by about $1.078 million at a cost of about $940,000, the company's net worth increased by about $138,000. This change, however, merely reflects the fact that the bonds were listed on the liability side of the balance sheet at their face amount, while the cash was shown at full value. If the company's assets and liabilities to creditors had been valued at their fair market values, the company's net worth would have been the same before and after the repurchase.

Finally, the statement in the opinion that the discount repurchase "made available . . . assets previously offset" by the repurchased bonds has been a continual source of confusion. This comment cannot be squared with the Court's concern with the whole transaction because, whether it refers to the fact that the repurchase reduced liabilities by more than it reduced assets or to the fact that the taxpayer borrowed more than it paid back, it is based on a fact also present in *Kerbaugh-Empire*.

A particularly troublesome legacy of the above passage has been a tendency of some courts to read *Kirby Lumber* as holding that the freeing of assets on the cancellation of indebtedness, rather than the cancellation itself, results in a taxable gain. In actuality, income results from the discharge of indebtedness because the taxpayer has received more than is paid back, not because assets are freed of offsetting liabilities on the balance sheet. Thus, if a taxpayer borrows $15,000 in cash and the debt is later

---

[15] Vukasovich, Inc. v. CIR, 790 F2d 1409 (9th Cir. 1986) (discharge of indebtedness income recognized when loan satisfied for less than face amount, even though loan obtained in transaction in which taxpayer had overall loss; *Kerbaugh-Empire* inconsistent with later Supreme Court decisions and should not be followed).

[16] Burnet v. Sanford & Brooks Co., 282 US 359 (1931), discussed infra ¶105.1.4. For discussion of the relationship between *Sanford & Brooks, Kerbaugh-Empire*, and *Kirby Lumber*, see Magill, Taxable Income 245–54 (Ronald Press, rev. ed. 1945).

canceled, the taxpayer should be taxed on $15,000 whether or not he was personally liable for the debt. Concentrating on the freed-assets rationale of *Kirby Lumber*, however, the Tax Court has held that a debtor who is not personally liable recognizes income only to the extent that collateral is freed as a result of a cancellation.[17]

Since borrowed funds are obviously worth their face amount and assets acquired on credit in an arm's length transaction are also worth what the buyer agrees to pay, a taxpayer who ultimately pays back less than he received enjoys a financial benefit whether the funds were invested successfully, lost in a business venture, spent for food and clothing, or given to charity. Were we blessed with perfect foresight, it would be possible to exclude borrowed funds from gross income only to the extent of the ultimate repayment and to tax at the outset the amount that will not be repaid. In the absence of perfect prevision, however, a second best solution is required. One alternative would be to tax the entire amount borrowed and to allow deductions only when, as, and if the debt is repaid. Since most loans are paid in full and taxing the receipt would impose a heavy front-end burden on debt financing, a better alternative is the existing system of excluding borrowed funds from gross income and requiring the taxpayer to account for any gain if he succeeds in settling the debt for less than the amount due.[18]

The tax treatment of below-face debt discharges would have been much simpler if, from the outset, the courts had recognized this as its basis; because borrowed funds are excluded from gross income on the assumption they will be repaid, a tax adjustment is required when this assumption proves erroneous, regardless of the use to which the taxpayer put the borrowed funds. Unfortunately, *Kerbaugh-Empire* linked the tax treatment of the debt discharge to the fate of the borrowed funds, and *Kirby Lumber* carried this idea forward by distinguishing rather than repudiating *Kerbaugh-Empire*, seeming thereby to invite an open-ended inquiry into the debtor's financial history in order to determine whether a discharge of a debt generates gain. In a tortuous series of later decisions, examined below, the courts have held that such things as the nature of the obligation, the

---

[17] Collins v. CIR, 22 TCM (CCH) 1467 (1963). See infra ¶6.4.2, text accompanying notes 33–35, for more on nonrecourse debt.

Focusing on the freeing of assets, rather than on the gain to the debtor on cancellation of its indebtedness, might also have contributed to anomalous or debatable results in other areas. See infra ¶6.4.3 (modification of original obligation and substitution of new obligations; exchange of stock for debt), ¶6.4.6 (effect of debtor's insolvency).

[18] For other situations in which an offsetting adjustment is required when the assumption underlying an exclusion, deduction, or other tax allowance ultimately proves erroneous, see supra ¶5.5.3 (unclaimed deposits, etc.), ¶5.7 (tax benefit doctrine).

mode of discharge, the creditor's objective in agreeing to the settlement, the absence of prior tax benefits, and the debtor's financial condition may, in particular circumstances, shield the taxpayer from the result reached in *Kirby Lumber*.[19]

Despite this tangled net of judicial rules, Congress has remained largely quiescent. Since 1954, the statute has explicitly included "income from discharge of indebtedness" in gross income,[20] but the statute leaves to the courts the task of determining when the discharge of a debt produces income. Until 1986, §§108 and 1017 allowed business taxpayers to avoid realizing income on a discharge of a debt by electing to reduce the basis of their assets or other tax attributes, but a 1986 amendment limits these provisions to insolvent and bankrupt taxpayers.[21] Sections 108 and 1017, further, apply only if the taxpayer realizes income under the judicially prescribed rules. The other instances of legislative intervention involve similarly limited issues rather than basic principles.[22]

Finally, application of the *Kirby Lumber* principle is complicated by the fact that debts are often described as having been discharged for less

---

[19] See generally Bittker & Thompson, Income From the Discharge of Indebtedness: The Progeny of *United States v. Kirby Lumber Co.*, 66 Calif. L. Rev. 1159 (1978); Blattner, Debt Cancellation, 30 NYU Inst. on Fed. Tax'n 237 (1972); Eustice, Cancellation of Indebtedness and the Federal Income Tax: A Problem of Creeping Confusion, 14 Tax L. Rev. 225 (1959); Powell, A Review of the Judicial Exceptions to the *Kirby Lumber* Rule, 30 U. Fla. L. Rev. 94 (1977); Stone, Cancellation of Indebtedness, 34 NYU Inst. on Fed. Tax'n 555 (1976); Wright, Realization of Income Through Cancellations, Modifications, and Bargain Purchases of Indebtedness: I and II, 49 Mich. L. Rev. 459, 667 (1951). Older articles of continuing interest are Darrell, Discharge of Indebtedness and the Federal Income Tax, 53 Harv. L. Rev. 977 (1940); Surrey, The Revenue Act of 1939 and the Income Tax Treatment of Cancellation of Indebtedness, 49 Yale LJ 1153 (1940); Warren & Sugarman, Cancellation of Indebtedness and Its Tax Consequences, I and II, 40 Colum. L. Rev. 1326 (1940) and 41 Colum. L. Rev. 61 (1941).

[20] IRC §61(a)(12).

[21] See infra ¶6.4.7.

[22] For provisions relating to bankrupt taxpayers, see infra ¶6.4.6; for the cancellation of parent-subsidiary debts under §337(b), see infra ¶93.8.3.

In 1954, the House of Representatives proposed to legislate comprehensively in this area by codifying the *Kirby Lumber* doctrine and its major exceptions, and by making the exceptions inapplicable to the cancellation of liabilities previously deducted with tax benefit. See H. R. Rep. No. 1337, 83d Cong., 2d Sess. 12, A28, A35, A267 (1954). The Senate Finance Committee recommended against accepting the House proposal because "of considerable doubt as to its meaning and effects," and favored leaving the situation "to be settled according to rules developed by the courts." S. Rep. No. 1622, 83d Cong., 2d Sess. 13–14, 186, 425 (1954). The Senate decision was accepted when the matter went to conference. Conf. Rep. No. 2543, 83d Cong., 2d Sess. 23 (1954) (determination of whether discharge of debt results in gross income "will be made, as under existing law, by applying the general rules for determining gross income").

than their face amount, when in fact they have been paid in full. Assume an employee borrows $50 from his employer, instructing that this amount be deducted from his next paycheck. When the deduction is made, the debt is paid, even though no cash changes hands. The employee has $50 of income, not because his debt has been canceled but because this is the agreed upon method for the employer to pay for the employee's services. *Kirby Lumber* is not relevant to such a situation. There are many other examples of this phenomenon of debts that, superficially viewed, have been canceled without payment but that on analysis are found to have been fully paid in a medium other than cash. Unfortunately, the courts have sometimes confused these spurious cancellation of indebtedness cases with the genuine article.[23]

¶6.4.2 Nature of the Debt

Income from discharge of indebtedness should depend not on the type of debt, but only on the spread between the amount received by the debtor and the amount paid by him to satisfy his obligation.[24] Encouraged, however, by *Kirby Lumber*'s failure to overrule *Kerbaugh-Empire* and its reference to "freed assets," the courts have grafted several exceptions onto *Kirby Lumber* that depend on apparently irrelevant considerations, such as whether the debtor was personally liable on the debt and whether the debt was incurred for cash or other assets.

1. *Nature and amount of consideration.* The bonds in *Kirby Lumber* were issued in exchange for the taxpayer's preferred stock with dividends in arrears, but the case has often been thought to involve bonds issued for cash, perhaps because the Court said that the taxpayer, on issuing the bonds, "received their par value."[25] Despite this misconception, the *Kirby Lumber* principle has been regularly applied to bonds issued or assumed by the taxpayer to acquire business assets,[26] but obligations arising in other noncash transactions have sometimes been held outside the reach of that

---

[23] The term "spurious" is not intended to imply doubt about the legal effectiveness of the discharge; what is spurious is the implication that the debt was discharged for less than its face amount. See infra ¶6.4.4.

[24] The courts have held, for example, that a homeowner with a low-interest mortgage has discharge of indebtedness income if he prepays pursuant to the mortgagee's offer to accept a discounted amount equal to the present value of the obligation. Sutphin v. US, 14 Cl. Ct. 545, 88-1 USTC ¶9269 (1988); Michaels v. CIR, 87 TC 1412 (1986).

[25] US v. Kirby Lumber Co., 284 US 1, 2 (1931); see also Bittker, supra note 10.

[26] See, e.g., Helvering v. American Chicle Co., 291 US 426 (1934) (purchase for less than face of a predecessor company's bonds, which had been assumed by the taxpayer on purchasing its assets).

case. Thus, in *CIR v. Rail Joint Co.*,[27] it was held that the taxpayer did not realize income on repurchasing certain bonds for less than their face amount that it had previously distributed as a dividend to its shareholders because the distribution did not increase the taxpayer's assets. The distribution of the bonds, however, served the same function as a distribution of cash, and could properly have been analogized to a sale of the bonds for their face amount, followed by a distribution of the proceeds as a dividend. Viewed in this light, the bonds gave the distributing corporation the same corporate benefits as a distribution of cash, and a later discharge of the bonds for less than this amount should have been taxed in the same way as a redemption of bonds issued for cash.[28]

In *Kirby Lumber*, the repurchased bonds had been issued by the taxpayer at par. For this reason, it is customary to describe the case as holding that the taxpayer realizes income on discharging a debt for less than its face amount.[29] The computation is more complicated, however, if the taxpayer gets more or less than face amount on incurring an obligation. When bonds are issued at a premium or discount, the premium is an indirect way of reducing the nominal interest rate, while the discount is an indirect way of increasing the nominal interest. If a $1,000 bond is issued for $1,100, for

---

[27] CIR v. Rail Joint Co., 61 F2d 751 (2d Cir. 1932). The courts have disagreed on whether discharge of indebtedness income can arise on a redemption of bonds issued in exchange for shares of the taxpayer's stock. Compare Fashion Park, Inc. v. CIR, 21 TC 600 (1954) (nonacq.) (holding *Kirby Lumber* inapplicable to bonds issued for preferred stock with arrearages) with U.S. Steel Corp. v. US, 11 Cl. Ct. 375, 848 F2d 1232 (Cl. Ct. 1986) (on retirement of bonds issued in exchange for taxpayer's preferred stock, cancellation of indebtedness income recognized equal to excess of (1) value of preferred stock when received in exchange for bonds over (2) amount paid in retirement of bonds; *Fashion Park* not followed). See also Bradford v. CIR, 233 F2d 935 (6th Cir. 1956) (note issued to bank to obtain reduction of debt owed by taxpayer's husband; taxpayer is described as issuing her note "without receiving any consideration in return," although it might have been treated as an indirect way of getting cash to reduce the husband's debt).

[28] The bonds in *Kirby Lumber Co.* were issued in part to satisfy dividend arrearages on the taxpayer's preferred stock, yet their discharge for less than face was held to constitute taxable income. See Bittker, supra note 10.

Also, under §312(a)(2), a corporation's earnings and profits account is reduced by the principal amount of obligations distributed to shareholders. Assume a corporation distributes a $100 bond as a dividend, and sometime later, after interest rates have risen, the corporation redeems the bond for $80. The corporation is out of pocket $80, but its earnings and profits have been reduced by $100. If $20 of discharge of indebtedness income is recognized on the redemption, however, this income generates additional earnings and profits that square the earnings and profits account with the economics of the transaction. The earnings and profits rule, in other words, implies that discharge of indebtedness is recognized on a repurchase at less than face of a bond distributed as a dividend.

[29] See, e.g., Reg. §1.61-12(a).

example, $100 of the amount received for the bond will never be repaid as principal, but is effectively repaid through the interest payments; the issuer must recognize the premium as income in periodic installments over the bond's term in order to offset the deduction for the portion of each interest payment that is in substance a repayment of principal.[30] Conversely, if a $1,000 bond is issued for $900, the last $100 paid at maturity is in substance interest rather than principal; because interest accrues economically at a constant rate, the issuer is allowed to amortize the $100 discount as additional interest deductions over the bond's term.[31] On discharging a premium or discount obligation, the taxpayer's gain under the *Kirby Lumber* principle is the excess of (1) the issue price, plus any previously deducted discount or minus any premium previously reported as income, over (2) the amount paid on repurchase.[32] In the ensuing discussion, the first of these amounts—issue price plus or minus previously amortized discount or premium—is variously referred to as the principal or face amount of the obligation.

Discharge of indebtedness income is not recognized if the taxpayer would have been allowed to deduct a payment of the discharged liability.[33] Assume a cash basis taxpayer falls behind on payments on a mortgage, and, in recognition of the taxpayer's straightened circumstances, the mortgagee agrees to accept payment of 90 percent of the principal of the mortgage loan in full satisfaction of the taxpayer's obligations with respect to principal and interest. If a payment of the accrued but unpaid interest would have been fully deductible, the taxpayer's discharge of indebtedness income is limited to the forgiven 10 percent of principal; because a payment of the interest would have been deductible, the discharge of the interest obligation is not income.

2. *Nonrecouse debts.* If the taxpayer borrows on a nonrecourse basis (that is, if he is not personally liable and the lender's only recourse is against the property that secures the loan), a discharge for less than the amount owing should generate income in the same manner as a discharge of a debt for which he is personally liable. The crucial facts—that the debtor excludes the borrowed funds from income when received and ultimately pays less than the excluded amount—are the same whether or not he has personal liability.

Influenced by the freed-asset rationale of *Kirby Lumber*, however, the courts have held that when a nonrecourse debt is discharged at less than face, the excess of the face amount over the amount paid for the discharge is

---

[30] See infra ¶56.9.
[31] See infra ¶56.3
[32] IRC §108(e)(3). For an illustrative computation, see Reg. §1.61-12(c)(5).
[33] IRC §108(e)(2).

not included in the debtor's gross income, but is instead applied in reduction of the basis of the property that secures the debt.[34] Assume T purchases Blackacre, paying $50 down and taking the property subject to a mortgage of $100, as to which T does not assume personal liability. Because the mortgage bears interest at a rate below the current market rate, the mortgagee subsequently agrees to take $95 in full payment of the mortgage. Because T is not personally liable on the mortgage, the $5 discount is not discharge of indebtedness income but is instead subtracted from T's basis for the property, reducing the basis from $150 (the sum of the $50 down payment and the original $100 principal balance on the mortgage) to $145. The basis reduction occurs when the liability reduction occurs, and depreciation previously taken on the property is thus unaffected.[35]

Because the basis reduction increases subsequent gain on sale or indirectly increases operating income by reducing depreciation deductions, this rule usually has the effect of deferring recognition of the debt discharge income. If the discharged liability exceeds the basis of the encumbered property, however, the excess may permanently escape taxation.[36]

3. *Liabilities assumed or taken subject to.* The *Kirby Lumber* rule sometimes has an unfortunate and probably unintended effect when taxpayers acquire property subject to mortgages and other encumbrances. In this context, the rule sometimes taxes to the present owner gain that accrued to a prior owner of the property. The prior owner also recognizes this gain, but often as capital gain.

Assume S buys Blackacre for $150, paying $50 down and financing the remainder of the price with a mortgage loan of $100. Because of a subsequent rise in interest rates, the present value of the mortgage obligation falls to $90. That is, after this rise, the lender would be indifferent between an

---

[34] Fulton Gold Corp. v. CIR, 31 BTA 519 (1934). See also Stanley Co. v. CIR, 12 TC 1122 (1949) (five judges dissenting without opinion), rev'd sub nom. CIR v. Stanley Co., 185 F2d 979, 981 (2d Cir. 1951) ("even if the *Kirby* rule must be restricted, as the Tax Court thought, to a case where the taxpayer . . . is personally liable," restriction inapplicable because taxpayer effectively assumed personal liability); Mendham Corp. v. CIR, 9 TC 320 (1947); Collins v. CIR, 22 TCM (CCH) 1467 (1963). But see Gershkowitz v. CIR, 88 TC 984 (1987) (where nonrecourse debt discharged for cash payment less than face amount, excess of face over payment is discharge of indebtedness income; court rejects implication of freeing-of-assets rationale that income limited to fair market value of security, but does not consider reduction of basis alternative). See generally Green & Sparkman, Consequences of Discharges of Nonrecourse Indebtedness, 67 J. Tax'n 18 (1987).

[35] Blackstone Theater Co. v. CIR, 12 TC 801 (1949). See also Mayerson v. CIR, 47 TC 340 (1966) (basis for depreciation includes entire amount of nonrecourse mortgage even though mortgage instrument includes provision for payment at discount in specified circumstances and discount payment occurs in subsequent year).

[36] The Supreme Court referred to this possibility in CIR v. Tufts, 461 US 300, 310 n.11 (1983), but did not endorse it.

immediate pay off for $90 and the payments of interest and principal called for under the mortgage instrument. *S* sells the property to *B*, when the property is worth $160. The price is $70 in cash plus *B*'s assumption of the $100 mortgage. Because the present value of the mortgage obligation is only $90, the price is effectively $160, the sum of $70 of cash and $90 of debt assumption, and thus equals the property's fair market value. *S*'s amount realized in the sale is $170 (the sum of the cash and the principal amount of the mortgage), and her gain is $20 (the excess of the amount realized over her adjusted basis of $150). The gain, all of which is treated as gain on sale of Blackacre, consists economically of $10 of appreciation in the value of Blackacre and the $10 decline in the value of the mortgage liability.

Assume the mortgage lender subsequently accepts $90 from *B* in full satisfaction of the $100 mortgage. Under *Kirby Lumber*, *B* has discharge of indebtedness income of $10. Economically, however, he has no income or gain. He purchased property worth $160 and has now expended $160 (the sum of $70 and $90) to acquire unencumbered ownership. *B* has taxable income without gain. Because *S* has already been taxed on the *Kirby Lumber* gain, which accrued while he held the property subject to the mortgage, the tax on *B* is a second tax on a single economic gain.

B probably will not be overtaxed in the long run because he has a basis for the property of $170, which exceeds the economic purchase price by the amount of the *Kirby Lumber* gain. The recovery of this excess basis, however, will rarely coincide in time with the recognition of the discharge of indebtedness income. If the property is depreciable, the excess basis might be recovered through depreciation before the income is recognized. If the property is land and the mortgage pay off occurs soon after *B* buys the property, the income may be recognized years before any tax benefit is derived from the excess basis.

An adequate solution to this problem comes quite by accident in one context. As previously explained,[37] when a nonrecourse liability is satisfied at less than face, the discount is subtracted from the property's basis rather than included in the debtor's gross income. Assume *B* in this example purchases Blackacre subject to the mortgage, but does not assume personal liability. When *B* pays off the $100 mortgage for $90, the $10 discount is applied to reduce his basis for the property to $160, an amount equal to the true purchase price.

It is by accident that the rule for nonrecourse debt produces the right answer. The problem has nothing to do with whether the debt is with or without recourse; the problem is that the *Kirby Lumber* rule, if applicable, taxes *B* on a gain that accrued to *S* and has already been taxed to him. Even within its bailiwick, the nonrecourse rule does not always produce the

---

[37] See supra text accompanying notes 33–35.

correct result; it would also apply if *B*'s payment of the mortgage occurred some time after his purchase of Blackacre, and the $10 discount accrued while *B* held the property. The nonrecourse rule also applies when a nonrecourse debt is an original borrowing by the taxpayer, not an indebtedness taken subject to in a property purchase, and in this context it provides a benefit unrelated to the problem discussed here.

4. *Disputed liabilities.* The regulations under §108 define "indebtedness" as "an obligation, absolute and not contingent, to pay on demand or within a given time, in cash or another medium, a fixed amount."[38] Although not explicitly applicable to the term "indebtedness" as used in §61(a)(12), this definition has effectively been adopted by the courts in applying the *Kirby Lumber* principle.

Settlement of a claim for less than the creditor seeks therefore does not generate income under §61(a)(12) if the debtor disputes the claim.[39] Such a claim is not for "a fixed amount," as the regulations require; the amount payable is, in a realistic sense, whatever the parties agree upon in their settlement. For this reason, discharge of the debt does not increase the taxpayer's net worth, as required by the *Kirby Lumber* principle.

If the debtor acknowledges liability for a portion of the creditor's claim, but contests the remainder of it, a settlement for less than the acknowledged liability (because, for example, the debtor has suffered financial reverses) could properly be regarded as both (1) a nontaxable cancellation of the disputed amount and (2) a discharge of the balance of the claim for less than the amount due, subject to the *Kirby Lumber* principle. There appear to be no reported cases, however, in which a transaction was bifurcated in this way.

5. *Discharge of purchase-money debt.* If debt arising in a sale on credit is canceled or reduced, the amount discharged is usually treated as an adjustment of the purchase price, and is therefore applied in reduction of the buyer's adjusted basis for the property, rather than included in gross income as discharge of indebtedness income. In a particular case, this result can derive from any one of three rules.

First, if the discharge is in settlement of a dispute over the amount owing by the purchaser, the amount is freed of the *Kirby Lumber* principle by the disputed liability rule discussed in the preceding paragraphs. If business equipment is bought for $1,000 on credit and the buyer refuses to pay

---

[38] Reg. §1.108(b)-1(c) (issued under §108(b), repealed in 1976). See also infra ¶91.10.4.

[39] See N. Sobel, Inc. v. CIR, 40 BTA 1263 (1939) (nonacq.). The no-income result presupposes a bona fide dispute but not necessarily a valid defense. See also Exchange Security Bank v. US, 345 F. Supp. 486 (ND Ala. 1972) (taxpayer has burden of establishing that debt was not owing), rev'd on other grounds, 492 F2d 1096 (5th Cir. 1974).

because of an alleged misrepresentation or breach of warranty, for example, a settlement of the debt for $750 is not a taxable event but rather a retroactive reduction of the purchase to $750; this amount, rather than the original price of $1,000, is the taxpayer's basis for computing depreciation on the property and gain or loss when it is disposed of.[40]

Second, in a line of anomalous cases, the disputed liability principle has been stretched to encompass a discharge of a purchase-money mortgage if the value of the property declines and the debtor induces the creditor to accept less than the amount due.[41] Since there is no dispute about liability in this situation, the theory that *Kirby Lumber* does not apply because the transaction is a retroactive reduction of the price for the property is not persuasive.[42] Perhaps in implicit recognition of the weakness of this rationale when there is no dispute about liability, the courts have refused to apply it if the (1) debt is discharged in an open market transaction rather than in face-to-face dealings with the creditor, (2) parties do not focus on the property in their negotiations, (3) property is worth more than the unpaid balance of the debt, or (4) creditor is not the person from whom the taxpayer purchased the property.[43]

The scope of this rule, however, was made largely irrelevant by the addition in 1980 of §108(e)(5), which provides that a reduction of debt is treated as a reduction of purchase price, rather than discharge of indebtedness income, if the (1) discharged or reduced obligation is "debt of a pur-

---

[40] CIR v. Sherman, 135 F2d 68 (6th Cir. 1943).

[41] Helvering v. A.L. Killian Co., 128 F2d 433 (8th Cir. 1942). This and several comparable cases were cited by the Supreme Court in Helvering v. American Dental Co., 318 US 322 (1943), but they were described as entailing an irrational distinction by Judge Jerome Frank in Fifth Ave.-Fourteenth St. Corp. v. CIR, 147 F2d 453, 457 (2d Cir. 1945). See also Delman's Est. v. CIR, 73 TC 15 (1979) (repossession from debtor-taxpayer of property purchased with funds borrowed on nonrecourse basis gave rise to gain on transfer of property, not to income from cancellation of debt; insolvency exception to *Kirby Lumber* not applicable).

[42] The *Killian* case (supra note 41) and its compatriots also rest in part on the *Kerbaugh-Empire* "overall loss" theory (supra note 5), but that case must be stretched to the breaking point to cover unrealized depreciation in an asset that has not been sold and whose value may bounce back to its original level or above.

[43] Fifth Ave.-Fourteenth St. Corp. v. CIR, supra note 41; CIR v. Coastwise Transp. Corp., 71 F2d 104 (1st Cir.), cert. denied, 293 US 595 (1934); Denman Tire & Rubber Co. v. CIR, 14 TC 706, 714–15 (1950) (acq.), aff'd, 192 F2d 261 (6th Cir. 1951); L.D. Coddon & Bros. v. CIR, 37 BTA 393 (1938); see also Edwards v. CIR, 19 TC 275 (1952) (acq.); B.F. Avery & Sons v. CIR, 26 BTA 1393, 1399–1400 (1932) (gain on discharge of debt might have been applied to reduce basis of property if it had occurred in the year the property was purchased but must be reported as income when realized many years later, by which time the original cost of the property had been largely written off against income); Gwinn v. CIR, ¶44,208 P-H Memo TC (1944) (reduction of purchase price principle applies only if property is worth less than the remaining debt, if any, after the adjustment).

chaser of property to the seller of such property which arose out of the purchase of such property," (2) taxpayer is not insolvent or in bankruptcy when the reduction occurs, and (3) reduction would, apart from this rule, be discharge of indebtedness income. Section 108(e)(5) was enacted "to eliminate disagreements between the Internal Revenue Service and the debtor" about the application of the disputed liability and purchase-money debt rules herein described.[44]

The statutory rule, however, is subject to limitations that might not apply to the earlier common law rules. Section 108(e)(4) does not apply if "the debt has been transferred by the seller to a third party . . . or if the property has been transferred by the buyer to a third party."[45] Assume *A* sells Blackacre on credit to *B*. The statutory exception does not apply if *A* sells *B*'s note to *C*, and the adjustment of the debt is by agreement between *B* and *C*. Neither does the rule apply if *B* sells the property to *D*, who assumes *B*'s obligation as part of the purchase price, and the renegotiation of the debt is between *A*, the original creditor, and *D*, the substituted debtor. Also, the statutory rule only applies to reductions by agreement between buyer and seller, and not, for example, to a discharge resulting from "the running of the statute of limitations on enforcement of the obligation."[46]

6. *Deductible items.* Section 108(e)(2) provides that discharge of indebtedness income is not recognized on the cancellation or reduction of a debt if the taxpayer would have been allowed a deduction had he paid the item. Assume an employer using the cash method of accounting owes an employee $1,000 for salary, but employer and employee agree to settle the obligation for a cash payment of $700. The employer is allowed a deduction for the payment, subject to the usual limitations on deductions for salary, and the $300 reduction of the debt is not debt discharge income. The only tax consequence of nonpayment of the $300 is loss of the deduction the employer would otherwise have been allowed on a payment of this amount.

7. *Student loans.* To encourage young people to work in underrepresented professions and areas, student loans are sometimes granted under programs that forgive all or a portion of the loans when borrowers pursue the subsidized professional avenues. The IRS initially ruled that discharge of indebtedness income is recognized when a former student qualifies for forgiveness under such a program.[47] Congress, however, took a

---

[44] S. Rep. No. 1035, 95th Cong., 2d Sess. 16–17, reprinted in 1980-2 CB 620.

[45] Id. This disqualification obtains even if the related transferee is related to the transferor. Id.

[46] Id.

[47] Rev. Rul. 73-256, 1973-1 CB 56, as modified by Rev. Rul. 74-540, 1974-2 CB 38 (cancellation of student loan when debtor works for specified period in rural or other deprived area is taxable quid pro quo, not a tax-free scholarship).

different view. Section 108(f), enacted in 1984,[48] exempts debt discharge income if the indebtedness is a student loan and the discharge is pursuant to a provision of the loan program that said the loan would be forgiven in whole or part in the event "the individual worked for a certain period of time in certain professions for any of a broad class of employers."

The term "student loan" indicates a loan made by a qualified lender to assist the borrower in attending an educational institution that has a regular student body, faculty, and curriculum.[49] A lender is qualified if it is an agency of the federal government or a state or local government.[50] The student's school, college, or university can also be a qualified lender, but only when it lends funds provided under an agreement with a federal, state, or local government.

¶6.4.3　Effect of Method by Which Debt Is Discharged

In most debt cancellation cases, including *Kirby Lumber*, the taxpayer used cash to extinguish its debt at less than face. There are other ways to eliminate, scale down, or modify debts, and these alternatives introduce further complications.

1. *Modifications of original obligation and substitution of new obligations.* Debtors and creditors sometimes agree to extend the time for payment, reduce the interest rate, release collateral, or eliminate restrictions imposed by a loan agreement, without reducing the principal amount due. However extensive these modifications may be, they neither reduce the debtor's obligation to repay the amount received when the debt was incurred nor increase his net worth. For this reason it is generally assumed that changes of this type do not generate income under the *Kirby Lumber* principle, even if the fair market value of the new obligation is less than the face amount of the old debt and the latter is discharged in exchange for the new obligations.[51]

---

[48] Section 108(f) applies to discharges occurring after 1982. Similar treatment for earlier periods was, however, provided by §2117 of the Tax Reform Act of 1976 and §162 of the Revenue Act of 1978. See Joint Comm. on Tax'n, 95th Cong., 2d Sess., General Explanation of the Revenue Act of 1978, at 120 (1979).

[49] IRC §108(f)(2).

[50] The District of Columbia, Puerto Rico, the possessions of the United States, and political subdivisions of the foregoing also qualify. IRC §108(f)(2)(B). Also, a charitable organization that has taken over a state, county, or municipal hospital qualifies if its employees are considered public employees under state law. IRC §108(f)(2)(C).

[51] See Eustice, supra note 19, at 238–42; see also Rev. Rul. 58-546, 1958-2 CB 143 (on bond-for-bond exchange, which changed interest rates and maturities but

Since the debtor would have to recognize income under *Kirby Lumber* if the new obligation were sold for cash at its fair market value and the proceeds were then used to discharge the old obligation for that amount, it may seem anomalous to exempt the debtor who engages in a direct exchange having the same economic result. An actual sale of the new obligation, however, would fix its value by an arm's length transaction, while an exchange does not.[52] If exchanges were treated as equivalent to selling the new bonds and paying the old ones with the proceeds, further, debtors would be impelled to avoid "exchanges" of obligations while achieving similar relief by "modifications" easing the terms of, without discharging, the old debt. This ploy could be frustrated by treating modifications as exchanges, but recognition of income on the making of a minor modification probably is not fair when debtors with sufficient foresight to fashion agreements that never require modification are not taxed on mere declines in the value of their obligations.

If there is a reduction in the amount due, however, as distinguished from a change in the maturity date, interest rate, or other terms of the obligation, the resulting increase in the taxpayer's net worth brings the *Kirby Lumber* principle into play, whether there is an exchange of obligations or simply an agreement by the creditor to accept a scaled down amount.[53] Although there appear to be no cases in point, the most appropriate treatment of a reduction in the debt's face amount would be to bifurcate the transaction by treating the difference between the face amount of the old debt and the fair market value of the new debt as discharge of indebtedness income, to be taxed immediately, with any difference between the fair market value and the face amount of the new debt being viewed as premium or discount to be amortized over the life of the new obligation. This bifurcated approach is illustrated by the three cases set out in Example 6-2. A disadvantage is that this method requires the new debt to be valued, unlike an approach that takes account solely of the difference between the face amounts of the old and new debts.[54]

---

not face amount, obligor realized gain only to extent of canceled liability for accrued interest previously deducted with tax benefit).

[52] In CIR v. National Alfalfa Dehydrating & Milling Co., 417 US 134 (1974), the Court held that no original issue discount arose on the issuance of debentures in exchange for the taxpayer's preferred stock, resting this conclusion in part on the difficulty of estimating the fair market value of the debentures and the preferred stock. It observed that an estimate was particularly difficult because the exchange was "insulated from market forces." Id. at 150.

[53] See Rev. Rul. 77-437, 1977-2 CB 28 (obligor realizes income on exchange of convertible bonds for new convertible bonds with lower face amount).

[54] For whether the reduction should be reported when agreed upon or treated as a premium on the new obligation to be amortized over its life, see CIR v. Stanley

Example 6-2

**Reduction in Face Amount of Existing Obligation—
Cancellation of Indebtedness Income vs.
Bond Premium or Discount**

	A	B	C
1. Original obligation			
a. Face amount	$1,000	$1,000	$1,000
b. Fair market value	$700	$700	$700
2. Reduced obligation			
a. Face amount	$700	$650	$750
b. Fair market value	$700	$700	$700
3. Cancellation of debt income (line 1a minus line 2b)	$300	$300	$300
4. Bond premium (discount) (line 2b minus line 2a)	–0–	$50	($50)

2. Issuance of stock in retirement of debt. The courts and the IRS initially held that when a corporate debtor issues stock to a creditor in exchange for the corporation's obligation, discharge of indebtedness income is not recognized because the substitution of stock for debt "does not effect a cancellation, reduction, or discharge of indebtedness but rather amounts to a transformation from a fixed indebtedness to a capital stock liability."[55] Congress, however, chipped away at this rule in 1980 and 1984 and largely eliminated it in 1986.

Under §108(e)(10), which was enacted in 1984 and expanded in 1986,[56] a corporation issuing stock in satisfaction of debt is treated as though it had paid the debt with cash equal to the fair market value of the stock, and any excess of the principal amount of the debt over this constructive cash payment is discharge of indebtedness income. If a corporation issues stock

---

Co., 185 F2d 979 (2d Cir. 1951) (reduction taxable under *Kirby Lumber* in year of exchange); Eustice, supra note 19, at 241–42.

[55] Rev. Rul. 59-222, 1959-1 CB 80. See Motor Mart Trust v. CIR, 4 TC 931 (1945) (acq.), aff'd, 156 F2d 122 (1st Cir. 1946). See also CIR v. Fender Sales, Inc., 338 F2d 924 (9th Cir. 1964), cert. denied, 381 US 935 (1965) (stock issued by corporation to shareholder-employees in settlement of liability for unpaid salaries; held, taxable to shareholder-employees, but no discharge of indebtedness income to corporation); but see Claridge Apartments Co. v. CIR, 138 F2d 962 (7th Cir. 1943), rev'd on other grounds, 323 US 141 (1944).

[56] The 1984 enactment contained an exception in §108(e)(10)(C) for stock for debt exchanges made in certain "workouts" of cash flow and credit problems. This exception was repealed for exchanges occuring in 1986 and thereafter. Pub. L. No. 99-514, §621(f)(2)(A), 100 Stat. 2085 (1986).

worth $700 in exchange for a $1,000 bond previously issued by the corporation, for example, it has $300 of discharge of indebtedness income. The prior common law exception continues to be available only if the taxpayer is insolvent or is in Chapter 11 bankruptcy proceedings.[57]

3. *Use of property to discharge debt.* The debtor may use property other than cash to effect a settlement of his debt. If the property is worth less than the face amount of the debt, a transfer to the creditor in discharge of the debt raises a *Kirby Lumber* problem. If the debtor's basis for the property differs from its fair market value, the transaction simultaneously raises an issue of gain or loss on the disposition of appreciated or depreciated property.

Assume a debtor transfers property worth $100 in satisfaction of a $100 debt. In this case, the debt is not discounted, and the only tax consequence should be recognition of gain on the disposition equal to the difference between $100 and the adjusted basis of the property. If the basis is $70 for example, capital gain of $30 is recognized.

Assume, alternatively, that property worth $70 and with an adjusted basis of $70 is transferred in satisfaction of a $100 debt. In this case, there is no gain on the disposition of the property because the value received in the transfer equals the property's basis. The debtor, however, has been discharged from $30 of debt without payment, and discharge of indebtedness income of $30 could appropriately be recognized.

Assume a third alternative, property worth $90 and a basis of $70 is transferred in satisfaction of a $100 debt. If the debt discharge issue is separated from the capital gain or loss issue, the debtor in this case recognizes $10 of discharge of indebtedness income (excess of $100 principal

---

[57] IRC §108(e)(10)(B). Even in insolvency and bankruptcy exchanges, the common law rule is limited by §108(e)(8), which provides that in two cases, "the stock for debt exception shall not apply," and the recognition rule of §108(e)(10) presumably applies instead. The first of these cases is where only "nominal or token shares" are issued in exchange for debt. If, for example, stock worth $1 is issued by an insolvent corporation in discharge of a $1,000 debt, the discharge of indebtedness income of $999 is not protected by the insolvency exception. The second is where the stock is issued to unsecured creditors in partial satisfaction of their claims pursuant to a workout of an insolvent or bankrupt taxpayer's affairs. In this latter case, a ratio is computed for each unsecured creditor equal to (1) the value of the stock received, divided by (2) the principal amount of the debt that is either discharged or exchanged for debt in the workout. If the ratio for a particular creditor is less than 50 percent of the ratio for all unsecured creditors considered as a group, discharge of indebtedness income is recognized on the stock for debt exchange with that creditor. Although the role for this provision is now quite limited, during the period between its enactment in 1980 and the enactment of §108(e)(10) in 1984, it was the only exception to the common law rule, and applied to all taxpayers, not only to those who were insolvent or in Chapter 11 bankruptcy.

amount over value of consideration given in payment) and $20 of capital gain (excess of $90 value received on disposition of property less $70 basis).

The courts, however, have not unbundled these transactions in this way, but have ordinarily treated them as sales of the property for the face amount of the canceled debt,[58] an approach that results in $30 of capital gain and no debt discharge income in each of the three alternatives.

4. *Transfers of encumbered property.* When encumbered property is transferred to a buyer or other transferee who assumes or takes the property subject to the debt, the amount of the debt is included in the transferor's amount realized in the transaction and thus enters into his gain or loss.[59] Although the transferor is effectively relieved of liability on the debt, there usually is no discharge of indebtedness income, even if the transfer is a foreclosure or a transfer to the lien holder in lieu of foreclosure and extinguishes the debt.[60] The regulations make a limited exception from this principle: If the transferor is personally liable on the debt and if the debt exceeds the fair market value of the encumbered property, the excess of debt over fair market value is discharge of indebtedness income, and the amount realized on the transfer includes debt only in an amount equal to the property's fair market value.[61]

Assume T holds property worth $60 (adjusted basis, $20) that is encumbered by a mortgage of $75 on which T is personally liable; the mortgagee forecloses. If the foreclosure extinguishes T's liability on the mortgage, the $15 excess of the mortgage over the fair market value of the property is

---

[58] Unique Art Mfg. Co. v. CIR, 8 TC 1341 (1947) (acq.); Eustice, supra note 19, at 232–35. See Spartan Petroleum Co. v. US, 437 F. Supp. 733 (DSC 1977) (gain on transfer of appreciated property to pay debt; no discharge of debt income, hence no right to make election allowed under pre-1986 version of §108); but see Bialock v. CIR, 35 TC 649, 661 (1961) (acq.) (transfer of property to discharge debt with face amount in excess of property's value generated debt discharge income). While it is unclear whether the IRS has ever pushed for bifurcation in an appropriate case, the regulations appear to recognize that where a debt is cancelled in exchange for property, a portion of the resulting gain may be pure debt discharge income: "Whenever a discharge of indebtedness is accomplished by a transfer of the taxpayer's property in kind, the difference between the amount of the obligation discharged and the fair market value of the property transferred is the amount which may be applied in reduction of basis [under §1017]." Reg. §1.1017-1(b)(5).

[59] See infra ¶43.5.

[60] If property subject to nonrecourse indebtedness is abandoned, the abandonment is treated as a transfer of the property in exchange for extinguishment of the debt. Cozzi v. CIR, 88 TC 435, 445 (1987) (abandonment deemed to occur "the moment it becomes clear that a debt will never have to be paid;" test "requires a practical assessment of the facts and circumstances relating to the likelihood of payment;" "an overt act may be sufficient to fix the time of the abandonment . . . but such an act is not required").

[61] Reg. §§1.1001-2(a)(2), (c)(8) Ex. 8.

discharge of indebtedness income. The remaining $60 is an amount realized on the foreclosure transfer, and T's gain on the disposition of the property is therefore $40 ($60 amount realized less $20 adjusted basis). If T had no personal liability on the mortgage, in contrast, the gain on the disposition would be $55 ($75 amount realized, less $20 basis), and there would be no discharge of indebtedness income.[62]

5. *Three-party transactions.* If a creditor sells a claim against a debtor to a third party for less than its face amount, the debtor has no income under the *Kirby Lumber* principle because the liability is not altered except for the subsitution of a new creditor. This suggests the possibility that a debtor, believing that his creditor will accept less than face to settle a claim but not wanting to report the spread under *Kirby Lumber*, might induce a friendly third party to buy the obligation and keep it alive in order to defer the recognition of discharge of indebtedness income. If the new creditor uses funds advanced by the debtor and agrees to discharge the debt on request, the plan is a sham, possibly fraudulent,[63] and the purchase should be imputed to the debtor, the obligation being treated as discharged when the original creditor is paid off. In the absence of such shenanigans, closely related persons, even husband and wife, are entitled to be treated as independent if their transactions can survive close scrutiny, and the courts held that the purchase by one of the other's obligations should be no exception to this principle.[64] The same was true of a purchase by a corporation of a related corporation's obligations.[65]

Congress decided in 1980, however, that such a factually based approach to the problem is not adequate, and enacted §108(e)(4) to authorize the Treasury by regulation to treat an acquisition of an obligation by a person related to the debtor as an acquisition by the debtor if the previous holder of the obligation was not related. The purpose for the acquisition is irrelevant under this rule. The rule, however, only applies "for purposes of

---

[62] CIR v. Tufts, 461 US 300 (1983); Reg. §1.1001-2(c) Ex. 7.

[63] Even if the use of an intermediary serves a nontax purpose, the fact that he is acting for the debtor is controlling for tax purposes. See Bradford v. CIR, 233 F2d 935 (6th Cir. 1956), where an intermediary was used and the parties acknowledged that he acted as an agent, not as a principal.

[64] Forrester v. CIR, 4 TC 907 (1945) (acq.); but see Briarcliff Inv. Co. v. CIR, 90 F2d 330 (5th Cir.), cert. denied, 302 US 731 (1937) (taxpayer's principal shareholder purchased $150,000 of its debt for $130,000 and promptly transferred debt to taxpayer for same amount; *Kirby Lumber* applied, possibly because shareholder was viewed as taxpayer's agent in repurchasing its debt rather than as shareholder making contribution to capital).

[65] Peter Pan Seafoods, Inc. v. US, 417 F2d 670 (9th Cir. 1969); see also American Packing & Provision Co. v. CIR, 36 BTA 340 (1937) (income realized by parent when its bonds were purchased by subsidiary with which it filed consolidated tax returns and then sold to parent at less than face).

determining income of the debtor from discharge of indebtedness,"[66] and therefore is presumably inapplicable if the related purchaser pays a price at least equal to the obligation's principal amount. Related persons include family members, entities and their greater than 50 percent owners, and entities joined by common ownership of more than 50 percent.[67] Assume a $1,000 corporate bond previously held by an unrelated person is purchased for $900 by an individual holding 60 percent of the issuer's stock. The purchase is deemed made by the corporation, and it therefore has $100 of discharge of indebtedness income.

The Treasury is instructed to make appropriate adjustments in subsequent transactions for the recognition of this income. According to the legislative history, when the debt in this example is subsequently paid, the holder's gain on receipt of the payment ($1,000 received less $900 basis, or $100) is a dividend.[68] The theory for this treatment is apparently that because the debtor is deemed to have retired the obligation when the related person acquires it, subsequent payments to the related holder must be treated as something other than debt payments.[69] Although the legislative history is silent on the point, this theory would also characterize as a dividend any interest paid on the bond after the related person's acquisition.

If the related acquiror and the debtor are related in a way other than as shareholder and corporation, subsequent payments must be characterized with reference to the nature of the relationship. If an obligation is acquired by a family member of the debtor, for example, the holder's gain on subsequent payment is probably an excludable gift. Assume an individual debtor's $1,000 note is purchased by his mother for $900. The debtor has discharge of indebtedness income of $100 at the time of his mother's purchase, but the mother has no gain or loss when the note is paid.

---

[66] IRC §108(e)(4)(A).

[67] An individual's family consists of his spouse, children, grandchildren, and parents, and the spouses of his children and grandchildren. IRC §108(e)(4)(B). Also, two entities are considered related if they would be treated as one in determining the qualification of a pension, profit sharing, or stock bonus plan adopted by either. IRC §108(e)(4)(C). In all other respects, the related person definitions of §§267(b) and 707(b)(1) are adopted by reference. IRC §108(e)(4)(A). See infra ¶78.3 for §267(b) and ¶86.5 for §707(b)(1).

[68] S. Rep. No. 1035, 96th Cong., 2d Sess. 19 (1980), reprinted in 1980-2 CB 620, 630.

[69] If this theory were rigorously applied, the shareholder might have a dividend of $1,000 on the theory that the $900 paid for the bond should be added to the basis of the shareholder's stock as a capital contribution and that the $1,000 should therefore be treated as a payment with respect to the stock—that is, as a dividend to the extent of the corporation's earnings and profits.

¶6.4.4 Spurious Cancellations of Indebtedness

The classic case for application of the *Kirby Lumber* principle is a financial adjustment in which a creditor accepts less than the face amount of a debt because of doubts about the debtor's ability to pay in full or because the interest rate for comparable loans has gone up, making the old debt worth less than par. In these circumstances, the creditor seeks to get as much as he can for his claim, while the debtor pursues the corresponding strategy of paying as little as possible.

Debts are often canceled, however, not to effect a financial adjustment of the debtor-creditor relationship but as an indirect way of achieving a much different objective. An example, as suggested earlier, is the employee who borrows $50 from his employer, with the understanding that the debt will be deducted from his next paycheck. When this occurs, the debt is paid in full even though no cash changes hands. The employee must report the $50 as income, not because the debt has been canceled for less than its face amount within the meaning of the *Kirby Lumber* case, but because he has been paid for his services.[70] For this reason, the $50 should be classified as earned income, not as income from the discharge of indebtedness.[71]

There are many instances of such spurious cancellations, where careful analysis discloses that the debt was not discharged for less than its face amount but was paid, albeit indirectly, in full. The risk of confusion is increased by the fact that spurious and genuine cancellations can occur together. Assume an architect borrows $25,000 from a bank and, when there is doubt about his financial ability to pay in full, agrees to perform services worth $10,000 for the bank in return for a full discharge. The arrangement is best viewed as generating $10,000 of earned income plus $15,000 of income from the discharge of indebtedness, so that each component can be taxed in accordance with its true nature. In the litigated cases, however, transactions of this type are usually assigned to one broad category or the other. This result, however rough and ready, is understandable if both the taxpayer and the government disregard the possibility of bifurcating the transaction and argue for an all-or-nothing tax result, possibly because the relevant values are difficult to establish or fragmentation would not, in the particular case, alter the actual tax liability.

---

[70] Supra ¶6.4.1. See Denny v. CIR, 33 BTA 738 (1935) (acq. and nonacq. on other issues); but see Watson's Est. v. CIR, 3 TCM (CCH) 1108 (1944) (cancellation of employee's debt at specified rate per month of service held, on unusual facts, not to be compensation).

[71] The term "earned income" is defined in §911(b) and plays a role in several provisions. For example, the amounts of the credit for dependent care (IRC §21) and the earned income credit (IRC §32) are defined with reference to the taxpayer's earned income.

The distinction between genuine cancellations of indebtedness for less than the face amount and spurious cancellations can be illustrated by analyzing the tax treatment of the creditor. If the creditor accepts less than the amount due in a *Kirby Lumber* situation, he is ordinarily entitled to deduct the difference between the amount due and the amount received as a loss or worthless debt. By contrast, a creditor who agrees to a spurious cancellation (for example, an employer who cancels the employee's debt by docking his pay) is not entitled to a bad debt deduction because no loss has been suffered.[72]

Some of the major areas in which spurious cancellations occur are described below.

1. *Contributions to capital.* When a corporation is indebted to a principal shareholder, cancellation of the debt for less than its face amount, or for nothing, is often a way to strengthen the corporation's financial condition by increasing its capital. If the debt is fully collectible, cancellation in these circumstances has the same effect as a payment in full coupled with a transfer of the proceeds as a contribution to the corporation's capital. Since contributions to capital are not taxed to the corporation,[73] the regulations and cases hold that no income is realized when a contribution to a corporation's capital is effected by a cancellation of its debt.[74] In 1980, Congress effectively confirmed this exemption by enacting an exception that requires the corporation to recognize as discharge of indebtedness income any excess of the principal amount over the shareholder's adjusted basis for the obligation.[75]

---

[72] The employer can usually deduct the cancelled debt as a business expense if the services are rendered by a business employee, but not if the employee is a domestic servant. See also Perlman v. CIR, 252 F.2d 890 (2d Cir. 1958) (cancellation of debt for unpaid salary held a contribution to capital by shareholder; not deductible by him as loss); Johnson, Drake & Piper, Inc. v. Helvering, 69 F2d 151 (8th Cir.), cert. denied, 292 US 650 (1934); but see Giblin v. CIR, 227 F2d 692 (5th Cir. 1955) (bad debt deduction allowed where corporate debtor was insolvent both before and after cancellation); contra Lidgerwood Mfg. Co. v. CIR, 229 F2d 241 (2d Cir.), cert. denied, 351 US 951 (1956).

[73] See IRC §118, discussed infra ¶91.9

[74] Reg. §1.61-12(a); CIR v. Auto Strop Safety Razor Co., 74 F2d 226 (2d Cir. 1934). See also Sheraton Plaza Co. v. CIR, 39 TC 697 (1963) (acq.); but see Briarcliff Inv. Co. v. CIR, 90 F2d 330 (5th Cir.), cert. denied, 302 US 731 (1937) (taxpayer's principal shareholder purchased $150,000 of its debt for $130,000 and promptly transferred debt to taxpayer for same amount; *Kirby Lumber* applied, possibly because shareholder viewed as taxpayer's agent in repurchasing debt rather than as shareholder making contribution to capital). Compare Arlington Metal Indus., Inc. v. CIR, 57 TC 302 (1971) (release of claims by shareholders against corporation and vice versa; taxable event, not contribution to capital).

[75] See infra ¶6.4.5.

Although often regarded as a variance from the *Kirby Lumber* principle, the exemption of capital contributions really acknowledges that for practical purposes the debt has been paid rather than canceled. Sometimes, however, the transaction might appropriately be fragmented into a capital contribution of part of the debt and a genuine cancellation of the balance, reflecting doubts about the corporation's ability to pay or a reduction in the value of the claim below its face amount because the interest rate is less than the current rate on comparable loans. Viewed separately, the contributed component would be tax free as to the debtor and would serve to increase the shareholder-creditor's basis for his stock, while, as to the cancellation component, the creditor would be allowed a bad debt deduction, and the debtor would report the same amount as debt discharge income. The cases, however, usually apply the capital contribution analysis to the entire transaction.[76]

Without such a bifurcation, the capital contribution rule and the rule for stock for debt exchanges effectively offer a choice of tax consequences. If a shareholder surrendering corporate debt receives additional shares of the corporation worth an amount equal to the fair market value of the debt, the corporation has discharge of indebtedness income under §108(e)(10) equal to the excess of the principal amount over the fair market value of the stock.[77] If the shareholder receives no additional stock, the capital contribution rule allows the corporation to escape debt discharge income.[78]

Assume a sole shareholder holds a $1,000 bond of his corporation that is worth only $700. If the bond is transferred to the corporation for stock worth $700, the corporation has $300 of discharge of indebtedness income. If the corporation receives the bond as a contribution to capital, the debt discharge income disappears. Since the shareholder owns 100 percent of the stock whether the transaction is structured as a stock for debt exchange or as a contribution to capital, the recognition rule of §108(e)(10) works as a trap for the unwary in this context.

2. *Dividends to shareholder-debtors.* Another example of a spurious cancellation of indebtedness, the mirror image of the transaction just described, is the cancellation by a corporation of a debt owed to it by a

---

[76] In Putoma Corp. v. CIR, 66 TC 652, 670 (1976), aff'd, 601 F2d 734 (5th Cir. 1979), the Tax Court held that a shareholder's cancellation of a corporate debt was a nontaxable contribution to capital, although there was such doubt about collectibility that "the improvement of the corporation's prospects as a result of the cancellation was more symbolic than real." If the shareholder's claim was wholly worthless, however, the cancellation could be viewed as an acceptance of the inevitable rather than a contribution by the shareholder. See generally Hutton, An Asymmetrical Shell Game, 3 J. Corp. Tax'n 349, 352 (1976).

[77] See supra text accompanying notes 56–57.

[78] It is assumed here that the shareholder's basis for the obligation equals or exceeds the principal amount. See infra ¶6.4.5.

shareholder. If the claim is fully collectible, the act of cancelling it has the same effect as the payment of a formal dividend, which the shareholder then uses to pay off the debt. Viewed as a constructive dividend, the transaction generates income for the shareholder, not by virtue of the *Kirby Lumber* case but because dividends are taxable receipts under §§61(a)(7) and 301(c)(1).[79] The principal significance of this distinction is that a distribution to a shareholder is a taxable dividend only to the extent of the corporation's earnings and profits, a limitation inapplicable to debt discharge income.

3. *Gifts.* Creditors sometimes forgive their claims as an indirect way of making gifts to relatives, friends, and nonprofit organizations. If a proud grandparent who loaned money to a favorite grandchild for college tuition is overcome by emotion on graduation day, tears up the promissory notes, and announces that the debt is forgiven, the transaction is so clearly outside the proper ambit of *Kirby Lumber* that even the most assiduous revenue agent is not likely to assert that the grandchild has income on the cancellation of the debt. The transaction is tantamount to a gift by the grandparent to the grandchild of enough cash to enable the latter to pay the debt in full, and bears no resemblance to the financial adjustments that give rise to debt discharge income.

Against this background, the *Kirby Lumber* doctrine was dramatically, although temporarily, narrowed by the Supreme Court's 1943 decision in *Helvering v. American Dental Co.*,[80] holding that a routine financial adjustment between a debtor and his creditors could qualify as a tax-exempt gift to him, although the trial court had found that the creditors "acted for purely business reasons and did not forgive the debts for altruistic reasons or out of pure generosity." Despite this seemingly conclusive rebuttal of the taxpayer's claim that the transaction was a gift to him of the difference between the amount owing and the amount paid, the Supreme Court reversed, saying: "The fact that the motives leading to the cancellations were those of business or even selfish, if it be true, is not significant. The forgiveness was gratuitous, a release of something to the debtor for nothing, and sufficient to make the cancellations here gifts within the statute."[81]

---

[79] For cases holding that a corporation's cancellation of a shareholder's indebtedness is a constructive dividend to the shareholder, see Shephard v. CIR, 340 F2d 27 (6th Cir.), cert. denied, 382 US 813 (1965); Cohen v. CIR, 77 F2d 184 (6th Cir.), cert. denied, 296 US 610 (1935). For the treatment of constructive distributions in excess of the corporation's earnings and profits and the proper treatment of non pro rata constructive distributions when there are two or more shareholders, see infra ¶92.2.

[80] Helvering v. American Dental Co., 318 US 322, 331 (1943).

[81] Id.

What was surprising about *American Dental* was not its recognition that a tax-free gift could be effected by cancelling a debt; that point, illustrated every day by cancellations of intrafamily debts, was never in doubt. Rather, the opinion is surprising in its willingness to treat a purely commercial settlement as a gift. The validity of its conclusion can be tested by asking whether the debtor in *American Dental* should have thanked his creditors, after the settlement, for their generosity. The answer is almost certainly no. The creditors collected all they could get and displayed no generosity.

Since the only obvious distinction between the facts of *Kirby Lumber* and *American Dental* was that the former involved repurchases of the debt on the open market while the debtor in *American Dental* dealt directly with his creditors, the Court's endorsement of a gift rationale in the latter case implies that face to face negotiations are a hallmark of a tax-free gift. Within six years, however, the Court rejected this notion, properly so. In *CIR v. Jacobson*, a gift exclusion was denied to a debtor who had dealt directly with his creditors in repurchasing his bonded indebtedness from them.[82] *Jacobson* presented the issue in an especially neat way; the debtor had purchased some of his bonds through a bondholders' committee and two security firms and others directly from bondholders with whom he was personally acquainted. The Tax Court held that the former purchases generated debt discharge income because they resembled the open market transactions in *Kirby Lumber*, but that his gains on the bonds purchased from the bondholders personally were tax-free gifts under *American Dental*. The Supreme Court, however, rejected the latter conclusion:

> Although the sales price was less than the face of the bond and less than the original issuing price of the bond, there was nothing to indicate that the seller was not getting all that he could for all that he had. There is nothing in the evidence or findings to indicate that he intended to transfer or did transfer something for nothing. . . . It is conceivable, although hardly likely, that a bondholder, in the ordinary course of business and without any express release of his debtor, might have sold part of his claims on the bonds he held at the full face value of those parts and then have made a gift of the rest of his claims on those bonds to the same debtor "for nothing." It is that kind of extraordinary transaction that the respondent asks us, as a matter of law, to read into the simple sales which actually took place and from which he derived financial gains. We are unable to do so on the findings before us. . . .
>
> The situation in each transaction is a factual one. It turns upon whether the transaction is in fact a transfer of something for the best

---

[82] CIR v. Jacobson, 336 US 28 (1949).

price available or is a transfer or release of only a part of a claim for cash and of the balance "for nothing." The latter situation is more likely to arise in connection with a release of an open account for rent or for interest, as was found to have occurred in *Helvering v. American Dental Co.* . . . than in the sale of outstanding securities . . . as presented in this case. For these reasons we hold that the Commissioner was justified in finding a taxable gain, rather than an exempt gift, in each of the transactions before us.[83]

Although the Court refrained from overruling *American Dental*, and, indeed, ostensibly preserved the theory that the cancellation of a debt in a wholly commercial context can qualify as a tax-free gift to the debtor, its observation that such an "extraordinary transaction" is "hardly likely" has proved to be a requiem for the *American Dental* doctrine.[84]

When the commercial aspect of the debtor-creditor relationship is overshadowed by affection or other personal impulses, however, the cancellation of a debt can be a gift, notwithstanding the short shrift that *Jacobson* gave to *American Dental*. But this possibility does not depend on the validity of *American Dental*, which was concerned with a debtor who had no personal links with his creditors. As pointed out elsewhere in this work,[85] it is always difficult to classify a payment by one person to another if they have a business relationship but are also bound together by ties of friendship, blood, or marriage. To qualify as a gift, the transaction must stem from "detached and disinterested generosity . . . affection, respect, admiration, charity or like impulses."[86] If (but only if) the debt cancellation is attributable to motives of this type, the tax exemption accorded to gifts by §102 prevails over the *Kirby Lumber* principle.

Unless *American Dental* is unexpectedly resurrected, then, a personal relationship between debtor and creditor appears to be a necessary condition for gift classification. But it is not a sufficient condition, since in each case the trial court must go on to decide whether the creditor agreed to

---

[83] Id. at 50–52.

[84] Reynolds v. Boos, 188 F2d 322 (8th Cir. 1951), is sometimes cited as a post-*Jacobson* case that relies on the *American Dental* case. But the decision, which does not refer to *Jacobson*, rested on a finding that the cancellation was a gift, and the trial court's opinion suggests that the context might have included a personal as well as a commercial relationship between the debtor and the creditor; the opinion refers to "a close and harmonious relationship between the taxpayer and [the creditor]," and the formal cancellation of the debt (which might have merely ratified an earlier informal forgiveness) occurred at the instigation of the debtor's auditor. See Boos v. Reynolds, 84 F. Supp. 185 (D. Minn. 1949). For general discussion, see Chommie, The Debt Release: Gift or Increase in Net Worth, 4 Utah L. Rev. 36 (1954).

[85] Infra ¶10.2.1.

[86] CIR v. Duberstein, 363 US 278, 285 (1960), discussed infra ¶10.2.1.

accept less than the amount due because that was the best he could get or because he placed personal considerations above his financial interest.[87] Moreover, if there is objective evidence of the value of his claim and he receives that much or more (but less than the face amount due), his action can hardly be attributed to affection or similar impulses. Accepting the inevitable may be praiseworthy, but it exhibits realism, not generosity.

¶6.4.5 Effect of Prior Deductions—Tax Benefit Principles

When an accrual basis taxpayer deducts a liability for a business expense such as wages, business supplies, or interest, but later succeeds in discharging the debt for less than the amount deducted, it could be argued that the forgiven amount must be included in income because the deduction presupposed ultimate payment of the accrued liability. Had *Kirby Lumber* gone the other way, such a tax benefit theory might have developed to prevent taxpayers from getting tax benefit from disappearing liabilities.[88] This potential line of growth, however, was swallowed up by *Kirby Lumber*'s broader principle, which applies even if the taxpayer did not receive a tax benefit from the borrowing transaction and never will—for example, an individual who borrows money to finance personal expenditures and then settles the debt for less than its face amount.

A tax benefit rule has, however, sprung up in the debt-discharge rules' back garden. Under §108(e)(6), if a shareholder transfers an obligation of his corporation to the corporation as a contribution to capital, the corporation is treated as having satisfied the debt for cash equal to the shareholder's adjusted basis for the obligation. Any excess of the principal amount of the obligation over this deemed payment is discharge of indebtedness income to which the usual exclusion for capital contributions is inapplicable.[89]

---

[87] See Bosse v. CIR, 29 TCM (CCH) 1772 (1970) (employer's forgiveness of employee's debt constituted gift, where personal considerations were paramount); Clem v. Campbell, 62-2 USTC ¶9786 (ND Tex. 1962) (not officially reported) (same). See also Canton v. US, 226 F2d 313, 316–18 (8th Cir. 1955), cert. denied, 350 US 965 (1956) (cancellation of debt by taxpayer's brother; held, issue of gift vs. income was properly submitted to jury in criminal tax fraud case); Reynolds v. Boos, 188 F2d 322 (8th Cir. 1951); Capitol Coal Corp. versus CIR, 26 TC 1183 (1956), aff'd, 250 F2d 351 (2d Cir. 1957) (despite friendly relationships, three cancellations were not gifts, but a fourth, by brother of 50 percent shareholder, was).

[88] The courts have applied the tax benefit doctrine when a liability for a deducted item is avoided altogether. See supra ¶5.7.2.

[89] See infra ¶91.9.1 for the rule excluding capital contributions from gross income.

The enactment of §108(e)(6) followed upon an earlier unsuccessful attempt by the IRS to achieve this result judicially. Dwyer v. US, 439 F. Supp. 99 (D. Ore. 1977) (no income on shareholder's cancellation of interest owed him by controlled corporation); Putoma Corp. v. CIR, 66 TC 652 (1976), aff'd, 601 F2d 734 (5th Cir. 1979).

Section 108(e)(6) applies whenever a shareholder has a basis of less than face for a debt canceled as a capital contribution, but the principal goal of the provision's authors was to reach accrued liabilities to cash basis shareholders.[90] Assume a corporation accrues a deduction for $1,000 of salary to a shareholder-employee, but does not make payment to the shareholder; the shareholder, who uses the cash method of accounting and therefore does not report the accrued amount as gross income, forgives the corporation's debt in a later year as a contribution to capital. Because the shareholder has not reported the salary as gross income, his adjusted basis for the claim for payment is zero. The corporation therefore has debt discharge income of $1,000 when the shareholder makes his capital contribution.[91] The $1,000 deduction taken when the salary accrued is thereby recouped.

See also Rev. Rul. 76-316, 1976-2 CB 22 (solvent accrual method corporation taxable when sole shareholder forgave interest claims that corporation had deducted with tax benefit). Helvering v. Jane Holding Corp., 109 F2d 933 (8th Cir.), cert. denied, 310 US 653 (1940) (holding that a corporation realized income when its sole shareholder cancelled about $2.5 million of accrued interest in a transaction that was tantamount to a contribution to capital, is of doubtful validity today).

[90] The applicability of the provision in other contexts is sharply limited by §108(e)(4), which provides that when a debtor's obligation is acquired from an unrelated person by a person related to the debtor, the acquisition is deemed made by the debtor. See supra ¶6.4.3. For this purpose, a corporation is related to any person holding more than 50 percent of its stock. Assume one of a corporation's $1,000 bonds is purchased by its majority shareholder for $900. The purchase is deemed made by the corporation, which immediately recognizes $100 of discharge of indebtedness income. If the shareholder later contributes the obligation to the corporation, the rule described in the text does not apply, even though the shareholder's adjusted basis is less than the obligation's face amount, because the obligation has already been accounted for under the debt discharge rules. S. Rep. No. 1035, 99th Cong., 2d Sess. 19 n.23 (1980), reprinted at 1980-2 CB 820, 830.

Congress explicitly cut off the application of the rule in one context. If a shareholder's share of an S corporation's losses exceed the adjusted basis of his stock, the excess is allowed to the extent of the adjusted basis for obligations of the corporation held by the shareholder (IRC §1366(d)(1)(B)), and the bases of the obligations are reduced in like amount (IRC §1367(b)(2)). If the shareholder subsequently contributes the obligations to the corporation's capital, §108(e)(6) would give the corporation debt discharge income equal to the amount of this basis adjustment. Congress decided this result was inappropriate; the effect of a capital contribution of an obligation is to merge the obligation into the shareholder's stock, and corporate losses would have been allowed without this collateral consequence if the obligations in the example had been cast as stock rather than debt at the outset. For purposes of §108(e)(6), a shareholder's basis of corporate obligations is therefore determined without regard to the basis adjustments made to reflect corporate losses. IRC §108(d)(7)(C).

[91] See S. Rep. No. 1035, supra note 90, at 18 n.21, 1980-2 CB at 827.

One might quarrel with the policy choice made by Congress in enacting §108(e)(6). The corporation would realize no income if it paid the debt in full and the shareholder then turned the same amount over to the corporation as a contribution to its capital. The appropriate target in this situation is not the corporation but the shareholder. If he did not report the item when it was accrued by the corporation because he reported on the cash basis, it would be proper to treat the amount as constructively received when the shareholder makes the contribution to capital. Section 108(e)(6) does the opposite; it cancels out the earlier deduction and leaves the shareholder with no income, effectively treating the parties as though they had rescinded the transaction from which the original accrual arose.

Section 108(e)(6) usually does not apply if the corporation's deduction on the accrual of the item was denied or deferred; §108(e)(2) provides that debt discharge income is not realized if a payment of the discharged debt would have been deductible.[92] Under §267(a)(2), when a corporation accrues an item payable to a greater than 50 percent shareholder who uses the cash method of accounting, the corporation's deduction is delayed until the shareholder includes the item in gross income, usually on payment.[93] If the shareholder cancels the obligation as a contribution to capital without having included the item in gross income, the corporation has no income under §108(e)(6), notwithstanding the shareholder's zero basis for the obligation, because a payment would have been deductible.

One consequence of the placement of §108(e)(6) in the debt discharge context is that where a deduction has been allowed for an accrued item, income is recognized on a capital contribution of the obligation whether or not the deduction produced tax benefit. When the government was pursuing the issue in the courts before the enactment of §108(e)(6), it conceded that the exclusionary aspect of the tax benefit rule was available to the taxpayer.[94] Thus, on the cancellation of accrued interest, the debtor was allowed to exclude its gain from gross income to the extent that the prior deductions failed to reduce its taxes, leaving only the balance of the canceled liability subject to *Kirby Lumber*.[95] Now that the rule has been stated statutorily in terms of debt discharge income, such an exclusion is probably not available.

---

[92] See supra ¶6.4.2 for §108(e)(2).

[93] See infra ¶78.2.

[94] See supra ¶5.7.3.

[95] Warner Co. v. CIR, 11 TC 419 (1948), aff'd per curiam, 181 F2d 599 (3d Cir. 1950); Retail Properties, Inc. v. CIR, 23 TCM (CCH) 1463 (1964). In 1967, the IRS ruled that under the version of §108 then in effect, a taxpayer could elect not to recognize income from a below face discharge of a liability for accrued interest to the extent that there had been no tax benefit. Rev. Rul. 67-200, 1967-1 CB 15; see also Rev. Rul. 70-406, 1970-2 CB 16.

Section 108(e)(6) only applies if a shareholder-held corporate obligation is discharged by the shareholder's contribution of the obligation to the corporation's capital. Whether a shareholder's discharge of such an obligation is a capital contribution is an issue of fact. It is so characterized, according to the legislative history, if "the shareholder's action in cancelling the debt [is] related to his status as a shareholder," but not if "the shareholder-creditor acts merely as a creditor attempting to maximize the satisfaction of a claim."[96]

¶6.4.6   Effect of Debtor's Bankruptcy or Insolvency

Under §§108(a) and (b), an amount that would otherwise be debt discharge income is excluded from gross income and is instead applied in reduction of various of the taxpayer's tax attributes if the discharge occurs in a bankruptcy proceeding or when the taxpayer is insolvent.[97] These rules apply to a complete or partial discharge of any debt as to which the taxpayer is personally liable or that encumbers the taxpayer's property.[98]

1. *Taxpayers subject to reduction of tax attributes.* The reduction-of-tax-attributes rules apply in three situations. First, a taxpayer that is the subject of a bankruptcy proceeding must apply the rules to any "discharge of indebtedness [that] is granted by the court or is pursuant to a plan approved by the court."[99] Second, the rules apply to any discharge of indebtedness that occurs when the taxpayer is insolvent. A taxpayer is insolvent when its liabilities exceed the fair market value of its assets.[100] Liabilities and assets are measured for this purpose immediately before the discharge. Third, the rules sometimes apply to discharge of indebtedness incurred in a farming business, even if the taxpayer is solvent at the time of the

---

[96] S. Rep. No. 1035, supra note 90, at 19 n.22, 1980-2 CB 630. An example of the latter situation is "where the stock and bonds are publicly held and the creditor simply happens also to be a shareholder." Id.

[97] These rules, which were enacted in 1980, are exclusive and supersede earlier rules developed by the courts and the IRS. IRC §108(e)(1). Under prior law, an insolvent or bankrupt taxpayer realized no income on a discharge of indebtedness and suffered no reduction in any tax attribute. This rule originated in a 1923 ruling (IT 1564, II-1 CB 59 (1923)), and was carried into the regulations in 1935 (Reg. 86, §22(a)-14 (1935)). See Rev. Rul. 69-43, 1969-1 CB 310 (declaring the 1923 ruling obsolete).

[98] IRC §108(a)(1), (d)(1).

[99] IRC §108(d)(2). More completely, such a discharge is covered if the "case [is] under title 11 of the United States Code (relating to bankruptcy), but only if the taxpayer is under the jurisdiction of the court in such case." Id.

[100] IRC §108(d)(3).

discharge.[101]

The rules never apply to partnerships. The rules, in other words, are applied at the partner rather than the partnership level.[102] All debt discharge income of a partnership is included in the distributive shares of the partners. The reduction-of-tax-attributes rules apply to a particular partner's share of this income if the partner is insolvent or the subject of a bankruptcy proceeding.[103] The rules apply to bankrupt and insolvent S corporations, but some adaptations of the rules are made to coordinate them with subchapter S.[104]

When an individual enters bankruptcy under Chapter 7 or 11 of the bankruptcy laws, the bankruptcy estate is usually treated as a separate taxpayer that inherits the bankrupt's tax attributes.[105] The reduction-of-tax-attributes rules apply in this case to the estate, not the bankrupt individual.[106]

2. *Application of reduction procedure.* When the reduction-of-tax-attributes rules apply, the taxpayer's debt discharge income is applied against various items that could otherwise produce tax benefit for the taxpayer in the future. The effect of the rules, in other words, is to relieve the taxpayer of immediate recognition of debt discharge income, but at the cost of a forfeiture of an equal amount of potential tax benefit. The debt discharge income is applied against specified tax attributes in a statutorily prescribed order, beginning with the taxpayer's net operating losses and continuing if necessary with its general business credit carryovers, net capital losses, asset bases, and foreign tax credits.

If these attributes are insufficient to absorb all of the debt discharge income, the unabsorbed amount is not included in gross income and is ignored.[107] In this situation, §§108(a) and (b) preserve an anomaly from the

---

[101] The rules apply in this context if three tests—one relating to the lender, another to the indebtedness, and a third to the taxpayer—are met. IRC §108(g)(1). The lender qualifies if (1) it "is actively and regularly engaged in the business of lending money" and (2) it is neither a person who sold to the taxpayer property encumbered by the debt, a person who received a fee in connection with the taxpayer's investment in the property, nor a person related to the taxpayer or such a seller or fee-receiver. IRC §§46(c)(8)(D)(iv), 108(g)(3). The indebtedness qualifies if the taxpayer incurred it in the business of farming. IRC §108(g)(2). The taxpayer qualifies if farming was the source of at least 50 percent of his average annual gross receipts for the three years preceding the taxable year in which the discharge occurs. Id.

[102] IRC §108(d)(6).

[103] See S. Rep. No. 1035, 96th Cong., 2d Sess. 21, reprinted in 1980-2 CB 620, 631.

[104] IRC §108(d)(7).

[105] See infra ¶82.5.

[106] IRC §108(d)(8).

[107] S. Rep. No. 1035, supra note 103, at 13.

law predating their enactment in 1980, when a bankrupt or insolvent taxpayer was excused from recognizing debt discharge income and suffered no collateral consequence. Assume an individual borrows $10,000, spends it on riotous living, and is then discharged in bankruptcy. If the individual has no loss or credit carryovers and emerges from bankruptcy with no property, he pays no price for the exemption of his debt discharge income. If the same $10,000 of personal expenses had been financed with $10,000 of unreported income (or reported income on which the tax was not paid), the individual would be subject to tax, the government's claim would have a high priority in the distribution of assets in bankruptcy, and any unpaid tax liability would survive the discharge in bankruptcy of his other debts and be collectible from assets acquired thereafter.

This curious dichotomy is less common for business and investment debts. An investment of $10,000 of borrowed funds in business assets usually produces either net operating losses, basis in property, or one of the other tax attributes subject to reduction. When borrowed funds are used to pay expenses incurred in a loss year, for example, deductions for the expenses add to a net operating loss. If the borrowed funds are used to pay expenses incurred while the taxpayer has profits, the deductions for the expenses reduce taxes, but only because they are taken against gross income items represented by cash receipts or accounts receivable that have bases subject to reduction under these rules. A bankrupt corporation usually has more debt discharge income than attributes subject to reduction only if dividends were distributed to shareholders while the corporation was insolvent, an occurrence that often entitles creditors to insist that the distributed funds be brought back into the bankruptcy estate. Similarly, an individual's income from discharge of business debt usually exceeds the tax attributes of the business only if cash from the business is used for personal consumption while the business is insolvent.

The ordering rules are described more fully below.

a. *Net operating losses.* A bankrupt's or insolvent's debt discharge income is first subtracted from its net operating loss, if any, for the taxable year in which the discharge occurs; if the amount exceeds this loss, the excess is applied in reduction of net operating loss carryovers to that year.[108] The theory underlying this reduction is as follows: By reason of the debt

---

[108] IRC §§108(b)(2)(A), (4)(B). If carryovers come from more than one year, the reduction is made in the order the losses were incurred, starting with the earliest loss year. IRC §108(b)(4)(B). Tax for the current year is determined before the reduction of tax attributes. IRC §108(b)(4)(A). Carryovers from prior years are thus applied first as deductions against current taxable income, and only the carryovers remaining after this application are reduced under the rule described in the text. See infra ¶25.11 for net operating losses generally.

discharge, losses sustained by the taxpayer have been borne by the taxpayer's creditors. Normally, this would be reflected by requiring that the taxpayer recognize gross income in the year of the discharge to offset its earlier deductions of the shifted losses. Because the losses have not yet yielded tax benefit, however, this rule simply shaves down the loss deductions to eliminate the portions not ultimately borne by the taxpayer. This reduction, in fact, often has the same effect as if the debt discharge were recognized as gross income.[109]

b. *General business credits.* If the discharged debt exceeds the sum of the taxpayer's current net operating loss and all net operating loss carryovers to the year, the excess is applied in reduction of general business credit carryovers. The general business credit is the sum of the investment credit, targeted jobs credit, alcohol fuels credit, research credit, and low-income housing credit allowable to the taxpayer.[110]

Whereas each $1 of debt discharge income offsets $1 of net operating loss, it takes $3 of debt discharge income to eliminate $1 of business credit.[111] This three-to-one rule is apparently based on the idea that because (given a 34 percent corporate rate) credits are approximately three times as potent as deductions, credits should disappear under these rules only one third as fast as deductions.[112] The theory, however, is unsound. By the discharge of debt, the economic burden of expenditures made by the taxpayer is thrust on creditors. Because $1 of expenditure generated each $1 of business credit carryover, a dollar-for-dollar offset is appropriate when amounts spent for creditable items are treated as having been shifted to creditors.[113]

---

[109] That is, debt discharge income recognized for the year of the discharge would also be offset first by current losses and then by net operating loss carryovers to that year, starting with the oldest such carryover. See S. Rep. No. 1035, supra note 103, at 13 n.13 (1980).

[110] See infra ¶27.11 for the general business credit.

[111] IRC §108(b)(3). For taxable years beginning before 1987, the ratio is $1 of business credit offset for each $2 of debt discharge income. IRC §108(b)(3)(B) (before amendment in 1986).

The following ordering rules apply: Business credits for the year of the discharge are first applied against the tax on any positive taxable income for the year. IRC §108(b)(4)(A). If these credits exceed the tax, the excess is carried back to prior years under the usual business credit carryback rules. IRC §39. Business credit carryovers to the current year are then applied against debt discharge income under the three-for-one rule, starting with the oldest carryover and proceding to the newest. IRC §§108(b)(2)(B), (b)(4)(C). If all of these carryovers are exhausted, the three-for-one rule is applied to any business credit that would otherwise be carried from the current year to succeeding years. Id.

[112] See S. Rep. No. 1035, supra note 103, at 12 n.12 (1980).

[113] With respect to business credits, the three-for-one rule could be defended as a device to preserve to the bankrupt or insolvent taxpayer the incentive provided by

c. *Capital losses, basis, and foreign tax credits.* If debt discharge income remains unabsorbed after the application of the rules for net operating losses and business credits, the excess is applied next against capital loss carryovers, then against the basis of the taxpayer's property, and finally against foreign tax credit carryovers.[114] The offset of capital loss carryovers works like the net operating loss offset described above,[115] and foreign tax credit carryovers are absorbed under the rules provided for business credits.[116]

Several special rules are provided for reductions of basis. If the taxpayer's liabilities are not completely discharged, the debt discharge income applied in reduction of basis is limited to the excess of (1) the sum of the bases of the taxpayer's property immediately after the discharge over (2) the sum of the taxpayer's post-discharge liabilities.[117] Assume that immediately after an insolvency adjustment, a taxpayer has assets with an aggregate basis of $190 and liabilities of $100. No more than $90 of the debt discharge income from the insolvency adjustment can be applied in reduction of the basis of the taxpayer's assets. The basis reduction rule, in other words, leaves the taxpayer with a basis for its assets no smaller than its liabilities.

Also, if the taxpayer is an individual, no reduction is made in the basis of property that is exempted from creditor's claims under the bankruptcy laws.[118] Further, when the reduction-of-tax-attributes procedure applies to a solvent farmer, the amount to be applied against basis is applied first against the basis of property other than land used in farming and then, after the basis of such other property has been reduced to zero, to the land.

Unless the IRS consents to the use of a different method or a different ordering is required by the statutory rules, the amount of a basis reduction is allocated among the taxpayer's assets according to an elaborately prescribed hierarchy set up by the regulations.[119] Briefly stated, the order is (1)

---

the credit. Given a 34 percent rate, a $1 deductible expense reduces taxes by 34 cents, and thus effectively costs the taxpayer 66 cents; a credit, in contrast, provides $1 of tax savings for each $1 of expenditure and thus reduces the after-tax cost to zero. The tax incentive provided by the credit, in other words, is 66 cents for each $1 spent. Ignoring the discrepancy between one third and 34 percent, the three-for-one rule effectively reclaims the 34 cents and leaves the taxpayer with the 66 cents. The flaw in this analysis, however, is that the three-for-one rule also applies to the foreign tax credit, in which context it tends to favor foreign over domestic investment, something Congress is usually loath to do.

[114] IRC §§108(b)(2)(C), (D), and (E).
[115] IRC §§108(b)(2)(C), (4)(B).
[116] IRC §§108(b)(2)(E), (4)(C).
[117] IRC §1017(b)(2).
[118] Specifically, the individual must treat the property as exempt under 11 USC §522. IRC §1017(c)(1).
[119] Reg. §1.1016-7; S. Rep. No. 1035, supra note 103, at 14 (1980). For permission to depart from the general rules, see Reg. §1.1016-8.

property (other than inventory or receivables) for whose purchase the indebtedness was incurred, (2) property (other than inventory or receivables) used to secure the indebtedness, (3) all other property of the debtor (other than inventory and receivables), and (4) inventory and receivables.

Basis reductions occur as of the beginning of the taxable year following the year in which the debt discharge occurs.[120] A basis reduction under these rules is not treated as a disposition and thus does not trigger recognition of appreciation or depreciation in asset values or a recapture of investment credits.[121] On a subsequent disposition of property whose basis has been reduced, however, gain is characterized as ordinary income, regardless of the character of the asset, up to the amount of the basis reduction.[122]

d. *Election to reduce basis first.* The taxpayer can elect to alter the foregoing ordering in one respect:[123] An electing taxpayer applies debt discharge income first against the adjusted basis of its depreciable property.[124] This is done as of the first day of the taxable year following the year in which the discharge occurs. All basis adjustments for depreciation and other items are thus made for the year of the discharge before the basis reduction occurs. The rule that normally limits basis adjustments to the aggregate excess of liabilities over basis does not apply to a taxpayer making this election, and an electing taxpayer's basis can thus be reduced to zero.[125] If the debt discharge income exceeds the adjusted basis of the depreciable property, the excess is applied in reduction of other tax attributes under the ordering rules described above.

The term "depreciable property" refers to property subject to the allowance for depreciation, but only to the extent a reduction in adjusted basis

---

[120] IRC §1017(a). "If basis reduction is required in respect of a discharge of indebtedness in the final year of a bankruptcy estate, the reduction is to be made in the basis of assets acquired by the debtor from the estate at the time so acquired.". S. Rep. No. 1035, supra note 103.

[121] IRC §1017(c)(2); S. Rep. No. 1035, supra note 103, at 20. See Rev. Rul. 74-184, 1974-1 CB 8 (elective basis reduction under pre-1981 version of elective rule described in ¶6.4.7 caused investment credits to be recaptured).

[122] This is accomplished by requiring that the depreciation recapture rules of §§1245 and 1250 be applied as though (1) the basis reductions were adjustments to reflect depreciation deductions and (2) nondepreciable property subject to basis reduction were depreciable. IRC §1017(d). See infra Ch. 55 for the depreciation recapture rules.

[123] IRC §108(b)(5). The election usually must be made on the taxpayer's return for the year in which the discharge occurs, and, once made, can only be revoked with IRS approval. IRC §108(d)(9).

[124] The election is provided to allow a bankrupt the flexibility to keep its net operating loss carryovers at the cost of giving up asset basis. S. Rep. No. 1035, supra note 103, at 10 (1980).

[125] IRC §1017(b)(2).

reduces depreciation deductions.[126] If property is depreciated under a method limiting aggregate depreciation to the excess of cost over salvage value, for example, a portion of the adjusted basis equal to salvage value is not considered depreciable. The taxpayer can elect to treat as depreciable property any real property that it holds for sale to customers in the ordinary course of its business.[127]

If the taxpayer is a partner in a partnership, a look-through rule can be applied under which the taxpayer's partnership interest is treated as depreciable property to the extent of his indirect interest in the partnership's depreciable property.[128] The look-through rule only applies, however, if the partnership agrees to reduce the basis of its depreciable property in an amount equal to the basis reduction applied to the partnership interest.[129]

e. *Application of rules to S corporations.* If the taxpayer is an S corporation, several adjustments are made to reflect the special treatment of these corporations and their shareholders. Because an S corporation's losses are usually allowed directly on its shareholder's returns, it is not allowed the net operating loss deduction.[130] Debt discharge income of an insolvent or bankrupt S corporation is thus applied against current losses (capital as well as operating) to the extent shareholders' deductions for the losses are barred,[131] but there are no net operating or capital loss carryovers to absorb the income. An S corporation's credits also pass through to shareholders, thus precluding carryovers from arising at the corporate level. Except to the

---

[126] IRC §§108(d)(5), 1017(b)(3)(B).

[127] IRC §1017(b)(3)(E). The election must usually be made on the taxpayer's return for the year of the discharge and, once made, can only be revoked with IRS consent. Id.

[128] IRC §1017(b)(3)(C).

[129] Subsequent allocations of partnership income and deduction must be made in a way that thrusts on this particular partner the burden of the partnership-level basis reduction. S. Rep. No. 1035, supra note 103, at 22 (1980). This is accomplished by the same procedures as are applied to the basis adjustments reflecting a sale of an interest in a partnership that has made an election under §754. Id. See infra ¶86.6 for the §754 election.

A similar rule applies when the basis reduction procedure applies to a corporation (the parent) that holds stock in another corporation (the subsidiary) with which it files a consolidated return for the year of the debt discharge; the parent's stock is treated as depreciable property if the subsidiary agrees to reduce the basis of its depreciable property in an amount equal to the parent's reduction in its stock basis. IRC §1017(b)(3)(D). "This rule can be applied successively through a chain of corporations so long as the lowest tier subsidiary reduces its basis in actual depreciable property." S. Rep. No. 1035, supra, at 13 n.15.

[130] IRC §§703(a)(2)(D), 1363(b)(2), and 1366(a)(1).

[131] IRC §108(d)(7)(B). Section 1366(d)(1) limits a shareholder's deduction for his share of the corporation's loss to the sum of the adjusted bases of his stock and obligations of the corporation he holds.

limited extent absorbed by undeductible current losses, the reduction rule thus points to the S corporation's adjusted basis for its assets.

f. *Limitation in insolvencies.* One distinction is drawn between bankruptcy proceedings and insolvency adjustments. The reduction-of-tax-attributes procedure applies to all debt discharged in bankruptcy. In an insolvency adjustment, in contrast, this procedure is limited to the amount of the taxpayer's negative net worth immediately before the discharge, and gross income must be reported equal to the taxpayer's positive net worth immediately after the discharge.[132] A negative net worth is an excess of the taxpayer's liabilities over the fair market value of its assets, measured immediately before the discharge.[133]

¶6.4.7 Election for Years Prior to 1987 to Exclude Income From Discharge of Indebtedness and Reduce Basis of Property

Until 1987, a solvent taxpayer realizing debt discharge income with respect to "qualified business indebtedness" could elect to reduce the basis of his assets by the amount discharged rather than including this amount in gross income.[134] For individuals, the term "qualified business indebtedness" included any indebtedness "incurred or assumed . . . in connection with property used in his trade or business"; all indebtedness of corporations was qualified.[135]

A pre-1987 election usually postpones realization of debt discharge income rather than excluding it permanently because the reduced basis will

---

[132] IRC §§108(a)(2), (3).

[133] IRC §108(d)(3).

[134] IRC §§108(a)(1)(C), (c) (before repeal in 1986). The repeal of the election is effective for debt discharges occurring in 1987 and succeeding years. Pub. L. No. 99-514, §822(c), 100 Stat. 2085 (1986). See Montgomery v. CIR, 65 TC 511, 520 (1975) (re requirement of timely election); Magill v. US, 70 TC 465 (1978) (delinquent election not effective).

[135] IRC §108(d)(4) (before repeal in 1986). An individual's indebtedness does not qualify merely because it was secured by business property; the facts of each case must be considered, and a debt qualifies if the proceeds were used to purchase, improve, or repair business property. Reg. §1.108(a)-1(a)(2).

The statute only refers to corporations and individuals. When a partnership has discharge of indebtedness income, §§108(a) and (b) are applied at the partner rather than the partnership level (IRC §108(d)(6)), thus making the election rule turn on whether a partner is a corporation or an individual. See Rev. Rul. 72-205, 1972-1 CB 37 (under pre-1980 law, partnerships can elect to defer recognition, but cancellation viewed as distribution of money to partners, reducing basis of partnership interest). It is unclear whether the election is available to trusts and estates.

When first enacted, the election rule only applied to corporations "in an unsound financial condition" and only if the debt was evidenced by a "security" issued before June 1, 1939. See Surrey, supra note 19.

result in lower depreciation deductions for depreciable property and more taxable gain (or a smaller deductible loss) on a subsequent sale of the property. The postponement is usually attractive to a taxpayer, however, and prior to 1981, it often permitted some or all of the gain to be reported as long-term capital gain when the property was sold, as compared with the ordinary income status of debt discharge income.[136]

The principal areas requiring attention under the election and basis reduction rules are:

1. *Scope of election.* A pre-1987 election can only be made if the taxpayer realized income "by reason of the discharge, in whole or in part . . . of any indebtedness for which the taxpayer is liable, or subject to which the taxpayer holds property."[137] If a discharge occurs in circumstances not generating income (e.g., as a gift from the creditor),[138] the taxpayer has no reason to make an election and can preserve intact the basis of his property. On the other hand, if the debt is discharged as an indirect method of paying compensation or distributing a dividend to the debtor,[139] the debtor's income does not arise "by reason of the discharge" of the debt and does not qualify for exclusion.[140]

---

[136] For elections made for the years 1981 through 1987, ordinary income treatment of the eventual recognition of the deferred income is insured by §1017(d). See Rev. Rul. 69-613, 1969-2 CB 163 (income from cancellation of debt is ordinary income, not capital gain, since not realized on a "sale or exchange").

[137] IRC §108(a).

[138] Supra ¶6.4.4.

[139] For these spurious cancellations, see supra ¶6.4.4.

[140] The regulations state that if a debt is satisfied by a transfer of property, the amount to be applied in reduction of the basis of other property is the difference between the amount of the debt and the value of the transferred property, thus implying that the difference (if any) between the adjusted basis of the property and its fair market value is not subject to these rules but is instead to be treated as the amount realized on the disposition of the property. Reg. §1.1017-1(b)(5). See also Spartan Petroleum Co. v. US, 437 F. Supp. 733 (DSC 1977) (election only applies to income from cancellation of debt, not income from other sources paid by canceling a debt); Rev. Rul. 84-176, 1984-2 CB 34 (rationale of *Spartan Petroleum* applied to creditor's agreement to forgive taxpayer's debt in exchange for release of taxpayer's contract claim against creditor; §108 not applicable when debt forgiveness is "only a medium for some other form of payment"). Compare Colonial Sav. Ass'n v. CIR, 85 TC 855 (1985) (interest forfeiture on early withdrawal from thrift institution not discharge of indebtedness income of institution; cancellation of obligation to pay previously accrued interest was merely a medium for compensating the institution for revenue lost by early withdrawal) and Rev. Rul. 83-60, 1983-1 CB 39 (same as *Colonial Sav.*) with Centennial Sav. Bank v. US, 88-1 USTC ¶9153 (ND Tex. 1988) (not officially reported) (finding cancellation of indebtedness income on same facts as *Colonial Sav.*).

2. *Order in which basis reduced.* For the years 1981 through 1986, an electing taxpayer is required to apply debt discharge income in reduction of depreciable property only, and the reduction takes effect as of the beginning of the taxable year following the year in which the debt discharge occurs.[141] For earlier years, the amount of a basis reduction is applied according to an elaborately prescribed hierarchy set up by the regulations.[142] Briefly stated, the order for pre-1981 elections is (1) property (other than inventory or receivables) for whose purchase the indebtedness was incurred, (2) property (other than inventory or receivables) used to secure the indebtedness, (3) all other property of the debtor (other than inventory and receivables), and (4) inventory and receivables. If an individual is required to reduce basis by an amount exceeding his aggregate basis for property in the foregoing categories, the excess is applied first against the basis of property held for the production of income but not used in a trade or business, and finally against the basis of all other property.

3. *Income in excess of aggregate basis of property.* If the debt discharge income covered by a pre-1987 election exceeds the aggregate adjusted basis of the taxpayer's property before reduction, the excess cannot be used to reduce basis because the exotic concept of negative basis is excluded by the regulations.[143] The IRS, not surprisingly, requires the unallocated excess to be reported as income in the year of the discharge.[144] The statutory authority for this position is not clear, but it is a more reasonable result than the alternative of permanently immunizing this part of the taxpayer's gain from tax.

4. *Conditional consents.* If the taxpayer believes that the discharge of his debt occurred in circumstances immunizing him from the *Kirby Lumber* principle (e.g., as a gift), but is not sure of his ground, can he preserve this primary contention but file an election as a secondary defense? The regulations do not explicitly authorize a conditional election, but there is no sound reason to treat such a reservation of rights as a waiver, nor is the election likely to mislead the government so as to justify estopping the taxpayer from pressing his claim that no income was realized on the discharge. Thus, if the taxpayer actually effects the required reductions in

---

[141] IRC §§1017(a), (b)(3)(A) (before amendment in 1986). The definition of "depreciable property" and other aspects of this limitation are described above in ¶6.4.6, text accompanying notes 123–29.

[142] Reg. §1.1017-1. For permission to depart from the general rules, see Reg. §1.1017-2. Also, the insolvency rules require departures from this ordering in various circumstances described above in ¶6.4.6.

[143] Reg. §1.1017-1(a) (final sentence). See infra ¶42.7 for more on negative basis.

[144] Rev. Rul. 67-200, 1967-1 CB 15, as clarified by Rev. Rul. 70-406, 1970-2 CB 16 (forgiveness by creditor of accrued interest). Taken literally, however, the statute permits the taxpayer to exclude all of his debt discharge income if he consents to the adjustment of basis required by the regulations under §1017.

basis, computing and paying his taxes accordingly, and then claims refunds for the post-discharge years on the ground that the discharge did not generate any income, it is hard to see how the government would be injured.[145]

¶6.5 INCOME FROM UNLAWFUL ACTIVITIES

As explained earlier,[1] taxpayers do not ordinarily realize income on receiving money or other property that must be returned or repaid, since the transaction does not produce any gain. If property is obtained unlawfully and the taxpayer intends to disregard his legal obligation to make restitution, however, he is ordinarily not allowed to use the offsetting liability as a shield against tax liability; he resembles the parricide who asks for mercy because he is an orphan. Instead, the unlawful receipts are included in gross income, and the wrongdoer may take a deduction only if and when he reimburses the victim for the loss.

This result was reached only after a series of confusing and conflicting Supreme Court decisions.[2] The story begins with the Revenue Act of 1913, which taxed income from a variety of sources, including "any lawful business carried on for gain or profit."[3] Three years later Congress eliminated the word "lawful" without giving a reason for the change.[4] With the advent of Prohibition, however, the Treasury relied on the change in prosecuting bootleggers for failing to report income from unlawful sales of liquor, arguing that it manifested a legislative intent to tax the profits of illegal as well as lawful activities. One judge expressed the view, however, that taxing an unlawful activity seemed inconsistent with prohibiting it and that it was degrading for the government to become a silent partner in an unlawful business by taxing its profits.[5]

In *United States v. Sullivan*, the Supreme Court exhibited no such embarrassment, saying: "We see no reason . . . why the fact that a busi-

---

[145] See Eustice, supra note 19, at 262 (conditional consents under 1939 Code).

[1] Supra ¶6.4.1.

[2] See generally Bittker, Taxing Income From Unlawful Activities, 25 Case W. Res. L. Rev. 130 (1974).

[3] Revenue Act of 1913, Pub. L. No. 16, §IIB, 38 Stat. 114, 167.

[4] Revenue Act of 1916, Pub. L. No. 271, §2(a), 39 Stat. 756, 757.

[5] See Steinberg v. US, 14 F2d 564, 569 (2d Cir. 1926) (concurring opinion by Judge Manton, who by extraordinary irony of fate was later held liable for fraud penalties for failing to report amounts received as bribes while serving as senior circuit judge of Court of Appeals for Second Circuit; Manton v. CIR, 7 TCM (CCH) 937 (1948)). But see US v. Stafoff, 260 US 477, 480 (1923) (upholding excise tax on liquor prohibited by National Prohibition Act: "Of course Congress may tax what it also forbids").

For the question of whether the real objective of tax prosecutions is to punish the defendant for other crimes, see infra ¶114.4.

ness is unlawful should exempt it from paying the taxes that if lawful it would have to pay."[6] Mr. Justice Holmes, writing for the Court, went on to dispose of the defendant's claim that the Fifth Amendment exempted him from filing a return:

> Most of the items [called for by the return] warranted no complaint. It would be an extreme if not an extravagant application of the Fifth Amendment to say that it authorized a man to refuse to state the amount of his income because it had been made in crime. But if the defendant desired to test that or any other point he should have tested it in the return so that it could be passed upon. He could not draw a conjurer's circle around the whole matter by his own declaration that to write any word upon the government blank would bring him into danger of the law.[7]

Although the *Sullivan* case was decided in 1927, the scope of the privilege against self-incrimination, so far as tax returns are concerned, remains unclear to this day.[8] When income from unlawful activities is reported, the taxpayer often supplies his name, address, and net income (usually in round figures, with such laconic labels as "miscellaneous income" or "income from various sources"), leaving the rest of the return blank. Returns like these invite intensive scrutiny by the IRS, but taxpayers are rarely prosecuted for failing to supply more information, either because the Fifth Amendment is thought to protect them against making further disclosures or because juries are thought unlikely to convict for mere silence. Instead, revenue agents endeavor to verify the accuracy of the reported amounts by reconstructing the taxpayer's financial history from purchases, investments, loans, and so on.[9]

The *Sullivan* case did not discuss the taxability of illegal receipts received under circumstances that entitle the victim to compel the wrongdoer to disgorge the fruits of the crime. Can an embezzler be said to realize income, in view of his obligation to pay back whatever he has taken? Are embezzled funds like borrowed funds, which are excluded from gross income because the receipt is offset by a liability of equal amount? The Supreme Court did not address this issue until 1946, when it accepted the borrower analogy in *CIR v. Wilcox*,[10] holding (with one Justice dissenting) that embezzled funds are not taxable:

---

[6] US v. Sullivan, 274 US 259, 263 (1927).
[7] Id. at 263–64.
[8] See infra ¶112.2.2.
[9] See infra ¶112.2.4 (self-incrimination), ¶114.4 (prosecution for failure to supply information), ¶107.1 (indirect methods of computing income).
[10] CIR v. Wilcox, 327 US 404 (1946).

> [T]axable income [does not] accrue from the mere receipt of prop-
> erty or money which one is obliged to return or repay to the rightful
> owner, as in the case of a loan or credit. . . . Moral turpitude is not a
> touchstone of taxability. The question, rather, is whether the taxpayer
> in fact received a statutory gain, profit or benefit. That the taxpayer's
> motive may have been reprehensible or the mode of receipt illegal has
> no bearing on the application of [the taxing statute].[11]

The Court left open the possibility that the embezzler might subsequently
be taxable if his obligation to repay were terminated by the statute of
limitations or by an act of forgiveness on the part of the victim.

Wilcox was often invoked by shareholder-officers who had pocketed
the proceeds of sales by family corporations. If the IRS alleged an understatement of the corporation's taxable income, the corporation's defense
was that the funds had been embezzled, so that it was entitled to a deduction for a loss by theft equal to, and hence offsetting, the amount omitted
from its gross receipts. If, on the other hand, the IRS alleged a wrongful
omission from the shareholder-officer's personal tax returns of the funds
taken by him from the corporation, he relied on the Wilcox case to negate
tax liability. On the whole, the courts resisted these attempts, sometimes on
the theory that a shareholder cannot embezzle from his wholly owned corporation, sometimes on finding that the corporation suffered no loss because the shareholder was financially able to make restitution. In an ironic
turn of the screw, the Tax Court refused to accept a taxpayer's claim that he
was an embezzler partly because his admission that he had engaged in fraud
made him unworthy of belief.[12]

Six years after deciding Wilcox, the Supreme Court had to decide
whether the defendant in Rutkin v. United States was taxable on $250,000
extorted by threats of violence from an ex-partner in a "high seas venture"
(bootlegging).[13] In theory, extortion resembles embezzlement because the
extortioner, like the embezzler, is liable to his victim for restitution. In

---

[11] Id. at 408. For the loan theory of embezzlement, see James v. US, 366 US
213, 251 (1961), where Mr. Justice Whittaker (concurring in part and dissenting in
part) observed that an embezzler is "indebted to his victim in the full amount taken
as surely as if he had left a signed promissory note at the scene of the crime." The
simile would be more accurate if amended to read "a signed promissory note that is
not intended to be, and almost certainly will not be, honored."

[12] See Davis v. US, 226 F2d 331 (6th Cir. 1955) (stockholder cannot embezzle
from wholly owned corporation), cert. denied, 350 US 965 (1956); Kann v. CIR, 18
TC 1032 (1952), aff'd, 210 F2d 247 (3d Cir. 1953), cert. denied, 347 US 967 (1954);
but see Dix's Est. v. CIR, 223 F2d 436 (2d Cir.), cert. denied, 350 US 894 (1955)
(president, who was not sole shareholder and who had deceived only other responsible executive, held to have embezzled from family corporation; Wilcox applied).

[13] Rutkin v. US, 343 US 130, rehearing denied, 343 US 952 (1952).

practice, an extortioner is less likely to be asked for repayment; if the victim's fear of exposure or violence keeps him from complaining to the police when he is first approached, he will probably remain silent thereafter. For this reason, the Supreme Court held in *Rutkin* that extorted funds are taxable:

> An unlawful gain, as well as a lawful one, constitutes taxable income when its recipient has such control over it that, as a practical matter, he derives readily realizable economic value from it. . . . That occurs when cash, as here, is delivered by its owner to the taxpayer in a manner which allows the recipient freedom to dispose of it at will, even though it may have been obtained by fraud and his freedom to use it may be assailable by someone with a better title to it.[14]

This decision evoked a vigorous dissent by four of the nine Justices, who could see no distinction between embezzled and extorted funds. The dissenters were not prepared, however, to extend the borrower analogy to criminal activity that was sufficiently sustained and regular to constitute a business. Acknowledging that "some states have laws which under special circumstances permit some particular groups to assert a legal claim for recovery of gambling losses or money paid for bootleg liquor," they asserted that "bootleggers and gamblers are engaged in going businesses and make regular business profits which should be taxed in the same manner as profits made through more legitimate endeavor." The dissenting Justices argued that in this situation, the theoretical obligation to repay should be recognized only by allowing a deduction for restitution actually made to victims (just as ordinary businessmen can deduct refunds to customers victimized by false advertising or other improper business practices). They would, however, have excluded the "sporadic loot of an embezzler, an extortioner or a robber" from taxable income, on the theory that the commission of these felonies does not comprise a business.[15]

The distinction drawn by the majority in *Rutkin* between embezzled funds (held nontaxable in *Wilcox*) and extorted funds (held taxable in *Rutkin*) lasted for less than 10 years. In *James v. United States*, involving a union official who had embezzled more than $700,000 from his union and a related insurance company, the Supreme Court overruled *Wilcox*, holding that income from illegal activity is taxable despite the recipient's legal obligation to make restitution.[16] The offsetting liability should be disregarded, according to Mr. Chief Justice Warren, because the taxpayer does not intend to honor this obligation and because, "as a practical matter," he has

---

[14] Id. at 137.
[15] Id. at 140–41.
[16] James v. US, 366 US 213 (1961).

enough control over the funds to derive economic value from them. The majority in *James* went on to suggest that if the taxpayer actually made restitution to his victim, he would be entitled to a deduction in the year of repayment.[17] The taxpayer's indictment for tax evasion was dismissed, however, on the ground that "willfulness," indispensable to a criminal conviction under §7201, could not be established for the period when *Wilcox* was in force. This nonretroactive application of *James* was later extended to civil tax penalties requiring proof of fraudulent intent.[18]

The *James* case apparently embraces all illegal receipts, even if the culprit promises restitution, although an exception should be left for malefactors whose victims agree, before the end of the taxable year, to treat the improper taking as a loan.[19] The theft-loan dichotomy is also encountered if a taxpayer purports to borrow funds for legitimate business transactions, but is actually swindling the lenders. If the investment facade is given credence, the receipts are nontaxable borrowed funds, but if the intent to cheat is dominant, they are taxable fruits of larceny or embezzlement.[20]

---

[17] Id. at 220–22. See Rev. Rul. 65-254, 1965-2 CB 50 (repayment of embezzled funds is loss deductible under §§165(a) and (c)(2), relating to transactions entered into for profit); but see Chumbook v. CIR, 36 TCM (CCH) 487 (1977) (no income where converted property returned to true owner in same taxable year). See also McKinney v. US, 76-2 USTC ¶9728 (WD Tex. 1976) (not officially reported), aff'd on another issue, 574 F2d 1240 (5th Cir. 1978), cert. denied, 439 US 1072 (1979) (repayment of embezzled funds creates no net operating loss under §172 because activities not a "business"); Yerkie v. CIR, 67 TC 388 (1976) (§1341 not applicable because embezzled funds not received under claim of right); Fox v. CIR, 61 TC 704 (1974) (acq.) (surrender of stock by embezzler to victim results in ordinary loss, not capital loss, because surrender is not "sale or exchange").

[18] Kahr's Est. v. CIR, 414 F2d 621 (2d Cir. 1969); but see McGee v. CIR, 519 F2d 1121 (5th Cir. 1975), cert. denied, 424 US 967 (1976) (civil fraud penalties applied to pre-*James* embezzlement where there was evidence of fraudulent intent other than mere failure to report income); Geiger's Est. v. CIR, 352 F2d 221 (8th Cir. 1965), cert. denied, 382 US 1012 (1966) (civil tax liability on pre-*James* embezzlement receipts upheld; taxpayer's intent not material when fraud not an issue).

[19] Gilbert v. CIR, 552 F2d 478 (2d Cir. 1977) (despite guilty plea in grand larceny case, taxpayer had no income from unauthorized withdrawals of corporate funds because he acknowledged obligation to repay and intended to do so). But see Quinn v. CIR, 524 F2d 617 (7th Cir. 1975) (embezzler taxed despite giving promissory note to victimized bank in same year); Buff v. CIR, 496 F2d 847 (2d Cir. 1974) (bookkeeper taxed on embezzled funds despite promise in same year to make restitution, embodied in confession of judgment; judgment "not worth the paper it was written on"); Mais v. CIR, 51 TC 494 (1968) (embezzler's confession and acknowledgment of obligation to repay are not "a consensual agreement between him and his victim which would justify treating the embezzled funds as in any way similar to borrowed funds"). None of these cases involve a decision by the victim to convert the misappropriation into a loan.

[20] See In re Diversified Brokers Co., 487 F2d 355 (8th Cir. 1973) (receipts in Ponzi pyramiding scheme treated as loans to corporate borrower rather than as

If the Supreme Court, in deciding *James*, had perpetuated the distinction between embezzlement and extortion, the line would have become increasingly difficult to police with every passing year, since taxpayers engage in a much wider range of unlawful activities than the bootlegging, embezzlement, and extortion that came before the Supreme Court in the *Wilcox*, *Rutkin*, and *James* cases. A taxpayer may derive economic benefit from peripheral misconduct in a business that is entirely lawful (such as a corporate officer's illegal use of inside information in purchasing his company's stock), from an unlawful enterprise that could be conducted legally but would then be less profitable (such as a mail order business that persistently engages in false advertising), or from behavior that is wholly unrelated to any legitimate enterprise (such as murder for hire). The unlawful activity might be confined to a single act of misconduct, which the taxpayer does not intend to repeat; it may consist of behavior that would have been repeated if it had not been detected by the police; or it may constitute a continuous business. The profits may, or may not, be refundable to the victim; if neither party to an unlawful act is innocent (e.g., bribery of a public official), the government may have a right to the fruits of the crime; in other cases, the status of an unlawful profit might not be defined by law. The behavior may be punishable by fine and imprisonment, or it may be unlawful only in the sense that the courts will order restitution or impose civil penalties. In many cases the full range of the taxpayer's activities is not known; sometimes the source of a taxpayer's income can only be inferred from the fact that his expenditures substantially exceeded the amount reported on his tax returns and that he is reputed to be a gambler, thief, corrupt public official, or loan shark.

For these reasons, it would be very difficult to administer a distinction between one type of illegal income and another, whether based on the regularity of the receipts, the relative morality of the behavior, the existence of a legal duty to make restitution, the public's attitude toward the taxpayer's activities, or the severity of the penalties. On the other hand, a blanket exemption for all unlawful income would embrace not only the neighborhood thief and bootlegger but also a much broader range of taxpayers (including businessmen whose profits are attributable to violations of antitrust and price control laws, of health, safety, environmental, labor, and racial standards, and of other governmental regulations). It is therefore not surprising that the Supreme Court decided in *James* to tax all income from unlawful activities.

---

embezzled funds); Moore v. US, 412 F2d 974 (5th Cir. 1969) (Billy Sol Estes operations treated as swindle resulting in taxable income, not as investments); US v. Rochelle, 384 F2d 748, 751 (5th Cir. 1967), cert. denied, 390 US 946 (1968) (money obtained in the form of loans but under fraudulent pretenses and without intent to repay held taxable).

Will disclosure of the illegal activities make it impossible for the tax-payer to get a fair trial, at least in a tax evasion prosecution? Dissenting in *Rutkin*, Mr. Justice Black argued that the tax evasion issue in that case was obfuscated by irrelevant evidence of the defendant's criminal history and associations, and that "the fantastic story of supposed extortion . . . would probably never have been accepted by a jury if presented in a trial uncol-ored by the manifold other inflammatory matters which took up 887 of the 900 pages in this 'tax evasion' case."[21]

Although real enough, the danger to the defendant's right to a fair trial does not justify a tax exemption for all income from unlawful activity. To begin with, a tax evasion trial may require only a minimal reference to the defendant's illegal behavior or even none at all. If, for example, the govern-ment's case consists of evidence that the taxpayer spent more money than his reported income made available to him and that he had a likely source of unreported income from which the unreported funds might have come,[22] there is rarely a need for extensive details about the source, and the judge can reduce the possibility of prejudice by firm instructions to the jury.

Sometimes, however, more extensive or lurid evidence of the defen-dant's misconduct is properly offered by the government or must be intro-duced by the defendant himself, and he must rely on the judge, acting under the principles established by the appellate courts, to exert his authority over the jury in an effort to insure a fair trial. Mr. Justice Black himself was prepared to tolerate the risk of unfairness in the case of bootleggers, profes-sional gamblers, and other "businessmen," whose income he regarded as fair game for the tax collector.[23] He suggested no reservations about taxing persons whose income derives from false advertising, black marketing, usu-rious loans, over-ceiling rental charges, and violations of other regulatory laws, even though juries, especially in urban centers, may well think that these white-collar crimes are as abhorrent as extortion and robbery.[24]

Even if prejudice to the defendant cannot be adequately checked by a searching voir dire and by the judge's control of the courtroom, it does not necessarily follow that exempting all illegal income from tax is the most

---

[21] Rutkin v. US, 343 US 130, 147, rehearing denied, 343 US 952 (1952). Mr. Justice Black also feared that Washington would get "more and more power to punish purely local crimes."

[22] For indirect methods of reconstructing income, see infra ¶107.1.

[23] Rutkin v. US, supra note 21, at 140–41.

[24] Disallowance of deductions can also entail proof by the government that the defendant engaged in activities that a jury might disapprove. For example, in US v. Lillehei, 357 F. Supp. 718, 724 (D. Minn. 1973), deductions for "additional profes-sional secretarial and maid help" were shown by the government to reflect payments to three women "whose testimony indicated . . . a rather personal relationship with the defendant." See also US v. Windham, 489 F2d 1389 (5th Cir. 1974) (in tax evasion prosecution of physician, reference to abortions not prejudicial).

appropriate remedy. A more limited corrective would be to abandon the use of criminal sanctions in such cases, leaving the defendant subject to the normal civil remedies of liability for the tax itself, interest, and penalties for negligence or deliberate disregard of the regulations. There would be a residue of unavoidable prejudice even in civil proceedings, but a regime of blanket immunity from the rules of government for everyone who might be treated unfairly by a jury would be intolerable.

A final problem in the taxability of income from unlawful activities is the plight of the victim. When it held in *Wilcox* that embezzled funds were not includable in income, the Court asserted that the victim's chance of recovering from the wrongdoer would be jeopardized if the wrongdoer were required to pay part of the embezzled funds to satisfy his tax liability.[25] In point of fact, the defendant in *Wilcox* had dissipated the embezzled funds in gambling and was probably judgment proof. While this may be typical, sometimes the guilty party may still have possession of the victim's property or hold other assets that can be reached. The issue then is whether the victim or the government has the superior claim.

In general, if the victim can trace and identify his property, as in the case of a stolen work of art, he can get it back, even if the thief has nothing left to pay his taxes. If the property cannot be traced (if it is, for example, currency whose serial numbers are not known), the victim is ordinarily familiar with the facts sooner than the government, and this prior knowledge usually enables him to establish an enforceable claim against any assets that can be discovered in the criminal's possession before the government's tax lien takes hold. But situations can also be imagined in which the victim's right to reimbursement is subordinated to the government's right to collect taxes on the unlawful income.[26] This possibility is offensive, but a corrective could be provided by Congress without going so far as to confer a blanket tax exemption on unlawful receipts.[27]

Section 90, added in 1987, effectively uses the income tax to penalize recipients of one type of illegal income. The provision applies to a taxpayer

---

[25] CIR v. Wilcox, 327 US 404, 410 (1946).

[26] In US v. Rochelle, 384 F2d 748 (5th Cir. 1967), cert. denied, 390 US 946 (1968), a swindler engaged in a fraudulent loan scheme left a briefcase full of money in an airport locker. The government got wind of the existence of the briefcase, promptly terminated the swindler's taxable year, assessed tax, and levied against the briefcase. Victims of the swindler had previously commenced involuntary bankruptcy proceedings against him. The government's levy, however, had priority over the unsecured claims of the victim-creditors, a conclusion so clear in the circumstances that litigation over the matter related solely to whether the swindled funds were gross income. See supra note 20.

[27] Congress could protect the victim, for example, by adding his claim against the wrongdoer to the list of favored claims in §6323. See infra ¶111.5.4 for federal tax liens.

who receives, but does not pay for, water made available to farmers under a federal reclamation or irrigation project. Such a taxpayer must include in gross income the excess of the amount required to be paid for the water over the amount actually paid. In this, the provision is a straightforward application of the *James* principle. The statute goes on, however, to deny any deduction for the amount included in gross income. If the water is used in the taxpayer's business, it is a cost of doing business, and the inclusion of its value in gross income without an offsetting deduction causes the taxpayer to be taxed on gross income that is used to pay business expenses—a consequence that is inconsistent with the basic concept of the tax as a net income tax.

PART
2

Exclusions From Gross Income

CHAPTER

10

Property Acquired by Gift and Inheritance

¶10.1 INTRODUCTORY

Since 1913, the value of property acquired by gift, bequest, devise, or inheritance has been excluded from the recipient's gross income.[1] Like many other durable features of the federal income tax, however, this exclusion (now embodied in §102) entered the law without formal congressional explanation, and this deficiency has not been remedied in the decades since its enactment. When the sixteenth amendment was still young, there were doubts about the power of Congress to tax gifts and bequests to the recipient without apportioning the tax among the states in proportion to population. When the Supreme Court indicated in *Eisner v. Macomber* (1920) that income could only be derived from capital, labor, or both combined, some legal scholars thought that gifts and bequests could not be treated as income because they were not generated by the donees' labor or capital.[2]

---

[1] The statutory language stating the exclusion has varied little over the years. From 1913 to 1926, the statute referred to property acquired by "gift, bequest, devise or descent". In 1926, "descent" was replaced by "inheritance" because the latter "more appropriately [refers to] both real and personal property." S. Rep. No. 52, 69th Cong., 1st Sess. (1926), reprinted in 1939-1 (Part 2) CB 332, 347; H.R. Rep. No. 356, 69th Cong., 1st Sess. (1926), reprinted in 1939-1 (Part 2) CB 361, 364. Sections 102(a) and (b)(1) are slightly modified versions of the language in force since 1913. Section 102(b)(2) and the second sentence of §102(b) date from 1942; they are discussed in ¶10.4. The third sentence of §102(b), added in 1954, was not intended to effect a substantive change (H.R. Rep. No. 1337, 83d Cong., 2d Sess. A32 (1954)); it is discussed in ¶10.4. Section 102(c), which denies the §102 exclusion to transfers from employer to employee, was enacted in 1986 (Pub. L. No. 99-514, §122(b), 100 Stat. 2085); it is discussed in ¶10.2.3.

The 1894 federal income tax law, held unconstitutional in Pollock v. Farmers Loan & Trust Co., 158 US 429 (1895) (supra ¶1.2.2), defined income to include "money and the value of all personal property acquired by gift or inheritance." 28 Stat. 509, 553 (1893). Real property was excluded from the definition on the theory that a tax on a gift or devise of such property would be a direct tax requiring apportionment among the states under the direct tax clause of the Constitution, discussed in ¶1.2.2. See 26 Cong. Rec. 6820–25 (1894).

For convenience, the phrase "gifts and bequests" is sometimes used in the text as an abbreviation for "gift, bequest, devise, or inheritance."

[2] See, e.g., Magill, Taxable Income 406 (Ronald Press, rev. ed. 1945); Maguire, Capitalization of Periodical Payments by Gift, 34 Harv. L. Rev. 20, 21 n.8, 47 (1920); see also Wilner v. US, 195 F. Supp. 786, 788 n.7 (SDNY 1961). The direct tax theory was rejected in 1929 by Bromley v. McCaughn, 280 US 124 (1929), which upheld an unapportioned gift tax. By then, however, the income tax exclusion for gifts was deeply entrenched.

For more on the constitutionality of taxing gifts and bequests as income, see Federal Estate and Gift Taxes: Hearings Before the House Ways and Means Comm., 94th Cong., 2d Sess., Pt. 1, at 485 (1976) (statement of John K. McNulty); Sneed, The Configurations of Gross Income 131 n.4 (Ohio State U. Press 1967); Del Cotto, The Trust Annuity as Income: The Constitutional Problem of Taxing Gifts and

Quite aside from the constitutional question, taxing gifts and bequests as income might have seemed objectionable to the legislators because gratuitous receipts do not increase the aggregate stock of goods and services available for consumption but simply transfer wealth from one person to another. Thus, if (1) Smith inherits $100 from his parents, (2) he gives the legacy to his wife for Christmas, (3) she uses the funds to purchase a bicycle as a birthday gift for one of their children, and (4) the donee gives the bicycle to a younger brother or sister, an outside observer might doubt that this chain of events should be treated as creating $400 of income, even though each of the four participants experienced an accession to his or her wealth.

Once it is decided that gifts and bequests should not be taxable to both donor and donee, however, there remains the question of whether donor or donee is the proper taxpayer. The present system effectively taxes the donor by providing no deduction for gifts or bequests and explicitly exempts the donee. This system might be defended on the ground that ability to pay taxes is best measured by a taxpayer's command over goods and services and is not diminished by a taxpayer's voluntary decision to transfer some of this power to a donee. The difficulty with this argument is that it leads most comfortably to taxing both donor and donee because a gift or bequest bestows a power to consume on the donee and thus increases his ability to pay under this theory.

The alternative system (allowing the donor a deduction for gifts and bequests, and including them in the gross income of the donee) might be adopted on the theory that a person's actual consumption, not what he could have consumed,[3] is the best measure of the ability to pay taxes. This theory, however, is subject to the objection that it argues for the substitution of a consumption tax for the income tax, rather than delimiting the concept of income. Moreover, if gifts were taxed to the recipient, it would be necessary either to draw a line between taxable gifts and tax-free family support or to require the minor children and other members of a household to report the value of the right to occupy the family residence and dine at the family table.[4] Finally, the early legislators might have refrained from

---

Bequests as Income, 23 Tax L. Rev. 231 (1968); Klein, An Enigma in the Federal Income Tax: The Meaning of the Word "Gift," 48 Minn. L. Rev. 215 (1963).

[3] An adherent of this theory might find the present system acceptable, believing that (1) most gifts and bequests are made to close relatives, (2) the family is the appropriate taxpayer unit, and (3) donors, typically being senior members of their families, are acceptable taxpayer surrogates for the family unit. See Andrews, Personal Deductions in an Ideal Income Tax, 86 Harv. L. Rev. 309, 348–51 (1972).

[4] For the distinction between taxable gifts and tax-free support under the federal gift tax, see Rev. Rul. 68-379, 1968-2 CB 414; see also Surrey, Pathways to Tax Reform 286 n.6 (Harvard U. Press 1973); Klein, supra note 2, at 226 n.50; cf. Simons, Personal Income Taxation 135–36 (U. of Chicago Press 1938).

treating gifts and bequests as income lest amounts received irregularly or only once in a lifetime be taxed at a capriciously high rate.

These concerns are not overwhelmingly persuasive, and their force could be deflected by income averaging, exempting de minimis amounts and intraspousal transfers, and other measures. It is, however, easy to see why, when the income tax was still in its infancy, Congress might have wanted to avoid these issues by granting a blanket exclusion for gifts and bequests.

Many tax theorists have critized this legislative decision on the ground that a taxpayer's economic well-being is improved as much by a gift or bequest as by the fruits of his own labor or capital.[5] Most tax reformers, however, have avoided a direct assault on §102, preferring to push for peripheral changes in existing law (e.g., taxing unrealized appreciation when property is transferred by gift or at death) and for a separate system of taxing gratuitous receipts.[6] As a result, few provisions of existing law resemble their 1913 antecedents as much as §102.

Neither Congress nor the Treasury has promulgated a definition of the terms "gift," "bequest," "devise," and "inheritance," as used in §102. In practice, there has only been one major source of persistent difficulty in applying these terms: the fact that voluntary payments sometimes reflect affection or charitable impulses while simultaneously compensating the recipient for services previously rendered to the donor or testator. As will be seen, the courts have had great difficulty in determining when payments by employers to the families and estates of deceased employees are tax-free gifts rather than taxable compensation.[7] (Congress responded in 1986 by barring the application of the gift exclusion to any transfer to or for the

---

[5] See, e.g., Commission to Revise the Tax Structure, Reforming the Federal Tax Structure 18 (Fund for Public Policy Research 1973); 3 Report of the Royal Commission on Taxation ("Carter Commission Report") 467–519 (1966); Simons, supra note 4, at 56–58, 125–47; Dodge, Beyond Estate and Gift Tax Reform: Including Gifts and Bequests in Income, 91 Harv. L. Rev. 1177 (1978); McNulty, supra note 2. These critics, while subjecting gifts and bequests to income taxation, would simultaneously abolish the estate and gift taxes. But see Goode, The Individual Income Tax 98–100 (Brookings, rev. ed. 1976); Vickrey, Agenda for Progressive Taxation 198–202 (Ronald Press 1947).

[6] See, e.g., Break & Pechman, Federal Tax Reform: The Impossible Dream? 110–16 (Brookings 1975); Pechman, Federal Tax Policy 235 (Brookings, 5th ed. 1987); Surrey, supra note 4, at 19 n.7, citing Kurtz & Surrey, Reform of Death and Gift Taxes: The 1969 Treasury Proposals, the Criticisms, and a Rebuttal, 70 Colum. L. Rev. 1365 (1970).

The tax expenditure budget (supra ¶3.6) treats the exclusion of gifts and bequests as a structural feature of the federal income tax rather than as a tax expenditure. See U.S. Office of Management and Budget, Special Analyses, Budget of the United States Government, Fiscal Year 1977, Special Analysis F, at 116, 120 (1976).

[7] See infra ¶10.2.4.

benefit of an employee.) A similar problem of classification arises when an executor receives a "bequest" in lieu of the fees and commissions to which he would be entitled for administering the testator's estate.[8]

While excluding from gross income the value of property acquired by gift, bequest, devise, or inheritance, §102 does not exempt the income produced by the property after the transfer.[9] Were it not for this limitation, set out in §102(b)(1), the income from a family fortune would be immunized from tax for all time, once the property passed from the person who created the fortune to his donees or heirs. The application of §102(b)(1) is simple enough in the case of ordinary gifts of money or investment property; the recipient is not taxed on receipt, but must report income flowing from the property thereafter. The matter is more complex if the donor or testator creates divided interests in the property (e.g, income to *A* for life, remainder to *B*); the full benefit of the exclusion seemingly goes to the remainderman because the life tenant is required to report all of the income, even though he may be the primary target of the donor's generous impulse.[10]

If the subject of the gift or bequest is not money but securities, real estate, or other property, the new owner must ascertain his or her adjusted basis for the property in order to compute gain or loss on a subsequent sale, depreciation, if the property is a wasting asset used in the transferee's business, and other tax allowances. Although gifts and bequests are equally tax-free when received, they are subject to entirely different rules so far as basis is concerned. In the case of lifetime transfers, the donee, in general, takes over the donor's basis,[11] with the consequence that unrealized gain or loss accruing during the transferor's ownership can become taxable to the donee when the property is sold.

---

[8] See infra ¶10.3.2.

[9] IRC §102(b)(1).

[10] Infra ¶10.4. In fact, the §102 exclusion applies to the life beneficiary also; it is §102(a) that excludes the value of the life interest from gross income at the time this interest is created. Although the split-interest situation is more complex factually than an outright gift, the rules apply equally in both cases. Section 102(a) insulates a donee or legatee from tax when a gift or bequest is made. Under the basis rules described in the immediately following paragraph of the text, a subsequent tax-free recovery is allowed equal to the donor's investment in the property (in the case of a gift) or the value of the property when transferred (in the case of a bequest). Everything else is taxed when realized according to the normal tax realization rules. If a life beneficiary is mistreated, it is by the rule that assigns to the remainderman the entire benefit of the property's basis. If a portion of the basis were given to the life beneficiary, however, a special computational mechanism would be needed for amortizing this basis against receipts that would otherwise be taxable, a procedure that would be complex and would effect a partial deferral of the taxes that would be imposed if the property were held outright by one person.

[11] IRC §1015, discussed infra ¶41.3.1.

The status of inherited property in the hands of the decedent's estate and heirs, however, is quite different. Property received by will or intestate succession, along with nonprobate property included in the decedent's gross estate for federal estate tax purposes, takes a new basis equal to the property's value on the date of death.[12] The new basis is often called a "stepped-up" basis because the date of death value in a period of inflation and economic growth is usually higher than the decedent's own basis, but a stepped-down basis is also possible. In either event, the decedent's unrealized gain or loss (the difference between his basis and the value of the property at his death) is disregarded for income tax purposes. In 1976, Congress undertook a brief flirtation with a rule requiring a decedent's estate and heirs to use the decedent's basis, with certain adjustments, in many situations. The change was controversial, and Congress' enthusiasm for it quickly waned; the carryover basis rules were repealed in 1980, and the old date of death rules were reinstated.[13]

The rules prescribing the basis of transferred property are subject to important qualifications, which are discussed in detail in a later chapter.[14]

¶10.2 EXCLUSION OF GIFTS FROM GROSS INCOME

¶10.2.1 Introductory

Neither Congress nor the Treasury has ever promulgated a definition of the term "gift" as used in §102(a), preferring to leave the task of interpreting the naked statutory language to the courts. In *CIR v. Duberstein*, decided in 1960, the Supreme Court also declined to announce a comprehensive definition. It summarized the decisional law as follows:

> The Government suggests that we promulgate a new "test" in this area [namely, that gifts are "transfers of property made for personal as distinguished from business reasons"] to serve as a standard to be applied by the lower courts and by the Tax Court in dealing with the numerous cases that arise. We reject this invitation. We are of [the] opinion that the governing principles are necessarily general and have already been spelled out in the opinions of this Court, and that the problem is one which, under the present statutory framework, does not lend itself to any more definitive statement that would produce a talisman for the solution of concrete cases. . . .

---

[12] IRC §1014, discussed infra ¶41.4.1.
[13] See supra ¶5.2; infra ¶41.5.
[14] Infra ¶¶41.3.1, 41.4.1.

The course of decision here makes it plain that the statute does not use the term "gift" in the common-law sense, but in a more colloquial sense. This Court has indicated that a voluntary executed transfer of his property by one to another, without any consideration or compensation therefor, though a common-law gift, is not necessarily a "gift" within the meaning of the statute. For the Court has shown that the mere absence of a legal or moral obligation to make such a payment does not establish that it is a gift. . . . And, importantly, if the payment proceeds primarily from "the constraining force of any moral or legal duty," or from "the incentive of anticipated benefit" of an economic nature, . . . it is not a gift. And, conversely, "where the payment is in return for services rendered, it is irrelevant that the donor derives no economic benefit from it." . . . A gift in the statutory sense, on the other hand, proceeds from a "detached and disinterested generosity," . . . "out of affection, respect, admiration, charity or like impulses." . . . And in this regard, the most critical consideration . . . is the transferor's "intention." . . . "What controls is the intention with which payment, however voluntary, has been made."[1]

The Court went on to comment on a series of principles or presumptions offered by the government in support of its proposed test:

The Government derives its test from such propositions as the following: That payments by an employer to an employee, even though voluntary, ought, by and large, to be taxable; that the concept of a gift is inconsistent with a payment's being a deductible business expense; that a gift involves "personal" elements; that a business corporation cannot properly make a gift of its assets. The Government admits that there are exceptions and qualifications to these propositions. We think,

---

[1] CIR v. Duberstein, 363 US 278, 284–86 (1960) (citations omitted). The earlier cases cited by the Court as spelling out the governing principles are Old Colony Trust Co. v. CIR, 279 US 716 (1929) (corporation's payment of income taxes on officer's salary was taxable compensation, not tax-free gift); Bogardus v. CIR, 302 US 34 (1937) (selling shareholders directed payment of about $600,000 of the sales proceeds as "a gift or honorarium" to 64 employees and other associates of their company in appreciation of their loyalty; held (four Justices dissenting), payments, stemming from "spontaneous generosity," were tax-free gifts); Robertson v. US, 343 US 711 (1952) (composer taxed on $25,000 award for best symphonic work by native-born composer; payment was "for services rendered" even though donor derived no economic benefit therefrom); and CIR v. LoBue, 351 US 243 (1956) (employee realized income on exercising stock option granted in recognition of his contribution to employer's success — "none of the earmarks of a gift" were present, and "company was not giving something away for nothing").

For a review of the pre-*Duberstein* cases, see Chommie, Payments to Employees: Gifts of Compensation for Services, 31 Taxes 620 (1953).

to the extent they are correct, that these propositions are not principles of law but rather maxims of experience that the tribunals which have tried the facts of cases in this area have enunciated in explaining their factual determinations. Some of them simply represent truisms; it doubtless is, statistically speaking, the exceptional payment by an employer to an employee that amounts to a gift. Others are overstatements of possible evidentiary inferences relevant to a factual determination on the totality of circumstances in the case: it is doubtless relevant to the overall inference that the transferor treats a payment as a business deduction, or that the transferor is a corporate entity. But these inferences cannot be stated in absolute terms. Neither factor is a shibboleth. The taxing statute does not make nondeductibility by the transferor a condition on the "gift" exclusion;[2] nor does it draw any distinction, in terms, between transfers by corporations and individuals, as to the availability of the "gift" exclusion to the transferee. The conclusion whether a transfer amounts to a "gift" is one that must be reached on consideration of all the factors.[3]

The Court's concern with "all the factors" resulted in its placing great weight on the conclusions of the trial court and narrowing the range of appellate review:

> The nontechnical nature of the statutory standard, the close relationship of it to the data of practical human experience, and the multiplicity of relevant factual elements, with their various combinations, creating the necessity of ascribing the proper force to each, confirm us in our conclusion that primary weight in this area must be given to the conclusions of the trier of fact. . . .
> One consequence of this is that appellate review determinations in this field must be quite restricted. Where a jury has tried the matter upon correct instructions, the only inquiry is whether it cannot be said that reasonable men could reach differing conclusions on the issue. . . . Where the trial has been by a judge without a jury, the

---

[2] When *Duberstein* was decided in 1960, the Code did not connect the transferor's right to deduct the payment with the transferee's right to exclude it from gross income as a gift. In 1962, however, §274(b) was enacted, limiting the transferor's deduction for "business gifts" to $25 for any donee during a taxable year. The treatment of the transferor under §274(b) follows from the treatment of the transferee, however, not vice versa. See infra ¶21.3.1. See Abdella v. CIR, 46 TCM (CCH) 1602 (1983) (exclusion allowed for payment to employee by major stockholders of employer upon profitable sale of corporate stock; that payors deducted payment does not preclude exclusion if payment "in fact a gift").

[3] CIR v. Duberstein, supra note 1, at 287–88.

judge's findings must stand unless "clearly erroneous."[4]

Finally, the Court applied these principles to the facts of the two cases under review. In *Duberstein* itself, the Tax Court held that a Cadillac automobile received by the taxpayer from a businessman to whom he had occasionally given the names of potential customers was not a tax-free gift under §102(a), even though the taxpayer insisted that the transferor "owed him [nothing]" and the latter said that the car was "a present." The Tax Court's judgment was reversed by the court of appeals but was reinstated by the Supreme Court:

> [I]t cannot be said that the conclusion of the Tax Court was "clearly erroneous." It seems to us plain that as trier of the facts it was warranted in concluding that despite the characterization of the transfer of the Cadillac by the parties and the absence of any obligation, even of a moral nature, to make it, it was at bottom a recompense for Duberstein's past services, or an inducement for him to be of further service in the future. We cannot say with the Court of Appeals that such a conclusion was "mere suspicion" on the Tax Court's part. To us it appears based in the sort of informed experience with human affairs that fact-finding tribunals should bring to this task.[5]

The Court had more difficulty with a companion case (*Stanton v. United States*), which involved an employee of a church's real estate subsidiary who received a "gratuity" of $20,000 on resigning to enter business for himself. The trial court held that the transfer was a gift, but the court of appeals reversed, noting that there was "no evidence that personal affection enter[ed] into the payment." The appellate court also noted that the resolution authorizing the payment required the employee to release any pension and retirement benefits, even though there was undisputed testimony that this proviso reflected an abundance of caution because the employee had no such rights.[6] Two Justices agreed with the appellate court's judgment that the payment was taxable, while two others wanted to reinstate the trial court's judgment that it was a tax-free gift. A majority of the Court voted to remand the case to the trial court for further findings because the simple conclusion that the transfer was a gift made it impossible to determine

---

[4] Id. at 289–91. See Griswold, Foreword: Of Time and Attitudes — Professor Hart and Judge Arnold, 74 Harv. L. Rev. 81, 88–91 (1960) (criticizing *Duberstein* for "excessive deference to the triers of fact" and for failing to provide a more reliable guide for tax planners).

[5] CIR v. Duberstein, supra note 1, at 291–92.

[6] Stanton v. US, 268 F2d 727 (2d Cir. 1959), vacated and remanded, 363 US 278 (1960).

whether the trial court had applied the proper legal standards to the facts.[7] On remand, the district court made detailed findings of fact, again concluding that the payment was a gift, and its judgment was affirmed on appeal on the ground that the findings were not clearly erroneous.[8]

As the foregoing extracts from the *Duberstein* case suggest, the common law meaning of the term "gift" has not played a significant role in judicial interpretations of §102(a). The common law elements of an effective gift (donative intent, delivery, and acceptance),[9] although ordinarily present in transfers that satisfy §102(a), are rarely missing in the disputed cases. These traditional requirements, developed in order to confirm the transferor's intent to rid himself of the property, are used primarily to determine whether property was effectively transferred during the owner's life or continued to be owned by him until death so as to form part of his probate estate.[10] In federal tax cases, however, the effectiveness of the transfer is ordinarily conceded;[11] the issue is not whether the transferee owns the property but whether the circumstances of acquisition constitute a gift within the meaning of §102(a).

In addition to holding that §102(a) does not use the term gift in its common law sense, the courts have held that the statutory term does not necessarily have the same meaning that it has for federal estate and gift tax purposes. This inspired Judge Jerome N. Frank to suggest that the terms "gift," "gaft," and "geft" might be used to denote the separate income, gift, and estate tax usages.[12]

---

[7] CIR v. Duberstein, supra note 1, at 292–93.

[8] Stanton v. US, 186 F. Supp. 393 (EDNY 1960), aff'd per curiam, 287 F2d 876, 877 (2d Cir. 1961). Compare Ruestow v. CIR, 37 TCM (CCH) 639 (1978), aff'd, 79-1 USTC ¶9173 (2d Cir. 1979) (severance pay taxable where payment was in part motivated by employer's desire to retain employee's goodwill and to create impression that it was a good firm to work for).

[9] See Edson v. Lucas, 40 F2d 398 (8th Cir. 1930); 7 Powell, The Law of Real Property ¶971A (Rohan, rev. ed. 1976).

[10] See generally Gulliver & Tilson, Classification of Gratuitous Transfers, 51 Yale L J 1 (1941).

[11] Occasionally, however, it is necessary to determine *when* a transfer that was effected in several steps became an effective gift. For example, if the property is sold, it must be known whether the transferor made a gift of property, which was subsequently sold by the transferee, or sold the property and then made a gift of the proceeds. In situations of this type, the date when the common law requirements were satisfied may be significant. See Edson v. Lucas, supra note 9; Merner v. CIR, 32 BTA 658 (nonacq.), appeal dismissed per curiam, 79 F2d 985 (9th Cir. 1935) (gift made before December 31, 1920, the effective date of the statutory predecessor of §1015); see also Eaton v. CIR, 36 TCM (CCH) 354 (1977) (transferor lacked mental capacity to make gift; hence, §102 not applicable and taxpayer taxable on receipts).

[12] See Farid-Es-Sultaneh v. CIR, 160 F2d 812 (2d Cir. 1947) (concerned with "gift" as used by §1015, but presumably same approach would apply to §102); CIR v. Beck's Est., 129 F2d 243 (2d Cir. 1942) ("gift," "gaft," and "geft").

The overwhelming bulk of disputes in this area is concentrated in a few areas that are discussed further below.

¶10.2.2 Tips

For many years, Treasury regulations have provided that tips must be included in gross income, and the courts have sustained this rule.[13] The basic principle (which is broad enough to embrace honoraria received by professors and marriage fees contributed to clergymen) is well established, and most disputes in this area involve the validity of estimates by the IRS of the amount received by hotel and restaurant employees, taxi drivers, and other persons failing to keep accurate records of their receipts.[14]

Recipients of tips almost always regard them as a normal component of their compensation, but the emphasis in the *Duberstein* case on the intention of the transferor suggests that a tip could qualify as a tax-free gift on proof that the patron was motivated by "detached and disinterested generosity" rather than by a desire to pay for services or avoid an embarrassing insult.[15] In practice, however, taxpayers in jobs where tips are customary have rarely tried to divide their receipts between taxable tips and tax-free gifts, probably in tacit acknowledgment that pure generosity is seldom encountered in this setting and, even when it occurs, is difficult to prove.[16]

If the link between the parties is not the rendition of services by one to the other in a context normally calling for tips, there is a stronger case for excluding the payment under §102(a), but it is still far from conclusive. Thus, the courts have determined that "tokes" or "side money" given by successful gamblers to casino dealers is gross income despite the argument

---

[13] Reg. §1.61-2(a)(1); see Reg. 45, Art. 32, which dates from 1919; Roberts v. CIR, 176 F2d 221 (9th Cir. 1949) (1943 regulation upheld). Marriage fees and other contributions received by a clergyman for services are also viewed as gross income under §1.61-2(a)(1) of the regulations, the antecedent of which is Reg. 45, Art. 32 (prelim. ed.).

[14] See infra ¶107.1 (indirect methods of computing income).

For employers' problems in this area, see infra ¶111.1.9 (requirements for employer reporting of employees' tips) ¶111.4.2 (application of wage withholding to tips).

[15] See Roberts v. CIR, supra note 13 (history of tipping; "there is an element of compulsion in tipping"); US v. McCormick, 67 F2d 867 (2d Cir. 1933), cert. denied, 291 US 662 (1934) (tax evasion conviction of city clerk for failing to report "contributions" by bridegrooms wanting to obtain marriage certificates promptly and without embarrassment; some payments "were practically extorted"). See also Killoran v. CIR, 42 TCM (CCH) 1662 (1981), aff'd, 709 F2d 31 (9th Cir. 1983) (rejecting cabdriver's argument that tips must be gifts because state statute forbade driver from charging more than amount shown on meter).

[16] But see Johnson v. CIR, 31 TCM (CCH) 884 (1972) (transfer from elderly person to nurse was gift, excludable under §102).

that the dealers' services are performed in an impartial and impersonal fashion precluding the rendition of favors to the patrons who reward them.[17] If the payments are not made to reward or elicit special treatment or to avoid embarrassment, a test that focuses on the attitude of the payor tends to weight the scales in favor of tax-free gifts; on the other hand, it is obvious that the recipient views them as supplemental compensation, although from a sporadic source.

The same tension is characteristic of birthday and Christmas "gifts" received by entertainers and other public personalities from their fans. The donors get no special services since the same performance is rendered to the entire audience. The performers, however, surely consider the receipts a welcome supplement to their regular compensation—a perquisite of stardom.[18] In some situations, it may be possible to classify the patrons by motive, treating some as generous donors of tax-free gifts and the others as customers paying for services. In deciding, for example, whether a union official was taxable on the profits of a testimonial dinner in his honor (sponsored by his union and financed by selling banquet tickets and advertising in a souvenir program to trade associations and employers in the same industry, lawyers and physicians associated with the union, and fellow employees and friends), the Tax Court distinguished between participants who purchased banquet tickets and advertising for business reasons and those who did so out of friendship and affection. It concluded that about 20 percent of the amount received reflected tax-free gifts and that the balance was includable in gross income.[19]

---

[17] See Olk v. US, 536 F2d 876 (9th Cir.), cert. denied, 429 US 920 (1976) (payments taxable because "contributed by those with whom the taxpayers have some personal or functional contact in the course of performance of . . . services"); Bevers v. CIR, 26 TC 1218 (1956) (dealer taxed on winning bets made for him by patrons; profit "came to him in his capacity of dealer, and therefore, we can only conclude that it represented gains derived from his labor as a dealer"; no reference in opinion to intent of patrons).

[18] See Webber v. CIR, 219 F2d 834, 836 (10th Cir. 1955) (radio minister taxed on amounts received in response to solicitation; although amounts were larger on taxpayer's birthday and wedding anniversary, there was "no evidence tending to show that the contributions were referred to [by the contributors] as gifts; or that any of the contributors knew the petitioners personally or had any personal relationship with them that would form the basis for personal gifts as distinguished from contributions to the perpetuation of the programs that the contributors enjoyed and desired to support financially"); Publishers New Press, Inc. v. CIR, 42 TC 396 (1964) (acq.) (newspaper taxed on contributions solicited from readers to continue publication).

[19] Kralstein v. CIR, 38 TC 810 (1962) (acq.); see also Wright v. CIR, 30 TC 392 (1958) (acq.) (funds raised by testimonial dinner sponsored by Japanese community to honor lawyer who represented Japanese alien without fee in case testing constitutionality of California alien land acts; held, tax-free gift).

¶10.2.3 Payments to Employees and Other Providers of Services

Section 102(c)(1), added in 1986, provides that a transfer from employer to employee cannot qualify for exclusion under §102(a). Before enactment of this provision, payments to employees and others providing services to the putative donors were a fertile ground for litigation under §102(a). The pre-1986 case law is described first below, and the 1986 statute is discussed thereafter.

1. *Pre-1986 case law.* *Stanton v. United States*, decided as a companion case with *Duberstein*, involved a "gratuity" paid by an employer to an employee resigning to enter business for himself; as described above, the Supreme Court was divided on the proper treatment of the payment.[20] This division has been characteristic of the judicial response to payments to employees at or after retirement—payments that would not have been made except for the employee's faithful services, but that are often also motivated by personal affection and esteem. In an early case, *Bogardus v. CIR*, involving bonuses paid by the acquiring corporation in a reorganization to 64 former and current employees of the acquired corporation in gratitude for their aid in building up the business, a majority of the Supreme Court held that the payments were excludable from gross income because they were neither intended to compensate for past or future services nor paid under legal or other compulsion, but stemmed instead from "spontaneous generosity."[21] Four dissenting Justices would have remanded the case to the trial court to determine whether the payments were made "with the intention that services rendered in the past shall be requited more completely" or "to show good will, esteem, or kindliness toward persons who happen to have served, but who are paid without thought to make requital for the services." In their view, the payment was exempt only if the payor's intention met the latter standard.

The Supreme Court later observed that the difference between the majority and dissenters in *Bogardus* lay more in the weight given to the trial court's findings of fact than in disagreement about the relevant substantive principles.[22] Since *Duberstein*, the courts have focused on the employer's

---

[20] Supra ¶10.2.1.

[21] Bogardus v. CIR, 302 US 34 (1937). See also Goethals v. US, 147 F. Supp. 757 (Ct. Cl. 1957), and Dewling v. US, 101 F. Supp. 892 (Ct. Cl. 1952), involving annuities granted by Congress to military personnel and civilians who had worked on construction of the Panama Canal. A civilian recipient was allowed to exclude the payments in *Dewling* because the court determined the annuity to be "a token of gratitude for services faithfully rendered." In *Goethals*, however, the exclusion was denied to a retired army officer; *Dewling* was distinguished "on the ground of the remoteness of the payment," which was not authorized until 1944.

[22] CIR v. Duberstein, 363 US 278, 286, 289 ns. 9, 11 (1960).

intent, but there have been few cases,[23] perhaps because §274(b) limits the payor's deduction to a maximum of $25 if a payment is excludable from the recipient's income as a gift.[24] Since this restriction is of no concern to tax-exempt organizations (unless the employment is in activities generating unrelated business taxable income), a few cases continue to arise in this sector.[25]

Perhaps on the supposition that members of religious communities have a special affection for their spiritual shepherds, the IRS ruled in 1955 that payments by congregations to retiring clergymen are excludable gifts if the following requirements are met: (1) The payment must not be made pursuant to an enforceable agreement, established plan, or past practice; (2) the recipient must not undertake to perform further services for the congregation and must not be expected to do so; (3) there must be a closer personal relationship between the recipient and the congregation than is characteristic of secular employment; (4) the amount paid must be determined in light of the congregation's financial position and the recipient's needs; and (5) the pastor must already have been adequately compensated for past services.[26]

The IRS once allowed an exclusion for "the value of a turkey, ham or other item of merchandise of similar nominal value, distributed by an employer to an employee at Christmas, or a comparable holiday, as part of a general distribution to employees engaged in the business of the employer as a means of promoting their good will."[27] The exclusion was allowed "in view

---

[23] An employee succeeded in Brimm v. CIR, 27 TCM (CCH) 1148 (1968) (payment by school on ceasing operations "in appreciation and recognition of [professor's] past services and achievements"). The exclusion was denied, in contrast, in Nattrass v. CIR, 33 TCM (CCH) 1389 (1974) ("severance payments" by dissolved corporation's parent to subsidiary's employees); Rev. Rul. 76-516, 1976-2 CB 24 (payments to retired volunteer firemen or widows); Rev. Rul. 72-342, 1972-2 CB 36 (on merger, successor corporation paid part of dissolved corporation's surplus to officers dropped from payroll).

[24] For §274(b), see infra ¶21.3.

[25] See, e.g., Sweeney's Est. v. CIR, 39 TCM (CCH) 201 (1979) (retired physician-founder taxable on amounts received from camp for diabetic children, although directors were circularized and asked to state whether payments were authorized to compensate past services or "to show good will, esteem or kindness," and all checked latter alternative).

[26] Rev. Rul. 55-422, 1955-1 CB 14. But see Perkins v. CIR, 34 TC 117 (1960) (payments to retired minister by a conference of churches to which several congregations contributed; requirements of Rev. Rul. 55-422 not met).

[27] Rev. Rul. 59-58, 1959-1 CB 17. The ruling goes on to hold that the cost of these items is deductible by the employer as a business expense under §162.

In addition to acknowledging that the employer can be Santa Claus, the IRS ruled that amounts contributed by an employer for the rehabilitation of employees suffering personal injury or property damage as the result of a tornado are not

of the small amounts involved, and since it may reasonably be contended in many cases that such items constitute excludable gifts." The IRS position has subsequently been codified in part and superseded in whole. In 1984 and 1986, Congress enacted a detailed set of rules on employee fringe benefits that provide limited exclusions for such benefits (including an exclusion for de minimis benefits such as the Christmas turkey), but further state that fringe benefits not explicitly excluded are gross income.[28] Also, §102(c)(1), discussed immediately below, precludes these items from being excluded as gifts.

2. *Statutory rule.* Section 102(c)(1) states that the §102(a) exclusion is inapplicable to "any amount transferred by or for an employer to, or for the benefit of, an employee."[29] The legislative history of the provision is scant.[30] It is intended to bar the exclusion for any transfer arising out of the employment relationship.

The existence of such a relationship, however, does not preclude an exclusion if the motivation for the transfer is extraneous to the employment relationship. The House committee report states: "Of course, gifts between individuals made exclusively for personal reasons (such as birthday presents) that are wholly unrelated to an employment relationship are not includible in the recipient's gross income merely because the gift-giver is the employer of the recipient."[31] This concession, however, was intended as only the smallest of openings. The reference to "gifts between individuals" is probably meant to imply that a transfer by an entity cannot qualify unless it is made on behalf of a shareholder or partner in his personal capacity, where it would be treated as having first been distributed by the entity to the shareholder or partner and then transferred by the shareholder or partner to the donee. Also, "a transfer between personal acquaintances will not be considered to have been made exclusively for personal reasons if reflecting any employment-related reason (e.g., gratitude for services rendered) or any anticipation of business benefit."[32] The report notes, finally, that a transfer

---

taxable to the employees if the payments are measured by need rather than by services rendered or length of service. Rev. Rul. 131, 1953-2 CB 112.

[28] See supra ¶14.1 for the fringe benefit rules.

[29] Section 102(c)(1) applies to transfers after December 31, 1986. Pub. L. No. 99-514, §§122(b), 151(c), 100 Stat. 2085 (1986).

[30] It was enacted together with a provision allowing an exclusion for certain employee achievement awards (see infra ¶14.1), and the purpose was apparently to make the achievement award rules the exclusive means of obtaining exclusion for a payment given in appreciation of an employee's services. See P.L. No. 99-514, supra note 29, at §112(a).

[31] H.R. Rep. No. 426, 99th Cong., 2d Sess. 106 n.5 (1986), reprinted in 1986-3 CB (vol.3) 1, 106 n.5.

[32] Id.

to an employee qualifying as an excludable gift cannot be deductible by the employer.

The statutory rule does not apply to transfers to persons providing services in a capacity other than as employee, and the pre-1986 jurisprudence continues to apply in these cases.[33]

¶10.2.4 Employee Death Benefits

Upon the death of an employee, employers sometimes pay death benefits to the decedent's surviving spouse and children. As in the case of transfers to employees in appreciation of their services, these payments may reflect personal affection, but simultaneously serve to acknowledge the employee's services. Before *CIR v. Duberstein*, death benefits were usually excluded from gross income as gifts under §102(a), partly under the influence of an IRS ruling that authorized the employer to deduct a "salary" paid to an employee's "widow or heirs, in recognition of the services rendered" by the decedent, but also allowed the recipient to exclude the payment from gross income.[34] In *Hellstrom's Estate v. CIR*, a leading pre-*Duberstein* case, the court concluded that the corporate employer's "principal motive" in paying benefits to a deceased employee's widow was a "desire to do an act of kindness" for her. The court found five factors to be controlling:

> [T]he payment was made to petitioner and not to her husband's estate; . . . there was no obligation on the part of the corporation to pay any additional compensation to petitioner's husband; it derived no benefit from the payment; petitioner performed no services for the corporation and . . . those of her husband had been fully compensated for.[35]

After *Duberstein* the Tax Court, concluding that the Supreme Court had adopted a more restrictive construction of the term "gift," made "an abrupt swerve"[36] toward taxability, while the federal district courts, believ-

---

[33] See Rev. Rul. 87-119, 1987-46 IRB 10 (volunteer worker on political campaign taxed on cash award from campaign).

[34] IT 3329, 1939-2 CB 153, modified by IT 4027, 1950-2 CB 9 ("the essential factor [in excluding payments from gross income] is whether services were rendered to the employer, not, as indicated in IT 3329, . . . whether services were rendered by the recipient"). The Tax Court relied on IT 3329 in Aprill v. CIR, 13 TC 707 (1949) (acq., later withdrawn), to exclude payments to a widow; but it refused to follow IT 4027 in Hellstrom's Est. v. CIR, infra note 35.

[35] Hellstrom's Est. v. CIR, 24 TC 916, 920 (1955). Accord, Luntz v. CIR, 29 TC 647 (1957) (acq.) (payment to widow of amount equivalent to two years' salary of deceased corporate officer held to be tax-free gift).

[36] Carter's Est. v. CIR, 453 F2d 61, 65 (2d Cir. 1971). One judge dissented from the reversal of the Tax Court in *Carter's Estate*, arguing that *Duberstein* required

ing that the *Hellstrom* five-factor test was consistent with *Duberstein*, continued to apply it. In an extended review of the post-*Duberstein* cases, the Court of Appeals for the Second Circuit observed that as of 1971, "the Tax Court seems to have found almost uniformly that payments to survivors constituted income" except in "unusual circumstances demonstrating compassion," but that the federal district courts have "rather consistently" found such payments to be gifts unless the corporation was dominated by the decedent's family, or there was a plan (whether formal or informal) for making such payments, or the payments were characterized by the employer as compensation.[37] Of particular importance to closely held corporations is the possibility that when payments are made to persons owning (directly or by inheritance) a controlling block of stock, the transaction may be treated as a constructive dividend.[38]

Since death benefits paid to a deceased employee's beneficiaries or estate are excludable from the recipient's gross income under §101(b) up to $5,000,[39] the protection accorded to gifts by §102(a) is only needed for amounts in excess of $5,000. If the recipient successfully invokes §102(a) to exclude the excess over $5,000, the employer's deduction is largely denied by §274(b), which limits deductions for business gifts to $25 annually per payee.[40] The employer thus may buttress its claim for a deduction by explicitly characterizing the payment as additional compensation. While neither the label nor the claim of a deduction is conclusive, a corporate resolution or letter couched in terms of compensation inevitably weakens the recipient's case for exclusion under §102(a).[41]

---

greater deference to the trial court, even at the cost of disparities between one trial court and another. See also the Fifth Circuit's review of the post-*Duberstein* cases in Jensen v. US, 511 F2d 265 (5th Cir. 1975), commenting that the five factors listed in *Hellstrom* and reiterated in Poyner v. CIR, 301 F2d 287 (4th Cir. 1962), are neither the only relevant factors in determining whether a transfer is a gift nor of equal relevance in all cases.

[37] Carter's Est. v. CIR, supra note 36, at 66–67. For the significance of control of a corporate employer by the recipient of the payment, see Poyner v. CIR, supra note 36 (payment may be tantamount to taxable dividend); see also Jensen v. US, supra note 36 (plan as denoting taxable payment); Pearson v. US, 519 F2d 1279 (4th Cir. 1975) (same).

[38] Poyner v. CIR, supra note 36.

[39] For §101(b), see infra ¶12.6. The IRS formerly asserted that the explicit exclusion of $5,000 by §101(b) manifested, by negative pregnant, a legislative intent to deny recourse to §102(a) for any excess over $5,000, but this position, after being rejected by the courts, was withdrawn by the IRS, as explained in ¶12.6.5.

[40] See infra ¶21.3.1.

[41] Compare Carter's Est. v. CIR, 453 F2d 61, 65 (2d Cir. 1971) (exclusion of death benefits from gross income) with Bank of Palm Beach & Trust Co. v. US, 476 F2d 1343 (Ct. Cl. 1973) (deduction by *Carter* employer allowed for year before §274(b) enacted).

The excludability of these payments is apparently unaffected by §102(c)(1), added in 1986, which denies the §102(a) exclusion to any payment by "an employer to, or for the benefit of, an employee." If a payment to survivors is not pursuant to an agreement or plan existing while the employee lived—a condition probably prerequisite to even a colorable claim for exclusion under §102(a)—the payment can hardly be said to be for the employee's benefit.

¶10.2.5 Employer, Governmental, and Institutional Charity

In *Duberstein*, the Supreme Court quoted with approval from an earlier decision that described "gifts" for purposes of §102(a) as payments generated by "affection, respect, admiration, *charity* or like impulses."[42] In most of the litigated cases described above, the taxpayer relied primarily on a claim that the payment was motivated by affection, respect, or admiration rather than by "charity." When the facts sustain an inference of charitable benevolence, however, the taxpayer's case is substantially enhanced. These instances of tax-free institutional charity include benefits provided by both private and public benefactors.

Whether a particular payment is motivated by charity, however, is often not obvious. For example, if employees are assisted through difficult days by strike benefits paid by their union, the tax status of the payments depends on the relative weight of imponderables similar to those that before 1986, determined whether payments by the employer were taxable. On the one hand, unions pay benefits to their members (and sometimes to nonmembers) to insure solidarity and reduce defections from the cause—objectives that point toward taxability; on the other hand, the motivation may be compassion, which is a hallmark of a tax-free gift. In *United States v. Kaiser*, a companion case to *Duberstein*, the Supreme Court was concerned with a union's payment of rent and food vouchers to striking workers who established a need for aid. The taxpayer received assistance before joining the union and without being expected to picket the employer. Although he subsequently joined and engaged in picketing, the trial court found that the union had not encouraged either action.[43]

A jury found that the payments were gifts. The Supreme Court declined "to speculate as to what conclusion we would have drawn had we sat in the jury box," and held that the jury could properly have concluded that the "assistance, rendered as it was to a class of persons in the community in economic need, proceeded primarily from generosity or charity, rather than

---

[42] CIR v. Duberstein, 363 US 278, 285 (1960) (emphasis added).
[43] US v. Kaiser, 363 US 299 (1960).

from the incentive of anticipated economic benefit."[44] A later Tax Court case holding strike benefits taxable summarized the factors to be considered as follows:

> whether the union calling the strike was under a moral or legal obligation to make the payments; whether the payments were made upon a consideration of the recipient's financial status and need, and as a corollary, whether the benefits continued during the strike regardless of whether the recipient worked elsewhere; whether the recipient was a member of the striking union; whether the payments required the recipient to perform any strike duties such as picketing, and if not, whether or to what extent the recipient was under a moral obligation to participate in such strike activities; and finally, whether any restrictions were placed on the use of the payments, particularly in regard to whether the benefits were restricted to payment of basic necessities such as food and shelter or whether the recipient had unfettered control over use of the funds.[45]

A broad range of governmental disbursements made "in the interest of the general welfare" has been excluded from gross income, including social security benefits, disaster relief, and payments to families with low income or to persons who are elderly or disabled.[46] (The exclusion for social security

---

[44] Id. at 304 (opinion by Mr. Justice Brennan, in which three other Justices joined). A concurring opinion by Mr. Justice Frankfurter, with one other Justice, extensively reviewed earlier IRS rulings involving subsistence aid, rejected the taxpayer's contention that these rulings required an exclusion of strike benefits, and concluded that while the question was "very close," there was sufficient evidence to support the theory that the union was engaged in "a wholly charitable function" in making the payments.

[45] Colwell v. CIR, 64 TC 584, 587 (1975) (union's payments to nonmember honoring picket line, in amount based on wages, included in gross income). See Hagar v. CIR, 43 TC 468, 485 (1965) (strike benefits to enable union members to continue the strike held taxable); Rev. Rul. 61-136, 1961-2 CB 20 (strike payments in cases similar to *Kaiser* are gifts).

[46] One ruling suggests that exclusion is appropriate whenever a government makes payments "from a general welfare fund in the interest of the general welfare." Rev. Rul. 76-144, 1976-1 CB 17. See Rev. Rul. 78-170, 1978-1 CB 24 (state financed credits against winter energy bills of elderly low-income individuals); Rev. Rul. 76-373, 1976-2 CB 16 (urban relocation payments); Rev. Rul. 76-229, 1976-1 CB 19 (payments to workers who are unemployed because of foreign competition); Rev. Rul. 76-144, supra (federal payments to needy victims of major disasters); Rev. Rul. 74-153, 1974-1 CB 20 (state payments to adoptive parents, based on financial need); Rev. Rul. 74-74, 1974-1 CB 18 (victims of crime); Rev. Rul. 73-87, 1973-1 CB 39 (federally funded experimental antipoverty program); Rev. Rul. 70-217, 1970-1 CB 12 (social security benefits); Rev. Rul. 68-158, 1968-1 CB 47 (state bonuses to veterans); Rev. Rul. 57-102, 1957-1 CB 26 (payment by state to blind persons).

benefits has been partially eliminated by statute.)[47] Also, several rulings hold
that payments compensating taxpayers for invasions of personal rights (e.g.,
Nazi persecution) are excludable from gross income, not because the payments manifest a charitable impulse but because they merely make the
taxpayer whole by remedying an injury.[48]

In a series of pre-1978 rulings, the IRS exempted federal and state
unemployment benefits from tax but held that benefits under private plans
are taxable to the extent they exceed the recipient's contributions.[49] In 1978,

---

Compare Rev. Rul. 76-75, 1976-1 CB 14 (federal payment of mortgage interest
owed by limited-profit corporation on low-income housing project is gross income)
with Rev. Rul. 75-271, 1975-2 CB 23 (federal payment of mortgage interest of low-
income families excluded).

But see Foley v. CIR, 87 TC 605, 609 (1986) (payments by West Berlin government to persons living and working in the city, made under law designed to encourage residence and employment in city, are gross income because "not predicated
on need [or] made in furtherance of a social program sponsored by the United
States"); Rev. Rul. 85-39, 1985-1 CB 21 (payments by State of Alaska to its residents
out of state's mineral income are gross income; payments not general welfare payments because not "restricted to those in need"); Rev. Rul. 76-230, 1976-1 CB 19
(payments under IRS work-study program taxable); Rev. Rul. 62-179, 1962-2 CB 20
(benefits in the nature of social security received from foreign governments are gross
income absent treaty provision to contrary).

Sometimes the IRS giveth with one hand and taketh away with the other. If an
excludable government benefit compensates the taxpayer for medical expenses or
casualty losses, the tax benefit of the exclusion is offset by a denial of deductions
under §165(c)(3) (casualty losses) and §213 (medical expenses) on the ground that
these items have been compensated for "by insurance or otherwise." See Rev. Rul.
76-144, supra; see also Londagin v. CIR, 61 TC 117 (1973) (earthquake relief in form
of reduction of taxpayer's mortgage debt held taxable to extent of casualty loss
deducted in prior year with tax benefit).

For the tax treatment of governmental subsidies to farmers, ship owners, and
other business taxpayers, see Edwards v. Cuba R.R., 268 US 628 (1925) (subsidy
payments from Cuban government excludable as contributions to capital); Deason v.
CIR, 590 F2d 1377 (5th Cir. 1979) (payments by Dep't of Labor under Manpower
Act taxable); Stafford & Co. v. Pedrick, 171 F2d 42 (2d Cir. 1948) (payments under
Agricultural Adjustment and Soil Conservation Acts are income); US v. Hurst, 2 F2d
73 (D. Wyo. 1924) (mineral interest received as gift); Rev. Rul. 60-32, 1960-1 CB 23
(Soil Bank Act payments taxable); IRS Pub. No. 225, Farmer's Tax Guide 8 (1979
ed.) (payments to farmers in cash or materials are income).

For statutory exclusion of federal payments under a variety of cost-sharing
conservation and other programs, see IRC §126. See also IRC §621 (exclusion from
income of payments to encourage exploration, etc., for defense purposes).

[47] See infra ¶14.10.
[48] For these rulings, see supra ¶5.6.
[49] Compare Rev. Rul. 76-63, 1976-1 CB 14 (federal unemployment compensation exempt) with Rev. Rul. 71-70, 1971-1 CB 27 (union's payment of unemployment benefits to unemployed members taxable) and Rev. Rul. 59-9, 1959-1 CB 232
(unemployment benefits funded by recipients taxable to extent of excess over recipient's contribution).

Congress reduced this disparity by enacting §85, which initially provided for a phaseout of the exemption of governmental unemployment benefits for taxpayers whose adjusted gross income exceeded a specified ceiling ($20,000 or, if a joint return was filed, $25,000). This limitation was explained as follows:

> The Congress believes that a portion of unemployment compensation benefits paid under government programs should be includible in gross income because such benefits are, in substance, a substitute for taxable wages and are equivalent to unemployment benefits paid pursuant to private plans, which are includible in gross income to the extent that they exceed the recipient's prior contributions. The Congress also believes that the prior total exclusion of unemployment compensation benefits paid under government programs tended to create a work disincentive in that it increased the incentive to remain unemployed.[50]

In 1986, Congress took these thoughts to their logical conclusion by amending §85 to include all unemployment benefits in gross income, regardless of the size of the taxpayer's adjusted gross income.[51]

¶10.2.6 Intrafamily Transfers

The elusiveness of the concept "gift" is illustrated by an example from a family context where one would least expect any difficulty: allowances paid by parents to their minor children. These payments are customarily omitted from the recipients' gross income even if they file tax returns reporting their income from babysitting for neighbors. If asked whether this practice is justified, most tax advisers, after expressing astonishment at the question, would probably say that a child's weekly allowance is a tax-free gift, perhaps supporting this conclusion by pointing to the legal presumption that children performing household chores do so without compensation.[52]

---

[50] Joint Comm. on Tax'n, 95th Cong., 2d Sess., General Explanation of the Revenue Act of 1978, at 58–59 (Comm. Print 1979). See also Rev. Rul. 79-299, 1979-2 CB 32 (certain federal benefits are "unemployment compensation" under §85(c)).

[51] See Staff of Joint Comm. on Tax'n, 99th Cong., 2d Sess., General Explanation of the Tax Reform Act of 1986, at 29 (Comm. Print 1987).

[52] Supra ¶5.3.2. See, e.g., Krug v. Miller, 159 Md. 670, 152 A. 493 (1930); see also Restatement of Restitution, §107, Comment (1937) (promise of compensation for services may be rebutted by close relationship of parties).

In Loveland's Est. v. CIR, 13 TC 5 (1949), concerning the federal estate tax consequences of an agreement by a chronically ill husband to pay his wife for caring

Even if this common law principle applies in an affluent society, it would be fatuous to assert that their allowances do not help to elicit services. If a payment can qualify as a gift only if there is no "anticipated benefit," no return in the form of services rendered, and no "moral duty" to make the payment—the indicia endorsed by *Duberstein*—conscientious parents may have some difficulty in characterizing their payments as gifts within the meaning of §102(a). Threats to reduce or stop an allowance if children neglect their domestic chores are common, and the payments often stem not from spontaneous generosity but from social if not moral compulsion: "Billy's parents give him *five* dollars a week, and he doesn't even have to wash the dishes!"

In holding that tips to waiters are not tax-free gifts, the courts have referred to the scowls and insults vented on patrons who leave nothing.[53] A repetition of these transitory stigmata can be avoided by eating in a different restaurant. By contrast, parents who withdraw their child's allowance have no easy refuge from allegations of niggardly behavior. Yet, if a revenue agent attempted to deny an exclusion for children's allowances, the courts somehow would certainly bring them within the shelter of §102(a).[54]

Other intrafamily transfers are also regularly treated as tax free even though their excludability under the *Duberstein* criteria is arguable. A promise to pay a student's college tuition and living expenses on condition that the recipient maintain a specified scholastic average or refrain from drinking or smoking may be stimulated by affection, but it also exacts a quid pro quo and imposes a moral—in some situations a legal—duty to make the payment if the condition is satisfied.[55] Amounts paid by breadwinners to support their spouses and minor children are routinely excluded from the beneficiaries' gross income, but to the extent paid pursuant to legal compulsion, these amounts would not qualify as gifts if the *Duberstein* criteria were

---

for him, the court in effect treated the agreement as a promise to make a gift because the services were the normal consequences of marriage; had payments been made, presumably they would have been excludable from the wife's gross income under §102.

[53] See Roberts v. CIR, 176 F2d 221 (9th Cir. 1949); US v. McCormick, 67 F2d 867 (2d Cir. 1933).

[54] If the child works in a parent's business, however, the compensation can qualify for deduction by the parent and is taxable to the child. See infra ¶75.2.8 (salaries to children), ¶75.4.3 (earnings of minor children); see also infra ¶37.1 (compensation to certain related persons disqualified for credit under §21).

[55] See Hamer v. Sidway, 124 NY 538, 27 NE 256 (1891) (promise to pay $5,000 to nephew if he refrained from drinking, smoking, and swearing until age 21 held enforceable). See also Robertson v. US, 341 US 711 (1952) (prize taxable even though donor derived no economic benefit from recipient's prizewinning entry); Smith v. CIR, 249 F2d 218 (5th Cir. 1957) (parent's transfer of farmland to son for abandoning plans to play professional baseball, completing school, and endeavoring to develop the land).

pushed to their logical extreme.[56] Despite this, intrafamily transfers of this type can be properly viewed as excludable by a higher authority than the language of §102(a)—a supposition, so obvious that it does not require explicit mention in the Code, that Congress never intended to tax them.[57]

The principal case touching at least tangentially on the nature of such intrafamily transactions is *Farid-Es-Sultaneh v. CIR*, involving the basis to the taxpayer of stock received from her fiancé as security in case he died before their contemplated marriage. The stock was received under an antenuptial agreement by which she released her prospective dower and other marital rights.[58] When the taxpayer sold the stock after her divorce, the Commissioner argued that she had received it as a gift, but the Court of Appeals for the Second Circuit determined that the taxpayer had paid "a fair consideration" for the stock, thus establishing a basis equal to its fair market value at acquisition.[59] The IRS subsequently ruled that a wife is not required to include in income property received at the time of divorce in exchange for dower rights.[60] The taxpayer in *Farid-Es-Sultaneh* would enjoy a comparable exclusion for the stock, since it was received in exchange for the dower rights she would otherwise have acquired on marriage, but such an exclusion is hardly consistent to the court's holding that the antenuptial arrangement was equivalent to an arm's length purchase.

¶10.2.7 Payments for Companionship, Etc.

Transfers of cash and property by a taxpayer to a companion or sexual partner have been classified in a few litigated cases as tax-free gifts or taxable compensation, depending on whether the recipient appears to be a beneficiary of generosity or a purveyor of services.[61] The increased frequen-

---

[56] CIR v. Duberstein, 363 US 278, 285 (1960); see also Paulsen, Support Rights and Duties Between Husband and Wife, 9 Vand. L. Rev. 709, 717 (1956) (obligation terminates if spouse fails to perform marital duties).

[57] The Supreme Court asserted in CIR v. Glenshaw Glass Co., 348 US 426, 430 (1955), that Congress intended "to tax all gains except those specifically exempted [by statute]," but this statement is clearly too sweeping. See supra ¶5.5.1.

[58] Farid-Es-Sultaneh v. CIR, 160 F2d 812 (2d Cir. 1947). See also infra ¶41.3 (basis of property acquired by gift).

[59] See Farid-Es-Sultaneh v. CIR, supra note 58.

[60] Rev. Rul. 67-221, 1967-2 CB 63.

[61] See Pascarelli v. CIR, 55 TC 1082 (1971), aff'd without published opinion, 485 F2d 681 (3d Cir. 1973) (male friend gave taxpayer large sums of money and a house, which they occupied for over 20 years, and she assisted him in business "with the same spirit of cooperation that would motivate a wife to strive to help her husband advance in his business"; held, tax-free gifts); Jones v. CIR, 36 TCM (CCH) 1323 (1977) (taxpayer must report funds received from person who, according to taxpayer's testimony, "was getting his money's worth"); Starks v. CIR, 25 TCM (CCH) 676 (1966) (amounts received from friend excludable, even though payments

cy and social acceptability of informal alliances make it likely that financial arrangements between consenting adults will ordinarily be regarded as a sharing of resources, comparable to marital support, and that only blatant commercial traffic will be characterized as compensatory.

¶10.3 EXCLUSION OF INHERITED PROPERTY FROM GROSS INCOME

¶10.3.1 Bequest or Compensation for Services?

The exclusion from gross income accorded since 1913 by §102(a) to gifts also encompasses property acquired by "bequest, devise, or inheritance."[1] This long-standing statutory parallelism between transfers during life and transfers at death is mirrored by the litigated cases: As is true of gifts, the principal source of dispute in the case of property acquired from a decedent is the shadowy borderline between the exercise of benevolence and the discharge of a moral or legal obligation. The frequency of these disputes may be reduced by the enactment in 1986 of a provision barring the §102(a) exclusion for transfers from employer to employee; but the application of the provision in this context may not be entirely clear, and cases will continue to arise in contexts where the performer of the services is not an employee.

As early as 1923, in its first pronouncement on the subject, the Supreme Court held in *United States v. Merriam* that testamentary bequests to the decedent's executors in lieu of commissions were tax-free bequests:

> The distinction to be drawn is between compensation fixed by will for services to be rendered by the executor and a legacy to one upon the implied condition that he shall clothe himself with the character of executor. In the former case he must perform the service to earn the compensation. In the latter case he need do no more than in good faith

---

were made "to insure the [taxpayer's] companionship" and as "personal investment in the future"); Brizendine v. CIR, 16 TCM (CCH) 149 (1957) (cash and house received from taxpayer's friend were "in consideration of her forbearance to refrain from engaging in prostitution"; held, taxable); Blevins v. CIR, 14 TCM (CCH) 840 (1955), aff'd per curiam, 238 F2d 621 (6th Cir. 1956) (payments of cash by taxpayer's male friend taxable, not gifts in contemplation of marriage; he was already married and not considering divorce). The exclusion of gifts presumably embraces recoveries in cases like Marvin v. Marvin, 18 Cal. 3d 660 (1976) (agreements between nonmarital partners enforced unless they rest on "unlawful meretricious consideration").

See also infra ¶30.3.2 (dependency exemption disallowed by §152(b)(5) in case of illicit relationship).

[1] For the statutory history of this phrase, see supra ¶10.1 note 1.

comply with the condition in order to receive the bequest; and in that view the further provision that the bequest shall be in lieu of commissions is, in effect, nothing more than an expression of the testator's will that the executor shall not receive statutory allowances for the services he may render.[2]

Although never overruled, the *Merriam* case inspired little judicial enthusiasm[3] and rests on an unpersuasive interpretation of the decedent's will. It is difficult to imagine why a decedent would want a person to "clothe himself with the character of executor" except to perform the customary fiduciary services, nor is it likely that such a person would be entitled to receive or retain the legacy if he promptly resigned, for he would not yet have cloaked himself "with the character of executor." The Court's reference to a "good faith" compliance with the "condition" of qualifying as executor is puzzling because it implies a right to receive the legacy without performing the duties of the office. If the executor intended to perform but became disabled or died before he could do so, he would probably be entitled to receive the legacy; but the claim would rest on the theory that the legacy was promised in exchange for the executor's implied agreement to perform the fiduciary services to the best of his ability, and, were it not for *Merriam*, this would imply taxability. In any event, it is clear that the executor is taxable on a purported bequest in lieu of statutory compensation if he is *required* to perform the services, and this condition is probably the expectation of testators leaving such bequests.[4]

---

[2] US v. Merriam, 263 US 179, 187 (1923).

[3] In Bank of N.Y. v. Helvering, 132 F2d 773 (2d Cir. 1943), a legacy was held to be tax free to the extent that it exceeded statutory commissions (the taxpayer having reported the latter amount). The court, however, implied discontent with the *Merriam* rationale ("if it is to be overruled, the Supreme Court, not we, must overrule it") and went further in Wolder v. CIR, 493 F2d 608 (2d Cir.), cert. denied, 419 US 828 (1974), asserting that *Merriam* reflected an outmoded respect for form and that *Duberstein* embodied "an entirely different viewpoint from *Merriam*" in interpreting the term "gift" in §102(a).

[4] See Grant v. Rose, 39 F2d 338 (5th Cir.), cert. granted, 282 US 821 (1930), cert. dismissed, 283 US 867 (1931) (taxable compensation); Ream v. Bowers, 22 F2d 465 (2d Cir. 1927) (decedent "contemplated payment for the . . . entire [fiduciary] service"); Murray v. CIR, 38 BTA 26 (1938) (acq.) (executors and trustees of testamentary trust received percentages of trust's income; two of the six fiduciaries received income interests of approximately one third each, the other four, interests of 1 percent each; to treat all six fiduciaries as receiving bequests in lieu of commissions was "an absurdity"); but see Rev. Rul. 57-398, 1957-2 CB 93 (legacy to former employee "in appreciation of [her earlier] service" and for acting as executor; not being "contingent upon her performing the duties of executrix," legacy was tax free).

A legacy to an executor is deductible from the decedent's gross estate under §2053(a)(2) if the testamentary clause is interpreted as fixing the executor's compensation, but not if the payment is viewed as a bequest in lieu of commissions. See Reg.

Difficult though it is, the task of determining whether bequests to executors in lieu of statutory commissions are taxable or not requires, under *Merriam*, no more than an interpretation of the testamentary language. An even larger category of litigated cases—those where the issue is whether a legacy is a tax-free transfer under §102(a) or belated compensation for services rendered by the legatee to the decedent during his life—entails a comprehensive examination of facts that are often hard to reconstruct. If intended as compensation, the payment is taxable even though it is a bequest under state law, which no more controls the meaning of "bequest" as used in §102(a) than it controls the scope of the term "gift."[5]

The distinction between a tax-free bequest and a testamentary payment of belated or supplemental compensation is difficult to administer, especially in the case of domestic servants and trusted advisers whose personal relationships with the decedent often ripen into intimate friendship and who sometimes become virtual members of the family. If the decedent did not agree to leave anything by will to the beneficiary, a legacy ordinarily qualifies as a tax-free bequest; the absence of a legal obligation seems to have more significance in classifying testamentary transfers than in the case of analogous inter vivos transfers, which are often denied the §102(a) exclusion even though wholly voluntary.[6] If the bequest discharges a promise to reward the employee by will, an exclusion under §102(a) is inconsistent with the rationale of *Duberstein*.[7] It is likely, however, that many oral arrange-

---

§20.2053-3(b)(2); Jones v. CIR, 23 TCM (CCH) 235 (1964) (executor received both bequest, not in lieu of commissions, and statutory commissions; bequest nondeductible and commissions deductible). See also Bath v. US, 480 F2d 289, 292 n.3 (9th Cir. 1973) (in substance, Commissioner alternatively asserted that estate's payment to taxpayer, who claimed he performed services for decedent before his death, was tax free to taxpayer or deductible from gross estate, but not both).

[5] CIR v. Duberstein, 363 US 278 (1960) (regarding "gifts"); Lyeth v. Hoey, 305 US 188 (1938) (statutory term "acquired by . . . inheritance" has special federal meaning); Wolder v. CIR, supra note 3; but see US v. Merriam, supra note 2.

[6] There appear to be no cases in which the IRS attempted to deny tax-free status to a bequest to an employee in appreciation of services, unless the decedent was obligated by agreement to make such a bequest. See also Jones v. CIR, supra note 4; Rev. Rul. 57-398, supra note 4. For cases holding that voluntary inter vivos payments to retired employees or their families are taxable compensation rather than tax-free gifts, see supra ¶10.2.3.

[7] See Wolder v. CIR, supra note 3 (bequest to decedent's attorney pursuant to formal agreement by which he agreed to render legal services without charge; held, taxable); Rev. Rul. 67-375, 1967-2 CB 60 (bequest pursuant to written agreement to care for decedent held taxable; "bequest" as used in §102(a) "generally implies bounty, gift, or gratuity"). But see McDonald v. CIR, 2 TC 840 (1943) (acq.) (bequest "in appreciation" of employee's services tax free; employer "frequently stated to petitioner that he was going to see that she received something through his will"; government asserted this was oral agreement to pay additional compensation, but court did not directly respond).

ments for the care of elderly persons by children or younger relatives in return for a promised bequest escape notice.[8] The more vague and informal the understanding, the more it resembles a garden variety bequest by a lonely testator, who rewards a relative providing solace in the form of personal attention in preference to other relatives who contented themselves with verbal professions of affection.

When a taxpayer makes a claim against the estate alleging the decedent breached an agreement to leave him a legacy as compensation for services, a payment in satisfaction of the claim is invariably held taxable. Exclusion under §102(a) is denied in these cases because the decedent's promise— and, even more clearly, the breach of promise—is inconsistent with an attitude of benevolence, and the amount paid by the estate, whether under a judgment or in settlement of the claim, can hardly be regarded as anything other than compensation.[9]

In 1986, Congress enacted §102(c)(1), which states that the §102(a) exclusion cannot apply to "any amount transferred by or for an employer to, or for the benefit of, an employee."[10] The suggestion has been made that the provision might not apply to an employer's bequest to an employee because the employment relationship terminates with the employer's death.[11] The words "by or for an employer," however, seem sufficient to reach a payment made at an employer's direction growing out of an employment relationship, even when the direction is carried out after the employer's death. The provision, however, does not apply when services are performed in a capacity other than as employee, and, in this context, the issue of whether services are performed as employee or as independent contractor or volunteer might be as difficult as those dealt with in the earlier cases. The legislative history indicates, further, that the bar on the §102(a) exclusion

---

[8] If the decedent fails to leave the anticipated bequest, however, the arrangement will come to light when the disappointed relative sues the estate for breach of contract. See infra note 9.

[9] See Braddock v. US, 434 F2d 631 (9th Cir. 1970) (oral agreement to leave entire estate in return for taxpayer's agreement to cook, clean, and help with decedent's farm work); Cotnam v. CIR, 263 F2d 119 (5th Cir. 1959) (judgment against intestate decedent's administrator based on oral contract to leave taxpayer one fifth of estate if she would serve as "attendant or friend"); Mariani v. CIR, 54 TC 135 (1970) (son taxed on amount received in settlement of claim that decedent-father had agreed to leave son one third of estate in recognition of his services). Cf. Bath v. US, 480 F2d 289 (9th Cir. 1973) (life tenant of testamentary trust asserted claim for compensation; jury determination that amount received acquired by bequest rather than as compensation upheld, on showing that taxpayer's claim was insubstantial and that primary purpose of settlement (embodied in state court judgment) was to avoid family friction).

[10] Section 102(c)(1) applies to transfers after December 31, 1986. Pub. L. No. 99-514, §§122(b), 151(c), 100 Stat. 2085 (1986).

[11] Rhodes, Are Employer Bequests Income? 36 Tax Notes 1305 (1987).

does not apply if the transfer flows from motives unrelated to the services relationship. The provision is described in more detail in connection with its application to gifts.[12]

¶10.3.2 Settlement of Will Contests

In *Lyeth v. Hoey*, the Supreme Court held that an amount received in settlement of a will contest was "acquired by . . . inheritance" within the meaning of §102(a).[13] As an intestate successor of his grandmother, the taxpayer objected to the probate of her will, asserting lack of testamentary capacity and undue influence. Under a compromise agreement among all claimants, the will was admitted to probate, but the residuary bequest was disregarded so that a substantial amount could be paid to the taxpayer and other heirs. Under local law, the amount received by the taxpayer was not subject to the state inheritance tax because his rights were "contractual and not testamentary," but a contrary rule applies to this situation in some other states.

Given this division at the state level, the Court held that the phrase "acquired by . . . inheritance" in §102(a) should not be defined by local characterizations,[14] that the words "bequest, devise, [and] inheritance" were used by Congress as "comprehensive terms embracing all acquisitions in the devolution of a decedent's estate," and that the amount received by the taxpayer was excludable from income.

> Petitioner was concededly an heir of his grandmother under the Massachusetts statute. It was by virtue of that heirship that he opposed probate of her alleged will that constituted an obstacle to the enforcement of his right; save as heir he had no standing. Seeking to remove that obstacle, he asserted that the will was invalid because of want of testamentary capacity and undue influence.
>
> [The government] agrees that the word "inheritance" as used in the federal statute is not solely applicable to cases of complete intestacy. The portion of the decedent's property that petitioner obtained under the compromise did not come to him through the testator's will. That portion he obtained because of his heirship and to that extent he took in spite of the will and as in case of intestacy. The fact that petitioner received less than the amount of his claim did not alter its

---

[12] Supra ¶10.2.3.

[13] Lyeth v. Hoey, 305 US 188 (1938). See generally Kemp, Federal Tax Aspects of Will Contests, 23 U. Miami L. Rev. 72 (1968); Paul, The Federal Tax Status of Will Contestants, in Paul, Selected Studies in Federal Taxation 305 (Callaghan, 2d ser. 1938).

[14] See supra ¶4.1.4 on the role of state law in federal tax cases.

nature or the quality of its recognition through the distribution that he did receive.[15]

In effect, the Supreme Court held that in applying §102(a), property acquired in settlement of a claim should be treated as it would have been if the taxpayer's claim had been honored rather than disputed.[16] This principle has been applied to an amount received in settlement of a will contest by a taxpayer claiming under a prior will[17] and is also encountered in other contexts.[18]

In *Lyeth v. Hoey*, the taxpayer's status as an heir of the decedent was conceded, but the same principle has been applied when the claimant's right to take in intestacy was in doubt.[19] This approach makes it necessary to determine in the federal tax case whether the taxpayer was in fact an heir or legatee under a prior will. The judgment or settlement, however, is ordinarily a sufficient guaranty that the claim was not wholly spurious.[20]

---

[15] Lyeth v. Hoey, supra note 13, at 195–97.

[16] In *Lyeth v. Hoey*, the property received by the taxpayer was distributed to him by the estate against which his claim was made. In Harrison v. CIR, 119 F2d 963 (7th Cir. 1941), where property used to settle the taxpayer's claim was made available by the residuary legatee pending distribution under the will, an exclusion under §102(a) was conceded by the government, and the court commented that "Lyeth v. Hoey . . . is exactly in point." See also Quigley v. CIR, 143 F2d 27 (7th Cir. 1944) (where taxpayer withdrew threat to contest father's will in return for brothers' agreement to pay her specified amounts of income from testamentary trusts created for their benefit, value of contract rights excludable under §102(a) in year of settlement, but subsequent receipts of trust income taxable); Hopkins v. CIR, 13 TC 952 (1949) (nonacq.) (§102(a) not applicable to amounts paid to taxpayer by trust created by her mother in settlement of threat to contest her father's estate).

[17] Keller v. CIR, 41 BTA 478 (1940) (acq.) (taxpayer petitioned for revocation of probate of later will on grounds of incompetency and undue influence; she received payments under settlement agreement and withdrew objections; held, tax free).

[18] See Kemp, supra note 13.

[19] US v. Gavin, 159 F2d 613 (9th Cir. 1947) (payment to person claiming as decedent's illegitimate child held tax free, although claimant agreed to refrain from asserting her paternity in the future and consented to probate decree finding against the relationship). See also Harrison v. CIR, supra note 16 (taxpayer's claim was that antenuptial agreement with her husband was invalid because of his failure to make full disclosure of his financial resources, so that under state law she had right to renounce provision made for her by his will); but see Rev. Rul. 70-60, 1970-1 CB 11 (consideration received by taxpayer for interest in an expected inheritance from her father, who was living at time of sale and had not drawn a will, is includable in gross income).

[20] But see White v. Thomas, 116 F2d 147 (5th Cir. 1940), cert. denied, 313 US 581 (1941), where a payment of $125,000 in settlement of a claim against executors and testamentary trustees was based on the decedent's alleged inter vivos gift to the claimant of a ranch that was then devised to the trustee by the decedent's will. The court implied that the taxpayer's claim was fraudulent ("a business venture in litiga-

A corollary of the origin-of-the-claim theory in *Lyeth v. Hoey* is that if the original claim would have generated taxable income had it been paid in due course (if it is, for example, a claim for compensation for services), the amount paid to settle the claim is also taxable.[21]

¶10.4 GIFTS AND BEQUESTS OF INCOME, REMAINDERS, AND OTHER DIVIDED INTERESTS

The §102(a) exclusion does not embrace income from property acquired by gift, bequest, devise, or inheritance.[1] This restriction, embodied in §102(b)(1), prevents the permanent immunization of investment income from family fortunes. In its absence, children of wealthy parents not only would be free of tax on the receipt of their patrimony, but would also receive its subsequent investment yield tax free. Their descendants would enjoy the same privilege to the end of time—or at least until they succeeded in dissipating both the exempt income and the capital from which it sprang.

The application of §102(b)(1) to an outright gift or bequest of income producing property is quite straightforward: The recipient is not taxed on receiving the property itself, but must report the dividends, interest, rents, or other investment income generated by the property thereafter. If the transferor does not rid himself of all incidents of ownership, however, he may be required to report the income under the assignment-of-income doctrine and related principles, discussed elsewhere in this work.[2]

The distinction between donated property and income from the property is more complicated if the donor transfers the right to receive the income to one donee and a remainder interest in the property to a different donee. Assume property is given in trust with directions that income be

---

tion"), but also advanced a less tenable ground for denying an exclusion under §102(a)—that the claim was settled for cash rather than for "a part of the very thing [the ranch] claimed." See also Howard v. CIR, 447 F2d 152 (5th Cir. 1971) (claim should be taken as made, unless a mere "naked threat"); Grossman v. Campbell, 368 F2d 206 (5th Cir. 1966) (estate tax case interpreting *Lyeth v. Hoey* as requiring "a good faith, bona fide settlement of a valid dispute"); Jones v. CIR, 17 TCM (CCH) 952 (1958).

[21] See Parker v. US, 573 F2d 42 (Ct. Cl. 1978) (settlement of will contest allocated between claim for inheritance, which was excludable, and claim for income from inherited property, which was taxable); Jones v. CIR, supra note 20.

[1] From 1913 through 1941, the statutory language was more affirmative, providing explicitly that income from donated or inherited property was includable in gross income. Since 1942, the statute has stated only that the exclusion for gifts and bequests does not embrace income from the transferred property, which leaves open the possibility, not available under the earlier language, that the income qualifies under another exclusion (e.g., §103, relating to state and municipal bonds).

[2] See generally infra ¶75.1.

distributed to *A* for life and that the corpus be distributed to *B* on *A*'s death. From 1913 to 1942, the relevant statutory provisions were similar to §102(a) (excluding from gross income "the value of property acquired by gift, bequest, devise, or inheritance") and §102(b)(1) (denying the exclusion to "the income from any [such] property").[3] In *Irwin v. Gavit*, a landmark decision under pre-1942 law, a life tenant argued that the "property" that he acquired by inheritance was the right to collect the income and that his periodic receipts were therefore excludable from gross income.[4] The Supreme Court disagreed, saying:

> The [statutory] language . . . leaves no doubt in our minds that if a fund were given to trustees for A for life with remainder over, the income received by the trustees and paid over to A would be income of A under the statute. It seems to us hardly less clear that even if there were a specific provision that A should have no interest in the corpus, the payments would be income none the less, within the meaning of the statute and the Constitution, and by popular speech. In the first case it is true that the bequest might be said to be of the corpus for life, in the second it might be said to be of the income. But we think that the provision of the act that exempts bequests assumes the gift of a corpus and contrasts it with the income arising from it, but was not intended to exempt income properly so-called simply because of a severance between it and the principal fund.[5]

Irwin v. Gavit reached its conclusion under what is now §102(b)(1). In 1942, Congress explicitly confirmed interpretation by enacting what is now §102(b)(2).[6]

---

[3] As of 1941, §22(b)(3) of the 1939 Code provided for the exclusion from gross income of "the value of property acquired by gift, bequest, devise, or inheritance (but the income from such property shall be included in gross income)."

[4] Irwin v. Gavit, 268 US 161 (1925).

[5] Id. at 167. The issue in this case was complicated by the fact that trusts and estates were not taxed as separate entities during the years before the Court (1913 through 1915), with the result that their income was taxed to no one if the beneficiaries were exempted. See Smietanka v. First Trust & Sav. Bank, 257 US 602 (1922). Despite this, both lower courts held in favor of the taxpayer. Irwin v. Gavit, 295 Fed. 84 (2d Cir. 1923); Gavit v. Irwin, 275 Fed. 643 (NDNY 1921). See also Maguire, Capitalization of Periodical Payments by Gift, 34 Harv. L. Rev. 20 (1920).

[6] S. Rep. No. 1631, 77th Cong., 2d Sess., reprinted in 1942-2 CB 504, 558. For discussion of this and other 1942 changes in §102, see Hopkins v. CIR, 13 TC 952, 967–68 (1949) (nonacq.).

This treatment of the life tenant is confirmed by §273, denying life tenants the right to amortize the value of the life estate, and by §1001(e), denying them any basis on a sale of the interest except in conjunction with a sale by the remainderman. See infra ¶41.8.6.

Because the amounts received by the taxpayer in *Irwin v. Gavit* were explicitly payable from trust income, the Court was not required to pass on the status of amounts payable without regard to the amount of income generated by the transferred property. The Court later held in *Burnet v. Whitehouse* that such receipts are excludable from gross income under §102(a) whether paid from income or not, provided they are payable out of corpus if necessary.[7] In 1942, however, Congress rejected this rule by enacting the second sentence of §102(b), which denies the exclusion to periodic payments to the extent they are paid, credited, or distributed from income. The *Whitehouse* case is still applicable to lump sum payments, however, as distinguished from amounts paid "at intervals."[8]

The final sentence of §102(b), enacted in 1954, gives subchapter J (relating to trusts and estates) precedence over §102, so that amounts included in the gross income of a beneficiary of a trust or estate under §652, 662, or 667 cannot be excluded under §102.[9]

¶10.5 GIFTS AND INHERITED PROPERTY—ANCILLARY TAX PROBLEMS

¶10.5.1 Indirect Transfers and Bargain Sales

Although most transfers by gift or at death are straightforward gifts or bequests of property, indirect gratuitous transfers—especially by gift—are also possible. Instead of giving a donee a check for $100, for example, the donor may sell to him for $400 property with a fair market value of $500, or give him the free use of property with a rental value of $100, or cancel a $100 debt, or pay the donee's $100 debt to a department store, or take other action increasing the donee's net worth by $100. If the transaction is motivated by "detached and disinterested generosity" or by "affection, respect, admiration, charity or like impulses,"[1] it qualifies as an excludable item regardless of its form.

---

[7] Burnet v. Whitehouse, 283 US 148 (1931) (annuity payable without regard to income). See Coleman v. CIR, 151 F2d 235 (3d Cir. 1945) (extended discussion of post-*Whitehouse* cases and legislation); see also infra ¶81.4.

[8] Lindau v. CIR, 21 TC 911 (1954) (acq.).

[9] See Reg. §1.102-1(d); infra ¶¶81.1.1, 81.4.7; Ferguson, Freeland & Stephens, Federal Income Taxation of Estates and Beneficiaries 501–09 (Little, Brown 1970).

For the treatment of amounts received from an estate or trust that do not constitute distributions under subchapter J, see US v. Folckemer, 307 F2d 171 (5th Cir. 1962) (interest on legacy taxable under §61(a) without regard to §662); Rev. Rul. 73-322, 1973-2 CB 44 (accord).

[1] CIR v. Duberstein, 363 US 278, 285 (1960), discussed supra ¶10.2.1.

In some circumstances, however, an indirect gift may have collateral consequences for the donor. For example, if he puts a friend or relative on his business payroll, intending to make a gift because no services are to be performed, the payment cannot be deducted as a business expense; if the business is conducted in corporate form, the payment ordinarily constitutes a constructive distribution, taxable to the shareholder who directed the action.[2]

When a taxpayer is allowed to purchase property for less than its fair market value, the spread can be excluded from gross income if the bargain sale exhibits the normal characteristics of a gift, but not if it is a mode of compensating the purchaser for services to the vendor.[3] Bargain sales often contain a genuinely gratuitous element if the transferee is a charitable organization or a member of the vendor's family, in which event computation of the vendor's gain or loss on the sale is affected by special rules, discussed elsewhere in this work.[4]

¶10.5.2 Basis of Property Acquired by Gift or Inheritance

As explained elsewhere in this work,[5] a recipient's adjusted basis for donated or inherited property for computing gain or loss on a later sale (or depreciation if the property is used in the recipient's business) depends on whether it was acquired by gift or at death. In general, property received by gift continues to have the same basis in the hands of the donee that it had in the hands of the donor. Property transferred at death, however, ordinarily acquires a new basis, equal to its value on the date of the decedent's death.

¶10.5.3 Deduction of Business Gifts

In *CIR v. Duberstein*, the Supreme Court held that "it is doubtless relevant to the over-all inference [that a transaction is or is not a gift] that the transferor treats a payment as a business deduction."[6] It decided, however, that this action is not conclusive and that the transferee's right to an exclusion under §102 should not become a "trial of the tax liability" of the transferor. Although the Court did not expand on these points, it might have added that an effort by the transferor to deduct a particular payment as a business expense might be erroneous or even fraudulent, so that the

---

[2] For constructive dividends, see infra ¶92.2. If the alleged salary is deducted, the misrepresentation may be civil or criminal fraud.

[3] See infra ¶60.4.1.

[4] Infra ¶41.3.5.

[5] Infra ¶41.3 (gifts), ¶41.4 (bequests).

[6] CIR v. Duberstein, 363 US 278 (1960).

naked claim does not prove that the transferor made the payment for business rather than personal motives.

Moreover, even if the deduction is justified, it may be consistent with a decision that the payment was a tax-free gift to the recipient. Just as ordinary business usage sanctions or even mandates some charitable contributions, so it encompasses occasional transfers to business associates that are motivated by generosity, affection, or similar impulses rather than by business objectives. The IRS long recognized this by administrative practice,[7] and it is also tacitly acknowledged by §274(b), which limits to $25 per donee per year (but does not forbid) the deduction of amounts paid for gifts that are excluded from the recipient's gross income by §102.[8] If the transferor not only deducts the disputed payment but also describes it as compensation, however, this representation is relevant evidence of a noncharitable motive, even though it may not be conclusive. Cases involving payments to employees' survivors, for example, often refer to the label used by the employer to describe the payment in directors' resolutions, internal records, or tax returns.[9]

---

[7] See supra ¶10.2.3.
[8] See infra ¶21.3.
[9] See supra ¶10.2.4.

this exclusion has always been subject to several requirements in addition to that imposed by the language quoted above.[8] In 1986, Congress further narrowed the exclusion by providing that even when all other requirements are satisfied, a meritorious achievement award is included in gross income unless the recipient assigns it over to charity. Congress decided that because "a prize or award . . . increases the recipient's net wealth and ability to pay taxes to the same extent as the receipt of . . . wages, dividends, or . . . a taxable award," it should be taxable except where the recipient relinquishes it to charity.[9]

The meritorious achievement standard of §74(b) was intended to deny the exclusion to door prizes and awards in radio and television giveaway shows, which had sometimes qualified as tax-free gifts under pre-1954 law.[10] It also disqualifies many other receipts. For example, the terms "artistic" and "civic" have been held not to encompass athletic achievement.[11] As used in §74(b), the term "civic" has been held to imply "positive action, exemplary, unselfish, and broadly advantageous to the community," and to exclude a display of skill as a fisherman, despite "the rhapsodies uttered in praise of the delights and virtues of the piscatorial pastime."[12] The court could think of only one "genuine civic achievement" that a fisherman might accomplish—the capture of a killer whale terrorizing the local coastline, particularly if the taxpayer acted "at considerable risk to himself." Also, the IRS has ruled the exclusion unavailable when a family is given an award for "typif[ying] a certain average family routine" or when wage earners are honored by their labor union for serving more than 25 years in the same

---

fish in Third Annual American Beer Fishing Derby; §74(b) requires "genuinely meritorious achievement"); Cass v. CIR, 86 TC 1275 (1986) (fellowship grant not excludable under §74(b) and thus taxable to extent not excluded by §117); Rev. Rul. 72-163, 1972-1 CB 26 (award by National Foundation on the Arts and Humanities to established author to assist in completion of literary work in progress; held, not excludable under §74(b) because not for past achievement, but qualifies as a fellowship under §117).

[8] The form in which the award is paid, however, is irrelevant to the issue of its excludability. Rev. Rul. 84-9, 1984-1 CB 22 (award payable over 10-year period, another for recipient's life, held excludable).

[9] Staff of Joint Comm. on Tax'n, 99th Cong., 2d Sess., General Explanation of Tax Reform Act of 1986, at 31 (Comm. Print 1987) [hereinafter 1986 Bluebook].

[10] Reg. §1.74-1(a); S. Rep. No. 1622, 83d Cong., 2d Sess. 13, 178–79 (1954). For pre-1954 law, see Washburn v. CIR, 5 TC 1333 (1945) (prize on Pot O'Gold radio giveaway program excludable from gross income as gift).

[11] See Wills v. CIR, 411 F2d 537 (9th Cir. 1969) (automobile awarded to "most popular Dodger" of 1962 baseball season and S. Rae Hickok belt for the outstanding professional athlete of the prior year), citing unenacted legislative bills to amend §74 to cover athletic activity; Hornung v. CIR, 47 TC 428 (1967) (same).

[12] Simmons v. US, 308 F2d 160 (4th Cir. 1962).

company's employ.[13]

An award for educational, civic, or other meritorious achievement is not disqualified under §74(b) by the fact that the prizewinner's accomplishments occurred in the course of employment, provided the grantor is not the employer.[14] Although the statute does not explicitly disqualify payments by an employer, the regulations do, and this interpretation is supported by the legislative history.[15] A related point is that the award must be made "primarily" in recognition of the taxpayer's achievement—a requirement that has been held to disqualify an award to an inventor on condition that he assign the commercial rights in his discovery to the grantor, since this condition indicates that the donor was more interested in obtaining the royalty-free license than in honoring the achievement per se.[16]

In addition to meritorious achievement, the taxpayer must display the virtue of humility, or at least patience, since a prize is only exempt under §74(b) if the recipient "was selected without any action on his part to enter the contest or proceeding." This requirement excludes contests, like the one involved in *Robertson*, where the entrants submit essays or other projects.[17] It also disqualifies contests where nothing need be submitted but entrants

---

[13] Rev. Rul. 58-354, 1958-2 CB 36 (representative families); Rev. Rul. 58-277, 1958-1 CB 41 (long service).

[14] Rev. Rul. 62-89, 1962-1 CB 19 (Rockefeller Public Service Award to outstanding federal employees); Rev. Rul. 61-92, 1961-1 CB 11, modified by Rev. Rul. 62-89, 1962-1 CB 19 (same); see also Denniston v. CIR, 41 TC 667, 673 n.7 (1964), aff'd per curiam, 343 F2d 312 (DC Cir. 1965).

[15] Reg. §1.74-1(a); S. Rep. No. 1622, 83d Cong., 2d Sess. 13, 179 (1954) (§74(b) "is not intended to exclude prizes or awards from an employer to an employee in recognition of some achievement in connection with his employment, such as having the largest sales record or best production record during a certain period"). The Senate committee comment seems to exclude any employment-related achievement if the grantor employs the grantee, presumably because the award in such cases may be a kind of contingent compensation. In many cases, awards to employees do not meet the meritorious achievement test, but since that requirement applies to all awards, regardless of the relationship between grantor and recipient, it seems incidental to the committee's principal purpose of disqualifying awards to employees. See Jones v. CIR, 743 F2d 1429 (9th Cir. 1984) (exclusion allowed for award by National Aeronautics and Space Administration to one of its employees for contribution to "conduct of NASA programs" and for "advancement of scientific knowledge;" neither statute nor regulations should be construed to preclude exclusion of award received from taxpayer's employer); Denniston v. CIR, supra note 14 (incentive award to government employee held taxable); Rev. Rul. 86-31, 1986-1 CB 75 (IRS will not follow *Jones*); but see infra note 26 for the possibility that some employee awards may qualify as tax-free gifts under pre-1986 law.

[16] Rogallo v. US, 475 F2d 1 (4th Cir. 1973).

[17] The Senate committee report states that §74 was intended to reject the exemption granted under pre-1954 law by McDermott v. CIR, 150 F2d 585 (DC Cir. 1945) (ABA essay contest), which was also overturned by Robertson v. US, discussed supra in text accompanying notes 3–4.

must nominate themselves or otherwise bring their achievements to the attention of the judges.[18] If the entrant is not too pushy, however, the award may qualify under IRS rulings permitting candidates who are selected in a preliminary screening without action on their part to appear for a personal interview or fill out a biographical form before the final selection occurs.[19]

Further, a prize may not be excluded as a meritorious achievement award if it is conditioned on the recipient's rendition of substantial future services. The IRS has held that this restriction disqualifies the winner of a beauty contest who was required to participate in a commercial pageant, pose for photographs, and engage in personal appearances for a one-year period.[20] On the other hand, a personal appearance to accept an award is not a disqualifying service.[21]

Finally, for taxable years after 1986, a prize or award that meets the foregoing tests is only excludable if the recipient instructs that it be paid to a unit of government or to a religious, educational, or other charitable organization that qualifies to receive deductible gifts under §170(c)(2).[22] Such a designation can be made before or after the recipient takes possession of the prize, but the exclusion is lost if the recipient "uses" the item awarded to him.[23] If the award is paid in money, a disqualifying use occurs if the recipient "spends, deposits, invests, or otherwise uses the money."[24] An exuberant award-winner should be warned against waving the check in the air. Also, any use "with the permission of the taxpayer or by one associated with the taxpayer (e.g., a member of the taxpayer's family)" disqualifies the award if a similar use by the recipient would have this effect.[25]

-----

[18] See Isenbergh v. CIR, 31 TC 1046 (1959) (acq.) (selection process initiated by taxpayer's application with resume and proposed course of study; held, award not qualified for exclusion under §74(b) but partly excludable as a fellowship under §117).

[19] Rev. Rul. 57-67, 1957-1 CB 33 (award to students for academic and citizenship achievement held exempt; students selected by their high school faculties and judged on regional basis after filling out forms and appearing for personal interviews); but see Rev. Rul. 72-163, 1972-1 CB 26 (writer invited to apply for grant; held, submission of resume and summary of project is excessive "action on his part").

[20] Rev. Rul. 68-20, 1968-1 CB 55 (beauty contest). Although the ruling refrains from saying so, demonstration of "talent, charm, and grooming" by a prizewinner hardly constitutes "artistic" or "civic" achievement. See also Mueller v. CIR, 338 F2d 1015 (1st Cir. 1964) (awards to scientists expected to work in tax-exempt grantor institute's laboratory; held, taxable).

[21] Rev. Rul. 58-89, 1958-1 CB 40.

[22] IRC §74(b)(3).

[23] 1986 Bluebook, supra note 9, at 34.

[24] Id.

[25] Id.

2. *Employee achievement awards.* Under §74(c), an award by an employer to an employee in recognition of the employee's length of service or safety achievement is excluded from gross income if several requirements are met.[26] The award, for example, must be given at a ceremony that is "a meaningful presentation."[27] Also, the "conditions and circumstances" must not suggest "a significant likelihood of the payment of disguised compensation."

The award is fully excludable by the employee only if the cost for the award does not exceed the employer's deduction for it,[28] which is closely regulated.[29] If the cost exceeds the deduction, the employee is taxed on the excess of the cost over the amount of the deduction or, if greater, the amount by which the award's value exceeds the employer's deduction.[30]

3. *Determining amount of taxable prize.* If a taxable prize is paid in goods or services rather than money, the regulations provide that it is to be valued at its fair market value.[31] In a case involving an automobile for which the grantor paid about $4,500, however, the Tax Court held that the taxpayer realized only $3,900 of income because "it is common knowledge, of which we may take notice, that when an automobile has been purchased from a dealer the purchaser cannot, on a sale of the car, normally realize the price which he paid for the car, even though it has not been actually used."[32] On the other hand, the amount taxable to the winner should not be less than he could realize on a sale, even if the grantor purchased it for less than that amount because it was entitled to a dealer or quantity discount.

---

[26] These requirements are described more fully in connection with the limits on the employer's deduction for such an award. Infra ¶21.3.

Section 74(c) applies to awards granted after 1986. Pub. L. No. 99-514, §§122(a)(1)(D), 151(c), 100 Stat. 2085 (1986). Before the 1986 amendments, §274(b) implied that an award by an employer to an employee for safety achievement could qualify as a tax-free gift under §102. IRC §274(b)(1)(C) (before repeal in 1986).

[27] IRC §§74(c)(1), 274(j)(3)(A).

[28] If the employer is exempt from tax on income from the activity in which the employee works (if the employer, for example, is a charity), the deduction amount is the amount the employer would be allowed to deduct if it were taxable. IRC §74(c)(3).

[29] See infra ¶21.3.

[30] IRC §74(c)(2). In either case, the taxable amount cannot exceed the value of the award. Id.

[31] Reg. §1.74-1(a)(2).

[32] McCoy v. CIR, 38 TC 841, 844 (1962) (acq.) (taxpayer disposed of automobile for $3,600 after driving it from place of award to his home; the court attributed $300 of depreciation to this use of the automobile, concluding that its value was $3,900 when received). See also Wills v. CIR, 411 F2d 537 (9th Cir. 1969) (belt taxable at stipulated value, though it was a trophy that would not ordinarily be sold; court envisions tax on value of Olympic medals as IRS' next step).

If a prize is in the form of goods or services that the taxpayer must either use personally or forfeit (e.g., a trip), the inability to convert it into cash does not prevent taxation of its value. A substantial discount from the retail price or fair market value of identical transferable property may be warranted, however, if the prize does not take the place of goods or services the taxpayer would have purchased in any event.[33] Moreover, if a taxpayer finds a prize unappealing and is unwilling to run the valuation gauntlet, he can decline the award and thereby avoid the risk of a tax assessment exceeding his personal estimate of the prize's worth.[34]

In order to moderate the impact of tax progression on recipients, most of whom use the cash method of reporting income, large cash awards are sometimes payable in installments. Under the usual principles of cash accounting, a stretch-out of payments is ordinarily effective unless the obligor's promise to pay is buttressed by an escrow or similar security arrangement or is evidenced by negotiable promissory notes.[35]

¶11.2 SCHOLARSHIPS AND FELLOWSHIPS

¶11.2.1 Introductory

Section 117 excludes a scholarship or fellowship grant from gross income if it covers tuition for the taxpayer's course of study as a degree candidate or is used for related expenses other than living expenses.[1] Schol-

---

[33] See Turner v. CIR, 11 TCM (CCH) 604 (1954) (steamship tickets with retail value of $2,220 used by taxpayer; held, under pre-1954 law, $1,400 taxable).

[34] Rev. Rul. 57-374, 1957-2 CB 69 (no tax when prizewinner refused to accept all-expense-paid trip). Tax would likely be imposed, however, if a taxpayer's refusal to accept the award served to divert it to a member of his family. See the dissenting opinions in Teschner v. CIR, 38 TC 1003 (1962) (nonacq.).

[35] See Rev. Rul. 67-203, 1967-1 CB 105 (minor who won Irish Sweepstakes must report present value of winnings deposited with Irish court, to be held until he comes of age); Rev. Rul. 62-74, 1962-1 CB 68 (winner taxed on discounted value of right to receive prize in installments, where full amount was deposited in noninterest-bearing escrow account by sponsor).

[1] Section 117 and the policy issues underlying it have attracted considerable interest among scholars. A representative sample of their work, all written before the 1986 overhaul of §117, would include: Sneed, The Configurations of Gross Income 160–69 (Ohio State U. Press 1967); Gordon, Scholarship and Fellowship Grants as Income: A Search for Treasury Policy, 1960 Wash. ULQ 144; McNulty, Tax Policy and Tuition Credit Legislation: Federal Income Tax Allowances for Personal Costs of Higher Education, 61 Calif. L. Rev. 1 (1973); Myers, Tax Status of Scholarships and Fellowships, 22 Tax Lawyer 391 (1969) (written before *Bingler v. Johnson* , discussed infra ¶11.2.2, but contains a useful summary of legislative history of §117); Stuart, Tax Status of Scholarship and Fellowship Grants: Frustration of Legislative Purpose and Approaches to Obtain the Exclusion Granted by Congress, 25 Emory LJ

arships and fellowships that do not qualify for the §117 exclusion are taxable under §74(a), which provides that a prize or award must be included in gross income unless excluded by §117 (scholarships and fellowships), §74(b) (awards for meritorious achievement), or §74(c) (employee achievement awards).[2]

Before §117 was enacted in 1954, no statutory provision explicitly governed the tax treatment of scholarships and fellowships, and they could be excluded from income only if they were considered gifts within the meaning of the predecessor of §102. The principal pre-1954 IRS ruling held that a grant was an excludable gift if it provided "for the training and education of an individual, either as a part of his program in acquiring a degree or in otherwise furthering his educational development, no services being rendered as consideration therefor."[3]

Grants to postdoctoral fellows were more troublesome, however, because of the grantor's expectation or requirement that the grantee pursue the research project that elicited the grant, which led the IRS to view the grant as compensation for services rendered.[4] Moreover, in 1952, the validity of the basic exclusionary ruling was threatened for scholarships and fellowships awarded to competition winners, when the Supreme Court held in *Robertson v. United States* that an award to the winner of a contest is paid pursuant to the sponsor's contractual obligation and is, therefore, "in no sense a gift."[5] Before the ramifications of the *Robertson* case were delineated by the courts, however, Congress enacted §§74 and 117, thereby ousting §102's jurisdiction over scholarships and fellowships, except for grants by individuals stimulated by family or philanthropic motives.[6]

---

357 (1976); Tucker, Federal Income Taxation of Scholarships and Fellowships: A Practical Analysis, 8 Ind. L. Rev. 749 (1975); Wolfman, Federal Tax Policy and the Support of Science, 114 U. Pa. L. Rev. 171 (1965).

[2] For §74, see supra ¶11.1. See Rev. Proc. 88-24, 1988-20 IRB 33 (procedures for withholding tax under §1441(b) from taxable scholarships and fellowships paid to foreign students and grantees with F, J, and M visas).

The regulations state that the taxability of scholarships and fellowships is governed "solely" by §117, so that a fellowship grant exceeding the dollar limit of the pre-1987 version of §117(b)(2) could not qualify for full exemption under the meritorious achievement rule of §74(b), presumably on the theory that grantees of fellowships are expected to pursue their studies and that this constitutes disqualifying "substantial future services" within the meaning of §74(b). See Reg. §1.117-1(a); Cass v. CIR, 86 TC 1275 (1986) (following the regulation).

[3] IT 4056, 1951-2 CB 8, declared obsolete by Rev. Rul. 69-43, 1969-1 CB 310.

[4] IT 4056, supra note 3, holding that "when the recipient of a grant or fellowship applies his skill and training to advance research, creative work, or some other project or activity, the essential elements of a gift . . . are not present."

[5] Robertson v. US, 343 US 711 (1952), discussed in ¶11.1.1.

[6] Section 1.117-3(a) defines the term "scholarship" to exclude "any amount provided by an individual to aid a relative, friend, or other individual in pursuing his

The 1954 legislative committee reports observe that pre-1954 law failed to provide a "clear-cut method of distinguishing between taxable and nontaxable grants [so that] the tax status of these grants presently must be decided on a case-by-case method." The reports, however, supply little justification for the new statutory rules (which have proved no more clear than the pre-1954 rules), nor do they explain why any scholarships and fellowships should be excluded from income. The comments in the relevant committee reports on these issues consist of brief statements to the effect that grants to students "generally are of small amount and are usually received by individuals who would have little or no tax liability in any case," that salary payments to persons on leave from their regular work ought to be taxed, and that grants to scholars who have completed their formal education and are engaged in teaching or research as part of their lifework should be excluded only if the grant is merely a supplement to the individual's own funds to make it possible for him to carry on research or further his educational development.[7]

As enacted in 1954, §117 excluded scholarships for study at educational institutions and fellowships for nondegree study and research. In either case, an excludable scholarship or fellowship could include amounts received to cover costs of travel, research, clerical help, or equipment. For nondegree candidates, the exclusion was limited to grants from educational and other charitable organizations, and could not exceed $300 per month for no more than 36 months in any individual's lifetime.

The provision was sharply curtailed in 1986.[8] No longer is the exclusion available for nondegree candidates. "Congress . . . determined that, in the case of grants to nondegree candidates for travel, research, etc., that would be deductible as ordinary and necessary business expenses, an exclusion for such expenses is not needed, and that an exclusion is not appropri-

---

studies where the grantor is motivated by family or philanthropic considerations." This is a sensible view because Congress certainly did not intend to subject intrafamily payments to the tests of §117, and the same can be said with almost equal conviction about payments by a generous patron to a deserving scholar, even if the grantor uses the word "scholarship" or "fellowship" to characterize his bounty. As the Supreme Court pointed out in Bingler v. Johnson, 394 US 741, 751 (1969), it would be erroneous to assume that §117 applies to "*all funds* received by students to support them during the course of their education."

[7] H.R. Rep. No. 1337, 83d Cong., 2d Sess. 16–17 (1954). The Senate Finance Committee's report did not repeat these observations, but seemingly endorsed them tacitly, even though the Senate bill was not identical with the House bill. S. Rep. No. 1622, 83d Cong., 2d Sess. 17–18 (1954).

[8] New §117 applies in 1987 and succeeding years. Pub. L. No. 99-514, §151(d), 100 Stat. 2085 (1986). For the application of the new and old rules to scholarships awarded in 1986 but paid in 1987 or thereafter, see Notice 87-31, 1987-1 CB 475.

ate if the expenses would not be deductible."[9] For degree candidates, further, the exclusion is only available for amounts covering tuition and fees and expenses incurred in their course work; a scholarship used for living expenses is gross income. "Congress concluded that the exclusion for scholarships should be targeted specifically for the purpose of educational benefits, and should not encompass other items that would otherwise constitute nondeductible personal expenses."[10]

¶11.2.2 The Meaning of "Scholarship" and "Fellowship Grant"

Congress has not defined the terms "scholarship" and "fellowship grant." The regulations say a scholarship is an amount paid or allowed to (or for the benefit of) a student, whether an undergraduate or graduate, to aid him in the pursuit of his studies; a "fellowship grant" is a similar amount to aid an individual in the pursuit of study or research.[11] A scholarship or fellowship can be in cash or in kind,[12] and qualifies whether, in the grantor's descriptions, it is "designated as a scholarship or by some other name (e.g., 'allowance')."[13] These definitions are not wholly consistent with academic usage (which usually reserves the term fellowship for graduate students and postdoctoral scholars),[14] but they sufficiently identify the subject matter of §117 to create no difficulties for most academic stipends.

---

[9] Staff of Joint Comm. on Tax'n, 99th Cong., 2d Sess., General Explanation of the Tax Reform Act of 1986, at 40 (Comm. Print 1987) [hereinafter 1986 Bluebook].
[10] Id.
[11] Reg. §§1.117-3(a), (c).
[12] The regulations state that a scholarship or fellowship grant can include not only cash but also the value of room, board, and other services and accommodations, tuition and other fees furnished or remitted to the grantee, and family allowances. Reg. §1.117-3(d). See Rev. Rul. 77-263, 1977-2 CB 47 (athletic scholarship held excludable under §117 where limited to value of tuition and fees, room and board, and books and supplies necessary for studies, less value of any other scholarship received and any wages earned during school year). Although the 1986 revisions of §117 deny the exclusion to room, board, and other living expenses, the principal point—that an excludable scholarship or fellowship may be in cash or in kind—surely remains valid.
[13] 1986 Bluebook, supra note 9, at 42.
[14] Section 117(a) specifies that a scholarship must be "at an educational institution" (as defined), and the Senate Finance Committee's report on §117 treats this as an indispensible condition: "In the case of a scholarship, in order for the exclusion to apply, the scholarship must be at an educational institution" S. Rep. No. 1622, supra note 7, at 188.
Before 1987, the term "fellowship grant," although used interchangeably with "scholarship," was not subject to this condition. IRC §117(a)(1)(B) (before amendment in 1986). The regulations say the term "fellowship grant" can be applied to students as well as to postdoctoral and nondegree scholars. Reg. §1.117-3(c). In short, the reference to "educational organizations" in §117(a) seemingly had no operative

The principal definitional problem under §117 has been distinguishing excludable scholarships and fellowships from taxable compensation for services. The scope of this problem has been reduced by two aspects of the 1986 amendments. First, the exclusion formerly allowed for individuals who are not degree candidates has been eliminated, thus cutting off the claims of a host of researchers, interns, medical residents, and others. Second, for degree candidates, the 1986 amendments deny the exclusion to any amount "which represents payment for teaching, research, or other services by the student required as a condition for receiving the [award]."[15] Prior law had allowed an exclusion for such payments when the services were required of all candidates for the degree.[16]

In the paragraphs below, the authorities on the scholarship versus compensation issue are discussed first; the pre-1987 exclusion for services required of all degree candidates and an exclusion added in 1984 for scholarships provided to employees of educational institutions and their spouses and dependents are discussed thereafter.

1. *The basic definition.* The issue most commonly arises when a business, nonprofit, or governmental organization provides a grant to a student engaged in vocational, graduate, and professional training where the student (1) is committed or expected to accept or resume employment with the grantor or, (2) while a student, renders personal services (e.g., as a hospital resident or as apprentice teacher) that advance his educational objectives and simultaneously relieve the grantor of the expense of hiring others to perform the same tasks. The Treasury staked out a position in the regulations: First, an amount representing "compensation for past, present, or future employment services or . . . payment for services which are subject to the direction or supervision of the grantor" cannot qualify as scholarships or fellowships even though paid to enable the grantee to pursue his studies or research. Second, a parallel disqualification applies if the grantee's studies or research is "primarily for the benefit of the grantor."[17]

---

significance before 1987. The present statute eliminates this anomaly by clearly requiring that all scholarships and fellowship grants be at educational institutions.

[15] IRC §117(c); H.R. Rep. No. 841, 99th Cong., 2d Sess. II-16 (Conf. Rep. 1986). It is not intended, however, that a student receiving payment for such a service should be categorically barred from enjoying the §117(a) exclusion. "If an amount representing reasonable compensation (whether paid in cash or as tuition reduction) for services performed by an employee is included in the employee's gross income and wages, then any additional amount of scholarship award or tuition reduction remains eligible for the . . . exclusion." 1986 Bluebook, supra note 9, at 43.

[16] See infra text accompanying notes 33–34.

[17] Reg. §1.117-4(c). The scope of the second paragraph of §1.117-4(c) (studies or research "primarily for the benefit of the grantor") is described in Bingler v. Johnson,

In line with the first of these interpretations, the Tax Court has held that compensation for services does not become a scholarship or fellowship merely because the recipient's objective is professional training:

> Petitioner maintains . . . that his principal objective in accepting an appointment as a resident physician [at a university hospital with an extensive training program] at great financial sacrifice was to obtain training in his profession—to have the opportunity to consult with staff physicians on a variety of medical problems. There can be no serious doubt that work as a resident physician provides highly valuable training, particularly in preparing for specialties in the various fields of medicine. Yet virtually all work as an apprentice, whether in medicine or law, carpentry or masonry, provides valuable training. Nothing in Section 117 requires that an amount paid as compensation for services rendered be treated as a nontaxable fellowship grant, merely because the recipient is learning a trade, business or profession. Whatever training petitioner received during the years of his residency —and we do not deny that it was substantial—was merely "incidental to and for the purpose of facilitating the *raison d'etre* of the Hospital, namely, the care of its patients." . . . We conclude that petitioner was an employee of University Hospital and was paid the stipend as compensation for the services which he rendered.[18]

For taxable years after 1986, the Tax Court's conclusion is underscored by the rules denying the exclusion unless the recipient is a candidate for a degree and can show that the services were not required as a condition of receiving the award.

The second disqualifying condition set out in the regulations (study or research for the grantor's benefit) is mitigated by two minor concessions: (1) It does not apply if the "primary purpose" of the studies or research is to further the training of the recipient in his individual capacity, provided the amount paid does not represent compensation or payment for his services;[19] and (2) incidental benefits to the grantor are not fatal, nor is a requirement that the grantee submit progress reports to the grantor.

The regulations were attacked as inconsistent with the 1954 legislation. This claim was based on the statutory rule disqualifying compensation for some part-time teaching and research services by candidates for degrees,[20] which would have been unnecessary if a broader restriction were inherent in

---

394 US 758 n.32 (1969) (bargained-for arrangements that do not create an employer-employee relationship, as in the case of an independent contractor).

[18] Proskey v. CIR, 51 TC 918, 924–25 (1969).

[19] See Rev. Rul. 75-280, 1975-2 CB 47.

[20] See infra text accompanying notes 34–35.

the concepts of "scholarships" and "fellowship grants." Proponents of this view also relied on the announced 1954 legislative intent to avoid case-by-case examinations of the grantor's motive.

The Supreme Court rejected these arguments in 1969, when it held in *Bingler v. Johnson* that a grant by a business corporation to enable an employee to work on a doctoral dissertation, on condition that he return to the company's employ at the end of a leave of absence, was not a scholarship within the meaning of §117(a).[21] Acknowledging that the legislative history was not clear, the Court concluded that the regulations were a reasonable contemporaneous interpretation of the statutory language:

> The difficulty with [the taxpayer's] position . . . lies in its implicit assumption that [the explicit limitations in §117] are limitations on an exclusion of *all funds* received by students to support them during the course of their education. Section 117 provides, however, only that amounts received as "scholarships" or "fellowships" shall be excludable. And Congress never defined what it meant by the quoted terms. As the Tax Court has observed:
>
> "[A] proper reading of the statute requires that before the exclusion comes into play there must be a determination that the payment sought to be excluded has the normal characteristics associated with the term 'scholarship.'" *Reese v. CIR*, 45 TC 407, 413, aff'd, 373 F.2d 742.
>
> The regulation here in question represents an effort by the Commissioner to supply the definitions that Congress omitted. . . . Here, the definitions supplied by the Regulation clearly are prima facie proper, comporting as they do with the ordinary understanding of "scholarships" and "fellowships" as relatively disinterested, "no-strings" educational grants, with no requirement of any substantial *quid pro quo* from the recipients. . . . The thrust of the provision [of the regulations] dealing with compensation is that bargained-for payments, given only as a *quo* in return for the *quid* of services rendered—whether past, present, or future—should not be excludable from income as "scholarship" funds.[22]

In the years since *Bingler v. Johnson* was decided, few grants by employers to current or prospective employees have avoided the stigma of being a "quo" for past, present, or future services, except (for years before 1987) by meeting the test of former §117(b)(1) (payments to candidates for degrees for services required of all candidates for the same degree).[23] In

---

[21] Bingler v. Johnson, 394 US 741 (1969).

[22] Id. at 749, 751, 757–58.

[23] This escape hatch is discussed in the text accompanying notes 34–35.

many situations, the disqualification results from the performance of services that while advancing the taxpayer's educational objective, also relieve the grantor of the expense of hiring others to perform the same tasks. In others, the grantee's studies or research does not enable the grantor to reduce its staff or avoid hiring other persons, but—like the grant in *Bingler v. Johnson*—serves to upgrade the skills or increase the supply of qualified persons who are required or expected to work for the grantor. The quid pro quo test of *Bingler v. Johnson* can apply to trainees in any occupation, but the most persistent losers have been hospital interns and residents, nurses, and teachers.[24]

The statute denies the exclusion to "that portion of any amount received which represents payment for teaching, research, or other services by the student required as a condition for receiving the [award]."[25] Although similar language has been found in the statute since 1954, until 1986 it was focused on "services in the nature of part-time employment."[26] The elimination of the reference to part-time work allows this language to become the fulcrum of the scholarship versus compensation dichotomy. For years after 1986, the *Bingler v. Johnson* test should be reformulated as three questions:

---

[24] See Logan v. US, 518 F2d 143 (6th Cir. 1975) (teaching assistant); Willie v. CIR, 57 TC 383 (1971) (teacher in desegregation program); Marquette Univ. v. US, 58 AFTR2d 5929 (ED Wis. 1986) (not officially reported) (summer research grants given by university to its faculty); Adams v. CIR, 71 TC 477 (1978) (hospital intern taxed; divided court); Rev. Rul. 82-57, 1982-1 CB 24 (grants by Veterans Administration to graduate students serving as staff assistants at VA hospitals as condition of receiving university degree); Rev. Rul. 70-648, 1970-2 CB 21 (hospital ministerial interns); Rev. Rul. 70-220, 1970-1 CB 26 (nurses and sanitarians). But see Burstein v. US, 79-1 USTC ¶9354 (Ct. Cl. Trial Judge 1979) (not officially reported), aff'd, 622 F2d 529 (Ct. Cl. 1980) (hospital residents allowed to exclude grants received from hospital that separated salaries from grants—a rare exception to a "near unanimous group" of over 50 cases denying exclusions to hospital residents). Compare Mizell v. US, 663 F2d 772 (8th Cir. 1981) (jury verdict that hospital residents' stipends were scholarships or fellowships and not compensation for services held supported by evidence; divided court) with Yarlott v. CIR, 717 F2d 439 (8th Cir. 1983) (Tax Court decision taxing students in clinical residency/advanced degree joint program affirmed). See also Olick v. CIR, 73 TC 479, 485 (1979) (teacher's aide rendered services only when related to current academic courses, not when needed by regular teacher; "services were dispensable in that his absence would not create any additional burden for the permanent teachers"); Bieberdorf v. CIR, 60 TC 114 (1973) (acq.) (20–25 percent of time spent in clinical work by taxpayer in academic medicine field held "incidental," as work was primarily educational and taxpayer did not treat patients on own initiative); Bailey v. CIR, 60 TC 447 (1973) (acq.) (incidental services; mere possibility of future employment is insufficient to disqualify); Rev. Rul. 71-538, 1971-2 CB 97 (activities of research fellows did not discharge duties of staff or provide a "net benefit" to grantor institution).

[25] IRC §117(c).

[26] IRC §117(b)(1) (before amendment in 1986).

(1) Did the student render services? (2) If so, were the services a condition for receiving the award? (3) If so, was the award payment for the services? If all three questions are answered affirmatively, the award is taxable compensation. The compensation stigma is avoided, in contrast, if any of the three is answered no.

Although §117 was enacted to provide clear-cut criteria for determining the excludability of educational grants,[27] the cases and revenue rulings have employed a case-by-case approach, examining all the circumstances under which the grant was made.[28] This approach continues to be appropriate for years after 1986, even if the test is recast as suggested in the preceding paragraph.

Where research or teaching assistantships are involved, the key factors include the extent of faculty supervision, freedom of the grantee to pursue individual goals, consideration of financial need in making grants, existence of equivalent research or teaching requirements for all similarly situated students, the university's treatment of the grant, the receipt of degree-related academic credit, and the extent to which the student's activities are tied to the needs of the university.[29] When studies are subsidized by an ordinary employer, the grants are almost always income to the employee, save in extraordinary circumstances where the possible benefits to the employer are nominal.[30] Moreover, even if the grant is unrelated to past, present, or future employment, exemptions are regularly denied if the grantor receives preferential rights to the results of the grantee's research, such as patents or copyrights.[31]

---

[27] H.R. Rep. No. 1337, 83d Cong., 2d Sess. 16 (1954).

[28] See, e.g., Zolnay v. CIR, 49 TC 389, 395 (1968) ("each case must turn upon its own particular facts and circumstances"); Rev. Rul. 72-263, 1972-1 CB 40.

[29] See generally Stuart, supra note 1; Tucker, supra note 1.

[30] See, e.g., Ehrhart v. CIR, 470 F2d 940 (1st Cir. 1973) (living allowances paid for employees while attending university taxable despite absence of obligation to return; company's primary object was that graduates would remain as employees and "hearts can be won as well as coerced"); but see Broniwitz v. CIR, 27 TCM (CCH) 1088 (1968) (full-time student not taxed where student directed own course of study, was under no obligation to work for employer after graduation, and was separately paid for work for employer during summer). For the possibility of deductions for employer financed education, see infra ¶22.1; see also infra ¶14.4 (exclusion of benefits under employer's educational assistance program qualified under §127).

[31] See Utech v. CIR, 55 TC 434 (1970) (project for benefit of National Bureau of Standards); Rev. Rul. 75-490, 1975-2 CB 50 (potential benefits to employer from taxpayer's research); Rev. Rul. 74-95, 1974-1 CB 39 (rights to publication); Rev. Rul. 73-564, 1973-2 CB 28 (right to patents and inventions arising out of research grant); Rev. Rul. 72-263, 1972-1 CB 40 (right to patents and royalty-free use of copyrighted materials); but see Krupin v. US, 439 F. Supp. 440 (ED Mo. 1977) (retained copyright and patent privileges were at best speculative and insufficient to deny §117 exclusion).

When funds are provided by one entity to another (e.g., as a grant by a federal agency to a tax-exempt hospital), it may be debatable whether one or the other is the grantor. The recipient's claim to an exclusion, however, is likely to be denied if he fails the quid pro quo test of *Bingler v. Johnson* with regard to either the immediate payee or the original source of the funds. Thus, research funds cannot be laundered by passing them through a disinterested institution;[32] conversely, payments for services cannot be excluded under §117 merely because the funds are furnished by a disinterested source to the institution for which the services are performed.[33]

If a grant to a student is found to include compensation for services, the §117 exclusion is not necessarily lost entirely, particularly if the grantor and receipient of the services is the educational institution at which the student studies. Assume a graduate student receives a $10,000 grant from his university and is required to perform various duties as a graduate assistant. At least in theory, if the student can show that the value of his services is, say, $6,000, the remaining $4,000 of the grant is excludable under §117.

This approach is most credible when the grantor is an educational institution that makes grants to students that clearly qualify as scholarships. There is no reason to suppose that the university in this example divides grantees into two rigid categories: (1) scholarship recipients who do no work for their grants and (2) student-employees who get fair pay for their work, no more and no less. It is reasonable to assume that the university might wish to provide for a student's financial needs with a combination of pay for employment and true scholarship grants. This assumption, however, creates the difficult task of allocating a student's grant between compensation and scholarship. If the school splits the grant between the two categories, is this allocation determinative? If so, the rule is greatly compromised because the school is usually as eager to maximize the scholarship component as the student.[34] If not, how is the value of the student's services to be

---

[32] See Rev. Rul. 73-564, supra note 31 (foundation made funds available to college to pay designated professor while on leave, indirectly controlled his research, and had preferential right to patents and inventions; held, foundation is grantor); Rev. Rul. 64-213, 1964-2 CB 40 (students working as newspaper interns were paid by university from funds contributed by newspapers; held, newspapers were grantors).

[33] Carroll v. CIR, 60 TC 96 (1973) (both provider of funds and actual payor are grantors where both benefit from taxpayer's activities); Turem v. CIR, 54 TC 1494 (1970) (same); Johnson v. CIR, 37 TCM (CCH) 418 (1978) (board of education held to be grantor where it selected recipient of grant and provided her with employee benefits; irrelevant that board was reimbursed by federal agency and institution).

[34] The school, for example, owes employment taxes on the compensation element, but not the scholarship element. Also, the school's ability to provide for students' financial needs is diminished when students are taxed on their grants. If the

determined? What, for example, is the market rate of pay for grading a professor's exam papers?

The issue of allocation is less likely to arise when the grantor is not the educational institution at which the grantee studies. If a business corporation makes a grant to an employee to finance the employee's study at a university, for example, the grant is usually considered to consist of compensation only.

2. *Former exclusion for teaching and research services.* Until 1987, the scholarship exclusion was allowed for compensation for some teaching and research services. While stating that compensation for such services generally did not qualify, former §117(b)(1) went on to exclude the compensation when similar services were required of all candidates for the degree, "whether or not [they are] recipients of scholarships or fellowship grants."

The statutory language was unsatisfactory. First, it contains an inherent ambiguity: If all candidates for the degree must engage in part-time teaching and receive the same stipend, are all exempt? Or does the statutory relief for such payments require that some candidates for the same degree perform the identical services without payment? Second, by disqualifying payments for services performed by candidates for degrees while failing to refer to such payments in former §117(b)(2), relating to persons who are not candidates for degrees, did Congress implicitly grant the latter group of taxpayers an exemption for payments that would be taxable if received by degree candidates?

3. *Scholarships for employee's dependents.* Business corporations often establish and finance private foundations to grant scholarships to children of their employees. Although grants can be compensatory even though the recipients are members of the employees' families rather than the employees themselves, the IRS' policy is to allow the §117 exclusion if the grants are "controlled and limited by substantial nonemployment factors to such an extent that the preferential treatment derived from employment does not continue to be of any significance beyond an initial qualifier."[35]

---

student in the example needs $10,000 after taxes to make ends meet, this need can be met by a tax-free grant of $10,000 or (assuming a tax rate of 28 percent) a taxable grant of $13,889. If the larger sum must be paid, the school has $3,889 less to provide for the financial need of other students.

[35] Rev. Proc. 76-47, 1976-2 CB 670, amplified by Rev. Proc. 77-32, 1977-2 CB 541, amended by Rev. Proc. 83-36, 1983-1 CB 763. The leading case on the issue is Armantrout v. CIR, 67 TC 996 (1977), aff'd per curiam, 570 F2d 210 (7th Cir. 1978) (employee taxed on assignment-of-income grounds on benefits paid by employer's trust established by employer to defray educational expenses of children of key employees). See Wheeler v. US, 768 F2d 1333 (Fed. Cir. 1985) (*Armantrout* followed on similar facts); Saunders v. CIR, 720 F2d 871 (5th Cir. 1983) (same); Grant-Jacoby, Inc. v. CIR, 73 TC 700 (1980) (same). See generally Blum, The Educational Benefit Trust as a Lesson in Taxation, 56 Taxes 600 (1978).

Under the IRS rules, the taint arising from the fact that the parent's employment is a threshold qualifying factor is dispelled if the program satisfies specified conditions, including use of an independent selection committee and such objective criteria as the candidate's academic performance and financial need, and also including a percentage test designed to disqualify grants that are a relatively automatic consequence of the parent's status as an employee.

4. *Special exclusion for employees of educational institutions and their dependents.* Since 1984, §117(d) has excluded from gross income a "qualified tuition reduction" allowed to an employee of an educational institution for the benefit of himself or a spouse or dependent.[36] A tuition reduction can only qualify if the plan under which it is provided does not discriminate in favor of highly compensated employees.[37] If this requirement is met, the "reduction" can apparently consist of a true reduction or a cash payment.[38] Assume an employee at *X* College has a child in school. The exclusion under §117(d) can apply if (1) the child is enrolled in *X* College and the college reduces tuition for the child under a nondiscriminatory plan for employees of the college or (2) the child is enrolled in some other school and *X* College pays a portion of the child's tuition under a nondiscriminatory employee benefit plan.

This exclusion, however, is not available for a stipend or tuition remission provided to a student who performs teaching, research, or other ser-

---

For the exclusion of educational benefits from gross income when provided under an employer's educational assistance program, see infra ¶14.4.

[36] The regulations previously provided an exclusion for plans under which educational institutions remit tuition charges for faculty children. Reg. §1.117-3(a) (last sentence). A Treasury proposal to tax the parents on these benefits was floated in 1976 and withdrawn in 1977. See Prop. Reg. §§1.117-3(a), -4(c), 41 Fed. Reg. 48,132 (1976), withdrawn Jan. 13, 1977.

The regulation exclusion only applied where the institution participated in a plan where "the tuition of a child of a faculty member of such institution is remitted by any other participating educational institution attended by [the] child." Reg. §1.117-3(a). Faculty have not fared well under plans following neither this model nor the requirements of the statutory exclusion enacted in 1984. Marquette Univ. v. US, 58 AFTR2d 5929 (ED Wis. 1986) (not officially reported) (university plan allowed employees to elect to have university pay tuition for dependents and deduct amounts paid from employees' paychecks; held, amounts taxable to employees); Western Reserve Academy v. US, 619 F. Supp. 394 (ND Ohio 1985), aff'd, 801 F2d 250 (6th Cir. 1986) (payments of college tuition for children of teachers at private secondary school taxable to parents; employer not liabile for withholding and FICA taxes with respect to payments because taxability of payments unclear when made (1976 and 1977)).

[37] IRC §117(d)(3).

[38] Staff of Joint Comm. on Tax'n, 98th Cong., 2d Sess., General Explanation of the Revenue Provisons of the Deficit Reduction Act of 1984, at 860 (Comm. Print 1984).

table, educational, and similar organizations),[49] a foreign government, an international organization,[50] the United States (or an instrumentality or agency thereof), a state, territory, or possession of the United States or political subdivision thereof,[51] or the District of Columbia. The legislative committee reports do not set out a rationale for this limitation, but presumably the primary legislative purpose was to disqualify grants by ordinary business corporations to past, present, or prospective employees. Since few grants of this type satisfy the administrative criteria approved by *Bingler v. Johnson*, however, the restriction had less work to do than was contemplated when it was enacted.[52]

Second, former §117(b)(2)(B) imposed a dollar limitation, under which (1) the exclusion for any one taxable year could not exceed $300 times the number of months for which grants were received and (2) no exclusion was allowed after the taxpayer had been permitted to exclude amounts for 36 months (whether or not consecutive) when he was not a candidate for a degree. All funds paid to the grantee are included in computing the $300 limit unless specifically designated to cover expenses for travel, research, clerical help, or equipment.[53]

In applying the $300 limit, the number of months *for which* the recipient received amounts was controlling, not the number of months *in which* payments were received. Thus, a qualified fellowship of $4,500 for a nine-month academic year spanning two calendar years results in an exclusion of $2,700 (9 × $300), even if paid in a single sum. If the recipient received less than the allowable limit (if, say, $1,800 was received for a nine-month period), the shortfall could not be carried forward to be used in a later year when the grantee got a more generous fellowship. Nor could an exclusion to which the grantee was entitled be renounced in such a case in order to avoid exhausting the lifetime 36-month limit.

---

[49] See infra ¶100.2.1.
[50] See Rev. Rul. 63-19, 1963-1 CB 28 (NATO qualifies as international organization).
[51] For taxable years after 1982, an Indian tribal government is treated as a state for this purpose. IRC §7871. See Rev. Proc. 83-87, 1983-2 CB 606, modified by Rev. Proc. 86-17, 1986-1 CB 550 (list of Indian tribal governments).
[52] See Williamsen v. CIR, 32 TC 154(1959) (taxpayer bears burden of proving that private corporation making grant was agent of United States and not independent contractor); Rev. Rul. 62-205, 1962-2 CB 43 (funds originated with government agency, but exclusion depends on status of institution running program); Rev. Rul. 61-66, 1961-1 CB 19 (where university was conduit for grant from one individual to another, individual is grantor; no exclusion under §117).
[53] See Rev. Rul. 71-344, 1971-2 CB 94 (amount specifically designated for expenses held excludable); Rev. Rul. 67-85, 1967-1 CB 25 (contra for amount not specifically designated for expenses); Rev. Rul. 55-554, 1955-2 CB 36 (supplemental amount for dependents includable in computing $300 limit).

It is not inconceivable that a career academician might endeavor to treat a borderline grant as taxable compensation if it is received when the resulting tax would be minimal (or zero), in order to save the 36-month exclusion for use in later years, when he expected to be in a higher tax bracket. This is a dangerous strategy, however, because the exclusion applies to the first 36 months to which the taxpayer is "entitled" to it. If an earlier receipt is reported as gross income and the statute of limitations on refunds for that year runs before the inclusion is tested, a finding that the inclusion is improper causes the exclusion for at least some of the 36 months to be lost.[54]

---

[54] For an example of this misfortune, see Chang v. US, 82-1 USTC ¶9199 (Ct. Cl. 1982) (not officially reported).

CHAPTER

12

Life Insurance, Annuity, and Endowment Contracts and Employee Death Benefits

¶12.1 LIFE INSURANCE, ANNUITY, AND ENDOWMENT CONTRACTS: IN GENERAL

¶12.1.1 Introductory

Several important exclusions from gross income are authorized for amounts received under life insurance, annuity, and endowment contracts. The labyrinth of rules governing these contracts is discussed in detail hereafter, but can be summarized as follows:

1. *Death benefits.* Amounts paid under a life insurance contract on the death of the insured are ordinarily excluded from gross income by §101(a).[1] In effect, these payments are treated like bequests, which are also excluded from the recipient's gross income. Section 101(a) embraces both lump sum and installment payments, but the latter are ordinarily apportioned between the amount that would have been paid at the date of death, which is excluded from income, and postdeath earnings, which are ordinarily taxed.

2. *Annuities.* An annuity payment is divided by §72(b) into two components. A portion is excluded from gross income as a return of capital (the cost of the contract), and the balance is gross income under §72(a) since it is income earned by the taxpayer's investment in the contract.[2] The division between income and capital is made by allocating the investment in the contract ratably among the payments expected to be received under the annuity. If the payments received precisely equal the number and amount

---

[1] See infra ¶12.2.
[2] See infra ¶12.3.

of the payments predicted at the outset, this procedure allows full recovery of the investment in the contract and yet taxes every dollar of economic gain. If fact differs from expectation (as typically happens when an annuity is payable for the life of one or more persons), an adjustment is necessary: If the payments cease before the investment is fully recovered (e.g., if the annuitant under a life annuity dies prematurely), a deduction is allowed for the unrecovered amount. Conversely, once the investment is fully recovered, each subsequent annuity payment is fully included in gross income.[3]

Although "annuity" in layman's language connotes payments measured by the life of one or more individuals, the statutory scheme also covers amounts payable for a fixed period of years.[4]

3. *Other payments.* Other amounts paid under life insurance, annuity, and endowment contracts are treated by §72(e) either as tax-free refunds of the taxpayer's premiums or as profit on his investment in the contract.[5] This treatment is applicable to a wide and divergent array of receipts, including dividends, the maturity value of endowment policies, variable annuities in excess of an allocated part of the cost, guaranteed refunds under annuity policies if the annuitant dies prematurely, the cash surrender value of life insurance policies, and other payments.

The application of the foregoing rules can be complicated by many factors, including the following:

1. *Combination of components.* Some contracts combine features usually found in contracts of different types. Life insurance policies, for example, often provide for installment payments for the duration of the beneficiary's life rather than a lump sum payment, or contain a settlement option under which the beneficiary can, in effect, purchase an annuity contract on terms fixed when the policy was issued or in force at the time of the election. Conversely, an annuity contract may provide death benefits if the annuitant dies prematurely. Sometimes a policyholder can obtain a lump sum in partial redemption of the contract, while preserving the death benefit or annuity features of the contract at a reduced level. In these instances, two or all three of the rules described above may apply to the same contract. Conversely, when two ostensibly separate contracts are written by the insurer only in combination, they might be viewed as a unit in determining the characterization and proper treatment of a particular payment. These issues

---

[3] See infra ¶12.3.2.

[4] Between 1949 and 1954, the regulations provided that the phrase "amounts received as an annuity," as used in §22(b)(2)(A) of the 1939 Code, was restricted to amounts payable for a period determined by reference to life expectancy or mortality tables, excluding payments for a term certain. See Brawerman, Income Tax Problems of Non-Business Life Insurance, 1952 S. Cal. Tax Inst. 267, 284–87.

[5] See infra ¶12.4.

are developed more fully in the discussion that follows.[6]

2. *Noncommercial contracts.* Both §72 and §101 are primarily concerned with contracts written by regulated insurance companies, and this
focus accounts for the trade jargon used in the Code and regulations. Many
other contracts, such as agreements by employers to pay death benefits and
annuities to employees, are treated as life insurance and annuity contracts if
they sufficiently resemble commercial policies.[7] On the other hand, some
private and noncommercial transactions are excluded from §§72 and 101.
Thus, a transfer of property by parents to their children in return for a
promise of lifetime support is like an annuity contract, but the courts have
held that the uncertainty of payment and other aspects of these transactions
require different treatment.[8] Similarly, a contract for the sale of property
may resemble an annuity contract in providing for deferred periodic payments, but it is not so treated for tax purposes.[9]

3. *Overlapping statutory provisions.* Finally, §§72 and 101 are primarily
concerned with individuals who purchase life insurance, annuity, or endowment contracts to provide for their own well-being or the support of their
dependents. The statutory provisions are not confined to this standard
situation, but departures from it may trigger the application of other statutory provisions altering the tax results that would be reached if §§72 and
101 had sole jurisdiction over the transaction. Thus, annuity payments
received as alimony, reimbursement for personal injuries, or compensation
for personal services performed while a bona fide resident of a foreign
country may be entitled to a broader exclusion than is allowed by §72(b)
because the contract is merely a vehicle to accomplish a larger purpose that
qualifies for a special statutory allowance.[10]

¶12.1.2 The Tax Advantages of Life Insurance, Annuity, and Endowment Contracts

Owners and beneficiaries of life insurance, annuity, and endowment
contracts benefit from many dispensations under the Code. Perhaps most
prominent is the exemption beneficiaries are given for the proceeds of life
insurance. Of equal or greater interest to financial planners and policy
analysts is the rule that a policyholder is not taxed on an increase in the cash
surrender value of a life insurance, annuity, or endowment contract. The

---

[6] E.g., infra ¶12.2.3 (effect of settlement options in life insurance policies),
¶12.3.4 (effect of original annuitant's death).

[7] See infra ¶¶12.2.2, 12.7.4.

[8] See infra ¶12.3.5.

[9] See infra ¶106.1.

[10] See infra ¶12.3.6 (special rules), ¶12.3.2 note 34 (compensation for pre-1963
foreign service).

major tax advantages of these contracts is evaluated in the following paragraphs.

1. *Exclusion of death benefits.* Under §101(a)(1), amounts received under a life insurance contract, if paid by reason of the death of the insured, are ordinarily excluded from gross income. This exclusion, in force since 1913, may have originally reflected doubts about the constitutional validity of taxing the proceeds of life insurance, but the exclusion is now based on a legislative policy judgment rather than on a perception of constitutional compulsion.[11]

The exclusion of life insurance proceeds has much in common with the statutory exclusion of bequests;[12] indeed, for many families life insurance and social security benefits are the only significant assets left by breadwinners to their surviving spouses and children. If the decedent had saved the premiums instead of purchasing life insurance, the savings plus the accumulated yield could have been transferred to the survivors as a tax-free bequest. The analogy to bequests is not perfect. The proceeds of life insurance have nothing in common with a bequest, for example, when paid to an employer as compensation for the business loss suffered on the death of an officer or employee.

The analogy between life insurance proceeds and bequests is also weakened by the possibility of mortality gains and losses, which are unique to life insurance: If the insured dies in a plane crash after buying flight insurance at the airport, his beneficiaries receive far more than the amount paid for the policy; conversely, the insurance paid on the death of a long-lived decedent may be less than his family would have received if the premiums had been invested in securities or deposited in a savings account.[13]

---

[11] In US v. Supplee-Biddle Hardware Co., 265 US 189 (1924), the Court held that the exclusion granted by the Revenue Act of 1918 embraced corporate beneficiaries of life insurance as well as individuals, saying that life insurance proceeds "are not usually classed as income" and reserving judgment about whether "Congress could call the proceeds of such indemnity, income, and validly tax it as such." Since 1926, however, certain transferees of life insurance policies have been taxed on the proceeds to the extent that they get more than they paid for the policy (infra ¶12.2.4); and this treatment was upheld as constitutional in James F. Waters, Inc. v. CIR, 160 F2d 596 (9th Cir.), cert. denied, 332 US 767 (1947).

[12] See supra ¶10.1.

[13] For discussion of the policy issues in the tax treatment of life insurance, see Sneed, The Configurations of Gross Income 189–204 (Ohio State U. Press 1967); McClure, The Income Tax Treatment of Interest Earned on Savings in Life Insurance, in The Economics of Federal Subsidy Programs, Compendium of Papers Submitted to the Joint Economic Committee, 92d Cong., 2d Sess. 370–405 (1972); Goode, Policyholders' Interest Income From Life Insurance Under the Income Tax, 16 Vand. L. Rev. 33 (1962).

The exclusion of mortality gains realized through life insurance is probably explained by the fact that premiums for nonbusiness insurance are treated as personal expenditures rather than investments. If flight insurance were considered an investment, the beneficiaries (or perhaps the decedent on his final return) would be taxed in the event the plane goes down on the excess of the proceeds over the premium paid, and, in the event of a safe trip, the premium would be allowed as a deduction. Current law, however, treats the premium as a personal expense, allowing no deduction if nothing is collected and, as an appropriate corollary, the proceeds, if collected, are tax free. A purchaser of life insurance is treated like a purchaser of an old washing machine; whether the machine breaks down with the first load or lasts 10 years, providing washing services worth 20 times the price paid, is no concern of the tax collector.[14]

2. *Exemption or deferral of inside buildup.* Life insurance policies frequently have a cash surrender value that accumulates while the policy is outstanding and can be obtained from the insurer during the insured's lifetime by cashing in the policy. Annuity and endowment policies nearly always have cash surrender value. Under a policy with cash surrender value, a portion of each premium payment is allocated to cash surrender value, and cash surrender value also increases by the addition of interest on accumulations. Cash surrender value, in other words, is like a savings account buried within the policy.

During the insured's lifetime, the savings element in life insurance with cash surrender value grows without being currently taxed to the policyholder. The same is true of income accruing on the cash surrender value of an annuity prior to the time payments to the annuitant begin. For life insurance, this income often escapes the income tax permanently because the proceeds payable at death, including the portion thereof representing income accumulated on cash surrender value, are excluded from the recipient's gross income. For annuities, tax on income accruing on cash surrender value is more commonly deferred rather than exempted because a portion of each annuity payment, representing accrued income, is taxed to the annuitant. The exemption or deferral of inside buildup is attacked by tax theorists and reformers as a departure from the principles applied generally to investment income.[15]

Current taxation is also avoided by other investments whose growth in value consists of unrealized appreciation rather than taxable interest or dividends.[16] The growth in a policy's value resembles unrealized apprecia-

---

[14] See supra ¶5.8.1 for a similar explanation of why an insured under a liability insurance policy is not taxed when the insurer pays his liability.

[15] See, e.g., 2 Treasury Dept., Tax Reform for Fairness, Simplicity, and Economic Growth 259–60 (1984).

[16] See supra ¶5.2.

tion in one sense: If the policyholder realizes on the growth in cash surrender value by cashing in the policy, the benefits of keeping it in force are relinquished, and this entails a significant change in investments and perhaps a substantial sacrifice if the insured is no longer insurable at standard rates; cashing in a policy, in other words, is a closing out of an investment similar to a sale of a stock or bond.

Most policies, however, entitle the owner to take out policy loans on terms that resemble withdrawals from savings accounts. Interest continues to accrue on cash surrender value for the benefit of the policyholder, but interest also accrues to the company's benefit on the policy loan. Because these interest accruals roughly cancel each other out and because the choice of whether and when to repay the loan is largely left to the policyholder, the effect is essentially that the amount of the loan has been withdrawn, subject to the policyholder's right to reinvest it in the insurance contract. The preferential treatment of the loan feature is most obvious in the case of a policyholder who takes out a policy loan; he is generally allowed a deduction for interest on the loan from the company, but is not taxed on the compensating interest accrual on cash surrender value.

The broader issue, however, is whether the availability of policy loans under such circumstances should cause all inside buildup to be taxed to policyholders as it accrues. Under the doctrine of constructive receipt, income is taxed when "it is credited to his account . . . so that he may draw upon it at any time."[17] Under current law, this doctrine is not applied to increases in cash surrender value because policy loans are treated as loans, not as withdrawals of the taxpayer's own money, a treatment that some find formalistic and not reflective of economic substance.

The favorable treatment of inside buildup, further, encourages insurers to devise contracts that are meant primarily as investment vehicles, but are cloaked in the garb of life insurance to give buyers the tax advantages provided for life insurance. The attractiveness of this garb, in other words, leads taxpayers to try to fit as much as possible within it, including some contracts that vary greatly from those envisioned when the life insurance rules were developed. Congress responded to this development in 1984 by enacting rules that tax inside buildup on life insurance as it accrues when investment features predominate over insurance features.[18] A somewhat broader approach was taken for annuity contracts, where a series of rules was enacted to channel benefits into the annuitant's retirement years.

3. *Sales and dispositions.* The exclusion of life insurance benefits from gross income applies only to payments by reason of the insured's death; if the policy is cashed in during the insured's lifetime, the amount received is

---

[17] Reg. §1.451-2, discussed infra ¶105.2.3.
[18] See infra ¶12.5.

taxed to the extent that it exceeds the owner's cost.[19] The method used to measure this gain provides another advantage for policies with cash surrender. When life insurance protection is provided by term insurance (i.e., by a policy without cash surrender value), the unlucky insured who survives the end of a policy year has nothing to show for the premium paid and gets no loss deduction or other tax allowance for the premium. A purchaser of term insurance, in other words, must pay the premium from after-tax income. Under a policy with cash surrender value, a portion of each premium payment goes to purchase current life insurance protection and is not unlike a term premium; the remainder is added to the cash surrender accumulation. If the policy is later cashed in, however, the policyholder's gain is limited to the excess of the cash surrender value over the sum of all premiums paid, including the portions of the premiums used to pay for pure insurance protection for periods now elapsed. The inclusion of these portions of the premiums in the policy's cost basis has the effect of allowing the insurance protection to be paid for with pretax income.

4. *Ratable cost recovery for annuities.* When payments are received on an annuity, each payment is split between income and a recovery of the taxpayer's investment in the contract, the former being taxed and the latter being excluded from gross income. This is accomplished by prorating the taxpayer's investment among the payments expected to be received under the annuity. As pointed out later in this chapter,[20] the ratable cost recovery regime has the effect of deferring tax on some of the income accruing to the annuitant during the early years of the payout period. The deferral of tax on inside buildup, in other words, continues for part of the income accruing after the payout period begins.

¶12.2 LIFE INSURANCE PROCEEDS PAID AT DEATH

¶12.2.1 Introductory

Section 101(a) excluded from gross income the amounts payable under a life insurance contract "by reason of the death of the insured."[1] If the proceeds of the policy are paid a substantial time after the insured's death, however, postdeath interest or earnings are ordinarily taxable, the exclusion being limited to the date-of-death value of the future payments.[2] Also, the

---

[19] See infra ¶12.4. But see Rev. Rul. 79-87, 1979-1 CB 73 (exclusion covers amounts paid under variable life insurance policy, where benefits may increase or decrease depending on investment results, but not below a specified minimum).

[20] Infra ¶12.2., text accompanying notes 25-26.

[1] See infra ¶12.2.2.

[2] See infra ¶12.2.3.

exclusion is denied to purchasers of a policy and other transferees for value, who are treated in effect as investors and taxed if they receive more than they paid for the policy.[3] These rules are described in more detail below.

¶12.2.2 Amounts Paid by Reason of Insured's Death

The proceeds of life insurance paid by reason of the death of the insured are excluded from gross income by §101(a), whether payment is made to the insured's estate, to individual beneficiaries, or to a corporation or partnership, and whether the amount is paid directly or in trust.[4] The exclusion applies to installment payments as well as to lump-sum settlements, except that the interest component of amounts paid after the insured's death is ordinarily subject to tax.[5]

The regulations interpret the statutory phrase "amounts received . . . under a life insurance contract" to embrace death benefit payments "having the characteristics of life insurance proceeds," including payments under workmen's compensation insurance contracts, endowment contracts, and accident and health insurance policies.[6] The contract, however, must exhibit the risk-shifting and risk-distribution characteristics of insurance; a purported policy of life insurance is not subject to §101(a) if written only in combination with another contract that negates the insurer's normal actuarial risk. An ostensible life insurance payment under an insurance-annuity package, for example, does not qualify for the benefits of §101(a) if the insured's early death would produce a gain for the insurer on the annuity contract offsetting its loss on the insurance policy, while a long life would produce a gain on the insurance contract offsetting the insurer's loss on the annuity contract.[7]

---

[3] See infra ¶12.2.4.

[4] Reg. §1.101-1(a)(1).

[5] See infra ¶12.2.3.

[6] Reg. §1.101-1(a)(1). See Atlantic Oil Co. v. Patterson, 331 F2d 516 (5th Cir. 1964) (§101(a) exclusion denied to trucking company that insured lives of its drivers for its own benefit; for want of insurable interest, policy treated as wagering contract).

Variable life insurance policies guarantee that a basic amount will be paid on the death of the insured but contain an investment feature that may generate an additional amount if experience warrants. For discussion, see Gallian & Baylor, Federal Taxation Aspects of Variable Life Insurance, 8 USFL Rev. 523, 526–31 (1974).

[7] Kess v. US, 451 F2d 1229 (6th Cir. 1971) (single-premium life insurance policy and annuity contract issued without evidence of insurability because the company's commitments offset each other); see also Helvering v. LeGierse, 312 US 531 (1941) (similar estate tax result). Taking as given that the contract in Kess was not life insurance, it is not clear that the beneficiary should be taxed, as she was in that case. Should the amount received at the insured's death be treated as a bequest

Contracts having the requisite insurance characteristics can qualify, however, even if not written by regulated insurance companies, under judicial decisions holding that §101(a) covers death benefits paid by a state civil service system (financed by contributions to a fund by both the employee and the state) and by a trade association's gratuity program (financed by assessments against its members).[8] Although the risks were not reinsured in either case with an independent insurance company, the payments were made by funds that were somewhat separate from the sponsoring groups, thus distinguishing them from payments by a self-insuring employer financing payments from its regular resources.[9] It is not easy to stake out a boundary between these two situations, and this presages difficulties in deciding when death benefits paid under an employer's plan to a deceased employee's family qualify as life insurance under §101(a) and when they fall outside its jurisdiction.[10]

In addition to being paid "under a life insurance contract," the proceeds must be "paid by reason of the death of the insured" to qualify for exclusion under §101(a). Designed primarily to separate death benefits from such lifetime payments as dividends or cash surrender values, this requirement rarely creates interpretative difficulties.[11] When life insurance is used in a business setting to secure or fund an obligation, however, it may be necessary to decide which of several parties to the agreement received the

---

or inheritance (excludable under §102(a)) or as a final payment under an annuity contract whose cost has been fully recovered (taxable under §72(a))? See also Barnes v. US, 801 F2d 984 (7th Cir. 1986) (death benefits under employer's "Survivors Insurance Benefit" plan not life insurance; risk shifting absent because (1) employees entitled to return of their contributions with interest on retirement or termination of employment other than by death and (2) employer's obligation to contribute not dependent on mortality experience).

[8] Ross v. Odom, 401 F2d 464 (5th Cir. 1968) (actuarially sound and determinable obligation); Moyer's Est. v. CIR, 32 TC 515, 535 (1959) (benefits excludable under §101(a); fund was a mutual insurance company for federal tax purposes). See also Epmeier v. US, 199 F2d 508 (7th Cir. 1952), construing the statutory phrase "accident or health insurance" to include a self-insured employer's plan for employees, which led to the enactment of §105, discussed infra ¶13.2.1.

[9] See Essenfeld v. CIR, 311 F2d 208 (2d Cir. 1962) (employer-employee retirement contract not "life insurance contract"); Davis v. US, 323 F. Supp. 858 (SD W. Va. 1971) (West Virginia state retirement system did not meet criteria of Ross v. Odom, supra note 8; Tighe v. CIR, 33 TC 557 (1959) (acq.) (payment in settlement of partnership buy-out contract not life insurance).

[10] For the relationship between the exclusion of life insurance proceeds under §101(a) and the exclusion of employee death benefits up to $5,000 by §101(b), see infra ¶12.6.4.

[11] See Rev. Rul. 55-63, 1955-1 CB 227 (employer purchased life insurance on employees' lives, naming itself as beneficiary pursuant to program for payment of death benefits to employee's estate or beneficiaries; held, employer only a conduit and recipients entitled to exclusion).

proceeds "by reason of the death of the insured" since the nominal beneficiary may not be the real party in interest. For example, if a policy of life insurance is pledged as security for a debt, payment of the proceeds to the creditor on the debtor's death inures to the benefit of the debtor's estate by reducing the debt; the creditor is interested in the policy only as security for the debt and normally holds any surplus for the debtor's estate. For this reason, the latter is entitled to the exclusion under §101(a). By contrast, the creditor, even if irrevocably designated as the beneficiary, gets the proceeds not "by reason of the death of the insured," but in payment of the debt.[12] The IRS has ruled this principle applies to creditor life insurance, purchased by dealers engaged in retail installment sales in amounts equal to the unpaid balance of the customer's debt.[13]

On the other hand, if the taxpayer owns an insurance policy on someone else's life and can receive and use the proceeds for his own purposes, he is entitled to the exclusion even if the policy facilitates payment of an obligation or some other financial objective, such as acquisition of the insured's business interest under a buy-sell agreement or payment of a death benefit to the insured's family.[14] When the proceeds of a policy are used to

---

[12] See Reg. §1.101-1(b)(4) (§101 inapplicable to amounts received by pledgee of a policy); Landfield Fin. Co. v. US, 418 F2d 172 (7th Cir. 1969) (creditor designated as irrevocable beneficiary and co-owner of insurance on debtor's life, but with obligation to pay any balance to debtor after discharge of debt); Tennessee Foundry & Mach. Co. v. CIR, 399 F2d 156 (6th Cir. 1968) (proceeds of insurance on life of employee received by employer as restitution of embezzled funds, not by reason of death of insured); but see L.C. Thomsen & Sons v. US, 484 F2d 954 (7th Cir. 1973) (taxpayer wrote off debt owed to it by deceased insured, but held entitled to exclude proceeds because insurance was keyman coverage, not insurance against bad debt).

In Durr Drug Co. v. US, 99 F2d 757 (5th Cir. 1938), a creditor was held entitled to exclude the proceeds of insurance on the life of a debtor, but the government only argued that the insurance (taken out by the debtor) had been transferred for valuable consideration to the creditor (see §101(a)(2), discussed infra ¶12.2.4), not that the proceeds were received by virtue of the unpaid debt rather than by reason of the debtor's death. Compare McCamant v. CIR, 32 TC 824, 833–35 (1959) (acq.) (creditor denied exclusion for proceeds of insurance on debtor's life; Durr Drug Co. distinguished on the theory creditor there was entitled to proceeds whether debt was unpaid or not). For extended discussion, see Federal Nat'l Bank of Shawnee v. CIR, 16 TC 54 (1951) (nonacq.).

[13] Rev. Rul. 70-254, 1970-1 CB 31 (citing Landfield Fin. Co., supra note 12). In the ruling, the amount payable on the insured's death could not exceed the unpaid balance of his debt. If a surplus were possible, it presumably would not be excludable by the creditor as life insurance, but would instead be (1) uncollectible for want of an insurable interest, (2) held for the benefit of the customer's estate, or (3) taxed to the creditor as the fruits of a gambling contract (supra note 6).

[14] See Mushro v. CIR, 50 TC 43 (1968) (nonacq.) (surviving partners held to have received insurance proceeds on life of deceased partner although his widow was nominal beneficiary, because proceeds satisfied their obligation to purchase decedent's partnership interest under buy-sell agreement; issue before court was their

settle a dispute about ownership of the contract, however, it is often difficult to determine whether the recipient has been paid by reason of the
insured's death or because of an extraneous claim for damages, lost profits,
unpaid wages, or the like. The issues may be further complicated by a
question of insurable interest under state law.[15] The crucial importance of
beneficial ownership is also illustrated by the common situation of insurance that is paid for by closely held corporations, whose officers and controlling shareholders often fail to make clear whether the corporation is to
receive the proceeds in its own right or as a conduit for the insured's
family.[16]

¶12.2.3 Settlement Options

The general rule of §101(a) excludes life insurance death benefits
whether paid "in a single sum or otherwise." When payments are made over
a period of time after the insured's death, however, the exclusion embraces
only the principal and not the interest or other increments added by the
insurer to compensate the beneficiary for the delay. This division between
principal and income is required whether deferral is mandated by the policy, directed by the insured, or elected before or after the insured's death by
the beneficiary, and occurs whether the settlement provides for installment
payments over a period of time or a lump sum at a specified future date.[17]

The simplest situation of this type is an agreement under which the
insurer holds the proceeds after the insured's death, pays interest to the
beneficiary, and pays over the principal at a designated date or on the
beneficiary's request or death. Under §101(c), the interest is includable in

---

basis for partnership interests, but presumably they were also entitled to §101(a)
exclusion). See also Rev. Rul. 55-63, 1955-1 CB 227 (conduit treatment).

[15] See Salmonson v. US, 63-1 USTC ¶9481 (ED Wash. 1963) (not officially
reported) (deceased employee's widow received taxable employment benefits, not
excludable proceeds of keyman insurance); Harrison v. CIR, 59 TC 578 (1973) (acq.)
(keyman insurance, with ownership and insurable interest disputed; taxpayer's receipts in settlement of interpleader action held excludable despite concurrent debt
owed by deceased to taxpayer).

[16] See, e.g., Rhodes v. Gray, 59-2 USTC ¶9646 (WD Ky. 1959) (not officially
reported) (proceeds received by widow excludable under §101(a); corporate payment
of premiums was additional compensation to insured during his lifetime); Doran v.
CIR, 246 F2d 934, 937 (9th Cir. 1957) ("parties . . . did not have a clear concept of
what they were trying to do and of the difference between the acts of a corporation as
an entity and of the acts of the stockholders as individuals"; looking through form to
substance, policy held by officers as trustees for shareholders, not for corporation).

[17] If, however, the aggregate amount to be paid cannot exceed the amount
payable at the date of death (a poor bargain for the beneficiary), all payments are
fully excluded. Reg. §1.101-4(a)(1)(i).

the recipient's gross income,[18] but the principal, when received, qualifies for exclusion under §101(a). Such an interest-only arrangement resembles, and is taxed like, a deposit of funds in a savings account.

Although the periodic yield under interest-only options has been taxed by §101(c) and its predecessors since 1926, there was until 1954 no provision covering options under which the beneficiary receives income and capital in installments payable for his life or a term certain. In the absence of statutory guidance, the courts held that the phrase "amounts . . . held by the insurer under an agreement to pay interest thereon," as used by the pre-1954 version of §101(c), referred only to arrangements under which the capital sum was held intact for a period of time, and that installment payments exhausting the capital sum during the beneficiary's life or a specified period of years were excludable from gross income in their entirety, even though they included interest.[19]

In 1954, Congress enacted §101(d), requiring the interest component of installment payments to be separated from the principal and included in gross income.[20] Thus, the §101(a) exclusion now embraces only the amount payable at death or the value at that time of the future payments if the policy does not provide for a lump-sum settlement. The excludable amount is prorated over the installments as they are received, and the beneficiary is taxed on the excess of what is received over the excluded amount.[21] This

---

[18] If the payments do not reduce the capital sum to be paid at a later date, §101(c) applies whether they are labeled interest or an annuity. See Hunt v. US, 241 F. Supp. 147 (ND Okla. 1965) (statutory predecessor of §101(c) applicable to so-called annuities and whether interest option was elected by insured or beneficiary). Under §1.101-3(a) of the regulations, a settlement is treated as an interest-only option unless the periodic payments result in a "substantial diminution" of the principal.

[19] CIR v. Pierce, 146 F2d 388 (2d Cir. 1944).

[20] For a detailed explanation of the 1954 changes, see S. Rep. No. 1622, 83d Cong., 2d Sess. 14–15, 179–82 (1954). For discussion of the 1954 legislation, see Forster & Frost, Changes in Taxation of Life Insurance, Endowment, and Annuity Contracts, 1955 S. Cal. Tax Inst. 557; Goldstein, Tax Aspects of Corporate Business Use of Life Insurance, 18 Tax L. Rev. 133 (1963); Lawthers, Some Murky Blessings of the New Tax Code, 8 J. Am. Soc'y CLU 329 (1954).

In some situations, a single payment is subject to both §§101(c) and (d). For a detailed explanation of their interplay in the case of a so-called family income rider, see Reg. §1.101-4(h); see also Rev. Rul. 65-284, 1965-2 CB 28 (periodic installment election, subject to §101(d), is permissible after an interest-only option).

[21] The 1954 rules originally allowed a surviving spouse an additional exclusion of up to $1,000 of the interest per year if payments were in installments subject to §101(d) rather than under an interest-only option. IRC §101(d)(1)(B) (before amendment in 1986). This exclusion has been repealed for amounts payable under policies on insureds who die after October 22, 1986. Pub. L. No. 99-514, §§1001(a), (d), 100 Stat. 2085 (1986).

system resembles the tax treatment of annuities.[22]

When a settlement option provides for installment payments for a specified period of years, the amount held by the insurer is prorated among the installments. Assume (1) a life insurance contract pays $150,000 on the death of the insured, but (2) the beneficiary elects to receive this amount in 10 annual installments of $18,494 each (based on a guaranteed interest rate of 4 percent), plus such excess earnings as may be realized and declared by the insurer. In a year in which there are no excess earnings, the taxable amount income is $3,494, the excess of $18,494 over $15,000.

If payments are to continue only so long as the beneficiary lives (with no refund in the event of an early death), the amount held by the insurer is prorated over the beneficiary's life expectancy, and the amount allocated to each year is subtracted from the payments received in that year.[23] The amount remaining after this subtraction is gross income. Thus, the amount excluded from gross income over the beneficiary's life will equal the amount that would have been payable at death if, but only if, the beneficiary's life corresponds exactly to his or her expectancy. A short-lived beneficiary will be taxed even though the date-of-death amount is not recovered, while a long-lived beneficiary will exclude more than that amount over his or her lifetime.[24]

Under the spousal exclusion, qualification as a "surviving spouse" (who could be either male or female) was determined as of the date of death and was not forfeited by remarriage. IRC §101(d)(3) (before amendment in 1986); Rev. Rul. 72-164, 1972-1 CB 28. Payments under two or more policies on the same decedent were aggregated in applying the $1,000 annual limit. Reg. §1.101-4(a)(1)(ii).

There appears to be no authority distinguishing between (1) a surviving spouse who receives, constructively or actually, the proceeds of a life insurance policy and uses them to purchase an annuity that will be taxed under §72 (which never provided a $1,000 exclusion for interest) and (2) a spouse who elects an annuity under a settlement option allowing the beneficiary to choose any annuity contract that the company is selling to the public when the insured dies.

[22] See infra ¶12.3.

[23] For payments on account of an insured's death occurring after October 22, 1986, life expectancy is determined under mortality tables to be prescribed for this purpose by the Treasury. IRC §101(d)(2)(B)(ii); see Staff of Joint Comm. on Tax'n, 99th Cong., 2d Sess., General Explanation of the Tax Reform Act of 1986, at 576 (Comm. Print 1987) ("such tables will not distinguish among individuals on the basis of sex"); Reg. §1.72-9 (unisex mortality expectancy tables used in allocating annuity payments between income and principal, which do distinguish on basis of sex). For payments on account of deaths before October 23, 1987, the insurer's mortality tables are used.

[24] Until 1986, this phenomenon also occurred with purchased annuities. In 1986, however, the annuity rules were amended to (1) allow a loss deduction if the annuity terminates before cost is recovered and (2) include 100 percent of the payments in gross income once cost has been recovered. See infra ¶12.5.2. Congress' failure to include similar provisions in §101(d) is probably an oversight.

If the policy benefits are expressed in terms of a periodic payment and no lump-sum death benefit is specified in the policy, the excludable amount is the present value of the payments when the insured dies.[25] Present value is determined with a discount rate equal to "the interest used by the insurer in calculating payments under the agreement." If the payments are dependent on the lives of one or more persons, the life expectancies of these persons also enters into the calculation.[26]

Assume (1) a policy provides for an annual payment of $5,000 to the insured's surviving spouse for life, beginning at the insured's death, without a refund feature, and no principal sum is stated in the policy, (2) the present value of these payments at the decedent's death, determined using the insurance company's interest rate and the Treasury's mortality tables, is $60,000, and (3) the spouse's life expectancy is 20 years. The excludable portion of each $5,000 payment is $3,000 ($60,000 divided by 20), and the spouse includes $2,000 in gross income each year.[27]

Annuities payable for the beneficiary's life often contain a refund feature, such as a guarantee that payments will be made for at least a specified number of years or until the payments aggregate the amount that would have been paid in a lump sum on the insured's death, protecting the beneficiary against loss in the event of premature death. The regulations require a refund feature to be valued separately and deducted from the "amount held by the insurer" before it is prorated over the payments to the first beneficiary.[28] If the first beneficiary dies early and payments are made to his or her estate or to a secondary beneficiary pursuant to the refund feature, they are excluded from the recipient's gross income.

There is a curious interplay between the secondary beneficiary's right to exclude all refund payments and the primary beneficiary's obligation to include in gross income part of every installment payment. If the primary beneficiary dies during the guarantee period, the aggregate amount paid by the insurer to both beneficiaries is the same regardless of when the primary beneficiary dies, but the longer the primary beneficiary lives during the guarantee period, the more he includes in gross income. Conversely, if the first beneficiary lives beyond the guarantee period and the second benefici-

---

[25] The term "amount held by an insurer" is defined by §101(d)(2) and §1.101-4(b) of the regulations.

[26] Mortality tables are prescribed by the Treasury for cases where the insured dies after October 22, 1987; the insurer's mortality tables are used if the insured died earlier. See supra note 23.

For the computations where the annuity is for more than one life, see Reg. §§1.101-4(d), (g) Exs. 4–6.

[27] If the insured had died before October 23, 1986, an additional $1,000 would be excludable each year, and the spouse's gross income would only be $1,000. See supra note 21.

[28] Reg. §1.101-4(e).

ary receives nothing, the portion of the capital sum allocated to the latter goes unused, and the aggregate of the exclusions allowed never is as large as the present value of the settlement option when the insured died. It would be more rational to provide a single exclusion ratio, based on the value of all rights under the option, which would apply to all amounts received by both beneficiaries.

The effect of a refund feature is illustrated by the following example: Assume (1) A, the primary beneficiary of a $65,000 life insurance policy, elects a settlement option paying her $3,500 per year for life, with a guarantee that any part of the $65,000 that is not paid during her lifetime will be paid to a secondary beneficiary, B, or to B's estate; (2) A's life expectancy is 25 years; and (3) the present value at the insured's death of B's rights under the settlement option is $15,000. The portion of each $3,500 payment to be included in A's gross income is $1,500, as shown in Example 12-1.

Example 12-1

Single-Life Annuity With Refund Feature

1. Amount received $3,500
2. Exclusion
   a. Amount held by insurer $65,000
   b. Less: Value at insured's death of refund feature .. 15,000
   c. Amount to be prorated... $50,000
   d. Prorated amount ($50,000/25) 2,000
3. Amount includable in A's gross income $1,500

Apart from the anomalies in its application to options with refund features, the proration rule of §101(a) is advantageous to taxpayers because it has the effect of deferring the recognition of earnings on the sum held by the insurer. Assume a life insurance contract gives the beneficiary a choice between a lump sum of $150,000 and 10 annual payments of $18,494 each (computed to include interest at 4 percent). If the beneficiary chooses the installment option, gross income is recognized on each payment of $3,494 (the excess of $18,494 over one tenth of the principal amount of $150,000). Alternatively, the beneficiary could put himself in the same economic position by taking the $150,000 as a lump sum, depositing it in a bank account paying 4 percent interest, and withdrawing $18,494 from the account at the end of each year; the account, like the settlement option annuity, would be fully exhausted after 10 years. If this were done, however, the interest for the first year would be $6,000 (4 percent of $150,000), and would decline annually thereafter. For the second year, for example, it would be $5,500 (4 percent of the excess of $150,000 over the principal of $12,494 withdrawn in the first year).

Under the settlement option, as under the bank account alternative, economic interest is highest in the first year because all of the $150,000 is then on deposit, and declines annually thereafter to reflect the gradual withdrawal of principal. If the bank account alternative is chosen, the beneficiary is taxed on the economic interest as it accrues. Under the proration rule applied to the settlement, in contrast, the taxable amount is level over the period of the payout, and this has the effect of deferring until later years the taxation of portions of the income earned in earlier years. In the first year in the example, when economic income is $6,000 and taxable income is $3,494, tax on $2,506 of accrued income is avoided. This amount will be taxed near the end of the 10-year payout, however, when the remaining principal is low and economic income is far less than $3,494.[29]

¶12.2.4 Transferees for Value

With some exceptions, transferees for value of life insurance contracts are taxed on the proceeds, less the sum of the amounts paid to acquire the policy and later premiums and other payments, and the §101(a) exclusion is limited in this context to the policyholder's cost. Congress suggested no rationale for this restriction, now set out in §101(a)(2), when it was enacted in 1926.[30] A reasonable inference is that the bequest analogy that may have stimulated the exclusion for life insurance proceeds[31] did not seem appropriate if the beneficiary was a purchaser of the policy speculating on the insured's early death.

If a policy is purchased as an investment in a commercial setting, taxing the purchaser's gain does seem more appropriate than an exclusion. If this was its objective, however, §101(a)(2) is both too broad and too narrow. It denies the exclusion if an existing policy is sold by the insured to

---

[29] This deferral opportunity is not allowed for interest-only options, where §101(c) taxes accrued interest annually. In order to prevent interest-only settlements from posing as installment options by paying out a nominal amount of capital along with the interest, the regulations restrict §101(d) to cases where a "substantial diminution" of the principal amount occurs as a consequence of the payments. Reg. §1.101-3(a).

[30] See S. Rep. No. 52, 69th Cong., 1st Sess. (1926), reprinted in 1939-1 (Part 2) CB 332, 347. The House deleted the transfer for value provision in 1954, but the Senate Finance Committee, concerned that this would "result in abuse in encouraging speculation on the death of the insured," reinstated the provision, but with an exemption, granted by §101(a)(2)(B), for contracts "which have been transferred for certain legitimate business reasons rather than for speculation purposes." S. Rep. No. 1622, 83d Cong., 2d Sess. 14 (1954).

[31] See supra ¶12.2.1.

a member of his family, even if the transaction is an estate planning device rather than a business arrangement.[32] On the other hand, §101(a)(2) does not deny an exclusion to the proceeds of a policy serving an exclusively commercial function if it is taken out by (rather than transferred to) the beneficiary.[33]

Section 101(a)(2) applies "in the case of a transfer for a valuable consideration, by assignment or otherwise, of a life insurance contract or any interest therein." The regulations construe this language to embrace "any absolute transfer for value of a right to receive all or part of the proceeds of a life insurance policy," but not the assignment of a policy as collateral security.[34] In a few cases, the apparent breadth of the transfer for value concept has been mitigated by exempting transfers that did not effect a significant change in the beneficial ownership of a policy, as in the case of a policy sold by the insured to his employer for its cash surrender value and transferred by the employer to a pension plan whose trustee is required to pay the proceeds on the insured's death to a beneficiary designated by him.[35] More commonly, the disqualification is strictly applied, resulting in a denial of the exclusion in situations involving technical transfers where there was no risk of speculation on the death of the insured.[36]

To limit these severe interpretations of the 1926 provision, Congress intervened in later years to exempt two categories of transactions.

1. *Transferred basis.* Section 101(a)(2)(A) exempts a transfer to a transferee whose basis for determining gain or loss is determined in whole or in part by reference to the transferor's basis, such as a transfer by gift or in a tax-free corporate reorganization.[37] Although the language of §101(a)(2)(A)

---

[32] See Hacker v. CIR, 36 BTA 659 (1937) (no implied exemption from transfer for value rule for transfer to member of insured's family having "a special claim upon his bounty").

[33] But see Johnson v. CIR, 66 TC 897 (1976), aff'd per curiam, 574 F2d 189 (4th Cir. 1978) (proceeds of keyman insurance, although receivable tax free, compensated recipient for a loss, on a showing that the purpose of the policy was to provide such compensation; as a result, otherwise deductible loss disallowed).

[34] Reg. §1.101-1(b)(4).

[35] See Rev. Rul. 73-338, 1973-2 CB 20; Rev. Rul. 74-76, 1974-1 CB 30 (similar transfer, but by employee himself, for cash surrender value).

[36] See James F. Waters, Inc. v. CIR, 160 F2d 596 (9th Cir.), cert. denied, 332 US 767 (1947) (insured's transfer of policy to corporation controlled by insured).

[37] The statutory predecessor of §101(a)(2)(A) was enacted in 1942, evidently to overrule cases applying the transfer-for-value disqualification to policies transferred in mergers and other tax-free corporate reorganizations. See James F. Waters, Inc. v. CIR, supra note 36; S. Rep. No. 1631, 77th Cong., 2d Sess., reprinted in 1942-2 CB 504, 558.

The transferred basis exemption covers part-gift, part-sale transfers. Rev. Rul. 69-187, 1969-1 CB 45. But see Pritchard v. CIR, 3 TCM (CCH) 1125 TC (1944)

suggests that any transaction entailing a transferred basis is liberated from the transfer for value rule, the regulations deny the exemption if there was an earlier transfer for value. Thus, if a policy is sold by *A* to *B* and subsequently given by *B* to *C, C* is subject to the transfer for value rule and can exclude only the amount paid by *B* for the policy, plus any premiums paid by *B* and *C* to keep it in force after the transfer to *B*.[38]

2. *Transfers to insured and certain others.* The second category of exempt transfers for value, described by §101(a)(2)(B), consists of transfers to the insured,[39] a partner of the insured, a partnership of which the insured is a member, or a corporation of which the insured is a shareholder or officer. This exception, which was enacted in 1954 to protect policies transferred for "legitimate business reasons rather than for speculation,"[40] is of particular importance for buy-sell contracts affecting the interests of key persons in closely held enterprises on their deaths.

Despite its broad objective, §101(a)(2)(B) does not reach transfers among shareholders of a closely held corporation or transfers by the insured's corporation to one of his co-shareholders, although transfers among partners and from partnership to partner are covered.[41] Also, §101(a)(2)(B) does not immunize transfers to the spouse or children of the insured. If a family transferee receives a policy by gift from a person qualified under §101(a)(2)(B), however, the proceeds can be excluded under the transferred basis rule of §101(a)(2)(A).[42]

(carryover basis denied to part-gift, part-sale transfer because it was made in contemplation of death, but proceeds excluded from transferee's income under §102, relating to bequests); Bean v. CIR, 14 TCM (CCH) 786 (1955) (§102 inapplicable).

[38] Reg. §§1.101-1(b)(3), (b)(5) Ex. 6; see also James F. Waters, Inc. v. CIR, supra note 36 (after transfer for value, gratuitous transferee stands in shoes of his donor). If, however, a transfer for value is followed by a transfer to the insured or other person listed in §101(a)(2)(B), the proceeds qualify for exclusion. See infra note 43.

[39] See Swanson v. CIR, 518 F2d 59 (8th Cir. 1975), holding that a transfer for value to a grantor trust created by the insured (who was taxable on trust income under §674 (infra ¶80.6)) was equivalent to a transfer to the insured himself; because he had contributed 91 percent of the trust property and was taxed on 91 percent of its income, the same percentage of the proceeds was exempt under §101(a)(2)(B).

[40] S. Rep. No. 1622, supra note 30. Although the exemptions of §101(a)(2)(B) are limited to persons having a business relationship to the insured, it does not require the transfer to serve a business purpose.

[41] See generally Ben-Horin, Use of Life Insurance to Fund Buy-Out Agreements, 28 NYU Inst. on Fed. Tax'n 819 (1970); Wojta, Life Insurance Funding of Stock Purchase Agreements, 48 Neb. L. Rev. 961 (1969).

[42] But see Rath's Est. v. US, 608 F2d 254 (6th Cir. 1979) (on facts, policy transferred for value by insured's company to his widow, rather than sold to him and given by him to widow; exclusion denied).

On being transferred to a transferee qualifying under §101(a)(2)(B), a policy is purged of any taint from a prior transfer for value.[43] Thus, if *A* sells a policy on his life to *B*, and *B* subsequently sells it back to *A* or to a corporation of which *A* is a shareholder, the disqualification arising from the first transfer disappears. As pointed out above, §101(a)(2)(A) is construed more narrowly in the case of successive transfers.[44]

¶12.2.5 Life Insurance as Alimony

When life insurance proceeds are includable in the gross income of a spouse or former spouse under §71 (relating to alimony) or §682 (relating to the income of an estate or trust in case of divorce), their tax status is determined not by the rules discussed above, but by the statutory provisions relating to alimony and similar payments, which are discussed elsewhere in this work.[45]

¶12.3 ANNUITY PAYMENTS

¶12.3.1 Introductory

The tax treatment of amounts received under an annuity contract is prescribed by §72. Because this provision addresses a complicated financial arrangement that has provoked differing statutory rules over the years, a description of the basic transaction and a brief review of the legislative history are essential to an understanding of current law.[1]

Assume a 56-year-old individual pays $5,000 to an insurance company, either in a lump sum or in installments, for an annuity contract under which he is to be paid $1,000 a year, starting at age 65 and continuing for the rest of his life, with no refund if he should die before reaching 65 or thereafter but before receiving as much as the $5,000 paid in.[2] Assume the company bases the payments on mortality tables indicating the average 65-year-old will live 20 more years. If the taxpayer lives exactly as long as predicted, he will receive a total of $20,000, and the annuity will function like a savings account into which the individual deposited $5,000 and then makes annual withdrawals of $1,000 each commencing at age 65. If the annuitant's life is

---

[43] See Reg. §§1.101-1(b)(3)(ii), (b)(5) Exs. 5, 7.

[44] Supra note 38.

[45] IRC §101(e); for the tax treatment of alimony, see infra ¶77.2.2.

[1] See generally Caplin, Taxing Tax-Deferred Annuities: A Critique of the 1978 Carter Proposal, 56 Taxes 315 (1978).

[2] An annuity contract without a cash value or refund feature is unusual and is prohibited by some states; the example is simplified to illustrate the basic principles. Example 12-8 illustrates the impact of a refund feature.

longer or shorter than the average, however, he will reap a mortality gain or suffer a mortality loss. This phenomenon would not be duplicated by the hypothetical savings account, which would be exhausted during the depositor's lifetime if he lived longer than average but would have a balance if he died prematurely. An annuity, in other words, is an insurance contract as well as a savings device.

Before 1934, an annuitant recovered the cost of an annuity contract tax free from the earliest receipts; everything received thereafter was includable in gross income.[3] This cost recovery system was highly favorable to annuitants, who reported no income in the early years even though income accrues economically each day the insurance company holds any of the annuitant's money. In 1934, this approach was replaced by a rule that initially taxed an annuitant annually on the lesser of the payments received during the year or an amount equal to 3 percent of the contract's cost (a percentage based on the investment assumptions of insurance companies at that time). The balance of the payments were excluded from gross income as a return of the annuitant's investment. The payments became taxable in full as soon as the excluded amounts equaled the annuitant's cost. In the example, under the 1934 rule, the annuitant would report $150 of gross income (3 percent of $5,000) and exclude $850 for each of the first five years. In the sixth year, having already excluded $4,250 (5 × $850) of his $5,000 investment, he would exclude $750 and reported $250 of gross income. Thereafter, all amounts received would be gross income.

For long-lived annuitants, the 1934 change accelerated the annuitant's recognition of gross income and slowed down the recovery of his investment, but usually did not alter the aggregate amounts included and excluded over the long haul. For a short-lived annuitant, however, the 1934 legislation made it more likely that the excluded amounts would fall short of his investment because some of each payment was taxable from the outset.

This feature of the 1934 law led to an attack on its constitutionality in *Egtvedt v. United States*,[4] where a 45-year-old (with a life expectancy of 20 years) could not have recovered his investment tax free unless he lived to 98 —an unlikely event, despite the assurance in *Poor Richard's Almanac* that

---

[3] Klein v. CIR, 6 BTA 617 (1927) (acq.) (allocation between income and return of capital under pre-1926 law). See generally Brawerman, Income Tax Problems of Non-Business Life Insurance, 1952 S. Cal. Tax Inst. 267, 280 et seq.; see also Magill, Taxable Income 426–34 (Ronald Press, rev. ed. 1945); Treasury Dept., The Income Tax Treatment of Pensions and Annuities, reprinted in Hearings on Proposed Revisions of the Internal Revenue Code Before the House Ways and Means Committee, 80th Cong., 1st Sess., Pt. 5, at 4001–04 (1947).

[4] Egtvedt v. US, 112 Ct. Cl. 80, 48-2 USTC ¶9381 (1948). See also Raymond v. CIR, 114 F2d 140 (7th Cir.), cert. denied, 311 US 710 (1940). The risk of death before recovering the investment tax free was unusually great in the *Egtvedt* case because payments started immediately after the contract was purchased.

"pensioners never die; annuitants live forever." The court rejected the tax-payer's claim that the 1934 provision was an unconstitutional direct tax on his property rather than a tax on income, partly on the ground that he had failed to prove "what part of the payments [received by him] during the taxable years actually represent[ed] earnings on the amounts paid by him as consideration for the policies and what part was simply a return of capital."[5] Also, the court expressed the view that Congress was entitled to a certain amount of elbowroom in deciding how to tax annuity payments, which are composed of a complex mixture of invested capital, income, and mortality gains and losses. Without going so far as to say that Congress could tax these payments without any allowance for the taxpayer's cost, the court held out little hope for a successful attack on any scheme taxing "a fair approxima-tion" of the income component of the average annuity, however strange the result might be in particular cases.[6]

Notwithstanding this affirmation of its constitutionality, the 1934 rule elicited criticism for reasons summarized by the Senate Finance Committee in 1954:

> This present rule is objectionable because it is erratic. Where the amount paid for the annuity represents a large proportion of its value at the time payments begin, the present rule does not return to the annuitant on a tax-free basis the amount he paid for the annuity during his lifetime. On the other hand, where the amount the annuitant paid for the annuity represents a small proportion of its value at the time payments begin, the exclusion is used up rapidly. In such cases the annuitant finds that after being retired for a few years and becoming accustomed to living on a certain amount of income after tax, he suddenly has to make a sizable downward adjustment in his living standard because, when his exclusion is used up, the annuity income becomes fully taxable.[7]

---

[5] Egtvedt v. US, supra note 4, at 93.

[6] Id. at 95–96.

[7] S. Rep. No. 1622, 83d Cong., 2d Sess. 11 (1954); see also H.R. Rep. No. 1337, 83d Cong., 2d Sess. 10 (1954). The 1934 scheme was doubly flawed. First, the taxable amount was an invariable 3 percent of cost, whereas, economically, the income accruing on an annuitant's investment steadily declines as more and more of that investment is returned to the annuitant. If the annuity was purchased many years before payments began, this defect was offset by the second flaw in the statuto-ry mechanism—the taxable amount (3 percent of cost) took no account of income accrued on the annuity between the date of purchase and the date payments began. If payments began shortly after the annuity was purchased, however, the first defect, unmitigated by the second, prevented the annuitant from fully recovering his cost tax free unless he lived to an extraordinarily ripe age.

To avoid these features of the 1934 rule, Congress in 1954 adopted a substantially different method, which spreads the tax-free portion of the annuity income evenly over the annuitant's lifetime. This method was fine-tuned in 1986 to ensure that the aggregate of the exclusions and deductions for cost always equals the investment in the contract. The 1986 amendments, further, limited the general rule of §72(a) to annuities held by individuals; an entity owning an annuity is usually taxed annually on income accruing within the annuity.[8]

Since 1982, a penalty tax has been imposed on distributions under annuity contracts that Congress found inconsistent with its policy to restrict the favorable tax treatment of annuities to contracts used for retirement savings. This penalty usually applies to amounts not received as an annuity and is discussed in that context;[9] it can, however, apply to an amount received as an annuity.

¶12.3.2 Computation of Excludable Portions of Amounts Received as Annuity

Section 72 distinguishes between "amounts received as an annuity" under an annuity, endowment, or life insurance contract and other amounts received under such contracts.[10] The distinction is not elucidated by the statute, but the regulations provide that payments qualify as "amounts received as an annuity" only if (1) they are received on or after the "annuity starting date,"[11] (2) they are payable in periodic installments at regular intervals, and (3) the aggregate amount payable can be determined either directly from the contract (e.g., $10,000, payable in quarterly installments of $1,000 each) or indirectly by the use of mortality tables or compound interest computations (e.g., $1,000 annually for the annuitant's life, or $500 quarterly until $10,000 plus interest of 6 percent on the declining balance is exhausted).[12]

----

[8] See infra ¶12.3.7.

[9] Infra ¶12.4.1.

[10] Section 72's jurisdiction is not limited to contracts issued by regulated insurance companies but includes some noncommercial contracts as well. See infra ¶12.3.5.

See generally Forster & Frost, Changes in Taxation of Life Insurance, Endowment, and Annuity Contracts, 1955 S. Cal. Tax Inst. 557; Snell, Settlement Options and Annuity Problems, 15 NYU Inst. on Fed. Tax'n 191 (1957).

[11] For the definition of "annuity starting date," see infra text accompanying note 29.

[12] The regulations provide minor exceptions to the principles set out in the text for certain employee annuities, dividends, refunds, and commitments to pay a higher rate if the issuer's earnings warrant, as well as a more important exception for variable annuities. Reg. §1.72-2(b)(2). For variable annuities, see infra ¶12.3.3.

Payments meeting these standards are subject to the "exclusion ratio" of §72(b)(1), under which a uniform fraction of the "amount received as an annuity" is excluded from gross income as a recovery of the annuitant's investment in the contract, while the balance of the payment is gross income unless it qualifies for exclusion under some other provision of law.[13] All other payments, which the Code lumps together under the catchall phrase "amounts not received as an annuity," are allocated between income and cost recovery under a set of rules in §72(e), which is described elsewhere in this work.[14] Section 72(e) applies to such diverse items as dividends, the maturity value of endowment policies, payments on partial surrender, variable annuity payments in excess of an allocated part of the cost, and guaranteed refunds under annuity policies if the annuitant dies prematurely.[15]

The exclusion ratio applied to "amounts received as an annuity" (1) is the "investment in the contract" (the premiums[16] or other consideration paid, adjusted for any tax-free recoveries before the annuity starting date and for any refund feature) divided by (2) the "expected return" (the aggregate amount to be received, computed under actuarial tables prescribed by the Treasury if the payments depend on the life expectancy of one or more individuals).[17] The annuity payments received during the taxable year are multiplied by the exclusion ratio; the product is the portion of the payments that is excluded, and the remainder is gross income under §72(a).

Assume an individual pays $10,000 for an annuity contract that will pay $1,250 per year for 10 years, an aggregate of $12,500. The exclusion ratio is 80 percent (the $10,000 investment in the contract divided by the expected return of $12,500). The excludable portion of each payment is thus $1,000 (80 percent of $1,250), and $250 is included in gross income.

If the annuity is dependent on the life of one or more persons, the expected return is the annual annuity payment, multiplied by the annuitant's life expectancy, expressed in years, as given by tables found in the

---

[13] Such an amount could be excluded, for example, as an accident or health benefit excludable under §104 or §105. See infra ¶12.3.6.

[14] Infra ¶12.4.1.

[15] For amounts paid by reason of the death of the insured, see supra ¶12.2. See also Price v. US, 459 F. Supp. 362 (D. Md. 1978) (excess contributions taxed when returned, but exclusion ratio remains stable).

[16] If a discount is allowed for prepayment of premiums, it is includable in the annuitant's income (Rev. Rul. 66-120, 1966-1 CB 14; Rev. Rul. 65-199, 1965-2 CB 20), so that the full amount of the premium, not the discounted amount actually paid, is taken into account in applying §72(c)(1)(A).

[17] IRC §72(c)(1) (defining "investment in the contract"), §72(c)(3) (defining "expected return"). The regulations expand upon the statutory definitions. Reg. §§1.72-5, -6.

regulations.[18] Assume an individual who is 71 years old pays $11,995 for a single life annuity paying $100 per month, starting immediately and continuing until her death. According to the Treasury's tables, the life expectancy of a 71-year-old is 15.3 years. The expected return under the annuity is thus $18,360 ($100 × 12 × 15.3), and the exclusion ratio is 65.33 percent (the $11,995 investment in the contract divided by the expected return of $18,630). For each year in which 12 monthly payments of $100 each are received, the excludable amount is $784 (65.33 percent of $1,200), and $416 is included in gross income.

If the number of payments is not fixed at the outset (e.g., if the annuity is payable for the life of one or more persons), this exclusion procedure does not automatically match the aggregate of the exclusions with the annuitant's investment. For annuities that entered pay status before 1987, however, the exclusion ratio continues unchanged throughout the life of the contract, and the aggregate amount excluded thus is either more or less than the annuitant's investment unless the payments continue for exactly the period projected at the annuity starting date.[19]

If annuity payments begin after 1986, in contrast, adjustments are made to ensure that the aggregate amount excluded always equals the investment in the contract. First, once the unrecovered investment in the contract falls to zero, the recovery exclusion drops by the wayside, and payments are fully taxable.[20] Second, a deduction equal to the unrecovered investment is allowed if (1) the annuitant dies after the annuity starting date, (2) annuity payments cease "by reason of" the annuitant's death, and (3) exclusions provided by the exclusion ratio have not brought the unrecovered investment down to zero.[21] The deduction is allowed on the annuitant's final return or, if a payment under a refund feature is made to some other person, on that person's return for the year in which the payment is

---

[18] If any of the premiums for the contract were paid after June 1986, the expected return multiple must be taken from Table V of §1.72-9 of the regulations. If the last premium was paid before July 1986, Table I is used.

[19] Reg. §1.72-4(a)(4). In permitting a tax-free recovery of more than the taxpayer's cost, the pre-1987 exclusion mechanism resembles percentage depletion. See infra ¶24.3.1.

If a policy subject to the pre-1987 rules is sold after the annuitant has excluded more than his investment in the policy, there is no recapture of the excess by virtue of §1021, which prevents the adjusted basis of the contract from being reduced below zero. See S. Rep. No. 1622, supra note 7.

For the denial of a loss deduction under the pre-1987 rules if the annuitant dies before recovering his investment, see infra ¶12.3.2.

[20] More technically, the excludable portion of any payment cannot exceed the unrecovered investment immediately before the payment is received. IRC §72(b)(2).

[21] IRC §72(b)(2).

received.[22] The term "unrecovered investment" refers to the excess of the investment in the contract as of the annuity starting date over the sum of the excludable portions of all annuity payments.[23]

Return to the example previously given (monthly payment, $100; investment in the contract, $11,995; exclusion ratio, 65.33 percent). The exclusion ratio only applies to the first 183 payments, after which the unrecovered investment is $39 (original cost of $11,995 less $100 × 0.6533 × 183). Of the 184th $100 payment, $39 is excluded, and $61 is gross income. One hundred percent of the 185th and succeeding payments are includable in gross income.

Assume the annuitant dies after receiving 120 monthly payments. The unrecovered investment as of the date of her death is $4,155 (original cost of $11,995 less $100 × 0.6533 × 120). A deduction of $4,155 is thus allowed on the annuitant's final return.

Essentially the same procedures apply if the annuity is payable for the lives of two persons. Assume a husband and wife who are age 70 and 67 pay $14,543 for a joint and survivor annuity providing for monthly payments of $100 until the death of the survivor of them. According to the Treasury's table, the survivor of a 70-year-old and a 67-year-old is expected to live for 21.7 years. The expected return under the annuity is thus $26,040 ($100 × 12 × 21.7), and the exclusion ratio is 55.85 percent ($14,543 divided by $26,040). For each year in which 12 $100 payments are received, the excludable amount is $670 (55.85 percent of $1,200), and $530 is included in gross income. As in the previous example, the exclusion will drop to zero if the annuity continues longer than the predicted period (in this case, 21.7 years). The deduction for unrecovered investment will be allowed only if the survivor dies within 21.7 years; no deduction is allowed on the first death because annuity payments do not then cease.

The computations in the foregoing examples must be adjusted if (1) payments are to be made quarterly, semiannually, or annually rather than monthly, (2) the contract provides for payments to an annuitant until his death or the expiration of a limited period, whichever occurs first ("temporary life" annuities), (3) the payment is to be increased or decreased during the life of the contract (e.g., a joint and survivor annuity with a reduced amount payable to the survivor), or (4) payments are to be made only while two persons are alive ("joint life" annuities).[24]

---

[22] The deduction is treated as a business deduction, thus allowing it to create a net operating loss carryback or carryover if it is very large in relation to current income. IRC §72(b)(3)(C).

[23] IRC §72(b)(3).

[24] See Reg. §1.72-5(a)(3) (payments other than monthly), §1.72-5(a)(3) ("temporary life" annuities), §1.72-5(b) (joint and survivor and joint life annuities).

The complexities of these rules might obscure a significant tax advantage allowed to annuitants. The constant exclusion ratio provided by §72(b) is not reflective of the way in which income accrues economically, and this difference has the effect of deferring an annuitant's recognition of income.[25] Assume (1) *A* pays $10,000 for an immediate annuity paying $111 per month for 10 years certain, and (2) *B* places $10,000 in a bank account paying 6 percent interest and proceeds to withdraw $111 at the end of each month until the account is exhausted at the end of 10 years. Economically, *A* and *B* are in nearly indistinguishable situations, but they are taxed very differently. Under §72, *A* recognizes gross income on the receipt of each payment of $28.[26] *B*, in contrast, has interest income for the first month of $50 (one twelfth of 6 percent of $10,000), and in steadily declining amounts thereafter as principal is withdrawn from the account. Under an annuity, like *B*'s bank account, income accrues economically to the annuitant in large amounts when the insurance company has all of the money paid for the annuity, and declines thereafter as this money is gradually returned to the annuitant through the annuity payments. The exclusion procedure of §72, by not recognizing this, allows a tax deferral to annuitants even after annuity payments have begun.

Other problems encountered in computing the exclusion ratio of §72(b) are:

1. *Investment in the contract.* An annuitant's "investment in the contract" is the aggregate amount of the premiums or other consideration paid,[27] less premium refunds, dividends, and any excludable amounts received under the contract before the annuity starting date.[28] "Annuity starting date" is defined as the first day of the first period for which an annuity payment is received.[29] Thus, if payments are to be made annually starting on

---

[25] See Thuronyi, The "New and Improved" Taxation of Annuities: A Response to Professors Kreiser and Domonkos, 66 Taxes 297 (1988).

[26] The investment in the contract is $10,000; the expected return is 120 times $111, or $13,322; the exclusion ratio is $10,000 divided by $13,322, or 75.06 percent; the excludable portion of each payment is 75.06 percent of $111, or $83; and the gross income on each payment is $111 less $83, or $28.

[27] For allocation of a lump sum payment for a contract containing two or more annuity elements, see Reg. §1.72-6(b); see also Forster & Frost, supra note 10, at 564 et seq. Under §1.72-2(a)(2) of the regulations, two or more annuity elements or obligations acquired for a single consideration comprise a single annuity contract for which a single exclusion ratio is determined under §1.72-4(e), and this ratio is applied to all amounts received as an annuity under any of the annuity elements.

[28] Reg. §1.72-6(a). The taxpayer's investment in the contract is also reduced by amounts excludable from gross income under the 3 percent rule of pre-1954 law, since the annuity starting date for a pre-1954 contract is January 1, 1954. See IRC §72(c)(4).

[29] IRC §72(c)(4). See also Reg. §1.72-4(b).

December 31, 1988, the annuity starting date is January 1, 1988. To avoid periodic changes in the exclusion ratio, dividends and other nonannuity amounts received after the annuity starting date are included in gross income rather than applied to reduce the taxpayer's investment in the contract.[30]

2. *Employer contributions.* Section 72 applies to all amounts received by an employee from an employer's qualified pension, profit sharing, stock bonus, or annuity plan, except for lump-sum distributions and certain distributions made by the United States to nonresident aliens.[31] The provision also applies to nonqualified annuities provided by employers for employees.

In computing the premiums or other consideration paid for the contract, amounts contributed by an employer usually enter into the employee's investment in an annuity only if they were includable in his gross income.[32] Generally, employer contributions to qualified plans are excluded from the employee's gross income, but contributions to nonqualified plans are immediately taxed; the latter, in other words, are not part of the employee's investment, but the former are.[33] The statute also allows an employer contribution to be included in the employee's investment if the contribution would have been excluded from the employee's gross income, had it been paid directly to him, but this provison rarely applies.[34] An employee's investment in a qualified annuity usually consists of his own nondeductible contributions, if any.[35]

3. *Adjustment for refund feature.* To protect against loss of the annuitant's investment if he dies prematurely, annuity contracts often contain a

---

[30] IRC §72(e)(2)(A).

[31] IRC §§402(a)(1), (2), (4); 403(a)(1), (2). These provisions are discussed in ¶61.5.

[32] IRC §72(f)(1). Section 1.72-16 of the regulations, however, provides special rules for the treatment of life insurance contracts purchased under qualified employee plans. In general, the cost of life insurance protection is includable currently in the insured's income and only the balance of any premium paid by the plan is treated as an amount contributed for the annuity. For treatment of the employee, see Reg. §1.72-16(b)(5) Ex. Section 1.72-16(c) of the regulations limits the exclusion of §101(a), discussed supra ¶12.2, to true life insurance proceeds received under such a plan.

[33] IRC §§403(a), (c).

[34] IRC §72(f)(2). For an example of this rare situation, see Reg. §1.72-8(a)(2) (compensation for certain foreign service before 1963). The rule as stated in the text is literally applicable if a cash payment of the employer contribution would have been foreign source income excluded by §911, but a special limitation statute denies the benefit of the rule in this situation. IRC §72(f)(2).

[35] By virtue of §72(m)(2), the investment in the contract does not include deductible contributions made by a self-employed individual; these contributions are effectively treated as employer rather than employee contributions. See Reg. §1.72-17(a).

refund feature, such as an agreement to make payments for 10 years even if the annuitant dies during this period, or to continue payments after the annuitant's death until the aggregate amount paid by the insurer equals the premiums received by it. Under §72(c)(2), the value of these guaranteed payments must be subtracted from the cost of the contract in computing the exclusion ratio.

Assume an individual, 71 years old, purchases an annuity for $11,340 that pays $100 per month for her life and guarantees payments for at least 10 years. The Treasury's tables require that for a 71-year-old annuitant with a 10-year minimum payout, 12 percent of the investment in the contract must be allocated to the refund feature.[36] The adjusted investment in the contract is thus $9,979 ($11,340 less 12 percent thereof). The expected return is $18,360 (the annual payout, $1,200, times the expected return for a single life annuity for a 71-year-old, 15.3), and the exclusion ratio is 54.35 percent ($9,979 divided by $18,360).

If an annuitant dies before a refund feature expires, the guaranteed payments to the annuitant's beneficiary or estate are taxable to the extent that they exceed the unrecovered investment in contract.[37] Any excess of the unrecovered investment over the guaranteed payments is deductible by the recipient of the payments.[38] For this purpose, the unrecovered investment consists of the premiums paid for the annuity, reduced by the amounts excluded by the primary annuitant but not by the portion of the investment assigned to the refund feature. If more than one payment is due under the refund feature, the payments are tax free until the unrecovered investment has been recovered, and thereafter are fully taxable.[39]

Assume the annuitant in the example dies six months after the annuity starting date. She receives six monthly payments of $100, of which $326 (54.35 percent of $600) is excludable from her gross income. When the annuitant dies, the unrecovered investment is thus $11,014 (the annuity's cost of $11,340, less the $326 already excluded). The secondary beneficiary receives $100 per month for nine years and six months (114 months), a total of $11,400. Of this total, the payments in the first 110 months following the annuitant's death are not taxable. They exhaust all but $14 of the investment in the contract, however, and the 111th payment thus consists of $14 of cost recovery and $86 of gross income. The remaining three payments are

---

[36] Reg. §1.72-9, Table VII. If no premiums are paid after June 1986, Table III is used instead of Table VII.

[37] A guaranteed payment is treated as an amount not payable as an annuity and thus is taxed under the rules described in ¶12.4.1.

[38] See supra text accompanying note 21.

[39] Reg. §1.72-11(c)(2) Ex. 1.

taxable in full.[40]

4. *Transferees.* For a donee or other transferee whose basis in an annuity contract is determined by reference to its basis in the hands of the transferor, the latter's premiums and other payments are included in determining the transferee's investment in the contract. Purchasers and other transferees for value stand on their own feet and may take into account only the amount paid for the contract and the premiums paid thereafter.[41]

5. *Employee contributions recoverable in three years.* To avoid complex computations for small exclusions, §72(d), before its repeal in 1986, allowed cost to be recovered before any income was reported if (1) part of the consideration for the contract was contributed by an employer and (2) the consideration contributed by the employee was recovered during the three-year period beginning with receipt of the first annuity payment.[42] When §72(d) applied, the employee (or, if he died before any annuity payment under the contract was made, his beneficiary) excluded from gross income all amounts received as an annuity until his contributions were recovered. Thereafter, all annuity payments were fully included in gross income.

¶12.3.3 Variable Annuities

If the amount to be paid under an annuity contract varies with the insurer's investment experience, a cost of living index, or some other fluctuating criterion, the "expected return" cannot be projected in the usual way, and this complicates computation of the exclusion ratio (annuitant's investment in the contract divided by expected return). The regulations cope with this problem by (1) dividing the investment in the contract (less the value of any refund feature) by the number of anticipated periodic payments, (2) excluding from gross income a portion of each payment equal to the result-

---

[40] See supra ¶12.2.3, text accompanying note 28, for parallel situations resulting from election of an annuity under a life insurance policy settlement option.

[41] IRC §72(g)(1); Reg. §1.72-10. See also IRC §72(g)(2) (reduction of consideration by amounts received tax-free by the transferee). Under §72(g), the transfer for value rule applies to the extent that the transferee's basis is not determined by reference to the transferor's basis; this may require an allocation for part-gift, part-sale transactions, with the transfer for value rule applying to the part of the contract allocated to the sale. The regulations do not address this point. By way of comparison, the transfer for value rule of §101(a)(2) does not apply if the life insurance contract in question has a basis to the transferee "determined in whole or in part by reference to" the transferor's basis. See supra¶12.2.4 note 37.

[42] Section §72(d) only applies if the annuity starting date is before July 2, 1986. Pub. L. No. 99-514, §§1122(c)(1), (h)(2)(A), 100 Stat. 2085 (1986). The start of the three-year period under §72(d), however, was the date on which an amount was received as an annuity, not the "annuity starting date." See supra text accompanying note 29 for the annuity starting date.

ing amount, and (3) including the remainder of each payment in gross income.[43] As in the case of fixed annuities, the exclusions stop once they aggregate to the amount of the annuitant's investment as of the annuity starting date, and a deduction is allowed for the unrecovered investment if the payments cease before the investment is fully recovered.[44]

Assume an individual whose life expectancy is 20 years pays $100,000 for an annuity for his life (without refund feature), which pays annual amounts equal to a specified dollar amount, adjusted for changes in the insurer's investment experience. Of each payment, $5,000 ($100,000 divided by 20) is excluded from gross income, and the remainder is taxed. Thus, if the first three annual payments are $5,000, $6,500, and $4,500, the annuitant has gross income of zero, $1,500, and zero, respectively.

Since the amount excluded in any taxable year is the lesser of the amount received or the ratable portion of the taxpayer's investment, an annuitant cannot fully recover his investment over his life expectancy if he receives less than the investment amount in any year (as in the third year in the example). To compensate for this, the regulations permit the annual exclusion to be recomputed for payments received after a shortfall.[45] In the example, after the third year, the unrecovered investment of $85,500 ($100,000 less $5,000, $5,000, and $4,500) can be reallocated by dividing it by the annuitant's life expectancy at that time. If the annuitant's life expectancy is then 17.6 years,[46] the election would not be made because it would reduce the annual exclusion to $4,858 ($85,500 divided by 17.6).[47]

---

[43] Reg. §§1.72-2(b)(3), -4(d)(3). This formulation is squared with the statutory regime by providing that (1) the amounts deemed received as an annuity are limited to the portions of the payments equal to the investment allocated to them, (2) the exclusion ratio applied to these amounts is 100 percent, and (3) everything in addition to the amount deemed received as an annuity is gross income. See IRC §72(e)(2)(A) (amount received after starting date other than as annuity is fully taxable).

[44] See supra ¶12.3.2. If the annuity starting date occurs before 1987, the fixed dollar amount continues to be excluded from each payment so long as payments continue, and no deduction is allowed for unrecovered investment when the payments cease. Reg. §1.72-4(a)(4).

[45] Reg. §1.72-4(d)(3)(ii).

[46] Reg. §1.72-9 Table V (life expectancies for 65- and 68-year-olds are 20 and 17.6 years, respectively).

[47] Because an individual's life expectancy declines by less than 12 months for each year elapsed, the recomputation has the effect of spreading the investment over a period extending beyond the original period of the expected return, and thus is advantageous only if the shortfall is large enough to offset this effect and more. In the example, the recomputation spreads the investment over a period ending 20.6 years after the annuity starting date and is not advantageous because the small amount of the shortfall ($500) is swallowed up by the lengthening of the period. See Reg. §1.72-4(d)(3) Ex.

Variable annuity contracts giving policyholders control over the insurer's investment decisions are not viewed by the IRS as genuine annuity contracts subject to §72, but as custodial accounts generating income that is includable in the policyholder's gross income as realized.[48] The IRS has issued several rulings involving so-called wraparound annuity contracts that require premiums to be invested by the insurance company in specified assets apart from its general reserves and provide variable annuity payments tied to the performance of those investments. In some of the rulings, the contracts are found to be annuities and the wrapped investments are considered merely part of the reserves of the insurance company; in others, where the contract allows choices of investments available outside the annuity format, the wrapped investments are taxed as though they were owned directly by the owner of the annuity contract.[49]

¶12.3.4 Effect of Original Annuitant's Death

If the beneficiary of a single life annuity without a refund feature dies while receiving annuity payments, the issuer's obligation ceases and there is nothing for the annuitant's estate or beneficiaries. If the contract provides a joint and survivor annuity or includes a refund feature, the payments continue for the agreed period, and their value is included in the decedent's gross estate for federal estate tax purposes.[50]

The decedent's beneficiaries, however, do not get a date of death basis for their rights under the contract; instead, they inherit the decedent's exclusion ratio and basis.[51] The amounts includable in the survivor's gross

---

[48] See Rev. Rul. 77-85, 1977-1 CB 12; but see Investment Annuity, Inc. v. Blumenthal, 442 F. Supp. 681 (DDC 1977) (Rev. Rul. 77-85 invalid), rev'd, 609 F2d 1 (DC Cir. 1979) (district court lacked jurisdiction).

[49] Rev. Rul. 82-54, 1982-1 CB 11 (insurance company considered owner of mutual fund shares purchased with wraparound annuity premiums where shares cannot be purchased by general public, even though policyholder can choose among three mutual funds in which premiums will be invested; ability to choose among general investment strategies not inconsistent with annuity classification); Rev. Rul 81-225, 1981-2 CB 12, clarified by Rev. Rul 82-55, 1982-1 CB 12 (policyholder considered owner of mutual fund shares purchased by insurance company with wraparound annuity premiums where mutual fund investments not controlled by insurance company or where mutual fund shares can be purchased by investors other than through annuity contracts); Rev. Rul. 80-274, 1980-2 CB 27 (where wraparound annuity premiums deposited in savings accounts, interest taxed directly to policyholders); Christoffersen v. US, 749 F2d 513 (8th Cir. 1984) (Rev. Rul. 81-225 followed).

[50] IRC §2039.

[51] IRC §1014(b)(9)(A). See Rev. Rul. 79-335, 1979-2 CB 292 (variable annuity contracts subject to §72(e) and to exclusion of §1014(b)(9)(A); excess of lump sum payment to beneficiary over consideration paid includable in gross income).

income are thus subject to both estate and income taxation. To ameliorate this, §691(d) treats the taxable portions of amounts received as an annuity during the period of survivor's life expectancy as income in respect of a decedent under §691(a), a characterization that permits the survivor to take a deduction for an allocable portion of the death taxes resulting from inclusion of the contract in the first annuitant's estate.[52]

¶12.3.5 Noncommercial and Private Annuities

Although §72 applies to all contracts that "are considered to be life insurance, endowment, and annuity contracts in accordance with the customary practice of life insurance companies," the issuer need not be an insurance company,[53] and §72 encompasses some contracts issued by persons who are not subject to state insurance regulations and who do not pool the mortality risks of a large number of lives. Thus, the rules of §72 can reach noncommercial annuity contracts issued by governmental agencies, charitable institutions, closely held corporations, and even private individuals.[54]

If the policy is not purchased for cash, however, but with appreciated property, it is necessary to take account of the purchaser's gain on the transfer. Before 1969, the acquisition of the policy was treated as an open transaction, and gain on the transferred property was not recognized until the untaxed portion of the annuity payments equaled the adjusted basis of the transferred property.[55] Revenue Ruling 69-74 supplanted this approach with a more complicated method,[56] under which the transferor's gain, com-

---

[52] See Reg. §1.691(d)-1 (illustrating deduction and limiting it to period of survivor's life expectancy); see also infra ¶83.2.

[53] Reg. §1.72-2(a)(1).

[54] See Reg. §1.72-2(a)(3)(iii); Heard v. CIR, 40 TC 7 (1963), aff'd, 326 F2d 962 (8th Cir.), cert. denied, 377 US 978 (1964) (§72 applies to annuities under Federal Civil Service Retirement Act; extensive discussion); Rev. Rul. 72-438, 1972-2 CB 38, amplified by Rev. Rul. 84-162, 1984-2 CB 200 (policyholder's investment in noncommercial contract determined by reference to cost of comparable contract issued by insurance companies); De Canizares v. CIR, 32 TC 345 (1959) (acq.) (investment in contract issued by closely held corporation is amount paid, where less than cost of comparable commercial contract); Rev. Rul. 70-15, 1970-1 CB 20 (excess of amount paid to charity for annuity over cost of comparable commercial policy not part of annuitant's investment in policy but deductible as charitable contribution).

[55] Rev. Rul. 239, 1953-2 CB 53; CIR v. Kann's Est., 174 F2d 357 (3d Cir. 1949); but see Rev. Rul. 62-136, 1962-2 CB 12 (denying cost recovery treatment to annuities by organizations issuing such contracts "from time to time"). For pre-1969 law, see generally Goldberg, Annuities, A Comparative Analysis: Intra-Family, College-Type, Commercial, 22 NYU Inst. on Fed. Tax'n 1213 (1964).

[56] Rev. Rul. 69-74, 1969-1 CB 43. See Bell's Est. v. CIR, 60 TC 469 (1973) (excess of annuity's fair market value over taxpayer's adjusted basis realized in year

puted by subtracting the adjusted basis of the transferred property from the present value of the annuity, is taxed ratably over the annuitant's life expectancy. This result is accomplished by using the property's adjusted basis rather than its value in determining the exclusion ratio, so that the annuitant's tax-free recovery is limited to the property's adjusted basis. If the transferred property was a capital asset, the taxable portion of each annuity payment is divided between ordinary income and capital gain until the capital gain has been recognized in full; thereafter, the taxable portions of the annuity payments are taxed as ordinary income in their entirety.[57]

The issues affecting the issuer of a private annuity are less well developed.[58]

¶12.3.6 Special Rules

The general rules prescribed by §72 are qualified in a variety of circumstances, the most important of which are the following:

1. *Interest.* Section 72 presupposes periodic payments that gradually exhaust the annuitant's investment in the contract. Payments that represent only an investment yield on the premiums, leaving the investment substantially intact for subsequent payment to the policyholder or his beneficiaries,

---

of exchange); Sams, Private Annuities: Revenue Ruling 69-74—Its Significance, Effect, and Validity, 23 Vand. L. Rev. 675 (1970); Kanter, Recent Tax Court Decisions Shed Further Light on Private Annuity Transactions, 42 J. Tax'n 66 (1975). See also La Fargue v. CIR, 689 F2d 845 (9th Cir. 1982) (transfer of assets to trust newly created by transferor in exchange for annuity is bona fide sale, not a grantor trust transaction and not a sham to be disregarded); Benson v. CIR, 80 TC 789 (1983) (*La Fargue* followed under *Golsen* rule (infra ¶115.6)); Horstmier v. CIR, 46 TCM (CCH) 738 (1983) (purported transfer of assets to trust in exchange for annuity disregarded; transaction a sham or, alternatively, grantor trust rules apply).

[57] Although a transfer of property in exchange for a private annuity fits the definition of installment sale in §453(b)(1), the legislative history of the installment sales rules indicate they do not "deal directly with this type of arrangement." S. Rep. No. 1000, 96th Cong., 1st Sess. 12 n.12, reprinted in 1980-2 CB 494, 500. See Reg. §15a.453-1(c) (dealing extensively with installment sales under contracts providing contingent payments, apparently without affecting private annuities). See Ginsberg, Future Payment Sales After the 1980 Revision Act, 39 NYU Inst. on Fed. Tax'n ch. 43 (1981); Manning & Hesch, Private Annuities After the Installment Sales Revision Act of 1980, 6 Rev. Of Tax'n of Individuals 20 (1982). See infra ¶106.2 for the installment sales rules.

[58] See Perkins v. US, 701 F2d 771 (9th Cir. 1983) (distinguishing between annuity given for property, where payments are added to basis of property acquired, and annuity given in exchange for cash or cancellation of indebtedness, where payments in excess of consideration received may be losses deductible under §165(c)).

are treated as interest rather than as payments under §72.[59]

2. *Alimony.* Section 72 does not apply to payments includable in a spouse's gross income under §71 (relating to alimony and separate maintenance payments) or §682 (relating to income of an estate or trust in case of divorce).[60]

3. *Accident and health benefits.* Section 72 does not apply to amounts received as accident or health benefits, which are governed by §§104 and 105, discussed elsewhere in this work.[61] When amounts are received from an employer established plan that provides both distributions taxable under §72 and distributions that may be excludable from gross income under §104 or §105 as accident and health benefits, employee contributions allocable to the latter are excluded in determining the employee's investment in the contract and the exclusion ratio applicable to amounts received as an annuity.[62]

4. *Employee death benefits.* If by reason of an employee's death the employee's beneficiary receives payments to which §72 applies, the investment in the contract includes amounts excludable from the beneficiary's gross income under §101(b).[63] The beneficiary thereby receives the benefit of the §101(b) exclusion by way of the annuity rules.

5. *Annuities paid by trusts.* An individual purchasing an annuity contract from a trust is taxed in accordance with §72, unless, in substance, the transaction is a transfer in trust subject to a reservation of income. In the latter situation, the payments are taxed as trust distributions under the rules of subchapter J rather than as annuity payments.[64] Subchapter J also governs the tax treatment of periodic payments received by an income benefici-

---

[59] Rev. Rul. 75-255, 1975-2 CB 22 ("Life Annuity and Death Benefit Contract," providing for periodic payments and guaranteeing repayment of entire consideration on request by the policyholder during his life or on his death to his designated beneficiaries).

[60] IRC §72(k). For §§71 and 682, see infra ¶¶77.1 and 77.4.4. Conversely, if §§71 and 682 do not apply to payments received by a former spouse under an annuity contract, §72 does. See Bernatschke v. US, 364 F2d 400 (Ct. Cl. 1966) (payments subject to §72 rather than §71 where annuity for ex-wife not purchased because of obligation to support her).

[61] Infra ¶¶13.1, 13.2.

[62] Reg. §1.72-15(c). Although self-employed individuals are generally not employees under §104(a)(3) or §105, they may be subject to §72 on receiving accident or health benefits from such a plan, unless the benefits are provided through an insurance contract or an arrangement having the effect of insurance, in which case §104(a)(3) applies. See Reg. §1.72-15(g).

[63] Reg. §1.72-8(b); see Reg. §1.101-2(a)(2) (third sentence); IRC §101(b)(2)(D) (amount excluded determined by reference to date of death value). For §101(b), see infra ¶12.6.

[64] See, e.g., Lazarus v. CIR, 513 F2d 824 (9th Cir. 1975).

ary of a trust or estate whose interest was acquired by gift, devise, bequest, or inheritance.

6. *Retired serviceman's family protection or survivor benefit plan.* Under §72(n), a special rule applies to certain annuities paid pursuant to a retired serviceman's family protection or survivor benefit plan. The rule is discussed elsewhere in this work.[65]

¶12.3.7 Annuities Held by Entities

Under §72(u), enacted in 1986, an entity owning an annuity is taxed each year on the income accruing on the annuity during the year.[66] The principal purpose of the provision is to prevent employers from funding "on a tax-favored basis, significant amounts of deferred compensation for employees" through a medium that is not subject to the many requirements imposed on qualified pension plans.[67] The rule, however, applies to any annuity holder that is not a "natural person."[68]

When the rule applies, the owner must annually report "the income on the contract" for the year as ordinary income.[69] This amount is (1) the sum of the net surrender value of the contract at year-end and all distributions received since the contract was purchased, less (2) the sum of the net premiums paid under the contract in all years and the amounts included in gross income under this rule for prior years.[70] In other words, the income on

---

[65] Infra ¶14.7.

[66] Section 72(u) is effective with respect to annuity premiums paid after February 1986. Pub. L. No. 99-514, §1135(b) 100 Stat. 2085 (1986).

[67] Staff of Joint Comm. on Tax'n, 99th Cong., 2d Sess., General Explanation of the Tax Reform Act of 1986, at 658 (Comm. Print 1987) [hereinafter 1986 Bluebook]. See infra Ch. 61 for qualified pension plans.

[68] If a "trust or other entity" holds an annuity "as an agent for a natural person," the annuity is deemed owned by a natural person. IRC §72(u)(1). The legislative history suggests this rule should be applied broadly:

> In the case of a contract the nominal owner of which is a person who is not a natural person (e.g., a corporation or a trust), but the beneficial owner of which is a natural person, the contract is treated as held by a natural person. For example, if an employer holds a group policy to satisfy State group policy requirements, but has no right to any amounts contributed to the contract and all amounts contributed are employee contributions, the employer is merely the nominal holder of the contract and the contract is not treated as held by a nonnatural person.

1986 Bluebook, supra note 67, at 658.

[69] IRC §72(u)(1).

[70] IRC §72(u)(2)(A). The term "net premiums" refers to the excess of premiums paid over policyholder dividends. IRC §72(u)(2)(B). The IRS may use the "fair market value of the contract" in place of its "net surrender value" if "necessary to prevent the avoidance" of §72(u). IRC §72(u)(2)(A).

the contract is the total value held at the end of the year and previously received under the contract, reduced by the amounts paid for the contract and reduced further by the accretions previously taxed to the owner. This amount should equal the sum of current distributions and the increase in the contract's value during the year. The income on the contract is essentially reported on an accrual basis, whether the taxpayer's normal method of accounting is cash or accrual.

A few exceptions are provided.[71] A single premium annuity is excepted from §72(u) if it commences within a year of purchase. This exception suggests that the principal purpose of the rule is to catch inside buildup accruing before the annuity starting date. An annuity held by an estate is excepted if it was acquired from the decedent, probably because an estate is only a transitory entity standing between an individual owner and his legatees. Additional exceptions are provided for annuities held by a qualified pension, profit sharing, stock bonus, or annuity trust, annuities received by an employer in connection with the termination of a qualified trust, tax sheltered annuities qualifed under §403(b), and individual retirement annuities (IRAs).[72] An annuity within any of these exceptions is governed by the general rules of §72.

¶12.4 OTHER RECEIPTS UNDER LIFE INSURANCE, ANNUITY, AND ENDOWMENT CONTRACTS

¶12.4.1 "Amounts Not Received as an Annuity"

Section 72(e) prescribes the tax treatment of amounts received under a life insurance, annuity, or endowment contract that are not subject to either §101(a) (life insurance proceeds "paid by reason of the death of the insured") or §72(b) ("amounts received as an annuity").[1] The provision encompasses a motley assortment of payments, including policy dividends, partial and complete cash surrender payments, the maturity value of endowment policies, variable annuities in excess of an allocated portion of the cost,[2] and guaranteed refunds payable when an annuitant dies prematurely. These receipts—the residue remaining after the more specialized rules of §§101(a) and 72(b) have exerted jurisdiction over their respective territories —are collectively designated "amounts not received as an annuity." Section

---

[71] IRC §72(u)(3).

[72] See infra Ch. 61 for pension, profit sharing, stock bonus, and annuity plans, ¶62.5 for IRAs, and ¶62.7.3 for tax deferred annuities.

[1] For §§101(a) and 72(b), see supra ¶¶12.2 and 12.3. For other exceptions to the general rule of §72, see supra ¶12.3.6.

[2] See supra ¶12.3.3.

72(e), further, has been extended in recent years to cover many transactions — including policy loans and gifts of annuity contracts — that do not involve actual distributions under the contracts.

Until 1982, the operation of §72(e) was relatively simple. Nonannuity amounts received after the annuity starting date were included in gross income even if the taxpayer's investment had not yet been recovered.[3] The reason for this rule, which remains in present law, is that the exclusion ratio, which is the method of recovering the investment once annuity payments have begun, is computed as of the annuity starting date;[4] if subsequent nonannuity receipts were treated as tax-free recoveries of the annuitant's cost, it would be necessary to recompute the exclusion ratio every time that such a payment was received.

Under the pre-1982 rules, nonannuity amounts received before the annuity starting date were treated first as tax-free recoveries of investment and were taxable only after they had exhausted the owner's investment.[5] This rule was highly favorable to policyholders and encouraged insurance companies to develop annuity contracts that were designed as tax-favored investments, rather than as a means of providing for retirement. Until annuity payments begin, a policyholder is usually not taxed on the income earned by his investment in the contract. Under many annuity contracts, however, cash withdrawals and partial surrenders can be made before the annuity starting date. The pre-1982 rule, in combination with the general deferral of tax on inside buildup, allowed a contract owner to invest in an annuity, watch it build up in value tax free, and then withdraw his original investment tax free, leaving accrued income in place to earn still more nontaxable income.[6]

---

[3] IRC §72(e)(1)(A) (before amendment in 1982); see also supra ¶12.3.2 text accompanying note 29 (meaning of "annuity starting date"). This exception was itself subject to the qualification set out in former §72(e)(2) (payments in full discharge of contract or on surrender, redemption, or maturity subject to general rule of former §72(e)(1)(B)).

[4] See supra ¶12.3.2.

[5] The Senate Finance Committee report on the 1954 version of §72(e) states that a refund to a beneficiary on the death of the annuitant "is to be exempt from tax." S. Rep. No. 1622, 83d Cong., 2d Sess. 11 (1954). While this was ordinarily true, §72(e)(1) clearly required refunds to be included in gross income once the investment in the contract was fully recovered. See Moseley v. CIR, 72 TC 183 (1979) (acq.) (distribution from special reserve tax free because less than aggregate premiums paid for policy).

See generally Lawthers, Some Murky Blessings of the New Tax Code, 8 J. Am. Soc'y CLU 329 (1954).

[6] Staff of Joint Comm. on Tax'n, 97th Cong., 2d Sess., General Explanation of the Revenue Provisions of the Tax Equity and Fiscal Responsibility Act of 1982, at 361 (Comm. Print 1982) [hereinafter 1982 Bluebook].

Section 72(e) was restated in 1982, principally to eliminate this opportunity. The restated provision was amended in 1984 and 1986. Presently, the general rule is that amounts received under an annuity contract, but not as an annuity, are gross income. This rule, however, is subject to numerous qualifications, which are described below.

As before 1982, a nonannuity amount received after the annuity starting date is gross income.[7] When such an amount is received before the annuity starting date, it is gross income to the extent of the excess of "the cash value of the contract" just before the receipt over the investment in the contract.[8] The investment in the contract is the sum of the premiums and other consideration paid for the contract up to the date of the nonannuity receipt, reduced by all prior receipts that were excluded from gross income.[9] If the amount received exceeds the gross income amount, it is a tax-free recovery of investment in the contract.[10]

A loan against an annuity contract is generally treated as a nonannuity receipt under the contract.[11] This rule applies to a loan against cash value obtained from the issuer of the policy, but also reaches the proceeds of a loan from an unrelated lender if the contract is assigned or pledged to secure the loan. The use of the loan proceeds is irrelevant. Assume *A*, who owns an annuity issued by an insurance company, borrows $100 from his local bank, pledging the annuity as security for the loan. *A* is deemed to have received $100 under the contract other than as an annuity, even if the insurance company and the bank are unrelated and even if the loan proceeds are used to repair the leaky roof on *A*'s house.

If an annuity contract is transferred by gift, the donor is usually taxed on all income accrued under the contract up to the date of the gift.[12] This is

---

[7] IRC §72(e)(2)(A).

[8] IRC §§72(e)(2)(B), (3)(A). Cash value is "determined without regard to any surrender charge." IRC §72(e)(3)(A)(i).

[9] IRC §72(e)(6).

[10] IRC §72(e)(3)(B). A detailed example illustrating the application of these rules is given in 1982 Bluebook, supra note 6, at 362–63.

[11] IRC §72(e)(4)(A). Section 72(p), also added in 1982, provides specially for loans secured by an employee's interest in a qualified pension, profit sharing, stock bonus, or annuity plan or in a tax deferred annuity qualifying under §403(b). See infra ¶61.5.1.

Before the enactment of §§72(e)(4) and (p), the IRS ruled that loan proceeds were a §72(e) distribution if (1) a loan was obtained from the issuer of a §403(b) annuity and (2) the terms of the policy entitled the policyholder to take the loan and did not prescribe a time for the loan to be repaid; "in substance, the transaction is a return of consideration and not a loan." Rev. Rul. 81-126, 1980-1 CB 206. But see Drake v. US, 597 F. Supp. 1271 (MDNC 1984) (Rev. Rul. 81-126 rejected; policy loan treated as loan); Minnis v. CIR, 71 TC 1049 (1979) (earlier statement of IRS position rejected; same result as in *Drake*).

[12] IRC §72(e)(4)(C).

accomplished by treating the donor as having received a nonannuity amount under the contract equal to the excess of the contract's cash value at the time of the gift over the donor's investment in the contract. To avoid double taxation, the donee is considered to have an investment in the contract equal to the sum of the donor's investment and the income recognized by the donor on the gift. The gift rule applies whenever the holder of an annuity "transfers it without full and adequate consideration." If a contract is the subject of a part-gift, part-sale transaction, for example, all income accrued under the contract is taxed—not just the excess of the price paid over adjusted basis—and it is taxed as ordinary income, not as gain on a sale. A transfer between spouses or between former spouses incident to divorce, however, is excepted from the rule.

Several broad exceptions are allowed. Although policy dividends paid to the contract owner are subject to the rules described above, a dividend is excluded from gross income if the insurer keeps it in payment of premiums under the contract.[13] Also, the pre-1982 ordering—capital recovery first and income second—continues to apply in several situations:[14] (1) to nonannuity amounts received during the lifetime of the insured under a life insurance or endowment policy;[15] (2) to an amount received in complete discharge of the issuer's obligation when the policy is cashed in, matures, or is terminated for some other reason; and (3) to amounts received under contracts made before August 14, 1982.[16]

---

[13] IRC §§72(e)(1)(B), (4)(B). The portion of a premium paid by a retained dividend is not included in the policyholder's investment in the contract; the dividend is essentially treated as a premium reduction. 1982 Bluebook, supra note 6, at 361.

[14] IRC §72(e)(5).

[15] The Treasury, however, is expected to issue regulations subjecting a life insurance or endowment contract to the post-1982 ordering rule "when the amount at risk . . . is sufficiently minimal that the contract should be treated as an annuity." 1982 Bluebook, supra note 6, at 363.

[16] If no premiums or other consideration is paid under the policy after August 13, 1982, the old ordering rule applies to all nonannuity amounts under the contract. If the investment in the contract is increased after that date, in contrast, the contract is bifurcated, and the new ordering applies to nonannuity amounts attributable to premiums paid after August 13, 1982. IRC §72(e)(5)(B). More completely, the ordering rule where post-1982 premiums have been paid on a pre-1982 contract is: "first, from investments prior to August 14, 1982, next from income accumulated with respect to such investments [including income accumulated both before and after August 14, 1982], then from income accumulated with respect to investments after August 13, 1982, and finally from investments after August 13, 1982." 1982 Bluebook, supra note 6, at 363. Amounts treated as income are usually treated the same whether earned on pre- or post-1982 investment. When this is so, the second and third of these categories can be collapsed into one, making the ordering first from investment before August 14, 1982, second from income on the contract (measured as the excess of cash value over investment just before the withdrawal), and third from investment after August 13, 1982. The division of income between accruals on

A third scheme for allocating nonannuity receipts between income and capital applies, further, to qualified pension, profit sharing, stock bonus, or annuity plans, tax deferred annuities under §403(b), and individual retirement annuities.[17] A nonannuity distribution from one of these sources is prorated. The portion treated as tax-free recovery of investment is the amount of the distribution multiplied by a fraction whose numerator is the taxpayer's investment and whose denominator is his account balance or accrued benefit under the plan.[18] The remainder of the receipt is gross income. For example, if an employee's account under a profit sharing plan is $100, $15 of which consists of nondeductible employee contributions, 15 percent of a nonannuity receipt from the plan is a recovery of basis and 85 percent is gross income.

For this purpose, the account balance or accrued benefit does not include an amount as to which the taxpayer's rights are not vested. If an employee is 60 percent vested in an account balance of $167, for example, his account balance is deemed to be $100 for purposes of this rule. Also, in a defined contribution plan, an employee's contributions and the income earned through investments of these contributions are treated as a separate contract.[19] The latter rule is doubly significant because an employee's investment in a qualified plan usually includes only his own nondeductible contributions, and nonannuity withdrawals from the plan are limited to this source in many circumstances. A further significance is that "if an employee

---

pre-and post-1982 investment, however, is necessary if the distribution triggers the penalty tax on premature distributions because income on investment made before August 14, 1982 is exempted from this tax. See infra ¶12.4.2 note 31.

[17] IRC §72(e)(8). These rules apply to distributions after 1986. Pub. L. No. 99-514, §§1122(c)(3), (h)(1), 100 Stat. 2085 (1986). Earlier distributions are subject to the pre-1982 ordering rule (capital recovery first). IRC §72(e)(5)(D).

Also, a transitional rule is provided: If, as of May 5, 1986, a plan allowed employees to withdraw their own contributions before separation from service, the pre-1982 ordering rule (capital recovery first) applies to distributions before the annuity starting date until the total of these distributions equals the investment in the contract as of the end of 1986. For example, if, on December 31, 1986, an employee's account under such a plan includes employee contributions of $100, the first $100 received from the plan thereafter is a tax-free recovery of these contributions.

In addition, the income-first-investment-second rule applies if 85 percent or more of the contributions to a plan are made by employees. IRC §72(e)(7).

[18] The Treasury can "prescribe appropriate rules for estimating the amounts [in this fraction] if precise calculation would be unjustifiably burdensome." Staff of Joint Comm. on Tax'n, 99th Cong., 2d Sess., General Explanation of the Tax Reform Act of 1986, at 723 (Comm. Print 1987) [hereinafter 1986 Bluebook].

[19] It was intended that this rule also apply where employee contributions to a defined benefit plan are held in a separate account, essentially as an employee-funded defined contribution plan within an employer-funded defined benefit plan. 1986 Bluebook, supra note 18, at 724.

withdraws all amounts attributable to employee contributions and such amount is less than the total employee contributions, the employee may recognize a loss."[20]

¶12.4.2 Penalty on Early Withdrawal

Section 72(q) imposes a penalty on distributions and withdrawals from annuities that Congress determines to be premature.[21] The penalty is 10 percent of the gross income recognized on receipt of such a distribution. The penalty is one of several expressions of a policy, adopted in 1982, that the tax advantages of annuity contracts should be fully allowed only when the contracts are held "to meet long-term investment and retirement goals," and that "their use for short-term investment and income tax deferral should be discouraged."[22]

The penalties apply to all distributions and withdrawals except those that fall within one or more of nine excluded categories.[23] Several of the exceptions focus directly on the retirement and income security objectives Congress intended not to impede. The penalty is excused, for example, if the distribution is received after the taxpayer reaches the age of 59 1/2 or is made after the policyholder dies[24] or becomes disabled. An individual is disabled for this purpose "if he is unable to engage in any substantial gainful activity by reason of any medically determinable physical or mental impairment which can be expected to result in death or to be of long-continued and indefinite duration."[25]

Also, distributions under standard life annuities are not penalized. More specifically, a distribution is excepted from the penalty if it is "a part of a series of substantially equal periodic payments . . . made for the life . . . of the taxpayer or the joint lives . . . of such taxpayer and his benefi-

---

[20] Id.

[21] In the form described here, §72(q) applies only to distributions received after 1986. Pub. L. No. 99-514, §§1123(b), (e)(1), 100 Stat. 2085 (1986). When §72(q) was enacted in 1982, the penalty rate was 5 percent. The 1982 version exempted most of the distributions exempted by present law, and also exempted distributions allocable to investment in the contract made more than 10 years prior to the distribution. IRC §72(q) (before amendment in 1984). Amendments made in 1984 eliminated the 10-year rule for contracts issued after January 18, 1985. Pub. L. No. 98-369, §222, 98 Stat. 494 (1984). The penalty rate was raised to 10 percent by the 1986 amendments.

[22] 1982 Bluebook, supra note 6.

[23] IRC §72(q)(2). The tax can apply, for example, to policy dividends paid to the policyholder rather than retained in payment of premiums. 1982 Bluebook, supra note 6, at 364.

[24] If the policyholder is not an individual, this exception applies to any distribution after the death of the primary annuitant. IRC §72(q)(2)(B).

[25] IRC §§72(m)(7), (q)(2)(C).

ciary."[26] An annuity of $100 per month for the annuitant's life, for example, is not subject to the penalty even if the annuity begins long before the taxpayer reaches 59 1/2 or becomes disabled. An annuity for a fixed term can also qualify if, at the annuity starting date, the term equals the annuitant's life expectancy or the joint life expectancies of the annuitant and his beneficiary. In either case, the requirement of periodic payments is only satisfied if payments are made annually or more frequently. The requirement that the payments be "substantially equal" is met by a variable annuity if "the number of units withdrawn to make each distribution is substantially the same."[27] To protect against evasion of the substantially equal requirement, a special tax is imposed if the amounts of the payments change before the taxpayer reaches age 64 1/2.[28]

All distributions under an annuity issued for a single premium are exempted if the annuity starting date is within one year after the annuity is purchased.[29] The congressional target, in other words, is the situation where significant inside buildup occurs before annuity payments begin.

Other exceptions are provided for more specialized reasons. The penalty is inapplicable to distributions under qualified pension, profit sharing, stock bonus, and annuity plans, tax deferred annuities qualifying under §403(b), and individual retirement annuities. This exception is only allowed, however, because early distributions from these plans are subject to a similar penalty scheme specially designed for them.[30] Also, a transition rule excepts distributions "allocable to investment in the contract before August 14, 1982."[31]

When the penalty applies, it is 10 percent of the gross income recognized on receipt of the distribution.[32] If a $100 distribution consists of $85 of gross income and $15 of tax-free cost recovery, for example, the penalty is $8.5. The penalty is an addition to the taxpayer's income tax for the year and is not allowed as a deduction or credit in determining the regular tax. If regular tax is imposed at 28 percent, for example, the penalty has the effect of increasing the tax on the distribution to 38 percent.

---

[26] For taxable years before 1987, this exemption applies to any distribution "which is one of a series of substantially equal periodic payments made for the life of a taxpayer or over a period extending for at least 60 months after the annuity starting date." IRC §72(q)(2)(D) (before amendment in 1986).

[27] 1982 Bluebook, supra note 6, at 364.

[28] IRC §72(q)(3). This special tax only applies in taxable years after 1986. Pub. L. No. 99-514, §1123(b), 100 Stat. 2085 (1986).

[29] IRC §§72(q)(2)(I), (u)(4). This exemption applies only in taxable years after 1986. Pub. L. No. 99-514, §1123(b), 100 Stat. 2085 (1986).

[30] IRC §72(t), discussed infra ¶61.4.

[31] IRC §72(q)(2)(F). For the allocation of distributions between pre- and post-1982 investment, see supra ¶12.4.1 note 16.

[32] IRC §72(q)(1).

¶12.4.3 Constructive Receipt of Lump Sum

Under pre-1954 law, the doctrine of constructive receipt was some-times applied to a policyholder who was entitled to receive a lump-sum settlement in full discharge of the issuer's obligations under the contract, even though he elected to take the proceeds in a series of annuity or other installment payments.[33] By virtue of §72(h), enacted in 1954, the taxpayer is not required to include the lump sum in gross income if an option to receive an annuity is exercised within 60 days after the lump sum first becomes payable. The regulations seem to interpret this provision to include agreements to take an annuity in lieu of the lump sum even if the specific option elected is not contained in the original contract.[34] When §72(h) is inapplicable because the optional settlement is not an annuity, the applicability of the doctrine of constructive receipt evidently depends on the developing case law.

¶12.4.4 Sales and Other Dispositions of Policies

If a policyholder sells or otherwise disposes of a life insurance, endowment, or annuity policy other than by electing a settlement option, the transaction is subject to the general rules of §1001, relating to gain or loss on a disposition of property.[35] If the contract is a capital asset in the owner's hands, any excess of the amount received over the premiums or other consideration paid for the contract is capital gain, unless the transaction is not a "sale or exchange" of the contract,[36] is a device to convert ordinary income into capital gain,[37] or otherwise falls outside the intended range of

---

[33] For constructive receipt, see infra ¶105.2.3; see also Brawerman, Income Tax Problems of Non-Business Life Insurance, 1952 S. Cal. Tax Inst. 267, 289–93.

[34] See Reg. §1.72-12 (exercises option or "irrevocably agrees" to take an option).

[35] For §1001, see infra ¶40.2. There is no explicit comprehensive exemption for settlement options, but it is usually assumed that the election of a particular option is not a sale or other disposition of the policyholder's other rights under the contract, by analogy to Rev. Rul. 72-265, 1972-1 CB 222 (gain or loss not recognized on conversion of debenture in accordance with its terms into stock of issuer). But see Barrett v. CIR, 348 F2d 916 (1st Cir. 1965) (election to take paid-up life insurance policy on maturity of endowment policies is taxable event under §72(e) (supra ¶12.4.1), although option included in original policies).

For restrictions on the deductibility of losses in this area, see infra ¶12.5.2.

[36] See Hawkins v. CIR, 3 TCM (CCH) 1135 (1944), rev'd on another issue, 152 F2d 221 (5th Cir. 1945) (surrender of insurance policies to issuer for cash value not a sale or exchange; gain taxable as ordinary income); see generally infra ¶52.1.

[37] See CIR v. Phillips, 275 F2d 33, 36 n.3 (4th Cir. 1960) (paid-up endowment policy sold by taxpayer to his law partners 12 days before maturity; held, ordinary income); Arnfeld v. US, 163 F. Supp. 865 (Ct. Cl. 1958), cert. denied, 359 US 943 (1959). See also infra ¶52.1.8.

the capital gain and loss provisions.[38] These exceptions leave little room for capital gains treatment save for the sale of a policy at a gain attributable to the insured's supervening ill health.

Section 1035, enacted in 1954, exempts certain exchanges of life insurance, endowment, and annuity contracts from the basic principle that gain or loss is recognized on a sale or other disposition of property. Granted on the ground that such transactions do not produce cash or serve tax-avoidance purposes, this nonrecognition treatment applies to the exchange of (1) a life insurance contract for a life insurance, endowment, or annuity contract, (2) an endowment contract for an annuity contract or for an endowment contract whose payments begin no later than payments under the surrendered contract, or (3) an annuity contract for another annuity contract.[39] The regulations require that both contracts relate to the same insured,[40] but the IRS has ruled that the contracts can be issued by different companies.[41]

If an exchange qualifies under §1035 except for the fact that the transferor receives cash or other property in addition to a policy that can be received tax free, the tax consequences of the transaction are determined under §§1031(b) and (c). Under these provisions, examined in more detail elsewhere in this work,[42] gain is recognized to the extent of the disqualified property (boot) received, but loss is not recognized. The transferor's basis for the contract received is the same as the basis of the transferred contract, with an adjustment for the boot and gain (if any) recognized on the exchange.[43] Tax characteristics other than basis carry over from the old to the new contract, including the status of the old contract under various transition rules pertaining to contracts issued or investment made before specified dates.[44]

---

[38] See Gallun v. CIR, 327 F2d 809 (7th Cir. 1964) (assignment of income theory). It is not clear whether the Tax Court, which denied capital gain treatment in *Gallun* because the seller's profit was primarily attributable to accumulated income, would have reached a different result if the profit had been attributable to some other factor, such as the insured's ill health at the time of the sale.

[39] See S. Rep. No. 1622, 83d Cong., 2d Sess. 110–11 (1954). Athough the rationale for §1035 primarily concerns transactions generating gain, it also provides for nonrecognition of loss. See generally Pyle, Income, Estate and Gift Taxation of Life, Accident and Sickness Insurance and Annuities Under the 1954 Code, 5 Tul. Tax Inst. 467, 481–92 (1956); Widdowson, Taxation of Policy Changes, 18 J. Am. Soc'y CLU 171 (1964); Young, Tax-Free Alteration of Insurance Policies, 45 Taxes 649 (1967).

[40] Reg. §1.1035-1.

[41] Rev. Rul. 72-358, 1972-2 CB 473.

[42] See infra ¶44.1.2.

[43] See IRC §1031(d), discussed infra ¶44.2.5.

[44] 1982 Bluebook, supra note 6, at 365 ("money that was grandfathered under one contract continues to be grandfathered . . . under the new contract").

Since §1035 does not apply to exchanges of endowment or annuity contracts for life insurance contracts or to exchanges of annuity contracts for endowment contracts, gain or loss is recognized on such an exchange under the basic rule of §1001.

¶12.5 TAXATION OF INSIDE BUILDUP

Normally, the owner of a life insurance contract with cash surrender value is not taxed on increases in cash surrender value.[1] Since 1984, however, §7702 has provided a detailed definition of life insurance, applicable throughout the Code, whose purpose is to restrict the tax exemption for inside buildup so that contracts that are primarily investment media, but include life insurance as an incidental aspect, do not qualify.[2] If a contract is life insurance under state law, but does not satisfy the tax definition, the owner is taxed annually on increases in cash surrender value, thereby taking away one of the two principal advantages of cash surrender value life insurance. The other advantage, exclusion of the death benefit, is retained. The sum of the premiums added to surrender value, and the amount taxed to the owner over the life of the policy, is received tax free at death as a return of capital. The remainder of the death benefit is excluded under §101(a) as though it were life insurance.

The tax on inside buildup is not restricted to recently developed life-insurance/investment products. "Certain contracts that have been traditionally sold by life insurance companies, such as endowment contracts [are no longer] classified as life insurance contracts because of their innate investment orientation."[3]

To be life insurance under §7702, a contract must be life insurance under state or foreign law, and must meet one of two tests, a cash value accumulation test or a guideline-premium/cash-value-corridor test.[4] These tests are described below.

1. *Cash value accumulation test.* The cash value accumulation test asks the question, "Will there ever come a time during the life of the insured when an astute policyholder would discover that he could cash the policy in, buy a single premium policy providing the same death benefit, and have

---

[1] See supra ¶12.1.2.

[2] The definition applies to contracts issued after 1984. Pub. L. No. 98-369, §221(a), 98 Stat. 494 (1984). An interim solution devised in 1982 remains in §101(f), but applies only to "flexible premium contracts" issued before 1985.

[3] Staff of Joint Comm. on Tax'n, General Explanation of the Revenue Provisions of the Deficit Reduction Act of 1984, at 647 (Comm. Print 1984) [hereinafter 1984 Bluebook].

[4] IRC §7702(a).

money left over?" If the answer to this question is yes, the policy is not life insurance. Generally, a policyholder's decision to cash in a policy reflects a change in circumstances or estate planning objectives. A contract that fails the cash value accumulation test, however, is structured so that it can be seen at the outset that cashing in the policy will eventually become the wise thing to do. When this is so, the policy is primarily a vehicle for savings and provides life insurance protection only incidentally in the case of premature death. The cash value accumulation test is usually satisfied, in contrast, by "traditional whole life policies, with cash values that accumulate based on reasonable interest rates."[5]

Specifically, the cash value accumulation test is applied as follows: When the policy is issued, the rise in cash surrender value is plotted out over the possible life span of the insured, and the cash value at each point in time is compared with the premium that would have to be paid at that time for a single premium policy providing the same benefits. The test is failed if cash value will ever rise above the contemporaneous single premium amount.[6]

Several rules are provided for projecting cash surrender values.[7] First, premiums are split between the portions charged by the insurer for pure insurance coverage and the portions added to cash surrender value. The term "cash surrender value" refers to "any amount to which the policyholder is entitled upon surrender and, generally, against which the policyholder can borrow."[8] Cash surrender accumulations equal the premiums paid, less "the mortality charges specified in the contract (or, if none is specified, the mortality charges used in determining the statutory reserves for such contract)." If the contract provides other benefits (e.g., an accidental death or disability benefit or a waiver of premiums in the event of disability), any charge specified in the contract for this benefit is also allocated to pure insurance rather than cash surrender value. Second, inside buildup is projected using a rate of interest on accumulations equal to the greater of 4 percent or the rate guaranteed in the contract. Third, cash surrender value is the sum of accumulations from premiums and interest accumulations, unreduced by surrender charge or policy loan. Also, cash surrender value does not include policyholder dividends left on deposit to accumulate interest or reasonable termination dividends.[9]

---

[5] 1984 Bluebook, supra note 3, at 647.
[6] IRC §7702(b)(1).
[7] IRC §7702(b)(2).
[8] 1984 Bluebook, supra note 3, at 647.
[9] Id. at 649. Interest on a policyholder dividend left on deposit is taxable without regard to these rules because the deposit is not considered part of an insurance contract.

2. *Guideline-premium/cash-value-corridor test.* The guideline-premium/cash-value-corridor test consists of two requirements, both of which must be satisfied to meet the test.

The first of these requirements, the guideline premium requirement, is satisfied if the sum of the premiums under the contract will never exceed a limitation prescribed by statute.[10] This limitation is applied by plotting out aggregate premiums, year by year over the potential life of the policy, and comparing each such aggregate with the greater of two figures, a single premium amount and a guideline level premium. If the aggregate of actual premiums will ever exceed the applicable testing amount, the contract fails this test.

The single premium amount is the single premium that would be charged when the policy is issued to provide the future benefits under the contract. The guideline level premium is the aggregate of the premiums that would have been paid, up to the date the test is being applied, if the premiums were computed on a level basis ending with the insured's death or, should the insured live so long, at age 95.

The second of the two requirements of the guideline-premium/cash-value-corridor test, the cash value corridor requirement, is satisfied if the death benefit always equals or exceeds a prescribed multiple of cash surrender value.[11] For years in which the insured is under age 40, the death benefit must always be at least 250 percent of cash surrender value. That is, during these years, cash surrender value can never exceed 40 percent of the death benefit. The required multiple declines year by year after age 40 until it reaches 100 percent at age 95. At no time before age 95, in other words, can cash surrender value be as large as the death benefit.

¶12.6 DEDUCTIBILITY OF PREMIUMS AND LOSSES

¶12.6.1 Deductibility of Premiums

Since no statutory provision explicitly authorizes a deduction for premiums paid for life insurance, annuity, or endowment policies, a deduction is permissible only when the cost fits within a broader class of deductible expenditures (e.g., business expenses). Even if the premiums seem at first to be covered by such a provision, a deduction may be barred by other statutory provisions or tax principles. Thus, taxpayers seeking deductions find that the road bristles with obstacles and that premiums are seldom deductible. The principal barriers are the following:

---

[10] IRC §7702(b).
[11] IRC §7702(c).

1. *Nondeductibility of personal expenditures.* When a life insurance, annuity, or endowment contract is purchased to provide financial security for the policyholder's retirement years and for his family after his death, the premiums are "personal, living and family expenses," which, by virtue of §262, cannot be deducted except pursuant to express statutory authority.[1] This restriction bars a deduction for virtually all premiums paid for policies serving personal objectives, except for (1) limited classes of contributions to IRAs and qualified pension, profit sharing, stock bonus, and annuity plans[2] and (2) premiums paid as alimony or as charitable contributions where the contract belongs to a former spouse or charitable donee and the expenditure serves the same function as a transfer of cash to the owner of the policy.[3]

2. *Business expenses.* Ordinary and necessary business expenses are usually deductible under §162, and §212 allows individuals to deduct similar expenses incurred in connection with income-producing property.[4] Thus, if an employer augments an employee's salary by paying premiums on the employee's life insurance, annuity, or endowment policy, the premiums are deductible business expenses if the premiums, when added to other forms of compensation to the employee, do not exceed reasonable compensation for the employee's services.[5]

If the employer is the owner or beneficiary of the policy, however, attention must be given to the capital outlay and other obstacles discussed below, which may bar a deduction even though the premiums are paid for business reasons. Also, business expenses can be deducted only if "ordinary and necessary" — a phrase that has been applied several times, not entirely convincingly, to disallow deductions for life insurance premiums when the insured was not closely connected with the taxpayer, even though the latter

---

[1] For §262, see infra ¶30.1. See also Reg. §1.262-1(b)(1) (premiums paid by insured for life insurance are not deductible); Kelsey v. CIR, 27 TCM (CCH) 337 (1968), aff'd per order, 69-2 USTC ¶9619 (2d Cir. 1969) (not officially reported) (premiums allocable to life insurance component of combination policy held nondeductible personal expenses); Rev. Rul. 86-80, 1986-1 CB 79 (contributions by member of board of trade to "gratuity fund" providing death benefits to beneficiaries of deceased members are nondeductible life insurance premiums, even though contributions required of all members below age 55).

[2] For the treatment of qualified plans and individual retirement accounts, see infra ¶¶61.1, 62.5. Contributions by employees to civil service and other retirement plans, even though mandatory, are nondeductible personal expenses.

[3] See infra ¶77.2.2 (insurance premiums as alimony), ¶35.1 (charitable contributions).

[4] For §§162 and 212, see infra ¶¶20.1 and 20.5.

[5] See Champion Trophy Mfg. Co. v. CIR, 31 TCM (CCH) 1236 (1972); Hubert Transfer & Storage Co. v. CIR, 7 TCM (CCH) 171 (1948). For the treatment by the employee of premiums paid by the employer on group term life insurance, see §79, discussed infra ¶14.2.

would suffer financially from the death of the insured.[6]

3. *Capital outlay.* Premiums paid for the savings component of life insurance, annuity, and endowment contracts are nondeductible if paid by the owner of the policy because they are a capital outlay. This barrier applies even if the policy is purchased for business reasons.[7] Thus, premiums paid by a business enterprise for an endowment policy to compensate for an anticipated loss on the retirement of a key employee are nondeductible investments rather than deductible business expenses.

For policies held for personal rather than business reasons, further, the capital outlay rationale is often a better explanation of the lack of a deduction than the "personal, living, and family expenses" theory of §262. Under an annuity, for example, the annuitant is allowed a tax-free recovery of his investment in the contract, and the same is true when a life insurance policy is surrendered for its cash value or sold.[8] These cost recovery rules imply that premiums are investments, not personal expenses.

4. *Expenses allocable to exempt income.* Section 265(1) bars a deduction for amounts allocable to income that is "wholly exempt" from income taxation, even if a deduction is otherwise allowable. Although the proceeds of life insurance policies are ordinarily exempt from tax when received by beneficiaries, there are exceptions to this principle;[9] nevertheless, it has been held that §265(1) applies to premiums paid for life insurance, presumably on the theory that the proceeds are ordinarily "wholly exempt."[10]

Section 265(1) seems to disallow deductions only if the exempt income accrues to the benefit of the taxpayer otherwise entitled to the deduction. For this reason, it does not bar a deduction for premiums paid by an employer to compensate an employee for services, even though the proceeds paid on the employee's death will be "wholly exempt" from taxation in the hands of the employee's beneficiaries. This result can be reconciled with the language of §265(1) on the theory that the premiums are "allocable" to the compensation (which is taxable to the employee) rather than to the exempt

---

[6] Goedel v. CIR, 39 BTA 1, 12 (1939) (premiums paid by stock dealer on life of President of the United States, whose death might disrupt the stock market); Rev. Rul. 55-714, 1955-2 CB 51 (manager denied deduction for insurance on lives of entertainers whom he represented for percentage of their gross income). See infra ¶20.3.2 ("ordinary and necessary" test).

[7] For discussion of the capital outlay restriction on business expenditures, see infra ¶20.4. See also Chism Ice Cream Co. v. CIR, 21 TCM (CCH) 25 (1962), aff'd on other issues sub nom. Chism's Est. v. CIR, 322 F2d 956 (9th Cir. 1963) (premiums on retirement income policy were nondeductible capital investment).

[8] See supra ¶¶12.2.1, 12.3.2.

[9] See supra ¶12.1.1.

[10] Jones v. CIR, 231 F2d 655 (3d Cir. 1956). See also Reg. §1.264-1(a) (last sentence).

proceeds received by the beneficiaries.[11]

5. *Premiums paid by beneficiary of business life insurance.* Section 264(a)(1) disallows any deduction for life insurance premiums paid on policies covering the life of any officer, employee, or person financially interested in the taxpayer's trade or business if the taxpayer is directly or indirectly a beneficiary under the policy. This specialized provision is both broader and narrower than the general restriction imposed on deductions by §265(1)—broader in applying whether the proceeds are exempt from income taxation or not, narrower in being confined to premiums paid in a business context.[12] The statutory predecessor of §264(a)(1) was enacted in 1918 because of a Treasury complaint that "large stockholders of corporations were utilizing the corporations to take over and handle their insurance for them."[13] Thus, the objectionable practice that gave rise to §264(a)(1) (deducting premiums paid for policies whose proceeds were received tax free on the death of the insured) is a subspecies of the more general practice at which §265(1) is aimed. Both provisions employ the same remedy, a disallowance of the expenses incurred in producing the exempt income.

The phrase "any officer or employee" of the taxpayer as used by §264(a)(1) has not generated serious interpretative problems, but the phrase "any person financially interested in any trade or business carried on by the taxpayer" is less clear. It embraces insurance on the life of a partner if the firm or its partners are beneficiaries and pay the premiums.[14] It also covers the case where the person paying the premiums is both the insured and the sole owner of the business;[15] to be sure, "any person financially interested in any trade or business carried on by the taxpayer" is a cumbersome way to describe the taxpayer himself, but the Code has never won an award for stylistic grace.

To trigger the disallowance of deductions under §264(a)(1), the taxpayer must be "directly or indirectly a beneficiary under [the] policy." This phrase has been broadly construed to encompass policies pledged as collat-

---

[11] See Reg. §1.264-1(b) (second sentence), assuming deductibility of the premiums when paid as compensation.

[12] Because of the historic link (discussed infra ¶20.5) between §162, relating to business expenses, and §212, relating to expenses incurred by individuals in connection with income-producing property, it has been held that §264(a)(1) applies to both classes of expenses. See Meyer v. US, 175 F2d 45 (2d Cir. 1949).

[13] 56 Cong. Rec. 10,419 (1918).

[14] See Reg. §1.264-1(b); Yarnall v. CIR, 9 TC 616 (1947), aff'd per curiam, 170 F2d 272 (3d Cir. 1948) (premiums paid by creditor-partner to insure debtor-partner's life under policy naming creditor-partner beneficiary disallowed under the predecessor to §264(a)(1)); Keefe v. CIR, 15 TC 947 (1950) (acq.); McKay v. CIR, 10 BTA 949, 952–53 (1928).

[15] Rodney v. CIR, 53 TC 287, 318 (1969) ("so apparent it needs no further comment"); see also Reg. §1.264-1(a) (first sentence).

eral for the taxpayer's debts,[16] policies in which the taxpayer's interest is limited to a specified fractional or dollar amount,[17] and policies on the lives of employees if the employer is entitled to the cash surrender value on termination of employment.[18]

Although premiums paid by debtors on insurance policies pledged to secure their obligations are disallowed by §264(a)(1), creditors who pay premiums to keep pledged policies in force are not subject to the same constraint because the insured is not financially interested in the creditor's business.[19] If the creditor has a contractual or implied right to be reimbursed for the premiums (whether by the debtor or from the proceeds of the policy), the IRS evidently regards the payments as nondeductible capital outlays unless the right to reimbursement is worthless.[20] In a litigated case, however, the court permitted the creditor to deduct the premiums even though they could be recouped from the resulting increase in the policy's cash surrender value.[21]

---

[16] See Rev. Rul. 68-5, 1968-1 CB 99 (policies on life of officer of taxpayer corporation, pledged to secure Small Business Administration loan); Rodney v. CIR, supra note 15.

[17] Desks, Inc. v. CIR, 18 TC 674, 679 (1952) (acq.) (taxpayer entitled to proceeds in excess of debt owed by predecessor); Rev. Rul. 66-203, 1966-2 CB 104 (premiums disallowed in whole, although taxpayer's interest limited to policy's cash surrender value and declined by 10 percentage points each year). The principle has been applied to deny employers' deductions for premiums paid on so-called split dollar insurance—an arrangement where an employer pays premiums on insurance on the life of an employee and is entitled on the employee's death to a share of the proceeds equal to the policy's cash surrender value just before the employee died, the remainder going to the employee's beneficiary. Rev. Rul. 64-328, 1964-2 CB 11, amplified by Rev. Rul. 66-110, 1966-1 CB 12 (split dollar premiums nondeductible); Rev. Rul. 78-420, 1978-2 CB 67 (amplifying and illustrating Rev. Rul. 64-328); Sercl v. US, 684 F2d 597 (8th Cir. 1982) (although Rev. Rul. 64-328 applies prospectively only, assignment of policy after effective date of ruling was a novation that made ruling applicable). If the employee-insured is a shareholder of the employer, premium payments are sometimes treated as dividends to the shareholder-employee. Johnson v. CIR, 74 TC 1316 (1980); Rev. Rul. 79-50, 1979-1 CB 138.

[18] Rev. Rul. 70-148, 1970-1 CB 60.

[19] Rev. Rul. 75-46, 1975-1 CB 55; Rev. Rul. 70-254, 1970-1 CB 31 (creditor's payment of premiums on credit life insurance deductible).

[20] Rev. Rul. 75-46, supra note 19; see also First Nat'l Bank & Trust Co. of Tulsa v. Jones, 143 F2d 652, 653 (10th Cir. 1944) ("advancements made for insurance premiums, without reasonable hope or expectancy of repayment," deductible as ordinary and necessary business expenses if justified as "proper business precaution").

[21] CIR v. Charleston Nat'l Bank, 213 F2d 45 (4th Cir. 1954) (cash values insufficient to reimburse for premiums paid and principal of debt).

¶12.6.2 Losses

If a life insurance policy expires during the life of the insured, the owner of the policy cannot deduct the cost of the policy as a loss. As the IRS has said, "the purchased protection was provided during the years for which the premium was paid so that no loss results."[22] If a premium on flight insurance is paid by a business enterprise to protect itself against loss from a key employee's death en route to an important appointment, for example, the premium is not a loss; it is a cost of doing business that is nondeductible by virtue of §265(1) because the proceeds will be excludable if the plane crashes.

The no-loss principle has also been employed to deny a deduction when a policyholder surrenders or sells a life insurance policy for its cash value and receives less than the premiums paid for the policy.[23] In effect, the excess of premiums paid over cash surrender value is viewed as the cost of the life insurance protection provided while the policy was in force. Premiums on a term policy are not deductible just because the insured does not die during the policy's term, and the cost of term protection under a cash surrender policy must similarly be nondeductible even though this cost and increments to cash value are bundled together in the premiums.

On this theory, a loss is suffered only if the taxpayer receives less than the policy's cash surrender value. If this occurs because of the insurer's insolvency or for some other reason, the taxpayer should ordinarily be able to establish that it arose in a transaction entered into for profit within the meaning of §165(c)(2), since the savings component of life insurance (reflected by its cash surrender value) is comparable to a savings account or an investment in securities or other assets.[24] The loss allowed in this case, however, should not exceed the policy's cash surrender value, even if this amount is exceeded by the aggregate of the premiums.

From 1954 through 1986, mortality gains and losses sustained by beneficiaries of annuity contracts were treated somewhat the same as the mortality gains and losses of life insurance beneficiaries.[25] Annuitants who outlived their life expectancies were not taxed on their mortality gains, but short-lived annuitants were not successful in establishing that a mortality loss should be deductible. Their claims were rejected because the annuity con-

---

[22] Rev. Rul. 56-634, 1956-2 CB 291.

[23] London Shoe Co. v. CIR, 80 F2d 230 (2d Cir. 1935), cert. denied, 298 US 663 (1936) (surrender to insurer); Century Wood Preserving Co. v. CIR, 69 F2d 967 (3d Cir. 1934) (sale to taxpayer's officers; "no effort to show the reserve carried by the insurer").

[24] See Cohen v. CIR, 44 BTA 709 (1941) (acq.) (loss attributable to insurer's financial difficulties incurred in transaction entered into for profit, one judge dissenting). For §165(c)(2), see infra ¶25.3.

[25] See supra ¶12.3.2.

tract was not purchased in a transaction entered into for profit, because the taxpayer suffered no loss since he got what he bargained for (guaranteed income for life), or for both reasons.[26] In a leading case, the Court of Appeals for the Third Circuit, disallowing a loss deduction in the case of a short-lived annuitant, said:

> Whether an annuitant lives a longer or shorter time than his expectancy is immaterial to the question of the value of the annuity. Elements of value other than the right to receive payments for life are present in an annuity, e.g. security, assurance of income, regularity of payments and relief from responsibility of attending to investment. The experience which actually develops for the annuitant, whatever that may be, extinguishes both the annuity's cost and its expected returns as a capital investment.[27]

Amendments made to §72(b) in 1986 now allow the deduction sought by the taxpayer in the foregoing case, but also tax annuitants fully on their receipts once exclusions under §72 have provided full recovery of their investments. After 1986, in other words, annuitants are effectively taxed on mortality gains and allowed deductions for mortality losses.

Even before these amendments, however, the IRS permitted an annuitant's unrecovered cost to be deducted on surrender of the policy to the insurer for a cash lump sum.[28] The rationale of the ruling, which is based on the regulations, may be that a refund annuity cannot be viewed merely as an arrangement to get a guaranteed income for life, since the refund feature is explicitly intended to protect short-lived annuitants against mortality losses. If this is the theory, however, it suggests that an annuitant suffers a loss only if, and to the extent that, the amount received is less than the premiums allocable to the refund component of the contract.

---

[26] Industrial Trust Co. v. Broderick, 94 F2d 927 (1st Cir.), cert. denied, 304 US 572 (1938); Rev. Rul. 72-193, 1972-1 CB 58; Arnold v. US, 180 F. Supp. 746 (ND Tex. 1959) (exchange of annuity contracts for lump sum).

[27] Evans v. Rothensies, 114 F2d 958, 961–62 (3d Cir. 1940). The "security" and "relief from responsibility" points are red herrings; these reasons animate many investments and are not inconsistent with deducting losses if the taxpayer disposes of the investment for less than its cost.

[28] Rev. Rul. 61-201, 1961-2 CB 46; see also Rev. Rul. 72-193, supra note 26.

¶12.7 EMPLOYEE DEATH BENEFITS

¶12.7.1 Introductory

Under §101(b)(1), the beneficiaries or estate of a deceased employee may exclude from gross income certain death benefits paid by an employer by reason of the decedent's death, up to an aggregate amount of $5,000. When enacted in 1951, this provision was intended to parallel the exclusion of life insurance payments under §101(a)(1), but with a $5,000 limit "to prevent abuses."[1] Both exclusions are restricted to amounts paid "by reason of the death" of the insured person or employee. Moreover, §101(b) originally applied only to payments pursuant to a contract,[2] a restriction paralleling the reference in §101(a)(1) to life insurance contracts. This requirement, however, was eliminated in 1954. Although Congress gave no reason for this liberalization, it may have been intended to reduce litigation over the proper treatment of widow's allowances paid voluntarily by employers by permitting such payments, up to $5,000, to be excluded even if they were belated compensation and could not qualify as tax-free gifts under §102(a).[3]

Except for the $5,000 limitation, the exclusion granted by §101(b)(1) is extremely broad. It is available whether the benefits are paid in a single sum or in installments,[4] outright or in trust, to the deceased employee's beneficiaries or to his estate, directly by the employer or indirectly on his behalf, by one employer or several, and whether the employee was on active duty or retired at the time of death.[5] The exclusion does not embrace income payable to the employee during his life, such as salary for the pay period during which the employee died, accumulated leave payments, other amounts to which he had a nonforfeitable right immediately before his death, and certain annuity payments.[6]

---

[1] S. Rep. No. 781, 82d Cong., 1st Sess., reprinted in 1951-2 CB 458, 493. See Hess v. CIR, 271 F2d 104, 107 (3d Cir. 1959). The abuses to be curtailed by the $5,000 limit were not specified by the congressional committees. They may have feared attempts to exclude large amounts of belated compensation paid by closely held companies to insiders; the statutory restriction to amounts paid "by reason of the death of the employee" might have been thought an inadequate safeguard against disguised dividends. See infra text accompanying note 12.

[2] For the scope of the term "contract" as used in the 1951 provisions, see Robinson v. CIR, 42 TC 403, 408 (1964) (acq.).

[3] For discussion of widow's allowances, see supra ¶10.2.4.

[4] If the benefit is held by the employer under an agreement to pay interest, however, the exclusion only covers the capital amount, not the interest payments. See IRC §101(c); Reg. §1.101-3. For discussion, see supra ¶12.2.3.

[5] Reg. §1.101-2(a).

[6] Id. See also infra notes 16, 17.

The status of an "employee" is determined by the usual common law rules,[7] which do not embrace independent contractors. Self-employed persons are generally excluded, but this limitation is relaxed to allow the exclusion, subject to the same restrictions that apply to common law employees, for distributions from qualified pension, profit sharing, stock bonus, and annuity plans.[8] Arguably, the exclusion is more generally available to the beneficiaries of partners receiving guaranteed payments for services under §707(a).[9]

Since the exclusion cannot exceed $5,000 per employee, it must be allocated if benefits aggregating more than $5,000 are paid to two or more beneficiaries of the same deceased employee. The regulations prorate the excludable amount among the beneficiaries in proportion to the amounts paid or payable.[10]

The application of §101(b)(1) is occasionally complicated by the limitations imposed by §101(b)(2) and by the provision's ambiguous relationship to several other statutory exclusions. The principal problem areas are discussed below.

¶12.7.2 Nonforfeitable Rights in Employee During Life

Under §101(b)(2)(B), the exclusion does not embrace amounts that the employee had a nonforfeitable right to receive while living.[11] The purpose of this restriction is not entirely clear, but it may have been intended to buttress the statutory requirement that the payment be made "by reason of the death of the employee," thus disqualifying amounts that would have been payable regardless of death.[12] As interpreted by the regulations, how-

---

[7] Rev. Rul. 54-547, 1954-2 CB 57. See also infra ¶111.4.2.

[8] IRC §101(b)(3). This exclusion, however, is only allowed with respect to employees dying after 1983. Pub. L. No. 99-514, §713(e), 100 Stat. 2085 (1986); Pub. L. No. 97-248, §239, 96 Stat. 317 (1982).

[9] See Armstrong v. Phinney, 394 F2d 661 (5th Cir. 1968) (partner an employee for §119 purposes); infra ¶86.5.

[10] Reg. §1.101-2(c). For examples, see Reg. §§1.101-2(c)(2) Ex., (e)(2) Exs. 1(ii), 2; Rev. Rul. 72-555, 1972-2 CB 44.

[11] For the meaning of "nonforfeitable," see Pollnow v. CIR, 35 TC 715 (1961) (acq.) (forfeiture of rights on conviction of crime or willful disloyalty to employer); Rev. Rul. 71-361, 1971-2 CB 90 (rights forfeited if employee quit before retirement, was discharged for cause, or engaged after retirement in competition with employer); Rev. Rul. 59-255, 1959-2 CB 36 (forfeiture on withdrawing contributions); McKinney, The Meaning of Forfeitability Under the 1954 Code, 50 Taxes 114 (1972).

[12] The statutory language dates from 1954, but similar language was found in the regulations under the 1951 provision. See Hess v. CIR, 271 F2d 104 (3d Cir. 1959), which links the restriction to the fact that the proceeds of life insurance excludable under §101(a) arise only by reason of the insured's death and cannot be collected by him during life. The analogy is defective, however, because insurance

ever, it disqualifies not only accrued salary, unpaid leave, bonuses, and other items of compensation that would have been paid in due course to the employee, but also amounts that he would have been able to collect only on retirement or termination of his employment.[13] Assume a noncontributory profit sharing plan provides that the amount accumulated in an employee's account vests at the rate of 10 percent per year and thus is fully vested after 10 years; the entire account balance, however, is payable to the employee's beneficiaries if he dies within these 10 years. If an employee dies after six years with an account balance of $10,000, the exclusion is only $4,000—the $10,000 received, less $6,000, the amount the employee would have received if his employment had terminated immediately before his death.[14]

This disqualification is not applicable, however, to lump-sum distributions by qualified pension, profit sharing, stock bonus, and annuity plans.[15] The full $5,000 exclusion is allowed in the example in the preceding paragraph, for instance, if the profit sharing plan is qualified and the $10,000 benefit is paid as a lump sum. The details of the basic disqualification and of these exceptions are described and illustrated at great length by the regulations.[16]

¶12.7.3 Annuity Payments

Death benefits do not qualify for the exclusion if received by the employee's survivor under a joint and survivor annuity contract after the employee himself has received an annuity payment.[17] This limitation is similar to the disqualification of benefits to which the employee had a nonforfeitable right during his life because the employee would have received the entire amount payable under the joint and survivor annuity if he had outlived the secondary beneficiary.

---

proceeds are fully excludable under §101(a) even though the insured could have taken the cash surrender value during life.

[13] See Reg. §1.101-2(d)(1)(i).

[14] Id. at Ex. 5.

[15] IRC §101(b)(2)(B). Lump sum distributions from annuities qualified under §403(b) are similarly treated to the extent the distributions come from employer contributions. Id.

[16] Reg. §1.101-2(d).

[17] IRC §101(b)(2)(C). This disqualification also applies if the employee is living on the annuity starting date ("the first day of the first period for which an amount was received as an annuity"), but dies before the first payment is received. Id.; Reg. §1.101-2(e)(1)(ii). If a joint and survivor annuity is payable annually commencing with 1988, for example, the exclusion is lost if the employee dies during 1988, even though his death occurs before the payment is received. See Rev. Rul. 81-121, 1981-1 CB 43 (election by disabled federal employee under §105(d)(6) to treat disability retirement income as annuity income precludes death benefit exclusion for surviving spouse).

If a qualifying benefit is paid as an annuity that is not tripped by the foregoing hurdle, the §101(b) exclusion is treated as the cost of the contract in applying §72, the provision governing the taxation of annuities.[18] As a result, part of each annuity payment is excluded from gross income by the beneficiary, but the interest component is subject to tax.

¶12.7.4 Employee Death Benefits as Tax-Free Proceeds of Life Insurance

Although employee death benefits were analogized by Congress to the proceeds of life insurance when §101(b) was enacted in 1951, the death benefit exclusion was subjected to a $5,000 cap that does not apply to life insurance.[19] The beneficiaries or estate of an employee is therefore advantaged if benefits received from an employer can qualify as the proceeds of "life insurance" within the meaning of §101(a).[20] The exclusion for life insurance proceeds is not limited to payments under a conventional policy issued by a regulated insurance company, but embraces all "death benefit payments having the characteristics of life insurance payable by reason of death,"[21] regardless of the payor's business. There is therefore a troublesome area of overlap between §§101(a) and 101(b). The scope of the crucial phrase "payments having the characteristics of life insurance" is examined elsewhere in this work.[22]

¶12.7.5 Employee Death Benefits as Tax-Free Gifts

When paid voluntarily by the employer, employee death benefits occasionally qualify as gifts under §102(a), in which event they are excluded from the recipient's gross income, regardless of the dollar amount.[23] The IRS formerly asserted that the $5,000 limit on the exclusion of employee death benefits should be interpreted as a congressional determination to tax

---

[18] IRC §101(b)(2)(D); Reg. §§1.101-2(a)(2) (third sentence), (e). For §72, see supra ¶12.3.

The nonforfeitable disqualification of §101(b)(2)(B) also applies to annuity payments. For a special rule applicable to servicemen's annuities, see §101(b)(2)(D) (last sentence); infra ¶14.7.

[19] Supra note 1.

[20] See supra ¶12.2.

[21] Reg. §1.101-1(a)(1).

[22] Supra ¶12.2.2. See also Ross v. Odom, 401 F2d 464 (5th Cir. 1968) (benefits under Georgia program for survivors of civil servants qualified for unlimited exclusion of §101(a), not merely for $5,000 exclusion of §101(b)(1)); Treanor, Code Section 101: The Thin Line Between Life Insurance and Employee Death Benefits, 37 J. Tax'n 176 (1972).

[23] For discussion of this possibility, see supra ¶10.2.4.

all amounts above this limit, but it subsequently abandoned this theory; the government now argues only that the 1954 extension of §101(b)(1) to non-contractual payments[24] is evidence that Congress endorsed the IRS theory that payments to employees' survivors are "generally" not tax-free gifts.[25] In practice, the existence of §101(b)(1) provides a safe harbor for the first $5,000 of employee death benefits, but it does not seem to reduce the taxpayer's chance to prove that amounts in excess of $5,000 are excludable gifts under §102.

Section 102(c)(1), added in 1986, states that the gift exclusion can never apply to "any amount transferred by . . . an employer to, or for the benefit of, an employee." The general standard applied under §102(a), however, is that a payment is not a gift unless it proceeds from detached and disinterested generosity and is not compensation for services. A payment to an employee's survivors that passes this test could hardly be said to be "for the benefit of [the] employee."

If the survivors succeed in obtaining gift treatment, however, the employer's deduction for the gift is limited to $25 per donee per year by §274(b). This restriction encourages employers to describe death benefits in excess of $5,000 as belated compensation rather than as acts of disinterested generosity.[26]

¶12.7.6 Employee Death Benefits as Income in Respect of Decedents

Benefits paid to the survivors of employees may be considered employee death benefits subject to §101(b), limiting the excludable amount to $5,000, rather than life insurance fully excludable under §101(a), even if the payments have some or all of the characteristics of life insurance. Section 101(b) takes over if the payments are income in respect of a decedent under §691, in the nature of deferred compensation or a continuation of the decedent's salary. This characterization is particularly likely if the survivor's benefits are periodic payments related to the decedent's Otcompensation, but it may also apply to lump-sum payments.[27] Payments of this type have the salient characteristics of income in respect of a decedent,[28] and they retain their compensatory character in the hands of the recipient. Thus, the payments qualify for the $5,000 exclusion of §101(b)(2)(A), but

---

[24] See supra note 2.

[25] Rev. Rul. 62-102, 1962-2 CB 37; see also Fanning v. Conley, 357 F2d 37 (2d Cir. 1966) (benefits above first $5,000 qualified as tax-free gifts); Paschkes v. CIR, 28 TCM (CCH) 1318 (1969).

[26] For discussion of §274(b), see infra ¶21.3.

[27] See Treanor, supra note 22.

[28] See generally infra ¶83.1.2 (income in respect of decedents).

any excess is includable in gross income, subject to the usual remote possibility of being excluded as gifts from the employer to the employee's survivor.[29]

---

[29] Rev. Rul. 68-124, 1968-1 CB 44 (bonuses income in respect of decedent, subject to $5,000 death benefit exclusion); see Nilssen's Est. v. US, 322 F. Supp. 260 (D. Minn. 1971) (payments to employee's surviving spouse under retirement contract subject to §691, despite inclusion of value of contract for federal estate tax purposes). For deduction of an appropriate portion of the federal estate tax under §691(c), see infra ¶83.1.4.

CHAPTER

13

Compensation for Personal Injuries and Sickness

¶13.1 COMPENSATION FOR PERSONAL INJURIES AND SICKNESS

¶13.1.1 Introductory

Compensation for personal injuries and sickness is excluded from gross income by §104(a), subject to qualifications examined below. The exclusion embodies a legislative policy that goes back to the Revenue Act of 1918, when many doubted that the proceeds of accident insurance and of tort suits for personal injuries constituted "gains or profits and income" satisfying the Supreme Court's constitutional definition of income.[1] These doubts have long since dissipated,[2] but the exclusion has persevered, although with important changes in detail. The imposition of an income tax on compensation received by persons who have been seriously injured by accident would no doubt be regarded as heartless, unless recoveries from tortfeasors were correspondingly increased. The exclusion, however, also embraces less emotionally charged receipts, such as compensation for loss of wages during absences from work if paid under a workmen's compensation act or recovered in a tort suit; this immunity is inconsistent with the usual practice of taxing substitutes for amounts that would be includable in gross income if received in the normal course of events.[3] If the level of these payments is currently based on the premise that the recipient will not be taxed, however, a change in the tax law would be unfair unless it induced appropriate increases in the payments themselves.

The §104(a) exclusion is subject to two major qualifications. First, amounts received under accident or health insurance provided by an employer are subject to the relatively restrictive rules of §105, rather than §104(a).[4] Second, an otherwise excludable receipt is gross income if it reimburses the taxpayer for medical expenses deducted in prior years under §213 (relating to medical expenses in excess of 7.5 percent of the taxpayer's

---

[1] See Revenue Act of 1918, §213(b)(6), 40 Stat. 1066; H.R. Rep. No. 767, 65th Cong., 2d Sess. (1918), reprinted in 1939-1 (Part 2) CB 86, 92; 31 Op. Att'y Gen. 304 (1918) (proceeds of accident insurance not gains, profits, or income as defined by Supreme Court); TD 2747, 20 Treas. Dec. 457 (1918) (same as to personal injury recoveries by suit or compromise). See also Cochran, Should Personal Injury Damage Awards be Taxed? 38 Case W. Res. L. Rev. 43 (1987) (arguing that §104(a) has no sound theoretical or policy basis); Schlenger, Disability Benefits Under Section 22(b)(5), 40 Va. L. Rev. 549 (1954); Comment, Taxation of Employee Accident and Health Plans Before and Under the 1954 Code, 64 Yale LJ 222 (1954).

[2] See supra ¶5.6.

[3] See Raytheon Prods. Corp. v. CIR, 144 F2d 110 (1st Cir.), cert. denied, 323 US 779 (1944).

[4] See infra ¶13.2.

adjusted gross income).[5] This limitation reflects the tax benefit concept, which requires that a recovery of a previously deducted item be taxed even though, absent the deduction, it could be received tax free.[6] The exclusion may apply, however, to amounts received for medical expenses that have not been deducted (because not yet paid or because below the deductible floor) and to advance payments for future medical expenses. When the taxpayer pays these expenses, however, they cannot be deducted under §213, which only applies to uncompensated medical expenditures.[7]

In the following discussion, attention is given first to the exclusion under §104 of compensation for personal injuries or sickness when received (1) under a workmen's compensation act;[8] (2) as a pension, annuity, or similar allowance as a result of active service in the armed forces of any country, in the U.S. Foreign Service, or in certain other federal agencies;[9] (3) as damages in tort actions (whether by suit or agreement);[10] or (4) as accident or health insurance benefits not provided by an employer.[11] Thereafter, attention is given to employer's accident and health plans, including both insured and uninsured plans.[12]

¶13.1.2 Workmen's Compensation

Compensation for personal injuries and sickness is excluded from gross income under §104(a)(1) if received under a "workmen's compensation act."[13] Recognizing that this phrase is hazy around the edges, the regulations reach out to encompass any "statute in the nature of a workmen's compensation act which provides compensation to employees for personal injuries or sickness incurred in the course of employment," a liberalization applied by the IRS to many compensation plans for public employees.[14] The regula-

---

[5] See Rev. Rul. 75-230, 1975-1 CB 93 (in absence of express allocation by parties, settlement of personal injury suit allocated first to previously deducted medical expenses). For §213, see infra ¶36.1.

[6] See supra ¶5.7 for the tax benefit doctrine.

[7] Rev. Rul. 75-232, 1975-1 CB 94 (payment for future medical expenses excludable but will reduce amounts deductible under §213).

[8] See infra ¶13.1.2.

[9] See infra ¶13.1.3.

[10] See infra ¶13.1.4.

[11] See infra ¶13.1.5.

[12] See infra ¶13.2.

[13] The exclusion does not apply to amounts attributable to medical expenses allowed as deductions under §213. See supra ¶13.1.1 text accompanying note 5.

[14] Reg. §1.104-1(b); Rev. Rul. 75-500, 1975-2 CB 44; Rev. Rul. 72-291, 1972-1 CB 36. See Dyer v. CIR, 71 TC 560 (1979) (acq.) (New York City ordinance establishing plan for teachers is "statute" as term is used by regulations); Rev. Rul. 83-91, 1983-1 CB 38 (exclusion applies to occupational disability retirement payments by state teachers' retirement system where payments discharge liability under

tions also extend the exclusion to payments to the survivors of employees killed in the line of duty.[15] Disabled employees whose workmen's compensation benefits continue even if they are able to find other employment do not lose the exclusion.[16]

Adhering to the original concept of workmen's compensation, the regulations deny the exclusion to retirement benefits determined by reference to the employee's age, length of service, or prior contributions, even though retirement is occasioned by occupational injury or sickness.[17] A rationale for this distinction has been suggested by the Court of Appeals for the District of Columbia:

> We would not be justified in assimilating pay for retirement due to disability to compensation for personal injuries or sickness under a Workmen's Compensation Act. Legislation of the latter character has a purpose of fixing and making certain the payment of some compensation for injury, free of the risks of litigation based on negligence. The amount of compensation depends upon the nature of the injury, which

---

workmen's compensation act); Rev. Rul. 81-47, 1981-1 CB 55 (payments by county to police officer injured in line of duty were received under statute in nature of workmen's compensation act, where payments required by collective bargaining agreement incorporated by reference into county code); Rev. Rul. 80-14, 1980-1 CB 33 (benefits paid to survivor of fire fighter who was retired for disability and died before reaching normal retirement age qualify for exclusion). But see Gallagher v. CIR, 75 TC 313 (1980) (payments under Air Traffic Controller's Act for retraining in second career not in nature of workmen's compensation because, although triggered by disability, payments not intended to compensate for disability); Rev. Rul. 73-346, 1973-2 CB 24 (voluntary child-allotment payments to disabled policeman or fireman under municipal ordinance not excludable). In Blackburn v. CIR, 15 TC 336 (1950), a California provision for continuation of state trooper's regular wages during temporary disability was held not excludable under §104(a)(1) because the state also had a separate compensation plan resembling workmen's compensation, but this holding was seemingly rejected by Revenue Ruling 68-10, 1968-1 CB 50, following a reinterpretation of California law by a local court.

The regulations deny the exclusion to occupational injury or sickness payments "to the extent that they are in excess of the amount provided in the applicable workmen's compensation act or acts." Reg. §1.104-1(b). This restriction, however, has been watered down by the IRS. Rev. Rul. 59-269, 1959-2 CB 39, modified by Rev. Rul. 83-91, 1983-1 CB 38 (§104(a)(1) applies to supplemental payments in lieu of workmen's compensation, even though in excess of those payable under ordinary workmen's compensation act).

[15] Reg. §1.104-1(b); but see Robinson v. CIR, 42 TC 403 (1964) (acq.) (death not in line of duty; exclusion denied).

[16] Rev. Rul. 72-44, 1972-1 CB 31 (Question 4).

[17] Reg. §1.104-1(b). See Rev. Rul. 80-44, 1980-1 CB 34 (benefit for occupational disability defined as larger of (1) life annuity equal to 60 percent of final pay or (2) pension for nonoccupational disability, which depended on years of service; held, where latter paid, exclusion limited to 60 percent of final pay).

is translated into the degree of loss of earning power. Appellant, however, receives pay on retirement because of services previously performed and as part of a system for maintaining an efficient service. This is so notwithstanding that the occasion of appellant's retirement was disability rather than age, under the provisions of the statute which permits disability to accelerate the time of retirement in advance of the normal retirement age. The two types of legislation are not the same. Both have long been commonly known. Retirement pay is not known as workmen's compensation, nor is the latter known as the former.[18]

If an employee compensation plan combines disability and retirement elements (as is true of many plans for public employees), benefits qualify for exclusion under §104(a)(1) only to the extent they are attributable to personal injury or sickness incurred in the course of employment and are not determined with reference to the employee's age, length of service, or prior contributions.[19]

The regulations also provide that compensation for nonoccupational injuries or sickness is not excludable under §104(a)(1). This limitation has frequently been applied to benefits received by public employees following retirement for disabilities that did not occur in the line of duty.[20] Some state

---

[18] Waller v. US, 180 F2d 194, 196 (DC Cir. 1950).

[19] Reg. §1.104-1(b); Rev. Rul. 72-44, supra note 16 (where service-disabled firemen received one half of regular salary if employed for less than 20 years but full salary if employed for 20 years or more, latter group can exclude only amount determined without regard to length of service, i.e., one half of regular salary). For discussion of the application of §104(a)(1) to combined disability-retirement plans, see Frye v. US, 72 F. Supp. 405 (DDC 1947) (District of Columbia plan for firemen and policemen qualifies in part under §104(a)(1)). For problems arising if benefits are based on the employee's age or length of service when disability could have been an alternative ground, see Simms v. CIR, 196 F2d 238 (DC Cir. 1952) (§104(a)(1) not applicable in absence of determination of disability by relevant local board).

Failure to qualify under §104(a)(1) does not preclude the possibility of an exclusion under §104(a)(3) (health and accident insurance), §104(a)(4) (payments to members of armed forces, etc.), or §105 (certain employer-financed health and accident payments).

[20] Haar v. CIR, 78 TC 864 (1982), aff'd per curiam, 709 F2d 1206 (8th Cir. 1983) (disability retirement payments to federal employee not excludable because payable whether or not disability related to job); McDonald v. CIR, 33 TC 540 (1959) (insufficient evidence of service connection); Golden v. CIR, 30 TCM (CCH) 691 (1971) (despite "valiant effort" by retired municipal judge to show that hypertension was service-connected, §104(a)(1) not applicable); Rev. Rul. 85-104, 1985-2 CB 52 (annuities paid under District of Columbia law to policemen and firemen disabled by nonoccupational injury or disease do not qualify for exclusion); Rev. Rul 83-77, 1983-1 CB 37 (payments to police officer injured in line of duty not excludable because made under ordinance providing for compensation on account of sickness or injury whether or not incurred on job). Compare Take v. CIR, 804 F2d 553 (9th Cir. 1986) (ordinance raising irrebuttable presumption that "heart, lung and

workmen's compensation acts have been expanded in recent years to cover nonoccupational disabilities resulting in unemployment.[21] The IRS has ruled that even though a state "placed its nonoccupational benefits provisions within the confines of its Workmen's Compensation Law," the term "workmen's compensation act" as used in §104(a)(1) has "been understood to encompass only occupational disability or injuries," so that nonoccupational benefits cannot be excluded under §104(a)(1).[22]

Despite this static view of the term "workmen's compensation act," the IRS has not endeavored to confine the concept of an injury "arising out of and in the course of employment" to its scope as of 1918, when the statutory predecessor of §104(a)(1) was enacted. For example, workmen's compensation payments for injuries resulting from horseplay in the plant or accidents while driving to work are excludable under §104, even if no service connection would have been perceived in 1918. It seems likely that the tax exclusion will continue to expand with the concept of service-connected injuries, which a commentator described in 1969 as follows:

> Except under the most strained process of interpretation, the causal definition [of the term "arising out of and in the course of employment," as used in state workmen's compensation acts] has for some time now been stretched to include cases without the bounds of the original theory of workmen's compensation. The time does not appear to be far off when there will be little, if any, relation to a particular occupation as a basis for determining compensable injuries under workmen's compensation. More striking is that this entire transition should take place without any legislative intervention to change the language of the statutes.[23]

Finally, if workmen's compensation benefits are applied in reduction of a social security benefit to which the taxpayer would otherwise be entitled, a portion of the workmen's compensation benefits equal to the reduction is treated as a social security benefit, one half of which is usually

---

respiratory system" illnesses of firemen are "occupational disabilities" precludes benefits for these conditions from being excludable workmen's compensation) with Rev. Rul. 85-105, 1985-2 CB 53 (exclusion can apply where statute creates rebuttable presumption that disability is employment related).

[21] See Henderson, Should Workmen's Compensation Be Extended to Nonoccupational Injuries? 48 Tex. L. Rev. 117 (1969).

[22] Rev. Rul. 72-191, 1972-1 CB 45, amplified by Rev. Rul. 75-499, 175-2 CB 43, modified by Rev. Rul. 81-192, 1981-2 CB 50 (benefits may qualify as excludable proceeds of health and accident insurance or unemployment compensation).

[23] See Henderson, supra note 21, at 122. For an illustration of the expansive contemporary view of workmen's compensation coverage, see Beauchesne v. David London & Co., 375 A2d 920 (RI 1977) (employee got drunk at office Christmas party and fell out of window; held, compensable).

subject to tax under §86.[24]

¶13.1.3 Military Disability Pensions

Pensions, annuities, and similar allowances for personal injuries or sickness resulting from active service in the armed forces of any country or the U.S. Public Health Service, U.S. Coast and Geodetic Survey, or U.S. Foreign Service are excludable under §104(a)(4),[25] subject to severe restrictions imposed in 1976. The statutory predecessor of §104(a)(4) was enacted in 1942.[26]

Like the exclusion of workmen's compensation benefits under §104(a)(1), §104(a)(4) was intended to apply only to service related disabilities. The principal difference in language between the two provisions is that §104(a)(4) explicitly covers an amount received as a "pension." Congress concluded in 1976 that this invited abuse:

> Criticism of the exclusion of armed forces disability pensions from income focuses on a number of cases involving the disability retirement of military personnel. In many cases, armed forces personnel have been classified as disabled for military service shortly before they would have become eligible for retirement principally to obtain the benefits of the special tax exclusion on the disability portion of their retirement pay. In most of these cases the individuals, having retired from the military, earn income from other employment while receiving tax-free "disability" payments from the military. The committee questions the equity of allowing retired military personnel to exclude the payments they receive as tax-exempt disability income when they are able to earn substantial amounts of income from civilian work, despite disabilities such as high blood pressure, arthritis, etc.[27]

---

[24] See infra ¶16.5.

[25] The exclusion does not apply to reimbursements for medical expenses previously deducted under §213. See supra ¶13.1.1 text accompanying note 5.

See Haar v. CIR, 78 TC 864 (1982), aff'd per curiam, 709 F2d 1206 (8th Cir. 1983) (§104(a)(4) inapplicable to disability pension paid to federal nonmilitary employee who retired on account of injury sustained during earlier tour of duty in military; pension paid because of inability to do nonmilitary job, not because disability incurred in military); Rev. Rul. 77-318, 1977-2 CB 45 (same).

[26] The 1942 provision embraced members of the armed forces; the other federal services were brought within §104(a)(4) in later years. For the status of employees of the Public Health Service before they were added, see Waller v. US, 180 F2d 194 (DC Cir. 1950). The reference to the Coast and Geodetic Survey embraces the National Oceanic and Atmospheric Administration.

[27] S. Rep. No. 938, 94th Cong., 2d Sess., reprinted in 1976-3 CB (Vol. 3) 49, 176–77. See also Bittker, Tax Reform and Disability Pensions—The Equal Treatment of Equals, 55 Taxes 363 (1977).

To remedy this problem, Congress enacted §104(b) in 1976, terminating the §104(a)(4) exclusion except for (1) combat-related injuries (defined to include personal injury or sickness from armed conflict, extrahazardous service, simulated war exercises, or instrumentalities of war) and (2) amounts the taxpayer could receive by applying to the Veterans Administration for disability compensation.[28] The latter amounts were probably regarded as comparable to workmen's compensation benefits available to nonfederal employees. Two grandfather clauses preserve the pre-1976 exclusion for taxpayers who, on or before September 24, 1975, were entitled to receive excludable amounts or were members of or subject to a binding written commitment to join one of the affected federal services.

The principal litigation under §104(a)(4) has concerned the excludability under the pre-1976 rules of pensions received by members of the armed forces who were retired for length of service when they might have been retired for disability. If the appropriate retirement board has made no determination of disability, an exclusion is not warranted even if the taxpayer offers to prove that disability existed and could have been found by the board.[29] If the board erroneously fails to find the taxpayer disabled, however, a later correction of its action qualifies the payments for exclusion, retroactively to the date when the finding of disability should have been made.[30] These principles remain applicable to the residual situations in

---

[28] Veterans Administration (VA) disability benefits are excludable from gross income under 38 USC §3101(a). For the treatment of retroactive disability compensation, see Rev. Rul. 80-9, 1980-1 CB 11.

[29] Simms v. CIR, 196 F2d 238 (DC Cir. 1952); Pangburn v. CIR, 13 TC 169 (1949). But see Prince v. US, 119 F. Supp. 421 (Ct. Cl. 1954) (retirement based on length of service treated as based on disability).

[30] Strickland v. CIR, 540 F2d 1196 (4th Cir. 1976) (exclusion allowed despite administrative delay in granting disability status); Rev. Rul. 78-161, 1978-1 CB 31 (retroactive determination of service-connected disability by VA accepted, following *Strickland*; earlier contrary ruling revoked); Rev. Rul. 74-582, 1974-2 CB 34 (retroactive change effective where original retirement for length of service was erroneous; but if taxpayer elected to retire for length of service, subsequent change is effective only prospectively). But see Sidoran v. CIR, 640 F2d 231 (9th Cir. 1981) (retirement pay not excludable even though VA found taxpayer 40 percent disabled); Berger v. CIR, 76 TC 687 (1981) (taxpayer received "readjustment pay" on being discharged from Army in reduction-of-force program, but was later found entitled to disability pay; held, readjustment pay not excludable even though 75 percent of it subtracted from disability amounts otherwise payable); Cleary v. CIR, 60 TC 133 (1973) (exclusion denied despite finding of disability by VA subsequent to retirement for length of service). See also supra note 20 for a similar problem arising under §104(a)(1).

In Ray v. US, 453 F2d 754 (Ct. Cl. 1972), a nontax case, the government was held liable to a retired officer for taxes erroneously withheld by the Air Force as a result of his erroneous retirement for length of service rather than disability.

which the exclusion of §104(a)(4) is still available after the 1976 changes.[31]

In limited circumstances, disability payments to servicemen and other government employees that are outside the ambit of §104(a)(4) may qualify for exclusion under §105(d), relating to payments for permanent and total disability received before the age of 65.[32] The status of benefits to members of the armed forces and the other organizations listed in §104(a)(4) is also affected by special provisions in the statutes regulating their retirement and other benefits.[33]

Proof that the Code keeps abreast of international events is found in §104(a)(5), enacted in 1976, which permits government employees injured in a terrorist attack while abroad in the performance of official duties to exclude disability income attributable to the injuries from gross income.[34]

¶13.1.4 Damages

Since 1918, §104(a)(2) and its statutory predecessors have excluded from gross income damages received, whether by suit or agreement, on account of personal injuries or sickness.[35] The rationale for the exclusion, which is interpreted by the regulations to embrace claims based on "tort or tort type rights,"[36] is presumably that the recovery does not generate a gain or profit but only makes the taxpayer whole by compensating for a loss.[37]

---

[31] See DePaolis v. CIR, 69 TC 283 n.4 (1977); see also Espenshade v. CIR, 354 F2d 332 (Ct. Cl. 1965) (military personnel allowed by Career Compensation Act to choose between retirement for disability and retirement for age).

[32] Reg. §1.104-1(e); Rev. Rul. 59-26, 1959-1 CB 29, declared obsolete by Rev. Rul. 76-565, 1976-2 CB 449; Rev. Rul. 58-43, 1958-1 CB 45; infra ¶13.2.6.

[33] See Reg. §1.104-1(e), listing the applicable nontax statutes.

[34] See S. Rep. No. 938, 94th Cong., 2d Sess. 704 (1976). See also Hostage Relief Act of 1980, Pub. L. No. 96-449, 94 Stat. 1967 (exclusion for compensation to American hostages in Iran).

[35] Like other items excludable under §104(a), damage recoveries are includable in gross income to the extent attributable to medical expenses previously deducted under §213. See supra ¶13.1.1 text accompanying note 5.

[36] Reg. §1.104-1(c). For receipts under no-fault insurance policies, see Rev. Rul. 73-155, 1973-1 CB 50; see also US v. Garber, 589 F2d 843 (5th Cir. 1979) (amounts received by commercial blood donor not damages for personal injuries).

[37] For a series of early IRS rulings excluding recoveries for wrongful death, alienation of affections, breach of promise to marry, and libel and slander from gross income because they do not represent gain, see supra ¶5.6. Later rulings exempting reparations paid to victims of Nazi persecution and to prisoners of war also use this "reimbursement" rationale rather than §104(a)(2), perhaps because a tort action against a sovereign power, even though a defeated enemy, would not have been successful. See supra ¶5.6 note 16. On the other hand, §104(a)(2) is cited in Revenue Ruling 68-649, 1968-2 CB 52, holding that damages received from the Israeli government by the widow of a naval officer pursuant to a claim submitted by the United States following the sinking of the U.S.S. Liberty were excludable from gross income.

The exclusion, however, embraces compensation for lost wages if occasioned by personal injury or sickness, despite the usual principle that recoveries are taxable if they compensate for amounts that would have been taxable if received in due course.[38] The IRS once ruled that punitive awards qualify for the exclusion if attributable to personal injuries or sickness;[39] this ruling has been revoked,[40] but one court found the revocation to be "an unwarranted administrative amendment of the clear language [of the statute]."[41] Also, although the exclusion does not embrace income accruing on an award of damages (e.g., interest on damages held by a court for the benefit of a minor),[42] damages received "as periodic payments" are fully excludable, even if they include implicit compensation for the delay in payment.[43]

The exclusion from the recipient's gross income of recoveries for personal injuries and wrongful death is deeply entrenched in private tort law, and juries are often instructed that plaintiffs are not taxed on their awards.[44]

---

[38] See supra note 3.

[39] Rev. Rul. 75-45, 1975-1 CB 47 (damages, "whether compensatory or punitive," received on account of personal injuries or sickness are excludable from gross income).

[40] Rev. Rul. 84-108, 1984-2 CB 32 (for payments under wrongful death statutes only allowing recovery of punitive damages, revocation not applicable to settlements made before July 16, 1984). See also Rev. Rul. 58-418, 1958-2 CB 18 (punitive component of settlement of libel action taxable as income). Revenue Ruling 58-418 was cited in CIR v. Glenshaw Glass Co., 348 US 426, 432 n.8 (1955), discussed supra ¶5.5.1, where the Court observed that punitive damages "cannot be considered a restoration of capital for taxation purposes." When the taxpayer relies on §104 rather than a restoratiom of capital theory, however, this comment seems inapplicable.

[41] Burford v. US, 642 F. Supp. 635 (ND Ala. 1986). See Morrison, Getting a Rule Right and Writing a Wrong Rule: The IRS Demands a Return on All Punitive Damages, 17 Conn. L. Rev. 39 (1984).

[42] Rev. Rul. 76-133, 1976-1 CB 34; Rev. Rul. 65-29, 1965-1 CB 59.

[43] The statute was amended in 1982 to include the words "whether as lump sums or as periodic payments." The IRS had previously followed the same rule. Rev. Rul. 79-313, 1979-2 CB 75 (installment payments settling tort action for personal injuries excludable in full, despite inclusion of interest factor); Rev. Rul. 79-220, 1979-2 CB 74 (similar result where installment obligation funded by obligor's purchase of annuity contract, of which it retained exclusive ownership). See S. Rep. No. 646, 97th Cong., 2d Sess 3–4 (1982), reprinted in 1983-1 CB 514, 515 (amendment "intended to codify, rather than change, present law," and applies "only if the recipient taxpayer is not in constructive receipt of or does not have the current economic benefit of the sum required to produce the periodic payments").

[44] See Norfolk & W. Ry. v. Liepelt, 445 US 972 (1980) (tax-free status of award under Federal Employers' Liability Act and effect of taxes on employee's future earnings admissible); Blake v. Delaware & Hudson Ry., 484 F2d 204, 208 (2d Cir. 1973) (instruction proper but not mandatory, one judge dissenting); McWeeney v. New York, N.H. & H.R.R., 282 F2d 34, 39 (2d Cir.), cert. denied, 364 US 870 (1960)

Thus, a repeal of §104(a)(2) would create shock waves throughout the personal injury area and would no doubt lead to larger verdicts and higher insurance premiums.

The phrase "personal injuries or sickness" as used in §104(a)(2) embraces emotional distress, libel, slander, and other nonphysical wrongs.[45] A split has developed between the IRS on the one hand, and the Tax Court and the Court of Appeals for the Ninth Circuit on the other, about the treatment of recoveries for damages to business or professional reputation.

The IRS holds that a recovery for injury to personal reputation is excludable, but a recovery for injury to business reputation is not.[46] Under this view, the allegations and evidence in the libel action must be examined to determine the basis for the recovery. If allegations of damage to both personal and business reputation are made and the recovery is not explicitly bifurcated, the entire recovery is excluded if damage to personal reputation is the primary basis, or is taxed if damage to business reputation is

---

(same). But see Burlington N., Inc. v. Boxberger, 529 F2d 284, 295–98 (9th Cir. 1975) (upon request, instruction re tax exclusion must be given); Domeracki v. Humble Oil & Ref. Co., 443 F2d 1245, 1248–51 (3d Cir.), cert. denied, 404 US 883 (1971) (same); Crick, Taxes, Lost Future Earnings, and Unexamined Assumptions, 34 Nat'l Tax J. 271 (1981); Frolik, The Convergence of I.R.C. §104(a)(2), *Norfolk & Western Railway Co. v. Liepelt* and Structured Tort Settlements: Tax Policy "Derailed," 51 Fordham L. Rev. 565 (1983); Kahane & Yoran, Compensation for Loss of Income and Its Taxation, 32 Nat'l Tax J. 117 (1979); Note, Income Taxes and the Computation of Lost Future Earnings in Wrongful Death and Personal Injury Cases, 29 Md. L. Rev. 177 (1969).

[45] Bent v. CIR, 87 TC 236 (1986) (amount received in settlement of claim under 42 USC §1983 for violation of First Amendment rights held excludable; excludability of amount received in settlement "depends on the *nature* of the claim which was the actual basis for settlement, not the *validity* of the claim"); Seay v. CIR, 58 TC 32 (1972) (acq.) (exclusion allowed for $45,000 of $105,000 received by ex-employee in settlement of claims for breach of contract and wrongful discharge, designated as "compensation for . . . personal embarrassment, mental and physical strain and injury to health and personal reputation in the community"); Wolfson v. CIR, 37 TCM (CCH) 1847 (1978), aff'd, 651 F2d 1228 (6th Cir. 1981) (damages found to be for injury to professional reputation; court raises but leaves open the possibility that such damages constitute nontaxable return of capital because issue not argued by taxpayer). But see Knuckles v. CIR, 349 F2d 610 (10th Cir. 1965) (taxpayer paid for release of rights under employment contract; claim for personal injuries only afterthought); Agar v. CIR, 290 F2d 283 (2d Cir. 1961) (settlement with ex-employer was in nature of severance pay, not compensation for alleged slander); Hodge v. CIR, 64 TC 616 (1975) (award of back pay in settlement of case alleging racial discrimination in violation of Civil Rights Act of 1964 not excludable). See generally Barkan, An Analysis of the Tax Treatment of Post-Termination Personal Injury Settlements, 41 J. Tax'n 306 (1974).

[46] Rev. Rul. 85-143, 1985-2 CB 55.

primary.[47]

The Ninth Circuit view, in contrast, is that excludability depends on whether the recovery is for personal or nonpersonal injury.[48] Under this view, a recovery for injury to personal reputation is excludable even if only the taxpayer's business or professional reputation is harmed, and a libel recovery is taxable only if the injury is not to the taxpayer's person, but is, for example, an injury to the reputation of the taxpayer's products. State law is consulted in determining whether the recovery is for a personal or nonpersonal injury.

The Tax Court followed this approach in holding excludable a recovery for malicious prosecution of a civil action, including a portion of the recovery allocated by settlement agreement to damages to professional reputation.[49] "Exclusion under section 104," in the Tax Court's view, is "appropriate if compensatory damages are received on account of any invasion of the rights that an individual is granted by virtue of being a person in the sight of the law."[50] In affirming, the Court of Appeals for the Sixth Circuit said that "the personal nature of an injury should not be defined by its effect"; a recovery for an injury to a taxpayer's arm is fully excluded even if it includes compensation for loss of income, and, similarly, "the injury to a taxpayer's reputation [is] a personal injury . . . even though it affected his professional pursuits."[51]

In *Bent v. CIR*, the Court of Appeals for the Third Circuit has taken the Ninth Circuit's theory a step or two further. It applied §104(a)(2) to exclude a public school teacher's recovery from his employer grounded on an allegation that the employer had abridged the teacher's first amendment rights.[52] The court allowed the exclusion for the entire recovery, including a portion compensating the taxpayer for lost wages. The exclusion arises because the recovery was for an invasion of a personal right, the court held, and is not affected by the fact that it was measured in part by lost wages.

While agreeing that a civil rights recovery is excludable, even if measured by lost wages,[53] the Tax Court has denied the exclusion for a recovery

---

[47] Earlier authorities indicate an apportionment can be made in any case, but the taxpayer has the burden of establishing a reasonable basis for the division. See Seay v. CIR, supra note 45 (allocation accepted); Wallace v. CIR, 35 TCM (CCH) 954 (1976) (taxpayer failed to allocate recovery between injury to personal reputation and injury to business reputation). See also Fono v. CIR, 79 TC 680 (1982) (allocation of amounts received in settlement of claims under employment contract and contract for assignment of patent and trade secrets).

[48] Roemer v. CIR, 716 F2d 693 (9th Cir. 1983).

[49] Threlkeld v. CIR, 87 TC 1294 (1986), aff'd, 848 F2d 81 (6th Cir. 1988).

[50] 87 TC 1308.

[51] 848 F.2d at 84.

[52] Bent v. CIR, 835 F2d 67 (3d Cir. 1987).

[53] Metzger v. CIR, 88 TC 834 (1987).

of back wages under the federal Equal Pay Act:

> The Equal Pay Act requires that an employer pay equal wages for equal work regardless of sex. . . . If an employer violates this obligation placed on it, it is required . . . to pay the back pay "owing" to the employee doing the equal work. . . . In our view, an amount paid as back pay under this provision is more in the nature of a payment for a contract violation than for a tort-type right.[54]

The exclusion has been denied, further, to payments for agreeing to a future invasion of the taxpayer's privacy (e.g., depicting the taxpayer's family in a motion picture).[55] It seems equally clear that a person engaged in a hazardous calling, such as a motion picture stunt actor, cannot use §104(a)(2) to shield amounts received for a release of the right to sue for injuries that might be sustained in the future.

¶13.1.5 Taxpayer-Financed Accident or Health Insurance

Payments for personal injuries or sickness received through accident or health insurance are excludable from gross income under §104(a)(3).[56] However, this exclusion does not embrace amounts received by an employee if the amounts are paid by an employer or are received under an insurance policy or other arrangement whose cost is paid by the employer and is not included in the employee's gross income.[57] Payments under employer-financed arrangements are not necessarily taxable, but their status is gov-

---

[54] Thompson v. CIR, 89 TC 632, 646 (1987). In addition to back pay, the taxpayer received "liquidated damages," which the court excluded as being equivalent to a recovery under a civil rights statute.

[55] Roosevelt v. CIR, 43 TC 77 (1964) (extended discussion of issue and relevant cases); see also Reg. §1.104-1(c) (exclusion embraces "damages" based on "tort or tort type rights").

[56] The exclusion does not cover amounts attributable to medical expenses previously deducted under §213. See supra note 5.

For the status of receipts under two or more policies covering the same medical expenses, see Rev. Rul. 69-154, 1969-1 CB 46 (excess indemnification excludable under §104(a)(3) if attributable to premiums paid by taxpayer, but not if attributable to nontaxable contributions by employer).

[57] In the case of self-employed persons, certain contributions deductible under §404 (relating to qualified pension, profit sharing, or annuity plans, discussed infra ¶62.2) are treated by the last sentence of §104(a) as made by the employer, so that distributions under the plan to the self-employed person cannot be treated as the proceeds of accident or health insurance and excluded under §104(a)(3). Moreover, by virtue of §105(g), these amounts are not covered by §105. As a result, jurisdiction over these amounts is vested in §72(m) rather than in §§104 and 105. See Reg. §§1.104-1(d) (last sentence), 1.105-1(a).

erned by §105,[58] rather than by §104(a)(3). If contributions are made by both employer and employee, benefits must be apportioned so that amounts attributable to the employer's contributions can be subjected to §105, while the employee-financed amounts are governed by §104(a)(3).[59]

The primary function of §104(a)(3) is to exempt from taxation amounts received under ordinary accident and health insurance policies that pay medical expenses, lump-sum amounts for bodily injury, per diem amounts during hospitalization, amounts related to the taxpayer's wage level or length of incapacity during recuperation, and perhaps other benefits. It also embraces amounts received by a sole proprietor as compensation for income lost as a result of disability or sickness and similar payments received by a corporation as compensation for a key employee's absence from work because of disability.[60] Moreover, the exclusion is not limited to payments under formal policies issued by commercial insurance companies, but also encompasses funds or other plans that spread the risk of loss by indemnifying participants.[61] Payments by a company-wide fund maintained by employee contributions, for example, can qualify as "insurance" payments under §104(a)(3).[62]

¶13.2 EMPLOYER-FINANCED ACCIDENT AND HEALTH PLANS

¶13.2.1 Introductory

Before 1954, the status of wage continuation payments received by a sick employee depended on whether they were "amounts received through

---

[58] See infra ¶13.2.

[59] Reg. §§1.104-1(d), 1.105-1(c). Compare Rev. Rul. 63-181, 1963-2 CB 74 (allocation of receipts under employer-employee contributory group insurance policy in proportion to percentages of premiums paid) with Conroy v. CIR, 41 TC 685 (1964), aff'd per curiam, 341 F2d 290 (4th Cir. 1965) (entire amount attributed to employer contributions where taxpayer failed to establish proper allocation).

[60] Rev. Rul. 58-90, 1958-1 CB 88 (sole proprietor); Castner Garage, Ltd. v. CIR, 43 BTA 1 (1940) (acq.) (exclusion available to anyone with insurable interest in person suffering injury or sickness); but see Peoples Fin. & Thrift Co. v. CIR, 184 F2d 836 (5th Cir. 1950) (exclusion denied to creditor holding accident insurance policy as security for loan); Rev. Rul. 55-264, 1955-1 CB 11 (exclusion not applicable to reimbursement for business overhead expenses during prolonged disability due to injury or sickness).

Revenue Ruling 73-155, 1973-1 CB 50, provides that disability benefits received by an injured automobile passenger from the owner's insurer under a no-fault provision are excludable under §104(a)(3). It is not clear why the IRS cited §104(a)(3) (insurance) rather than §104(a)(2) (damages) as authority for excluding the benefits from gross income.

[61] Haynes v. US, 353 US 81 (1957), discussed infra ¶13.2.1 note 2.

[62] Reg. §1.104-1(d). For the term "plan," see §105(e), discussed infra ¶13.2.2.

accident or health insurance for personal injuries or sickness" within the meaning of the statutory predecessor of §104(a)(3).[1] When the Court of Appeals for the Seventh Circuit held in *Epmeier v. United States* that a company's elaborate wage continuation plan for its employees was "accident or health insurance,"[2] the IRS announced that it would not follow the decision "in the absence of further clarification from the Congress,"[3] fearing that it would encourage closely held corporations to allow their executives and shareholder-employees to go to Florida on sick leave every winter and to treat their salaries as excludable insurance receipts.

In 1954, Congress responded to *Epmeier* by transferring jurisdiction over employer-financed accident and health insurance benefits from §104(a)(3) to a new §105. This shift was effected by making §104(a)(3) inapplicable to accident or health payments received by an employee if paid by the employer or attributable to employer contributions not includable in the employee's gross income.[4] Under §105(a), payments under employer-financed plans must be included in the employee's gross income unless they meet the special tests of §105(b), (c), or (d), which, as enacted in 1954, allowed exclusions for amounts that (1) reimbursed the employee for medical expenses, (2) compensated for permanent bodily injury, or (3) qualified as "sick pay."

The first two of these grounds for exclusion have generated little controversy. The exclusion of sick pay, however, was a prolific source of litigation and criticism. It was severely pruned in 1976 by amendments that (1) confined the exclusion to taxpayers who were permanently and totally disabled, were under the age of 65, and met other tests, and (2) phased out the exclusion when adjusted gross income exceeded $15,000. In even this limited form, the exclusion only lasted through 1983; for taxable years after 1983, the sick and disability pay rules have been repealed.

The foregoing rules are buttressed by §105(e), which in effect endorses the *Epmeier* construction of the term "accident or health insurance" by applying it to various "plans" and "funds." Also, §106(a) provides that employees are not taxable on employer contributions to accident or health plans compensating them for personal injuries or sickness.

---

[1] See supra ¶13.1.5. The parenthetical limitation of §104(a)(3), disqualifying payments under employer-financed plans, was added in 1954.

[2] Epmeier v. US, 199 F2d 508 (7th Cir. 1952). Although established by a life insurance company, the *Epmeier* plan did not involve conventional insurance. The Supreme Court later reached the same result as to a plan created by a utility company for its employees. Haynes v. US, 353 US 81 (1957).

[3] IR 047 (Mar. 26, 1953), 1953 P-H Fed. Taxes ¶76,437.

[4] See supra ¶13.1.5. For allocation of benefits if the plan is financed jointly by employees and their employer, see supra ¶13.1.5 note 59.

For each year after 1984, an employer maintaining an accident or health plan must file an information return showing the number of the employer's employees, the number of employees eligible to participate in the plan, the number actually participating, the number of highly compensated employees in each of the foregoing categories, the plan's cost for the year, and other such information.[5]

¶13.2.2 Accident and Health Insurance

Section 105 applies to "amounts received by an employee through accident or health insurance for personal injuries or sickness,"[6] and §105(e)(1) states that "an accident or health plan for employees" shall be treated as "insurance."[7] This explicit reference to "plans," which need not be insured or funded, carries forward the *Epmeier* theory that an indemnification arrangement can be "insurance" even though not backed by a formal policy issued by a commercial insurance company.[8] Moreover, when enacting §105(e) in 1954, Congress deliberately refrained from requiring employer-financed plans to meet the elaborate standards that must be satisfied by qualified pension and profit sharing plans.[9] This tolerance eventually ended with the enactment in 1976 of §105(h), which denied the exclusion of §105(b) for benefits under self-insured plans that discriminated in favor of

---

[5] IRC §6039D(a). The return is filed on Form 5500, 5500-C, or 5500-R.

[6] By virtue of §105(g), the term "employee" does not embrace self-employed individuals, so their accident and health insurance benefits are not covered by §105. But see Rev. Rul. 85-121, 1985-2 CB 57 (laid-off worker is employee for purposes of §105); Rev. Rul. 82-196, 1982-2 CB 53 (benefits paid surviving spouse and dependents of deceased employee under employer-financed health and accident plan are governed by §105).

[7] Section 105(e)(2) spreads the same umbrella over sickness and disability funds for public employees.

[8] See supra note 2.

[9] See S. Rep. No. 1622, 83d Cong., 2d Sess. 185 (1954):

The House [version of the 1954 Code] confined exclusions to benefits paid under qualified plans satisfying requirements designed to prevent discrimination as to coverage or benefits in favor of highly compensated as compared with rank and file employees. The [Senate amendment] eliminates these qualification requirements. However, it specifies that the exemption is to be granted only to benefits paid out under an arrangement that constitutes a plan.

For the possibility that a plan subject to §105 may be encapsulated within a qualified pension or profit sharing plan, see Wood v. US, 590 F2d 321 (9th Cir. 1979); Rev. Rul. 69-141, 1969-1 CB 48. See also Caplin v. US, 718 F2d 544 (2d Cir. 1983) (taxpayer failed to prove that profit sharing plan included accident or health plan; *Wood* distinguished); Paul v. US, 88-1 USTC ¶9138 (ED Mich. 1988) (not officially reported) (profit sharing plan found not to include accident and health plan even though distribution to taxpayer was triggered by disability).

highly compensated employees. Congress tightened the nondiscrimination requirements even further in 1986 by replacing §105(h) with §89, which broadly prohibits such discrimination in all health plans.[10]

The vague term "plan" opened the door to abuse. This risk was increased by the regulations, which provide that a plan may cover "one or more employees,"[11] that different plans may be established for "different employees or classes of employees," that the plan need not be in writing, that a "program, policy, or custom having the effect of a plan" suffices,[12] and that an employee's rights need not be enforceable, provided notice or knowledge of the plan is reasonably available to the employee when injury or sickness is sustained.[13] This flabby concept of a "plan," however, eventually found disfavor with Congress, which in 1986 enacted §89(k) to limit the §105 exclusion to benefits under written plans that provide legally enforceable rights and satisfy several other requirements.[14]

Even before the enactment of §89, further, the courts implied some limits from the word "plan":

> [The legislative] use of "plan" signifies something more than merely one or more *ad hoc* benefit payments. Had Congress intended to exclude from gross income all *ad hoc* benefit payments arbitrarily made at the complete discretion of the employer in the absence of any sort of prior arrangement or practice, the use of the term "plan" would scarcely have been necessary.[15]

In addition to surmounting the "ad hoc" hurdle, an accident or health plan must be for the benefit of "employees" to qualify under §105.[16] This criterion does not preclude a plan that benefits shareholder-employees, but they must be included by virtue of their status as employees rather than as

---

[10] For §§105(h) and 89, see infra ¶13.2.7 and ¶13.2.8.

[11] For plans whose only participant was one key employee, see Kuhn v. US, 258 F2d 840 (3d Cir. 1958); Rev. Rul. 58-90, 1958-1 CB 88.

[12] Reg. §1.105-5(a).

[13] Id.

[14] See infra ¶13.2.8.

[15] Kaufman's Est. v. CIR, 35 TC 663, 666 (1961), aff'd per curiam, 300 F2d 128 (6th Cir. 1962). See also Chism's Est. v. CIR, 322 F2d 956 (9th Cir. 1963) (plan not reduced to writing, employees not formally notified of plan, and any rights they might have had were subject to change without their consent; held, Tax Court could properly conclude that no plan existed); Lang v. CIR, 41 TC 352, 356–57 (1963) (term "plan" "presupposes a predetermined course of action under prescribed circumstances," not merely the "favorable exercise of discretion by the employer when sickness arises"; no plan where employee could not "really count on his salary being continued if he became ill" and could not anticipate how long any payments that might be made would continue).

[16] Self-employment does not qualify. See supra note 6.

shareholders. Thus, "there must be some rational basis other than owner-ship of the business to justify discrimination among employees,"[17] and the inclusion of some nonshareholding employees does not rescue an otherwise invalid plan if it benefits them "only incidentally and sporadically."[18] If payments are made not because the recipient is an employee but in his capacity as a shareholder, they are taxable distributions of corporate profits rather than excludable proceeds of an accident or health plan.[19] Moreover, even if there is a plan for employees, disproportionate payments to share-holder-employees may be treated as paid outside the plan rather than pursu-ant to it.[20]

Most of the litigated disputes regarding the existence of a "plan" have involved wage continuation payments to shareholder-employees rather than reimbursement of medical expenses or compensation for permanent bodily injury. Before 1976, the sick pay exclusion was especially attractive to corporate insiders, even though limited to $100 per week, because the payments could continue for the duration of a protracted illness if the employer's plan so provided.[21] For the controlling shareholders of closely held enterprises, it was tempting to describe Florida vacations as periods of convalescence from illness and to pension off relatives on the pretext of physical disability. These claims were difficult for the IRS to police without offensive intrusions into the private lives of the allegedly sick recipients. The audit problem was exacerbated by the possibility that a dominant shareholder, allegedly "absent from work on account of personal injuries or

---

[17] Levine v. CIR, 50 TC 422, 427 (1968). See American Foundry v. CIR, 536 F2d 289 (9th Cir. 1976) ("rational basis" standard; medical expense reimbursement to corporate officers qualified, but not salary continuation payments); Epstein v. CIR, 31 TCM (CCH) 217 (1972) (plan for employee-shareholders satisfied "rational basis" test); see also Giberson v. CIR, 44 TCM (CCH) 154 (1982) (plan qualified despite more favorable benefits for shareholder-employee than for other employees); Seidel v. CIR, 30 TCM (CCH) 1021 (1971) (plan qualified where corporation had only two employees, each owning one half of stock).

[18] Larkin v. CIR, 394 F2d 494, 495 (1st Cir. 1968); John H. Kennedy, Inc. v. CIR, 36 TCM (CCH) 878 (1977) (plan to benefit sole shareholder only not qualified).

[19] Leidy's Est. v. CIR, 34 TCM (CCH) 1476 (1975), aff'd per curiam, 549 F2d 798 (4th Cir. 1976) (payments to controlling shareholder and mother treated as constructive dividends). See infra ¶92.2 for more on constructive distributions.

[20] See Kaufman's Est. v. CIR, 35 TC 663, 667 (1961), aff'd per curiam, 300 F2d 128 (6th Cir. 1962) ("petitioners have not, in our opinion, established that the payments in question were made pursuant to any accident or health plan it may have had"); Levine v. CIR, supra note 17 (payments to taxpayer for more than five years; on basis of employer's financial circumstances, court concluded that payments to ordinary employees would have been restricted to shorter periods and that taxpayer's payments continued only because he was controlling shareholder).

[21] The exclusion, however, terminated when the employee reached normal re-tirement age. See infra ¶13.2.5.

sickness,"[22] was in fact running the enterprise with a poolside telephone at a resort hotel in a benign climate.[23]

The possibility of abuse was drastically reduced in 1976, when Congress restricted the sick pay exclusion to employees afflicted with permanent and total disability and provided for a phaseout of even this limited exclusion if the employee's adjusted gross income exceeded $15,000.[24] These restrictions did not apply to the exclusion of reimbursed medical expenses and payments for permanent bodily injury under §§105(b) and (c), but these items are more easily verified than sick pay, and the amounts are ordinarily subject to reasonable ceilings. The attack on abuse advanced in 1978, with the addition of §105(h), which denied the exclusion for reimbursements of medical expenses when provided to a highly compensated employee under a discriminatory plan. Although §105(h) was repealed for taxable years after 1988, it has been replaced by §89, which bundles accident and health plans into a broad-based package of employee benefits subject to a uniform antidiscrimination rule.[25]

¶13.2.3 Reimbursed Medical Expenses

Accident and health insurance payments made directly or indirectly to an employee to reimburse expenses incurred for "medical care" of the taxpayer or the taxpayer's spouse or dependents are excludable from the employee's gross income under §105(b), unless attributable to deductions allowed under §213 (relating to the deduction of medical expenses) in prior taxable years.[26] The term "dependent" is defined by §152; the exclusion of §105(b) is allowed if the sick or injured person is a "dependent" of the taxpayer, whether or not the additional requirements for a "dependency exemption" are met.

There is no dollar limit on the amount of medical expenses that may be reimbursed, and the payor is not required to demand proof of the taxpayer's

---

[22] IRC §105(d) (before amendment in 1976).

[23] See Reg. §1.105-4(a)(5); Laverty v. CIR, 523 F2d 479 (9th Cir. 1975) (business executive with no formal workday was not "away from work" despite need for therapeutic exercises occupying 25 percent of each working day); Kaufman's Est. v. CIR, supra note 20 (compensation, not sick pay, where, after suffering stroke, managing officer of bank continued as consultant, drawing undiminished salary).

[24] See infra ¶13.2.6.

[25] For the effective date of the repeal of §105(h) and the enactment of §89, see infra note 49.

[26] "Indirect" payments include amounts paid to a physician or hospital or to the employee's spouse or dependents. See Reg. §1.105-2.

For the definition of "medical care" under §213(e), see infra ¶36.1.2. As to amounts "attributable" to prior deductions, see supra ¶13.1.1 note 5. For the requirement of nondiscrimination, see infra ¶¶13.2.7, 13.2.8.

actual expenditures. Amounts in excess of actual expenses do not qualify, however, because the exclusion only applies to amounts "paid specifically to reimburse the taxpayer for the prescribed medical expenses."[27]

¶13.2.4 Payments for Permanent Bodily Injury

Section 105(c) excludes payments for permanent bodily injury incurred by an employee or his spouse or dependents,[28] provided the amount is computed by reference to the nature of the injury and (in the case of a benefit for the employee) without regard to the length of his absence from work.[29] By virtue of the latter restriction, periodic payments terminating at the employee's normal retirement age evidently do not qualify for exclusion, even if paid to compensate for permanent bodily injury; and the IRS has ruled that this disqualification extends to a lump-sum commutation of payments that would terminate at age 65.[30] If computed without regard to the taxpayer's absence from work, however, payments for permanent bodily injury can be excluded whether paid in a lump sum or installments.[31]

Section 105(c) covers payments for the permanent loss or loss of use of a member or function of the body, or for permanent disfigurement. The regulations provide that "disfigurement" shall be given "a reasonable interpretation in the light of all the particular facts and circumstances," and that disfigurement or loss of use of a member or function of the body "shall be considered permanent when it may reasonably be expected to continue for the life of the individual."[32]

---

[27] H.R. Rep. No. 2543, 83d Cong., 2d Sess. 25 (1954) (no dollar limit on exclusion); Reg. §1.105-2.

[28] For the scope of the term "dependent," see supra text accompanying note 26.

[29] See Beisler v. CIR, 787 F2d 1325 (9th Cir. 1986) (benefits computed "with reference to the nature of the injury" only if they "vary according to the type or severity of a person's injury"; benefit paid to every employee retired on account of permanent disability, in amount based on years of service, not excludable under §105(c)). But see Rosen v. US, 646 F. Supp. 97 (WD Va. 1986) (payments on account of permanent and total disability are necessarily computed without regard to period of absence from work because recipient will never return to work; this conclusion not affected by provision allowing benefit only when absence from work exceeds six months because provision is standard limitation meant as part of definition of disability).

[30] Rev. Rul. 74-603, 1974-2 CB 35.

[31] Reg. §1.105-3 (penultimate sentence).

[32] Reg. §1.105-3; see Rev. Rul. 63-181, 1963-2 CB 74 (lump-sum payment on account of permanent and total disability due to acute cancer is payment for permanent loss of use of member or function of the body); see also Watts v. US, 703 F2d 346 (9th Cir. 1983) (on record presented, hypertension not a permanent loss or loss of use of function of body); Hines v. CIR, 72 TC 715 (1979) (payments to commercial airline pilot not excludable; damage from heart attack not permanent loss of or

The §105(c) exclusion does not apply to workmen's compensation payments or to death benefits, but these amounts are ordinarily excludable from the recipient's gross income under §104(a)(1) or §101, respectively.[33]

¶13.2.5 Pre-1976 Sick Pay

From 1954 through 1983, §105(d) permitted an exclusion for sick or disability pay. Until 1976, the provision allowed employees to exclude wages or payments in lieu of wages, up to a weekly rate of $100, for periods of absence from work on account of personal injuries or sickness. This exclusion was restricted to cases of total and permanent disability for the taxable years 1977 through 1983,[34] and was repealed for taxable years after 1983.

Application of the 1954–1976 exclusion of sick pay created difficulties in various areas. The question of whether a payment is pursuant to a plan, although raised by all of the §105 exclusions, has been most troublesome under the sick pay exclusion.[35] Two areas of dispute peculiar to the sick pay exclusion are described below:

1. *"Absent from work."* Old §105(d) encompasses wage continuation payments only for periods "during which the employee is absent from work on account of personal injuries or sickness." The concept of "absence from work" is difficult to apply to executives and shareholders of closely held corporations, whose working days are flexible and who can often conduct business activities from their homes or hospital beds.[36] Pre-1976 law also raised problems in computing the period of disability if the employee was ill during a weekend, holiday, or vacation, and would not have been at work in any event.[37]

In the case of protracted or permanent disability, the IRS tried at one time to terminate the exclusion when the taxpayer reached the earliest age at which retirement without loss of benefits was permissible, on the theory that absence from work thereafter was no longer the result of injury or sickness. After a series of litigation losses, however, the Treasury amended

---

loss of use of member or function of body, and payments not computed with reference to nature of injury); Laverty v. CIR, 61 TC 160 (1973), aff'd per curiam, 523 F2d 479 (9th Cir. 1975) (permanent bodily injuries established, but no evidence that any part of continued wages was "payment" for injuries).

[33] Reg. §1.105-3 (last sentence). For §§104(a)(1) and 101, see supra ¶¶13.1.2 and 12.2.1.

[34] For §105(d) as amended in 1976, see infra ¶13.2.6. The 1976 legislation was effective for taxable years beginning after December 31, 1976.

[35] See supra ¶13.2.2.

[36] See supra note 23.

[37] Reg. §§1.105-4(a)(3)(ii), (b).

the regulations in 1975 to provide that the exclusion would terminate when the employee reached the employer's mandatory retirement age or, in the absence of such a requirement, the later of age 65 or the age at which the employer customarily terminated employment for the employee class to which the taxpayer belonged.[38]

2. *Seven-day and 30-day waiting periods.* The pre-1976 version of §105(d) imposed a ceiling of $100 per week on the exclusion of sick pay. Also, if the sick pay for the first 30 calendar days of absence from work exceeded 75 percent of the taxpayer's regular weekly wage rate, no exclusion was allowed for these 30 days. If the sick pay did not exceed the 75 percent bench mark, there was a seven-day waiting period (unless the taxpayer was hospitalized for at least one of the seven days), following which an exclusion of $75 weekly was allowed for the balance of the 30-day period. The waiting periods and the dollar and percentage limitations raised numerous niggling questions, which are addressed in detail and illustrated by the regulations.[39]

¶13.2.6 Pre-1984 Payments for Permanent and Total Disability

In 1976, Congress repealed the sick pay exclusion provided in 1954, and substituted a much narrower exclusion, embracing wage continuation payments only if the taxpayer (1) retired on disability when permanently and totally disabled, (2) is absent from work on account of permanent and total disability, and (3) has not attained age 65 before the close of the taxable year.[40] The disability exclusion has been repealed for years after 1983, thus ending all exclusions for sick or disability pay.[41]

The requisite permanent disability exists if the taxpayer is unable to engage in any substantial gainful activity by reason of a medically determinable physical or mental impairment that has lasted or can be ex-

---

[38] Reg. §§1.105-4(a)(3), -6 (employees retired before January 1, 1975); Rev. Proc. 76-12, 1976-1 CB 552. For earlier rules, see Brooks v. US, 473 F2d 829 (6th Cir. 1973); Rev. Rul. 57-76, 1957-1 CB 66, superseded by Rev. Rul. 68-385, 1968-2 CB 53, declared obsolete by Rev. Rul. 76-565, 1976-2 CB 449.

[39] Reg. §1.105-4(e), (f).

[40] The first and second of these requirements overlap in part, but are independently significant in that the employee must not only be permanently disabled at retirement, but must continue to be absent from work because of the disability. If there is an unexpected remission, the employee does not satisfy the second requirement.

Recipients of payments to which both §105(d) and the annuity rules of §72 would otherwise apply are subject solely to §105(d) until attaining age 65 or until an irrevocable election is made to rely on §72. IRC § 105(d)(6) (before repeal in 1983). See Rev. Rul. 81-121, 1981-1 CB 43 (where §105(d)(6) election made by disabled employee, survivors benefits disqualified for §101(b) exclusion under rule denying that exclusion where decedent received annuity).

[41] Pub. L. No. 98-21, 97 Stat. 65 (1983).

pected to last for a continuous period of 12 months or more or to result in death.[42]

Even if these onerous standards are satisfied, the taxpayer is not showered with gold. The exclusion is limited to a weekly rate of $100, and is phased out, dollar for dollar, if the taxpayer's adjusted gross income (including the disability income) exceeds $15,000.[43] Thus, an employee who is disabled throughout a taxable year gets no exclusion if adjusted gross income exceeds $20,200. Lest a disabled taxpayer with an employed spouse file a separate return to mitigate the adjusted gross income limitation, the exclusion is conditioned on the filing of a joint return unless the husband and wife "live apart at all times during the taxable year."[44] If the couple gets divorced, however, the $15,000 phaseout applies only to the disabled spouse's own income, even if they continue to live together.[45]

¶13.2.7 Discriminatory Medical Expense Reimbursement Plans — Rules for 1980 Through 1988

As explained above, employees can exclude from gross income amounts received as reimbursement for their medical expenses (as well as those of the employee's spouse and dependents) if paid under an employer's accident or health plan.[46] To qualify, the benefits must be paid pursuant to a "plan for employees," rather than merely on an ad hoc basis.[47] Section 105(h), enacted in 1978 and applicable to the taxable years 1980 through 1988, limits the blanket exclusion of benefits paid under an employer's self-insured medical reimbursement plan in order to deny the §105(b) exclusion to highly compensated employees covered by plans that discriminate in their favor.[48] The provision has been replaced for years after 1988 with the addition of §89, which subjects accident and health plans to a uniform

---

[42] IRC §105(d)(4) (before repeal in 1983).

[43] For the computation of adjusted gross income, see supra ¶2.1.3.

[44] See DeMars v. CIR, 79 TC 247 (1982) (rules do not unconstitutionally discriminate against married persons).

[45] But see Rev. Rul. 76-255, 1976-2 CB 40 (tax-induced divorce followed by remarriage disregarded); see also infra ¶111.3.6.

[46] IRC §§105(b) and (e), discussed supra ¶13.2.3.

[47] For the limited restrictions imposed on plans by the regulations and case law, see supra ¶13.2.2.

[48] See generally Joint Comm. on Tax'n, 95th Cong., 2d Sess., General Explanation of the Revenue Act of 1978 (Comm. Print 1979) [hereinafter 1978 Bluebook]; Colvin, Coping With the Anti-Discrimination Requirement of Medical Reimbursement Plans, 50 J. Tax'n 104 (1979); James & Lowe, Reassessing Medical Reimbursement Plans After Changes in the Law and Regulations, 54 J. Tax'n 80, 89 (1981).

nondiscrimination rule applicable to many employee benefits.[49] Section 89 is discussed below.[50]

The heart of the 1978 legislation is §105(h)(1), providing that if a self-insured medical reimbursement plan is discriminatory as to eligibility or benefits, the normal exclusion from gross income allowed by §105(b) does not apply to any "excess reimbursement" paid to a "highly compensated individual." This rule is backed up by several definitions.

1. *Nondiscriminatory plans.* A plan is discriminatory unless it satisfies both an eligibility and a benefits test.

The eligibility test is met if the plan benefits (1) at least 70 percent of all employees, (2) at least 80 percent of the eligible employees if at least 70 percent are eligible, or (3) such employees as qualify under a classification established by the employer and found by the IRS not to discriminate in favor of highly compensated employees.[51] These alternative eligibility standards, which resemble those applicable to qualified pension and profit sharing plans,[52] are relaxed by rules permitting the exclusion of employees with less than three years of service, employees under age 25, part-time and seasonal employees, employees covered by certain collective bargaining agreements, and certain nonresident aliens.

The benefits test requires all benefits for highly compensated individuals to be provided for all other participants.[53]

2. *Excess reimbursement.* The term "excess reimbursement," which determines the taxable amount in the case of a highly compensated individual's benefits under a discriminatory plan, is given a twofold meaning by §105(h)(7).

First, the entire amount is an excess reimbursement if the benefit is available to a highly compensated individual but not to a "broad cross-section" of employees. A plan can be discriminatory, but nevertheless provide a benefit of a particular type, such as emergency medical care and ambulance service, to a broad cross section of employees. Such benefits are not disqualified, even if paid to highly compensated individuals.

Second, in the case of benefits not disqualified by the broad cross-section test, a payment to a highly compensated individual is an excess reimbursement in an amount determined by multiplying the individual's

---

[49] Section 89 supercedes §105(h) for taxable years beginning after the earlier of (1) the date three months after the promulgation of regulations under §89 or (2) December 31, 1988. Pub. L. No. 99-514, §1151(k), 100 Stat. 2085 (1986).

[50] Infra ¶13.2.8.

[51] IRC §105(h)(3) (before repeal in 1986).

[52] See infra ¶61.2; see also IRC §105(h)(8) (before repeal in 1986) (employees of all members of controlled group, as defined by §414(b) or (c), treated as employed by a single employer).

[53] IRC §105(h)(4) (before repeal in 1986).

reimbursements for the plan year by a fraction, the numerator of which is the total amount reimbursed to highly compensated individuals and the denominator is the total amount reimbursed to all employees under the plan. For example, if rank-and-file employees receive only one third of the total benefits for a plan year, only one third of a highly compensated individual's benefits qualify for the exclusion because the other two thirds is an excess reimbursement.

3. *Highly compensated individuals.* The highly compensated group consists of (1) the five highest paid officers, (2) shareholder-employees owning (directly, indirectly, or constructively) more than 10 percent of the employer's stock, and (3) the highest paid 25 percent of all employees (other than nonparticipating employees excluded by rule excluding employees with less than three years of service, employees under age 25, and a few others). Employees outside this prohibited group are not taxed on benefits, even if the plan discriminates in their favor.

4. *Regulations.* Section 105(h)(9) authorizes the Treasury to prescribe "such regulations as may be necessary" to carry out the provisions of §105(h), a noncommital mandate that, according to legislative history, is expected to result in an exemption of reimbursement for such diagnostic procedures as medical examinations and X-rays.[54]

5. *Relationship to medical expense deduction.* For highly compensated individuals who itemize their personal deductions the impact of §105(h) is sometimes mitigated by a medical expense deduction under §213 offsetting the inclusion of excess reimbursements in gross income.[55] When a medical reimbursement is included in an employee's gross income, the reimbursed amount should be treated as additional compensation that is first received by the employee and then paid over as a medical expense; this constructive payment should be deductible subject to the usual limitations of §213, including the deduction floor of 3, 5, or 7.5 percent of adjusted gross income.

If the taxpayer's unreimbursed medical expenses exceeded the floor on the medical deduction, an excess reimbursement thus was simply added to gross income and deducted from adjusted gross income, leaving taxable income unaffected. Indeed, an occasional generous taxpayer could even benefit from §105(h) because it increased adjusted gross income and thus correspondingly raised the limit on the charitable contribution deduction.[56] These effects, however, were not inconsistent with §105(h)'s policy, which was essentially to treat discriminatory payments to highly compensated

---

[54] See 1978 Bluebook, supra note 48, at 223.

[55] For §213(a)(1), see generally infra ¶36.1.5.

[56] For the percentage limits on the deduction of charitable contributions, see §170(b), discussed infra ¶35.3.

employees as additional compensation, subjecting them to the same limitations as apply to medical expenses paid from any other portion of the employees' income.

The floor on the medical deduction, moreover, rose during the period §105(h) was in effect (from 3 percent of adjusted gross income for years before 1983 to 5 percent for the years 1983 through 1986, and to 7.5 percent for 1987 and 1988). As a consequence, the denial of the exclusion became more and more likely to have a tax cost to the employee.

¶13.2.8 Discrimination in Accident and Health Plans After 1988

Under §89, which generally applies for taxable years after 1988,[57] a highly compensated employee is taxed on any "excess benefit" provided to him under a discriminatory accident or health plan.[58] A plan is considered discriminatory unless it complies with a detailed set of rules designed to test whether the plan discriminates in coverage or benefits in favor of highly compensated employees. Congress decided that the exclusions for medical and other fringe benefits are only appropriate "if such benefits fulfill important social policy objectives, such as increasing health insurance coverage among taxpayers . . . who otherwise would not purchase or could not afford such coverage."[59] Section 105(h), the prior nondiscrimination rule for health plans, was found inadequate because it "did not require sufficient coverage of nonhighly compensated employees" and did not define clearly the class of employees in favor of whom discrimination was forbidden.[60] Section 89 is intended to "require employers to cover nonhighly compensated employees to an extent comparable to the coverage of highly compensated employees," while allowing some "flexibility in designing employee benefit programs."[61]

---

[57] See supra note 49 for more detail on the effective date of §89. See generally Kelly, How Will the Welfare Benefit Plan Nondiscrimination Rules Apply? 69 J. Tax'n 76 (1988).

[58] The term "accident and health plan" is shortened to "health plan." IRC §89(j)(2).

Section 89 also applies to group-term life insurance plans (infra ¶14.2.2), and an employer can elect to apply it to a group legal services plan, educational assistance program, or dependent care assistance program. IRC §89(i); see infra ¶14.3 (group legal services plans), ¶14.4 (educational assistance programs), ¶14.9 (dependent care assistance programs). When this election is made, §89 supersedes the nondiscrimination rules that normally apply to such plans and programs. IRC §89(j)(7).

[59] Staff of Joint Comm. on Tax'n, 99th Cong., 2d Sess., General Explanation of the Tax Reform Act of 1986, at 780–81 (Comm. Print 1987) [hereinafter 1986 Bluebook].

[60] Id. at 781.

[61] Id.

Section 89 applies to all health and accident plans, whether or not insured. When a plan is found to be discriminatory, §89 limits both the §105(b) exclusion for reimbursed medical expenses and the §105(c) exclusion for payments for the loss of use of a portion or function of the body.

To avoid being classified as discriminatory, a plan must meet two sets of requirements, eligibility requirements and a benefit requirement.[62] Also, the exclusion of benefits under a nondiscriminatory plan is denied if the plan is not set out in writing satisfying detailed requirements. These rules are described more fully below.

1. *Eligibility requirements.* There are three eligibility requirements.[63] First, at least 90 percent of the employer's employees who are not highly compensated must be eligible to participate. To be counted toward satisfying this 90 percent test, a rank-and-file employee must, if he elects to participate, receive a benefit through employer contributions that is at least 50 percent as large as the largest employer-provided benefit enjoyed by any highly compensated employee.[64] The term "employer-provided benefit" means the value of the coverage for the employee, to the extent attributable to employer contributions under the plan.[65] All of the employer's medical plans are aggregated in applying this 90 percent/50 percent test.[66] If an employee can participate in two health plans, for example, his employer-provided benefit is the sum of the benefits from employer contributions

---

[62] IRC §89(c).

[63] IRC §89(d).

[64] In determining the qualification of a health plan, an employer can elect to apply this 50 percent test separately with respect to employee coverage on the one hand, and spouse and dependent coverage on the other. IRC §89(g)(6). If this election is made, only employees having spouses or dependents are taken into account in applying the test to spouse and dependent coverage.

[65] IRC §89(g)(5)(A). For a plan other than an accident, health, or group-term life insurance plan, the employer-provided benefit is the value of the benefits that come from employer contributions.

The value of health coverage will be determined under regulations that give values for standard coverage and provide rules for adjusting these values for the particulars of an employer's plan. IRC §89(g)(3)(B). The value of group-term life coverage is determined under regulations prescribed under §79(c) (see infra ¶14.2), making the arbitrary assumption that all employees are 40 years old. IRC §89(g)(3)(C).

A benefit paid for by salary reductions is considered employer-provided. IRC §89(g)(3)(D).

[66] Similarly, when §89 is applied to a group-term life insurance plan, group legal services plan, educational assistance program, or dependent care assistance program, all plans of the same type are aggregated.

available through the two plans.[67]

The second requirement is stated in the alternative. The requirement is satisfied, first, if no more than 50 percent of the employees eligible to participate in the plan are highly compensated employees. Alternatively, it is met if the ratio of eligible employees to all employees in the class is no higher for highly compensated employees than for other employees. Assume an employer has 20 employees, 15 of whom are highly compensated and all of whom are eligible to participate in the employer's health plan. The 50 percent test is not met because more than 50 percent of those eligible are highly compensated; the alternative test is satisfied, however, because the percentage of highly compensated employees who are eligible (100 percent) is no greater than the percentage of rank-and-file employees who are eligible (also 100 percent).[68]

In determining eligibility percentages under either of these alternatives, two or more "comparable" health plans of an employer can be aggregated, at the employer's option. Plans are comparable if the least advantaged participant in the aggregated plans receives employer-provided benefits that are at least 95 percent as large as those provided to the most favorably treated highly compensated employee.[69]

---

[67] 1986 Bluebook, supra note 59, at 783. If an employee is allowed to choose between two or more plans, the most valuable of the benefits open to him is his employer-provided benefit. Id.

[68] Id.

[69] IRC §89(g)(1). The comparability test requires a precise definition of the term "plan"; if an employer has more than one plan, the comparability test must be applied, and each separate plan that falls outside the 95 percent range is considered discriminatory unless it meets the 50 percent test on its own.

For this purpose, "each option or different benefit [is] a separate plan." IRC §89(j)(11). For example, an employer has two plans if it offers a choice between health insurance or membership in a health maintenance organization (HMO). Each HMO, further, is a separate plan. 1986 Bluebook, supra at 785. Individual and family coverage constitute two plans if either can be elected without the other. Id. If more than one kind of family coverage is offered, each is a separate plan. "For example, if an employer offers 'employee plus 1 family member' health coverage and 'employee plus 2 or more family members' health coverage, there are 3 plans: (1) employee coverage, (2) coverage of 1 family member, and (3) coverage of additional family members." Id.

On the other hand, plans that are in fact separate are treated as one if they are identical in all respects except that they cover different groups of employees. Also, a group-term life insurance program is not considered more than one plan merely because the insurance benefit is proportional to compensation. IRC §89(j)(4). A program that provides group-term life insurance for each employee with a death benefit equal to the employee's annual salary, for example, is one plan. 1986 Bluebook, supra at 786.

Further, a health plan can be considered one plan even if the employer's contribution is reduced proportionately for employees who work less than 30 hours

The third of the eligibility requirements is that the plan can contain no provision relating to eligibility that discriminates in favor of highly compensated employees, either "by its terms or otherwise." This test is directed at "discrimination that is not quantifiable."[70] Asssume an employer has a plan for salaried employees (many of whom are highly compensated) that is measurably better than a plan the employer maintains for hourly employees (none of whom are highly compensated). This difference might cause the plans to fail the first eligibility test or the benefit requirement; if the difference between the two plans can be quantified, however, it does not violate the third of the eligibility requirements. A plan that provides unusual coverage for a rare disease that the owner of the business suffers from, on the other hand, might exhibit a nonquantifiable discrimination in favor of a highly compensated employee that violates this requirement.[71]

2. *Benefit requirement.* The benefit requirement is satisfied if the average employer-provided benefit for rank-and-file employees is at least 75 percent of the average benefit for highly compensated employees.[72] The average benefit for each class (highly compensated employees and all other employees) is a fraction, whose numerator is the aggregate of the employer-provided benefits for employees of that class and whose denominator is the number of employees in that class, including those who do not participate in the plan. The averages are computed annually.

---

per week. IRC §89(j)(5). These proportionate reductions can be in steps: a 25 percent reduction if the employee works 22 1/2 or more hours per week, and a 50 percent reduction if the employee works less. 1986 Bluebook, supra at 786. Assume an employer provides health coverage worth $1,100 per employee, and normally requires employees to pay $100 of this cost. Employees who customarily work 20 hours per week can be required to pay $600 (leaving the employer contribution at $500, 50 percent of the $1,000 contribution for a full-time employee). Id. This rule only applies, however, if the average work week of employees counted in applying the §89 tests is at least 30 hours.

[70] 1986 Bluebook, supra note 59, at 783–84.

[71] Id. This requirement is also meant to catch a plan that provides benefits for rank-and-file employees that have a high value in the Treasury's valuation tables, but are not very valuable because of a special circumstance not reflected in the tables—a scheme, in other words, to exploit a weakness in the tables. Id.

[72] IRC §89(e). Plans of the same type (health plan, group-term life plan, etc.) are aggregated in applying the benefits requirement, but plans of different types usually must satisfy the requirement independently. If, however, an election is made to apply §89 to a group legal services plan, educational assistance program, or dependent care assistance program, the employer can further elect to aggregate two or more plans and programs covered by the election (whether or not of the same type) in applying the benefit requirements. IRC §89(g)(4). A group-life insurance plan can also be included in this aggregation. Although a health plan must satisfy the requirements independently, it may be aggregated with plans of other types in determining whether the latter plans meet the test.

An employer can elect to refine the benefit computations to reflect better the family status of employees and coverage available through the plans of other employers.[73] When the election is made, a nonparticipating employee is excluded from the denominator of the relevant fraction if the employee and his spouse and dependents are covered under a plan of another employer that provides "core benefits."[74] This exclusion could apply if the employee opts not to participate in the employer's plan because he and his family are covered under a plan of his spouse's employer. It could also apply if the employee has two jobs. Further, an electing employer computes each of the fractions separately for employee coverage on the one hand, and coverage for spouses and dependents on the other, excluding from the latter fraction employees who do not have spouses or dependents and employees whose spouses and dependents are covered by plans of other employers.[75] A married employee would be excluded from the family coverage fraction, for example, if he and his spouse each had individual coverage under their respective employer's plan.

An employer who uses either of these alternatives must collect "adequate sworn statements" showing whether (1) employees have core benefits under plans of other employers, (2) employees have spouses or dependents, and (3) spouses and dependents are covered under plans of other employers. In the absence of these statements, presumptions are made that make it difficult to meet the benefit requirement.[76]

3. *Alternative to eligibility and benefit requirements.* An alternative test is provided in lieu of the eligibility and benefit requirements: A plan satisfies these requirements for a plan year if (1) at least 80 percent of the employer's rank-and-file employees are covered under the plan during the year and (2) the plan does not contain any provision that discriminates in favor of highly compensated employees.[77] An employee is counted toward the required 80 percent only if covered by the plan; eligibility to participate without actual particpation is not enough. This test applies only to insured plans, not to a plan self-insured by the employer.[78] Comparable plans are

---

[73] IRC §§89(g)(1), (2). This rule only applies to health plans.

[74] IRC §89(g)(2)(A).

[75] IRC §89(g)(2)(A)(ii).

[76] A rank-and-file nonparticipant is included in the computations, but a highly compensated nonparticipant is excluded; a rank-and-file participant who does not have family coverage is included in the spouse and dependent fraction, but a highly compensated employee in the same position is excluded. IRC §89(g)(2)(D).

[77] IRC §89(f). This alternative is not available when §89 is applied to a group legal services, educational assistance, or dependent care assistance program.

[78] 1986 Bluebook, supra note 59, at 784. It can apply to a group-term life insurance plan, but not to a group legal services, educational assistance, or dependent care assistance program.

aggregated for this purpose.[79]

4. *Excluded employees.* Several classes of employees are excluded in applying the several requirements described above.[80] An employee who is not eligible to participate in a plan[81] is ignored in applying the requirements if he (1) has completed less than one year of service with the employer,[82] (2) is under age 21, or (3) normally works less than 17 1/2 hours per week or during fewer than 6 months each year. Another exclusion is made for ineligible employees covered by a collective bargaining agreement if benefits of the type provided in the plan were the subject of good faith bargaining. Finally, a nonresident alien employee is excluded if none of his compensation from the employer is from U.S. sources.

5. *Definition of "employee" and "highly compensated employee."* The term "employee" is used in §89 to include both common law employees and self-employed persons.[83] A sole proprietor is treated as his own employee, and a partnership is treated as the employer of each partner who has earned income from the partnership.

The purpose of §89 is to discourage employers from having plans that discriminate in favor of highly compensated employees, and many of the rules turn on the classification of employees as highly compensated or not. A detailed definition of highly compensated is provided in the statute.[84] Generally, an employee is highly compensated if he is paid more than $75,000 or owns more than 5 percent of the employer's stock. The definition is developed in more detail elsewhere.[85]

6. *Separate lines of business.* If an employer has more than one line of business, §89 can be applied separately to each line of business, provided that eligibility under each plan is defined in a way that does not discrimi-

---

[79] See supra note 69 for the meaning of comparable plan.

[80] IRC §89(h)(1).

[81] An employee is considered ineligible if he cannot participate in any plan of the same type. IRC §89(h)(3). An employee is ineligible under a health plan, for example, if the employer provides no health coverage for the employee under any plan. A health plan may, however, provide different waiting periods "for core and noncore benefits." Id. Also, if a separate plan is provided for employees who do not meet a minimum age or service requirement, this plan and the plan for other employees are tested separately; the former by taking into account only those who do not meet the age or service requirement, and the latter excluding those employees from consideration. IRC §89(h)(5).

[82] For "core benefits" under a health plan, the maximum waiting period is reduced to six months. IRC §89(h)(1)(A). Once the one year or six months of service has been completed, the waiting period must end as of the beginning of the following calendar month.

[83] IRC §89(j)(6). See IRC §401(c)(1) for the definition of self employed.

[84] IRC §§89(j)(1), 414(q).

[85] Infra ¶61.2.2.

nate in favor of highly compensated employees.[86]

7. *Consequences of failure to satisfy eligibility and benefit requirements.* If a plan fails the eligibility or benefit requirements, each highly compensated employee covered by the plan is taxed on his "excess benefit" under the plan.[87] The excess benefit is the value of the employer-provided benefit for the employee, less the "highest permitted benefit."[88] The highest permitted benefit, in turn, is the benefit the employee would have enjoyed if plan benefits for highly compensated employees were shaved down sufficiently to meet the eligibility and benefit requirements. This hypothetical reduction of benefits begins with the employees enjoying the largest benefits under the plan.

8. *Requirement that plan be in writing and satisfy other procedural requirements.* A plan subject to §89 must be in writing and must further satisfy all of the following requirements:[89] Each employee's rights under the plan must be legally enforceable; employees must be given reasonable notification of the benefits the plan provides to them; the plan must be maintained for the exclusive benefit of the employees; and the employer must intend, when the plan is adopted, to keep it in effect indefinitely. If these requirements are not met, every employee must report as gross income the entire value of his employer-provided benefits under the plan.

¶13.2.9 Exclusion of Employer Contributions From Employee's Gross Income

Section 106(a) excludes "employer-provided coverage under an accident or health plan" from an employee's gross income; but for this exclusion, an employer's payment of premiums to an insurer or contributions to a disability fund would be additional compensation to the employee, unless the amount attributable to individuals could not be ascertained or the employee's rights were too tenuous to constitute income.[90] Section 106(a)

---

[86] IRC §§89(g)(5), (h)(4). This rule is meant to allow "employee benefit structures in [the various] line[s] of business [to] differ because of historical trends within each industry," without allowing a circumvention of the "premise that highly compensated employees should not be permitted to exclude employee benefits unless the employer's plan benefits a nondiscriminatory group of the employer's employees." 1986 Bluebook, supra note 59, at 781. For the definition of "line of business," see §414(r), discussed infra ¶61.2.

[87] IRC §89(a)(1). The excess benefit for each plan year is included in the employee's gross income for the taxable year that includes the last day of the plan year. IRC §89(a)(2).

[88] IRC §89(b)(1).

[89] IRC §89(k).

[90] According to S. Rep. No. 1622, 83d Cong., 2d Sess. 185, (1954) pre-1954 law was interpreted to tax employees on premiums paid by the employer on individual

functions in conjunction with §§104(a)(3) and 105(a); if the employer's contributions are not includable in the employee's gross income, benefits under the plan are subject to §105(a) rather than to §104(a)(3).

Since §106(a) only applies to contributions to "accident or health plans," premiums paid for a combination of accident and health coverage and other benefits must be unbundled.[91] Amounts attributable to other benefits are not excludable under §106, but might qualify for exclusion under some other provison (e.g., §79, relating to group-term life insurance).[92] Section 106(a) is also inapplicable to premiums paid for independent contractors and others who are not employees.[93]

¶13.2.10 Employer-Financed Accident and Health Benefits Paid Without Regard to a "Plan"

Section 105(a) provides, as a general rule, that amounts received by an employee through employer-financed accident or health insurance for personal injuries or sickness are taxable, unless the exclusions of §105(b), (c), or (d) apply. For this purpose, as explained earlier, the term "insurance" includes accident and health plans for employees that employers self-insure. Thus, §105 is an exhaustive provision for the payments described by §105(a).

Section 105 has no jurisdiction over accident and health benefits paid by an employer to an employee in the absence of "insurance" or a "plan." The status of such sporadic benefits can only be determined by an analysis of the circumstances leading to the payment itself. Among the possibilities are the following:

1. Additional compensation, taxable to the employee as such.[94]
2. A gift, excludable under §102 if motivated by affection or similar impulses rather than by a profit making purpose.[95]

---

policies, but not on premiums for group policies or contributions to state disability funds. See also Rev. Rul. 210, 1953-2 CB 114 (salesmen taxed on premiums paid by employer for individual accident insurance policies, where employer retained no incidents of ownership); Gordon, Tax Effects of Union Welfare Funds, 6 Tax L. Rev. 1, 46 et seq. (1950).

[91] Reg. §1.106-1. See supra ¶13.1.5 note 59.

[92] For §79, see infra ¶14.2.

[93] Rev. Rul. 56-400, 1956-2 CB 116 (employee status of commission salesmen determined by common law concepts or §7701(a)(20), relating to full-time life insurance salesmen). But see Rev. Rul. 85-121, 1985-2 CB 57 (laid-off worker is employee for this purpose); Rev. Rul. 82-196, 1982-2 CB 53 (exclusion allowed to retired employees and spouses and dependents of deceased employees).

[94] See Charlie Sturgill Motor Co. v. CIR, 32 TCM (CCH) 1336 (1973) (employer's payment of medical expenses treated as additional compensation).

[95] For §102, see supra ¶10.2.1.

3. Damages, excludable under §104(a)(2).[96]
4. A constructive dividend, if paid to a shareholder-employee or a shareholder's relative.[97]
5. An employee death benefit, excludable to the extent provided by §101(b).[98]

¶13.2.11 Continuation Coverage

Section 106(b), enacted in 1986, requires that employees covered by a group health plan and their covered spouses and dependents must be entitled to purchase a continuation of their coverage when events occur that would otherwise terminate the coverage.[99] Most commonly, the right to continuation coverage arises when an employee leaves an employer's service. Because the period of continuation is brief (18 or 36 months), a continuation of coverage under these rules serves as a bridge to coverage under some other plan or policy, not as an entitlement to remain in the employer's plan indefinitely. If a plan does not allow coverage continuation in all of the circumstances required, the employer loses its deduction for contributions to the plan,[100] and highly compensated employees are taxed on employer contributions made for their benefit.[101]

The requirements for continuation coverage are described below.

1. *Group health plan.* The coverage continuation requirement applies to any "group health plan," defined as a plan maintained by an employer (or a plan to which the employer contributes) that provides medical care for employees or their families through insurance, reimbursements, or otherwise.[102]

2. *Qualifying events and beneficiaries.* Continuation coverage must be offered in several situations.[103] If an employee's coverage would cease because of the termination of his employment or a reduction of his hours, the employee must be allowed to elect to continue his coverage; if the employee's spouse or dependents are covered by the plan, the election must apply

---

[96] For §104(a)(2), see supra ¶13.1.4.

[97] See Leidy's Est. v. CIR, 34 TCM (CCH) 1476 (1975), aff'd per curiam, 549 F.2d 798 (4th Cir. 1976).

[98] For §101(b), see supra ¶12.6.

[99] The requirements usually apply for plan years beginning after June 30, 1986. Pub. L. No. 99-272, §§1001(b), (e)(2), 100 Stat. 82 (1986). See generally Hamburger, New Law Makes Substantial Changes in Private Health Insurance Coverage Plans, 65 J. Tax'n 34 (1986).

[100] IRC §162(i)(2).

[101] IRC §106(b)(1).

[102] IRC §162(i)(3).

[103] IRC §§162(k)(1), (3), (7).

to their coverage as well.[104] A covered spouse or dependent must be offered continuation coverage if the employee dies or is divorced from the spouse. A continuation election must be available to a child who attains the age or status that would normally cause coverage to cease. If coverage for a dependent normally continues so long as the dependent is under age 21 or a full-time student, for example, the election must be available when the dependent becomes 21 or ceases being a student. Finally, a spouse or dependent is entitled to continuation coverage if the employee becomes entitled to Medicare benefits. There can be no requirement of insurability for any person entitled to continuation coverage.

3. *Nature of coverage.* If a qualifying employee, spouse, or dependent elects a continuation of coverage, the coverage must be identical to what would have been available under the plan if the event giving rise to the entitlement to continuation had not occurred.[105] The continuation must be available for at least 18 months if that event is termination of the employee's employment or a reduction of his hours; in other cases, coverage must be available for 36 months.[106] Coverage may cease, however, when the employee, spouse, or dependent (1) becomes a covered employee under some other group health plan, (2) is covered under a plan in which a new spouse participates, or (3) becomes eligible for Medicare benefits. Premiums may be charged for continuation coverage, and the coverage may be ended prematurely for failure to pay the premiums.

4. *Premiums.* The premiums charged for continuation coverage may not exceed 102 percent of the premiums in effect for equivalent coverage available to active employees. If the employer contributes for active employees, a purchaser of continuation coverage can be required to pay both the employer's and the employee's share of the premium. The purchaser must be allowed to pay the premiums in monthly installments.

5. *Election procedures.* A person eligible for continuation coverage must be allowed at least 60 days to elect the coverage,[107] and must be allowed at least 45 days after the election is made to pay the first premium.[108]

6. *Exception for small employers and churches.* A plan is excused from the coverage continuation requirement if, on "a typical business day during the preceding calendar year," the employer had no more than 20 employ-

---

[104] Continuation need not be allowed, however, if an employee is discharged "by reason of the employee's gross misconduct." IRC §162(k)(3)(B).

[105] IRC §162(k)(2).

[106] If the plan provides an option to convert to individual coverage, this option must be available to a purchaser of continuation coverage at the end of the 18- or 36-month period. IRC §162(k)(2)(E).

[107] IRC §162(k)(5).

[108] IRC §162(k)(2)(C).

ees.[109] Also, exemptions are provided for plans of governments, government agencies, churches, and conventions of churches.[110]

---

[109] IRC §§106(b)(2)(A), 162(i)(2)(B). If the plan is maintained by more than one employer, the 20-employee limit applies to them in the aggregate. Id.

[110] Id.

CHAPTER

14

Miscellaneous Employee Benefits

¶14.1 FRINGE BENEFITS

¶14.1.1 Introductory

According to §61(a)(1), all "compensation for services, including . . . fringe benefits" is gross income, "except as otherwise provided in this subtitle." The reference to fringe benefits was added in 1984, when Congress also enacted §132 to itemize those fringe benefits not swept into gross income. Section 132 excludes a fringe benefit from gross income if it consists of (1) a service that the employer regularly sells to its customers and is enjoyed by the employee without additional cost to the employer, (2) a discount on goods or services sold by the employer in the ordinary course of its business, (3) favorable working conditions, or (4) a benefit whose cost is too small to justify the burden of accounting for it. Subsequent sections of this chapter describe other exclusions for employee benefits.[1] A fringe benefit not excluded by §132 or some other explicit exclusionary rule is gross income.

Examples of taxable fringe benefits are employer-provided automobiles, airplane flights, country club memberships, and tickets to entertainment events that do not fit into any of the statutory exclusions.[2] The inclusionary rule of §61(a)(1) is not limited to benefits received by common law employees; it also applies to benefits provided to independent contractors and corporate directors who are not common law employees.[3] A taxable fringe benefit of an employee is treated as wages for withholding and other employment tax purposes.[4]

The amount of a taxable fringe benefit is its fair market value, less any amount the employee pays for it. If the benefit is partially excluded by §132 or some other statutory rule, a subtraction is also made for the excludable amount.[5] Generally, fair market value is the amount that would be paid for the benefit between unrelated parties dealing at arm's length.[6] The employee's subjective valuation of the benefit is not relevant even if the benefit's value to him is such that he uses it when provided for nothing but would not otherwise buy it. "The fair market value of a benefit may be substantially

---

[1] For other exclusions, see supra ¶11.2.1 (scholarship awards for employees of educational institutions and their spouses and dependents).

[2] Reg. §1.61-2T(a)(1).

[3] Reg. §1.61-2T(a)(4).

[4] Staff of Joint Comm. on Tax'n, 98th Cong, 2d Sess., General Explanation of the Revenue Provisions of the Deficit Reduction Act of 1984, at 843 (Comm. Print 1984) [hereinafter 1984 Bluebook].

[5] Reg. §1.61-2T(b)(1).

[6] Reg. §1.61-2T(b)(2).

greater than the cost to the employer of providing the benefit."[7] The regulations, however, provide mechanical rules for determining the values of some common benefits, including automobiles,[8] meals at an eating facility,[9] and airplane flights.[10]

A taxable fringe is taxable to "the person performing the services in connection with which the fringe benefit is provided."[11] If an employer provides an automobile for the personal use of a child of an employee, for example, the use value of the automobile is taxed to the employee, not the child.

Prior to the 1984 amendments, the tax status of fringe benefits furnished to employees and other persons performing personal services was veiled in uncertainty. On the one hand, the Supreme Court held in *CIR v. Glenshaw Glass Co.* that Congress intended "to tax all gains except those specifically exempted," and the regulations have long provided that if compensation for services is received in a form other than in money, the fair market value of the property or services must be included in income.[12] On the other hand, the IRS ruled as long ago as 1920 and 1921 that "supper

---

[7] 1984 Bluebook, supra note 4, at 864. However, "the inclusion of the fair market value amount in the employee's income does not allow the employer to deduct any amount in excess of the employer's cost of providing the benefit." Id.

[8] Three alternatives are provided for valuing an employee's personal use of an automobile furnished by his employer. First, the value of the use can be determined under a table based on the fair market value of the automobile when first made available to the employee. Reg. §1.61-2T(d). Second, if an automobile's fair market value does not exceed $12,800, the use value can be computed on a cents-per-mile basis. Reg. §1.61-2T(e); Notice 88-17, 1988-7 IRB 54. The value per mile under this alternative is the standard mileage allowance established for deduction purposes, less 5.5 cents per mile if the employee supplies the fuel. See infra ¶21.4.4 for the standard mileage allowance. Third, a flat $1.50 for each one-way commute may be used if (1) an employer supplies an automobile that for noncompensatory business reasons must be used by an employee in commuting to and from work and (2) the employee's personal use of the automobile is limited to commuting. Reg. §1.61-2T(f). See generally Brown & Smith, Valuation of Personal Use of Company Car Under Standard Mileage Allowance Rules, 64 J. Tax'n 348 (1986).

[9] Meals provided to employees at an eating facility operated by an employer can be valued at 150 percent of the direct costs incurred by the employer in providing the meals. Reg. §1.61-2T(j).

[10] Valuation rules are provided for flights on both commercial and noncommercial airplanes. Reg. §§1.61-2T (g), (h); Rev. Rul. 88-40, 1988-22 IRB 18 (Standard Industry Fare Level cents-per-mile rates and terminal charges used in valuing noncommercial flights on employer-provided aircraft).

[11] Reg. §1.61-2T(a)(4).

[12] CIR v. Glenshaw Glass Co., 348 US 426, 430 (1955), discussed supra ¶5.1; Reg. §1.61-2(d)(1). See also CIR v. Smith, 324 US 177, 181 (1945) (statutory predecessor of §61(a) "is broad enough to include in taxable income any economic or financial benefit conferred on the employee as compensation, whatever the form or mode by which it is effected").

money" paid to employees working overtime and travel passes issued to railroad employees and their families were not taxable.[13] Thus began an administrative practice under which, as the government has acknowledged, the value of employee fringe benefits "has not generally been considered income to the employees even if the employer's sole reason for providing them is to confer a benefit upon the employees — *e.g.*, provision of parking facilities, medical services, swimming pools, libraries, courtesy discounts, etc.," despite the absence of any express statutory exclusion for such receipts.[14]

This relaxed administrative approach to fringe benefits was never embodied in an official statement of the applicable rules or a catalog of excludable items. Only a few isolated rulings and litigated cases explicitly exempted fringe benefits from taxation, and they were matched in number by cases holding other benefits taxable.[15] The formal rulings and cases were only the tip of the iceberg. Most fringe benefits are not exposed to view. University life is especially rich in untaxed perquisites of office, supplied either without charge or at fees that, being subsidized by the employer, are below the

---

[13] OD 514, 2 CB 90 (1920) (supper money, not "considered additional compensation" or charged to salary account, is "paid for the convenience of the employer and for that reason does not represent taxable income to the employee"); OD 946, 4 CB 110 (1921) (railroad passes not provided pursuant to contracts of employment considered as gifts). In CIR v. Kowalski, 434 US 77 (1977), the Supreme Court cast doubt on, but left unsettled, the current validity of OD 514. The Court described OD 946 as "questionable" because it was "inconsistent with the position the Service has taken with regard to other economic benefits to employees or shareholders and their families," in Joint Comm. on Internal Revenue Tax'n, Examination of President Nixon's Tax Returns for 1969 Through 1972, H.R. Rep. No. 966, 93d Cong., 2d Sess. 159 (1974).

[14] Brief for US at 39, Rudolph v. US, 370 US 269 (1962), discussed infra ¶21.1.9. See also the preamble to a discussion draft on proposed regulations regarding fringe benefits, published in 1975, observing that the Code "does not provide specific rules for determining which economic benefits provided to employees by their employers are required to be included in gross income," and that "administrative practice over the years has permitted certain items to be excluded from the employees' income." 40 Fed. Reg. 41,118–19 (1975). The discussion draft was withdrawn in 1976.

[15] For exempted fringe benefits, see Rev. Rul. 59-58, 1959-1 CB 17 (value of turkey, ham, or other merchandise of nominal value distributed at Christmas or other holidays to employees to promote good relations not taxable; rule not applicable to cash, gift certificates, and other items with readily convertible cash value); Rev. Rul. 131, 1953-2 CB 112 (disaster relief to employees, based on need). With Rev. Rul. 59-58, compare Hallmark Cards, Inc. v. US, 200 F. Supp. 847 (WD Mo. 1961) ($15 and $25 merchandise certificates distributed to employees held tax-free gifts). For interest-free loans by employers to employees, see Crown v. CIR, 585 F2d 234 (7th Cir. 1978) (interest-free loans not subject to gift tax); Keller, The Tax Consequences of Interest-Free Loans From Corporations to Shareholders and From Employers to Employees, 29 BCL Rev. 231 (1978).

cost of comparable commercial facilities: meals in college dining halls and at faculty meetings; faculty club memberships; travel; family use of gymnasiums and other recreational facilities; parking lots; scholarships for children;[16] medical services; low-interest mortgage loans; low-rent faculty apartments and houses; course auditing privileges for spouses; personal use (authorized, tolerated by custom, or improper) of secretarial services, duplicating facilities, telephones, and postage; and tickets to concerts and sports events.[17]

The tension between the uncompromisingly broad language of the *Glenshaw Glass Co.* opinion and the facts of life resulted in an uneasy truce that occasionally broke into open conflict. A dramatic instance was the 1974 examination of President Nixon's tax returns by the Joint Committee on Internal Revenue Taxation, which led the Committee's staff to conclude that Mr. Nixon should have reported the value of the personal use of government planes by his family and friends, even if they occupied seats that would otherwise have been empty, and that the appropriate measure of value was the first-class commercial fare rather than charter rates or the actual cost of operating the government planes.[18] In reaching this conclusion, the staff report cited *Glenshaw Glass Co.*, acknowledged that "there is not presently an announced uniform official policy" regarding the personal use by employees of employer-owned facilities, and described as "questionable" the 1921 IRS ruling, which held that railroad employees realize no income when they or their families make use of free passes issued by the employer.

In 1975, the Treasury issued a "discussion draft" of proposed regulations governing the tax status of fringe benefits.[19] The draft, which might

---

[16] Reg. §1.117-3(a) (remitted tuition qualifies as scholarship); see supra ¶11.2.

[17] A few of these items, if included in gross income, might qualify as deductible business expenses if the employee itemizes deductions. Not being reported, however, they were rarely exposed to the rigors of audit.

[18] H.R. Rep. No. 966, supra note 13, at 157–68. The report also cites constructive distribution cases involving the use of corporate property by shareholders (see infra ¶92.2), as well as cases and rulings taxing employees and shareholders on economic benefits enjoyed by their friends and members of their families.

[19] Supra note 14. See statement of Donald C. Lubick, Assistant Secretary of the Treasury for Tax Policy, before the House Ways and Means Comm. (Task Force on Employee Fringe Benefits), 95th Cong., 2d Sess. (Aug. 14, 1978); Popkin, The Taxation of Employee Fringe Benefits, 22 BCL Rev. 439 (1981); Wasserman, Principles in Taxation of Nonstatutory Fringe Benefits, 32 Tax Lawyer 137 (1978); Note, Federal Income Taxation of Employee Fringe Benefits, 89 Harv. L. Rev. 1141 (1976); see also Macaulay, Fringe Benefits and Their Federal Tax Treatment (Columbia U. Press 1959) (survey of industrial practice and economic effects); ABA Tax Section, Recommendation No. 1979-7, 32 Tax Lawyer 468 (1978); Bittker, The Individual as Wage Earner, 11 NYU Inst. on Fed. Tax'n 1147 (1953); Guttentag, Leonard & Rodewald, Federal Income Taxation of Fringe Benefits: A Specific Pro-

have been impelled in part by the reference in the Nixon report to the absence of a comprehensive official policy in this area, would have confirmed the exclusion of employee fringe benefits where facilities, goods, or services made available to employees were (1) owned or controlled by the employer for business reasons unrelated to personal use or consumption by the employees, (2) available to employees on terms involving no substantial additional cost to the employer, and (3) available to employees generally or to groups of employees classified by reference to the nature of their work, seniority, or similar factors and not primarily limited to highly compensated employees. Benefits not meeting these conditions for exclusion could be excluded under a de minimis rule (embracing any amount "so small as to make accounting for it unreasonable or administratively impractical") or if all the facts and circumstances indicated that the benefit was not compensation. The "facts and circumstances" standard was augmented by a list of factors militating against taxability, such as the inability to identify the cost attributable to the benefit and the use of the benefit during business hours.

Caught in a heated cross fire between critics who found the proposed regulations too lenient and those who thought they were too severe, the Treasury withdrew its draft in 1976.[20] Congress responded by temporarily forbidding the Treasury to issue regulations on fringe benefits,[21] and a Task Force of the House Committee on Ways and Means was commissioned to propose legislation.[22]

Interest in the issue was heightened by the increased visibility of executive fringe benefits resulting from SEC disclosure rules, which embrace a broad spectrum of management perquisites, as indicated by the following 1977 SEC amendment:

Among the benefits received by management which the [SEC] believes should be reported as remuneration are payments made by registrants for the following purposes: (1) Home repairs and improvements; (2) housing and other living expenses (including domestic service) provided at principal and/or vacation residences of management

---

posal, 6 Nat'l Tax J. 250 (1953); Newman, Transferability, Utility, and Taxation, 30 U. Kan. L. Rev. 27 (1981).

[20] Withdrawal notice, 41 Fed. Reg. 56,334 (Dec. 20, 1976). For background see Hickman, The Outlook for Fringe Benefits, 1977 S. Cal. Tax Inst. 459.

[21] Pub. L. No. 95-427, 92 Stat. 963 (1978). The regulations freeze initially continued through 1980, but it was kept in effect until the enactment of the 1984 amendments. See Pub. L. No. 96-167, 93 Stat. 1275 (1979) (extending freeze through May 31, 1981); Pub. L. No. 97-34, 95 Stat. 172 (1981) (extending freeze through December 31, 1983); Ann. 84-5, 1984-4 IRB 31 (no regulations "altering the tax treatment of nonstatutory fringe benefits [to be issued] prior to January 1, 1985"; "present administrative practice will not be changed during this period").

[22] See H.R. Rep. No. 1232, 95th Cong., 2d Sess., reprinted in 1978-2 CB 365.

personnel; (3) the personal use of company property such as automobiles, planes, yachts, apartments, hunting lodges or company vacation houses; (4) personal travel expenses; (5) personal entertainment and related expenses; and (6) legal, accounting and other professional fees for matters unrelated to the business of the registrant. Other personal benefits which may be forms of remuneration are the following: the ability of management to obtain benefits from third parties, such as favorable bank loans and benefits from suppliers, because the corporation compensates, directly or indirectly, the bank or supplier for providing the loan or services to management; and the use of the corporate staff for personal purposes.

Certain incidental personal benefits which are directly related to job performance may be omitted from aggregate reported remuneration provided they are authorized and properly accounted for by the company. Parking places, meals at company facilities and office space and furnishings at company-maintained offices are a few examples of personal benefits directly related to job performance.[23]

¶14.1.2 Excludable Fringe Benefits

Section 132(a) excludes a fringe benefit from gross income if it is a "no-additional-cost service," "qualified employee discount," "working condition fringe," or "de minimis fringe."[24] Elsewhere within §132, an exclusion is provided for on-premises athletic facilities. These exclusions are described below.

1. *No-additional-cost service.* Section 132(a)(1) provides an exclusion for a "no-additional-cost service"—a service that meets the following requirements.[25] First, the service must be one offered for sale to customers in the ordinary course of the employer's business. The rule, for example, could apply to a seat on a commercial airline flight if the employer is a commercial airline, but a ride on an executive aircraft of an employer not in the airline business is not excluded, even if the flight would occur whether or not the employee were on board and even if the employee occupies a seat that would otherwise be vacant.

---

[23] 42 Fed. Reg. 43,060 (Aug. 18, 1977).
[24] See generally Shaller, The New Fringe Benefit Legislation: A Codification of Historical Inequities, 34 Cath. UL Rev. 425 (1985).
[25] IRC §132(b).

Second, the employee must be employed in the line of the employer's business in which this service is provided.[26] If an employer operates a commercial airline and also owns and operates hotels, for example, a trip on an airline flight provided to an employee of the hotel business cannot be a no-additional-cost service. "If an employee provides services that directly benefit more than one line of business of the employer, then the individual is treated as performing services in all such lines of business."[27] An example is a headquarters employee, who can receive no-additional-cost services from all of his employer's lines of business. "The purpose of the line of business limitation is to avoid . . . the competitive imbalances and inequities which would result from giving the employees of a conglomerate or other large employer with several lines of business a greater variety of tax-free benefits than could be given to the employees of a small employer with only one line of business."[28]

Finally, the employer must not incur any substantial additional expense or forgo any revenue in providing a no-additional-cost service to the employee.[29] The expense limitation is violated if "a substantial amount of time is spent by employees in providing a service for other employees," but not if the work done by other employees is "merely incidental to services provided to nonemployee customers."[30] An example of the latter are "in-flight services provided to an airline employee traveling on a standby ba-

---

[26] See Reg. §1.132-4T for more on the concept of line of business. Also, §§132(h)(6) and (g) provide specially for the application of the line of business requirement to airlines and their affiliates.

Some employers can elect to pay an excise tax under §4977 in lieu of complying with the line of business requirement. This election is available if, as of January 1, 1984, the employer furnished a no-additional-cost service produced in one of its lines of business to "substantially all" of its employees, including employees in other lines of business.

The excise tax on an electing employer is 30 percent of the employer's "excess fringe benefits." IRC §4977(a). Excess fringe benefits are computed by adding together the values of the no-additional-cost services and qualified employee discounts that are provided by the employer in ways that qualify for exclusion from employee gross income under §§132(a)(1) and (2) or that would so qualify but for the line of business requirement. From this sum is subtracted 1 percent of the taxable compensation paid by the employer to its employees. The result is "excess fringe benefits." IRC §4977(b). In effect, an electing employer is excused from the line of business requirement, but is subject to a penalty tax when the value of the fringe benefits normally subject to this requirement exceed 1 percent of payroll. Once made, an election under §4977 remains in effect until revoked by the employer, but IRS consent to a revocation is not needed. IRC §4977(d).

[27] 1984 Bluebook, supra note 4, at 846.

[28] Id. at 845.

[29] See Reg. §1.132-2T(a)(5) for more detail on the no additional-cost or forgone revenue rule.

[30] 1984 Bluebook, supra note 4, at 845.

sis."[31] The forgone revenue rule limits the exclusion to situations where employees are allowed "the benefit of excess capacity which otherwise would have remained unused because nonemployee customers would not have purchased it."[32] The rule can be satisfied by airlines, railroads, and subways that give employees seats "in such a way that nonemployee customers are not displaced."[33] Other employers who can comply with the rule are hotels that allow employees to use unrented rooms, and "telephone companies that provide telephone service to employees within existing capacity."[34]

When the foregoing requirements are met, "the exclusion applies whether the no-additional-cost service is provided directly for no charge or at a reduced price, or whether the benefit is provided through a cash rebate of all or part of any amount paid for the service."[35]

The exclusion is denied to a highly compensated employee unless the service is available to other employees on a nondiscriminatory basis. To satisfy this rule, the service must be "available on substantially the same terms to each member of a group of employees which is defined under a reasonable classification . . . which does not discriminate in favor of highly compensated employees."[36] An employee is considered highly compensated if he (1) is paid more than $75,000, (2) is among the most highly paid 20 percent of the employer's employees and receives an annual salary exceeding $50,000, or (3) has a greater than 5 percent equity interest in the employer as shareholder, proprietor, or partner.[37]

Whether a classification is reasonable and free of the prohibited discrimination depends on the facts and circumstances. "A classification that, on its face, makes benefits available only to . . . highly compensated employees . . . is per se discriminatory," however.[38] A classification might pass muster in a particular case, in contrast, if it is "based on certain appropriate factors, such as seniority, full-time vs. part-time employment, or job description."[39] In testing a classification, several classes of employees made ineligible by the classification are ignored, including any employee who (1) has worked less than a year for the employer, (2) works part-time, or (3) is under age 21.[40] If a no-additional-cost service is available to all em-

---

[31] Id.
[32] Id. at 844.
[33] Id. at 845.
[34] Id.
[35] Id. at 844.
[36] IRC §132(h)(1).
[37] IRC §§132(h)(7), 414(q). The definition of highly compensated is described more fully in ¶61.2.
[38] 1984 Bluebook, supra note 4, at 861.
[39] Id.
[40] Id.; IRC §89(h). See supra ¶13.2.8 for more detail on these exclusions.

ployees except those with less than one year of service, for example, the service is deemed available to all employees, and the nondiscrimination test is passed.

The exclusion for no-additional-cost services can include services received from a person other than the employer if the services are provided pursuant to a reciprocal agreement between the employer and the provider of the service.[41] If a group of airlines agrees to let all employees ride free in vacant seats on each other's flights, for example, the exclusion can apply when an employee of one of the airlines rides on a flight of another airline participating in the arrangement. Generally, the exclusion applies in such a case if it would apply were the flight on the employee's own airline. Among other things, the service must be in the same line of business as the employer for whom the employee works. The exclusion cannot be made available, for example, by a reciprocal arrangement between an airline and a hotel chain.

The exclusion only applies to benefits provided to employees. Section 132(f), however, defines the term "employee" to include several classes of persons who are not actually employees. A retired employee, for example, is treated as an employee in the line of business of the employer he worked for just before retirement. A surviving spouse of an employee or retired employee is also treated as an employee in the line of business in which the employee last worked. The regulations further provide that a partner who performs services for his partnership is considered an employee.[42]

Also, a service provided to a spouse or dependent child of an employee is treated as though it had been furnished to the employee.[43] If an employee's spouse rides free on the airline that the employee works for, the flight is considered a benefit to the employee, and this benefit is excluded if an identical benefit to the employee would be excludable. Further, a use of air transportation by a parent of an employee is treated as the employee's use.[44]

2. Qualified employee discount. Section 132(a)(2) excludes a qualified employee discount from an employee's income. This exclusion is provided because "employers often have valid business reasons, other than simply providing compensation, for encouraging employees to avail themselves of the products which those employees sell to the public."[45] A retail clothing

---

[41] IRC §132(g)(2).

[42] Reg. §1.132-1T(b)(1).

[43] IRC §132(f)(2). A child is a dependent if the employee is entitled to a dependency exemption under §151(c). See infra ¶30.3 for dependency exemptions. A child of divorced parents, however, is considered a dependent of both parents if either parent is entitled to the exemption. A deceased employee's orphan child is considered a dependent for this purpose until he reaches age 25.

[44] IRC §132(f)(3).

[45] 1984 Bluebook, supra note 4, at 840.

business, for example, probably benefits when sales personnel wear its clothing, rather than that of its competitors. In a particular case, however, the exclusion is available whether or not any such benefits to the business can be shown.

To be qualified, an employee discount must satisfy several requirements. First, it must be allowed in a purchase of goods or services of a type that the employer offers for sale in the ordinary course of its business.[46] The exclusion is not allowable on goods or services that an employer sells regularly, but primarily to employees.

Also, a discount on a purchase of goods or services is only qualified if the employee is employed in the line of business in which the item is ordinarily sold.[47] For this purpose, a department store is considered to have only one line of business, and an employee working in catalogue sales is in the same line of business as those selling on the floor, and vice versa.[48] The exclusion can apply even if the employer does not sell at retail. A worker on an assembly line, for example, can have a qualified employee discount on assembled goods that normally are only sold to wholesalers.

The nondiscrimination rule described previously for no-additional-cost services also applies to qualified employee discounts.[49] "For example, if an employer offers a 20-percent discount . . . to rank-and-file employees and a 35-percent discount to the highly compensated group, the entire value of the 35-percent discount (not just the excess over 20 percent) is includible in gross income."[50]

Finally, the employee discount exclusion can never apply to discounts on employee purchases of real property and property usually held for investment.[51] The exclusion is thus inapplicable to "discounts on any employee purchases of securities, commodities, . . . residential real estate, commercial real estate, or interests in mineral-producing property."[52] This ban does not apply, however, to services in connection with the purchase of an investment asset or real property. If an employer in the business of selling such property on commission allows employees to purchase commission

---

[46] IRC §§132(c)(3), (4). If a section of a department store is leased to an independent operator whose separate identity is not readily apparent to customers, employees of the department store may have excludable discounts on purchases in the leased section, and employees of the lessee who work in the leased space can have excludable discounts in the department store. 1984 Bluebook, supra note 4, at 855; Reg. §1.132-3T(d).

[47] Section 4977 sometimes allows employers to elect to pay an excise tax in lieu of complying with the line of business requirement. See supra note 26.

[48] 1984 Bluebook, supra note 4, at 851.

[49] See supra text accompanying notes 36–40.

[50] 1984 Bluebook, supra note 4, at 861.

[51] Id. at 849; Reg. §1.132-3T(a)(2).

[52] 1984 Bluebook, supra note 4, 849–50.

Section 132(f)'s expansive definition of "employee," discussed above in connection with no-additional-cost services, applies as well to employee discounts.[59] The rule allowing employers to reciprocate in providing no-additional-cost services, however, has no analogue in the employee discount rules.

3. *Working condition fringe.* Section 132(a)(3) excludes a "working condition fringe" from an employee's gross income. An item of property or a service provided by an employer is a working condition fringe if the employee could deduct or depreciate the cost of the property or service had the cost been paid by the employee rather than the employer.[60] An employee's use of an employer-owned automobile (or corporate jet) in the course of the employee's duties is an example of a working condition fringe. If an employer furnishes an automobile for an employee to use for both business and personal purposes, in contrast, the working condition exclusion only applies to the business use.[61] Other examples of excludable working condition fringes are subscriptions to business periodicals for employees, reimbursements of dues for professional organizations, and on the job training and travel.[62] Examples of benefits not excludable as working condition fringes are the payment of a real estate broker's commission in a house sale made in connection with a move to a new work location, and supper money and cab fare for employees working overtime.[63]

Where a product produced by the employer is used by an employee for the purpose of testing or evaluating the product, the working condition fringe exclusion applies, but only if an elaborate set of requirements is satisfied.[64] For example, the employer must be able to deduct the costs of the testing as a business expense other than employee compensation, the tested item (if not consumed in the test) must be available for the employee's use

---

[59] See supra text accompanying notes 42–44.

[60] IRC §132(d). Thus, any substantiation requirement that would apply to an employee expenditure (e.g., under §162, §274(d), or §280F) must also be satisfied if an employer expenditure is to be excluded as a working condition fringe. 1984 Bluebook, supra note 4, at 855; Reg. §§1.132-5T(c), (e)(1)(i). See infra ¶¶20.19 and 21.4 for substantiation requirements.

[61] See Reg. §1.132-5T(b) for allocation rules used in such a case. "Merely incidental personal use of a company car, such as a small detour for a personal errand while on a business trip, might qualify for exclusion as a de minimis fringe, but regular personal use (e.g., after business hours or on weekends) or use on vacation trips cannot qualify for an exclusion." 1984 Bluebook, supra note 4, at 856.

[62] Id.

[63] Id. In the real estate commission case, the employee might get a deduction under §217 (infra ¶22.4). Also, "occasional supper money, taxi fare, or parking expense reimburements because of overtime work may be excludable as de minimis fringes." 1984 Bluebook, supra note 4, at 856.

[64] Id. at 856–57; Reg. §1.132-5T(n).

only so long as the test requires, and the employee must submit detailed reports on his use of the product.

The statute bends the basic definition of working condition fringe in a few cases. Employee parking "on or near the business premises of the employer" is a working condition fringe, even though an employee's parking expense, if he paid it himself, would be a nondeductible commuting expense.[65] Also, if a full-time automobile salesperson has the use of an automobile, the use may be considered a working condition fringe, even if the car is sometimes used outside the course of the employee's work. This extension of the rule applies if (1) the use is limited to the "sales area in which the automobile dealer's sales office is located," (2) the use is provided "primarily to facilitate the salesman's performance of services for the employer," and (3) there are "substantial restrictions" on personal use.[66]

The exclusion for working condition fringes is not limited by a nondiscrimination rule. Parking for executives, for example, is an excludable fringe benefit even if parking is not furnished to rank and file employees.

An excludable working condition fringe cannot be provided to a person other than an employee. The term "employee," however, is defined to include partners performing services for their partnerships; for some fringes, corporate directors who are not common law employees and independent contractors who perform services are also treated as employees.[67]

4. *De minimis fringe.* Section 132(a)(4) excludes a "de minimis fringe" from employee gross income. An employer-provided benefit is a de minimis fringe if the value of the benefit is "so small as to make accounting for it unreasonable or administratively impracticable."[68] In comparing a benefit's value with the burden of accounting for it, the frequency "with which similar fringes are provided by the employer" is taken into account. Some examples of de minimis fringes:

> the occasional typing of personal letters by a company secretary, occasional personal use of the company copying machine, transit passes or tokens provided at discounts not exceeding a total of $15 per

---

[65] IRC §132(h)(4). See Reg. §1.132-5T(p).

[66] IRC §132(h)(3). See Reg. §1.132-5T(o). "For example, if an auto salesperson is required to have a car available for showing to customers during working hours, is required to drive the make of car which the auto dealer sells, is limited in the amount of miles he or she may drive the car, may not store personal possessions in the car, and is prohibited from using the car for vacation trips, then use of the car in the described sales area qualifes as a working condition fringe." 1984 Bluebook, supra note 4, at 858.

[67] Reg. §1.132-1T(b)(2). Independent contractors are not eligible for the parking exclusion, and neither independent contractors nor nonemployee corporate directors can exclude the use of consumer goods under a product testing program. Id.

[68] IRC §132(e)(1).

month . . . occasional company cocktail parties or picnics for employees, occasional supper money or taxi fare because of overtime work, traditional gifts on holidays of tangible personal property having a low fair market value (e.g., a turkey given for the year-end holidays), occasional theatre or sporting event tickets, and coffee and doughnuts furnished to employees.[69]

Any such benefit, however, can lose its exclusion if provided too frequently —if, for example, "traditional holiday gifts are provided to employees each month, or if sandwiches are provided free-of-charge to employees on a regular basis."[70]

Under certain circumstances, an employer's subsidization of an eating facility for employees can be a de minimis fringe. The exclusion applies to such a facility if (1) the employer charges for meals, (2) its revenues from the facility annually equal or exceed direct operating costs, and (3) the facility is available to all employees on a nondiscriminatory basis or to a group defined without discrimination in favor of highly compensated employees.[71] The facility can be operated with the employer's employees or by a food service business under contract with the employer.[72]

The de minimis exclusion only applies to benefits provided in kind. A cash payment to an employee does not qualify for the exclusion, regardless of how small it is or how difficult accounting for it can be.[73] Only employees may receive de minimis fringes; this exclusion may not apply to a benefit to a former employee, or a spouse or dependent of a present or former employee. Except in its application to eating facilities, however, the exclusion is not limited by a nondiscrimination rule; a fringe only provided to executives can qualify as de minimis fringe.

5. *On-premises athletic facilities.* The use value of an employer-provided gym or other athletic facility is excluded from an employee's gross income if (1) the facility is located on the premises of the employer, (2) the facility is operated by the employer,[74] and (3) substantially all of the use of the facility is by employees, spouses, and dependents.[75] Examples of facili-

---

[69] 1984 Bluebook, supra note 4, at 858–59.

[70] Id. at 859.

[71] Reg. §1.132-7T. The nondiscrimination rule is applied by aggregating all employees who work at or near the premises of the eating facility, including employees of related employers. Reg. §1.132-8T(b)(2).

[72] 1984 Bluebook, supra note 4, at 859 n.87.

[73] Reg. §1.132-6T(d).

[74] An employer is the operator of an athletic facility if it "operates the facilities through its own employees, or . . . contracts out the actual operation (e.g., maintenance and supervision of exercise equipment) to an outside business." 1984 Bluebook, supra note 4, at 859 n.88.

[75] IRC §132(h)(5). See Reg. §1.132-1T(e).

ties that can qualify are "swimming pools, gyms and exercise rooms, tennis courts, and golf courses."[76] The premises-of-the-employer requirement demands only that the employer be the owner or lessee of the facility, not that the facility be located on the business premises of the employer. This requirement is not met, however, by "a facility for residential use" or a country club membership.[77]

6. *Requirement of written plan.* For years after 1988, a fringe benefit otherwise excludable under §132 is taxed unless the benefit is provided under a written plan that satisfies all of the following requirements:[78] Each employee's rights under the plan must be legally enforceable; employees must be given reasonable notice of the plan's benefits; the plan must be maintained for the exclusive benefit of the employees; and the employer must intend, when the plan is adopted, to keep it in effect indefinitely.

¶14.2 GROUP-TERM LIFE INSURANCE

¶14.2.1 Introductory

Section 79 excludes from an employee's gross income the cost of up to $50,000 in group-term life insurance on the employee's life under a policy carried directly or indirectly by the employer; it requires, however, that the cost of employer-provided coverage in excess of $50,000 be reported as gross income.[1] Because the §79 exclusion is confined to insurance on the life of "an employee," it does not embrace insurance on partners, self-employed persons, or members of the employee's family.[2] The exclusion can, however,

---

[76] 1984 Bluebook, supra note 4, at 860.

[77] Id.

[78] IRC §89(k).

[1] See Rev. Rul. 73-174, 1973-1 CB 43 (employee taxed on amounts paid by employer for coverage above $50,000, despite irrevocable assignment of rights under policy).

Enacted in 1964, the limited exclusion of §79 replaced an unlimited exclusion previously allowed under the regulations. Reg. §1.61-2(d)(2) (as of 1963). See S. Rep. No. 830, 88th Cong., 2d Sess., reprinted in 1964-1 (Part 2) CB 505, 549; Conf. Rep. No. 1149, 88th Cong., 2d Sess., reprinted in 1964-1 (Part 2) CB 774, 794. See generally Bruttomesso, Group-Term Life Insurance Plans, 46 J. Tax'n 182 (1977).

[2] See Reg. §1.79-0 (incorporating by reference the employer-employee relationship rules of §3401(c), discussed infra ¶111.4.2, and excluding independent contractors and self-employed persons); Reg. §1.79-3(f)(2) (cost of insurance on life of employee's spouse or other relatives not exempted by §79); Enright v. CIR, 56 TC 1261 (1971) (director-employee taxed on premiums paid on directors' group-term life insurance by corporation having separate plan for employees); but see Reg. §1.61-2(d)(2)(ii)(b) (cost of no more than $2,000 of coverage on life of employee's spouse or child disregarded as "incidental").

apply to coverage for a former employee.[3]

Since 1983, §79 has been qualified by rules, described in the next section of this chapter, which deny the §79 exclusion, in whole or part, when a group-term life insurance discriminates in favor of key or highly compensated employees. Apart from the nondiscrimination rules, the principal features of §79 are:

1. *Group-term insurance.* The regulations define the term "group-term life insurance" to mean insurance that (1) provides a death benefit qualifying for exclusion under §101(a),[4] (2) covers a group of employees, (3) is provided under a policy carried by the employer, directly or indirectly, and (4) is in an amount determined without "individual election."[5] The last of these requirements does not demand that coverage in an identical dollar amount be provided for every participant in the plan; coverage in amounts determined by a formula is acceptable if the formula is "based on factors such as age, years of service, compensation, or position."[6] The amount of insurance can also vary depending on whether the employee chooses to contribute toward its cost.

If the plan does not provide coverage for at least 10 full-time employees at some time during the calendar year, it must meet still stricter standards:[7] Insurance must be provided to all employees who satisfy the policy's insurability standards, excepting employees with less than six months of service, part-time and seasonal employees who work less than 20 hours per week or five months per year, those over age 65, and nonparticipants who chose not to make contributions required for participation.[8] Insurability must be determined by a medical questionnaire, without a physical examination. The amount of insurance for each employee must either be a uniform percentage of compensation or must be based on "coverage brackets

---

[3] IRC §79(e). This rule applies for taxable years after 1983.

[4] See supra ¶12.2.1.

[5] Reg. §1.79-1(a). See Whitcomb v. CIR, 81 TC 505 (1983), aff'd, 733 F2d 191 (1st Cir. 1984) (plan providing $1 million of insurance for any president or retired president with at least 25 years of service did not preclude individual selection because only one person qualified or could reasonably be expected to qualify); Towne v. CIR, 78 TC 791 (1982) (plan providing insurance of $525,000 for president and lesser of one year's salary or $25,000 for other employees failed individual selection test).

[6] Reg. §1.79-1(a).

[7] Reg. §1.79-1(c). These additional requirements do not apply to insurance sponsored by a union or professional organization if it is provided under a common plan of two or more employers and insurability is not a criterion for participation. Reg. §1.79-1(c)(3). See Rev. Rul. 80-220, 1980-2 CB 35 (finding plan covering fewer than 10 employees not qualified).

[8] Reg. §§1.79-1(c)(2), (4), (5).

established by the insurer."[9]

2. *Term life insurance.* Since §79 applies only to "term life insurance," the cost of providing cash surrender values, paid-up insurance, and similar benefits does not qualify for the exclusion; nor does the cost of insuring against hazards other than death, such as accidents and sickness.[10] A provision permitting employees to convert or continue their term insurance after the employer ceases to pay the premiums, however, does not result in disqualification.

Further, a policy providing permanent insurance can qualify under §79 if the policy or the employer designates the portion of the death benefit that is group-term life insurance.[11] In this case, the cost of the permanent benefit is computed by a complex formula given in the regulations, and is included in the employee's gross income.[12] The portion of the death benefit designated as group-term life insurance must equal or exceed the difference between the entire death benefit and the amount determined to be permanent insurance under the regulation's formula.

3. *Employee contributions.* When employer and employee both contribute toward the cost of group-term coverage, §79 only applies to the employer's contribution; the employee's contribution is a consumption purchase that has no tax consequence. An employee contribution is applied first against the coverage above $50,000.[13] Thus, if a $75,000 policy costs $1,500 per year, of which the employee pays $200, the employer's payment of the remaining $1,300 is tax free to the extent of $1,000 (the cost of $50,000 of coverage) and taxable to the extent of $300 ($500, the cost of the excess $25,000 of insurance, less the employee's $200 contribution, which is wholly allocated to this portion of the policy).

4. *Unlimited coverage.* An unlimited exclusion is provided for three classes of group-term life insurance policies: (1) insurance on the lives of employees who retired on disability;[14] (2) policies whose proceeds are paya-

---

[9] Reg. §1.79-1(c)(2).

[10] Reg. §1.79-3(f). See also Rev. Proc. 79-29, 1979-1 CB 571 (procedure for separating excludable cost of qualifying term coverage from taxable cost of permanent benefits).

For the exclusion of the cost of accident and health insurance from the employee's gross income under §106, discussed supra ¶13.2.7, see Reg. §1.79-3(f)(3).

[11] Reg. §1.79-1(b). For the distinction between term and permanent life insurance, see Rev. Rul. 71-360, 1971-2 CB 87; Rev. Rul. 75-91, 1975-1 CB 39.

[12] Reg. §1.79-1(d).

[13] See Reg. §1.79-3(e).

[14] Before 1984, the statute allowed the unlimited exclusion for all retired employees. The 1984 amendments, however, also added §79(e), which defines "employee" to include former employees. A retired employee thus can be covered under a group-term plan, but is subject to the same $50,000 cap as active employees unless he is disabled.

ble to the employer or a qualified charitable organization; and (3) insurance that is part of an asset of a qualified employee pension or profit sharing plan.[15]

5. *Cost of excess coverage.* If an employee's coverage under a group-term life insurance exceeds $50,000, the premium cost of the excess is gross income. The cost of the excess is determined under a table prescribed by the Treasury, and need not equal the employer's actual cost.[16] The table costs were formerly substantially less than actual costs, and thus effectively provided a partial exclusion for the cost of the coverage over $50,000. Congress, however, directed in 1982 that "the tables be periodically revised to reflect current group-term life insurance costs."[17] The present table was promulgated in 1983 in response to this directive.

6. *Requirement of written plan.* For years after 1988, a group-term life insurance plan must be in writing and must further satisfy all of the following requirements:[18] Each employee's rights under the plan must be legally enforceable; employees must be given reasonable notification of the plan's benefits; the plan must be maintained for the exclusive benefit of the employees; and the employer must intend, when the plan is adopted, to keep it in effect indefinitely. If these requirements are not met, every employee must report as gross income the entire value of his benefits under the plan.

¶14.2.2 Nondiscrimination Rules

For taxable years after 1983, the §79 exclusion is denied, in whole or part, to key or highly compensated employees participating in group-term plans that discriminate in their favor. For years after 1988, group-term life insurance plans are subject to the nondiscrimination rules of §89, which are summarized briefly below and are described more fully elsewhere.[19] For the years 1984 through 1987, nondiscrimination rules are provided by §79(d),

---

Under a liberal transition rule, the unlimited exclusion continues to apply indefinitely to a nondisabled retired employee if he (1) retired before 1984, (2) attained age 55 before 1984, retired before 1987, and receives his coverage under a plan that was in effect during 1983, or (3) attained age 55 before 1984, retires after 1986, and is covered by a plan that existed during 1983 and meets the nondiscrimination rules in all years after 1986. See Reg. §1.79-4T(A-1).

[15] IRC §79(b). See Whitcomb v. CIR, 81 TC 505 (1983), aff'd, 733 F2d 191 (1st Cir. 1984) (§79(b) only applies if insurance provided under plan satisfying regulation's definition of group-term life insurance).

[16] IRC §79(c); Reg. §1.79-3(d)(2).

[17] Staff of Joint Comm. on Tax'n, 97th Cong., 2d Sess., General Explanation of the Revenue Provisions of the Tax Equity and Fiscal Responsibility Act of 1982, at 328 (Comm. Print 1982).

[18] IRC §89(k).

[19] Supra ¶13.2.8.

which is described below. No nondiscrimination rules apply for years prior to 1984.

1. *Rules for 1984 through 1987.* For the taxable years 1984 through 1987, a key employee who is covered by a discriminatory group-term life insurance plan must report the entire cost of his coverage as gross income.[20] The cost of the coverage, further, is the greater of actual cost or cost determined under the table usually used for determining coverage cost under §79.[21]

A group-term life insurance plan exhibits the forbidden discrimination if it discriminates in favor of key employees in defining either the classes of employees eligible to participate or the type or amount of benefits.[22] The term "key employee" includes any employee who, during the current year or one of the preceding four years, was (1) an officer whose compensation exceeds $45,000, (2) an owner of more than 5 percent of the employer's stock, or (3) a greater than 1 percent shareholder with compensation exceeding $150,000.[23]

A plan is considered nondiscriminatory as to eligibility if it meets one of four tests.[24] Specifically, a plan passes muster in this respect if (1) it covers at least 70 percent of the employer's employees, (2) at least 85 percent of the participants in the plan are not key employees, (3) the plan sets up eligibility criteria that are found not to discriminate in favor of key employees, or (4) the group-term coverage is provided in a cafeteria plan that meets all requirements for cafeteria plans.[25] In applying these tests, several categories of employees can be excluded from consideration, including (1) those with less than three years of service with the employer, (2) part-time and seasonal employees,[26] and (3) unionized employees whose collective bargaining representative has bargained with the employer on the subject of group-term life insurance benefits.

To be free of the forbidden discrimination as to benefits, any benefit available to a key employee must be available to all participants who are not

---

[20] IRC §79(d)(1) (before amendment in 1986). For more detail on the effective date of these rules, see Reg. §1.79-4T.

[21] Rules for determining actual cost are given in Reg. §1.79-4T(A-6).

[22] IRC §79(d)(2) (before amendment in 1986). For rules requiring an aggregation of separate policies on key employees in certain cases, see Reg. §1.79-4T(A-5).

[23] IRC §79(d)(6) (before amendment in 1986); §416(i). This definition is described more fully in ¶61.2.12.

[24] IRC §79(d)(3) (before amendment in 1986).

[25] See infra ¶14.9 for cafeteria plans.

[26] An employee is part-time if his customary work week is 20 hours or less, or is seasonal if he customarily works for no more than five months each year. Staff of Joint Comm. on Tax'n, 97th Cong, 2d Sess, General Explanation of the Revenue Provisions of the Tax Equity and Fiscal Responsibility Act of 1982, at 328 (1982).

key employees.[27] The amount of insurance, however, need not be constant for all employees; it is not discriminatory for a plan to provide death benefits that are proportional to compensation, and compensation can be defined as total compensation or the basic or regular rate of compensation.[28] A nondiscriminatory plan might, for example, provide a death benefit equal to two times the employee's annual compensation. Also, if a plan allows employees to purchase additional coverage above a minimum prescribed for all participants, the additional coverage is ignored if the employees pay its full cost.[29]

The plans and employees of commonly controlled employers are aggregated in applying the foregoing rules.[30] If the plan covers former employees, in contrast, the rules are applied separately to former and present employees, but the entire plan fails if it is discriminatory in its application to either group.[31]

2. *Rules for years after 1988.* For taxable years after 1988, a group-term life insurance plan must meet the detailed nondiscrimination rules found in §89.[32] These rules include several eligibility requirements and a benefit requirement. The eligibility requirements demand that plan benefits be made available to nearly all employees at levels no less than one half of those provided to the most favored highly compensated employee. If not all eligible employees participate in the plan, at least half of the participants must not be highly compensated or, if this test cannot be met, participation rates must be no higher for highly compensated employees than for the others. The benefit requirement is that the average plan benefit for nonhighly compensated employees must be at least 75 percent of the average benefit for the highly compensated. All employees, including those who do not participate in the plan, are included in computing these averages.

If the eligibility and benefit requirements are not satisfied, otherwise excludable benefits of highly compensated employees are taxed, in whole or in part. The taxable amounts are determined by asking, "How much would benefits for the highly compensated employees have to be reduced to bring the plan into compliance with the nondiscrimination rules?" Each highly compensated employee is taxed on the cost of the portion of his plan benefit that is eliminated in this hypothetical reduction, even if this cost would otherwise be excluded under §79.

---

[27] IRC §79(d)(4) (before amendment in 1986).

[28] IRC §79(d)(5) (before amendment in 1986).

[29] Reg. §1.79-4T(A-10).

[30] IRC §79(d)(7) (before amendment in 1986).

[31] IRC §79(d)(8) (before amendment in 1986); Reg. §1.79-4T(A-7).

[32] Section 89 is described more fully in ¶13.2.8 in its application to accident and health plans.

¶14.3 GROUP LEGAL SERVICES

As an incentive to the establishment of prepaid legal services plans, Congress enacted §120 in 1976, which excludes from a participating employee's gross income both his employer's contributions to a qualified group legal services plan and benefits received under the plan. These benefits can consist of legal services performed for the employee or his spouse or dependents, or they can be payments of the employee's legal bills or reimbursements of the employee's payments. A qualified plan must conform to rules designed to "prohibit discrimination and minimize the possibility of abuse of the tax incentive by . . . plans to channel otherwise taxable compensation through a plan providing a tax-free fringe benefit."[1] The §120 exclusion does not embrace direct payments from employer to employee, nor does it affect an employer's right to deduct contributions to a legal services plan (whether qualified under §120 or not) as business expenses under §162.[2]

Section 120 expired by its terms at the end of 1987.[3] The provision was enacted for a five-year trial period (1977 through 1982), but its life was subsequently extended three times.[4] The last extension was enacted in 1986 "to permit Treasury to complete its evaluations of the effect of these exclusions based on the information reports that employers are . . . required to file [for years after 1984]."[5] A resurrection of the provision is distinctly possible.

To qualify under §120, a group legal services plan must meet the following conditions:

1. *Coverage.* The arrangement must be a "separate written plan of an employer for the exclusive benefit of his employees or their spouses or dependents"[6] to "provide personal legal services" through an employer's prepayment of legal fees or other advance provision for such services. The term "personal legal services" implies a distinction between personal and

---

[1] Staff of Joint Comm. on Tax'n, 94th Cong., 2d Sess., General Explanation of the Tax Reform Act of 1976, reprinted in 1976-3 CB (Vol. 2) 681. See generally Litwin, Designing a Qualified Group Legal Services Plan, 56 Taxes 123 (1978).

[2] For the deductibility of compensation for personal services, see infra ¶22.2.

[3] IRC §120(e).

[4] See Pub. L. No. 97-34, §802(a), 95 Stat. 170 (1981) (extending §120's life through 1984); Pub. L. No. 98-612, §1(a), 98 Stat. 3180 (1984) (extending through 1985); Pub. L. No. 99-514, §1162(b), 100 Stat. 2085 (1986) (extending through 1987).

[5] Staff of Joint Comm. on Tax'n, 99th Cong., 2d Sess., General Explanation of Tax Reform Act of 1986, at 818 (Comm. Print 1986). For the information reporting requirement, see infra text accompanying note 18.

[6] "Dependent" is used by §120 as defined by §152. IRC §120(d)(4). As explained in ¶30.3.1, the term can include many persons for whom the taxpayer is not entitled to claim a dependency exemption. "Spouse" is not defined, but see §143.

business problems, but is not otherwise defined. The term "employee" is defined to include partners and proprietors who have earned income from their partnerships and proprietorships.[7] A plan of a partnership or proprietorship thus can cover its owners if they are active in the business, as well as the common law employees of the business. Also, a plan can cover the employees of two or more employers.

2. *Discrimination and eligibility.* A qualified group legal services plan cannot discriminate in either contributions or benefits in favor of highly compensated employees.[8] An employee is considered highly compensated if he (1) is paid more than $75,000, (2) is among the most highly paid 20 percent of the employer's employees and receives an annual salary exceeding $50,000, or (3) has a greater than 5 percent equity interest in the employer as shareholder, proprietor, or partner.[9] Also, the plan must either benefit all employees or set up eligibility critera that the IRS finds free of discrimination in favor of the highly compensated.[10] In lieu of complying with these rather general proscriptions, an employer can elect to subject its plan to an elaborate set of nondiscrimination rules found in §89, which are described elsewhere in this work.[11]

3. *Contributions for shareholders and their relatives.* Not more than 25 percent of the amounts contributed during a taxable year may be provided for shareholder-employees, partners, or proprietors holding greater than 5 percent equity interests in the employer. Amounts contributed for spouses and dependents of these owner-employees are also counted against the 25 percent cap. Stock ownership is determined with the constructive ownership rules of §§1563(d) and (e), and the Treasury is authorized to promulgate similar rules for determining the ownership of unincorporated businesses.[12]

The 25 percent restriction limits qualification, not the amount that can be deducted by the employer; if violated, the contributions and benefits do not qualify for exclusion under §120, but the entire amount might be de-

[7] IRC §§120(d)(1), 401(c)(1). For this purpose, a partnership is the employer of its partners, and a sole proprietor is his own employer. IRC §120(d)(2).

[8] IRC §120(c)(1). For taxable years before 1988, the provision bans discrimination in favor of officers, shareholders, self-employed persons, or highly compensated employees.

[9] IRC §§120(c)(1), 414(q). The definition of highly compensated is described more fully in ¶61.2.2.

[10] For comparable but much more elaborate prohibitions on discrimination by qualified pension and profit-sharing plans, see infra ¶61.2.1.

[11] Supra ¶13.2.8.

[12] IRC §120(d)(6). For constructive ownership, see infra ¶93.1.7. The rules of §§1563(d) and (e) are modified to disregard §1563(e)(3)(C), relating to stock owned by employee benefit trusts.

ductible as a business expense if reasonable relative to the services rendered by the favored employees.

4. *Disposition of contributions.* Benefits under a qualified group legal services plan cannot be paid directly to employees; contributions must be paid to an intermediary that either performs legal services or pays legal costs incurred by participating employees. Specifically, employer contributions must be paid to one or more of the following: (1) an insurance company, (2) an organization providing personal legal services for prepayment, (3) an organization providing indemnification against the cost of legal services for a premium, or (3) a tax-exempt organization that serves as intermediary between employers and organizations providing group legal services or indemnification against the costs of these services.[13]

5. *Requirement of written plan.* For years after 1988, a group legal services plan must be in writing, and must further satisfy all of the following requirements:[14] Each employee's rights under the plan must be legally enforceable; employees must be given reasonable notification of the plan's benefits; the plan must be maintained for the exclusive benefit of employees; and the employer must intend, when the plan is adopted, to keep it in effect indefinitely. If these requirements are not met, every employee must report as gross income the entire value of his benefits under the plan.

6. *Notification.* The plan must apply to the IRS for recognition as a qualified group legal services plan.[15] If notice is given after the prescribed time, the organization does not qualify under §120 for the period prior to the notice.[16]

7. *Reporting requirement.* For each year after 1984, an employer maintaining a qualifed group legal services plan must file an information return showing the number of its employees, the number of employees eligible to participate in the plan, the number actually participating, the number of highly compensated employees in each of the foregoing categories, the plan's cost for the year, and various other information.[17]

¶14.4 EDUCATIONAL ASSISTANCE PROGRAMS

Under §127, employees can exclude educational assistance received from their employers if the benefits are furnished under an "educational assistance program."[1] The exclusion, however, is limited to $5,250 for each

---

[13] IRC §120(c)(5).
[14] IRC §89(k).
[15] IRC §120(c)(4).
[16] IRC §120(d)(7).
[17] IRC §6039D(a). The return is filed on Form 5500, 5500-C, or 5500-R.
[1] The provision of this exclusion is not meant to limit the tax treatment of nonqualifying benefits under other provisions. Specifically, §127 does not affect

calendar year.[2] Further, the exclusion is lost altogether if benefits under the program are an alternative to additional cash compensation or other benefits that are taxable to the employee.[3]

An educational assistance program can be a program for an employer to put on courses directly for its employees, or it can be a plan for reimbursing employees for their expenses in taking courses from independent institutions. The program need not be funded; benefits can consist of cash reimbursements paid by the employer directly to the employee, cash payments to institutions providing education to employees, or other expenses incurred by the employer.[4]

The cost of job-related education can ordinarily be excluded from the employee's gross income if defrayed by the employer or be deducted as a business expense under §162 if paid by the employee.[5] The principal function of §127 is therefore to exclude two types of employer-provided educational benefits that are otherwise taxable to employees: (1) education (whether or not related to the employee's present job) that either satisfies the minimum educational requirements for qualification in the individual's occupation or qualifies him for a new occupation[6] and (2) education pursued for cultural or recreational reasons.[7] Since §127 is not limited to any particular type of education, however, it simplifies the treatment of all qualifying educational assistance by making it unnecessary to determine whether the benefits are job-related or not.

As enacted in 1978, §127 applied to the taxable years 1979 through 1983.[8] Its life, however, has been extended twice, most recently through the

---

whether an educational benefit is excludable as a scholarship under §117 or whether the inclusion of an employer-provided benefit in gross income might be offset by a deduction allowable to the employee under §162 or §212. IRC §127(c)(6). See supra ¶10.2 for the exclusion for scholarships, and ¶20.2.9 for deductions for educational expenses.

[2] IRC §127(a)(2). This limitation applies for taxable years after 1985. The dollar cap was $5,000 for 1984 and 1985, and there was no such limitation for prior years. See Pub. L. No. 99-514, §1162(a)(2), 100 Stat. 2085 (1986); Pub. L. No. 98-611, §1(b), 98 Stat. 3175 (1984).

[3] IRC §127(b)(4).

[4] IRC §127(b)(5).

[5] See infra ¶22.1.1

[6] For the nondeductibility of educational expenses of this type, and the employee's correlative obligation to report employer-defrayed expenses as income, see infra ¶22.1.3.

[7] Section 127 is superfluous even for these classes of educational benefits if they are scholarships qualifying for exclusion under §117. Payments by employers, however, rarely qualify for this exclusion. See supra ¶11.2.3.

[8] IRC §127(d) (before amendment in 1984).

end of 1987.[9] The most recent extension was enacted "to permit Treasury to complete its evaluation of the effect of [the] exclusion based on the information reports that employers are . . . required to file."[10] As of early 1988, the applicability of the exclusion for 1988 and subsequent years is uncertain.

To qualify, an educational assistance program must satisfy the following four requirements:

1. *Provision of educational assistance.* A qualified plan must provide "educational assistance," a term defined to include both the payment by the employer of expenses for the employee's education and courses of instruction provided by the employer directly.[11] Benefits can consist of tuition, fees, books, supplies, and equipment. They cannot, however, include (1) tools or supplies that can be retained by the employee after completion of the course of instruction, (2) meals, lodging, or transportation, or (3) courses or education involving hobbies, sports, or games.

2. *Benefits for employees only.* Excludable benefits can only be provided to employees. The term "employee," however, is defined to include both sole proprietors and partners who have earned income from their proprietorships and partnerships.[12]

3. *Nondiscrimination rule.* An educational assistance program must benefit employees qualifying under a classification found by the IRS not to be discriminatory in favor of highly compensated employees or their dependents.[13] An employee is considered highly compensated if he (1) is paid more than $75,000, (2) is among the most highly paid 20 percent of the employer's employees and receives an annual salary exceeding $50,000, or (3) has a greater than 5 percent equity interest in the employer as shareholder, proprietor, or partner.[14] Although benefits for employees' spouses and dependents do not qualify for exclusion under §127,[15] a qualified plan can

---

[9] Pub. L. No. 99-514, §1162(a)(1), 100 Stat. 2085 (1986) (reviving provision for 1986 and 1987); Pub. L. No. 98-611, 98 Stat. 3175 (1984) (extending it for 1984 and 1985).

[10] Staff of Joint Comm. on Tax'n, 99th Cong., 2d Sess., General Explanation of Tax Reform Act of 1986, at 818 (Comm. Print 1987). See infra text accompanying note 21 for the reporting rules.

[11] IRC §127(c)(1).

[12] IRC §§127(c)(2), (3); 401(c)(1).

[13] IRC §127(b)(2). For years prior to 1988, the provision bars discrimination in favor of employees who are officers, owners, or highly compensated.

[14] IRC §§120(c)(1), 414(q). The definition of highly compensated is described more fully in ¶61.2.2.

[15] But see Rev. Proc. 76-47, 1976-2 CB 670, amplified by Rev. Proc. 77-32, 1977-2 CB 541 and amended by Rev. Proc. 83-36, 1983-1 CB 763 (grants by employer-related private foundations to children of employees can qualify as tax-exempt scholarships under §117), discussed supra ¶11.2.1.

provide such benefits, and benefits for spouses and dependents must be taken into account in determining whether the program is discriminatory.

Various categories of employees can be excluded in testing for discrimination, including employees with less than one year of service, part-time and seasonal employees, employees under age 21, and union members whose collective bargaining representative has bargained with the employer about educational assistance benefits.[16] Further, a program is not considered discriminatory merely because different types of educational assistance are used to varying degrees by different classes of employees or because reimbursement is contingent upon satisfactory completion of a course or attainment of a prescribed grade.[17]

In lieu of meeting §127's rather loose prohibition of discrimination, an employer can elect to subject its educational assistance program to a detailed set of nondiscrimination rules found in §89, which are described elsewhere.[18]

4. *Limit on benefits for owner-employees.* Not more than 5 percent of the plan's cost to the employer for any taxable year can be provided to owner-employees and their spouses and dependents. For this purpose, a shareholder or partner is counted as an employee-owner only if he owns (directly or constructively) more than 5 percent of the employer's stock or a partnership interest representing more than 5 percent of the capital or profits interest in the employer.[19]

5. *Requirement that plan be in writing.* For years after 1988, an educational assistance plan must be in writing and must further satisfy the following requirements:[20] Employees' rights under the plan must be legally enforceable; employees must be given reasonable notification of the plan's benefits; the plan must be maintained for the exclusive benefit of employees; and the employer must intend, when the plan is adopted, to keep it in effect indefinitely. If these requirements are not met, every employee must report as gross income the entire value of his benefits under the plan.

6. *Information returns.* An employer maintaining an educational assistance program is required to file an annual information return showing the number of the employer's employees, the number of employees eligible to

---

[16] IRC §§89(h), 127(b)(2). The exclusions are described more fully in ¶13.2.8. The only such exclusion recognized by the pre-1988 version of §127(b)(2) is one for unionized employees where educational assistance benefits were subject to good-faith collective bargaining.

[17] IRC §127(c)(5).

[18] Supra ¶13.2.8. See IRC §89(i)(2) for the election.

[19] For the applicable constructive ownership rules, see §127(c)(5).

[20] IRC §89(k). For prior years, there is a requirement that employees be notified of the plan, but the remainder of the requirements described here do not apply. See IRC §127(b)(6) (before amendment in 1986).

participate in the plan, the number actually participating, the number of highly compensated employees in each of the foregoing categories, the plan's cost for the year, and various other information.[21]

¶14.5 MEALS AND LODGING FURNISHED TO EMPLOYEES FOR CONVENIENCE OF EMPLOYER

¶14.5.1 Introductory

Under §119, the value of meals and lodging furnished to employees and their spouses and dependents is excluded from gross income if the meals and lodging are furnished for the convenience of the employer on the employer's business premises and meet various other conditions discussed below. Enacted in 1954, §119 was "designed to end the confusion" that had arisen under a "convenience of the employer" doctrine developed by the IRS and the courts without an explicit statutory foundation.[1] During this prestatutory period, the IRS and courts gravitated between two polar theories: (1) that meals and lodging furnished by an employer were not income to the employee if they were not "considered" by the employer to be compensation for services and (2) that they were only excludable if furnished as a matter of business necessity to enable the employees to perform their duties properly.[2] In *CIR v. Kowalski*, decided in 1977, the Supreme Court held that §119 codified the business necessity rationale for the convenience-of-the-employer doctrine. The Court also held that §119 is limited to meals and lodging furnished in kind, excluding cash, and that it preempts the field, leaving no room for the exclusion of so-called noncompensatory cash allowances under either §119 or §61.[3]

---

[21] IRC §6039D(a). The return, which is required for years after 1984, is filed on Form 5500, 5500-C, or 5500-R.

[1] S. Rep. No. 1622, 83d Cong., 2d Sess. 19, 190–91 (1954).

[2] For the history of the convenience-of-the-employer doctrine, see CIR v. Kowalski, 434 US 77 (1977). See generally Kragen & Speer, IRC Section 119: Is Convenience of the Employer a Valid Concept? 29 Hastings LJ 921 (1978); McDavitt, Dissection of a Malignancy: The Convenience of the Employer Doctrine, 44 Notre Dame Law. 1104 (1969).

[3] CIR v. Kowalski, supra note 2. Congress responded to *Kowalski* by providing that it should not be applied retroactively to certain state police officers. See Rev. Proc. 79-13, 1979-1 CB 493, modified by Rev. Proc. 81-26, 1981-2 CB 547. An exclusion for cash subsistence allowances, limited to state troopers, was in force from 1954 to 1957, but was repealed in 1957. See CIR v. Kowalski, supra.

¶14.5.2 Convenience of the Employer

Neither meals nor lodging can be excluded from an employee's gross income under §119 unless they are furnished "for the convenience of the employer." Since virtually all benefits, including wages and salaries, serve the employer's "convenience" in the sense that they help to get the employer's work done, the statutory phrase must have been used in a narrower sense. In a pre-1954 case, cited with approval by the Supreme Court in *Kowalski*, the Tax Court said that meals and lodging are furnished for the employer's convenience when they resemble conditions of employment:

> The better and more accurate statement of the reason for the exclusion from the employee's income of the value of subsistence and quarters furnished in kind is found, we think, in *Arthur Benaglia*, 36 BTA 838, where it was pointed out that, on the facts, the subsistence and quarters were not supplied by the employer and received by the employee "for his personal convenience, comfort or pleasure, but solely because he could not otherwise perform the services required of him." In other words, although there was an element of gain to the employee, in that he received subsistence and quarters which he otherwise would have had to supply for himself, he had nothing he could take, appropriate, use, and expend according to his own dictates. Rather, the ends of the employer's business dominated and controlled, just as in the furnishing of a place to work and in the supplying of the tools and machinery with which to work. The fact that certain personal wants and needs of the employee were satisfied was plainly secondary and incidental to the employment.[4]

In the case of lodging, §119(a)(2) further limits the exclusion to where the employee "is required to accept such lodging . . . as a condition of his employment." Although separately stated, this requirement seems to add nothing to the convenience of the employer standard; both are satisfied by a showing that the employee must occupy the housing furnished by the employer in order to perform the duties of his employment properly. As interpreted by the cases and rulings, §119(a)(2) is satisfied if the lodging is furnished at an isolated location lacking alternative housing (e.g., a remote construction site)[5] or if the employee must be available for duty at all times

---

[4] Van Rosen v. CIR, 17 TC 834, 838 (1951).

[5] See Olkjer v. CIR, 32 TC 464, 468 (1959) (acq.) (construction site in Greenland where no other housing was available; "facilities so furnished were not only for the employer's convenience but were indispensable if any work was to be accomplished"); Stone v. CIR, 32 TC 1021 (1959) (acq.) (same result under pre-1954 law); Rev. Rul. 71-267, 1971-1 CB 37 (Navy employees at California offshore islands).

(e.g., a caretaker or hotel manager).[6] Round-the-clock obligations can some-times be adequately discharged if the employee lives in private housing close to the employer's place of business, but there is a tendency to allow the exclusion despite the availability of alternative housing if the employee is in fact on 24-hour call and occupies housing furnished by the employer.[7]

The statute does not say that excludable meals must be accepted as a condition of employment. Since employers do not ordinarily force-feed their employees, compulsion to accept meals could hardly be insisted on. The only employees who must accept meals are food critics and official tasters; others can usually bring their lunches to the job, cook on the prem-ises, or survive on seeds and nuts until they get back to civilization.

The regulations interpret §119(a)(1) as encompassing meals "furnished for a substantial noncompensatory business reason of the employer."[8] After stating that this amorphous standard is to be applied to "all the surrounding facts and circumstances," the regulations put some flesh on the skeleton by stating that "substantial noncompensatory business reasons" include (1) having the employee available for emergency call during the meal period, (2) a business need for restricting the employee to a short meal period when quick meals elsewhere are not feasible, and (3) an absence of sufficient eating facilities in the vicinity of the employer's premises.[9]

---

[6] Reg. §1.119-1(d) Ex. 5 (employee of state institution required to be available for duty at all times); Coyner v. Bingler, 344 F2d 736, 737–38 (3d Cir. 1965) (caretaker of building whose duties "made it a practical necessity for him and his wife to live there"); U.S. Junior Chamber of Commerce v. US, 334 F2d 660 (Ct. Cl. 1964) (official residence temporarily occupied by organization's presidents with one-year terms of office); Wilhelm v. US, 257 F. Supp. 16 (D. Wyo. 1966) (manager of cattle ranch); Lindeman v. CIR, 60 TC 609 (1973) (acq.) (hotel manager); Rev. Rul. 68-354, 1968-2 CB 60 (employees volunteering to live on premises of state mental hospital subject to 24-hour call, in exchange for free meals and lodging).

Cases denying exclusions include McDonald v. CIR, 66 TC 223 (1976) (mul-tinational corporation furnished western-style housing to executive stationed in Ja-pan; no proof that proper performance of duties required such facilities), and Hey-ward v. CIR, 36 TC 739 (1961), aff'd per curiam, 201 F2d 307 (4th Cir. 1962) (occasional entertainment and company policy of having employees live on quarry premises to protect it insufficient to justify exclusion).

[7] See Caratan v. CIR, 442 F2d 606, 610 (9th Cir. 1971) (if employee's duties require constant availability, it is not necessary to negate "access to feasible alterna-tive housing"); but see Peterson v. CIR, 25 TCM (CCH) 1002 (1966) (availability of alternative housing in nearby town casts doubt on bona fides of alleged demand by taxpayer's controlled corporation that he live in company housing).

[8] Reg. §1.119-1(a)(2)(i) (first sentence). See Bob Jones Univ. v. US, 670 F2d 167 (Ct. Cl. 1982) (no exclusion for meals provided by university to faculty and staff because no "substantial noncompensatory business reasons" shown).

[9] Reg. §1.119-1(a)(2)(ii)(c). See Rev. Rul. 71-411, 1971-2 CB 103 (exclusion allowed for employees subject to phone calls while eating at desks or in company dining area).

If there is a noncompensatory reason for furnishing meals during working hours, the exclusion also reaches meals furnished immediately after working hours to employees whose duties caused them to miss a meal during working hours.[10] Further, if a noncompensatory reason applies to substantially all of the employees, the remaining employees can take advantage of the exclusion too.[11] Bowing more to the clout of the hotel and restaurant industry and its unions than to anything in §119, the regulations give a special rule for employees of restaurants and other food service establishments: A meal for each meal period of work can be excluded whether it is furnished during, immediately before, or immediately after the employee's working hours.[12] Another rule allows employees who occupy lodgings for the employer's convenience to exclude all meals furnished without charge on the excludable premises.[13]

By contrast, meals furnished to promote employee morale or goodwill or to attract prospective employees do not meet the noncompensatory standard.[14] Meals furnished before or after the employee's work period "generally" do not qualify, and meals on nonworking days cannot qualify.

¶14.5.3 Business Premises

To qualify for the §119 exclusion, meals and lodging must be furnished on the employer's "business premises." This requirement, which was not part of the pre-1954 nonstatutory doctrine, is construed by the regulations to mean "the place of employment of the employee."[15] The courts have held that the term embraces "(1) living quarters that constitute an integral part of the business property or (2) premises on which the company carries on some of its business activities," as well as the employer's residence in the case of domestic servants even though no business is conducted there.[16] Meals furnished on property leased by the employer for business reasons (e.g., leased grazing lands) also qualify.[17]

A residence leased by the employer for an employee's use can be business premises of the employer, and hence the employee's place of employment, if a significant part of the employee's duties is performed there. It

---

[10] Reg. §1.119-1(a)(2)(ii)(*f*).

[11] Reg. §§1.119-1(a)(2)(ii)(*e*), (d) Ex. 9.

[12] Reg. §1.119-1(a)(2)(ii)(*d*).

[13] Reg. §1.119-1(a)(2)(ii)(last sentence).

[14] Reg. §§1.119-1(a)(2)(i), (iii).

[15] Reg. §1.119-1(c)(1). See also Conf. Rep. No. 2543, 83d Cong., 2d Sess. 27 (1954) ("business premises of the employer" as used in Senate bill intended to have same meaning, in general, as "place of employment" as used in House bill).

[16] Dole v. CIR, 43 TC 697, 707 (acq.), aff'd per curiam, 351 F2d 308 (1st Cir. 1965).

[17] See Reg. §1.119-1(c)(1).

does not acquire this character, however, merely because the employee receives phone calls or writes reports there after working hours or occasionally uses it for business entertaining.[18] Nor does ownership of the residence by the employer ensure that it qualifies as the employee's place of employment.[19]

Section 119(c) relaxes the business premises requirement for foreign work camps. It provides that lodging for employees in a foreign country is deemed to be on the employer's business premises, even if the employees' duties are entirely performed elsewhere, if (1) the employees using the lodging work "in a remote area where satisfactory housing is not available on the open market,"[20] (2) the lodging is "located in the vicinity" of where the employees work, or as near thereto as is "practicable," and (3) the lodging is in an enclave not open to the public that normally houses at least 10 employees.

¶14.5.4 Qualified Recipients

Section 119 refers to meals and lodging furnished to employees and their dependents and spouses. Although the exclusion can be claimed by shareholder-employees, it is necessary to determine in these cases whether the taxpayer receives the benefits as an employee or as shareholder of the employer.[21] Partners are not ordinarily employees of their firms, but one

---

[18] See CIR v. Anderson, 371 F2d 59 (6th Cir. 1966), cert. denied, 387 US 906 (1967) (residence two blocks from employer's motel not on business premises although occupied by manager on 24-hour call; extensive discussion); Winchell v. US, 564 F. Supp. 131 (D. Neb. 1983) (college president's house four miles away from campus not on employer's business premises because few job-related activities occurred there); McDonald v. CIR, 66 TC 223 (1976). Compare Adams v. US, 585 F2d 1060 (Ct. Cl. 1978) (residence owned by U.S. company and occupied by officer based in Japan qualifies as business premises of employer); Lindeman v. CIR, 60 TC 609 (1973) (acq.) (separate residence for manager on hotel property held to be on business premises because manager subject to 24-hour call could view hotel from, and made part-time business use of, residence).

A series of state trooper cases holds that public restaurants are the employer's business premises because state troopers have statewide law-enforcement jurisdiction, but they must be regarded as sui generis. See Kowalski v. CIR, 544 F2d 686 (3d Cir. 1976), rev'd on other grounds, 434 US 77 (1977); US v. Barrett, 321 F2d 911 (5th Cir. 1963). Compare Benninghoff v. CIR, 71 TC 216 (1978), aff'd per curiam, 614 F2d 398 (5th Cir. 1980) (policeman employed by Canal Zone government cannot treat entire Zone as employer's business premises).

[19] See CIR v. Anderson, supra note 18.

[20] See Reg. §§1.119-1(c)(2), (3).

[21] See Wilhelm v. US, 257 F. Supp. 16 (D. Wyo. 1966) (employee-shareholder of S corporation); Hatt v. CIR, 28 TCM (CCH) 1194 (1969), aff'd per curiam, 457 F2d 499 (7th Cir. 1972) (closely held corporation; exclusion allowed after "careful scrutiny of the arrangement"). But see Atlanta Biltmore Hotel Corp. v. CIR, 349 F2d 677

decision, which should probably be regarded as an aberration, held that a partner receiving payments for services without regard to the firm's income pursuant to §707(c) can qualify as an employee under §119.[22]

From its enactment in 1954 until 1978, §119 only referred to meals and lodging furnished to employees. There was a surprising dearth of authority on whether it encompassed housing occupied and meals consumed by members of the employee's family. Strictly speaking, the employer needs only the employee's presence on the job. If an unattached employee could perform the required services satisfactorily, it was arguable under pre-1978 law that meals and lodging for an employee's family were not furnished for the employer's convenience.

In 1978, before this issue was authoritatively resolved, Congress amended §119 by explicitly exempting meals and lodging furnished to an employee's spouse and dependents.[23] The convenience-of-the-employer test, however, applies to meals and lodging furnished to spouses and dependents, and a noncompensatory business reason for meals or lodging for an employee does not necessarily justify an exemption for a spouse or dependent. Where an employer furnishes family quarters to allow an employee to live on the employer's business premises, the convenience-of-the-employer test is usually satisfied for the family if it is satisfied for the employee. If the employee does not live on the business premises, however, meals for dependents and spouses are typically taxable because any noncompensatory business reason for furnishing meals to the employee rarely extends to meals for family members. Even if mom or dad must eat at work to be available for emergencies, the kids can just as well eat at home.

(5th Cir. 1965) (exclusion denied where major shareholder had no significant managerial duties).

[22] Armstrong v. Phinney, 394 F2d 661 (5th Cir. 1968).

[23] The amendment is effective for taxable years beginning after December 31, 1977. For the scope of the term "dependent" (which is not limited to persons for which the taxpayer is entitled to a dependency exemption), see §152(a), discussed infra ¶30.3.1. For the status of meals and lodging furnished to members of the taxpayer's family under pre-1978 law, see Rev. Rul. 59-409, 1959-2 CB 48 (value of meals and lodging supplied by boarding school to families of teachers includable in employee's gross income), withdrawn by Rev. Rul. 60-348, 1960-2 CB 41; see also Armstrong v. Phinney, 394 F2d 661 (5th Cir. 1968) (remand to determine whether employee's wife and child were also employees); Coyner v. Bingler, 344 F2d 736 (3d Cir. 1965) (caretaker and wife); Tougher v. CIR, 51 TC 737 (1969), aff'd per curiam, 441 F2d 1148 (9th Cir.), cert. denied, 404 US 856 (1971) (cost of groceries purchased at employer's commissary not "meals"; no need to decide whether they were furnished to employee).

¶14.5.5 Compensatory Character of Benefits

Whether furnished for the employer's convenience or not, meals virtually always confer economic benefit on the recipients. The same is usually true of employer-supplied housing, except for such employees as married sailors and lumberjacks whose family expenses are not reduced when they live at the job site. For this reason, the IRS sought before 1954 to confine the convenience-of-the-employer doctrine to benefits that were not "compensatory" in character.[24] Section 119 has been construed to reject this effort. Thus, the regulations state that meals furnished for a substantial noncompensatory business reason qualify for the exclusion "even though such meals are also furnished for a compensatory reason" and that lodging can satisfy the standards of §119(b)(1) even though "furnished as compensation" under the terms of an employment contract or statute.[25] Indeed, by accepting the business necessity rationale for §119,[26] and thereby downgrading the compensatory nature of the benefits, the regulations permit meals and lodging to be excluded from the employee's gross income even if they are the sole reward for the services rendered.[27]

In theory, if an employee bargains for more luxurious housing or meals than are necessary to do the job properly (e.g., a hotel manager who insists on a lavish suite), it would be possible to exclude the basic accommodation under §119 while treating the excess value as compensation. The statutory language is not well suited to such a bifurcation, however, and no rulings or litigated cases in point require an allocation of this type.

Section 119(b)(1) provides that in determining whether meals or lodging are furnished for the employer's convenience, the provisions of employment contracts and of state statutes "shall not be determinative of whether

---

[24] See Dietz v. CIR, 25 TC 1255 (1956) (apartment furnished to live-in janitor as sole compensation for services; taxable under pre-1954 law even if furnished for employer's convenience); Mim. 6472, 1950-1 CB 15 (now obsolete) (employer's-convenience doctrine not applicable if meals and lodging are compensation for services). But see Diamond v. Sturr, 221 F2d 264 (2d Cir. 1955) (Mim. 6472 theory rejected, at least for pre-1950 years).

[25] Reg. §1.119-1(a)(2)(i) (meals), §1.119-1(b) (lodging), §1.119-1(d) Ex. 5 (meals and lodging furnished to civil service employee on 24-hour call excludable although regarded as compensation under applicable state statute); Boykin v. CIR, 260 F2d 249 (8th Cir. 1958) (rental value of housing furnished to physician at V.A. hospital excludable under §119 although it was compensation); Rev. Rul. 59-307, 1959-2 CB 48, clarified by Rev. Rul. 84-86, 1984-1 CB 26 (accepting *Boykin* decision).

[26] See CIR v. Kowalski, 434 US 77 (1977).

[27] See Coyner v. Bingler, 344 F2d 736 (3d Cir. 1965) (caretaker whose sole compensation for extra duties was housing; value excluded from gross income); Rev. Rul. 68-354, 1963-2 CB 60 (meals and housing excludable although they were sole compensation for extra duties by employees volunteering to be on 24-hour call). Compare Dietz v. CIR, supra note 24 (contrary under pre-1954 law).

the meals or lodging are intended as compensation." This ill-phrased statement seems to imply (1) that employment contracts and state statutes, although not "determinative," may be evidence of a compensatory intent and (2) that if established, a compensatory intent shows that the meals and lodging are not furnished for the employer's convenience. Neither of these inferences has been adopted, and the provision is a virtual dead letter.

¶14.5.6 Miscellaneous Matters

1. *Cash allowances.* In *CIR v. Kowalski*, the Supreme Court held that §119(a)(1) applies only to meals furnished in kind and that cash allowances to reimburse employees for the cost of meals are gross income.[28] Strictly speaking, the allowances before the Court were not reimbursements because they were paid even if the employees brought their own meals to the job site or were on vacation or sick leave. The Court's decision, however, clearly disqualifies cash payments that merely reimburse an employee's out-of-pocket expenses. It is not clear, however, whether *Kowalski* would tax employees on the value of meals that they are authorized to charge to the employer's account or would instead treat this as an in-kind arrangement.

2. *Groceries as meals, restaurant meals.* The authorities are in conflict on whether groceries furnished by an employer qualify as "meals." One court allowed an exclusion for groceries, but another court and the IRS find a difference between the fixings for a meal and the meal itself.[29]

Also, there might be some doubt about whether a restaurant meal can be excludable.[30] This doubt was reduced in 1978, when the requirement that the meals and lodging be furnished "by" the employer was amended to require that they be furnished "by or on behalf of" the employer. The business premises and convenience-of-the-employer tests usually are an insurmountable obstacle to the exclusion of restaurant meals where the employer is not a restaurant operator. In the rare case where these obstacles are overcome, however, the fact that the meal was furnished by a restaurant should not be relevant.

---

[28] CIR v. Kowalski, supra note 26. See also Reg. §1.119-1(c)(2) (exclusion applicable only to meals and lodging furnished in kind; cash allowances includable in gross income if they are "compensation").

[29] Compare Jacob v. US, 493 F2d 1294 (3d Cir. 1974) (qualified) with Tougher v. CIR, 51 TC 737 (1969), aff'd per curiam, 441 F2d 1148 (9th Cir.), cert. denied, 404 US 856 (1971) (contra), and Rev. Rul. 77-80, 1977-1 CB 36, modified by Rev. Rul. 81-222, 1981-2 CB 205 (IRS takes *Tougher* position).

[30] Many of the meals involved in CIR v. Kowalski, supra note 26, were eaten in restaurants, but the Court found it unnecessary to decide whether this was a disqualifying fact. See Rev. Rul. 71-267, 1971-1 CB 37 (meals prepared by Navy contractor are furnished by Navy, where contractor did not function as independent enterprise and merely assisted Navy, which approved menus, set charges, etc.).

3. *Meals for which employees pay.* In 1978, Congress added §§119(b)(2) and (3), both concerned with charges for meals.[31] Section 119(b)(2) provides that in determining whether meals are furnished for the convenience of the employer, neither the fact that a charge is made nor that the employee may accept or decline the meals shall be taken into account. Prior to the enactment of §119(b)(2), these circumstances were viewed as inconsistent with the convenience-of-the-employer requirement because the charge, coupled with the employee's option to make independent arrangements for meals, suggests that the services could be properly performed even if meals were not furnished by the employer.[32]

Under §119(b)(3), where an employer requires an employee to pay a fixed charge for meals, whether he eats them or not, an amount equal to the fixed charge is excluded from gross income if the meals are furnished for the convenience of the employer. The exclusion applies whether the fixed charge is withheld from the employee's compensation or the employee pays it separately.[33]

4. *Value of taxable meals and lodging.* Section 119 provides that the value of qualified meals and lodging is excluded from gross income, but it says nothing about the treatment of items that fail to meet its standards. In general, the value of unqualified meals and lodging is includable in gross income. The fair market value of the items actually furnished is the measure of the income even if the taxpayer would have preferred more or less expensive facilities.[34] If the employee is away from home for business rea-

---

[31] Both provisions were given retroactive effect as though they had originally been included in the 1954 Code.

[32] See Reg. §1.119-1(a)(3)(i) (not amended to reflect 1978 changes) ("meals for which a charge is made by the employer will not be regarded as furnished for the convenience of the employer if the employee has a choice of accepting the meals and paying for them or of not paying for them and providing his meals in another manner").

[33] See Reg. §1.119-1(a)(3)(ii) (not amended to reflect 1978 changes) (amount of fixed charge for meals excluded, but value of meals included unless convenience-of-employer test met). See also Reg. §1.119-1(b) (same for lodging); Sibla v. CIR, 611 F2d 1260 (9th Cir. 1980) (under pre-1978 law, where fireman required to participate in mandatory organized mess at firehouse with charge for meals, cost could either be deducted as business expense or excluded under §119); Olkjer v. CIR, 32 TC 464 (1959) (acq.) (amounts deducted from wages excludable from gross income to extent allocable to meals and housing furnished for employer's convenience, but not amount allocable to laundry, medical services, etc.).

[34] See McDonald v. CIR, 66 TC 223 (1976) (corporate executive taxed on expensive Japanese housing, not on lesser amount spent by typical executives of similar rank for housing in United States); Heyward v. CIR, 36 TC 739 (1961), aff'd per curiam, 201 F2d 307 (4th Cir. 1962) (isolation of company-supplied housing affects its fair rental value); but see supra ¶11.1.2 notes 31–35 (re valuation of taxable prizes and awards).

sons, however, the amount included in gross income may qualify for deduction under §162.[35]

5. *Lodging for employees of educational institutions.* For years after 1985,[36] §119(d) provides a special exclusion for employees of schools, colleges, and universities[37] who rent housing from their employers at below-market rates. Specifically, the value of lodging furnished to such an employee on or in the vicinity of the employer's campus is excluded, in whole or in part, even if the convenience-of-the-employer test and other requirements normally imposed by §119 are not met. Generally, an employee has no gross income on account of such lodging if his annual rent equals or exceeds 5 percent of the lodging's appraised value, but is taxed on the shortfall if the rent is less than this amount. If a university leases an apartment worth $240,000 to one of its professors, for example, the professor has gross income from the arrangement only if and to the extent his monthly rental is less than $1,000 ($240,000 times 0.05 divided by 12). If the employer rents comparable facilities to tenants who are neither employees nor students, however, the employee avoids gross income by paying rent equal to the average rent paid by the unaffiliated tenants, even if that is less than 5 percent of fair market value. Assume the university in the example has unaffiliated tenants, and rent control laws keep the average unaffiliated rental for an apartment comparable to the professor's at $800. The professor has no gross income if his monthly rental is $800 or more. The exclusion applies to housing occupied by employees and their spouses and dependents.[38]

---

[35] See infra ¶21.1.2 ("away from home" expenses). See also CIR v. Kowalski, 434 US 77, 81 n.10, 95 n.30 (1977).

[36] For prior years, see Pub. L. No. 98-63, 97 Stat. 343 (1983) (IRS appropriation subject to condition that no funds be used to impose tax on value of campus lodging for an employee, spouse, or dependent); Bob Jones Univ. v. US, 670 F2d 167 (Ct. Cl. 1982) (value of lodging provided faculty and staff members not excludable, except for dormitory counselors; no evidence that faculty and staff who lived off campus were less able to perform duties than those who lived on campus in university housing).

[37] More technically, the exclusion applies to educational institutions described in §170(b)(1)(A)(ii), which refers to organizations that have regular faculties and curricula and normally have regularly enrolled students in attendance at the places of their educational activities. IRC §119(d)(4).

[38] If an employee lives in employer-provided housing with a person who is neither his spouse nor a dependent, he is apparently taxable on the rent discount on the portion of the apartment allocable to that person. How that portion might be ascertained is unclear.

¶14.6 HOMES AND HOUSING ALLOWANCES FURNISHED TO MINISTERS

Ministers are permitted by §107 to exclude from gross income the rental value of a home provided to them as part of their compensation, as well as housing allowances to the extent used to rent or provide a home. The exclusion of allowances dates from 1954, but the rental value of housing furnished by the employer in kind has been excludable by statute since 1921, presumably because parsonages can sometimes be analogized to premises supplied for the convenience of the minister's congregation.[1] In appropriate cases, a minister can exclude both types of benefits (e.g., the rental value of a house and a cash allowance earmarked for utility services).[2] Section 107, however, does not authorize a minister to deduct rental expenses defrayed from his own resources or to exclude any of his salary if none of it is designated by the employer as a rental allowance.[3] Although §107 refers to "a minister of the gospel," it embraces clergymen of all faiths.[4]

The cases and rulings confine the benefits of §107 to "duly ordained, commissioned, or licensed" clergymen, which seems to disqualify self-styled or self-appointed ministers, even if they perform sacerdotal functions.[5]

---

[1] Revenue Act of 1921, Pub. L. No. 98, §213(b)(11), 42 Stat. 239, which displaced OD 862, 4 CB 85 (1921) (rental value of parsonage includable in gross income). For the 1954 change, see S. Rep. No. 1622, 83d Cong., 2d Sess. 186 (1954). See also Williamson v. CIR, 224 F2d 377 (8th Cir. 1955) (rental allowance held excludable under pre-1954 convenience-of-employer doctrine and statutory predecessor of §107). See generally Taft, Tax Benefits for the Clergy: The Unconstitutionality of Section 107, 62 Geo. LJ 1261 (1974).

For the exclusion of meals and lodging furnished for the convenience of the employer under §119, which, unlike §107, applies to all employees, see supra ¶14.5.

[2] Rev. Rul. 59-350, 1959-2 CB 45.

[3] Reg. §1.107-1(b). See Eden v. CIR, 41 TC 605 (1964) (no official designation; exclusion denied); Rev. Rul. 78-324, 1978-2 CB 105 (designation of salary as "housing allowance" to extent actually used to rent or maintain home insufficient because amount not definite). But see Libman v. CIR, 44 TCM (CCH) 370 (1982) (oral designation sufficient). Compare Boyd v. CIR, 42 TCM (CCH) 1136 (1981) (where police chaplain worked under joint supervision of police department and church federation, designation by federation sufficient even though salary paid by police department) and Rev. Rul. 75-22, 1975-1 CB 49 (designation by national governing body having control of retirement held effective) with Rev. Rul. 62-117, 1962-2 CB 38 (national committee could not effectively designate amounts paid to local ministers employed and compensated by local congregation).

[4] Salkov v. CIR, 46 TC 190, 194 (1966) (acq.) (no legislative intent to exclude non-Christian faiths or persons who are equivalent to "ministers").

[5] The phrase "duly ordained, commissioned, or licensed" is found in §1402(e)(1), relating to self-employment taxation. Section 1.107-1(a) of the regulations defers to §1.1402(c)-5 in determining whether parsonages and rental allowances are furnished for "services which are ordinarily the duties of a minister of the gospel." This does not incorporate the "duly ordained, commissioned, or licensed"

There are no cases or rulings to this effect, however, and such a disqualification would be of doubtful constitutionality. Indeed, if a self-styled minister has followers, their acknowledgment of his leadership should be a sufficient commission or license if this is their only mode of vesting the individual with sacerdotal powers.[6]

The benefits of §107, however, are properly denied to an individual who belongs to a religious group with an ordination procedure but is not qualified to perform sacerdotal functions, even if he performs administrative, social welfare, or other secular functions on a par with ordained ministers.[7] On the other hand, if the religious body recognizes two or more levels of sacerdotal authority, persons who are authorized to perform some functions qualify as ministers even if they are not authorized to perform all religious functions.[8]

In addition to being a minister, the taxpayer must receive the home or rental allowance "as part of his compensation," which is construed by the regulations to mean "as remuneration for services which are ordinarily the duties of a minister of the gospel."[9] As examples of qualified duties, the regulations mention sacerdotal functions, conduct of religious worship, administration of religious organizations and their integral agencies, and

---

requirement quite as explicitly as the cases and rulings suggest. See Kirk v. CIR, 425 F2d 492 (DC Cir.), cert. denied, 400 US 853 (1970); Salkov v. CIR, supra note 4, at 196 ("reasonably clear" that "self-appointed ministers" do not qualify); Rev. Rul. 59-270, 1959-2 CB 44 ("ministers" of music and education who were not ordained, commissioned, or licensed as ministers of the gospel held not qualified).

[6] See Salkov v. CIR, supra note 4, implying that a congregation's selection of its leader constitutes a commission or license.

[7] See Kirk v. CIR, supra note 5.

[8] Salkov v. CIR, supra note 4 (Jewish cantor commissioned by recognized national body and installed by local congregation with power to perform certain religious functions; qualified under §107 even though he cannot perform all functions of ordained rabbi); Silverman v. CIR, 73-2 USTC ¶9546 (8th Cir. 1973) (not officially reported) (same, with extensive discussion of Judaism's "dual ministry"). But see Lawrence v. CIR, 50 TC 494, 495 (1968) (taxpayer designated by local church as "Commissioned Minister of the Gospel in Religious Education [so] that he may receive benefits of laws relative to the Social Security Act and Internal Revenue Services"; held, "nothing more than paperwork procedure" that does not qualify under §107); Rev. Rul. 65-124, 1965-1 CB 60 (religious workers engaged in educational, musical, and organizational activities, whose denomination provides for ordination, do not qualify despite resolution designating them as ministers of the gospel, since it did not invest them with ecclesiastical authority of ordained ministers), modified by Rev. Rul. 78-301, 1978-1 CB 103 (qualification to exercise substantially all religious functions is sufficient).

[9] Reg. §1.107-1(a). See also Rev. Rul. 63-156, 1963-2 CB 79 (retired minister may exclude rental allowance received as compensation for past services); but see Rev. Rul. 78-448, 1978-2 CB 105 (rental allowance not excludable where it exceeded reasonable compensation for services).

teaching and administration at theological seminaries. If they perform these functions, ministers employed by federal, state, and local governments qualify, but chaplains in the armed forces are excluded, presumably because they participate in the more comprehensive program of tax allowances for military personnel.[10] In practice, the distinction between religious and secular activities is difficult to draw,[11] and it runs the risk of offending religious sensibilities, since some denominations regard the "social gospel" as central to their calling.

Finally, the statutory exemption for a "home" encompasses a dwelling place, furnishings, and such appurtenances as a garage.[12] Rental allowances qualify for the exclusion under §107 only to the extent used "to rent or provide a home," which the regulations construe to include the purchase of a home, but not the cost of food or domestic service.[13] If a rental allowance is used to purchase or rent a farm or other business property, only the part allocable to the home qualifies for the exclusion.

A minister's business expenses are nondeductible under §265(1) if allocable to income exempt from tax under §107.[14] Section 265(a)(6), however, provides that a minister does not lose the deduction for interest on a mortgage on his home or for real property taxes on the home merely because the interest or taxes are allocable to an excludable parsonage

---

[10] Reg. §1.107-1(a); see infra ¶14.7.

[11] See Flowers v. US, 82-1 USTC ¶9114 (ND Tex. 1981) (ordained minister working as professor in undergraduate religion department of church-related university not qualifed); Boyer v. CIR, 69 TC 521 (1977) (acq.) (minister teaching data processing in state college not qualified despite purported assignment by church); Toavs v. CIR, 67 TC 897 (1977) (ordained ministers administering nursing homes "affiliated in spirit" with but not "integral agencies" of Assemblies of God Church; not qualified); Colbert v. CIR, 61 TC 449 (1974) (ordained minister not qualified while serving with Christian Anti-Communism Crusade to combat communism by lectures, broadcasts, publications, evangelistic services, and other means); Tanenbaum v. CIR, 58 TC 1 (1972) (ordained rabbi employed by American Jewish Committee for public relations activities; not qualified); Rev. Rul. 78-172, 1978-1 CB 35 (minister not qualified while serving as president of exempt charitable corporation furnishing financial advice to churches). But see Libman v. CIR, 44 TCM (CCH) 370 (1982) (rabbi employed by United Jewish Appeal to perform rabbinical functions; qualified); Rev. Rul. 58-221, 1958-1 CB 53 (rabbi of community center and temple engaged in preaching, religious training and confirmation of children, etc.; qualified).

[12] Reg. §1.107-1(b).

[13] Reg. §1.107-1(c); Reed v. CIR, 82 TC 208 (1984) (excess of housing allowance over out-of-pocket housing costs is gross income). See also Rev. Rul. 59-350, 1959-2 CB 45 (cost of utilities qualifies for exclusion).

[14] Deason v. CIR, 41 TC 465 (1964) (acq.) (minister's salary of $1,300 was exempt under §107 to extent of $1,239; held, automobile expenses nondeductible to extent allocable to exempt portion).

allowance.[15]

¶14.7 HOUSING AND SUBSISTENCE FURNISHED TO MILITARY PERSONNEL

Members of the uniformed services are subject to the basic rules of the Code, but a few provisions prescribe special time limits and allowances to take account of the hazards, travel obligations, and other features of military life. Some of these provisions are found in the Code and tax regulations, but many of them are found outside the Code in legislation and regulations peculiar to the armed forces and other uniformed services.[1] Until 1986, neither the Code nor regulations contained a complete compendium of the relevant rules. Such a compendium was provided in 1986 in connection with the enactment of §134, which freezes non-Code tax benefits for military personnel under the law as it existed on September 9, 1986.

The principal allowances are:

1. *Quarters and subsistence allowances.* The basic compensation of uniformed personnel is subject to tax, but the value of their quarters and subsistence is excluded from income, along with cash allowances for subsistence, uniforms, and commutation of quarters.[2] The IRS has ruled that this exclusion encompasses allowances paid to military personnel to defray additional household expenses attributable to separation from their families for military reasons, as well as noncompensatory housing and cost-of-living allowances paid to members of the uniformed services while stationed abroad on certain training missions.[3] The exclusion does not embrace per diem allowances in lieu of subsistence or mileage allowances while in a travel status or on temporary duty away from the taxpayer's permanent

---

[15] The provision, enacted in 1986, ended an IRS flirtation with the opposite position. See Rev. Rul. 83-3, 1983-1 CB 72, modified by Rev. Rul. 85-96, 1985-2 CB 87 (denying deductions for such interest and taxes under §265(1), revoking earlier contrary ruling); Rev. Rul. 87-32, 1987-17 IRB 4 (new §265(a)(6) overrules Rev. Rul. 83-3 retroactively; taxpayers who followed the ruling in filing their returns entitled to refunds for years not barred by statute of limtations).

[1] See, e.g., Scott v. US, 74-1 USTC ¶9281 (DSC 1973) (not officially reported) (examining military statutes at length to ascertain status of retired officer teaching in Junior ROTC program). The statutory definition of the term "regular compensation" for members of the uniformed services includes "Federal tax advantages accruing to [service] allowances because they are not subject to Federal income tax." Pub. L. No. 93-419, 88 Stat. 1152 (1974).

[2] Reg. §1.61-2(b). See Scott v. US, supra note 1 (§1.61-2 does not apply to retired officer in JROTC); Rev. Rul. 60-65, 1960-1 CB 21 (contra as to National Guard).

[3] Rev. Rul. 70-281, 1970-1 CB 16 (family separation allowances); Rev. Rul. 61-5, 1961-1 CB 8 (cost-of-living allowance to defray excess quarters cost).

duty station.[4]

2. *Moving and storage expenses.* Under §§82 and 217, employees must include in gross income any amounts received as payment or reimbursement of the expense of moving from one residence to another, but can deduct these expenses, subject to detailed qualifications.[5] For members of the armed forces on active duty, §217(g) liberalizes the rules if the move is pursuant to military orders incident to a permanent change of station. The value of moving and storage services provided in kind and cash reimbursements and allowances (to the extent of the expenses paid or incurred) are excluded from gross income. Unreimbursed expenses can be deducted to the extent permitted by §217, but without regard to the minimum distance and time limits imposed on nonmilitary taxpayers.[6] If the taxpayer's spouse and dependents move to or from a different location, their moving expenses are also deductible under §217, as though the spouse commenced work as an employee at the new location, but without regard to the distance and time limits.

3. *Combat pay.* Pursuant to §112, compensation for any month during which a member of the armed forces served in a combat zone or was hospitalized because of wounds, disease, or injury incurred in a combat zone is excluded from gross income in its entirety for personnel below the grade of commissioned officer and subject to a $500-per-month limit for commissioned officers. The exclusion does not apply to retirement pay or pensions, and it is denied in the case of hospitalization for any month beginning more than two years after the termination of combatant activities in the relevant zone of operations. Section 112(d), enacted in 1972, permits members of the armed forces and civilian employees in a "missing status" during the Vietnam War to exclude from gross income their compensation for active service.[7]

4. *Mustering-out pay.* Under §113, mustering-out payments for service in the armed forces are excluded from gross income.

5. *Reductions in retirement pay to provide family annuities.* To put members of the uniformed services on a par with participants in qualified civilian pension plans, §122 was enacted in 1966 to exclude from gross

---

[4] Reg. §1.61-2(b). See Rev. Rul. 76-2, 1976-1 CB 82 (temporary lodging allowance includable in gross income, but deductible as provided by §217, discussed infra ¶22.4).

[5] See infra ¶22.4.

[6] IRC §217(c).

[7] See Reg. §1.112-1. See also Reynolds v. CIR, 31 TCM (CCH) 331 (1972) (civilian pilot flying planes chartered by armed forces does not qualify under §112); Fagerland v. CIR, 30 TCM (CCH) 583 (1971) (same as to civilian commercial pilot flying military personnel to and from Vietnam); Rev. Rul. 73-187, 1973-1 CB 51 (accrued leave pay attributable to combat service qualifies for exclusion under §112).

income reductions in retired or retainer pay to purchase annuities for surviving spouses and children. If, for example, a serviceman eligible to receive retirement pay of $500 per month elects to receive $400 per month in order to obtain an annuity for his wife of $200 per month after his death, he is taxed only on the $400 actually received during his life.[8] Starting with his death, the $200 monthly received by his wife is taxed to her in full; thus, her annuity is treated as having a zero cost, since the $100 withheld from his pay to compensate for the extended annuity was excluded from his gross income.

As a transitional rule, §122(b) provides that reductions in retirement or retainer pay before 1966 for such annuities (which were not excluded in computing gross income since §122(a) was not yet in force) can be excluded from gross income in reporting the serviceman's post-1965 pay. This tax-free recovery principle also applies to certain payments by servicemen to the Treasury on electing to receive veterans' benefits in lieu of retirement pay. If these amounts are not fully excluded by the serviceman from his retirement pay during his lifetime, the balance is excluded from the annuitant's gross income under §72(n).

Under a related provision, annuities purchased by reductions in retirement pay are ineligible for the employee death benefit exclusion of §101(b) if the serviceman died after attaining retirement age.[9] If he retired because of disability and died before the normal retirement age, however, the death benefit exclusion is allowed; the excludable amount is treated as consideration paid by the serviceman for the annuity under §101(b)(2)(D) (second sentence) and can be excluded by the beneficiary from gross income under §72(n).

6. *Abatement of taxes on death.* Under §692, members of the armed forces who die while serving in a combat zone or because of wounds, disease, or injury incurred in combat are exempted from income taxes for the year of death and any prior taxable year ending on or after the first day of combat service. In addition, taxes for prior years that are unpaid at the date of death are forgiven. To ameliorate the financial circumstances of families of missing servicemen, §692 applies until a determination of death is made under Title 37, Section 556 of the U.S. Code, subject, except for those in the Vietnam conflict, to the two-year period specified by §112.

8. *Non-Code allowances.* Section 134 freezes the non-Code rules for military benefits. It excludes from gross income any "qualified military benefit," a term defined to include a cash allowance or in-kind benefit

---

[8] See H.R. Rep. No. 1118, 89th Cong., 1st Sess. (1965), reprinted in 1966-1 CB 429, 433. Under current law, the serviceman's retired pay is reduced to provide an annuity unless the serviceman elects to take the larger alternative amount. See Conf. Rep. No. 1280, 93d Cong., 2d Sess, reprinted in 1974-3 CB 547.

[9] IRC §101(b)(2)(D) (last sentence). See generally supra ¶12.6.

received by a member or former member of the uniformed services or dependent of such member or former member, subject to two conditions. First, the benefit must be received "by reason of such member's status or service as a member of such uniformed services." Second, on September 9, 1986, the item must have been authorized by law and excludable "under any provision of law or regulation thereunder."[10] An example of a benefit that does not meet the second requirement, and is therefore taxable, is "personal use of a vehicle provided to military personnel."[11]

A statutory provision enacted after September 9, 1986 may not be the basis of an exclusion of a military benefit unless it is found in the Internal Revenue Code or in a revenue act.[12] If a qualified military benefit is modified or adjusted after September 9, 1986, further, the modified or adjusted benefit does not qualify unless the adjustment merely reflects "fluctuation in cost, price, currency, or other similar index."[13]

The legislative history gives the following list of qualified military benefits, which, subject to correction by the Treasury, is intended to be exclusive:[14]

	United States Code Authorization	
Benefit	Title	Section
Annual round trip for dependent students	37	430
Burial and death services	10	1481–82
Combat zone compensation and combat related benefits	37	310

---

[10] IRC §134(a), (b)(1). This rule is intended to embrace any "income benefits which were authorized by law, regulation, or administrative practice on September 9, 1986, and which were excludable from income on such date." Staff of Joint Comm. on Tax'n, 99th Cong., 2d Sess., General Explanation of the Tax Reform Act of 1986, at 828 (Comm. Print 1987) [hereinafter 1986 Bluebook].

[11] 1986 Bluebook, supra note 10, at 830.

[12] IRC §134(b)(2). Because no Congress can bind its successors, this prohibition against lodging tax benefits for military personnel in nontax legislation is like a New Year's resolution; it is only applicable to the body that established it, and that body's willpower is the only enforcement mechanism. Where it is unclear whether a subsequent nontax enactment is intended to create a tax exemption or deduction, the prohibition might be a useful tool for resolving the ambiguity against the exemption or deduction, but where a new non-Code tax benefit is clearly expressed, Congress's later action in creating the benefit prevails over its earlier promise never to do such a thing.

[13] IRC §134(b)(3).

[14] H.R. Rep. No. 841, 99th Cong., 2d Sess., at II-549 (Conf. Rep. 1986). Apart from the direction to add benefits inadvertently omitted, the Treasury has no power to expand the list. Id.

Benefit	United States Code Authorization	
	Title	*Section*
Death gratuities	10	1475–80
Defense counsel	10	133, 801–940, 1181–87
Dental care for military dependents	10	1074, 1078
Dependent education	20	921
	10	7204
Disability benefits	10	chapter 61
Educational assistance	10	141
	37	203, 209
Emergency assistance	10	133
	37	chapter 1
Evacuation allowances	37	405a
Family counseling services	10	133
Family separation allowances	37	427
Group term life insurance	38	404–12
Housing allowances	37	403, 403a, 405
Interment allowances	10	1481–82
Medical benefits	50	2005
	10	1071–83
Moving and storage	37	404–12
Mustering out payments	37	771a(b)(3)
Overseas cost-of-living allowances	37	405
Premiums for survivor and retirement protection plans	10	1445–47
Temporary lodging in conjunction with certain orders	37	404a
Travel in lieu of moving dependents during ship overhaul or inactivation	37	406b
Travel for consecutive overseas tours	37	411
Travel for consecutive overseas tours (dependents)	37	411b
Travel of dependents to a burial site	37	411f
Travel to a designated place in conjunction with reassignment in a dependent-restricted status	37	406
Uniform allowances	37	415–18
Veterans benefits	28	3101

¶14.8 COMMUTER TRANSPORTATION

To encourage conservation in the use of energy, §124, which applied for the years 1979 through 1985, excluded from gross income the value of "qualified transportation" furnished by employers between an employee's residence and place of employment.[1] To qualify under §124, (1) the transportation had to be provided under a separate written plan that did not discriminate in favor of officers, shareholders, or highly compensated employees,[2] (2) the plan had to provide that the transportation was supplied in addition to any other compensation otherwise payable to the employee, and (3) the vehicle had to have a seating capacity of at least eight adults in addition to the driver, and its reasonably expected use had to have been a prescribed fraction of its full capacity.[3] The exclusion did not cover transportation furnished to self-employed individuals.[4]

Congress intended that no inference be drawn from §124 regarding the inclusion in gross income of other fringe benefits, such as transportation to and from work by nonqualifying cars or limousines.[5]

¶14.9 DEPENDENT CARE ASSISTANCE

Section 129, added in 1981, excludes from an employee's gross income the costs of certain dependent care assistance provided by his employer.[1] This exclusion can apply to child care provided in facilities owned and operated by the employer, and can also apply to an employer's reimbursements of child care expenses incurred by employees. An employer reluctant to adopt a plan discriminating in favor of employees with children can provide dependent care assistance on a salary reduction basis; that is, participation can be conditioned on an employee's agreement that his salary will be reduced by the employer's costs for the assistance provided to him. The assistance can be provided by direct employer payments of expenses incurred for dependent assistance; no advance funding is required.[2] The

---

[1] See S. Rep. No. 529, 95th Cong., 2d Sess., reprinted in 1978-3 CB (Vol. 2) 251; S. Rep. No. 1324, 95th Cong., 2d Sess., reprinted in 1978-3 CB (Vol. 2) 325.

[2] IRC §124(c). See S. Rep. No. 1324, supra note 1 (§124(c) requires satisfaction of antidiscrimination requirements of §401(a)(4), relating to qualified pension and profit sharing plans); for §401(a)(4), see infra ¶61.2.3.

[3] S. Rep. No. 1324, supra note 1, at 326.

[4] IRC §§124(b); 46(c)(6)(B)(i), (ii).

[5] S. Rep. No. 1324, supra note 1.

[1] See generally N.Y. Times, Jan. 18, 1987, at A25, col. 1 (Labor Department study of employers with more than 10 employees shows that 2 percent of employers sponsor day care centers and an additional 3 percent provide other forms of financial help for child care).

[2] IRC §129(d)(5).

requirements for a dependent care assistance program and some limitations on the §129 exclusion are described below.

1. *Benefits qualifying for exclusion.* The exclusion is only allowed for "dependent care assistance," a term defined to include any service the cost of which would qualify for the dependent care credit if paid by the employee.[3] The §129 exclusion for employer-provided dependent care is thus intended as a rough parallel to the credit allowed to employees who bear their own work-related dependent care costs. This definition covers costs of (1) caring for dependents who are under age 15 or who are physically or mentally unable to care for themselves and (2) household services, but only if the costs are incurred to enable the employee to be gainfully employed while he has one or more dependents who are under age 15 or disabled.

2. *Eligible participants.* A dependent care assistance program can make benefits available to all employees with dependents, including shareholder-employees and, if the employer is not incorporated, partners or the proprietor of the business.[4]

3. *Nondiscrimination rules and limitations on benefits to owners.* A dependent care assistance program must satisfy three requirements designed to prevent the program from excessively benefiting highly paid employees and the owners of the business. First, the assistance plan must either be open to all employees with qualifying dependents or eligibility must be extended to classes of employees defined in a way that does not discriminate in favor of highly compensated employees.[5] An employee is considered highly compensated if he (1) is paid more than $75,000, (2) is among the most highly paid 20 percent of the employer's employees and receives an annual salary exceeding $50,000, or (3) has a greater than 5 percent equity interest in the employer as shareholder, proprietor, or partner.[6] In evaluating a plan's eligibility requirements, however, several groups of employees can be ignored, including employees with less than a year of service, part-time and seasonal employees, employees who are under age 21, and unionized employees whose collective bargaining agent has bargained with the employer about dependent care assistance.[7]

---

[3] IRC §§21(b)(2); 129(a)(1), (d)(1), (e)(1). See infra ¶31.1 for the dependent care credit.

[4] IRC §§129(e)(3), (4).

[5] IRC §129(d)(3).

[6] IRC §§125(d), 414(q). The definition of highly compensated is described more fully in ¶61.2. For years before 1986, the discrimination rules forbid plans favoring "employees who are officers, owners, or highly compensated." IRC §§129(d)(2), (3) (before amendment in 1986).

[7] IRC §§89(h), 125(b)(3). The excludable classes are described more fully in ¶13.2.8. For years before 1986, the only exclusion is for unionized employees. IRC §129(d)(3).

Second, a dependent care assistance program must not discriminate in favor of highly compensated employees in either contributions or benefits.[8] A related rule additionally requires that the average benefits for rank-and-file employees must be at least 55 percent of the average benefits for highly compensated employees.[9]

Third, the costs incurred under the plan for the benefit of employees who are 5 percent or greater shareholders, partners, or proprietors of the employer cannot exceed 25 percent of total costs.[10] Broad attribution rules are used in determining participants' stockholdings and partnership interests.[11]

4. *Requirement of written plan.* For years after 1988, a dependent care assistance program qualifies for the exclusion only if it is provided under a written plan that meets all of the following requirements:[12] Each employee's rights under the plan must be legally enforceable; employees must be given reasonable notification of the benefits the plan provides to them; the plan must be maintained for the exclusive benefit of the employees; and the employer must intend, when the plan is adopted, to keep it in effect indefinitely. If these requirements are not met, every employee must report as gross income the entire value of his benefits under the plan.

5. *Dollar limits on exclusion.* The §129 exclusion is subject to two caps. First, the annual exclusion may not exceed the employee's earned income or, if the employee is married at the end of the year, the lesser of the employee's earned income or the spouses's earned income.[13] A special rule is provided to keep this rule from reducing the exclusion to insignificance when one spouse is unemployed or minimally employed because he is a student or is physically or mentally incapable of caring for himself: The earned income of a spouse who is a full-time student or is disabled is deemed to be the greater of actual earned income or a statutorily prescribed amount. The latter amount is (1) $200 per month if the family includes one person who either is a dependent under age 15 or is a dependent or spouse

---

[8] IRC §129(d)(2).

[9] IRC §129(d)(7)(A). This test only applies for years after 1985. In applying the test to a plan that provides benefits through salary reduction agreements with participating employees, employees earning less than $25,000 per year are excluded from consideration. IRC §129(d)(7)(B). Nonparticipants are apparently excluded in determining average benefits; §129(e)(6) says that none of the qualification requirements can be failed "merely because of utilization rates for different types of assistance made available under the program."

[10] IRC §129(d)(4).

[11] IRC §129(e)(5).

[12] IRC §§89(k), 129(d)(1).

[13] IRC §129(b). An employee's earned income does not include benefits under the dependent care assistance plan, even if the earned income limitation causes some of the assistance to be taxed. IRC §129(e)(2).

physically unable to care for himself or (2) $400 per month if the family includes more than one such person.[14] Assume a family consists of one spouse employed at an annual salary of $20,000, one spouse who is a full-time student and has no income, and a three-year-old child. The exclusion is limited to $2,400 (12 × $200) because the lesser of the earned incomes of the two spouses is the deemed income of $200 per month of the student-spouse. If the unemployed spouse is disabled, in contrast, the deemed income is $400 per month because the family includes two qualifying individuals (the child and the disabled spouse), and the maximum annual exclusion is therefore $4,800.

Also, for years after 1986, the maximum exclusion is $5,000.[15] If the taxpayer is married and files a separate return, the limitation is usually reduced to $2,500. Special dispensation is made, however, for employees who do not live with their spouses. Specifically, a married employee is treated as not married (and thus eligible for a $5,000 exclusion on a separate return) if the employee is (1) legally separated from his spouse under a decree of separate maintenance or (2) informally separated from his spouse during the last half of the year and maintains a household that is the principal residence of a dependent.[16]

To aid employees in applying the two dollar limitations, the employer must provide an annual statement to each participant itemizing the employer's cost in providing dependent assistance for the employee during the year.[17]

6. *Services provided by relatives.* The exclusion is wholly denied for dependent care services that are paid for by an employer, but are provided by a member of the employee's family.[18] For this purpose, the employee's family includes the employee's children under age 19 and any other person for whom either the employee or the employee's spouse is entitled to a

---

[14] IRC §§21(d)(2), 129(b)(2).

[15] IRC §129(a)(2). The $5,000 ceiling is imposed to provide rough equivalence to the dependent care credit, which is even more sharply limited. Staff of Joint Comm. on Tax'n, 99th Cong., 2d Sess., General Expanation of the Tax Reform Act of 1986, at 818–19 (Comm. Print 1987).

If the employer provides dependent care services in kind through on-site facilities, the exclusion cap applies to the value of the services. IRC §129(e)(8). Also, a child care benefit is taken into account for the year in which the child care services are provided, not the year in which the employer pays for the benefit. Notice 88-3, 1988-2 IRB 27. For example, if an employee is reimbursed in 1987 for child care expenses incurred in 1986, the reimbursement is treated as a 1986 benefit, and thus is not subject to the limit because the limiting rule did not become effective until 1987.

[16] IRC §§21(e)(3), (4); 129(a).

[17] IRC §129(d)(6). The statement is due by January 31 of the following year.

[18] IRC §129(c).

dependency exemption for the year. If an employer hires an employee's 18-year-old son to look after the employee's 10-year-old daughter while the employee is at work, for example, the employer's payment of the son's salary is taxable to the employee.

7. *Reporting requirement.* For each year after 1984, an employer maintaining a dependent care assistance plan must file an information return showing the number of the employer's employees, the number of employees eligible to participate in the plan, the number actually participating, the number of highly compensated employees in each of the foregoing categories, the plan's cost for the year, and various other information.[19]

¶14.10 EMPLOYEE-CHOSEN BENEFITS ("CAFETERIA PLANS")

Under §125, enacted in 1978, an otherwise nontaxable fringe benefit does not become taxable merely because it is provided under a "cafeteria plan" that permits the employee to choose among benefits, which may include cash.[1] For example, if an employee can choose between cash and group-term life insurance coverage of not more than $50,000 and selects the insurance policy, the exclusion under §79 for the insurance is not affected by the fact that the taxpayer could have taken cash instead. Section 125 thus supersedes the pervasive nonstatutory principle that taxpayers who choose nontaxable benefits in lieu of cash must be viewed as though they had taken the cash and used it to purchase the benefits actually chosen.[2] The requirements of §125 are described below.

1. *Definition of "cafeteria plan."* To qualify as a "cafeteria plan," a plan must meet several requirements. First, the plan must limit participation to employees.[3] Shareholder-employees may be participants, but sole proprietors and partners may not be. The legislative history indicates, however, that former employees may be participants and that a plan may provide

---

[19] IRC §6039D(a). The return is filed on Form 5500, 5500-C, or 5500-R.

[1] See generally Staff of Joint Comm. on Tax'n, 95th Cong., 2d Sess., General Explanation of the Revenue Act of 1978 (Comm. Print 1979) [hereinafter 1978 Bluebook]. For the complicated status of cafeteria plan benefits for pre-1979 taxable years, see id. at 79.

Excludable benefits under a cafeteria plan are not wages for withholding, social security, and unemployment tax purposes. IRC §§3121(a)(5), 3306(b)(5).

[2] See supra ¶5.8.1 (indirect receipts). See also infra ¶60.2 (deferred compensation where employer would have been willing to pay cash); 1978 Bluebook, supra note 1, at 80 (implying that controlling shareholders are not taxable on receiving otherwise tax-free benefits from their corporation merely because they could have caused it to pay cash instead).

[3] IRC §125(c)(1).

benefits for beneficiaries of participants.[4]

Second, the plan must allow all participants a choice between two or more benefits.[5] The benefits may be cash and one or more "qualified benefits," or they may be two or more qualified benefits. A qualified benefit is an employee benefit that apart from the elective feature of the plan, is excluded by statute from the employee's gross income.[6] Accident and health benefits, group-term life insurance, group legal services, and dependent care benefits are examples of benefits that may be offered in a cafeteria plan. Group-term life insurance qualifies, regardless of the amount of coverage, even though the cost of coverage in excess of $50,000 is taxable under §79(a). Group-term life insurance coverage on spouses and children of employees can also qualify.[7] Paid vacation days are a permissible benefit if days unused during a plan year may neither be carried to another year nor compensated for with additional cash.[8] Several types of benefits, however, may not be offered, including fringe benefits excluded by §132, scholarships under §117, and educational assistance excludable under §127.[9] Also, a benefit of one of the permitted types may not be offered if it is provided by a plan that does not satisfy antidiscrimination or other qualification rules applicable to benefits of that type.[10]

Generally, deferred compensation is not a permissible benefit under a cafeteria plan, but two exceptions are made.[11] First, if an employer maintains a profit sharing or stock bonus plan that qualifies as a cash-or-deferred arrangement, employer contributions to the profit sharing or stock bonus plan are a permissible cafeteria benefit.[12] Second, postretirement coverage under a group life insurance policy may be offered under a cafeteria plan for employees of a school, college, or university if all contributions for the insurance must be made before retirement and the insurance has no cash

---

[4] See 1978 Bluebook, supra note 1, at 79.

[5] IRC §125(c)(1).

[6] IRC §125(e).

[7] Reg. §1.125-2T(a).

[8] Id.

[9] These exclusions apply for years after 1984. See supra ¶14.1 (fringe benefits under §132), ¶11.2 (scholarships under §117), ¶14.4 (educational assistance excludable under §127). For 1985, the disqualification also embraced vanpooling benefits excludable under §124, but §124 expired at the end of 1985. See supra ¶14.8.

Further, according to the regulations, meals and lodging excludable under §119 are ineligible for inclusion in a cafeteria plan because the election feature of a cafeteria plan is inconsistent with the convenience-of-the-employer test of ¶119. Reg. §1.125-2T(a). See supra ¶14.5 for §119.

[10] Reg. §1.125-2T(b).

[11] IRC §125(c)(2).

[12] The cash-or-deferred option was not originally available in a cafeteria plan, but was added in 1980.

surrender value.[13] The employer can obtain this post-retirement coverage either by using preretirement contributions to purchase paid-up coverage for the period after the employee's projected retirement or by placing these contributions in separate accounts that are used after retirement to purchase the coverage.[14]

For years after 1988, a cafeteria plan must be in writing and must further satisfy all of the following requirements:[15] Each employee's rights under the plan must be legally enforceable; employees must be given reasonable notification of the benefits the plan provides to them; the plan must be maintained for the exclusive benefit of the employees; and the employer must intend, when the plan is adopted, to keep it in effect indefinitely. If these requirements are not met, every employee must report as gross income the entire value of his benefits under the plan.

According to the IRS, a so-called reimbursement plan cannot qualify as a cafeteria plan.[16] Under such a plan, an employee who incurs an expense covered by the plan submits proof of it to the employer, who then recharacterizes a portion of the employee's salary as reimbursement for the expense. If cash is an option under a cafeteria plan, the IRS requires that participating employees taking nontaxable benefits must designate at the beginning of each year an amount to be used for these benefits, and any portion of this amount that is not expended under the plan during the year must be forfeited.

2. *Nondiscrimination rule.* A cafeteria plan must either be open to all employees or must extend eligibility to a class of employees that is defined in a way that does not discriminate in favor of highly compensated employees.[17] An employee is considered highly compensated if he (1) is paid more than $75,000, (2) is among the most highly paid 20 percent of the employ-

---

[13] IRC §125(c)(2). If these requirements are met, the insurance is treated as group-term life insurance for purposes of §79, even though the permanent feature of the insurance disqualifies it under the usual definition of term insurance. This means that (1) employees are entitled to no exclusion for employer contributions for the insurance unless the qualification criteria of §79 are met and (2) satisfaction of these criteria wins for the employees an exclusion for only the first $50,000 of coverage. See supra ¶14.2 for group-term life insurance.

This rule applies for years after 1988. Employers were intended to be given an election to apply it for any plan year beginning after October 22, 1986, but this intention is not expressed in the statute. 1986 Bluebook, supra note 1, at 822.

[14] 1986 Bluebook, supra note 1, at 822.

[15] IRC §§89(k), 125(c)(1).

[16] Ann. 84-24, 1984-10 IRB 39.

[17] IRC §125(b)(1). For years prior to 1988, discrimination in benefits or contributions is also forbidden. IRC §125(b)(1) (before amendment in 1986). Discrimination as to benefits is tested by comparing nontaxable benefits and total benefits for the highly compensated with those for the rank-and-file; similarly, in testing for discrimination in contributions, both contributions for nontaxable benefits and con-

er's employees and receives an annual salary exceeding $50,000, or (3) has a greater than 5 percent equity interest in the employer as shareholder, proprietor, or partner.[18] In evaluating a plan's eligibility requirements, however, several groups of employees may be ignored, including employees with less than a year of service, part-time and seasonal employees, and employees who are under age 21.[19]

Two special rules are provided for unionized employees. First, a plan maintained under a collective bargaining agreement is automatically considered nondiscriminatory.[20] Conversely, unionized employees excluded from eligibility are ignored in testing for discrimination if cafeteria plan benefits have been the subject of good faith bargaining between the employer and the employee's collective bargaining representative.[21]

If a plan exhibits the forbidden discrimination, a highly compensated employee who participates in the plan is taxable on all benefits he receives under the plan, including those that would otherwise be nontaxable.[22] Although the present statute is not clear on the point, participants who are not highly compensated apparently do not lose the exemption for noncash benefits.[23]

3. *Limitation on benefits for key employees.* The §125 exclusion is denied to a key employee if more than 25 percent of all nontaxable benefits under the plan go to key employees.[24] The term "key employee" includes any employee who, during the current year or one of the preceding four years, was (1) an officer whose compensation exceeds $45,000, (2) an owner of more than 5 percent of the employer's stock, or (3) a greater than 1 percent shareholder with compensation exceeding $150,000.[25] Although the statute

---

tributions for total benefits are considered. IRC §125(c) (before amendment in 1986).

[18] IRC §§125(d), 414(q). The definition of highly compensated is described more fully in ¶61.2. For years before 1989, the term "highly compensated" is defined to include officers, shareholder-employees owning more than 5 percent of the employer's stock, employees who are "highly compensated," and spouses and dependents of the foregoing. IRC §125(e) (before amendment in 1986).

[19] IRC §§89(h), 125(b)(3). The excludable classes are described more fully in ¶13.2.8.

[20] IRC §125(f).

[21] IRC §§89(h)(1), 125(b)(3).

[22] IRC §125(a)(2)(B).

[23] This ambiguity only arises under the version of the statute enacted in 1986, which generally applies for years after 1988. Pub. L. No. 99-514, §§1151(d), (k), 100 Stat. 2085 (1986). The statute applicable to prior years is explicit that discrimination only causes the highly compensated to be taxed. IRC §125(b)(1) (before amendment in 1986).

[24] IRC §125(b)(2). In applying this test, the cost of group-term life insurance coverage in excess of $50,000 is not counted. Id.

[25] IRC §416(i). This definition is described more fully in ¶61.2.12.

is not explicit on the point, a key employee participating in a plan failing the 25 percent test is apparently taxed on the fair market value of all noncash benefits under the plan.

4. *Reporting requirement.* For each year after 1984, an employer maintaining a cafeteria plan must file an information return showing the number of the employer's employees, the number of employees eligible to participate in the plan, the number actually participating, the number of highly compensated employees in each of the foregoing categories, the plan's cost for the year, and various other information.[26]

---

[26] IRC §6039D(a). The return is filed on Form 5500, 5500-C, or 5500-R.

CHAPTER

15

Interest on Federal, State, and Local Obligations

¶15.1 FEDERAL OBLIGATIONS

From 1913 to 1917, interest on federal obligations was excluded from the obligee's gross income. In 1917, this blanket exemption was replaced by a more selective approach, providing for an exemption only to the extent granted by the law authorizing particular obligations to be issued. Thereafter, no wholly exempt federal obligations were issued. In some instances, however, a partial tax exemption was granted under which the interest was exempt from the federal "normal" income tax but not from the "surtax."[1] When the distinction between the normal tax and surtax was eliminated for individuals in 1954, Congress enacted a credit, formerly §35, to honor its commitment to investors in partially tax-exempt federal obligations.[2] This provision was repealed in 1976 as unnecessary since no such bonds remained outstanding.[3] Thus, interest on federal obligations no longer enjoys any tax immunity.

¶15.2 STATE AND LOCAL OBLIGATIONS—IN GENERAL

¶15.2.1 Introductory

Since 1913, interest on obligations of states and their political subdivisions has been excluded from the obligee's gross income. When this provision, now §103(a), was first enacted, it was widely thought that taxing the recipients of such income would impose an unconstitutional burden on the borrowing power of state and local governments.[1] With the waning of the

---

[1] For the distinction between the normal tax and the surtax, see supra ¶1.1.3 note 17.

[2] See S. Rep. No. 1622, 83d Cong., 2d Sess. 164 (1954).

[3] Staff of Joint Comm. on Tax'n, 94th Cong., 2d Sess., General Explanation of the Tax Reform Act of 1976, reprinted in 1976-3 CB (Vol. 2) 483. For an anachronistic vestige of partially tax-exempt federal obligations, see §1.661(c)-2 Ex. of the regulations.

[1] Supra ¶1.2.8.

doctrine of intergovernmental tax immunity, the exemption has been preserved by Congress as a kind of revenue sharing, which enables states and cities to borrow at interest rates lower than those on taxable obligations of similar quality.[2]

The benefit derived by a bondholder from the exemption depends on the investor's marginal tax rate and the differential between the interest rates on exempt and taxable bonds. Assume all state and local bonds are purchased by corporations that would otherwise be taxed on the interest at 34 percent, the highest marginal rate applied to any taxpayer in 1988. At a time when comparable private obligations carry an interest rate of 10 percent, exempt issuers would have to pay only 6.6 percent (or a shade more) to float their securities; this is because a 6.6 percent exempt yield would equal the after-tax yield on a 10 percent taxable bond (10 percent, less 34 percent thereof, is 6.6 percent). If this were so, the entire benefit of the tax exemption would pass through to the governmental units issuing exempt bonds. Investors would be indifferent as between exempt and taxable bonds; although they claim the exemption, they would only be conduits through which the benefit would pass to the borrowers.

Interest rates on exempt and taxable bonds, however, are not related in this way in real life.[3] In recent years, cities and states have flooded the market with tax-exempt obligations. The supply of bonds is so great that there are not enough top-bracket purchasers to buy them all, and state and local governments have responded by offering higher interest rates to appeal to taxpayers in ever lower tax brackets. When the rate on taxable bonds is 10 percent, for example, an investor in the 28 percent bracket loses on an exempt bond unless it pays at least 7.2 percent (10 percent, less 28 percent thereof), and an investor in the 14 percent bracket must have at least 8.6

---

[2] See Davie & Zimmerman, Tax-Exempt Bonds After the South Carolina Decision, 39 Tax Notes 1573, 1575–78 (1988) (describing the history of proposals to abolish the exemption and presenting an economic argument for the exemption).

[3] It was estimated in 1976 that yields on tax-exempt issues were about 70 percent of those on comparable taxable bonds. Joint Economic Comm., 94th Cong., 2d Sess., Changing Conditions in the Market for State and Local Government Debt 57 (1976). The gap between tax-exempt and taxable rates narrowed in the period 1976 to 1986. Staff of Joint Comm. on Tax'n, 99th Cong., 2d Sess., General Explanation of the Tax Reform Act of 1986, at 1151 (1987) [hereinafter 1986 Bluebook].

The Tax Reform Act of 1986 made two changes that are likely to affect this differential. The rules allowing state and local governments to issue tax-exempt bonds to finance privately used facilities were sharply curtailed, in part for the purpose of reducing interest rates on exempt issues by restraining the volume of exempt bonds in the marketplace. Id. The 1986 Act, however, also reduced tax rates, which diminishes the benefit of the tax exemption and leads bondholders to demand higher yields.

percent on an exempt bond.[4]

When exempt interest rates are pegged to attract investors in lower tax brackets, however, top-bracket investors get a windfall because all tax-exempt bonds, not merely the ones offered to lower-bracket investors, must pay the higher rates. The tax benefit effectively trickles up. In theory, investors in the lowest bracket should get no benefit because the market should price the issue to equate the interest rate on the exempt bonds with the after-tax yields they would have on taxable bonds. Any investor subject to higher marginal tax rates, however, does better than his after-tax yield on taxable bonds, and the amount of this benefit rises with income.[5]

Even the top-bracket taxpayers, however, do not get the full benefit of the exclusion; so long as exempt yields are less than taxable yields, they share the benefit with the cities and states issuing the bonds.

¶15.2.2 Obligations Eligible for Exemption

Although §103 is often described as an exclusion for state and municipal bond interest, it is broader in scope, encompassing interest paid on "obligations," whether evidenced by bonds or not, including ordinary commercial debts incurred by state and local governments for services and supplies. Also, the exemption extends to obligations of states, territories, U.S. possessions, and their political subdivisions, as well as the District of Columbia. Certain "private activity bonds" and "arbitrage bonds," however, are disqualified.[6] Moreover, the exclusion is offset to some extent by provisions denying deductions for interest on debts incurred or continued to purchase or carry exempt obligations,[7] as well as expenses otherwise qualifying for deduction under §212 if allocable to exempt interest.[8]

Given the dollar amounts involved, §103(a) (as distinguished from statutory limitations on its scope) has generated surprisingly few interpreta-

---

[4] This differential is less dramatic now than it was formerly. Between 1962 and 1982, when the highest marginal rate was 70 percent, an exempt yield of just 30 percent of the yields on comparable taxable bonds was sufficient to attract investors in the highest bracket. For these investors, for example, 3 percent exempt bonds were equivalent to 10 percent taxable bonds. To draw investors in the 40 percent bracket, however, the exempt yield had to be doubled—from 3 percent to 6 percent to compete with 10 percent taxable bonds.

[5] For more on the trickle-up phenomenon, see Bittker, Equity, Efficiency, and Income Tax Theory: Do Misallocations Drive Out Inequities? 16 San Diego L. Rev. 735 (1979).

[6] For private activity bonds, see infra ¶15.3; for arbitrage bonds, see infra ¶15.5.

[7] IRC §265(a)(2), discussed infra ¶31.2.1.

[8] IRC §265(a)(1), discussed infra ¶15.7.

tive issues.[9] In the overwhelming bulk of situations, its applicability is so clear that purchasers of state and local obligations can routinely rely on opinions of bond counsel that their interest is excludable from federal income taxation under current law.[10] Also, the consequences of a loss of exemption are typically so severe as to discourage litigation. When a bond issue has been sold to a large group of investors who have invested millions of dollars in reliance on the exemption, the IRS is like a prosecutor who can win conviction only by persuading a jury to impose the death penalty; the prosecutor is reluctant to prosecute where the penalty is obviously excessive, and everyone avoids behavior that could possibly be the basis for a successful prosecution. A few questions, however, have been litigated:

1. *Is the obligor a "political subdivision" of a state, territory, or possession?* In *CIR v. Shamberg's Estate*,[11] a landmark decision, the IRS argued that the Port of New York Authority, created by a compact between New York and New Jersey, was not a "political subdivision" within the meaning of §103. Its theory was that the Authority, not being authorized to exercise traditional political functions, was not within the legislative intent underlying the exemption, which was allegedly to exempt interest only if it was constitutionally immune to federal taxation. The Court of Appeals for the Second Circuit rejected this claim, pointing out that the 1913 legislative debate manifested a desire by Congress to avoid arousing "the antagonism of any of the states" by taxing items thought at that time to be of minor economic importance, not merely to avoid creating "any constitutional question."[12] The court also cited several opinions of the Attorney General ruling that the exclusion was not limited to a "true governmental subdivision such as a county, township, etc.," but extended as well to "any subdivision of the state created for a public purpose although authorized to exercise a portion of the sovereign power of the state only to a limited degree," such as assessment districts for the construction of streets, sewage disposal, irri-

---

[9] For declaratory judgments to determine whether proposed bond issues qualify under §103(a), see §7478, discussed infra ¶115.2.5. For procedures for obtaining a ruling on the qualification of an issue for exemption, see Rev. Proc. 88-32, 1988-25 IRB 46 and Rev. Proc. 88-33, 1988-25 IRB 48.

[10] See Reg. §1.103-13(a)(2)(iii) (if face amount of issue not in excess of $2.5 million, unqualified opinion of counsel that bonds are not arbitrage bonds fully protects investors on this issue unless opinion unreasonable or given in bad faith).

[11] CIR v. Shamberg's Est., 144 F2d 998 (2d Cir. 1944), cert. denied, 323 US 792 (1945). See also CIR v. White's Est., 144 F2d 1019 (2d Cir. 1944), cert. denied, 323 US 792 (1945) (same result as to Triborough Bridge and Tunnel Authority). Judge Jerome N. Frank dissented at length in *Shamberg's Estate* (but with the prefatory remark that "I would not go to the stake to vindicate my position") and, more briefly, in *White's Estate*.

[12] CIR v. Shamberg's Est., supra note 11, at 1003–04.

gation, flood control, harbor improvements, and the like.[13] More recently, the term "political subdivision" has been defined as a unit of government that has "more than an insubstantial amount" of "the power to tax, the power of eminent domain, [or] the police power (in the law enforcement sense)."[14]

Also, long-standing Treasury regulations allow exempt obligations to be issued "by or on behalf of" a state or political subdivision.[15] The words "on behalf of", the *Shamberg* court observed, must have been intended to refer to bonds "issued by a state agency to carry out a public purpose where the [state] is not named as obligor."[16] In the court's view, this included the bonds in the case before it, which were serviced by revenues collected by the Port Authority from users of its facilities, since it had no power to levy taxes or assessments.

Special rules allow volunteer fire departments and Indian tribal governments to issue exempt bonds. Under a rule added in 1981, a volunteer fire department is treated as a political subdivision of a state in applying §103 to obligations issued to finance a firehouse or fire truck if the organization is bound by agreement to furnish fire fighting or emergency services to an area not otherwise provided with such services.[17] Under a rule enacted in 1982, an Indian tribal government is treated as a state for purposes of §103, but cannot issue exempt bonds for any purpose other than an "essential governmental function."[18]

2. *Does the payment constitute "interest" on an "obligation"?* Interest on an obligation of a state or political subdivision qualifies for exclusion even if the obligation is not evidenced by bonds or promissory notes in conventional form. The IRS has ruled, for example, that interest on a debt evidenced only by an ordinary written agreement of purchase and sale

---

[13] Id.

[14] 1986 Bluebook, supra note 3, at 1157. "State universities, hospitals, and . . . public benefit corporations" can be political subdivisions if they exercise these powers. Id. But see Philadelphia Nat'l Bank v. US, 666 F2d 834 (3d Cir. 1981), cert. denied, 457 US 1105 (1982) (Temple University, which is state-related and partially state-supported and controlled, is not a political subdivision of a state).

[15] Reg. §1.103-1(b). See Rev. Rul. 63-20, 1963-1 CB 24 (conditions that must be met to establish that obligations of nonprofit corporations are issued "on behalf of" a state or political subdivision within meaning of §1.103-1(b)); Rev. Proc. 82-26, 1982-1 CB 476 (procedures for obtaining a ruling on the issue). This principle has been reaffirmed under the 1986 revisions of §103. H.R. Rep. No. 841, 99th Cong., 2d Sess., at II-686 n.3 (Conf. Rep. 1986).

[16] CIR v. Shamberg's Est., 144 F2d 1005–06 (2d Cir. 1944).

[17] IRC §150(e). Volunteer fire departments had previously been held ineligible to issue exempt bonds. Seagrave Corp. v. CIR, 38 TC 247, 250–51 (1962).

[18] IRC §§7871(a)(4), (c). The IRS previously took the position that an Indian tribe could not issue exempt bonds. Rev. Rul. 68-231, 1968-1 CB 48, declared obsolete by Rev. Rul. 86-44, 1986-1 CB 376.

qualifies under §103(a).[19]

The shield of §103(a), however, extends only to interest paid by a state or political subdivision on obligations incurred in the exercise of its borrowing power.[20] The exemption does not apply to interest on condemnation awards, and possibly to obligations arising in other involuntary transactions, because the congressional objective to avoid burdening the state's "borrowing power" is not inconsistent with a tax on interest that the recipient must accept whatever interest rate the state chooses to prescribe by statute.[21]

The obligations, however, need not be secured by the issuer's general credit or taxing power; tax-exempt interest can be payable out of special funds or revenues derived from particular property.[22] If property acquired for public purposes is subject to preexisting indebtedness, interest on the debt is exempt under §103(a) whether the public body assumes the debt or takes subject to it, since either arrangement is similar to the conventional exercise of the agency's borrowing power.[23] To be sure, the acquisition of property subject to an existing mortgage creates no liability to the mortga-

---

[19] Rev. Rul. 60-179, 1960-1 CB 37. See also H.R. Rep. No. 841, supra note 15, at II-686 n.4 ("installment purchase agreements, finance leases, and other evidences of debt issued pursuant to the borrowing power of a qualified governmental unit are treated as bonds"); Marsh Monument Co. v. US, 301 F. Supp. 1316 (ED Mich. 1969) (commercial contract with implicit interest held qualified for exclusion).

[20] See Power Equip. Co. v. US, 748 F2d 1130 (6th Cir. 1984) (no exemption for interest on installment debt arising in sale by taxpayer to local governments made without proper governmental authorization; although unauthorized debt probably enforceable, it was not issued in exercise of borrowing power); Fox v. US, 397 F2d 119 (8th Cir. 1968) (interest on certificates of deposit issued by a state bank not exempt); Rev. Rul. 87-116, 1987-46 IRB 7 (no exemption for interest on bond that is not legally enforceable obligation of issuer); Rev. Rul. 78-140, 1978-1 CB 27 (no exclusion for "interest" on lottery prize paid in annual installments).

[21] Stewart v. CIR, 714 F2d 977 (9th Cir. 1983) (interest at statutory rate on obligation incurred by local government in a condemnation action not exempt). See also Stewart v. CIR, 739 F2d 411 (9th Cir. 1984) (interest on installment obligations received in sale to a local government under threat of condemnation not exempt); Drew v. US, 551 F2d 85 (5th Cir. 1977) (same); King v. CIR, 77 TC 1113 (1981) (acq.) (same as to interest on notes issued in deferred payment sale under threat of condemnation, but interest on notes issued in payment for land not subject to power of eminent domain but sold voluntarily held excludable); Newman v. CIR, 68 TC 433 (1977) (interest included in state retirement annuity under pension plan for civil service employees not excludable).

[22] Reg. §1.103-1(b) (special assessments); Independent Gravel Co. v. CIR, 56 TC 698 (1971) (special tax bills issued as payment for street and sewer improvements, assessed against adjacent landowners), and cases therein cited; Rev. Rul. 58-452, 1958-2 CB 37, modified by Rev. Rul. 71-594, 1971-2 CB 91 (bonds of water district, payable from revenues and insured by federal agency).

[23] Kings County Dev. Co. v. CIR, 93 F2d 33 (9th Cir. 1937), cert. denied, 304 US 559 (1938) (prearranged assumption of debt).

gee; but if the payments are not made, the state or municipality will forfeit its equity in the property. Thus, the acquisition is tantamount to a borrowing to be repaid solely out of the revenues produced by the property purchased from the loan proceeds.

On the other hand, tax-exempt status has been denied to interest paid by a public agency as guarantor of third-party indebtedness, even though the lender would have been unwilling to advance funds without the guaranty, on the ground that "the obligation to pay the principal of the loans is not the obligation of the State or a political subdivision thereof" but is instead the obligation of the private borrower.[24] Since the guaranty was simply a device to raise funds for a program that the governmental body would otherwise have had to finance by issuing conventional exempt obligations, the distinction is more formal than real.

Also, the exclusion does not apply to payments that are called interest, but that really are compensation for services.[25] Nor does it apply to penalties paid by an issuer for failing to redeem bonds at maturity within the scope of §103(a).[26] On the other hand, the exemption covers the proceeds of insurance purchased by investors in exempt obligations to indemnify themselves against the loss of interest on default.[27]

3. *Registration requirement.* Generally, the §103(a) exemption is only allowed for bonds that are registered.[28] Exceptions from the registration requirement are, however, provided for three categories of bonds: (1) bonds of a type not offered to the public, (2) bonds maturing within one year of issue, and (3) bonds issued to foreigners subject to limitations designed to keep them out of the hands of U.S. persons.[29] Registration can be accomplished by a mere entry on the books of the issuer or a transfer agent if the person the books show as owner is entitled to all payments of principal and

---

[24] State Bank of Albany v. US, 389 F2d 85, 86 (2d Cir. 1968) (student loans guaranteed by New York Higher Education Assistance Corporation); Rev. Rul. 69-171, 1969-1 CB 46 (same).

[25] Rev. Rul. 73-27, 1973-1 CB 46 (portion of interest on municipal loans retained by commercial bank as compensation for servicing pool of investments is not excludable from bank's gross income). See also Rev. Rul. 58-536, 1958-2 CB 21 ("Class B" bond coupons intended as compensation to underwriters of municipal bonds not exempt); American Nat'l Bank v. US, 573 F2d 1201 (Ct. Cl. 1978) (bank was true owner of exempt securities, rather than dealers obligated to purchase them; interest excludable).

[26] Bryant v. CIR, 2 TC 789, 794 (1943) (acq.). See also Rev. Rul. 80-135, 1980-1 CB 18 (taxpayer lending municipal bonds to broker not entitled to exclude payments from broker equal to interest taxpayer would have received on bonds).

[27] Rev. Rul. 76-78, 1976-1 CB 25.

[28] IRC §149(a)(1). South Carolina v. Baker, 108 S. Ct. 1355 (1988) (registration requirement constitutional), discussed supra ¶1.2.8.

[29] IRC §§149(a)(2), 163(f)(2)(B).

interest.[30]

4. *Non-Code exemptions.* Section 149(c) purports to deny effect to any statutory exemption of interest that is not found in the Code or a revenue act. A grandfather rule preserves the effectiveness of non-Code exemptions that were in effect on January 6, 1983, treating bonds issued under these exemptions as though they were §103(a) bonds. Some bonds issued under pre-1983 non-Code exemptions need comply only with the non-Code authorizing legislation. This treatment applies to (1) bonds issued by the governments of Puerto Rico and the Virgin Islands in compliance with the law as in effect on October 22, 1986, (2) bonds issued before June 19, 1984 under §11(b) of the Housing Act of 1937, and (3) bonds issued under the Northwest Power Act, as it existed on July 18, 1984. Bonds issued under other pre-1983 non-Code provisions must additionally comply with "the appropriate requirements" of the Code provisions on state and local obligations.[31]

The basic rule of §149(c) nullifying post-1983 exemptions that are not in the Code or a revenue act has little legal effect, if any, because future Congresses have the power to enact non-Code rules that override all previously enacted provisions of law, including §149(c). The rule serves principally as an expression of disgruntlement by the tax committees of Congress over others treading on their turf.

¶15.2.3 Bond Discount and Premium

If a state or municipal obligation is issued at a discount, the difference between the issue price and the amount paid at maturity is "interest" qualifying for exclusion under §103(a).[32] Original issue discount accrues on a constant interest basis over the term of the obligation.[33] Under a constant interest method, some portion of the original issue discount accrues at least once each year. In each period, the accrual of discount and stated interest equals the outstanding balance of the indebtedness (including previously accrued original issue discount) multiplied by an accrual rate that remains constant over the bond's term. The accrual of discount is the excess of the total accrual over stated interest for the period. Because the accruals are the product of a constant rate and an ever-rising indebtedness figure, the dollar amount of each accrual is larger than the previous one. The principal significance of the accrual procedure is that the accruals are added to the holder's

---

[30] IRC §149(a)(3)(A).

[31] IRC §149(c)(2)(B). Prior law was more explicit in specifying the Code provisions that must be satisfied. IRC §103(m)(1) (before repeal in 1986).

[32] Rev. Rul. 72-587, 1972-2 CB 74. But see Rev. Rul. 80-143, 1980-1 CB 19 (if discount bond redeemed before maturity, exclusion applies to original issue discount accrued prior to redemption, but unaccrued discount taxable as gain on disposition).

[33] IRC §1288.

basis for the obligation.[34]

Discount income is not exempt unless it arises on original issue. If a bond issued at par is purchased on the market for less than par, the resulting market discount is not exempt interest because it is a consequence of interest rate fluctuation after the bond's issuance and does not reflect the cost to the obligor of borrowing money. Market discount is realized by the holder as gain when the bond is redeemed at par or sold for an amount exceeding the holder's cost, and this gain is includable in gross income—as a capital gain if the bond is a capital asset.[35]

Moreover, any premium paid upon retirement of an exempt security, whether or not issued at a discount, is treated as an amount received in exchange for the security, not as exempt interest, on the theory that it is not compensation for the use of the borrowed funds.[36]

If exempt bonds are issued or purchased for more than par, the premium cannot be amortized by a deduction against income, as is permitted by §171(a) in the case of taxable securities, because the premium is paid for the exempt interest and in effect reduces the net amount thereof. A portion of the premium must be applied annually in reduction of the taxpayer's basis for the security under §1016(a)(5), however, to reflect the fact that the premium is recovered in annual installments as interest accrues or is received.[37] The annual accrual of premium is usually determined on a constant interest basis.[38] The constant interest method works as follows: Some portion of the premium accrues at least once each year. For each period, the accrual of premium and stated interest equals the outstanding balance of the indebtedness multiplied by a constant percentage. The outstanding indebtedness is the taxpayer's cost for the bond, reduced by prior accruals of premium. The constant percentage is the yield to maturity on the taxpayer's investment. The premium accrual for a particular period is the excess of the

---

[34] See Lokken, The Time Value of Money Rules, 42 Tax L. Rev. 1, 15, 284–86 (1986). Prior to 1984, original issue discount on an exempt bond accrued ratably over the bond's term. Rev. Rul. 73-112, 1973-1 CB 47. This procedure increased the basis of a bond faster than the bond's value rose (absent a decline in prevailing interest rates), thus allowing artificial losses to be realized on sales of tax-exempt discount bonds before maturity.

[35] IRC §1232(a)(1) (sale or exchange treatment); M.C. Parrish Co. v. CIR, 147 F2d 284 (5th Cir. 1945); Rev. Rul. 73-112, supra note 34; Rev. Rul. 60-210, 1960-1 CB 38, modified by Rev. Rul. 60-376, 1960-2 CB 38. For the somewhat different treatment of market discount under taxable bonds, see Lokken, The Time Value of Money Rules, 42 Tax L. Rev. 1, 251–72 (1986).

[36] District Bond Co. v. CIR, 1 TC 837 (1943); Rev. Rul. 72-587, supra note 32.

[37] For special rules applicable to premium on tax-exempt bonds held by dealers in securities, see §75, discussed in detail in Brown v. US, 426 F2d 355 (Ct. Cl. 1970). See also S. Rep. No. 1983, 85th Cong., 2d Sess., reprinted in 1958-3 CB 922, 934.

[38] IRC §171(b)(3).

interest payment for the period over the accrual determined under the procedure just described. Because the accruals are the product of a constant rate and an ever-declining indebtedness figure and because interest payments are constant, the dollar amount of each accrual of premium is smaller than the previous one.

In the case of bonds that can be called at gradually reducing prices on different dates, the premium is amortized to the redemption price for the earliest call date; if that date passes without a call, any remaining premium is similarly amortized to the next date, and so on.[39] Thus, only the unrecovered part is reflected in the taxpayer's basis. Because of adjustment for the premium, the bond's basis will equal its face amount at maturity.

¶15.2.4 Exempt-Interest Distributions by Mutual Funds

To enable small investors to invest in diversified portfolios of exempt securities, the rules governing distributions by regulated investment companies permit the flow-through of tax-exempt bond interest to their shareholders.[40] To qualify, the fund must invest at least 50 percent of the value of its assets in tax-exempt securities and distribute at least 90 percent of both its investment company taxable income and its net income from exempt securities. Correlative provisions of §265 prevent shareholders from deducting interest paid on debt to purchase or carry shares making exempt-interest distributions, and disallow deductions by the fund itself to the extent allocable to its exempt income.[41] These restrictions put the shareholders in substantially the same position that they would have occupied had they purchased the exempt securities directly.

¶15.2.5 Reporting Requirements

Reporting requirements are imposed on both issuers and holders of tax-exempt bonds.

1. *Reporting by issuers.* An issuer must submit a statement on an exempt bond issue soon after the bonds are issued. The statement reports a variety of information about the issue, including the issue date, the stated interest rate, term, and face amount of each bond, the net proceeds of the issue, the portion of the gross proceeds held as a reserve fund, and issuance

---

[39] See Rev. Rul. 60-17, 1960-1 CB 124.

[40] IRC §852, discussed infra ¶95.7.1. See also Joint Comm. on Taxation, 94th Cong., 2d Sess., General Explanation of the Tax Reform Act of 1976, reprinted in 1976-3 CB (Vol. 2) 690.

[41] IRC §265(a)(3) (deductions by fund), §265(a)(4) (interest on shareholder's debt). See also infra ¶15.5.

costs.[42] If the bonds are private activity bonds, the statement must also include a description of how the public approval requirement was satisfied, various information about the users of the facilities financed by the issue, and a certification by the appropriate state official that the issue does not exceed the issuer's volume cap. Any property financed by the issue proceeds must be described. The Treasury or IRS can require additional information or waive the requirement of some of the information required by statute where the information is "not necessary to carry out the purposes" of the reporting rules. Also, the Treasury is directed to provide regulations allowing simplified, consolidated statements for small governmental issues where full, separate reporting for each issue would create hardship.[43]

The statement is due by the fifteenth day of the second calendar month after the calendar quarter in which the bonds were issued. For bonds issued during the first three months of a calendar year, for example, the statement is due by May 15. The IRS can prescribe a later time for portions of the statement, and has the power to forgive lateness when there is "reasonable cause" for untimeliness.[44]

If the statement is not timely filed and the time for filing is not extended, the §103(a) exclusion is denied to all interest on the bonds.

2. *Reporting by holders.* Under §6012(d), every person who is required to file an income tax return for a taxable year after 1986 must show in the return the amounts of tax-exempt interest received or accrued during the year.

¶15.3 PRIVATE ACTIVITY BONDS

¶15.3.1 Introductory

Once it was decided in *Shamberg's Estate* that bond interest could qualify for the §103(a) exemption even though payment depended on revenues to be received by an obligor having no power to levy taxes or assess-

---

[42] IRC §149(e). The requirements described in the text apply to bonds issued after August 15, 1986. Pub. L. No. 99-514, §1301(b), 100 Stat. 2085 (1986). Similar requirements were imposed by prior law, but only with respect to private activity bonds.

The statement must be filed on Form 8038 (for private activity bonds), Form 8038-G (for governmental issues), or 8038-GC (a consolidated statement for certain small issues). Procedures for obtaining an extension of the filing date or remedying an overlooked filing date are given in Revenue Procedure 88-10, 1988-4 IRB 29.

[43] 1986 Bluebook, supra note 3, at 1223–24.

[44] IRC §149(e)(3). Congress intends that an extension be allowed when a failure to file a timely statement is "not due to willful neglect." 1986 Bluebook, supra note 3, at 1223.

ments,[1] it was only a short step to the issuance of tax-exempt bonds financing wholly private facilities and activities. These obligations were originally known as industrial development bonds, but were relabeled "private activity bonds" in 1986. An example is a bond issue by a state-owned corporation to finance the construction of a factory or other business facility, which is then leased to a private enterprise whose rental payments are used by the issuer-landlord to pay the interest and eventually retire the bonds.

Until 1968, the statutes contained no explicit limitation on the use of tax-exempt bond proceeds for private purposes. The expanding volume and uses of industrial development and other private activity bonds, however, took the §103(a) exemption far beyond what Congress had originally contemplated. The revenue bonds issued by the Port of New York Authority (the issuer in *Shamberg's Estate*) and similar agencies usually finance facilities used by a multitude of patrons, while the issuer of private activity bonds often looks to a single patron, which is committed to use the facility throughout its useful life. When the cost of funds borrowed by the Port of New York Authority and similar agencies is reduced by tax exemption, the benefit inures to the vast and anonymous mass of persons who use its bridges, highways, and tunnels. By contrast, when private activity bonds are issued to construct a facility for a single occupant, the interest savings attributable to the tax exemption may result in reduced rental costs for business facilities that are not normally provided by public agencies. State and local governments often justify the use of their borrowing powers for private activity bonds on the ground that the projects financed by the bonds create jobs, but the effects of private activity bonds on employment have never been substantiated.

The IRS initially adopted a benign attitude toward the increasing volume of industrial development bonds issued after World War II,[2] but the Treasury became restive as the device came to be used as a financing arrangement for ordinary business facilities, with state and local governments acting merely as complaisant conduits. Recognizing that the public agency was only a middleman in these transactions, a few state courts held that the bonds were not public debts in applying statutory debt ceilings and other restrictions on local borrowing. The SEC adopted rules requiring the private company's obligation to be registered, despite the exemption grant-

---

[1] CIR v. Shamberg's Est., 144 F2d 998 (2d Cir. 1944), cert. denied, 323 US 792 (1945), discussed supra ¶15.2.2.

[2] See, e.g., Rev. Rul. 63-20, 1963-1 CB 24 (denying qualification on particular facts but providing blueprint to facilitate qualification); Rev. Rul. 54-106, 1954-1 CB 28; Nelson, Tax Considerations of Municipal Industrial Incentive Financing, 45 Taxes 941 (1967); Spiegel, Financing Private Ventures With Tax-Exempt Bonds: A Developing "Truckhole" in the Tax Law, 17 Stan. L. Rev. 224 (1965).

ed by the Securities Act of 1933 for state and municipal securities.[3]

In 1968, Congress responded by enacting detailed rules regulating the issuance of industrial development bonds.[4] The subject, however, again became a controversial one in the 1980s, when the rules were repeatedly amended, most commonly to further restrict the categories of tax-exempt bonds that could be issued for purposes other than the financing of essential governmental activities and facilities.

The rules were overhauled and restated in 1986. The 1986 rules retire the term "industrial development bond," and coin a broader term, "private activity bond." Very generally, a private activity bond is a bond whose proceeds are used to finance nongovernmental projects and activities. Interest on a private activity bond is not exempt under §103(a) unless the bond is a qualified bond. Qualified bonds are bonds financing nongovernmental projects and activities that Congress has found appropriate subjects for tax-exempt financing. Even qualified bonds, however, can only be issued within dollar ceilings prescribed by statute.

The major thrust of the 1986 changes was to narrow the categories of private activity bonds that qualify for exemption—to "restrict tax-exempt financing for private activities without affecting the ability of state and local governments to issue bonds for traditional governmental purposes."[5] Congress noted that tax-exempt financing of private activities increased in the period 1975 through 1985 from $8.9 billion to $116.4 billion, from 29 percent of state and local borrowing to 53 percent.[6] This "indirect Federal subsidy to private activities" was found to be inefficient and disruptive of the equity of the tax system.[7] The growth in tax-exempt financing tended to push up interest rates on all tax-exempt bonds, including those issued to finance government operations. As a consequence, "the additional bond

---

[3] Ritter, Federal Income Tax Treatment of Municipal Obligations: Industrial Development Bonds, 25 Tax Lawyer 513 (1972); SEC Rule 131 (Securities Act of 1933); SEC Rule 3b-5 (Securities Exchange Act of 1934); SEC Release Nos. 33-4921, 33-5055.

[4] Congress was galvanized into action by the Treasury's announcement that it was about to revoke a series of favorable IRS rulings and would issue proposed regulations providing that industrial development bonds were obligations of the private corporation occupying the facilities rather than of the state or political subdivision ostensibly issuing them. TIR 972 (March 6, 1968), reprinted in Senate Finance Comm., Hearings on Tax Adjustment Act of 1968 (H.R. 15414), 90th Cong., 2d Sess. 94–95 (1968). The proposed regulations (33 Fed. Reg. 4950) presaged the main features of the statutory rules as well as some of the examples in the regulations thereunder. See generally Ritter, supra note 3, at 513.

[5] Staff of Joint Comm. on Tax'n, 99th Cong., 2d Sess., General Explanation of the Tax Reform Act of 1986, at 1151 (Comm. Print 1987) [hereinafter 1986 Bluebook].

[6] Id.

[7] Id.

volume caused by nongovernmental use . . . increases the cost of financing essential government services."[8] Also, tax-exempt rates rose to be nearly as high as rates on taxable issues, diminishing the interest savings obtained by the issuers and causing the benefit of the exemption to flow increasingly to investors. Further, tax-exempt financing of private activities is economically inefficient because it causes activities to be undertaken that are not sufficiently profitable to compete successfully for capital in the absence of a governmental subsidy.

The narrowing of tax-exempt financing for private use was accomplished in two ways. First, the portion of the proceeds of a governmental issue that can be used for private purposes was reduced. Under prior law, as much as 25 percent of the proceeds of a governmental issue could be used for private purposes. The 1986 amendments classify an issue as private activity bonds if more than 5 or 10 percent of the proceeds are so used.[9] Second, the categories of private activity bonds that qualify for exemption have been restricted.

There are two broad categories of private activity bonds—bonds that meet a private business test and bonds that meet a private loan financing test—and a third, narrower category consisting of bonds financing electric, gas, and other utility facilities.[10] Under the private business test, which usually applies when the issuer owns the facilities financed by an issue, bonds are private activity bonds if more than a small percentage of the proceeds (5 or 10 percent) is used to finance facilities to be used by persons other than state and local governments. The private business test catches the traditional industrial development bond issue used to finance a factory building to be constructed for lease to a private business. The private loan financing test attaches the private activity taint to an issue if more than 5 percent of the proceeds are reloaned to nongovernmental borrowers or used to finance loans to such borrowers. Bonds issued to raise funds for student or home mortgage loans are private activity bonds under the private loan financing test, but the test also applies to bonds issued to finance facilities if the financing is structured as a loan of the bond proceeds to a private owner of the financed facilities. These rules are described in more detail below.

---

[8] Id. Senator Ribicoff predicted this when he proposed in 1968 that the exemption be repealed for interest on industrial development bonds: "As more and more tax-exempt bonds are issued the interest rate on all tax-exempt bonds, including school bonds, water and sewer bonds, will increase in order to make the total supply of exemption bonds attractive to lower bracket taxpayers. Thus, the cost of local government goes up." Hearings on Tax Adjustment Act of 1968, supra note 4, at 81.

[9] The 10 percent leeway is given so that "de minimis or incidental usage of government facilities and services by private users [does not] cause interest on an issue to be taxable." 1986 Bluebook, supra note 5, at 1152.

[10] IRC §141(a).

¶15.3.2 Private Business Rule

A bond is a private activity bond under the private business rule if it is part of an issue that meets both a private business use test and a private security or payment test.[11] Generally, these tests are met if more than 10 percent of the bond proceeds are applied for a nongovernmental use and more than 10 percent of the interest and principal payments under the bonds is secured by or will be paid from revenues from the nongovernmental use. A special rule, however, reduces the 10 percent leeway allowed by this rule to 5 percent if the nongovernmental uses of the proceeds are not related to government activities. These rules are described in more detail below.

1. *Private business use.* The private business use test is met if more than 10 percent of the proceeds of the issue are to be used for private business uses.[12] A "private business use" is a "use . . . by any person other than a governmental unit."[13] A private business use might result from the issuer's lease to a nongovernmental user of property purchased with the issue proceeds or from a contract under which a person other than a governmental unit agrees to manage such property.[14] Because the term "private

---

[11] IRC §141(a)(1). The private business rule has been criticized for focusing on the identity of the users of the financed facilities rather than on whether the use is public or private. Davie & Zimmerman, Tax-Exempt Bonds After the South Carolina Decision, 39 Tax Notes 1573 (1988). For example, if bonds are issued to finance a jail that is operated by a private company under contract with a city or county government, the bonds are private activity bonds because the user of the facility (the operator of the jail) is private. On the other hand, bonds issued to finance an electric generating facility of a government-owned electric system are not necessarily private activity bonds. Arguably, the results in these situations should be reversed because the jail financing serves a public purpose whereas the bonds for the generating facility finance a business.

[12] IRC §141(b)(1); H.R. Rep. No. 841, 99th Cong., 2d Sess., at II-687 n.8 (Conf. Rep. 1986).

[13] IRC §141(b)(6)(A). An "industrial customer" can be a member of the general public for this purpose. 1986 Bluebook, supra note 5, at 1159. Bonds financing public roads are not private activity bonds, for example, even though private companies will use the roads in pursuit of their businesses.

[14] H.R. Rep. No. 841, supra note 12, at II-687. The Conference Report also mentions "incentive payment" contracts and "take-or-pay or other output-type" contracts as arrangements that involve private business uses. Id. at II-688.
Congress decided, however, that because governments can sometimes "achieve significant cost efficiencies through joint public-private partnerships that utilize private management skills to assist in the provision of governmental services, . . . properly restricted private management contracts" should not be considered private uses. 1986 Bluebook, supra note 5, at 1153. Specifically, a management contract with a nongovernmental entity is not a private use if (1) the contract's term is no longer than five years, (2) at least one half of the manager's compensation is "on a periodic,

business use" is defined as any nongovernmental use, the term encompasses uses by nonprofit organizations.[15] A private business use occurs, for example, if property is leased to a charity for use in its charitable activities. A use by the federal government or one of its agencies is also considered a private rather than a governmental use.[16]

A use "as a member of the general public," however, is not a private business use.[17] Bonds financing public roads are not private activity bonds, for example, even though private companies will use the roads in pursuit of their businesses.

Generally, the private business use test is applied to the ultimate use of the proceeds.[18] The test is not always met, however, when proceeds wind up in private hands. It is not met, for example, if bond proceeds are used to pay for services and property purchased by a governmental unit in the course of its general operations. When a computer is purchased for use by a governmental unit, for example, the computer company is not deemed to be the user of bond proceeds used to pay the price. Also, salaries of government employees or a court judgment against a governmental unit could be paid from the proceeds without tainting bonds as private activity bonds.

Moreover, where an area under development constitutes a special tax or utility district and the district issues bonds to finance streets, municipal utility extensions, and other "facilities for essential government functions," the proceeds are not deemed applied indirectly for a private use, even if the area is owned by a small number of developers.[19] The developer or developers, however, must be "proceeding with all reasonable speed to develop and sell the land to members of the general public for residential or commercial use."[20]

The private business use taint can attach, in contrast, to quite indirect private uses. A private business use occurs, for example, if an electric generating facility financed with bond proceeds is operated by a govern-

---

fixed fee basis" and none of it is based on net profits, and (3) the governmental unit making the contract can terminate it without penalty after three years. Id. at 1161–62.

Also, a cooperative research arrangement between a State university and private business does not bring the private business use taint to the university's research facilities if certain restrictions are observed. Id. at 1162–63.

[15] IRC §141(b)(6)(A). Also, an investment use is a business use. If the proceeds of an issue finance property held by a partnership as an investment, for example, the business use test is met.

[16] IRC §150(a)(2).

[17] IRC §141(b)(6)(A). An "industrial customer" can be a member of the general public for this purpose. 1986 Bluebook, supra note 5, at 1159.

[18] Id. at 1160.

[19] Id. at 1160–61.

[20] Id.

mental agency, but the electricity produced by the facility is sold to a business under an output contract.[21]

2. *Private security or payment.* Even if the proceeds of an issue will finance a private business use, bonds are not private activity bonds under the private business use tests unless the private security or payment test is also met. This test is satisfied if (1) the bonds are secured by privately used facilities or by rental, loan, or other payments due from private users of facilities and (2) this security interest stands behind 10 percent or more of the interest and principal payments under the bonds.[22] The private security or payment test is also met if 10 percent or more of the principal or interest will be paid "from payments (whether or not to the issuer) in respect of property, or borrowed money, used or to be used for a private business use."[23] The test is satisfied, for example, if at least 10 percent of the funds expected to be used to pay interest and principal on an issue will come from rents paid by private users of facilities financed by the issue or from repayments of loans made from the bond proceeds.

The 10 percent payment test is applied by comparing the present value of the payments to come from private business uses with the present value of all payments under the bonds.[24] Present values are determined as of the issue date using a discount rate equal to the yield on the issue.

Such security or payments can be direct or indirect. "For example, payments made by a lessee of bond-financed property to a redevelopment agency are considered under the test even though the city, as opposed to the redevelopment agency, actually issues the bonds and does not receive the payments from the redevelopment agency."[25] This test can be met, further, even if bonds are secured by and nominally paid from tax revenues. For example, "if a facility is leased to a nongovernmental user and receipts from a tax are formally pledged as security, lease payments from the private user are considered [dedicated to bond repayments], even if the tax revenues [are] the direct source for repayment."[26]

3. *Special rule for private uses that are unrelated to or overshadow government uses.* The 10 percent threshold in the private business use and

---

[21] Sales and exchanges of electric power under pooling and swapping arrangements between investor-owned and public utilities, in contrast, usually do not make the public utilities' facilities private use property. 1986 Bluebook, supra note 5, at 1164.

[22] IRC §141(b)(2)(A).

[23] IRC §141(b)(2)(B).

[24] Notice 87-69, 1987-2 CB 378. Total payments include "credit enhancement fees taken into account in computing the yield on the issue under section 148," but do not include payments to be made from a reserve fund constituted from the issue proceeds. Id.

[25] 1986 Bluebook, supra note 5, at 1161.

[26] Id.

private security or payment tests is lowered to 5 percent if the private business uses are unrelated to government uses or if private business and government uses are related but the private predominate.[27] A fine distinction is drawn between private uses that are and are not related to government uses.[28] A newsstand in a courthouse is related to the government use of the courthouse, but a separate building for lawyers' offices across the street is not. A privately operated cafeteria in a school building is related, but an office building for the catering company that runs the cafeteria is not.

The 5 percent test is applied as follows: If any portion of the issue proceeds is used for a private business use that is related to a government use, there is subtracted from this portion an amount equal to the issue proceeds used in the related government use. If a positive number remains, it is added to (1) similar excesses of private over government use proceeds for other mixed projects financed by the issue and (2) all of the proceeds devoted to private business uses that are not related to government uses. The private business use test is met if this sum is 5 percent or more of the issue proceeds.

If the private business use test is met in this way, an examination is made of security and payment arrangements with respect to the portion of the issue represented by the sum computed under the rules described in the preceding paragraph. This portion of the issue is here referred to as the private business use portion. The private security or payment test is met if 5 percent or more of the issue is made up of (1) portions of the private business use portion of the issue that are secured by property held for private business use or payments with respect to such property and (2) portions of the private business use portion that will be paid from amounts to be received by the issuer as rents on private use property or as payments on loans that finance private use property.

4. *Special rule where private business use and payment or security exceeds $15 million.* A special rule applies if the 5 or 10 percent threshold under the private business tests exceeds $15 million.[29] The rule works as follows: A computation is made of (1) the portion of the issue proceeds to be used for private business uses and (2) the portion of the issue that is secured by or is to be paid from property used in private business uses. The special rule does not apply unless both of these figures exceed $15 million. If they do, the bonds are private activity bonds unless the issuer allocates to the issue a portion of its annual volume cap for qualified private activity bonds equal to the excess of the smaller figure over $15 million.[30] This rule does

---

[27] IRC §141(b)(3). The term "government use" is defined as any use that is not a private business use. IRC §141(b)(7).

[28] See 1986 Bluebook, supra note 5, at 1165–66.

[29] IRC §141(b)(5).

[30] See infra ¶15.4.9 for the volume cap.

not apply to output facilities.[31]

¶15.3.3 Private Loan Financing Test

If a bond is part of an issue that does not meet one or both of the private business tests, the bond is nevertheless a private activity bond if the issue meets a private loan financing test. This test applies if some portion of the proceeds of the issue is lent to borrowers that are not governmental units or is used to finance loans to such borrowers. The test is met if this portion exceeds the lesser of $5 million or 5 percent of the proceeds of the issue.[32]

Whether proceeds are used to make or finance "loans" is determined by the substance of transactions, not their form.[33] A transaction that purports to be a lease or a management or output contract, for example, is treated as a loan if the transaction shifts the significant benefits and burdens of ownership to the lessee, manager, or output purchaser.[34]

A loan does not count against the $5-million-or-5-percent cap, however, if it finances the borrower's payment of a "tax or assessment of general application [that is imposed] for a specific essential governmental function."[35] Another exception allows, free of this limitation, a loan that is a "nonpurpose investment," i.e., an investment that is acquired from the proceeds of the issue but for a purpose other than "the governmental purpose of the issue."[36] A use of bond proceeds to make a market purchase of a corporate bond is an example of a nonpurpose investment. An issuer that makes a nonpurpose investment must, however, be prepared to tangle with the rules on arbitrage, which are described elsewhere.[37]

¶15.3.4 Bonds Financing Output Facilities

Bonds issued to finance utility facilities are sometimes private activity bonds even if the private business use and private security or payment tests are not met. This rule applies when a significant portion of the bond proceeds are used for an "output facility (other than a facility for the furnishing of water)." The term "output facility" is defined as "property used in the

---

[31] See infra ¶15.3.4 for output facilities.

[32] IRC §141(c)(1).

[33] 1986 Bluebook, supra note 5, at 1166.

[34] Advance ruling guidelines were issued under a pre-1986 provision raising a similar issue. Rev. Proc. 82-14, 1982-1 CB 459; Rev. Proc. 82-15, 1982-1 CB 460.

[35] IRC §141(c)(2)(A). For additional detail on these obligations, called "tax-assessment bonds," see 1986 Bluebook, supra note 5, at 1166-67.

[36] IRC §§141(c)(2)(B); 148(f)(6)(A).

[37] Infra ¶15.5.

generation, transmission, or distribution of electric energy, gas, [or] district heating or cooling."[38] Also, the output facilities rule only applies if (1) the output facilities financed by the bond proceeds are used in significant part by private users other than utility customers from the general public or (2) the proceeds finance an acquisition of investor-owned utility facilities. The foregoing rules and limitations are described in more detail below.

1. *Private use rule.* An issue is classified as private activity bonds under the output facilities rule if (1) 5 percent or more of the proceeds of the issue is "used with respect to" an output facility and (2) the "nonqualified amount" of the issue proceeds exceeds $15 million.[39] The nonqualified amount is the portion of an issue that is used for a private business use or, if less, the portion of the issue to be paid from rents from property used in a private business use or from payments on loans to private business users.[40] For this purpose, a use is private only if it differs from the general public's use of the facility.[41] This rule does not apply, for example, merely because businesses are among the customers of a government-owned bond-financed utility that serves both businesses and residences within a defined district.

Assume an electric generating facility is to be owned 90 percent by a governmental unit and 10 percent by an investor-owned utility. Bonds issued by the governmental unit to finance the facility are private activity bonds if more than $15 million of the proceeds are used to finance the private utility's 10 percent interest, regardless of what percentage $15 million might be of the proceeds. Because 100 percent of the issue proceeds are used to finance an output facility, the 5 percent test is necessarily met. The private utility's use of its 10 percent interest in the facility is a private use even if it sells electricity from the facility to a broad base of business and residential customers, and the $15 million test is thus met if the issue finances more than $15 million of the private utility's interest in the facility.[42]

2. *Acquisitions from investor-owned utilities.* An issue constitutes private activity bonds under the output-facilities rule if a significant portion of the proceeds is used by a governmental unit to acquire "nongovernmental output property."[43] The portion used for this purpose is considered substantial if it exceeds the lesser of 5 percent of the issue proceeds or $5 million.

---

[38] H.R. Rep. No. 391, 100th Cong., 2d Sess. 1138 (1987); 1986 Bluebook, supra note 5, at 1163.
[39] IRC §141(b)(4). The $15 million figure is reduced by the nonqualified amounts of prior tax-exempt issues used in the same project. Id.
[40] IRC §141(b)(8).
[41] 1986 Bluebook, supra note 5, at 1163.
[42] Id.; H.R. Rep. No. 841, supra note 12, at II-690.
[43] IRC §141(d).

Output property is "nongovernmental output property" if, at any time after October 13, 1987, the facility was used or held for use by a person other than a governmental unit. The rule applies, for example, if a state floats bonds to raise funds to buy out a private electric company. The rule also covers "property which was constructed by or for an investor-owned utility with the expectation that it would be placed in service by an investor-owned utility but that is not actually placed in service before its acquisition by a governmental unit."[44] In the latter case, it is irrelevant "whether the investor-owned utility actually placed the property in service."[45] The rule applies, for example, if a state government floats a bond issue to buy and mothball a troubled nuclear power plant that has never been operated.

The rule was enacted in 1987 in response to a surge of interest by state and local governments in acquiring existing electric and gas generating and transmission systems. "Financing the purchase of such investor-owned facilities with tax-exempt bonds effectively substitutes tax-exempt securities for taxable securities."[46] Although the substitution might reduce utility costs for consumers, the reduction would come from federal tax revenues rather than from any increase in efficiency or paring of real costs, and thus would "effectively remove control of Federal Government revenues from Congress."[47] Congress therefore decided to subject these bonds to the volume limitations and other restrictions on private activity bonds.

The rule applies whether bond proceeds are used to acquire outright ownership of physical facilities or merely an interest in these facilities. A bond-financed purchase of stock or debt of an investor-owned utility, for example, is subject to the rule, as is a purchase of a fractional interest in a generation or transmission facility.[48] Also,

> the acquisition of power or other output pursuant to an output, capacity, or similar arrangement that is different from the basis on which the output is made available to the public generally is treated as acquisition of an interest in the underlying property unless the contract is of short duration and for wheeling of excess capacity.[49]

The rule does not apply, however, to facilities purchased by a governmental unit for use in serving its existing utility customers. Specifically, output property acquired from a nongovernmental user is not nongovernmental output property if at least 95 percent of the output from the facility

---

[44] H.R. Rep. No. 391, supra note 38, at 1138.
[45] H.R. Rep. No. 495, 100th Cong., 1st Sess. 1011 (Conf. Rep. 1987).
[46] H.R. Rep. No. 391, supra note 38, at 1137.
[47] Id.
[48] H.R. Rep. No. 495, supra note 45, at 1011.
[49] H.R. Rep. No. 391, supra note 38, at 1138.

will be used in an area throughout which the governmental purchaser has provided service of the same kind at all times since October 13, 1987.[50] An area must be "actively served" to qualify under this exception; it is not enough for the government agency to have merely been "authorized to provide service."[51]

For example, under the 95 percent rule, if a governmentally owned utility authority providing electric service throughout a city issues bonds to finance the purchase of a generating plant from a private utility company, the bonds are not private activity bonds unless more than 5 percent of the plant's output will be used outside the city. The utility authority might previously have been only a distributor of electricity, the acquisition being its first venture into generation facilities. The exception could also apply if the authority has long owned generating facilities and makes the acquisition to increase its capacity to meet enlarged demand, including "reasonable projected future demand."[52]

A fine distinction must sometimes be drawn if a government-owned utility has been in business since October 13, 1987, but has expanded its service area since that time. Assume a manufacturer builds a plant outside the existing service area of a city-owned electric utility but contracts with the utility for electricity. Bonds subsequently floated to purchase an investor-owned generating plant are private activity bonds if the plant is purchased to meet demand created by the contract with the manufacturer, but not if the purchase is made to meet demand within the historical service area.[53]

If a governmental unit in a utility business annexes a contiguous area "for general governmental purposes" after October 13, 1987, the area can sometimes be treated as part of the government's historical service area for purposes of the 95 percent test.[54] This rule could apply, for example, when the annexing government, in connection with the annexation, acquires a private utility company providing service to the annexed area. For an annexed area to qualify as part of the historical service area, two requirements must be met. First, output from the acquired property must be made available to all members of the public in the annexed area. The exception cannot

---

[50] After October 13, 1997, the required period of service will be the 10-year period preceding the acquisition.

[51] H.R. Rep. No. 495, supra note 45, at 1009.

[52] Id.

[53] Id.

[54] An annexation occurs for "general governmental purposes if it involves the transfer of voter registration and property tax rolls as well as responsibility for extension of general governmental services (e.g., police and fire protection and sewer and water services) on the same basis as those services are provided to other residents of the governmental unit." Id. at 1008.

apply, for example, to an "acquisition of output capacity to serve a single, or limited group of, industrial users either directly or through wheeling arrangements with another provider currently serving those users."[55] Second, the annexed area cannot be more than 10 percent larger than the government's existing utility service area. Alternatively, the second requirement is met if the capacity of the output property acquired for the annexed area is no greater than 10 percent of the capacity of output property held for the historical service area, exclusive of the annexed area. The comparison of existing with annexed territory or capacity is made as of the last day of the calendar year preceding the year of the acquisition.[56] The rule for annexations cannot apply, in contrast, if a government unit first enters the utility business through a post-1987 acquisition of a utility serving an annexed area. For the rule to apply, the unit must have "served a core area within its total area of actual service with the same type of service" since October 13, 1987.[57]

The 95 percent requirement is not met if more than 5 percent of an acquired facility's output is sold outside a utility's historical service area or qualified annexed service area. If a plant larger than presently needed is acquired to meet reasonably anticipated future needs, for example, the excess capacity does not disqualify the acquisition, but a plan to sell excess output to other utilities does if the excess is expected to exceed 5 percent. The legislative history indicates that power sales under some swapping arrangements and spot sales are not counted against the 5 percent margin.[58]

A further exception is provided for cases where governments purchase output property from nongovernmental users, but then convert it to uses other than providing utility output. The nongovernmental-output-property rule does not apply, for example, to "the acquisition by a governmental unit of land, easement[s], office buildings, or used vehicles from an investor-owned utility" if the governmental unit does not use the acquired property

---

[55] Id. at 1009.

[56] The conference report states that "the 10-percent restrictions [are] to be applied separately with regard to each such annexation." Id. at 1009. The statute, however, says that annexations within any calendar year are tested separately from annexations of other years, thus allowing a government-owned utility to increase its territory or capacity by up to 10 percent per year, on a compound basis.

[57] Id. at 1009.

[58] The purpose of a qualifying swapping arrangement must be to enable participating "utilities to satisfy differing peak load demands or to accommodate temporary outages." Id. at 1010. Each year, the power sold must be approximately balanced by power purchased under the arrangement. A qualifying swapping arrangement, in other words, cannot be a means of regularly unloading excess output. A spot sale outside the service area is ignored if it is "pursuant to a single agreement that is limited to no more than 30 days' duration (including renewal periods)." Id.

in providing utility services.⁵⁹ Another example covered by the exception is where a garage used by an investor-owned utility for its service vehicles is purchased by a government authority for use as a bus garage.⁶⁰ This exception, however, cannot apply to a nuclear power plant. If a governmental unit makes a bond-financed purchase of a privately owned nuclear plant with the intention of mothballing it, for example, the bonds are private activity bonds.

If several governmental units join in purchasing an output facility, the rules described above are applied to each participant in the purchase by treating its interest in the acquired facility as a separate facility. If a governmental unit purchases a 10 percent interest in a nuclear power plant and uses its 10 percent share of the plant's output to serve existing electricity customers, for example, the 95 percent test can be satisfied even though 90 percent of the plant's output is used outside its service area.

¶15.4 QUALIFIED BONDS

¶15.4.1 Generally

Interest on a private activity bond cannot be exempt under §103(a) unless the bond is a "qualified bond." There are seven types of qualified bonds: exempt facility bonds, qualified mortgage bonds, qualified veterans' mortgage bonds, qualified small issue bonds, qualified student loan bonds, qualified redevelopment bonds, and qualified 501(c)(3) bonds.¹ Most of these bonds are subject to a "volume cap" that restricts the aggregate amount of qualified bonds that can be issued by an issuer during any calendar year.² The seven types of qualified bonds and the volume cap are described in succeeding sections. Some requirements applicable to all qualified bonds are described immediately below.

1. *Public approval.* Qualified bonds can usually be issued only after a public hearing or a referendum.³ Generally, the public approval require-

---

⁵⁹ H.R. Rep. No. 391, supra note 38, at 1138.
⁶⁰ H.R. Rep. No. 495, supra note 45, at 1011.
¹ IRC §141(d)(1).
² See infra ¶15.4.9.
³ IRC §147(f)(1). An issue that refunds a prior issue need not have public approval if (1) the prior issue was publicly approved, (2) the maturity date of each bond of the new issue is no later than that of the bond it replaces, and (3) the new issue is not an advance refunding. IRC §147(f)(2)(D). See infra ¶15.6 for advance refundings.

If more than one bond issue is made to finance a facility, approval of a plan for the financing of the facility can suffice as approval of all bonds issued under the plan within three years after the first issue. IRC §147(f)(2)(C). Substantially all of the

ment applies to the governmental unit that issues the bonds and to each other governmental unit within whose jurisdiction is located any facility to be financed by the issue.[4] This approval can be given by voter referendum or by an "applicable elected representative."[5] The applicable elected representative of a state is its legislature, governor, attorney general, or other elected official designated by the governor or state law.[6] The applicable elected representative of a local government is its elected legislative body, chief elected executive officer, or other elected officer designated by the chief elected executive officer or state law.[7] Elected representatives, however, can act only after the matter has been aired at a public hearing that is preceded by "reasonable public notice."

2. *Issuance costs.* Issuance costs can be paid from the proceeds of a qualified bond issue, but the amount so paid is usually restricted to 2 percent of the face amount of the issue.[8] If the face amount of an issue of qualified mortgage bonds or qualified veterans' mortgage bonds does not exceed $20 million, however, as much as 3.5 percent of the aggregate face amount can be spent for issuance costs. The costs treated as issuance costs are underwriters' spreads, attorneys' and accountants' fees, fees of financial advisers, rating agency fees, trustee fees, printing costs, notice and hearing costs incurred in obtaining public approval for an issue, and costs of engineering and feasibility studies relating to the issuance of the bonds (but not

---

proceeds of each issue made under the plan, however, must be expended for the facility or to refund prior issues under the plan.

[4] IRC §147(f)(2)(A). If more than one governmental unit has jurisdiction over all of the area in which a facility is located, only one of the units need give its approval. Id. A facility located within a city, for example, need not be approved by both the city and the county that includes the city. The statute does not indicate which unit is the appropriate one to give approval, but regulations under prior law indicate that either will do. Reg. §5f.103-2(c)(3).

If an issue finances facilities at an airport owned or operated by the issuer, the issuer is the only level of government at which approval is needed. IRC §147(f)(3).

[5] IRC §147(f)(2)(B).

[6] IRC §147(f)(2)(E)(i).

[7] Id. If a governmental unit has no elective legislative body or elected official, its applicable elected representative is the applicable elected representative of the next highest unit of government. IRC §147(f)(2)(E)(ii).

[8] IRC §147(g). The definitions of the various categories of qualified bonds require that 95 percent of the net proceeds of the issue be expended for the purpose justifying the exemption. The term "net proceeds" is defined as the issue proceeds, exclusive of any portion set aside as a reserve or replacement fund. IRC §150(a)(3). If issuance costs are paid from the proceeds, they thus count against the 5 percent that need not be expended for the exempt purpose (the so-called bad money portion). See Staff of Joint Comm. on Tax'n, General Explanation of the Tax Reform Act of 1986, at 1154 (Comm. Print 1987) [hereinafter 1986 Bluebook].

to the completion of the project financed with the bonds).[9]

3. *Economic life limitation.* The average maturity of an issue of qualified bonds cannot exceed 120 percent of "the average reasonably expected economic life" of the facilities financed by the bond proceeds.[10] If an issue consists of bonds with more than one maturity date, average maturity is an average of the periods the bonds are scheduled to remain outstanding, weighted according to the bonds' issue prices. The "average reasonably expected economic life" of the financed facilities is an average of the anticipated economic lives of the facilities, weighted by the costs of the facilities.[11] Economic life is determined as of the time the facilities will be placed in service or, if later, as of the issue date of the bonds.[12] The statute provides no guidance on how to measure the economic useful life of a facility, but the legislative history indicates that the class lives prescribed for depreciation purposes can be used as a safe harbor.[13] The economic life limitation is only suitable for bonds financing physical assets, and is therefore made inapplicable to qualified mortgage bonds, qualified veterans' mortgage bonds, qualified student loan bonds, and some bonds used to finance FHA mortgages.[14]

Also, a special elective rule is provided for applying the limitation to qualifed 501(c)(3) bonds issued to fund a revolving loan pool for §501(c)(3) organizations.[15] Each loan from the pool must be made on terms that would satisfy the economic useful life test if the loan were a separate bond issue. The maturity dates of the bonds, however, can be fixed without regard to the test, and principal payments on the loans thus can be used to make qualified loans to other organizations, rather than being used to retire bonds. More completely, the economic life limitation is deemed satisfied if (1) at least 95 percent of the net proceeds of the issue is reloaned to two or more §501(c)(3) organizations or governmental units within one year after the bonds are issued, (2) these loans are made to finance acquisitions of property to be used in the borrowers' activities, (3) any portion of the net proceeds not reloaned to §501(c)(3) organizations and governments within one year of issue is used within 18 months of the issue date to redeem bonds of the issue, (4) each loan to a §501(c)(3) organization would meet the

----

[9] 1986 Bluebook, supra note 8, at 1216–17. Reasonable premiums on bond insurance, letter of credit fees, and costs of other "credit enhancement" devices can be treated as interest costs rather than as issuance costs. Id.

[10] IRC §147(b)(1).

[11] IRC §147(b)(2)(B). Normally, land is not included in the average. If more than 25 percent of the net proceeds is used for land, however, the land is averaged in as though its economic life were 30 years. IRC §147(b)(3)(B).

[12] IRC §147(b)(3)(A).

[13] 1986 Bluebook, supra note 8, at 1217.

[14] IRC §147(h)(1).

[15] IRC §147(b)(4).

economic useful life limitation if the loan were treated as a separate bond issue, (5) a survey taken before the bonds were issued shows a demand for financing exceeding 120 percent of the net proceeds of the issue, (6) none of the bonds will mature more than 30 years after issue, and (7) the issuer elects to be governed by this rule.

4. *Restrictions on property financed with qualified bonds.* Several types of property cannot be financed from the proceeds of qualified bonds. They are described below.

a. *Out-of-state facilities.* Generally, qualified bonds cannot be issued to finance facilities located outside the state that is the issuer of the bonds or the state in which the issuer is located.[16] Bonds that finance water, sewage, solid waste disposal, or hazardous waste facilities are exempted from this prohibition, but only if the facility or its output will be used wholly within the issuing state or, in the case of shared facilities, only if the bonds issued by the state to finance the facility pay for no more than the state's share of the facility.

b. *Land acquisitions.* Generally, no more than 25 percent of the net proceeds of a qualified bond issue can be used for the acquisition of land, and none of the net proceeds can be used for farmland.[17] These restrictions do not apply to qualified mortgage bonds, qualified veterans' bonds, and qualified 501(c)(3) bonds.[18]

An exemption from the restrictions is also provided for land acquired in connection with an airport, mass commuting facility, dock, or wharf.[19] To be so exempted, the land must be acquired by the issuer of the bonds or another governmental unit, and must be acquired for noise abatement or wetland preservation or for future use as an airport or other transportation facility. Also, the land can have no "other significant use."

A further exception allows tax-exempt bonds to be issued to finance loans of up to $250,000 each to persons new to the business of farming to enable them to buy farms.[20] An issuer can finance first-time farmer loans by making the loans itself or by purchasing loans made by other lenders. Each borrower and lending transaction, however, must meet several requirements, described below.

First, the borrower must be a "first-time farmer." A borrower is not a first-time farmer if either he or his spouse or minor children have previously had "any direct or indirect ownership interest in substantial farmland"

---

[16] IRC §146(k).
[17] IRC §147(c)(1).
[18] IRC §147(h).
[19] IRC §147(c)(3).
[20] IRC §147(c)(2)(A).

and if any of them "materially participated" in the operation of this land.[21] A parcel of land is "substantial farmland" if (1) it is at least 15 percent as large as the median farm size in the county in which it is located or (2) it is or was worth more than $125,000 at any time while the borrower held it.

Second, first-time farmer financing must be provided in connection with the borrower's acquisition of land or of land, buildings and other improvements, and equipment. This property, further, must be purchased to be used for "farming purposes."[22] The term "farming" is defined broadly to include nearly all agricultural and horticultural endeavors.[23] As long as some land is acquired, the portion of the loan proceeds that can be used to acquire improvements and new equipment is unlimited. No more than $62,500, however, can finance used equipment.[24] Also, the borrower must become "the principal user" of the land, and must "materially and substantially participate . . . in the operation of [the] farm."[25] This material and substantial participation must occur "on the farm."[26]

Third, no more than $250,000 of the proceeds of an issue can be used for the benefit of one individual and his spouse and minor children.[27] This $250,000 cap is reduced by any first-time farmer financing provided to the family from any prior issue.

c. *Existing facilities.* Generally, only new facilities can be financed with the proceeds of qualified bonds. More technically, when an acquisition of property is financed from the proceeds of a qualified issue, the "first use" of the property must be "pursuant to such acquisition."[28] Exceptions from this requirement, however, are made for qualified mortgage bonds, qualified veterans' mortgage bonds, qualified 501(c)(3) bonds, and bonds that finance first-time farmer loans.[29]

---

[21] IRC §§147(c)(2)(C)(i)(I), (ii). A farmer whose previous ventures have gone broke is given a fresh start. Specifically, an individual who has previously owned a farm is considered a first-time farmer if (1) the prior farm was disposed of while the individual was insolvent and (2) debts encumbering the farmland were discharged at less than face in bankruptcy or an insolvency arrangement. IRC §147(c)(2)(C)(iii).

[22] IRC §147(c)(2)(B)(i).

[23] Specifically, the term includes "stock, dairy, poultry, fruit, fur-bearing animal, and truck farms, plantations, ranches, nurseries, ranges, greenhouses or other similar structures used primarily for the raising of agricultural or horticultural commodities, and orchards." IRC §§147(c)(2)(D), 6420(c)(2).

[24] IRC §147(c)(2)(F). This cap is reduced by any financing provided from prior issues to the borrower, his spouse, or minor children. Id.

[25] IRC §147(c)(2)(B).

[26] Id.

[27] IRC §§147(c)(2)(C)(i)(II), (ii).

[28] IRC §147(d)(1).

[29] IRC §§147(c)(2)(A), (h).

A more complex exception is provided for rehabilitations.[30] Under this exception, funds raised by a qualified bond issue can be used to finance an existing building and its equipment if the building or equipment is of a type that qualifies where new and if a rehabilitation is undertaken at a cost that equals or exceeds 15 percent of the portion of the acquisition cost that is financed from the issue proceeds. Existing structures other than buildings can also be financed from a qualified issue, but only if rehabilitation costs are at least 100 percent of the financing provided from the issue to acquire the structure. If two or more buildings or structures are purchased and rehabilitated as a single "project," the 15 or 100 percent requirement must be met by the project as a whole, and need not be met for each building or structure.[31]

The term "rehabilitation cost" includes any cost that (1) is a capital expenditure, (2) is made by the person who acquires the building or structure in the transaction financed by the bond issue, and (3) is made in connection with the property's rehabilitation.[32] If equipment was used in an "integrated operation" conducted in a building prior to its acquisition, costs of rehabilitating or replacing the equipment are also counted as rehabilitation expenditures. Costs incurred in expanding a building, however, are not. The 15 or 100 percent requirement must be satisfied by expenditures incurred within two years after the building or structure is acquired or, if later, within two years after the issue date of the bonds.

d. *Forbidden property.* No portion of the proceeds of a qualified bond issue can be used to finance an "airplane, skybox or other private luxury box, health club facility, facility primarily used for gambling, or store the principal business of which is the sale of alcoholic beverages for consumption off premises."[33] Exceptions from this requirement are made for health club facilities financed by qualified 501(c)(3) bonds, but only if the facilities are related to the exempt purpose of the organization financed by the issue.[34]

5. *User-owned bonds.* Interest on a qualified bond loses its tax exemption during any period the bond is owned by a person "who is a substantial user of the facilities" financed by the issue of which the bond is part. The disqualification also applies while the bond is held by a person related to

---

[30] IRC §147(d)(2).

[31] IRC §147(d)(4).

[32] IRC §147(d)(3)(A). An expenditure is deemed made by the financed purchaser if it is actually made by (1) the seller in the financed purchase pursuant to the contract of sale or (2) a person who subsequently purchases the property from the financed purchaser. Id.

[33] IRC §147(e).

[34] IRC §147(h)(2); 1986 Bluebook, supra note 8, at 1218.

such a substantial user.[35] The rule is apparently meant to disqualify a bond held by any person who is a major beneficiary of the financing provided by the issue. Regulations under prior law define "substantial user" as a "person who regularly uses a part of such facility in his trade or business."[36] The rule would typically apply, for example, if an airline purchased a bond from an issue whose proceeds financed improvements at the airport that is the airline's principal base of operations. Qualified mortgage bonds, qualified veterans' mortgage bonds, and student loan bonds, however, are exempted from the disqualification,[37] thus allowing such a bond to retain its exemption while held by a borrower under the program financed by the bonds.

¶15.4.2 Exempt Facility Bonds

An "exempt facility bond" that satisfies the requirements described above is a qualifed bond. An issue constitutes exempt facility bonds if at least 95 percent of the net proceeds of the issue are "to be used to provide" one of the following types of facilities:[38] an airport, a dock or wharf, mass commuting facilities, facilities for "the furnishing of water,"[39] sewage facili-

---

[35] IRC §147(a)(1). A bondholder is considered related to a substantial user if (1) a loss in a sale or exchange between the two would be disallowed by §267(a)(1) or §707(b), (2) they belong to the same controlled group of corporations, (3) they are a partnership and a partner or spouse or minor child of a partner, or (4) they are an S corporation and a shareholder or spouse or minor child of a shareholder. IRC §147(a)(2).

[36] Reg. §1.103-11(b). If a facility is constructed, reconstructed, or acquired for a particular person, that person is a substantial user. A person not reached by the foregoing rule is a substantial user only if (1) his revenues from his use of the facility exceed 5 percent of the revenues of all users or (2) the person occupies more than 5 percent of the usable area of the facility. Id.

[37] IRC §147(h)(1). Qualified 501(c)(3) bonds are also exempted from the disqualification by §147(h)(2), but the exemption is of limited significance because a §501(c)(3) organization's general tax exemption would usually shelter interest on any bond that lost its §103 exemption.

[38] IRC §142(a). The term "net proceeds" refers to the proceeds remaining after any set aside as a reasonable reserve or replacement fund. IRC §150(a)(3). Issuance costs, if paid from the issue proceeds, must be paid from the 5 percent that need not be expended for the exempt purpose. 1986 Bluebook, supra note 8, at 1175.

[39] IRC §142(a)(4). Two additional requirements are imposed for bonds financing a facility for "the furnishing of water." First, water from the facility must be available to the "general public," a term defined to include electric utilities, and "industrial, agricultural, [and] commercial users." IRC §142(e)(1). Second, if the facility is not operated by a government unit, water rates must be "established or approved" by a federal, state, or local government or government agency ("a public service or public utility commission," for example). IRC §142(e)(2).

ties, solid waste disposal facilities,[40] a qualified residential rental project, "facilities for the local furnishing of electric energy or gas,"[41] "local district heating or cooling facilities,"[42] or "qualified hazardous waste facilities."[43]

The property financed by an exempt activity issue can include not only a primary facility of any of the foregoing types, but also "property that is functionally related and subordinate to [the] exempt facility."[44] An office, however, cannot be financed by exempt activity bonds unless (1) it is "located on the premises of [an exempt] facility" that is financed by the issue and (2) the functions to be carried on in the office are usually "directly related to the day-to-day operations at such facility."[45] "Thus, a separate office building, or an office wing of a mixed-use facility, is not treated as functionally related and subordinate to an exempt facility."[46] The directly related test, however, can be met, even though unrelated activities are carried on in the office, if these activities are de minimis in both size and cost.

Special rules for bonds financing airports, docks, wharves, mass commuting facilities, and residential rental projects are described first below. A restriction on private users' deductions for items related to facilities financed with exempt facility bonds is described thereafter.

---

[40] Solid waste disposal facilities include facilities "for the processing of solid waste or heat into usable form, but not [facilities] for further processing that converts the resulting materials or heat into other products (*e.g.*, for turbines or electric generators)." 1986 Bluebook, supra note 8, at 1170–71.

[41] IRC §142(a)(8). A facility is not "local" unless all of its customers are within a city and one contiguous county or within two contiguous counties. IRC §142(f).

[42] IRC §142(a)(9). Such a facility must be "used as an integral part of a local district heating or cooling system." IRC §142(g)(1). To qualify, a system must consist of "a pipeline or network . . . providing hot water, chilled water, or steam to 2 or more users for (i) residential, commercial, or industrial heating or cooling, or (ii) process steam." IRC §142(g)(2). Also, the area served by the system must lie entirely within a city and one contiguous county.

[43] IRC §142(a)(10). To qualify under this heading, a facility must be for "the disposal of hazardous waste by incineration or entombment," and must meet two additional requirements. IRC §142(h). First, the facility must be "subject to final permit requirements under subtitle C of title II of the Solid Waste Disposal Act (as in effect on [October 22, 1986])." IRC §142(h)(1). Second, the exempt financing must be used to provide hazardous waste disposal for persons other than the owner and operator of the facility and persons related to them. Specifically, if the owner, operator, or related persons will use the facility, the portion of the facility that is financed by the exempt facility bond issue cannot exceed "the portion of the facility which is to be used by persons other than the owner or operator of such facility" and persons related to the owner or operator. IRC §142(h)(2). See infra note 139 for the definition of relatedness used for this purpose.

Facilities for disposal of radioactive waste are not eligible for financing by exempt activity bonds. 1986 Bluebook, supra note 8, at 1170.

[44] Id. at 1175.

[45] IRC §142(b)(2); 1986 Bluebook, supra note 8, at 1175.

[46] 1986 Bluebook, supra note 8, at 1175.

1. *Airports, docks and wharves, and mass commuting facilities.* The proceeds of an issue for an airport, dock, wharf, or mass commuting facility can usually be used for any portion of the facility, including "storage or training facilities directly related to" the primary facility.[47] Such an issue, however, is not an exempt facility bond unless "all of the property financed by the net proceeds of the issue is to be owned by a governmental unit."[48]

The government ownership requirement usually can be met even if the property is privately used. An airport terminal can be financed by exempt activity bonds, for example, even though private airlines might be considered the primary users of the terminal. Some categories of property, however, cannot be financed by exempt activity bonds if the property is leased to a nongovernmental lessee for use in the lessee's trade or business or is operated as a trade or business by a person other than a governmental unit. The types of property subject to this prohibition are (1) lodging facilities, (2) retail facilities outside the terminal, (3) office buildings used by persons other than employees of governmental units and the operating authority for the facility, and (4) industrial parks and manufacturing facilities.[49] Retail facilities located within a terminal are exempt from the ban, but only if they are not larger than is necessary to serve passengers and employees.[50]

If a governmental unit holds title to property but leases it to others, there can be a question of whether the property is government-owned in substance as well as form. The ownership requirement is not met unless a governmental unit is the owner in substance. General tax principles determine who is the owner of property in substance. Under these principles,

---

[47] IRC §142(c)(1). See Rev. Rul. 88-51, 1988-25 IRB 5 (vehicles not considered part of mass commuting facility).

[48] IRC §142(b)(1). If such a facility passes out of government ownership, the nongovernmental owner is allowed no deductions for interest on indebtedness financed by the bond issue. IRC §150(b)(5).

[49] IRC §142(c)(2). The bar against leased retail facilities located outside the terminal applies to car rental lots, but not to public parking facilities. 1986 Bluebook, supra note 8, at 1168.

When a terminal or other facility is used in part for a qualifying purpose and in part for an ineligible purpose, the cost of the facility must be allocated, and bond proceeds may be used only for the portion of the cost that qualifies. The ineligible costs can be limited to costs of "the structural components required for the nonqualified portion of the facility (*e.g.*, interior walls, partitions, ceilings, and special enclosures) and the interior furnishings of that facility (*e.g.*, additional plumbing, electrical, and decorating costs)," and need not include "the general components of the terminal or . . . facility, such as land, structural supports, and exterior walls." Id.

[50] People "meeting or accompanying persons arriving and departing on flights to and from [an] airport" are considered passengers for this purpose. 1986 Bluebook, supra note 8, at 1168 n.69.

the owner of property is required to possess meaningful burdens and benefits of ownership. For example, where property is leased, the lessor has to suffer or benefit from fluctuations in the value of the property, in order to be treated as the owner for tax purposes. Thus, lease treatment may be denied, and the lessee treated as the owner, where, *e.g.*, the lessee has the option to obtain title to the property at the end of the lease term for a price that is nominal in relation to the value of the property at the time the option may be exercised, or for a price that is relatively small compared with total lease payments. A lessee also may be treated as the tax owner in certain situations where the lessor has a contractual right to require the lessee to purchase the property at the end of the lease. In determining tax ownership of property, the form of a transaction is not disregarded simply because tax considerations are a significant motive, as long as the transaction also has a *bona fide* business purpose and the person claiming tax ownership has significant burdens and benefits of ownership.[51]

A safe harbor rule is provided. Under this rule, property is considered owned by a governmental lessor if (1) the lessee elects not to claim depreciation or the investment credit with respect to the property, (2) this election binds the lessee and all successors in interest, (3) the lease term does not exceed 80 percent of the "reasonably expected economic life of the property," and (4) any option the lessee may have to purchase the property provides an option price equal to the property's fair market value when the option is exercised.[52] The safe harbor, unfortunately, was drafted so conservatively as to be of little practical value.

Congress also anticipated that property nominally owned by a governmental unit might not be owned by it in substance if the property is covered by "management contracts and similar types of operating agreements," but directed that the safe harbor rule for leases be adapted for application where a governmental unit has made such an agreement.[53]

2. *Qualified residential rental projects.* A qualified residential rental project can be financed with an issue of exempt facility bonds. Very generally, a qualified residential rental project is a multifamily housing project dedicated in significant part to low-income tenants.[54]

---

[51] 1986 Bluebook, supra note 8, at 1176. See also supra ¶¶4.4.2, 4.4.3.

[52] IRC §142(b)(1)(B). For purposes of the third of these requirements, the term of a lease includes periods covered by options to renew, and two or more successive leases are treated as one if they are part of the same transaction. Id.; IRC §168(i)(3).

[53] IRC §142(b)(1)(B).

[54] Generally, a project qualifies under these rules only if the occupants of the residential units will be renters rather than owners. A limited equity cooperative housing project can qualify, however, if the cooperative corporation elects this treatment when the bonds are issued. A cooperative is a limited equity project if (1)

More specifically, a qualified residential rental project must meet either a 20-50 test or a 40-60 test.[55] The 20-50 test is met if "20 percent or more of the residential units in such project are occupied by individuals whose income is 50 percent or less of area median gross income."[56] To meet the 40-60 test, "40 percent or more of the residential units in such project [must be] occupied by individuals whose income is 60 percent or less of area median gross income."[57] The income levels of the other 80 or 60 percent of the tenants is not regulated.

One of these tests must be designated by the issuer when the bonds are issued. The designated test must be met throughout the "qualified project period", which begins when 10 percent of the residential units are occupied and continues for at least 15 years after the first date on which 50 percent of the residential units are occupied. After these 15 years have elapsed, the qualified project period continues until (1) no tax-exempt private activity bonds issued for the project are outstanding and (2) assistance to the project under §8 of the U.S. Housing Act of 1937 has ceased.[58]

In applying the 20-50 or 40-60 test, tenants' incomes and "area median gross income" are determined "in a manner consistent" with the income and median determinations made under §8 of the 1937 Act.[59] This means, among other things, that the income level required to qualify a tenant as a low-income tenant depends on the size of the tenant's family.[60]

Whether a tenant's income exceeds the applicable income limit (50 or 60 percent of area median gross income) must be redetermined "at least annually on the basis of [his] current income."[61] If a tenant's income is within the limit when he takes possession of his unit or in any subsequent annual determination, however, his income is generally deemed not to

---

tenants-stockholders are generally precluded from profiting on sales of their stock and (2) appreciation in the value of the project is dedicated to public or charitable uses. IRC §143(k)(9).

[55] IRC §142(d)(1).

[56] IRC §142(d)(1)(A).

[57] IRC §142(d)(1)(B). For projects in New York City, the 40-60 test is met if at least 25 percent of the units are rented to persons with incomes not exceeding 60 percent of area median gross income. IRC §142(d)(6). If any other city with a population greater than five million divides itself into five boroughs, it will also qualify for this dispensation.

[58] IRC §142(d)(2)(A).

[59] IRC §142(d)(2)(B).

[60] 1986 Bluebook, supra note 8, at 1172. If the project uses the 20-50 test, a family of four is counted as low income if its income is no greater than 50 percent of area median gross income, but this percentage is lowered to 45 for a family of three, 40 for a family of two, and 35 for a single person. Under the 40-60 test, the qualifying percentages are 60 for a family of four, 54 for a family of three, 48 for a family of two, and 42 for a single person. Id.

[61] IRC §142(d)(3)(A).

exceed the limit so long as his tenancy continues, regardless of how high his income might go.[62] This rule, however, is subject to one exception: A qualifying tenant whose income rises above 140 percent of the limit in any subsequent determination ceases to be counted as being within the limit if, before a still later determination when his income is again below 140 percent of the limit, a unit of comparable or smaller size is rented to a person whose income exceeds 100 percent of the limit.[63] Much of the complexity in this rule results from Congress's desire that the required percentage of low-income tenants be maintained through rentals of vacant apartments rather than by evictions of newly affluent tenants.[64] When a tenant's income rises above 140 percent of the low-income threshold, in other words, he continues to be counted as a low-income tenant until a comparable or smaller apartment opens up that can be rented to a person who will replace him on the low-income roll. The foregoing requirements are further relaxed for a "deep rent skewed project."[65]

Transient housing, including "hotels, dormitories, hospitals, nursing homes, retirement homes, and trailer parks," cannot be qualified residential rental projects.[66] Also, each unit must contain "separate and complete facili-

---

[62] IRC §142(c)(3)(B).

[63] Id.

[64] 1986 Bluebook, supra note 8, at 1172.

[65] The 140 percent threshold is raised to 170 percent for a deep rent skewed project, but any qualified tenant in such a project whose income exceeds 170 percent of the limit in the most recent determination ceases to be qualified if any "low income unit" is let to a new resident whose income exceeds 40 percent of the area median gross income. IRC §142(d)(4)(A). The low income units of a project are the 20 or 40 percent that must be occupied by low income tenants in order to meet the 20-50 or 40-60 test. IRC §§142(d)(4)(C)(i), (5). See also 1986 Bluebook, supra note 8, at 1173.

A project is deep rent skewed if (1) the owner elects to have it so classified and, (2) throughout the qualified project period (supra text accompanying note 58), the project meets the following requirements: First, tenants occupying at least 15 percent of the low income units in the project must have incomes not exceeding 40 percent of area median gross income. Second, the gross rent for each low income unit must be capped at 30 percent of the income limit for the unit. The income limit is 40 percent of area median gross income for the units that meet the 15-40 test of the first requirement described above, and is 50 or 60 percent of the median for the remaining 5 or 25 percent of the units that are income restricted to satisfy the 20 or 40 percent requirement of the 20-50 or 40-60 test, whichever is elected for the project. Finally, the gross rent for a low-income unit cannot exceed one third of the average rent for units in the project of comparable size that are occupied by tenants whose incomes exceed the applicable income limit. IRC §142(d)(4)(B). For purposes of the second and third of these rules, "gross rent" includes payments under §8 of the United States Housing Act of 1937 and "any utility allowance determined by the Secretary after taking into account such determinations under such section 8." IRC §142(d)(4)(C)(ii).

[66] 1986 Bluebook, supra note 8, at 1171.

ties for living, sleeping, eating, cooking, and sanitation."[67] If a building includes both residential rental units and space used for nonresidential purposes, the proceeds of exempt facility bonds can be used to finance only the residential units, but the presence of nonresidential space in the building does not disqualify the project.[68]

If the qualification criteria are not met for any part of the qualified project period,[69] the operator's deductions for payments to the issuer are disallowed for so long as the criteria are not satisfied. If the issuer has reloaned the issue proceeds to a private owner of the project, for example, the owner is allowed no deduction for interest accruing during a year in which the criteria are not met.[70] If the issuer owns the facility and leases it to a private operator, the operator's deductions for rent accruing in such a year are denied.[71] Failure to meet the qualification criteria for any year does not jeopardize the §103(a) exclusion for interest on the bonds.

The operator of a qualified residential rental project, whether it be owner, lessee, or manager of the project, must annually report to the IRS on whether the project continues to satisfy the qualification criteria elected for the project. Failure to supply the report subjects the operator to a penalty of $100, but does not affect the tax exemption of interest on the bonds.[72]

3. *Limitation on private users' deductions.* If a facility financed with exempt facility bonds is privately owned or used, the owner or user is allowed deductions for payments to the issuer only so long as the facilities are used for a purpose permitted by the exempt facility rules. If the issue proceeds are re-lent to a private owner of the financed facility, for example, the owner is allowed no deduction for interest on the loan accruing during any period the property is not used for a permitted purpose.[73] If the facilities are governmentally owned but leased to a private user, rent or other user charges accruing while the property is impermissibly used are nondeduct-

---

[67] Id.

[68] IRC §142(d)(1). "The costs of such a mixed-use facility must be allocated according to a reasonable method that properly reflects the proportionate benefit to be derived, directly or indirectly, by the residential rental units and the nonqualifying property." 1986 Bluebook, supra note 8, at 1171.

[69] See supra text accompanying note 58 for the definition of "qualified project period."

[70] IRC §150(b)(2).

[71] IRC §150(c)(2). If the rent exceeds the interest accruing on the bonds, however, the deduction for the excess is not denied. Id.

[72] IRC §§142(d)(7), 6652(j).

[73] IRC §150(b)(4). Whether a use is permissible or not is determined by the law in effect when the bonds are issued. Id. If a facility is used in part for a permitted purpose and in part for an impermissible purpose, the deduction is lost only for interest on the portion of the mortgage allocable to the latter part of the facility. IRC §150(c)(4).

ible.[74] These rules do not apply to qualified residential rental projects, which are subject to a similar disallowance rule described above.[75]

¶15.4.3 Qualified Mortgage Bonds

Interest on a qualified mortgage bond is exempt under §103(a). Very generally, a qualified mortgage bond is a bond issued to finance mortgages, home improvement loans, and rehabilitation financing for middle income homeowners. Specifically, such a bond qualifies if it is issued before December 31, 1988 as part of a "qualified mortgage issue."[76] To qualify an issue under this rule, an issuer must use all of the proceeds remaining after issuance costs and "a reasonably required reserve" to make qualifying mortgage loans and provide other financing to owner-occupants of residential property.[77] Also, the issue must avoid being caught by the private business tests of §141(b),[78] and must comply with numerous requirements described below.

1. *Owner occupancy and location.* Every loan made from the proceeds of a qualified mortgage bond issue must be "financing" for a "residence which can reasonably be expected to become the principal residence of the mortgagor within a reasonable time after the financing is provided."[79] The term "financing" is meant to cover purchase money mortgages, home improvement loans, rehabilitation loans, and other loans to homeowners. Normally, the financed residence must be a single family residence, but buildings with two, three, or four residential units and cooperatives sometimes qualify.[80] Also, the residence must be "located within the jurisdiction of the

---

[74] IRC §150(c)(2). "For example, if a governmentally owned airport terminal were converted to an office or retail complex, each nongovernmental user of the converted property would be denied deductions for rent and other user fees with respect to the property, to the extent of the interest payments on an allocable portion of the bonds." 1986 Bluebook, supra note 8, at 1220.

[75] See infra notes 69–71 and accompanying text.

[76] IRC §143(a)(1).

[77] IRC §143(a)(2)(A)(i). In the statute, the terms "mortgage" and "owner-financing" are used interchangeably. IRC §143(k)(1). That usage is followed here.

[78] IRC §143(a)(2)(A)(iii). See supra ¶15.3.2 for the private business tests.

[79] IRC §§143(c)(1)(A), (2).

[80] A multiple unit building other than a co-op qualifies if (1) the property is entirely residential and contains no more than four units, (2) one of the units is occupied by the owner, and (3) the building has been occupied for at least five years before the mortgage loan is made. IRC §143(k)(7).

Generally, loans to cooperative corporations are allowed under the rules for single family houses, applied with two fictions: Each dwelling unit in the cooperative is treated as though it were owned by the shareholder entitled to occupy it, and each shareholder is treated as borrower with respect to the portion of the loan that is

authority issuing the bond."[81]

2. *Types of permissible loans.* At least 95 percent of the net proceeds of a qualified mortgage issue must be reloaned to home buyers and other homeowners in one or more of four types of home loans.

First, loans can be made from this 95 percent to home buyers "who had no present ownership interest in their principal residences" during the three years before the loans are made to them.[82] Purchase money mortgages of first-time home buyers qualify within this category.

Second, loans can be made to finance "targeted area residences."[83] A targeted area residence is one that is located in either "a qualified census tract" or "an area of chronic economic distress."[84] A qualified census tract is a census tract where the incomes of at least 70 percent of the families are 80 percent or less of "the statewide median family income."[85] An area of chronic economic distress is an area designated as such under standards established and applied by the state in which it is located; both the IRS and the Department of Housing and Urban Development (HUD) must approve this designation.[86]

Third, loans from the required 95 percent can include "qualified home improvement loans," defined as a loan of not more than $15,000 that finances "alterations, repairs, and improvements" to the borrower's existing

---

allocable to the shareholder's unit. IRC §143(k)(8)(A). A bond issue financing a cooperative housing project, however, is governed by the rules for qualified residential rental projects (see supra notes 54–72) rather than the rules for qualified mortgage issues if (1) the cooperative corporation elects this treatment when the bonds are issued, (2) tenants are precluded from profiting on sales of their stock, and (3) appreciation in the value of project is dedicated to public or charitable uses. IRC §143(k)(9).

[81] IRC §§143(c)(1)(B), (2).

[82] IRC §§143(d)(1), (3).

[83] IRC §143(d)(2)(A).

[84] IRC §143(j)(1).

[85] IRC §143(j)(2). The most recent available data from a decennial census is used in applying this definition. Id.

[86] IRC §143(j)(3)(A). The term "state" includes the District of Columbia, Puerto Rico, and possessions of the United States. IRC §§103(c)(2), 7701(d). In evaluating a state's designation of an area of chronic economic distress, the IRS and HUD must look to (1) "the condition of the housing stock [in the area], including the age of the housing and the number of abandoned and substandard resident[ial] units," (2) factors such as "low per capita income, a high percentage of families in poverty, a high number of welfare recipients, and high unemployment rates" that indicate a "need of area residents for owner-financing" through tax-exempt bonds, (3) the potential for exempt-bond financing improving "housing conditions in the area," and (4) whether there is "a housing assistance plan which provides a displacement program and a public improvements and service program." IRC §143(j)(3)(B). See Rev. Proc. 88-31, 1988-25 IRB 45 (procedures for obtaining approval of a state's designation).

residence which "substantially protect or improve the basic livability or energy efficiency of the property."[87]

Finally, the required 95 percent can include "qualified rehabilitation loans," defined as loans satisfying the following requirements.[88] The building must be at least 20 years old when "the physical work on [the] rehabilitation begins." Rehabilitation costs must amount to at least 25 percent of the mortgagor's adjusted basis after the rehabilitation. If a mortgagor's basis for his home is $75,000 before rehabilitation, for example, a rehabilitation loan can qualify only if rehabilitation costs are at least $25,000 (25 percent of the post-rehabilitation basis of $100,000). Also, in the rehabilitation, (1) 50 percent or more of the original external walls must be left as external walls, (2) at least 75 percent of the original external walls must be retained as external or internal walls, and (3) 75 percent or more of the original "internal structural framework" must stay in place. If a rehabilitation qualifies, a qualified rehabilitation loan can be made to finance the rehabilitation or to finance a purchase of the rehabilitated residence by a mortgagor who becomes the first resident after the rehabilitation.[89]

3. *Purchase price.* Except for qualified home improvement loans,[90] loans from the proceeds of a qualified mortgage issue can be made only to homeowners who acquire their residences at costs not exceeding 90 percent of "the average area purchase price."[91] The average area purchase price is "the average purchase price of . . . residences (in the statistical area in which the residence is located)."[92] The average is based on purchases "dur-

---

[87] IRC §§143(d)(2)(B), (k)(4).

[88] IRC §§143(d)(2)(B), (5)(B).

[89] IRC §143(k)(5)(A).

[90] See supra text accompanying note 87 for the definition of qualified home improvement loan.

[91] IRC §§143(e)(1), (6). Average area purchase prices are given in Revenue Procedure 87-20, 1987-1 CB 713, modified by Rev. Proc. 88-30, 1988-24 IRB 30.

If the residence is located in a targeted area, the 90 percent cap is raised to 110 percent. IRC §143(e)(5). See supra text accompanying notes 83–86 for the definition of "target area residence."

A residence's cost is "the cost of acquiring the residence as a completed residential unit," exclusive of "usual and reasonable settlement or financing costs," the value of work done by the mortgagor and members of his family in constructing the residence, and the cost of land held by the mortgagor for more than two years before construction begins. IRC §143(k)(3). If the loan is a qualified rehabilitation loan (supra text accompanying notes 88–89), rehabilitation costs are considered acquisition costs even if the mortgagor purchased the rehabilitated building long before the rehabilitation is done. Id.

[92] IRC §143(e)(1). The term "statistical area" generally means a metropolitan statistical area as defined by the Commerce Department. If the residence is not within such an area, the statistical area is the county in which the residence is located or the portion of the county that is not within a metropolitan statistical area. Where

ing the most recent 12-month period for which statistical information is available" when the loan commitment is given or, if earlier, when the borrower purchases his residence. The Treasury is authorized to provide separate averages for single family, two family, three family, and four family residences.[93] For each such category for which averages are supplied, separate averages must be given for new and used housing.[94]

4. *Limitation on borrowers' incomes.* Usually, the family income of each borrower under a program financed by a qualified mortgage issue cannot exceed 115 percent of "the applicable median family income."[95] "[A]pplicable median family income" is the greater of (1) area median gross income for the area in which the residence is located or (2) statewide median gross income.[96] This requirement, however, is relaxed for targeted area residences.[97]

5. *Arbitrage limitations.* Two sets of rules sharply limit the extent to which an issuer can profit from a qualified mortgage issue.[98] First, "the effective rate of interest" on the mortgages financed by the issue cannot exceed "the yield on the issue" by more than 1.125 percentage points.[99] If bonds are issued to yield 8 percent, for example, the effective rate of interest on the mortgages cannot exceed 9.125 percent.

The effective rate of interest on the mortgages is the yield to maturity of the mortgages taken as a whole. The interest on the mortgages includes both stated interest and original issue discount. That is, the excess of all principal and interest payable under the mortgages over the amounts loaned to the mortgagors is considered interest.[100] This excess is deemed to accrue

---

recent data for a county is inadequate, the Treasury can specify a larger area as the statistical area. IRC §143(k)(2).

[93] IRC §143(e)(4).

[94] IRC §143(e)(3).

[95] IRC §143(f)(1).

[96] IRC §143(f)(4). Borrowers' family incomes and area median gross income are determined by the IRS "taking into account" regulations under §8 of the United States Housing Act of 1937. IRC §143(f)(2). The same median applies to families of all sizes. 1986 Bluebook, supra note 8, at 1182.

[97] The income limitation is wholly inapplicable to one third of the portion of a qualified mortgage issue that is re-lent as mortgages on targeted area residences, and in applying this limitation to the other two thirds, the 115 percent cap is raised to 140 percent. IRC §143(f)(3). A targeted area residence is a residence located in a low-income or economically distressed area. See supra text accompanying notes 83–86 for a fuller definition.

[98] IRC §143(g)(1). These requirements are in addition to the arbitrage limitations of §148, discussed below at ¶15.5.

[99] IRC §143(g)(2)(A).

[100] For this purpose, the amounts loaned to mortgagors are reduced by fees and charges borne by mortgagors, including points (whether nominally paid by the mortgagor or the mortgagor's seller), origination fees, and "similar charges." IRC

at a constant rate over the terms of the mortgages.[101] This constant rate is the effective rate of interest on the mortgages.

The yield on the issue is determined similarly. The interest is the sum of stated interest on the bonds and original issue discount (i.e., any excess of the stated redemption price of the bonds at maturity over the issue price paid by the original buyers of the bonds).[102] This interest is deemed to accrue over the term of the issue at a constant rate, which is the yield on the issue.[103]

Second, if any portion of the issue proceeds is invested in property other than qualified mortgages (i.e., if the issuer holds "nonpurpose investments") and if the rate of return on this property exceeds the yield on the issue, the excess must be paid to the mortgagors under the qualified mort-

---

§§143(g)(2)(B)(i), (ii). Assume property is purchased under an agreement by which the seller agrees to pay four points on the buyer's mortgage. If the buyer's mortgage is $100 and the seller pays the mortgage lender $4 as points, the amount loaned is $96, and the $4 excess of the mortgage principal over the amount loaned is original issue discount.

Another reduction of the amount loaned is required if fees are charged to subsequent buyers assuming mortgages financed by a tax-exempt issue and if these fees exceed "the usual and reasonable acquisition costs of a person acquiring like property" where financing is not provided through tax-exempt bonds. In this case, the excess of the fees to be received over the usual and reasonable charges is estimated, and this estimate is treated as a reduction of the amounts loaned to mortgagors. IRC §143(g)(2)(B)(ii)(II).

The amounts loaned are not reduced by application, survey, or credit report fees or by insurance charges if the amounts of these fees and charges do not exceed customary charges for these items in lending transactions not financed by tax-exempt bonds. IRC §143(g)(2)(B)(iii)(II). If the mortgagor in the example pays, say, $1 for credit report fees and title insurance, the amount loaned is still $96, and is not reduced to $95 by the $1 of fees.

The amounts payable by mortgagors is not reduced by anticipated rebates of arbitrage profits under the rules described below in the text accompanying notes 107–08. IRC §143(g)(2)(B)(iii)(I).

[101] Because mortgages are often paid before maturity, it is not realistic to base this calculation on the terms stated in the mortgage instruments. The period the mortgages will be outstanding therefore must be estimated by taking prepayments into account. The prepayment rate assumed must be the rate given "in the most recent applicable mortgage maturity experience table published by the Federal Housing Administration," and the yield to maturity is calculated assuming that principal prepayments will be received on the last days of the months indicated by the prepayment assumption. IRC §143(g)(2)(B)(iv).

[102] IRC §143(g)(2)(C)(i). The stated redemption price and issue price are determined under §§1273 and 1274. Id.

[103] The length of the bonds' term is determined taking into account early payments on the bonds that will be made if the mortgages are prepaid at the rate assumed in determining the effective interest rate on the mortgages. IRC §143(g)(2)(C)(ii). See supra note 101 for mortgage prepayment assumptions.

gages or to the federal government.[104] Also, if this excess is invested pending the required distribution, all of the earnings on these investments must be paid to the mortgagors or the federal government. The earnings subject to this rule include both periodic returns and gains and losses on dispositions.[105] If the excess of the mortgages' yield over the issue's yield is less than the 1.125 percentage points allowed by the rule described above, however, the issuer is allowed to keep some of the earnings otherwise distributable.[106]

The excess earnings subject to the foregoing rule must go to mortgagors under the qualified mortgages unless the issuer elects before the bonds are issued to deliver the earnings to the federal government. When the mortgagors are the beneficiaries, the excess earnings must be paid to them or credited against their obligations under the mortgages, in either case "as rapidly as may be practicable."[107] If the federal government is the beneficiary, 90 percent of the excess earnings must be paid to the government at least once every five years, and a final payment, bringing the sum of the payments to 100 percent of the excess earnings, must be made within 60 days after the last bond is retired.[108]

6. *Targeted area requirement.* A portion of the proceeds of a qualified mortgage issue must be set aside for mortgages on targeted area residences (generally, residences in low-income neighborhoods).[109] The minimum amount required to be so dedicated is usually 20 percent of the amount loaned as qualified mortgages from the issue proceeds. If this amount exceeds 40 percent of average annual residential mortgage lending by all lenders in all targeted areas within the issuer's jurisdiction, however, the set-aside is limited to this 40 percent.[110]

---

[104] IRC §§143(g)(3)(A), (F); 148(f)(6)(A). All of the proceeds remaining after the payment of issue costs must be re-lent as qualified mortgages or held as "a reasonably required reserve." IRC §143(a)(2)(A)(i). The rule described in the text applies to investments of the reserve.

[105] IRC §143(g)(3)(B).

[106] The amount that can be retained equals the excess of (1) the difference between interest on the mortgages and interest on the bonds that would exist if the mortgage interest were high enough to provide the full 1.125 point spread over (2) the actual difference. IRC §143(g)(3)(C). This amount is determined when the bonds are issued.

[107] IRC §143(g)(3)(A).

[108] IRC §143(g)(3)(D).

[109] IRC §143(h). See supra text accompanying notes 83–86 for the definition of "targeted area residences."

[110] The average annual residential mortgage lending in all of the issuer's targeted areas is an average of the principal amounts of the mortgage loans made within these areas during the three calendar years preceding the year in which loans are first offered from the issue proceeds. IRC §143(h)(2). Only loans on single family residences are included in the average. See Rev. Proc. 87-31, 1987-1 CB 774 (average annual mortgage originations, state by state, for the period 1983–1986).

The issuer must exercise "reasonable diligence" to loan the set-aside to targeted area borrowers within 12 months. If some of the set-aside remains unloaned after 12 months, notwithstanding this reasonable diligence, the remainder is then freed to be loaned to any qualified borrower.

7. *New mortgage requirement.* Generally, the proceeds of a qualified mortgage issue must be used to make new loans, and cannot be used to purchase or refinance existing mortgages.[111] Exceptions from this prohibition are made, however, for loans that replace "construction period loans" and "bridge loans or similar temporary initial financing." Also, refinancings of existing mortgages are permitted in connection with qualified rehabilitations.[112]

8. *Assumptions.* A mortgage from a qualified mortgage issue must be made under an instrument providing that the mortgage cannot be assumed by a buyer or other transferee of the mortgaged property unless several of the requirements for new mortgages are met.[113] Specifically, a subsequent owner can assume such a mortgage only if he satisfies the principal residence requirement,[114] the first-time home owner requirement,[115] the purchase price limitation,[116] and the income limitation,[117] just as though he were obtaining a new mortgage from the issue proceeds.

9. *Good faith failure to meet requirements.* The tax exemption for interest on an issue intended to be a qualified mortgage issue is not necessarily lost if one or more of the foregoing requirements are not strictly observed. Recognizing the difficulties of meeting these numerous requirements in every loan made from an issue and further recognizing the drastic consequences of a disallowance of the exemption, Congress provided a little breathing space.[118] Specifically, a failure to meet the arbitrage limitations[119] or the targeted area requirement[120] is not disqualifying if (1) "the issuer in good faith attempted to meet all such requirements" and (2) lapses were "due to inadvertent error after taking reasonable steps to comply with such

---

If bonds are issued to finance a housing cooperative that is not located in a targeted area, this requirement can be met by aggregating the issue with other issues. IRC §143(k)(8)(B).

[111] IRC §143(i).

[112] For the definition of "qualified rehabilitation," see supra text accompanying notes 88–89.

[113] IRC §143(i)(2).

[114] See supra text accompanying notes 79–81.

[115] See supra text accompanying notes 82–89.

[116] See supra text accompanying notes 90–94.

[117] See supra text accompanying notes 95–97.

[118] The statutory provisions are largely a codification of regulations issued under prior law. Reg. §6a.103A-2(c).

[119] See supra text accompanying notes 98–108.

[120] See supra text accompanying notes 109–10.

requirements."[121] A slip from full compliance with one of the other requirements is excused if (1) the issuer tries "in good faith" to meet all of the requirements when the mortgage loans are made, (2) at least 95 percent of the amounts loaned to mortgagors from the issue proceeds is loaned under mortgages that meet all of the requirements, and (3) the failure at full compliance is "corrected within a reasonable period after such failure is first discovered."[122]

10. *Borrowers' interest deductions.* Generally, interest on a mortgage loan financed by a qualified mortgage bond issue is deductible under §163(a) under the rules applicable to home mortgage interest generally.[123] This deduction, however, is denied if, for a continuous period of a year or more, the mortgaged property is not the mortgagor's residence.[124] The IRS can waive the residence requirement where it would cause "undue hardship" because the mortgagor's nonresidence results from "circumstances beyond [his] control."[125] A waiver would be appropriate, for example, if a mortgagor's house burns down and it takes more than a year to rebuild it or if the mortgagor dies and the residence is thereafter occupied by his minor children.[126]

¶15.4.4 Qualified Veterans' Mortgage Bonds

The §103(a) exemption is allowed for interest on a qualified veterans' mortgage bond. Several requirements must be met to qualify a bond under this heading, including requirements that effectively bar local governments and all but five state governments from issuing these bonds.

First, at least 95 percent of the net proceeds of the issue of which the bond is part must be reloaned to qualified veterans as home loans.[127] A veteran is qualified if (1) he served on active duty and at least part of this service occurred before 1977 and (2) his application for a loan from the

---

[121] IRC §143(a)(2)(C).

[122] IRC §143(a)(2)(B).

[123] See IRC §163(h), discussed infra ¶31.3.

[124] IRC §150(b)(1). The denial applies to interest accruing during all of the continuous period of nonresidence, including the first year. If there is more than one mortgagor, the deduction is preserved if any one of them uses the property as his principal residence. Where a mortgage loan on a multiple unit building is made from the proceeds of a qualified mortgage bond issue, the mortgagor's occupancy of one of the units satisfies the principal residence requirement for the entire mortgage. 1986 Bluebook, supra note 8, at 1221.

The term "principal residence" has the same meaning here as under §1034. Id. See infra ¶44.5.2 for meaning of the term under §1034.

[125] IRC §150(b)(1)(B).

[126] 1986 Bluebook, supra note 8, at 1221.

[127] IRC §143(b)(1).

issue proceeds is made within 30 years after the end of his active duty.[128]

Second, the bond must be issued by a state that issued qualified veterans' mortgage bonds before June 22, 1984. Only five states issued such bonds before this date, and all other states are barred from issuing this type of qualified bond.[129] Also, both interest and principal must be a general obligation of the state, and all issues of qualified veterans' mortgage bonds by the state during the calendar year must be within an annual volume cap.[130] The cap essentially limits the state to issuing such bonds at the rate it issued them during the period 1979 through 1984.[131]

Third, the bonds must not be caught by the private business tests of §141(b). Fourth, the bonds must satisfy several of the requirements for qualified mortgage bonds, including the owner occupancy and location requirements,[132] the arbitrage limitations,[133] and the new mortgage requirement.[134] Finally, the deduction for interest on a mortgage financed by a qualified veterans' mortgage bond issue is lost if the mortgagor fails to occupy it as his principal residence.[135]

---

[128] IRC §§143(*l*)(1), (4). Veterans whose active duty ended before January 31, 1955 were allowed until January 31, 1985 to make application for a loan under these rules. IRC §143(*l*)(4)(b)(ii).

A nonveteran can assume a loan financed by qualified veterans' mortgage bonds if such an assumption is permitted by the program under which the veterans' loan was first made. 1986 Bluebook, supra note 8, at 1221 n.197.

[129] Id. at 1180.

[130] IRC §§143(b)(2), (*l*)(2), (*l*)(3). Some refundings of qualified veterans' mortgage bonds are exempted from the cap. IRC §143(*l*)(3)(C); 1986 Bluebook, supra note 8, at 1180–81. Also, some short-term bonds issued to finance veterans' payments of property taxes count against the cap only to the extent of one fifteenth of their principal amounts. IRC §143(*l*)(5).

[131] The cap is computed as follows: The aggregate amount of such bonds issued during the period January 1, 1979 through June 22, 1984 is added together, excluding the bonds issued during the calendar year in which volume was smallest. The cap is usually one fifth of this aggregate. If the bonds issued during the period January 1, 1979 to June 22, 1984 were issued in fewer than five calendar years, however, the cap is determined by dividing the 1979 through 1984 volume by the number of calendar years in which the bonds were issued. IRC §143(*l*)(3)(B).

[132] See supra text accompanying notes 79–86.

[133] See supra text accompanying notes 98–108.

[134] See supra text accompanying notes 111–17. The good faith rules described in the text accompanying notes 118–22 also apply in this context.

[135] This rule is described more fully in its application to mortgages financed by qualified mortgage bonds. See supra notes 123–26 and accompanying text.

¶15.4.5 Qualified Small Issue Bonds

Interest on qualified small issue bonds is exempt under §103(a).[136] The principal requirements for a qualified small issue are: (1) The issue must not exceed a dollar cap, which is either $1 million or $10 million and (2) at least 95 percent of the net proceeds of the issue must be used either to acquire, construct, or improve land or depreciable property or to redeem bonds previously issued for this purpose. The land or depreciable property can be leased to an industrial or other private user, but no more than 5 percent of the net proceeds can be used for residential units for families.[137] The qualified small issue rules, which are scheduled to expire at the end of 1989, are described in greater detail below.

1. *$1 million cap.* Except where the $10 million limit described below is elected, "the aggregate authorized face amount" of a qualified small issue cannot exceed $1 million.[138] Under an aggregation rule intended to block evasion of the cap, two or more issues are treated as one if (1) the proceeds of the issues are to be used "primarily with respect to facilities" within one municipality or within the unincorporated portions of one county, (2) the same person (or a group of related persons) will be the user of all of the facilities,[139] and (3) each of the issues would qualify as a small issue in the absence of the aggregation.[140] When the aggregation causes the cap to be exceeded, all bonds issued after the cap is reached are disqualified. The aggregation rule can apply even if the issuers of the several issues are not the same.

2. *Alternative $10 million cap.* A $10 million limitation can be substituted for the $1 million cap at the issuer's election. When it is elected, however, the $10 million is applied against a larger aggregate. Very generally, the expanded limitation is not satisfied unless the total cost of the project

---

[136] IRC §144(a)(1). A bond that would otherwise be a qualified small issue bond, however, is not so classified if interest on the bond is exempt under any other provision. IRC §144(a)(7).

[137] IRC §144(a)(5).

[138] IRC §144(a)(1).

[139] Two or more corporations are related for purposes of this rule if they are members of a controlled group joined together in a parent-subsidiary or brother-sister relationship (or a combination of both) with stock ownership of more than 50 percent at each level. IRC §144(a)(3). Also, individuals and entities of any sort are deemed related if a loss in a sale or exchange between them would be disallowed by §267 or §707(b). See infra ¶¶78.1 and 86.5 for §§267 and 707(b).

[140] IRC §144(a)(2). An earlier issue is not taken into account in determining the qualification of a later issue, however, if (1) the proceeds of the later issue are to be used to redeem all or a portion of the earlier issue and (2) the later issue and the redemption are not an advance refunding. Id. See infra ¶15.6 for advance refundings.

financed by the issue, including the portion of the cost that is financed with nongovernmental borrowing or paid by the private owner or user of the project, is no greater than $10 million.

The expanded limitation is applied as follows: The issue is first aggregated with other issues caught by the aggregation rule described above in the description of the $1 million cap. To this aggregate is added all capital expenditures made (and reasonably expected to be made) during the six-year period consisting of the three years preceding and the three years following the issue date of the bonds, but including only those expenditures that (1) are not financed by tax-exempt bonds and (2) are made for facilities that are principally used by the same user (or related persons) and are located within the same municipality or the unincorporated portions of the same county. An expenditure that meets these requirements is included regardless of who makes it. The broad reach of this aggregation is mitigated, however, by the exclusion of capital expenditures that are not a planned addition to the user's investment in the community and of a few other categories of expenditures.[141]

If an issue exceeds the $10 million ceiling because of expenditures made after the bonds are issued, the disqualification takes effect only when the expenditures are paid or incurred. Congress intended that private owners and users who exceed the cap not be allowed deductions for interest or rent accruing to the issuer under any mortgage or lease pertaining to the financed property.[142] This intention, however, is not adequately expressed in the statutes.

3. *Other aggregation and disaggregation rules.* An issue far larger than $1 million or $10 million can qualify as a small issue if more than one project is financed by the proceeds and if the proceeds of "separate lots of bonds" are used to finance separate projects for different beneficiaries.[143]

---

[141] The cost of replacing property destroyed or damaged by casualty is included only to the extent it exceeds the fair market value of the property before the casualty. If fire destroys a factory worth $100 million and the factory is rebuilt at a cost of $110 million, for example, the $10 million limitation is not exceeded. Also, an expenditure is excluded from the aggregate if it is necessitated by a change after the bonds are issued in any federal, state, or local law, ordinance, or regulation of general application. An exclusion is also allowed for up to $1 million of expenditures resulting from "circumstances which could not be reasonably foreseen" when the bonds were issued or from "a mistake of law or fact." Further, amounts spent for certain in-house research and development are excluded. IRC §144(a)(4)(C). An additional $10 million exclusion is allowed for expenditures of any kind if the facilities are subsidized by an urban development action grant. IRC §144(a)(4)(F).

[142] 1986 Bluebook, supra note 8, at 1220.

[143] IRC §144(a)(6). Two facilities are separate projects for this purpose unless one person or a group of related persons is the principal user of both facilities. A person who does not actually use a facility, however, is treated as the principal user for this purpose if the person (1) provides a franchise, trademark, trade name, or

When this is done, each lot is treated as a separate issue in the application of the small issue rules.

Conversely, in applying the foregoing rule and the $1 million and $10 million limitations described earlier, bonds and issues are aggregated and treated as one if the net proceeds are used to finance "a single building, an enclosed shopping mall, or a strip of offices, stores, or warehouses using substantial common facilities."[144]

4. *Use of proceeds.* Generally, the proceeds of a qualified small issue can be used to acquire, construct, or improve land or depreciable property or to redeem bonds previously issued for this purpose.[145] The issuer can re-lend the proceeds to a person who uses them to buy, construct, or improve land or depreciable property, or the issuer can hold title to the property and lease it to a nongovernmental user. Some types of property, however, cannot be financed with a qualified small issue,[146] and expenditures for other types of property are limited to 25 percent of the net proceeds.[147] Also, an additional dollar cap applies to an issue if any portion of the net proceeds are to be used for farm equipment or farm buildings.[148]

---

other property to the actual user and (2) participates in the issuance of the bonds by guaranteeing the user's obligations, paying issuance costs, or otherwise giving assistance. If a franchisor arranges an issue of bonds to finance separate facilities for several franchisees, for example, the facilities are considered principally used by one person, the franchisor, and the whole issue is subject to the $1 million or $10 million cap.

Also, a group of related persons is considered the principal user if its members provide property to the actual user and participate in the issue. A unit of government, however, is not considered to be a principal user under this rule. The benefits of the separate lot rule are lost, further, if the facilities financed by the proceeds of an issue are located in more than one state.

[144] IRC §144(a)(9).

[145] IRC §144(a)(1).

[146] The facilities covered by this prohibition are "any private or commercial golf course, country club, massage parlor, tennis club, skating facility . . . , racquet sports facility . . . , hot tub facility, suntan facility, or racetrack." IRC §144(a)(8)(B).

[147] The facilities subject to this 25 percent limitation are restaurants, bars, car dealerships, and recreation and entertainment facilities not covered by the outright prohibition described in the preceding note. IRC §144(a)(8)(A).

[148] No more than $250,000 of the net proceeds of a qualified small issue can be used to finance "depreciable farm property" to be used principally by any one person or by two or more persons that are related to one another. (See supra note 139 for the definition of related person.) Property is subject to this limitation if it is of a depreciable character and is used in a farming business.

"The $250,000 is a lifetime limit." 1986 Bluebook, supra note 8, at 1178. If the principal user of the property (or a related person) is the principal user of depreciable farm property financed by a prior small issue, the $250,000 cap is reduced for the present issue by the amount of this prior financing. IRC §144(a)(11). The reduction occurs whether the prior issue got its tax exemption under present or prior law and

5. *Per owner or user limitation.* A small issue is disqualified if a non-governmental owner or user of facilities financed by the issue is the beneficiary of $40 million or more of financing outstanding under this and prior tax-exempt issues. This cap is applied as follows:

The previously issued bonds taken into account are exempt facility bonds, qualified small issue bonds, qualified redevelopment bonds, and bonds that qualify as industrial development bonds under the pre-1986 rules.[149] Such a bond, however, is taken into account only if (1) it is outstanding on the issue date of the small issue being tested and (2) it is allocated to the beneficiary of that issue.[150]

A person is considered a beneficiary of the small issue being tested if the person owns or is a principal user of facilities financed by the issue at any time during the three years following the date the facilities are placed in service or, if later, the issue date of the bonds.[151] The statute is not explicit on how the beneficiaries of prior issues are identified. The regulations could most reasonably fill this gap by providing that a person is a beneficiary of a prior issue in two circumstances.[152] First, a prior issue should be traced to the beneficiary of the small issue being tested if, on the issue date of the small issue, the person is an owner or principal user of facilities financed by the prior issue. Second, a person should be considered such a beneficiary if the person becomes an owner or principal user of these facilities within three years after the issue date of the prior issue or, if later, within three years of the date the facilities financed by the prior issue are placed in service. If a beneficiary owns or is the principal user of only a portion of the facilities financed by the present issue or a prior issue, a ratable portion of the issue is allocated to the beneficiary, determined by the ratio of the portion of the facility owned or principally used by the person to the entire facility.[153]

The portion of the small issue that is allocated to each beneficiary is added to the amounts allocated to that beneficiary from other bonds taken into account in this determination. If the sum so computed for any beneficiary exceeds $40 million, the small issue fails to qualify.[154]

---

apparently occurs whether or not the prior issue is still outstanding. See supra text accompanying notes 20–27 for additional limitations on financing for farmers.

[149] IRC §144(a)(10)(B)(ii).

[150] IRC §144(a)(10)(B)(i). Outstanding bonds are excluded, further, if (1) they will be redeemed from the proceeds of the small issue being tested and (2) the issue and redemption are not an advance refunding. Id. See infra ¶15.6 for the definition of advance refunding.

[151] IRC §144(a)(10)(D).

[152] See Prop. Reg. §1.103-10(i).

[153] IRC §144(a)(10)(C).

[154] IRC §144(a)(10)(A).

For purposes of the foregoing rules, all persons that are related to one another are treated as one person.[155] The portions of various issues allocated to a person thus are combined with the portions allocated to related persons. If a small issue would push this sum over $40 million, no member of the related group is an eligible beneficiary of the issue.

6. *Termination rules.* The rules for qualified small issue bonds generally apply only to bonds issued before 1987 or, for bonds financing manufacturing facilities, before 1990. Bonds issued before the relevant expiration date, however, can be refunded at any time under certain circumstances.

The rules expired at the end of 1986 for all new bonds except those that finance manufacturing facilities and certain farm property, and as to the excepted bonds, the rules' life is only extended through 1989.[156] A manufacturing facility is a facility "used in the manufacturing or production of tangible personal property" and in "processing resulting in a change in the condition of such property."[157] A farm is treated as a manufacturing facility for this purpose if the bond issue finances an acquisition of the farm by a first-time farmer.[158]

A refunding can be a qualified small issue if the issuer observes several limitations meant to assure that no new financing is obtained after the expiration of the rules for new bonds.[159] The bonds retired in a refunding must have been issued before the relevant expiration date for new bonds. The maturity date of the refunding bonds can be no later than the maturity date of the bonds redeemed in the refunding, and the amount of the refunding bonds cannot exceed the outstanding amount of the redeemed bonds. The interest rate on the new bonds must be lower than the interest rate on the old bonds. Further, no more than 90 days can elapse between the issue of the new bonds and the use of the proceeds to redeem the old bonds.

¶15.4.6 Qualified Student Loan Bonds

The §103(a) exemption extends to interest on a "qualified student loan bond," a term that includes two types of financing for student loans—financing that operates in conjunction with federal guaranteed student loan programs and financing of supplemental loan programs that operate independently of federal programs.[160] Such bonds can be issued by a state or

---

[155] IRC §144(a)(10)(E). See supra note 139 for the definition of related person.

[156] IRC §§144(a)(12)(A)(i), (B).

[157] IRC §144(a)(12)(C).

[158] 1986 Bluebook, supra note 8, at 1177. For the definition of first-time farmers and various limitations on tax-exempt financing for such farmers, see infra text accompanying notes 20–27.

[159] IRC §144(a)(12)(A)(ii); 1986 Bluebook, supra note 8, at 1177–78.

[160] IRC §144(b).

local government or by a qualified scholarship funding corporation. A qualified scholarship funding corporation is a corporation organized by a state or local government for the purpose of issuing bonds and using the proceeds for student loans.[161]

Qualified student loan bonds can be issued to finance Guaranteed Student Loan (GSL) and Parent Loan for Undergraduate Student (PLUS) programs. A GSL or PLUS is a loan made to a student or a student's parent by a lender other than the federal government, but with a federal guarantee of the borrower's obligation and usually with a federal interest subsidy. Bonds issued to finance GSL or PLUS loans are qualified student loan bonds if at least 90 percent of the net loan proceeds of the issue is used for student loans under a program that satisfies the requirements of the Higher Education Act of 1965 for GSLs and PLUSs. These requirements include annual and lifetime limits on the amounts loaned with respect to each student and limits on the interest rates that can be charged. Further, student loans financed by the bonds must be of kinds that qualify for an interest subsidy, called special allowance payments, under §438 of the Higher Education Act. These payments are sometimes denied to loans financed with tax-exempt bonds, but the loans must be of a type that would qualify for the payments in the absence of this bar. Also, the program cannot discriminate on the basis of the location of students' schools. That is, if the program is restricted to students residing in the state issuing the bonds, students must be eligible whether they attend school within the state or in another state. If the program is open to students attending school within the state, regardless of place of residence, a student attending a school anywhere in the state must be eligible. Students attending school outside the United States, however, need not be eligible.

Qualified student loan bonds can also finance student loans other than GSLs and PLUSs. Such bonds qualify if at least 95 percent of the net proceeds of the issue is used for student loans under a program sponsored by the issuer. The loan to each student can be no greater than the excess of "the total cost of attendance" over "other forms of student assistance . . . for which the student borrower may be eligible."[162] The role of such a supplemental loan program, in other words, is to narrow or close the gap between a student's total costs and the funds available through GSLs, loans and scholarships provided by the school the student attends, and other

---

[161] Income of such a corporation must either be used to purchase additional student loans or be paid over to the federal government. 1986 Bluebook, supra note 8, at 1158.

[162] PLUS loans are not counted as available student assistance for this purpose. Also, student assistance available under subpart I or part C of title VI of the Public Health Service Act is ignored in measuring the student's eligibility under a state's supplemental loan program. IRC §144(b)(1)(B).

private sources of student aid. The rule prohibiting discrimination on the basis of school location does not apply to such a program, but the program must be one of "general application."

A student is an eligible borrower under either type of qualified student bond program if he resides in the state issuing the bonds or attends school in the state.

¶15.4.7 Qualified Redevelopment Bonds

Exemption is allowed under §103(a) for interest on a "qualifed redevelopment bond," defined as a bond that is part of an issue at least 95 percent of the net proceeds of which is dedicated to "redevelopment purposes in any designated blighted area."[163] Qualified redevelopment bonds must be issued under a state law authorizing bond issues for the redevelopment of blighted areas, and the issue must be part of the redevelopment plan adopted for the particular area to be redeveloped with the proceeds.[164]

A designated blighted area is an area identified as such "by the governing body of a local general purpose govenmental unit in the jurisdiction of which such area is located."[165] The appropriate unit of government is the smallest general purpose government having jurisdiction over the redeveloped area—generally a city or, for an unincorporated area, a county.[166] A designation could be made, for example, by a city council or board of county commissioners, but not by a planning board or a redevelopment agency.

A designation must be based on "the substantial presence of factors such as excessive vacant land on which structures were previously located, abandoned or vacant buildings, substandard structures, vacancies, and delinquencies in payment of real property taxes."[167] The assessed value of real property within this and other designated blight areas cannot exceed 20 percent of the assessed value of all real property within the jurisdiction of the governmental unit making the designation.[168] A designated blighted area,

---

[163] IRC §144(c)(1).

[164] IRC §144(c)(2)(A).

[165] IRC §144(c)(4)(A).

[166] 1986 Bluebook, supra note 8, at 1190.

[167] IRC §144(c)(4)(B).

[168] IRC §144(c)(4)(C). In applying this test, a previously designated blighted area is treated as though it had not been so designated if none of the proceeds of an outstanding qualified redevelopment issue has been used in the area and no future redevelopment bond issue is contemplated by the redevelopment plan for the area. Id.

If more than one designation is made, the percentage for each designation is fixed when it is made. 1986 Bluebook, supra note 8, at 1191–92. If, for example, a city makes a designation in 1987 of an area then containing 15 percent of the city's

further, must be "contiguous and compact," and must usually consist of at least 100 acres.[169] The governmental unit making the designation must adopt a redevelopment plan for the area before any bonds are issued.[170] All of the designated area should be slated for redevelopment, and the Treasury is expected to disallow an "artificial" expansion of a designated area in order to make tax-exempt financing available for "one or a few specific facilities that happen to be located" in the vicinity of an area to be redeveloped.[171]

The redevelopment purposes that may be pursued with the proceeds of a qualified redevelopment issue include (1) acquisition of real property in the designated blighted area by a governmental unit having the power of eminent domain, (2) the clearing of land so acquired and its preparation for redevelopment, (3) rehabilitation of buildings acquired as part of the real property, and (4) relocation of occupants of the real property.[172] Bond proceeds can also be used to rehabilitate buildings acquired by foreclosure of tax liens.[173] Rehabilitations are the only improvements that can be financed from a qualified issue; none of the proceeds can be used for new construction or enlargements of existing buildings.[174] Persons purchasing land or buildings from the redevelopment agency, however, are not limited in their further development of the property. No more than 25 percent of the net proceeds can be used to purchase land, and none of the proceeds can be used for several types of facilities.[175] When property acquired from the proceeds of a qualified issue is sold to a person other than a unit of govern-

---

assessed value, an additional designation can be made some time in the future of an area containing property which, at the time of the subsequent designation, is assessed at up to 5 percent of total assessed value. It is not relevant that the assessed value of the first area at the time of the second designation is likely more or less than 15 percent of total assessed value.

[169] IRC §144(c)(4)(D)(i). The 100-acre minimum is reduced to 10 acres if no more than 25 percent of the area to be financed by the bonds is to be provided to one person or one group of related persons other than a developer who will hold it "on a short-term interim basis." IRC §144(c)(4)(D)(ii).

[170] IRC §144(c)(2)(A)(ii).

[171] 1986 Bluebook, supra note 8, at 1192.

[172] IRC §144(c)(3).

[173] 1986 Bluebook, supra note 8, at 1191.

[174] Tax-exempt financing for new or expanded buildings in a redeveloped area might, however, be obtainable through mortgage revenue bonds, exempt facility bonds for low-income rental projects, or qualified small issues. Id.

[175] IRC §144(c)(6). It is forbidden to use any part of the proceeds for a "private or commercial golf course, country club, massage parlor, hot tub facility, suntan facility, racetrack or other facility used for gambling," or liquor store. Id. Neither can the proceeds be used to provide land for any such facility.

ment, the price received must equal the property's fair market value.[176]

Payment of principal and interest on the bonds must usually be "primarily secured by taxes of general applicability imposed by a general purpose governmental unit."[177] Alternatively, the primary security for payment can be a commitment that increases in property tax revenues from enhancements in assessed value caused by the redevelopment will be used first for debt service on the issue. The purpose of the security rules is to require "a direct and substantial financial commitment by the issuer of the bonds," and they are considered not met if the commitment is diluted by agreements with private developers or buyers of the redeveloped property.[178] An excessive dilution of the issuer's commitment occurs, for example, if a developer has

(1) entered into a special agreement with the city that the redevelopment site will be considered to have an assessed value for local property tax purposes of not less than a prescribed amount, until such time as the bonds are repaid, (2) agreed to be personally liable to pay the difference between the amount of real property taxes levied against the site and the amount of debt service on the bonds, or (3) agreed to finance the cost of credit enhancement for the bonds.[179]

In each of these situations, the bonds are disqualifed because their "repayment . . . is indirectly secured by payments derived from [the developer] or property used in the developer's business."[180]

Also, special financial burdens cannot be placed on owners and users of property within the portion of the designated blighted area in which the proceeds of the issue are to be used.[181] Specifically, no such owner or user can be subject to any charge or fee while the bonds are outstanding unless the charge or fee is also imposed on the owners and users of similarly situated property of the same type that is located elsewhere within the jurisdiction of the governmental unit that designated the blighted area. Also, real property tax assessment methods and rates must be the same within and without the area of the proceeds' use.

---

[176] IRC §144(c)(2)(C). If future use of the property is limited by restrictions and covenants imposed by the issuer, these restrictions and covenants are taken into account in determining fair market value. 1986 Bluebook, supra note 8, at 1191.

[177] IRC §144(c)(2)(B).

[178] 1986 Bluebook, supra note 8, at 1189.

[179] Id. at n.124.

[180] Id.

[181] IRC §§144(c)(2)(D), (5)(A), (7).

¶15.4.8 Qualified 501(c)(3) Bonds

Interest on a qualified 501(c)(3) bond is exempt from tax under §103(a). The principal qualification criterion for such bonds is that the bond proceeds must be used for the benefit of charities, educational organizations, other §501(c)(3) organizations, and governments.[182]

More specifically, all property financed with the net proceeds of a qualified 501(c)(3) bond issue must be owned by governmental units and by organizations that are described in §501(c)(3) and are exempt from tax under §501(a).[183] Further, at least 95 percent of the net proceeds of the issue must be used to finance property that will be used by units of government or by §501(c)(3) organizations in their exempt activities.[184] That is, an issue cannot be qualified 501(c)(3) bonds if more than 5 percent of the net proceeds is used to finance property used by §501(c)(3) organizations in unrelated trades or businesses or by persons who are neither charities nor governments. A bond issue for a hospital is not a qualified 501(c)(3) issue, for example, if more than 5 percent of the net proceeds will be used to finance a laundry facility that will serve many hospitals (an unrelated trade or business) or to finance an office building for use by physicians in their private practices (a noncharitable private use).[185] Cost of issuance paid from

---

[182] The reason for the inclusion of units of government among the permissible beneficiaries of a qualified 501(c)(3) issue is not clear. Issues for the benefit of governmentally owned hospitals and universities are treated as governmental bonds, and thus need not comply with any of the requirements for private activity bonds, including those for qualified 501(c)(3) bonds. 1986 Bluebook, supra note 8, at 1185. Also, if bond proceeds are used in part for governmental purposes and in part for §501(c)(3) organizations, the issue can be treated as a composite issue, classified in part as a governmental issue and in part as a qualified 501(c)(3) issue. Id. at 1184–85.

If an issue qualifies both under these rules and those for exempt facility bonds or qualified redevelopment bonds, the issuer can elect to make the qualified 501(c)(3) bond rules inapplicable. IRC §145(d).

For an unsuccessful effort of a community organization of a large unincorporated development to qualify as a §501(c)(3) organization in order to be able to be the beneficiary of an issue of qualifed 501(c)(3) bonds, see Columbia Park & Recreation Ass'n v. CIR, 88 TC 1 (1987).

[183] IRC §145(a)(1). The owner of property is identified for this purpose "using general tax concepts of ownership." 1986 Bluebook, supra note 8, at 1184.

[184] IRC §145(a)(2).

[185] 1986 Bluebook, supra note 8, at 1184. If some portions of facility will be used by a §501(c)(3) organization in exempt activities, but other portions will be used in an unrelated trade or business or by a noncharitable private user, the former portions can be financed with qualified 501(c)(3) bonds. Id. "[T]he costs of such mixed-use facilities (including common elements)" can be allocated by "any reasonable method that properly reflects the proportionate benefit to be derived, directly or indirectly, by the various users of the facility." Id.

the issue proceeds also count against this 5 percent, typically reducing the amount available for nonexempt uses to something in the neighborhood of 3 percent.

Except for certain bonds financing hospitals, one §501(c)(3) organization can be the beneficiary of no more than $150 million of qualified 501(c)(3) bonds outstanding at any particular time.[186] This limitation is applied as follows: A §501(c)(3) organization is considered a beneficiary of a bond issue if proceeds of the issue are used to finance facilities that are owned or principally used by the organization at any time during a test period consisting of the three years beginning with the date the facilities are placed in service or, if later, the date the bonds are issued.[187] If some but less than all of the net proceeds of an issue are so used, an apportionment is made.[188] The bonds that count against the limit are prior issues of qualified 501(c)(3) bonds and some bonds issued under the pre-1986 rules.[189] The portions of these bonds that remain outstanding and are allocable to the §501(c)(3) organization are added to the portion of the new issue that is allocable to the organization.[190] If this sum exceeds $150 million, the newly issued bonds cannot be qualified 501(c)(3) bonds.

Qualified hospital bonds—bonds at least 95 percent of the net proceeds of which "are to be used with respect to a hospital"—are exempted from the $150 million cap, and are not taken into account in applying the cap to other bonds.[191] If a private university operates a hospital, for example, there is no limit on the amount of qualified 501(c)(3) bonds that can be issued for the hospital, and the bonds issued for the benefit of university functions other than the hospital can go as high as $150 million.

Various tax benefits are withdrawn if ownership of a facility financed by a qualified 501(c)(3) issue is transferred to a person other than a §501(c)(3) organization or governmental unit or if such a facility is used by

---

[186] IRC §145(b)(1). Two or more organizations "under common management or control" are treated as one for this purpose. IRC §145(b)(3).

[187] IRC §§144(a)(10)(D), 145(b)(4).

[188] The apportionment is made under rules set out in §144(a)(10)(C), which is described above in the text accompanying note 153. IRC §145(b)(4).

[189] IRC §145(b)(2)(B). The prior-law bonds taken into account are those that would have been industrial development bonds under the pre-1986 rules, but for the exemption of bonds for §501(c)(3) organizations from the industrial development rules. Id.

[190] An outstanding bond allocable to the §501(c)(3) organization is excluded from this sum if it is to be redeemed from the proceeds of the new issue and if the issue and redemption are not an advance refunding. IRC §145(b)(2)(A)(ii). See infra ¶15.6 for the definition of advance refunding.

[191] IRC §§145(b)(1), (c). See also IRC §145(b)(2)(C). "[N]ursing homes, day care centers, medical school facilities, research laboratories, [and] ambulatory care facilities" are not considered hospitals for this purpose. 1986 Bluebook, supra note 8, at 1188.

a noncharitable private user. These benefits are also lost if ownership or use is transferred to a §501(c)(3) organization that would not have qualified as an initial borrower. An organization is not a permitted transferee, for example, if other bonds have exhausted the $150 million cap on financing for the organization.[192]

The first of these benefit-denial rules provides that if the financed facility ceases to be owned by a qualifying §501(c)(3) organization or governmental unit, no deduction is allowed for interest accruing after the change in ownership on loans financed from the issue proceeds.[193] Assume the proceeds of a qualified 501(c)(3) issue are reloaned to a §501(c)(3) organization and are used by the organization to acquire a building used in carrying on its exempt activities. If the building is later sold to a for-profit corporation that assumes the obligation to the issuer of the bonds, the corporation is allowed no deduction for interest on that obligation.

If the facility continues to be owned by a §501(c)(3) organization but is used in a trade or business of a person that is neither a charity nor a government, the facility is treated as an unrelated trade or business of the charitable owner.[194] Rents or other compensation received from the noncharitable user is thus included in unrelated business taxable income. In computing unrelated business taxable income, further, the owner's gross income is deemed to be not less than the fair rental value of the premises, and the owner is allowed no deduction for interest on loans financed from the bond proceeds.

¶15.4.9 Volume Cap

An issuer of tax-exempt private activity bonds is subject to a volume cap on the aggregate face amount of such bonds that can be issued during any calendar year.[195] The volume cap is the principal technique adopted by Congress in 1986 to "control the total volume of tax-exempt bonds issued for [private] activities."[196] The cap, it was hoped, will cause issuers to scrutinize proposed issues more carefully, and better target the proceeds "to serve those persons and activities for which the [qualified bonds] are intended."[197]

---

[192] Id. at 1221.

[193] IRC §150(b)(5).

[194] IRC §150(b)(3). If only a portion of the facility is so used, only that portion is considered an unrelated trade or business. Id.

[195] IRC §146(a).

[196] 1986 Bluebook, supra note 8, at 1153.

[197] Id.

Separate volume caps, based on population,[198] are computed annually for each state or possession and its agencies and for each unit of local government. An aggregate volume cap, however, is first determined for a state or possession, its agencies, and all units of local government within the state. For a state, the annual cap is $50 for each resident or, if greater, $150 million.[199] The ceiling is similarly computed for Puerto Rico and the possessions, except that the $150 million floor is lowered for possessions.[200]

The statewide cap can be allocated by the state legislature in whatever way it sees fit.[201] In the absence of such an allocation, it is allocated by default, one half to the state and its agencies and one half to local government. The default ceiling for a state and its agencies is thus $25 for each resident of the state or, if more, $75 million.[202] For a unit of local government, the default cap is 50 percent of the statewide limitation for the year multiplied by a fraction whose numerator is the population within that unit's jurisdiction and whose denominator is the population of the state.[203]

The ceiling for a particular issuer applies to all private activity bonds it issues during the year, except qualified veterans' mortgage bonds, qualified 501(c)(3) bonds, exempt facility bonds that finance airports or docks and wharves, some exempt facility bonds that finance solid waste disposal facili-

---

[198] Population figures are taken from the most recent census estimate of the Census Bureau. IRC §146(j).

[199] IRC §§146(b)(1), (2). For 1987, the limitation is $75 per person or $250 million, whichever is greater. Id.

[200] The per person ceiling applies to a possession unless its population is less than that of the least populous state. For a possession whose population falls below that mark, the minimum cap is $150 million (or, for 1987, $250 million) multiplied by a fraction whose numerator is the population of the possession and whose denominator is the population of the least populous state. IRC §§146(d)(1), (4).

[201] IRC §146(e)(1).

[202] IRC §146(b)(1). The limitations are $37.50 per person or $125 million for 1987. Id.

If more than one agency of a state issues tax-exempt private activity bonds during a calendar year, the state-level cap must be shared by these agencies. IRC §146(b)(2).

[203] IRC §146(c)(1). If a particular area is within the jurisdiction of two units of local government (e.g., a city and a county), the population of the area is usually counted in determining the cap for the smaller unit (the city in this case). IRC §146(c)(2). A smaller unit, however, can surrender part of its area to the next larger unit. Id. A city, for example, can allow a portion of its population to be counted in determining the ceiling for the county rather than the city.

The cap is doubled for constitutional home rule cities in Illinois, but this doubling is partially compensated for by a lowering of the ceilings for the state and other units of local government. IRC §146(d)(3). Further, the allocation to Illinois constitutional home rule cities cannot be altered by the state under the reallocation procedures described above. IRC §146(e)(3).

ties, and bonds that refund previously issued bonds.[204] Qualified 501(c)(3) issues are excepted from the volume cap because the services of §501(c)(3) organizations financed by such an issue are provided to the general public rather than to the residents of a particular state or locality.[205] Solid waste disposal issues are excepted so as not to distinguish between facilities owned and operated by government units (which can be financed with governmental issues not subject to the cap) and publicly financed, but privately operated, facilities (which are usually financed by private activity bonds).[206]

If an issuer exceeds its cap for any year, the bonds issued first during the year qualify for exemption, and the issue that pushes the aggregate over the limit and subsequent issues during the year are disqualified.[207] If the aggregate face amount of the tax-exempt private activity bonds issued in any calendar year is less than the issuer's volume cap for the year, the issuer can elect to carry the unused portion of the cap to succeeding years.[208] The election must designate the purpose or purposes for which the carryover will be used, and, if more than one purpose is designated, must specify the amount of the carryover to be used for each purpose. The permitted uses of carryovers are (1) exempt facility bonds, (2) qualified mortgage bonds or mortgage credit certificates, (3) qualified student loan bonds, and (4) qualified redevelopment bonds. A carryover expires unless it is used within three years after the year in which it arises.

¶15.5 ARBITRAGE BONDS

¶15.5.1 Introductory

Since 1969, Congress has denied the §103(a) exemption to interest on "arbitrage bonds." Arbitrage bonds previously enabled state and local governments to use the exemption as a tool for profit. Assume a municipality issues $1 million of bonds at the favorable interest rate fostered by §103(a)

---

[204] IRC §§146(a), (g). A refunding issue is exempted from the cap only if it does not exceed the outstanding amount of the bonds to be redeemed and is not an advance refunding. IRC §§146(i)(1), (4). Special restrictions are imposed on a refunding of qualified student loan bonds or qualified mortgage bonds. Generally, such a refunding is exempt only if the new bonds mature no later than the maturity date of the refunded bonds. Alternatively, the new bonds can extend the maturity to a date no later than 17 years (for qualified student loan bonds) or 32 years (for qualified mortgage bonds) after the issue date of the original bonds prior to all refundings. IRC §§146(i)(2), (3).

[205] 1986 Bluebook, supra note 8, at 1153.

[206] Id. at 1154.

[207] IRC §146(a).

[208] IRC §146(f).

(say, 7 percent) and invests the proceeds in federal obligations bearing the higher rate required by their taxable status (say, 10 percent). The margin between the interest received on the federal securities ($100,000) and interest paid on the tax-exempt bonds ($70,000) would, in the absence of the arbitrage limitations, be profit to the issuer. By pledging the federal obligations to secure payment of interest and principal on the bonds, further, the issuer could assure the bondholders of the best of all possible worlds—the security of the federal government and the tax exemption of a local bond. There was, therefore, no reason to stop with an issue of $1 million; the sky was the limit. This all occurred solely at the federal government's expense because the transactions made no sense apart from the §103 exemption.[1]

At its most blatant, the device promised to self-destruct because the IRS could argue with some hope of success that the municipality's promises to invest in federal obligations and apply the interest to service the arbitrage bonds were not obligations of the type intended by Congress to be encompassed by §103(a). However, sometimes the arbitrage was only a by-product, achieved by floating construction or refunding bonds earlier than the cash was required and investing the proceeds in the interim or by issuing bonds in a larger amount than required by a particular project and placing the excess in escrow as security for the debt. It was doubtful that these modest or inadvertent arbitrage operations could be controlled by the strictest interpretation of §103(a).

The Treasury, therefore, called in 1968 for a legislative solution to the problem.[2] Many state and local governments sympathized with the Treasury's effort because a flooding of the market with arbitrage bonds would

---

[1] "Arbitrage transactions have no economic substance, but are made profitable solely through the ability to borrow at tax-exempt rates." Staff of Joint Comm. on Tax'n, 99th Cong., 2d Sess., General Explanation of the Tax Reform Act of 1986, at 1154–55 (Comm. Print 1987) [hereinafter 1986 Bluebook]. Also:

> The ability to earn and retain arbitrage profits provides a substantial incentive for qualified governmental units to issue more bonds, to issue them earlier, and to leave them outstanding longer than they otherwise would. Arbitrage is an inefficient alternative to additional borrowing, because it is more costly to the Federal Government in terms of foregone tax revenue than the additional borrowing that would be necessary to produce the same amount of proceeds. It also may become a means for inflating bond financing beyond the intended volume limits.

Id. at 1155.

[2] See Letter from Assistant Secretary of the Treasury Surrey to Senator Long, Chairman, Senate Finance Comm. (Jan. 23, 1968), reprinted in Senate Finance Comm., Hearings on Tax Adjustment Act of 1968 (H.R. 15414), 90th Cong., 2d Sess. 90 (1968). In 1966, the IRS announced a no rulings policy as to certain arbitrage bonds. TIR 840 (Aug. 11, 1966), reprinted id. at 79. See Lewis & Loftis, The Tax Exempt Status of Local Government Bonds Used in Arbitrage Transactions, 35 Geo. Wash. L. Rev. 574 (1967).

force up interest rates on exempt bonds, and this effect would have its most devastating consequences on bond issues for schools, highways, and other public facilities because investors would see these issues as riskier than arbitrage bonds.

Congress responded to the Treasury's call by enacting arbitrage rules as part of the Tax Reform Act of 1969. Originally, these rules denied the §103 exemption to a bond issue if any major portion of the proceeds was expected to be invested in taxable securities.[3] Exceptions were provided, however, for temporary investments held until the proceeds were needed for the nonarbitrage purpose for which the obligations were issued and for investments of reasonably required reserve or replacement funds.

The arbitrage rules were amended in 1980 and 1984 and were revised and restated in 1986 to further limit the circumstances in which arbitrage profits could be realized by issuers of exempt bonds. The 1986 amendments added an additional device meant to deny all arbitrage to issuers; if an issuer realizes arbitrage profits in the limited situations where investments in taxable securities are permitted, the profit must usually be paid over to the federal government.

The statutory definition of "arbitrage bond" is discussed first below, and succeeding sections describe the exceptions to the arbitrage ban and the rule requiring that arbitrage profit be rebated to the federal government.

¶15.5.2 Definition of Arbitrage Bond

A bond is a nonexempt arbitrage bond if, when the bond is issued, some portion of the proceeds of the issue of which it is part is "reasonably expected . . . to be used directly or indirectly . . . to acquire higher yielding investments, or . . . to replace funds which were used directly or indirectly to acquire higher yielding investments."[4] An issue constitutes arbitrage bonds, for example, if proceeds of the issue are expected to be used to acquire taxable Treasury notes or if the issuer previously bought Treasury notes and issues the bonds as a means of recovering its investment in the notes. The arbitrage bond taint also applies if such a use is not anticipated when the bond is issued, but the issuer subsequently "intentionally uses"

---

[3] See generally Peaslee, The Limits of Section 103(c): Municipal Bond Arbitrage After the Invested Sinking Fund, 34 Tax L. Rev. 421 (1979).

[4] IRC §148(a). Regulations under substantially identical provisions of prior law provide that a sinking fund accumulated to retire an issue is deemed to consist of proceeds of the issue, with the consequence that investments of the sinking fund are arbitrage investments. Reg. §1.103-13(g)(1). See City of Tucson v. CIR, 820 F2d 1283 (DC Cir. 1987) (holding regulation invalid).

some portion of the proceeds for either of the prohibited purposes.[5]

The term "higher yielding investments" refers to "investment property which produces a yield over the term of the issue which is materially higher than the yield on the issue."[6] The yield on a debt instrument held as an investment or on a bond issue is the effective rate of interest, determined by giving appropriate effect to any discount or premium on the instrument or bonds.[7] Generally, the yield on an investment is materially higher than the yield on the issue if it exceeds the issue's yield by more than 0.125 percentage points.[8] For example, if the proceeds of 7 percent municipals (issued at par) are used to purchase 9 percent Treasury notes (purchased at par), the notes are higher yielding investments because their yield is materially higher than the yield on the municipals.

Only "investment property" can be a higher yielding investment. The term "investment property" includes corporate stock, debt instruments other than tax-exempt bonds, and, more generally, "investment-type property," including, for example, annuities.[9] The arbitrage ban, in other words, goes far beyond the original gambit of investing bond proceeds in federal securities.

Investment property can be a higher yielding investment even if it is acquired to serve the governmental purpose of the issue. If the governmental purpose is to use the proceeds to build a facility for lease to a private user, for example, the facility might be a higher yielding investment if rents produce a yield to the issuer that is materially higher than the interest yield on the bond issue. If applied in this context, the arbitrage limitations would

---

[5] IRC §148(a). A loss of exemption on account of an intentional use of bond proceeds for arbitrage is retroactive to the date of issue. 1986 Bluebook, supra note 1, at 1201. The intentional use rule is meant to codify rulings under prior law holding that "subsequent deliberate and intentional acts to produce arbitrage occurring after bonds were issued" caused bonds to be arbitrage bonds. Id. at 1143, 1201.

[6] IRC §148(b)(1).

[7] More specifically, total interest consists of stated interest, increased by any original issue or market discount (i.e., any excess of the face amount over the issue or purchase price), and decreased by any premium (i.e., any excess of the issue or purchase price over the face amount). The yield is a rate of interest, which when applied periodically to the outstanding indebtedness (including accrued but unpaid interest) produces interest in the aggregate equal to the total interest. See IRC §148(h).

The issue price of the bond issue is reduced (and original issue discount and yield are increased) by "credit enhancement fees," such as bond insurance premiums and letter of credit fees, that reduce the stated interest rate demanded by the market on the issue. 1986 Bluebook, supra note 1, at 1202–03. These credit enhancement fees, however, must "arise from an arm's-length transaction and [must] represent a reasonable charge for transfer of credit risk." Id. at 1203.

[8] Id. at 1201–02.

[9] IRC §148(b)(2).

have the effect of restricting the rents charged to private users of facilities financed with the bond issue and thereby requiring that the interest savings from the §103(a) exemption be passed along to these users. Tangible property is not investment property, however, if it is "acquired for reasons other than investment (*e.g.*, a courthouse or other public facilities . . .)."[10]

¶15.5.3 Permitted Higher Yielding Investments

In three circumstances, issue proceeds can be invested in higher yielding investments without causing bonds to become arbitrage bonds. These circumstances—temporary investments, investments of reserve funds, and investments of minor portions of the issue proceeds—are described more fully below.

1. *Temporary investments.* A bond is not an arbitrage bond merely because issue proceeds are invested in higher yielding investments "for a reasonable temporary period until such proceeds are needed for the purpose for which such issue was issued."[11]

The length of this "reasonable temporary period" is arbitrarily limited in a few situations. If bonds are issued to create a loan pool (i.e., if a purpose of an issue is to make or finance loans to two or more borrowers), the proceeds dedicated to this purpose cannot be held in temporary investments for more than six months.[12] Also, if a loan made or financed from the proceeds of an issue is repaid or sold and if, in furtherance of the original purpose of the issue, the amount collected or received in the sale is to be reloaned or used to finance other loans, the collection or sale proceeds can be held in higher yielding investments for no more than three months.[13] Neither of the foregoing rules applies to qualified mortgage bonds and qualified veterans' mortgage bonds because special arbitrage rules are built into the definitional requirements for these bonds.[14]

---

[10] 1986 Bluebook, supra note 1, at 1202.

[11] IRC §148(c)(1).

[12] IRC §148(c)(2)(A). Generally, bonds are considered issued to finance a loan pool if "the proceeds of [the issue] are to be used to make loans, as opposed to . . . financ[ing] a specific project that will be jointly owned by more than one entity." 1986 Bluebook, supra note 1, at 1203.

The six-month grace period is extended to 18 months for qualified student loan bonds issued before the end of 1988 to fund federally guaranteed student loans. IRC §148(c)(2)(B).

[13] IRC §148(c)(2)(C).

[14] IRC §148(c)(2)(D); 1986 Bluebook, supra note 1, at 1203–04. See supra ¶¶15.4.3 and 15.4.4 for qualified mortgage bonds and qualified veterans' mortgage bonds.

2. *Reserve and replacement funds.* A bond does not become an arbitrage bond merely because a portion of the proceeds of the issue of which it is part is set aside as "a reasonably required reserve or replacement fund" and invested in higher yielding investments.[15] A reserve or replacement fund, however, cannot exceed 10 percent of the proceeds unless the issuer satisfies the IRS that a larger amount is necessary.[16]

Two additional requirements are imposed on reserve and replacement funds for most private activity bonds (other than qualified 501(c)(3) bonds).[17] First, investments that are unrelated to the purpose of the issue and produce yields "materially higher than the yield on the issue" cannot, at any time during a bond year, exceed 150 percent of the debt service on the issue for the year.[18] The debt service on an issue is "the scheduled amount of interest and amortization of principal payable for such year" on bonds of the issue that are outstanding at the beginning of the year.[19] If interest and principal payments on an issue for a particular year are $100, for example, unrelated higher yielding investments must be capped at $150 throughout the year. Second, investments unrelated to the purpose of the issue must be "promptly and appropriately reduced" as bonds are redeemed.[20]

Neither of the foregoing requirements applies, however, to "temporary investment periods related to debt service."[21] Also, an issuer is exempted from these requirements for any period during which they could be satisfied only by selling investments at a loss that exceeds the arbitrage profits required to be rebated under the rebate rules described below.[22]

3. *Investments of minor portions of issue proceeds.* Higher yielding investments in excess of the amounts allowed for temporary investments

---

[15] IRC §148(d)(1).

[16] IRC §148(d)(2). This 10 percent cap only applies to the portion of the issue proceeds that is placed in a reserve or replacement fund and does not limit amounts the issuer might add to such a fund from other sources. 1986 Bluebook, supra note 1, at 1204.

[17] IRC §148(d)(3).

[18] IRC §§148(d)(3)(A), (B)(i).

[19] IRC §148(d)(3)(D).

[20] IRC §§148(d)(3)(A), (B)(ii).

[21] IRC §148(d)(3)(C)(ii). An exemption from these requirements is also provided for amounts "invested for an initial temporary period until such proceeds are needed for the governmental purpose of the issue." IRC §148(d)(3)(C)(i). This exemption is probably meant to exclude amounts subject to the rules for temporary investments (supra text accompanying notes 11–14) from the additional limitations on reserve and replacement funds.

[22] IRC §148(d)(3)(E). The rebate rule is described in ¶15.5.4. For qualified mortgage bonds and qualified veterans' mortgage bonds, the exemption applies if the loss would exceed the amounts required to be rebated to mortgagors under the special rebate rules for these bonds. See ¶15.4.3 and ¶15.4.4 for qualified mortgage bonds and qualified veterans' mortgage bonds.

and reserve and replacement funds are permitted so long as they do not exceed $100,000 or, if less, 5 percent of the issue proceeds.[23]

¶15.5.4 Rebates of Arbitrage Profits

Generally, issuers of exempt bonds must pay their arbitrage profits over to the federal government. If an issuer fails to do this, its bonds are arbitrage bonds even though they are not caught by the general definition of arbitrage bond and the issuer limits its higher yielding investments to those permitted by the rules described above. The arbitrage-remittance requirement was adopted as an alternative to outright prohibition of arbitrage; allowing issuers to make arbitrage investments in limited circumstances, subject to a requirement that they give up the resulting profits, was considered to be more flexible than, but "substantively equivalent to," a complete prohibition.[24]

Arbitrage profits are computed as follows:[25] The issuer's nonpurpose investments are first identified. An item of property is a nonpurpose investment if (1) it is a stock, bond other than a tax-exempt bond, or other "investment-type property," (2) it is acquired from the gross proceeds of the bond issue, and (3) the issuer's purpose in acquiring the investment is not "to carry out the governmental purpose of the issue."[26] Identifying nonpurpose investments can be complicated if the issuer commingles bond proceeds with tax and other revenues. The requirement to rebate arbitrage profits is not defeated by such a commingling. The Treasury, however, is expected to "prescribe simplified methods of accounting" for commingled proceeds.[27]

Next, earnings from all nonpurpose investments (including gains and losses on dispositions) are aggregated, and from this sum is subtracted the income the nonpurpose investments would have earned if their yields equaled the yield on the issue.[28] This remainder (the excess income) does not

---

[23] IRC §148(e).

[24] 1986 Bluebook, supra note 1, at 1155.

[25] IRC §148(f)(2).

[26] IRC §§148(b)(2), (f)(6)(A). An investment is deemed purchased from the gross proceeds of an issue if the purchase price comes from "the original proceeds of the bonds, the investment return on obligations acquired with the bond proceeds (including repayment of principal), and amounts to be used or to be available to pay debt service on the issue." 1986 Bluebook, supra note 1, at 1206. See also Reg. §1.103-15AT(a)(6) (similar expansive definition of "gross proceeds" under comparable provisions of pre-1986 law).

[27] Id. at 1207.

[28] A "bona fide debt service fund" and income earned by the fund are usually excluded from this calculation for any bond year in which this income is less than $100,000, unless the issuer elects to include it. IRC §148(f)(4)(A)(ii). An election to

include income earned by the issuer on investments of the excess income. Income on investments of excess income, however, is added to the excess income, and the resulting sum is arbitrage profit. The effect of this addition is that while income on nonpurpose investments of the issue proceeds is rebatable only to the extent it exceeds the yield on the issue, 100 percent of any income earned by investing the rebatable amount is added to that amount. No reduction of this profit is made for "costs associated with nonpurpose investments or with the bond issue itself (including issuance costs and underwriter's discount)."[29]

Arbitrage profits must be calculated annually, and must be remitted to the federal government at least once every five years.[30] Each remittance must be in an amount that brings the aggregate of all remittances to at least 90 percent of the arbitrage profits earned since the bonds were issued.[31] A payment sufficient to bring the aggregate to 100 percent of the profits must be made within 60 days after the last bond of the issue is redeemed.[32]

No rebate is required if arbitrage profits arise from temporary investments of the issue proceeds and the gross proceeds are expended for the governmental purpose of the issue within six months of the issue date.[33] The

---

forgo this exclusion must be made no later than the issue date of the bonds, and, once made, is irrevocable. 1986 Bluebook, supra note 1, at 1208. Also, an exclusion is allowed for some income from nonpurpose investments of the proceeds of qualified student loan bonds that are issued before the end of 1988 to finance student loans guaranteed by the federal government. IRC §148(f)(4)(D).

[29] 1986 Bluebook, supra note 1, at 1206.

[30] IRC §148(f)(3).

[31] By basing each five-year computation on cumulative arbitrage profits and remittances from the date of issue and by limiting remittances to 90 percent of cumulative profits, Congress intended to accommodate the possibility that nonpurpose investments might yield arbitrage profits in some periods and arbitrage losses in others. 1986 Bluebook, supra note 1, at 1208.

The Treasury is expected to promulgate regulations allowing an issuer to establish an annual accounting date for all issues on which interim remittances of arbitrage profits come due within the year. Id. at 1207.

[32] If an issuer has numerous issues of notes coming due within 60 days of issue, issues falling within any six-month period can be aggregated in computing arbitrage rebates. 1986 Bluebook, supra note 1, at 1207.

[33] The proceeds of an issue of tax or revenue anticipation bonds are deemed to have been expended for governmental purposes when "the cumulative cash flow deficit to be financed by such issue exceeds 90 percent of the aggregate face amount of such issue." IRC §148(f)(4)(B)(iii). The cash flow deficit is the excess of (1) the issuer's expenses paid during the period beginning with the issue date of the bonds to the extent the expenses "would ordinarily be paid out of or financed by anticipated tax or other revenues over (2) the aggregate amount available (other than from the proceeds of the issue) during this period for the payment of the expenses." Id. If any of the bonds matures less than six months after the issue date, further, the safe-harbor period for expending the proceeds expires on the first maturity date. See Notice 87-42, 1987-1 CB 501.

requirement that the "gross proceeds" be expended for the governmental purpose means that this exception is unavailable if a reserve or replacement fund is maintained from the gross proceeds after the six-month period or if any of the proceeds are used to redeem bonds rather than for the governmental purpose of the issue.[34] For bonds that are not private activity bonds or tax or revenue anticipation bonds, the six-month grace period is extended to one year if the proceeds remaining unexpended at the end of six months are no greater than $100,000 or, if less, 5 percent of the proceeds.[35]

Another exception from the arbitrage rebate rules is provided for governmental units that do not issue more than $5 million of bonds annually.[36] To qualify for this exception, an issuer must possess general taxing powers. The excepted bonds, further, cannot be private activity bonds, and at least 95 percent of the net proceeds must be used for "local government activities" of the issuer or a subordinate governmental unit.[37] The exception applies, finally, only to bonds issued during a calendar year during which the issuer restricts its bond issues to $5 million.[38] The $5 million cap is exceeded with respect to an issue if the issue, bonds issued earlier in the year, and bonds "reasonably expected" to be issued later in the year go beyond that figure. Bonds of subordinate units are combined with those of the issuer in applying this rule.

If an issuer fails to make timely remittances of arbitrage profits under a private activity bond issue (other than an issue of qualified 501(c)(3) bonds), the bonds lose their tax exemption. For other bonds, the IRS is authorized to accept a penalty in place of the loss of tax exemption if a late payment or erroneous calculation is "due to reasonable cause and not to willful neglect."[39] Normally, the penalty is 50 percent of the amount not

---

[34] 1986 Bluebook, supra note 1, at 1208. See supra note 26 for the definition of "gross proceeds." A "bona fide debt service fund," however, can be set aside from the gross proceeds without forfeiting the exemption. IRC §148(f)(4)(B)(i). See supra note 28 for the requirements for such a fund.

[35] IRC §148(f)(4)(B)(ii). Qualified 501(c)(3) bonds are also eligible for this extended grace period. Id.

A redemption of some of the bonds during the second six-month period is a permissible use of the de minimis $100,000 or 5 percent. 1986 Bluebook, supra note 1, at 1209.

[36] IRC §148(f)(6)(C).

[37] "A governmental unit may be subordinate to any issuer if, for example, its budget is subject to control by the issuer. The performance of purely ministerial functions such as attesting to the legality of a bond issue, however, would not by itself create a subordinate relationship." 1986 Bluebook, supra note 1, at 1209.

[38] For this purpose, bonds issued by the issuer and all subordinate units and entities are aggregated. Private activity bonds and bonds to be refunded by an issue included in the aggregate, however, are excluded from the aggregate.

[39] IRC §148(f)(7).

timely remitted, plus interest at the rate for tax underpayments.[40] The IRS, however, is allowed to reduce the penalty or waive it altogether.

¶15.6 ADVANCE REFUNDINGS

Advance refundings of exempt bonds issued by state and local governments are restricted. A refunding is an issuance of bonds for the purpose of redeeming outstanding bonds. A refunding is an advance refunding if any bond is issued more than 90 days before the redemption of the bond it refunds.[1] Bonds are considered redeemed for this purpose when they are "called in such a manner that no further interest accrues on the bonds."[2]

The evils of advance refundings have been described as follows:

> Issuers of certain tax-exempt bonds . . . frequently advance refunded (*i.e.*, refunded outstanding bonds without retiring the old debt) at virtually no cost or risk, since the proceeds of an advance refunding may be invested in Federal securities at a guaranteed yield equal to that of the refunding issue. Advance refunding resulted in multiple issues of bonds being outstanding simultaneously, and thereby in multiple indirect Federal subsidies attributable to a single activity. For example, bonds for a single project costing $50 million might be advance refunded two or more times, so that the Federal Government would be subsidizing $150 million or more in tax-exempt bonds for one $50 million project. . . . The ability to advance refund bonds also encouraged tax-exempt borrowers to agree to covenants and other terms (*e.g.*, call protection) that other borrowers would reject.[3]

The rule for bonds issued to advance refund private activity bonds other than qualified 501(c)(3) bonds is simple: Any use of the issue proceeds in such an advance refunding forfeits the §103(a) exemption for all bonds in the issue.[4]

The exemption is also denied to interest on bonds that advance refund governmental or qualified 501(c)(3) bonds unless several requirements are met.[5] First, the number of times an issue can be refunded is limited. Bonds originally issued after 1985 can be refunded only once, and bonds issued

---

[40] See infra ¶114.1 for the rates of interest on underpayments.

[1] IRC §149(d)(5). The grace period is 180 days for bonds issued before 1986. Staff of Joint Comm. on Tax'n, 99th Cong., 2d Sess., General Explanation of the Tax Reform Act of 1986, at 1213 (Comm. Print 1987) [hereinafter 1986 Bluebook].

[2] Id.

[3] Id. at 1156.

[4] IRC §§149(d)(1), (2).

[5] IRC §149(d)(3).

earlier cannot be refunded more than twice.[6]

Second, there is usually a limitation on the length of the period the old bonds can be left outstanding after the refunding bonds are issued. Refunded bonds issued before 1986 need not be redeemed until the first date on which they can be redeemed at par or at a premium of not more than 3 percent. In contrast, if the bonds being refunded were issued after 1985 and if the refunding produces an interest savings for the issuer (i.e., if the present value of the debt service is less under the new bonds than under the old bonds), the old bonds must be called for redemption at the earliest date permitted by their terms or, if later, within 90 days of the issuance of the new bonds.[7] This call requirement would not apply, however, if a post-1985 low-interest issue were refunded with a higher-interest issue in order to relieve the issuer of covenants in the old issue or to restructure debt service because, in such a case, the present value of debt service is increased rather than reduced by the refunding.[8]

Third, the reasonable temporary period during which bond proceeds can be invested in higher yielding investments without running afoul of the disqualification for arbitrage bonds is shortened for advance refundings. This period is limited to 30 days for the new bonds, and ends for the bonds to be redeemed no later than the issue date of the new bonds.[9] Also, proceeds of the refunding issue that may be invested in higher yielding investments are limited to a reasonably required reserve, plus a minor portion of the proceeds.

Even if an advance refunding of a governmental or qualifed 501(c)(3) issue meets the foregoing requirements, the refunding bonds are disqualified if the refunding is a device to realize arbitrage profits rather than to obtain savings attributable to lower interest rates or other nontax financial advantages.[10] If, for example, refunding bonds are issued to raise funds for debt service on a prior issue, but adequate provision for this debt service

---

[6] For purposes of the two-refundings rule, refundings before and after the effective date of the 1986 changes are counted, but a special transition rule allows one additional refunding for bonds issued before 1986 that were refunded two or more times before March 15, 1986. IRC §149(d)(6).

[7] "[I]ssuance and administrative costs" are not taken into account in determining the present value of debt service. 1986 Bluebook, supra note 1, at 1213.

[8] Id. at n.177.

[9] See supra ¶15.5.3 for the rule on reasonable temporary periods. Also, if the old bonds were issued before 1986, the refunding subjects the old bonds to a rule enacted in 1986 restricting the size of so-called minor portions of issue proceeds that can be invested free of arbitrage restrictions. See supra ¶15.5.3.

[10] IRC §149(d)(4). An advance refunding done to relieve the issuer of burdensome bond covenants or inconvenient scheduling of debt service is not prohibited by this rule, notwithstanding the lack of an interest savings, if the refunding is not a device to obtain arbitrage. 1986 Bluebook, supra note 1, at 1216.

already exists in a debt service fund maintained under the prior issue, the refunding frees the fund for arbitrage; if the fund is so used, the new bonds are disqualified."[11] Also, if new bonds are issued to pay costs that were to be paid from the proceeds of a prior issue and if the proceeds of the prior issue that would have been used for these costs are instead placed in a reserve fund for debt service in future years, the new bonds are treated as a refunding issue, and are disqualified if the substitution facilitates arbitrage.[12]

¶15.7 NONDEDUCTIBILITY OF INTEREST AND INVESTMENT EXPENSES ATTRIBUTABLE TO TAX-EXEMPT INTEREST

Without directly attacking the exclusion of interest on state and local obligations from gross income, §265(a) disallows certain otherwise allowable deductions related to the taxpayer's ownership of tax-exempt securities. The most important of these restrictions is §265(a)(2), providing that interest on indebtedness "incurred or continued to purchase or carry [tax-exempt] obligations" may not be deducted. Section 265(a)(2) is discussed in another chapter.[1] Less important because the amounts are usually nominal is the disallowance by §265(a)(1) of deductions otherwise allowable under §212 to the extent allocable to tax-exempt interest. Sections 265(a)(1) and (2) can apply, however, whether or not the taxpayer is *currently* receiving interest from tax-exempt securities or had a tax-avoidance motive in purchasing them.[2] Although both these restrictions encompass all interest that is "wholly exempt" from federal income taxation,[3] in practice they apply primarily to interest on state and local obligations exempt under §103(a).

Section 265(a)(1), which disallows amounts otherwise deductible under §212 (relating to expenses for the production of income) if allocable to exempt interest,[4] applies to such items as payments for investment advice, safe deposit and custodial facilities, clerical assistance, fiduciary services,

---

[11] Id. at 1215.

[12] Id.

[1] Infra ¶31.2.1

[2] See Illinois Terminal R.R. v. US, 375 F2d 1016 (Ct. Cl. 1967) (deduction disallowed although no interest was received during taxable year); Clyde C. Pierce Corp. v. CIR, 120 F2d 206 (5th Cir. 1941) (same, re defaulted bonds held by dealer for sale); Denman v. Slayton, 282 US 514 (1931) (exempt securities purchased for sale, not for yield).

[3] For interpretations of the term "wholly exempt" as used in the first clause of §265(a)(1) (relating to exempt income other than interest), see infra ¶22.7.

[4] For §212, see generally infra ¶20.5. Section 265(a)(1) also disallows all otherwise allowable deductions if allocable to exempt income other than interest. For this aspect of §265(a)(1), see infra ¶22.7.

and legal advice.[5] If the taxpayer's portfolio includes both exempt and taxable securities, §212 expenses must be allocated between the two classes, ordinarily in proportion to the amount of income derived from each. Being limited to amounts whose deductibility depends on §212, §265(a)(1) does not affect deductions allowed by other statutory provisions, such as §162 (trade and business expenses), §164 (taxes), and §167(a)(2) (depreciation of property held for production of income).[6] There is, therefore, a curious gap within §265(a)(1), which disallows all deductions allocable to exempt income *other than interest*, but only the taxpayer's §212 deductions as to exempt interest.[7]

¶15.8 EXEMPTIONS FOR INTEREST ON NONGOVERNMENTAL OBLIGATIONS

Interest on obligations of debtors that are not governments is generally included in gross income. During the early 1980s, however, Congress provided two short-lived exemptions for interest on bank deposits and other nongovernmental obligations. These exemptions and a third that was repealed before it came into effect are described below.

1. *Section 116 exclusion.* For the year 1981, an exclusion was allowed for up to $200 of interest income ($400 on a joint return). The exclusion was provided by §116, which until its repeal in 1986 provided a limited exclusion for dividends, and the $200 or $400 exclusion for 1981 was shared by the taxpayer's dividends and interest.[1] The exclusion, in other words, was of dividends and interest up to the dollar cap. Within this limitation, a broad range of interest income was excluded, including interest

---

[5] See Whittemore v. US, 383 F2d 824 (8th Cir. 1967) (parenthetical reference in §265(a)(1) to "expenses for the production of income" seems to refer only to §212(1), but §212(2) expenses are also subject to disallowance; fiduciary commissions and attorney fees relating to trust assets, consisting of taxable and exempt securities, disallowed in part); Jamison v. CIR, 8 TC 173 (1947) (acq.) (investor's office expenses); Weil's Est. v. CIR, 13 TCM (CCH) 653 (1954) (legal and other fees relating to appointment of committee for incompetent); Mallinckrodt v. CIR, 2 TC 1128 (1943) (acq.), aff'd on other grounds, 146 F2d 1 (8th Cir.), cert. denied, 324 US 871 (1945) (cost of investment advice, custodial and collection services, financial secretary, and bookkeeping and auditing services); Rev. Rul. 73-27, 1973-1 CB 46 (management fee).

[6] Early v. CIR, 52 TC 560 (1969), rev'd on other grounds, 445 F2d 166 (5th Cir.), cert. denied, 404 US 855 (1971) (amortization of life estate under §167(a)(2) not disallowed by §265(a)(1)); Rev. Rul. 61-86, 1961-1 CB 41 (state income taxes).

[7] See Rev. Rul. 61-86, supra note 6 (state income taxes disallowed under §265(a)(1) to extent allocable to exempt income other than interest, but not as respects exempt interest).

[1] See infra ¶92.4 for §116.

on bank deposits, certificates of deposits with banks, corporate bonds, and Treasury securities.

2. *All-savers certificates.* During the years 1981 through 1983, §128 provided a limited exclusion from gross income for interest on certain certificates of deposit known as all-savers certificates. To qualify as an all-savers certificate, a certificate had to (1) be issued during the period October 1, 1981 through December 31, 1982 by a bank, thrift institution, or credit union, (2) have a maturity of one year, (3) pay interest at a rate equal to 70 percent of the average rate on comparable Treasury bills, and (4) be available in denominations of $500. Also, the bank receiving the deposit had to use the funds to finance residential and agricultural loans.[2] The exclusion was subject to a lifetime ceiling of $1,000 ($2,000 on a joint return). If an otherwise qualified certificate was redeemed before maturity or pledged for a loan, the exclusion was lost retroactively; not only was the exclusion denied for interest accruing in the year of the redemption or pledge, but the taxpayer was required to include previously excluded amounts in gross income.[3]

Although §128 remains in the Code, the rule limiting the exclusion to one-year certificates issued before the end of 1982 prevents it from having any effect for any year after 1983.

3. *Net interest exclusion.* The 1981 legislation establishing the exclusion for interest on all-savers certificates provided that for 1985 and succeeding years, a new §128 would come into existence allowing an exemption for up to $3,000 of interest income ($6,000 on a joint return). This exclusion was known as a net interest exclusion because it would have been allowed only for interest income in excess of the taxpayer's interest expense (exclusive of interest on a home mortgage). The net interest exclusion, however, was repealed in 1984, and never came into effect.[4]

---

[2] See Rev. Rul. 82-113, 1982-1 CB 78; Rev. Rul. 81-218, 1981-2 CB 43.

[3] See Rev. Rul. 82-58, 1982-1 CB 27 (disqualification applied even when taxpayer becomes incompetent after issuance of certificate and redemption is effected by representative).

[4] See Staff of Joint Comm. on Tax'n, 98th Cong., 2d Sess., General Explanation of the Revenue Provisions of the Deficit Reduction Act of 1984, at 23–24 (Comm. Print 1984).

CHAPTER

16

Other Exclusions From Gross Income

¶16.1 LESSEE IMPROVEMENTS ON LESSOR'S PROPERTY

Under §109, if a building or other improvement constructed by a lessee of real property reverts to the lessor on termination of the lease, the value of the improvement is not gross income to the lessor unless it is "rent." Under a related provision, §1019, the lessor's basis for the building is neither increased nor decreased by the excluded amount. Taken in combination, these provisions have the effect of postponing recognition of the lessor's windfall profit. If he uses or rents the property, his gross income will reflect the value of the tenant's improvements but will not be reduced by depreciation attributable thereto; if the property is sold, the sales proceeds will include payment for the value of the tenant's investment, with no offsetting increase in the lessor's basis.

Sections 109 and 1019 were enacted in 1942 to overrule *Helvering v. Bruun,* in which the Supreme Court held that a building constructed by a lessee was income to the lessor to the extent of its value when the lessor regained possession of the property on forfeiture of the lease for nonpayment of rent.[1] Under *Bruun*, the amount taxed to the lessor increased his adjusted basis for the property and hence diminished his income in later years when the property was used, rented, or sold.

Section 109 does not apply to "rent," a qualification interpreted by the regulations to deny the exclusion to the value of buildings or improvements representing "a liquidation in kind of lease rentals."[2] The principal interpretative problem under §109 is the distinction between taxable rent and excludable windfalls. If the tenant is required to construct a building or make improvements of a specified character with an estimated useful life exceeding the term of the leasehold, the landlord's anticipated benefit on the termination of the lease is probably "rent," but it is not clear whether the proper time is when the improvements are made, when the lease terminates, or in installments between these two dates.[3] Moreover, the waters are muddied by an observation by the Supreme Court in *M.E. Blatt Co. v. United States*, decided in 1938, that improvements by a tenant "will not be deemed rent unless [the] intention that they shall be is plainly disclosed," which has sometimes been interpreted to refer to the subjective intent of the parties rather than the objective fact of anticipated economic benefit.[4]

Section 109 only applies to "buildings . . . or other improvements," and hence does not encompass cash received by a lessor on the termination of a lease (e.g., forfeiture of a security deposit).[5]

---

[1] Helvering v. Bruun, 309 US 461 (1940), discussed supra ¶5.2; S. Rep. No. 1631, 77th Cong., 2d Sess., reprinted in 1942-2 CB 504, 564–65. See generally Bartlett, Tax Treatment of Replacements of Leased Property and of Leasehold Improvements Made by a Lessee, 30 Tax Lawyer 105 (1976); Burford, Tax Treatment of Tenant-Added Leasehold Improvements, 1964 S. Cal. Tax Inst. 183.

[2] Reg. §1.109-1(a). For the tenant's right to depreciate the cost of leasehold improvements, see infra ¶23.1.5.

[3] See Reg. §1.61-8(c) (whether tenant's improvements are rent to lessor depends on intention of parties, disclosed either by terms of lease or by surrounding circumstances).

For uncertainty regarding the time when rent in the form of improvements is taxable to the lessor, see Burford, supra note 1, at 189–90.

[4] M.E. Blatt Co. v. US, 305 US 267, 277 (1938). See Reg. §1.61-8(c); Porter v. US, 63-1 USTC ¶9441 (not officially reported) (WD Tenn. 1963) ("intention" submitted to jury); Neel v. US, 57-1 USTC ¶9430 (not officially reported) (MD Ga. 1957) (same); see also CIR v. Cunningham, 258 F2d 231 (9th Cir. 1958) (rent not intended because specialized lessee improvements were not expected to have value to lessor on termination of lease).

[5] Reg. §1.109-1(b) Ex.; see also Boston Fish Mkt. Corp. v. CIR, 57 TC 884 (1972) (§109 not applicable to payment by tenant in settlement of obligation to restore premises to original condition); Satterfield v. CIR, 34 TCM (CCH) 872 (1975) (§109 not applicable to increased rent allegedly paid to reimburse lessor for improvements made at tenant's request; excess over cost of improvements taxed as capital gain); but see Tobias v. CIR, 40 TC 84 (1963) (acq.) (heavy machinery and equipment installed by tenant qualified as "other improvements" under §109).

¶16.2 REIMBURSEMENT OF LIVING EXPENSES AND OTHER NONDEDUCTIBLE AMOUNTS

Section 123 provides that an individual whose principal residence is damaged or destroyed by fire or other casualty can exclude from gross income amounts received under an insurance contract to reimburse the resulting additional living expenses, to the extent that they exceed the expenses that would have been incurred for the taxpayer and other members of the taxpayer's household during the period that the residence cannot be used or occupied. The exclusion is also allowed if access to the residence is denied by government action attributable to a casualty or threat thereof.

In computing the amount qualifying for exclusion, the taxpayer must take into account both increases and decreases in expenses incurred after the casualty in maintaining the normal standard of living of the taxpayer's household, such as rent, transportation, food, utilities, and miscellaneous services. Amounts unaffected by the casualty (mortgage payments) are disregarded. Assume A's principal residence is uninhabitable for one month because of a fire; living expenses incurred in maintaining A's household as a result of the loss of occupancy are (1) rent of $450 for temporary quarters, (2) restaurant meals costing $600, as compared with normal food expenses at home of $300, (3) utility expenses of $20, as compared with normal expenses of $100, (4) laundry expenses of $50, as compared with detergents and other supplies costing $10 when at home, and (5) bus fares in commuting to and from work of $80, as compared with normal commuting expenses of $90. On these facts, the limit on the amount A can exclude from gross income under a qualifying insurance policy[1] is $700, as shown by Example 16-1.

Example 16-1

Exclusion of Insurance Proceeds Reimbursing Taxpayer for Additional Living Expenses Attributable to Casualty

	Actual Expenses Following Casualty	Normal Expenses Not Incurred	Increase (Decrease)
1. Housing	$ 450	—	$450
2. Meals	600	$300	300
3. Utilities	20	100	(80)
4. Laundry	50	10	40
5. Transportation	80	90	(10)
Totals	$1,200	$500	$700

---

[1] For the allocation of lump sum payments covering increased living expenses, property damage, and loss of rental income, see Reg. §1.123-1(a)(4)(ii).

If the taxpayer in the example were a tenant instead of a homeowner and had been relieved of normal rental expenses of $300 while the damaged residence was being repaired, the excludable amount would be limited to $400—$700 as computed above, less unincurred normal rental expense of $300.

The legislative committee report on §123, which was enacted in 1969, states that the excluded amounts "merely reimburse the taxpayer for a real casualty loss,"[2] but the report does not explain why taxpayers who are not covered by excess living expense insurance are not allowed to deduct their losses. It might be, as suggested in a case involving pre-1969 insurance, that uncompensated taxpayers sometimes get the equivalent of a deduction because the reduction in the residence's value—the measure of the casualty loss deduction allowable under §165(c)(3)—reflects the fact that it cannot be used until the damage has been repaired.[3] There are situations, however, where the taxpayer's loss is not reflected even in this roundabout fashion— where, for example, the residence is completely destroyed, has a very low basis (which limits the amount of the taxpayer's casualty loss), or is rented rather than owned by the taxpayer. The casualty loss deduction, further, is only allowed to the extent casualty losses exceed 10 percent of gross income, a limitation not found in §123.[4] Moreover, §123 applies only if the taxpayer's principal residence is damaged or destroyed and only if the taxpayer is reimbursed by insurance, although the economic loss is just as genuine if the property is a vacation home or the compensation is paid by the taxpayer's employer.

Section 123 permits qualifying amounts to be excluded from gross income, but it does not speak to the treatment of amounts that exceed the taxpayer's increased living expenses, are received from sources other than an insurance company, or compensate for the loss of use of property other than a principal residence, such as a vacation home or automobile. The committee report recommending enactment of §123 is equally silent on the status of these nonqualifying amounts. The regulations, however, state that any insurance recovery for increased living expenses in excess of the limit prescribed by §123 is includable in gross income.[5] This construction is supported by several pre-1969 cases holding that amounts of this type are

---

[2] S. Rep. No. 552, 91st Cong., 1st Sess., reprinted in 1969-3 CB 423, 596.

[3] See Conner v. US, 439 F2d 974, 981 (5th Cir.), supplemented per curiam, 442 F2d 1349 (5th Cir. 1971) (fair market value of house after casualty "would contain, in any rational buyer's mind, a discount amount for loss of use while the house was being restored to a livable condition"; held under pre-1969 law, reimbursement applied in reduction of casualty loss).

[4] See infra ¶34.1 for the casualty loss deduction.

[5] Reg. §1.123-1(a)(5).

gross income.[6] The Tax Court observed that "the pivotal question . . . is whether the proceeds should be included because they have no basis, or excluded because they are a substitute for a nontaxable type of income [the rental value of an owner-occupied residence]." It decided that the lack of an offsetting basis was fatal and required the insurance proceeds to be included in gross income.[7]

These cases and the regulations under §123 seem to imply that all amounts reimbursing the taxpayer for nondeductible expenses are taxable unless explicitly excluded from gross income by a specific statutory provision, such as §123 or §102, relating to gifts. In a series of rulings, however, the IRS has held that reimbursements for expenses incurred on behalf of other persons or organizations are not taxable, even if unreimbursed expenses of the same type could not be deducted.[8] Moreover, it is assumed, so universally that the issue has never been litigated, that payments under an automobile liability policy to persons injured by the taxpayer's negligence are not includable in the taxpayer's gross income.[9] Although these amounts are paid to the victim rather than to the taxpayer, they inure to his economic benefit unless he is judgment-proof. Also, amounts paid directly to injured persons by drivers who are uninsured or whose liability exceeds the policy limits are personal living expenses and may not be deducted if the accident occurs while driving for pleasure.

¶16.3 ALIMONY, SEPARATE MAINTENANCE, AND SUPPORT PAYMENTS

Alimony, separate maintenance, and support payments by one spouse to the other are ordinarily deductible by the payor and taxable to the recipient. When the payments do not meet certain statutory conditions, however, they cannot be deducted by the payor and, as a corollary, are excluded from the recipient's gross income. Because of the reciprocal treatment of the two parties, this area is examined in more detail in the section

---

[6] Millsap v. CIR, 387 F2d 420 (8th Cir. 1968); Arnold v. US, 289 F. Supp. 206 (EDNY 1968); McCabe v. CIR, 54 TC 1745 (1970); but see Taylor v. US, 72-1 USTC ¶9109 (ND Ala. 1964) (not officially reported) (contra); Conner v. US, supra note 3.

[7] McCabe v. CIR, supra note 6, at 1748.

[8] See Rev. Rul. 80-99, 1980-1 CB 10 (reimbursement by political organizations); Rev. Rul. 63-77, 1963-1 CB 177 (expenses incurred in attending interviews with prospective employers); Rev. Rul. 55-555, 1955-2 CB 20 (car pool expenses).

For the status of reimbursed moving expenses, see §217, discussed infra ¶22.4.5.

[9] See supra ¶5.8.1.

of this work dealing with transactions between related parties.[1]

¶16.4 GOVERNMENT SUBSIDIES

Government subsidies are ordinarily includable in gross income, unless they qualify for exclusion under a particular statutory provision, such as §102 (exclusion of gifts), which has been construed to embrace federal disaster aid and similar assistance, or §1032 (contributions to a corporation's capital).[1]

In addition to these broad exclusions, which do not explicitly refer to government subsidies, §126(a) lists several federal and state subsidies that are excluded from gross income if, and to the extent, they (1) are "made primarily for the purpose of conserving soil and water resources, protecting or restoring the environment, improving forests, or providing a habitat for wildlife," as determined by the Secretary of Agriculture and (2) do not substantially increase the annual income derived from the property, as determined by the IRS. A similar exclusion is allowed by §621 for subsidies for the exploration, development, or mining of strategic minerals.[2] No deduction or credit is allowable for expenditures financed by these excludable subsidies, and they cannot be included in the basis of the benefited property.[3]

On a sale or other disposition of property acquired, improved, or otherwise modified by expenditures financed with the excluded amounts, §1255 requires a recapture, on a sliding scale, of these amounts, subject to rules similar to those applicable to the recapture of depreciation under §1245.[4] The recapture rule works by characterizing gain on the disposition as ordinary income up to the amount of (1) the §126 exclusion, reduced by (2) 10 percent for every year in excess of 10 years that the taxpayer held the property following receipt of the excludable amount.

The recapture rule could put the taxpayer in a less favorable position than would have obtained in the absence of §126. For example, if excludable subsidies are used to finance otherwise deductible expenses, §126 puts the taxpayer in no better position than he would have had with a gross income inclusion matched by a deduction. If the recapture rule applies,

---

[1] Infra ¶77.1.
[1] See supra ¶10.2.5 (institutional charity); infra ¶91.9 (contributions to capital). For agricultural support payments, see §77, discussed infra ¶105.5.2. See also Deason v. CIR, 590 F2d 1377 (5th Cir. 1979) (payments under federal contract to hire and train unemployed workers are gross income, not contribution to S corporation's capital).
[2] See infra ¶26.2.1.
[3] IRC §§126(d),(e).
[4] For §1245, see infra ¶55.2.

however, the taxpayer might pay for the meaningless exclusion by recognizing ordinary income in a transaction that would otherwise yield capital gain. To alleviate this unfairness, §126(b)(2), added in 1980, provides that subsidies properly associated with deductions for the same taxable year are not excludable.[5] The inclusion of these amounts in gross income, coupled with the deduction for the expenses, produces a wash and negates recapture under §1255. Also, §126(c) allows taxpayers to elect out of §126 for any otherwise excludable amount, or portion thereof, an option that can have a beneficial effect by, for example, increasing a net operating loss carryback or carryover.

¶16.5 SOCIAL SECURITY BENEFITS

Under §86, a recipient of monthly social security benefits must usually include one half of the benefits in gross income.[1] Section 86, enacted in 1983, reverses a long-standing administrative practice of treating social security benefits as nontaxable.[2] Congress concluded in 1983 that "social security benefits are in the nature of benefits received under other retirement systems" and, like other retirement benefits, should be taxed to the extent they exceed the recipient's nondeductible contributions.[3] Because social security benefits are financed by taxes imposed in equal amounts on employers and employees, one half of a social security benefit was excluded as the equivalent of a recovery of employee contributions. The full rigor of the analogy to private pensions was not accepted, however; a social security benefit is wholly excludable if the taxpayer's income does not exceed a base amount ($25,000 for unmarried taxpayers and $32,000 on a joint return). This assures that "lower-income individuals, many of whom rely upon their benefits to afford basic necessities, will not be taxed on their benefits."[4]

The details of §86 are described below.

---

[5] S. Rep. No. 498, 96th Cong., 1st Sess. 79 (1979).

[1] Section 86 only applies to citizens and residents of the United States receiving U.S. social security benefits. A social security benefit received by a citizen or resident from a foreign government is fully included in gross income. S. Rep. No. 23, 98th Cong., 2d Sess. 26, reprinted in 1983-1 CB 326; Rev. Rul. 62-179, 1962-2 CB 20. Conversely, unless a more lenient treatment is required by treaty, a U.S. social security benefit received by a nonresident alien is subject to a tax of 15 percent of the total amount (30 percent of one half of the benefit), and the tax is withheld by the paying agency from the benefit checks. IRC §871(a)(3). See infra ¶66.2 for the taxation of nonresident aliens.

[2] Rev. Rul. 70-217, 1970-1 CB 12.

[3] S. Rep. No. 23, supra note 1, at 25.

[4] Id. at 26.

1. *Definition of "social security benefit."* The term "social security benefit" includes a monthly benefit under the Old-Age, Survivors, and Disability Insurance (OASDI) provisions of the Social Security Act.[5] It also includes a "tier 1 railroad retirement benfit," which is defined as a portion of a railroad employee's retirement annuity under the Railroad Retirement Act of 1974 equal to the social security benefit he would have received if his railroad employment had been covered by social security.[6]

If Medicare premiums are deducted from a taxpayer's social security checks, the gross amount of the benefit, before the deduction, is used in applying §86.[7] The same rule applies if attorneys' fees incurred in establishing a right to the benefit are deducted from benefit checks. Social security benefits are sometimes reduced by the recipient's benefits under a workmen's compensation statute. When this occurs, a portion of the workmen's compensation benefits equal to the reduction is treated as a social security benefit.[8]

A social security benefit is treated as a benefit of the person "who has the legal right to [it]."[9] A child's benefit, for example, is taken into account in applying §86 to the child.[10]

If a social security benefit is required to be paid, the repayment is offset against benefits received during the year of repayment, and the amount remaining after the offset is treated as the benefit for the year.[11] If the repayment exceeds current benefits, the excess is allocated between the portions that were taxed and those that were exempt when received, and the former portions are deductible under §165.[12] In some cases, an alternative tax computation under §1341 might be permitted in lieu of the deduction.[13]

Normally, under the cash method of accounting used by nearly all individuals, a taxpayer's social security benefits for a year include those received during the year. A benefit for a particular month is usually paid at the beginning of the next month. For each year, a calendar year taxpayer thus usually reports the benefits for the months of December of the preceding year through November of the current year. A special rule allows this

---

[5] IRC §86(d)(1).
[6] IRC §86(d)(4).
[7] S. Rep. No. 23, supra note 1, at 26.
[8] IRC §86(d)(3).
[9] S. Rep. No. 23, supra note 1.
[10] Also, if a parent's benefit would have been reduced because of earnings in excess of the amount allowed to recipients of full benefits, but the reduction is not made because it would result in an increase in a child's benefit, an amount equal to the reduction that would have been made, but for the child, is treated as the child's benefit. Rev. Rul. 84-173, 1984-2 CB 16.
[11] IRC §86(d)(2).
[12] S. Rep. No. 23, supra note 1, at 27.
[13] See supra ¶6.3.4 for §1341.

sequence to be observed even if the December check is received in December rather than early January.[14] Under this rule, for example, the check for December 1988 is treated as a 1989 benefit even if it is received in December 1988.

2. *Taxpayers subject to §86.* A recipient of social security benefits is subject to §86 if an expanded income figure exceeds a base amount (usually, $25,000 for unmarried taxpayers and $32,000 for married couples). Very generally, social security benefits are wholly exempt if the taxpayer's economic income is no greater than the base amount.

The expanded income figure is the sum of (1) one half of the social security benefits received during the year and (2) the taxpayer's "modified adjusted gross income" for the year.[15] The term "modified adjusted gross income" is defined as the taxpayer's adjusted gross income (exclusive of social security benefits), increased by the following items: (1) interest on state and local bonds that is excluded from gross income under §103;[16] (2) interest income that is exempt under any other provision; (3) earned income from foreign sources that is excluded under §911; and (4) income of a resident of Puerto Rico, Guam, American Samoa, or the Northern Mariana Islands that is excluded by §931 or §933.[17]

The base amount is $25,000 for an unmarried taxpayer and $32,000 on a joint return.[18] The base amount for a married person filing separately is usually zero, but the $25,000 base amount is allowed on a separate return if the spouses live apart throughout the taxable year.

These rules are illustrated by a married couple whose income for a particular year consists of a private pension of $12,000, social security benefits of $8,000, taxable interest and dividends of $2,000, and $11,000 of interest on municipal bonds. It is assumed that the couple has no deductions allowable in determining adjusted gross income. If the couple files a joint return, social security benefits are fully excluded from gross income because the base amount is not exceeded, as shown in Example 16-2.

---

[14] IRC §86(d)(5). If the taxpayer uses a taxable year ending with a month other than December, the rule applies to any check for the last month of a taxable year that is received during that month. This rule only applies, however, where the early delivery occurs under §708 of the Social Security Act.

[15] IRC §86(b).

[16] "This provision does not affect the exclusion for interest on tax-exempt obligations. Rather, it merely includes that interest in the base for the purpose of determining the amount of an individual's social security benefits that will be taxed." S. Rep. No. 23, supra note 1, at 27.

[17] IRC §86(b). For taxable years before 1987, the deduction under §221 for two-income couples is also eliminated in determining modified adjusted gross income. IRC §86(b)(2)(A) (before amendment in 1986).

[18] IRC §86(c).

Example 16-2

Determining Whether Base Amount Exceeded

1. Modified adjusted gross income:
   a. Adjusted gross income (sum of $12,000 pension and $2,000 of taxable interest and dividends).. $14,000
   b. Plus tax-exempt interest.................................... 11,000 $25,000
2. Plus one half of social security benefits 4,000
3. Expanded income $29,000
4. Base amount on joint return... $32,000
5. Excess of expanded income over base amount......................... 0

3. *Phase-in rule.* If expanded income exceeds the base amount, the inclusion for social security benefits is the lesser of (1) one half of these benefits or (2) one half of the excess of expanded income over the base amount. For example, if the married couple in Example 16-2 had received social security benefits of $18,000 rather than $8,000, then $1,000 of the benefits would be gross income, as shown in Example 16-3.

Example 16-3

Application of Phase-In Rule

1. Modified adjusted gross income
   a. Adjusted gross income (sum of $12,000 pension and $2,000 of taxable interest and dividends).. $14,000
   b. Plus tax-exempt interest.................................... 11,000 $25,000
2. Plus one half of social security benefits 9,000
3. Expanded income $34,000
4. Base amount on joint return... $32,000
5. Excess over base amount .... $ 2,000
6. Lesser of:
   a. One half of social security benefits..................... $ 9,000
   b. One half of excess over base amount (one half of line 5) .... 1,000 $ 1,000

By halving two figures, this rule has the effect of phasing in income recognition above the base amount at the rate of 25 cents for each dollar of social security benefits. Assume a married couple's modified adjusted gross income is $32,000, an amount equal to the base amount. If they receive $1,000 of social security benefits, they are taxed on $250, as shown in Example 16-4. When modified adjusted gross income is below the base amount, in contrast, each dollar of social security benefits pushes expanded income 50 cents closer to the base amount. It is not clear why Congress chose to slow the pace of the phase-in by one half once the base amount is reached.

Example 16-4

Application of Phase-In Rule When Modified Adjusted Gross Income Exceeds Base Amount

1. Modified adjusted gross income		$32,000
2. Plus one half of social security benefits		500
3. Expanded income		$32,500
4. Base amount on joint return		$32,000
5. Excess over base amount		$500
6. Lesser of:		
a. One half of social security benefits	$500	
b. One half of excess over base amount (one half of line 5)	250	$250

4. *Special rule for lump-sum payment of arrears.* The foregoing rules are normally applied to all social security benefits received during the taxable year, including benefits for a prior year that for one reason or another are received during the current year. If, however, a taxpayer receives "a lump-sum payment" attributable in any part to prior years, an election may be made to compute the taxable amount of the payment as though it had been received in monthly installments in the years to which it is attributable.[19] If this election is made, the base and phase-in determinations are redone for the prior years, adding the portion of the lump sum attributable to each year to the social security benefits actually received during that year. The additional taxable amounts for all prior years resulting from these recalculations are added together, and the sum is the taxable amount of the portion of the lump sum that is attributable to prior years. This sum is added to gross income for the current year. Any portion of the lump sum attributable to the current year is taken into account in applying §86 for the current year.

---

[19] IRC §86(e). When a lump-sum payment is made, the Social Security Administration or Railroad Retirement Board is supposed to notify the recipient of the amounts attributable to various years. S. Rep. No. 23, supra note 1, at 28.

5. *Reporting requirements.* The Social Security Administration and Railroad Retirement Board are each required to make an annual report to the IRS with respect to each recipient of social security benefits from the agency.[20] The information reported includes (1) the individual's name and address, (2) the aggregate social security benefits paid to the individual during the year, (3) any repayments made by the individual, and (4) any reductions of the individual's benefits to reflect workmen's compensation benefits. By January 31 of the following year, the agency must furnish the recipient a statement with the same information.

---

[20] IRC §6050F.

PART
3

Business and Profit-Oriented Deductions and Credits

CHAPTER

20

Expenses Incurred in Business and Profit-Oriented Activities

¶20.1 INTRODUCTORY

¶20.1.1 Statutory Framework

In determining the taxable income of taxpayers engaged in business or profit-oriented activities, the Code focuses on net profits rather than on gross receipts or gross income. The central importance of net profits is illustrated by Example 20-1, involving a merchant with sales of $1 million, cost of goods sold of $800,000, and selling and other business expenses of $150,000. On these assumptions, business profits are $50,000, as shown by Example 20-1.

Example 20-1

Computation of Gross Receipts, Gross Income, and Business Profits

1.	Gross receipts (sales)......................	$1,000,000
2.	Less: Cost of goods sold	800,000
3.	Equals: Gross income......................	$ 200,000
4.	Less: Business expenses...................	150,000
5.	Equals: Business profits	$ 50,000

For a taxpayer who engages in no other relevant transactions for the taxable year, these business profits are its taxable income if it is a corporation or adjusted gross income if he is an individual. In the latter case, adjusted gross income is reduced by itemized deductions (charitable contributions, medical expenses, interest, etc.) or the standard deduction and the taxpayer's personal and dependency exemptions to reach taxable income, the statutory base on which tax is imposed.[1]

Taxpayers receiving salaries and wages are also taxed on net profits rather than on gross receipts or gross income, but the spread is usually much smaller for them than for merchants and manufacturers. Gross receipts and gross income are often identical if the taxpayer does not sell goods, and gross income is often reduced by only a few minor items (e.g., union dues, costs of business periodicals) in arriving at net profits. In the same vein, when determining the taxable income of a taxpayer who sells securities, a personal residence, or other appreciated assets, the profit realized, rather than the sales proceeds, is taxed.

Whatever the nature of the taxpayer's economic activities, Congress has chosen to allow virtually all expenses incurred in business or profit-oriented transactions to be deducted. This stands in sharp contrast to the legislative treatment of taxpayers' personal activities, which give rise to only a few circumscribed deductions. Unlike the cost of living, the cost of earning a living is ordinarily fully deductible.

---

[1] These steps are described in more detail in ¶2.1.

Tax allowances for the cost of earning income are not required by the Constitution,[2] but instead express a fundamental legislative decision to tax net rather than gross income. Business-related payments are not automatically deductible, however. Like personal expenditures, they can be deducted only if and to the extent authorized by statute. The difference between the two categories is that the provisions allowing deductions for business and profit-oriented expenses are expressed in very broad terms, while the itemized personal deductions cover only a few of the manifold items comprising the cost of living and are subject to tight limits.[3]

The broad—but not unqualified—principle of taxing net income rather than gross receipts or gross income is affected by the following statutory provisions:

1. *Business expenses.* Section 162 allows taxpayers to deduct "all the ordinary and necessary expenses paid or incurred during the taxable year in carrying on any trade or business."[4]

2. *Depreciation.* Section 167 authorizes annual depreciation deductions for buildings, equipment, and other assets that wear out or become obsolete while used in the taxpayer's business or profit-oriented activities.[5] Because assets of this type contribute to income over extended periods, their costs cannot be deducted under §162 at the time of purchase, but the annual allowance for depreciation reflects the gradual erosion of the taxpayer's investment in them.

3. *Losses.* Section 165 permits losses to be deducted if incurred in the taxpayer's business or in a transaction entered into for profit.[6] If the taxpayer purchases nondepreciable property with an extended life for business use (e.g., goodwill or land), the purchase price cannot be deducted under §162 when the property is purchased and no depreciation deductions under §167 are allowed. If the asset is sold at a loss or abandoned on retirement from service, however, the loss is then deductible under §165. In the case of depreciable property, the loss on abandonment is the undepreciated balance of the property's cost or other basis.

---

[2] See supra ¶1.2.

[3] See also §262, forbidding the deduction of "personal, living, or family expenses" except as otherwise expressly provided, discussed infra ¶30.1.

[4] See infra ¶¶20.2 et seq. The taxable year in which business expenses may be deducted depends on whether the taxpayer uses the cash or accrual method of computing income. See infra ¶105.1.5.

[5] See infra ¶23.1.

[6] Strictly speaking, §165(c) imposes the "trade or business" and "transaction entered into for profit" qualifications on the deductibility of losses only as to individual taxpayers. For uncertainties in the application of the same principles to corporations, see infra ¶25.3.

For the distinction between expenses and losses, see infra ¶25.8.5.

4. *Expenses of producing income.* Section 212 authorizes the deduction of all ordinary and necessary expenses paid or incurred during the taxable year for the production or collection of income or the management, conservation, or maintenance of property held for the production of income.[7] For historical reasons described elsewhere in this work, §212 applies only to individuals, trusts, and estates, and is primarily concerned with expenses attributable to marketable securities and other passive investments, such as the cost of investment advice and custodial services. When incurred by corporations, expenses of this type generally qualify as business expenses under §162.[8]

5. *Hobbies.* Section 183 authorizes the deduction of expenses incurred in hobbies and other "activities not engaged in for profit" (defined as activities not meeting the standards of §162 or §212), but the deductions, roughly speaking, cannot exceed the gross income generated by the activity.[9] Thus, a hobby can generate a taxable gain or a break-even result for the taxpayer, but not a deductible loss.

6. *Cost of goods sold.* A manufacturer, retailer, or other producer of or dealer in goods subtracts its cost of goods sold from gross receipts in computing gross income. The cost of goods sold is determined by keeping inventory accounts, as prescribed by regulations under §471.[10]

7. *Specialized provisions.* In addition to the foregoing provisions, there are several more specialized deductions, limited to particular business activities or industries. Examples are §174, permitting research and experimental expenditures to be deducted as incurred or amortized over a period of not less than 60 months, and §263(c), permitting the deduction of intangible drilling and development costs of oil and gas wells.

Viewed as a whole, this network enables taxpayers to deduct virtually all business and profit-oriented expenditures at some time during the life of the enterprise—when the cost is paid or incurred, during the asset's useful life, when it is sold, or when the business venture is terminated. The few exceptions to this basic principle of deductibility, which are discussed below, were mandated by Congress primarily to curb exaggerated claims and other forms of tax abuse.

---

[7] See infra ¶20.5. The confusing label "nonbusiness expenses" is sometimes applied to §212 items. See infra ¶20.5.1.

[8] See infra ¶20.1.2; supra ¶2.5.

[9] For §183, which only applies to individuals and S corporations, see infra ¶22.5.

[10] Infra ¶105.4. See also Reg. §1.61-3(a) ("In a manufacturing, merchandising, or mining business, 'gross income' means the total sales, less the cost of goods sold, plus any [incidental or investment] income").

¶20.1.2 Business and Profit-Oriented Expenses

Although the §162(a) deduction for the ordinary and necessary expenses incurred "in carrying on any trade or business" is the Code's most fundamental allowance, the term "trade or business" is not defined by the statute or the regulations; neither is there an authoritative judicial definition.[11] Indeed, the Supreme Court's principal contribution to a definition was the announcement in 1941 that its own 1911 definition of "business" as used in the Corporation Tax Law of 1909—"a very comprehensive term [that] embraces everything about which a person can be employed"—was not controlling under the statutory predecessor of §162(a).[12] Although it has no greater claim to authenticity, a substantially identical definition with the same provenance—"that which occupies the time, attention, and labor of men for the purpose of a livelihood or profit"—continues to be quoted,[13] which may prove the difficulty of killing off a vacuous remark.

Another much-quoted definition—that "carrying on any trade or business" as used in §162(a) "involves holding one's self out to others as engaged in the selling of goods or services"—was floated by a solo concurring opinion in 1940.[14] It seems to imply, erroneously, that a taxpayer working throughout his life for a single employer is not engaged in a trade or business because he does not hold himself out to serve all comers in the manner

---

[11] Just prior to the enactment of the Tax Reform Act of 1986, the term "trade or business" appeared in at least 492 subsections of the Code and 664 provisions of the regulations. Boyle, What Is a Trade or Business? 39 Tax Lawyer 737 (1986) (extensively discussing the meaning of the term). Compare Saunders, "Trade or Business," Its Meaning Under the Internal Revenue Code, 1960 S. Cal. Tax Inst. 693 (as of 1960, "trade or business" appeared more than 170 times in at least 60 different sections of the Code).

[12] Higgins v. CIR, 312 US 212, 217 (1941), commenting on Flint v. Stone Tracy Co., 220 US 107, 171 (1911), which in turn cited two law dictionaries and an 1861 decision of the New York Court of Appeals. The Court later looked more favorably on the *Stone Tracy* definitions in CIR v. Groetzinger, 480 US 23, 31 (1987), citing the earlier case for the proposition "that, to be sure, the statutory words are broad and comprehensive."

The first clause of §162(a) ("there shall be allowed as a deduction all the ordinary and necessary expenses paid or incurred during the taxable year in carrying on any trade or business") dates from the Revenue Act of 1918. From 1913 to 1918, the statutory language for individual taxpayers was "the necessary expenses actually paid in carrying on any business or trade," except that "or trade" did not appear in the Revenue Act of 1913. As for corporations, the statutory language from 1913 to 1918 was "all the ordinary and necessary expenses paid within the year in the maintenance and operation of its business and properties." See 1 Barton's Federal Tax Laws Correlated 90–93, 192–93 (J. Byrne & Co., 2d ed. 1925).

[13] Marlin v. CIR, 29 TCM (CCH) 1425 (1970). Since this definition would embrace an investor, it is clearly repudiated by the *Higgins* case, supra note 12.

[14] Deputy v. Du Pont, 308 US 488, 499 (1940) (Mr. Justice Frankfurter).

of a merchant, independent contractor, or professional person.[15] The hold-ing-out test was expressly disavowed by the Court in 1987, when it held that a full-time gambler could be considered engaged in the business of gam-bling.[16] More broadly, the Court suggested that an activity is a trade or business if it is "pursued full time, in good faith, and with regularity, [for] the production of income for a livelihood, and is not a mere hobby."[17] This definition was not meant to be all-encompassing, however; a part-time activity can be a trade or business even if it is the source of only a small portion of the taxpayer's income.

The Court's most restrictive application of the term was evoked by an aspect of §162 that became obsolete in 1942, when §212 was enacted. Before then, the courts had to determine whether the activities of individuals in managing their investments could be a trade or business, so that expendi-tures for investment advice, clerical assistance, safe-deposit rentals, and similar services could be deducted under the predecessor of §162. In *Hig-gins v. CIR*, decided in 1941, the Supreme Court held that the management of one's own securities, even on a scale large enough to require an office and staff, was not a trade or business.[18] Since the taxpayer in *Higgins* was allowed to deduct losses on sales of securities, as well as both the expenses and the losses of his real estate investments, the disallowance of deductions for the expenses of his securities transactions was anomalous and was in-consistent with the basic principle of taxing only net income.

Congress almost immediately overruled *Higgins* to permit taxpayers to deduct ordinary and necessary expenses incurred for the production or

---

[15] See Noland v. CIR, 269 F2d 108, 111 (4th Cir.), cert. denied, 361 US 885 (1959) ("every person who works for compensation is engaged in the business of earning his pay," so that expenses essential to continuance of employment are de-ductible under statutory predecessor of §162(a)). See also Steffens v. CIR, 707 F2d 478 (11th Cir. 1983) (retired executive serving as corporate director and part-time consultant for former employer was engaged in trade or business for purposes of tax imposed by §1401 on earnings from self-employment, even though he served on no other board of directors); Hornaday v. CIR, 81 TC 830 (1983) (same as to retired executive serving as consultant to former employer); Rev. Rul. 82-210, 1982-2 CB 203 (same); Rev. Rul. 82-178, 1982-2 CB 59 (employee's repayment to employer of layoff benefits, required as condition of restoration to prelayoff seniority, deductible under §165(c)(1) as loss incurred in trade or business).

[16] CIR v. Groetzinger, supra note 12.

[17] Id. at 35.

[18] Higgins v. CIR, 312 US 212, 217 (1941). See Moller v. US, 721 F2d 810 (Fed. Cir. 1983) (taxpayers who spent 40 to 42 hours each week managing their securities portfolios and had no income from other sources, except pensions and social secu-rity, not engaged in business, and thus not entitled to deduction for home office; although trading in securities can be a business, trader's activities must be directed to short-term transactions, and income must be principally from sales of securities; taxpayers not traders because they held securities for long-term growth).

collection of income or for the management, conservation, or maintenance of property held for the production of income. This result was achieved by the enactment in 1942 of the statutory predecessor of §§212(1) and (2).[19]

With the enactment of §212, it was no longer necessary to distinguish between business and profit oriented (or investor) expenses in deciding whether a deduction is permissible.[20] If the taxpayer is an individual, both types of expenses are deductible. Except in special circumstances,[21] it is not necessary to decide whether the deduction rests on §162 or §212. Section 212 applies to individuals, estates, and trusts.[22] Congress' failure to include corporations in §212 suggests that the term "trade or business" as used by §162 was thought to be broad enough to embrace a corporation's activities in managing its own investments.[23]

Neither §162 nor §212 applies, however, unless the activity giving rise to the expense is conducted for profit rather than pleasure. Activities not engaged in for profit, usually described as hobbies, may produce income as a by-product, but these incidental profits, even if large in amount, do not qualify the activity as a business under §162 or as an income producing activity under §212.

For many years, the line between §162 and §212 activities and hobbies was pricked out by the courts case by case, subject to special legislation for activities producing losses of $50,000 per year for five consecutive years.[24] In an effort to deal more systematically with this area, Congress enacted §183 in 1969. Discussed in more detail below,[25] §183 distinguishes between activities that are, and those that are not, engaged in for profit. The regulations identify nine factors that are relevant in determining whether an activity is "engaged in for profit."[26] Because the function of these regulations is to exclude activities engaged in for profit from §183's rules, they are discussed below in conjunction with §183 itself. They are, however, useful

---

[19] See infra ¶20.5. See also the simultaneous change in §167, relating to depreciation, discussed infra ¶23.2.1.

[20] The distinction between business and investment activities remains crucial, however, in applying the capital gain and loss provisions and certain other statutory provisions. See, e.g., infra ¶20.5.1.

[21] See infra ¶20.5.1.

[22] Id.

[23] This is not to say that all of a corporation's expenses are necessarily deductible. See, e.g., Savarona Ship Corp. v. CIR, ¶42,596 P-H Memo TC (1942) (no deduction for expenses of yacht constructed primarily for principal shareholder's pleasure); Black Dome Corp. v. CIR, 5 TCM (CCH) 455 (1946) (same as to country estate); see also Smith v. CIR, 38 TCM (CCH) 1246 (1979) (corporate expenses in raising Lipizzan horses held deductible, but only after activity found to be profit-oriented).

[24] IRC §270 (before repeal in 1969), discussed infra ¶22.5.

[25] Infra ¶22.5.

[26] Reg. §1.183-2. For discussion of the Nine Big Factors, see infra ¶22.5.

guideposts to §§162 and 212 as well, since an exclusion from §183 virtually ensures that the activity is either a trade or business within the meaning of §162 or a profit-oriented activity within the meaning of §212.

¶20.1.3 Relation to Itemized Deductions

It is not unusual for expenses qualifying for deduction under §162 or §212 to qualify also under other provisions, such as §163 (interest) and §164 (taxes), that do not require the item to arise in a business or profit-oriented activity.[27] In general, these twice-blessed deductions are viewed as business expenses if this classification is most favorable to the taxpayer. Mortgage interest and real property taxes paid with respect to an individual taxpayer's place of business, for example, can be deducted as business expenses under §62(a)(1) in computing adjusted gross income, so that taxpayers can, for example, take these deductions in addition to the standard deduction.[28]

Moreover, §§162 and 212 ordinarily take precedence over the more specific itemized deductions when the latter are subject to special restrictions. For example, §164, allowing certain taxes to be deducted whether or not they are incurred in a business or profit-related activity, does not encompass any federal tax, but if a federal tax qualifies as an expense under §162 or §212, it is deductible even though it is not listed in §164(a).[29] Section 162, however, sometimes plays second fiddle. Section 162(b), for example, provides that charitable contributions in excess of the percentage limitations imposed by §170, relating to the deduction of charitable contributions, may not be deducted under §162.[30]

In no event, however, does the fact that an expenditure is deductible under more than one statutory provision permit it to be deducted twice.[31]

¶20.1.4 Expenses Paid on Behalf of Another Person

Section 162 authorizes the deduction of the ordinary and necessary expenses of carrying on "any" trade or business, without explicitly requiring that the enterprise belong to the taxpayer, and §212 similarly fails to state that expenses, to be deductible, must arise in *the taxpayer's* income-oriented activities. Nevertheless, it is well established that expenses can be deducted under §162 or §212 only if they are incurred in the taxpayer's

---

[27] For §163 and §164, see infra Chs. 31 and 32, respectively.

[28] For the standard deduction, see infra ¶30.5.

[29] See infra ¶32.2.3.

[30] Section 162(b) also applies to the dollar limitations and timing requirements of §170. See infra ¶¶20.1.7, 35.1.

[31] Reg. §1.161-1.

business or profit-oriented activities.[32]

This sound principle is sometimes said to prohibit a taxpayer from deducting "the expenses of another taxpayer's business" or "expenses incurred for the benefit of another person."[33] The term "expense" in the "expense of another" cases sometimes refers to an amount that would be a deductible expense if paid directly by the person for whose benefit it was paid by the taxpayer. Sometimes it refers merely to a debt of the other party, which might or might not have been deductible if paid by the debtor and which, if deductible, might have already been deducted (although not paid) if the debtor used the accrual method of accounting.

When properly employed, the expense-of-another notion is less a rule of law than a tool of analysis, directing attention to the reason why the item was paid by the taxpayer claiming the deduction. If an individual pays his barber's rent to keep him in business during a period of financial distress, for example, the individual cannot deduct the payment, but the reason for the denial is not that the expense arose in the barber's business but rather that it did not arise in any business or profit-oriented activity of the payor. By contrast, if a university requires its professors to wear academic robes in the classroom, the resulting expense to each professor arises in his trade or business and qualifies for deduction under §162, even though incurred at the university's instigation and to satisfy its sense of academic propriety. The professor's deduction, in other words, is not undermined by the fact that the expense was for the employer's benefit. Instead, this fact strengthens the claim for deduction by establishing that the expense was a necessary expense of engaging in the professor's own occupation.

In *Deputy v. Du Pont*, the leading expense-of-another case, the taxpayer wished to assist the Du Pont Company, of which he was a principal shareholder, in cementing its relationship with a group of young executives by giving them a financial stake in the enterprise.[34] Because the company could not legally sell them stock, the taxpayer agreed to do so. Not having sufficient shares in his own portfolio, he borrowed shares under an agreement

---

[32] See Reg. §1.162-1(a).

[33] The expense-of-another problem arises in the itemized deduction area when, for example, a taxpayer seeks to deduct interest or taxes paid for another person. See infra ¶¶31.1.5, 32.1.2. The parallel is not complete, since taxpayers seeking to deduct interest under §163 or taxes under §164 must establish that the payments are, as to them, interest or taxes rather than rent, loans, or gifts. By contrast, the cost of travel or entertainment may be a business expense as to either the employee or the employer.

See generally Lee, Command Performance: The Tax Treatment of Employer Mandated Expenses, 7 U. Rich. L. Rev. 1, 39 et seq. (1972); Lempert, Who Can Deduct a Business Expense? 11 Tax L. Rev. 433 (1956); Note, Deductibility of Expenses Incurred for the Benefit of Another, 66 Harv. L. Rev. 1508 (1953).

[34] Deputy v. Du Pont, 308 US 488 (1940).

requiring him to replace them at a later date and to pay the lender an amount equal to the dividends received in the interim. On claiming a deduction for the dividends reimbursed, the taxpayer was forced to rely on the statutory predecessor of §162 because the taxable year preceded the enactment in 1942 of §212, authorizing expenses to conserve or maintain income producing property to be deducted.[35]

The Court assumed arguendo that the taxpayer's activities in managing his large estate was a business,[36] but it held that the expenses were nevertheless not deductible. First, the Court held that the taxpayer's expenses "proximately result[ed] not from the taxpayer's business but from the business of the Du Pont Company," since the transactions "had their origin in an effort by that company to increase the efficiency of its management by selling its stock to certain of its key executives."[37] Citing cases holding that shareholders of closely held corporations cannot deduct their corporations' losses on their personal returns,[38] the Court prohibited any "blending" of the corporation's business with those of its stockholders. The Court acknowledged, however, that the taxpayer engaged in the transactions "to the end that his beneficial stock ownership in the Du Pont Company might be conserved and enhanced," and it would have had more difficulty with this aspect of the case if it had involved a taxable year after the enactment of §212(2), authorizing the deduction of ordinary and necessary expenses paid or incurred "for the management, conservation, or maintenance of property held for the production of income."

---

[35] For §212, see infra ¶20.5.1. The taxpayer also argued that payments for the borrowed stock were interest, deductible under the statutory predecessor of §163, but this claim was rejected because he had not borrowed any money.

[36] In Higgins v. CIR, 312 US 212 (1941), decided the following year, the Court held to the contrary.

[37] Deputy v. Du Pont, supra note 34, at 494.

[38] Dalton v. Bowers, 287 US 404 (1932) ("under the general rules for tax purposes, a corporation is an entity distinct from the stockholders"); Burnet v. Clark, 287 US 410 (1932) (same); Rink v. CIR, 51 TC 746, 751 (1969) (acq.) (dominant shareholder cannot deduct taxes and fees paid for dormant corporation, which was still a viable entity). See also Interstate Transit Lines v. CIR, 319 US 590 (1943) (parent corporation cannot deduct amounts paid to subsidiary under contract to reimburse latter for its operating deficits); Young & Rubicam, Inc. v. US, 410 F2d 1233 (Ct. Cl. 1969) (allocation of expenses among affiliated corporations, with review of prior decisions); Austin Co. v. CIR, 71 TC 955 (1979) (parent's payment of Mexican subsidiary's Mexican taxes not sufficiently related to parent's own business to be deductible); Nalco Chem. Co. v. US, 561 F. Supp. 1274 (ND Ill. 1983) (disallowing deduction for payment to subsidiary under agreement to hold subsidiary harmless for foreign exchange loss on loan from subsidiary to another company in which taxpayer had 49 percent interest; payment made as shareholder, not in taxpayer's own business); Dinardo v. CIR, 22 TC 430 (1954) (acq.) (physicians who contracted to meet operating deficits of private hospital to preserve ability to practice there allowed to deduct payments; *Interstate Transit Lines* distinguished).

After enunciating its antiblending principle, the Court went on to hold that the expenses incurred by the taxpayer were not "ordinary"—a barrier to deductions not only under §162 but also, had it been in force, under §212. This aspect of *Deputy v. Du Pont* was ultimately factual. In the absence of evidence "that stockholders or investors, in furtherance of enhancing and conserving their estates, ordinarily or frequently lend such assistance to employee stock purchase plans of their corporations," the Court held that the taxpayer's expenses could not "be placed in the same category as typically ordinary expenses of such activities, e.g., rental of safe deposit boxes, cost of investment counsel or of investment services, salaries of secretaries and the like."[39]

Deputy v. Du Pont does not prohibit the deduction of the expenses of another person, but merely required that the taxpayer stand on his own feet. Evidence that the transactions enhanced the company's business operations was not enough to establish that they advanced any business conducted by the taxpayer or that, if they did, they were "ordinary" expenses.[40] Moreover, if viewed as expenditures to conserve and enhance the value of the taxpayer's stock, the payments resembled nondeductible capital outlays to achieve long-term benefits, rather than currently deductible expenses of carrying on business.[41] Indeed, although not alluded to in its opinion, this would have been the soundest rationale for the decision.

The factual basis of *Deputy v. Du Pont* was recognized, and appropriately distinguished, by the Tax Court in *Gould v. CIR*.[42] The taxpayer in *Gould* was the president and sole shareholder of a failing corporation (GPH) and was simultaneously an employee and minority shareholder of a successful corporation (IMC) in the same industry. Under pressure from the directors of IMC, who feared damage to their company's reputation if GPH went into bankruptcy, the taxpayer paid about $30,000 to settle obligations of GPH for which he had no personal liability. The Tax Court allowed a §162 deduction for the payment:

---

[39] Deputy v. Du Pont, 308 US 496–97. Although the Court did not say so, the expenses in *Du Pont* might have been thought extraordinary because the taxpayer, who owned only 16 percent of the stock, bore the entire cost of a stock purchase plan benefiting all shareholders.

[40] See infra ¶20.3.

[41] A purchaser paying his seller's accrued but unpaid expenses, for example, must capitalize the payments as part of the purchase price of the property, rather than as deductible expenses. See, e.g., Bennet Land Co. v. CIR, 70 TC 904 (1978) (expenses attributable to seller's summer fallowing of farmland); M. Buten & Sons v. CIR, 31 TCM (CCH) 178 (1972); infra ¶20.4.2. See also Rev. Rul. 84-68, 1984-1 CB 31 (parent's payment of bonuses to subsidiary's employees treated as nondeductible contributions to subsidiary's capital and potentially deductible payments by the subsidiary to its employees).

[42] Gould v. CIR, 64 TC 132 (1975).

Ordinarily, a shareholder may not deduct a payment made on behalf of the corporation, but must treat it as a capital expenditure. *Deputy v. DuPont*, 308 U.S. 488 (1940). . . . However, such rule is not invariable; the payment may be deducted if it is an ordinary and necessary expense of a trade or business of the shareholder. . . . During 1968, Mr. Gould was an employee of IMC, in addition to being the sole shareholder of GPH. His employment with IMC constituted a business, and he is entitled to deduct expenditures that have the requisite relationship to such employment. . . .

Although IMC's other directors did not threaten to fire Mr. Gould unless he satisfied the creditors of GPH, he believed his position with IMC was in jeopardy. The Commissioner argued that the payments by Mr. Gould were deductible only if he would have lost his job had the payments not been made. However, the petitioner is only required to carry his burden of proving that his motive for making the payments was to protect his job with IMC, and we are satisfied that he has carried that burden.[43]

The expense-of-another problem arises with some frequency when executives deduct travel and entertainment expenses incurred in promoting an employer's business. In *Schmidlapp v. CIR*, a leading early case involving a bank officer whose employer "expected that as part of [the taxpayer's] duties he would entertain at his own expense visitors whose favor the bank desired," Judge Learned Hand held that the officer could deduct the expenses "so far as they really were to drum up business for the bank, though it was proper to be extremely suspicious as to how far that was their purpose."[44] Since this evidentiary burden was satisfied, Judge Hand did not regard the expense-of-another principle as a barrier to a deduction:

---

[43] Id. at 134–36. See also Gudmundsson v. CIR, 37 TCM (CCH) 1249 (1978) (teacher allowed to deduct expenses of trips for handicapped students, although employer did not require trips); Conley v. CIR, 36 TCM (CCH) 1644 (1977) (payment of wholly owned corporation's debts to protect taxpayer's business reputation; deduction allowed). For cases involving different but analogous facts, see infra ¶20.4.7 note 85.

For the converse situation, where a corporation pays an expense of a shareholder-employee, see Jack's Maintenance Contractors, Inc. v. CIR, 703 F2d 154 (5th Cir. 1983) (payment of legal expenses in defense of criminal prosecution of president and sole shareholder was constructive dividend; personal benefit to individual in staying out of jail far outweighed benefit to corporation's business); Graphic Business Sys., Inc. v. CIR, 43 TCM (CCH) 957 (1982) (deduction by corporation allowed for payment in settlement of lawsuit against shareholder-employees by former employer because actions complained of were in pursuit of corporation's business).

[44] Schmidlapp v. CIR, 96 F2d 680, 681–82 (2d Cir. 1938). See Henricks v. CIR, 8 TCM (CCH) 993 (1949), where an employee's claim for deduction was bolstered by the following memorandum to the advertising staff of Time, Inc.:

It is no answer to say that [the expenses] were for the bank's benefit; so were all the taxpayer's services; if it did in fact give him to understand that he was to extend a factitious hospitality in its interest, the cost of it was a necessary expense of his office.[45]

Some later cases have suggested that the employer's failure to reimburse the employee for such expenses is evidence that they serve personal rather than business purposes.[46] This theory presupposes that it is abnormal for salesmen and executives to pursue their trade at their own expense. As *Schmidlapp* recognizes, however, employers sometimes prefer to pay higher salaries and shift the burden of these expenses to employees, an arrangement that may be more economical than allowing employees to charge entertainment expenses to the employer and less abrasive than requiring the expenditures to be approved in advance or after the fact. From the employee's viewpoint, financial success—whether in the direct form of commissions or the indirect form of movement up the business ladder—can often be promoted by entertaining the employer's customers or advertising the employer's goods and services. Indeed, the targets of the employee's expenditures are often described as the employee's customers, even though they purchase the employer's goods.

These realities of business life are so commonplace that one is surprised to find them disregarded by some of the expense-of-another cases. The source of the difficulty seems to be a fear that expenses may be "transferred," especially by closely held companies, from the employer to the employee "so that [they] may be deducted in the highest brackets."[47] If the expenses are animated by business objectives rather than personal preferences, however, the Treasury comes out the same, whether the employer (1) pays a base salary and defrays the expenses or (2) increases the salary by the

---

Mr. Luce and other Management officers have often emphasized that TIME salesmen are paid high salaries because selling is not a routine job and makes demands on a man's time and money that cannot be accounted for minute-by-minute or penny-by-penny. There are many expenses incidental to selling which the salesman is not expected to recover from the Company on top of his salary.

For cases disallowing deductions for entertainment expenses paid by shareholder-employees of closely held corporations, see Jergens v. CIR, 17 TC 806 (1951) (acq.); Roach v. CIR, 20 BTA 919 (1930) (nonacq.). In both cases, a business connection, even at the corporate level, was debatable, and there was evidently no effort to relate the expenditures to the taxpayer's own occupation.

[45] Schmidlapp v. CIR, supra note 44, at 682.

[46] Noland v. CIR, 269 F2d 108, 113 (4th Cir.), cert. denied, 361 US 885 (1959). The court in *Noland* may have meant only that an adverse inference arises if an employer whose practice is to reimburse all appropriate entertainment expenses explicitly declines to reimburse the one in dispute.

[47] Id. at 111.

amount of anticipated expenses and requires the employee to pay them. The proof is in Example 20-2, which assumes that an employee incurs $5,000 of expenses and that the employer either (1) pays a base salary of $25,000 and reimburses the employee for the expenses or (2) pays a gross salary of $30,000, from which the employee defrays the expenses. In either case, the employer can deduct $30,000, and the employee's taxable income (disregarding other income, deductions, and personal exemptions) is $25,000.

Example 20-2

**Comparison of Salary-Expense Arrangement With
Expanded Salary Without Reimbursement**

	Salary/ Expense Arrangement	Expanded Salary Without Reimbursement
1. Employer pays and deducts:		
Salary	$25,000	$30,000
Expenses	5,000	–0–
Total	$30,000	$30,000
2. Employee receives and deducts:		
Gross income	$25,000	$30,000
Business expenses	–0–	5,000
Taxable income	$25,000	$25,000

There is a genuine problem in this area, but it is the creation of unwarranted deductions, not the transfer of legitimate deductions. The remedy for this problem, however, is vigilance in reviewing the facts, as counseled by Judge Hand in the *Schmidlapp* case, not a rigid expense-of-another principle.

The basic IRS ruling in this area offers the following temperate summary:

[A] corporate officer who claims deductions for traveling and entertainment expenses incurred on behalf of a corporation must bear the burden of proof that he is entitled to such deduction. Reimbursement for such expenses to the corporation officer or a resolution requiring the assumption of such expenses by him would tend to indicate that they are a necessary expense of his office. Although the presence of such evidence does not conclusively determine that the expenses are deductible, neither does the absence of such evidence of itself necessarily result in the disallowance of deductions, provided it can be established otherwise that the expenses are a necessary expense of the office.[48]

The ruling properly treats an employer's resolution requiring employees to defray their own traveling and entertainment expenses as neither indispensable nor conclusive. Commission salesmen, for example, do not need to be advised that travel and entertainment can serve their financial interests by promoting the employer's goods and services. Conversely, a formal declaration by the employer may be a shabby attempt to furnish a fringe benefit to the employee at the expense of the Treasury, rather than a genuine statement of business policy.

The expense-of-another rationale has been used in a few cases to disallow the deduction of entertainment expenses by an employee who was entitled to be reimbursed by the employer but who failed to press the claim.[49] The result may be justified by the circumstances of the particular cases. An employee's failure to enforce a right of reimbursement, however, is neutral; what is material is the reason for the failure.

If the employee is careless or lazy in failing to request reimbursement, the payment is not a business expense. It might, however, be deductible as bad debt if and when the right to be reimbursed expires, rather like a debt that becomes worthless because the taxpayer is not vigilant and lets the statute of limitations run.

If the right to be reimbursed is not pursued because the employee fears resistance by the employer, this may indicate that the employee has decided to bear the expense personally rather than jeopardize his continued employ-

---

[48] Rev. Rul. 57-502, 1957-2 CB 118. See Rev. Rul. 72-192, 1972-1 CB 48 (involving chamber of commerce dues of three corporate presidents, *A, B,* and *C; A's* dues were paid by his employer; *A* and *B* were required by their employers to join the organization, but *C* was not; held, *A's* dues are deductible by employer; *B* and *C* may deduct their dues on showing that membership was a means of carrying out substantive duties of their employment). See also Horowitz v. CIR, 38 TCM (CCH) 108 (1979) (majority shareholder-officer denied deduction for certain corporate expenses; reimbursement contract not probative of necessity of expenditures, absent true bargaining and in light of substantial reimbursements and minimal and irregular salary); Richardson v. CIR, 37 TCM (CCH) 1335 (1978) (reduction in salary on promotion to chairman of board evidence that taxpayer was not required or expected to entertain at own expense for corporation's benefit; corporate resolution re such expenses during tenure as president and general manager might have supported deduction of similar expenses then).
See generally Malloy & Bratton, Unreimbursed Expenses—A Problem Area, 55 Taxes 257 (1977).

[49] Heidt v. CIR, 274 F2d 25 (7th Cir. 1959); Brown v. CIR, 446 F2d 926, 929 n.5 (8th Cir. 1971). See also infra ¶¶20.2.12, 20.3.2 note 28 (re expenses of public officials and government employees), ¶25.5 (effect of failure to press claim on loss deduction); ¶34.4.3 (effect failure to press claim against insurer on casualty deduction).

ment or the level of his salary. The salesman may be right in thinking that his success depends on results, that the expenditure helps to produce the results expected by the employer, and that it is better to absorb the expense —as an offset to his salary—than to insist on enforcing a reimbursement arrangement. It is common business practice to refrain from enforcing indisputable rights. Department stores, for example, often let customers return goods despite an announced policy of "no refunds—no returns" or "all sales final," even if the returned merchandise cannot be resold except at a sacrifice.

On the other hand, a salesman may refrain from requesting reimbursement because he anticipates and fears a dispute with the employer over whether the expenditure served business or personal objectives. That is a datum to which appropriate weight should be given, but it is not necessarily conclusive—the boss may be wrong.

A right to be reimbursed is a more solid barrier to a deduction if the reimbursement is not payable until some time in the future, but there is no business reason why the taxpayer should not press the claim when it matures. Taxpayers often incur expenses on behalf of customers, clients, or other persons under reimbursement arrangements that allow a substantial lag between the time the expenses are incurred and the time when reimbursement is due. In this context, the taxpayer's expenditure is better viewed as a loan or advance to the party on whose behalf the payment is made than as a deductible expense of the taxpayer's business.[50] If the taxpayer's right to be reimbursed becomes worthless, the loss will be reflected by a bad debt deduction.

¶20.1.5 "Reasonableness" Standard—Transactions Between Related Parties

It is sometimes asserted that expenses must be "reasonable" in amount to be deducted under §162(a) or §212. Explicit statutory limitations of this type appear in §162(a)(1) ("reasonable allowance for salaries or other com-

---

[50] Flower v. CIR, 61 TC 140, 152 (1973) (promotional expenses paid by sales representative pursuant to reimbursement agreement nondeductible even though reimbursement long delayed and no interest provided; "we must assume [taxpayer] received something else of value under the agreement that compensated him for the deferral in reimbursement without interest"). See also Burnett v. CIR, 356 F2d 755 (5th Cir.), cert. denied, 385 US 832 (1966) (attorney's advances to or on behalf of clients, subject to reimbursement on successful completion of litigation, nondeductible despite slight risk of nonpayment); Boccardo v. US, 12 Cl. Ct. 184, 87-1 USTC ¶9288 (1987) (no deduction for law firm's advances for litigation expenses on clients' behalf; because firm had right of reimbursement, advances were in the nature of loans; that reimbursement contingent on success in litigation does not justify deduction because firm took only cases where success was probable).

pensation for personal services actually rendered") and §162(a)(2) (amounts expended for meals and lodging not deductible if "lavish or extravagant under the circumstances").[51] It has been held, however, that "the element of reasonableness is [also] inherent in the phrase 'ordinary and necessary.'"[52] In practice, the concept of reasonableness adds little if anything to the statutory requirement that expenses must be "ordinary and necessary."[53] If the amount of an otherwise deductible expense is determined by an impersonal market or fixed in arm's length bargaining between the taxpayer and an independent supplier, there is no reason to pare it down for tax purposes. Indeed, the best evidence that an amount is reasonable is that it was paid by the taxpayer to an independent party for the goods or services in question.

On the other hand, payments between related parties, such as members of the same family, may serve personal as well as business or profit motives. Since payments are deductible if they are genuine expenses but not if they are gifts, it is entirely appropriate for the IRS and the courts to scrutinize the amount paid in determining whether the expense is what it purports to be. If the amount is excessive, the payment is pro tanto not an expense of carrying on a business or of conserving and maintaining income producing property, but is a gift, dividend, loan, or other nondeductible item. Even if the related parties are not linked by emotional ties but are instead coldly calculating parent-subsidiary corporations or other affiliated business entities, a showing that a payment is excessive may establish that the transaction is, in whole or in part, a dividend or capital contribution rather than a bona fide payment for goods or services.

¶20.1.6 Temporary Suspension vs. Abandonment of Business Activities

By authorizing the deduction of expenses paid or incurred "in carrying on" a trade or business, §162(a) impliedly disqualifies expenditures to enter a business (e.g., the cost of attending law or medical school), a disqualifica-

---

[51] See infra ¶22.2 ("reasonable" compensation for services), ¶21.1.1 ("lavish and extravagant" restriction on travel expenses), ¶21.2.3 (same as to entertainment expenses).

[52] CIR v. Lincoln Elec. Co., 176 F2d 815, 817 (6th Cir.) (one judge dissenting), cert. denied, 338 US 949 (1949); see also Bingham's Trust v. CIR, 325 US 365, 370 (1945) (same as to "ordinary and necessary" as used in §212); Reg. §1.212-1(d) (to be deductible under §212, expenses "must be reasonable in amount"), §1.162-2(a) (same for traveling expenses).

[53] See infra ¶22.2.1; see also Palo Alto Town & Country Village, Inc. v. CIR, 565 F2d 1388 (9th Cir. 1977) (expense of maintaining plane on 24-hour standby basis for business use deductible, reversing Tax Court, which had limited deduction to normal charter rate for periods of actual use, on ground that standby expense was not "reasonable in amount in relation to its purpose").

tion that also encompasses expenses to shift from an existing occupation to a new trade or business.[54] On the other hand, a slack season or period of temporary unemployment does not terminate a taxpayer's business status. It is sometimes necessary to decide whether a taxpayer has terminated his business (so that expenditures to reenter the area are not incurred in "carrying on" the business) or has only suspended business activities temporarily, in which event the taxpayer's status continues for purposes of §162(a). This problem, which can arise with respect to any type of business expense, has been especially troublesome for taxpayers incurring expenses in seeking employment or in pursuing an extended program of business related education; the applicable principles are analyzed elsewhere in this work in the discussion of these subjects.[55]

The statute might be read to disallow the deduction of an expense paid in a taxable year in which the taxpayer was not carrying on a trade or business, even though the expense was incurred in a business conducted in a previous year. Following several judicial decisions, however, the IRS has ruled that a cash basis taxpayer may deduct ordinary and necessary business expenses when they are paid, even if payment is made after the business has been terminated.[56] Conversely, expenses incurred by a cash basis taxpayer before entering a business should not be deductible merely because they are paid after the taxpayer is engaged in or has embarked on a business or other profit-oriented activity.[57]

---

[54] See infra ¶22.1.3.

[55] See infra ¶¶20.4.6, 22.1.5.

[56] Rev. Rul. 67-12, 1967-1 CB 29. See Ditmars v. CIR, 302 F2d 481 (2d Cir. 1962) (legal expenses in settling claims arising out of taxpayer's former brokerage business); Flood v. US, 133 F2d 173 (1st Cir. 1943) (income of trust established to pay pensions to former employees); Ward v. CIR, 20 TC 332 (1953) (acq.), aff'd on other issues, 224 F2d 547 (9th Cir. 1955) (payment for care of former secretary).

[57] Kales v. CIR, 101 F2d 35 (6th Cir. 1939) sometimes cited as supporting the transmutation of such payments, does not so hold. Deciding that expenses incurred in 1919 could be deducted when paid in 1928 and 1930, the court said that disallowance "would mean that business expenses . . . could never be deducted, no matter how ordinary or how necessary they might be to the carrying on of a business unless they were paid for the taxable year within which the use or service was required by the business." Thus, *Kales* belongs with the cases cited in the preceding note involving belated payment of expenses incurred while the taxpayer was engaged in a trade or business. See also IRC §166(d)(2) (defining, for a limited purpose, the term "business debt" to mean a debt created or acquired in connection with the taxpayer's trade or business or a debt whose loss from worthlessness is incurred in the taxpayer's trade or business; discussed infra ¶33.6).

¶20.1.7 Charitable Contributions as Business Expenses

Section 162(b) disallows deductions under §162(a) for contributions that would be deductible as charitable gifts were it not for the percentage limitations or time-of-payment requirements imposed by §170 on the charitable deduction.[58] Before 1935, corporations were not ordinarily allowed to deduct charitable contributions as such, but some corporate taxpayers successfully established that gifts to charitable organizations were ordinary and necessary business expenses.[59] A 1935 amendment permitted corporations to deduct charitable contributions up to a specified percentage of income, and the statutory predecessor of §162(b) was enacted shortly thereafter to prevent outflanking the percentage limitation by a claim that particular contributions were business expenses.[60] Later amendments expanded §162(b) to cover all taxpayers and to buttress the dollar limitations and time-of-payment requirements of §170, as well as its percentage limitations.[61]

Section 162(b) only applies to payments that are "in fact contributions or gifts to organizations described in Section 170."[62] Thus, payments to a hospital in consideration for the hospital's agreement to provide services and facilities to the taxpayer's employees are deductible without regard to the limitations of §162(b) because they are not contributions.[63] However, the merely incidental benefit to the taxpayer's business resulting from a pay-

---

[58] For these restrictions under §170, see infra ¶¶35.1.4, 35.3.

[59] See, e.g., Yamhill Elec. Co. v. CIR, 20 BTA 1232 (1930) (acq.) (contribution to college endowment fund to assure its continuation as a substantial patron).

[60] See H.R. Rep. No. 1860, 75th Cong., 3d Sess. (1938), reprinted in 1939-1 (Part 2) CB 728, 740.

[61] For historical details, see Marquis v. CIR, 49 TC 695, 698–700 (1968) (acq.) (travel agent's cash payments to charitable organizations booking tours through her office deductible under §162).

[62] Reg. §1.162-15(a)(2).

[63] Id. For examples of payments held not to be charitable contributions, see Reg. §1.162-15(c) (labor union and trade association dues); Jefferson Mills, Inc. v. US, 259 F. Supp. 305 (ND Ga. 1965), aff'd per curiam, 367 F2d 392 (5th Cir. 1966) (contractual payments to board of education to maintain schools at level enabling taxpayer to attract and hold employees); Rev. Rul. 72-314, 1972-1 CB 44 (stock brokerage firm's payment to charitable organization organized to reduce neighborhood tensions and combat community deterioration, emphasized in firm's advertisements); Rev. Rul. 63-73, 1963-1 CB 35 (payments to charitable organization for use of its name and cooperation in taxpayer's advertising program). For payments not made as part of a contractual arrangement, see Marquis v. CIR, supra note 61, at 695 (where travel agent did large business with charities, annual payments to charities based on amount, character, and profitability of business not contributions). See generally infra ¶35.1.3 (benefit to taxpayer as barring charitable deduction under §170).

ment to a charity is not sufficient to support a §162 deduction.[64]

The factual nature of this distinction is illustrated by a pair of rulings involving operators of racetracks. The IRS ruled in 1972 that an operator having "charity days," the proceeds of which were distributed to a charitable foundation without expectation of a commensurate economic return, had contributed the proceeds to the charity within the meaning of §170, and was not entitled to a §162 deduction.[65] In a 1977 ruling involving another racetrack, however, the IRS held that where charity days were held to obtain and ensure retention of the taxpayer's license and favorable racing schedule, §162(b) did not bar a §162 deduction because "the payments to the benefited charities bear a direct relationship to the taxpayer's business and are made with a reasonable expectation of a financial return commensurate with the amount of the payments."[66]

Section §162(b) is inapplicable to a gift to a donee not qualified to receive deductible contributions under §170 because the provision is exclusively concerned with contributions that would be deductible under §170 save for its percentage or dollar limitations or its time-of-payment requirements. Thus, contributions to nonqualifying foreign charities are deductible if they constitute ordinary and necessary expenses of the taxpayer's business.[67]

¶20.1.8 Business and Profit-Oriented Expenses as Capital Losses

Amounts deductible under §§162 and 212 are almost always applied against ordinary income; indeed, they are classic examples of "ordinary" deductions. Occasionally, however, a deduction under §162 or §212 is closely linked to a current or prior transaction involving a capital asset. An example is a payment by the taxpayer to settle a claim for misrepresentation or fraud in the sale of securities in an earlier year. Since payments of this type are most realistically viewed as reducing the capital gain on the related

---

[64] Hartless Linen Serv. Co. v. CIR, 32 TC 1026 (1959) (payments to churches and religious societies; no attempt to measure resulting benefits in dollar terms or in terms of business obtained); Brooks v. CIR, ¶51,335 P-H Memo TC (1951) (benefits from surgeon's payments to hospital were "incidental and certainly not commensurate with the amount of the payments").

[65] Rev. Rul. 72-542, 1972-2 CB 37. See also Rev. Rul. 72-293, 1972-1 CB 95 (status of payments to 1972 US Transportation Exposition depends on all facts and circumstances of each case).

[66] Rev. Rul. 77-124, 1977-1 CB 39, 40.

[67] See Reg. §1.162-15(b); B. Manischewitz Co. v. CIR, 10 TC 1139 (1948) (acq.) (contribution by manufacturer of kosher food to B. Manischewitz Yeshiva in Palestine, not an eligible recipient of charitable contributions, held ordinary and necessary business expense).

transaction (or increasing the capital loss), they are treated as capital losses under principles discussed elsewhere in this work.[68]

The converse of this phenomenon is the occasional transformation of a taxpayer's loss on the sale of a capital asset from a capital loss into a deduction from ordinary income because the transaction was an integral part of the taxpayer's business operations, rather than the type of investment activity that the capital gain and loss provisions were designed to encompass. An example is a loss incurred by a manufacturing company on selling the stock of a supplier, if the stock was purchased in order to ensure a source of supply in a period of scarcity and was sold when the business need terminated.[69]

¶20.1.9 Estimating and Substantiating Deductible Amounts

In addition to establishing that an expenditure was paid or incurred for business or profit-oriented purposes within the meaning of §162 or §212, the taxpayer must prove the amount spent for qualified purposes. If the actual amount of an expenditure cannot be established by such documentary evidence as an invoice, paid bill, or canceled check, oral testimony by the taxpayer or other persons may suffice; self-serving declarations, however, are closely scrutinized.

Sometimes, taxpayers are enormously aided by the rule promulgated in 1930 by the Court of Appeals for the Second Circuit in *Cohan v. CIR*, on appeal from the Board of Tax Appeals.[70] The Board found that George M. Cohan, in conducting his business as a Broadway producer, "was required to and did spend large sums of money in traveling and entertaining," but it upheld the IRS' disallowance of Cohan's deductions because "the amounts claimed are bare estimates unsupported by any vouchers or bookkeeping entries of any kind" and because "we do not know what part of the amounts expended were for personal expenses."[71] In an opinion by Judge Learned Hand, the appellate court reversed, holding that the Board should have made the best estimate possible in the circumstances:

> In the production of his plays Cohan was obliged to be free-handed in entertaining actors, employees, and, as he naively adds, dramatic critics. He had also to travel much, at times with his attorney. These expenses amounted to substantial sums, but he kept no account and probably could not have done so. At the trial before the Board he estimated that he had spent eleven thousand dollars in this fashion

---

[68] See infra ¶¶20.4.2, 51.10.6.
[69] See infra ¶51.10.3.
[70] Cohan v. CIR, 11 BTA 743 (1928), rev'd, 39 F2d 540 (2d Cir. 1930).
[71] Id. at 761.

during the first six months of 1921, twenty-two thousand dollars, between July first, 1921, and June thirtieth, 1922, and as much for his following fiscal year, fifty-five thousand dollars in all. The Board refused to allow him any part of this, on the ground that it was impossible to tell how much he had in fact spent, in the absence of any items or details. The question is how far this refusal is justified, in view of the finding that he had spent much and that the sums were allowable expenses. Absolute certainty in such matters is usually impossible and is not necessary; the Board should make as close an approximation as it can, bearing heavily if it chooses upon the taxpayer whose inexactitude is of his own making. But to allow nothing at all appears to us inconsistent with saying that something was spent. True, we do not know how many trips Cohan made, nor how large his entertainments were; yet there was obviously some basis for computation, if necessary by drawing upon the Board's personal estimates of the minimum of such expenses. The amount may be trivial and unsatisfactory, but there was basis for some allowance, and it was wrong to refuse any, even though it were the traveling expenses of a single trip. It is not fatal that the result will inevitably be speculative; many important decisions must be such.[72]

Judge Hand's assertion that the taxpayer probably could not have kept detailed records of his expenditures may have been right for the taxable years before the court, 1921 and 1922. Since then, the process of evolution —nudged along by the Code—has produced a more docile race of taxpayers, with record-keeping habits that more freehanded earlier generations would have thought demeaning. A case can be made for restricting the *Cohan* doctrine to areas in which record keeping remains counter-cultural,[73] and for refusing to apply it to areas in which documentary evidence is customarily requested and retained by the average taxpayer, unless its absence is satisfactorily explained (e.g., destruction by casualty).

Despite its outdated premise that record-keeping is not a customary part of everyday business life, *Cohan* has been expanded to cover virtually the entire corpus of the tax law.[74] Although ousted from jurisdiction over

---

[72] Cohan v. CIR, supra note 70, 39 F2d at 543–44.

[73] Lewis v. CIR, 44 TCM (CCH) 887 (1982) (*Cohan* applied to allow moving van operator deduction for estimate of wages paid to temporary help in loading and unloading trucks; one reason for lack of records was that workers were recruited from "underground economy" in which transactions were in cash and names were not recorded).

[74] See generally Gluck, How *Cohan* Works: Allowance of Business Expense Deductions When No Exact Records Are Kept, 6 Rutgers L. Rev. 375 (1952); Kramer, Estimated Income and Expense in the Tax Law, 32 Taxes 906 (1954).

travel and entertainment expenses by the enactment in 1962 of §274,[75] it remains a major factor in the allowance of virtually all other deductions under §162.[76] It should be noted, however, that the Board of Tax Appeals was reversed in *Cohan* "only because [it] found that the taxpayer had made *some* allowable expenditures, yet had granted no relief therefor."[77] Taxpayers relying on *Cohan*, therefore, must make a threshold showing that they spent more for deductible items than was allowed by the IRS. Moreover, if the *Cohan* principle was applied by the IRS in determining a deficiency, it need not be applied again by the trial court to allow an additional amount if the IRS' application of *Cohan* adequately recognized the taxpayer's right to an estimated deduction.[78] Finally, *Cohan* does not require a partial allowance for an item that is either wholly deductible or wholly nondeductible, no matter how difficult it is to categorize the item. *Cohan*, in other words, does not establish a comprehensive split-the-difference principle.

In 1954, the IRS addressed the problem of verifying claims for business deductions based on "small items [that] often are not susceptible of complete substantiation by documentary evidence," and announced:

> In connection with the determination of factual matters of this type, due consideration should be given to the reasonableness of the taxpayer's stated expenditures for the claimed purposes in relation to his reported income, to the reliability and accuracy of his records in connection with other items more readily lending themselves to detailed record-keeping, and to the general credibility of his statements in the light of the entire record in the case. Disallowing amounts claimed for such items merely because there is available no documentary evidence which will establish the precise amount beyond any reasonable doubt ignores commonly-recognized business practice as well as the fact that proof may be established by credible oral testimony. On the other hand, it is not Service policy to allow a percentage or other

[75] Infra ¶21.4.

[76] See, e.g., Bruce v. CIR, 45 TCM (CCH) 916 (1983) (deduction allowed under *Cohan* for portions of taxpayer's payments of living expenses for live-in friend and her son and dog where taxpayer agreed to provide support in exchange for work in taxpayer's business of owning and operating rental residential property).

[77] Oates v. CIR, 316 F2d 56, 59 (8th Cir. 1963) (emphasis added). See also US v. Didio, 76-1 USTC ¶9261 (ED Pa. 1976) (not officially reported) (taxpayer "must first prove some deductible expenses before the fact-finder can indulge in estimates or approximations"); Metas v. CIR, 43 TCM (CCH) 376 (1982) (no deduction under *Cohan* rule for gambling losses because evidence indicated unreported gambling winnings).

[78] See Havas v. CIR, 29 TCM (CCH) 1461 (1970), aff'd per mem. order, 73-2 USTC ¶9561 (9th Cir. 1973) (not officially reported) ("question really is whether respondent's application of *Cohan* is, considering the evidence, fair and adequate").

arbitrarily-computed portion of deductions of this character merely for the purpose of settlement.[79]

Deficiencies based on approximations by the IRS are entitled to the usual presumption of correctness even if the basis for the agent's estimate is not established, so that the taxpayer has the burden of proving that a larger deduction is allowable.[80] If the IRS has already applied *Cohan* in allowing the claimed deduction in part, it may be very difficult to establish that a more generous estimate is required. By contrast, the taxpayer in *Cohan*, whose deductions had been disallowed in toto, became entitled to an estimate on showing that something had been spent for deductible items.

Dissatisfaction with the results under *Cohan* led Congress in 1962 to enact §274(d), discussed later in this work,[81] which supersedes the *Cohan* doctrine by requiring the taxpayer, under penalty of losing the deduction entirely, to substantiate the amount, business purpose, and other aspects of (1) travel expenses, (2) expenses for entertainment and similar activities, (3) business gifts, and (4) expenses relating to business use of passenger automobiles, computers, and a few other types of property. Expenses not covered by §274(d), however, remain subject to the *Cohan* principle.

¶20.2 THE BUSINESS-PERSONAL BORDERLINE

¶20.2.1 Introductory

Most expenses can be readily classified as purely personal or purely business, but many others serve personal purposes while simultaneously advancing the taxpayer's business or profit-oriented pursuits. Ranging from expenditures that are "personal with a tinge of business" to those that are "business with a personal tinge,"[1] numerous items fall between the two extremes. Common examples are uniforms, meals and lodging during business travel, and medical care required by occupational disease. In deciding whether to allow expenses along the business-personal borderline to be deducted under §162 or §212 as ordinary and necessary expenses of carrying

---

[79] Rev. Rul. 54-195, 1954-1 CB 47 (*Cohan* not cited!), superseded as to travel and entertainment expenses by §274, discussed infra ¶21.4. See also Fisher v. CIR, 23 TC 218, 225–26 (1954) (acq.), aff'd as to other issues, 230 F2d 79 (7th Cir. 1956) (applying *Cohan* case against IRS when it, having affirmatively raised an issue in the Tax Court, had burden of proof.

[80] See Walker v. CIR, 362 F2d 140 (7th Cir. 1966); United Aniline Co. v. CIR, 316 F2d 701 (1st Cir. 1963).

[81] See infra ¶21.4.

[1] CIR v. Doak, 234 F2d 704, 709 (4th Cir. 1956). For wages paid by parents to their minor children for services in a family business, see infra ¶75.2.8.

on the taxpayer's business or profit-oriented activities or to disallow them under §262, prohibiting any deduction for "personal, living, or family expenses" unless otherwise expressly allowed, the IRS, courts, and Congress have vacillated between four main approaches:

1. *Inherently personal.* Some expenses are nondeductible because they are considered "inherently personal" even though they may also serve business purposes or needs. As a minimum, this concept prohibits deductions for expenses essential to life itself. Otherwise, as pointed out by the Tax Court, the basic cost of living would be deductible:

> The fee to the doctor, but for whose healing service the earner of the family income could not leave his sickbed; the cost of the laborer's raiment, for how can the world proceed about its business unclothed; the very home which gives us shelter and rest and the food which provides energy, might all . . . be construed as necessary to the operation of business and to the creation of income. Yet these are the very essence of those "personal" expenses the deductibility of which is expressly denied [by §262].[2]

The expenses cited by the court are incurred whether the taxpayer works or not, but in the case itself, the inherently-personal concept was used to disallow deductions claimed by a young couple for the care of their infant child while they both were at work—expenses that would not have been incurred but for their employment. In the same vein, expenses are often viewed as inherently personal, and therefore nondeductible, even though they exceed the level that the taxpayer would have incurred in the absence of pressure from employers or customers, such as the excess cost of clothing when stylish dress is expected in the taxpayer's occupation.

---

[2] Smith v. CIR, 40 BTA 1038, 1038–39 (1939), aff'd per curiam, 113 F2d 114 (2d Cir. 1940) (amounts spent by two-job married couple for care of young child during working hours not deductible). Although a credit is now allowed by §21 for certain expenses of this type (see infra ¶37.1), *Smith* is still a barrier to deductions under §162 for analogous expenses. See also Fred W. Amend Co. v. CIR, 454 F2d 399 (7th Cir. 1971) (businessman's use of Christian Science practitioner as consultant is inherently personal); Sparkman v. CIR, 112 F2d 774 (9th Cir. 1940) (dentures to correct radio actor's speech defect nondeductible); Callender v. CIR, 75 TC 334 (1980) (no deduction for cost of maintaining personal checking account even though account also served as record of financial transactions for tax purposes; functions so intertwined that allocating cost between personal use and use for keeping tax records would be "an administrative impracticality"); Bakewell v. CIR, 23 TC 803 (1955) (cost of maintaining lawyer's hearing aid nondeductible); Rev. Rul. 82-168, 1982-2 CB 56 (no deduction for cost of wristwatch purchased to satisfy employer's requirement that taxpayer know time of day whenever on duty); Rev. Rul. 78-128, 1978-1 CB 39 (no deduction for health spa expenses of law-enforcement officer required to keep in top physical condition).

In 1978, the Tax Court rejected the claim that a taxpayer's living expenses were a cost of selling labor, analogous to a merchant's cost of goods sold:

> Labor . . . is, in the current context, behavior performed by human beings in exchange for compensation. One's living expenses simply cannot be his "cost" directly in the very item sold, i.e., his labor, no matter how much money he spends to satisfy his human needs and those of his family. Of course we recognize the necessity for expenditures for such items as food, shelter, clothing, and proper health maintenance. They provide both the mental and physical nourishment essential to maintain the *body* at a level of effectiveness that will permit its labor to be productive. We do not even deny that a certain similarity exists between the "cost of doing labor" and the "cost of goods sold" concept. But the sale of one's labor is not the same creature as the sale of property, and whether the distinction comports with petitioners' philosophical rationalization for their argument, it is recognized for Federal income tax purposes. . . . One's gain, ergo his "income," from the sale of his labor is the entire amount received therefor without any reduction for what he spends to satisfy his human needs.[3]

2. *Excess cost.* A second approach is to allow a deduction only if, and to the extent that, the expense was increased by the exigencies of the taxpayer's business or profit-oriented activities. This approach was adopted in 1920 by the Treasury in dealing with the cost of meals and lodging incurred by taxpayers on business trips, but was abandoned when Congress enacted the statutory predecessor of §162(a)(2), permitting these expenses to be deducted in full.[4] The excess cost theory was endorsed by the Supreme Court in *Fausner v. CIR*, involving a commercial airline pilot's expenses of getting to and from his place of employment with his flight equipment and overnight bag.[5] Holding that the expenses were personal because they would have been incurred even if the taxpayer had no occupational baggage, the Court indicated that a deduction would have been in order for any additional expenses incurred to transport job-required tools and materials.

3. *Allocation.* Third, expenses can be allocated between their business and personal components, with only the amount assigned to the business function being deductible. This approach is often applied to expenditures

---

[3] Reading v. CIR, 70 TC 730, 733–34 (1978).

[4] Infra ¶21.1.3.

[5] Fausner v. CIR, 413 US 838 (1973), discussed infra ¶21.1.3. See also Sutter v. CIR, 21 TC 170 (1953) (acq.) (cost of businessman's lunches at meetings of chamber of commerce, etc. not deductible in absence of evidence that they exceeded his normal lunch expense); Fenstermaker v. CIR, 37 TCM (CCH) 898 (1978) (same as to cost of lunches with other company executives).

for dual-purpose facilities, when business and personal uses can be separated by reference to the amounts of time, space, etc. devoted to each, such as an automobile used for both business and pleasure.[6]

4. *Primary purpose.* Finally, a deduction is sometimes allowed for the full amount of an expense if it is incurred primarily for business or profit-oriented activities, and the personal benefit is a mere by-product.[7] This approach is characteristic of cases and rulings permitting taxpayers to deduct educational expenses and the cost of business entertainment, where personal benefits are usually inevitable despite the primacy of the taxpayer's business goal.

Neither the bare language nor the legislative history of §162, 212, or 262 supplies a firm basis for choosing among these conflicting principles, and there is no possible way to reconcile all of the cases and rulings.[8] There is, unfortunately, no theoretically satisfactory boundary between business expenses that provide incidental personal benefits and personal expenditures that incidentally serve business purposes. No matter how generously the Code defines business expenses, there will always be nondeductible items that contribute in some way to the production of income, whether it is the basic cost of living—one cannot work, after all, unless one is fed and housed—or the cost of luxuries that contribute to the taxpayer's willingness to work and to his initiative and reliability while on the job.[9] On the other hand, no matter how narrowly business expenses are defined, many items that confer personal benefits will qualify. Taxpayers might be forbidden to deduct entertainment expenses because they are suspected of enjoying dinners and theater parties with their business customers, for example, but even the most puritanical definition of business expense is not likely to prevent self-employed taxpayers from deducting the cost of air-conditioning

---

[6] See Sapp v. CIR, 36 TC 852 (1961) (acq.), aff'd per curiam, 309 F2d 143 (5th Cir. 1962) (depreciation and maintenance of physician's automobile allocated between personal and business mileage, even though he was always on call). See also International Artists, Ltd. v. CIR, 55 TC 94 (1970) (acq.) (allocation of Liberace's home-studio between personal and business uses; pre-IRC §280A); infra ¶22.6 (re home offices).

[7] See, e.g., LaForge v. CIR, 53 TC 41, 51 (1969) (acq.), modified as to other issues, 434 F2d 370 (2d Cir. 1970) (physician's expenses in entertaining professional associates and wives at "quiet business meals" deductible); infra ¶21.2 (entertainment).

[8] See generally Halperin, Business Deductions for Personal Living Expenses: A Uniform Approach to an Unsolved Problem, 122 U. Pa. L. Rev. 859 (1974).

[9] See Henderson v. CIR, 46 TCM (CCH) 566 (1983) (assistant state attorney general not allowed to deduct cost of decorating office in which consultations with attorneys and others from private sector sometimes took place); Bistrup v. CIR, 40 TCM (CCH) 1289 (1980) (corporate officers denied deductions for cost of chairs purchased for their own comfort).

their offices, upholstering their swivel chairs, or adding gadgets to their telephones, even if they derive personal pleasure from these amenities.

When an excess cost or apportionment approach is not feasible, the issue is whether a substantial business connection should be sufficient to draw an expense into the deductible category or whether a substantial personal benefit should push the expense out of this category. One writer has suggested that the latter approach is most consistent with the conceptual foundation of the income tax. Tax theorists usually define personal income as the sum of the taxpayer's consumption and accumulation of wealth during the taxable year.[10] A true business expense reduces income under this definition because the amount paid for the expense is not available to be spent on consumption or accumulated. A deduction for a consumption expenditure, in contrast, eats into the basic grist of the tax. "[I]f we think of the tax as having ultimately to do with consumption, then a deduction should be disallowed if the personal benefit from the expenditure is clear and substantial, whatever its business utility."[11]

The most common categories of borderline expenses have produced their own bodies of administrative practice and case law, which are summarized below. As will be seen, the personal-business issue is sometimes complicated by the statutory requirement that expenses, to be deductible, must be "ordinary and necessary,"[12] as well as by disputes over whether particular expenditures are currently deductible expenses or nondeductible capital outlays.[13] Moreover, in a few areas Congress has not been satisfied with the tax results reached by the general rules of §§162 and 212 and has intervened with special legislation.

¶20.2.2 Food and Shelter

With the exception of meals and lodging while the taxpayer is away from home on a business or profit-oriented trip, which are deductible under special rules discussed below,[14] food and shelter are quintessential nondeductible personal expenses.[15] Yet it would be too dogmatic to assert that

---

[10] See supra ¶3.1.1.

[11] Andrews, Personal Deductions in an Ideal Income Tax, 86 Harv. L. Rev. 309, 381 (1972).

[12] See infra ¶20.3.

[13] See infra ¶20.4.

[14] Infra ¶21.1.

[15] See Moss v. CIR, 758 F2d 211 (7th Cir. 1985) (disallowing deduction for cost of daily lunches of law firm, during which work assignments were made and problems were discussed); Duggan v. CIR, 77 TC 911 (1981) (fireman on 24-hour shifts allowed no deduction for contributions for groceries used in common mess); Moscini v. CIR, 36 TCM (CCH) 1002 (1977) (policeman cannot deduct excess cost of restaurant meals over home-prepared meals, even though departmental regulations prohib-

they can never qualify for deduction under §162 or §212. Although there are no rulings or litigated cases on the point, freelance professional food tasters or restaurant critics, for example, have a reasonably solid case for deducting the excess cost of their meals, if not the entire amount. As for shelter, expenses allocable to residential areas occupied by taxpayers and their families cannot be deducted under §162 or §212, but facilities within the taxpayer's home used for business purposes can generate deductions, subject to the limitations of §280A.[16]

¶20.2.3 Clothing and Personal Grooming

The basic IRS ruling on expenditures to acquire and maintain uniforms provides that they are business expenses if they are (1) specifically required as a condition of employment and (2) not suitable for ordinary wear.[17] The latter requirement is evidently satisfied by a showing that the uniform is distinctive; any uniform takes the place of ordinary clothing while the employee is on duty, and the ruling does not condition deductions on proof that the uniform exposes the employee to public ridicule or scorn. Thus, the disallowance of deductions for uniforms that are suited to ordinary usage is presumably intended to forestall claims by bankers, lawyers, sales clerks in fashionable stores, and others who dress expensively at the actual or imagined insistence of their employers or customers.[18] By confin-

---

ited carrying bag lunch or eating in patrol car). But see Christey v. US, 841 F2d 809 (8th Cir. 1988) (state troopers allowed to deduct cost of meals eaten on duty; because they were required to eat in restaurants adjacent to highways to show public presence and because they were frequently interrupted while eating, troopers were subject to restrictions sufficient to convert personal expense to business); Sibla v. CIR, 611 F2d 1260 (9th Cir. 1980) (fireman allowed deduction for mandatory contributions to organized mess at firehouse); Green v. CIR, 74 TC 1229 (1980) (taxpayer in business of selling blood plasma allowed to deduct excess cost of high-protein diet).

[16] See infra ¶22.6.

[17] Rev. Rul. 70-474, 1970-2 CB 34 (re police officers, firemen, letter carriers, nurses, bus drivers, and railroad employees). See also Sanner v. CIR, 28 TCM (CCH) 476 (1969) (employer-prescribed grey gabardine suit, required of state driver's license examiners, not a uniform because not distinctive in appearance). For the early history of this area, see Comment, Deductibility of Uniform and Clothing Expenses by Employees, 36 Calif. L. Rev. 452 (1948).

For expenditures by the military, see Reg. §1.262-1(b)(8) (uniforms not deductible, except by reservists); Rev. Rul. 67-115, 1967-1 CB 30 (military fatigues deductible if local military regulations forbid off-duty use). The disallowance of deductions for military uniforms when comparable civilian uniforms are deductible may be built into the military pay structure, rather than reflect a coherent tax theory.

[18] See Pevsner v. CIR, 628 F2d 467 (5th Cir. 1980) (manager of boutique not allowed to deduct cost of fashionable clothes and accessories because clothing could be used for normal wear); Stiner v. US, 524 F2d 640 (10th Cir. 1975) (airline stewardess denied deduction for cost of accessories to uniform); Hynes v. CIR, 74

ing its scope to "uniforms," further, the ruling impliedly disqualifies over-alls and other heavy-duty clothing worn by blue-collar workers, even if specially chosen to withstand the conditions of employment.[19] When its twin conditions are satisfied, the ruling permits a deduction for the entire cost of procuring and maintaining the uniform, even if it does not exceed the cost of ordinary clothing.

The ruling's insistence on employer compulsion disregards the possibility that a uniform might be an ordinary and necessary expense of the taxpayer's occupation, whether pursued as an employee or otherwise. The courts, however, have held that self-employed persons can deduct the cost of uniforms required by the nature of their occupations.[20]

Although TV entertainers, circus clowns, and similar performers can no doubt deduct the cost of cosmetics, hairstyling, etc., grooming expenses are normally nondeductible costs of living, even if mandated by employers accustomed to obedience, like the United States Army. In *Drake v. CIR*, the Tax Court so held in a case involving an enlisted man who was required to have his hair cut at least every two weeks:

> Expenses for personal grooming are inherently personal in nature; e.g., in *Sparkman v. CIR*, . . . the cost of dentures used to aid an actor's enunciation was not deductible, and in *Paul Bakewell, Jr.*, . . . the cost of a hearing aid used by a lawyer both in his trade or business and for personal purposes was not deductible as a business expense. The fact that the Army may have required such grooming does not

---

TC 1266 (1980) (television newsman denied deduction for clothes worn only when on-camera, even though restricted in choice of colors and patterns); Kosmal v. CIR, 39 TCM (CCH) 651 (1979), aff'd, 670 F2d 842 (9th Cir. 1982) (no deduction for cost of clothes worn by government prosecutor aspiring to become "big time Beverly Hills personal injury attorney"); Jackson v. CIR, ¶54,341 P-H Memo TC (1954) (depreciation denied for mink coat allegedly required by married couple's public relations business); but see Yeomans v. CIR, 30 TC 757 (1958) (nonacq.) (high-fashion clothing required by fashion coordinator's job deductible, but amounts claimed severely limited because allocation between business and personal use not clearly established by taxpayer).

[19] See Donnelly v. CIR, 262 F2d 411 (2d Cir. 1959) (heavy-duty work clothing not deductible; Judge Learned Hand, dissenting, observed, "I can see no reason for limiting [deductions for clothing] to uniforms prescribed by the employer; to me that is an entirely arbitrary and capricious line to draw"); Drill v. CIR, 8 TC 902 (1947) (because clothing was not specifically required by employer and was adaptable to general wear, no deduction even though clothing soiled with plaster, cement, mud, and grease at work); Rev. Rul. 57-143, 1957-1 CB 89 (painter's work clothing, required by his union, not a uniform); but see Bushey v. CIR, 30 TCM (CCH) 651 (1971) (specially designed work clothing, special work shoes, and safety glasses, all required in taxpayer's employment, held deductible).

[20] Mortrud v. CIR, 44 TC 208, 216 (1965) (independent contractor operating wholesale dairy route); Harsaghy v. CIR, 2 TC 484 (acq.) (1943) (private-duty nurse).

make the expenses therefor any less personal. The evidence showed that the Army's requirement was directed toward the maintenance by the petitioner of a high standard of personal appearance and not toward the accomplishment of the duties of his employment. In setting standards for personal grooming, the Army is not unique. Many employers, expressly or otherwise, establish standards to which their employees are expected to conform. Men are to be clean shaven and are often required to wear suits, ties, and clean shirts, and women are expected to be dressed attractively. To conform to these requirements, employees must make expenditures which would not be required if they were at home or not on the job. Nevertheless, such expenditures for general personal grooming are inherently personal in nature and cannot be considered as business expenses.[21]

The court was not called upon to decide whether a recruit realizes income when the Army gives him a free haircut.

¶20.2.4 Medical Expenses

Medical expenses, even if occasioned by occupational injuries or required to perform business services properly, are rarely deductible under §162, but they may qualify as itemized deductions under §213, discussed elsewhere in this work,[22] subject to its percentage limitations.

¶20.2.5 Care of Taxpayer's Dependents During Working Hours

In *Smith v. CIR*, the Tax Court held that a two-job married couple could not deduct, as a business expense under §162, the cost of nursemaids employed to care for their young child during working hours.[23] Although Congress subsequently enacted a deduction for expenses of this type, which was later converted into the credit now allowed by §21, the principle of the *Smith* case remains in force except where superseded by this legislation.[24]

---

[21] Drake v. CIR, 52 TC 842, 844 (1969) (acq.). See also Reg. §1.212-1(f) (expenses to improve personal appearance not deductible under §212); Fryer v. CIR, 33 TCM (CCH) 122 (1974) (pilot's cost of complying with airline's hair rules nondeductible).

[22] See infra ¶36.2.4.

[23] Smith v. CIR, 40 BTA 1038 (1939), aff'd per curiam, 113 F2d 114 (2d Cir. 1940).

[24] See infra ¶37.1.1. As to two-job married couples, see generally Bittker, Federal Income Taxation and the Family, 27 Stan. L. Rev. 1389, 1431–44 (1975).

¶20.2.6 Commuting, Travel, and Moving Expenses

Although the cost of getting to and from work is incurred only by taxpayers who work and not by those who live on investment income or are supported by others, it has long been established that commuting expenses are not deductible business expenses.[25] A 1919 ruling by the IRS gave the following explanation of the principle:

> [The taxpayer] fixes [his personal residence] according to his personal convenience and inclinations, as a matter separate and apart from business. Any expense, therefore, incident to such residence as fixed by the individual is a matter personal to him. If he prefers, for personal reasons, to live in a different city from that in which his business or employment is located, any expense incident to so doing is the result of a decision based upon personal convenience and preference, and it is not the result of anything undertaken for business purposes and, therefore, is not a business expense.[26]

In actuality, there is sometimes no housing to be had at any price within walking distance of the taxpayer's place of employment; more often, none is available at a price commensurate with the taxpayer's wages. But despite the weakness of its rationale, the nondeductibility of commuting expenses remains a cardinal principle.[27]

Subject to qualifications discussed in detail below, however, the disallowance of commuting expenses is not applicable to the expense of getting to and from temporary job sites.[28] Similarly, taxpayers can deduct transportation expenses incurred between the primary place of business and secondary business locations (e.g., a physician's travel between the office and a hospital).[29] Deductions are also allowed for travel expenses (including the cost of meals and lodging) while away from home on a business or profit-oriented trip.[30]

The cost of moving to a new principal place of business, once governed exclusively by §162 or §212, is now subject to §217, enacted in 1964, which is discussed below.[31]

---

[25] Reg. §§1.162-2(e), 1.212-1(f), 1.262-1(b)(5). For cogent criticism of this principle, see Klein, Income Taxation and Commuting Expenses: Tax Policy and the Need for Nonsimplistic Analysis of "Simple" Problems, 54 Cornell L. Rev. 871 (1969).

[26] SM 1048, 1 CB 101 (1919).

[27] See infra ¶21.1.3.

[28] Infra ¶21.1.4.

[29] Infra ¶21.1.3.

[30] Infra ¶21.1.1.

[31] Infra ¶22.4.

¶20.2.7 Entertainment Expenses

Of all dual-purpose items, entertainment expenses are the most susceptible to exaggeration and fraud. For this reason, their deductibility is governed not only by the usual standards of §162 or §212 but also by a network of special rules, discussed in detail below.[32]

¶20.2.8 Business Use of Personal Residences

Another area particularly subject to abuse is the alleged business and profit-oriented use of the taxpayer's personal residence. By virtue of §280A, enacted in 1976 and discussed below,[33] deductions for depreciation and maintenance of home offices, vacation homes held for part-time rental purposes, and similar properties are severely restricted.

¶20.2.9 Education

Education to fulfill the taxpayer's cultural aspirations is a nondeductible cost of living.[34] Many educational courses, however, serve both personal and business objectives, and some training has a purely vocational function. To qualify for deduction under §162 or §212, educational expenses not only must avoid being classified as living expenses under §262, but must also qualify as current expenses rather than long-term capital expenditures. Further discussion of this subject follows an examination of the capital expenditure issue.[35]

¶20.2.10 Litigation Expenses

Like educational expenses, litigation costs can be deducted under §162 or §212 only if, under principles discussed below,[36] they can avoid being

---

[32] Infra ¶21.2.

[33] Infra ¶22.6.

[34] See infra ¶22.1.

[35] Infra ¶20.4.

[36] For litigation expenses, see infra ¶20.2.11 (litigation involving taxpayer's personal or business reputation), ¶20.2.12 (contested elections), ¶20.4.2 (litigation involving acquisition or disposition of property and clearing title), ¶20.5.2 (litigation involving divorce settlements), ¶22.7 notes 2, 3 (litigation involving tax-exempt income). See also Kopp's Co. v. US, 636 F2d 59 (4th Cir. 1980) (legal expense deduction allowed corporation for claim resulting from use of company car by president's son because corporation would be directly liable); West v. CIR, 71 TC 532 (1979) (legal fees incurred in unsuccessful litigation to avoid active duty in the Navy not deductible since origin of claim was personal decision to defer service while in medical school).

classified either as personal expenses (e.g., the cost of getting a divorce) or as capital expenditures (e.g., the cost of clearing title to property).

¶20.2.11 Expenses to Protect Taxpayer's Reputation

In a tangled group of cases, the courts have distinguished payments, legal fees, and other expenditures to protect the taxpayer's personal reputation, which are nondeductible living expenses, from outlays to protect the taxpayer's business reputation, which are deductible under §162 or §212 unless classified as capital expenditures. Spillover effects are common, however, so that preservation or rehabilitation of personal repute often enhances the taxpayer's business or occupational standing, and vice versa.

In deciding whether such payments are deductible, the courts frequently look to the nature of the events giving rise to the payments. Thus, an accountant who pleaded nolo contendere in a criminal tax evasion case was denied a deduction for the cost of his unsuccessful defense in a professional disciplinary proceeding because it was caused by personal misconduct rather than by his business activities.[37]

On the other hand, if the claim affecting the taxpayer's reputation originates in the taxpayer's business activities, the expenses are ordinarily deductible, even if the claim adversely affects the taxpayer's personal repu-

---

See generally Wegher, Deductibility of Fees for Professional Services—Accountant or Attorney; Divorce and Separation; Estate Planning; Tax Advice; Title Matters, Etc., 34 NYU Inst. on Fed. Tax'n 163 (1976).

[37] Bell v. CIR, 320 F2d 953 (8th Cir. 1963). See also McDonald v. CIR, 592 F2d 635, 638 (2d Cir. 1978) (no deduction for lawyer-beneficiary's expenses in settling will contest in which he was charged with exerting undue influence on client to make him beneficiary; "settlement of a dispute with regard to inheritance is virtually the paradigm of a personal concern"); Dyer v. CIR, 352 F2d 948 (8th Cir. 1965) (expenses of proxy fight and corporate lawsuits nondeductible because origin was taxpayer's personal crusade against management); Lewis v. CIR, 253 F2d 821 (2d Cir. 1958) (fees to defend incompetency proceeding nondeductible, despite possible adverse effect on taxpayer's status as author); Bonney v. CIR, 247 F2d 237 (2d Cir.), cert. denied, 355 US 906 (1957) (payments to silence ex-wife, whose allegations would damage taxpayer's professional reputation nondeductible); Rollins v. CIR, 38 TCM (CCH) 1274 (1979) (payments to liquidate debts of taxpayer's dishonest uncle not deductible; insufficient evidence that disgrace would adversely affect taxpayer's business, despite same family name); Rev. Rul. 68-662, 1968-2 CB 69 (legal expenses paid by corporate officer in defending tax fraud case deductible as business expenses to extent allocable to corporate taxes; amounts allocable to evasion of personal income taxes deductible only under §212(3)). But see Draper v. CIR, 26 TC 201 (1956) (acq.) (deduction allowed for legal expenses to prosecute libel suit against person alleging performer was Communist; disapproved by the *Lewis* case).

If the origin of the claim was an earlier transaction involving a capital asset, the expense may be deductible only as a capital loss. See Kimbell v. US, 490 F2d 203 (5th Cir.), cert. denied, 419 US 833 (1974) (fraud claim re oil and gas leases).

tation as well as his business standing.[38] In an unpersuasive opinion, however, the Court of Appeals for the First Circuit held that a lawyer who assured a client's creditors that funds for a settlement would be forthcoming could not deduct his personal payment of the promised amount when the client failed to make good.[39] The court said that it was "no part of a lawyer's business to take on a personal obligation to make payments which should come from his client," and that the payment was voluntary and satisfied a moral rather than a legal obligation. While true, these points seem to rest on an erroneous premise—that payments to redress mistakes in the conduct of a business or profession cannot be ordinary and necessary business expenses.

Even if the payments have an exclusively business origin and objective, the taxpayer must prove that they are current expenses rather than capital expenditures, since outlays of the latter type must be capitalized and are taken into account only when the resulting goodwill is abandoned or sold.[40] The capital outlay hurdle is especially difficult in the case of payments of a predecessor's debts, since this action may indicate that the taxpayer is seeking to establish a business reputation on entering an occupation rather than to protect an existing reputation. The leading case in this area is *Welch v. Helvering*, disallowing deductions for a taxpayer's payments of unpaid debts of his former employer, which were made after the employer became bankrupt and the taxpayer entered the same business as an individual proprietor.[41] The taxpayer's activities as an employee of the prior company might have been amalgamated with his later business activities in his individual capacity, in which event the payments could plausibly have been viewed as expenses to preserve an existing business reputation.[42] Deductions

---

[38] Lohrke v. CIR, 48 TC 679 (1967) (payments by patent licensor of losses incurred by customer of related corporation due to defective goods held deductible as expenses of his personal licensing business); Pepper v. CIR, 36 TC 886 (1961) (acq.) (deduction allowed for lawyer's payments to clients who invested funds on his recommendation in another client's business, on discovering that latter was engaged in fraud). But see Webb v. US, 560 F. Supp. 150 (SD Miss. 1982) (taxpayer, who sold all of corporation's shares to its employees while corporation was disputing state tax and related penalty, later paid penalty "to protect his reputation"; held, no deduction because taxpayer, who retired after stock sale, had no business when payment made).

See generally Tucker, When Can a Taxpayer Deduct Expenses Made to Protect His Personal Business Reputation? 39 J. Tax'n 36 (1973).

[39] Friedman v. Delaney, 171 F2d 269 (1st Cir. 1948), cert. denied, 336 US 936 (1949).

[40] See infra ¶23.2.6 (goodwill as nondepreciable asset).

[41] Welch v. Helvering, 290 US 111 (1933), discussed infra ¶20.3.2.

[42] For similar cases in which deductions were allowed, see M.L. Eakes Co. v. CIR, 686 F2d 217 (4th Cir. 1982) (corporation's payments to creditors of insolvent related corporation; payments necessary to secure credit and were common local practice in industry involved); Lutz v. CIR, 282 F2d 614 (5th Cir. 1960) (payment of

under §162 are not warranted, however, if payment of the other enterprise's debts is not proximately related to the taxpayer's business reputation.[43]

¶20.2.12 Expenses of Public Officials

In *McDonald v. CIR*, the Supreme Court held that a judge holding a temporary appointment could not deduct expenses incurred in an unsuccessful campaign for election to a full term on the same bench.[44] The plurality opinion pointed out that the taxpayer was a candidate for election rather than reelection, but also said that a distinction between the two situations would be "unsupportable in reason."[45] Although the taxpayer in *McDonald* was defeated in the election, the case has been applied to prevent winners from either deducting or amortizing their campaign expenses.[46] While in office, however, a public official may deduct unreimbursed current expenses, including the cost of contesting a recall election.[47]

---

debts of corporations organized by taxpayer to facilitate investments by employees); Dunn & McCarthy, Inc. v. CIR, 139 F2d 242 (2d Cir. 1943) (payments by corporation to employees who lent funds to its former president, who died insolvent); Milbank v. CIR, 51 TC 805 (1969) (investment banker's payment of client's debts to protect personal reputation for integrity). But see Fischer v. US, 490 F2d 218 (7th Cir. 1973) (corporate president's sale of stock below fair market value to settle suit by debenture holders against corporation; held, nondeductible expense for benefit of company, although litigation threatened his status and reputation as corporate executive; one judge dissenting).

[43] See Nicholson v. CIR, 13 TC 686, 688 (1949) (businessman who headed war bond campaign made up deficit caused by employee's theft; case "difficult to decide, because the heart goes one way and the law the other," but payment nondeductible because of insufficient relationship to taxpayer's business; query possibility of charitable contribution deduction).

[44] McDonald v. CIR, 323 US 57 (1944). See also infra ¶20.4.6 (expenses of seeking employment).

[45] McDonald v. CIR, supra note 44, at 63.

[46] Levy v. US, 535 F2d 47 (Ct. Cl.), cert. denied, 429 US 885 (1976). See also Rockefeller's Est. v. CIR, 762 F2d 264 (2d Cir. 1985) (nominee for Vice Presidency of United States not entitled to deduct costs incurred in confirmation hearings because job was a trade or business different from other public offices held by nominee); Martino v. CIR, 62 TC 840 (1974) (*McDonald* applied to disallow expenses of defending victory in contested election); Arditto v. CIR, 30 TCM (CCH) 866 (1971), aff'd by unpublished opinion (9th Cir., Feb. 11, 1974) (lawyer denied advertising expense deduction for political campaign expenses).

[47] See IRC §7701(a)(26) ("trade or business" includes performance of functions of public office); Diggs v. CIR, 715 F2d 245 (6th Cir. 1983) (congressman could deduct expenses incurred in attending National Black Political Conference where he could learn about his constituents' problems, but not those of attending national party convention since attendance there primarily advanced reelection campaign and was only secondarily related to trade or business as legislator); Rev. Rul. 84-110, 1984-2 CB 35 (city council member allowed deductions for salaries, office rent, and

On the ground that labor union elections are analogous to political campaigns, at least so far as the influence of money is concerned, *McDonald* has been applied to deny deductions for expenses incurred by the president of a large union in seeking reelection.[48]

¶20.2.13   Hobbies and Other Activities Not Engaged in for Profit

Although not engaged in for profit, hobbies and other recreational activities sometimes produce income. Since a sale of a personal asset generates gain only if and to the extent the amount realized exceeds the taxpayer's adjusted basis for the property,[49] it seems reasonable to tax income from a hobby only if it exceeds the taxpayer's related expenses. Before 1969, the IRS followed the practice of taxing only the net income of hobbies, but since the activity was neither a business within the meaning of §162 nor a profit-oriented activity under §212, there was no statutory foundation for this

---

office supplies even though these expenses consistently exceeded salary and expense allowance provided by city; under §7701(a)(26), public office is trade or business whether or not carried on for profit); Rev. Rul. 78-373, 1978-2 CB 108 (congressman's expense of lunch with constituents to discuss problems with government agency deductible; if lunch involves social visit or campaign matters, nondeductible; cost of parties for staff or constituents not deductible where atmosphere not conducive to business); Rev. Rul. 71-470, 1971-2 CB 121 (recall election); Rev. Rul. 73-356, 1973-2 CB 31 (amounts expended by congressman for newsletters, etc., to constituents); Rev. Rul. 74-394, 1974-2 CB 40 (legal expenses of judge charged with misconduct in office); infra ¶21.1.7 (travel expenses of legislators); infra ¶20.3.2 note 27 (re expenses of official duties voluntarily defrayed by government employees); infra ¶102.5 (re disposition of excess political contributions). See also Frank v. US, 577 F2d 93 (9th Cir. 1978) (Senate staff member who received nominal Senate pay but traveled extensively as fact finder at own expense engaged in trade or business and allowed to deduct travel expenses); Rev. Rul. 78-265, 1978-2 CB 107 (government employee can deduct cost of subscribing to agency's official work manual, used extensively while in travel status). But see Rev. Rul. 86-3, 1986-1 CB 81 (state legislator indicted on charge of vote buying while working as volunteer in county-level campaign; held, expense of defending against charge is nondeductible because litigation originated with an activity, expenses of which are nondeductible); Rev. Rul. 76-64, 1976-1 CB 45 (legislator's expenses of attending party convention as participant on panel discussing law enforcement not deductible).

[48] Carey v. CIR, 56 TC 477 (1971) (acq.), aff'd per curiam, 460 F2d 1259 (4th Cir.), cert. denied, 409 US 990 (1972). See also Rev. Rul. 83-181, 1983-2 CB 39 (expenses incurred in successful campaign for president of labor union not deductible; deduction allowed for expenses incurred after election in assisting employees in presenting grievances to employer, even though no compensation received for serving as president); Note, Cost of Union Executive's Campaign for Reelection Nondeductible as Business Expense Under Section 162(a), 24 Vand. L. Rev. 1305 (1971).

[49] See IRC §1001(a), discussed infra ¶40.1.

sensible administrative practice.[50] By enacting §183, discussed below,[51] Congress supplied a statutory framework for taxing only the net income of hobbies and other activities not conducted for profit.

¶20.2.14 Correlation Between Exclusions and Deductions

In general, taxpayers whose employers or customers furnish them with dual-purpose items (e.g., work clothing or travel expenses) can exclude these items from gross income if the expenses could have been deducted under §162 or §212 had they been incurred and paid by the taxpayer.[52] Conversely, the receipts should be included in gross income if direct payments would not have been deductible.

There are exceptions to this principle of parity. Meals and lodging furnished in kind for the employer's convenience are excluded from the employee's gross income by §119, for example, but cannot be deducted if procured and paid for by the employee, even if they serve the identical function of facilitating performance of the taxpayer's duties.[53] The result is an anomalous distinction that depends more on the form of the transaction than its substance.

A distinction between employer-paid and employee-paid expenses also characterizes several areas in which favoritism to corporate insiders and highly compensated employees is reduced or avoided by allowing expenses to be deducted only if paid by the employer pursuant to a nondiscriminatory plan. Qualified pension plans are the most important example of this dichotomy, but there are some less dramatic illustrations, such as employer-financed programs for educational assistance, group legal services, and com-

---

[50] See infra ¶22.5.

[51] Infra ¶22.5.

[52] The same result could be reached by requiring the taxpayer to include the item in income but allowing an offsetting business expense deduction, and indeed this view has played a role in the development of the law regarding employer-reimbursed expenses of employees. See Lee, Command Performance: The Tax Treatment of Employer Mandated Expenses, 7 U. Rich. L. Rev. 1, 53 et seq. (1972). Even where the inclusion-deduction alternative is the norm, however, the regulations allow employees to exclude the item if they properly account to the employer. See Reg. §1.162-17; Rev. Rul. 76-71, 1976-1 CB 308 (employer reimbursement of tuition paid for business educational expense); Rev. Rul. 76-65, 1976-1 CB 46 (tuition fees paid directly by employer not compensatory because they would have been deductible if paid by employees).

[53] For §119, see supra ¶14.5. Also, §132 excludes various fringe benefits from employees' gross income even though an employee's cost in providing similar benefits for himself would not be deductible. See supra ¶14.1 for §132.

muter bus transportation.[54] Employer contributions to such a plan or program are not included in employees' gross income, even though they would not be allowed to deduct the cost of similar programs undertaken on their own initiative. In the case of qualified pension plans, the benefits are taxable to the employees when received, but benefits under the other group programs mentioned above are never taxable to the employees.

¶20.3 "ORDINARY AND NECESSARY" AND SIMILAR QUALIFICATIONS ON DEDUCTIBILITY OF BUSINESS AND PROFIT-ORIENTED EXPENSES

¶20.3.1 Introductory

Section 162(a) allows a deduction for all "ordinary and necessary expenses" paid or incurred during the taxable year in carrying on any trade or business, and §212 similarly provides for the deduction of "ordinary and necessary expenses" paid or incurred for the production or collection of income or for the management, conservation, or maintenance of property held for the production of income. The "ordinary and necessary" qualification has been present since the Revenue Act of 1913,[1] but its scope has never been authoritatively delineated and remains uncertain to this day. In the discussion below, the pertinent rulings and cases are grouped together for purposes of analysis into six categories:

1. "Ordinary and necessary" expenses as the antithesis of unusual and extraordinary expenses, personal and living expenses, payments excessive in amount, and capital expenditures.[2]
2. Payments whose deduction would contravene public policy.[3]

---

[54] See infra ¶61.1.1 (qualified pension and profit-sharing plans); supra ¶14.3 (group legal services), ¶14.4 (educational assistance programs), ¶14.8 (commuter bus transportation).

[1] From 1913 to 1918, corporations were authorized to deduct "all the ordinary and necessary expenses paid within the year in the maintenance and operations of [their] business and properties." The corresponding deduction for individual taxpayers referred to "the necessary expenses actually paid in carrying on any business [or trade]," the bracketed words having been added by the Revenue Act of 1916. The Revenue Act of 1918 adopted, for both individuals and corporations, the current phraseology ("all the ordinary and necessary expenses paid or incurred during the taxable year in carrying on any trade or business"). See 1 Barton's Federal Tax Laws Correlated 90–93, 192–93 (J. Byrne & Co., 2d ed. 1925). Section 212 has contained the "ordinary and necessary" phrase since its enactment in 1942; see infra ¶20.5.

[2] See infra ¶20.3.2.

[3] See infra ¶20.3.3.

3. Fines and penalties.[4]
4. Bribes, kickbacks, and similar illegal payments.[5]
5. Treble damages under the federal antitrust laws.[6]
6. Lobbying expenses.[7]

As will be seen, the importance of the statutory "ordinary and necessary" standard as a restriction on the deductibility of items in category 1 has waned in recent years, as more explicit and comprehensive judicial rationales have been developed to achieve substantially the same results. The "ordinary and necessary" phrase has also declined in importance as respects items in categories 2–6; although it formerly provided the statutory support for disallowing them as deductions, this function has been taken over by legislation dealing explicitly with these types of payments.

¶20.3.2 Scope of "Ordinary and Necessary"

To qualify for deduction under §162 or §212, an expense must be both "ordinary" and "necessary."[8] The most widely quoted definition of "ordinary" appears in *Welch v. Helvering*, an opinion by Mr. Justice Cardozo that does not offer much in the way of precision:

> Now, what is ordinary, though there must always be a strain of constancy within it, is none the less a variable affected by time and place and circumstance. Ordinary in this context does not mean that the payments must be habitual or normal in the sense that the same taxpayer will have to make them often. A lawsuit affecting the safety of a business may happen once in a lifetime. The counsel fees may be so heavy that repetition is unlikely. None the less, the expense is an ordinary one because we know from experience that payments for such a purpose, whether the amount is large or small, are the common and accepted means of defense against attack. . . . The situation is unique in the life of the individual affected, but not in the life of the group, the community, of which he is a part. At such times there are norms of conduct that help to stabilize our judgment, and make it certain and objective. The instance is not erratic, but is brought within a known type. . . .

---

[4] See infra ¶20.3.4.
[5] See infra ¶20.3.5.
[6] See infra ¶20.3.6.
[7] See infra ¶20.3.7.
[8] CIR v. Lincoln Sav. & Loan Ass'n, 403 US 345, 353 (1971) ("ordinary and necessary" is used in conjunctive sense).

Here, indeed, as so often in other branches of the law, the decisive distinctions are those of degree and not of kind. One struggles in vain for any verbal formula that will supply a ready touchstone. The standard set up by the statute is not a rule of law; it is rather a way of life. Life in all its fullness must supply the answer to the riddle.[9]

Another much cited definition of "ordinary" appears in *Deputy v. Du Pont*, decided by the Supreme Court a few years after *Welch v. Helvering*:

Ordinary has the connotation of normal, usual, or customary. To be sure, an expense may be ordinary though it happen but once in the taxpayer's lifetime. . . . Yet the transaction which gives rise to it must be of common or frequent occurrence in the type of business involved. . . . Hence, the fact that a particular expense would be an ordinary or common one in the course of one business and so deductible under [§162] does not necessarily make it such in connection with another business. . . . One of the extremely relevant circumstances is the nature and scope of the particular business out of which the expense in question accrued. The fact that an obligation to pay has arisen is not sufficient. It is the kind of transaction out of which the obligation arose and its normalcy in the particular business which are crucial and controlling.[10]

As for the statutory term "necessary," *Welch v. Helvering* suggests that it requires no more than that expenses be "appropriate and helpful"[11] in developing the taxpayer's business. This "minimal requirement"[12] implies that the expenses need not be indispensable or unavoidable. Moreover, the courts have tended to accept the taxpayer's judgment of the business value of expenditures, since otherwise they would have to assume, or to authorize

---

[9] Welch v. Helvering, 290 US 111, 113–15 (1933).

[10] Deputy v. Du Pont, 308 US 488, 495–96 (1940). See also Salt v. CIR, 18 TC 182, 185 (1952) (expense can be "ordinary" even though it is "unusual").

[11] Welch v. Helvering, supra note 9, at 113, citing McCulloch v. Maryland, presumably for its latitudinarian interpretation (see 17 US (4 Wheat.) 316, 411–15 (1819)) of article I, section 8, clause 18 of the Constitution, authorizing Congress to make "all Laws which shall be necessary and proper for carrying into Execution the foregoing Powers."

[12] CIR v. Tellier, 383 US 687, 689 (1966) ("our decisions have consistently construed the term 'necessary' as imposing only the minimal requirement that the expense be 'appropriate and helpful' for 'the development of the [taxpayer's] business'"). See also Mason & Dixon Lines, Inc. v. US, 708 F2d 1043 (6th Cir. 1983) (rejecting argument that expense was not "necessary" because it could have been avoided by exercise of greater care); US v. Tauferner, 407 F2d 243 (10th Cir.), cert. denied, 396 US 824 (1969) ("'necessity,' of course, has gradations from the absolute out in all directions to 'advisable,' to 'preferred,' or to 'convenient'").

the IRS to assume, the role of "business efficiency experts reviewing the commercial decisions of the taxpayer."[13]

Although Mr. Justice Cardozo acknowledged in *Welch v. Helvering* that it would be "a futile task" to attempt to harmonize all the cases applying these generalities to what he called "life in all its fullness,"[14] a few major functions assigned by the courts to the words "ordinary and necessary" can be identified:

1. *Capital expenditures.* In *CIR v. Tellier*, the Supreme Court said: "The principal function of the term "ordinary" in §162(a) is to clarify the distinction, often difficult, between those expenses that are currently deductible and those that are in the nature of capital expenditures, which, if deductible at all, must be amortized over the useful life of the asset."[15] Viewed as a prohibition against deductions for capital expenditures, however, the phrase "ordinary and necessary" is a handkerchief thrown over something that is already covered by a blanket.[16] This is because §263(a), denying any deduction for amounts paid for the acquisition, improvement, or betterment of property, explicitly embodies "the basic principle that a capital expenditure may not be deducted from current income" and takes precedence over §162.[17] Moreover, the distinction between deductible expenses and nondeductible capital expenditures is inherent in both the term "expenses" and the statutory phrase "in carrying on" any trade or business. In an earlier day, to be sure, "ordinary" was used as a touchstone to distinguish current expenses from capital expenditures; *Welch v. Helvering*, for example, does not cite the statutory predecessor of §263(a). In recent years, however, "ordinary" as a standard has been more of a buttress than a foundation for the principle that capital expenditures cannot be deducted.

2. *Personal expenses.* The "ordinary and necessary" standard is occasionally invoked to disallow deductions for personal expenses. An example is *Henry v. CIR*, in which the Tax Court held that a tax lawyer-accountant

---

[13] See Comment, Business Expenses, Disallowance and Public Policy: Some Problems of Sanctioning With the Internal Revenue Code, 72 Yale LJ 108, 113 n.20 (1962), quoted with approval by Texas Instruments, Inc. v. US, 551 F2d 599, 605 (5th Cir. 1977), stating that an expense is "ordinary and necessary" if "a hardheaded businessman, under the circumstances, would have incurred the expense." See also Welch v. Helvering, supra note 9, at 113 ("we should be slow to override [the taxpayer's] judgment" as to whether an expense is "necessary").

[14] Welch v. Helvering, supra note 9, at 115.

[15] CIR v. Tellier, supra note 12, at 689–90.

[16] See Paul, Federal Estate and Gift Taxation 92 (Little, Brown, 1946 supp.) (commenting on the 1916–1950 presumption that transfers made within two years of death were gifts in contemplation of death for federal estate tax purposes); see generally infra ¶20.4.

[17] See CIR v. Idaho Power Co., 418 US 1, 16 (1974) (§263(a) takes precedence over §167(a) under the priority directive of §161).

could not deduct the cost of maintaining a yacht, despite his claim that its red, white, and blue pennant bearing the numerals "1040" stimulated inquiries and brought him clients:

> In determining that which is "necessary" to a taxpayer's trade or business, the taxpayer is ordinarily the best judge on the matter, and we would hesitate to substitute our own discretion for his with regard to whether an expenditure is "appropriate and helpful," in those cases in which he has decided to make the expenditure solely to serve the purposes of his business. . . . But where, as in this case, the expenditure may well have been made to further ends which are primarily personal, this ordinary constraint does not prevail; petitioner must show affirmatively that his expenses were "necessary" to the conduct of his professions. . . . We do not think petitioner has shown that the expenses of acquiring and maintaining a yacht were "necessary" to the conduct of his professions.[18]

The same result could have been reached, without reference to the term "necessary," by relying on (1) §262, prohibiting the deduction of "personal, living, or family expenses," (2) the fact that expenses are deductible under §162 only if paid or incurred "in carrying on any trade or business," and (3) the basic principle that taxpayers have the burden of proving entitlement to deductions.[19] Although harmless, the use of "ordinary and necessary" as a barrier to the deduction of personal expenses, like its use to disallow capital expenditures, adds nothing of substance to the government's primary safeguards.

3. *Frustration of public policy.* Largely in reliance on the "ordinary and necessary" standard, the courts disallowed deductions whose allowance "would frustrate sharply defined national or state policies proscribing particular types of conduct."[20] Starting in 1969, however, this judicially created doctrine was supplanted by legislation disqualifying specified expenditures as deductions under §162, so that the "ordinary and necessary" standard

---

[18] Henry v. CIR, 36 TC 879, 884 (1961). See also Brown v. CIR, 446 F2d 926 (8th Cir. 1971) (expense of photographic safari not a "necessary" expense of corporate executive's occupation, although films used to advertise employer's product); Greenspon v. CIR, 229 F2d 947 (8th Cir. 1956) (cost of maintaining horticultural showplace not "ordinary and necessary" business expense); Korth v. CIR, 42 TCM (CCH) 866 (1981) (expense of glider and aerobatic airplane not deductible by commercial jet pilot).

[19] See generally supra ¶20.2.

[20] See Tank Truck Rentals, Inc. v. CIR, 356 US 30, 33 (1958) (finding of "necessary" cannot be made if allowance of the deduction would frustrate sharply defined public policy).

has become functus officio in this area.[21]

4. *Reasonableness of amount.* The regulations under §212 state that the phrase "ordinary and necessary" limits the deduction to expenses that are "reasonable in amount."[22] The same constraint has been imputed to the phrase in §162(a).[23] As pointed out elsewhere in this work, however, "reasonableness" is used primarily as a test to determine whether payments between related parties are what they purport to be.[24] If an alleged payment for goods or services is excessive, the excess may well be a disguised gift, dividend, or other item, rather than a bona fide expense. Once again, the ordinary and necessary standard is excess baggage.

5. *Ordinary vs. extraordinary.* In a troublesome use of the phrase "ordinary and necessary," the courts sometimes contrast "ordinary" expenses with "extraordinary" ones on the theory that §§162 and 212 do not permit unusual, idiosyncratic, or unique expenditures to be deducted, even if they are helpful or appropriate in carrying on the taxpayer's business or profit-oriented activities. The distinction derives from *Welch v. Helvering,* where the Supreme Court suggested that allowing extraordinary expenses to be deducted would "open the door to many bizarre analogies." The Court there was primarily worried about attempts to deduct personal expenses and capital expenditures, however, and it conceded that the term "ordinary" does not require payments to be "habitual or normal in the sense that the same taxpayer will have to make them often."[25]

In a few subsequent cases, taxpayers have been denied deductions for payments that served business purposes and were not capital expenditures, on the ground that the payments were unusual or extraordinary. In *Goedel v. CIR,* for example, a stock dealer was denied a deduction for premiums on insurance on the life of the President of the United States, whose death he feared would disrupt the stock market:

> Where, as here, the expenditure is so unusual as never to have been made, so far as the record reveals, by other persons in the same business, *when confronted with similar conditions,* . . . then we do not think the expenditure was ordinary or necessary, so as to be a deductible business expense within the intendment and meaning of the statute.[26]

---

[21] See infra ¶20.3.3.

[22] Reg. §1.212-1(d).

[23] CIR v. Lincoln Elec. Co., 176 F2d 815 (6th Cir. 1949).

[24] See supra ¶20.1.5.

[25] Welch v. Helvering, 290 US 111, 114 (1933).

[26] Goedel v. CIR, 39 BTA 1, 12 (1939) (emphasis in original). See also Rev. Rul. 55-714, 1955-2 CB 51 (manager of entertainer entitled to percentage of latter's gross income cannot deduct premiums for insurance on entertainer's life in absence of evidence that practice is customary in the industry).

Other cases in this category have disallowed deductions for services performed by a minister who advised the taxpayer and his employees about business problems, using prayer rather than business skill; for hush money paid by an attorney to silence an accuser whose derogatory charges adversely affected his professional reputation; and for kickbacks to a customer's purchasing agent.[27] Several cases have disallowed deductions for occupation-related expenses incurred voluntarily by public officials and employees to improve performance of their official duties, perhaps on a theory that government agencies provide all that is required for the efficient discharge of the employee's duties, that voluntary expenditures put improper pressure on other employees to follow suit, and that gifts to government agencies must be proffered and officially accepted in a prescribed manner.[28]

---

[27] Trebilcock v. CIR, 64 TC 852 (1975) (acq.), aff'd, 557 F2d 1226 (6th Cir. 1977) (spiritual advice); Bonney v. CIR, 247 F2d 237 (2d Cir.), cert. denied, 355 US 906 (1957) (hush money); United Draperies, Inc. v. CIR, 41 TC 457, aff'd, 340 F2d 936 (7th Cir. 1964), cert. denied, 382 US 813 (1965) (kickbacks). Compare Raymond Bertolini Trucking Co. v. CIR, 736 F2d 1120 (6th Cir 1984) (deduction allowed for payments by subcontractor to officer of contractor to secure continuing business; taxpayer never made any other such payments; no evidence that such payments were usual in construction business; principal function of "ordinary" is to distinguish capital expenditures from currently deductible expenses) with Car-Ron Asphalt Paving Co. v. CIR, 758 F2d 1132 (6th Cir. 1985) (on facts similar to *Bertolini*, payments held not "necessary" because neither appropriate nor helpful for taxpayer's business; *Bertolini* distinguished on ground that government conceded payments were necessary there) and Kelley-Dempsey & Co. v. CIR, 31 BTA 351, 354–55 (1934) (payments by contractor to customer's inspectors to avoid groundless faultfinding; not "ordinary" or "necessary" because taxpayer could have sued to enforce its rights under contract).

See also Pantages Theatre Co. v. Welch, 71 F2d 68 (9th Cir. 1934) (disallowing deduction for payments by corporation to defray legal expenses incurred by its president in defense of rape case arising out of "interview" with applicant for employment); Maness v. CIR, 54 TC 1602 (1970) (lawyer may not deduct expenses of running for political office despite resulting benefit to his legal practice); Reffett v. CIR, 39 TC 869 (1963) (contingent fees paid to witnesses in taxpayer's action against labor union for damages not ordinary); Haverhill Shoe Novelty Co. v. CIR, 15 TC 517 (1950) (60 percent of expenses of wedding reception for majority shareholder's daughter deducted by corporation on claim that 60 percent of guests were persons "who would not have been invited were it not for the ordinary and necessary advertising policy of the corporation"; deduction disallowed because not "ordinary and necessary" for corporation to act as "father of the bride").

[28] Wells v. CIR, 36 TCM (CCH) 1698 (1977) (expenses incurred by public defender in entertaining staff not deductible; "not something that the usual civil servant could afford"); Wheatland v. CIR, 23 TCM (CCH) 579 (1964) (public school teacher allowed no deduction for cost of scientific equipment purchased for use in classroom); Rev. Rul. 55-201, 1955-1 CB 269 (expenditures by National Guard officers to increase morale, etc., not deductible unless authorized by military regulations; in latter case, deductible as charitable contributions rather than business expenses). Compare CIR v. Motch, 180 F2d 859 (6th Cir. 1950) (army officer

In some of these cases, there was at least a suspicion that the expenditure either served personal rather than business objectives or contravened public policy. To the extent that they rest solely on the theory that unusual or extraordinary payments are not deductible even if helpful and appropriate in carrying on the taxpayer's business, however, they are anomalous. There is no sound reason to deny a deduction merely because the taxpayer is unusually imaginative or innovative, and the paucity of cases resting on this ground attests to the impossibility of enforcing any such policy systematically.

In any event, there is no type of business expenditure, however distinctive or unique when viewed in isolation, that is wholly alien to a larger group; to find that a solitary aristocrat has hordes of plebeian relatives, one need only descend down the evolutionary tree from species to genus, from genus to family, and, if need be, from family to order. The Hometown Bank of Sauk Center may be the first in its neck of the woods to distribute bubble

---

stationed in Washington could not deduct expense of using personal car on official business because "it is not the ordinary practice for army officers and other government officials to supply and use their own vehicles"; personal car not "necessary" because taxpayer could have waited for bus or official vehicle) with IT 4012, 1950-1 CB 33 (court misunderstood government's position in *Motch*, which will not be followed to extent it disallows expenses in excess of per diem allowances incurred by U.S. employees in performing official duties) and Rev. Rul. 70-559, 1970-2 CB 36 (U.S. employees operating private automobiles on official business may deduct standard mileage allowance, despite option of using government cars without charge), both declared obsolete (by Rev. Rul. 69-43, 1969-1 CB 310, and Rev. Rul. 76-565, 1976-2 CB 449, respectively), evidently on procedural rather than substantive grounds. See also Rev. Rul. 78-265, 1978-2 CB 107 (federal employee may deduct cost of subscribing to manual used in official work, helpful because he travels and is often distant from agency's office where manual is available).

At one time, the IRS disallowed research expenditures by professors on the theory that they were personal or not necessary to the taxpayer's occupation, but a 1963 ruling abandoned these claims and held that research expenses, including travel expenses, are ordinary and necessary business expenses. Rev. Rul. 63-275, 1963-2 CB 85; see also Reg. §1.162-5 (research costs deductible if part of business education expenses); Wesenberg v. CIR, 69 TC 1005 (1978) (nonacq.) (physician's expenses in writing book on chest disorders in infants deductible, apparently under §212 since book produced income); Drury v. CIR, 36 TCM (CCH) 835 (1977) (expense of publishing scientific article deductible by research associate); Rev. Rul. 64-272, 1964-2 CB 55 (home office expenses deductible, but note subsequent enactment of §280A, discussed infra ¶22.6). For limitations on deductibility, see Osborn v. CIR, 3 TC 603 (1944) (research expenditures incurred to increase prestige and obtain employment not deductible); Wolfson v. CIR, 37 TCM (CCH) 1847-14 (1978), aff'd on other issues, 651 F2d 1228 (6th Cir. 1981) (no deduction allowed practicing physician for expenses of research activities, without commercial applications, conducted at home); Feldman v. CIR, 26 TCM (CCH) 444 (1967) (research on solar eclipses not related to teaching of high school physics). See generally Wolfman, Professors and the "Ordinary and Necessary" Business Expense, 112 U. Pa. L. Rev. 1089 (1964).

gum to kiddies whose parents open new accounts, but it is probably not the first bank in America to do so; if, mirabile dictu, no other American bank ever thought of the idea, the Sauk Center bank is assuredly not the first American business to peddle its wares in a lurid or undignified manner. As Mr. Justice Cardozo recognized in *Welch v. Helvering*, "the instance is not erratic, but is brought within a known type."[29]

Moreover, the fear voiced in *Welch v. Helvering* of "bizarre analogies" is misdirected. The fisc is threatened not by genuine business expenses that happen to be unusual or extraordinary but by commonplace payments (gifts, loans, personal expenses, capital outlays, etc.) camouflaged as business expenses. To deduct a payment under §162 or §212, the taxpayer must prove that it was an "expense," that it was paid or incurred "in carrying on [the taxpayer's] trade or business" or profit-oriented activities, that it was not a "personal, living or family expense," and that it was not a capital outlay. If these filters are too coarse, the IRS needs additional legislation, not a doctrine disallowing unusual or extraordinary payments.

¶20.3.3 Frustration of Public Policy

In an important series of cases involving taxable years before 1970, the courts disallowed deductions—usually for unlawful payments and bribes—whose allowance, it was thought or assumed, would frustrate public policy by encouraging unlawful conduct. The principal rationale was that it is neither "ordinary" nor "necessary" to violate the law.[30] At a high level of abstraction, this proposition is undeniably true. At a more mundane level, however, fines for violations of law are sometimes unavoidable (e.g., for traffic infractions by companies operating fleets of taxis or trucks, despite sedulous efforts to discipline careless drivers). It is also notorious that professional gamblers and bootleggers cannot operate unless they lubricate the local political machine with cash.

Recognizing that fines and unlawful payments are sometimes necessary for an enterprise to continue in business but feeling that it is distasteful, if not shocking to the conscience, to allow bribes and some other payments to be deducted, the courts vacillated between the impulse to measure net income accurately regardless of moral considerations and a more demanding frustration-of-public-policy doctrine. As early as 1924, when the Board of Tax Appeals was in its first year, the Board disallowed a deduction for the cost of defending a perjury charge growing out of testimony given by the

---

[29] Welch v. Helvering, supra note 25, at 114.
[30] See generally Taggart, Fines, Penalties, Bribes, and Damage Payments and Recoveries, 25 Tax L. Rev. 611 (1970); Tyler, Disallowance of Deductions on Public Policy Grounds, 20 Tax L. Rev. 665 (1965); Comment, supra note 13.

taxpayer in an investigation of payoffs to officers of construction unions, with the comment:

> Manifestly the commission of perjury can, under no circumstances, be recognized as part of a taxpayer's business; and so the expense incident to such criminal activity can likewise not be recognized. We must regard this as written into every statute, especially as to such common crimes as are prohibited generally throughout the land—those *mala in se*, which have immemorially been regarded as contrary to public welfare. It would be an anachronism to say that such an act, so inimical to the public interest as to justify punishment for its commission, may at the same time be so recognized that the expense involved in its commission is sanctioned by the revenue law as an ordinary and necessary expense of carrying on a business. . . . We do not believe that it is in the interest of sound public policy that the commission of illegal acts should be so far protected or recognized that their cost is regarded as a legitimate and proper deduction in the computation of net income under the revenue laws of the United States.[31]

In later cases, however, the seemingly simple line drawn by the Board of Tax Appeals proved difficult to apply. Thus, the Supreme Court held that fines paid by a trucking company for violations of state maximum-weight laws were nondeductible even if the offenses were inadvertent; that an illegal gambling enterprise, by contrast, could deduct wages and rental payments even though both types of expenditures violated state law; that opticians making payments to eye doctors who referred patients to them could deduct the payments because they did not violate any "sharply defined national or state policies," although the contracts were unenforceable under local law as a matter of public policy; and that the deduction of legal fees paid in unsuccessfully defending a prosecution for fraud in the sale of securities did not frustrate public policy either.[32]

---

[31] Backer v. CIR, 1 BTA 214, 216–17 (1924). The idea that it would be shocking to allow deductions incurred in the course of criminal behavior is reminiscent of the notion—long since abandoned—that taxing the profits of crime would make the government a partner in criminal behavior. See supra ¶6.5.

Deductions for legal fees incurred in defending against charges of criminal misconduct in the taxpayer's business were later permitted by the Supreme Court in CIR v. Tellier, 383 US 687 (1966).

[32] Tank Truck Rentals, Inc. v. CIR, 356 US 30 (1958) (violations of state maximum-weight laws); Hoover Motor Express Co. v. US, 356 US 38 (1958) (same, inadvertent violations); CIR v. Sullivan, 356 US 27 (1958) (gambling enterprise); Lilly v. CIR, 343 US 90 (1952) (payments to eye doctors); CIR v. Tellier, supra note 31 (legal fees in prosecution for fraud in sale of securities).

These decisions and others by the lower federal courts left many issues unsettled, such as the status of payments that violated trade practices, administrative rules, or civil statutes but were not punishable by fine or imprisonment; the effect of an absence of criminal intent, resulting in a reduced level of punishment; and the deductibility of payments to settle private lawsuits involving conduct in violation of law, including the punitive portion of treble-damage actions.

These inconsistencies and uncertainties derive from a basic flaw in the frustration-of-public-policy doctrine. The Supreme Court, for example, said that allowing a trucking company to deduct fines paid for violating the Pennsylvania maximum-weight law would "encourage continued violations of state law by increasing the odds in favor of noncompliance. This could only tend to destroy the effectiveness of the State's . . . laws."[33] These statements are not correct. In the absence of an income tax, a business motivated solely by profit would choose an illegal means of pursuing the business if it produces greater net profit than the most profitable legal alternative. If profits are $150 under an illegal alternative and $100 under the legal alternative, an amoral, untaxed business chooses the former. Assume a tax of 34 percent is imposed. If all costs are deductible, the choice between the alternatives is unaffected by the tax; after-tax profits are $99 ($150 less 34 percent thereof) and $66 ($100 less $34), and the illegal alternative is still 50 percent more profitable than the legal alternative. Assume, in contrast, that the illegal alternative causes the business to be subject to a penalty of $200, and the penalty is nondeductible. Under this alternative, taxable income is now $350 (the sum of the $150 profit and the $200 penalty), the tax is $119 (34 percent of $350), and after-tax income is $31 ($150 less $119). Denial of the deduction thus makes the legal alternative more profitable.

Denial of the deduction, in other words, is not needed to preserve the sting of the penalty, but rather is a tax penalty in addition to the original penalty. While a company violating the law to increase its profits has a weak claim for sympathy, the dilemma created by the frustration-of-public-policy approach is that as a penalty imposed through the tax laws, denial of one deduction is as effective as the denial of any other. A state's policy against overweight trucks, for example, would be aided as much by denying a deduction for a truck driver's salary as by the nondeductibility of a fine for driving overweight. Once the Court decided to allow deductions for some expenses of businesses carried on illegally, it was left without any principled means of defining the scope of the frustration-of-public-policy doctrine.

Another uncertainty was the relevance of empirical evidence that a tax deduction would or would not encourage violations of law. According to the

---

[33] Tank Truck Rentals, Inc. v. CIR, supra note 32, at 35.

record in *Tank Truck Rentals*, the company violated the Pennsylvania weight limits on about 50,000 trips during 1951, paying 764 fines and related costs totaling about $40,000, so that the average cost of violating the law was about 60 cents per trip if the fines were deductible and about 80 cents otherwise. On these facts, a link between deductibility and actual behavior is unlikely, and this may well have been the conclusion of the Pennsylvania authorities themselves, since the fines were treated as operating expenses under the accounting system used for rate-making purposes by the Pennsylvania Public Utility Commission.[34]

Rather than leave the many uncertainties in the frustration doctrine to be decided case by case, Congress preempted the field in 1969 by amending §162 to disallow deductions for specific categories of payments, stating that the new provisions are "intended to be all inclusive" and that "public policy, in other circumstances, generally is not sufficiently clearly defined to justify the disallowance of deductions."[35] As amended in 1971, the 1969 rules are embodied in §162(c) (illegal bribes, kickbacks, and other payments), §162(f) (fines and penalties), and §162(g) (treble damages under the antitrust laws), discussed in more detail below.[36]

The legislative intent to preempt the frustration-of-public-policy doctrine, as restated by the regulations, seems to apply to both §§162 and 212.[37]

---

[34] Id., Record at 116a–120a, 129a–130a.

[35] S. Rep. No. 552, 91st Cong., 1st Sess., reprinted in 1969-3 CB 423, 597. The 1969 legislation carried forward a 1958 provision, now §162(c)(1), disallowing payments to officers and employees of foreign governments if the payment would be unlawful under U.S. law. The 1958 legislation, however, was not intended to be all-inclusive.

For another approach, see the World War II Price Control Act, authorizing the President to prescribe the extent to which over-ceiling wage and salary payments should be disregarded "in determining the costs or expenses of any employer," pursuant to which the President issued an executive order providing that such payments should not be allowed for income tax purposes. In Weather-Seal Mfg. Co. v. CIR, 16 TC 1312 (1951), aff'd per curiam, 199 F2d 376 (6th Cir. 1952), this action was held constitutional, even where the disallowed wage payments were, pursuant to customary accounting practice, part of the taxpayer's cost of goods sold. See also N.A. Woodworth Co. v. Kavanaugh, 202 F2d 154 (6th Cir. 1953). For a similar disallowance of overceiling payments by the Defense Production Act of 1950, see Pedone v. US, 151 F. Supp. 288 (Ct. Cl.) (over dissent), cert. denied, 355 US 829 (1957); IT 4105, 1952-2 CB 93, declared obsolete by Rev. Rul. 68-100, 1968-1 CB 572.

[36] Infra ¶¶20.3.4, 20.3.5, 20.3.6. Also §280E, added in 1982, disallows any deduction or credit for amounts paid or incurred in a business consisting of trafficking in controlled substances if the activities of the business are prohibited by state or federal law.

[37] Reg. §§1.162-1(a), 1.212-1(p). The latter statement is not as explicit as the former, but it seems to have the same objective. For recognition of the preemptive effect of the 1969 legislation, see Ostrom v. CIR, 77 TC 608 (1981) (deduction

The regulations also provide that gross income is to be determined without subtraction of amounts that cannot be deducted under §162(c), (f), or (g).[38] The 1969 rules, however, may have left some crevices to be filled by the otherwise outmoded frustration doctrine. The IRS has ruled, for example, that §165, relating to losses, does not permit a deduction for a loss resulting from seizure and forfeiture of a taxpayer's slot machines when his possession became unlawful for nonpayment of the federal tax on coin-operated gaming devices, and the Tax Court similarly disallowed deductions to a taxpayer whose vehicles were confiscated because they were used to transport marijuana.[39]

¶20.3.4　Fines and Penalties

Section 162(f), enacted in 1969 as part of the legislative program to codify and limit the frustration doctrine,[40] bars the deduction under §162(a) of "any fine or similar penalty paid to a government for the violation of any law." As respects fines, §162(f) codifies the Supreme Court's decisions in *Tank Truck Rentals* and *Hoover Motor Express*, disallowing any deduction

---

allowed for payment in satisfaction of judgment for fraud; claim arose from taxpayer's misrepresentation in course of business as corporate officer); Rev. Rul. 80-211, 1980-2 CB 57 (same for punitive damages paid in action for breach of contract and fraud in conduct of business activities); Rev. Rul. 74-323, 1974-2 CB 40 (advertising expenses deductible although in violation of Civil Rights Act of 1964).

[38] Reg. §1.61-3(a). See also infra note 52.

[39] Rev. Rul. 77-126, 1977-1 CB 47 (public-policy doctrine not codified or limited as respects §165). See Holmes Enters., Inc. v. CIR, 69 TC 114 (1977) (loss disallowed under §165 without reaching government's contention that §162(f) precluded deduction, where petitioner's sole shareholder used vehicle to transport marijuana); Holt v. CIR, 69 TC 75 (1977) (similarly where taxpayer used own truck). See also Mazzei v. CIR, 61 TC 497 (1974) (denying theft loss on public policy grounds to taxpayer defrauded by his confederates in scheme to manufacture counterfeit currency; although case involved a pre-1970 year, IRS would presumably contend for same result in later years, since deduction claimed under §165 rather than §162); Rev. Rul. 81-24, 1981-1 CB 79 (no deduction under §165 for loss of building burned down by taxpayer); Rev. Rul. 82-74, 1982-1 CB 110 (when insurance proceeds are refunded upon discovery of arson, deduction limited to amount of gain recognized when proceeds received; owner's payment to arsonist not added to basis as demolition cost). The Tax Court has also held that when a §162 deduction is denied by §162(c), (f), or (g), the item cannot be deducted under any other provision. Medeiros v. CIR, 77 TC 1255, 1261 n.7 (1981) (no §165 deduction); Arrigoni v. CIR, 73 TC 792, 801 n.9 (1980) (no bad debt deduction under §166). But see Lafayette Extended Care, Inc. v. CIR, 37 TCM (CCH) 995 (1978) (capital gain deduction under §1202 not disallowed although sale involved sham employment contract designed to exploit Medicare reimbursement rules).

[40] See supra note 35.

whether the violation was deliberate or inadvertent.[41]

Regarding the ambiguous term "similar penalty" in §162(f), the Senate Finance Committee said in 1971:

> In connection with the proposed regulations relating to the disallowance of deductions for fines and similar penalties (sec. 162(f)), questions have been raised as to whether the provision applies only to criminal "penalties" or also to civil penalties as well. In approving the provisions dealing with fines and similar penalties in 1969, it was the intention of the committee to disallow deductions for payments of sanctions which are imposed under civil statutes but which in general terms serve the same purpose as a fine exacted under a criminal statute. . . .
>
> On the other hand, it was not intended that deductions be denied in the case of sanctions imposed to encourage prompt compliance . . . with [tax return] filing or other requirements which are really more in the nature of late filing charges or interest charges than they are fines. It was not intended that this type of sanction be disallowed under the 1969 action.[42]

After initially proposing regulations consistent with these comments, the Treasury reversed itself and issued regulations subjecting penalties in the nature of late filing charges or interest to disallowance under §162(f).[43]

---

[41] Supra notes 20, 32.

[42] S. Rep. No. 437, 92d Cong., 1st Sess. (1971), reprinted in 1972-1 CB 559, 600. See Rev. Rul. 78-196, 1978-1 CB 45 ("liquidity deficiency penalty" imposed by federal banking agency on savings and loan association for failure to maintain prescribed level of liquid assets held nondeductible). See Taggart, supra note 30, at 638–55 (discussion of §162(f) before 1971 Senate Finance Committee report issued).

[43] Reg. §1.162-21; see also Reg. §1.212-1(p) (same under IRC §212). For cases finding payments to be nondeductible fines or penalties, see Adolph Meller Co. v. US, 600 F2d 1360 (Ct. Cl. 1979) (penalty for customs violation); Waldman v. CIR, 88 TC 1384 (1987), aff'd per curiam, 850 F2d 611 (9th Cir. 1988) (restitution paid to victim as condition of suspension of prison sentence for theft); Uhlenbrock v. CIR, 67 TC 818 (1977) (addition to tax for late filing of estate tax return); Henson Robinson Co. v. CIR, 48 TCM (CCH) 508 (1984) (amount paid in settlement of claim for civil penalty); Conley v. CIR, 36 TCM (CCH) 1644 (1977) (penalties for failure to pay withholding taxes); Rev. Rul. 78-196, 1978-1 CB 45 (interest-like deficiency penalty imposed by federal loan agency). For cases finding various payments not to be fines or penalties, see Mason & Dixon Lines, Inc. v. US, 708 F2d 1043 (6th Cir. 1983) ("liquidated damages" paid to state by trucking company as result of overweight operations, in addition to and separately from fines); True v. US, 603 F. Supp. 1370 (D. Wyo. 1985) (civil oil spill penalties imposed without fault and used to clean up oil spills; meant to be remedial rather than punitive); S&B Restaurant, Inc. v. CIR, 73 TC 1226 (1980) (payments by taxpayer discharging sewage waste, under agreement with state environmental agency, until central sewer

¶20.3.5 Bribes, Kickbacks, and Similar Payments

Section 162(c), enacted in 1958 and amended in 1969 and 1971,[44] disallows deductions under §162(a) for three categories of payments:

1. *Illegal payments to government officials or employees.* Section 162(c)(1) disallows deductions for amounts paid directly or indirectly to a governmental official or employee if the payment is an illegal bribe or kickback. If the recipient is an official or employee of a foreign government, a payment is nondeductible if it is an illegal bribe or kickback under the law applicable to the payment and the official receiving it or if it violates the Foreign Corrupt Practices Act of 1977.[45] For this purpose, a foreign revolutionary group that has not been accorded diplomatic recognition is treated as a foreign government.[46] The burden of proving that a payment is an illegal bribe or kickback rests with the IRS, which must prove this issue by clear and convincing evidence.[47]

---

became available); Rev. Rul. 88-46, 1988-24 IRB 5 ("nonconformance penalty" imposed on truck manufacturer failing to conform to emission standards); Rev. Rul. 80-334, 1980-2 CB 61 (payment under consent order relating to federal petroleum pricing rules precluding criminal or civil penalties). Compare Barone v. CIR, 85 TC 462 (1985) (trucking company allowed deduction for amount withheld from pay owing to owner-operator of truck to reimburse taxpayer for fine imposed because of inadequacy of lease with owner-operator) with Tucker v. CIR, 69 TC 675 (1978) (school teacher must include in gross income amounts withheld from salary for participation in illegal strike; §162(f) prohibits deduction of penalty).

See generally Westin, Fines and Penalties in the Nature of Interest, 57 Taxes 110 (1979).

[44] For the legislative history of §162(c), see S. Rep. No. 1983, 85th Cong., 2d Sess., reprinted in 1958-3 CB 922, 937; S. Rep. No. 552, supra note 35; S. Rep. No. 437, supra note 42.

[45] The Foreign Corrupt Practices Act "makes it illegal for U.S. persons or their agents to make, offer, or authorize . . . payments to foreign government officials, foreign political parties, or foreign political candidates with the intent of influencing official action in order to obtain business." Staff of Joint Comm. on Tax'n, 97th Cong., 2d Sess., General Explanation of the Revenue Provisions of the Tax Equity and Fiscal Responsibility Act of 1982, at 422 (1982). The Act, however, does not forbid "facilitating payments"—"payments made to government officials to facilitate routine administrative actions that are not discretionary on their part." Id. at 423. "Thus, payments to a customs official to expedite goods through customs are allowed as a deductible payment." Id.

For payments before September 3, 1982, the test is whether the payment would be unlawful under U.S. law if U.S. law were applicable to the payment and the official receiving it. IRC §162(c)(1) (before amendment in 1982).

[46] Reg. §1.162-18(a)(3).

[47] Reg. §1.162-18(a)(5). More specifically, the government bears the same burden of proof on this issue as it does on the issue of fraud. See infra ¶114.3.4 for the burden of proof of fraud. See also Adak Carting, Inc. v. CIR, 46 TCM (CCH) 1229

In the late 1970s, so-called questionable payments, especially to officials of foreign governments, evoked a massive audit program by the IRS, as well as extensive investigations by the SEC and other federal authorities.[48] Gathering proof of the amounts, and discerning their nature, purpose, and ultimate beneficiaries is obviously difficult, not only because of the difficulties encountered by taxpayers and the IRS in getting nonresident aliens to testify here, but also because perjury is standard operating procedure when thieves try to save their skins. In addition, since §162(c) is concerned only with the deductibility of "payments," its application requires a threshold determination of whether particular amounts were "paid," directly or indirectly, by a U.S. taxpayer to a proscribed recipient, or instead (1) were a division of profits among members of a joint venture or (2) if disbursed by a foreign associate of the U.S. taxpayer, were paid on behalf of the associate rather than on behalf of the taxpayer.[49]

2. *Other illegal payments.* Section 162(c)(2) disallows direct or indirect payments to any person if the payment is an illegal bribe, illegal kickback, or other illegal payment under any U.S. law subjecting the payor to a criminal penalty or to the loss of a license or privilege to engage in a trade or business. A payment illegal under a state law imposing either of these sanctions is also disallowed, but only if the state law is "generally enforced,"[50] a requirement that echoes several cases under pre-1970 law hold-

---

(1983) (gifts to city dump operators to obtain preferential treatment for taxpayer's disposal operations held deductible because IRS failed to show gifts illegal).

[48] See generally ABA Tax Section, Letter to Commissioner of Internal Revenue on Revision of "11 Questions," 32 Tax Lawyer 7 (1978); Chu & Magraw, The Deductibility of Questionable Foreign Payments, 87 Yale LJ 1091 (1978); Hickman, Tax Aspects of "Sensitive Payments," 54 Taxes 865 (1976); Special Subcommittee of the Committee on Practice and Procedure, New York State Bar Association Tax Section, Report on the Internal Revenue Service "Slush Fund" Investigation, 32 Tax L. Rev. 161 (1977).

[49] See Nunez v. CIR, 28 TCM (CCH) 1150 (1969) (taxpayer, acting as conduit, not taxed on kickbacks passed on to other persons); Diamond v. CIR, 56 TC 530, 541–42 (1971), aff'd, 492 F2d 286 (7th Cir. 1974) (recognizing conduit principle, but holding taxpayer was not mere conduit, was required to include kickbacks in income, and could not deduct amounts paid out by him because they were not "ordinary and necessary" expenses). Compare Farnsworth v. CIR, 32 TCM (CCH) 902 (1973) (payments by independent contractor not imputed to taxpayer in applying §162(c)(1)) with Reg. §1.162-18(a)(2) (contra where independent contractor's payment inures to taxpayer's benefit).

See also Special Subcommittee, supra note 48, at 176–77, for the possibility of including illegal payments in computing the basis of property or the cost of goods sold.

[50] Compare Boucher v. CIR, 77 TC 214 (1981), aff'd per curiam, 693 F2d 98 (9th Cir. 1982) (deduction for insurance premium discounts denied; rebate statute forbidding such discounts "generally enforced" even though enforcement program not aggressive) with Custis v. CIR, 43 TCM (CCH) 1511 (1982) (allowing deduction

ing that public policy was not frustrated by deductions for payments unlawful under a state law that was not enforced.[51] Section 162(c)(2) provides that kickbacks include payments for the referral of a client, patient, or customer. Like §162(c)(1), it places the burden of proving illegality on the IRS.

In applying §162(c), the Tax Court has distinguished between (1) unlawful discounts or rebates under an agreement for the sale of goods or services and (2) unlawful payments made in other contexts. Allowances of the first type are customarily treated as reductions of gross income, rather than as deductions, and are thus affected by neither the pre-1969 frustration-of-public-policy doctrine nor its statutory codification in §162(c).[52] Payments of the second type, on the other hand, have been disallowed both before and after 1969.[53]

---

on facts similar to *Boucher* because IRS failed to discharge burden of proving statute generally enforced). See Rev. Rul. 82-74, 1982-1 CB 110 (payment to arsonist not deductible because illegal under generally enforced state law subjecting payor to criminal penalties).

[51] Sterling Distribs., Inc. v. Patterson, 236 F. Supp. 479 (ND Ala. 1964) (Alabama law against rebates by beer distributors "has become a dead letter").

[52] See Max Sobel Wholesale Liquors v. CIR, 630 F2d 670 (9th Cir. 1980) (where taxpayer secretly transferred extra liquor to customers, cost of extra liquor included in cost of goods even though transfers violated minimum price law; §162(a)(2) inapplicable in determining cost of goods sold); Haas Bros. v. CIR, 73 TC 1217 (1980) (acq.) (illegal rebates to customers allowed in determining cost of goods sold; not disallowed by §162(c)(2). But see Reg. §1.61-3(a) (amounts described in §162(c) not includable in cost of goods sold; held invalid in *Max Sobel*); Rev. Rul. 82-149, 1982-2 CB 56 (IRS will follow *Max Sobel*). For pre-§162(a)(2) cases, see Pittsburgh Milk Co. v. CIR, 26 TC 707 (1956) (acq.) (milk sold for net prices below legal minimum with books showing sales at legal minimum and reduction charged to advertising); Atzingen-Whitehouse Dairy, Inc. v. CIR, 36 TC 173 (1961) (acq.) (illegal rebates to milk purchasers treated on books as selling expenses involving sales promotion); Rosedale Dairy Co. v. CIR, 16 TCM (CCH) 1121 (1957) (same, treated on books as freight and hauling expense).

[53] See Alex v. CIR, 628 F2d 1222 (9th Cir. 1980) (insurance agent's illegal payments to customers not deductible; neither can they be applied in reduction of gross income as a rebate or discount because insurance agent not the seller of the policies); Kreisberg v. CIR, 39 TCM (CCH) 337 (1979) (insurance agent's allowances to clients were nondeductible kickbacks, not discounts or reductions of premiums paid by clients to insurance companies). See generally Note, The Tax Treatment of Illegal Payments After *Alex v. Commissioner*, 79 Colum. L. Rev. 579 (1979).

Prior to §162(c), illegal payments not part of a sale transaction were disallowed under the judicial frustration doctrine. Coed Records, Inc. v. CIR, 47 TC 422 (1967) (record company disallowed deduction of illegal payments to disc jockeys and other radio station employees to give its records preference on the air); Boyle, Flagg & Seaman, Inc. v. CIR, 25 TC 43 (1955) (acq.) (insurance agency disallowed deduction of illegal payments to auto dealers for soliciting insurance on behalf of auto purchasers); cf. United Draperies, Inc. v. CIR, 41 TC 457, 465, aff'd, 340 F2d 936 (7th Cir. 1964), cert. denied, 382 US 813 (1965) (illegal kickbacks to employees of customers).

3. *Kickbacks, rebates, and bribes under Medicare and Medicaid.* Section 162(c)(3), added in 1971, denies any deduction for kickbacks, rebates, or bribes by physicians, suppliers, and other providers of goods or services in connection with Medicare and Medicaid, including payments for the referral of clients, patients, or customers.[54] Unlike §§162(c)(1) and (2), §162(c)(3) does not require the payment to be unlawful. No reason was given by Congress for singling out payments under these programs for special treatment, but the context was a series of highly publicized investigations into Medicare and Medicaid abuses.

¶20.3.6 Treble-Damage Payments Under Federal Antitrust Laws

Section 162(g) disallows deductions under §162(a) for two thirds of any damages paid under the Clayton Antitrust Act, whether the action is settled or goes to judgment, if the taxpayer is convicted or pleads guilty or nolo contendere to an indictment or information charging a violation of the antitrust laws. Enacted in 1969, §162(g) overrules an IRS ruling allowing payments to be deducted in full.[55] Section 162(g) does not come into play if the only proceedings against the taxpayer are private antitrust actions or civil proceedings by the government, presumably on the theory that the government's failure to institute a criminal prosecution betokens a milder degree of misconduct; nor does it apply if the taxpayer is the target of a criminal prosecution but is acquitted. It disallows only two thirds of the payment on the theory that the balance is restitution of gains previously received and included in the taxpayer's gross income.

¶20.3.7 Lobbying Expenses and Other Political Activities

In 1918, relying on the "ordinary and necessary" requirement of the predecessor of §162, the Treasury promulgated regulations disallowing any deduction for expenditures for lobbying, the promotion or defeat of legisla-

---

[54] Section 162(c)(3) was a conference committee substitute for a Senate proposal imposing criminal penalties on persons engaging in kickbacks, bribes, and rebates under the Social Security Act. See Conf. Rep. No. 553, 92d Cong., 1st Sess. (1971), reprinted in 1972-1 CB 644, 663. The operative statutory language refers broadly to payments under the Social Security Act, but the title refers only to Medicare and Medicaid.

[55] Rev. Rul. 64-224, 1964-2 CB 52, declared obsolete by Rev. Rul. 83-122, 1983-2 CB 271 (damages paid to private parties are deductible, but not amounts paid to the United States, which, "although resembling restitution, are in effect punishment for injury to the public occasioned by the violation of law"). For discussion of the policy issues, see Boland, Income Tax Treatment of Antitrust Damages, 22 Tax L. Rev. 47 (1966); Wright, A Tax Formula to Restore the Historical Effects of the Antitrust Treble Damage Provisions, 65 Mich. L. Rev. 245 (1966).

tion, and political contributions.[56] With minor changes in language, this restriction has been carried forward to the present day, except as modified since 1962 by §162(e). Alluding to the "insidious influences" of money on politics, the Supreme Court held in *Textile Mills Securities Corp. v. CIR* that the regulation was a reasonable interpretation of the statutory phrase "ordinary and necessary" and that the taxpayer could not deduct the cost of lobbying for legislation authorizing the return to German business interests of properties seized by the United States during World War I under the Trading with the Enemy Act.[57]

In *Cammarano v. United States*, the Supreme Court held that the regulation applied to expenses incurred by beer and liquor dealers in publicity campaigns urging voters to defeat state initiative measures that would have put them out of business.[58] Rejecting the taxpayer's claim that the restriction violated the First Amendment, the Court said:

> Petitioners are not being denied a tax deduction because they engage in constitutionally protected activities, but are simply being required to pay for those activities entirely out of their own pockets, as everyone else engaging in similar activities is required to do under the provisions of the Internal Revenue Code. Nondiscriminatory denial of deduction from gross income to sums expended to promote or defeat legislation is plainly not "aimed at the suppression of dangerous ideas." . . . Rather, it appears to us to express a determination by Congress that since purchased publicity can influence the fate of legislation which will affect, directly or indirectly, all in the community, everyone in the community should stand on the same footing as regards its purchase so far as the Treasury of the United States is concerned.[59]

In 1962, following the issuance of revised regulations based on *Cammarano*, Congress intervened by enacting §162(e), which permits the deduction of certain expenses related to proposed or existing legislation "of direct interest" to the taxpayer, but preserves the restrictive rules of prior law in other respects. These restrictions were buttressed in 1966, when Congress enacted §276, prohibiting the deduction of amounts spent for political advertising or for admission to political dinners and similar events. Thus, the status of expenditures for political purposes now depends on three sets of

---

[56] For the early history of the anti-lobbying regulation, see Textile Mills Sec. Corp. v. CIR, 314 US 326, 337 (1941).

[57] Id. at 338–39.

[58] Cammarano v. US, 358 US 498 (1959). See Comment, Deducting Business Expenses Designed to Influence Governmental Policy as "Ordinary and Necessary:" *Cammarano v. U.S.*, and a Bit Beyond, 69 Yale LJ 1017 (1960).

[59] Cammarano v. US, supra note 58, at 513.

rules:[60]

1. *Appearances and statements regarding legislation.* Section 162(e)(1)(A) authorizes the deduction of all ordinary and necessary expenses paid or incurred in direct connection with (1) appearances before and statements to individual members and committees of Congress and state and local legislative bodies with respect to legislation or proposed legislation of direct interest to the taxpayer and (2) the communication of information between taxpayers and organizations to which they belong if similarly related to legislation of direct interest to the taxpayer. For this purpose, the term "ordinary and necessary expenses" includes, but is not limited to, travel expenses, the cost of preparing testimony, and dues attributable to both types of activities. The Senate Finance Committee offered the following explanation for these principles:

> The regulations issued by the Treasury Department in 1959 brought to a head many administrative and enforcement problems and uncertainties which have plagued both the Government and taxpayers. The difficulty in allowing trade or business expenses generally, but isolating expenses relating to legislative matters and denying deductions for them, stems in part from the difficulty in segregating and classifying such expenses. This is a form of detailed recordkeeping to which taxpayers are not accustomed. Moreover, in the case of many expenses which may primarily be incurred to inform the business itself as to the application of certain proposed legislation, when such information is also made available to legislators it is difficult to determine how an allocation of the expense should be made between legislation and mere planning of the company. . . . .
>
> More important than the administrative and enforcement problems, however, are the policy considerations involved in denying expenses with respect to legislative matters. It appears anomalous, for example, that expenses incurred in appearing before legislative bodies or before legislators are not deductible while appearances before executive or administrative officials with respect to administrative matters, or before the courts with respect to judicial matters, are deductible where the expenses otherwise qualify as trade or business expenses. Your committee believes that the present bar on deductions with respect to legislative matters must be modified to place presentations to the legislative branch of Government on substantially the same footing

---

[60] Whether these rules also apply to deductions under §212 is unclear. See Reg. §1.212-1(p) (making the frustration-of-public-policy principles of §§162(c), (f), and (g) applicable to §212, but containing no reference to §162(e)).

in this respect as that which obtains in the other two coordinate branches of Government.

It also is desirable that taxpayers who have information bearing on the impact of present laws, or proposed legislation, on their trades or businesses not be discouraged in making this information available to the Members of Congress or legislators at other levels of Government. The presentation of such information to the legislators is necessary to a proper evaluation on their part of the impact of present or proposed legislation. The deduction of such expenditures on the part of business also is necessary to arrive at a true reflection of their real income for tax purposes. In many cases making sure that legislators are aware of the effect of proposed legislation may be essential to the very existence of a business.[61]

The term "legislation or proposed legislation" as used by §162(e) is defined broadly by the regulations to include any bill or resolution introduced in the legislative body, as well as oral or written legislative proposals submitted to the body or one of its committees or members. The regulations further provide that legislation or proposed legislation is of direct interest to the taxpayer if it will, or may reasonably be expected to, affect his trade or business either positively or negatively.[62] The effect need not be immediate, but speculative and remote effects do not satisfy the direct-interest test. Legislation or proposed legislation is not of direct interest to the taxpayer merely because it may affect business in general or the taxpayer's personal, living, or family activities or expenses. The direct-interest test is satisfied with respect to a membership organization if the legislation or proposed legislation is of direct interest to the organization itself or to at least one of its members.[63]

The regulations provide a number of examples of legislation of direct interest to particular taxpayers—such as proposals that would increase or decrease the enterprise's taxes, costs, earnings, administrative burdens, or competition. They also state that "if legislation or proposed legislation has such a relationship to a trade or business that the expenses of any appearance or communication in connection with the legislation meets the ordinary and necessary test of Section 162(a), then such legislation ordinarily meets the direct interest test of Section 162(e)."[64] On the other hand, legisla-

---

[61] S. Rep. No. 1881, 87th Cong., 2d Sess., reprinted in 1962-3 CB 707, 728–29. See generally Boehm, Taxes and Politics, 22 Tax L. Rev. 369 (1967).

[62] Reg. §§1.162-20(c)(2)(ii)(a), (b).

[63] Id.

[64] Reg. §§1.162-20(c)(2)(ii)(*b*)(1)(i), (ii). See also Jordan v. CIR, 60 TC 770 (1973) (acq.) (employment benefits for Georgia Highway Department employees of direct interest to one such employee).

tion relating to presidential succession would only have a remote and speculative effect on business, and the cost of legislative appearances to oppose an appropriation bill in the interest of general governmental economy would not be deductible for similar reasons.[65] A taxpayer does not have a direct interest in "matters such as nominations, appointments, or the operation of the legislative body,"[66] although professional lobbyists can presumably have a direct interest in any other actual or proposed legislation of direct interest to their clients.[67]

The regulations provide special rules for appearances or communications by experts. Legislation or proposed legislation is of direct interest to an employee who specializes in the field of the legislation and appears on his own "if it is customary for individuals in his type of employment to publicly express their views in respect of matters in their field of competence."[68] An example is a university professor teaching money and banking who testifies on his own behalf regarding proposed banking legislation. A similar rule applies to employees and self-employed persons invited to provide expert testimony.[69]

The last clause of §162(e)(1) allows taxpayers to deduct a membership organization's dues to the extent attributable to activities described in §§162(e)(1)(A) and (B). Dues paid to labor unions and other organizations engaging in grass-roots lobbying and political campaigns, the expenses of which do not qualify for deduction by virtue of §162(e)(2), can only be deducted if and to the extent the taxpayer clearly establishes the portion attributable to the direct legislative activities described by §162(e)(1).[70]

2. *Other political expenditures.* Lobbying and political expenditures not within the §162(e)(1) categories are generally not deductible.[71] In particular, §162(e)(2) disallows as business expenses any expenditures for participation or intervention in a political campaign[72] or in connection with an

---

[65] Reg. §1.162-20(c)(2)(ii)(*b*)(1)(ii).
[66] Reg. §1.162-20(c)(2)(ii)(*b*)(3).
[67] See Rev. Rul. 68-414, 1968-2 CB 74. For prior law, see Black v. US, 129 F. Supp. 956 (Ct. Cl. 1955).
[68] Reg. §1.162-20(c)(2)(ii)(*b*)(2)(i).
[69] Reg. §1.162-20(c)(2)(ii)(*b*)(2)(ii).
[70] See Reg. §1.162-20(c)(3) (labor unions and trade associations exempt from tax under §§501(c)(5) and (6)). See also Rev. Rul. 67-163, 1967-1 CB 43 (same rule as to "action" organizations exempt under §501(c)(4)).
For restrictions on the political activities of tax-exempt charitable organizations, see infra ¶¶100.2.5, 100.2.6.
[71] See Reg. §1.162-20(c)(1).
[72] The Code only refers to campaigns on behalf of candidates for public office, but expenditures for campaigns in opposition to a candidacy are also within the intended reach of the statute. See S. Rep. No. 1881, supra note 61, at 730. For special rules regarding the bad debts or worthless securities of political parties, see §271, discussed infra ¶33.8.4.

attempt to influence the general public with respect to legislative matters, elections, or referendums. The Senate Finance Committee elaborated on the latter category of disallowed expenditures:

> Thus, except to the extent allowed by existing law, no deduction is intended to be allowed for expenses incurred in connection with what is usually called "grassroot" campaigns intended to develop a point of view among the public generally which in turn is directed toward the legislators. However, your committee does not intend that this limitation should have any effect upon the deductibility of dues, contributions or other payments to organizations whose activities consist primarily of gathering and disseminating factual information, data and statistics. For example, a nonprofit organization would not be affected by the limitation if it were organized and operated for the purpose of studying governmental affairs, Federal, State, or local (which might include analysis of legislation or proposed legislation) and of publishing and distributing to its members and the public factual reports and information on such governmental affairs. Such factual reports might contain data which could be used by subscribers and others to promote or defeat legislation, but so long as the organization itself did not engage in lobbying activities to promote or defeat legislation, payments to such organization will continue to be deductible to the same extent as under existing law.[73]

Nice questions can arise as to the distinction between nondeductible attempts to influence the public with respect to legislative matters and deductible advertising expenses. In a 1974 ruling, the IRS disallowed a corporation's expenses for preparing, printing, and distributing to its shareholders a pamphlet describing proposed legislation that would affect its tax liability and suggesting they contact their Congressmen to express their views.[74] Other expenditures disallowed under prior law included newspaper advertisements opposing implementation of a comprehensive power plan threatening the taxpayer's business, contributions to a campaign to defeat a prohibition referendum, and advertising to influence voters to continue

---

[73] S. Rep. No. 1881, supra note 61, at 730. For elucidation of the term "grassroot lobbying" in the context of activities of a tax-exempt trade association, see Rev. Rul. 78-113, 1978-1 CB 43; Rev. Rul. 78-114, 1978-1 CB 44. See generally Krebs, Grassroots Lobbying Defined: The Scope of IRC Section 162(e)(2)(B), 56 Taxes 516 (1978).

[74] Rev. Rul. 74-407, 1974-2 CB 45 (noting that Congress had considered and rejected a proposal to allow deduction of such expenses). See also Rev. Rul. 78-111, 1978-1 CB 41 (same as to cost of printing and distributing to shareholders corporate president's testimony before legislature explaining opposition to bill).

pari-mutuel betting.[75] In contrast, expenditures for institutional or goodwill advertising that keep the taxpayer's name before the public are allowable if "related to the patronage the taxpayer might reasonably expect in the future." As examples, the regulations refer to the cost of encouraging contributions to the Red Cross and the purchase of U.S. savings bonds and advertising presenting general economic, financial, and social views not involving specific proscribed matters.[76]

3. *Advertising in political publications, admission to political events, etc.* Section 276(a) disallows three types of political expenditures: (1) advertising in a political party's convention program or in any other publication if the proceeds are intended to, or do, directly or indirectly inure to or for the use of a political party or candidate; (2) admission to a dinner or program whose proceeds are intended to, or do, directly or indirectly inure to or for the use of a political party or candidate; and (3) admission to an inaugural ball, gala, parade, or concert or to any similar event identified with a political party or a political candidate. This provision, originally enacted in 1966, represents a congressional attempt to disallow deductions for political contributions disguised as advertising expenses.[77]

In harmony with the legislative design, the regulations construe §276 broadly. Advertising in a political party's convention program, regardless of who publishes it or profits therefrom, is disallowed. A program is any "written publication . . . distributed or displayed in connection with or at a political convention, conclave or meeting," including "a book, magazine, pamphlet, brochure, flier, almanac, newspaper, newsletter, handbill, billboard, menu, sign, scorecard, program, announcement, radio or television program or announcement, or any similar means of communication."[78] Even if the publication is not a convention program, an improper political beneficiary taints the cost of advertising therein. Deductions are also disallowed for the cost of dinners or programs, including a "gala, dance, ball,

----

[75] Southwestern Elec. Power Co. v. US, 312 F2d 437 (Ct. Cl. 1963) (power plan); Cammarano v. US, 358 US 498 (1959) (prohibition of liquor); Revere Racing Ass'n v. Scanlon, 232 F2d 816 (1st Cir. 1956). See also Rev. Rul. 58-255, 1958-1 CB 91 (re constitutional amendment relating to selection of state judges).

[76] Reg. §1.162-20(a)(2). But see Rev. Rul. 78-112, 1978-1 CB 42 (corporation may not deduct cost of advertising its objections to legislation in state and regional newspapers).

[77] See S. Rep. No. 1010, 89th Cong., 2d Sess., reprinted in 1966-1 CB 476, 504–05, 508–10. In 1968, Congress exempted presidential nominating convention programs whose proceeds were used solely to defray convention expenses, but the exception was eliminated in 1974 with the authorization of the Dollar Check-off Fund. See Conf. Rep. No. 1533, 90th Cong., 2d Sess., reprinted in 1968-2 CB 801, 813–14; Conf. Rep. No. 1237, 93d Cong., 2d Sess., reprinted in 1974-2 CB 428, 432; Rev. Rul. 76-29, 1976-1 CB 85 (application of repealed provision).

[78] Reg. §§1.276-1(b), (c).

theatrical or film presentation, cocktail or other party, picnic, barbecue, sporting event, brunch, tea, supper, auction, bazaar, reading, speech, forum, lecture, fashion show, concert, opening, meeting, gathering, or any similar event."[79] The foregoing may also constitute inaugural or equivalent events, whose costs are disallowed regardless of sponsorship or beneficiary, if held in connection with the inauguration or installation of any official.[80]

Section 276(b)(1) defines "political party" for this purpose in the same manner as §271, relating to bad debts owed by political organizations.[81] The term "political candidate" includes not only persons already selected or nominated by a political party for an elective office, but also anyone "generally believed, under the facts and circumstances at the time of the event or publication, by the persons making expenditures in connection therewith to be an individual who is or who in the reasonably foreseeable future will be seeking selection, nomination, or election to any public office."[82]

In the case of expenditures for advertising in a publication other than a convention program or for dinners or programs other than inaugural events or their equivalents, the intended or actual use of the proceeds determines deductibility. In general, proceeds inure to or for the use of a political party or candidate if (1) the party or candidate can order the disposition of any part thereof, regardless of its actual ultimate use, or (2) any part of the proceeds is used for the benefit of the party or candidate.[83] This is true in the case of a political party even if the use of the proceeds is restricted to a particular purpose, such as a nonprofit political research program, or is to pay the actual cost of a dinner or program.[84] The taint, however, does not extend to benefits "so remote as to be negligible or merely a coincidence of the relationship of a political candidate" to a business profiting from the expenditure, such as advertising in a newspaper endorsing a candidate.[85]

Section 276(b)(2) provides that proceeds are treated as inuring to or for the use of a political candidate only if (1) they may be used directly or indirectly to further his candidacy for selection, nomination, or election to any elective public office and (2) they are not received by him in the ordinary course of a trade or business other than that of holding elective

---

[79] Reg. §1.276-1(d). All charges for attendance or participation are subject to §276(a)(3), including separate charges for transportation. Reg. §1.276-1(f)(4).

[80] Reg. §1.276-1(e).

[81] See Reg. §1.276-1(f)(1); Reg. §1.271-1(b)(1), discussed infra ¶33.8.4.

[82] Reg. §1.276-1(f)(2) (persons making expenditures presumed to believe incumbents will run for reelection or for other office).

[83] Reg. §1.276-1(f)(3)(i).

[84] Reg. §1.276-1(f)(3)(ii).

[85] Reg. §1.276-1(f)(3)(i).

public office.[86] Proceeds of a post-election event that may be used to pay a former candidate's campaign loans or expenses are deemed to inure to or for the use of the candidate.[87] Reg. §1.162-20(c)(2)(ii)(*b*)(2)(i).

¶20.4 CAPITAL EXPENDITURES

¶20.4.1 Introductory

A cost that would otherwise be deductible under §162 or §212 cannot be deducted immediately if it is a capital expenditure. Very generally, a capital expenditure is a cost that will yield benefits in future years in the taxpayer's business or income producing activities. Obvious examples are the costs of buildings and equipment.

The principal provisions on capital expenditures are §§263 and 263A. Section 263A, enacted in 1986, applies to property that is produced by the taxpayer or is purchased for resale, and requires the capitalization of the direct costs of such property and any indirect costs allocable to the production, acquisition, and holding of the property. Manufacturers, wholesalers, and retailers, for example, are subject to §263A; for them, capitalization is usually accomplished by including the capitalized costs in their inventory accounts. Section 263A also applies when taxpayers produce property for use in their own businesses or income producing activities. In this context, a capitalized cost is added to the taxpayer's basis for the property. If a partnership constructs an apartment building and thereafter operates it as rental property, for example, §263A requires that the direct and indirect costs of constructing the building be added to the building's basis, rather than being deducted as incurred or paid. Because §263A is intimately connected with inventory accounting, it is discussed elsewhere in this work in connection with inventories.[1]

Section 263(a)(1) provides that no deduction shall be allowed for "any amount paid out for new buildings or for permanent improvements or betterments made to increase the value of any property or estate," and §263(a)(2) denies deductions for amounts "expended in restoring property or in making good the exhaustion thereof for which an allowance is or has

---

[86] Proceeds received by a candidate in exchange for goods or services of substantially lesser fair market value are not received in the ordinary course of his trade or business. Reg. §§1.276-1(f)(3)(iii), (iv) Ex. 4.

[87] Reg. §1.276-1(f)(3)(iii). See also IRC §527(d), relating to the disposition of excess political contributions, discussed infra ¶102.5.

[1] See infra ¶105.4. See generally Lee & Murphy, Capital Expenditures: A Result in Search of a Rationale, 15 U. Rich. L. Rev. 473 (1981).

been made."[2] As interpreted by the regulations, §263 prohibits any deduction for "the cost of acquisition, construction, or erection of buildings, machinery and equipment, furniture and fixtures, and similar property having a useful life substantially beyond the taxable year," or for "amounts paid or incurred (1) to add to the value, or substantially prolong the useful life, of property owned by the taxpayer, such as plant or equipment, or (2) to adapt property to a new or different use."[3]

Much of the terrain formerly occupied by §263 has been captured by §263A. Section 263, however, continues to be important. It requires the capitalization of the purchase price of property not acquired for resale whose useful life extends substantially beyond the year of purchase. It also governs a host of costs incurred after property is acquired and costs pertaining to intangibles. Section 263 is the principal subject of the discussion in the pages that follow.

As explained by the Supreme Court in *CIR v. Idaho Power Co.*: "The purpose of §263 is to reflect the basic principle that a capital expenditure may not be deducted from current income. It serves to prevent a taxpayer from utilizing currently a deduction properly attributable, through amortization, to later tax years when the capital asset becomes income producing."[4] Capital expenditures subject to §263 either constitute or are added to the basis of the acquired or improved property. If the property is subject to exhaustion or obsolescence, a capitalized cost is often deducted in installments in future years as depreciation, depletion, or amortization. If the property is sold before the end of the depreciation, depletion, or amortization period, the undeducted portion of the cost is subtracted in computing gain or loss on the sale.[5] This offset against the sales proceeds is usually the only tax allowance for capital expenditures relating to land and other property not subject to exhaustion through use. The effect of these rules, however, is usually to defer the allowance for a capital expenditure. Although the period of deferral is sometimes very long, rarely is a taxpayer left with no possibility of a deduction or offset for such an expenditure.[6] Thus, the basic difference between business expenses and capital expenditures is that expenses are deducted when paid or incurred, while capital expenditures are

---

[2] The allowances for exhaustion referred to by §263(a)(2) include depreciation, amortization, and depletion. Reg. §1.263(a)-1(a)(2). See infra ¶23.1.1.

[3] Reg. §§1.263(a)-1(b), -2(a).

[4] CIR v. Idaho Power Co., 418 US 1, 16 (1974) (taxpayer must capitalize depreciation on equipment used to construct its own capital facilities); see also infra ¶20.4.3. The term "capital asset" is used by the Court in *Idaho Power* as a synonym for "capital expenditure," not in its technical sense as defined by §1221.

[5] Infra ¶23.1.1.

[6] The principal exception is the treatment of the costs of education, which are permanently disallowed when they are categorized as nondeductible capital expenditures. See infra ¶22.1.

written off over a longer period of time.[7] In layman's language, amounts used to defray expenses are spent; amounts used for capital expenditures are invested.

The fundamental distinction between deductible expenses and nondeductible capital expenditures is inherent in the concept of an expense as a cost of current operations. Moreover, in *CIR v. Tellier*, the Supreme Court observed that the principal function of the term "ordinary" as used in §162(a) "is to clarify the distinction, often difficult, between those expenses that are currently deductible and those that are in the nature of capital expenditures, which, if deductible at all, must be amortized over the useful life of the asset."[8] The same basic principle is embodied in §446(b), requiring use of an accounting method that "clearly reflects income"—a standard that imposes the following requirement: "Expenditures made during the year shall be properly classified as between capital and expense. For example, expenditures for such items as plant and equipment, which have a useful life extending substantially beyond the taxable year, shall be charged to a capital account and not to an expense account."[9] Indeed, it can be said that "capitalization is a basic principle of income taxation rather than a technical requirement imposed by specific statutory language."[10]

Often, nondeductible capital expenditures are readily identifiable. When a taxpayer purchases land, equipment, or a new building, the expenditure serves to "create or enhance . . . what is essentially a separate and distinct additional asset"[11] whose value is obviously not properly allocable to the current taxable year.

In many other situations, however, the usual criteria of a capital expenditure are either over-inclusive or under-inclusive. The "separate and distinct additional asset" and "useful life beyond the current year" criteria, if applied rigorously, would classify numerous purchases of minor items as

---

[7] For discussion of the way current deductions and depreciation or amortization deductions would converge if the taxpayer's business activities were on a steady-state plateau, see infra ¶23.1.2.

[8] CIR v. Tellier, 383 US 687, 689–90 (1966), quoted with approval in CIR v. Lincoln Sav. & Loan Ass'n, 403 US 345, 353 (1971) (financial institution's contributions to federal insurance agency must be capitalized rather than deducted as business expenses). Although *Tellier* refers only to §162(a), presumably the Court would have ascribed the same function to the term "ordinary" in §212.

[9] Reg. §1.446-1(a)(4)(ii). See also Reg. §§1.461-1(a)(1), (2) (re assets with a useful life "which extends substantially beyond the close of the taxable year"); Jack's Cookie Co. v. US, 597 F2d 395 (4th Cir. 1979) (application of one-year rule to preclude deduction of reserve payments to bank to ensure that lease proceeds would be adequate to service bonds).

[10] Gunn, The Requirement That a Capital Expenditure Create or Enhance an Asset, 15 BC Indus. & Com. L. Rev. 443, 450 (1974).

[11] CIR v. Lincoln Sav. & Loan Ass'n, supra note 8, at 354, discussed by Gunn, supra note 10.

capital expenditures—an accountant's fountain pen, a carpenter's screwdriver, a welder's goggles. The regulations explicitly permit farmers to deduct the cost of "ordinary tools of short life or small cost, such as hand tools, including shovels, rakes, etc."; and professional taxpayers are allowed to deduct the cost of "books, furniture, and professional instruments and equipment, the useful life of which is short."[12] In a similar vein, the Court of Claims, recognizing that the fundamental issue in this area is whether the taxpayer's income is clearly reflected, has held that a railroad may deduct the cost of items costing less than $500, regardless of the asset's expected useful life, if this practice is consistently followed and is used by the Interstate Commerce Commission for rate-making purposes.[13]

This emphasis on the long-run consequences of the taxpayer's accounting practice acknowledges that a rule of reason is essential. If every cost contributing to the profits of future periods were to be disallowed, it would be necessary to divide almost every salary and advertising expense between its immediate impact on the customer and its contribution to the company's long-lived goodwill. Recognizing this, the Supreme Court has said that "the presence of an ensuing benefit that may have some future aspect is not controlling; many expenses concededly deductible have prospective effect beyond the taxable year."[14] As will be seen, even the most routine repairs often have a long-term impact but are, nevertheless, classified as deductible expenses rather than as nondeductible capital expenditures.[15]

In addition to being over-inclusive with respect to minor items, the conventional criteria of a capital expenditure are sometimes—although less frequently—under-inclusive. Thus, a vocational course qualifying the tax-

---

[12] Reg. §1.162-12 (farmers), §1.162-6 (professional expenses); see also Reg. §1.162-3 (incidental materials and supplies can be deducted when purchased if inventories and records of consumption are not kept, provided taxable income is clearly reflected); Beaudry v. CIR, 150 F2d 20 (2d Cir. 1945) (distinguishing between professional books and periodicals with a temporary value and those with more permanent value, and requiring costs of latter to be capitalized); Sharon v. CIR, 66 TC 515, 526–27 (1976), aff'd per curiam, 591 F2d 1273 (9th Cir. 1978) (dictum: $25 state fee for license to practice law deductible when paid, despite capital nature, by analogy to deduction allowed for inexpensive tools). If supplies are expensed and subsequently transferred in a tax-free transaction prior to the expiration of their useful life, the tax benefit rule may require recapture of part of the deduction. See supra ¶5.7.

[13] Cincinnati, N. & Tex. Pac. Ry. v. US, 424 F2d 563 (Ct. Cl. 1970) (purchases of less than $500 each for assets other than land, track, and railroad cars, treated as operating expenses under ICC accounting rules, can be deducted as business expenses under §162). But see Rev. Rul. 84-24, 1984-1 CB 89 (telephone company required to capitalize wiring costs even though FCC rules required that they be expensed).

[14] CIR v. Lincoln Sav. & Loan Ass'n, 403 US 354 (1971).

[15] Infra ¶20.4.8.

payer to embark on a new career does not create a "separate and distinct additional asset" in the ordinary sense. The cost of the educational program is nevertheless a nondeductible capital expenditure rather than a currently deductible business expense.[16] Also, costs incurred in obtaining a loan (including appraisal, abstract, and recording fees) must be capitalized and amortized as deductions over the life of the loan.[17] As with the danger of over-inclusion, the best remedy against an under-inclusive application of the capital expenditure concept is to focus on whether income will be better reflected by deducting or by capitalizing the amount in question. This is obviously not an easy standard to apply, but it has the virtue of emphasizing the basic objective of the relevant statutory provisions rather than secondary guideposts.

Real estate developers often donate part of a tract under development to a governmental or nonprofit organization as a site for a school or recreation center or dedicate part of the tract to public uses, such as roads, to obtain zoning or division approval of their development plans. Attempts to deduct these transfers as charitable contributions under §170 usually fail because of the developer's commercial motivation.[18] Attempts to deduct

---

[16] See Sharon v. CIR, supra note 12, at 525–26, discussed infra ¶22.1.1, disallowing amortization of the cost of law school and a bar review course on the theory that they serve both personal and business purposes. This is debatable and surely not accurate as applied to many vocational courses, which are better viewed as capital expenditures than as personal or living expenses. See also David R. Webb Co. v. CIR, 708 F2d 1254 (7th Cir. 1983) (payment of liability assumed as part of purchase price of going business must be capitalized, regardless of whether prior owner could have deducted it). Other instances of nondeductible capital expenditures that do not create separate assets in the conventional sense are cited and discussed by Gunn, supra note 10, at 466–69.

[17] Enoch v. CIR, 57 TC 781 (1972). See also S&L Bldg. Corp. v. CIR, 19 BTA 788 (1930) (acq.) (unamortized loan expenses deductible when borrower sells the property securing the loan to a purchaser who assumes the obligation); Rev. Rul. 86-67, 1986-1 CB 238 (if borrower dies before loan expenses fully amortized, unamortized portion deductible on decedent's final return).

[18] See, e.g., In re Drage, 78-2 USTC ¶9632 (MD Fla. 1978) (not officially reported) (no charitable deduction for transfer of parcel to city as site for public park and fire station where transfer was made so city would provide water and sewage connections); Forkan v. CIR, 36 TCM (CCH) 798 (1977) (trailer park owner denied charitable deduction for easement dedicated to county in expectation of approval of request to expand trailer park). But see Collman v. CIR, 511 F2d 1263 (5th Cir. 1975) (charitable deduction allowed for tract dedicated to county for construction of adjoining roads in absence of evidence that taxpayer knew they were necessary for rezoning and petition for rezoning was filed more than 17 months after dedication; deduction offset by cost of roads); Citizens & S. Nat'l Bank v. US, 243 F. Supp. 900 (WDSC 1965) (land donated for construction of highway; charitable contribution where no agreement by state highway commission to build highways). See also infra ¶35.1.3.

them as business expenses under §162 have also failed, on the theory that
transfers of this type are business expenditures of a capital nature, comparable to the cost of obtaining a license or franchise of indefinite duration.[19]
Rather than treat the transfer as a taxable disposition of the property for
benefits equal to its fair market value at the time of the transfer, the courts
simply deny a deduction and assign the basis of the transferred property to
the remaining property.[20]

¶20.4.2 Expenditures to Acquire, Clear Title to, and Dispose of Property

Among the examples of capital expenditures listed in the regulations
are the cost of acquiring property, the cost of defending or perfecting title
thereto, and commissions paid in purchasing securities.[21] Costs incurred in
defending or perfecting title to property are easily viewed as capital expenditures, since the elimination of a disputed claim or cloud on the taxpayer's
title increases its value.[22]

---

[19] See Lots, Inc. v. CIR, 49 TC 541 (1968), aff'd per curiam on other issues sub
nom.; Christie v. CIR, 410 F2d 759 (5th Cir. 1969); Eggert v. CIR, 36 TCM (CCH)
1071 (1977). See also Chicago & Northwestern Ry. v. CIR, 114 F2d 882 (7th Cir.
1940), cert. denied, 312 US 692 (1941) (land conveyed to municipality for street,
resulting in permanent protection of petitioner's property); Eggert v. CIR, supra
(land conveyed to Conservation Trust to obtain building permits and subdivision
approval); Oliver v. CIR, 35 TCM (CCH) 656 (1976), aff'd per curiam, 553 F2d 560
(8th Cir. 1977) (easement conveyed to obtain zoning approval for shopping center
development); Sevier Terrace Realty Co. v. CIR, 21 TCM (CCH) 1289 (1962), aff'd
per curiam, 327 F2d 999 (6th Cir. 1964) (lots transferred to taxpayer's subdivision
for social and recreation center).

[20] See, e.g., Country Club Estates, Inc. v. CIR, 22 TC 1283 (1954) (acq.) (cost of
land donated to nonprofit country club for benefit of purchasers of subdivision lots
allocated to basis in lots); Ackerman Buick, Inc. v. CIR, 32 TCM (CCH) 1061 (1973)
(cost of dedicated roadway added to taxpayer's basis in remaining lots); Rev. Rul.
68-478, 1968-2 CB 330 (cost of land, golf course, and recreational facility transferred
to nonprofit club included in cost of lots on pro rata basis).

[21] Reg. §§1.263(a)-2(a), (c), (e). See also Nagy v. CIR, 37 TCM (CCH) 1326
(1978) (payment of incentive compensation to employees of taxpayer's corporation
to increase net corporate earnings and thus entitle taxpayer to more stock under
merger agreement; held, capital expense of acquiring stock). Compare Briggs v. CIR,
75 TC 465 (1980), aff'd, 694 F2d 614 (9th Cir. 1982) (mandatory union dues
collected for building fund not deductible because taxpayers received certificates in
fund that were redeemable under certain circumstances) with Rev. Rul. 82-15, 1982-
1 CB 29 (deduction allowed for portion of dues allocated to trade association's loan
fund for members; because eligibility for loans was unrelated to amount of dues paid,
dues did not give members an interest in property, but merely entitled them to
benefits of membership, including loans from fund).

[22] The cost of defending title is properly capital only if the cloud on the taxpayer's title arises from facts existing when the taxpayer acquired the property; in this

Expenses in connection with the acquisition of property sometimes seem, at least at first, to qualify either as business expenses under §162 or, in the case of individuals, as expenses of managing, conserving, or maintaining property under §212; and if they do not increase the value of the property, they do not seem to be disallowed as capital expenditures by §263. The problem can be illustrated by assuming that A and B each purchase 50 percent of the stock of a corporation, that A employs an appraiser to advise him on the value of the stock, that B relies on his own judgment, and that they pay the same amount for their half interests. Since A's stock is worth no more than B's, can the appraiser's fee paid by A be properly characterized as a capital expenditure—as an improvement or betterment "made to increase the value of any property"—within the meaning of §263(a)(1)?

Whatever might be the answer if the issue were presented de novo, numerous cases hold that expenditures for legal, brokerage, accounting, and similar services in the acquisition of assets are nondeductible capital expenditures.[23] In *Woodward v. CIR*, the Supreme Court treated the principle as self-evident: "The law could hardly be otherwise for such ancillary expenses . . . are as much part of the cost of [the] asset as is the price paid for it."[24] The issue in *Woodward* was the deductibility of expenses incurred in litigation under a state statute requiring shareholders voting in favor of the perpetual extension of a corporate charter to purchase all dissenting stock at "its real value." Since there was no dispute regarding their obligation to

---

case, a successful defense gives the taxpayer something he never had before, and is similar to an acquisition cost. Costs of defending against threats to a taxpayer's property or status that arise from facts subsequent to acquisition have usually been held deductible. See BHA Enters., Inc. v. CIR, 74 TC 593 (1980) (expenses incurred in resisting FCC's attempt to revoke license held to be deductible business expense rather than capital outlay); infra ¶20.4.8 (costs of defending business reputation). Similarly, expenses incurred in defending title against a claim based on adverse possession, for example, should be deductible. There are, however, no authorities in the title area recognizing this distinction.

[23] See, e.g., Ellis Banking Corp. v. CIR, 688 F2d 1376 (11th Cir. 1982) (expenditures incurred by acquiring corporation in examining books of target company and obtaining requisite governmental approvals capitalized as part of basis of target's stock even though incurred before acquisition agreement); Nicolazzi v. CIR, 79 TC 109 (1982), aff'd per curiam, 722 F2d 324 (6th Cir. 1983) (costs incurred in choosing parcels of land for which filing would be most advantageous and then filing applications for Bureau of Land Management noncompetitive lottery mineral leases must be capitalized in cost of acquiring leases); Rev. Rul. 84-35, 1984-1 CB 31 (amounts paid seller for maintenance of cattle for period between grant to taxpayer of right to purchase the cattle and taxpayer's exercise of the right are part of purchase price, not deductible business expenses). But see Dunlap v. CIR, 74 TC 1377 (1980), rev'd on another issue, 670 F2d 785 (8th Cir. 1982) (overhead expenses in acquiring banks were incidental to taxpayer's business of holding and managing banks; only costs directly associated with stock acquisitions must be capitalized).

[24] Woodward v. CIR, 397 US 572, 576 (1970).

purchase the dissenting stock, the taxpayers argued that the expenses were incurred not in acquiring the stock or defending or perfecting title to it but solely in determining its value. Despite this, the Court held that the expenditures had to be capitalized as part of the cost of the acquired stock:

> In one sense, any law-suit brought against a taxpayer may affect his title to property—money or other assets subject to lien. The courts, not believing that Congress meant all litigation expenses to be capitalized, have created the rule that such expenses are capital in nature only where the taxpayer's "primary purpose" in incurring them is to defend or perfect title. . . .
>
> Taxpayers urge that this "primary purpose" test, developed in the context of cases involving the costs of defending property, should be applied to cost incurred in acquiring or disposing of property as well. And if it is so applied, they argue, the costs here in question were properly deducted, since the legal proceedings in which they were incurred did not directly involve the question of title to the minority stock, which all agreed was to pass to taxpayers, but rather was concerned solely with the value of that stock.
>
> We agree with the Tax Court and the Court of Appeals that the "primary purpose" test has no application here. That uncertain and difficult test may be the best that can be devised to determine the tax treatment of costs incurred in litigation that may affect a taxpayer's title to property more or less indirectly, and that thus calls for a judgment whether the taxpayer can fairly be said to be "defending or perfecting title." Such uncertainty is not called for in applying the regulation that makes the "cost of acquisition" of a capital asset a capital expense. In our view application of the latter regulation to litigation expenses involves the simpler inquiry whether the origin of the claim litigated is in the process of acquisition itself.
>
> A test based upon the taxpayer's "purpose" in undertaking or defending a particular piece of litigation would encourage resort to formalisms and artificial distinctions. For instance, in this case there can be no doubt that legal, accounting, and appraisal costs incurred by taxpayers in *negotiating* a purchase of the minority stock would have been capital expenditures. . . . Under whatever test might be applied, such expenses would have clearly been "part of the acquisition cost" of the stock. . . . Yet the appraisal proceeding was no more than the substitute that state law provided for the process of negotiation as a means of fixing the price at which the stock was to be purchased. Allowing deduction of expenses incurred in such a proceeding, merely on the ground that title was not directly put in question in the particu-

lar litigation, would be anomalous.[25]

With *Woodward*, the Court decided a companion case, *United States v. Hilton Hotels Corp.*, involving fees paid in an appraisal proceeding brought by shareholders of a controlled subsidiary who dissented to its merger into the taxpayer.[26] The taxpayer relied heavily on the fact that title to the dissenting shares vested in the subsidiary as soon as the dissenters registered their opposition to the merger, giving them the status thereafter of creditors. The Court, however, held that this difference provided no distinction:

> The functional nature of the appraisal remedy as a forced purchase of the dissenters' stock is the same, whether title passes before or after the price is determined. Determination and payment of a price is no less an element of an acquisition by purchase than is the passage of title to the property. In both *Woodward* and this case, the expenses were incurred in determining what that price should be, by litigation rather than by negotiation. The whole process of acquisition required both legal operations—fixing the price, and conveying title to the property —and we cannot see why the order in which those operations occurred under applicable state law should make any difference in the characterization of the expenses incurred for the particular federal tax purposes involved here.[27]

The Court did not allude to the point, but a contrary result in *Woodward* and *Hilton Hotels* would have permitted the taxpayers to deduct their expenses from ordinary income under §162 or §212, although profits on a subsequent sale of the stock would be capital gains.[28] Thus, both decisions helped to reduce the disparity between ordinary income and capital gains. At best, however, their contribution is a limited one. Costs of investment advice, custodial services, safe-deposit box rentals, and similar expenses are deductible under §162 or, in the case of individual investors, §212, even if the taxpayer invests only in capital assets and seeks long-term appreciation rather than current yield.

The Supreme Court acknowledged in *Woodward* that it would be diffi-

---

[25] Id. at 576–78.

[26] US v. Hilton Hotels Corp., 397 US 580 (1970).

[27] Id. at 584.

[28] For the leading case linking expenses with a related transaction involving a capital asset, see Arrowsmith v. CIR, 344 US 6 (1952), discussed infra ¶51.10.6. See also Sharples v. US, 533 F2d 550 (Ct. Cl. 1976), linking *Arrowsmith* with *Woodward* and *Hilton Hotels* in refusing to extend the capitalization principle to §212(3), relating to fees incurred in determining tax liabilities.

cult in borderline cases to determine "whether the origin of particular litigation lies in the process of acquisition,"[29] so as to require capitalization of the expenditures. In subsequent cases, the origin-of-the-claim principle has been applied to litigation expenses incurred in enforcing a corporate buy-sell agreement;[30] but when the dispute involved both the ownership of property and the right to income therefrom, only the amount allocable to the former aspect of the litigation has been capitalized.[31] In series of appellate cases, however, it has been held that payments by corporate insiders to settle claims under §16(b) of the Securities Exchange Act of 1934 are wholly allocable to the stock transaction (and hence deductible only as capital losses), even if payment was made in part to avoid adverse publicity and damage to the taxpayer's business reputation.[32]

In a case concluding that an allocation of litigation expenses was required, the Tax Court described the nature of the inquiry required by *Woodward* as follows:

> Quite plainly, the "origin-of-the-claim" rule does not contemplate a mechanical search for the first in the chain of events which led to the litigation but, rather, requires an examination of all the facts. The inquiry is directed to the ascertainment of the "kind of transaction" out of which the litigation arose. . . . Consideration must be given to the issues involved, the nature and objectives of the litigation, the defenses asserted, the purpose for which the claimed deductions were expended,

---

[29] Woodward v. CIR, 397 US 578 (1970).

[30] Ransburg v. US, 440 F2d 1140 (10th Cir. 1971). See also Clements v. CIR, 42 TCM (CCH) 1144 (1981) (on advice of counsel, taxpayer purchased stock rather than assets of a corporation, a choice that resulted in needlessly high taxes; held, legal expenses incurred in suing counsel for damages are nondeductible capital expenditures because origin of claim was transaction in which stock was acquired; the "amount of additional taxes paid is merely a measure of damages").

[31] Boagni v. CIR, 59 TC 708 (1973) (acq.) (expenses to establish ownership of royalty interest capitalized; expenses to establish taxpayer's share of accumulated royalties deductible). See also Southland Royalty Co. v. US, 582 F2d 604 (Ct. Cl. 1978) (distinguishing between litigation involving title and claim to income—"tree" and "fruit" analogy—with extensive citations); Eisler v. CIR, 59 TC 634 (1973) (acq.) (dispute involving discharged employee's ownership of stock, right to compensatory damages, and counterclaim by employer alleging negligence; settlement payment and legal fees allocated between stock claim and threatened negligence claim).

[32] See Brown v. CIR, 529 F2d 609 (10th Cir. 1976), and cases therein cited. See also Rev. Rul. 80-119, 1980-1 CB 40 (out-of-court payment to settle actual and threatened claims under §10(b) of Securities Exchange Act of 1934 is capital expenditure attributable to acquisition of capital asset, even though, in order to protect business reputation, taxpayer paid more than amount that might have been awarded in litigation).

the background of the litigation, and all facts pertaining to the controversy. . . .

Situations arise where the litigation is rooted, in part, in the defense or perfection of title (nondeductible) and, in part, in the collection of income or for the management of property (deductible). In these circumstances, Section 1.212-1(k), Income Tax Regs., contemplates that an allocation should be made.[33]

Appraisal litigation and similar expenses must also be capitalized under a series of cases involving dispositions of property. While it has long been established that selling commissions cannot be deducted (except by dealers) but must be offset against the amount realized in computing the taxpayer's gain or loss on a sale of property,[34] it was less clear until *Woodward* that the same principle applies to other expenses incurred in a sale of property. But *Woodward* referred interchangeably to "the acquisition or disposition of property" in stating that legal, brokerage, accounting, and similar expenses must be capitalized,[35] and the later cases have followed suit.[36]

---

[33] Boagni v. CIR, supra note 31, at 713.

[34] Reg. §1.263(a)-2(e); Spreckels v. Helvering, 315 US 626 (1942); Jordan v. US, 344 F. Supp. 87 (WD Ark. 1972) (same as to commissions to sell commodity futures contracts); Black v. CIR, 60 TC 108 (1973) (same as to commission to sell real property); Hunt v. CIR, 47 BTA 829, 839 (1942) (acq. as to this issue) (same result as to commissions to sell real estate, despite absence of a specific regulation). See also Allstate Sav. & Loan Ass'n v. CIR, 600 F2d 760 (9th Cir. 1979) (selling expenses incurred in foreclosure sales taken into account in determining bank's reserve for bad debts).

[35] Woodward v. CIR, 397 US 572, 576 (1970).

[36] See Baier's Est. v. CIR, 533 F2d 117 (3d Cir. 1976) (dispute over terms of disposition of capital asset); Brown v. US, 526 F2d 135 (6th Cir. 1975) (litigation to obtain information about closely held corporation in order to evaluate offer to buy taxpayer's stock); Madden v. CIR, 514 F2d 1149 (9th Cir. 1975), cert. denied, 424 US 912 (1976) (expenses of opposing condemnation in unsuccessful effort to get public agency to take an easement rather than title); Meade's Est. v. CIR, 489 F2d 161 (5th Cir.), cert. denied, 419 US 882 (1974) (legal fees to enforce antitrust claim, received by taxpayer on corporate liquidating distribution); Munn v. CIR, 455 F2d 1028 (Ct. Cl. 1972) (proceeding to collect proceeds of sale; expenses capitalized even though sale was at loss); Third Nat'l Bank v. US, 427 F2d 343 (6th Cir. 1970) (expenses incurred by minority shareholders in appraisal proceeding following dissent to merger); Helgerson v. US, 426 F2d 1293 (8th Cir. 1970) (litigation relating to stock held in escrow pending sale); Plym v. US, 338 F. Supp. 717 (WD Mich. 1971) (amount paid to settle claim for finder's fee relating to corporate merger). But see Newark Morning Ledger Co. v. US, 539 F2d 929 (3d Cir. 1976) (deduction allowed for expenses of suing to prevent controlling shareholders from siphoning off earnings of corporation in which taxpayer had minority interest); Sharples v. US, 533 F2d 550

In acquisition cases, the effect of capitalizing an expenditure is often to hold it in abeyance until the property is sold. Thus, the *Woodward* principle affects both the timing of the allowance for the expenditure and whether it will reduce ordinary income or capital gain. By contrast, disposition cases do not ordinarily involve a timing issue. Since the disputed expenses are usually paid or incurred when the gain or loss on the disposition is recognized, the issue is whether the expenses can be deducted from ordinary income or must be used as an offset in computing the taxpayer's capital gain or loss. If the expenditures are paid or incurred after the disposition is completed, however, they cannot be used as an offset against the sales price and can hardly be viewed as a "capital expenditure" for property that the taxpayer no longer owns. The rationale of *Arrowsmith v. CIR*, discussed elsewhere in this work, requires the taxpayer to treat such expenditures as capital losses rather than deduct them from ordinary income.[37]

¶20.4.3 Self-Constructed Assets — Pre-1987 Law

It has long been established that when a taxpayer uses its own equipment, facilities, and staff to construct or improve a long-lived asset to be used in the taxpayer's business or to be held by the taxpayer for investment, direct construction costs, such as tools, materials, and labor, must be charged to capital account, rather than being currently deducted.[38] In *CIR v. Idaho Power Co.*, the Supreme Court held that the same principle applies to depreciation on the company's construction equipment. For costs incurred

---

(Ct. Cl. 1976) (*Woodward* inapplicable to §212(3), permitting deduction of fees relating to determination of tax liability); Wagner v. CIR, 78 TC 910 (1982) (seller of stock must capitalize cost of defending buyer's suit for damages based on misrepresentations violating §10(b) of Securities Exchange Act of 1934; purpose of suit was to modify sales price, and origin of claim was sale of stock); Leigh v. US, 611 F. Supp. 33 (ND Ill. 1985) (same result even if taxpayer counterclaims for selling price). See also McMullan v. US, 78-2 USTC ¶9656 (Ct. Cl. Trial J. Op. 1978) (not officially reported) (forest management expenses deductible even though partly related to sale of timber treated under §631 as a capital asset); Von Hafften v. CIR, 76 TC 831 (1981) (costs of defending action for breach of contract, specific performance, and fraud relating to proposed sale of house must be capitalized because attributable to interest in property); Rev. Rul. 78-389, 1978-2 CB 125 (expenses incurred to invalidate ordinance prohibiting taxpayer from installing equipment to expand business not deductible; expenses incurred to invalidate ordinance prohibiting operation of taxpayer's business deductible).

[37] See Arrowsmith v. US, 344 US 6 (1952). See also Arthur H. DuGrenier, Inc. v. CIR, 58 TC 931, 939 n.9 (1972).

[38] CIR v. Idaho Power Co., 418 US 1, 12–13 (1974); Chevy Chase Motor Co. v. CIR, 36 TCM (CCH) 942 (1977) (corporate executive supervised construction of real estate investments; portion of salary capitalized).

after 1986, these principles are stated in §263A, which is discussed elsewhere in this work.[39] Pre-1987 law, however, continues to apply to costs incurred before 1987, and also provides important background for §263A; it is therefore discussed here.

The Court explained its decision in *Idaho Power* as follows:

> Construction-related depreciation is not unlike expenditures for wages for construction workers. The significant fact is that the exhaustion of construction equipment does not represent the final disposition of the taxpayer's investment in that equipment; rather, the investment in the equipment is assimilated into the cost of the capital asset constructed. Construction-related depreciation on the equipment is not an expense to the taxpayer of its day-to-day business. It is, however, appropriately recognized as a part of the taxpayer's cost or investment in the capital asset. . . .
>
> An additional pertinent factor is that capitalization of construction-related depreciation by the taxpayer who does its own construction work maintains tax parity with the taxpayer who has its construction work done by an independent contractor. The depreciation on the contractor's equipment incurred during the performance of the job will be an element of cost charged by the contractor for his construction services, and the entire cost, of course, must be capitalized by the taxpayer having the construction work performed.[40]

The Court rejected the taxpayer's theory that §263, denying deductions for amounts "paid out" for new buildings or permanent improvements or betterments, was inapplicable because depreciation is not "paid out." The Court pointed out that the cost of the construction equipment was paid out when it was acquired. Given the purpose of §263 "to reflect the basic principle that a capital expenditure may not be deducted from current income," the Court held that it encompasses depreciation, which "is simply the means of allocating the payment [for the construction equipment] over the various accounting periods affected."[41] Although the point was not essential to the result, the taxpayer in *Idaho Power* was required by federal

---

[39] See infra ¶105.4.

[40] CIR v. Idaho Power Co., supra note 38, at 13–14.

[41] Id. at 16–17. In this context, the Court held that the "priority-ordering directive" of §§161 and 261 requires that §263 take precedence over §167(a), which allows the deduction for depreciation.

For cases and rulings holding that depreciation is not "paid" within the meaning of §§170 and 213, relating respectively to charitable contributions and medical expenses, see infra ¶35.1.4 (charitable contributions), ¶36.1.2 (medical expenses).

and state regulatory commissions to capitalize its construction-related depreciation, leading the Court to observe that such a compulsory accounting method is "almost presumptively controlling of federal income tax consequences" if it also clearly reflects income.[42] If tax depreciation is taken by an accelerated method, all of the depreciation actually taken, not merely an amount computed on a straight line basis, must be capitalized if the *Idaho Power* principle applies.[43]

By requiring that depreciation on construction equipment be capitalized as part of the basis of the constructed property,[44] *Idaho Power* has the effect of requiring that this depreciation be spread over the depreciation recovery period for the constructed property or, if attributable to land or other nondepreciable property, of requiring it to be held in abeyance until the property is disposed of, at which time it will reduce the gain or increase the loss on the disposition. Assume construction equipment with an adjusted basis of $30,000 and a recovery period of three years is employed for one year to construct a building with a recovery period of 50 years. If the straight line method is used in computing depreciation on the equipment, $10,000 of depreciation on the equipment is capitalized, and this amount, together with all of the other costs of the building, is deducted over 50 years by whatever depreciation method is applicable to the building.

On the authority of *Idaho Power* and §446(b), requiring use of an accounting method that clearly reflects income, taxpayers have been required to capitalize a variety of indirect construction-related expenses, including vacation pay, payroll taxes, health and welfare benefits,[45] general

---

[42] CIR v. Idaho Power Co., supra note 38, at 14–15. But see Rev. Rul. 77-325, 1977-2 CB 67 (capitalized depreciation to be computed on basis of depreciation method and useful lives used for tax purposes, regardless of method and lives used for financial accounting purposes).

[43] Pacific Power & Light Co. v. US, 644 F2d 1358 (9th Cir. 1981). See also Rev. Rul. 83-67, 1983-1 CB 74 (under *Idaho Power*, depreciation on irrigation system required to be capitalized until grove that is to be irrigated becomes productive).

[44] In determining the investment credit, however, capitalized depreciation has been excluded from the basis of self-constructed property if the investment credit was allowed on the taxpayer's purchase of the construction equipment. United Telecommunications, Inc. v. CIR, 589 F2d 1383 (10th Cir.), cert. denied, 442 US 917 (1979); Rev. Rul 81-1, 1981-1 CB 18. An inappropriate doubling of the credit would occur, it is thought, if any portion of the cost of construction equipment were included in determining the credit for both the construction equipment and the constructed property.

[45] Louisville & Nashville RR v. CIR, 66 TC 962 (1976) (vacation pay, holiday pay, payroll taxes, health and welfare benefits, and cost of transporting construction materials on taxpayer's own tracks required to be capitalized); Rev. Rul. 67-75, 1967-1 CB 41 (vacation pay attributable to construction project capitalized).

overhead costs,[46] and, in some instances, executive salaries.[47] The full reach of *Idaho Power* has not yet been determined, however, and precise boundaries as to what overhead expenses should be capitalized cannot be delineated.[48] Overhead costs are probably subject to capitalization only if they bear a direct and close relationship to the taxpayer's construction activity, as judged by generally accepted accounting practices. There may be room for a de minimis exception if the taxpayer's internal construction and replacement activity is not substantial.[49]

Because capitalized construction-related depreciation becomes part of the basis of the new or improved property under §1016(a), it must be charged against the basis of the construction equipment. Without such a charge, the same amount would both be used to reduce the taxpayer's gain (or increase the loss) on disposition of the construction equipment, and be included in depreciation deductions on the constructed property. Since §1016(a)(2), the usual rule for reducing basis for depreciation, only refers to amounts that are allowed or allowable as deductions in computing taxable income, the adjustment should probably be made under §1016(a)(1), relating to amounts "properly chargeable to capital account."

---

[46] Adolph Coors Co. v. CIR, 519 F2d 1280 (10th Cir. 1975), cert. denied, 423 US 1087 (1976) (method of accounting whereby only direct construction costs are capitalized and overhead is charged to cost of goods sold does not clearly reflect income; IRS warranted in requiring capitalization of overhead); but see Fort Howard Paper Co. v. CIR, 49 TC 275 (1967) (no overhead required to be capitalized where construction was performed by regular employees in slack times and no increase in overhead costs can be directly identified with self-constructed assets; taxpayer's method clearly reflects income).

[47] Acer Realty Co. v. CIR, 132 F2d 512 (8th Cir. 1942) (acq.) (officer's salary attributable to construction supervision not ordinary and necessary expense but capital expenditure); Perlmutter v. CIR, 44 TC 382 (1965), aff'd, 373 F2d 45 (10th Cir. 1967) (portion of officer's salary, as part of overhead expense, capitalized); Chevy Chase Motor Co. v. CIR, 36 TCM (CCH) 942 (1977) (salary of president-shareholder of real estate development firm capitalized to extent of time devoted to supervising construction); Rev. Rul. 81-150, 1981-1 CB 119 (management fees paid to managing partner for supervision of construction of drilling rig must be capitalized).

[48] See Aboussie v. US, 779 F2d 424 (8th Cir. 1985), which held that interest and taxes accruing during the period of a building's construction need not be capitalized under §163 or *Idaho Power*. Since 1976, Congress has provided separate rules for the capitalization of construction period interest and taxes. These rules, originally found in §189 and since 1986 in §263A(f), are discussed in ¶105.4.2.

[49] See generally Fox & Jackson, Internal Revenue Service Reevaluates the Deductibility of Construction-Related Overhead Expenses, 4 J. Corp. Tax'n 354 (1978); Travostino, *Idaho Power*: The Capitalization of Depreciation, 28 Tax Lawyer 149 (1974).

¶20.4.4　Expenditures to Investigate, Start, Enter, or Expand a Business

The principle that the cost of acquiring a long-lived asset is a capital expenditure rather than a current business expense also applies to intangibles acquired on purchasing an existing business as a going concern, such as goodwill, know-how, franchises, staff experience, and favorable contracts with employees and suppliers.[50] Expenditures in investigating a potential acquisition, as well as commissions, legal fees, and other expenses incurred in consummating the transaction, are also capital expenditures, includable in the cost basis of the acquired assets, rather than deductible expenses under §162 or §212.[51]

If the investigation does not result in a consummated transaction, the expenses ought to be deductible in order to reflect accurately the net economic results of the taxpayer's business or profit-oriented activities, but the courts and the IRS have been unreasonably severe in denying deductions for expenses incurred in unsuccessful investigations of business and investment opportunities. The leading case is *Frank v. CIR*, which held that travel and legal expenses in searching for a newspaper or radio station to purchase and operate, were not deductible under (1) §162 because the taxpayers were not engaged in any trade or business, (2) §212 because they had no interest in an income-producing asset, or (3) §165(c)(2), relating to losses on transactions entered into for profit, because they decided not to enter into any transaction after the preliminary investigation.[52] There is, to be sure, a

---

[50] See Reg. §1.263(a)-2(h). For problems in allocating a lump-sum purchase price among the various tangible and intangible assets acquired on the purchase of a going concern, see infra ¶51.9.

[51] See Woodward v. CIR, 397 US 572 (1970) and US v. Hilton Hotels Corp., 397 US 580 (1970), discussed supra ¶20.4.2; Plym v. US, 338 F. Supp. 717 (WD Mich. 1971). See also Payte v. US, 492 F. Supp. 518 (ND Tex. 1979), aff'd per curiam, 626 F2d 400 (5th Cir. 1980), cert. denied, 450 US 995 (1981) (because interest on promissory note given in purchase of partnership interest was attributable to acquisition of capital assets, it could not be treated as trade or business deduction in computing net operating loss carryback).

[52] Frank v. CIR, 20 TC 511 (1953). See also Akers v. CIR, 42 TCM (CCH) 1548 (1981) (where taxpayer investigated several business sites and then chose one, cost of investigating all sites added to basis of selected site); Bick v. CIR, 37 TCM (CCH) 1591 (1978) (expenses of European trip to investigate investment opportunities in German vineyards or Swiss housing disallowed), collecting prior cases and articles; Stroope v. CIR, 34 TCM (CCH) 1524 (1975) (expenses incurred in search for possible future real estate investments not deductible); Rev. Rul. 57-418, 1957-2 CB 143 (expenditures in search of a business or investment are deductible "only where the activities are more than investigatory and the taxpayer has actually entered into a transaction for profit and the project is later abandoned"); Rev. Rul. 77-254, 1977-2 CB 63 (amplifying Rev. Rul. 57-418). But see Seed v. CIR, 52 TC 880 (1969) (acq.) (deductible loss under §165(c)(2) for legal and other expenses on abandonment of

danger of fictitious claims for travel[53] and the expenses of hobbies, but the appropriate remedy for abuse is a skeptical eye, not a rigid rule of law. Indeed, some of the cases disallowing deductions for abortive investigations are best explained on failure-of-proof grounds.[54]

Since taxpayers who purchase a business as a going concern must capitalize the purchase price, including amounts allocable to its goodwill and industrial know-how, it is not surprising that the IRS contends that taxpayers creating an enterprise from scratch must capitalize expenditures incurred in training the staff during the start-up or preoperating period. In *Richmond Television Corp. v. United States*, the Court of Appeals for the Fourth Circuit upheld this requirement, summarizing the relevant cases as follows:

> The uniform teaching of these several cases is that, even though a taxpayer has made a firm decision to enter into business and over a considerable period of time spent money in preparation for entering

---

business venture following denial of application for charter); Rev. Rul. 73-580, 1973-2 CB 86 (expenses of conglomerate's acquisition staff must be capitalized, but if a merger or acquisition plan is abandoned, expenditures are deductible as losses under §165(a)).

[53] In "Europe's Lighter Side," N.Y. Herald-Tribune, July 20, 1954, at 21, Art Buchwald reported that many Europeans were puzzled by promising business deals that, after being discussed with them by vacationing Americans, were never closed: "The only way we've been able to appease the Europeans is to explain that the Americans weren't malicious. They were just trying to deduct their trip from their income tax. After it's explained, the European is always mollified. If there's one thing a European understands, it's tax evasion."

See Kinney v. CIR, 66 TC 122 (1976) (travel expenses incurred by investor to make on-site investigations of plants and retail outlets of corporations in which he was buying and selling stock, allegedly part of "his overall investment technique," not deductible; insufficient evidence of relationship to investment activities); Haft v. CIR, 40 TC 2, 7 (1963) (acq.) (three-month sojourn in Florida resort at height of winter season was either personal or, if related to investigating purchase of business interest or real estate, not deductible); Rev. Rul. 56-511, 1956-2 CB 170 (no deduction for trips by investor to attend shareholders' meetings of corporations in which he owned stock); Rev. Rul. 55-237, 1955-1 CB 317 (investor in independently produced motion pictures could not deduct expense of trip to Europe "to explore the general possibilities of making more favorable investments in films there" because he did not possess "an existing right or interest resulting in the production of income"). See also infra ¶20.5 (nonbusiness expenses), ¶21.1.9 (combined business-pleasure trips).

[54] See, e.g., Myers v. CIR, 38 TC 658, 666 (1962) (taxpayer failed to show what portion of time on South American trip was devoted to business activities); Walet v. CIR, 31 TC 461, 471 (1958), aff'd per curiam, 272 F2d 694 (5th Cir. 1959) ("vagueness of the testimony . . . left us with a sense of unreality" about proposed business deals); Downs v. CIR, 49 TC 533 (1968) (acq.) (failure to establish reasonable expectancy of making a profit).

that business, he still has not "engaged in carrying on any trade or business" within the intendment of Section 162(a) until such time as the business has begun to function as a going concern and performed those activities for which it was organized.[55]

The distinction between preoperating and operating expenses implicit in this principle was readily applied in *Richmond Television Corp.*, which involved costs incurred before the taxpayer was legally licensed to engage in its projected broadcasting business. Several of the precedents cited by the court also involved prelicense expenditures by television stations. In analogizing these threshold expenditures to the purchase price of a "turnkey" operation, the IRS can point to the principle that expenses incurred by a taxpayer in constructing its own facilities must be capitalized.[56] Another familiar example is the cost of gaining entry to a licensed occupation, such as expenditures for professional education, review courses, and license fees.[57]

As applied to the generality of businesses, however, the *Richmond Television* principle beckons the IRS and taxpayers alike into a quagmire. The demarcation between a business that is getting ready to operate and one

---

[55] Richmond Television Corp. v. US, 345 F2d 901, 907 (4th Cir.), rev'd and remanded on another issue, 382 US 68, decision on remand, 354 F2d 410 (4th Cir. 1965). See Madison Gas & Elec. Co. v. CIR, 633 F2d 512 (7th Cir. 1980) (denying deduction for pre-operating expenses incurred by taxpayer in connection with interest in nuclear power plant, owned jointly with other utility companies). See also Fishman v. CIR, 837 F2d 309 (7th Cir. 1988), cert. denied, 108 S. Ct. 2902 (1988) (partnership organized to develop and operate shopping center required to capitalize mortgage commitment fee and ground rents for period before center completed); Johnsen v. CIR, 794 F2d 1157 (6th Cir. 1986) (partnership organized to construct and operate apartment building required to capitalize fees for tax and legal advice, loan commitment fees, and management and guaranty fees incurred before building rented to tenants); Aboussie v. US, 779 F2d 424 (8th Cir. 1985) (on facts similar to *Johnsen*, no deduction for mortgage insurance premium for coverage before project ready for rental). But see Blitzer v. US, 684 F2d 874 (Cl. Ct. 1980) (deduction allowed for expenses incurred by real estate partnership after construction began but before completion). For discussion of the preoperating/operating distinction, see Lee, A Blend of Old Wines in a New Wineskin: Section 183 and Beyond, 29 Tax L. Rev. 347, 454 et seq. (1974); Ludtke, Vitek & Witt, Tax Aspects of the Formation and Initial Operation of a Real Estate Limited Partnership, 39 Tax Lawyer 195, 196–210 (1986).

In Snow v. CIR, 416 US 500 (1974), the Supreme Court held that research and experimental expenditures were incurred "in connection with [the taxpayer's] trade or business" within the meaning of §174 (infra ¶26.4.1) even though the business was in the preoperating stage, observing that §162 is "more narrowly written" than §174. See Lee, Pre-Operating Expenses and Section 174: Will *Snow* Fall? 27 Tax Lawyer 381 (1974) (before reversal by Supreme Court of appellate decision in *Snow*).

[56] See CIR v. Idaho Power Co., 418 US 1 (1974), discussed supra ¶20.4.3.

[57] See infra ¶22.1.3.

that is already operating is usually indistinct, and becomes even more murky when the issue is whether a going concern is preparing to enter a new line of business or is merely expanding its existing operations.[58] In the latter situation, despite a foundation in theory for distinguishing between advertising and similar expenditures to preserve the taxpayer's goodwill and expenditures to enhance it,[59] no serious effort has ever been made to enforce the distinction. The IRS has sought to apply the preoperating/operating distinction almost exclusively to taxpayers entering into new lines of business.

The difficulty of identifying new lines of business can be illustrated by a series of cases in which the IRS unsuccessfully sought to disallow deductions to banks for expenditures associated with entry into the consumer credit card field. The start-up costs, including computer programming, credit evaluations, and promotional activities, have been allowed by the courts as business expenses under §162 on the theory that banks have always engaged in the business of making loans and that "the credit card system enables a bank to carry on an old business in a new way" rather than to enter a "new business."[60] In another leading case, *Briarcliff Candy Corp. v. CIR*, the Court of Appeals for the Second Circuit held that expenditures by a candy manufacturer to create a franchise division in order to expand its sales in suburban drugstores and other retail outlets were deductible under "the long recognized principle that expenditures for the protection of an existing investment or the continuation of an existing business or the preservation of existing income from loss or diminution, are ordinary and necessary [expenses] within the meaning of §162 and not capital in na-

---

[58] See, e.g., Malmstedt v. CIR, 578 F2d 520 (4th Cir. 1978) (rejecting distinction between residential and commercial real estate businesses); York v. CIR, 261 F2d 421 (4th Cir. 1958) (rejecting distinction between industrial real estate business and residential and commercial real estate business).

[59] For an early recognition of the distinction between current and long-term advertising and promotional activities, in which the taxpayer, not the IRS, argued for capitalization, see Northwestern Yeast Co. v. CIR, 5 BTA 232 (1926) (acq.). As implied by the court in Briarcliff Candy Corp. v. CIR, 475 F2d 775 (2d Cir. 1973), this distinction has long been a dead letter for want of any legislative or regulatory guideposts. See also infra ¶20.4.5 (re advertising expenses).

[60] Iowa-Des Moines Nat'l Bank v. CIR, 592 F2d 433 (8th Cir. 1979); Colorado Springs Nat'l Bank v. US, 505 F2d 1185, 1190 (10th Cir. 1974). In both cases, a one-time membership fee paid to join a Master Charge association was held to be a capital expenditure. See also Equitable Life Ins. Co. of Iowa v. CIR, 36 TCM (CCH) 1184 (1977) (expense of registering variable annuity contracts with SEC held deductible; although new type of contract was involved, taxpayer was already engaged in business of selling insurance and annuity contracts).

See generally Brown & Lee, Deductibility of Start-Up Expenditures Under Section 162—The "Clear-Reflection-of-Income" Test, 61 Cornell L. Rev. 618 (1976).

ture."[61] Pointing out the difficulty of applying the preoperating/operating distinction to taxpayers already engaged in business, the court observed:

> The interpretation and application of the statutes and regulations with regard to tangibles in deciding whether a particular expenditure is for repairs or for a capital addition or improvement are sometimes difficult, but guidelines have been established which give a taxpayer clues as to what is correct and what is not.
>
> In the realm of intangibles, however, the rulings and decisions are in a state of hopeless confusion particularly where the issue concerns an intangible contribution (such as a salesman's work-product) to an intangible asset (such as his company's position in the market). Many decisions in this area rest upon administrative fiat, fortified by the requirement that the taxpayer show clear error. The Commissioner in the present case resorted to such nebulous phrases as "an intensive campaign to get new customers" and "an ambitious new distribution program" to define what a capital asset was in the circumstances of the case. But practically all businesses are constantly seeking new customers and pursuing a distribution program. When are the wages and salaries of its employees who take care of these things capital expenditures and nondeductible and when are they current expenses and deductible under §162? The taxpayer, who may be exposed to interest and penalties for guessing wrong, is entitled to reasonably clear criteria or standards to let him know what his rights and duties are.[62]

---

[61] Briarcliff Candy Corp. v. CIR, supra note 59, at 487. In reaching this conclusion, the court relied in part on the theory that CIR v. Lincoln Sav. & Loan Ass'n, 403 US 345 (1971), brought about a "radical shift in emphasis" by requiring capital expenditures to be capitalized only if they create or enhance "a separate and distinct additional asset." This overstates the significance of this phrase in *Lincoln Savings*, but the result in *Briarcliff* is independently persuasive. See also Southland Royalty Co. v. US, 582 F2d 604 (Ct. Cl. 1978) (cost of consultant's study of taxpayer's oil and gas reserves deductible; even if useful beyond taxable year, not a "separate and distinct asset" and similar to salaries of employees engaged in ordinary management planning); Funkhouser Indus., Inc. v. CIR, 16 TCM (CCH) 890 (1957) (taxpayer allowed to deduct cost of survey "to find new products and new markets").

[62] Briarcliff Candy Corp. v. CIR, 475 F2d 785 (2d Cir. 1973). For cases in which existing enterprises were held to have expanded into new lines of business, see Cleveland Elec. Illuminating Co. v. US, 7 Cl. Ct. 220, 85-1 USTC ¶9128 (1985) (electric utility required to capitalize expenses of training employees for its first nuclear plant and public relations expenses incurred in connection with the licensing of the plant; similar expenses with respect to construction of additional conventionally powered plants held deductible); Mid-State Prods. Co. v. CIR, 21 TC 696, 713–14 (1954) (acq.) (company engaged in buying shell eggs and selling frozen eggs required to capitalize expenditures to enter business of producing and selling dried eggs; taxpayer had classified expenditures as "deferred development and preoperating expense" on its books). Compare Central Tex. Sav. & Loan Ass'n v. US, 731 F2d

At bottom, difficulties in this area stem not from any weakness in the theory that preoperating expenditures to create intangibles should be capitalized but from the impossibility of systematically administering this principle.

Some confusion has arisen, however, over the theory. Is the only bar to the deduction of preoperating expenses the fact that the taxpayer is not engaged in a trade or business when the expenses are incurred, or is the deduction also precluded because the costs are capital expenditures? The question is most important for individuals, who might be allowed to deduct the expenses under §212 as expenses incurred for the production of income if the lack of a trade or business is the only reason for denying the §162 deduction. If the costs are capital expenditures, in contrast, §212 provides no relief because the requirement of capitalization applies to §212 as well as to §162. The latter is the sounder approach because the only persuasive reason for denying the deduction is that the costs pertain to future revenues. The courts, however, have split on the issue.[63]

When a newly organized entity incurs expenses in starting up its business, the expenses are usually considered nondeductible preoperating costs under the foregoing authorities even if the new entity is closely related to another entity that is presently engaged in a similar business.[64] The application of these authorities thus can be importantly affected by whether a new

---

1181 (5th Cir. 1984) (savings and loan association must capitalize costs incurred in starting up new branches, including costs of making market evaluations and obtaining licenses) with NCNB Corp. v. US, 684 F2d 285 (4th Cir. 1982) (en banc 8-1 decision) (current deductions allowed for bank's costs in finding new locations, studying feasibility, obtaining government permissions, and opening new branches). See also Houston Natural Gas Corp. v. CIR, 90 F2d 814 (4th Cir.), cert. denied, 302 US 722 (1937) (cost of driving competitor out of business not deductible).

[63] Compare Hoopengarner v. CIR, 80 TC 538 (1983) (rental payments on lease of undeveloped land on which taxpayer planned to construct office building are not deductible under §162 because no trade or business when payments made, but are deductible under §212 because leasehold held for production of future income and payments did not result in acquisition of asset continuing after end of year; eight judges dissenting), with Johnsen v. CIR, 794 F2d 1157 (6th Cir. 1986) (no deduction under §212 for preoperating expenses nondeductible under §162).

[64] Bennett Paper Corp. v. CIR, 78 TC 458 (1982), aff'd, 669 F2d 450 (8th Cir. 1983) (newly formed member of affiliated group filing consolidated returns must capitalize preoperating costs because they cannot be regarded as incurred in continuation or extension of similar businesses of other members of group, even if group files consolidated returns); Goodwin v. CIR, 75 TC 424 (1980), aff'd without opinion, 691 F2d 490 (3d Cir. 1982) (limited partner in construction firm not allowed to deduct his distributive share of partnership's preoperating costs, even though he had personal history of construction activities). But see Duffy v. US, 690 F2d 889 (Ct. Cl. 1982) (on facts, taxpayer was personally in business of hotel development, construction, and operation, notwithstanding use of corporations to conduct certain activities; loan commitment fee related to new project was deductible expense of this continuing business).

venture is carried on by a new corporation or partnership or as a division of an entity with a history in the same type of business.

Until 1980, capitalized preoperating costs usually could not be amortized over the taxable years in which the new venture was conducted,[65] and the ultimate choice was between deducting the costs when paid or incurred and holding them in abeyance for deduction only when the venture is terminated. It is far from clear that the former distorted taxable income more than the latter. In 1980, Congress largely remedied this deficiency by enacting §195, which permits taxpayers to elect to amortize start-up expenses over a period of 60 months or longer.[66]

¶20.4.5 Advertising Expenses

Efforts by taxpayers in the early years of income taxation to capitalize the costs of large-scale advertising campaigns and to amortize the capitalized amounts over a period of years were consistently opposed by the IRS, on the ground that allocating advertising expenditures between current expenses and capital outlays was not feasible. This insistence by the IRS on the deduction of advertising expenditures when paid or incurred produced a string of victories that, in the light of hindsight, must be classified as Pyrrhic.[67] In a leading early case, for example, the Board of Tax Appeals rejected the taxpayer's claim that the cost of free samples, distributed in its early years to promote and expand a regional business into a national enterprise, constituted part of its invested capital in determining its liability under a tax on excess wartime profits:

> There can be little doubt in the minds of reasonable men fairly acquainted with modern business that promotion expenditures like those before us have a significance similar to the investment in more tangible assets. They fertilize the field for new production. The free distribution of samples at the state fair is justified only if it lures a new

---

[65] For the entrenched principle that expenditures for goodwill cannot be amortized and can be deducted only when the business is sold or abandoned, see infra ¶23.2.6.

[66] See infra ¶26.4.2.

[67] See E.H. Sheldon & Co. v. CIR, 214 F2d 655 (6th Cir. 1954), and cases therein cited; Consolidated Apparel Co. v. CIR, 17 TC 1570, 1582 (1952) (acq.), modified as to other issues, 207 F2d 580 (7th Cir. 1953) (no statutory requirement or authorization for allocating advertising expenses over a period of years). *Sheldon* allowed the taxpayer to deduct costs incurred in publishing a trade catalogue having a useful life in excess of one year. Neither the Tax Court nor the IRS currently follows *Sheldon*. See Best Lock Corp. v. CIR, 31 TC 1217 (1959); Rev. Rul. 68-360, 1968-2 CB 197. As advertising costs not resulting in tangible assets like catalogues, however, the rationale of *Sheldon* still prevails.

customer. It was not to the housewife already convinced that the petitioner planned to give away its samples of yeast year after year, but to one who would become a new unit in its expanding business. In this way it was risking new capital in the business in the hope of future profits—making an investment. Whether this investment is to be called good will or trade name or trade-mark, or something else, is unimportant. It may not need a name, except for accounting purposes, in order to reflect the expenditure and yet not ignore its investment significance.

Generally and theoretically, therefore, it is safe to say that some part of the cost of a campaign or system of promotion may be of permanent significance and may be regarded as a capital investment rather than a deductible expense. But how far in a given case the recognition of this doctrine may require the capitalization of some expenditures and the charging off of others is hard to say. Clearly, when the question is submitted for judicial consideration, it may not be answered *ab inconvenienti* by an arbitrary rule. . . .

[The wide variations in expenditures] lead one, in the absence of any further knowledge, to doubt that there was any consistent policy of investment or any satisfactory way of determining a fair allocation. Perhaps it would be reasonable to believe that as time went on and the business grew the proportion of capital decreased and current maintenance increased. But as to this the Board has no knowledge of the probabilities and there is no proof. It is not a matter of judicial notice, and we are not permitted to guess. If anyone has any evidence upon which an allocation can be predicated, such evidence must be produced by the petitioner.[68]

Although the courts did not entirely foreclose the propriety of capitalizing some advertising expenditures, they were never satisfied in the litigated cases with the taxpayer's allocation between current and long-term benefits. In time, this insistence on evidence hardened into a rule of law that capitalization is proper only if the taxpayer can establish "with reasonable certainty the benefits resulting in later years from the expenditure."[69] If the IRS went on the warpath by disallowing current deductions for advertising, the tax-

---

[68] Northwestern Yeast Co. v. CIR, 5 BTA 232, 237–38 (1926) (acq.). For a vestige of the relationship of advertising to taxation of excess wartime profits, see Reg. §1.162-14.

[69] E.H. Sheldon & Co. v. CIR, supra note 67, at 659. See also A. Finkenberg's Sons v. CIR, 17 TC 973, 982–83 (1951) (acq.) (taxpayer must show that future benefits "can be determined precisely"). But see Durovic v. CIR, 542 F2d 1328 (7th Cir. 1976) (cost of free samples must be capitalized; amortization denied in absence of proof of limited useful life).

payer would have to bear—and would probably fail to carry—the burden of establishing the currently deductible component of the expenditure. The IRS, however, has eschewed this tactic,[70] and its long acquiescence in the deduction of advertising costs may have been implicitly ratified by congressional silence.

The result, as a practical matter, is that advertising expenses are deductible (assuming a sufficient nexus between the expenditure and the taxpayer's business),[71] even if long-term benefits are the taxpayer's primary objective. The only significant exceptions are that (1) taxpayers who elected to capitalize advertising expenditures in computing their liability under the long-defunct wartime excess profits taxes must follow a consistent practice for subsequent expenditures[72] and (2) the expense of advertising in a political party's convention program and certain other political publications cannot be deducted.[73] Occasional judicial comments to the effect that advertising costs may be nondeductible capital expenditures either involve expenditures for physical assets with an extended life (catalogues, billboards, etc.)[74] or are reminders that a sleeping dog exists, but they are not loud enough to wake him up or cause him to bite. Thus, advertising expenditures to construct goodwill are deductible business expenses, unlike expenditures to purchase goodwill or to construct tangible assets.

---

[70] Reg. §1.162-20(a)(2) (expenditures for institutional and goodwill advertising to keep taxpayer's name before the public are deductible if related to "the patronage the taxpayer might reasonably expect in the future"). See also Rev. Rul. 68-561, 1968-2 CB 117, concerning a public utility's campaign to encourage the construction of homes using gas heat and conversion of existing homes to gas systems. The ruling holds that cash allowances to builders and homeowners must be capitalized, but advertising expenses "are less directly and significantly productive of intangible assets having a value extending beyond the taxable years in which they were paid or incurred" and may be deducted. (Those who believe in this distinction will believe anything.) Also see IT 3581, 1942-2 CB 88 (guideposts to deductibility of wartime advertising to preserve customer loyalty), declared obsolete by Rev. Rul. 68-100, 1968-1 CB 572.

[71] See Burrous v. CIR, 36 TCM (CCH) 1465 (1977) (accountant did not establish link between his practice and alleged advertising by racing stock and midget cars; remote or incidental connection between racing activities and taxpayer's business insufficient).

[72] IRC §263(b); Reg. §1.162-14. See supra note 67.

[73] See IRC §276(a)(1), discussed supra ¶20.3.7.

[74] See Best Lock Corp. v. CIR, 31 TC 1217 (1959) (cost of catalogues with useful life of more than one year must be capitalized); Rev. Rul. 68-360, 1968-2 CB 197 (same); French Broad Ice Cream Co. v. US, 57-2 USTC ¶9972 (ED Tenn. 1957) (not officially reported) (same as to signs); Alabama Coca-Cola Bottling Co. v. CIR, 28 TCM (CCH) 635 (1969) (same as to cost of signs, clocks, and scoreboards with useful lives of more than one year).

¶20.4.6 Expenses of Finding Employment

The preoperating/operating distinction has a counterpart for employees in the tax treatment of expenditures incurred in seeking or finding employment.[75] The most frequently cited case in this area is *McDonald v. CIR*, in which the Supreme Court held that a state judge appointed to fill a term could not deduct his campaign expenses in seeking election to a regular term, since they "were not expenses incurred in being a judge but in trying to be a judge for the next ten years."[76] The relevance of the case to ordinary employees, however, is complicated by the difficulty of envisioning "judgeship" as a continuing occupation if reelection is necessary to continue in office, as well as by the Court's obvious concern in *McDonald* with the prickly relation between money and politics. In any event, after failing in reliance on *McDonald* to persuade the courts that expenses incurred by employees in seeking new jobs are deductible only if the employee actually secured employment, but not if the effort was unsuccessful, the IRS conceded in 1975 that the distinction was untenable.[77] Ruling that the expenses are deductible regardless of success if the search is for employment in the taxpayer's existing trade or business, the IRS relied on the familiar principle that an employee is engaged in the business of providing services to various employers, not merely in the business of working for his or her current employer.

If the employee is seeking employment for the first time, however, the 1975 ruling disallows any deduction even if employment is actually secured, and the same principle applies if the taxpayer seeks employment in a new trade or business.[78] The basis for this conclusion is not explicitly stated, but it presumably rests on the theory that the expenses are not incurred "in carrying on" the taxpayer's trade or business, as required by §162(a). In

---

[75] For the preoperating/operating distinction, see supra ¶20.4.4. See also infra ¶¶22.1.2 and 22.1.3, regarding educational expenses, where a similar distinction is made between education to qualify for entry into an occupation and education to preserve one's skills after entry.

[76] McDonald v. CIR, 323 US 57, 60 (1944), discussed supra ¶20.2.12 (re expenses of public officials).

[77] See Rev. Rul. 75-120, 1975-1 CB 55, reviewing the earlier rulings and litigated cases. See also McKinley v. CIR, 37 TCM (CCH) 1769 (1978) (electrician allowed to deduct cost of traveling to union halls to seek employment); Rev. Rul. 78-93, 1978-1 CB 38 (career counseling expense allowed attorney and part-time law professor who secured full-time teaching position).

[78] Rev. Rul. 75-120, supra note 77. See also Rev. Rul. 77-16, 1977-1 CB 37 (relation of Revenue Ruling 75-120 to computation of adjusted gross income). The IRS, however, does not appear to apply this distinction where a prospective employer reimburses an interviewee's expenses in connection with an interview conducted at the employer's invitation. See Rev. Rul. 63-77, 1963-1 CB 177 (reimbursements not includable in interviewee's gross income; no mention of previous employment).

practice, it often is not easy to draw the distinction between an existing trade or business and a new one.

The 1975 ruling also deals with the status of currently unemployed taxpayers. They are viewed as still engaged in the business of providing the type of services performed for the prior employer unless "there is a substantial lack of continuity between the time of [the employee's] past employment and the seeking of the new employment."[79] Although not confined to students, the "hiatus" theory has been most frequently applied to taxpayers leaving their employment for graduate work or other training. As developed in this area, the applicable principles have been summarized as follows by the Tax Court:

> We have held that a taxpayer who temporarily ceases active participation in a trade or business during a transition period between leaving one position and obtaining another may be "carrying on" a trade or business during the transition period. . . . Likewise, a taxpayer who leaves his position temporarily to attend school full time may be "carrying on" a trade or business while in school. . . . These cases [citations omitted] establish that a leave of absence is not essential to carry on a trade or business while attending school, nor is it essential to return to the same position after completing the course of study undertaken.
>
> However, when a taxpayer leaves his trade or business for a prolonged period of study with no apparent continuing connection with either his former job or any clear indication of an intention to actively carry on the same trade or business upon completion of study, the taxpayer is not "carrying on" his trade or business while attending school.[80]

---

[79] Rev. Rul. 75-120, supra note 77, at 56.

[80] Sherman v. CIR, 36 TCM (CCH) 1191 (1977) (business manager held to be carrying on trade or business while attending graduate school for two years, although he was denied leave of absence by former employer and took job with another employer on completing studies). As examples of interruptions terminating taxpayers' business status, *Sherman* cited Canter v. US, 354 F2d 352 (Ct. Cl. 1965) (nurse discontinued nursing activities for more than four years while obtaining degrees in nursing), and Corbett v. CIR, 55 TC 884 (1971) (teacher discontinued teaching and commenced full-time study leading to Ph.D.; at time of trial four years later, was still full-time student). See also Dickman v. CIR, 46 TCM (CCH) 1102 (1983) (unemployed research scientist who had abandoned search for employment not engaged in trade or business, despite some effort to make himself proficient as technical translator); Rev. Rul. 77-32, 1977-1 CB 38 (physician who suspended practice "indefinitely" because of increase in cost of malpractice insurance cannot deduct educational expenses to maintain professional skills in preparation for return to practice at indefinite future date); infra ¶22.1.5 (interruption of business activities by education). But see Picknally v. CIR, 36 TCM (CCH) 1292 (1977) (educational adminis-

¶20.4.7 Expenditures to Create or Preserve Taxpayer's Business Reputation

The deductibility under §162 of expenditures relating to the taxpayer's business reputation depends on whether they are incurred to create a reputation or to preserve an existing reputation; the former must be capitalized, while the latter can be deducted. This distinction can be traced back to *Welch v. Helvering*, where the Supreme Court held that the taxpayer could not deduct amounts he paid to reimburse customers of a family business, with which he had been connected, for their losses when the company went into bankruptcy and received a discharge from its debts.[81] His purpose in paying off the discharged debts was to reestablish his standing, credit, and relations with the customers of the prior business on going into business for his own account.

In holding these expenditures not deductible, the Court hinted that they were personal rather than business expenses by comparing them to payments to the victims of an ancestor's thefts in order to clear the taxpayer's family name.[82] This analogy, however, had no support in the record, and the trial court had disallowed the expenditures solely because the taxpayer was "seeking to *build up* a business," citing earlier cases holding that "the payment of discharged obligations for the purpose of reestablishing credit resulted in the acquisition of an intangible capital asset, in the nature of good will, which had a probable life coextensive with the business."[83] Viewed as a whole, the Supreme Court opinion in *Welch v. Helvering* rests primarily on the conclusion that the expenditures were capital outlays rather than ordinary and necessary business expenses.

Viewing *Welch v. Helvering* as involving "a capital outlay to acquire good will for a new business,"[84] the courts have subsequently allowed taxpayers to deduct similar payments on showing that they served to preserve and protect the goodwill or reputation of an existing business. In *Dunn & McCarthy, Inc. v. CIR*, for example, a corporation was permitted to deduct amounts paid to employees who had lent funds to its former president, who had lost the money gambling at the racetrack and died insolvent. The court did not think the payments were "extraordinary:" "It was the kind of outlay which we believe many corporations would make, and have made, under

---

trator who sought work while studying and held fellowship and instructorship at other schools allowed to deduct cost of Ph.D. course in educational administration), collecting earlier cases.

[81] Welch v. Helvering, 290 US 111 (1933).

[82] For the distinction between personal and business reputation, see supra ¶20.2.11.

[83] Welch v. CIR, 25 BTA 117, 119 (1932).

[84] Dunn & McCarthy, Inc. v. CIR, 139 F2d 242, 244 (2d Cir. 1943).

similar circumstances."[85]

¶20.4.8 Repairs vs. Improvements and Replacements

The regulations under §162 provide that (1) the cost of incidental repairs that neither materially increase the value of property nor appreciably prolong its life, but simply keep it in an ordinarily efficient operating condition, may be deducted as business expenses, provided the basis of the property is not increased by the amount expended, but that (2) repairs in the nature of replacements, to the extent that they arrest deterioration and appreciably prolong the property's life, must be capitalized and depreciated.[86] The regulations under §263 similarly distinguish between "incidental repairs" and capital expenditures that add to the value or substantially prolong the useful life of property or adapt it to a new or different use.[87]

In an early and much-quoted decision, the Board of Tax Appeals elaborated on the distinction between repairs and replacements as follows:

------

[85] Id. at 244. See Gould v. CIR, 64 TC 132 (1975) (rejecting theory that similar payments were nondeductible because they were paid expenses of another taxpayer, discussed supra ¶20.1.4); Pepper v. CIR, 36 TC 886 (1961) (lawyer allowed to deduct payments to reimburse clients for losses suffered through another client's dishonesty); Rev. Rul. 76-203, 1976-1 CB 45 (moving and storage company may deduct payments to reimburse uninsured customers for fire losses, where made to preserve its goodwill and protect business reputation); Rev. Rul. 56-359, 1956-2 CB 115 (insurance broker reimbursed customers for losses when insurance company he represented failed; held, deductible expenses of protecting business by preserving confidence of customers). But see Dodd v. CIR, 298 F2d 570 (4th Cir. 1962) (advances to enable failing corporation to pay its debts not deductible expenses of preserving taxpayer's business reputation; extensive review of earlier cases); Carl Reimers Co. v. CIR, 211 F2d 66 (2d Cir. 1954) (payment of bankrupt predecessor's debts to qualify for admission to a business association; held, capital expenditure to get into new field); supra ¶20.2.11 (expenses of protecting personal reputation).

See also Anderson v. CIR, 480 F2d 1304 (7th Cir. 1973) (corporate insider's repayment of profits on stock transaction violating §16(b) of Securities Exchange Act only deductible as capital loss under *Arrowsmith* principle (supra note 28), even if purpose of payment was to protect taxpayer's business reputation); Bradford v. CIR, 70 TC 584 (1978) (insider's repayment of profits on stock transactions alleged to violate §10(b) of the Securities Exchange Act was capital expenditure because origin of claim was stock purchase, not protection of business reputation). While *Bradford*'s application of the origin-of-the-claim test, discussed supra ¶20.4.2, produces a result similar to that of *Arrowsmith, Bradford* is notable for its express rejection of the primary purpose test previously applied in this area.

[86] Reg. §1.162-4. Replacements can, in the alternative, be charged to the depreciation reserve. See also Jones v. US, 279 F. Supp. 772 (D. Del. 1968) (applying repair-capital expenditure distinction to deny deduction under §212). For the nondeductibility of reserves for future repair/replacement expenditures, see World Airways, Inc. v. CIR, 62 TC 786 (1974), aff'd, 564 F2d 886 (9th Cir. 1977).

[87] Reg. §1.263(a)-1(b).

In determining whether an expenditure is a capital one or is chargeable against operating income, it is necessary to bear in mind the purpose for which the expenditure was made. To repair is to restore to a sound state or to mend, while a replacement connotes a substitution. A repair is an expenditure for the purpose of keeping the property in an ordinarily efficient operating condition. It does not add to the value of the property, nor does it appreciably prolong its life. It merely keeps the property in an operating condition over its probable useful life for the uses for which it was acquired. Expenditures for that purpose are distinguishable from those for replacements, alterations, improvements, or additions which prolong the life of the property, increase its value, or make it adaptable to a different use. The one is a maintenance charge, while the others are additions to capital investment which should not be applied against current earnings.[88]

In a later case, the Tax Court observed that it "is none too easy" to apply this distinction.[89] Seldom has a court applied so mild a label to a chimera.

The most frequently cited criteria for distinguishing repairs from replacements are:

1. *Material increase in property's value.* The principle that expenditures materially adding to an asset's value are capital expenditures is closely related to the principle that expenditures creating or enhancing an asset with a useful life of more than one year must be capitalized.[90] In *Hotel Kingkade v. CIR*, for example, the Court of Appeals for the Tenth Circuit held that payments for carpets, refrigerators, repairs, and similar rehabilitation expenditures to replace a hotel's worn-out and discarded equipment were capital outlays.[91] Rejecting the taxpayer's contention that the expenditures merely kept the hotel in a reasonably efficient operating condition, the court said: "Some were for repairs of a permanent nature which materially

---

[88] Illinois Merchants Trust Co. v. CIR, 4 BTA 103, 106 (1926) (acq.) (deduction allowed for cost of shoring up walls and repairing foundation of building threatened by lowering of water level). See generally Cook, Repairs Expense Versus Capital Expenditures, 13 Tax L. Rev. 231 (1958); Shugerman, Basic Criteria for Distinguishing Revenue Charges From Capital Expenditures in Income Tax Computations, 49 Mich. L. Rev. 213 (1950).

[89] Midland Empire Packing Co. v. CIR, 14 TC 635, 640 (1950) (acq.) (cost of oilproofing a leaking basement to prevent contamination of the taxpayer's meat products held deductible).

[90] Reg. §§1.263(a)-1(b), -2(a).

[91] Hotel Kingkade v. CIR, 180 F2d 310 (10th Cir. 1950). In US v. Times-Mirror Co., 231 F2d 876 (9th Cir. 1956), the court held, over a persuasive dissent, that the cost of microfilming a newspaper's collection of back issues as a precaution in the event of bombing was deductible because it did not create any "capital asset or capital value."

added to the value of the property and appreciably prolonged its life as an operating hotel; and others were for replacements of furnishings and equipment having a useful life in excess of one year."[92]

Recognizing that "any properly performed repair adds value as compared with the situation existing immediately prior to the repair," however, the Tax Court has stated that "the proper test is whether the expenditure materially enhances the value, use, life expectancy, strength, or capacity [of the property] as compared with the status of the asset prior to the condition necessitating the expenditure."[93] Applying this standard, the courts have frequently allowed major expenditures to be deducted when necessitated by casualties, distinguishing these unexpected outlays from the cost of replacing or rehabilitating assets that have become exhausted or obsolescent in normal use.[94]

This concession to casualties has not been extended to changes required by governmental regulations. In *Hotel Sulgrave, Inc. v. CIR*, for example, the cost of installing a sprinkler system in a hotel, as required by a local housing agency, was held to be a nondeductible capital expenditure: "While it may not have increased the value of the hotel property or prolonged its useful life, the property became more valuable for use in the [taxpayer's] business by reason of compliance with the city's order."[95] The

---

[92] Hotel Kingkade v. CIR, supra note 91, at 312. See also Reg. §1.263(a)-1(a)(2) (amounts spent to make good exhaustion for which depreciation allowances were allowed must be capitalized).

[93] Oberman Mfg. Co. v. CIR, 47 TC 471, 483 (1967) (acq.) (insertion of expansion joint in roof to prevent leaks deductible). See also Lavery v. CIR, ¶78,901 P-H Memo TC (1978) ("cheap, expedient, fix-up job" in lieu of more costly replacement or restoration suggests repair); Hudlow v. CIR, 30 TCM (CCH) 894 (1971) (issue 9 — use of cheapest expedient to correct defect is indicative of repair).

[94] See Plainfield-Union Water Co. v. CIR, 39 TC 333 (1962) (cement lining of water pipes to reduce invasion by "aggressive" waters); Southern Ford Tractor Corp. v. CIR, 29 TC 833, 844–45 (1958) (acq.) (grading of lot to correct faulty drainage after neighboring drainage ditch was blocked); Midland Empire Packing Co. v. CIR, 14 TC 635 (1950) (acq.); American Bemberg Corp. v. CIR, 10 TC 361 (1948) (nonacq.), aff'd per curiam, 177 F2d 200 (6th Cir. 1949) (drilling and grouting of building foundations, required by subsoil cave-ins). Compare Phillips & Easton Supply Co. v. CIR, 20 TC 455, 459 (1953) (new floor installed to replace worn-out floor, not because of accelerated deterioration due to sudden external condition; held, capital expenditure).

See also Rev. Rul. 71-161, 1971-1 CB 76, 77 (cost of debris removal and repairs following deducted casualty loss "in the nature of replacement of the part of the property that was damaged" should be capitalized). Perhaps temporary repairs with a useful life of less than one year would be currently deductible if otherwise constituting an ordinary and necessary business expense.

[95] Hotel Sulgrave, Inc. v. CIR, 21 TC 619, 621 (1954). See also Russell Box Co. v. CIR, 208 F2d 452 (1st Cir. 1953) (fence installed to protect defense plant against wartime sabotage; held, nondeductible); Connally Realty Co. v. CIR, 81 F2d 221

court also rejected the taxpayer's secondary argument that the excess cost of installing the system in an old building over the cost of installing a similar system in a new building was a deductible repair:

> Its position in the main is based upon the fact that the cost of the sprinkler system was considerably in excess of what it would have been had it been installed during the construction of a new building. However, that fact cannot convert a capital item or any portion of it into a current expense. In the course of events there may be many circumstances that require an increased capital outlay. In the construction of a building, for example, a variety of factors may increase the normal expected cost, such as changes in plans, workmen's mistakes, errors in design or plan, overtime pay in order to meet a deadline, and the like. . . . Yet all such increases . . . in the *cost* of the capital asset . . . enter into the total cost which is to be depreciated over the life of the asset; they are not in the nature of current expenses.[96]

2. *Material increase in property's life.* Expenditures materially prolonging the property's life, especially as part of a general rehabilitation program, are ordinarily classified as capital expenditures.[97] In this context, the capitalization requirement extends even to minor items that, in isolation, would qualify as repairs. On the other hand, the fact that materials and supplies used to effect repairs have a long life does not preclude their classification as current expenses; otherwise, every nail, shingle, and pane of glass would

---

(5th Cir. 1936) (structural changes adjusting to city's change in street level; held, capital expenditures).

[96] Hotel Sulgrave, Inc. v. CIR, supra note 95, at 621–22. For the nondeductibility of overtime and similar payments to expedite construction and thus avoid interruptions in current business operations, see Rev. Rul. 70-332, 1970-1 CB 31, and cases therein cited.

[97] Mountain Fuel Supply Co. v. US, 449 F2d 816 (10th Cir. 1971), cert. denied, 405 US 989 (1972) (rehabilitation of pipeline that substantially prolonged life of reconditioned segments); Stoeltzing v. CIR, 266 F2d 374 (3d Cir. 1959) (reconversion of neglected building to commercial use by concentrating in one year repairs that prior owner should have made as a matter of good housekeeping over a period of time); Jones v. CIR, 242 F2d 616 (5th Cir. 1957) (reconstruction of historic but uninhabitable building in French Quarter of New Orleans, which could not be demolished under regulations of local preservation agency). See US v. Wehrli, 400 F2d 686 (10th Cir. 1968) (jury to be instructed that incidental repairs are not deductible if integrated into a general plan of capital improvement). See also Harrah's Club v. US, 661 F2d 203 (Ct. Cl. 1981) (so-called excess restoration expenses incurred in preparing antique cars for display in museum adjacent to taxpayer's casino not deductible even though total investment exceeded market value of restored cars).

have to be capitalized.[98]

3. *Repairs in the nature of replacements.* The regulations classify "repairs in the nature of replacements" as capital expenditures if they arrest deterioration and appreciably prolong the life of the property, contrasting these items with "incidental repairs."[99] In practice, this amorphous dichotomy usually results in capitalizing major replacement items (e.g., the roof, floor, or wall of a building), but structural alterations sometimes qualify as repairs.[100] The Tax Court has summarized the distinction as follows:

> It is evident that the distinction between the terms "repair" and "replacement" is one of fine degree. However, we think that a repair involves something more in the nature of a substitution of new parts or restoration of certain parts of a given whole, whereas in the instant case the entire structural unit was replaced and a new one substituted therefor without relation to the original physical facility.[101]

Another useful judicial summary of the applicable principles:

> It is, of course, true that the distinction between the terms used in the Regulations ("repair" and "replacement") is one of degree rather than of kind. We must draw the line without too much help from the definition of the two terms. Most repairs would necessarily involve substitution of new parts or ingredients for old. If the substitution is of a major unit or structural part of the nature of a floor, wall or roof, or large part thereof, so that the building as a whole may be considered to have gained appreciably in expectancy of useful life, it is a substitution so great in degree that we may well place it on the "replacement" side of the line.
>
> Where the substitutions, though numerous, are of relatively minor proportions of the physical structure and of any of its major parts, even

---

[98] See US v. Wehrli, supra note 97, at 689 ("replacement of a broken windowpane, a damaged lock, or a door, or even a periodic repainting of the entire structure, may well be treated as a deductible repair expenditure even though the benefits endure quite beyond the current year").

[99] Reg. §1.162-4.

[100] Compare Phillips & Easton Supply Co. v. CIR, 20 TC 455 (1953) (floor), Alexander Sprunt & Son v. CIR, 24 BTA 599 (1931) (acq.), rev'd on other grounds, 64 F2d 424 (4th Cir. 1933) (wall), and Rev. Rul. 82-12, 1982-1 CB 52 (telephone company's replacement of overhead wire with buried cable) with Farmers Creamery Co. v. CIR, 14 TC 879 (1950) (acq.) (replacement of less than one half of deteriorated building's walls, ceilings, and floors; deductible), Midland Empire Packing Co. v. CIR, 14 TC 635 (1950) (acq.) and American Bemberg Corp. v. CIR, 10 TC 361 (1948) (nonacq.), aff'd per curiam, 177 F2d 200 (6th Cir. 1949).

[101] Red Star Yeast & Prods. Co. v. CIR, 25 TC 321, 349 (1955) (acq.) (new sewer and drains were capital expenditures).

though high in cost, where the building as a whole may not be considered to have gained appreciably in expectancy of useful life over its expectancy when built, it falls more naturally on the "repair" side of the line . . . [102]

Another judicial statement stresses the relationship between the items replaced and the larger structure of which they are components:

Expenditures for small parts of a large machine, in order to keep that machine in an efficient working condition, under the facts of this case, are, in our opinion, ordinary and necessary expenses and are not capital expenditures. The machine as a whole was repaired by replacing the worn out parts, while the parts when they were acquired as a part of the machine were, of course, a part of the capital acquisition. The replacing of the small parts as they wear out, under such circumstances, is properly expense. When a building is erected the flooring, nails and other small supplies of course enter into the capital cost of the building, yet when a building is repaired, the cost of replacing planks in the floor, and the cost of nails in making repairs, while it might be a considerable item, is entirely different from the ordinary cost of such things when the building is being erected. As in the case of the locomotive involved in this appeal, expenditures to replace certain worn out parts, as worn out tubes, broken parts, wheels, etc., merely keep the machine in operating condition.[103]

4. *Adaptation to new or different use.* Alterations adapting a building or machine to a new or different use are capital expenditures, in the nature of improvements or betterments.[104]

5. *ADR allowances.* Taxpayers electing to depreciate their business assets under the asset depreciation range (ADR) are entitled to compute deductions for repairs under a formula, discussed elsewhere in this work,[105] that reduces the need to distinguish between "repairs" and "replacements." The ADR election is generally available for tangible personal property placed in service during the period 1971 through 1980.

---

[102] Buckland v. US, 66 F. Supp. 681, 683 (D. Conn. 1946) (expenditures amounting to 35 percent of value of building to correct leaky walls and roof; deductible, where no major unit was wholly replaced).

[103] Libby & Blouin, Ltd. v. CIR, 4 BTA 910, 914 (1926).

[104] See Coors Porcelain Co. v. CIR, 52 TC 682, 696–97 (1969), aff'd on other issues, 429 F2d 1 (10th Cir. 1970) (conversion of machine from oscillating to rotary action); West Virginia Steel Corp. v. CIR, 34 TC 851, 859–60 (1960) (rewiring of factory and adjacent storage area to rearrange equipment for more efficient operations). See also the rehabilitation cases, supra note 97, which usually involve adapting a building to a different or upgraded use.

[105] Infra ¶23.6.6.

¶20.4.9 Expenditures to Raise Equity Capital

Under a long-entrenched line of cases, a corporation's cost of raising equity capital, such as fees and commissions paid by a corporation to underwriters for selling its stock and the related legal, accounting, and printing expenses, cannot be deducted as business expenses. The principle has been extended by statute to syndication costs of partnerships.[106] Costs incurred in obtaining borrowed funds must also be capitalized,[107] although, as noted below, there is an important difference in the treatments of capitalized costs associated with equity and debt capital, respectively.

In *Emerson Electric Manufacturing Co. v. CIR*, a 1926 decision of the Board of Tax Appeals, the rule for stock issuance costs was explained as follows:

> Expenses incurred by a corporation in selling its capital stock, the proceeds from which are to be permanently invested in property or otherwise used in the operation of the business, subject to all its risks and hazards, are not deductible expenses for the reason that such expenses are incurred in connection with a capital transaction. The only effect of expenses of this character, as in the case of discount at which the shares of stock may be sold, is to reduce the capital available to the corporation, and they can not be used to reduce the income from operations. They represent a capital expenditure which should be charged against the proceeds of the stock and not recouped out of operating earnings. Further, it is clear to us that the revenue of a day or a year should not be burdened with the cost of acquiring additional capital, the benefits from which will inure [to] the corporation over a long period of years. This is the doctrine generally recognized and adopted in the treatment of expenses incident to the procuring of temporary capital through the flotation of bonds and other term securities, and in such cases the expenses are written off over the life of the indebtedness.[108]

---

[106] IRC §709(a), discussed infra ¶86.1.2.

[107] See infra ¶105.4.2.

[108] Emerson Elec. Mfg. Co. v. CIR, 3 BTA 932, 935 (1926). See General Bancshares Corp. v. CIR, 326 F2d 712 (8th Cir.), cert. denied, 379 US 832 (1964) (expenses of issuing nontaxable stock dividends not deductible; comparable to cost of raising equity capital). See also National Can Corp. v. US, 687 F2d 1107 (7th Cir. 1982) (excess of value of stock over face amount of debentures received in exchange not deductible by taxpayer parent corporation that exchanged its stock for bonds of subsidiary pursuant to bondholders' conversion privilege); Tandy Corp. v. US, 626 F2d 1186 (5th Cir. 1980) (no deduction for accrued interest and unamortized bond premium when bond converted into stock); Rev. Rul. 72-348, 1972-2 CB 97 (same for unamortized bond discount).

By analogizing the cost of raising equity capital to the cost of floating a bond issue, the court seemed to imply that the disallowed expenses could be deducted or amortized at some later time — for example, over the life of the assets acquired with the funds, over the corporation's life if it is restricted to a definite period by charter or statute, or when the corporation is dissolved. While the cost of raising borrowed funds can be amortized over the life of the loan and organizational expenses can be either amortized over the period prescribed by §248 or deducted as a loss when the corporation dissolves,[109] these analogies have been rejected for the cost of raising equity capital on the theory that "money paid out to acquire capital does not result in the acquisition of any asset other than the capital itself," so that there is nothing to be amortized or deducted as worthless.[110] Yet, over the long haul, expenses incurred to raise equity capital are as much a cost of earning income as expenses incurred to float a bond issue or to acquire a corporate charter.[111]

In a curiously restricted 1973 ruling, the IRS held that a mutual fund can deduct the cost of issuing stock, except for expenses incurred during its initial 90-day stock offering period, because the shareholders' unrestricted power to demand that their shares be redeemed "leads to the conclusion that continuous capital raising efforts by the company after the initial stock offering period is an essential part of its day-to-day business operations."[112] The ruling is on the right track. The fund's withdrawable capital and its permanent capital, however, are comparable, except for the length of time for which the capital is expected to be used in the company's business. The expenses of raising its withdrawable capital can be properly viewed as costs

---

[109] For the amortization of expenses related to borrowed funds and organizational expenses, see infra ¶¶105.4.2 and 90.2.4.

[110] Van Keuren v. CIR, 28 BTA 480, 487 (1933), and cases therein cited. See also Reg. §1.248-1(b)(3)(i) (expenses of issuing stock not amortizable under §248).

[111] Arguably, debt and equity capital differ in this respect because, while a borrower is legally obligated to repay the principal amount of a loan, a corporation's ultimate obligation to shareholders is to distribute to them what remains after the satisfaction of all creditors. If expenses of $2 are incurred in obtaining a $100 loan, for example, the $2 represents a cost of using the remaining $98 because it must be repaid at maturity. If a corporation incurs $2 of expense in issuing $100 of common stock, in contrast, the shareholder's liquidation rights consist of the sum of $98 and the corporation's net earnings on that $98. Since the $2 of issue expense need not be repaid, it is not a cost of using the shareholder's capital.

This argument suggests a distinction should be drawn between common and preferred stock. Assume a corporation incurs $2 of expense in issuing preferred stock with a liquidation preference of $100. On liquidation, the preferred shareholder is entitled to $100, not the net issue proceeds of $98. The $2 difference comes from the common shareholders' residue and effectively is a cost incurred by the common shareholders in hiring the preferred shareholder's capital.

[112] Rev. Rul. 73-463, 1973-2 CB 34.

of day-to-day operations, as the ruling holds, but the expenses of raising the permanent capital are just as clearly attributable to the corporation's operations over the long haul—and should be deductible when and if the enterprise is wound up or abandoned.

The disallowance of any deduction for the expenses of raising equity capital is partially redressed by the fact that the basis of the shares in the hands of the shareholders to whom they are issued is the amount they pay for the shares, even if the corporation nets a smaller amount. If a corporation liquidates immediately after its organization, for example, the shareholders have a loss equal to the corporation's stock issuance expenses. This is not, however,a valid reason for disallowing the expenses at the corporate level. If a corporation liquidates after earning an amount exactly equal to its stock issuance costs, for example, the earnings are taxable to the corporation and the shareholders have a loss equal to the tax, even though, before taxes, the venture broke even. More generally, the denial of any deduction for stock issuance costs has the effect of imposing a corporate tax on amounts that will ultimately be distributed to shareholders as a return of their capital. Only if a corporation is viewed as an entity divorced from its shareholders does the argument for disallowance have any credence at all.[113]

¶20.4.10 Deduction and Rapid Amortization of Certain Capital Expenditures

If a business outlay is classified as a capital expenditure, it cannot be deducted when paid or incurred, but instead must either be depreciated over its useful life or, in the case of land, goodwill, and other assets that are not exhausted by use, be held in abeyance until the property is sold or abandoned, at which time its cost can be offset against the amount realized in computing gain or loss on the sale or deducted as an abandonment loss. In a few situations, however, capitalized expenditures can never be deducted. The principal example is the cost of preparing to enter an occupation. Contrary to the usual practice of taking all business and profit-oriented expenses into account in computing taxable income, either currently or over the long haul, the IRS and the courts have not allowed taxpayers to deduct the cost of vocational and professional education, either during their productive years or on retirement or death.[114]

---

[113] Arguably, this view is appropriate. Some economists believe that the corporation income tax is passed on to consumers as higher prices or to employees as lower wages. See supra ¶3.3.3. If this is so, the tax has no effect on returns to shareholders, and the comparisons made in the text are irrelevant.

[114] See infra ¶22.1.3. Other examples are (1) the cost of investigating a business prospect, if incurred by an individual who does not enter into an actual transaction and (2) the costs of raising equity capital. See supra ¶¶20.4.4, 20.4.9.

Expenditures that are wholly disregarded in determining taxable income are very uncommon and most of them are anomalous exceptions to the basic statutory scheme of taxing net income. By contrast, in many situations, Congress has authorized immediate deductions or amortization over arbitrary periods of years for many capital expenditures. The most important of these specialized statutory deductions, most of which are discussed elsewhere in this work, are the following:

1. Section 162(d), requiring capital contributions to the Federal National Mortgage Association ("Fanny Mae") to be deducted to the extent they exceed the fair market value of the stock evidencing the contribution.[115]

2. Section 173, permitting expenditures to establish, maintain, or increase the circulation of newspapers, magazines, and other periodicals to be deducted.[116]

3. Section 174, permitting research and experimental expenditures to be deducted when paid or incurred or to be amortized over a period of not less than 60 months.[117]

4. Sections 175 and 180 permitting farmers to deduct or amortize expenditures for soil and water conservation or to prevent erosion of farming land, and to deduct expenditures for fertilizer and other soil conditioners.[118]

5. Section 190, permitting the deduction of expenditures to remove architectural and transportation barriers to the handicapped and elderly.[119]

6. Sections 248 and 709(b), permitting corporate and partnership organizational expenditures to be amortized over a period of not less than 60 months.[120]

7. Section 263(c), permitting the deduction of intangible drilling and development costs of oil and gas wells.[121]

8. Section 616, requiring expenditures in developing mines and other natural deposits (other than oil and gas wells) to be deducted or, at the taxpayer's option, to be treated as deferred expenses deductible

---

[115] See Reg. §1.162-19. See also IRC §1054 (basis adjustment to reflect deduction); Eastern Serv. Corp. v. CIR, 650 F2d 379 (2d Cir. 1981) (fair market value of FNMA stock equals mean between bid and asked prices on over-the-counter market; no discount to reflect requirement that taxpayer retain stock so long as it services mortgages held by FNMA).

[116] See infra ¶26.6.6.

[117] See infra ¶26.4.

[118] See infra ¶105.5.

[119] See infra ¶26.6.4.

[120] See infra ¶90.2.4 (corporations), ¶86.1.2 (partnerships).

[121] See infra ¶26.1.

on a ratable basis as the ores or minerals are sold.[122]

9. Section 188, permitting employer expenditures for child care facilities to be amortized over 60 months.[123]

¶20.4.11 Capitalization of Carrying Charges

Pursuant to regulations discussed elsewhere in this work, taxpayers are allowed to capitalize taxes and other carrying charges, primarily on real property while in an unimproved state or under construction.[124]

¶20.5 NONBUSINESS PROFIT-ORIENTED ACTIVITIES OF INDIVIDUALS

¶20.5.1 Introductory

Sections 212(1) and (2), enacted in 1942, allow individuals to deduct all ordinary and necessary expenses paid or incurred for the production or collection of income or for the management, conservation, or maintenance of property held for the production of income.[1] With minor exceptions,[2] therefore, it does not matter whether a taxpayer's profit-oriented activities are a trade or business within the meaning of §162; if they are, the expenses can be deducted as business expenses under §162, but if not, they can be deducted under §§212(1) and (2). In either case, the individual's tax liability is based on net rather than gross income.

In the early days of the income tax, the IRS recognized this parallel between business and other profit-oriented expenses by allowing both types to be deducted.[3] Until 1942, the only statutory foundation for the deduction of profit-oriented expenses was the predecessor of §162, relating to expenses incurred in carrying on a trade or business, and the IRS eventually abandoned its early tolerance by ruling that expenses were not deductible unless

---

[122] See infra ¶26.2.

[123] See infra ¶26.6.2.

[124] See infra ¶42.2.

[1] See generally Lang, The Scope of Deductions Under Section 212, 7 Rev. Tax'n Individuals 291 (1983).

[2] See infra notes 16–25.

[3] See, e.g., OD 537, 2 CB 175 (1920) (expense of estate for collection of income), OD 877, 4 CB 123 (1921) (investor expenses), IT 2238, IV-2 CB 49 (1925) (trustee's commission deductible from trust gross income), IT 2751, XIII-1 CB 43 (1934) (expenses with respect to management, conservation, and protection of income-producing property)—all of which were revoked by IT 3452, 1941-1 CB 205 and IT 3492, 1941-2 CB 187.

the taxpayer's profit-making activities were a trade or business.[4] This interpretation of pre-1942 law was of primary importance to individuals' expenses in managing their investments in securities, such as fees for clerical, advisory, and custodial services. The disallowance of these expenses for the lack of a trade or business was endorsed by the courts, most notably by the Supreme Court in *Higgins v. CIR*, decided in 1941.[5] Although the taxpayer in *Higgins* devoted a considerable part of his time to the management of his investments and incurred substantial expenses for clerical assistance and office space, the Supreme Court refused to overrule the trial court's finding that he was not engaged in a trade or business:

> The [taxpayer] merely kept records and collected interest and dividends from his securities, through managerial attention for his investments. No matter how large the estate or how continuous or extended the work required may be, such facts are not sufficient as a matter of law to permit the courts to reverse the decision of the Board [of Tax Appeals].[6]

Although the *Higgins* case could be defended as an exercise in statutory construction, its practical results were anomalous. Under the statutory predecessor of §165(c)(2), individuals could deduct losses incurred "in any transaction entered into for profit," even though not connected with a trade or business. Thus, the taxpayer in *Higgins* could deduct losses on sales of his securities but not expenses of investment advice, safe-deposit rental, and bookkeeping services related to the same securities. Moreover, it was admitted by the Treasury that his real estate activities constituted a trade or business, so that the expenses of those activities were deductible. It thus was not surprising that Congress decided to extend the same treatment to expenses of investing or speculating in stocks or bonds and other profit-seeking activities, which it did in 1942 by enacting the statutory predecessor of §§212(1) and (2).[7] The function of these provisions, in short, was "to

---

[4] IT 3492, supra note 3; IT 3452, supra note 3. See Kane v. CIR, 100 F2d 382 (2d Cir. 1938) (commissions paid for bookkeeper and office rental and to collect income from investments not deductible business expenses under Revenue Act of 1928).

[5] Higgins v. CIR, 312 US 212 (1941).

[6] Id. at 218. For the distinction between investors and dealers in securities under §1221, relating to capital assets, see infra ¶51.2.2. For the possibility that a securities "trader" might be engaged in a trade or business, see Levin v. US, 597 F2d 760 (Ct. Cl. 1979) (small-scale trader subject to §166(d), relating to nonbusiness bad debts).

[7] See S. Rep. No. 1631, 77th Cong., 2d Sess., reprinted in 1942-2 CB 504, 570; Diamond, Allowance of Deductions for Non-Trade or Non-Business Expenses, 3 NYU Inst. on Fed. Tax'n 241, 242-43 (1944); Brodsky & McKibbin, Deduction of Non-Trade or Non-Business Expenses, 2 Tax L. Rev. 39, 40–44 (1946). For the

remedy the inequity inherent in the disallowance [by the *Higgins* case] of expense deductions in respect of such profit-seeking activities, the income from which was nonetheless taxable."[8]

Within three years thereafter, the Supreme Court was called upon to render its first interpretation of §212. In *Bingham's Trust v. CIR*, involving the deductibility of legal fees incurred by the trustees of a testamentary trust in connection with the payment of certain legacies, the Court upheld the trial court's determination that the fees were deductible.[9] In deciding that the expenses were incurred by the trust in managing property held for the production of income, even though they did not directly produce any income, the Court stressed the parallelism between §§162 and 212:

> Section 23(a)(2) [now §§212(1) and (2)] is comparable and *in pari materia* with §23(a)(1) [now §162(a)], authorizing the deduction of business or trade expenses. Such expenses need not relate directly to the production of income for the business. It is enough that the expense, if "ordinary and necessary," is directly connected with or proximately results from the conduct of the business. . . . The effect of §23(a)(2) was to provide for a class of nonbusiness deductions coextensive with the business deductions allowed by §23(a)(1), except for the fact that, since they were not incurred in connection with a business, the sections made it necessary that they be incurred for the production of income or in the management or conservation of property held for the production of income.[10]

The Court's use of the phrase "nonbusiness deductions" is misleading in suggesting that §212 encompasses expenses incurred in personal activities. Although the "nonbusiness" label is entrenched in tax usage,[11] it is simply an abbreviated way of referring to profit-oriented activities that are not sufficiently frequent and continuous to be a trade or business.

In keeping with the parallelism between §§162 and 212(1) and (2), the term "ordinary and necessary" as used in both provisions is interpreted in the same manner.[12] The same is true of such issues as whether an expense is reasonable in amount, personal in character, or a nondeductible capital

---

parallel enactment of the statutory predecessor of §167(a)(2) (depreciation of property held for production of income), see infra ¶23.2.1.

Section 212(3), authorizing the deduction of expenses incurred in connection with the determination, collection, or refund of taxes, was added in 1954. See infra ¶20.5.4.

[8] US v. Gilmore, 372 US 39, 45 (1963).

[9] Bingham's Trust v. CIR, 325 US 365 (1945).

[10] Id. at 373–74.

[11] See, e.g., Reg. §1.212-1, headed "Nontrade or nonbusiness expenses."

[12] See infra ¶20.5.2.

outlay.[13] A similar parallelism characterizes the rulings and cases on the deductibility of expenses for travel, entertainment, education, hobbies, home offices, and vacation homes.[14]

The parallelism between §§162 and 212(1) and (2) is not complete because some statutory provisions explicitly distinguish between the two, although it is not always clear whether the legislative distinction was deliberate or inadvertent. If a reference to business expenses seems to overlook §212 items by mistake, the IRS may put them back on a plane of equality by administrative action.[15] When there is an operational difference, however, it is necessary to determine whether the taxpayer's profit-oriented activities are a trade or business. The principal areas generating distinctions or interpretative problems include the following:

1. Section 212 refers only to "individuals." Because trusts and estates determine taxable income by the rules for individuals, they also benefit from the provision.[16] Also, individual partners can deduct their respective shares of a partnership's §212 expenses.[17] Although corporations are not covered by §212, the paucity of litigation concerning corporate investment expenses suggests that corporations regularly deduct under §162 expenses of the type that individuals are authorized to deduct under §§212(1) and (2) and that the IRS does not undertake to disallow these expenses even if the

---

[13] See Reg. §§1.212-1(d) and (f) and supra ¶20.2 (personal items); Reg. §1.212-1(n) and supra ¶20.4 (capital outlays).

[14] For travel, see Lowrey v. CIR, 24 TCM (CCH) 1078 (1965) (expenses of travel to look after out-of-state investment property allowed under §212(2)); Kanelos v. CIR, 2 TCM (CCH) 806 (1943) (same re cost of traveling to Dublin to collect proceeds of lottery ticket in Irish Sweepstakes); Rev. Rul. 84-113, 1984-2 CB 60 (standards developed under §162 used in determining deductibility of travel expenses under §212); Rev. Rul. 74-473, 1974-2 CB 21 (educator who organized and led People-to-People tour to foreign country allowed to deduct expenses, including meals and lodging under §212(1)). But see Shiosaki v. CIR, 475 F2d 770 (9th Cir.), cert. denied, 414 US 830 (1973) (continued gambling losses showed absence of profit motive); Dicker v. CIR, 22 TCM (CCH) 345 (1963) (expenses of profitable trip to Las Vegas disallowed, presumably on the assumption that taxpayer was lucky rather than truly profit-oriented); Rev. Rul. 56-511, 1956-2 CB 170 (shareholder's cost of attending company's shareholders' meeting not deductible). See also infra ¶22.1 (education), ¶22.5 (hobbies, etc.), ¶22.6 (home offices and vacation homes).

To put §162 and §212 deductions for travel and entertainment on a plane of equality so far as substantiation is concerned, §274(a)(2)(B) provides that §212 activities shall be treated as a trade or business.

[15] See, e.g., infra ¶21.1.1 note 4 (meals and lodging while away from home); supra ¶20.3.3 note 37 (frustration of public policy).

[16] IRC §641(b); Bingham's Trust v. CIR, 325 US 365 (1945).

[17] Reg. §§1.702-1(a)(8), 1.703-1(a)(2)(vi); Rev. Rul. 75-523, 1975-2 CB 257 (pass through of §212 items to members of investment club partnership).

corporate activities are not a trade or business.[18] It is virtually certain, for example, that personal holding companies regularly deduct investment expenses without objection by the IRS because a practice of disallowing these expenses would undoubtedly have stimulated litigation.

2. Except for most employee business expenses, trade and business expenses are deductible from gross income in computing the adjusted gross income of individuals. Section 212 expenses, in contrast, can be deducted in determining adjusted gross income only if attributable to property held for the production of rents or royalties.[19] This distinction has several consequences. Most obviously, §212 deductions not allowable in determining adjusted gross income are denied unless the taxpayer elects to itemize deductions in lieu of taking the standard deduction.[20] Also, several deductions are subject to limits computed with reference to adjusted gross income. The deduction for medical expenses, for example, is restricted to the amount by which these expenses exceed 7.5 percent of adjusted gross income. Most §162 deductions lower this floor, but a §212 deduction does not if it is not allowable in computing adjusted gross income.[21] Further, such a §212 deduction is an item of tax preference that might cause the taxpayer to be liable for the alternative minimum tax.[22]

3. Trade and business expenses enter into the computation of net operating losses under §172 regardless of amount and, hence, can be carried over to other years, but §212 expenses are taken into account in computing net operating losses only to the extent of the taxpayer's nonbusiness income.[23]

4. Section 280A, restricting deductions for home offices, vacation homes, and other dwelling units, contains exceptions for certain trade or business uses but not for use of the property in activities covered by §212.[24]

---

[18] For an unenacted recommendation that the 1942 legislation explicitly embrace corporations, see Senate Finance Comm., Hearings on Revenue Act of 1942, 77th Cong., 2d Sess., Vol. 2., at 1734 (1942). For implicit recognition of the propriety of corporate deductions for investment expenses of the type covered by §212, see Reg. §1.861-8(e)(4) (re expenses of "stewardship" or "overseeing" functions undertaken for a corporation's "own benefit as an investor" in subsidiaries and other related corporations). See also Reg. §1.864-3(a) Ex. 2 (supervision of foreign corporation's investments not a trade or business); Howell v. CIR, 57 TC 546, 553 (1972) (acq.) ("nothing unique or improper about a corporation engaging in exclusively investment activity"). For expenses incurred by corporations that cannot be deducted because the activity is not profit-oriented, see Black Dome Corp. v. CIR, 5 TCM (CCH) 455 (1946); Savarona Ship Corp. v. CIR, 1 TCM (CCH) 89 (1942).

[19] See IRC §§62(1) and (2), discussed infra ¶30.5.

[20] See infra ¶30.5 for the standard deduction.

[21] See infra ¶36.1 for the medical deduction.

[22] See infra ¶111.3.12 for the alternative minimum tax.

[23] See IRC §172(d)(4), discussed infra ¶25.11.2.

[24] See IRC §§280A(c)(1), (2), and (4), discussed infra ¶22.6.

5. Expenses allocable to tax-exempt interest cannot be deducted under §212, but they can be deducted under §162 if they qualify as business expenses.[25]

¶20.5.2 Standards for Deduction

1. *Proximate relationship to profit-oriented activity.* Echoing the Supreme Court's language in *Bingham's Trust v. CIR*, the regulations provide that, to be deductible under §212(1) or (2), expenses "must be reasonable in amount and must bear a reasonable and proximate relation to the production or collection of taxable income or to the management, conservation, or maintenance of property held for the production of income."[26] In using the phrase "reasonable and proximate relation" in *Bingham's Trust*, the Court rejected the IRS' claim that expenses can only be deducted under §§212(1) and (2) if they produce income directly. Too relaxed a construction of the phrase, however, could permit deductions for expenses clearly outside the intended scope of §212. In *Lykes v. CIR*, for example, the Supreme Court held that legal expenses incurred in contesting a gift tax deficiency of about $150,000 did not become deductible under §212 merely because the taxpayer would have to use income-producing property to pay the deficiency if he lost the case.[27] The particular issue before the Court in *Lykes* would now be decided differently under §212(3), which was enacted in 1954, but the principle enunciated by the Court is still valid.

A contrary rule, as the Court pointed out, would permit taxpayers to deduct the cost of defending an action for damages caused by the taxpayer's negligence in driving an automobile for pleasure. Under *Lykes*, the deductibility of expenses under §212 turns on their "immediate purposes" rather than on "the more remote contributions they might make to the conservation of a taxpayer's income-producing assets by reducing his general liabilities."[28] It has not been easy, however, for courts to decide whether particular expenses exhibit the "reasonable and proximate relation" required by *Bingham's Trust* and the regulations or make only a "remote contribution" to the taxpayer's income-producing activities—particularly since "proximate" in this context is not construed as strictly as "proximate cause" in tort law.[29]

---

[25] IRC §265(1), discussed infra ¶22.7.

[26] Reg. §1.212-1(d); Bingham's Trust v. CIR, 325 US 365, 370 (1945) (ordinary and necessary requirement implies that expenses "must be reasonable in amount and must bear a reasonable and proximate relation to the management of property held for the production of income").

[27] Lykes v. CIR, 343 US 118 (1952). See also Reg. §1.212-1(m).

[28] Lykes v. CIR, supra note 27, at 125.

[29] See Surasky v. US, 325 F2d 191, 195 (5th Cir. 1963).

The regulations acknowledge that expenses can be incurred to produce income and that property can be held for the production of income even though no income is currently being received.[30] This necessarily implies that expenses can be deducted by taxpayers anticipating that the property will produce income in the future or be sold at a profit, even though their expectations ultimately turn to ashes. Moreover, the regulations provide that expenses can be deducted if related to income received in prior years or to investment property held merely to minimize a loss.[31] Although the cases and rulings have not explicitly developed a concept of "reasonable investment judgment" to epitomize the requirements of §§212(1) and (2), such a parallel to the reasonable business judgment concept used in applying §162 is implicit.

2. *Origin-of-the-claim test.* The requirement enunciated in *Bingham's Trust* that expenses must bear a "reasonable and proximate relation" to a profit-oriented activity was buttressed by *United States v. Gilmore*, where the Supreme Court held that §212(2) did not allow a taxpayer to deduct legal expenses incurred in a divorce proceeding.[32] The expenses were disallowed even though attributable to the taxpayer's successful resistance to his wife's claim that certain assets, primarily controlling stock interests in three automobile dealerships, were community property—a claim that if upheld might have resulted in the loss of his salaried posts with the companies and in the cancellation of their franchises. After reviewing *Bingham's Trust, Lykes,* and other cases interpreting §212, the Court summarized the governing rules as follows:

> The principle we derive from these cases is that the characterization, as "business" or "personal," of the litigation costs of resisting a claim depends on whether or not the claim *arises in connection with* the taxpayer's profit-seeking activities. It does not depend on the *consequences* that might result to a taxpayer's income-producing property from a failure to defeat the claim, for, as *Lykes* teaches, that "would carry us too far" and would not be compatible with the basic lines of expense deductibility drawn by Congress. . . .
>
> For these reasons, we [take] the view that the origin and character of the claim with respect to which an expense was incurred, rather than

---

[30] Reg. §1.212-1(b).

[31] Id. See also Hartford v. US, 265 F. Supp. 86, 88 (WD Wis. 1967) (income under §212 means "an inflow of money or gross receipts," as distinguished from Code concept of "taxable income"). But see Hart v. CIR, 338 F2d 410 (2d Cir. 1964) (expenses of tax-avoidance scheme, with no expectation of financial gain except through reduction of tax liability, not incurred "for production of income"); Knetsch v. US, 348 F2d 932 (Ct. Cl. 1965), cert. denied, 383 US 957 (1966) (same result under §212(2)).

[32] US v. Gilmore, 372 US 39 (1963).

its potential consequences upon the fortunes of the taxpayer, is the controlling basic test of whether the expense was "business" or "personal" and hence whether it is deductible or not under [§§212(1) and (2)].[33]

Applying these principles to the facts of the case, the Court found the expenses nondeductible:

> In classifying [the taxpayer's] legal expenses the court below did not distinguish between those relating to the claims of the wife with respect to the *existence* of community property and those involving the *division* of any such property. . . . Nor is such a breakdown necessary for a disposition of the present case. It is enough to say that in both aspects the wife's claims stemmed entirely from the marital relationship, and not, under any tenable view of things, from income-producing activity. This is obviously so as regards the claim to more than an equal division of any community property found to exist. For any such right depended entirely on the wife's making good her charges of marital infidelity on the part of the husband. The same conclusion is no less true respecting the claim relating to the existence of community property. For no such property could have existed but for the marriage relationship. Thus none of respondent's expenditures in resisting these claims can be deemed "business" expenses, and they are therefore not deductible under [§212(2)].[34]

In referring to "business expenses" in the final sentence of this extract, the Court obviously used the label as shorthand for "nonbusiness expenses within the meaning of §212."

In a companion case, *United States v. Patrick*, the Court held that legal expenses incurred by a husband in arranging a property settlement incident to a divorce could not be deducted, even though "the fees were incurred not to resist a liability, but to arrange how it could be met without depriving the taxpayer of income-producing property, the loss of which would have destroyed his capacity to earn income."[35] Pointing out that the settlement "served ultimately to protect [the taxpayer's] income-producing property from an assertion of his wife's latent marital rights," the Court held that "it would be unsound to make deductibility turn on the nature of the measures taken to forestall a claim rather than the source of the claim itself."[36]

---

[33] Id. at 48–49.

[34] Id. at 51–52. See generally Gibbs, Post-*Gilmore*—Recent Trends in the Deductibility of Professional Fees, 23 Sw. LJ 644 (1969).

[35] US v. Patrick, 372 US 53, 56 (1963).

[36] Id. at 57. For other nondeductible expenses incurred in connection with separation and divorce, see Fleischman v. CIR, 45 TC 439 (1966) (defending action

In both *Gilmore* and *Patrick*, the Court mentioned but did not pass on the government's alternative argument that the expenses in dispute were nondeductible capital outlays. In a sequel to *Gilmore*, however, the taxpayer was allowed to add the disallowed expenses to the basis of the stock in computing gain on a later sale, and the IRS evidently accepts this otherwise debatable practice.[37]

Although its career was launched in a case construing §212(2), the origin-of-the-claim standard has not been confined to that provision,[38] but has also been used in disallowing deductions claimed under §162. In *Nadiak v. CIR*, for example, a commercial airline pilot was denied a deduction under §162 for legal expenses incurred in successfully defending criminal prosecutions for assault, battery, and grand larceny, despite his contention that conviction would have resulted in the revocation of his pilot's license.[39] *Gilmore* was applied because the prosecutions and resulting legal expenses grew out of an exacerbated relationship between the taxpayer and his ex-wife. If a claim has two origins of differing characters, litigation expenses

---

to declare antenuptial contract void); Neill v. CIR, 42 TC 793 (1964) (suit to set aside property settlement agreement incident to divorce); McDonald v. CIR, 32 TCM (CCH) 488 (1973) (defending suit for child support arrearages and suing for custody); Kozak v. CIR, 30 TCM (CCH) 717 (1971) (adjusting property after annulled marriage).

[37] Gilmore v. US, 245 F. Supp. 383 (ND Cal. 1965). See George v. US, 434 F2d 1336 (Ct. Cl. 1970); Spector v. CIR, 71 TC 1017 (1979).

[38] For application of the origin-of-the-claim standard in a nondivorce context, see Wallace v. CIR, 56 TC 624, 633 (1971) (taxpayer sought son's hospitalization as mentally ill after son threatened to kill him; held, settlement payments and legal expenses incurred in defending damage action brought by son nondeductible under either §162 or §212 because origin was taxpayer's fear for personal safety). See also Woodward v. CIR, 397 US 572, 577–78 (1970) (origin-of-the-claim standard used in determining whether legal expenses were attributable to acquisition of additional stock or managing existing stock).

[39] Nadiak v. CIR, 356 F2d 911 (2d Cir. 1966). See also Serino v. US, 252 F. Supp. 717 (DSC 1966) (mother's legal expenses in successfully defending suit brought by son's creditors on theory she was son's partner; held, nondeductible because claims were based on her informal familial assistance to son and his unauthorized action in listing her as partner on credit statements, not on any financial interest in business), and cases therein cited. For converse cases, see Tolzman v. CIR, 43 TCM (CCH) 1 (1981) (deduction allowed for attorney's fees for litigation concerning corporate notes guaranteed by taxpayer; although consequence of success would have been to save taxpayer's home, which secured notes, origin of guaranty was taxpayer's investment in corporation and his trade or business as employee of corporation); Cox v. CIR, 42 TCM (CCH) 1229 (1981) (attorney's fee for filing petition in bankruptcy deductible under §162(a) in proportion of business debts to total debts; although consequences of bankruptcy discharge—protection of household goods and of portion of equity in home—were primarily personal, origin of bankruptcy was primarily business).

must be apportioned between the two.[40]

In both contexts, however, the origin-of-the-claim rationale has severe limits. If, for example, the wife in the *Gilmore* case had succeeded in establishing that the assets in dispute were community property and that she was entitled to alimony, she would undoubtedly have been entitled in later years to deduct legal expenses incurred in collecting delinquent alimony payments and custodial fees incurred in safeguarding the stock or other investment property—even though her claim to alimony and to a share in the community assets arose solely from the marital relationship. Indeed, investment expenses deducted by individuals are frequently attributable to inherited wealth and, hence, would not have been incurred save for the taxpayer's ancestry.

3. *Production or collection of income.* Expenses can be deducted under §§212(1) and (2) if paid or incurred either (1) for the production or collection of income or (2) for the management, conservation, or maintenance of property held for the production of income. It is not necessary in particular cases to assign expenses to one of these functions rather than the other, and many expenses serve both functions simultaneously. In illustrating the scope of §212, for example, the regulations refer to such investment expenses as custodial and advisory fees, clerical help, and office rent,[41] which ordinarily serve both to produce income and to manage income-producing property. Similarly, expenses incurred in administering the property of estates, trusts, and minors—also explicitly mentioned by the regulations[42] — ordinarily serve both functions at the same time. The cases and rulings, however, sometimes emphasize §212(1) rather than §212(2), or vice versa, and they are therefore separated for the purpose of discussion here.

Although §212 was enacted to permit investment expenses of the type involved in *Higgins v. CIR* to be deducted,[43] the reference in §212(1) to the "production or collection of income" is not restricted to investment income. Taxpayers have been allowed, for example, to deduct expenses incurred in

---

[40] McKeague v. US, 788 F2d 755 (Fed. Cir. 1986) (suit brought to protect employment relationship and realize a fair price on sale of stock of employer).

[41] Reg. §1.212-1(g).

[42] Reg. §1.212-1(j).

[43] Higgins v. CIR, 312 US 212 (1941).

collecting alimony,[44] lottery prizes,[45] damages for copyright infringement,[46] and claims for wrongful discharge from employment.[47]

The principal bone of contention under §212(1) is the distinction— developed primarily under §162 but equally applicable to §§212(1) and (2) —between currently deductible expenses and nondeductible capital outlays, such as expenditures to create or acquire a new investment or to add to or improve an existing one.[48] In some circumstances, expenditures are disqualified as both capital outlays and personal expenses. To illustrate these restrictions, the regulations provide that §212 does not allow the deduction of commuting expenses, expenses in seeking employment or placing oneself in a position to begin rendering personal services for compensation, campaign expenses of candidates for political office, and bar examination fees and similar expenses incurred to secure the right to practice a profession.[49]

4. *Management of property held for production of income.* To qualify for deduction under §212(2), expenses must be paid or incurred for the management, conservation, or maintenance of property held for the production of income. This statutory standard embodies two independent requirements: (1) The property must be held for the production of income and (2) the expense must entail management, conservation, or maintenance of the property.

In applying the first of these requirements, it is necessary to exclude property held for recreation, pleasure, or other personal uses, such as the taxpayer's residence. Property, however, can be converted from nonqualify-

---

[44] See Reg. §1.262-1(b)(7); Wild v. CIR, 42 TC 706 (1964) (divided court) (discussion and review of prior cases); Hesse v. CIR, 60 TC 685 (1973) (acq.), aff'd by unpublished opinion (3d Cir., Mar. 10, 1975), cert. denied, 423 US 834 (1975) (legal fees for obtaining alimony); Elliott v. CIR, 40 TC 304 (1963) (acq.) (legal fees for collecting alimony from recalcitrant husband). But see Hunter v. US, 219 F2d 69 (2d Cir. 1955) (husband cannot deduct legal fees incurred in renegotiating and reducing alimony payable by him); Wolfson v. CIR, 47 TC 290 (1966) (expenses of obtaining alimony pendente lite not deductible because joint return filed); Swenson v. CIR, 43 TC 897 (1965) (expenses of recovering child support arrearages not deductible because amounts not includable in wife's income). Expenses attributable to separation and divorce proceedings may have to be allocated in determining the deductible portion. See, e.g., Howard v. CIR, 34 TCM (CCH) 751 (1975) (allocation between deductible portion attributable to alimony and nondeductible portion attributable to property settlement and child support payments); Jernigan v. CIR, 34 TCM (CCH) 615 (1975) (allocation by agreement between parties to divorce).

[45] Kanelos v. CIR, 2 TCM (CCH) 806 (1943).

[46] Rose v. CIR, 1 TC 24 (1942) (acq.).

[47] Rev. Rul. 60-188, 1960-1 CB 28. See also Helvering v. Stormfeltz, 142 F2d 982 (8th Cir. 1944) (interest element in recovery against former guardian).

[48] For the distinction between expenses and capital outlays, see generally supra ¶20.4.

[49] Reg. §1.212-1(f).

ing to qualifying uses (or vice versa),[50] and an allocation of expenses is appropriate in the case of such dual-use property as an automobile used by an investor to visit his rental properties as well as for personal transportation.[51] These distinctions are frequently drawn in applying §§162 and 167, relating to business expenses and depreciation, respectively, and they also apply under §212(2).[52]

The second requirement—that the expenses be incurred for the management, conservation, or maintenance of property—also echoes the case law under §162 by implicitly precluding the deduction of capital outlays, such as expenses incurred in improving property and in defending, perfecting, or quieting title.[53] As pointed out by the Court of Appeals for the Fifth Circuit in *Brown v. CIR*, any expenditure to defend or perfect title to income-producing property necessarily helps to assure that the income flow will continue,[54] but the greater swallows up the lesser—if incurred to defend or perfect title, the expenditure cannot be deducted as a conservation expense. Thus, expenses incurred to assert the taxpayer's rights as an heir, legatee, or beneficiary of a trust are not deductible unless the proceeding also involves the recovery of interest, rents, damages, or other amounts includable in income, in which event an appropriate portion of the expenses can be deducted under §212(1) because they were incurred for the collection of income.[55]

---

[50] For the conversion of personal residences to business or investment status, see Reg. §1.212-1(h); infra ¶23.2.1 notes 12.

[51] For special restrictions on expenses incurred in relation to home offices and vacation homes, see §280A, discussed infra ¶22.6.

[52] See supra ¶20.2 (business expenses); infra ¶23.2.1 (depreciation). See also Yanow v. CIR, 44 TC 444 (1965), aff'd per curiam, 358 F2d 743 (3d Cir. 1966) (property rented to related corporation at below-market rate not held for production of income but for "production of deductions"); Prince Trust v. CIR, 35 TC 974 (1961) (principal beneficiary allowed to occupy trust-held residential property rent-free); Nicath Realty Co. v. CIR, 25 TCM (CCH) 1260 (1966) (home provided to daughter's family at low rental, despite extensive capital improvements).

[53] Reg. §1.212-1(k). See also Burgwin v. CIR, 31 TC 981 (1959) (nonacq.), rev'd on another issue, 277 F2d 395 (3d Cir. 1960) (expense of life beneficiary's suit claiming right to distribution of shares of stock received by trust in tax-free reorganization not deductible because incurred to acquire interest); Jones v. US, 279 F. Supp. 772 (D. Del. 1968) (repair-capital expenditure distinction under §212); Scott v. CIR, 38 TCM (CCH) 115 (1979) (same; cost of sprinkler system for apartment building held deductible as repair expense).

[54] Brown v. CIR, 215 F2d 697, 699 (5th Cir. 1954) ("when property is held for the production of income, any expenditure which relates to the perfection or defense of the taxpayer's title to the property can, in one sense, be said to have been an expenditure for the *conservation* of the property").

[55] See Reg. §1.212-1(k); Helvering v. Stormfeltz, 142 F2d 982 (8th Cir. 1944) (unliquidated claim not held for production of income; expenses not for maintenance, etc., of any specific property since taxpayer sued for money, but portion

When acknowledging that expenses to recover income are deductible, the regulations curiously couple such actions with actions to recover "investment property."[56] This suggests that the expenses of recovering any investment property can be deducted, at least if title is not disputed. Arguably, however, such expenses are only deductible if the recovery is includable in gross income because, for example, the property's adjusted basis was deducted in a prior taxable year.[57]

¶20.5.3 Common Categories of Nonbusiness Expenses

The enactment of §§212(1) and (2) was triggered by the decision in *Higgins v. CIR* involving expenses incurred by an investor in managing a large portfolio of marketable securities,[58] but the provision is not confined to expenses of this type and has been construed to encompass a diversity of expenses incurred in profit-oriented activities. Although it is impossible to describe the outer limits of §§212(1) and (2) except in vague terms, most cases and rulings involve expenses incurred in the three contexts discussed below.

1. *Investments in securities.* In applying §§212(1) and (2), investment expenses of the type involved in *Higgins v. CIR* (custodial and clerical expense, rent, etc.) are clearly deductible, as pointed out earlier in this discussion.[59] Although fees paid to investment advisers are deductible, tax-

---

allocable to recovery of interest deductible). But see Ruoff v. CIR, 277 F2d 222 (3d Cir. 1960) (expense of contesting alien property custodian's seizure of income-producing property held deductible because incurred to "conserve" property by getting it back); Cruttenden v. CIR, 644 F2d 1368 (9th Cir. 1981) (expense of recovering stock loaned to enable borrower to obtain bank loan; held, deductible because no dispute over title).

[56] Reg. §1.212-1(k).

[57] See Cruttenden v. CIR, 70 TC 191, 205 (1978) (dissenting opinion), aff'd, 644 F2d 1368 (9th Cir. 1981). For the tax benefit doctrine, see supra ¶5.7.

[58] Higgins v. CIR, 312 US 212 (1941), discussed supra ¶20.5.1.

[59] Supra ¶20.5.2. See Reg. §1.212-1(g) (advisory and custodial fees, clerical help, office rent, and similar expenses); Wiesler v. CIR, 6 TC 1148 (1946) (acq.), aff'd on other issues, 161 F2d 997 (6th Cir.), cert. denied, 332 US 842 (1947) (salaries of secretary-bookkeeper and researcher and office expenses); Mallinckrodt v. CIR, 2 TC 1128 (1943) (acq.), aff'd on other issues, 146 F2d 1 (8th Cir.), cert. denied, 324 US 871 (1945) (investment advice, custodial and collection services, financial-secretary, etc., to extent not allocable to exempt income); Abrams v. CIR, 23 TCM (CCH) 1546 (1964) (expense of moving investment office); Milner's Est. v. CIR, 1 TCM (CCH) 513 (1943) (safe-deposit box, legal and auditing expenses); Rev. Rul. 75-548, 1975-2 CB 331 (bank service charge paid by participants in automatic investment service); Rev. Rul. 70-627, 1970-2 CB 159 (same as to automatic dividend reinvestment plan); Rev. Rul. 70-544, 1970-2 CB 6, modified by Rev. Rul. 74-300, 1974-1 CB 169 (servicing, custodian, and guaranty fees paid by holders of GNMA-guaranteed mort-

payers who supervise their own investments may encounter skepticism if they deduct large travel expenses in attending to relatively modest assets, since personal pleasure may overshadow the profit-oriented activity.[60] Since 1986, further, the statute has barred the deduction under §212 of the costs of attending any "convention, seminar, or similar meeting."[61] This prohibition applies, for example, to expenses incurred in attending a seminar on investments.

After losing several cases involving expenses incurred by shareholders in proxy fights, the IRS agreed that they are deductible under §212 if "proximately" related either to the production or collection of income or to the management, conservation, or maintenance of property held for the

---

gage-backed certificates); Rev. Rul. 62-21, 1962-1 CB 37 (premium for indemnity bond required to replace lost stock certificates). See also Picker v. US, 371 F2d 486 (Ct. Cl. 1967) (cost of investment advice deductible even when not followed); Kelly v. CIR, 23 TC 682, 689 (1955) (acq.), aff'd on other issues, 228 F2d 512 (7th Cir. 1956) (failure to report any investment income does not preclude deduction of safe-deposit box rental). But see Rev. Rul. 82-59, 1982-1 CB 47 (fees for checks written for personal purposes on interest-bearing account are nondeductible personal expenses because fee is for privilege of writing checks, not for maintaining interest-bearing account). For sponsored investment plans, compare Rev. Rul. 55-23, 1955-1 CB 275 (custody fee cannot be capitalized) with Rev. Rul. 3, 1953-1 CB 37 (creation fees must be capitalized as cost of shares acquired; custody fees deductible).

[60] See Kinney v. CIR, 66 TC 122, 127 (1976) (shareholder's travel to visit corporate plants; no evidence of "rationally planned, systematic investigation"; taxpayer did not negate disguised personal motive for the travel or establish that cost was reasonable relative to size of investment); Kingsbury v. CIR, 34 TCM (CCH) 875, modified, 34 TCM (CCH) 1537 (1975) (claimed travel to visit broker's office and to pick up *Wall Street Journal* not credible); Walters v. CIR, 28 TCM (CCH) 22 (1969) (transportation to watch stock ticker at broker's office held nondeductible because activity served as entertainment; insufficient showing of relationship to taxpayer's investment activities); Rev. Rul. 56-511, 1956-2 CB 170 (travel to attend shareholders' meetings nondeductible; insufficient relationship to taxpayer's investment activities). But see IRC §274(h)(7) (no deduction under §212 for costs of attending convention or seminar; discussed infra ¶21.1.1); Steckel's Est. v. CIR, 26 TC 600 (1956), aff'd on other issues, 253 F2d 267 (6th Cir. 1958) (deduction allowed for attorney's fees allocable to watching corporate affairs on daily basis; not capital expenditure but expense of protecting investment); Gustin v. CIR, 46 TCM (CCH) 1505 (1983) (deduction allowed for travel to conventions of association of investment clubs because trips were part of systematic investigation, costs were reasonable in proportion to portfolio, and personal benefits were secondary to investment benefits); Stranahan v. CIR, 43 TCM (CCH) 883 (1982) (minority shareholder and director of corporation allowed to deduct costs incurred in attending directors' meetings and meetings with other minority shareholders and directors; case "in the realm of nuance [where] we search for the line of demarcation"); Henderson v. CIR, 27 TCM (CCH) 109 (1968) (transportation to bank, broker's office, and safe-deposit box and to meet with manager of custodial account held deductible).

[61] IRC §274(h)(7).

production of income.[62] This standard should be readily satisfied if the dispute concerns corporate business or financial policies, even if the company's dividend practices are not directly involved.[63]

Controlling shareholders of closely held corporations must be prepared to show that unusual expenses are attributable to managing, conserving, or maintaining their investment, and are not expenditures in the nature of capital contributions to increase the value of their stock.[64]

2. *Real estate.* Because the holding of real estate for rental is usually considered to be a trade or business even if management activities are modest in scale,[65] real estate owners can usually deduct their expenses under §162, and hence need not rely on §§212(1) and (2). Some rental property falls below the "business" threshold, however. When it does, §§212(1) and (2) allows deductions for management expenses, repairs, travel to visit the properties, and clerical assistance (1) provided they are not capital outlays and (2) subject to allocation or other restrictions if the property is devoted to both personal and rental purposes.[66] Similar expenses incurred in holding

---

[62] Rev. Rul. 64-236, 1964-2 CB 64, following Graham v. CIR, 326 F2d 878 (4th Cir. 1964), rather than the more relaxed business judgment standard of Surasky v. US, 325 F2d 191 (5th Cir. 1963), discussed supra text accompanying note 29. See also Nidetch v. CIR, 37 TCM (CCH) 1309 (1978) (expenses of proceeding to substitute trustee of trust holding stock in anticipation of proxy fight deductible, although change of corporate policy precluded actual battle).

[63] But see Dyer v. CIR, 352 F2d 948 (8th Cir. 1965) (expenses of proxy fight in nature of personal vendetta not deductible).

[64] For cases denying deductions in this context, see Fischer v. US, 490 F2d 218 (7th Cir. 1973) (shareholder payment to settle claim against corporation); Hewett v. CIR, 47 TC 483 (1967) (shareholder payment to salesman for selling corporate stock); Bautzer v. US, 207 Ct. Cl. 1038, 75-2 USTC ¶9769 (1975) (shareholder's payment of corporation's legal expenses; court adopted trial judge's recommended opinion (75-1 USTC ¶9246 (1975)), which contains extended analysis and collects earlier cases); Harrison Succession v. US, 392 F. Supp. 1067 (ED La. 1975) (expenses of managing oil properties transferred to corporation nondeductible despite reservation of ownership in shareholder); Kaplan v. CIR, 21 TC 134 (1953) (acq.) (travel and entertainment paid for by shareholder).

For the status of payments by corporate insiders to settle claims of impropriety in the purchase or sale of corporate shares, see infra ¶51.10.6. See also US v. Wheeler, 311 F2d 60 (5th Cir. 1962), cert. denied, 375 US 818 (1963) (payment in compromise of suit for breach of contract to sell controlling stock interest in three corporations; held, nondeductible capital expenditure to defend title to stock).

[65] For example, in Higgins v. CIR, 312 US 212 (1941), the government conceded that the taxpayer's expenses in real estate activities constituted a trade or business. For current law on this issue, see infra ¶51.3.

[66] See, e.g., Jones v. US, 279 F. Supp. 772 (D. Del. 1968) (cost of maintaining roads to rental properties); Disney v. US, 267 F. Supp. 1 (CD Cal. 1967), aff'd on other issues, 413 F2d 783 (9th Cir. 1969) (salary of secretary overseeing rental of house); Hartford v. US, 265 F. Supp. 86 (WD Wis. 1967) (insurance, legal expenses, and depreciation); Coors v. CIR, 60 TC 368 (1973) (acq.) (amount paid agency to

property for capital appreciation or future development are also deducti-ble;[67] but, unlike expenses in connection with rental property, these expenses are not deductible from gross income in computing adjusted gross income, and thus are only allowed if the taxpayer itemizes deductions.[68]

Brokerage commissions paid to purchase or sell property cannot be deducted, but must instead be added to the cost of the acquired property or offset against the selling price of the property disposed of, as the case may be.[69]

3. *Trusts and estates.* The regulations permit the deduction of the reasonable administration expenses of trusts and estates, including fiduciary fees and legal expenses incurred in performing the duties of administration, provided the amounts are not allocable to tax-exempt income[70] and are not taken as federal estate tax deductions.[71] In the case of grantor trusts, however, the expenses pass through for deduction by the grantor.[72] Moreover, the usual rules of tax accounting apply, so that administration ex-

---

manage and rent condominium unit); Scott v. CIR, 38 TCM (CCH) 115 (1979) (sprinkler system for apartment building; repair not capital expenditure); Horowitz v. CIR, 38 TCM (CCH) 108 (1979) (local transportation and parking); Nelson v. CIR, 37 TCM (CCH) 1204 (1978) (advertising and maintenance of condominium); Lord v. CIR, 10 TCM (CCH) 521 (1951) (payments for abandoned leasehold while seeking sublessee). See also Hilton v. CIR, 30 TCM (CCH) 444 (1971) (travel and lodging to collect rent); Tschupp v. CIR, 22 TCM (CCH) 466 (1963) (payments to taxpayer's sons for janitorial and repair service).

For home offices, vacation homes, etc., see infra ¶22.6.

[67] See, e.g., Harris v. CIR, 37 TCM (CCH) 1370 (1978) (expenses to keep unimproved land free of trash and debris); Markward v. CIR, 37 TCM (CCH) 1306 (1978) (repairs and maintenance on farm bought as investment). See also Connell v. CIR, 11 TCM (CCH) 771 (1952) (expenses in connection with development of property deductible under either §162 or 212).

[68] See IRC §62(a)(4), discussed supra ¶2.1.3.

[69] See infra ¶41.2.3 (purchase commissions), ¶43.1 (selling expenses). But see Braznell v. CIR, 16 TC 503 (1951) (damages for breach of obligation to pay broker's commission deductible, when property sold through different broker).

[70] Reg. §1.212-1(i). See also Bingham's Trust v. CIR, 325 US 365 (1945) (expenses incurred between termination of testamentary trust and distribution of assets to remaindermen deductible); New York Trust Co. v. US, 115 F. Supp. 661 (SDNY 1953) (executors' commissions paid by testamentary trustee that was in effect a successor trustee or administrator with will annexed; held, deductible from trust income to the extent paid on income of property turned over to trustee by executors).

[71] IRC §642(g), discussed infra ¶81.2.6.

[72] Rev. Rul. 58-53, 1958-1 CB 152. See also Rev. Rul. 76-498, 1976-2 CB 199 (fees paid to trustees of decedent's grantor trust for services rendered to date of death deductible by estate). With this exception, expenses properly allocable to estates and trusts cannot be deducted on the personal returns of fiduciaries or beneficiaries. See Erdman v. CIR, 315 F2d 762 (7th Cir. 1963) (trust beneficiary); Carrington v. US, 66-2 USTC ¶9626 (MD Fla. 1966) (not officially reported) (remainderman); Mac-Donough's Est. v. CIR, 17 TCM (CCH) 53 (1958) (legatees); Henderson v. CIR, 11

penses for an extended period into the future must be spread out and deducted in the years to which they are properly allocable rather than in the year of payment,[73] and expenditures to acquire, perfect, or defend title to trust assets are nondeductible capital outlays.[74]

The regulations similarly authorize the deduction of reasonable amounts paid or incurred for the services of guardians and committees for wards and minors and other ordinary and necessary expenses in connection with the production or collection of the ward's or minor's income or the management, conservation, or maintenance of the ward's or minor's property held for the production of income.[75] Although involuntary, these expenses are in effect treated as §212 expenses incurred by the wards or minors for the collection of their income or management of their property.[76]

Fiduciaries often incur expenses in earning their fees, commissions, or other compensation. Professional fiduciaries can deduct these expenses under §162, and nonprofessional fiduciaries can treat them as expenses of producing income under §212(1).[77] The IRS, however, has successfully resisted efforts by nonprofessional fiduciaries to deduct legal fees and settlement payments in defending suits alleging mismanagement or negligence in

---

TCM (CCH) 419 (1952) (executor); Rev. Rul. 55-190, 1955-1 CB 275 (executor or administrator).

Payment of the expense by the beneficiary may preclude the estate or trust from deducting it. See Henderson v. CIR, supra (executor's personal funds); Tolfree v. CIR, 13 TCM (CCH) 493 (1954) (legal expenses of estate paid by sole residuary legatee). See also Shertzer Trust v. CIR, 10 TC 1126, 1131 (1948) (legatees' payment of fees in connection with partition proceeding offered as reason for disallowing trust's deduction).

[73] Rev. Rul. 58-53, supra note 72.

[74] See Moore Trust v. CIR, 49 TC 430 (1968) (acq.).

[75] Reg. §1.212-1(j). See Kohnstamm v. Pedrick, 66 F. Supp. 410 (SDNY 1946) (expenses of committee for incompetent in proceeding for court instructions on whether to elect to bypass will); Morgan's Est. v. CIR, 37 TC 31 (1961), modified as to other issues, 332 F2d 144 (5th Cir. 1964) (fees allocable to incompetency proceedings of person with substantial income-producing property); McHenry v. CIR, 6 TCM (CCH) 1027 (1947) (fees and expenses paid by trustee to guardians and their counsel in litigation as to distribution of trust income).

[76] For the returns of minors, incompetents, etc., see infra ¶¶82.4.3, 82.4.4.

[77] See Rev. Rul. 72-316, 1972-1 CB 96 (nonprofessional trustee can deduct premiums for indemnification insurance under §212); Rev. Rul. 55-447, 1955-2 CB 533 (inexperienced nonprofessional executor allowed to deduct payments to coexecutors for special assistance). See also Leaf's Est. v. CIR, 23 TCM (CCH) 1497 (1964) (legal fees in will contest allocable to commissions as executrix deductible). Compare Crawford v. CIR, 5 TC 91 (1945) (acq.) (deduction allowed for attorney's fees in successful suit to establish right to act as coexecutor and receive compensation), with Statler v. CIR, 25 TC 1175, 1177 (1956) (fees and court costs to secure appointment as trustee not deductible because taxpayer seeking to obtain income "by the creation of some new interest"). For expenses of obtaining employment, see supra ¶20.4.6.

performing their fiduciary duties.[78] To the extent that these decisions rest on the view that a defense against a charge of negligence or mismanagement is inherently personal rather than profit-oriented or that the expenses are not "necessary" because negligence is not inevitable, their authority was undermined by the Supreme Court's later decision in *CIR v. Tellier*, allowing a securities dealer to deduct the legal expenses of an unsuccessful defense in a criminal prosecution for securities fraud and mail fraud arising out of his business activities.[79]

A principle of fundamental importance to heirs and to beneficiaries of trusts and estates is stated with surprising brevity and bluntness by the regulations: "Expenses paid or incurred in protecting or asserting one's rights to property of a decedent as heir or legatee, or as beneficiary under a testamentary trust, are not deductible."[80] Although the regulation only refers to testamentary trusts, taxpayers seeking to establish their rights under inter vivos trusts are subject to the same restriction.[81] The rationale for disallowance of the expenses is that they are incurred to establish or defend the claimant's rights, rather than to produce income or conserve existing property; the disputed claim is not itself viewed as property held for the production of income.[82]

Income beneficiaries have fared better because their expenses can be viewed as incurred for the production or collection of income within the

---

[78] See Fayen v. CIR, 34 TC 630 (1960), and cases therein cited.

[79] CIR v. Tellier, 383 US 687 (1966), discussed supra ¶20.3.2.

[80] Reg. §1.212-1(k).

[81] See, e.g., Lucas v. CIR, 388 F2d 472 (1st Cir. 1967). See also Martin v. US, 249 F. Supp. 204 (DSC 1966) (grantor/income-beneficiary's legal expenses of setting aside trust to regain corpus); but see Matthews v. US, 425 F2d 738 (Ct. Cl. 1970) (primary purpose test applied to allow deduction of legal fees incurred to revoke grantor trust).

[82] See, e.g., Burch v. US, 698 F2d 575 (2d Cir. 1983) (remainder beneficiary); Bliss v. US, 373 F2d 936 (Ct. Cl. 1967) (attempt to upset will); Hartt v. US, 65-2 USTC ¶9547 (D. Wyo. 1965) (not officially reported) (effort to obtain statutory share and testamentary share; origin-of-the-claim test applied); Perret v. CIR, 55 TC 712 (1971) (expenses of disinherited son to acquire share of estate); Davis' Est. v. CIR, 79 TC 503 (1982) (legal fees incurred in establishing rights as heir and protecting already-owned property from entanglement in estate litigation); Grabien v. CIR, 48 TC 750, 753 (1967) (residuary beneficiary); Hendrick v. CIR, 35 TC 1223 (1961) (acq.) (legal fees incurred to probate copy of will where original lost); Kelce v. CIR, 37 TCM (CCH) 1851-79 (1978) (expenses of establishing dower rights); Leaf's Est. v. CIR, 23 TCM (CCH) 1497 (1964) (defense of status as sole residuary legatee). See also Franklin v. CIR, 39 TC 192 (1962) (legal expenses to reduce liability for legal fees in connection with will contest); Delp v. CIR, 30 TC 1230 (1958) (payments for promise not to contest will); Rippey v. CIR, 25 TC 916 (1956) (payment by beneficiary of testamentary trust of federal estate tax deficiency made on behalf of the decedent's estate).

meaning of §212(1)[83]—a statutory support that cannot be employed by remaindermen or other beneficiaries whose rights, if established, produce amounts excludable from gross income. In keeping with this rationale, the Court of Appeals for the Third Circuit has held that §212(1) does not allow an income beneficiary of a testamentary trust to deduct legal expenses incurred in an effort to compel distribution of trust assets that, if distributed, would have been received tax free.[84] The court also rejected the taxpayer's alternative claim under §212(2), on the ground that the expenses were not "conservatory in nature" because they were incurred "not to vindicate [the taxpayer's] fully recognized basic interest in the trust estate which entitled her to current income, but rather to establish an additional equitable claim to a partial distribution of the corpus."[85]

Another qualification on the sweeping language of the regulations[86] is illustrated by a Tax Court case holding that a remainderman of a trust can deduct expenses incurred in maintaining surveillance of the fiduciary's administration of the corpus under §212(2), on the ground that they are expenses of conserving property—the taxpayer's remainder interest—held for the production of income.[87] Without explicitly rejecting the regulations, this and similar decisions limit the flat-footed disallowance of deductions for "protecting" one's rights as a beneficiary under a testamentary trust.

¶20.5.4 Expenses in Connection With the Determination, Collection, or Refund of Taxes

Section 212(3), enacted in 1954, permits individuals to deduct all the ordinary and necessary expenses paid or incurred in connection with the determination, collection, or refund of any tax, whether federal, state, local,

---

[83] See Geary v. CIR, 9 TC 8 (1947) (acq.) (fees paid by life beneficiary challenging trustee's charges to income); Tyler v. CIR, 6 TC 135 (1946) (acq.) (fees paid to establish share of annual income of estate); Mann v. CIR, 24 TCM (CCH) 855 (1965) (cost of investigating business in which trust owned stock to convince trustee that income distributions should be increased). But see Ramos v. CIR, 38 TC 820 (1962) (income beneficiary denied deduction for amount paid to settle litigation challenging his status).

[84] Burgwin v. CIR, 277 F2d 395 (3d Cir. 1960); see also Munn v. US, 455 F2d 1028 (Ct. Cl. 1972) (same as to expenses incurred by beneficiary to enforce right to receive tax-free distribution resulting from sale of trust assets).

[85] Burgwin v. CIR, supra note 84, at 397.

[86] Reg. §1.212-1(k).

[87] Hendrick v. CIR, 35 TC 1223 (1961) (acq.). See also Rowe v. CIR, 24 TC 382, 384 (1955) (acq.) (legal fees to conserve remainder interest); Fairman v. CIR, 23 TCM (CCH) 1381 (1964) (contra for contingent remainderman); Fletcher v. CIR, 10 TCM (CCH) 793 (1951) (cost of hiring attorney to protect taxpayer's income and remainder interest under trust while in military service).

or foreign.[88] Since the expenses need not be related to business or profit-oriented activities and can be deducted whether or not the tax is deducti-ble,[89] §212(3) is properly viewed as a personal deduction, comparable to the deductions for charitable contributions and medical expenses, rather than a profit-oriented deduction like §§212(1) and (2). It was enacted to fill a gap in §§212(1) and (2) and is conveniently examined in this context. Like §§212(1) and (2), §212(3) applies not only to individuals, but also to trusts and estates and to partners' distributive shares of partnership expenses; it does not encompass corporations, but they can deduct their tax-related expenses under §162.[90]

Before the enactment of §212(3), expenses incurred in determining or contesting taxes could be deducted by individuals under §162 if related to a trade or business (e.g., legal fees in determining liability for a manufactur-er's excise tax) or if §212(1) or (2) applied. Section 212(2) applied if the tax related to income-producing property (e.g., real property taxes on the tax-payer's rental property), and §212(1) applied to refund actions, regardless of the nature of the tax, to the extent that the expense was allocable to the recovery of interest. In *Bingham's Trust v. CIR*, the Supreme Court expand-ed the first category by permitting a trust to deduct legal expenses incurred in contesting an income tax deficiency arising from its use of appreciated property to satisfy a pecuniary legacy, on the ground that the expenses "were a proximate result of the holding of the [trust assets] for income."[91] In *Lykes v. CIR*, however, the Supreme Court held that expenses incurred by a donor in contesting a gift tax deficiency were not deductible under §212(1) or (2) because the gifts and related expenses did not serve to produce income or to manage or conserve property held for the production of in-come.[92] In so holding, the Court distinguished *Bingham's Trust* on the theory that the expenses in that case "were integral parts of the management or conservation of the trust property for the production of income."[93]

Two years after *Lykes* was decided, Congress enacted §212(3) without explaining why expenses related to taxes attributable to wholly personal activities, such as gifts and purchases of consumer goods, should be deducti-ble.[94] Perhaps, the implicit rationale was that the deductibility of tax-related

---

[88] See Reg. §1.212-1(1) (federal, state, and municipal taxes); Sharples v. US, 533 F2d 550 (Ct. Cl. 1976) (inclusion of foreign taxes assumed without discussion); Rev. Rul. 62-9, 1962-1 CB 35 (same).

[89] For the deduction of taxes under §164, see infra ¶32.1.

[90] See supra note 18.

[91] Bingham's Trust v. CIR, 325 US 365, 376 (1945).

[92] Lykes v. CIR, 343 US 118 (1952).

[93] Id. at 124.

[94] S. Rep. No. 1622, 83d Cong., 2d Sess. 34, 218 (1954).

expenses would encourage resistance to arbitrary determinations by the tax bureaucracy and thus contribute to a sense of fairness in the tax process.

In keeping with the broad language of §212(3) and the reference in the Senate Finance Committee's 1954 report to "any expenses incurred in contesting any liability collected as a tax or as part of the tax," the regulations state that taxpayers can deduct not only the expenses of tax counsel and of preparing returns but also expenses paid or incurred in proceedings to determine or contest the extent of tax liability.[95] Since it covers expenses "in connection with" the determination, collection, or refund of taxes, §212(3) permits taxpayers to deduct such associated expenses as appraisal fees to determine the amount of a charitable contribution or casualty loss[96] and legal fees incurred in civil or criminal proceedings for tax evasion.[97]

However, all good things have limits. A graduate of New York University's LL.M. program in taxation was informed in 1979 by the Tax Court that he could not deduct the cost of a year's tuition, meals, and lodging as an expense of preparing his federal income tax returns.[98] The opinion does not state whether this lacuna in his education was caused by inattention in class or faulty instruction; in any event, the additional lesson cost him nothing, since he appeared pro se.

---

[95] Reg. §1.212-1(1); S. Rep. No. 1622, supra note 94, at 218.

[96] Rev. Rul. 67-461, 1967-2 CB 125 (charitable contribution); Rev. Rul. 58-180, 1958-1 CB 153 (casualty loss). But see Stein v. CIR, 31 TCM (CCH) 663 (1972), aff'd by unpublished opinion (7th Cir., Mar. 4, 1974) (suggesting nondeductibility of appraisal expense if incurred in pressing insurance claim).

Taxpayers have not had much luck in deducting record keeping costs. See Callander v. CIR, 75 TC 334 (1980) (cost of checking account used to pay personal bills not deductible, even though account also served as tax record of financial transactions; functions so intertwined that determination of portion attributable to tax records "would create an administrative impracticality"); Hill v. CIR, 41 TCM (CCH) 700 (1981) (same as to cost of storing "personal records" even though required to be kept by government).

[97] See Rev. Rul. 68-662, 1968-2 CB 69 (expenses incurred by corporate officer in unsuccessful defense of criminal case charging evasion of personal and corporate taxes; held, deductible because disposition affects issue of tax liability); query whether this rationale would apply to tax-related criminal proceedings in which the government does not have to show that any tax was actually due, such as prosecutions for filing false statements or bribing a government official. For tax-related crimes, see generally infra ¶114.4. See also Johnson v. CIR, 72 TC 340 (1979) (legal fees incurred in defense of criminal prosecution for filing fraudulent tax refund claims deductible under §212(1) as expenses paid for the production of income!).

[98] Wassenaar v. CIR, 72 TC 1195 (1979) ("it strains our credulity to conclude that the petitioner's total expenses of $2,781 incurred while attending NYU . . . bear any reasonable relationship to the preparation of his tax return").

The principal areas of dispute in the application of §212(3) are:

1. *Divorce planning.* The IRS initially tried to confine §212(3) to expenses related to taxes resulting from past or settled facts, as distinguished from advice about the molding of events so as to minimize future tax liabilities, but was largely unsuccessful in defending this position in court.[99] After this restrictive reading was abandoned, a comprehensive ruling was issued relating to legal fees incident to divorce proceedings. The ruling generally allows deductions for the cost of advice relating to such matters as the federal income tax consequences of a proposed property settlement agreement, the federal income, gift, and estate tax consequences of an alimony trust, and the right to dependency exemptions for future years for the taxpayer's children.[100] The deduction is only allowed, however, if the fees attributable to the tax advice are properly substantiated and separated from amounts attributable to nontax matters.

2. *Estate planning.* The present-future distinction also arises in the context of estate planning; but, while tax advice in separation and divorce matters is ordinarily incidental to the taxpayer's obligation to make financial arrangements for his or her spouse, estate planning is almost wholly voluntary. In *Merians v. CIR*, however, decided by the Tax Court in 1973, the IRS conceded that legal fees for estate planning are deductible to the extent allocable to tax advice, even though the plan entails the molding of future events and does not grow out of any current compulsion.[101] The court, treating the case as involving allocation rather than the underlying issue of deductibility, said:

---

[99] Carpenter v. US, 338 F2d 366 (Ct. Cl. 1964) (divided court) (tax consequences of divorce and separation). For a case applying the present-future distinction, see Kaufman v. US, 227 F. Supp. 807 (WD Mo. 1963), appeal dismissed per stipulation, 328 F2d 619 (8th Cir. 1964) (cost of obtaining ruling on corporate reorganization deductible to extent allocable to tax liability in year of reorganization but not to extent allocable to basis of stock in determining gain or loss if and when sold).

[100] Rev. Rul. 72-545, 1972-2 CB 179. See also Munn v. US, 455 F2d 1028 (Ct. Cl. 1972) (expenses attributable to tax advice estimated); Hall v. US, 78-1 USTC ¶9126 (Ct. Cl. Trial Judge 1977), aff'd, 578 F2d 1389 (Ct. Cl. 1978) (no showing that tax advice expense exceeded de minimis amount).

For ethical problems in allocating legal fees, see Darrell, Conscience and Propriety in Tax Practice, 17 NYU Inst. on Fed. Tax'n 1, 20–21 (1959).

[101] Merians v. CIR, 60 TC 187 (1973) (acq.). See generally Allington, Deductibility of Estate Planning Fees, 60 ABAJ 482 (1974); Vogen & Halperin, Has Dentist Merians Pulled the Teeth From Section 212(3)? 27 Tax Lawyer 435 (1974); Note, Federal Income Tax Deductions for Estate Planning Advice: *Sidney Merians* Divides the Tax Court, 42 Geo. Wash. L. Rev. 568 (1974).

A complete analysis of an estate involves more than a consideration of tax consequences; in fact, it is basically concerned with transferring the client's property to the persons he wishes to receive it. The client's financial condition, the nature of his property, the extent to which he wants various persons to share in his estate, the needs and capacity of each intended beneficiary, the details of State law, and the need for flexibility are among the multitude of factors which are considered in establishing a plan to dispose of a client's wealth. . . . We realize that in establishing the estate plan, the attorney considered the tax implications of his actions, but we cannot accept the proposition that he considered only such implications, especially since his client did not retain separate counsel for advice on the nontax aspects of the estate plan. We also recognize that in establishing an estate plan, choices made for personal nontax reasons may have tax implications, but the consideration of such implications does not convert into tax advice the advice given concerning nontax problems.[102]

On the basis of vague testimony, the court estimated that 20 percent of the legal fee in dispute was allocable to tax advice. Although *Merians* was decided by a sharply divided court, the IRS has acquiesced in the decision, an action that seems to formalize the concession made there.

Some estate planning expenses may be deductible apart from §212(3), such as the expense of creating a revocable trust to facilitate management of the taxpayer's income-producing property,[103] but most such expenses, if not deductible under *Merians*, either are personal expenses incurred in transferring assets to objects of the taxpayer's bounty or are capital expenditures.

3. *Capital expenditures.* The IRS has argued on several occasions that expenses for tax advice should be disallowed if they are related to a capital expenditure. Although rejected in an important Court of Claims case,[104] this theory cannot be written off as yet, especially in the light of *CIR v. Idaho Power Co.*, where the Supreme Court indicated that when a provision authorizing a deduction conflicts with §263, prohibiting deductions for capital

---

[102] Merians v. CIR, supra note 101, at 189.

[103] For the cost of creating trusts, see Vest v. CIR, 57 TC 128 (1971), modified as to other issues, 481 F2d 238 (5th Cir.), cert. denied, 414 US 1092 (1973) (payments to trustee of revocable trust deductible in part); Bagley v. CIR, 8 TC 130 (1947) (acq.) (fee for advice relating to rearrangement of income-producing property deductible). But see Luman v. CIR, 79 TC 846 (1982) (no deduction for cost of establishing so-called family trust; *Bagley* distinguished and limited; divided court); Contini v. CIR, 76 TC 447 (1981) (acq.) (same; deduction allowed for cost of tax book used to prepare tax return); Mathews v. CIR, 61 TC 12 (1973), rev'd on other issues, 520 F2d 323 (5th Cir. 1975), cert. denied, 424 US 967 (1976) (cost of creating irrevocable trust personal, since origin was gift motivation).

[104] Sharples v. US, 533 F2d 550 (Ct. Cl. 1976).

expenditures, the latter takes precedence.[105] In so holding, the Court referred only to the "priority-ordering directive" of §§161 and 261; but §211 seems to subordinate §212 to §263 in the same way that §161 subordinates §167, the provision involved in the *Idaho Power Co.* case.

4. *Sham and fraudulent transactions.* Payments for tax advice that turns out to be erroneous are deductible under §212(3). If the taxpayer knowingly pays for assistance in effecting a sham transaction or committing fraud, the expense should not be considered within the intended scope of §212(3), even though if the statutory language is taken literally, the payment can be described as occurring "in connection with the determination" of a tax. There is a paucity of authority in this area, since, when sham transactions do not entail forgery, the destruction of records, or other affirmative misconduct, it is difficult to distinguish between taxpayers bent on fraud and those who are merely gullible or reckless.[106]

5. *Taxes of another person.* Although §212(3) does not explicitly provide that expenses, to be deductible, must relate to the tax liability of the person paying or incurring them, this requirement is implicit; otherwise a deduction would be allowable for gifts effected by paying the bills of a relative's tax counsel. Thus, deductions have been denied to taxpayers paying for tax advice furnished to a spouse or controlled corporation.[107] On the

---

[105] CIR v. Idaho Power Co., 418 US 1, 17 (1974), discussed supra ¶20.4.3.

[106] Compare Dooley v. CIR, 332 F2d 463 (7th Cir. 1964) (deduction denied for advice on sham transaction); Zmuda v. CIR, 79 TC 714 (1982), aff'd, 731 F2d 1417 (9th Cir. 1984) (deduction denied for fee and "seminar" costs paid to organization that provided instructions and forms for establishing foreign trusts, which were "paper entities structured solely to avoid taxes") and Rev. Rul. 80-74, 1980-1 CB 137 (because "foreign tax haven double trust" is sham, no deduction for associated costs) with Ippolito v. CIR, 24 TCM (CCH) 894 (1965), aff'd as to other issues, 364 F2d 744 (2d Cir. 1966), cert. denied, 385 US 1005 (1967) (deduction allowed for advice on similar scheme). See Collins v. CIR, 54 TC 1656 (1970) (acq.) (advice on purchase transaction including sham indebtedness; expense allowed); Rev. Rul. 79-324, 1979-2 CB 119 (no deduction for transaction of type involved in Morgan v. CIR, 37 TCM (CCH) 1661 (1977)); see also Rev. Rul. 68-662, 1968-2 CB 69.

[107] Davis v. US, 370 US 65, 74 (1962) (fees of attorney for tax advice to taxpayer's spouse in separation and divorce proceeding); Biggs v. CIR, 27 TCM (CCH) 1177 (1968), aff'd on other issues, 440 F2d 1 (6th Cir. 1971) (advice re wife's separate tax return); Southern Ariz. Bank & Trust Co. v. US, 386 F2d 1002 (Ct. Cl. 1967), cert. denied, 391 US 967 (1968) (shareholder's expenses in connection with liability for corporate taxes under stock sales agreement; no discussion of deductibility as capital loss); Moyer v. CIR, 35 TCM (CCH) 304 (1976), aff'd by unpublished opinion (3d Cir., Oct. 27, 1977) (fees of tax counsel allocable equally to corporation and taxpayer-officer but paid in full by latter; held, only one-half deductible); Rev. Rul. 81-153, 1981-1 CB 387 (portion of limited partner's investment in tax shelter partnership paid to tax adviser who reviewed prospectus with investor; if viewed as paid by investor, amount not deductible under §212 because it discharged partnership's obligation rather than investor's).

other hand, persons who succeed to someone else's tax liability, such as a shareholder of a liquidating corporation or a donee whose donor failed to pay the gift tax, have been allowed to deduct expenses incurred in resisting secondary or transferee liability.[108] Moreover, the fact that particular tax-related expenses are not deductible under §212(3) because they concern someone else's taxes does not preclude deduction in appropriate cases under §162 if, for example, the expenses are incurred to compensate employees[109] or to persuade customers to buy insurance policies or invest in tax shelters.

Tax advice procured by one party to a transaction often covers the tax status of other parties to the same transaction. Although there are no cases or rulings directly on point, the expenses are presumably deductible in full if the advice relating to the other parties follows as a matter of course from or is ancillary to the advice given to the taxpayer. An allocation may be required in other circumstances.

----

[108] Sharples v. US, 533 F2d 550 (Ct. Cl. 1976) (transferee liability); Bonnyman v. US, 156 F. Supp. 625 (ED Tenn.), aff'd per curiam, 261 F2d 835 (6th Cir. 1958) (donee's liability for unpaid gift tax).

[109] See Rev. Rul. 73-13, 1973-1 CB 42 (financial counseling fees paid by corporation for executive and includable in executive's gross income as compensation are deductible by him under §212(3) to extent allocable to tax advice).

CHAPTER

21

Travel, Entertainment, and Business Gifts

¶21.1 TRAVEL AND TRANSPORTATION

¶21.1.1 Introductory

In 1921, the general rule of §162(a), allowing the deduction of expenses paid or incurred in carrying on a trade or business, was augmented by the statutory predecessor of §162(a)(2), allowing taxpayers to deduct traveling expenses while "away from home in the pursuit of a trade or business," including amounts expended for meals and lodging.[1] Since the business traveler's automobile expenses and plane fares would be deductible under the general rule of §162(a), the primary function of the special rule of §162(a)(2) is to allow the cost of meals and lodging incurred on business trips to be deducted. Before 1921, these expenses were deductible only if, and to the extent, they exceeded "any expenditures ordinarily required for such purposes when at home."[2] Difficulties in administering this excess cost principle led the Treasury, in 1921, to propose enactment of the predecessor of §162(a)(2), allowing the entire cost of meals and lodging incurred on a business trip away from home to be deducted.[3] Although there is no explicit authorization in §212 for the deduction of expenses for meals and lodging incurred on trips related to an investor's income-producing property, other statutory provisions assume that §§162 and 212 are parallel in this respect.[4]

---

[1] In addition to costs of transportation, meals, and lodging, travel expenses include such incidentals as sample rooms, telephone and telegraph charges, laundry and cleaning bills, parking fees, and tolls. See Reg. §1.162-2(a); Rev. Rul. 80-62, 1980-1 CB 63; Rev. Rul. 63-145, 1963-2 CB 86.

Travel expenses, like any other type of business or investment expenses, can be capital expenditures rather than currently deductible expenses. See supra ¶20.4.4 (expenses to investigate investment or purchase of business).

[2] TD 3101, 3 CB 191 (1920). See generally Hoff, Tax Treatment of Home-to-Work Trip Expenses, 6 Rev. Tax'n Individuals 40 (1982); Milton, Logan & Tallant, The Travelling Taxpayer: A Rational Framework for His Deductions, 29 U. Fla. L. Rev. 119 (1976); Note, A House Is Not a Tax Home, 49 Va. L. Rev. 125 (1963).

[3] Statement of Dr. T.S. Adams, Tax Advisor to Treasury Department, Senate Finance Comm., Hearings on H.R. Rep. 8245, 67th Cong., 1st Sess. 50, 234–35 (1921) (confidential print).

[4] See IRC §§274(c), (d), (h). See also Harris v. CIR, 37 TCM (CCH) 1370 (1978) (allowing deduction of cost of meals as travel expenses under §212); Moffit v. CIR,

For most taxpayers, the cost of lodging when on a business trip is a dead loss because the cost of maintaining the taxpayer's personal residence is not diminished. Meals on the road usually cost more than they would at home. Section 162(a)(2) applies, however, even if the travel does not entail an increase in the taxpayer's living expenses. In this situation, the deduction of the expenses resembles the exclusion allowed by §119 for meals and lodging furnished to an employee for the convenience of the employer.[5] Occasionally, however, the fact that a particular taxpayer did not incur any excess cost for meals or lodging is cited as a reason for not applying §162(a)(2), as in the case of "homeless" taxpayers who travel continuously and maintain no permanent place of abode.[6]

Congress has not retreated from the basic principle of the 1921 legislation, but in 1962 it qualified the statutory language of §162(a) to disallow amounts expended for meals and lodging "which are lavish or extravagant under the circumstances." The 1962 legislation also imposed substantiation requirements to cope with exaggerated and unfounded claims.[7] In addition, foreign travel is subject to special limitations.[8]

Although the statutory term "lavish or extravagant" appears only in §162(a)(2), relating to meals and lodging, the IRS ruled in 1963 that it also applies to entertainment expenses, but went on to construe it in an easygoing manner:

> *Question*: Will entertainment expenses be subject to disallowance on grounds of being lavish or extravagant merely because they exceed a fixed dollar amount or are incurred at deluxe restaurants, hotels, night clubs and resort establishments?
>
> *Answer*: No. An expense for entertainment will not be considered lavish or extravagant merely because it involves first class accommodations or services. An expense which, considering the facts and circumstances, is reasonable will not be considered lavish or extravagant.[9]

---

31 TCM (CCH) 910, 913 n.5 (1972) (deductions "also available for meal expenses under [§]212"); Rev. Rul. 74-473, 1974-2 CB 21 (educator who originated and led People-to-People tour to foreign country allowed to deduct expenses, apparently including meals and lodging, under §212(1)).

[5] See supra ¶14.5.

[6] Bochner v. CIR, 67 TC 824, 828 (1977) (to have a "home," taxpayer "must incur substantial continuing living expenses at a permanent place of residence"); Rosenspan v. US, 438 F2d 905, 906 (2d Cir.), cert. denied, 404 US 864 (1971). See also US v. Correll, 389 US 299 (1967) (citing increased expense as a reason for upholding "sleep or rest" rule, discussed infra ¶21.1.2).

[7] For the substantiation requirements, see §274(d), discussed infra ¶21.4.

[8] See IRC §274(c) (foreign travel) and §274(h) (foreign conventions), discussed infra ¶21.1.9.

[9] Rev. Rul. 63-144, 1963-2 CB 129, 136–37. See also Denison v. CIR, 36 TCM (CCH) 1759 (1977) (under ordinary and necessary test, chauffeured Cadillac legiti-

Given the antiquity—as the age of tax provisions is measured—of §162(a)(2), it is astonishing that we still do not know whether the term "home" in the statutory phrase "away from home" refers to the taxpayer's permanent place of abode or to his business headquarters. In an early case, the Board of Tax Appeals held that the 1921 provision was "intended to allow a taxpayer a deduction of traveling expenses while away from his post of duty or place of employment on duties connected with his employment,"[10] and this statement led the IRS to espouse the view that "home" ordinarily means the place where the taxpayer is employed or conducts his business, often called the taxpayer's "tax home."[11] Asserting, however, that the "plain, obvious and rational meaning of a tax statute is always to be preferred to any narrow or hidden sense that nothing but the exigency of a hard case justifies," other courts held that "home" was used by Congress in its normal and customary meaning of residence or place of abode.[12]

In 1946, the Supreme Court had an opportunity to resolve this debate when it decided *CIR v. Flowers*, involving a lawyer whose permanent residence was in Jackson, Mississippi, but who was employed as vice-president and general counsel of a railroad with its business headquarters in Mobile, Alabama, and who deducted the cost of getting from Jackson to Mobile and his meals and lodging while there.[13] Declining to take the bait, the Court construed §162(a)(2) as imposing three conditions on the deductibility of traveling expenses:

(1) The expense must be a reasonable and necessary traveling expense, as that term is generally understood. This includes such items as transportation fares and food and lodging expenses incurred while traveling.

(2) The expense must be incurred "while away from home."

(3) The expense must be incurred in pursuit of business. This means that there must be a direct connection between the expenditure and the carrying on of the trade or business of the taxpayer or of his

---

mate expenditure; rejecting attempt by IRS to create "per se exception of 'extravagance'").

[10] Bixler v. CIR, 5 BTA 1181, 1184 (1927) (taxpayer lived in Alabama but worked in Louisiana and Texas). The Board did not explicitly rule that "home" means business headquarters; indeed, the statement quoted in the text is substantially the same as the third condition in the subsequent *Flowers* decision, discussed below.

[11] GCM 4956, VII-2 CB 128 (1928), declared obsolete by Rev. Rul. 74-268, 1974-1 CB 367. For a later ruling adhering to the "tax home" theory, see Rev. Rul. 75-432, 1975-2 CB 60. The Tax Court also has generally followed this view. E.g., Daly v. CIR, 72 TC 190 (1979).

[12] Wallace v. CIR, 144 F2d 407, 410 (9th Cir. 1944).

[13] CIR v. Flowers, 326 US 465 (1946).

employer, and that the expenditure must be necessary or appropriate to the development and pursuit of the business or trade.[14]

After observing that "whether particular expenditures fulfill these three conditions . . . is purely a question of fact in most instances" and that the Tax Court's findings on such matters should ordinarily not be disturbed,[15] the Supreme Court held that the applicable principles had been properly applied by the Tax Court to the case under review:

> The facts demonstrate clearly that the expenses were not incurred in the pursuit of the business of the taxpayer's employer, the railroad. Jackson was his regular home. Had his post of duty been in that city the cost of maintaining his home there and of commuting or driving to work concededly would be non-deductible living and personal expenses lacking the necessary direct relation to the prosecution of the business. The character of such expenses is unaltered by the circumstance that the taxpayer's post of duty was in Mobile, thereby increasing the costs of transportation, food and lodging. Whether he maintained one abode or two, whether he traveled three blocks or three hundred miles to work, the nature of these expenditures remained the same.
>
> The added costs in issue, moreover, were as unnecessary and inappropriate to the development of the railroad's business as were his personal and living costs in Jackson. They were incurred solely as the result of the taxpayer's desire to maintain a home in Jackson while working in Mobile, a factor irrelevant to the maintenance and prosecution of the railroad's legal business. The railroad did not require him to travel on business from Jackson to Mobile or to maintain living quarters in both cities. Nor did it compel him, save in one instance, to perform tasks for it in Jackson. It simply asked him to be at his principal post in Mobile as business demanded and as his personal convenience was served, allowing him to divide his business time between Mobile and Jackson as he saw fit. Except for the federal court litigation, all of the taxpayer's work in Jackson would normally have been performed in the headquarters at Mobile. The fact that he traveled frequently between the two cities and incurred extra living expenses in Mobile, while doing much of his work in Jackson, was occa-

---

[14] Id. at 470. In setting out these conditions, the Court summarized the long-standing regulations, stating that they were "deemed to possess implied legislative approval and to have the effect of law." Id. at 469. See Reg. §1.162-2.

[15] The Court's description of the special status of the Tax Court in such matters was based on Dobson v. CIR, 320 US 489 (1943), which was rejected by Congress in 1948 when it provided that Tax Court decisions are reviewable to the same extent as decisions of the district courts. See infra ¶115.6.

sioned solely by his personal propensities. The railroad gained nothing from this arrangement except the personal satisfaction of the taxpayer.

Travel expenses in pursuit of business within the meaning of [the statutory predecessor of §162(a)(2)] could arise only when the railroad's business forced the taxpayer to travel and to live temporarily at some place other than Mobile, thereby advancing the interests of the railroad. Business trips are to be identified in relation to business demands and the traveler's business headquarters. The exigencies of business rather than the personal convenience and necessities of the traveler must be the motivating factors. Such was not the case here.[16]

The business exigency principle embodied in the third condition set out in *Flowers* would have barred any deduction for the taxpayer's meals and lodging in Jackson, whether or not it was viewed as his home because he was there as a matter of personal preference rather than for business reasons. If he traveled on business to a third city, however, the business exigency principle would be satisfied, and the second condition ("away from home") would also be satisfied whether "home" refers to the taxpayer's residence or business headquarters. This would permit him to deduct the cost of meals and lodging on a trip to Washington, D.C., for example, but the amount deductible for plane fares and other transportation expenses in getting to and from Washington would depend on whether his route was Mobile-Washington-Mobile or Jackson-Washington-Jackson. In the former situation, the transportation expenses would be entirely attributable to business exigencies, but in the latter case, the business-related expense would be the lesser of (1) the actual expenses and (2) the cost of a Mobile-Washington-Mobile trip.[17]

The taxpayer's inability in *Flowers* to satisfy the business exigency test made it unnecessary for the Court to decide whether his "home" was Jackson, where he and his family lived, or Mobile, where his business office was located. This unresolved aspect of the phrase "away from home" has contin-

---

[16] CIR v. Flowers, supra note 13, at 473–74. The Court did not explain why the taxpayer, who had practiced law in Jackson for many years and continued to maintain an office there where he conducted some legal work for his Mobile employer, was not a Jackson lawyer (rather than a Mobile employee) who was away from both his residence and his place of business while working in Mobile at the employer's place of business. This reading of the facts was alluded to by Mr. Justice Rutledge, who dissented, id. at 476. The Tax Court intimated that the result might have been different if the taxpayer had continued to represent other clients in Jackson. For the status of taxpayers who reside at a minor or secondary place of business, see infra ¶21.1.6.

[17] See Daly v. CIR, 662 F2d 253 (4th Cir. 1981) (en banc 6-3 decision) (computation of travel expenses when salesman with business headquarters in Philadelphia and home in Virginia traveled to other locations on business).

ued to trouble taxpayers, the IRS, and the lower courts in later cases. After an extensive review of the cases, Judge Friendly concluded in 1971 that this lingering conceptual confusion seldom affected the result in actual practice:

> Since the Commissioner's definition of "home" as "business head-quarters" will produce the same result as the third *Flowers* condition in the overwhelming bulk of cases arising under §162(a)(2), courts have often fallen into the habit of referring to it as a ground or an alternate ground of decision . . . . But examination of the string of cases cited by plaintiff as endorsing the "business headquarters" test has revealed almost none, aside from the unique situations involving military personnel . . . , which cannot be explained on the basis that the taxpayer had no permanent residence, or was not away from it, or maintained it in a locale apart from where he regularly worked as a matter of personal choice rather than business necessity.[18]

The crucial business exigency test, however, is difficult to apply in many situations. The principal areas of difficulty, which are examined below, are:

1. The status of expenses for commuting, transporting tools and bulky equipment between the taxpayer's residence and his place of employment, getting to and from distant temporary job sites, and traveling from one business location to another within the taxpayer's general residential area.[19]
2. Whether taxpayers living at a temporary job site while retaining a place of abode at a prior place of employment are away from home in the pursuit of a trade or business.[20]
3. The status of itinerant taxpayers who have no permanent place of abode.[21]
4. The status of taxpayers with two employers or places of employment or business[22] (including legislators),[23] and two-job married couples

---

[18] Rosenspan v. US, 438 F2d 905, 911 (2d Cir.), cert. denied, 404 US 864 (1971). In CIR v. Stidger, 386 US 287 (1967), the Court held that an officer in the Marine Corps was not "away from home" while at his permanent duty station, even though his family was required to reside elsewhere. This was not a ruling that "home" means "business headquarters" for the generality of taxpayers, however, because the Court relied heavily on the special circumstances of members of the armed forces, reflected by a statutory system of allowances for their living expenses.

[19] Infra ¶21.1.3.
[20] Infra ¶21.1.4.
[21] Infra ¶21.1.5.
[22] Infra ¶21.1.6.
[23] Infra ¶21.1.7.

whose places of employment or business are in different localities.[24]

5. The deductibility of travel expenses if the taxpayer engages in both business and nonbusiness activities while on the same trip.[25]

¶21.1.2 "Away From Home" — The "Sleep or Rest" Rule

As used by §162(a)(2), the phrase "away from home" seems to focus on the distance between the taxpayer's home and the place where meals and lodging are procured, suggesting a geographical test to determine whether taxpayers are at home or "away from home." However, the IRS has long given a chronological rather than geographical meaning to the phrase, asserting that it requires the taxpayer to be "away from home" overnight or, in a later more refined version, for a period requiring either sleep or rest.[26] In *United States v. Correll*, involving a traveling salesman who left home early in the morning on daily trips of 150 to 175 miles, ate breakfast and lunch en route, and returned home in time for dinner, the Supreme Court upheld the sleep or rest rule, saying:

> Any rule in this area must make some rather arbitrary distinctions, but at least the sleep or rest rule avoids the obvious inequity of permitting the New Yorker who makes a quick trip to Washington and back, missing neither his breakfast nor his dinner at home, to deduct the cost of his lunch merely because he covers more miles than the salesman who travels locally and must finance all his meals without the help of the Federal Treasury. And the Commissioner's rule surely makes more sense than one which would allow the respondent in this case to deduct the cost of his breakfast and lunch simply because he spends a greater percentage of his time at the wheel than the commuter who eats breakfast on his way to work and lunch a block from his office.
>
> The Court of Appeals nonetheless found in the "plain language of the statute" an insuperable obstacle to the Commissioner's construction. . . . We disagree. The language of the statute — "meals and lodging . . . away from home" — is obviously not self-defining. And to the extent that the words chosen by Congress cut in either direction, they tend to support rather than defeat the Commissioner's position, for the statute speaks of "meals and lodging" as a unit, suggesting — at least arguably — that Congress contemplated a deduction for the cost of meals only where the travel in question involves lodging as well.[27]

---

[24] Infra ¶21.1.8.

[25] Infra ¶21.1.9.

[26] For the history of this interpretation, see US v. Correll, 389 US 299, 302 (1967).

[27] Id. at 303–04.

Although the taxpayer in *Correll* was on the road for about 12 hours a day, the trips were not of sufficient duration to require sleep or rest. His meals, therefore, were not deductible under §162(a)(2) "regardless of how many cities a given trip may have touched, how many miles it may have covered, or how many hours it may have consumed."[28] Following *Correll*, in a ruling concerned with railroad employees but of wider import, the IRS made the sleep or rest principle more concrete:

> Accordingly, railroad employees who stop performing their regular duties (with their employer's tacit or expressed concurrence) at away-from-home terminals in order to obtain substantial sleep or rest prior to making a return run to the home terminal, are entitled to deduct their costs of meals and lodging (including expenses incident thereto, such as tips) as traveling expenses pursuant to section 162(a) of the Code.
>
> Further, such absence need not be for an entire 24-hour day or throughout the hours from dusk until dawn, but it must be of such duration or nature that the taxpayers cannot reasonably be expected to complete the round trip without being released from duty, or otherwise stopping (with their employer's tacit or expressed concurrence) the performance of their regular duties, for sufficient time to obtain substantial sleep or rest.
>
> However, the Service does not consider the brief interval during which employees may stop, or be released from duty, for sufficient time to eat, but not to obtain substantial sleep or rest, as being an adequate rest period to satisfy the requirement for deducting the cost of meals on business trips completed within one day. Thus, amounts incurred and paid for such meals are not deductible.[29]

---

[28] Id. at 302–03.

[29] Rev. Rul. 75-170, 1975-1 CB 60. See also Barry v. CIR, 435 F2d 1290 (1st Cir. 1970) (taxpayer on long trips napped in his car at side of road; held, sleep and rest rule not satisfied, even if it can be met by trips that are not overnight, "a matter on which we intimate no view"); Rev. Rul. 75-168, 1975-1 CB 58 (truck driver on round trips of several hundred miles may deduct cost of meals and lodging during layover of about eight hours during which employer tacitly agreed to release him from duties to obtain necessary sleep or rest). See generally Weissman & Solomon, Go, Stay and Don't Return Today—Ten Years Later, 56 Taxes 189 (1978).

¶21.1.3 Commuting and Transportation Expenses

As pointed out by *Flowers*, the cost of commuting between the taxpayer's residence and place of business is not deductible.[30] This entrenched principle is based on the theory that commuting expenses are incurred not for business reasons but because the taxpayer prefers to live at a distance from his place of employment or business. It encompasses not only corporate executives who enjoy life in the suburbs, but also city dwellers who could not find housing within walking distance of their job sites even if they wanted to. This aspect of the anticommuting rule was cited in *Sanders v. CIR*, where the Court of Appeals for the Ninth Circuit held that civilian employees working at an air force base could not deduct the cost of commuting between the nearest habitable community and the base:

> There is no convincing way to distinguish the expenses here from those of suburban commuters. Petitioner's hardships are no different than those confronting the many taxpayers who cannot find suitable housing close to their urban place of employment and must daily commute to work. We see no reason why petitioners in the case at bar should receive more favored tax treatment than their urban counterparts who also cannot live near their worksites.[31]

The Tax Court has applied the same rule to employees working at a nuclear test site in a remote area of the Nevada desert, located 65 miles from the nearest habitable community.[32]

---

[30] CIR v. Flowers, 326 US 465 (1946); see also supra ¶20.2.6 notes 25 and 26 and accompanying text. The anti-commuting rule may derive from British tax law. See Gilberg v. CIR, 55 TC 611, 616 (1971).

Reimbursed commuting expenses are includable in gross income. Ireland v. US, 621 F2d 731 (5th Cir. 1980); Monroe v. CIR, 38 TCM (CCH) 466 (1979). During the period 1979 through 1985, transportation provided by an employer in a "commuter highway vehicle" was excluded from gross income by §124. See supra ¶14.8.

See also Hall v. CIR, 41 TCM (CCH) 282 (1980), aff'd per curiam, 663 F2d 1067 (1st Cir. 1981) (no deduction for damages paid to settle claim for negligent driving while commuting). But see Green v. CIR, 74 TC 1229 (1980) (professional blood donor's cost of travel between home and hospital deductible transportation cost, not nondeductible commuting expense, because she "was the container in which her product was transported to market").

[31] Sanders v. CIR, 439 F2d 296, 299 (9th Cir.), cert. denied, 404 US 864 (1971) (quoting Tax Court's opinion with approval).

[32] Coombs v. CIR, 67 TC 426, 473–77 (1976), affirmed as to daily trips between the taxpayer's residence and the work site, but reversed as to the cost of lodging and extra meals when overtime work required overnight stays at the site, 608 F2d 1269 (9th Cir. 1979) (extensive analysis). See also Pilcher v. CIR, 651 F2d 717 (10th Cir. 1981) (pipe fitter employed at job site 67 miles from family residence allowed no

Congress has anticipated and disapproved another contention taxpayers might make in seeking deductions for commuting expense:

> Commuting is not used in a trade or business or for the production of income, regardless of whether work is performed during the trip. Thus, for example, a business telephone call on a telephone installed in an automobile made while the taxpayer is commuting to work does not transform the character of the trip from commuting to business. This is also true for a business meeting held in a car while the taxpayer is commuting to work.[33]

Although the classic commuter travels to and from the same office every day, the disallowance rule applies equally to taxpayers like nurses, office temporaries, and river pilots, who go to a different job site every day in response to instructions from an employer or central registry.[34] In 1976, after winning a series of cases based on *Corell*, the IRS ruled that transportation expenses in going between the taxpayer's residence and place of work are nondeductible commuting expenses, even though the job is a temporary one, regardless of the nature of the work, the distance traveled, the mode of transportation used, or the degree of necessity.[35] The ruling's effective date, however, was indefinitely suspended in 1977.[36] The suspension avoids a curious result that would be produced by the ruling: If the employee leaves his family at their regular place of abode and lives at the temporary job site, he is "away from home" within the meaning of §162(a)(2) and may therefore deduct the cost of meals and lodging at the site;[37] if the site is close enough so that he can live at home and commute, in contrast, the transportation expenses would be nondeductible under the suspended ruling.

---

deduction for transportation expense even though taxpayer could not find closer residence); Brown v. CIR, 47 TCM (CCH) 526 (1983) (no deduction for commuting costs incurred, taxpayers contended, because racial discrimination prevented them from finding home near work).

[33] Staff of Joint Comm. on Tax'n, 98th Cong., 2d Sess., General Explanation of Revenue Provisions of Deficit Reduction Act of 1984, at 566 (Comm. Print 1984).

[34] Steinhort v. CIR, 335 F2d 496 (5th Cir. 1964) (river pilots; extensive discussion); Marot v. CIR, 36 TC 238 (1961) (nurse on 24-hour call). But see McKinley v. CIR, 37 TCM (CCH) 1769 (1978) (cost of trips to union hiring halls deductible as expenses of seeking employment; apparently conceded by IRS).

[35] Rev. Rul. 76-453, 1976-2 CB 86. The ruling also holds that a reimbursement of such expenses by the employer constitutes wages includable in gross income.

[36] TIR 1884, 1977 P-H Fed. Taxes ¶55,898. Congress subsequently barred any application of Revenue Ruling 76-453 with respect to transportation expenses paid before June 1, 1981. See S. Rep. No. 433, 96th Cong., 2d Sess. (1979), reprinted in 1980-1 CB 488. Although the congressional moratorium has long expired, the IRS has never lifted the suspension of the ruling or otherwise revisited the issue. See Ellwein v. US, 778 F2d 506 (8th Cir. 1985).

[37] Infra ¶21.1.4 (temporary versus indefinite distinction).

The issue in daily commuting cases is only the cost of transportation (typically, automobile expenses and subway, bus, and train fares). Meals and lodging costs can only be deducted under §162(a)(2) if the taxpayer is away from home long enough to require sleep or rest.

In a few situations, these transportation expenses can be deducted under the general rule of §162(a) despite the anticommuting principle:

1. *Tools and bulky equipment.* In *Fausner v. CIR*, the Supreme Court held that an airline pilot could not deduct the cost of commuting by private automobile between his home and place of employment, even though he had to take two flight and overnight bags with him, because he would have traveled by private automobile regardless of whether he had to take the bags along.[38] Since the entire cost of commuting would have been incurred in any event, the Court held that no portion thereof became deductible merely "because by happenstance" the taxpayer was required to transport these items with him.

The Court stated in *Fausner* that an allocation would be permissible, however, if a taxpayer incurred additional expenses to transport job-required tools and materials to and from work. To illustrate this possibility, an IRS ruling describes a taxpayer who ceased to commute by public transportation and began to use an automobile and trailer when transportation of bulky equipment became essential.[39] In practice, taxpayers claiming de-

---

[38] Fausner v. CIR, 413 US 838 (1973); see also Fausner v. CIR, 38 TCM (CCH) 1365 (1979), appeal dismissed without opinion (9th Cir.), cert. denied, 449 US 993 (1980) (same result for later taxable years); Fausner v. CIR, 55 TC 620 (1971) (opposite result for years prior to those involved in other two cases).

See also McCabe v. CIR, 688 F2d 102 (2d Cir.), cert. denied, 459 US 906 (1982) (no deduction to policeman required to carry gun within limits of employer city, even when off duty, for additional commuting costs incurred to avoid violating gun laws en route to work from home outside city; costs resulted primarily from choice of place to live); Pollei v. CIR, 87 TC 869 (1986) (costs of police captains' travel between headquarters and home nondeductible even though captains required to have cars with radios and to maintain radio contact with headquarters while in their cars; "commuting is one of the expenses that is so inherently personal that it cannot qualify for deduction, irrespective of its role in the taxpayers' trade or business").

[39] Rev. Rul. 75-380, 1975-2 CB 59. The ruling limits the deduction to the cost of renting the trailer, excluding a deduction for the excess of the automobile expenses over the prior cost of traveling by public transportation. This severe interpretation of *Fausner* presumably rests on the theory that the hypothetical taxpayer obtained the personal convenience of automobile travel, even if that was not what he would have chosen in the absence of the need to transport the tools. See, however, Kallander v. US, 526 F2d 1131 (Ct. Cl. 1975), which assumes that the excess of automobile expenses over public transportation expenses can be deducted by a taxpayer who proves that he would have used public facilities except for the weight of his business equipment.

ductions for automobile expenses because they transport tools to work face a formidable problem of proof. As stated by a trial judge of the Court of Claims, in a case involving an airline pilot who had to carry about 50 pounds of equipment and clothing between his home and the airport and who used his own car although public transportation was available:

> In summary, plaintiff has the burden of describing an available public transportation system, so difficult and inconvenient as to render it impractical for a commuter laden with the above-described equipment and baggage; but at the same time so convenient and practical that it would be the preferred mode of travel by a commuter not so laden. That is a difficult burden, and it has not been met.[40]

2. *Transportation expenses between business sites.* In addition to commuting between their personal residences and business headquarters, many taxpayers must leave their headquarters during the day to see customers, patients, clients, and suppliers elsewhere in the same city. Although they are not "away from home" for a period requiring sleep or rest and hence cannot deduct the cost of meals while on these daily trips, their automobile expenses, taxi fares, and other transportation expenses are "ordinary and necessary expenses paid or incurred . . . in carrying on [the taxpayers'] trade or business" within the meaning of the general rule of §162(a).

This distinction between nondeductible commuting expenses and deductible transportation expenses is readily applied to taxpayers who routinely go from their residences to their business headquarters at the beginning of every working day and return home at the end of the day, so that their business-related travel, if any, is confined to trips between one business site and another. Some taxpayers, however, do not follow this pattern: They call on customers before going to the office in the morning or after leaving it at night, do not put in an appearance at the office on some days, or have no office other than the glove compartment of a car. In general, the IRS disallows as a commuting expense the cost of going from the taxpayer's residence to the first "work location" and of returning home from the last "work location" each day.[41] In some situations, however, the IRS disallows

---

[40] Kallander v. US, supra note 39, at 1135. See also Grayson v. CIR, 36 TCM (CCH) 1201 (1977) (electrician convinced court he would have used bus and hitchhiked were it not for necessity to transport tools).

[41] See, e.g., Bovington v. US, 78-1 USTC ¶9194 (D. Mont. 1977) (not officially reported) (doctor allowed all transportation expenses incurred in his medical practice except estimated cost of one daily round trip between home and office). Compare Curphey v. CIR, 73 TC 766 (1980) (taxpayer managing rental properties from home office allowed deductions for expenses of traveling between home and properties) with Hall v. CIR, 41 TCM (CCH) 282 (1980), aff'd per curiam, 663 F2d 1067 (1st Cir. 1981) (taking work home did not make residence a place of business); Shea

the cost of two round trips on the theory that both are commuting expenses; an example is where a taxpayer spends the day at his office, goes home, and returns for additional work in the evening.[42]

Substantially similar principles govern the deductibility of transportation expenses incurred by a taxpayer working for two employers. Even though the cost of getting from one business site to the other is not incurred in carrying on the business of either employer, it is an expense of the taxpayer's trade or business of rendering personal services for compensation.[43]

¶21.1.4 Temporary vs. Indefinite Employment

In applying §162(a)(2), the IRS has for many years distinguished between "temporary" employment and employment of "indefinite" or "indeterminate" duration, permitting employees employed temporarily at a distance from their places of abode to deduct the cost of meals and lodging at temporary job sites on the theory that they are "away from home" while there. By contrast, taxpayers who accept employment of indefinite or indeterminate duration at a distant location cannot deduct the cost of living at the site even if it is inconvenient to move their personal residences to the new location.

In *Peurifoy v. CIR*, involving construction workers who were employed at a job site for periods of 8 to 20 months, the Supreme Court expressed the view that the "temporary employment" rule was inconsistent with the business exigency principle of *CIR v. Flowers*, but because the IRS contested only the application of the rule and not its validity, the Court applied the rule to the case before it.[44] The Tax Court has offered the following rationale:

> The purpose of allowing the deduction of living expenses while a
> taxpayer is "away from home" is "to mitigate the burden of the taxpay-

---

v. CIR, 38 TCM (CCH) 1178 (1979) (physician allowed no deduction for cost of driving between home and office or hospital; home not a business location merely because taxpayer on 24-hour call), Buccino v. US, 83-2 USTC ¶9697 (Ct. Cl. 1983) (not officially reported) (similar to *Shea*).

[42] Rev. Rul. 76-453, 1976-2 CB 86.

[43] See Adelberg v. CIR, 30 TCM (CCH) 68 (1971); Rev. Rul. 55-109, 1955-1 CB 261, modified by Rev. Rul. 76-453, 1976-2 CB 86. For the status of traveling expenses, including the cost of meals and lodging, where two duty posts are widely separated, see infra ¶21.1.6.

[44] Peurifoy v. CIR, 358 US 59 (1958) (Tax Court finding of temporary employment reversed by court of appeals as clearly erroneous; held, court of appeals made fair assessment of record and is affirmed). For the business exigency principle as set out in CIR v. Flowers, see supra ¶21.1.1.

er who, because of the exigencies of his trade or business, must maintain two places of abode and thereby incur additional and duplicate living expenses." . . . In furtherance of this purpose, when a taxpayer with a principal place of employment goes elsewhere to take work which is merely temporary, he may deduct the living expenses incurred at the temporary post of duty, because it would not be reasonable to expect him to move his residence under such circumstances. . . . For this purpose, temporary employment is the type which can be expected to last for only a short period of time.[45]

Another rationale is that the employee is engaged in a trade or business of his own (rendering services in the field of his competence to various employers), and that the exigencies of this business require travel when he is on temporary assignments. This would equate employees with self-employed persons like lawyers and consultants, whose trips to visit clients are regularly attributed to the exigencies of their trade or business, without regard to whether the trip is required by the exigencies of the client's business or not.[46]

The courts have differed somewhat in verbalizing the temporary versus indefinite distinction. The Court of Appeals for the Ninth Circuit reversed a decision of the Tax Court in which it held a taxpayer's employment at a particular location is indefinite if "it could not be foreseen that termination would occur within a fixed or reasonably short period";[47] according to the Ninth Circuit, the proper test is whether "there is a reasonable probability *known to him* that he may be employed for a long period of time at his new station."[48]

To simplify application of the temporary-indefinite distinction, the IRS ruled in 1974:

In general, employment at a given location is treated as temporary if both its actual and anticipated duration is less than one year. However, an employment or stay of an anticipated or actual duration of a year or more at a particular location is viewed as strongly tending to indicate presence there beyond a temporary period.[49]

---

[45] Tucker v. CIR, 55 TC 783, 786 (1971). See also Rosenspan v. US, 438 F2d 905, 912 (2d Cir.), cert. denied, 404 US 864 (1971).

[46] See Rosenspan v. US, supra note 45, at 912, pointing out that the decisions do not foreclose applying the business exigency principle to the employee's own trade or business. For the relation of this possibility to the *Flowers* case, see supra note 16.

[47] Harvey v. CIR, 32 TC 1368, 1387 (1959), rev'd, 283 F2d 491 (9th Cir. 1960).

[48] Harvey v. CIR, 283 F2d at 495. Abbott v. CIR, 42 TCM (CCH) 646 (1981) (applying Ninth Circuit's test in case appealable to that court).

[49] Rev. Rul. 74-291, 1974-1 CB 42. For decisions on the factual issue, see Waldrop v. CIR, 36 TCM (CCH) 780 (1977), and cases therein cited; Guignard v. US, 78-2 USTC ¶9637 (SD Ohio 1978) (not officially reported) (nonresident alien

A later ruling holds that an actual or expected stay of two years or more is ordinarily considered indefinite, and that an actual stay of between one and two years is treated as temporary only if the taxpayer shows that (1) at the outset, there was a realistic expectation that, within two years, the temporary employment would terminate and the taxpayer would return to his claimed home and (2) the claimed home is the taxpayer's "regular place of abode" in a "real and substantial sense."[50]

A taxpayer with no business connections within the area of his permanent residence may have special difficulties in satisfying the temporary employment rule. In *Hantzis v. CIR*, the Court of Appeals for the First Circuit held that a married Harvard Law School student could not deduct living expenses incurred during temporary summer employment in New York City because the decision to maintain the Boston residence of herself and her husband was motivated by personal rather than business considerations.[51] The IRS argued that meals and lodging costs incurred at a temporary business location are not deductible unless the taxpayer previously had a trade or business in the locale of her permanent home. The court rejected this argument, but held "that continued maintenance of a first home [must] have a business justification." Further:

> If no business exigency dictates the location of the taxpayer's usual residence, then the mere fact of his taking temporary employment elsewhere cannot supply a compelling business reason for continuing to maintain that residence. Only a taxpayer who lives one place, works another and has business ties to both is in the ambiguous situation that the temporary employment doctrine is designed to resolve. . . . Thus, a taxpayer who pursues temporary employment away from the location of his usual residence, but has no business connection with that location, is not "away from home" for purposes of section 162(a)(2).[52]

---

allowed to deduct living expenses for period employed at laboratory, to terminate within one year, but not expenses in connection with subsequent university appointment that he knew would continue for at least two years).

[50] Rev. Rul. 83-82, 1983-1 CB 45 (whether last requirement is met depends on three factors relating to contacts with claimed home and home area, duplication of living expenses, and continuing use of claimed home by taxpayer or taxpayer's family). See Frederick v. US, 603 F2d 1292 (8th Cir. 1979) (commuting expenses of construction worker employed for three years at same job site were deductible because he reasonably expected to be employed for temporary period only); Rev. Rul. 80-333, 1980-2 CB 60 (IRS will not follow *Frederick*); Hendry v. CIR, 43 TCM (CCH) 232 (1981) (taxpayer not allowed to deduct living expenses for job at which he intended to remain two years but could remain longer).

[51] Hantzis v. CIR, 638 F2d 248 (1st Cir. 1981), cert. denied, 452 US 962 (1981).

[52] Id. at 255. See also CIR v. Janss, 260 F2d 99 (8th Cir. 1958) (college student who worked as construction laborer in Alaska during summer vacation does not satisfy temporary employment exception); Bochner v. CIR, 67 TC 824, 829 (1977)

In another case, the Tax Court held that a taxpayer who stubbornly kept his family in an area offering no employment opportunities in his field, while living at a distant temporary job site, did not meet the temporary employment test because his decision was motivated by "reasons of personal choice that were *despite*, rather than *because of*, the exigencies of his trade or business."[53]

The temporary employment rule has also been held inapplicable to seasonal employees who work for the same employer at the same location on a recurring basis.[54] Sometimes it is necessary to determine whether, even if the taxpayer's employment is temporary rather than indefinite in duration, the exception is inapplicable because the taxpayer's residence has been moved from its former location to the new job site.[55]

¶21.1.5 Homeless Taxpayers

From an early date, the IRS has maintained that an itinerant unmarried taxpayer with no permanent place of abode cannot deduct the cost of meals and lodging while on the road,[56] and this principle has been accepted by the courts.[57] For courts interpreting the term "home" as used in §162(a)(2) as referring to the taxpayer's place of abode, the rationale for disallowing the cost of meals and lodging incurred by itinerant taxpayers is that they have no home from which to be away. Courts equating "home" with business headquarters ("tax home") reach the same result, either by holding that an itinerant's home is wherever he is working at the moment or

---

(aerospace engineer cannot deduct expenses at temporary job site when old residence retained despite lack of local employment opportunities); Tucker v. CIR, 55 TC 783 (1971) (temporary employment rule not satisfied where taxpayer had no business ties to area of previously established residence).

[53] Tucker v. CIR, supra note 52, at 787.

[54] Wills v. CIR, 411 F2d 537 (9th Cir. 1969) (baseball player with Los Angeles Dodgers); Gardin v. CIR, 64 TC 1079 (1975) (professional football player), collecting prior cases; Dilley v. CIR, 58 TC 276 (1972) (seasonal employee of Florida racetrack). But see Horton v. CIR, 86 TC 589 (1986) (hockey player's employment at team's home base temporary where taxpayer only had a one season contract and no expectation of renewal); Boyer v. CIR, 36 TCM (CCH) 1329 (1977) (professional skaters away from home while on road with ice show).

[55] See Six v. US, 450 F2d 66 (2d Cir. 1971) (involving Ethel Merman's theatrical engagement in New York City; remanded to determine whether her residence was Colorado or New York City and, if Colorado, whether the engagement was of temporary or indefinite duration).

[56] OD 905, 4 CB 212 (1921), declared obsolete by Rev. Rul. 69-31, 1969-1 CB 307.

[57] Rosenspan v. US, 438 F2d 905 (2d Cir.), cert. denied, 404 US 864 (1971), and cases therein cited.

by giving the term "home" its conventional meaning for this limited class of taxpayers.[58] Whatever the rationale, an itinerant differs from a taxpayer with a permanent residence in that the latter's "travel costs represent a duplication of expense or at least an incidence of expense which the existence of his permanent residence demonstrates he would not incur absent business compulsion."[59] Despite the absence of duplicative expenses, however, a homeless taxpayer's meals and lodging in the aggregate may be far more expensive than the living expenses, even with duplications, of a taxpayer who travels intermittently and returns regularly to a permanent place of abode.

Taxpayers who travel continuously often keep personal belongings in a relative's home or maintain other permanent links with a particular locality. Whether the links create a place of abode for the taxpayer is a question of fact that can only be resolved by a detailed inquiry into the taxpayer's personal habits.[60] After acknowledging that the taxpayer's relationship to an alleged place of abode is ultimately subjective, the IRS summarized the salient factors in a 1973 ruling as follows:

(1) Whether the taxpayer performs a portion of his business in the vicinity of his claimed abode and uses such abode (for purposes of his lodging) while performing such business there;

---

[58] Id. at 908 (taxpayer had no home in the conventional sense); James v. US, 308 F2d 204 (9th Cir. 1962) (implying that "home" of taxpayer without fixed and permanent place of abode is located wherever taxpayer happens to be); Bochner v. CIR, 67 TC 824 (1977) (IRS argued that taxpayer "carried his tax home on his back").

[59] Rosenspan v. US, supra note 57, at 912. See also James v. US, supra note 58, at 208 (taxpayer has a "home" for tax purposes "only when it appears that he has incurred substantial continuing living expenses at a permanent place of residence"); Cook v. CIR, 37 TCM (CCH) 771 (1978) (traveling expenses of preachers disallowed because they incurred no substantial continuing living expenses at their rent-free permanent abode).

[60] For typical cases, see Hicks v. CIR, 47 TC 71 (1966), and cases there cited; Michael v. CIR, 37 TCM (CCH) 1847 (1978) (parents' home not taxpayer's home despite sincere contrary belief because she was only there two weeks every year); Cummins v. CIR, 35 TCM (CCH) 1280 (1976) (family residence ceased being tax home as of date of taxpayer's divorce); Kaye v. CIR, 33 TCM (CCH) 553 (1974). But see Rambo v. CIR, 69 TC 920 (1978) (cabin in Montana was tax home in light of taxpayer's various ties to area and actual presence there for four to six weeks during each of years at issue).

See also Bell v. US, 591 F2d 647 (Ct. Cl. 1979) (foreign service employee on home leave between assignments has no "home" to be away from). For remedial legislation, see §913(g) (prior to repeal in 1981) (deduction allowed for taxable years prior to 1982 for certain home leave travel expenses).

(2) Whether the taxpayer's living expenses incurred at his claimed abode are duplicated because his business requires him to be away therefrom; and

(3) Whether the taxpayer

(a) has not abandoned the vicinity in which his historical place of lodging and his claimed abode are both located, [or] (b) has a member or members of his family (marital or lineal only) currently residing at his claimed abode, [or] (c) uses his claimed abode frequently for purposes of his lodging.[61]

¶21.1.6 Taxpayers With Two Employers or Places of Business

Taxpayers with two employers or two places of business can deduct the cost of getting from one site to the other during the same day, on the theory that it is an ordinary and necessary expense of carrying out the taxpayer's combined trade or business of working at both locations.[62] Thus, the two-employer taxpayer is treated the same as an employee who is required by a single employer to travel from one branch office to another, even though the two-employer employee is not performing services for either employer while getting from one site to another.

Similarly, away-from-home travel expenses incurred by a taxpayer who travels between two widely separated jobs are deductible. The leading case is *Sherman v. CIR*, where the Tax Court stated:

> [A] taxpayer may have more than one occupation or business, and . . . where it is shown that the taxpayer has two occupations which require him to spend a substantial amount of time in each of two cities, he is entitled to the deduction of traveling and other ordinary and

---

[61] Rev. Rul. 73-529, 1973-2 CB 37 (tests to be applied only to taxpayer who has no regular or principal place of business; taxpayer failing to satisfy at least two factors regarded as itinerant whose home is wherever he happens to work and who thus cannot be "away from home" for purposes of §162(a)(2)). See also Rev. Rul. 80-212, 1980-2 CB 58 (Rev. Rul. 73-529 applied to taxpayer participating in employer's 12-month training program at various sites throughout country pending reassignment in new location).

[62] Curphey v. CIR, 73 TC 766 (1980); Adelberg v. CIR, 30 TCM (CCH) 68 (1971) (engineer drove from work to part-time teaching job; transportation expense deductible); Rev. Rul. 55-109, 1955-1 CB 261, modified by Rev. Rul. 76-453, 1976-2 CB 86. But see Green v. CIR, 59 TC 456 (1972) (where taxpayer had principal job in city and used den in suburban home for evening work, two-business rule does not allow deduction of commuting expenses). Compare Freedman v. CIR, 301 F2d 359 (5th Cir. 1962) (no deduction for expense of settling claim for accident caused by taxpayer while driving between sites of taxpayer's two separate businesses) with Dancer v. CIR, 73 TC 1103 (1980) (deduction allowed where accident occurred while driving between two locations of same business).

necessary business expenses incurred in connection with attendance upon the one removed from his residence.[63]

In *Sherman*, the taxpayer had a proprietorship in New York City and was employed in Worcester, Massachusetts. On finding that Worcester was his tax home, the Tax Court allowed a deduction for the expenses of traveling to and from New York City, including meals and lodging while there.

The extent to which a taxpayer with two employers can deduct overnight meal and lodging expenses (as in *Sherman*) depends on where his "tax home" is. The IRS considers the taxpayer's principal place of business during the tax year to be his tax home; if he maintains homes at both posts, he can deduct meal and lodging expenses at the minor post if properly attributable to the taxpayer's presence there in actual performance of his business duties.[64] This is so even if the taxpayer maintains his family at the minor post of duty.[65] The principal post is generally ascertained on an objective basis, considering the time spent at each location, the proportion of income and business generated by each, and other relevant factors.[66]

While the taxpayer's "tax home" must be identified in order to determine the deductibility of meals and lodging, the principal-minor distinction is not applied to transportation expenses, since they are deductible if incurred for business reasons whether the taxpayer is "away from home" or not.[67]

---

[63] Sherman v. CIR, 16 TC 332, 337 (1951) (acq.).

[64] Rev. Rul. 75-432, 1975-2 CB 60, superseding Rev. Rul. 54-497, 1954-2 CB 75; Rev. Rul. 63-82, 1963-1 CB 33, modified by Rev. Rul. 76-453, 1976-2 CB 86 (taxpayer can deduct overnight meal and lodging expenses at minor post of duty, plus transportation costs of trips between locations for business reasons whether or not overnight). See Puckett v. CIR, 56 TC 1092 (1971) (acq.) (meal and lodging expenses at minor post would have been deductible but for failure to meet substantiation requirement; transportation expenses allowed). But see Folkman v. US, 433 F. Supp. 1022 (D. Nev. 1977) (minor post held tax home; meals and lodging at other post attributable to performance of business duties deductible).

[65] Rev. Rul. 55-604, 1955-2 CB 49 (taxpayer's family at minor post of duty; deduction limited to portion of meals and lodging properly attributable to taxpayer's presence there while in actual performance of duties).

[66] See Markey v. CIR, 490 F2d 1249 (6th Cir. 1974); Sherman v. CIR, supra note 63. Compare US v. LeBlanc, 278 F2d 571 (5th Cir. 1960) (state supreme court justice required by constitution to maintain residence in home district allowed to deduct cost of apartment in state capital even though three fourths of his work done at capital) with Jones v. US, 648 F2d 1081 (6th Cir. 1981) (state justices could deduct costs of travel and living while in home district because required to work in both state capital and home district; state capital was "tax home" because two thirds of work done there; home district was "minor place of business"). For legislators, see infra ¶21.1.7.

[67] See Rev. Rul. 63-82, supra note 64. See also Powell v. CIR, 34 BTA 655 (acq.), aff'd on other issues, 94 F2d 483 (1st Cir. 1938) (business split between New

¶21.1.7 Federal and State Legislators

In *Lindsay v. CIR*, decided in 1936, the Board of Tax Appeals applied the "tax home" rationale to a member of the House of Representatives, holding that his living expenses in the District of Columbia were not deductible, partly because a federal statute specified that his office was to be "exercised" there.[68] As for the cost of trips to and from his congressional district, the Board ruled that "visiting his constituents in their places of assembly" was a nondeductible personal function and that he had failed to establish the amount of expenses incurred on official trips to his home district. Congress subsequently enacted the last sentence of §162(a), providing that a congressman's district "shall be considered his home" for travel-expense purposes, but that no more than $3,000 may be deducted for away-from-home living expenses per taxable year.[69]

In *Montgomery v. CIR*, the Court of Appeals for the Sixth Circuit held that a state legislator had two places of business, one at the state capital and the other in his home district. Applying the principal/minor-place-of-business rule, the court upheld the Tax Court's finding of fact that his principal post was at the state capital, which barred a deduction for his living expenses while there.[70]

Because of uncertainties in applying the principal/minor distinction and because of state-to-state variations in the length of legislative sessions, Congress enacted §162(h), applicable for taxable years after 1975, providing an elective scheme for state legislators who live more than 50 miles from their state capitol.[71] An electing legislator's home is deemed to be his place of residence within his district. His deduction for living expenses while away from home on legislative business is determined by formula. Under the formula, a daily allowance is provided equal to the greater of two amounts: (1) the per diem allowance for employees of the executive branch

---

York and Boston; travel, food, and lodging expenses allowed while away from home); Brown v. CIR, 13 BTA 832 (1928) (acq.) (taxpayer accepting government appointment in Washington, D.C., while retaining law practice in Ohio allowed to deduct meals and lodging in Washington; travel expenses deductible regardless of location of home).

[68] Lindsay v. CIR, 34 BTA 840 (1936).

[69] See Rev. Rul. 73-468, 1973-2 CB 77 (newly elected member of Congress may deduct moving expenses between home district and Washington under §217, discussed infra ¶22.4).

[70] Montgomery v. CIR, 532 F2d 1088 (6th Cir. 1976). See also Rev. Rul. 61-67, 1961-1 CB 25, modified by Rev. Rul. 76-453, 1976-2 CB 86 (whether state capital or home district is state legislator's principal duty post depends primarily on relative amount of time required to be spent for business purposes at the two posts).

[71] Section 162(h) was enacted in 1981, but it replaced an uncodified provision enacted in 1976 that allowed a similar election. For the 1976 legislation, see Rev. Rul. 82-33, 1982-1 CB 28; Chappie v. CIR, 73 TC 823 (1980).

of the federal government while traveling on government business or (2) the equivalent allowance for employees of the legislator's state, but not more than 110 percent of the federal allowance. An electing legislator's annual deduction is the applicable one of these two amounts, multiplied by the number of "legislative days" during the year. The term "legislative day" is defined to include (1) a day when the legislature is in session, (2) each day in a break of four days or less between days in session (i.e., weekend and long weekend breaks), and (3) any other day when "the [taxpayer's] physical presence . . . was formally recorded at a meeting of a committee of [the] legislature." The meals and lodging deduction of a legislator who is not eligible to elect or forgoes the election is determined under the case law.

¶21.1.8 Two-Job Married Couples

In a series of cases, the courts have held that when husband and wife are employed or conduct businesses in two widely separated locations, they cannot deduct living expenses incurred at either site.[72] When the husband is at his duty post, his living expenses are not attributable to business exigencies and hence do not satisfy the third condition set out in the *Flowers* case;[73] when he is at his wife's duty post, his living expenses are also personal rather than business expenses. The same is true, mutatis mutandis, for the wife. This barrier applies not only to their living expenses at both sites, but also to the cost of getting from one to the other, since the travel is animated by personal rather than business reasons.

¶21.1.9 Combined Business-Pleasure Travel

In practice, §162(a)(2) has been plagued by the fact that travel frequently entails both business and personal components.[74] Taxpayers tend to exaggerate the business reasons for trips that combine business with pleasure,

---

[72] See Foote v. CIR, 67 TC 1 (1976), and cases therein cited. In Wallace v. CIR, 144 F2d 407 (9th Cir. 1944), an actress domiciled with her husband in San Francisco, where he was employed, was allowed to deduct the cost of a three-month stay in Hollywood. This may have been a justified application of the temporary-employment principle (supra ¶21.1.4), but its broader implications are inconsistent with the business exigency aspect of the subsequently decided *Flowers* case. See Daly v. CIR, 662 F2d 253, 255 (4th Cir. 1981) (Murnaghan, J., concurring) (expressing the hope that Congress will make "rules detailing appropriate circumstances in which the one spouse's situation should play a significant role in ascertaining the situs of the other spouse's tax home").

[73] CIR v. Flowers, 326 US 465 (1946), discussed supra ¶21.1.1.

[74] For analysis of this issue, see Klein, The Deductibility of Transportation Expenses of a Combination Business and Pleasure Trip—A Conceptual Analysis, 18 Stan. L. Rev. 1099 (1966). For attempts by taxpayers to deduct vacation travel

while revenue agents naturally listen skeptically to taxpayers' explanations. In an effort to separate fact from fiction, the IRS, Congress, and the courts have addressed themselves to the following troublesome aspects of this area:

1. *Primary purpose.* The regulations provide that traveling expenses to and from a destination at which the taxpayer engages in both business and personal activities are deductible if the trip is "related primarily" to the taxpayer's trade or business, but not if it is "primarily personal in nature."[75] In the latter case, expenses at the destination are deductible to the extent properly allocable to the business activities conducted there; conversely, expenses at the destination properly allocable to personal activities cannot be deducted even if the trip was undertaken primarily for business reasons.[76] Whether a trip is primarily related to the taxpayer's business or is primarily personal in nature depends on all the facts and circumstances, especially the relative amounts of time devoted to the two categories of activities.[77]

2. *Foreign travel.* In addition to satisfying the basic tests for deductibility imposed by §162(a) or §212, travel outside the United States must run the gauntlet of §274(c), which disallows any deduction for expenses not allocable to business or profit-oriented activities.[78] Since expenses of sight-

---

expenses on the ground that they were investigating business opportunities, see supra ¶20.4.4 notes 53–54.

[75] Reg. §1.162-2(b)(1).

[76] Id. See also Cannon v. CIR, 24 TCM (CCH) 1074 (1965) (trip primarily to attend foreign business convention, combined with extensive sightseeing throughout Europe that also included some business activities; held, taxpayer can deduct cost of getting to and from convention, living expenses while there, and an estimated amount for business activities elsewhere, but not expenses attributable to sightseeing).

[77] Reg. §1.162-2(b)(2). See Buddy Schoellkopf Prods., Inc. v. CIR, 65 TC 640, 662 (1975) (acq. and nonacq. on other issues) (president's Alaskan Arctic hunt primarily personal, not to test cold-weather gear); Ballantine v. CIR, 46 TC 272 (1966) (acq.) (newspaper publisher's South American trip for personal satisfaction despite claim that it furnished newspaper with writing based on first-hand experience); Brotman v. CIR, 36 TCM (CCH) 279 (1977) (accountant's trip to California principally for personal enjoyment rather than finding clients); Stroope v. CIR, 34 TCM (CCH) 1524 (1975) (real estate salesman's Hawaiian trip predominantly for vacation rather than investigating real estate opportunities). For educational travel, see infra ¶22.1.4. For conventions, see infra text accompanying notes 84–98.

Employer-mandated "home leave" for foreign employees has been held to be business travel, at least for foreign service officers. Brewin v. CIR, 639 F2d 805 (DC Cir. 1981) (deduction allowed for expenses of foreign service officer's mandatory home leave); Rev. Rul. 82-2, 1982-1 CB 27 (IRS agrees with *Brewin*). For a short-lived statutory rule providing the same result, see §913(g) (enacted in 1978 but repealed in 1981).

[78] When enacted in 1962, §274(c) applied to domestic as well as foreign travel, but it was restricted to foreign travel in 1964. See S. Rep. No. 1881, 87th Cong., 2d Sess., reprinted in 1962-3 CB 707, 740; Conf. Rep. No. 1149, 88th Cong., 2d Sess.,

seeing and other personal activities on a business trip are not deductible in any event (whether the trip is within or without the United States),[79] the significance of §274(c) is that, when applicable, it disallows an appropriate fraction of the taxpayer's expenses in getting to and from the business destination. For example, if a taxpayer travels primarily for business purposes from New York City to London, flies to Paris for nonbusiness activities, and returns to New York City via London, the expenses of the London-Paris-London leg of the trip are nondeductible personal expenses without regard to §274(c), but if §274(c) applies, part of the cost of getting from New York City to London and back is also disallowed.[80]

Section 274(c) does not apply if the travel outside the United States does not exceed seven consecutive days, or if the time attributable to nonbusiness activities constitutes less than 25 percent of the total time.[81] The regulations also exempt travel expenses if (1) the taxpayer incurring the expenses did not have "substantial control over the arranging of the business trip" or (2) obtaining a personal vacation or holiday was not a major consideration in the decision to make the trip.[82] Moreover, §274(c) only applies to expenses incurred by the traveler, and does not affect the deductibility of travel expenses paid or incurred by the traveler's employer or client.[83]

A second statutory restriction on the deductibility of foreign travel is imposed by §274(h), relating to foreign conventions, which is discussed below.

3. *Conventions.* For conventions and other meetings, the test of deductibility prescribed by the regulations is "whether there is a sufficient relationship between the taxpayer's trade or business and his attendance at the convention or other meeting so that he is benefiting or advancing the

---

reprinted in 1964-1 (Part 2) CB 774, 805. The Senate version of the Revenue Act of 1964 would have repealed the provision entirely. S. Rep. No. 830, 88th Cong., 2d Sess., reprinted in 1964-1 (Part 2) CB 505, 585–86. See generally Lewis, Allocation of Travel Expenses, 46 Taxes 316 (1968); Klein, supra note 74. For a question-and-answer explanation of §274(c) (before the 1964 amendment), see Rev. Rul. 63-144, 1963-2 CB 129, 140–42.

[79] Supra text accompanying notes 75–77.

[80] See Reg. §1.274-4(g) Ex.7. But see Habeeb v. CIR, 559 F2d 435 (5th Cir. 1977) (contra; but not clear that issue was presented by either party). For computation of the disallowed amount, see Reg. §1.274-4(f).

[81] For the complex rules determining the length of the trip and the amount of time attributable to nonbusiness activities, see Reg. §§1.274-4(c), (d).

Section 274(c)(3) provides that travel between two points in the United States (e.g., a nonstop flight between Juneau and Seattle) is not foreign travel for purposes of §274(c). For problems in applying §274(c)(3), see Reg. §1.274-4(e).

[82] For these exemptions, see Reg. §§1.274-4(f)(5), (g).

[83] Reg. §1.274-4(a).

interests of his trade or business by such attendance."[84] The regulations also state that no distinction is made between employees and self-employed persons and that an employee's voluntary attendance or use of vacation or leave time to attend does "not necessarily" prohibit a deduction. Expenses of attending conventions for political, social, or other nonbusiness purposes cannot be deducted under §162(a).[85] If a trip made primarily to attend a business meeting includes some personal activities, the expenses attributable to the latter do not qualify for deduction, but the taxpayer's transportation expenses in getting to and from the business location are deductible in full unless the foreign travel restrictions of §274(c) apply.[86]

In *Rudolph v. United States*, the Supreme Court granted certiorari in a case involving convention expenses paid by the taxpayer's employer, which was thought to present important questions involving the meaning of "income" and "ordinary and necessary business expenses."[87] The trial court had held that the trip was regarded by the employer as compensation and by the employee as a pleasure trip in the nature of a vacation. Because these findings had been approved by the court of appeals as not "clearly erroneous," the Supreme Court dismissed the writ of certiorari as improvidently granted. Justices Douglas and Black dissented, arguing that the convention was a business trip, so that the employer's payments either were not income to the taxpayer or, if included in income, were offset by a business deduction of the same amount.[88]

---

[84] Reg. §1.162-2(d). See Rev. Rul. 63-266, 1963-2 CB 88 (agenda of convention need not deal specifically with duties and responsibilities of taxpayer's work; regulations satisfied if agenda is sufficiently related to taxpayer's position to show that attendance was for business purposes); Rev. Rul. 59-316, 1959-2 CB 57 (business purpose not established merely by showing that taxpayer was convention delegate). See also Reed v. CIR, 35 TC 199 (1969) (general practitioner's attendance at meeting in Yugoslavia of International Law Association not sufficiently related to his legal practice). See generally Postlewaite, Deductibility of Expenses for Conventions and Educational Seminars, 61 Minn. L. Rev. 253 (1977). See also Hoffman v. CIR, 19 TCM (CCH) 836 (1960), modified as to other issues, 298 F2d 784 (3d Cir. 1962) (manufacturer of body-building equipment allowed to deduct cost of attending Olympic Games, on showing that presence promoted sales).

[85] Reg. §1.162-2(d). For the possibility of deducting the expenses of travel as a charitable contribution, see infra ¶35.1.2 (out-of-pocket expenses of volunteer workers).

[86] Cannon v. CIR, 24 TCM (CCH) 1074 (1965).

[87] Rudolph v. US, 370 US 269 (1962).

[88] Id. at 278. See also Patterson v. Thomas, 289 F2d 108 (5th Cir.), cert. denied, 368 US 837 (1961) (insurance company's employee convention at resort hotel; employer pressure to attend but "business is secondary . . . main object is to give our people a good time"; held, company's payments to reimburse expenses of employee and spouse are includable in employee's gross income and not deductible except for nontransportation costs allocable to business part of meeting).

In 1976, the Senate Finance Committee concluded that the basic rules of §162(a) and the special rules applied to foreign travel by §274(c) were insufficient to cope with "the recent proliferation of [foreign] conventions, educational seminars, and cruises which are ostensibly held for business or educational purposes, but which it is believed are held at locations outside the United States primarily because of the recreational and sightseeing opportunities," epitomized by the claim of travel agencies "that they will find a convention for the taxpayer to attend in any part of the world at any given time of the year."[89] The legislative response was the enactment of §274(h), which was adopted in 1976 and rewritten in 1980, and has been amended repeatedly since. The present rules are as follows:

Costs incurred by an individual in attending "a convention, seminar, or similar meeting . . . outside the North American area" are deductible under §162 only if (1) the meeting is "directly related to the active conduct of [the taxpayer's] trade or business" and (2) "it is as reasonable for the meeting to be held outside the North American area as within the North American area."[90] The term "North American area" includes the United States, Canada, Mexico, Puerto Rico, the possessions of the United States, and the Trust Territory of the Pacific Islands.[91] A country within the Caribbean Basin is also considered part of the North American area if it has made a treaty with the United States for sharing information for tax enforcement purposes and the tax laws of the country do not discriminate against conventions held in the United States.[92] The reasonableness of holding a meeting outside the North American area is evaluated on the basis of such factors as the purpose of the meeting and the activities at the meeting, the purposes and activities of the convention sponsor, where the active members of the sponsoring organization live, and the location of other meetings of the organization.[93]

A second limitation applies to meetings held aboard cruise ships. To qualify for a §162 deduction for the costs of such a meeting, the taxpayer must show that (1) the meeting is "directly related to the active conduct of his trade or business," (2) the ship is registered in the United States, (3) all of the ship's ports of call are within the United States, its possessions, or

---

[89] S. Rep. No. 938, 94th Cong., 1st Sess., reprinted in 1976-3 CB (Vol. 3) 49, 194–95.

[90] IRC §274(h)(1).

[91] IRC §274(h)(3)(A). The possessions and the countries included within the Trust Territories are listed in Rev. Rul. 87-95, 1987-2 CB 79.

[92] IRC §274(h)(6). The countries qualifying for this treatment are Barbados, Jamaica, and Grenada. Rev. Rul. 87-95, supra note 91.

[93] IRC §274(h)(1).

Puerto Rico, and (4) a reporting requirement is satisfied.[94] The reporting requirement is that there must be attached to the return claiming the deduction (1) a statement by the individual attending the meeting describing the trip, the meetings held aboard ship, the amounts of time spent in business meetings, and a few other items and (2) a statement of an officer of the meeting sponsor giving a schedule of business activities and indicating the number of hours the attendee was present at these activities.[95] If all of these requirements are satisfied, deductions for meetings on cruise ships are further limited to $2,000 for all cruises taken by any one individual that begin within any calendar year.

The foregoing limitations apply whether the costs of an individual's attendance at a meeting are borne by the individual or someone else.[96] If an individual's expenses in attending a convention are partially reimbursed by his employer, for example, the limitations apply to the employer's deduction of the reimbursed amount and the employee's deduction of the unreimbursed portion. If the meeting is on a cruise ship, the $2,000 ceiling on deductions for such meetings is shared by employer and employee. One exception is recognized: If amounts paid by a person other than the attendee are included in the attendee's gross income, that person's deduction is not affected by §274(h),[97] but the attendee's deduction continues to be subject to the limitations.

The foregoing rules apply only to deductions claimed under §162(a). The rule for §212 deductions is much simpler; no deduction is allowable under §212 for the costs of a convention, seminar, or similar meeting.[98] Costs incurred in attending meetings are not deductible as investment expenses, for example, whether the meetings are held in the United States or abroad.

4. *Expenses of spouses.* The regulations provide that if a taxpayer is accompanied by his wife on a business trip, her travel expenses are deductible only if her presence serves a bona fide business purpose, a standard that is not satisfied by the performance of incidental services.[99] The same principle is applied by the regulations to other members of the taxpayer's family, and the IRS would be well advised to add the case of a husband who

---

[94] IRC §274(h)(2). The cruise need not be within the territorial waters of the United States or within the North American area. IRC §274(h)(3)(B).

[95] IRC §274(h)(5).

[96] IRC §274(h)(4)(A).

[97] IRC §274(h)(4)(B). The exemption is lost, however, if the person neglects his duty to report the amount on an information return. Id.

[98] IRC §274(h)(7).

[99] Reg. §1.162-2(c). See Rev. Rul. 56-168, 1956-1 CB 93 (spouse's presence not "necessary" despite performance of typing and similar services; if actual expenses are more than single rate but less than twice single rate, single rate may be deducted).

accompanies his wife when she travels on business. Acknowledging that the issue is a question of fact, the Tax Court has been skeptical of claims that the presence of the taxpayer's spouse served a business purpose,[100] but taxpayers seem to fare slightly better in the courts, especially if the taxpayer's employer encourages married couples to travel together on business trips and reimburses their combined expenses.[101]

5. *"Necessary" as "necessary," not merely "appropriate or helpful."* When travel expenses emit a mixed business-personal aroma, the courts sometimes disallow deductions on the ground that the expenses were not "necessary" to the taxpayer's business or profit-oriented activities, implying a shift from the usual meaning of "necessary" as "appropriate or helpful" to a stricter interpretation.[102] Judicial language of this type is best viewed as rhetorical flourish (like saying that the expenses must be "really helpful," not merely "helpful"). Administrative and judicial skepticism in this area is warranted, whatever the verbal formula may be.

¶21.1.10 Substantiation

Travel expenses, like expenses for entertainment and business gifts, must not only meet the substantive rules laid down by §§162(a), 212, and 274, but must also be substantiated as required by §274(d), discussed in detail later in this chapter.[103]

---

[100] See Rieley v. CIR, 23 TCM (CCH) 449 (1964); but see Bank of Stockton v. CIR, 36 TCM (CCH) 114 (1977) (employer allowed to deduct convention expenses of employees' wives; same result might have been reached on theory payments were added compensation, but this theory was not argued by taxpayer). For an extensive analysis of the relevant cases, see Lee, Command Performance: The Tax Treatment of Employer Mandated Expenses, 7 U. Rich. L. Rev. 1, 77 et seq. (1972).

[101] See US v. Disney, 413 F2d 783 (9th Cir. 1969) (employer "virtually insisted" on presence of executives' wives to enhance company's reputation for producing family entertainment), and cases therein cited. But see Rudolph v. US, 370 US 269 (1962); Patterson v. Thomas, 289 F2d 108 (5th Cir.), cert. denied, 368 US 837 (1961); Fenstermaker v. CIR, 37 TCM (CCH) 898 (1978) (spouse's services at annual trade convention "minimal at best"; expenses paid by employer taxable to employee and nondeductible despite employer's policy of sending spouses to convention, which does not establish bona fide business purpose for their attendance; earlier cases cited and analyzed). For cases disregarding alleged employer compulsion when the taxpayer is the employer's controlling shareholder, see Bank of Stockton v. CIR, supra note 100, at 117–18 n.5.

For the possibility that the expenses of an accompanying family member may be deductible as medical expenses if the taxpayer is infirm, see infra ¶36.1.2.

[102] See Lee, supra note 100, at 39–40; see also Henry v. CIR, 36 TC 879 (1961) (tax expert with yacht bearing "1040" burgee).

[103] See infra ¶21.4.

¶21.2 ENTERTAINMENT, AMUSEMENT, AND RECREATION

¶21.2.1 Introductory

The deductibility of entertainment expenses has long been a disaster area, producing results that do not satisfy taxpayers, practitioners, the IRS, Congress, or the general public. The roots of the problem are that a bright line cannot be drawn between business and pleasure, that administrators and judges are fallible human beings, and that any mechanical rule is bound to put numerous items on the wrong side of the line. Among the complicating factors are: (1) By joining in the merriment himself, the taxpayer who pays the bill usually derives personal benefits from the activity; (2) business guests are sometimes personal friends whom the taxpayer would have entertained in any event; (3) the type and level of entertainment are usually within the taxpayer's control, making it difficult to determine whether the expenditures are animated by business needs or personal preference; and (4) the taxpayer is sometimes the beneficiary of reciprocal entertainment, supplied (and deducted) by his guests in an informal but effective mutual back-scratching arrangement.

The long-standing practice of deducting the taxpayer's share of restaurant, nightclub, and theater expenses, as well as the amount attributable to business guests, led the Tax Court in 1953 to speak of

> the stubborn thread of a single problem which has never apparently been squarely and expressly passed upon . . . . When a taxpayer in the course of supplying food or entertainment or making other outlays customarily regarded as ordinary and necessary includes an amount attributable to himself or his family, such as the payment for his own meals, is that portion of the expenditure an ordinary and necessary business expense on the one hand or a nondeductible personal item on the other? . . . [W]e think the presumptive nondeductibility of personal expenses may be overcome only by clear and detailed evidence as to each instance that the expenditure in question was different from or in excess of that which would have been made for the taxpayer's personal purposes.[1]

In a 1963 ruling, the IRS summarized the decisions as holding that "a taxpayer cannot obtain a deduction for the portion of his meal cost which does not exceed an amount he would normally spend on himself," but said that it did not intend to depart from its practice of applying this rule "largely to abuse cases where taxpayers claim deductions for substantial

---

[1] Sutter v. CIR, 21 TC 170, 173 (1953) (acq.).

amounts of personal living expenses."[2] No reference was made in the ruling to the cost of theater tickets and other entertainment expenses.

The difficulty of deciding whether customers are friends or friends are customers has also been noted by the Tax Court:

> During 1945 petitioner elaborately entertained buyers and others connected with the jewelry business, personally spending about $7,000. In addition thereto approximately $2,000 was expended by his wife and employees on luncheons, drinks, weekend visits, conventions, suppers, theaters, and nightclubs. Approximately $3,400 of the $7,000 expended by petitioner personally was spent on suppers, theaters, and nightclubs and other forms of evening entertainment. On these occasions petitioner would bring his wife and the party or parties he was entertaining would also bring their wives. There is little to distinguish these occasions from the usual social gatherings among friends to renew acquaintanceship and enjoy a pleasant evening.[3]

In a later case the Tax Court pierced the corporate veil to disallow expenses incurred by a corporation to entertain business guests who were friends of the taxpayer's sole shareholder:

> [E]ven when guests having some "business" connection with [the corporate taxpayer] were aboard [its yacht], it is far from clear to us that their presence on the yacht in any particular instance was proximately related to [its] business . . . so as to form the basis for deduction. It is entirely normal for friendships to develop with some of those that one meets in business transactions, and we cannot say on this record that a number of the so-called "business" guests were not also social friends of [the corporation's sole shareholder] and were not invited on the yacht because [he] found them companionable and congenial, wholly apart from business reasons. The mere fact that they may have been "business" contacts as well would not render deductible the cost of entertainment if it in fact was furnished primarily for social or personal reasons.[4]

---

[2] Rev. Rul. 63-144, 1963-2 CB 129, 135. See also LaForge v. CIR, 434 F2d 370 (2d Cir. 1970) (taxpayer's meals not deductible except to extent of excess over normal amount; but court implies that full amount is deductible if taxpayer can show that IRS applies *Sutter* rule only to cases of abuse and that his case does not fall in that category); Fenstermaker v. CIR, 37 TCM (CCH) 898 (1978) (amounts received from the taxpayer's employer to reimburse cost of his meals at business lunches are includable in gross income without offsetting deduction).

[3] Schulz v. CIR, 16 TC 401, 405 (1951) (acq.).

[4] Challenge Mfg. Co. v. CIR, 37 TC 650, 659, 660 (1962) (acq.).

As for reciprocity in entertainment, a 1963 ruling of the IRS holds that turnabout is not fair play:

> *Question:* Where a group of businessmen make a practice of having lunch together primarily for personal reasons, and they alternate in paying for the lunch, does this make the cost deductible?
>
> *Answer:* This practice is not connected with the carrying on of a trade or business but is a personal or social arrangement. As under prior law, the cost of the lunch would not be an ordinary and necessary business expense, and is not deductible.[5]

In the years following World War II, abuses in the deduction of entertainment expenses became more common, more widely publicized, or both, leading to journalistic descriptions of the "expense account society" such as the following:

> In cities like New York, Washington and Chicago it is safe to say that at any given moment well over half of all the people in the best hotels, the best nightclubs and the best restaurants are charging the bill as an expense account item to their companies, which in turn are charging it to the government in the form of tax deductions.[6]

Another source of dissatisfaction with the growing amount of entertainment deductions was the degree of discretion vested in the subordinate employees of the IRS who pass on the propriety of such deductions. After an extended investigation in 1951–1952, a subcommittee of the House Ways and Means Committee reported:

> A second way to reduce possible corrupt practices in the [IRS] is to minimize the opportunities and temptation. For example, under a leading judicial decision [the *Cohan* case, discussed in ¶20.1.9], a taxpayer who claims large business deductions but has not kept any records to substantiate the claim is entitled to a reasonable allowance for the claimed expenses, which must be estimated by the Revenue Agent. Stricter requirements for keeping of reasonably detailed records by taxpayers would eliminate the necessity for discretionary determination of the proper expense deduction, and with it, any possible temptation for the Revenue Agent to allow an improperly large deduction in exchange for some private benefit extended to him by the taxpayer.

---

[5] Rev. Rul. 63-144, supra note 2, at 133.

[6] Life, Mar. 9, 1953, at 140. See also Buchwald, Europe's Lighter Side, N.Y. Herald-Tribune, July 20, 1954, at 21; Knowles, The Tax Treatment of Entertainment Expenses Under §274: Results Reviewed and Revisions Recommended, 13 Harv. J. Legis. 845, 846–50 (1976) (historical review).

This record-keeping proposal, aside from its tendency to eliminate opportunities for corruption in the Bureau, should reduce the risk that the great multitude of taxpayers who have no substantial business deductions may feel that some persons having such opportunity to claim deductions are not paying their fair share of taxes.[7]

Judge Learned Hand's opinion in *Cohan v. CIR*—holding that George M. Cohan was entitled to deduct entertainment expenses based on estimates where exact amounts and documentation were lacking—led a later federal circuit court judge to observe that the blame for abuse in this area started on Broadway and ended at the U.S. Courthouse in Foley Square.[8]

In 1961, President Kennedy proposed a series of drastic restrictions of entertainment deductions, urging that "the slogan—'It's deductible'—should pass from our scene."[9] In support of President Kennedy's proposals, the Treasury submitted an extended report to Congress, with the following introduction:

> Abuses through expense accounts take a variety of forms. Tax deductible entertainment allowances frequently are a means by which business provides tax-free compensation to favored employees or business associates. The seller invites the buyer to his yacht or hunting lodge, the buyer may reciprocate with lavish parties and nightclub entertainment, and both then charge it off as a business expense. Some of this is done because of the businessman's own desire to obtain such luxuries tax free; much of it is done in response to a competitive pressure which has in large measure been created by our tax law and not by the dictates of business. As a result, therefore, there are few of the luxuries of life, such as vacations at fancy resorts, club memberships, and cruises which a large number of taxpayers cannot in some way deduct on tax returns as business expenses. As the President stated, the time has come when our tax laws should cease to encourage luxury spending as a charge on the Federal Treasury.[10]

The Treasury report contained a summary of an audit of 38,000 returns to ascertain the magnitude of the entertainment problem, a report by the IRS on problems encountered in auditing deductions, a summary of judicial and

---

[7] Internal Revenue Investigation, Report to House Comm. on Ways and Means, Subcommittee on Administration of the Internal Revenue Laws 29 (1952).

[8] Dowell v. US, 522 F2d 708, 711 (5th Cir.), cert. denied, 426 US 920 (1976).

[9] President's Tax Message in Hearings on Tax Recommendations of the President, April 20, 1961, Before House Ways and Means Comm., 87th Cong., 1st Sess. 11, reprinted in Staff of House Ways and Means Comm., 90th Cong., 1st Sess., Legislative History of the Revenue Act of 1962, Pt. 1, at 135, 151 (1967).

[10] Id. at 38, reprinted at 178.

administrative decisions to illustrate the type of expenditures allowed as deductions under existing law, and a compilation of journalistic comments on expense account abuses.

As President Kennedy's proposals moved through successive stages of congressional consideration, they were whittled down in important respects,[11] but the outcome was a series of major changes in the tax treatment of expenditures for entertainment, amusement, and recreation, as well as limits on the deductibility of business-related travel expenses and business gifts.[12] To be deductible, expenditures for entertainment, amusement, or recreation must be "ordinary and necessary expenses" incurred in carrying on the taxpayer's business or profit-oriented activities, as required by §§162 and 212.[13] They must also satisfy the more severe business-relationship standards of §274(a),[14] and be substantiated in the manner required by §274(d).[15]

In 1978, President Carter urged that additional restrictions be imposed on the deductibility of entertainment expenses, symbolized by the "three-martini lunch," including disallowance of half of the cost. By the time the proposals emerged from the congressional mill, however, all that was left was a disallowance of deductions for entertainment facilities (e.g., hunting lodges, swimming pools, hotel suites, and yachts but not certain club dues).[16]

A more encompassing assault on these deductions occurred in 1986, when Congress (echoing President Carter's proposals on the three-martini lunch) limited most deductions for food, beverages, and business entertainment to 80 percent of their cost. The 1986 amendments also eliminated the deduction for such items entirely in cases where neither the taxpayer nor an employee is present when the items are furnished or where an entertainment expense consists of a skybox or a ticket purchased from a scalper.[17]

The proper classification of entertainment expenses can come into question in any of the following ways:

1. Claims may be made by self-employed taxpayers that entertainment expenses are deductible as ordinary and necessary business expenses under §162 or, less frequently, as profit-oriented expenses under §212.

---

[11] See Lipoff, Entertainment and Related Expenses Under Legislative Attack, 17 Tax L. Rev. 183 (1962).

[12] For travel expenses and business gifts, see supra ¶21.1 and infra ¶21.3.

[13] See supra ¶20.3.

[14] See infra ¶21.2.2.

[15] See infra ¶21.4.

[16] For details, see infra ¶21.2.3; for the proposals, see Treasury Department, The President's 1978 Tax Program: Detailed Descriptions and Supporting Analyses of the Proposals 182–211 (1978).

[17] See infra ¶21.2.2.

2. Employees may entertain customers, paying the bills out of their salaries, in which event they are in substantially the same boat as self-employed taxpayers.[18]

3. Some employees receive flat expense allowances, are reimbursed by the employer for specific entertainment expenditures, or are authorized to charge expenditures to the employer. If the employee's expenditures are scrutinized by a hard-nosed comptroller, approval may be weighty evidence that they served a business purpose. On the other hand, the employer may be interested only in the bottom line—salary plus expense allowances—and be willing to acquiesce in any allocation proposed by the employee, provided the aggregate amount paid is warranted by the employee's sales record. In this situation, the allocation may mean only that the employee is tax-conscious and the employer is not overly scrupulous; indeed, one can envision arrangements to split the fruits of a conspiracy against the Treasury.[19]

4. The employer, as just suggested, may view the aggregate amount paid to the employee as compensation, not caring how it is allocated for tax purposes between compensation and entertainment, provided the full amount can be deducted under one heading or the other. Thus, if reimbursed entertainment expenditures are taxed to the employee for want of a sufficient business connection, the employer ordinarily seeks to deduct the payments as additional compensation to the employee, even though they were originally classified on the employer's books as entertainment expenditures. The IRS and the courts sometimes accept the new label and allow the deduction if the aggregate amount does not exceed reasonable compensation for the employee's services,[20] but sometimes they are less tolerant of such a shift in the employer's claim.[21] Disallowance is most likely if the entertainment expenditures were incurred by a controlling shareholder-employee or by an employee who is closely related to a controlling shareholder; in this situation the corporation's payment may be viewed as a nondeductible constructive dividend to the shareholder rather than as a deductible payment of additional compensation.[22]

---

[18] But see supra ¶20.1.4, for discussion of the theory that employees who use their own funds to entertain their employer's potential customers are seeking to deduct "the expense of another taxpayer."

[19] See supra ¶4.4.4 (re splitting tax benefits between two parties).

[20] For the requirement that compensation be "reasonable" to be deducted, see infra ¶22.2.2.

[21] See Watson Elec. Constr. Co. v. CIR, 35 TCM (CCH) 8 (1976) (cost of facility allocated to personal use by taxpayer's president disallowed as compensation because not treated as such by taxpayer in accordance with §274(e)(3)).

[22] But see Tennessee Sec., Inc. v. CIR, 37 TCM (CCH) 1803 (1978), aff'd on other issues, 674 F2d 570 (6th Cir. 1982) (disallowance of expenses at corporate level under §274 did not result in constructive dividend to shareholders where payments

¶21.2.2 Entertainment, Amusement, and Recreation Activities; Business Meals

Section 274(a)(1)(A) provides that no deduction shall be allowed for an item with respect to an activity "which is of a type generally considered to constitute entertainment, amusement, or recreation," unless it is directly related to or associated with the active conduct of the taxpayer's business. For this purpose, activities described by §212, relating to expenses incurred for the production of income and other profit-oriented activities, are treated as a trade or business.[23] Also, rules added to §274 in 1986 limit deductions for costs of food and beverages, whether or not furnished in an entertainment setting; among the rules is a provision denying 20 percent of these costs, even when they satisfy all other requirements for deduction.

The salient features of the rules for entertainment activities and business meals are:

1. *Entertainment activities.* An expenditure for entertainment, amusement, or recreation is not deductible unless the taxpayer establishes that it was (1) "directly related to" the "active conduct" of the taxpayer's trade or business or (2) "associated with" the active conduct of the business and directly preceded or followed "a substantial and bona fide business discussion."

As examples of entertainment "directly related to" the active conduct of the taxpayer's business, the regulations cite the entertainment of business representatives and civic leaders at the opening of a hotel, the maintenance of a hospitality suite at a business convention where the taxpayer's products are displayed or discussed, and the award of vacation trips as prizes to the taxpayer's dealers.[24] By contrast, entertainment at theaters, nightclubs, and sporting events is said by the regulations not to be "directly related," unless the taxpayer clearly proves the contrary, and the same principles apply to entertainment at country clubs and cocktail lounges if the group includes persons other than business associates.[25]

---

otherwise qualified as ordinary and necessary business expenses). For the constructive dividend concept, see infra ¶92.2.

[23] IRC §274(a)(2)(B).

[24] Reg. §§1.274-2(c)(4), (5). See Berkley Mach. Works & Foundry Co. v. CIR, 623 F2d 898 (4th Cir. 1980) (weekend outings for employees of taxpayer and customers "were in the area of general business goodwill, exactly the type of expenditure the Congress intended to eliminate [by] the directly related test"); Hippodrome Oldsmobile, Inc. v. US, 474 F2d 959 (6th Cir. 1973) (entertainment on pleasure boat not directly related to active conduct of business where taxpayer refrained from initiating discussions in belief that "soft sell" was best approach).

[25] Reg. §1.274-2(c)(7).

If not "directly related to" the "active conduct" of the taxpayer's business, entertainment expenses are deductible only if the entertainment directly precedes or follows a substantial business discussion and is "associated with" the active conduct of the taxpayer's business. The regulations cite only two instances of "associated" entertainment: (1) entertainment at business conventions and similar meetings where a business program is the principal activity of the meeting and (2) entertainment on the day of a substantial business discussion or, if the persons entertained are from out of town, on the preceding or following evening.[26] The regulations provide that entertainment is "associated with the active conduct of the taxpayer's trade or business if the taxpayer establishes that he had a clear business purpose in making the expenditure, such as to obtain new business or to encourage the continuation of an existing business relationship."[27] If entertainment of business guests meets either the "directly related" or the "associated" test, expenses allocable to spouses (including the taxpayer's) are treated as "associated" with the active conduct of the taxpayer's business.[28]

2. *"Directly related to," "associated with," etc.* The regulations under §274(a) make an effort—valiant and comic, in about equal parts—to give meaning to such terms as "directly related to," "associated with," "active conduct," "directly preceding or following," "substantial and bona fide business discussion," and "primarily for the furtherance" of business.[29] It is hard to believe that these refinements can be effectively administered, or that Congress could not have achieved substantially the same results by simply requiring taxpayers to establish that entertainment expenses are clearly essential to the conduct of business or to prove their business relationship by a clear preponderance of the evidence. The Tax Court has said:

> While it is this Court's role to construe and apply the Code and
> regulations and not to intrude its own notions as to tax policy, the

---

[26] Reg. §1.274-2(d)(3). See Walliser v. CIR, 72 TC 433 (1979) (bank officer's expenses on vacation tours with customers neither directly related to nor associated with the active conduct of business, despite qualification under §162); Leon v. CIR, 37 TCM (CCH) 1514 (1978) (same for home dinner parties).

[27] Reg. §1.274-2(d)(2).

[28] Id.; Reg. §1.274-2(d)(4). See also LaForge v. CIR, 53 TC 41, 51–52 (1969) (acq.), modified as to other issues, 434 F2d 370 (2d Cir. 1970) (expenses attributable to spouses accompanying business guests at "quiet business meals" deductible under business meal exception of §274(e)(1)).

[29] Reg. §1.274-2(c) (directly related entertainment), §1.274-2(d) (associated entertainment), §1.274-2(c)(3) (directly related to active conduct), §1.274-2(d)(3) (directly preceding or following a substantial and bona fide business discussion), §1.274-2(e)(4) (primarily for the furtherance of business). See St. Petersburg Bank & Trust Co. v. US, 362 F. Supp. 674 (MD Fla. 1973), aff'd by unpublished opinion (5th Cir., Oct. 30, 1974), cert. denied, 423 US 834 (1975) (distinction between "directly related" and "associated" entertainment).

extremely laborious task cut out for us by the application to the facts of this case of an almost unbearably prolix and convoluted set of regulations makes it difficult to resist the observation that the average citizen to whom these regulations are applicable could not realistically be expected to comprehend and follow them in every precise detail, if they are construed in the most rigorous possible sense. The Court has accordingly attempted to give the regulations as common-sense a construction as the rather astounding wording permits.[30]

3. *Allocation.* Even if an item meets the standards of §274(a)(1)(A), the deduction may not exceed the portion that is directly related to or, as appropriate, associated with, the active conduct of the business.[31]

4. *Scope of "entertainment, amusement, or recreation."* Section 274(a)(1)(A) applies to activities "of a type generally considered to constitute entertainment, amusement, or recreation," and §274(a)(1)(B), discussed below,[32] applies to facilities used in connection with such activities. The regulations offer the following definition:

> For purposes of [§274], the term "entertainment" means any activity which is of a type generally considered to constitute entertainment, amusement, or recreation, such as entertaining at night clubs, cocktail lounges, theaters, country clubs, golf and athletic clubs, sporting events, and on hunting, fishing, vacation and similar trips, including such activity relating solely to the taxpayer or the taxpayer's family. The term "entertainment" may include an activity, the cost of which is claimed as a business expense by the taxpayer, which satisfies the personal, living, or family needs of any individual, such as providing food and beverages, a hotel suite, or an automobile to a business customer or his family. The term "entertainment" does not include activities which, although satisfying personal, living, or family needs of an individual, are clearly not regarded as constituting entertainment, such as (a) supper money provided by an employer to his employee working overtime, (b) a hotel room maintained by an employer for lodging of his employees while in business travel status, or (c) an automobile used in the active conduct of trade or business even though used for routine personal purposes such as commuting to and from work.[33]

The regulations also provide that the statutory phrase is to be interpreted in the light of the taxpayer's trade or business:

---

[30] Durgom v. CIR, 33 TCM (CCH) 276, 282 n.3 (1974).
[31] IRC §274(a)(1) (final sentence).
[32] Infra ¶21.2.3.
[33] Reg. §1.274-2(b)(1)(i).

Thus, although attending a theatrical performance would generally be considered entertainment, it would not be so considered in the case of a professional theater critic, attending in his professional capacity. Similarly, if a manufacturer of dresses conducts a fashion show to introduce his products to a group of store buyers, the show would not be generally considered to constitute entertainment. However, if an appliance distributor conducts a fashion show for the wives of his retailers, the fashion show would be generally considered to constitute entertainment.[34]

By embracing activities of a type that are "generally considered" as entertainment, amusement, or recreation, §274(a) requires its strict rules to be applied even if the events are, for the particular taxpayer, painful or boring business responsibilities rather than sources of pleasure.

Relying on the same statutory language, the regulations seek to prevent taxpayers from classifying expenditures as advertising or public relations rather than as entertainment:

An objective test shall be used to determine whether an activity is of a type generally considered to constitute entertainment. Thus, if an activity is generally considered to be entertainment, it will constitute entertainment for purposes of this section and section 274(a) regardless of whether the expenditure can also be described otherwise, and even though the expenditure relates to the taxpayer alone. This objective test precludes arguments such as that "entertainment" means only entertainment of others or that an expenditure for entertainment should be characterized as an expenditure for advertising or public relations.[35]

Acknowledging that the terms "travel," "business gift," and "entertainment"—all covered by §274, but subjected to different rules—can overlap, the regulations classify dual status items as "entertainment," except that expenditures for (1) packaged food or beverages to be consumed at a later time by the recipient are treated as gifts and (2) tickets of admission to a place of entertainment are treated as gifts if the taxpayer does not accompany the recipient to the event, unless the taxpayer elects to treat the expendi-

---

[34] Reg. §1.274-2(b)(1)(ii). See also S. Rep. No. 1881, 87th Cong., 2d Sess., reprinted in 1962-3 CB 707, 733 (hunting trip is recreation for a taxpayer in machine tool or clothing business but not for a professional hunter).

[35] Reg. §1.274-2(b)(1)(ii). See also Andress v. CIR, 51 TC 863 (1969), aff'd per curiam, 423 F2d 679 (5th Cir. 1970) (entertainment cannot be classified as "advertising" by lawyer merely because canons of ethics do not permit other types of advertising). For the type of situation that the objective test aims to correct, see U.S. Equip. Co. v. CIR, 22 TCM (CCH) 1309 (1963) (advertising expense deduction allowed for corporation's cost of maintaining racing boat used by sole shareholder).

ture as entertainment.[36] Expenditures for automobiles, airplanes, and other transportation facilities, however, are classified as "travel" rather than "entertainment" to the extent that the facility is used in business activities other than entertainment.[37]

5. *Requirements of §§162 and 212.* Section 274(a)(1) disallows deductions that are "otherwise allowable"; hence, it need not be consulted in the case of expenditures that do not qualify as ordinary and necessary expenses under §162 or §212. Conversely, the fact that an expenditure is not disallowed by §274(a) does not guarantee that it is allowable under §162 or §212; it may, for example, be a nondeductible capital expenditure.[38]

6. *"Lavish and extravagant" expenditures.* Section 274(k), added in 1986, denies any deduction for the costs of "food or beverages" that are "lavish or extravagant under the circumstances." Also, the regulations impose on entertainment expenses the "lavish and extravagant" limitation applied by §162(a)(2) to the taxpayer's meals and lodging while away from home on business.[39] This restriction has little bite under §162(a)(2),[40] and there is no evidence that it plays a livelier role under §274.

7. *Taxpayer presence requirement for business meals.* Section 274(k) also makes costs of "food or beverages" nondeductible if neither the taxpayer nor an employee is present when the food or beverages are furnished. The presence of an independent contractor (e.g., a lawyer or accountant) can be substituted for that of the taxpayer or an employee if the contractor "renders significant services to the taxpayer."[41] If an expense is reimbursed by another person, the rule applies to the person making the reimbursement, not the person receiving it.[42] If a lawyer passes the cost of a business meal on to a client, for example, the client's payment to the lawyer, not the lawyer's payment of the meal expense, is subject to the rule.

There are several exceptions. The rule does not apply, for example, to (1) food and beverages that are sold to customers or otherwise made available to the public (a restaurant's food and beverage costs, for example), (2) costs that are taxed as compensation to the recipient, or (3) food and beverages furnished at a meeting or convention of an exempt business league.[43] Also, the presence-of-the-taxpayer requirement does not apply to a

---

[36] Reg. §1.274-2(b)(1)(iii). When a dual status expenditure is classified as a gift rather than as entertainment, it escapes the strict business-relationship rules of §274(a) but becomes subject to the $25 limit of §274(b)—out of the frying pan into the fire.

[37] Reg. §1.274-2(b)(1)(iii)(c).

[38] Reg. §1.274-1.

[39] Id.

[40] See¶21.1.1 note 9.

[41] H.R. Rep. No. 841, 99th Cong., 2d Sess. II-26 (Conf. Rep. 1986).

[42] Id.

[43] See infra ¶21.2.4.

meal for a person traveling away from home who eats alone or with family members.[44] If a company reimburses the meal expenses of a prospective employee who is brought to the taxpayer's city for an interview, for example, the deduction for the meals is not lost merely because neither the taxpayer nor an employee is in attendance.

The deduction for a business meal that survives this test is limited to 80 percent of the cost under a rule described below.[45]

8. *Tickets to entertainment events and skyboxes.* If a taxpayer purchases an otherwise deductible ticket to an entertainment event, but pays a price in excess of the "face value" of the ticket, the excess cannot be deducted.[46] A premium paid to a ticket scalper, in other words, is nondeductible. An exception is allowed for an extra amount paid for a ticket to a sporting event organized for the benefit of charity where (1) the net proceeds of the event go entirely to charity and (2) substantially all of the work in putting on the event is performed by volunteers.[47]

Another rule provides that if "a skybox or other private luxury box is leased for more than 1 event," no deduction is allowed for the excess of its cost over the cost of a number of "nonluxury box seat tickets" equal to the number of seats in the box.[48] If nonluxury box seat tickets are offered at more than one price, the highest price can be used.[49] Also, if food and beverage costs are separately stated from the cost of a skybox, they are not limited by this rule.[50]

The portion of the cost of a ticket or skybox that is not made nondeductible by either of the foregoing rules is deductible only to the extent it passes muster under the other rules of §§162(a), 212, and 274, including the 80 percent rule described immediately below.

9. *Eighty percent rule.* Section 274(n), enacted in 1986, places an 80 percent cap on most deductions for food, beverages, and business entertain-

---

[44] H.R. Rep. No. 841, supra note 41.

[45] Infra text accompanying notes 51–55.

[46] IRC §274(*l*)(1)(A). This rule is effective for taxable years after 1986. Pub. L. No. 99-514, §151(a), 100 Stat. 2085 (1986).

[47] IRC §274(*l*)(1)(B). For charity events not covered by this exception, the excess is usually allowable as a charitable deduction, but subject to the percentage and other limitations on that deduction. See infra ¶35.3. The principal effect of the exception is thus to allow taxpayers to skirt the percentage limitation on the charitable deduction in the limited circumstances in which the exception applies.

[48] IRC §274(*l*)(2)(A). This rule is phased in over three years. For taxable years beginning in 1987, only one third of the excess cost of a skybox is denied; two thirds is nondeductible in 1988. IRC §274(*l*)(2)(B).

[49] H.R. Rep. No. 841, supra note 41, at II-28, II-29 n.4.

[50] Id.

ment.[51] The 80 percent rule applies to the portion of a meal or entertainment cost that is deductible under §162(a) or §212 and is not made nondeductible by any of the other rules of §274. Assume a $10 ticket to an entertainment event is purchased from a scalper for $15. None of the cost is deductible unless the taxpayer shows that the expense is directly related to his business or otherwise satisfies §274(a)(1)(A).[52] If this hurdle is overcome, the $5 premium paid the scalper is disallowed under the rule described above.[53] Finally, if the $10 face value of the ticket is otherwise deductible, the 80 percent rule limits the deduction to $8.

If an expense is reimbursed by another person, the 80 percent limitation applies to the person making the reimbursement, not the person receiving it.[54] If a lawyer passes the cost of a business meal on to a client, for example, the client's deduction for the payment to the lawyer, not the lawyer's deduction for the payment to the restaurant, is limited to 80 percent of the cost.

The 80 percent rule is qualified by several exceptions, which are described below.[55]

¶21.2.3 Entertainment, Amusement, and Recreation—Facilities

As enacted in 1962, §274(a) distinguished between activities constituting entertainment, amusement, or recreation, and facilities used in connection with the activities. Although the rules relating to facilities were more severe than the rules relating to activities, Congress decided in 1978 that they left too much room for abuse, and it imposed drastic additional limitations. The 1962–1978 rules were summarized as follows by the Joint Committee on Taxation:

> Expenses with respect to entertainment "facilities" were deductible under prior law if (1) they were ordinary and necessary, (2) the facility was used primarily for the furtherance of the taxpayer's business (i.e., more than 50 percent of the time that it was used), and (3) the expense in question was "directly related" to the active conduct of the taxpayer's business.

---

[51] The term "business entertainment" is used here as shorthand for the complete statutory description, "any item with respect to an activity which is of a type generally considered to constitute entertainment, amusement, or recreation, or with respect to a facility used in connection with such activity" (IRC §274(n)(1)(B)). See supra text accompanying note 35 for the meaning of the phrase "generally considered to constitute entertainment, amusement, or recreation."

[52] IRC §274(a)(1)(A).

[53] IRC §274(*l*)(1).

[54] IRC §§274(e)(4), (n)(2)(A); Notice 87-23, 1987-1 CB 467.

[55] Infra ¶21.2.4.

For this purpose, an entertainment facility was any item of personal or real property owned, rented, or used by a taxpayer during the taxable year for, or in connection with, any activity which was of a type generally considered to constitute entertainment, amusement, or recreation. For example, entertainment facilities included yachts, hunting lodges, fishing camps, swimming pools, tennis courts, bowling alleys, automobiles, airplanes, apartments, hotel suites, and vacation homes. However, a facility was not considered to be an "entertainment facility" if it was used only incidentally during a taxable year in connection with entertainment, and that use was insubstantial in relation to its business use. . . .

If an item of property was considered to be an entertainment facility, the expenditures subject to the special entertainment facility rules included depreciation, rent, utility charges, maintenance and repair expenses, insurance premiums, salaries for caretakers and watchmen, and losses realized on the sale or other disposition of the property. These expenditures also included dues and fees paid to any social, athletic, or sporting club or organization. However, expenditures were not treated as being made with respect to a facility if they were out-of-pocket expenses, e.g., nonoperating costs such as expenditures for food and beverages. In addition, expenses attributable to a nonentertainment use of a facility were not treated as being expenses with respect to an "entertainment" facility, e.g., the use of an automobile or airplane for business travel purposes. Finally, expenses which were deductible without regard to their connection with a taxpayer's trade or business were not considered to be expenditures with respect to an entertainment facility, e.g., taxes, interest, and casualty losses.

In determining whether an entertainment facility was used primarily for business purposes, all the ordinary and necessary business use of the facility could be taken into account even though the use was not "directly related to" or "associated with" the active conduct of the taxpayer's profit-seeking activities (Rev. Rul. 63-144, 1963-2 CB 129, 137). However, only the portion of the expenses which were "directly related" to the active conduct of the taxpayer's trade or business were deductible. Thus, the use of the facility in providing entertainment "associated with" the active conduct of a trade or business was taken into account in determining if the facility was used primarily for business purposes, but only those expenses attributable to a use which was "directly related" to the active conduct of a trade or business were deductible. For example, if 60 percent of the use of a yacht was for business entertaining but only 45 percent of the use satisfied the "directly related" test, only 45 percent of the facility expenditures would have been deductible.[56]

The 1978 legislation did not alter the rules for items paid or incurred before 1979. The deduction for depreciation on facilities acquired before 1979, for example, continues to be subject to the prior rules.

For items paid or incurred after 1978, §274(a)(1)(B) wholly disallows otherwise allowable deductions for facilities used in connection with an activity constituting entertainment, amusement, or recreation.[57] In applying this rule, dues and fees paid to social, athletic, and sporting clubs constitute items with respect to facilities.[58] The regulations, however, exempt clubs operated solely to provide lunches in circumstances conducive to business discussions, and an IRS ruling provides that dues paid to professional associations and civic organizations are also generally outside the jurisdic-

---

[56] Joint Comm. on Tax'n, 95th Cong., 2d Sess., General Explanation of the Revenue Act of 1978, at 205–06 (Comm. Print 1979). See Reg. §§1.274-2(e)(2), (3) (definition of entertainment facilities and of expenditures with respect to such facilities); Ireland v. CIR, 89 TC 978 (1987) (stock broker's beach-front property held to be entertainment facility because, although primary use was for business meetings, attendees at meetings sometimes brought their families); Finney v. CIR, 39 TCM (CCH) 938 (1980) (construction company's houseboat was entertainment facility, not "floating office"). See also Reg. §1.274-2(e)(4) (determination of primary use under 50 percent test); Rev. Rul. 72-273, 1972-1 CB 44 (country club dues for corporate membership, limited to dining facilities and used only to entertain prospective customers, negotiate business transactions, and conduct holiday and retirement parties; held, deductible if substantiation requirements of §274(d) are satisfied). In applying the 50 percent test, actual use (based on the time spent for business purposes or the number of business occasions) was controlling, not the facility's availability for business use or the taxpayer's primary purpose in acquiring the facility. See Kopowski v. CIR, 38 TCM (CCH) 1239 (1979) (computation of days of business use). See also D.A. Foster Trenching Co. v. US, 473 F2d 1398 (Ct. Cl. 1973) (taxpayer made fishing boat available to business guests; held, although IRS conceded that 50 percent standard was met, expenditures were not "directly related" or incurred in "clear business setting" in absence of taxpayer's officers, salesmen, etc.); Rev. Rul. 63-144, 1963-2 CB 129 (satisfying 50 percent test does not ensure deduction of at least 50 percent of expenditures for facility; all ordinary and necessary business entertainment is counted in applying 50 percent test, but only "directly related" entertainment may be deducted under §274(a)).

[57] See generally Bostock & Terr, How the 1978 Act Affects T & E Deductions for Facilities: Implications and Planning, 50 J. Tax'n 130 (1979). See Harrigan Lumber Co. v. CIR, 88 TC 1562, 1566 (1987) (lease granting taxpayer exclusive hunting rights in 6,000-acre tract is entertainment facility where taxpayer's use was for hunting and fishing trips for customers and suppliers; distinction between entertainment activity and entertainment facility depends on "whether the property used for the entertainment is occupied exclusively by the taxpayer for or during the recreation or entertainment").

[58] IRC §274(a)(2)(A).

tion of §274(a)(1)(B).[59] A further statutory exception lifts the no-deduction rule for clubs if the taxpayer establishes that the facility was used primarily for the furtherance of the taxpayer's business and that the item was related directly to the active conduct of the business—the same conditions that were formerly applicable to all types of facilities.[60]

The blanket disallowance imposed by §274(a)(1)(B) is also inapplicable to deductions that, apart from §274, are allowable whether or not connected with the taxpayer's business or profit-oriented activities. Thus, the owner of a hunting lodge can deduct real estate taxes and casualty losses even though the lodge's status as an entertainment facility bars deductions for depreciation and operating expenses.[61] Section 274(a)(1)(B) is also inapplicable in a variety of other circumstances that Congress did not view as fraught with abuse, summarized as follows by the Joint Committee on Taxation:

> In addition, the [rule] does not preclude a deduction for business meals or entertainment simply because the expense was incurred in a club with respect to which the taxpayer is not allowed a deduction for dues or fees, if the quiet business meal or associated with business test is satisfied for entertainment activities.

> Similarly, the [rule] does not disallow an otherwise allowable deduction for meal and lodging expenses incurred while away from home overnight. For example, [it] generally does not apply to travel expenses incurred by an individual away from home at a bona fide business, trade, or professional organization meeting or convention. These expenses, however, continue to be subject to the generally applicable rules relating to the deductibility of business travel, convention, and entertainment activity expenses. For example, if a salesman took a customer hunting for a day at a commercial shooting preserve, the expenses of the hunt, such as hunting rights, dogs, a guide, etc., would be deductible provided that the current law requirements of substantiation, adequate records, ordinary and necessary, directly related, etc. are met. However, if the hunters stayed overnight at a hunting lodge on the shooting preserve, the cost attributable to the lodging would be nondeductible but expenses for any meals would be deductible if they satisfied the requirements of current law. The shooting preserve should

---

[59] Reg. §1.274-2(e)(3)(ii) (luncheon clubs); Rev. Rul. 63-144, 1963-2 CB 129, 138–139 (professional organizations, etc.). See also Smith v. CIR, 24 TCM (CCH) 899 (1965) (business-related initiation fee was nondeductible capital expenditure).

[60] IRC §274(a)(2)(C).

[61] See, however, W.L. Schautz Co. v. US, 567 F2d 373 (Ct. Cl. 1977) (corporation denied loss deduction on sale of residential property held for personal use of shareholders). Compare IRC §§183(b), 280A(b) (taxes, interest, etc., attributable to hobbies and vacation homes may be deducted if allowable without regard to business or profit-oriented objective), discussed infra ¶¶22.5 and 22.6.

provide the taxpayer with an allocation of charges attributable to the overnight lodging for the taxpayer and guests.

The [rule is also] inapplicable to expenditures for tickets to sporting and theatrical events, regardless of whether the tickets are purchased individually, in a series or by the season, or by an equivalent fee which entitles the taxpayer to use a seat. Ticket costs generally remain subject to the provisions of present law relating to entertainment activities, or to those which govern the deductibility of business gifts.

In addition, the [1978 legislation] continues a number of the present statutory exceptions to the facility expense rules. Thus, for example, otherwise allowable deductions for expenditures relating to the following items are not covered by the [legislation]: (1) facilities located on the taxpayer's business premises and used in connection with furnishing food and beverages to employees, (2) certain employee recreational facilities, (3) facility expenses treated as employee compensation, (4) facilities made available to the general public, (5) facilities used in connection with a taxpayer's trade or business of selling entertainment for adequate and full consideration in bona fide transactions, and (6) facilities actively used in the taxpayer's business of selling such facilities. The [legislation] however, also continues any applicable present law limitations on these exceptions, including those pertaining to substantiation and allocation of expenses.[62]

Finally, expenses paid or incurred by individuals and S corporations for apartments, vacation homes, and other dwelling units—even if they satisfy all of the requirements of §274—are subject to the special disallowance rules imposed by §280A whenever personal use exceeds the greater of 14 days per year or 10 percent of the days during which the unit is rented.[63]

¶21.2.4 Exempted Expenses

Section 274(e) exempts a variety of expenses for entertainment, amusement, and recreation from the business-relationship and disallowance rules of §274(a). Many, but not all, of these exceptions also apply to the requirement that the taxpayer or an employee be present when food or beverages are furnished and to the 80 percent rule that denies 20 percent of the cost of business meals and entertainment that clear all other hurdles erected by §274. Further, the exempted items cannot be deducted unless they are

---

[62] Joint Comm. on Tax'n, supra note 56, at 207–08. For the exceptions referred to by this report, see Reg. §1.274-2(e)(3)(iii)(*a*) (out-of-pocket expenditures), §1.274-2(b)(1)(i), §1.274-2(b)(1)(iii)(*c*) (business travel). For the preexisting statutory exceptions listed in the report, see infra ¶21.2.4.

[63] For §280A, see infra ¶22.6.

ordinary and necessary expenses of carrying on the taxpayer's business or profit-oriented activities as required by §162 or §212, and they may be subject to the substantiation rules of §274(d).[64]

The exemptions granted by §274(e) are elaborated and qualified at such length by the regulations that it is impossible to do more than summarize their scope. They encompass the following expenses:

1. *Business meals.* For taxable years before 1987, expenses for food and beverages furnished in circumstances conducive to a business discussion, such as a life insurance agent's meeting with a client at lunch during a normal business day, were exempted.[65] Business luncheons or dinners that were part of a business program or sponsored by a trade association could also qualify, and meals or beverages served in the taxpayer's residence qualified "on a clear showing that the expenditure was commercially rather than socially motivated." The exemption, however, did not apply to nightclubs, sporting events, large cocktail parties, sizable social gatherings, and other events entailing "major distractions not conducive to business discussions."

This exception has been repealed for taxable years after 1986, and business meals must now meet the directly-related-to or associated-with test of §274(a), just like all other entertainment expenses. The principal effect of the repeal is that conduciveness to business discussion is no longer sufficient, and the more direct ties to business required by §274(a) must now be shown.

2. *Food and beverages furnished to employees.* Expenses for food and beverages furnished on the taxpayer's business premises primarily for employees are exempted, including expenses for related facilities, such as a company cafeteria or executive dining room.[66]

This exception lifts only the bar of §274(a). Costs of operating a facility primarily for employees, however, rarely fail to meet the requirement that the taxpayer or an employee be present. Also, another provision often excepts these costs from the 80 percent rule; an employer's costs for a de minimis fringe benefit are not subject to the 80 percent rule, and meals at an eating facility for employees on the employer's business premises are a

---

[64] The regulations exempt some expenses from the substantiation requirements as well as from the business-relationship tests. See Reg. §1.274-5(c)(7) (§§274(e)(1), (2), (7), and (8) expenses not subject to substantiation rules; §274(e)(4) expenses subject to limited substantiation requirements); infra ¶21.4.3.

[65] IRC §274(e)(1) (before amendment in 1986); Reg. §1.274-2(f)(2)(i)(*b*).

[66] IRC §274(e)(1); Reg. §1.274-2(f)(2)(ii). See Haman v. CIR, 31 TCM (CCH) 466 (1972), modified as to other issues, 500 F2d 401 (9th Cir. 1974) (commercial fisherman exempted under several of the §274(e) exceptions with respect to food and drinks used on his boat to feed his crew, restaurant meals for crew as reward for efficient performance, and Christmas parties for crew).

de minimis fringe benefit if charges for the meals at least cover the direct operating costs of the facility.[67]

3. *Expenses treated as compensation.* Expenses for goods, services, and facilities are exempted from §274(a), the presence-of-the-taxpayer requirement, and the 80 percent rule if the employer treats them as wages subject to withholding and the employee treats them as compensation.[68] An example of an item that should be covered by this rule is a vacation trip for outstanding performance in a sales contest.

A parallel exception applies to entertainment provided to a person who is not an employee of the taxpayer, but is nevertheless taxed on the value of the entertainment as compensation for services.[69] To gain the benefit of this exception, however, the taxpayer must report the item on an information return, even if its value falls below $600, the minimum amount covered by the reporting requirement that usually applies to such items.[70]

4. *Reimbursed expenses.* Expenses paid or incurred by the taxpayer in performing services for an employer or other person under a reimbursement or expense allowance arrangement are exempted in two situations.[71] If the services are performed as an employee, the exemption applies to expenses that are not treated as compensation. In other cases, reimbursed expenses are exempted if the taxpayer accounts to the person making the reimbursement as provided by §274(d). This exception applies to the presence-of-the-taxpayer requirement and the 80 percent rule, as well as to §274(a).[72]

As a consequence, these rules usually apply only once, either to the person making an expenditure or to the person bearing the expense, but not to both.[73] If an expenditure is incurred by an employee under a reimbursement or other expense allowance arrangement with his employer, the rules apply to the employer unless the employer's income tax return as originally filed treats the expense as compensation and wages subject to withholding; in the latter case, the rules apply to the employee.[74]

---

[67] IRC §§132(e)(2), 274(n)(2)(B). See supra ¶14.1 for the fringe benefit rules.

[68] IRC §274(e)(2); Reg. §1.274-2(f)(2)(iii).

[69] IRC §274(e)(9). The exception also applies if the nonemployee recipient can exclude the item as a prize. This aspect of the exception, however, rarely applies because, for taxable years after 1986, a prize to a person other than an employee cannot be excluded as a prize unless, among other things, it is turned over to charity. See supra ¶11.1.

[70] IRC §6041(a), discussed infra ¶111.1.9.

[71] IRC §274(e)(3); Reg. §1.274-2(f)(2)(iv).

[72] IRC §§274(k)(2), (n)(2)(A).

[73] Reg. §§1.274-2(f)(2)(iv)(*a*), (*b*).

[74] Id. The term "reimbursement or other expense allowance arrangement" has the same meaning as under §62(a)(2)(A), defining adjusted gross income, but without regard to whether there is an employer-employee relationship between the parties. For the treatment of independent contractors, see Reg. §1.274-2(f)(2)(iv)(*c*).

5. *Employee recreational activities.* Expenses for recreational, social, or similar activities, and for related facilities (e.g., employee picnics and baseball fields) are exempted if incurred primarily for the benefit of employees other than highly compensated employees.[75] An employee is "highly compensated" if (1) his compensation from the employer exceeds $75,000, (2) his compensation exceeds $50,000 and places him among the most highly compensated 20 percent of the employees, (3) he is a greater than 5 percent shareholder, partner, or proprietor of the employer, or (4) he is an officer receiving compensation above a prescribed level.[76]

6. *Business meetings of employees, etc.* Expenses directly related to meetings of the taxpayer's employees, shareholders, agents, or directors are exempted from §274(a), but not from the presence-of-the-taxpayer requirement or the 80 percent rule.[77] If a corporation serves tea and cookies at a meeting of its directors, for example, it need not satisfy the directly-related-to or associated-with test of §274(a), but only 80 percent of the expense is deductible.

7. *Meetings and conventions of business leagues.* Expenses directly related and necessary to attendance at a business meeting or convention of a business league, chamber of commerce, or other tax-exempt organization described by §501(c)(6) are exempted from §274(a).[78] The presence-of-the-taxpayer requirement and the 80 percent rule, however, apply to these expenses.[79]

8. *Items made available to the public.* Expenses for goods, services, and facilities made available by the taxpayer to the general public are exempted from §274(a), the presence-of-the-taxpayer requirement, and the 80 percent rule.[80] Examples of items covered by this exception are "expenditures for entertainment of the general public by means of television, radio, newspa-

---

For related but not identical rules determining which party to a reimbursement arrangement must substantiate expenditures under §274(d), see infra ¶21.4.4 (employees), ¶21.4.5 (independent contractors).

[75] IRC §274(e)(4); Reg. §1.274-2(f)(2)(v). See Termicold Corp. v. US, 2 Cl. Ct. 351, 83-1 USTC ¶9350 (1983) (expenses of company yacht, use of which was limited to executive employees, not covered by this exception).

[76] IRC §§274(e)(4), 414(q). See infra ¶61.2.2 for more on the definition of "highly compensated."

[77] IRC §274(e)(5); Reg. §1.274-2(f)(2)(vi).

[78] IRC §274(e)(6); Reg. §1.274-2(f)(2)(vii). For §501(c)(6), see infra ¶102.3.

[79] A transition rule that applies through 1988, however, exempts from the 80 percent rule food and beverages at a "convention, seminar, annual meeting, or similar business program" if (1) the cost of the food and beverages is not separately stated in the charge for the program, (2) more than one half of the participants in the program are away from home, (3) at least 40 people attend the program, and (4) there is a speaker at the function where the food and beverages are furnished. IRC §§274(n)(2)(D), (3).

[80] IRC §274(e)(7); Reg. §1.274-2(f)(2)(viii).

pers and the like," and "expenditures for maintaining private parks, golf courses and similar facilities, to the extent that they are available for public use."[81]

9. *Entertainment sold to customers.* Expenses for goods and services sold by the taxpayer in bona fide transactions for full value in money or money's worth are exempted from §274(a), the presence-of-the-taxpayer requirement, and the 80 percent rule.[82] This provision, inserted out of an excess of caution, ensures that expenses incurred by nightclubs, cruise ships, and other purveyors of entertainment in furnishing their services to customers are not subject to the special rules of §274. If a reductio ad absurdum of this kind of overly broad legislation is needed, it can be found in this exception, which assures the owners of resort hotels that they can deduct the salaries of nightclub performers even if "substantial and bona fide business discussions" cannot be conducted while the show is going on.

¶21.2.5 Substantiation

Even if they satisfy the substantive rules of §274(a), expenses for entertainment, amusement, and recreation can only be deducted if substantiated as required by §274(d), discussed later in this chapter.[83]

¶21.3 BUSINESS GIFTS

¶21.3.1 $25 Per Donee Limit

Most payments qualifying as business expenses under §162(a) are included in the recipient's gross income as compensation for services or payments for goods. In a few situations, however, the payor may be entitled to a deduction even though the payee can exclude the amount received from gross income under §102(a) as a gift. In 1962, as part of a broad campaign against deductions for entertainment and similar activities,[1] Congress enacted §274(b), under which no deduction is allowed under §162 or §212 for gifts to an individual in excess of $25 per donee per year.[2] For this purpose, the term "gift" means an item that (1) is excludable from the recipient's gross income under §102, relating to gifts, but (2) is not excludable under

---

[81] Reg. §1.274-2(f)(2)(viii).

[82] IRC §274(e)(8); Reg. §1.274-2(f)(2)(ix).

[83] See infra ¶21.4.

[1] See supra ¶21.2.1.

[2] Although the statute literally bars any deduction when the $25 limit is exceeded, it has been interpreted to disallow only the excess over $25. Feinstein v. CIR, 34 TCM (CCH) 830 (1975). For a question-and-answer explanation of §274(b), see Rev. Rul. 63-144, 1963-2 CB 129, 142–44.

any other statutory provision. Thus, a scholarship or the first $5,000 of an employee's death benefit is not subject to the $25 limit if it qualifies for exclusion from the recipient's gross income under §117 (scholarships and fellowships) or §101(b) (employee death benefits up to $5,000).[3]

Normally, a transfer is a gift for purposes of §102 only if it proceeds from detached and disinterested generosity.[4] Section 274(b), however, is mostly concerned with transfers that arise from motivations having to do more with business advantage than generosity. These transfers are excluded from the recipient's gross income under an unverbalized extension of the meaning of "gift," covering gratuitous transfers of items of small value. If an automobile dealer gives out calendars bearing the picture of a shiny new Cadillac, the calendars are excludable gifts, even if the dealer is a Scrooge who wouldn't part with a nickel without knowing precisely what he would get in return. In contrast, if the dealer gives a real Cadillac to a person who has been exceptionally helpful in developing the dealer's business, the recipient is probably taxed. The distinction turns on the value of the items, not the underlying motivation.

The $25 annual limit of §274(b), which is based on the cost of the donated item to the donor,[5] is computed on an aggregate basis for each donee. Thus, two gifts of $20 each to the same donee are combined and subjected to the $25 limit. Gifts are deemed made to a particular individual if made "directly or indirectly" to him. As interpreted by the regulations, this language imputes gifts to individuals having business connections with the taxpayer, even if the item is given to the individual's spouse or other family member.[6] In the same vein, gifts to a corporation or other business entity for eventual personal use by an employee, stockholder, or owner are treated as made to the ultimate individual beneficiaries. Gifts to a business organization for distribution to a large group of individuals, however, are not subject to this treatment unless it is reasonably practicable for the taxpayer to ascertain the ultimate beneficiaries.[7] If the beneficiaries of a

---

[3] Reg. §1.274-3(b)(1). See supra ¶11.2 (scholarships and fellowships), ¶10.2.4 (employee death benefits).

[4] See supra ¶10.2.

[5] Reg. §1.274-3(c) (incidental costs for engraving, packaging, and mailing are disregarded if they do not add substantial value to the gift).

[6] Reg. §1.274-3(d)(1). If the husband and wife are engaged in business together, however, a gift to one is not imputed to the other unless intended for the latter's use or benefit.

[7] Reg. §1.274-3(d)(2). See World Wide Agency, Inc. v. CIR, 42 TCM (CCH) 617 (1981) (taxpayer's reimbursement of costs of business gifts made by independent contractor not subject to §274(b) because it was a cost of obtaining contractor's services, not of business gifts; alternatively, if taxpayer was donor, it was not reasonably practicable for taxpayer to ascertain ultimate beneficiaries, who were chosen by independent contractor).

transfer to an entity are not reasonably ascertainable, an otherwise allowable deduction is not restricted by the $25 limit, since it applies only to individual donees.

In applying the $25 limit to donors, §274(b)(2) provides that a married couple is considered a single donor, whether joint or separate returns are filed, and that partnership gifts are subject to the $25 limit at both the partnership level and the level of the individual partners.[8] Thus, regardless of the number of partners, the deduction for a partnership gift cannot exceed $25 per donee, and this amount must be shared by the partners on their individual returns in proportion to their distributive shares of the partnership's income or loss.[9]

Because business gifts and entertainment are often alternative or intertwined modes of promoting the taxpayer's products, the regulations address, but only briefly, the problem of distinguishing between them. Expenditures that might generally be considered either gifts or entertainment are to be considered entertainment (a classification that brings into play the strict business-relationship and 80 percent rules of §274).[10] An expenditure for packaged food or beverages transferred to the donee for consumption at a later time, in contrast, is a gift.[11] Tickets to theaters and other places of entertainment are gifts rather than entertainment if the taxpayer does not accompany the recipient to the event, unless the taxpayer chooses to treat the item as entertainment.[12]

The enactment of §274(b) in 1962 significantly altered the stakes in determining whether borderline payments by employers to retired employees or the families of deceased employees constitute taxable compensation for services or tax-free gifts. The pre-1962 halcyon days when the employer could deduct such a payment under §162 with impunity, even though the recipient excluded it from gross income under §102, are gone.[13] An employer who is familiar with §274(b) is more likely to describe the payment as belated compensation than in the old days and is less likely to supply helpful letters or affidavits to the payees when their tax returns are audited. Congress took the matter a step further in 1986 by providing that a transfer to or for the benefit of an employee can never be an excludable gift, thus narrowing the field for dispute to transfers to relatives of deceased

---

[8] IRC §274(b)(2); Reg. §1.274-3(e).

[9] For the allocation of partnership income and loss, see infra ¶86.2.

[10] Supra ¶21.2.1.

[11] Reg. §1.274-2(b)(1)(iii)(*b*).

[12] Id. The rule denying deductions for scalpers' premiums and skyboxes, however, applies whether a ticket is classified as a gift or entertainment. See supra ¶21.2.3.

[13] See supra ¶10.2.4.

employees.[14]

¶21.3.2 Exempted Items

Section 274(b)(1) exempts two categories of items from the $25 limit: (1) items costing the taxpayer not more than $4 each, on which the taxpayer's name is imprinted and which are distributed generally (e.g., desk calendars, ballpoint pens, and similar advertising tokens); and (2) signs, display racks, and other promotional items to be used on the recipient's business premises. Although the exemption of these items from the $25 limit of §274(b) does not automatically establish that they are deductible, they ordinarily qualify as business expenses under §162.[15]

For taxable years before 1987, a third exception was allowed for items of tangible personal property awarded to employees for length of service, productivity, or safety achievements.[16] The exception applied only if the item cost the taxpayer less than $400 or was a "qualified plan award." An item was a "qualified plan award" if (1) the award was pursuant to a plan that did not discriminate in favor of officers, shareholders, or highly compensated employees, and (2) the average cost of all items awarded under the plan during the taxable year did not exceed $400. Although particular items awarded under the plan could have a cost exceeding $400 (so long as the average cost did not go above $400), any excess of an item's cost over $1,600 was not deductible.

The exception for employee awards was repealed in connection with Congress' decision in 1986 to deny gift treatment to all transfers to employees. In its place was enacted §274(j), a similar but more complex provision, which is described elsewhere in this work.[17]

¶21.3.3 Substantiation

Along with expenditures for entertainment and travel, business gifts must meet the substantiation requirements of §274(d), discussed below.[18]

---

[14] See supra ¶10.2.3.

[15] But see Lancaster Stone Prods. Corp. v. CIR, 28 TCM (CCH) 619 (1969) (deduction for cost of tickets to political dinners, allegedly distributed to customers, barred by §276, relating to indirect contributions to political parties).

[16] IRC §274(b)(3)(C) (before repeal in 1986). The provision described in the text applied to awards made before 1987 in taxable years ending after August 12, 1981. For prior years, the exception applied to awards costing no more than $100 made in recognition of length of service or for saftey achievement. IRC §274(b)(1)(C) (before amendment in 1981).

[17] Infra ¶22.2.5.

[18] Infra ¶21.4. Items exempted by §274(b)(1) from the $25 limit (supra ¶21.3.2) are not "gifts" within the meaning of §274(d) and, hence, are not subject to its

Given the $25 limit on deductions for business gifts, it is surprising to find that they are subject to the full panoply of documentation required for travel and entertainment deductions, which present much greater opportunities for exaggeration and fraud.

¶21.4 SUBSTANTIATION

¶21.4.1 Introductory

In order to deduct expenses for travel, entertainment, amusement, recreation, or business gifts or to deduct expenses of automobiles or home computers, the taxpayer must meet the stiff substantiation requirements of §274(d).[1] The substantiation requirements also apply to credits associated with entertainment facilities, automobiles, and home computers. These rules, which are elaborately amplified by the regulations, supersede the *Cohan* decision, which held that if a taxpayer incurs deductible expenses but cannot prove the exact amount, the trial court must make "as close an approximation as it can" rather than disallow the deduction entirely.[2] The regulations, with support from the legislative history, provide that "no deduction shall be allowed a taxpayer for [items subject to §274(d)] on the basis of such approximations or unsupported testimony of the taxpayer."[3] Section 274(d), however, only applies to travel, entertainment, and gift expenses, and to deductions and credits relating to automobiles, other vehicles, and computers and peripheral equipment; for other deductions and items, the *Cohan* doctrine remains in force.[4]

---

substantiation requirements. Reg. §1.274-5(a) (substantiation required for "gifts defined in section 274").

[1] For travel expenses, see supra ¶21.1; for entertainment expenses, see supra ¶21.2; for business gifts, see supra ¶21.3. See also Quinn v. CIR, 33 TCM (CCH) 310 (1974) (movie actor's photography expenses on trip in preparation for film not subject to §274(d) requirements).

See generally Eichel, The Missouri Rule—Substantiation Requirements for Travel and Entertainment Expenditures Under Section 274(d) of the Internal Revenue Code of 1954, 18 U. Miami L. Rev. 613 (1964).

[2] Cohan v. CIR, 39 F2d 540 (2d Cir. 1930), discussed supra ¶20.1.9.

[3] Reg. §1.274-5(a); S. Rep. No. 1881, 87th Cong., 2d Sess., reprinted in 1962-3 CB 707, 877 ("if the taxpayer fails to substantiate an item as required by [§274(d)] and the regulations thereunder, the item will be completely disallowed").

For a Treasury study documenting the administrative difficulties created by the *Cohan* doctrine, see President's Tax Message, H. Doc. No. 140, 87th Cong., 1st Sess. 177 (1961) (with supporting exhibits and documents, submitted by Secretary Dillon to the House Ways and Means Comm.).

[4] See Stewart v. CIR, 35 TCM (CCH) 1762 (1976) (in case arising before §274(d) extended to local transportation expenses, *Cohan* applied in determining deduction for such expenses); Freedman v. CIR, 35 TCM (CCH) 1531 (1976)

For most deductions and credits subject to §274(d), the taxpayer is required to substantiate, by adequate records or sufficient evidence corroborating his own statement, four aspects of the deducted or credited item: (1) its amount; (2) the time and place of the travel, entertainment, or use of the facility or the date and description of the gift; (3) the business purpose of the item; and (4) the business relationship between the taxpayer and the persons entertained, using the facility, or receiving the gift.[5] For automobiles, other vehicles, and computers and peripherals, the substantiation must show (1) the amount of each expenditure with respect to the property, including the purchase price, lease payments, and maintenance expenses; (2) the amount of the business or other profit-oriented use of the property for the taxable year and the amount of total use for the same period (for automobiles, measured in miles traveled); (3) the date of each expenditure and use; and (4) the business purpose of each expenditure or use.[6]

Because §274(d) is only concerned with substantiation, it does not come into play until the taxpayer establishes that the item is otherwise deductible under the substantive rules of §§162, 212, and 274(a). The mere fact that an item can be substantiated does not establish that it is deductible.

¶21.4.2 Items Subject to §274(d) Substantiation

Section 274(d) applies to the following four classes of deductions and credits: (1) deductions under §162 or §212 for traveling expenses, including meals and lodging while away from home; (2) entertainment costs, including both expenses of activities generally considered to be entertainment, amusement, or recreation and items relating to facilities used in connection with these activities; (3) deductible gifts; and (4) deductions and credits with respect to personal automobiles, other transportation equipment, computers, and computer peripherals.

(*Cohan* applied in allocating expenditures, which were disallowed as corporate deductions under §274(d), between constructive dividends to sole shareholder and nondeductible expenditures for corporation's own benefit); Evans v. CIR, 33 TCM (CCH) 1192 (1974), modified as to other issues, 557 F2d 1095 (5th Cir. 1977) (*Cohan* doctrine used to allocate expenditures among categories subject to §274(d) and other categories not subject to its substantiation rules).

[5] For an elaboration of these four elements of an expenditure, see Reg. §1.274-5T(b).

See Erickson v. CIR, 598 F2d 525 (9th Cir. 1979) (failure to substantiate entertainment expenses incurred by taxpayer's corporation, resulting in nondeductibility at corporate level, does not necessarily result in constructive distribution to shareholder-employee).

[6] Reg. §1.274-5T(b)(6).

The fourth of these categories, consisting principally of cars and home computers, was added in 1984. Previously, the statute, which always applied to "traveling expense (including meals and lodging while away from home)," was held inapplicable to deductions for local transportation expenses, including expenses of local usage of an automobile in business.[7] The purpose of the 1984 extension of §274(d) is to require substantiation of expenses on the personal-business borderline. Because an automobile, for example, is so susceptible to personal use, extra care is warranted to ensure that deductions for automobile expense reflect true business use. According to the regulations, the statute does not cover vehicles "not likely to be used more than a de minimis amount for personal purposes."[8] Examples of vehicles not covered are police cars, fire engines, moving vans, and cement mixers.

Although most items subject to substantiation are current out-of-pocket expenditures, items not involving current payments, such as depreciation on automobiles, computers, and entertainment facilities, are also burdened by the requirement.

¶21.4.3 Substantiating Evidence

In general, each of the four elements specified by §274(d), as previously summarized, must be substantiated by either "adequate records" or "sufficient evidence corroborating [the taxpayer's] statement."[9] The regulations elaborate on these requirements at some length.

1. *Adequate records.* To substantiate an item by adequate records, the taxpayer must maintain an account book, diary, statement of expense, or similar record in which each element of an expenditure is recorded "at or near the time of the expenditure."[10] An adequate record must include a written statement of business purpose, unless it is evident from the sur-

---

[7] Cobb v. CIR, 77 TC 1096 (1981); Rev. Proc. 63-4, 1963-1 CB 474, 475.

[8] Reg. §1.274-5T(d)(2)(i).

[9] Reg. §1.274-5T(c)(1). The regulations, however, empower the IRS to ask for even more information. See Reg. §§1.274-5T(c)(6)(iv), (d) (disclosure of information may be required on tax returns). These requirements were summarized in a 1980 Tax Court case as follows: "In laymen's terms, a taxpayer who seeks to deduct traveling expenses must prove by his records or by his testimony and records the amount he spent, when he spent it, where he spent it, and how the expenditure related to his business." Hatch v. CIR, 40 TCM (CCH) 110 (1980) (detailed analysis of taxpayer's travel expense diary).

[10] For the meaning of "at or near the time of the expenditure," see Reg. §1.274-5T(c)(2)(ii)(A). Confidential information need not appear in the account book or other similar record if it is recorded at or near the time of the expenditure and is available to the IRS for substantiation purposes. Reg. §1.274-5T(c)(2)(ii)(D).

rounding facts and circumstances, such as a salesman's travel to call on customers on an established sales route.[11]

For automobiles, other vehicles, computers, and computer peripherals, "the record must contain sufficient information as to each element of every business/investment use."[12] The amount of detail required, however, depends on the taxpayer's circumstances. If a truck is used for personal purposes and also for business deliveries along a standard route, for example, the only record necessary at or near the time of a business use might be a notation of the days on which the delivery trip was made; with this information, the deduction for business use can be determined from the length of each trip, the number of trips made during the year, and the number of miles the truck was driven during the year. A record of business use of an automobile or computer must usually be in writing, but can be made with "a computer memory device with the aid of a logging program."

For away-from-home lodging expenditures and other expenditures of $25 or more, the adequate records requirement can only be satisfied with documentary evidence (receipts, paid bills, etc.).[13] Documentary evidence should establish the amount, date, place, and essential character of the expenditure. A hotel receipt with the date of lodging and separate entries for charges such as lodging, meals, and telephone calls may be sufficient, but a canceled check with a bill from the payee might establish only the cost element.[14]

If a taxpayer substantially complies with the adequate records requirement, he may be permitted to establish a particular element of the substantiation with other "adequate evidence" instead of being required to produce full substantiation.[15]

In a case in which the taxpayer produced over 1,700 bills, chits, "and other memorabilia" to substantiate deductions under §274, the Court of Appeals for the Fifth Circuit held that the requirements of the regulations must be applied expenditure by expenditure and that a generalized finding of business purpose cannot take the place of a specific finding with respect to each item:

> The District Court found that the times, places and amounts of expenditures had been clearly provided by "a virtual blizzard of bills,

---

[11] Reg. §1.274-5T(c)(2)(ii)(B).

[12] Reg. §1.274-5T(c)(2)(ii)(C).

[13] Reg. §1.274-5T(c)(2)(iii). Documentary evidence is not required for transportation charges if not readily available. The exemption for expenditures of less than $25 each relieves the taxpayer of the need to substantiate the item with a receipt or paid bill, but does not waive the "account book" requirement. Reg. §§1.274-5T(c)(2)(i), (e)(2)(iii); Silverton v. CIR, 37 TCM (CCH) 142 (1978).

[14] Reg. §1.274-5T(c)(2)(iii).

[15] Reg. §1.274-5T(c)(2)(v).

chits and other papers relating to [the taxpayer's] meals with other persons." The District Court also determined that those elements for which adequate records had not been provided, namely, the business purpose and business relationship of those entertained, had been adequately substantiated by [the taxpayer's] own testimony as corroborated by the oral testimony of some twenty witnesses. . . .

The District Court's finding that the "blizzard" of bills, chits, etc. established the amounts, dates and places of expenditures misapprehended the specificity with which a taxpayer must substantiate each expenditure deducted under §274(d). It is apparent that the District Court was snowed under by the volume of paper in evidence and chose not to wade through it to make an expenditure-by-expenditure determination, instead making a general determination that the deductions were substantiated. Yet, this is just what §274(d) requires the District Court to do. A less stringent examination would echo the approach under the former *Cohan* rule and clearly defeat the purpose of §274(d). . . . The substantiation statute says "the"—not "a"—business relationship. [With respect to entertainment expense, for example,] the business relationship cannot be ascertained unless the taxpayer establishes the identity of his entertainee—whether by name, title or other specific designation. If such identification were not required, the element of business relationship would be redundant, since "business purpose" almost necessarily requires showing "a" business relationship.[16]

2. *Taxpayer's corroborated statement.* In lieu of adequate records, taxpayers may rely on their own written or oral statements, if corroborated by other evidence "sufficient to establish each element."[17] Spouses may corroborate each other's statements even if they file joint returns,[18] but a taxpayer may not corroborate oral testimony with an exhibit prepared by a secretary approximating the expenditures on the basis of the recollections underlying the taxpayer's oral testimony.[19] Direct corroborative evidence is required as to all elements of the expenditure except its business purpose and the

---

[16] Dowell v. US, 522 F2d 708, 714–15 (5th Cir. 1975), cert. denied, 426 US 920 (1976). See also Lennon v. CIR, 37 TCM (CCH) 751 (1978) (*Dowell* principle applied).

[17] Reg. §1.274-5T(c)(3)(i). As originally promulgated, the regulations required the taxpayer's statement to be in writing, but this requirement was held invalid in LaForge v. CIR, 434 F2d 370 (2d Cir. 1970) (taxpayer's oral testimony adequate if sufficiently precise and properly corroborated). Thereafter, the regulations were retroactively amended to permit either oral or written statements by the taxpayer. TD 7226, 1973-1 CB 153.

[18] Durgom v. CIR, 33 TCM (CCH) 276 (1974).

[19] Quinn v. CIR, 33 TCM (CCH) 310 (1974).

business relationship between the taxpayer and the persons entertained; these elements can be proved by circumstantial evidence.[20]

The corroboration method can be combined with the adequate records method by maintaining adequate records for part of the year and using these records to corroborate the taxpayer's statement as to the remainder of the year; the corroboration, however, must include evidence that the portion of the year for which records are maintained is representative of the entire year.[21] If a taxpayer keeps an adequate record showing that 75 percent of an automobile's use is for business over a three-month period during the taxable year and further shows that the level of business for those three months was similar to that during the remainder of the year, the combination method allows the car to be treated as used 75 percent for business during the whole year.[22] Alternatively, the business usage of the car could be established in this case by keeping a record of actual use for business during the first week of each month.[23] Although this sampling technique seems intended primarily for automobile expense, the regulations allow it for other items subject to substantiation under §274(d).

3. *Exceptional circumstances.* The foregoing requirements are relaxed by the regulations if the taxpayer is unable to meet them "by reason of the inherent nature of the situation in which an expenditure was made"[24] or because his records were lost through circumstances beyond his control.[25] In the first situation, the regulations require the taxpayer to present other evidence of each element required to be substantiated "which possesses the highest degree of probative value possible under the circumstances," while in the latter situation the deductions can be substantiated by a "reasonable

---

[20] Reg. §1.274-5T(c)(3)(i).

[21] Reg. §1.274-5T(c)(3)(ii)(A).

[22] Reg. §1.274-5T(c)(3)(ii)(C) Ex. 1.

[23] Reg. §1.274-5T(c)(3)(ii)(C) Ex. 2.

[24] Reg. §1.274-5T(c)(4).

[25] Reg. §1.274-5T(c)(5). This exception is strictly construed by the Tax Court. See, e.g., Gizzi v. CIR, 65 TC 342 (1975) (marital difficulties do not "sufficiently resemble floods or fire to be considered a casualty"); Rembusch v. CIR, 38 TCM (CCH) 310 (1979) (need to return records to employer not "loss" since taxpayer could have copied them); Miller v. CIR, 34 TCM (CCH) 1541 (1975) (loss of records on dissolution of predecessor corporation not comparable to casualty); Holderness v. CIR, 36 TCM (CCH) 13 (1977), aff'd per curiam, 615 F2d 401 (6th Cir. 1980) (same as to "vague" testimony regarding loss of records when business transferred); Freedman v. CIR, 35 TCM (CCH) 1531 (1976) (loss of records does not shift burden of reconstruction to IRS; taxpayer made no effort to obtain testimony of others who might have expanded or corroborated his testimony). For cases applying the lost-records rule, see Schneider v. CIR, 37 TCM (CCH) 1847 (1978) (tax diary mailed to IRS; lost either in mail or by IRS); Jackson v. CIR, 34 TCM (CCH) 1315 (1975) (records lost by IRS).

reconstruction" of the taxpayer's expenditures.[26]

4. *Separate or aggregated expenditures.* In applying the substantiation rules, each separate payment is a separate "expenditure," but concurrent or repetitive payments during a single event (e.g., several rounds of drinks in a cocktail lounge) are treated as a single expenditure.[27] The account book or diary entry must record each separate expenditure, except that (1) tips or gratuities may be aggregated with the expenses to which they relate and (2) travel expenses may be aggregated daily in reasonable categories (i.e., gasoline and oil, meals, and taxi fares).[28] Where several people participate in an event whose cost the taxpayer cannot allocate to each person, a pro rata allocation ordinarily suffices.[29]

A "round trip or uninterrupted business use" of an automobile or other vehicle can be aggregated.[30] A salesman who makes an extended trip away from home, for example, can account for automobile use as a single figure of miles traveled in the entire trip, and a delivery route can be accounted for as one trip even though there are stops at the business places of several customers. A business use is considered uninterrupted for this purpose even if it is broken up by "de minimis personal use (such as a stop for lunch on the way between two business stops)."

5. *Entertainment facilities.* For years prior to 1979 (when deductions were allowed for entertainment facilities if their primary use was for business),[31] a taxpayer claiming such expenses was required not only to maintain records as to each business use of the facility in accordance with the above requirements but also to maintain proper records as to the facility's non-business use.[32] Failure to maintain "adequate records" concerning a facility likely to serve personal purposes resulted in a presumption that its use was

---

[26] Reg. §1.274-5T(c)(4) ("inherent nature" exception), §1.274-5T(c)(5) (lost-records exception).

[27] Reg. §1.274-5T(c)(6)(i)(A).

[28] Reg. §1.274-5T(c)(6)(i)(B), §1.274-5T(b)(2) (travel), §1.274-5T(b)(3) (entertainment). As to tips, compare Moylan v. CIR, 27 TCM (CCH) 84 (1968) (allowing flat deduction of 15 percent of food and beverage bills) with Culwell v. Coard, 67-2 USTC ¶9508 (DNM 1967) (not officially reported) (disallowing similar computation for failure to satisfy substantiation requirements).

[29] Reg. §1.274-5T(c)(6)(ii). If an allocation is material (e.g., where business and personal guests are entertained at the same event), the taxpayer must establish the number of persons covered by the total expenditure.

[30] Reg. §1.274-5T(c)(6)(i)(C).

[31] See supra ¶21.2.3.

[32] Reg. §1.274-2(e)(4)(iii). See Berkley Mach. Works & Foundry Co. v. CIR, 623 F2d 898 (4th Cir. 1980) (requirements not met); Nicholls, North, Buse Co. v. CIR, 56 TC 1225 (1971) (acq.) (same).

primarily personal.[33]

6. *Contemporaneous records.* In 1984, in connection with the extension of the substantiation requirements to automobile expense, Congress enacted a short-lived amendment to §274(d) providing that only "contemporaneous" records would satisfy the requirements. Once the Treasury proposed regulations showing how this amendment would apply to automobile expense, Congress promptly restored the prior language allowing the requirements to be met by either "adequate records or . . . other sufficient evidence corroborating the taxpayer's own statement." In doing so, however, care was taken not to disapprove the Treasury's long-standing preference for contemporaneous written records.[34] In response, the following language, largely a repetition of language from earlier regulations, was included in the present regulations:

> A contemporaneous log is not required, but a record of the elements of an expenditure or of a business use of . . . property made at or near the time of the expenditure or use, supported by sufficient documentary evidence, has a high degree of credibility not present with respect to a statement prepared subsequent thereto when generally there is a lack of accurate recall. Thus, the corroborative evidence required to support a statement not made at or near the time of the expenditure or use must have a high degree of probative value to elevate such statement and evidence to the level of credibility reflected by a record made at or near the time of the expenditure or use supported by sufficient documentary evidence.[35]

7. *Standard mileage allowance and per diem allowances.* In lieu of accounting item by item for deductible expenses for automobiles or for meals while away from home on business, a taxpayer can take prescribed standard allowances. For automobile use, the standard allowance is a stipulated amount per mile.[36] For meal expenses, the standard amount is a fixed

---

[33] Reg. §1.274-5(c)(6)(iii) (last sentence). The regulations do not specify that the presumption is conclusive, and the language of §274(d) seems to allow rebuttal of the presumption by the taxpayer's corroborated statement.

[34] H.R. Rep. No. 34, 99th Cong., 1st Sess. (1985), reprinted in 1985-2 CB 35, 354.

[35] Reg. §1.274-5T(c)(1).

[36] Re. Proc. 85-49, 1985-2 CB 716 (for 1985 and subsequent years, standard allowance is 21 cents for each of first 15,000 miles of business use during taxable year, and 11 cents for each mile in excess of 15,000, in lieu of all operating and fixed costs, including depreciation, maintenance, repairs, gasoline, oil, insurance, and registration fees); Rev. Proc. 83-74, 1983-2 CB 593 (for 1983 and 1984, 20.5 cents for first 15,000 miles, and 11 cents thereafter); Rev. Proc. 82-61, 1982-2 CB 849 (for 1982, 20 cents for first 15,000, and 11 cents thereafter). A portion of the standard allowance must be treated as depreciation, and subtracted from the automobile's

daily allowance.[37]

¶21.4.4 Exempted Expenditures

The substantiation rules of §274(d) do not apply to items that are deductible without regard to their connection with a business or income-producing activity, such as home mortgage interest, certain taxes, and casualty losses.[38] The regulations also exempt:[39]

1. Expenses for food and beverage for employees, describe in §274(e)(1)".
2. Expenses treated as compensation, described in §274(e)(2).
3. Expenses for items made available to the general public, described in §274(e)(7).
4. Expenses for entertainment sold to customers, described in §274(e)(8).
5. Expenses for recreational and similar activities for employees, described in §274(e)(4), provided records or other evidence is kept to show that the activities or facilities were primarily for the benefit of employees other than highly compensated employees.

These items are also exempted from the substantive business-relationship rules of §274(a).[40] The two sets of exemptions, however, are not coextensive; some items (e.g., expenses of employee's recreational and social activities

---

adjusted basis under §1016(a). Rev. Proc. 87-49, 1987-2 CB 646 (depreciation rate is 10 cents per mile for 1987, 9 cents for 1986, 8 cents for 1983 through 1985, 7.5 cents for 1982, 7 cents for 1980 and 1981). If two or more automobiles are used alternately, the standard mileage rates apply to the total business mileage as though a single car were used.

A standard allowance is also provided for automobile use in various other contexts where a deduction is allowable. Rev. Proc. 85-49, 1985-2 CB 716 (for 1980 and subsequent years, standard allowance for automobile use in obtaining medical care or in connection with moving expense deduction is 9 cents per mile; for 1985 and thereafter, 12 cents per mile for automobile use in performing gratuitous services for charity). These rates are lower than the rates for business use because depreciation, general maintenance, general repairs, and liability insurance are not taken into account.

[37] Reg. §1.274-5T(g); Re. Proc. 83-71, 1983-2 CB 590 (the daily amount is $14 per day for travel requiring stay of less than 30 days in one general locality, or $9 per day for stay of 30 days or more; if elected, method must be used for all meal expenses during taxable year). See Rev. Proc. 88-3, 1988-1 IRB 29, at §3.01(15) (IRS will not rule on treatment of other fixed per day allowances).

[38] Reg. §1.274-6. See IRC §163 (interest), discussed infra ¶31.1; IRC §164 (taxes), discussed infra ¶32.1; IRC §165(c)(3) (casualty losses), discussed infra ¶34.1.

[39] Reg. §1.274-5T(c)(7).

[40] See supra ¶21.2.4.

and business meetings of employees and shareholders) are exempted from the business-relationship rules, but must be substantiated as required by §274(d).

¶21.4.5 Employee Expenses

When an employee incurs expenses solely for his employer's benefit and charges them to the employer or receives advances or reimbursements to cover them, he is partly relieved of the §274(d) substantiation burden if an adequate accounting to the employer is required and made.[41] The term "adequate accounting" means the submission to the employer of an account book or similar record with supporting documentary evidence, which together conform to the "adequate records" requirement discussed above.[42] The adequate accounting rule can be satisfied by more relaxed procedures in the event of exceptional circumstances or a loss of records due to circumstances beyond the employee's control, but it is not satisfied by his own statement even if corroborated by other evidence.[43]

If the employee satisfies the adequate accounting standard and the payments received from the employer equal his deductible expenses on his employer's behalf, he may omit both from his tax return.[44] If the payments received exceed the deductible expenses, however, he must include the excess in gross income.[45] In either case, the employee does not have to provide further substantiation of the expenses unless (1) he is related to his employer within the meaning of §267(b) or (2) the employer's accounting procedures are not adequate or cannot be determined to be adequate.[46] Whether the employer's procedures are adequate depends on all the facts and circumstances, including the use of proper internal controls, such as verification and approval of expense accounts by a responsible person other than the employee incurring the expenses.

---

[41] Reg. §1.274-5T(f). These expenses may also be exempted from the business-relationship rules of §274(a). See IRC §274(e)(4)(A); supra ¶21.2.4 notes 71–74.

[42] Reg. §1.274-5T(f)(4). The employee must account for all amounts received from the employer during the employee's taxable year, including amounts charged to the employer (on credit cards or otherwise). For the "adequate records" requirements, see supra ¶21.4.2.

[43] Reg. §1.274-5T(f)(4). For the more relaxed procedures, see Reg. §§1.274-5T(c)(3), (4).

[44] Reg. §1.274-5T(f)(2)(i). See also Rev. Rul. 66-78, 1966-1 CB 38 (where employer makes payment to one employee to cover expenses of group of employees, same result as to all individuals in group if adequate accounting given to employer).

[45] Reg. §1.274-5T(f)(2)(ii).

[46] Reg. §1.274-5T(f)(5). Relatedness is determined under §267(b), substituting 10 percent in place of the normal 50 percent in determining whether corporation and shareholder are related. For §267, see infra ¶78.3.

Although a proper accounting by an employee shifts the obligation to substantiate to the employer, it does not by itself ensure that the employee can exclude the reimbursement from gross income or deduct the expenses under §162. Reimbursements can be excluded from gross income only if they do not exceed the expenses "incurred by [the employee] solely for the benefit of his employer."[47] If reimbursements exceed allowable expenses, the excess is gross income, notwithstanding the adequacy of the employee's accounting.[48] In a 1977 case involving a taxpayer whose employer reimbursed 60 percent of residence-maintenance expenses because of partial business use, for example, the court held that even if the accounting to the employer under the reimbursement agreement relieved the employee of the obligation to substantiate the business use of the residence under §274(d), it did not establish the proper allocation of business-personal use under §162(a):

> [T]he taxpayer still has to justify his allocation between business and personal use as a matter of proving his entitlement under §162(a). In order to take these deductions, the taxpayer must meet the requirements of both §162(a) and §274. Nothing in the record supports the 60 percent allocation except the reimbursement agreement, and that agreement has little or no bearing on the problem. The company might have decided that the taxpayer was entitled to compensation for the inconvenience of having his home available at all times. That does not make such compensation nontaxable. The employer and the employee cannot, by agreement between themselves, convert part of the employee's compensation into a business expense for the employee.[49]

Although the employee's proof that the reimbursed amounts are not compensatory in character or that the expenses are bona fide business expenses need not satisfy the substantiation standards of §274(d), in practice the employee may have to produce rather similar details.

The substantive rules of §274(a) are applied only once, either to the person who makes the expenditures or to the person who bears the expense.[50] This does not preclude a double disallowance of deductions for reimbursed expenses. The employer may be denied a deduction for failure to satisfy §274(d), and the employee may fail to meet the standards of §162,

---

[47] Reg. §§1.274-5T(f)(2)(i), (iii).

[48] Reg. §1.274-5T(f)(2)(ii).

[49] Lewis v. CIR, 560 F2d 973, 978 (9th Cir. 1977). See also Noneman v. CIR, 37 TCM (CCH) 1195 (1978) (reimbursement by employer does not prove that expense was incurred solely for employer's benefit or was ordinary and necessary business expense of employee).

[50] Reg. §1.274-2(f)(2)(iv).

in which event the employee must include the reimbursed amounts in gross income under §61 without any offsetting deduction under §162.

An employee incurring deductible expenses on his employer's behalf in excess of the employer's reimbursements and other payments can deduct the excess only if he maintains records and evidence satisfying §274(d).[51] In this case, and in cases where the employer does not require an adequate accounting or the employee fails to make one, the employee must attach a statement to his tax return showing the total amount received from the employer (including charges to the employer), the nature of his occupation, the number of days away from home on business, and his business expenses broken down into categories such as transportation, meals and lodging, etc.[52]

An employer can meet his obligation to substantiate with respect to an automobile or other vehicle by treating the use of the vehicle for a particular period as all personal use by an employee or by satisfying certain conditions allowing use of the vehicle to be treated as all business. The use is treated as all personal by including in the employee's gross income "the value of the availability of the vehicle during the relevant period."[53] If a car owned by an employer is used exclusively by an employee for personal purposes, for example, the employer substantiates his deductions relating to the car by showing that the employee included the rental value of the car in his gross income.

A vehicle's use can be treated as all business use if the employer adopts and enforces a policy forbidding all personal use.[54] If the employer does this, employees need not keep records of their use of the vehicle. A policy forbidding personal use other than in commuting to and from work also relieves the employer of the §274(d) requirements, but only if (1) the employer has a bona fide noncompensatory business reason for having employees use his vehicles for commuting and (2) the employer accounts for the use in commuting as additional gross income to the employees. An employee complies with the substantiation rules in the latter case by including the value of the commuting use in gross income.

If a vehicle's use is not all personal or all business under the foregoing rules, an employer substantiates his automobile expense either by substantiating a business use or by including the value of the use in an employee's gross income.[55] A business use may be substantiated by an employee's adequate record of business use or by the employee's statement corroborated by other sufficient evidence.

---

[51] Reg. §1.274-5T(f)(2)(iii).

[52] Id.; Reg. §1.274-5T(f)(3). See Rev. Rul. 66-217, 1966-2 CB 107 (state judge receiving allowances for which he does not account to employer).

[53] Reg. §1.274-6T(c).

[54] Reg. §1.274-6T(a).

[55] Reg. §1.274-5T(e)(2).

Employees have an incentive to aid the employer in substantiating business use. Section 132 allows an employee to exclude the use value of an employer's vehicle from gross income if the cost, had it been incurred by the employee, would have been a deductible business expense.[56] Since the employee would have had to substantiate the deduction, had the cost been his, the exclusion for the employer's cost is lost if the employee fails to substantiate as required by §274(d).[57]

Another set of rules applies to vehicles used in farming.[58]

The regulations authorize the IRS to prescribe rules for treating per diem allowances and mileage allowances, "if in accordance with reasonable business practice," as equivalent to substantiation by adequate records for purposes of the basic substantiation requirements of §274(d) and as satisfying the adequate accounting requirement in the case of employees accounting to employers.[59] The IRS has provided such rules, and updates them from time to time. A per diem allowance for meals and lodging of not more than the greater of $44 per day or the maximum federal government per diem rate in the locality of the travel is currently approved on two conditions: (1) The employer must reasonably limit such expenses to those that are ordinary and necessary business expenses; and (2) the elements of time, place, and business purpose must be substantiated in accordance with the requirements of §274(d).[60] A standard mileage allowance, augmented by an allowance for parking fees and tolls, serves the same function for transportation expenses.[61] Employees related to the employer within the meaning of §267(b) may use the mileage allowance, but not the subsistence arrangements. In any event, an employee receiving a travel allowance in excess of his deductible traveling expenses must include the excess in gross income.[62] Although the standard allowances ease the burden of substantiating dollar amounts, taxpayers using them must still substantiate the other elements of

---

[56] See supra ¶14.1.

[57] Reg. §1.274-5T(e)(1).

[58] Reg. §1.274-6T(b).

[59] Reg. §1.274-5(g).

[60] Rev. Rul. 80-62, 1980-1 CB 63, modified by Rev. Rul. 87-93, 1987-2 CB 8 (also, arrangements must be reasonably limited by adequate internal controls and allowances must be reasonably accurate estimates of travel costs in relevant locality). See also Rev. Rul 84-164, 1984-2 CB 63 (if employer pays lodging expense or furnishes lodging or if employee incurs no lodging expense, substantiation and accounting requirements deemed met for reimbursements of meals costs if reimbursements do not exceed $14 per day for stays of less than 30 days and $9 per day for stays longer than 30 days).

[61] Rev. Rul. 87-93, supra note 60 (22.5 cents per mile for 1987 and subsequent years); Rev. Rul. 85-155, 1985-2 CB 89 (21 cents per mile for 1985 and 1986); Rev. Rul. 84-51, 1984-1 CB 90 (20.5 cents for 1983 and 1984); Rev. Rul. 80-203, 1980-2 CB 101 (20 cents for 1980 through 1982).

[62] Reg. §1.2745(g) (last sentence).

the deduction, including the time, place, and business purpose of the expense.[63]

In addition to the substantiation requirements of §274(d), regulations predating that provision continue to apply to expenses incurred by employees for their employer's benefit that are not subject to §274(d).[64] These regulations apply to expenses incurred before 1987 for local transportation, but not to such incidental expenses as "office supplies for the employer or local transportation in connection with an errand."[65] The substantiation rules under the earlier regulations resemble those under §274(d), but are less detailed. Since they are superseded by the §274(d) rules when inconsistent therewith, taxpayers who are not confident of the boundary line are well advised to comply with the latter rules.[66]

¶21.4.6 Independent Contractors

In general, independent contractors are required to substantiate each element of a travel or entertainment expenditure in the same manner as other taxpayers. Entertainment expenditures passed along to a client or customer, however, are exempted from the business relationship rules of §274(a) if the contractor accounts to the client or customer in the manner provided by §274(d).[67] If the contractor satisfies this requirement by submitting adequate records or other sufficient evidence, the burden of substantiating each element of the expenditure shifts to the client or customer. Unless the independent contractor also substantiates the reimbursed expenditures, however, the reimbursements must be included in gross income.[68]

The effect of this dual-substantiation rule is to impose on the client or customer the burden of satisfying the business relationship test of §274(a) when the independent contractor accounts for the expenditures, without relieving the independent contractor of the responsibility for showing that the reimbursements defrayed genuine business expenses and hence were not compensatory.

---

[63] Taylor v. CIR, 40 TCM (CCH) 1206 (1980).

[64] Reg. §1.162-17.

[65] Reg. §1.162-17(a) (incidentals need not be substantiated). The standard mileage allowance was permitted in lieu of substantiating costs of local transportation, even before these costs became subject to §274(d). E.g., Rev. Rul. 85-155, 1985-2 CB 89. See Rev. Rul. 76-71, 1976-1 CB 308 (payments by employer to reimburse employees for cost of noncompensatory vocational training not includable in employee's gross income).

[66] See Rev. Rul. 77-323, 1977-2 CB 18 (treatment of allowances and reimbursements to committees, members, and employees of Congress under both sets of substantiation and reporting rules).

[67] IRC §274(e)(3)(B); Reg. §1.274-5T(h)(3).

[68] Reg. §1.274-5T(h)(2).

CHAPTER

22

Specially Treated Business and Profit-Oriented Expenses

¶22.1 EDUCATIONAL EXPENSES

¶22.1.1 Introductory

Although neither §162 nor §212 contains special restrictions on the deductibility of educational expenses, they have evoked so much litigation and are subject to such elaborate regulations that the issue requires separate discussion.[1] Educational expenses can be divided into the following three categories:

1. *Personal expenses*, such as tuition paid by a practicing attorney to satisfy a cultural interest in the history of art by pursuing a course of study after the day's work. Expenses of this type are nondeductible both because they are "personal" or "living" expenses within the meaning of §262 and because they do not serve business or profit-oriented objectives as required by §§162 and 212.[2]

---

[1] See generally Mylan, Current Tax Treatment of Educational Costs, 32 U. Fla. L. Rev. 387 (1980); Schoenfeld, The Educational Expense Deduction: The Need for a Rational Approach, 27 Vill. L. Rev. 237 (1982).

[2] See Carroll v. CIR, 418 F2d 91 (7th Cir. 1969) (policeman pursuing college studies as philosophy major); Duffey v. CIR, 36 TCM (CCH) 609 (1977) (pressman's cost of taking college courses). See also Katz v. CIR, 27 TCM (CCH) 87 (1968) (CPA with a lifelong interest in flying who used private planes for personal and family

2. *Business expenses*, such as costs incurred by a practicing attorney or accountant in attending a tax institute to keep in touch with current developments, which are deductible under §162 because they are ordinary and necessary expenses of carrying on the taxpayer's trade or business.[3]

3. *Capital expenditures*, such as the cost of vocational or professional education undertaken in order to qualify for entry into a new occupation. Like other capital outlays, expenditures of this type may not be deducted. If their treatment were fully comparable to other capital outlays, the expenditure would either be (1) depreciable over the taxpayer's life expectancy or anticipated years of remunerative service or (2) held in abeyance and deducted as a loss on retirement, death, or irreversible failure to find employment in the chosen field. The IRS and the courts, however, permit neither of these methods and provide no means of recognizing that educational expenditures to enter an occupation constitute, over the long haul, an expense of earning a living.[4]

Since it is essential only to taxpayers wishing to enter the occupation in question, vocational education is not comparable to food, shelter, and clothing, which must be purchased by all taxpayers whether they are gainfully employed or not. Despite this distinction between living expenses and vocational expenses, they are given identical tax treatment.[5] This might account for the inaccurate description of educational expenditures to enter an occupation as "personal expenses," frequently encountered in both rulings and judicial opinions.[6] Since the ultimate tax results are unaffected by whether expenditures are viewed as capital expenditures or as personal expenses, the confusion is ordinarily harmless, but it may help to perpetuate the anomalous denial of deductions for depreciation or abandonment of the outlay during or at the end of its useful life.

---

travel; cost of flying lessons is nondeductible personal expense, notwithstanding claim that professional service to out-of-town clients was enhanced).

[3] Reg. §1.162-5(c)(1); Coughlin v. CIR, 203 F2d 307 (2d Cir. 1953). For §212, see infra note 16.

[4] See Denman v. CIR, 48 TC 439, 445–46 (1967) (acq.) (cost of education to qualify for occupation is a personal expense; nondeductible personal expenditures "are not made any less personal or transformed into [depreciable] business expenditures through the mechanics of capitalizing them"); Hall v. CIR, 29 TCM (CCH) 1363 (1970) (amortization over anticipated professional career disallowed).

[5] See Sharon v. CIR, 591 F2d 1273 (9th Cir. 1978), cert. denied, 442 US 941 (1979) (cost of attending law school and taking a bar review course cannot be deducted or amortized over taxpayer's anticipated professional life).

[6] See Rev. Rul. 69-292, 1969-1 CB 84 (expenses of taking review course in preparation for state CPA examination described as "nondeductible personal expenses"); Sharon v. CIR, supra note 5 (same as to law school and bar review expenses).

Many educational expenditures serve both personal and business objectives, thus falling into two or all three of the foregoing categories. Attending a liberal arts college, for example, serves cultural aspirations but is a prerequisite to entry into many occupations, and the cost could be viewed as a combination of personal expense and capital expenditure. An accountant who attends law school solely to improve skills in his current job could be viewed as incurring a business expense and simultaneously as making a capital expenditure facilitating entry into a new occupation should that be desired at a later time.

In theory, there is no barrier to an allocation of the amount spent for multifunction education among its components, but in practice this has not been thought possible unless the program can be divided on the basis of the time devoted to separable pursuits. When a single course of study simultaneously serves both personal and business objectives, the expenditure is ordinarily assigned entirely to its nondeductible element because the taxpayer cannot carry the burden of proving the portion qualifying as a current business expense.[7] The major exception to this application of the principle is for education required by an employer as a condition of retaining the taxpayer's established employment relationship; the regulations permit these expenses to be deducted, making no exception for taxpayers who derive personal pleasure from the course of study and would have incurred the expense even if it had not been required by the employer.[8]

Before 1958, the regulations under §162 were silent on the deductibility of educational expenses, and there were only a few rulings and cases in point.[9] In 1958, a comprehensive web of rules was issued by the Treasury, distinguishing between the costs of (1) education undertaken to maintain or improve the skills required by the taxpayer in his employment, other trade, or business or to meet requirements imposed by the employer, the applicable law, or regulations as a condition to retention of the taxpayer's salary, status, or employment, which were deductible, and (2) expenditures to obtain a new position, substantial advancement, or to fulfill the taxpayer's educational or other personal aspirations, which were nondeductible. In drawing this line, the 1958 regulations placed great stress on the taxpayer's "primary purpose" in incurring the expense.[10]

---

[7] See Reg. §1.162-5(b)(1) (no deduction for "an inseparable aggregate of personal and capital expenditures" even if the education maintains the taxpayer's skills in current occupation or employment). The *Cohan* principle, discussed supra ¶20.1.9, has played no role in this area, although it is not excluded by any rule of law.

[8] Reg. §1.162-5(c)(2), discussed infra ¶22.1.2.

[9] For pre-1958 law, see Wolfman, Professors and the "Ordinary and Necessary" Business Expense, 112 U. Pa. L. Rev. 1089, 1093–1101 (1964).

[10] See Fleischer v. CIR, 403 F2d 403, 405 (2d Cir. 1968) (under 1958 regulations, "the primary purpose of the taxpayer is central in determining the deductibili-

In 1967, however, new regulations were issued that substituted more objective standards for the primarily subjective test of the 1958 regulations and modified its rules in many other respects.[11] The 1967 regulations, much like their predecessor, permit taxpayers to deduct expenses (1) to maintain or improve skills required by the taxpayer's employment, other trade, or business or (2) to meet requirements imposed by the employer, applicable law, or regulations as a condition of retaining the taxpayer's established employment relationship, status, or rate of compensation.[12] The taxpayer, however, must also show that the expenses do not (3) meet the minimum educational requirements of the taxpayer's employment, other trade, or business or (4) constitute part of a program of study qualifying the taxpayer for a new trade or business.[13] Thus, the taxpayer must pass one of the two positive tests (the skill-maintenance or employer-mandate tests) and avoid both of the two negative tests (the entry-level and upward-bound tests).

The 1967 regulations deal only with expenditures by individuals for their own benefit. An employer's deduction for the cost of training employees or applicants for employment depends on whether, under the basic principles of §162, the cost is a current business expense, a capital expenditure, or some other kind of payment.[14]

The regulations are also limited to the effect of §162, and do not speak to the possibility of deducting educational expenses under other provisions, such as §§212(1) and (2) (expenses to produce income or conserve income-

---

ty of an educational expense"). For detailed analysis of the 1958 regulations and of the cases thereunder, see Shaw, Education as an Ordinary and Necessary Expense in Carrying on a Trade or Business, 19 Tax L. Rev. 1 (1963).

[11] Reg. §1.162-5. For comparisons of the 1958 and 1967 regulations, see Spencer, The Deductibility of Educational Expenses: Administrative Construction of Statute, 17 Buffalo L. Rev. 182 (1968); Webster, Education as a Trade or Business Expense Under Section 162(a), 27 Sw. LJ 674 (1973).

See also Taubman v. CIR, 60 TC 814, 817–18 (1973) (upholding Treasury's right to change regulations); Greenberg v. CIR, 45 TC 480, 488, rev'd, 367 F2d 663 (1st Cir. 1966) (Judge Tannenwald, dissenting: "It may well be that the [1958] primary purpose test, impregnated as it has become with the element of subjectivity, provides a haven for the skillful liar," but "we are not bereft of talent for determining truth from falsehood").

[12] See infra ¶22.1.2.

[13] See infra ¶22.1.3.

[14] But see Love Box Co. v. CIR, 842 F2d 1213 (8th Cir. 1988) (regulations applied to corporation's costs in putting on seminar for employees teaching "individual freedom, responsibility, hard work, thrift, honesty, truthfulness, and integrity;" no deduction because "the seminar expenses are more analogous to general education expenses which are too tenuous to the specific job skills of the Company to qualify for deduction under section 162"). See also Caledonian Record Pub. Co. v. US, 579 F. Supp. 449 (D. Vt. 1983) (corporation's payment of tuition and "salary" to son of controlling shareholder not deductible, and probably constructive dividend to shareholder).

producing property), §212(3) (expenses of determining tax liability), and §213 (medical expenses). For example, the cost of attending lectures on the management of income-producing property or on computing one's tax liability might, on appropriate facts, be deductible under §212. In 1986, Congress enacted a provision prohibiting the deduction under §212 of expenses incurred in attending a "convention, seminar, or similar meeting";[15] but the statutory language and its context suggest the intention was to reach meetings that involve travel (particularly travel to vacation spots), and educational expenses incurred closer to home might not be affected by the provison. Also, occupational therapy during convalescence from an injury or illness might qualify for deduction under §213, and payments to a fly-by-night school obtaining the taxpayer's money by false pretenses might be deductible casualty losses under §165(c)(3).[16]

Finally, the 1967 regulations do not define the term "education," leaving the status of payments for advice, counseling, and other functions to be decided under more general principles if the activity can be distinguished from "education." The Tax Court has held, however, that the term is not limited to formal programs of study, and may cover self-study.[17]

¶22.1.2 Maintaining Skills or Meeting Employer Requirements

An educational expenditure that does not violate the entry-level or upward-bound standard[18] can be deducted under §162 if it satisfies either the skill-maintenance or employer-mandate standard. That education can lead to a degree is not a disqualifying circumstance,[19] unless the entry-level or upward-bound standard is violated because the degree is a minimum educational requirement for entry into the taxpayer's occupation or qualifies the taxpayer for entry into a new occupation.

---

[15] IRC §274(h)(7).

[16] See Reg. §1.213-1(e)(1)(v)(a) (cost of attending special school for handicapped qualifies for medical expense deduction where resources of school for alleviating handicap are principal reason for attendance); Starrett v. CIR, 41 TC 877 (1964) (acq. in result only) (medical expense deduction allowed doctor for cost of psychoanalysis undertaken to cure mental disorder, although it also qualified him as student of psychoanalysis); infra ¶36.1.2 (re medical expenses). But see Dinsmore v. CIR, 36 TCM (CCH) 1008 (1977) (law school expenses not incurred to contest tax deficiencies but to obtain degree; not deductible under §212(3)); Schonhoff v. CIR, 22 TCM (CCH) 1072 (1963) (no casualty theft loss deduction for taxpayer who paid $8,800 for dancing lessons on implied representation he could date the instructors).

[17] Boser v. CIR, 77 TC 1124 (1981) (education-expense deduction allowed flight engineer for cost of operating his own light aircraft to extent of rental value of flying time required to maintain commercial pilot's license with instrument rating).

[18] See infra ¶22.1.3.

[19] Reg. §1.162-5(a)(1).

1. *The skill-maintenance standard.* The skill-maintenance standard is satisfied by education that "maintains or improves skills required by the individual in his employment or other trade or business."[20] The term "required," as construed by an IRS ruling, refers to skills that are "appropriate, helpful, or needed."[21]

The cost of maintaining the taxpayer's skills may be likened to the cost of keeping business equipment in "an ordinarily efficient operating condition," which is the hallmark of a deductible repair.[22] Costs of education improving the taxpayer's skills, by contrast, may be deducted even though it resembles a nondeductible expenditure increasing the value or prolonging the life of depreciable property. This tilt in favor of improvements to human capital can be viewed as partial atonement for the bias against allowing capitalized educational expenditures to be depreciated.[23]

The skill-maintenance standard is most obviously satisfied by refresher courses and other brief programs focusing on current developments in the taxpayer's chosen field.[24] The status of broader education is more problematical, especially if the course of study is protracted. The Tax Court has allowed a minister to deduct the cost of college courses in history, literature, psychology, English usage, and other subjects on finding that properly serving his congregation required skill "in public speaking, English, drama, accounting, psychology, history, education, and a host of other disciplines." These findings of fact, not being "clearly erroneous," were affirmed on appeal.[25] This decision goes to, if it does not overshoot, the verge of deductibility, and it must be contrasted with more typical cases holding that

---

[20] Reg. §§1.162-5(a)(1), (c)(1).

[21] Rev. Rul. 60-97, 1960-1 CB 69, 70. Although Revenue Ruling 60-97 was issued under the 1958 regulations and declared obsolete by Revenue Ruling 72-619, 1972-2 CB 630, after the 1967 regulations were promulgated, this principle is presumably still valid, since the 1967 regulations did not change the skill-maintenance standard.

[22] Reg. §1.162-4 (repairs), discussed supra ¶20.4.8.

[23] See Sharon v. CIR, 591 F2d 1273 (9th Cir. 1978), cert. denied, 442 US 941 (1979).

[24] Reg. §1.162-5(c)(1). See also Coughlin v. CIR, 203 F2d 307, 309–10 (2d Cir. 1953) (cost of attending NYU Institute on Federal Taxation "to keep sharp the tools [the taxpayer] actually used in his going trade or business" is deductible, in view of "the rather evanescent character of that for which the petitioner spent his money").

[25] Glasgow v. CIR, 31 TCM (CCH) 310 (1972), aff'd per curiam, 486 F2d 1045 (10th Cir. 1973); although based on the 1958 regulations, the findings of fact would support the same result under the skill-maintenance standard of the 1967 regulations. See also Iglesias v. CIR, 76 TC 1060 (1981) (acq.) (cost of hospital resident physician's psychoanalysis deductible because it maintained or improved skills required in present work of treating psychiatric patients); Voight v. CIR, 74 TC 82 (1980) (nonacq.) (cost of clinical social worker's psychoanalysis deductible because it improved diagnostic and treatment skills).

similarly generalized programs of study, although increasing the taxpayer's general level of competence, were only tenuously related to the skills required by the taxpayer's occupation rather than of direct proximate benefit.[26]

The difficulty of applying the skill-maintenance standard, and its ultimately factual character, are illustrated by a case involving a teacher of English, remedial reading, and social studies who attended a foreign university for a year to study linguistics and anthropology.[27] Holding that the expenses were deductible under the 1967 regulations, a majority of the Tax Court observed:

> It is our view that the petitioner's program of graduate study in anthropology and linguistics was appropriate and helpful, and did in fact improve his skills in teaching English, social studies, and Spanish. From the very nature of the courses petitioner took—anthropology, language and culture, and linguistics—it is quite apparent that there was more than a remote relationship between the courses and his work as a language and social studies teacher. . . . The lesson of the regulations, which clearly favors teachers, seems to be that, at least within broad subject-matter classifications (such as sciences and languages or sciences and humanities), a classroom teacher is a classroom teacher. Consequently, expenses of education, which directly maintain or improve skills in any of a variety of classroom subjects, are deductible.[28]

Six judges dissented. On appeal, the Court of Appeals for the Ninth Circuit affirmed: "Although reasonable minds can disagree with these findings—in fact, six judges of the Tax Court disagreed—we cannot say that the majority's findings were clearly erroneous, and we cannot set them aside."[29]

2. *The employer-mandate standard.* In lieu of satisfying the skill-maintenance standard, the taxpayer may rely on the employer-mandate standard

---

[26] See, e.g., Carroll v. CIR, 418 F2d 91 (7th Cir. 1969) (policeman pursuing college studies as philosophy major; although college education improves job skills of all students, this relationship insufficient to overcome barrier of §262); Takahashi v. CIR, 87 TC 126 (1986) (course in Hawaii on Hawaiian culture not sufficiently related to teaching science in California high school); Mullen v. CIR, 29 TCM (CCH) 925 (1970) (manager of engineering department; insufficient showing of relationship of courses in history and philosophy to occupational skills).

[27] Ford v. CIR, 56 TC 1300 (1971), aff'd per curiam, 487 F2d 1025 (9th Cir. 1973).

[28] Id. at 1306–07. The Tax Court also held (by a divided court) that the taxpayer, who had been pursuing doctoral studies while employed as a substitute teacher, was "carrying on" a trade or business before leaving for the foreign studies and that the departure marked temporary suspension rather than abandonment of his teaching status. For these issues, see supra ¶¶20.1.6, 20.4.6.

[29] Ford v. CIR, supra note 27, at 1026.

by establishing that the expenditures were for education meeting the employer's express requirements or the requirements of applicable law or regulations, imposed as a condition to retention of an established employment relationship, status, or rate of compensation.[30] In many situations, the skill-maintenance and employer-mandate standards cover the same ground, but if the education is required by the employer or applicable law, employees are relieved of the necessity of establishing that it contributes to their occupational sufficiency.

To avoid abuse, the regulations specify that the employer-mandate standard is only satisfied by educational requirements that are imposed for a bona fide business purpose of the employer. In the absence of this limitation, employers could impose specious educational requirements in order to provide education-thirsty employees with fringe benefits in the form of a tax deduction, at the Treasury's expense.[31] Also, the employer-mandate standard only applies to "the minimum education" necessary to retain the taxpayer's established employment relationship, status, or rate of compensation. The cost of education beyond this minimum, even if required by the employer, can be deducted only if it meets the skill-maintenance standard.[32]

The reference in the employer-mandate standard to the employer's "express requirements" is not satisfied by showing that the employer encouraged the taxpayer to embark on a program of studies or that the taxpayer thought he would lose his job if he did not make efforts to improve his performance.[33] These factors may be helpful in satisfying the skill-maintenance standard, but they do not establish that the education was undertaken

---

[30] Reg. §§1.162-5(a)(2), (c)(2). The phrase "retention by [the taxpayer] of an established employment relationship, status, or rate of compensation" was substituted by the 1967 regulations for "retention [of the taxpayer's] salary, status or employment," the language of the 1958 regulations. The employer-mandate standard originated in Hill v. CIR, 181 F2d 906 (4th Cir. 1950) (tuition deductible where teacher required by regulations to pursue college courses or pass examination for renewal of teaching certificate).

[31] Reg. §1.162-5(c)(2). Abuse is also restrained by the fact that employer-mandated education, like skill-maintenance education, must not violate the entry-level or upward-bound standard discussed in ¶22.1.3. See also Anaheim Paper Mill Supplies, Inc. v. CIR, 37 TCM (CCH) 403 (1978) (employer's payment of employee's education expenses not deductible under §162(a); tantamount to a nondeductible gift by "corporate father" in absence of showing of business relationship or compensatory purpose).

For tax-free benefits under employer financed educational assistance programs, see supra ¶14.4.

[32] Reg. §1.162-5(c)(2). See also Kandell v. CIR, 30 TCM (CCH) 1227 (1971) (no deduction for financial studies required by employer to qualify for promotion to account executive but not to retain job as clerk).

[33] See Bakken v. CIR, 51 TC 603, 610–11 (1969), aff'd per curiam, 435 F2d 1306 (9th Cir. 1971); Kinch v. CIR, 30 TCM (CCH) 502 (1971).

pursuant to the express requirements of the employer. The inclusion of applicable laws and regulations as a source of compulsion in the employer-mandate standard is particularly pertinent to public school teachers, who are frequently required by state statutes or regulations to take additional courses to preserve their accreditation. It also extends the employer-mandate standard to some self-employed persons, including lawyers and doctors who are required by local law to get educational booster shots from time to time in order to continue in practice.

¶22.1.3 Entry-Level and Upward-Bound Education

Even if the taxpayer meets the skill-maintenance or employer-mandate standard,[34] expenditures for education are not deductible under §162 if they violate either the entry-level or the upward-bound standard.

1. *Entry-level education.* The regulations disallow any deduction under §162 for education required to meet the minimum educational requirements for qualification in the taxpayer's employment or other trade or business. This barrier encompasses not only education required to enter the chosen occupation, but also education required of temporary employees or provisional appointees to preserve their status. On the other hand, taxpayers meeting the minimum educational requirements in force at the time of entry are treated as continuing to meet these requirements despite a subsequent increase in educational standards. Thus, expenditures to satisfy an upgraded standard are deductible employer-mandated expenses for existing employees, even though they are nondeductible entry-level expenditures for new employees.[35]

The distinction between temporary employees, who may not deduct costs of education required to obtain full status, and qualified employees who must pursue additional studies to retain their established status is not easily drawn. The regulations illustrate the distinction in typical situations encountered by public school teachers.[36] In the absence of normal requirements specifying the required minimum level of education required for a position in an educational institution, the regulations provide that a taxpayer is regarded as having met the requirements on becoming "a member of the faculty" under the institution's particular practices. This ordinarily oc-

---

[34] Supra ¶22.1.2.

[35] Reg. §§1.162-5(b)(2)(i), (iii) Ex. 1 (situation 4).

[36] See Reg. §1.162-5(b)(2)(iii) Ex. 1. The distinction between a bachelor's degree and the requisite 30 hours of professional educational courses, which leads to divergent results in situations 2 and 3 of this example, is puzzling. See also Garwood v. CIR, 62 TC 699, 702–03 (1974) (substitute teacher required to take additional courses to continue in that status; held, taxpayer had not previously met minimum educational requirements).

curs when he attains tenure or his service is counted toward tenure, the institution contributes to a retirement plan for his benefit (other than social security or a similar program), or he has a vote in faculty affairs.[37]

2. *Upward-bound education.* The second category of nondeductible expenses consists of education that "is part of a program of study . . . which will lead to qualifying [the taxpayer] in a new trade or business."[38] Under the 1958 regulations, the cost of education pursued for the "primary purpose" of maintaining or improving skills required by the taxpayer's current occupation could be deducted, even if a by-product of the program was qualification for entry into a new trade or business, particularly if the taxpayer did not intend to shift to the new area.[39] The objective standard of the 1967 regulations, in contrast, disallows deductions for education that in fact qualifies the taxpayer for entry into a new occupation, even if the taxpayer's purpose is to maintain or improve skills required in his existing employment or to satisfy requirements imposed by an employer as a condition to retention of an established relationship.[40] Because upward-bound education is equivalent to entry-level education for the new occupation, the expenses are disallowed even if they satisfy the skill-maintenance or employer-mandate standard.[41] The victims of this disqualification include many revenue agents who attended law school at night to improve their performance in their existing occupations and who might well have been entitled to deductions under the primary-purpose standard of the 1958

---

[37] Reg. §1.162-5(b)(2)(ii). See extended discussion in Jungreis v. CIR, 55 TC 581 (1970) (teaching assistant did not meet minimum educational requirements for faculty position). See also Diaz v. CIR, 70 TC 1067 (1978), aff'd per curiam, 607 F2d 995 (2d Cir. 1979) (paraprofessional in public school system had not met minimal educational requirements for teaching position); Davis v. CIR, 65 TC 1014, 1020 (1976) ("one has not met the minimum educational qualifications for a position in an educational institution until he is qualified to become a permanent member of the faculty"; social worker needed Ph.D. to qualify as permanent faculty member). But see Toner v. CIR, 623 F2d 315 (3d Cir. 1980) (Catholic elementary school teacher allowed deduction for costs of college education; even though bachelor's degree required for public school teaching position, degree did not meet minimum requirements for taxpayer's occupation or qualify for new trade or business).

[38] Reg. §1.162-5(b)(3)(i).

[39] See Charlton v. CIR, 23 TCM (CCH) 420 (1964) (CPA allowed to deduct expenses of attending law school, on showing that primary purpose was improvement of skills in practicing accountancy). See also Greenberg v. CIR, 367 F2d 663, 666–67 ns. 4, 5 (1st Cir. 1966), for extensive citations to cases on the deductibility of educational expenses relating to new occupations.

[40] Reg. §1.162-5(b)(3)(ii) Ex. 2 (engineer, accountant, etc., required by employer to obtain law degree cannot deduct expenses); Bodley v. CIR, 56 TC 1357, 1360 (1971) (law course).

[41] See supra ¶22.1.2.

regulations.[42]

The central interpretative problem in applying the upward-bound test is distinguishing education helping the taxpayer to qualify for a new trade or business from education that merely trains him for "new duties [involving] the same general type of work as is involved in the individual's present employment";[43] only the former category is disqualified. As examples of "changes in duties which do not constitute new trades or businesses," the regulations refer to shifts by classroom teachers from one subject to another and to changes in assignment from classroom teacher to guidance counselor or principal.[44] Treating the latter, rather drastic shift as no more than a change in duties is comparable to Napoleon's assertion that every private carries a marshall's baton in his knapsack.

Relying on the regulations statement that "all teaching and related duties" involve the same general type of work, the IRS ruled in 1968 that a college professor could deduct the cost of graduate work in order to remain on a state eligibility list for appointment to a college presidency.[45] However, when an accountant argued that it was an unconstitutional denial of equal protection to disallow his law school expenses while permitting teachers to deduct the costs of education qualifying them to become principals, the Tax Court declined to hold that the occupational distance between accountants and lawyers is no greater than that between classroom teachers and principals.[46]

After dealing with teachers, whose status under the regulations is probably sui generis,[47] the regulations illustrate the distinction between new occupations and new duties by ruling that law is a new occupation to an engineer or accountant, but that psychiatry and psychoanalysis are in the same boat.[48] In applying the distinction to other occupations, the Tax Court

---

[42] Weiler v. CIR, 54 TC 398 (1970). See Welsh v. US, 329 F2d 145 (6th Cir. 1964) (deduction allowed under 1958 regulations); see also Taubman v. CIR, 60 TC 814 (1973) (under 1967 regulations, accountant cannot deduct expense of attending law school).

[43] Reg. §1.162-5(b)(3)(i). The "new duties" exemption only refers to employees, but the same principle is presumably applicable to self-employed persons.

[44] Id.

[45] Rev. Rul. 68-580, 1968-2 CB 72.

[46] Taubman v. CIR, supra note 42. While the holding was based on the absence of any information or evidence on the occupational differences, it is not likely that the constitutional argument would succeed on a fuller record. See supra ¶1.2.

[47] See Ford v. CIR, 56 TC 1300, 1312 (1971) (Tannenwald, J., dissenting) ("arguable that respondent's regulations exhibit a favoritism toward the teaching profession that borders on discrimination"), aff'd per curiam, 487 F2d 1025 (9th Cir. 1973).

[48] Reg. §1.162-5(b)(3)(ii) Exs. 1, 2, 4. For the psychiatry-psychoanalysis distinction under prior law, see Greenberg v. CIR, 45 TC 480, 488, rev'd, 367 F2d 663 (1st Cir. 1966), and cases therein cited.

said in 1974:

> We have not found a substantial case law suggesting criteria for determining when the acquisition of new titles or abilities constitutes the entry into a new trade or business. . . . What has been suggested, and we uphold such suggestion as the only common sense approach to a classification, is that a comparison be made between the types of tasks and activities which the taxpayer was qualified to perform before the acquisition of a particular title or degree, and those which he is qualified to perform afterwards. . . . Where we have found such activities and abilities to be significantly different, we have disallowed an educational expense deduction, based on our finding that there had been qualification for a new trade or business.[49]

Employing these standards, the courts have found numerous occupations to be separate trades or businesses, including licensed public accountant and certified public accountant, intern pharmacist and registered pharmacist, member of the New York bar and member of the California bar, "tax expert" (employed as a revenue agent) and "tax attorney," and college teacher of mathematics and college teacher of law.[50]

---

[49] Glenn v. CIR, 62 TC 270, 275 (1974) (licensed public accountant cannot deduct cost of review course to qualify for CPA status).

[50] Id.; Sharon v. CIR, 591 F2d 1273 (9th Cir. 1978), cert. denied, 442 US 941 (1979) (bar review course taken by New York lawyer to prepare for California bar examination); Reisinger v. CIR, 71 TC 568 (1979) (licensed practical nurse and physician's assistant); Johnson v. CIR, 77 TC 837 (1981) (real estate agent and real estate broker); Diaz v. CIR, 70 TC 1067 (1978), aff'd per curiam, 607 F2d 995 (2d Cir. 1979) (educational paraprofessional and teacher); Grover v. CIR, 68 TC 598 (1977) (marine officer and judge advocate status); Burnstein v. CIR, 66 TC 492 (1976) (teacher of disabled children and social worker); Davis v. CIR, 65 TC 1014, 1020 (1976) (social worker with experience in research and as lecturer and author; cost of education leading to Ph.D. not deductible, since it would qualify taxpayer to meet minimum standards for college faculty appointment); Weiler v. CIR, 54 TC 398 (1970) (revenue agent and attorney; court rejects concept of "federal income tax expert" as unitary occupation; shift from "tax accountant" to "tax attorney" cannot be dismissed as "a lateral shift" not entailing a new business); Weiszmann v. CIR, 52 TC 1106 (1969), aff'd per curiam, 443 F2d 29 (9th Cir. 1971) (patent trainee and attorney); Roussel v. CIR, 38 TCM (CCH) 565 (1979) (ground school flying instructor of commercial pilots); Archie v. CIR, 37 TCM (CCH) 1759 (1978) (general accountant and CPA); Antzoulatos v. CIR, 34 TCM (CCH) 1426 (1975) (intern and registered pharmacist); Bouchard v. CIR, 36 TCM (CCH) 1098 (1977) (college teacher of mathematics and college teacher of law; expenses disallowed, since law degree qualified taxpayer to practice law as well as teach it). See also Vetrick v. CIR, 628 F2d 885 (5th Cir. 1980) (attorney who had not previously attended law school denied deduction for law school costs; without law degree, his only bar admission was in a distant state, which enabled him to practice in federal court in his home

Focusing as they do on publicly licensed occupations, these decisions suggest that taxpayers engaged in generalized clerical, administrative, or managerial activities might find it easier to establish that a new assignment is a lateral transfer involving changed or new duties, rather than an upward-bound entry into a new occupation. They may, however, find themselves hoisted on another petard: The education might not be sufficiently work-related to meet the skill-maintenance or employer-mandate standard because improvements in the taxpayer's ability to think logically, speak clearly, and work effectively with others serve "personal" rather than peculiarly business objectives.[51]

In imposing the upward-bound disqualification, the regulations refer to "education which is part of a program of study . . . which will lead to qualifying [the taxpayer] in a new trade or business."[52] The courts have rejected the ingenious but specious theory that this language does not embrace the cost of attending law school because passing the bar examination, not law school, is what qualifies a person to practice law.[53] If, however, a program of legal studies does not qualify the taxpayer to take a bar examination because the school is not accredited in any state, the upward-bound restriction does not apply.[54] It would presumably be equally inapplicable to legal or other professional studies if the program is limited in coverage and restricted to students whose current occupations will be enhanced by the training but who are not admitted to the school's full professional program.

On the other hand, a taxpayer's decision to take only a few skill-related courses and then drop out is probably insufficient, given the objective standard of the regulations, to establish that the courses are not "part of" a disqualifying program if the taxpayer is admitted as a full-fledged student who may continue in the program, grades permitting, until graduation.

---

state, but not in state courts; because degree enabled him to sit for local bar exam, it qualified him for new trade or business).

With Sharon v. CIR, supra, compare Rev. Rul. 71-58, 1971-1 CB 55 (qualified teacher may deduct educational expenses incurred to qualify for license in another state; change of employers and location is "merely a change of duties in the same general type of work as a classroom teacher") and Laurano v. CIR, 69 TC 723 (1978) (same result as to expenses incurred by teacher with Canadian license to obtain New Jersey certification).

[51] See Bakken v. CIR, 51 TC 603, 610 n.3 (1969), aff'd per curiam, 435 F2d 1306 (9th Cir. 1971) ("self-expression" and "logical reasoning" are not employment "skills" within meaning of skill-maintenance standard), and cases therein cited; Carrol v. CIR, 418 F2d 91 (7th Cir. 1969); Mullen v. CIR, 29 TCM (CCH) 925 (1970).

[52] Reg. §1.162-5(b)(3)(i).

[53] Weiszmann v. CIR, supra note 50; Dinsmore v. CIR, 36 TCM (CCH) 1008 (1977).

[54] Rev. Rul. 76-62, 1976-1 CB 12 (correspondence courses).

¶22.1.4 Educational Travel

For taxable years after 1986, "no deduction shall be allowed . . . for expenses for travel as a form of education."[55] This stricture was enacted because "allowing deductions for travel as a form of education could [permit] some individuals in particular professions to deduct the cost of a vacation, while most individuals must pay for vacation trips out of after-tax dollars, no matter how educationally stimulating the travel may be."[56] This disallowance, however, affects only cases where travel itself is claimed to be business education. An example is a French teacher's travel to France to absorb French culture.[57] Travel expenses incurred to get to a school or other place where business education is obtained, in contrast, can be deductible. An example not covered by the disallowance rule is "where a scholar of French literature travels to Paris in order to do specific library research that cannot be done elsewhere, or to take courses that are offered only at the Sorbonne, in circumstances such that the nontravel research or course costs are deductible."[58]

For years prior to 1987, the regulations allow a deduction for the travel as "a form of education" if the expenditures "are attributable to a period of travel that is directly related to the duties of the individual in his employment or other trade or business."[59] This condition is not satisfied unless "the major portion of the activities during such period is of a nature which directly maintains or improves skills required by the individual in [his] employment or other trade or business." Employer approval of the travel does not itself establish the required relationship between the travel "and the duties of the individual in his particular position."

The thinly veiled skepticism animating these conditions is understandable. In *Welch v. Helvering*, Mr. Justice Cardozo warned against specious deductions based on the claim that one can "practice his vocation with greater ease and profit if he has an opportunity to enrich his culture."[60] In a similar vein, the Court of Appeals for the Second Circuit disallowed a first grade teacher's deductions for foreign travel, even though her itinerary was approved by her school district under a regulation permitting sabbatical leave for "travel that will broaden the background of the teacher's experience," observing:

---

[55] IRC §274(m)(2).

[56] Staff of Joint Comm. on Tax'n, 99th Cong., 2d Sess., General Explanation of the Tax Reform Act of 1986, at 62 (Comm. Print 1987) [hereinafter 1986 Bluebook].

[57] H.R. Rep. No. 841, 99th Cong., 2d Sess. II-30 (Conf. Rep. 1986).

[58] 1986 Bluebook, supra note 56, at 72–73.

[59] Reg. §1.162-5(d). For comparison with the 1958 regulations, see Marlin v. CIR, 54 TC 560, 563–65 (1970).

[60] Welch v. Helvering, 290 US 111 (1933), discussed supra ¶20.4.7.

All travel has some educational value, but the test is whether the travel bears a direct relationship to the improvement of the traveler's particular skills. Such a relationship must be substantial, not ephemeral; the trip must be more than the "sightseeing" which [the] Regulations denote as "personal activity." . . . We do not have to say here whether a trip abroad or two-thirds around the world for a first grade teacher could ever directly and substantially relate to educational skills. Suffice it to say here that taxpayer's trip in 1967 was not sufficiently so related as a matter of law.[61]

Under pre-1987 law, the boundary between travel for business and travel for pleasure is especially murky in the case of teachers, who as a class are both especially likely to derive occupational benefits from travel and especially likely to travel for personal pleasure. Some teachers can demonstrate a special kinship between foreign travel and the needs of their own occupation; teachers of languages, anthropology, and art are prime examples.[62] Beyond this, virtually all teachers, and many other taxpayers, can assert that observing the techniques of foreign colleagues sheds light on their own occupational practices. For this reason, the results in litigated cases depend heavily on the trial court's assessment of the taxpayer's credibility and the validity of the asserted relationship between the sights seen on the trip and the taxpayer's daily work.[63]

---

[61] Krist v. CIR, 483 F2d 1345, 1351 (2d Cir. 1973). See also Cochran v. CIR, 32 TCM (CCH) 466 (1973) (second grade teacher; same result).

[62] See Takahashi v. CIR, 87 TC 126 (1986) (course in Hawaii on Hawaiian culture did not maintain or improve skills of California high school science teachers); Marlin v. CIR, supra note 59 (trip to France by married couple, both teachers; husband, who taught Latin, denied deduction despite visits to Roman ruins; wife, who taught history and collected slides and other teaching aids on trip, allowed to deduct her share of expenses); Gibbons v. CIR, 37 TCM (CCH) 366 (1978) (travel expenses of husband, a reading teacher, disallowed; expenses of wife, a school librarian and "an educational resource person," allowed, though "a very close case", method of allocating expenses illustrated); Sanders v. CIR, 19 TCM (CCH) 323 (1960) (teacher of art and geography; deduction allowed under 1958 regulations). But see Adelson v. US, 342 F2d 332 (9th Cir. 1965) (travel expenses incurred by teacher of English and journalism denied under 1958 regulations; trip resembled ordinary tourist's sightseeing trip); Schrimpf v. CIR, 36 TCM (CCH) 1275 (1977) (art teacher's expenses of travel to Soviet Union, Caribbean, and Hawaii disallowed; insufficient evidence of direct occupational benefits).

[63] See Postman v. CIR, 33 TCM (CCH) 649 (1974) (architect's foreign travel not deductible, despite claimed "new understanding and appreciation of various styles of architecture" useful in later work); Steinmann v. CIR, 30 TCM (CCH) 1251 (1971) (professor of management can deduct expenses of observing foreign business techniques); Dougherty v. CIR, 29 TCM (CCH) 186 (1970) (administrator who supervised teachers can deduct expenses of trip to observe foreign schools).

Even when the necessary link between the travel and the needs of the taxpayer's occupation has been established, it might be necessary under the pre-1987 rules to allocate travel expenses among the business component of the travel and personal side trips, expenses of the taxpayer's spouse, and other nonbusiness items.[64] Since expenditures for business-related educational travel are treated not merely as "expenses . . . in carrying on [the taxpayer's] trade or business" but also as "traveling expenses . . . while away from home in the pursuit of a trade or business," §162(a)(2) is brought into play. This permits the taxpayer to deduct amounts expended for meals and lodging (with the exception of amounts allocable to any personal component of the travel), but it also subjects the deduction to the "lavish or extravagant" restriction of §162(a)(2), to the substantiation and foreign travel limitations of §§274(c) and (h), and to the extensive body of law interpreting the phrase "away from home" in §162(a)(2).[65]

Under present law, as under the pre-1987 rules, when travel is undertaken not for its intrinsic educational value but as a means to an end (e.g., to attend lectures at a distance from the taxpayer's home and place of business), the deductibility of the expenses depends on §162(a)(2), relating to traveling expenses incurred while away from home in the pursuit of the taxpayer's trade or business. In effect, the travel expenses take their character from the underlying educational activities. Thus, a taxpayer who travels away from home "primarily to obtain education" may deduct not only the transportation expenses but also the cost of meals and lodging (except to the extent allocable to sightseeing, recreation, or other personal activities), provided the educational expenses are deductible.[66] On the other hand, if travel is primarily personal, transportation expenses are not deductible, and meals and lodging qualify for deduction only for the period spent in deductible

---

[64] See Marlin v. CIR, 54 TC 560, 563–65 (1970) (expenses of taxpayer's spouse; failure to substantiate some expenses as required by §274); Krist v. CIR, 31 TCM (CCH) 397 (1972) (20 percent of travel expenses held nondeductible personal expenses), rev'd, 483 F2d 1345 (2d Cir. 1973) (nothing deductible); Steinmann v. CIR, supra note 63 (expenses of taxpayer's spouse not deductible); James v. CIR, 23 TCM (CCH) 385 (1964) (taxpayer's allocation of 20 percent of expenses to personal travel approved); Neschis v. CIR, 22 TCM (CCH) 927 (1963) (50 percent of travel disallowed as ordinary sightseeing).

[65] See Marlin v. CIR, 54 TC 568 (1970); Rev. Rul. 64-176, 1964-1 (Part 1) CB 87 (general principles re travel expenses incurred by teachers); supra ¶21.1 (travel expenses), ¶21.4 (substantiation rules). For the status of transportation expenses incurred by taxpayers who pursue business-related educational programs after working hours or on nonworking days and who are not "away from home" within the meaning of §162(a)(2), see Boerner v. CIR, 30 TCM (CCH) 240 (1971); Burton v. CIR, 30 TCM (CCH) 243 (1971) (transportation expenses assimilated to commuting expenses, except for excess cost over trips between residence and primary place of business).

[66] Reg. §1.162-5(e).

educational pursuits.[67] In determining whether a trip is primarily to obtain education of a deductible character, the regulations provide that "all the facts and circumstances" are to be taken into account and that an important factor is the relative amounts of time devoted to educational pursuits as against personal activities.[68]

¶22.1.5 Interruption of Employment or Business Activities by Education

To deduct educational expenditures under §162(a)(2), the taxpayer must show that they are paid or incurred "in carrying on a trade or business." If the taxpayer's studies are pursued on a full-time basis for an extended period, rather than after working hours, the IRS sometimes argues that the taxpayer has abandoned his business and that the expenses are incurred to enter a business at an indefinite future time rather than to carry on an existing business. Moreover, part-time employment during an extended period of studies (e.g., as a college research or teaching assistant) may be viewed as a method of financing the studies rather than as an occupation to which the education is subsidiary.[69]

In Revenue Ruling 68-591, the IRS expressed the view that a suspension of business activities for a period of a year or less, if followed by a resumption of the same employment, trade, or business, is a temporary interruption rather than an abandonment of the taxpayer's business.[70] The ruling implies that a longer interruption, at least if the taxpayer is not on

---

[67] Id.

[68] Id. See Hoover v. CIR, 35 TC 566 (1961) (acq.) (expenses of "medical seminar cruise," involving a university-sponsored ocean cruise laced with a few lectures on medical subjects; held, physician's expenses deductible only to extent allocable to educational pursuits); James v. CIR, supra note 64; Neschis v. CIR, supra note 64. See also Weiman v. CIR, 30 TCM (CCH) 372 (1971) (world tour of teacher-librarian following summer course of study in Japan; held, only expenses directly involving course of study deductible); Bickel v. CIR, 25 TCM (CCH) 1037 (1966) (dentist who incidentally collected slides and gave lectures in his field during world tour; held, only minor expenses connected with lectures and slides deductible); Rev. Rul. 79-425, 1979-2 CB 81 (annual convention of local professional association held in foreign country, with several educational seminars; held, no expenses deductible except portion, if any, of registration fee and other items properly allocable to taxpayer's business while at convention site); Rev. Rul. 74-292, 1974-1 CB 43 (doctor who combined vacation abroad with brief professional seminars in each country arranged at no cost to him by sponsoring professional association; travel expenses disallowed in their entirety). For conventions generally, see supra ¶21.1.9.

[69] See Jungreis v. CIR, 55 TC 581 (1970), in which Judge Tannenwald, concurring, concluded (at 593) that "petitioner herein worked because he studied. He did not study because he worked."

[70] Rev. Rul. 68-591, 1968-2 CB 73. See also Rev. Rul. 77-32, 1977-1 CB 38.

leave of absence, is evidence that the taxpayer is no longer carrying on a trade or business. The litigated cases, however, make it clear that the distinction between temporary and indefinite suspensions requires an assessment of all the facts, not merely the elapsed time between periods of gainful activity.[71]

¶22.2 COMPENSATION FOR PERSONAL SERVICES

¶22.2.1 Introductory

Section 162(a)(1) specifies that the deduction for ordinary and necessary business expenses includes "a reasonable allowance for salaries or other compensation for personal services actually rendered." The term "allowance" is used deliberately, the provision having been added in 1919 to the statutory predecessor of §162 to permit closely held enterprises to deduct an allowance for services rendered by officers and proprietors in computing the World War I excess profits tax even if no salary was actually paid.[1] This function evaporated when the excess profits tax expired, and the statutory provision came to be interpreted as a disallowance of unreasonable amounts if paid rather than as an allowance for reasonable amounts that were not paid.[2]

---

[71] See Sherman v. CIR, 36 TCM (CCH) 1191 (1977) (taxpayer was carrying on business during two-year program at business school), and cases therein cited. See also Reisinger v. CIR, 71 TC 568 (1979) (five years of unemployment prior to enrollment of licensed practical nurse in educational program indicated she was not in the trade or business of being a nurse when she enrolled); Wyatt v. CIR, 56 TC 517, 520 (1971) (that taxpayer was member in good standing of profession by virtue of valid certificate or license does not by itself establish she was "carrying on" a business); Hitt v. CIR, 37 TCM (CCH) 333 (1978) ("as the period a taxpayer remains in school increases with no continuing connection to his former job or any clear indication of an intention to actively carry on the same trade or business upon completion of his studies, this begins to weigh as evidence that he is no longer 'carrying on' his trade or business while attending school"); supra ¶20.1.6 (temporary suspension versus abandonment of business activities), ¶20.4.6 (expenses of finding employment).

[1] The statutory provision ratified a Treasury practice announced in 1918. For a full account of this episode, see Griswold, New Light on "A Reasonable Allowance for Salaries," 59 Harv. L. Rev. 286 (1945).

[2] Even before the enactment of the statutory predecessor of §162(a)(1), the regulations provided that payments "in the guise of additional salaries or compensation, the amount of which is based upon or bears a close relationship to the stockholdings of such officers or employees or the capital invested by them in the business of the company, will be regarded as a special distribution of profits . . . in the nature of [nondeductible] dividends." Reg. 33 (rev.), Art. 138 (1918). For application of the "reasonable" standard to expenses other than compensation, see supra ¶20.1.5.

This "visitatorial power over salary payments through the medium of a disallowance of the deduction of payments actually made"[3] is almost never exercised unless the employer and employee are related or engage simultaneously in another transaction, such as a sale of property with a concomitant employment contract, where a purported payment for services may be in whole or part a disguised gift, loan, dividend, or payment for property. Since only genuine business expenses are deductible under §162(a), however, payments disguised as wages or salaries could be disallowed by the IRS even if the statutory reference to a "reasonable allowance" had not been enacted. There is no such specific limitation, for example, on the deduction of payments for materials, supplies, interest, rent, or other goods and services, nor does §212 explicitly restrict compensation payments to a reasonable amount, but the concept of an ordinary and necessary "expense," buttressed by the substance-over-form doctrine, forbids the deduction of payments inflated to disguise a nondeductible transfer.

To be sure, the regulations provide that "the test of deductibility in the case of compensation payments is whether they are reasonable *and* are in fact payments purely for services."[4] Referring to this regulation and related cases, the Tax Court has said that the test of deductibility is "two-pronged" (amount must be both reasonable and paid purely for services), but that the two prongs are "inextricably wed."[5] The court might have added that although the marriage was made on earth rather than in heaven, rarely is there a divorce. The same results would almost always be reached if the first prong of the test were eliminated and the IRS focused solely on whether the payments were "purely for services." Indeed, the regulations go on to refer to payments "in the form of compensation," "ostensible" salaries, and payments that "are a distribution of earnings,"[6] confirming a primary if not exclusive concern with amounts that are in fact not payments for services.

In principle, whether an amount is paid for services and whether it is reasonable in amount are separate issues, but in practice it is virtually impossible to analyze them separately. If the IRS disallowed compensation paid by employers who have no reason to inflate the amount paid, the question of reasonableness could be addressed in isolation. The acid test would be satisfied, for example, if the "unreasonable" portion of an employee's salary fixed by an arm's length contract between independent parties could be disallowed on proof that the employer agreed to pay more than the employee's services were worth because of stupidity, carelessness, or misinformation about the employee's experience and talents.

---

[3] Griswold, supra note 1, at 287.

[4] Reg. §1.162-7(a) (emphasis added).

[5] Nor-Cal Adjusters v. CIR, 30 TCM (CCH) 837 (1971), aff'd, 503 F2d 359 (9th Cir. 1974).

[6] Reg. §§1.162-7(b)(1), -8, -9.

In the litigated cases, however, the employer-employee relationship is almost always accompanied or overshadowed by another relationship (e.g., shareholder-corporation, parent-child, vendor-vendee) that supplies a motive for using compensation payments to camouflage some other objective. If there is no extraneous relationship between employer and employee, the amount fixed by them as payment for the services is almost always ipso facto reasonable, since they meet the willing-buyer, willing-seller criterion used in determining the fair market value of goods and services. The regulations virtually acknowledge this by stating that, in general, "reasonable and true compensation" is the amount that "would ordinarily be paid for like services by like enterprises under like circumstances."[7]

Although primary attention in reasonable-compensation cases is given to the employee's basic salary, deferred compensation and some other benefits must be aggregated with salary in evaluating the employer's claim for deduction.[8] This principle encompasses items that the employer classifies as noncompensatory, such as reimbursement of travel and entertainment expenses, but that are found to be compensation in substance. When items of this type are successfully challenged for want of a sufficient business relationship, the employer sometimes seeks to shift ground and deduct the same amount by reclassifying it as additional compensation.[9] This gambit requires at a minimum a showing that when added to the rest of the employee's compensatory package, the newly reclassified item is not the straw that

---

[7] Reg. §1.162-7(b)(3).

[8] See cases and rulings cited infra note 42.

[9] For limits on the extent to which a payment can be reclassified, however, see Paula Constr. Co. v. CIR, 58 TC 1055, 1058 (1972), aff'd per curiam, 474 F2d 1345 (5th Cir. 1973) (refusing to permit distributions to shareholder-employees by a faulty S corporation to be deducted as compensation despite their performance of substantial services without other compensation, "it is now settled law that only if payment is made with the intent to compensate is it deductible as compensation"), citing numerous cases. See also B.B. Rider Corp. v. CIR, 725 F2d 945, 951 (3d Cir. 1984) (travel and entertainment reimbursements not "salary because they were not made with compensatory intent"); Blake Constr. Co. v. US, 572 F2d 820 (Ct. Cl. 1978) (shareholder-officers accidentally paid themselves more than they had voted; held, excess not deductible as reasonable compensation, even if their services were worth total amount paid). The principle that compensation must be so intended to be deductible, however, does not prevent the deduction of amounts intended as compensation but erroneously described as something else. See A. Kreamer, Inc. v. US, 66 Ct. Cl. 308 (1928) (compensation entered on corporate books as charge against dividend account); L. Friedman Neckwear Corp. v. CIR, 15 BTA 61 (1929) (acq.) (amount designated "stock dividend" deductible as compensation); Benjamin Quillman Hardware Co. v. CIR, 11 BTA 1325 (1928) (amounts listed as gift on corporate books held deductible as compensation); Osborne & Clark Lumber Co. v. CIR, 8 BTA 382 (1927) (acq.) (compensation listed on books as purchase price of lumber); Henry Myer Thread Mfg. Co. v. CIR, 2 BTA 665 (1925) (acq.) (bonus paid salesman erroneously charged against salesman's drawing account).

breaks the camel's back by pushing the entire compensation package beyond reasonableness.

¶22.2.2 Criteria of Reasonableness

A useful and much-quoted summary of the relevant factors taken into account in reasonable compensation cases appears in *Mayson Manufacturing Co. v. CIR*, a 1949 opinion by the Court of Appeals for the Sixth Circuit:

> Although every case of this kind must stand upon its own facts and circumstances, it is well settled that several basic factors should be considered by the Court in [a] particular case. Such factors include the employee's qualifications; the nature, extent and scope of the employee's work; the size and complexities of the business; a comparison of salaries paid with the gross income and the net income; the prevailing general economic conditions; comparison of salaries with distributions to stockholders; the prevailing rates of compensation for comparable positions in comparable concerns; the salary policy of the taxpayer as to all employees; and in the case of small corporations with a limited number of officers the amount of compensation paid to the particular employee in previous years. The action of the Board of Directors of a corporation in voting salaries for any given period is entitled to the presumption that such salaries are reasonable and proper. . . . The situation must be considered as a whole with no single factor decisive.[10]

---

[10] Mayson Mfg. Co. v. CIR, 178 F2d 115, 119 (6th Cir. 1949). See also Owensby & Kritikos, Inc. v. CIR, 819 F2d 1315 (5th Cir. 1987); East Tenn. Motor Co. v. US, 71-1 USTC ¶9153 (ED Tenn. 1970) (not officially reported), aff'd, 453 F2d 494 (6th Cir. 1971) (jury instructions); R.J. Kremer Co. v. CIR, 39 TCM (CCH) 1212 (1980) (detailed examination of facts; limited relevance of comparisons in judging salaries paid by small businesses). These factors should be equally applicable in determining whether a family partnership agreement includes an "allowance of reasonable compensation" for a donor-partner's services under §704(e). In this situation, however, the forensic roles of taxpayers and the IRS are reversed, since the taxpayer ordinarily seeks to minimize the value of the dominant family member's services, while the IRS seeks to show that he is virtually indispensable. For this issue, see infra ¶85.2.

See generally Alvarez, The Deductibility of Reasonable Compensation in the Close Corporation, 11 Santa Clara L. Rev. 20 (1970); Brawerman & Racine, Corporate Compensation: The Client's Compensation Is More Reasonable Than He Thinks, 1981 S. Cal. Tax Inst. ¶1100; Brodsky, What Is Reasonable Compensation? 14 Tul. Tax Inst. 389 (1965); Comment, The Worth of a Man: A Study of Reasonable Compensation in Close Corporations, 38 S. Cal. L. Rev. 269 (1965); Ford & Page, Reasonable Compensation: Continuous Controversy, 5 J. Corp. Tax'n 307 (1979); Hoffman, Heeding Significant Factors Improves the Odds for Reasonable Compensation, 50 J. Tax'n 150 (1979).

Although less authoritative in the courts, the following list of factors in the IRS *Audit Techniques Handbook for Internal Revenue Agents* indicates the points that are likely to be persuasive at the administrative level:

    a. Duties performed and the character and amount of responsibility.

    b. Volume and complexity of business handled.

    c. Time required.

    d. Working conditions.

    e. Prevailing general economic conditions (wage levels, price levels, inflation).

    f. Future prospects.

    g. Living conditions of the particular locality.

    h. Individual ability.

    i. Previous technical training and experience of the employee.

    j. Profitableness to the employer of the services rendered.

    k. Number of available persons capable of performing the duties of the position.

    l. Corporation's dividend policies and history.

    m. Ratio of salaries to respective stockholdings.

    n. Compensation paid in prior years.[11]

Attempts to elaborate on the facts and circumstances relevant to ultimately factual determinations inevitably bog down in platitudes, but with this caveat, the relative weight of the factors listed by *Mayson Manufacturing*, can be summarized as follows:

    1. *Services performed.* Significant services contributing importantly to the taxpayer's financial success buttress a larger compensation deduction, especially if the employee has special qualifications, training, or experience.[12] Conversely, if the employee performs insignificant or part-time ser-

---

[11] IRS, Audit Techniques Handbook for Internal Revenue Agents ¶672(4)1 (1976) (IRM 4231), reprinted in 1 CCH Internal Revenue Manual ¶¶7239–7286 (hereinafter IRS). See Good Chevrolet Co. v. CIR, 36 TCM (CCH) 1157 (1977) (IRS agent's determination of deficiency not rendered arbitrary by failure to inquire into every factor listed in manual).

    See also Lewisville Inv. Co. v. CIR, 56 TC 770 (1971) (where compensation to members of two families was prescribed on a per-family basis by contract, reasonableness also judged on per-family basis); C.A. White Trucking Co. v. CIR, 601 F2d 867 (5th Cir. 1979) (contra in absence of contract fixing compensation by reference to two employees). The *Lewisville* case, it should be noted, concerns only the employer's deduction, not the allocation of the aggregate amount among the employees in determining the amount to be reported by each.

[12] See, e.g., Jones Bros. Bakery, Inc. v. US, 411 F2d 1282 (Ct. Cl. 1969); Baltimore Dairy Lunch, Inc. v. US, 231 F2d 870 (8th Cir. 1956); Wright-Bernet, Inc. v. CIR, 172 F2d 343 (6th Cir. 1949) (remanded because Tax Court ignored

vices or if the services require no special training or experience background, the compensation should be correspondingly smaller.[13]

2. *Comparison with other employees and other years.* The reasonableness of compensation is frequently supported by reference to amounts paid by similar taxpayers to similar employees, and the regulations, as pointed out above, encourage comparisons with the compensation "paid for like services by like enterprises under like circumstances."[14] The weight of such evidence depends on how comparable the two situations are,[15] although presumably the other enterprise should not be so similar that its salaries are also subject to challenge by the IRS as unreasonable.[16] Salaries paid to other employees of the taxpayer or to the same employee in a prior year are sometimes relevant if the taxpayer's entire salary scale is not out of line.[17]

---

unimpeached testimony as to experience, qualifications, ability, and industry of employees). See also Medical Collections Corp. v. CIR, 36 TCM (CCH) 1074 (1977) (IRS argued that corporation's success was attributable to improper and unethical practices, not to officer's talents; held, this would be relevant, but no evidence to support IRS' theory).

[13] See, e.g., Charles E. Smith & Sons Co. v. CIR, 184 F2d 1011 (6th Cir. 1950), cert. denied, 340 US 953 (1951) (simple, nontechnical nature of work a factor indicating compensation excessive); Charles Schneider & Co. v. CIR, 500 F2d 148 (8th Cir. 1974), cert. denied, 420 US 908 (1975) (similarly as to part-time work); General Roofing & Insulation Co. v. CIR, 42 TCM (CCH) 1697 (1981) (similarly as to officer-shareholder who worked 100 hours per year).

[14] See supra note 7.

[15] See, e.g., Pepsi-Cola Bottling Co. v. CIR, 528 F2d 176 (10th Cir. 1975) (industry study); Hammond Lead Prods., Inc. v. CIR, 425 F2d 31 (7th Cir. 1970) (evidence of salary paid by similar corporation inadequate because of different responsibilities); Jones Bros. Bakery, Inc. v. US, supra note 12; Dahlem Found., Inc. v. CIR, 54 TC 1566, 1579 (1970) (acq.) (real estate company's compensation validated in part by comparison with standard fees charged by outside brokers; amounts were small, and court impatiently commented "we are confident that [Commissioner] compensates his own employees on a more generous basis than he is apparently willing to permit petitioner to compensate its officers"); Ledford Constr. Co. v. CIR, 36 TCM (CCH) 858 (1977) (job offer by prospective purchaser of business).

[16] See Superior Motors, Inc. v. CIR, 33 TCM (CCH) 805 (1974) (auto dealer's profit sharing plan validated in part by comparison with similar plans used by other auto dealers; query whether comparable dealers were simultaneously seeking to validate their plans by comparison with taxpayer's challenged plan).

[17] See, e.g., Robert Louis Stevenson Apartments v. CIR, 337 F2d 681 (8th Cir. 1964) (that same amount paid same employee in prior years is evidence of reasonable compensation); Standard Asbestos Mfg. & Insulating Co. v. CIR, 276 F2d 289 (8th Cir.), cert. denied, 364 US 826 (1960) (increase in challenged salaries when less-well-paid officers did not get commensurate increase is evidence of unreasonable compensation). But see Giles Indus., Inc. v. US, 650 F2d 274 (Ct. Cl. 1981) (deductible compensation for executives not limited to amounts held reasonable for prior years; other factors enter into determination).

3. *Employer's earnings.* The employer's prosperity justifies a higher level of compensation,[18] but salaries tending to reduce dividends are suspect, especially if the dividends would go to the employees whose compensation is being challenged.[19] A high salary may be justified if the employee was hired to turn a losing company into a profitable one; by the same token, the employee's prior services in turning the business around may justify a higher salary in the current year.[20]

4. *Ownership.* Virtually all reasonable compensation cases involve family corporations or other closely held enterprises.[21] Salaries of employees who own stock or are related to controlling shareholders are the primary targets for disallowance, particularly if the amounts are roughly pro rata to stock ownership; proportionality inevitably suggests that part of the compensation is a disguised dividend to the employee or to the employee's parents or other relatives.[22] Compensation paid to persons who are neither owners nor related to the owners of the business is rarely challenged by the IRS.[23]

Stock ownership becomes less significant if control is divided between unrelated persons who can be expected, despite their association, to bargain

---

[18] See Nowland v. CIR, 244 F2d 450 (4th Cir. 1957) (large increase in compensation not justified where earnings showed no similar change).

[19] See, e.g., Charles McCandless Tile Serv. v. US, 422 F2d 1336 (Ct. Cl. 1970) (denying deduction because part of amount paid was disguised dividend, although compensation was otherwise reasonable); see cases and sources cited infra note 26.

[20] See Lucas v. Ox Fibre Brush Co., 281 US 115 (1930) (additional compensation for services in prior years deductible when paid, despite absence of prior agreement or legal obligation to make payment). See also R.J. Nicoll Co. v. CIR, 59 TC 37 (1972) (acq.) (amounts paid included reasonable compensation for both current services and prior services to employer's predecessors); but see Harry Fox, Inc. v. CIR, 37 TCM (CCH) 1847-53 (1978) (excessive portion of salary payments disallowed where authorizing resolution contained "no suggestion" that the payments were for past services).

[21] See IRS, supra note 11, at ¶672(7) (reasonableness usually considered only where stockholder-employee relationship exists).

[22] See Charles McCandless Tile Serv. v. US, supra note 19 (compensation in proportion to shareholdings). See also CIR v. R.J. Reynolds Tobacco Co., 260 F2d 9 (4th Cir. 1958) (public company, but compensation based on stock ownership).

[23] A 1948 case disallowing compensation paid to an employee who was neither a proprietor of the enterprise nor a relative of one, Patton v. CIR, 168 F2d 28 (6th Cir. 1948), is virtually unique. It may have been sucked into the bureaucratic machinery by a suspicion that the highly compensated but modestly endowed employee was kicking back part of his salary to his employers; portions of the record quoted in the trial court's opinion suggest such a theory, although no finding was made in support of it. Patton v. CIR, 6 TCM (CCH) 482 (1947) (cross-examination regarding employee's use of undeposited funds after cashing checks).

with each other at arm's length;[24] vigorous and even bitter negotiations sometimes take place between members of the same family over their relative financial rewards.

5. *Economic conditions.* The effect of improved general economic conditions on the appropriate level of compensation is ambiguous. On the one hand, higher costs of living can justify increased compensation, but improvements in the economy might account for a company's success more than the talents of its executives.[25]

6. *Employer's dividend policy.* A low level of dividends is sometimes cited as evidence of excessive compensation.[26] After reviewing prior case law, an IRS ruling issued in 1979 held that a closely held corporation's failure to pay more than an insubstantial portion of its earnings in dividends "is a very significant factor to be taken into account in determining the deductibility of compensation paid by the corporation to its shareholder-employees," but that deductions would not be denied on this ground alone if an examination of all facts and circumstances, including the corporation's dividend history, indicated that the compensation was reasonable compensation for services rendered.[27]

---

[24] See Albert Van Luit Co. v. CIR, 34 TCM (CCH) 321 (1975); Ziegler Steel Serv. Corp. v. CIR, 21 TCM (CCH) 311 (1962) (nothing to suggest that employee could dominate corporation through ownership of 50 percent of stock where balance was owned by unrelated persons).

[25] See, e.g., Petro-Chem Mktg. Co. v. US, 602 F2d 959 (Ct. Cl. 1979) (part of compensation unreasonable since large profits partly due to chaotic conditions in petrochemical industry); Charles E. Smith & Sons Co. v. CIR, 184 F2d 1011 (6th Cir. 1950), cert. denied, 340 US 953 (1951) (increased profits due to war contracts; compensation held unreasonable).

[26] Reg. §1.162-7(b)(1) ("ostensible salary paid by a corporation may be a distribution of a dividend on stock"); McCandless Tile Serv. v. US, 422 F2d 1336 (Ct. Cl. 1970) (payment deemed reasonable but held in part a disguised dividend); Logan Lumber Co. v. CIR, 365 F2d 846 (5th Cir. 1966); Charles Miles-Conley Co. v. CIR, 173 F2d 958 (4th Cir. 1949). But see Edwin's, Inc. v. US, 501 F2d 675, 677 n.5 (7th Cir. 1974) ("absence of dividends might be a red flag," but it does not require disallowance of compensation "demonstrated to be reasonable under all of the circumstances"); Isaacson, Rosenbaum, Spiegleman & Friedman, P.C. v. US, 79-2 USTC ¶9463 (Ct. Cl. 1979) (not officially reported) (state law characterization of payments as dividends not controlling); Schanchrist Foods, Inc. v. CIR, 36 TCM (CCH) 555 (1977) (same; poor dividend record explained by use of funds for substantial capital improvements); Laure v. CIR, 70 TC 1087 (1978) ("We doubt that section 162(a)(1) was intended to permit the Commissioner or the courts to so sit in judgment over whether dividends should be paid in lieu of reasonable compensation to employee-shareholders").

For comment on *Charles McCandless Tile Service*, see Coggin, The Status of the *McCandless* Doctrine, 55 Taxes 720 (1977), and articles therein cited.

[27] Rev. Rul. 79-8, 1979-1 CB 92.

The ruling is unsound in ascribing such great significance to dividend practices. Whether a corporation distributes its earnings as dividends or accumulates earnings says nothing about the reasonableness of compensation levels. No one would suggest that a publicly held corporation's policy of reinvesting earnings rather than distributing them as dividends is evidence that it pays its employees too much, and the suggestion has no greater plausibility for closely held corporations.

However, if a corporation pays substantial salaries to its shareholder-employees and, year after year, has no significant income after deducting these salaries, the lack of corporate income might reasonably be taken as evidence on the reasonableness of the salaries. When a person provides both capital and services to an enterprise over an extended period of time, it is most reasonable to suppose that a reasonable return is being provided for both aspects of the investment, and that a characterization of all fruits of the enterprise as salary is not a true representation of what is happening.[28] Even in this, however, great care must be exercised. When times are bad, corporate earnings usually fall or become losses before salaries are reduced; the lack of corporate income in a particular year thus has little probity on the issue of the reasonableness of the salaries. Also, taxable income is often a poor measure of the economic returns to shareholders.

7. *Contingent compensation.* While it is not easy to evaluate the reasonableness of fixed salaries, the inquiry becomes more difficult if compensation is paid under a long-term contract geared to sales, profits, or other variable factors, since the amount paid may skyrocket as a result of circumstances unrelated to the employee's contributions. The regulations provide as follows:

> The form or method of fixing compensation is not decisive as to deductibility. While any form of contingent compensation invites scrutiny as a possible distribution of earnings of the enterprise, it does not follow that payments on a contingent basis are to be treated fundamentally on any basis different from that applying to compensation at a flat rate. Generally speaking, if contingent compensation is paid pursuant to a free bargain between the employer and the individual made before the services are rendered, not influenced by any consideration on the part of the employer other than that of securing on fair and advantageous terms the services of the individual, it should be allowed as a deduction even though in the actual working out of the contract it may

---

[28] See Elliotts, Inc. v. CIR, 716 F2d 1241 (9th Cir. 1983) (rejecting "automatic dividend rule"; no statute requires profitable corporation to pay dividends), on remand, 48 TCM (CCH) 1245 (1982), aff'd without opinion (9th Cir. 1986) (reasonableness of return on equity nevertheless considered in determining reasonableness of bonus paid to sole shareholder).

prove to be greater than the amount which would ordinarily be paid.[29]

The regulations also provide that contracts for contingent compensation, like other compensation agreements, are to be judged by the circumstances "existing at the date when the contract for services was made, not those existing at the date when the contract is questioned."[30] Several cases hold, however, that agreements valid when made at arm's length may become unreasonable if the employee subsequently acquires control of the employing corporation.[31]

Since the litigated cases almost always involve closely held corporations, the "free bargain" theory of the regulations rarely conforms to reality. In a typical case of this kind, the Tax Court observed:

> We are not convinced . . . that this [profit-sharing] compensation arrangement was the result of an arm's-length free negotiation between unrelated parties. When this arrangement was entered into in 1947, 75 percent of the petitioner's stock was owned by Tracy [the officer whose compensation was questioned] and members of his family. The board of directors at that time consisted of Tracy, his wife, [petitioner's attorney, and two unrelated parties]. We believe these factors indicate the lack of an agreement freely negotiated at arm's-length.[32]

---

[29] Reg. §1.162-7(b)(2). See Rogers, Inc. v. US, 93 F. Supp. 1014 (Ct. Cl. 1950) (allowing large deduction on strength of regulations, although amount paid far exceeded amount anticipated at time of employment contract); McWane Cast Iron Pipe Co. v. Patterson, 63-1 USTC ¶9446 (ND Ala. 1963) (not officially reported), aff'd, 331 F2d 921 (5th Cir. 1964) (jury charge in accordance with principle of regulations). For bonuses, see Reg. §1.162-9.

[30] Reg. §1.162-7(b)(3).

[31] City Chevrolet Co. v. CIR, 13 TCM (CCH) 874 (1954), aff'd per curiam, 228 F2d 894 (4th Cir.), cert. denied, 351 US 939 (1956). See also Pepsi-Cola Bottling Co. v. CIR, 528 F2d 176 (10th Cir. 1975) (formula adopted in 1956 had become "unrealistic on the high side" by 1968–1970); but see Good Chevrolet v. CIR, 36 TCM (CCH) 1157 (1977) (contingent compensation deductible despite employee's acquisition of control after execution of contract).

[32] Alma Piston Co. v. CIR, 35 TCM (CCH) 464 (1976) (issue 2) (citing earlier cases), aff'd per order, 579 F2d 1000 (6th Cir. 1978). See also Northlich, Stolley, Inc. v. US, 368 F2d 272 (Ct. Cl. 1966) (bonuses to officer-shareholders in control of corporation partially disallowed even though officers unrelated to each other); Harolds Club v. CIR, 340 F2d 861 (9th Cir. 1965) (percentage-of-profits agreement for compensation of nonshareholder employee not result of "free bargain" where employee dominated shareholder sons; compensation partly disallowed); Kewaunee Eng'r Corp. v. CIR, 38 TCM (CCH) 672 (1979) (approval by outside minority shareholder not conclusive).

This conclusion may result in limiting the compensation deduction to a reasonable amount without regard to the incentive element in a bonus or profit sharing arrangement; "a bonus contract that might be reasonable if executed with an executive who is not a controlling shareholder may be viewed as unreasonable if made with a controlling shareholder, since incentive to the stockholder to call forth his best effort would not be needed."[33] Another opinion observes: "For a sole owner to pay himself a bonus as an incentive to do his best in managing his own business is nonsense."[34]

If made at arm's length between unrelated parties, compensation under a profit sharing contract may be reasonable even in bonanza years because the employee assumes the risk of lower earnings in poor years, taking the bitter with the sweet. If the employee is on both sides of the fence, however, the real reason for accepting a low salary in poor years might be to conserve corporate cash to protect his equity interest, rather than to get higher salaries in good years. Moreover, controlling shareholders can usually abrogate or revise their agreements if they become discontented with low salaries in lean years, so the theory that they accept the bitter with the sweet is unrealistic. Even so, the ultimate test of contingent compensation arrangements, like other employment contracts, is the reasonableness of the payments, and profit sharing agreements are often upheld in whole or in large part despite the absence of arm's length negotiations.[35]

8. *Other factors.* Other factors mentioned by the courts from time to time include efforts to avoid or evade tax, failure to pay the compensation

---

[33] Pepsi-Cola Bottling Co. v. CIR, supra note 31 (disallowing part of compensation under percentage-of-profits agreement), citing earlier cases. See Charles Schneider & Co. v. CIR, 500 F2d 148 (8th Cir. 1974), cert. denied, 420 US 908 (1975) (same). For profit sharing arrangements that have been upheld, see Kennedy v. CIR, 671 F2d 167 (6th Cir. 1982) (compensation calculated as share of profits found reasonable, reversing Tax Court; when compensation arrangement made, future of company uncertain); Quinn v. US, 77-1 USTC ¶9369 (D. Md. 1976) (not officially reported) (employee was "heart and soul" of controlled corporation, whose success "was almost totally attributable to his energy, initiative, creativity, and managerial talent"); Home Interiors & Gifts, Inc. v. CIR, 73 TC 1142, 1162 (1980) (salaries in excess of $1 million per year, based on percentage of sales, upheld as reasonable on analysis of facts and because "in these times of unparalleled inflation, our concept of reasonable compensation must take into consideration such inflation"); Neils v. CIR, 43 TCM (CCH) 982 (1982) (compensation of president and sole shareholder, based partly on profits, held reasonable); Allison Corp. v. CIR, 36 TCM (CCH) 689 (1977) (among other factors, service without compensation in prior years taken into account; also "extraordinary services such as guaranteeing corporate loans" — query, however, whether guarantee is hallmark of investor rather than employee). See also Superior Motors, Inc. v. CIR, 33 TCM (CCH) 805 (1974) (auto dealer's profit-sharing plan upheld in part).

[34] University Chevrolet Co. v. CIR, 16 TC 1452, 1455 (1951), aff'd, 199 F2d 629 (5th Cir. 1952).

[35] See cases cited supra note 32.

or to record it on the taxpayer's books, and the interests of minority share-holders. These additional factors, however, are on the whole of limited significance.[36]

The IRS instructs agents to check the time of year when compensation is set, on the theory that year-end determinations might betoken the distribution of profits.[37]

¶22.2.3 Services "Actually" Rendered

The reference in §162(a)(1) to a reasonable allowance for compensation for "services actually rendered" can give rise to misleading inferences. On the one hand, it may erroneously suggest that reasonable compensation for services that are in fact rendered is necessarily deductible. Under the general conditions of §162(a), however, compensation may not be deducted unless it is an ordinary and necessary business expense, and this standard incorporates the usual prohibitions against deducting personal expenses, capital expenditures, and illegal payments, even if the services actually rendered are worth the amount paid.[38]

At the other end of the spectrum, the statutory reference to "services actually rendered" may erroneously imply the automatic disallowance of payments to persons not currently performing services. In general, compensation may not be deducted if no consideration is received by the payor, and the deduction of salaries paid by closely held corporations to members of the controlling shareholder's family might be fraud if services are neither contemplated nor rendered. The statutory requirement of actual service, however, does not disqualify additional compensation for past services, even if the employee was adequately compensated when the services were

---

[36] See generally Annotation, Reasonableness of Compensation Paid to Officers or Employees, so as to Warrant Deduction Thereof in Computing Employer's Income Tax, 10 ALR3d 125, at §13 (1966).

[37] IRS, supra note 11, at ¶672(6).

[38] See, e.g., Richmond Television Corp. v. US, 345 F2d 901 (4th Cir.), rev'd and remanded on another issue, 382 US 68 (1965) (salaries paid for services in preparation for start of taxpayer's business must be capitalized); Bussabarger v. CIR, 52 TC 819 (1969) (payments by physician to former secretary made for personal reasons rather than business purposes; nondeductible); Chevy Chase Motor Co. v. CIR, 36 TCM (CCH) 942 (1977) (portion of executive salary, attributable to supervising construction of investment property, disallowed as capital expenditure); Maddas v. CIR, 40 BTA 572, 581–82 (1939), aff'd, 114 F2d 548 (1940) (protection money, now explicitly disallowed by §162(c)(1)). See generally supra ¶20.2 (personal expenses), ¶20.3.5 (unlawful payments), ¶20.4 (capital expenditures). See also IRC §267(a)(2) (nondeductibility of certain amounts payable by accrual-basis taxpayers to related cash-basis taxpayers), discussed infra ¶78.2. For compensation paid by parents to their children for business purposes, see infra ¶75.2.8.

rendered and there is no legal compulsion to augment the amount paid.[39]

The regulations state that contributions to qualified pension plans and other deferred compensation plans may be deducted under §404(a) only if the amount, when combined with other deductible compensation for the employee's services, does not exceed reasonable compensation for the services actually rendered.[40] But a variety of other items (e.g., payments on account of injuries, dismissal wages, unemployment benefits, guaranteed annual wages, vacation pay, and medical and recreational benefits) are not necessarily subject to the limitations of §404(a), and are deductible if they are ordinary and necessary business expenses.[41] While some of these fringe items may be part of a qualified pension plan or other deferred compensation plan and hence subject to §404(a), others are not; even so, their compensatory character ordinarily brings the criterion of reasonableness into play in determining whether the payment is deductible under §162.[42]

Compensation for services to be rendered during a specified future period may not be deducted when paid but must instead be treated as a capital expenditure and amortized over the period during which the services are rendered.[43] On the other hand, payments to an employee while on leave of absence for illness, occupational training, or military or public service may be currently deductible if the employee is not obligated to return to work and no future period can be identified as the years over which the anticipated services will be rendered.[44]

---

[39] Lucas v. Ox Fibre Brush Co., 281 US 115 (1930).

[40] Reg. §1.404(a)-1(b). See also Edwin's, Inc. v. US, 501 F2d 675 (7th Cir. 1974) (same, citing prior cases), and decision on remand, 77-1 USTC ¶9265 (WD Wis. 1977) (not officially reported); New York Seven-Up Bottling Co. v. CIR, 50 TC 391 (1968) (severance pay subject to §404(a) as deferred compensation).

[41] Reg. §1.162-10(a).

[42] See Reg. §1.162-9 (bonuses subject to reasonableness criterion); Willmark Serv. Sys., Inc. v. CIR, 368 F2d 359 (2d Cir. 1966) (employee death benefits); Ledford Constr. Co. v. CIR, 36 TCM (CCH) 858 (1977) (executive's medical and life insurance premiums, automobile, and club membership); Rev. Rul. 58-90, 1958-1 CB 88 (premiums for insurance providing sickness and disability protection for employees); Rev. Rul. 56-400, 1956-2 CB 116 (premiums for group life and hospitalization policies). See also Danskin, Inc. v. CIR, 40 TC 318 (1963), aff'd on other issue, 331 F2d 360 (2d Cir. 1964) (bargain element in bargain sale not deductible as compensation because, inter alia, not shown to be reasonable in amount).

[43] Maple v. CIR, 440 F2d 1055 (9th Cir. 1971); Farming Corp. v. CIR, 11 BTA 1413 (1928).

[44] See Rev. Rul. 71-260, 1971-1 CB 57 (payments to employee on military or governmental leave deductible as ordinary and necessary business expense where employee intended to return to employer). It is unclear whether a binding contract to return for a specified period would change the result.

Payments under a covenant not to compete may be deducted over the years to which the contract relates.[45] Even though they are not compensation for services actually rendered, a deduction under the general rule of §162(a) is warranted since they also serve who only stand and wait. In the same vein, a payment to insure the availability of consulting services can be deducted even if no services are requested or rendered,[46] provided the arrangement is not a disguised gift or payment for property. When bona fide, such payments are comparable to standby or commitment fees paid to insure that a loan will be forthcoming if and when needed.[47]

¶22.2.4 Status of Unreasonable Compensation

The regulations provide that a recipient's income tax liability for "an amount ostensibly paid to him as compensation, but not allowed to be deducted as such by the payor" depends on "the circumstances of each case":

> Thus, in the case of excessive payments by corporations, if such payments correspond or bear a close relationship to stockholdings, and are found to be a distribution of earnings or profits, the excessive payments will be treated as a dividend. If such payments constitute payment for property, they should be treated by the payor as a capital expenditure and by the recipient as part of the purchase price. In the absence of evidence to justify other treatment, excessive payments for salaries or other compensation for personal services will be included in [the] gross income of the recipient.[48]

Payments reclassified as dividends may be taxable to someone other than the recipient. If an ostensible salary paid to a controlling shareholder's child is viewed as a dividend, for example, it is taxable to the parent-shareholder on assignment-of-income principles,[49] and the child-employee is entitled to a refund of the tax paid on it. The regulations do not acknowledge that excess compensation might be a tax-free distribution of capital if

---

[45] See, e.g., Wilson Athletic Goods Mfg. Co. v. CIR, 222 F2d 355 (7th Cir. 1955) (buyer allowed to amortize cost of covenant not to compete); Rev. Rul. 68-636, 1968-2 CB 92 (payments on covenant deductible by subsidiary over life of covenant where subsidiary assumed parent's obligation thereunder). If a covenant not to compete given in connection with the sale of a business lacks economic substance, payments for the covenant may be allocated to goodwill or other acquired assets and fail to qualify for current deduction. See supra ¶4.4.4.

[46] Fumigators, Inc. v. CIR, 31 TCM (CCH) 29 (1972).

[47] See infra ¶31.1.3 for the treatment of standby fees.

[48] Reg. §1.162-8.

[49] See generally infra ¶92.2 (constructive distributions).

not covered by earnings and profits, and the IRS can be expected to resist this result, although it would be appropriate in some circumstances.[50] Reclassifying ostensible compensation as a payment for property can have the effect of qualifying it as a capital gain.[51]

The regulations quoted above presuppose a finding that the excess compensation is in reality a dividend or a payment for property. Courts, however, often disallow ostensible salary without giving it a new name, and even when opinions refer to the possibility that a payment is a disguised dividend, the ultimate finding is usually that the taxpayer has not carried the burden of proving that the amount was reasonable. In this situation, which probably characterizes most cases, the excess may in fact be reasonable compensation despite the employer's failure to prove its case. It is not surprising, therefore, that courts sometimes say that the excess remains "compensation" despite the disallowance. In *Sterno Sales Corp. v. United States*, for example, the Court of Claims held that the recipient of compensation for services was taxable thereon although a related corporation was not permitted to deduct the full amount:

> Compensation remains compensation even if it is held unreasonable in amount and, accordingly, not deductible as a business expense. The payment does not change in character solely because it is characterized as excessive or undue. The non-deductibility of the expense by the payer, because it is unreasonable in amount, does not transform the payment in the hands of the payee.[52]

While this does not preclude independent proof by the recipient that the excess amount should be reclassified as a tax-free corporate distribution, gift,[53] or payment for property, it clearly throws the burden of proving the proper category on the recipient. The IRS, however, may be the party to assert that an excessive salary is taxable to the recipient as a dividend, not compensation, in various circumstances where compensation income is treated more favorably than dividends.[54]

---

[50] See infra ¶92.2. But see IRS, supra note 11 (in absence of earnings and profits, unwarranted payments to shareholder's relatives may be classified as "other income" to shareholder).

[51] When the buyer wants to deduct part of the cost of the acquired assets, it is more common to use phantom covenants not to compete rather than employment contracts, but the same principle controls both devices. See supra ¶4.4.4.

[52] Sterno Sales Corp. v. US, 345 F2d 552, 554 (Ct. Cl. 1965).

[53] See Smith v. Manning, 189 F2d 345 (3d Cir. 1951) (disallowance of salaries paid by father to daughters as unreasonable in part does not establish that the excess amounts were tax-free gifts to recipients).

[54] Under §911, for example, foreign-source earned income of U.S. citizens residing abroad is excludable from gross income, subject to a dollar ceiling, but no parallel exclusion is provided for such a taxpayer's dividend income. See infra ¶65.4 for

Shareholder-employees sometimes agree with the employer to refund compensation that is disallowed as unreasonable. Under a 1969 ruling, the employee may deduct the refunded amount in the year of repayment if the agreement to refund was made before the payments were made and is enforceable under local law.[55] It has been suggested that such an agreement is an admission against interest, reflecting doubts by the parties that the agreed compensation is reasonable.[56] This is a highly debatable inference, however, given the fact, which a judge should know better than anyone, that litigation is chancy even if the taxpayer believes his case is airtight.

¶22.2.5 Additional Limitations on Deductions for Compensation

1. *Deferred compensation.* An employer's deduction for deferred compensation is subject to additional limitations found in §404, which is discussed elsewhere in this work.[57] Very generally, a contribution to a qualified pension, profit sharing, stock bonus, or annuity plan is deductible when made if it satisfies the deduction criteria of §162(a) and does not exceed the upper limit on contributions prescribed for plans of that type. Amounts payable by an employer under a nonqualified plan, in contrast, are only deductible when they are includable in the employees' gross income.

2. *Employee achievement awards.* Section 274(j), added in 1986, specially limits deductions for "employee achievement awards."[58] An employee achievement award is an item of tangible personal property that is awarded to an employee in recognition of service or safety achievement where (1) the award is given "as part of a meaningful presentation" and (2) the circumstances of the award suggest no "significant likelihood" that the award is

---

§911. Also, during the years 1971 through 1981, personal service income was taxed at a maximum rate of 50 percent, whereas the rates on unearned income, including dividends, rose to 70 percent. For the maximum tax on personal service income, see infra ¶111.3.10.

[55] Rev. Rul. 69-115, 1969-1 CB 50 (obligation imposed by resolution of directors and assumed by officer-shareholders), citing Oswald v. CIR, 49 TC 645 (1968) (acq.). See also Pahl v. CIR, 67 TC 286 (1976) (no deduction for reimbursed amounts where reimbursement agreement made after payments received by officer-employee). For the reimbursing employee's right to utilize the computational mechanism of §1341, see supra ¶6.3.4.

See generally Oshatz, Agreements to Repay Disallowed Deductions, 28 NYU Inst. on Fed. Tax'n 1145 (1970).

[56] Charles Schneider & Co. v. CIR, 500 F2d 148 (8th Cir. 1974), cert. denied, 420 US 908 (1975); Castle Ford Inc. v. CIR, 37 TCM (CCH) 692 (1978) ("an element which is entitled some consideration"; total compensation found unreasonable for this and other reasons).

[57] See infra ¶61.6.

[58] For prior years, deductions for employee awards are limited by the pre-1986 version of §274(b). See supra ¶21.3.2.

"disguised compensation."[59] An award qualifies as a service award if the recipient (1) has been employed at least five years and (2) has not received another service award from the employer during the current or preceding four taxable years.[60] An award qualifies as a safety achievement award if no more than 10 percent of the employer's employees have received such awards during the present taxable year and the recipient of the particular award is not "a manager, administrator, clerical employee, or other professional employee."[61]

Generally, the cost of an employee achievement award is only deductible to the extent that when added to the costs of all other employee achievement awards to the same employee in the same year, it does not exceed $400.[62] This limitation is raised to $1,600, however, if the award is made under a "qualified plan."[63] A qualified plan is a written plan for making employee achievement awards where (1) the plan does not discriminate in favor of highly compensated employees and (2) the average cost of all awards under the plan during the taxable year does not exceed $400.[64]

There is no limitation on deductions for awards to employees that fail to qualify as employee achievement awards. Employee achievement awards are excluded from gross income, however,[65] whereas nonqualifying awards are generally taxable to employees.[66]

3. *Golden parachutes.* Section 280G, added in 1984, limits deductions for payments, commonly called golden parachutes, to senior management of a company in the event of a corporate takeover.[67] These payments are usually justified as compensation to management for their expected ouster in the takeover, but corporations are often accused of entering into golden parachute agreements with management in order to make themselves less attractive to hostile suitors. Congress found this method of "hinder[ing] acquisition activity in the marketplace" to be inappropriate.[68] Conversely, it

---

[59] IRC §274(j)(3)(A).

[60] IRC §274(j)(4)(B). In applying the second of these limitations, an award excludable from the employee's gross income as a de minimis fringe benefit under §132(e) is ignored.

[61] IRC §274(j)(4)(C).

[62] IRC §274(j)(2)(A).

[63] IRC §274(j)(2)(B).

[64] IRC §274(j)(3)(B). In determining the average, awards "of nominal value" are ignored. Id.

[65] See supra ¶11.1.2.

[66] A nonqualifying award is taxable unless it is excludable under §132(e) as a de minimis fringe benefit. See supra ¶14.1 for §132.

[67] See generally Kaplan, A Study in Gold (*Les Parachutistes*), 15 J. Corp. Tax'n 58 (1988).

[68] Staff of Joint Comm. on Tax'n, General Explanation of the Revenue Provisions of the Deficit Reduction Act of 1984, 98th Cong., 2d Sess., at 199 (Comm. Print 1984) [hereinafter 1984 Bluebook].

was believed that golden parachute agreements, by holding out the prospect of handsome reward in the event of a takeover, could "encourage the executives and other key personnel involved to favor a proposed takeover that might not be in the best interests of the shareholders or others."[69] Whether a takeover is hostile or friendly, further, golden parachute payments tend to divert to management employees amounts that would otherwise be paid to shareholders for their stock. For all of these reasons, Congress decided that golden parachutes "should be strongly discouraged."[70] Congress' tool for discouraging these payments is to make them nondeductible to the payor and subject to an excise tax of 20 percent, in addition to the regular income tax, in the hands of the recipient.[71]

The rules are very complex.[72] They apply to a payment or series of deferred payments to an officer, shareholder, or highly compensated employee that (1) are contingent on a change in the ownership or effective control of the employer or a substantial portion of its assets and (2) have a present value of at least three times the recipient's average annual compensation from the company over the preceding five years. Compensation is presumed contingent on an acquisition, even in the absence of any explicit contingency, if it is provided under an agreement made during the year preceding the acquisition. The rules also apply if compensation is paid to an officer, shareholder, or highly compensated employee under an agreement that violates a securities law or regulation that is generally enforced.

The rules do not apply, in contrast, to any payment that is shown, "by clear and convincing evidence," to be reasonable compensation for services to be rendered after the acquisition.[73] If a company makes a long-term employment contract with an employee that is found to be contingent on an acquisition, for example, compensation under the contract for periods after the acquisition is a golden parachute only to the extent it exceeds reasonable compensation for the employee's services during those periods. In the absence of this exception, long-term employment contracts would be treated harshly. Assume an employee makes a five-year contract, found to be contingent on an acquisition, at the same salary the employee received during the preceding five years. At a discount rate of 10 percent, the present value of the compensation under the agreement is 379 percent of average annual compensation over the preceding five years; the golden parachute rules apply if this present value figure exceeds 300 percent. Even with the reason-

---

[69] Id.

[70] Id.

[71] "This innovative technique may be compared with dealing with the measles problem by taxing the spots." Kaplan, supra note 67, at 59.

[72] For more detail on the complexities, see 1984 Bluebook, supra note 68, at 200–07.

[73] IRC §280G(b)(4)(A).

able-compensation exception, long-term contracts might be seen as a bit risky because the 300 percent test is mechanical whereas the exception depends on the elusive test of reasonableness.

The rules are also inapplicable if, immediately before the acquisition, the employer is an S corporation or was eligible to elect to be an S corporation. A further exception is available to a corporation that has no publicly traded stock and obtains the approval of 75 percent of its shareholders for its golden parachute agreements.

If the rules apply, any excess of the payments over the recipient's average annual compensation is generally nondeductible. Although the limitation usually does not apply unless a golden parachute exceeds 300 percent of average annual compensation, once this threshold is crossed, the deduction is lost for the excess over 100 percent of average annual compensation.

The nondeductible amount is reduced, however, by any portion of it that is established "by clear and convincing evidence" to be reasonable compensation for services performed before the acquisition.[74] This rule, combined with the rule described above excepting payments clearly and convincingly shown to be reasonable compensation for future services, exempts a payment from disallowance if the requisite proof is given that it is reasonable compensation for services performed before or after the acquisition. The effect of golden parachute rules, in other words, is only to raise the taxpayer's burden of proof on the issue of reasonableness with respect to these payments.

Under §4999, the recipient must pay an excise tax of 20 percent of the amount the employer may not deduct.[75] The excise tax is nondeductible.[76]

¶22.3 RENTAL PAYMENTS

Under §162(a)(3), deductible business expenses include "rentals or other payments required to be made as a condition to the continued use or possession, for purposes of the trade or business, of property to which the taxpayer has not taken or is not taking title or in which he has no equity."[1]

---

[74] IRC §280G(b)(4)(B).

[75] For the effects of an agreement by the employer to reimburse the employee for this tax, see Kaplan, supra note 67, at 65–69.

[76] IRC §275(6).

[1] This provision, first enacted in 1916, was apparently aimed at preventing mortgagors from taking business deductions for mortgage payments. See Lukins, Tax Treatment of the Lease With Option to Purchase: Is Allocation the Answer? 11 Tax L. Rev. 65, 68 (1955).

There is no explicit counterpart in §212, but similar principles have been applied. Daniel v. CIR, 37 TCM (CCH) 1180 (1978) (option to purchase; §§162(a)(3) and 212 equivalent).

The affirmative message of this provision—that rents, royalties, and similar payments are deductible if incurred to use property for business purposes—is scarcely necessary; their deductibility is self-evident.[2] The negative message—that taxpayers cannot deduct capital outlays to purchase property—is also self-evident today,[3] although in 1916, when the "no equity" restriction was enacted, Congress evidently thought that an explicit warning was required to prevent taxpayers from deducting mortgage payments on business property. It is not uncommon for householders to refer to their monthly mortgage payments as rent, and perhaps businessmen were equally loose in their use of language in 1916. In any event, §162(a)(3) reinforces the basic principle that capital expenditures are not deductible.

Section 162(a)(3) is troublesome primarily in lease-option and sale-leaseback contexts, where taxpayers' relationships to property are ambiguous. If a taxpayer leases property for its fair market value, subject to an option to purchase at its estimated future value or for an amount to be determined by appraisal when the option is exercised, the rental payments while the option remains inchoate are deductible if the property is used for business purposes. On the other hand, if the rental payments exceed fair rental value and are applicable against the purchase price, the lessee's economic status may be virtually indistinguishable from that of a purchaser who finances acquisition of the property with a mortgage. In this case, rental payments may not be deducted but are instead recharacterized as interest and amortization on the hypothetical mortgage; the taxpayer may then deduct the interest component of the periodic payments and may depreciate the property over its estimated useful life. The same tax results follow if a sale-leaseback is recharacterized as a mortgage. The principles employed in determining whether a lease-option or sale-leaseback should be recharacterized as a financing arrangement, and the impact of the reclassifi-

---

[2] For the deduction of rent paid to a member of the lessee's family under a gift-leaseback arrangement, see infra ¶75.3.5. See Quinn v. US, 77-1 USTC ¶9369 (D. Md. 1976) (not officially reported) (reasonableness of rent paid to related parties subject to scrutiny to see if it is distribution of profits or other nondeductible payment disguised as rent and hence not "required to be made as a condition to continued use or possession . . . of property" within meaning of §162(a)(3)); Safway Steel Scaffolds Co. v. US, 590 F2d 1360 (5th Cir. 1979) (part of rental paid shareholder found to be nondeductible dividend). But see Carroll v. CIR, 37 TCM (CCH) 736 (1978) (sale-leaseback between corporation and sole shareholder valid; extensive collection of cases). See also Jack's Cookie Co. v. US, 597 F2d 395 (4th Cir. 1979) (extended analysis of rent deduction; payments to lessor to create reserve to pay lessor's bonds not deductible).

[3] See supra ¶20.4 (re capital expenditures). See also Velvet Horn, Inc. v. CIR, 41 TCM (CCH) 1445 (1981) (only "reasonable" rent deductible; rents under percentage lease found reasonable).

cation on the purported lessor, are discussed elsewhere in this work.[4]

The characterization problem just described arises most frequently in transactions involving real estate and business equipment, but the same legal issues are posed by royalty agreements involving trademarks, other intangible assets, and mineral property, where the licensee has an option to purchase and can apply the interim payments against the option price.[5]

Although §162(a)(3) does not explicitly deal with payments to acquire a leasehold for business purposes, the regulations provide that the cost is deductible in equal portions over the life of the lease. Section 178, discussed elsewhere in this work, contains rules determining whether renewal periods are to be taken into account in fixing the amortization period.[6] Section 178 also specifies the period over which improvements erected by the lessee are to be depreciated or amortized.[7]

¶22.4 MOVING EXPENSES

¶22.4.1 Introductory

Section 217 permits certain employees and self-employed individuals to deduct moving expenses paid or incurred in connection with the commencement of work at a new principal place of work. The allowance is subject to numerous limitations and qualifications, including principally: (1) The expenses must arise from a change in residences in connection with the taxpayer's employment at a new principal place of work that is at least 35 miles further from the taxpayer's former residence than was the old duty post, and (2) the taxpayer must be employed full-time in the vicinity of the new working place for at least 39 weeks during the 12-month period immediately following arrival there. For employees moving from one principal

---

[4] See supra ¶4.4.2.

[5] J. Strickland & Co. v. US, 352 F2d 1016 (6th Cir. 1965), cert. denied, 384 US 950 (1966) ("inordinately large" minimum royalty payments and large advertising and promotional campaign by "licensee," coupled with option to purchase in its controlling shareholders, indicated purported license of trademarks was purchase and sale); J.C. Cornillie Co. v. US, 298 F. Supp. 887 (ED Mich. 1968) ("commissions" for use of customer lists held purchase price; deduction denied); Chicago Stoker Corp. v. CIR, 14 TC 441 (1950) ("royalties" credited against purchase price of business if "buyer" opted to buy not deductible because they gave buyer equity in business); Goldfields of Am., Ltd. v. CIR, 44 BTA 200 (1941) (minimum royalties paid before production and applied to purchase price under option to buy not deductible), citing prior cases. See also Sanders v. CIR, 75 TC 157 (1981) (buyer under contract to purchase land paid fees to seller for dumping fill thereon; held, capital expenditures because fees applied against purchase price).

[6] Reg. §1.162-11(a); see infra ¶23.1.5.

[7] Reg. §1.162-11(b).

place of work to another, the deduction is available whether the taxpayer is changing employers or being transferred by an existing employer. The deduction is also available to persons entering the job market for the first time and to self-employed persons. Under §82, if moving expenses are paid or reimbursed by any other person and this payment or reimbursement is attributable to the taxpayer's employment or self-employment (e.g., if it is made by the taxpayer's employer), the payment or reimbursement is included in gross income as compensation for services. The inclusion under §82 is required whether or not the expenses are deductible under §217.

The statutory rules on moving expenses were enacted in 1964 (and elaborated in 1969, 1976, and 1978) to displace the prior case law.[1] Under pre-1964 law, the cost of moving the taxpayer's residence from one permanent place of business to another was a nondeductible personal expense. Amounts paid by employers to reimburse the moving expenses of an existing employee were viewed as incurred "primarily for the benefit of the employer," and hence were not includable in the employee's gross income, but similar amounts received by a new employee or a self-employed person were taxable.[2] These anomalous distinctions between reimbursed and unreimbursed expenses and between old and new employees were eliminated by the enactment of §§82 and 217.

The salient features of §§82 and 217, discussed below in more detail, are:

1. Work-commencement, minimum-distance, and duration-of-employment requirements that must be satisfied to qualify moving expenses for deduction under §217.[3]

---

[1] See Reg. §1.217-1(a)(1): "Except as provided in section 217, no deduction is allowable for any expenses incurred by the taxpayer in connection with moving himself, the members of his family or household, or household goods and personal effects."

For the 1964 legislation, see S. Rep. No. 830, 88th Cong., 2d Sess., reprinted in 1964-1 (Part 2) CB 505, 575; Hazelwood, Costs Incurred by an Individual Who Moves in Connection With His Employment: A Tax Analysis, 20 Tax L. Rev. 365 (1965). For the 1969 legislation, see S. Rep. No. 552, 91st Cong., 1st Sess., reprinted in 1969-3 CB 423, 492; De Salvo, Final Reg. on Moving Expense Allowance: A Complex Area Clarified by New Rules, 38 J. Tax'n 74 (1973). For the 1976 legislation, see S. Rep. No. 938, 94th Cong., 2d Sess., reprinted in 1976-3 CB (Vol. 3) 49, 178; S. Rep. No. 1236, 94th Cong., 2d Sess., reprinted in 1976-3 CB (Vol. 3) 807, 837.

[2] For exposition and analysis of the pre-1964 law, see Lee, Command Performance: The Tax Treatment of Employer Mandated Expenses, 7 U. Rich. L. Rev. 1, 11–29 (1972).

[3] Infra ¶22.4.2.

2. The scope of the term "moving expenses" and the dollar limits on the amounts that may be deducted.[4]

3. The relation between the deduction of moving expenses under §217 and the deduction of travel expenses while away from home under §162(a)(2).[5]

4. The treatment of amounts defrayed directly or reimbursed by the taxpayer's employer, customer, client, or other person.[6]

5. Special rules applicable to taxpayers whose principal places of work are outside the United States.[7]

Although expenses incurred in moving from one residence to another were branded as "personal" items by pre-1964 law and remain nondeductible when they fail to qualify under §217,[8] amounts deductible under §217 have a quasi-business character under various provisions. Section 217 deductions are included in computing net operating loss deductions on the theory that they are "attributable to the taxpayer's business,"[9] and the deduction is scaled down by §911 to the extent allocable to excludable foreign-source earned income.[10] Also, prior to 1987, the §217 deduction was allowed in computing adjusted gross income, and thus could be taken even if the taxpayer did not itemize personal deductions.[11]

¶22.4.2 Work-Commencement, Minimum-Distance, and Duration-of-Employment Requirements

To deduct moving expenses under §217, the taxpayer must meet the following tests:

1. *Work commencement.* The moving expenses must be incurred "in connection with the commencement of work by the taxpayer as an employee or as a self-employed individual at a new principal place of work."[12] The

---

[4] Infra ¶22.4.3.
[5] Infra ¶22.4.4.
[6] Infra ¶22.4.5.
[7] Infra ¶22.4.7.
[8] See supra notes 1, 2.
[9] Rev. Rul. 72-195, 1972-1 CB 95.
[10] Rev. Rul. 76-162, 1976-1 CB 197, and earlier rulings and cases therein cited. See also Roque v. CIR, 65 TC 920 (1976) (similar result under §933 in connection with income from Puerto Rico). See generally Kramer, Deductibility of Moving Expenses for the Expatriate American, 54 Taxes 654 (1976).
[11] The repeal of this provision is not necessarily a denial of the quasi-business character of deductible moving expenses because the same legislation made nearly all employee business expenses itemized deductions. For §62 and the adjusted gross income concept, see supra ¶2.1.3.
[12] IRC §217(a); see S. Rep. No. 552, reprinted in 1969-3 CB 493.

deduction, however, is not restricted to taxpayers moving under employer compulsion or primarily because the employment pastures are greener elsewhere. A move may be "in connection with the commencement of work" even if the taxpayer takes the new job because the locale promises a more benign climate, is closer to the taxpayer's relatives, or satisfies other personal desires. The change in work location, further, need not result from an employer's transfer of the taxpayer; §217 encompasses employees taking work with new employers, self-employed taxpayers changing locations, and persons beginning work for the first time.[13]

The regulations provide that "the move must bear a reasonable proximity both in time and place to [the commencement of work] at the new principal place of work."[14] In general, the time requirement is satisfied by moving expenses incurred within one year of the commencement of work; the facts and circumstances of each case[15] determine whether expenses incurred thereafter qualify. The requirement that the move be reasonably "proximate in place" to the commencement of work at the new location is not satisfied if the new duty post is closer to the old residence than to the new one, unless there are extenuating circumstances for the move, such as a decrease in commuting time or expense.[16] The unarticulated premise of the "proximate in place" standard is evidently that a move is not related to the commencement of work at the new duty post if the taxpayer could have remained, with equal convenience, at the old residence.

2. *Minimum distance.* Presumably on the theory that short residential moves are animated more by personal preferences than by business pressure, the new principal place of work is required to be at least 35 miles farther from the taxpayer's former residence than was the former principal place of work.[17] If the taxpayer had no former principal place of work, the

---

[13] Id. But see Taylor v. CIR, 71 TC 124 (1978) (moving expenses incurred in transfer from military post to university to complete graduate work not deductible).

[14] Reg. §1.217-2(a)(3).

[15] Id.; see id. Ex. 1 (expenses qualify where part was incurred during one-year period and balance was incurred thereafter, following completion by the taxpayer's children of their schooling at the old location).

[16] Id.

[17] IRC §217(c)(1). The minimum distance specified by the 1964 version of §217 was 20 miles; this was increased to 50 miles by the 1969 amendments and reduced to 35 miles in 1976. See Reg. §1.217-2(c)(2); Rev. Rul. 78-174, 1978-1 CB 77 (mileage measured from former principal place of work despite two months of unemployment prior to move).

For the terms "former residence" and "new residence," see Reg. §1.217-2(b)(8). A residence can include such offbeat dwellings as houseboats and trailers, but §217 is only concerned with moving expenses between principal residences, not with moving expenses involving vacation homes.

new work place must be at least 35 miles from the taxpayer's former residence.

The regulations deal at some length with the meaning of the term "principal place of work" as applied to taxpayers with several duty posts or several employers, and they caution against taking inconsistent positions by deducting travel expenses under §162 while allegedly "away from home" and simultaneously treating the place where the expenses are incurred as a new principal place of work under §217.[18]

3. *Duration of employment.* To prevent taxpayers from using temporary jobs as a pretext for deducting the expenses of moving for personal reasons from one residence to another, a duration-of-employment condition is imposed. It is met if the taxpayer is a full-time employee (not necessarily for a single employer) in the general location of the new principal place of work during at least 39 weeks of the 12-month period immediately following arrival there.[19] For self-employed taxpayers and employees who do not satisfy the 39-week, 12-month standard, an alternative is to be a full-time employee or perform services as a self-employed person on a full-time basis (or a combination of the two) during at least 78 weeks of the 24-month period starting with arrival, of which 39 weeks must occur during the first 12-month period.[20] These duration requirements are waived if the taxpayer is unable to satisfy the conditions by reason of death, disability, or certain other involuntary circumstances.[21]

Tax returns for a taxable year in which moving expenses are paid or incurred often come due before the duration-of-employment standards have been met. If it is still possible that the requirements will be satisfied, the taxpayer can elect to take the §217 deduction on the assumption that they will be met; if a taxpayer making this election ultimately fails to meet the requirements, however, the amount deducted must be included in gross income in the first subsequent taxable year in which it becomes evident that the requirements can never be satisfied.[22] If this election is not made, no §217 deduction may be taken in the return, as originally filed, for the year the expenses are paid or incurred, but when the taxpayer subsequently

---

[18] Reg. §1.217-2(c)(3). See infra ¶22.4.4.

[19] IRC §217(c)(2).

[20] Reg. §1.217-2(c)(4).

[21] IRC §217(d)(1); Reg. §1.217-2(d)(1). Waivers for involuntary separations from service are allowed for employees, but not self-employed persons, and for transfers for the convenience of the employer. See Muse v. CIR, 76 TC 574 (1981) (latter waiver does not apply where transfer initiated by employee); Rev. Rul. 88-47, 1988-24 IRB 9 (same).

[22] IRC §217(d)(2); Reg. §1.217-2(d)(2). The deduction must be taken for the year in which the moving expenses were paid or incurred, not in the year in which the duration-of-employment condition is ultimately satisfied. Meadows v. CIR, 66 TC 51 (1976).

meets the duration requirement, the deduction must be claimed by an amended return or claim for refund for the year in which the expenses were paid or incurred, not by taking the deduction for the year the duration requirements are satisfied.

¶22.4.3   Qualifying Expenses and Dollar Limits

Taxpayers eligible for the §217 deduction may deduct five categories of "moving expenses," subject to certain dollar limits, provided the amounts are "reasonable."[23] The five categories are:

1. *Household goods, etc.* The deduction is allowed for the cost of moving household goods and personal effects from the former residence to the new one, including expenses for packing, in-transit storage, and insurance but not penalties for breach of a lease, mortgage penalties, or losses of tuition fees or club dues.[24]

2. *Travel expenses.* The cost of traveling (including meals and lodging) between the two residences is deductible. Only one trip for the taxpayer and each family member qualifies, but they need not travel at the same time. Expenses incurred after arriving at the new place of residence and while waiting for the taxpayer's household goods to arrive are not covered, nor does this category include trips to sell the old residence or to find a new one or trips by the taxpayer to the old residence pending the family's move to the new residence.[25] Some of these expenses, however, fall within other deductible categories described below.

3. *House-hunting expenses.* The deduction includes the cost of traveling (including meals and lodging) between the old residence and the location of the new principal place of business, after obtaining employment, for the principal purpose of finding a new residence.[26] The number of qualifying house-hunting trips by the taxpayer and members of the taxpayer's family is not limited, and a trip can qualify even if it does not result in a lease or purchase of property.

---

[23] For the term "reasonable expenses," see Reg. §1.217-2(b)(2)(i) (moving must be by shortest and most direct route, excluding detours for scenic pleasure; meals and lodging must not be lavish or extravagant; etc.); Schwartz v. CIR, 41 TCM (CCH) 431 (1980), aff'd without opinion (8th Cir. 1981) (no deduction for expenses on detours off direct route).

[24] IRC §217(b)(1)(A); Reg. §1.217-2(b)(3). See Aksomitas v. CIR, 50 TC 679, 686 (1968) (no deduction for cost of moving 45-foot yacht); Repaci v. CIR, 39 TCM (CCH) 208 (1979) (auto registration and installation of carpet and dryer not qualified); Rev. Rul. 66-305, 1966-2 CB 102 (cost of moving household pets qualifies).

[25] IRC §217(b)(1)(B); Reg. §1.217-2(b)(4). Some travel expenses that fail to qualify in this category may fit in the third or fourth categories, subject to the dollar limits imposed thereon.

[26] IRC §217(b)(1)(C); Reg. §1.217-2(b)(5).

4. *Temporary quarters.* The deduction covers costs of meals and lodging while at temporary quarters in the general location of the new principal place of work during any period of 30 consecutive days after obtaining employment.[27] This allowance does not include laundry, entertainment, transportation, or other personal or living expenses at the new location or expenses attributable to temporary quarters in the vicinity of the taxpayer's former duty post.

5. *Qualified residence expenses.* Also deductible are "qualified residence sale, purchase, or lease expenses," an elaborately defined miscellany including commissions, attorneys' fees, and similar expenses incurred in selling the old residence or purchasing the new one and comparable expenses attributable to terminating or entering into residential leases.[28] Fixing-up expenses to facilitate a sale of the old residence and any loss incurred on an actual sale, however, do not qualify as moving expenses.

Moving expenses need not be attributable solely to the taxpayer to qualify for deduction. The deduction may include expenses within any of the first four of these categories that are attributable to a member of the taxpayer's household whose principal place of abode is both the former and the new residence.[29] This extension does not embrace a tenant or employee, however, unless he is a "dependent" of the taxpayer as defined by §152.[30] Expenses in the fifth category, in contrast, may only be deducted if attributable to the taxpayer or the taxpayer's spouse.

The expenses in the first two categories may be deducted regardless of amount, provided they are reasonable. The deduction for expenses in categories 3 and 4, however, is limited to $1,500, and the deduction for category 5 expenses may not exceed $3,000 less the amount deducted under categories 3 and 4.[31]

Some category 5 items, if not deducted under §217, are indirectly recognized, either by reducing the taxpayer's gain (or increasing loss) on the sale of the old residence or by increasing the basis of the new one. For this reason, it is advantageous to claim §217 deductions for expenses in catego-

---

[27] IRC §217(b)(1)(D); Reg. §1.217-2(b)(6). For post-1977 taxable years, this period is 90 consecutive days for foreign moves. IRC §217(h)(1)(A). See infra ¶22.4.7.

[28] IRC §§217(b)(1)(E), (2); Reg. §1.217-2(b)(7).

[29] IRC §217(b)(3)(C).

[30] Reg. §1.217-2(b)(10). For the term "dependent," which is not restricted to persons giving rise to a dependency exemption, see infra ¶30.3.1.

[31] IRC §217(b)(3). These dollar amounts are halved if separate returns are filed by a married couple. For the treatment of two-job married couples, see IRC §217(b)(3)(B); Reg. §§1.217-2(b)(9)(iv), (v) (commencement of work by both husband and wife at new principal place of work within same general location treated as only one commencement).

For certain moves to and from foreign work sites, the basic dollar amounts were increased to $4,500 and $6,000 by §217(h), enacted in 1978. See infra ¶22.4.7.

ries 3 and 4 to the extent possible before applying any category 5 items against the $3,000 limit. Section 217(e) makes it clear, however, that the taxpayer may not get a double benefit by deducting a §217 item and also using it in computing the amount realized on the sale of the old residence or in determining the basis of the new one.[32]

¶22.4.4 Moving Expenses and Travel Away From Home

Taxpayers may not deduct both moving expenses under §217 and the cost of meals and lodging at the new duty post under §162(a)(2). Moving expenses are not deductible under §217 unless the taxpayer will be employed at the new principal place of work on a permanent or indefinite basis, while §162(a)(2) permits living expenses at a duty post to be deducted only if the taxpayer's employment there is temporary.[33] If the taxpayer takes an inconsistent position in this respect, it is a question of fact whether §162(a)(2) or §217 applies.[34]

¶22.4.5 Reimbursed Moving Expenses

To eliminate the distinctions prevailing under prior law between taxpayers whose moving expenses were defrayed by their employers and those who paid their own expenses,[35] §82 was enacted in 1969 to require that a taxpayer include in gross income any other person's payment or reimbursement of the expenses of moving from one residence to another if the payment or reimbursement is attributable to the taxpayer's employment or self-employment.[36] For employees, these payments are usually made by employers, but §82 may also reach payments or reimbursements by clients or customers of a self-employed person. Taken in combination, §§82 and 217 force all taxpayers to comply with the conditions prescribed by §217 in order to deduct their moving expenses.

To achieve this objective, §82 is construed by the regulations to include not merely moving expenses qualifying for deduction under §217 but also those that do not qualify, whether because of the dollar limits or the taxpay-

---

[32] Reg. §1.217-2(e).

[33] See Goldman v. CIR, 497 F2d 382 (6th Cir.), cert. denied, 419 US 1021 (1974); Schweighardt v. CIR, 54 TC 1273, 1277 (1970). For temporary as distinguished from indefinite employment, see supra ¶21.1.4.

[34] Reg. §1.217-2(c)(3)(iii). See also Rev. Rul. 73-468, 1973-2 CB 77 (special rule for applying §§162 and 217 to newly elected Congressman).

[35] See supra notes 1, 2.

[36] Because §82 amounts are includable in gross income "as compensation for services," they are wages subject to withholding unless it is reasonable to believe that the employee will be entitled to an offsetting deduction under §217. IRC §3401(a)(15).

er's failure to satisfy the minimum-distance or duration-of-employment conditions or because the defrayed or reimbursed expenses are entirely excluded from §217 (e.g., losses incurred on the sale of furniture or the cost of refitting rugs or draperies).[37] In the same effort to achieve uniformity among taxpayers, the regulations interpret the statutory reference to "payment for or reimbursement of expenses" as including the fair market value of services furnished in kind, such as the use of an employer's facilities to move the taxpayer's belongings from the old residence to the new one.[38]

¶22.4.6 Members of the Armed Forces

Section 217(g), enacted in 1976, prescribes special rules for members of the armed forces on active duty who move under military orders incident to a permanent change of station.[39] They are not subject to the minimum-distance or duration-of-employment conditions of §217(c); moving and storage expenses furnished in kind (or covered by a reimbursement or allowance that is actually spent) are not includable in gross income; and certain expenses incurred in moving the taxpayer's spouse and dependents qualify for deduction even if the move is from or to a location different from the taxpayer's old or new location.

¶22.4.7 Foreign Work Sites

Special rules were enacted in 1978 for moving expenses incurred by (1) taxpayers commencing work outside the United States and (2) retirees returning after working abroad and surviving dependents of Americans who die while working abroad.[40] For taxpayers of the first type, the time and dollar limits on the deduction are relaxed, and a deduction is permitted for the costs of moving household goods and personal effects to and from

---

[37] Reg. §1.82-1(a)(5). For pre-IRC §82 law, see Bradley v. CIR, 39 TC 652, aff'd, 324 F2d 610 (4th Cir. 1963) (new employee reimbursed for difference between value and sale price of former residence; held, additional compensation, overruling Schairer v. CIR, 9 TC 549 (1947)); Keener v. CIR, 59 TC 302 (1972) (same, collecting prior cases); Rinehart v. CIR, 18 TC 672 (1952) (funds received from employer on relocation to enable taxpayer to buy house includable in gross income).

[38] Reg. §1.82-1(a)(2).

[39] See Reg. §1.217-2(g); Chamberlin v. CIR, 78 TC 1136 (1982) (deduction allowed for officer's move from Hawaii to California, where he served one week before retiring; no deduction for subsequent move because taxpayer never worked at new location). The enactment of §217(g) in 1976 was preceded by a moratorium on the application of §82 and prior §217(c) to members of the armed forces. See Rev. Proc. 75-55, 1975-2 CB 595.

[40] IRC §§217(h), (i). See Conf. Rep. No. 1798, 95th Cong., 2d Sess., reprinted in 1978-2 CB 432.

storage and of storing the goods while working at the foreign principal place of work.[41] Returning retirees and returning surviving dependents may deduct their expenses of moving back to the United States as if they were commencing work as employees at a new principal place of work in the United States.[42] To qualify, retirees must move from a foreign residence in connection with a bona fide retirement, and surviving dependents must begin their moves from the decedent's former residence within six months of the decedent's death.[43]

¶22.5 ACTIVITIES NOT ENGAGED IN FOR PROFIT

¶22.5.1 Introductory

Under §183, if an individual, partnership, or S corporation carries on an activity and if the primary objective of the activity is not profit, deductions attributable to the activity are only allowable to the extent of gross income from the activity. When the provision was first enacted, its principal application was to losses incurred in hobbies and other activities carried on primarily for recreation or pleasure. More recently, the provision has often been applied to losses from tax shelter investments, where the issue is whether the investor's primary objective is economic profit or tax benefits.

Although it has been clear from the inception of the federal income tax that costs incurred by a taxpayer in carrying on a hobby or other recreational activity do not qualify for deduction, it has never been easy to administer the distinction between business and profit-oriented activities on the one hand and not-for-profit activities on the other. In an early case, involving large losses incurred by a gentleman farmer, Judge Learned Hand directed a verdict in favor of the government, saying:

> It does seem to me that if a man does not expect to make any gain or profit out of the management of the farm, it cannot be said to be a business for profit, and while I should be the last to say that the making of a profit was not in itself a pleasure, I hope I should also be one of those to agree there were other pleasures than making a profit. Indeed, it makes no difference whether a man is engaged in a business which gives him pleasure, if it be a business. . . . But it does make a difference whether the occupation which gives him pleasure can honestly be said to be carried on for profit. Unless you can find that element it is

---

[41] See supra notes 27, 31. See also IRC §217(h)(3) (defining "foreign move"), §217(h)(4) (U.S. possessions not foreign).

[42] IRC §217(i)(1)(A). The duration-of-employment restrictions do not apply. IRC §217(i)(1)(B).

[43] IRC §217(i)(2) (retirees), §217(i)(3)(B) (surviving dependents).

not within the statute, and I cannot see in this case even the first intimation of a reason to suppose that [the taxpayer] in his lifetime carried on this farm with the hope of a profit, or that if he had not got anything else out of it except the money which he did get he would have kept on.[1]

Taxpayers with better prepared cases, however, managed to establish that their country estates, racing stables, and other costly pursuits were conducted for profit rather than for pleasure in a surprisingly large number of cases, especially if they had the good fortune to appear before judges less skeptical than Learned Hand. Commenting on these cases, Randolph Paul observed: "The American businessman has never appeared so indefatigably optimistic as in some of the cases on this point; taxpayers have earnestly contended (sometimes successfully) that they expected to reap an ultimate profit even though operating losses exceeded receipts with depressing regularity over a long period of years."[2] In one of these cases, the taxpayer was not only "indefatigably optimistic" but wryly defiant: Despite his bravado in naming his enterprise "Folly Farm," an admission against interest that was buttressed by 13 years of uninterrupted losses aggregating almost $700,000, his activities were found to be a business rather than a hobby.[3] Although the losses in cases like these were genuine enough, the issue was whether they constituted nondeductible costs of living or deductible costs of earning a living. The taxpayers uniformly testified that they were striving to make a profit, but this assertion can be both wholly honest and wholly immaterial: Whether one engages in a hobby or a business, it is obviously better to make money than to lose it.

Discontented with the outcome of these hobby-business cases, Congress enacted a provision in 1943, which became §270 of the 1954 Code, under which an individual whose losses from a trade or business exceeded the enterprise's gross income by $50,000 or more for each of five consecutive years could not deduct the excess losses. This statutory approach left the threshold question of whether the activity was a hobby or a business to be decided case-by-case with reference to all of the facts and circumstances. If the activity was found to be conducted for pleasure rather than for profit, the losses were entirely disallowed, but if the taxpayer succeeded in establishing that it was a business, §270 came into play to disallow losses in excess of $50,000 per year, subject to qualifications for drought, casualties,

---

[1] Thacher v. Lowe, 288 Fed. 994, 995 (SDNY 1922).
[2] Paul, Motive and Intent in Federal Tax Law, in Paul, Selected Studies in Federal Taxation 255, 281–82 (Callaghan, 2d ser. 1938).
[3] Ellsworth v. CIR, 21 TCM (CCH) 145 (1962). See also Farris v. CIR, 31 TCM (CCH) 821 (1972) (horse breeder conducted horse operation on trainer's premises, named "Fantasy Farm").

and some other special circumstances.[4]

Section 270 did not apply to corporations, an ironic exclusion since its enactment was supported by a number of legislators who thought that it would strike at Marshall Field, Jr., the publisher of the then controversial New York newspaper *PM*. Although §270 thus gained a popular name ("the Marshall Field amendment"), it did not apply to Mr. Field, whose publishing was carried on through corporations. Another bit of historical curiosa is that Mr. Field's father had been allowed to deduct his losses in running a racing stable, on the ground that they were incurred in a trade or business— losses that would have been disallowed in part by §270 if it had been in effect for earlier years.[5]

In 1969, Congress concluded that §270 had not worked well and replaced it with §183, a change that was explained as follows by the Senate Finance Committee:

> The hobby loss provision [§270] generally has been of very limited application. It is often possible for a taxpayer to slightly rearrange his income and deductions so as to break the required string of five [consecutive years with losses exceeding $50,000 a year]. In addition, the exclusion of certain specially treated deductions from the loss computations means that a number of expenses are not considered to give rise to a loss even though they are in fact deducted. Moreover, in the few cases in which the hobby loss provision has applied so as to disallow the deduction of the loss, the taxpayer has been faced in one year with a combined additional tax attributable to a five-year period.
>
> In addition to the hobby loss provision, some court cases have provided another basis on which the loss can be denied; namely, that the activity carried on by the taxpayer from which the loss results is not a business but is merely a hobby. The committee agrees with the House that this basic principle provides a more effective and reasonable basis for distinguishing situations where taxpayers are not carrying on a business to realize a profit, but rather are merely attempting to utilize the losses from the operation to offset their other income.
>
> [Proposed §183 provides] that in determining whether losses from an activity are to be allowed, the focus is to be on whether the activity is engaged in for profit rather than whether it is carried on with a reasonable expectation of profit. This will prevent the rule from being

---

[4] For details, see Reg. §1.270-1; Crouch, When Does a Business Become a "Hobby" for Tax Purposes: The Tax Dangers and How to Avoid Them, 1 Tax'n for Acct. 338 (1967).

[5] Field v. CIR, 26 BTA 116 (1932) (nonacq.), aff'd, 67 F2d 876 (2d Cir. 1933). The Field horses were evidently overshadowed by the Field newspapers and played no role in the legislative debate.

applicable to situations where many would consider that it is not reasonable to expect an activity to result in a profit even though the evidence available indicates that the activity actually is engaged in for profit. For example, it might be argued that there was not a "reasonable" expectation of profit in the case of a bona fide inventor or a person who invests in a wildcat oil well. A similar argument might be made in a case of a poor person engaged in what appears to be an inefficient farming operation. The committee does not believe that this provision should apply to these situations.[6]

The salient features of §183 are:[7]

1. It applies only to activities of individuals, partnerships, trusts, estates, and S corporations.[8]

2. If an activity is not engaged in for profit, deductions attributable to the activity are allowable only to the extent permitted by §183.[9] Because the "not engaged in for profit" determination must be made separately for each "activity" of the taxpayer, the regulations prescribe guideposts to determine whether a taxpayer's nonbusiness operations constitute a single activity or more than one.[10]

3. The allowable deductions are (1) those that are allowable under other statutory provisions without regard to whether an activity is engaged in for profit (e.g., casualty losses and certain taxes) plus (2) those allowable with respect to activities engaged in for profit, but only to the limited extent permitted by §183(b)(2).[11]

4. A protaxpayer presumption provides, in general, that an activity producing gross income in excess of its deductions for three or more taxable

---

[6] S. Rep. No. 552, 91st Cong., 1st Sess., reprinted in 1969-3 CB 423, 489–90.

[7] See generally Lee, A Blend of Old Wines in a New Wineskin: Section 183 and Beyond, 29 Tax L. Rev. 347 (1974).

[8] The statutory reference to "an individual" includes estates and trusts. Reg. §1.183-1(a). For the application of §183 to activities of partnerships, see infra text accompanying notes 44–45.

Although corporations other than S corporations are not subject to §183, the regulations state that no inference can be drawn from §183 or the regulations thereunder as to whether a corporation's activities are engaged in for profit. Reg. §1.183-1(a). Since the factors set forth in the regulations for determining whether an activity is carried on for profit are a distillation of prior case law, however, they seem equally applicable to corporations. See Smith v. CIR, 38 TCM (CCH) 1246 (1979) (corporate-owned Lipizzan horses held for profit, despite 20-year period of losses; analysis of facts similar to approach under §183 in cases involving individual taxpayers). The statutory presumption of §183(d) (infra ¶22.5.5) is clearly inapplicable to corporations.

[9] Infra ¶22.5.2.

[10] Infra ¶22.5.3.

[11] Infra ¶22.5.4.

years during a period of five consecutive years (two of seven in the case of horse breeding and racing) is engaged in for profit unless the IRS establishes the contrary.[12]

¶22.5.2 Activity "Not Engaged in for Profit"

The core of §183 is the concept of an "activity not engaged in for profit," which is defined by §183(c) as any activity other than one for which deductions are allowable under §162, relating to expenses in carrying on the taxpayer's trade or business, or §212(1) or (2), relating to expenses for the production or collection of income or for the management, conservation, or maintenance of property held for the production of income.[13] Although this definition necessarily incorporates the standards applied under §162 or §§212(1) and (2) to determine whether expenses of a particular activity qualify for deduction, the regulations under §183 lay down an independent set of interpretative principles to determine whether an activity is engaged in for profit. Because the §183 regulations are a distillation of the prior case law, however, the chance of conflict with the standards employed by §§162 and 212 is minimal.[14] As pointed out by the Tax Court:

> Although section 183 has clearly placed a gloss on post-1969 judicial profit-motive inquiries, we think pre-1969 case law in this area remains relevant. We say this for two reasons. First, section 183(c) defines an "activity not engaged in for profit" as an activity with respect to which deductions would not be allowable under section 162 or section 212(1) or (2). Thus, prior cases dealing with profit motive under these sections retain their vitality. Second, the so-called "relevant factors" set forth in the regulations are themselves derived from prior case law . . . and, therefore, we think such prior law has a role to play in their application.[15]

The regulations under §183 begin with a preamble drawn largely from the Senate Finance Committee's 1969 report:

> The determination whether an activity is engaged in for profit is to be made by reference to objective standards, taking into account all of

---

[12] Infra ¶22.5.5.

[13] For §§162 and 212, see supra ¶¶20.1 and 20.5.

[14] See Gregory v. US, 76-1 USTC ¶9220 (WD La. 1976) (not officially reported) (same result for pre- and post-§183 years); Benz v. CIR, 63 TC 375, 383 (1974) (same).

[15] Jasionowski v. CIR, 66 TC 312, 321–22 (1976). See also Hurd v. CIR, 37 TCM (CCH) 499 (1978) (same tests applied to taxable years before and after 1969 legislation).

the facts and circumstances of each case. Although a reasonable expectation of profit is not required, the facts and circumstances must indicate that the taxpayer entered into the activity, or continued the activity, with the objective of making a profit. In determining whether such an objective exists, it may be sufficient that there is a small chance of making a large profit. Thus it may be found that an investor in a wildcat oil well who incurs very substantial expenditures is in the venture for profit even though the expectation of a profit might be considered unreasonable. In determining whether an activity is engaged in for profit, greater weight is given to objective facts than to the taxpayer's mere statement of his intent.[16]

One message of these introductory remarks is a rejection of some prior cases that gave greater weight to the taxpayer's subjective intent than to objective adverse circumstances presaging continued failures.[17] Subjective intention, however, is still important. As said by one court: "The question is not whether . . . a particular mode of doing business is wise, but whether the taxpayer honestly believed that the method he employed would turn a profit for him. The test is the taxpayer's subjective intent, not whether a reasonable businessman would have done the same."[18]

The quoted passage from the regulations also underscores that an objective to profit is sufficient to avoid the application of §183(a); there is no requirement that the taxpayer entertain a reasonable expectation of profit. The focus on the taxpayer's objective rather than on whether a reasonable person would have expected a profit has two consequences. It tends to shift the inquiry to subjective intent, contrary to the congressional direction that objective factors have greater weight in the statutory calculus. It also raises an issue of what level of profit or probability of profitability the taxpayer must strive for. The Court of Appeals for the District of Columbia Circuit has said:

> [T]he objective, not the expectation, of making a profit is to govern determinations on whether a taxpayer is engaged in a business or a hobby . . . One may embark upon a venture for the sincere purpose of eventually reaping a profit but in the belief that the probability of financial success is small or even remote . . . Yet it cannot be gainsaid that "the activity actually is engaged in for profit"—that it was undertaken "with the objective of making a profit."[19]

---

[16] Reg. §1.183-2(a). See S. Rep. No. 552, supra note 6, at 490.

[17] See Lee, supra note 7, at 391–95.

[18] Cornfeld v. US, 797 F2d 1049, 1053 (DC Cir. 1986).

[19] Dreicer v. CIR, 665 F2d 1292, 1299 (DC Cir. 1981). Compare Eastman v. United States, 635 F2d 833, 837 (Ct. Cl. 1980) (issue is whether taxpayer "engaged

Taken literally, this statement would leave little within §183's clutches. If a "remote . . . probability of financial success" is all that need be shown to avoid the provision, a taxpayer's assertion that he had an objective to profit can be backed up by objective facts in all but the unusual case where not even a remote chance of profit existed. This standard, in other words, is wholly subjective. On remand, the Tax Court resolved this dilemma largely by ignoring the issue of probability:

> The purpose of the standard adopted by the Court of Appeals is to allow deductions where the evidence indicates that the activity is actually engaged in for profit even though it might be argued that there is not a reasonable expectation of profit. . . . However, a taxpayer's declaration of his motive to make a profit is not controlling. His motive is the ultimate question; yet, it must be determined by a careful analysis of all the surrounding objective facts, and greater weight is given to such facts than to his mere statement of intent. . . . Thus, although a reasonable expectation of profit is not required, the facts and circumstances must indicate that the taxpayer entered into the activity, or continued the activity, with the actual and honest objective of making a profit.[20]

The regulations state that in determining whether an activity is engaged in for profit, "all facts and circumstances with respect to the activity are to be taken into account."[21] This illuminating message is followed by a list, with discussion and illustrations, of nine "relevant factors" that "should normally be taken into account," along with a warning that neither a single one of the listed factors nor a majority of them is controlling and that

---

in the activity with the primary purpose of making a profit"); Lemmen v. CIR, 77 TC 1326, 1340 (1981) ("the courts have used words such as 'basic,' 'dominant,' 'primary,' 'predominant,' and 'substantial' to describe the requisite profit motive").

[20] Dreicer v. CIR, 78 TC 642, 644–45 (1982), aff'd without opinion, 702 F2d 1205 (DC Cir. 1983). See Cornfeld v. CIR, 797 F2d 1049 (DC Cir. 1986) (adopting Tax Court's test of "whether the taxpayer entertained an actual and honest profit objective," without citing appellate court's own opinion in *Dreicer*); Beck v. CIR, 85 TC 557, 569 (1985) (repeating the comment that triggered Court of Appeals to reverse first Tax Court decision in *Dreicer*: "While a reasonable expectation of profit is not required, petitioner's objective of making a profit must be bona fide"). Commenting in another case on the Court of Appeal's decision in *Dreicer*, the Tax Court observed: "The difference in the standard of 'objective of making a profit' and a 'bona fide expectation' of making a profit might be merely one of semantics." Brannen v. CIR, 78 TC 471 (1982).

[21] Reg. §1.183-2(b). See Giordan v. CIR, 35 TCM (CCH) 505 (1976) (taxpayer inheriting residence rented at a loss should be allowed a reasonable time within which to sell, renegotiate lease, or rent to another tenant; in effect, profit motive imputed for one year; §183 not in effect during grace period, but presumably same result under §183).

factors not explicitly specified may be relevant.[22]

The Big Nine Factors are:[23]

1. The manner in which the taxpayer carries on the activity, such as whether complete books and records are kept, unprofitable methods are abandoned, and operating procedures are comparable to those of profitable enterprises.[24]

2. The expertise of the taxpayer or his advisers, including whether a preparatory study is made of business, economic, and scientific practices or whether expert consultations are sought on these matters.[25]

3. The amount of time and effort devoted by the taxpayer to the activity.[26]

4. An expectation that assets used in the activity may appreciate in value, unless current operations and sales of the property (e.g., farmland) at a profit are separate activities.[27]

---

[22] Other factors that might be relevant are the taxpayer's advertising and plans to increase the activity's profitability, and the financial participation of other persons (e.g., a farm manager with a profit sharing arrangement). See Lee, supra note 7, at 444–47.

[23] For exhaustive annotations and discussion keyed to each of the nine factors, see Lee, supra note 7, at 397–444; Burns & Groomer, Effects of Section 183 on the Business/Hobby Controversy, 58 Taxes 195 (1980). See also Snyder v. US, 674 F2d 1359 (10th Cir. 1982) (extensive analysis of factors to be considered in determining whether attorney preparing book of photographs could deduct costs under §162 or 212); Churchman v. CIR, 68 TC 696 (1977) (application of regulations to artist; profit motive established); Ballich v. CIR, 37 TCM (CCH) 1851-40 (1978) (detailed analysis and application of factors to kennel operator; profit motive not established); Lindow v. CIR, 37 TCM (CCH) 1257 (1978) (same as to owner of Palm Beach condominium apartment).

[24] Reg. §1.183-2(b)(1). See Allen v. CIR, 72 TC 28 (1979) (taxpayers operated ski lodge in businesslike manner, experimenting with different modes of operating it in hope of making profit); Lyon v. CIR, 36 TCM (CCH) 979 (1977) (failure to maintain records and unbusinesslike approach; activity not "engaged in for profit"); Lee, supra note 7, at 397–407.

[25] Reg. §1.183-2(b)(2). See also Benz v. CIR, 63 TC 375 (1974) (taxpayer was "relative novice"; breeding activity held a hobby); Lee, supra note 7, at 407–12.

[26] Reg. §1.183-2(b)(3). See also Hawkins v. CIR, 38 TCM (CCH) 469 (1979) (publication of book of poetry not activity engaged in for profit; no evidence of continuous or repeated activity in literary field or intent to write with substantial regularity); Lee, supra note 7, at 412–16. But see Cornfeld v. CIR, 797 F2d 1049, 1052 (DC Cir. 1986) ("to have an honest profit objective a taxpayer need not run the business himself or have expertise in it; it suffices that he engage those who do"); Nickerson v. CIR, 700 F2d 402, 407 (7th Cir. 1983) (taxpayer engaged in farming for profit even though he had another full-time job and spent only his spare time on farm; taxpayer's efforts were "prodigious" and farm did not provide recreation).

[27] Reg. §1.183-2(b)(4). See Reg. §1.183-1(d) (definition of "activity"); infra ¶22.5.3. See also Bolaris v. CIR, 776 F2d 1428 (9th Cir. 1985) (depreciation and operating expense deductions allowed with respect to former principal residence that

5. The taxpayer's experience in converting other unprofitable activities into profitable enterprises.[28]

6. The taxpayer's history of income or losses in the activity, including whether losses were incurred in a start-up period, when they are to be expected, or have continued without adequate explanation thereafter or whether the losses were unforeseen consequences of drought, fire, or depressed market conditions. A series of profitable years is "strong evidence" that the activity is engaged in for profit.[29]

7. The amount of occasional profits, if any, that are earned, in relation to the losses and as compared to the amount invested by the taxpayer and the value of the assets used in the activity.[30]

8. The taxpayer's financial status (poor taxpayers are not oblivious to large losses; wealthy ones may be willing to accept them, especially if they generate offsetting tax, personal, or recreational benefits).[31]

9. Elements of personal pleasure or recreation in conducting the activity. While the derivation of pleasure from the activity does not negate a profit objective, the presence of recreational elements is an adverse factor. Conversely, that an activity "lacks any appeal other than profit" may denote a profit motivation.[32]

---

was rented pending sale; profit motive can exist even if gain on sale qualifies for nonrecognition); Dickson v. CIR, 47 TCM (CCH) 509 (1983) (expectation of profit from appreciation in value of sailboat was major factor in finding boat chartering activity engaged in for profit); Lee, supra note 7, at 416–18. But see Jasionowski v. CIR, 66 TC 312 (1976) (taxpayer's expectation of capital gains upon eventual sale of property not sufficient to supply profit motive for current lease of the property).

More broadly, it might be said that future as well as current profits and losses are considered in determining whether an activity is carried on for profit. See Landry v. CIR, 86 TC 1284, 1306 (1986) (rejecting IRS's argument that §183 applies where, notwithstanding a conceded intention to profit in the long run, a good faith intention to profit during the taxable year was lacking; §183 inapplicable if taxpayer "intended to make a profit within a reasonable time"); Lemmen v. CIR, 77 TC 1326 (1981) (acq.) (expectation of profit from herd of breeding cattle over long range established).

[28] Reg. §1.183-2(b)(5). See Lee, supra note 7, at 418–20.

[29] Reg. §1.183-2(b)(6). See Allen v. CIR, 72 TC 28 (1979) (ski lodge's losses explained by market saturation, low snowfall, and gasoline shortages); Lee, supra note 7, at 420–28; infra ¶22.5.5 (presumption arising from two successful years).

[30] Reg. §1.183-2(b)(7). See Lee, supra note 7, at 428–31.

[31] Reg. §1.183-2(b)(8). See Lee, supra note 7, at 431–36; Jasionowski v. CIR, supra note 27 (taxpayer's substantial income from other sources and other rental experience indicated that lease under which substantial losses, as distinguished from usual start-up losses, would be incurred for several years was not entered into for profit); Hurd v. CIR, 37 TCM (CCH) 499 (1978) (substantial outside income enabled taxpayers to absorb large losses from ranch; held, not operated for profit).

[32] Reg. §1.183-2(b)(9). See also Allen v. CIR, supra note 29 (taxpayers never used ski lodge for personal recreation); Lee, supra note 7, at 436–44.

While this catalogue of amorphous factors might be the best that can be done to illuminate the intractable issue of whether an activity is "engaged in for profit," it is obvious that some of the indicia (e.g., accurate books and records, preliminary investigations, consultations with experts, and use of businesslike operating techniques) might be no more than camouflage. The remarks of the Court of Appeals for the Third Circuit in a pre-§183 hobby/business case are still pertinent:

> The Tax Court, in seeking to determine motive, appears to have directed its inquiry to objective indications such as record-keeping, the general profit-potential of the activity and the actual results achieved by the taxpayer, and to have excluded his direct testimony regarding his motive. Objective factors are, of course, valuable evidence of a taxpayer's motive, although these are often burdened with the same infirmity as a taxpayer's testimony, since the meticulous observance of details which have been labeled as important objective signposts is of doubtful value once their observance becomes self-conscious.[33]

The evidentiary weight of an objective factor, in short, may depend on its subjective context.

In recent years, most of the cases under §183 have involved tax shelters, where the issue is whether an activity is carried on to generate tax benefits rather than economic profit, not whether the activity is a hobby rather than a venture carried on for profit. The regulations presage this development, stating: "Substantial income from sources other than the activity (particularly if the losses from the activity generate substantial tax benefits) may indicate that the activity is not engaged in for profit, especially if there are personal or recreational elements involved."[34] The courts have followed up this statement by holding that in cases involving tax shelters and other tax favored investments, a comparison of the relative amounts of economic profit and expected tax benefits is relevant in evaluating a taxpayer's expectations of profit.[35] Rather sophisticated analyses of the benefits of

---

[33] Imbesi v. CIR, 361 F2d 640, 645 (3d Cir. 1966); Jasionowski v. CIR, 66 TC 312 (1976).

[34] Reg. §1.183-2(b)(8).

[35] Baron's Est. v. CIR, 83 TC 542 (1984), aff'd, 798 F2d 65 (2d Cir. 1986) (tax shelter investor in master recording financed with large nonrecourse debt found not to have bona fide expectation of profit apart from tax consequences). See also Beck v. CIR, 85 TC 557, 570–71 (1985) (§183 applied where taxpayers "did not engage in the . . . activity with an actual and honest objective of making a profit but instead engaged in the transaction primarily, if not exclusively, to obtain tax deductions and credits and thereby reduce the tax [they] would otherwise have had to pay on their substantial income from other sources"); Elliott v. CIR, 84 TC 227 (1985), aff'd without opinion (3d Cir. 1986) (finding of no profit motive supported by facts that

tax deferral appear in some opinions.[36] An objective evaluation of the economic viability of the venture is sometimes made.[37]

An excessive purchase price for the activity's principal asset also suggests that tax benefits, not economic profit, are the primary motivation, particularly if a large portion of the price is paid by nonrecourse notes to the seller.[38] Further, where a venture is organized and promoted by persons other than the investors, a marketing effort focused almost exclusively on tax benefits is evidence of a lack of profit motive.[39]

The second of the Big Nine Factors—the extent and effectiveness of the taxpayer's study of the activity before investing—is especially important in tax shelter cases, but the focus in applying this factor is on the attention given to the possibility of economic profit apart from tax benefits.[40] The first factor—whether the activity is carried on in a businesslike

---

"promised tax benefits are suspiciously excessive" and that nonrecourse financing is large in relation to cash investment and is unlikely to be paid).

One court has taken the balancing approach used in *Baron's Est.* as a welcome departure in tax shelter cases from the usual rule that §183(a) applies unless the taxpayer's primary motive is economic profit:

> Economic and tax motives regularly operate side by side to influence business transactions, and it would be unfair and contrary to the realities of the marketplace to apply a "primary or dominant" test to them. [The appropriate test is that although] a primary or dominant profit motive is not required, . . . more than the "modicum" of profit necessary to avoid a finding of a "sham transaction" is necessary.

Johnson v. US, 86-2 USTC 9705 (Cl. Ct. 1986). None of the Tax Court opinions, however, say that anything less than a primary motive to make a profit suffices.

[36] Torres v. CIR, 88 TC 702 (1987) (economic profit and tax benefits evaluated by assuming cash flow and net tax savings each invested in sinking fund, and comparing sizes of sinking funds at end of economic life of investment). But see Taube v. CIR, 88 TC 464, 483–84 (1987) (projected cash flow compared with projected tax benefits without accounting for time value of money).

[37] West v. CIR, 88 TC 152 (1987) (lack of profit motive in motion picture tax shelter evidenced by poor quality of movie and purchase price inflated by excessive nonrecourse debt).

[38] Beck v. CIR, supra note 35; Elliott v. CIR, supra note 35. See also Soriano v. CIR, 90 TC 44 (1988) (where taxpayer leases rather than buys property, economic viability apart from taxes assessed by comparing present value of expected cash flows from property with present value of rental obligation).

[39] Simon v. CIR, 830 F2d 499 (3d Cir. 1987).

[40] See Simon v. CIR, supra note 39 (inadequate evaluation of venture's economic potential is evidence of lack of profit motive, as is taxpayer's failure to offer testimony of individuals who organized venture and carried on its activities); Beck v. CIR, 85 TC 557, 570–71 (1985) (inadequate evaluation where material furnished to taxpayer and advisor was riddled with inconsistencies and omissions); Elliot v. CIR, 84 TC 227 (1985) (failure to investigate economic feasibility of tax shelter evidence of lack of profit motive). But see Taube v. CIR, 88 TC 464 (1987) (presence of profit motive evidenced by general partner's preparation of detailed projections which

way—is also important, but here the focus is on whether the pursuit of economic profit is carried on effectively, not whether the tax shelter deal is organized and documented competently.[41]

An objective to realize economic profit apart from taxes is not always required. The IRS has ruled, for example, that §183 did not apply to an investment in a federally subsidized housing project, despite an expectation of losses for 20 years, because Congress intended to encourage the investment by allowing losses to be deducted.[42] The IRS is not likely to favor a broad application of the approach taken in the ruling. Tax shelters are often structured to take advantage of provisions enacted to encourage investments of various sorts. The tax shelter phenomenon, however, has been a target of congressional concern for at least 20 years. The IRS would probably limit the ruling's application to situations where Congress has indicated that the policies underlying a particular investment incentive override its usual distaste for tax shelters. The Tax Court has said:

> To some extent tax incentives, such as accelerated depreciation and investment tax credit, are designed to stimulate the formation of venture capital. Such incentives are not intended, however, to create a new economy consisting of paper transactions having no relationship to the real value of goods and services. Thus, the mere presence of a valid business enterprise at some levels of a transaction does not automatically entitle passive investors distant from day-to-day operations of the enterprise to the associated tax benefits.[43]

---

were "within, although perhaps at the outer boundaries of, reasonable estimates of the [activity's] potential for profit and cash-flow"); Tolwinsky v. CIR, 86 TC 1009 (1986) (close attention to economic viability demonstrated profit motive notwithstanding that "the presence of numerous, artificial stratagems and players . . . evidence[d] a strong intention to generate substantial tax losses"); Waddell v. CIR, 86 TC 848 (1986), aff'd, 841 F2d 264 (9th Cir. 1988) (careful examination of prospectus projecting economic profits showed profit motive notwithstanding obvious tax-motivated aspects of the deal, including prepaid royalties and excessive nonrecourse debt); Lemmen v. CIR, 77 TC 1326 (1981) (acq.) (profit motive shown where, before investing, cattle breeding investor studied prospectus carefully and visited farm where cattle would be managed).

[41] Brannen v. CIR, 722 F2d 695 (11th Cir. 1984) (unbusinesslike manner of arranging for distribution of motion picture; managing partners had little experience in motion picture business, and had losses in limited prior dealings in the business); Beck v. CIR, 85 TC 576 (1985) (taxpayer's argument that his businesslike manner was evidenced by agreements with shelter promoter "exalts form over substance to the extreme").

[42] Rev. Rul. 79-300, 1979-2 CB 112.

[43] Beck v. CIR, supra note 41, at 579–80. In a case involving the deductibility of a loss, the Tax Court has said:

> [M]any . . . tax-motivated transactions are congressionally approved and encouraged. We therefore relax our holding that section 165(c)(2) permits

Because tax shelters are commonly organized as partnerships, a recurring issue in these cases is, "Whose intention counts in determining whether a partnership activity is carried on for profit?" It is sometimes said that the relevant intention is that of the partnership, not that of the taxpayer claiming a share of partnership losses as a partner.[44] Partnerships, however, are artificial creations of the law, and do not exhibit such human characteristics as intention. A better statement is that "the proper focus is on the activities and intent of the individuals who 'actually ran all partnership affairs and whose expertise was relied on in making partnership decisions'".[45]

¶22.5.3 Scope of Term "Activity"

Although the term "activity" is not defined by §183, its meaning often has crucial importance. A taxpayer, for example, might wish to amalgamate two or more undertakings into a single activity if the resulting consolidated financial statement shows a profit because one of them, viewed in isolation, might be treated as an activity not engaged in for profit. Even if the taxpayer has no profitable activities to throw into the pool, the disallowance rules of §183(b) operate differently depending on whether the taxpayer's loss operations constitute a single activity or two or more separable activities.[46]

A similar problem existed under §183's predecessor, §270, except that the relevant statutory unit was a "trade or business" rather than an "activi-

---

loss deductions only from transactions entered into primarily for profit to allow for those essentially tax-motivated transactions which are unmistakably within the contemplation of congressional intent. The determination whether a transaction is one Congress intended to encourage will require a broad view of the relevant statutory framework and some investigation into legislative history. The issue of congressional intent is raised only upon a threshold determination that a particular transaction was entered into primarily for tax reasons.

Fox v. CIR, 82 TC 1001, 1021 (1984).

[44] Polakof v. CIR, 820 F2d 321, 303 (9th Cir. 1987) ("dominant economic motive of the partnership, not that of the individual investors . . . is determinative"); Tallal v. CIR, 778 F2d 275, 276 (5th Cir. 1985) ("the partnership's motive controls, not an individual partner's motive for joining the partnership"). See also Brannen v. CIR, 722 F2d 695, 703 (11th Cir. 1984) ("profit test should be applied at the partnership level"); Rev. Rul. 79-300, 1979-2 CB 112 (same).

[45] Simon v. CIR, 830 F2d 499, 507 (3d Cir. 1987). See also Deegan v. CIR, 787 F2d 825, 826 (2d Cir. 1986) ("where a general partner bears primary responsibility for managing the business of a limited partnership, the relevant inquiry is whether the general partners harbored 'an intent and objective of realizing a profit' through the investments"); Landry v. CIR, 86 TC 1284, 1303 (1986) ("proper focus is on the activities and intent of the general partners and promoters"); Fox v. CIR, 80 TC 972 (1983) (on facts, motive with reference to actions of promoter, in which nominal general partner acquiesced).

[46] For scope of the term "activity," see Reg. §1.183-1(d); Lee, supra note 7, at 365-80.

ty."[47] Although the latter term seems narrower in scope, it is not clear that the shift in terminology was intended to split operations that would have been a single business under prior law into several activities for purposes of §183, although it may have that effect in some situations. Without undertaking to define "activity," the regulations provide these guideposts:

> [W]here the taxpayer is engaged in several undertakings, each of these may be a separate activity, or several undertakings may constitute one activity. In ascertaining the activity or activities of the taxpayer, all the facts and circumstances of the case must be taken into account. Generally, the most significant facts and circumstances in making this determination are the degree of organizational and economic interrelationship of various undertakings, the business purpose which is (or might be) served by carrying on the various undertakings separately or together in a trade or business or in an investment setting, and the similarity of various undertakings. Generally, the Commissioner will accept the characterization by the taxpayer of several undertakings either as a single activity or as separate activities. The taxpayer's characterization will not be accepted, however, when it appears that his characterization is artificial and cannot be reasonably supported under the facts and circumstances of the case.[48]

To illustrate these principles, the regulations offer two examples. The first is drawn from the much-litigated country estate area:

> Where land is purchased or held primarily with the intent to profit from increase in its value, and the taxpayer also engages in farming on such land, the farming and the holding of the land will ordinarily be considered a single activity only if the farming activity reduces the net cost of carrying the land for its appreciation in value. Thus, the farming and holding of the land will be considered a single activity only if the income derived from farming exceeds the deductions attributable to the farming activity which are not directly attributable to the holding of the land (that is, deductions other than those directly attributable to the holding of the land such as interest on a mortgage secured by the land, annual property taxes attributable to the land and improvements, and depreciation of improvements to the land).[49]

---

[47] See Lee, supra note 7, at 366–67.

[48] Reg. §1.183-1(d)(1).

[49] Id. See Engdahl v. CIR, 72 TC 659 (1979) (where property purchased to breed and raise horses, land and horse-related activities were single activity); Rev. Rul. 78-22, 1978-1 CB 72 (horse racing conducted as sole proprietor and as member of partnership constituted two separate activities). See also Snyder v. CIR, 25 TCM (CCH) 1326 (1966) (deductions disallowed because farming activity not entered into

In another example the regulations take the position that the ownership of a beach house that is customarily rented for two months, occupied by the owner for one month, and vacant for nine months a year is a single activity.[50]

There are other contexts in which it is necessary to decide whether the taxpayer is engaged in two activities or only in one. In a number of cases, for example, taxpayers have claimed that distinctive recreational pursuits (e.g., sailing and car racing) served to advertise their occupations and hence to generate tax deductions. These claims are ordinarily evaluated under §§162 and 274, without reference to §183,[51] but it could make a difference whether the activity is amalgamated with a larger enterprise or must run the gauntlet of §183 by itself. In general, §§162 and 274 are concerned with discrete activities whose claim to deductibility depends on showing that they feed an acknowledged trade or business, while §183 is concerned with continuing activities whose tax status depends on whether, in and of themselves, they are carried on for profit. It is possible, however, that on failing to establish that a continuing activity like sailing or racing is a deductible expense of his primary trade or business, a taxpayer might be able to prove that, viewed in isolation, it is carried on for profit within the meaning of §183.

¶22.5.4 Allowable Deductions

Once it is determined that an activity is not engaged in for profit, deductions "attributable" to it are only allowed to the extent permitted by

---

for profit, although farm originally purchased as investment); Collins v. CIR, 34 TC 592 (1960) (nonacq.) (two professional football teams separate businesses for purposes of statutory predecessor of §270; held, Commissioner may not aggregate losses in applying $50,000 annual loss limit over five-year period); Comment, The Effect of Unrealized Appreciation in Determining Profit Motive in Farming Enterprises, 16 U. Kan. L. Rev. 529 (1968).

[50] Reg. §1.183-1(d)(3) Ex. Deductions attributable to vacation homes may be subject to the limitations of §280A, discussed infra ¶22.6. The application of §280A to a portion of a dwelling unit for a taxable year precludes application of §183 to the same portion for that year, but the year is taken into account in applying the five-year presumption of §183(d), discussed in ¶22.5.5. IRC §280A(f)(3). See also IRC §280A(g) (no income or deductions from rental of dwelling unit used by taxpayer as a residence if rented for less than 15 days during year).

[51] See Henry v. CIR, 36 TC 879 (1961) (tax expert allowed no deduction for expenses attributable to yacht with "1040" burgee); Sieber v. CIR, 38 TCM (CCH) 48 (1979) (builder of expensive homes not allowed to deduct cost of playing polo, despite incidental business contacts made thereby); Burrous v. CIR, 36 TCM (CCH) 1465 (1977) (accountant cannot deduct cost of racing midget cars). But see Sanitary Farms Dairy, Inc. v. CIR, 25 TC 463 (1955) (acq.) (cost of officer's African safari deductible as advertising expense).

§183(b), which clarifies an area that was previously quite murky.[52] Under pre-1969 law, if a country gentleman received $10,000 for agricultural products costing him $25,000 to raise and his farm was adjudged to be a hobby rather than a business, his gross receipts were ignored for tax purposes but he was not allowed to deduct the expenses. Thus, hobby cases were viewed as involving the deductibility of the taxpayer's net loss rather than the deductibility of the expenses. This result was approved by the regulations,[53] but it was difficult to see why the statutes did not require revenues from the activity to be included in gross income and the expenses to be disallowed in their entirety. As a matter of policy, further, it is debatable whether a hobbyist's receipts should be offset by his expenses, treated in part as taxable compensation for his time and effort in producing some salable products, or viewed as a taxable windfall on the theory that the activity was conducted solely for pleasure. It is also unclear whether different principles should be applied to not-for-profit activities that the taxpayer undertakes in the conscious expectation that part, although not all, of the expenses will be recouped by sales.

These issues are resolved by §183(b) in a way that is similar to the net-loss approach of prior law. Current law, however, is far more detailed. Deductions attributable to the activity are marshaled into three tiers,[54] which are then treated as follows:

1. Tier 1 consists of deductions that are allowable without regard to whether the activity is engaged in for profit, under such provisions as §163(h) (home mortgage interest), §164 (certain taxes), and §165(c)(3) (casualty losses in excess of the deduction floor on personal casualty losses). These items may be deducted in full.

2. Tier 2 consists of deductions that would be allowable if the activity had been conducted for profit but that do not result in adjustments to the basis of property, such as business expenses under §162(a) and profit-oriented expenses under §212(1) or (2). These items may be deducted, notwithstanding the finding that the activity was not conducted for profit, but only

---

[52] The term "attributable" is construed to embrace deductions that relate "directly or indirectly" to the activity. Rev. Rul. 73-219, 1973-1 CB 134 (interest on insurance policy loan taken out to purchase property is attributable thereto for purposes of §183).

[53] Reg. §1.162-12(b) (remains in force for taxable years beginning before 1970). See Imbesi v. CIR, 361 F2d 640, 645 (3d Cir. 1966); see also IRC §165(d) (gambling losses deductible only to extent of gambling winnings), discussed infra ¶25.9.

[54] Section 183(b) establishes only two categories, but the regulations split the second category into two subspecies. Reg. §1.183-1(b)(1). For the reason why tiers 2 and 3 are taken into account in that order, rather than the reverse, see Oshins, Proposed Regulations Provide New Rules for the Hobby Loss Game, 35 J. Tax'n 214 (1971).

to the extent the activity produced gross income in excess of its tier 1 deductions.

3. Tier 3 consists of deductions that would be allowable if the activity had been conducted for profit but that (unlike tier 2 deductions) result in basis adjustments. Depreciation is usually the principal tier 3 deduction, but this category also includes the portion of a casualty loss equal to the floor on the deduction for personal casualties, bad debts, and a few other items. These deductions are only allowable to the extent the activity's gross income exceeds the sum of its tier 1 and tier 2 deductions. If any tier 3 deductions are allowed, the property's basis is correspondingly adjusted, and this may result in a recapture of the deductions when the property is sold. If tier 3 deductions are attributable to two or more assets, the requisite basis adjustments are determined by a "basis adjustment fraction" prescribed by the regulations.[55]

These principles are illustrated by Example 22-1, which assumes that a taxpayer who races cars as a hobby receives a prize of $5,000 in a competition and incurs the following expenses, all with respect to a single car: (1) uninsured collision damage of $2,500, only $1,700 of which is deductible if the loss is not deemed incurred in a business or profit-oriented activity; (2) gasoline, oil, and repairs of $1,300; and (3) depreciation of $2,500. He is entitled to a deduction of $5,000 (line 4), and the car is subject to a basis adjustment of $2,000 (line 3e).

Example 22-1

Deductions as Limited by §183

1. Tier 1 deduction—casualty loss ($2,500 less
   nondeductible $800) $1,700
2. Tier 2 deductions
   a. Gross income from activity.................................. $5,000
   b. Less: Tier 1 deductions... 1,700
   c. Ceiling on Tier 2 deductions................................ $3,300
   d. Tier 2 deductions (those not affecting basis).......... $1,300
   e. Lesser of line 2c or line 2d...................................... 1,300
3. Tier 3 deductions
   a. Gross income from activity.................................. $5,000
   b. Less: Tier 1 and 2 deductions.............................. 3,000
   c. Ceiling on Tier 3 deductions................................ $2,000

---

[55] Reg. §§1.183-1(b)(2), (3).

d. Tier 3 deductions (depreciation and first $800 of
    casualty loss)... $3,300

e. Lesser of line 3c and 3d 2,000

4. Total deductions $5,000

The regulations deal at some length with the relationship between §183 and the deduction for capital gains allowed by §1202 for taxable years preceding 1987 to individual taxpayers. In general, the taxpayer must allocate a §1202 deduction among all activities producing an excess of net long-term capital gain over net short-term capital loss, so that the portion of the deduction properly allocable to an activity not engaged in for profit can be determined. The taxpayer must then treat this amount as a tier 1 deduction under §183(b)(1), thereby reducing pro tanto the gross income available to be offset by tier 2 and tier 3 deductions.[56]

As explained earlier, in applying the not-for-profit standard of §183(a), it is sometimes necessary to determine whether a taxpayer's operations constitute one activity or more than one.[57] The same problem can arise in applying the three-tier system to the taxpayer's deductions. Assume a taxpayer engages in enterprise A, which produces $1,000 of gross income and $1,000 of tier 2 deductions, and enterprise B, which produces no gross income and $1,000 of tier 1 deductions. If the enterprises are separate activities, the taxpayer must report $1,000 of gross income and can deduct the tier 2 deductions of $1,000 in respect of enterprise A and the tier 1 deductions of $1,000 in respect of enterprise B. If the enterprises constitute a single activity, however, the tier 1 deductions are offset against the gross income of $1,000, resulting in disallowance of the tier 2 deductions.

¶22.5.5 Presumption of For-Profit Operation

Under §183(d), if the gross income from an activity exceeds the deductions attributable to it for any three or more taxable years during the five-year period ending with the current taxable year, a rebuttable presumption arises that the activity was engaged in for profit during the taxable year.[58] For an activity consisting in major part of the breeding, training, showing, or racing of horses, however, the presumption arises if gross income exceeds

---

[56] Reg. §1.183-1(b)(4). See Lee, supra note 7, at 364–65.

[57] Supra ¶22.5.3.

[58] For taxable years beginning before 1987, profit need only be shown for two of these five years, not three. See Rev. Rul. 79-204, 1979-2 CB 111 (presumption period terminated with taxpayer's death; estate's profit in winding up activity not included).

deductions in two of the seven years ending with the current year; testimony to the extraordinary importance of horses in the American economy.

In applying this test, deductions are determined on the assumption that the activity is carried on for profit. The net operating loss deduction of §172, however, is not taken into account.[59] If gross income exceeds the deductions, so computed, for the requisite three of five or two of seven years, the activity is presumed to be conducted for profit during the third profit year (second for horses) and all subsequent years during the same five- or seven-year period.[60] A taxpayer's failure to get the benefit of the rebuttable presumption raises no inference that the activity is not carried for profit.

Section 183(e) permits taxpayers to elect to postpone a determination of whether the presumption applies until the close of the fourth taxable year (or the sixth year, for qualifying horse activities) following the first taxable year in which the taxpayer engages in the activity.[61] The effect of an election is that returns may be filed in the interim on the assumption that the activity is conducted for profit, and if there are three or two profitable years in the applicable five- or seven-year period, the presumption applies to all five or seven years, including years preceding the profit years. If the presumption does not come into force or is rebutted, however, the time for assessing deficiencies is extended by §183(e)(4).

¶22.6 RESIDENTIAL PROPERTY USED FOR BUSINESS AND PROFIT-ORIENTED PURPOSES—HOME OFFICES, VACATION HOMES, ETC.

¶22.6.1 Introductory

Section 280A, enacted in 1976, severely limits individuals, S corporations, trusts, and estates (including members of partnerships) in deducting expenses attributable to the business or profit-oriented use of a dwelling unit, whether owned or leased by the taxpayer, if the property is also used by the taxpayer as a residence during the taxable year.[1] Although aimed

---

[59] Also, the §1202 deduction for 60 percent of net capital gain, allowed for years prior to 1987, is ignored.

[60] Reg. §1.183-1(c)(1).

[61] For the formal requirements for an election, see Reg. §12.9.

[1] See generally Staff of Joint Comm. on Tax'n, 94th Cong., 2d Sess., General Explanation of the Tax Reform Act of 1976, reprinted in 1976-3 CB (Vol. 2) 148–58; De Guardiola, Home Office Deductions Under the New Section 280A of the Internal Revenue Code, 6 Fla. St. UL Rev. 129 (1978); Goff, Commingling Business and Personal Real Property: Severe Restrictions Under the 1976 Tax Reform Act, 13 Gonz. L. Rev. 493 (1978); Kaplan, Deductions for "Vacation Homes" Under the

primarily at deductions claimed for offices located in the taxpayer's residence and for vacation homes that are offered for rent when not occupied by the taxpayer, §280A also applies to dwelling units used for business entertainment or other profit-oriented purposes if the requisite amount of personal residential use occurs in the same taxable year. Moreover, because the crucial statutory reference to use of the property "by the taxpayer . . . as a residence" is defined to mean any use of a dwelling unit "for personal purposes" by the taxpayer, members of the taxpayer's family, or certain other persons, §280A can apply even if the taxpayer never sets foot on the premises and even if none of the tainted persons sleep there.

Before the enactment of §280A, the principles governing the deductibility of expenses attributable to property used both as the taxpayer's personal residence and as a place of business were uncertain, especially for employees. The IRS asserted that expenses attributable to an office in an employee's home could not be deducted under §162 unless maintaining the office was required by the employer as a condition of employment and the office was regularly used by the taxpayer in the performance of his duties.[2] The Tax Court adopted the more generous theory—conforming to the conventional construction of the term "ordinary and necessary" as used in §162(a)—that the expenses were deductible if the home office was "appropriate and helpful under all the circumstances" and was not maintained primarily for personal convenience.[3] Because of uncertainties in applying the "appropriate and helpful" standard and in allocating the taxpayer's expenses between business and personal uses, Congress decided in 1976 to impose the more severe tests of §280A on deductions for expenses of this type.

Similar problems in drawing a line between personal and business uses arise in the case of vacation homes that are put on the rental market when not occupied by the taxpayer, particularly since the rental activities may in fact be undertaken to minimize the expenses of holding the property for personal use, rather than to generate economic profit. Congress, therefore, applied the special rules of §280A to expenses attributable to the rental of dwelling units occupied by the taxpayer as a residence during the taxable

---

Tax Reform Act of 1976, 63 ABAJ 1302 (1977); Lang, When a House Is Not Entirely a Home: Deductions Under Internal Revenue Code §280A for Home Offices, Vacation Homes, etc., 1981 Utah L. Rev. 275; Rose, Home Office Deductions Under the Tax Reform Act of 1976, 63 ABAJ 559 (1977).

Regulations under §280A were proposed in 1980 and the proposal was amended in 1983, but no regulations have been adopted.

[2] Rev. Rul. 62-180, 1962-2 CB 52.

[3] Anderson v. CIR, 33 TCM (CCH) 234 (1974), aff'd per curiam, 527 F2d 198 (9th Cir. 1975) (appropriate and helpful standard applicable to investor). For a review of the cases, see Lucke v. CIR, 39 TCM (CCH) 478 (1979); see also infra note 31 (allocation of home office expenses).

year.[4] Although triggered by abuses in the rental of vacation homes, these rules also apply to all types of dwelling units, with a minor exception for certain rentals of the taxpayer's principal residence.

The structure of §280A is comparatively simple:

1. The general rule of §280A(a) flatly disallows all otherwise allowable deductions claimed by individuals and S corporations with respect to the use of a dwelling unit that is used during the taxable year by the taxpayer (or, in the case of an S corporation, any of its shareholders) as a residence, except as allowed by §280A itself, thus staking out a monopoly of the rules for this area.

2. Use of the property by the taxpayer as a residence is defined by §280A(d) to mean use of the unit for personal purposes for more than 14 days or more than 10 percent of the days for which it is rented at a fair rental, whichever is greater.[5]

3. Section 280A(b) exempts from the general disallowance rule of §280A(a) all deductions that are allowable without regard to business or income-producing activities, such as home mortgage interest, taxes, and casualty losses.[6]

4. Section 280A(c) exempts certain expenses for dwelling units used for specified business purposes, for rental, or to provide day care services, subject to the gross income limit of §280A(c)(5).[7]

5. The exemption of deductions attributable to rental use is qualified by §280A(e), which limits the deduction of rental expenses by a formula that takes into account the amount of personal use to which the unit is put during the taxable year.[8]

¶22.6.2 Definitions of "Dwelling Unit" and "Use as a Residence"

Absent an exception, the disallowance rule of §280A(a) applies to expenses of a "dwelling unit" if the unit is used "as a residence" during the taxable year. The meanings of the quoted words are discussed below.

---

[4] See infra ¶22.6.3.

[5] See infra ¶22.6.2.

[6] For analogies, see IRC §183(b)(1) (similar exemption for deductions attributable to hobbies and other activities not engaged in for profit), discussed supra ¶22.5.4; IRC §274(f) (same for deductions related to entertainment facilities, etc.); supra ¶21.2.3 and text accompanying note 61. The purpose of all of these provisions is to insure that a person who treads along the personal-business borderline does not fare worse than he would if the costs were clearly personal.

[7] See infra ¶22.6.3 (exempted uses), ¶22.6.4 (rental property), ¶22.6.5 (gross income limit).

[8] See infra ¶22.6.4.

1. *Dwelling unit.* The term "dwelling unit" is defined by §280A(f)(1)(A) to include not only houses but also apartments, condominiums, mobile homes, boats, and appurtenant structures and other property.[9] According to the proposed regulations, however, the term is limited to property that "provides basic living accommodations such as sleeping space, toilet, and cooking facilities."[10] The reference to "boats," for example, includes a large yacht but not a canoe. A dwelling unit used exclusively as a hotel, motel, inn, or similar establishment is exempted, but this exemption seems confined to taxpayers operating the property for use by the general public, so that hotel suites and similar accommodations leased by the taxpayer from the operator are subject to §280A.[11]

It is often necessary to determine whether particular property used for residential purposes consists of one dwelling unit or more than one. If a taxpayer lives in one portion of her house and rents out the remainder to an unrelated tenant at a fair rental, for example, §280A applies if the house constitutes one dwelling unit but not if the leased space is considered a separate unit. According to the proposed regulations, each portion of a structure that contains "basic living accommodations" is a separate dwelling unit.[12] If the space leased to the tenant in the example contains sleeping space, a toilet, and cooking facilities, it is a separate unit, and §280A is inapplicable.

2. *Use as residence.* Under §280A(d)(1), a dwelling unit is used as a residence if its use for personal purposes during the year exceeds the greater of 14 days or 10 percent of the number of days the unit is rented at a fair rental.

Use of the unit for any portion of a day counts as personal use. The proposed regulations, however, define the term "day" as "the 24-hour period for which a day's rental would be paid."[13] Assume a taxpayer arrives at her weekend retreat late Friday evening and leaves before daybreak on Monday morning. Probably, she is present for only three 24-hour rental periods (Friday–Saturday, Saturday–Sunday, and Sunday–Monday), even though she is present on four calendar days.

---

[9] IRC §280A(f)(1)(A). Compare §167(k)(3)(C) (defining "dwelling unit" for purposes of depreciation of rehabilitation expenditures for low-income housing). See Scott v. CIR, 84 TC 683 (1985) (separate structure in backyard used as home office was "appurtenant"); Haberkorn v. CIR, 75 TC 259 (1980) (mini-motorhome found to be dwelling unit).

[10] Prop. Reg. §1.280A-1(c)(1).

[11] IRC §280A(f)(1)(B). See Byers v. CIR, 82 TC 919 (1984) (exception for hotels did not apply to condominium that taxpayer used for 30 days each year and placed in a rental pool for the remainder of the year; exclusive use as hotel required).

[12] Prop. Reg. §1.280A-1(c)(1).

[13] Prop. Reg. §1.280A-1(f).

Personal use includes not only use by the taxpayer but also use by other persons who (1) have an interest in the property, (2) are members of the family (as defined by §267(c)(4)) of the taxpayer or another person having an interest in the property, (3) use the property under a reciprocal arrangement entitling the taxpayer to use another dwelling unit,[14] or (4) pay less than a fair rental.[15] Thus, a vacation home is caught by §280A(a) if the owners allow their child's college roommate to occupy it without charge for 2 months, even though it is rented to outsiders under an arm's length lease for the other 10 months of the taxable year. The statute says that where a dwelling unit is owned by an S corporation, use by a shareholder or a member of a shareholder's family counts as personal use, and the proposed regulations would follow the same approach for units owned by partnerships, trusts, and estates.[16]

A use, even by a member of the taxpayer's family, is not counted as a personal use, however, if the user pays a fair rental and uses the property as his personal residence.[17] If a parent rents a house to an adult child, for example, expenses relating to the house can be freed from §280A by complying with these limitations. A taxpayer who rents to a relative, however, should be cautious about accepting invitations to dinner because the proposed regulations warn: "If a taxpayer actually makes personal use of a unit on any such day, . . . that personal use is taken into account because it arises other than 'by reason of a rental arrangement.'"[18]

The proposed regulations state that a use for the purpose of repairs or maintenance is not considered a personal use. Specifically, a day on which the taxpayer or some other person is present in the unit is not counted as a day of personal use if, on that day, "the principal purpose of the use of the unit is to perform repair or maintenance work on the unit."[19] A day on which the taxpayer "engages in repair and maintenance of the unit on a substantially full-time basis" qualifies under this exemption, but in other cases its applicability depends on such factors as the amount of time devoted to repair and maintenance on that day, "the presence and activities of companions," and the number of repair and maintenance days claimed for

---

[14] For house swapping, see Rev. Rul. 80-55, 1980-1 CB 65.

[15] IRC §280A(d)(2). The requirement of a fair rental does not apply to use by an employee if the employee can exclude the use value from gross income under §119, relating to lodging furnished for the convenience of the employer. See supra ¶14.5 for §119.

[16] IRC §280A(f)(2); Prop. Reg. §1.280A-1(e)(5).

[17] IRC §280A(d)(3). This exception also applies to certain "shared equity financing" arrangements whereby two or more persons join in purchasing residential property under an agreement entitling each of them to use a portion of the property as his principal residence.

[18] Prop. Reg. §1.280A-1(e)(2).

[19] Prop. Reg. §1.280A-1(e)(6).

the year.[20]

¶22.6.3 Exempted Uses

Section 280A(c) exempts four categories of uses from the blanket disallowance of §280A(a): certain home office use, storage of inventory, rental, and day care services. Since §280A is only a limit on deductions otherwise allowable, however, the mere exemption of a particular use from §280A(a) does not insure that the expense is deductible; it must independently qualify under a substantive provision authorizing deductions, such as §162 (business expenses), §165 (losses), §167 (depreciation), or §212 (nonbusiness expenses of profit-oriented activities), and also satisfy any other applicable provision (e.g., §274, relating to substantiation of certain business expenses). The cost of adding a new room to the taxpayer's residence, for example, is a nondeductible capital expenditure even if the space is used exclusively for an exempted business use. Moreover, deductions allocable to exempted uses are subject to a gross-income limit described below.[21]

The four categories of exempted uses are:

1. *Certain home offices.* Section 280A(c)(1) exempts deductions allocable to portions of a dwelling unit used exclusively and regularly (1) as "the principal place of business for any trade or business of the taxpayer," (2) as a place of business to meet or deal with patients, clients, or customers in the normal course of the taxpayer's business, or (3) in the case of a separate structure that is not attached to the dwelling unit, in connection with the taxpayer's trade or business. These standards are clearly intended to disqualify residential offices, dens, studies, and other rooms used by investors to study stock market quotations and keep records, by business executives to read or prepare business reports, by teachers to prepare for class and grade examinations, and by most self-employed persons whose principal office is located elsewhere.

The exception for the taxpayer's principal place of business primarily accommodates self-employed persons working out of their homes and employees whose employers do not provide them with office space, but it also embraces taxpayers with two or more businesses, one of which is conducted from an office in the taxpayer's home. As originally enacted, this exception applied to "the taxpayer's principal place of business," language that was susceptible to the construction that it only reached the principal place of the taxpayer's sole or primary income-generating activity. The language quoted above was later substituted to make it clear that use as the principal place of

---

[20] Id.
[21] Infra ¶22.6.5.

a trade or business qualifies, even if this trade or business is a secondary activity of the taxpayer.[22] If a professor carries on a consulting business separately from her university job, for example, an office in her home can be the principal place of the consulting business even though an office on the university campus is the principal place of her business as professor.[23]

A frequent point of contention in the application of the principal place of business exception is whether a home office is a business' principal place of operations or only a secondary place.[24] Because the exception only applies to activities that constitute a trade or business, it creates one of the relatively rare situations where it makes a difference whether deductions are sought under §162(a), relating to trade or business expenses, or §212, relating to expenses of profit-oriented activities that do not rise to the level of a business.[25]

The exception for home offices in which the taxpayer meets patients, clients, and customers covers lawyers, physicians, salesmen, and other taxpayers with a secondary office at home, provided it is used regularly and the meetings occur in the normal course of business.[26] In theory, there is no justification for distinguishing these taxpayers from others with bona fide

---

[22] Pub. L. No. 97-119, §§113(c), (e), 95 Stat. 1642 (1982). See Green v. CIR, 78 TC 428 (1982), rev'd on other grounds, 707 F2d 404 (9th Cir. 1983) (amendment codified previous Tax Court interpretation). See generally Kulsrud, Recent Statutory and Judicial Developments Have Liberalized Home-Office Deductions, 56 J. Tax'n 344 (1982).

[23] See Prop. Reg. §1.280A-2(b)(2).

[24] See Meiers v. CIR, 782 F2d 75 (7th Cir. 1986) (laundromat manager's principal place of business was home office, not laundromat, because she "spent most of her time in the home office and performed what may be her most important functions as a manager there"); Weissman v. CIR, 751 F2d 512 (2d Cir. 1984) (college professor's home office was principal place of business because he spent 80 percent of his working time there and office space provided by college, which was shared with other professors, was not adequate; Tax Court wrong in adopting per se rule that principal business place of teacher or professor is at school or college); Drucker v. CIR, 715 F2d 67 (2d Cir. 1983) (principal place of business of members of Metropolitan Opera orchestra in home practice room, not at Met, because Met provided no place to practice); Jackson v. CIR, 76 TC 696 (1981) (real estate agent's principal place of business was office of licensed broker with whom she was associated, not home office); Baie v. CIR, 74 TC 105 (1980) (street vendor's principal place of business was his hot dog stand, not room in house used for bookkeeping or kitchen used to prepare food). See also Prop. Reg. §1.280A-2(b)(3).

[25] See Moller v. US, 721 F2d 810 (Fed. Cir. 1983) (exception inapplicable to investment activities); Curphey v. CIR, 73 TC 766 (1980) (same, but activities of dermatologist in managing six rental units from home office held to be a business).

[26] See Green v. CIR, 707 F2d 404 (9th Cir. 1983) (exception inapplicable to home office used to take telephone calls from customers; office "used" by customers only if they physically visit it); Prop. Reg. §1.280A-2(c) (same); Frankel v. CIR, 82 TC 318 (1984) (same). See also Jackson v. CIR, supra note 24 (real estate agent's sporadic meetings with clients not regular use).

secondary places of business at home, but the IRS can obviously separate genuine from fictitious claims with greater confidence if the taxpayer must establish that the office is used to meet with third persons.

Finally, the separate-structure exception is especially suited to artists and self-employed artisans with a secondary studio at home, but it also embraces other taxpayers using a separate structure exclusively and regularly in connection with a trade or business. Here again, enforcement is facilitated by the statutory standard.

The foregoing exceptions only apply if "a portion of the dwelling unit . . . is exclusively used on a regular basis" for the designated business purpose. The exclusive use requirement is not met, according to the proposed regulations, unless "there is no use of that portion of the unit at any time during the taxable year other than for business purposes."[27] Pity the poor child who comes into dad's home office looking for a small display of affection. The term "portion" refers to "a room or other separately identifiable space"; a permanent partition marking it off is not necessary.[28]

If the taxpayer is an employee, the foregoing standards are buttressed by a requirement that the exclusive use of the business area must be for the convenience of the employer. Expenses allocable to a separate structure used by an employee after working hours and on weekends as a matter of personal convenience do not qualify, for example, even if the space is used exclusively for business purposes. If the employee is expected or required to work at home when the employer's facilities are closed, the convenience-of-the-employer standard is presumably satisfied, but this is cold comfort in most cases because the employer's demands do not often bring the employee's home office within any of the exempted categories.

The natural tendency to refer to §280A(c)(1) as concerned with home offices, its principal target, should not obscure that it applies to any dwelling unit used by the taxpayer as a residence for the prescribed period. Thus, a taxpayer whose primary residence is in the suburbs, but who maintains an apartment in the city for the use of out-of-town employees and business entertainment, may lose his deductions for rental charges and maintenance expenses if he uses the space too often as a temporary shelter on missing the last train home after a late evening business conference or if he allows his children to use it when not needed for business purposes.

2. *Storage of inventory.* Section 280A(c)(2) exempts space within a dwelling if it is regularly used to store inventory for a business of selling products at retail or wholesale, but only if this is the sole fixed location of

---

[27] Prop. Reg. §1.280A-2(g)(1). But see Frankel v. CIR, 82 TC 318 (1984) (deduction allowed where home office used exclusively for business, but partially for a business purpose that fell within none of the exceptions).
[28] Id.

the business. This exception frequently overlaps the exception of §280A(c)(1)(A), relating to dwelling units used exclusively and regularly as the taxpayer's principal place of business, but it also covers door-to-door salesmen, whose homes are used for the storage of merchandise but arguably are not the taxpayer's principal place of business.

3. *Rental property.* Expenses attributable to the rental of dwelling units are exempted by §280A(c)(3) from disallowance under §280A(a), but are subject to special rules discussed below.[29]

4. *Day care services.* Section 280A(c)(4)(A), enacted in 1977, exempts items allocable to the regular use of a dwelling unit in a business of providing day care for children and persons who are over 65 or are physically or mentally unable to care for themselves, but only if the business is licensed as required by §280A(c)(4)(B). Exclusive use of the area for day care services is not required. In the case of a mixed use, however, the expenses are deductible under §280A(c)(4)(C) only in the proportion that the hours of day care use bear to the number of hours that the space is available for all uses. As interpreted by the Senate Finance Committee, the statutory formula assumes availability of the premises around the clock (168 hours per week), so that only one fourth of the expenses attributable to space used 42 hours a week for day care services qualify (42/168) if the space is used for any other purpose.[30] This is a curious result, since the expenses would evidently be deductible in full if the space were not put to any other use,[31] subject to the gross income limit of §280A(c)(5).

5. *Traveling expenses.* Section 280A is inapplicable to a deduction under §162(a)(2) for lodging expenses incurred while away from home in pursuit of business.[32] This exception would apply, for example, to an apartment maintained in a city the taxpayer frequently visits on business.

6. *Limitation on rental to employer.* Section 280A(c)(6) denies most of the foregoing exemptions where an employee leases a portion of his home to his employer. The provision was enacted in 1986 to close a loophole exposed by the decision in *Feldman v. CIR.*[33] Feldman used a room in his home as an office, but his use of the room was not within any of the

---

[29] Infra ¶22.6.4.

[30] S. Rep. No. 66, 95th Cong., 1st Sess., reprinted in 1977-1 CB 469, 498. See Prop. Reg. §1.280A-2(i)(4).

[31] For a similar problem in allocating expenses under pre-1977 law, see Gino v. CIR, 538 F2d 833 (9th Cir.), cert. denied, 429 US 979 (1976) (home office expenses allocated on 24-hour basis, where space served mixed purposes); Browne v. CIR, 73 TC 723 (1980) (contra; allocation based on ratio of business use to sum of business and personal use).

[32] IRC §280A(f)(4). See generally Caplin & Lent, Deducting Expenses Pertaining to Out-of-Town Residences Used as Business Accommodations, 58 J. Tax'n 270 (1983).

[33] Feldman v. CIR, 791 F2d 781 (9th Cir. 1986).

exceptions described in 280A(c)(1). He leased the room to his employer for use by Feldman in the course of his employment, and claimed expenses allocable to the room under §280A(c)(3), which lifts the deduction bar for expenses attributable to the renting of personal use property to others. The court recognized that this scheme might frustrate congressional designs, but held the claimed deductions were squarely allowed by the statute as it existed before §280A(c)(6) was enacted.

Section 280A(c)(6) reverses the *Feldman* decision by providing that none of the exceptions of §280A(c)(1) or (3) apply to an employee who leases to an employer. The provision sometimes puts such an employee in a worse position than an employee who uses his residence in his work and receives additional compensation in recognition of this use. Assume an employee uses a portion of his residence exclusively in meeting customers in the ordinary course of business. If this use is for the convenience of the employer, expenses of the residence allocable to the portion so used are deductible under §280A(c)(1). If the employee leases this portion to the employer and the portion is put to the same business use, however, the deduction is lost; in this case, the rent received from the employer is gross income, and can only be offset by deductions for interest and taxes that would be allowable if the house's use were strictly personal.

¶22.6.4 Rental Property

Items attributable to the rental of dwelling units are exempted from the blanket disallowance of §280A(a) by §280A(c)(3). These deductions, however, are subject to special restrictions that do not apply to deductions attributable to other exempted uses of dwelling units. Moreover, while the other exemptions only apply to use in the taxpayer's business, rental activity is exempted whether it is profit-oriented or not, and this makes it necessary to correlate the rules of §280A with those of §183 for hobbies and other activities not engaged in for profit.[34] Unfortunately, the statutory coordination is faulty, to speak charitably.

In analyzing the impact of §280A on dwelling units rented out, the following four categories can be examined separately:

1. *Dwelling units not used by the taxpayer for personal purposes at any time during the taxable year.* These units are not affected by §280A. Ordinarily, the taxpayer can deduct all expenses under §162, relating to trade or business expenses, or §212, relating to property held for the production of income. In the absence of a profit objective, however, the deductions are

---

[34] For §183, see supra ¶22.5.

subject to §183. A vacation home that is rented to minimize the expense of having it available for personal use is an example where §183 would apply.

2. *Dwelling units used for personal purposes, but for less than the period prescribed by the 14-day, 10 percent test of §280A(d)(1).*[35] These units are not subject to the disallowance rule of §280A(a), but expenses attributable to the rental period must be determined under §280A(e). This provision allows all deductions that are allowable without regard to the rental activity (usually, home mortgage interest, real property taxes, and casualty losses), but other deductions (depreciation, utilities, repairs, and maintenance) must be allocated in the proportion that the number of rental days (counting only those for which a fair rental is charged) bears to the total number of days that the unit is used for all purposes.[36] For example, if a vacation home is used for 100 days during the year, including 95 days of rental and 5 days of personal use, the deductions cannot exceed (1) the expenses deductible without regard to the rental activity plus (2) 95 percent of the other expenses.

Since §280A(e) limits "the amount deductible under this chapter" without explicitly allowing any deductions, the taxpayer's right to deduct class (2) items up to the prescribed cap depends on satisfying the standards of such substantive provisions as §162 (business expenses), §167 (depreciation), §212 (property held for production of income), and, if the activity is not engaged in for profit, §183.

3. *Dwelling units used for personal purposes for the period prescribed by §280A(d).* These units are subject to the allocation principles of §280A(e), described in the preceding paragraphs, and the amount allocated to rental use is further restricted by the overall limit prescribed by §280A(c)(5), described below.[37]

4. *Dwelling unit rented for less than 15 days.* If a dwelling unit is used by the taxpayer for the period prescribed by §280A(d) but is rented for less than 15 days during the same taxable year, §280A(g) excludes the rent from gross income and disallows all deductions attributable to the rental use. The taxpayer's right to deduct amounts allowable without regard to the rental activity (home mortgage interest, real property taxes, and casualty losses) is unaffected. This provision is a de minimis rule for cases where rental activity is insignificant relative to the taxpayer's personal use of the property, as in the case of a residence occupied by the taxpayer for most of the

---

[35] For this test, see supra ¶22.6.1.

[36] A day on which the unit's principal use is to do repair or maintenance work is not counted as a day of use for this purpose whether the work is done by the taxpayer or another person. Prop. Reg. §1.280A-3(c)(1). For the determination of when a use is for repair or maintenance, see supra text accompanying note 20.

The proposed regulations provide special rules for applying this procedure to rental pools and time sharing arrangements. Prop. Reg. §§1.280A-3(e), (f).

[37] Infra ¶22.6.4.

taxable year but rented for a week or two. It also applies, however, to vacation property that is used by the taxpayer for two weeks and rented to others for two weeks, even if the property produces a handsome profit because it is located in an area enjoying a short high season.

¶22.6.5 Overall Limit on Deductions

Under §280A(c)(5), if personal use of a dwelling unit is sufficient to invoke the disallowance rule of §280A(a) but one of the exemptions described above applies, deductions attributable to the exempted use are allowed, but their amount is limited to the excess of (1) the gross income earned by this use over (2) other expenses allocable to the income. The gross income figure probably includes all gross income from the trade or business in which the dwelling unit is used.[38] The other expenses taken into account are (1) interest expense and property taxes allocable to the portion of the dwelling used for business and (2) expenses of the business other than those of the dwelling itself. Assume a taxpayer uses 20 percent of his home exclusively as his principal place of business. Gross income of the business is $8,000. Interest and taxes on the home are $10,000, and deductions for salaries, supplies, and other items not directly connected with the residence are $5,000. Costs of the residence (other than interest and taxes) are deductible only to the extent of $1,000, computed as shown in Example 22-2.

Example 22-2

Deduction Limitation of §280A(c)(5)

1. Gross income from business conducted in home		$8,000
2. Less sum of:		
a. Mortgage interest and real property taxes allocable to business use	$2,000	
b. Business expenses not arising from use of residence with residence	5,000	7,000
3. Maximum deduction for residence expenses other than interest and taxes		$1,000

Regulations have been proposed that would require that where the business use of the dwelling unit continues for only a portion of the year, mortgage interest and property taxes must be allocated between business and personal use on the basis of the periods of actual use for each purpose

---

[38] See infra note 46.

during the year. Assume a lakeside home is rented for 90 days, used for personal purposes for 30 days, and left vacant for the remainder of the year. The proposed regulations would allocate to the rental use 75 percent (90/120) of the mortgage interest and property taxes on the property.[39] In *Bolton v. CIR*, however, the Court of Appeals for the Ninth Circuit held that the allocation must be based on the ratio of the number of days of rental use to the number of days in the taxable year.[40] In the example, the court would allocate to the rental use 90/365 of the mortgage interest and property taxes, thus providing a larger deduction ceiling by allocating against the rental use less of the amounts that are deductible in any event. The court's solution effectively treats the interest and taxes allocable to times when the property is vacant as a cost of carrying the property for personal use. Although this is not unreasonable, it conflicts with the scheme for allocating the deductions that are allowed only to the extent allocable to rental, where the allocation is based on actual use (ignoring periods of vacancy).[41] The court effectively gives the taxpayer the best of both worlds; in determining the deduction ceiling, the period of vacancy is considered personal (thus increasing the ceiling), but in calculating the deductions allowable against the ceiling, the period of vacancy is effectively split between rental and personal (thus increasing the deductions allocated to rental).

Expenses disallowed by §280A(c)(5) are carried forward and are allowed in any subsequent year to the extent the cap for that year exceeds current residence-related expenses subject to the deduction ceiling.

The limitation, as just described, applies for years after 1986. For prior years, the limitation is the excess of the gross income derived from the exempted use, reduced by the deductions allocable to the exempted use that are allowable without regard to a business connection (generally, home mortgage interest, real property taxes, and casualty losses).[42] The Treasury proposed regulations under the pre-1987 statute defining gross income from the business use of the dwelling unit as the gross income from the activity, reduced by expenses not directly connected with the use of the dwelling unit.[43] The latter subtraction was essentially the same as the reduction required by the present statute. The Tax Court, however, refused to follow the proposed regulations on this point, and the IRS acquiesced.[44] Also, under the proposed regulations, a taxpayer whose business income was derived from both the use of the dwelling unit and other facilities was required to

---

[39] Prop. Reg. §1.280A-3(d)(4) Ex.

[40] Bolton v. CIR, 694 F2d 556 (9th Cir. 1982).

[41] See supra text accompanying note 36.

[42] For a similar limit on deductions attributable to hobbies and other activities not engaged in for profit, see §183(b), discussed supra ¶22.5.4.

[43] Prop. Reg. §1.280A-2(i)(2)(iii).

[44] Scott v. CIR, 84 TC 683 (1985) (acq.).

"allocate the gross income from the business to the different locations on a reasonable basis," taking into account the time that each facility was used and the capital invested in each.[45] It is not clear whether Congress intended that this allocation be required under present law.[46]

The overall limit of §280A(c)(5) can have a drastic effect on taxpayers who put their residences on the rental market without finding a tenant or who are forced to rent for less than their out-of-pocket expenses plus depreciation, if they occupy the residence during the same year for the period specified by §280A(d)(1). Recognizing the unfairness of restricting deductions to the rent actually received when a residence is converted in good faith to rental property, Congress in 1978 added §280A(d)(3), exempting the taxpayer's principal residence from the overall limit if the deductions are attributable to a "qualified rental period" (ordinarily 12 consecutive months), as defined by §280A(d)(3)(B).[47] To prevent abuse, the exemption does not apply to vacation or other secondary homes but only to the taxpayer's principal residence.[48]

¶22.7 EXPENSES RELATED TO TAX-EXEMPT INCOME

Section 265(a)(1) disallows two categories of deductions allocable to tax-exempt income: (1) amounts otherwise deductible that are allocable to exempt income other than interest and (2) amounts otherwise deductible under §212 allocable to tax-exempt interest.

1. *Exempt income other than interest.* An otherwise deductible amount is disallowed if allocable to exempt income other than interest. The disallowance applies not only to otherwise deductible trade or business expenses, but also to taxes otherwise deductible under §164 and expenses otherwise deductible under §212.

---

[45] Prop. Reg. §1.280A-2(i)(2)(ii).

[46] The statutory language construed by the proposed regulation, "the gross income derived from such use for the taxable year," is the same under the pre-1987 and post-1986 versions of the statute. Under present law, however, this gross income is reduced by the deductions, not attributable to the dwelling unit, that are "allocable to the trade or business in which such use occurs," presumably including deductions relating to business facilities other than the dwelling unit. It would be unreasonable to reduce the gross income figure by amounts allocable to the use of other facilities and then subtract deductions relating to the other facilities from the reduced gross income figure. The "gross income derived from such use" should therefore be construed to include all gross income from the trade or business in which the use occurs.

[47] The exemption is retroactive to taxable years ending after 1975, the original effective date of §280A.

[48] "Principal residence" has the meaning ascribed by §1034, discussed infra ¶44.5. For the term "family," see §267(c)(4).

Section 265(a)(1) has been applied in diverse circumstances. Because educational assistance allowances provided to veterans by the Veterans Administration are exempt from tax, a veteran receiving such an allowance cannot deduct his educational expenses even if they would otherwise be deductible under §162(a) as, for example, costs of maintaining or improving his skills in his present employment.[1] Educational expenses financed by exempt gifts and fellowships are also caught by the provision.[2] A federal employee who received a cost of living adjustment (COLA) that was exempt from federal tax, but was subject to a state income tax, lost his deduction for the state tax attributable to the COLA.[3] An Indian exempt from tax on his farming income was denied deductions for his farming expenses.[4] Expenses attributable to foreign source income not taxed by the United States are usually nondeductible under §265(a)(1).[5] Premiums paid to purchase life

---

[1] Rev. Rul. 83-3, 1983-1 CB 72, modified by Rev. Rul. 87-32, 1987-1 CB 255 (lawyer taking advanced law courses to meet employer's requirements allowed to deduct costs of courses only to extent they exceeded exempt veterans allowances). The ruling has a tortured history. The IRS initially ruled that the receipt of an exempt veterans allowance did not affect a taxpayer's education-expense deduction. Rev. Rul. 62-213, 1962-2 CB 59. A subsequent ruling, however, held that a reimbursed educational expense could not be deducted if the reimbursement was tax exempt, and that the 1962 ruling only applied where the allowance was not in the form of a reimbursement. Rev. Rul. 80-173, 1980-2 CB 60. Section 265(a)(1) was not cited in either of these rulings. The position taken in the latter ruling was sustained in a Tax Court case affirmed on appeal; the appellate court followed the ruling in holding a reimbursed cost cannot be a deductible expense, but the Tax Court held more broadly that §265(a)(1) denied any deduction for expenses allocable to a tax-exempt veterans allowance. Manocchio v. CIR, 710 F2d 1400 (9th Cir. 1983), aff'g 78 TC 989 (1982). In response, the IRS issued the 1983 ruling cited above, revoking the 1962 ruling and adopting the Tax Court's approach. The 1983 ruling is only applied prospectively (generally for the 1983–1984 academic year and thereafter), but the 1980 ruling is not so limited. See Baker v. US, 748 F2d 1465 (11th Cir. 1984) (IRS abused its discretion in applying 1980 ruling retroactively); Becker v. CIR, 85 TC 291 (1985) (contra). See also Banks v. CIR, 17 TC 1386, 1393 (1952) (under 1939 Code provision, tuition and book expenses paid by Veterans Adminstration).

[2] Christian v. US, 201 F. Supp. 155 (ED La. 1962).

[3] Lapin v. US, 655 F. Supp. 1344 (D. Haw. 1987); Lapin v. US, 617 F. Supp. 167 (DDC 1985). See Curtis v. CIR, 3 TC 648 (1944) (acq.) (deduction denied for state income taxes and expenses of earning fees and salaries not taxed by virtue of Public Salary Tax Act of 1939); Rev. Rul. 61-86, 1961-1 CB 41 (no deduction for state income taxes allocable to exempt income other than interest).

[4] Rickard v. CIR, 88 TC 188 (1987) (because depreciation deduction denied, investment credit on farm equipment also unavailable).

[5] Rinehart v. US, 429 F2d 1286 (10th Cir. 1970) (Puerto Rican income taxes); Heffelfinger v. CIR, 5 TC 985 (1945) (Canadian taxes); Rev. Rul. 74-140, 1974-1 CB 50 (state income tax allocable to cost-of-living allowance exempt under §912); Rev. Rul. 62-9, 1962-1 CB 35 (§212(3) legal fees to contest foreign tax on income exempt under tax convention).

insurance policies have also been disallowed.[6]

Legal costs sometimes fall into the net of §265(a)(1). On finding that a recovery under a civil rights statute for a wrong occurring in a taxpayer's employment was an exempt recovery for personal injury, the Tax Court held costs incurred in obtaining the award were nondeductible under §265(a)(1).[7] Also, legal fees incurred in establishing a taxpayer's right to social security disability benefits are nondeductible to the extent allocable to the portion of the benefit not included in gross income under §86.[8]

Section 265(a)(6), added in 1986, exempts the deductions for home mortgage interest and real property taxes from disallowance under §265(a) whenever the disallowance rule would otherwise apply because of the receipt of an exempt military housing or parsonage allowance. The IRS issued a ruling in 1983 applying §265(a)(1) to a minister receiving a parsonage allowance exempt under §107.[9] The minister owned his own house and used the allowance (together with some of his other funds) to make a variety of payments relating to the house, including mortgage payments, real property taxes, and utilities. The ruling held that §265(a)(1) barred him from deduct-

---

Foreign compensation exempt from tax under §911 is embraced by §265(a)(1) as well as by the more specific disallowance of §911(d)(6). See Wells v. CIR, 26 TCM (CCH) 719 n.9 (1967) (deduction of German taxes denied under pre-1978 version of §911 without determining applicability of §265(a)(1)); see also Christensen v. CIR, 71 TC 328 n.4 (1978), aff'd per curiam, 601 F2d 75 (2d Cir. 1979) (deduction of expenses in connection with Puerto Rican tax audit denied under §933 without determining applicability of §265(a)(1)), citing prior cases; Roque v. CIR, 65 TC 920 (1976) (similar case involving moving expenses).

[6] Jones v. CIR, 25 TC 4 (1955), aff'd per curiam, 231 F2d 655 (3d Cir. 1956). See National Engraving Co. v. CIR, 3 TC 178 (1944) (same as to legal fees for litigation re tax-exempt insurance proceeds). For broader restrictions on deductions attributable to life insurance policies, see §264, disallowing deductions for certain premiums and interest, discussed supra ¶12.5.1.

[7] Bent v. CIR, 87 TC 236 (1986). See Church v. CIR, 80 TC 1104 (1983) (same for legal and other costs of obtaining exempt libel recovery). In an earlier case involving a recovery for personal injury arising out of an auto accident, the court intimated that related expenses might be disallowed under §265(a)(1), but it was not necessary to decide the issue because the expenses, being of a personal character, were not otherwise deductible. Murphy v. CIR, 48 TC 569 (1967).

[8] Rev. Rul. 87-102, 1987-41 IRB 5. For §86, see supra ¶16.5.

[9] Rev. Rul. 83-3, 1983-1 CB 72, modified by Rev. Rul. 87-32, 1987-1 CB 255. See supra ¶14.6 for §107. Congress made §265(a)(6) retroactively applicable to all prior years. Pub. L. No. 99-514, §144, 100 Stat. 2085 (1986). Any minister who followed the ruling thus received manna from the tax collector. For the IRS' earlier views on the matter, see Rev. Rul. 62-212, 1962-2 CB 41 (deduction of interest and taxes paid by minister in connection with parsonage not affected by §107 exclusion; no explanation or citation of §265(a)(1)). See also Deason v. CIR, 41 TC 465 (1964) (acq.) (auto expense incurred in earning parson's tax-free rental allowance disallowed).

ing his mortgage interest and property taxes, except to the extent they exceeded the parsonage allowance.

Whether income is "wholly exempt" from income taxes within the meaning of §265(a)(1) depends on its inherent character, not on whether it is subject to tax in a particular taxable year. Thus, otherwise qualified deductions attributable to income that is realized but not recognized by virtue of a nonrecognition provision are not disallowed by §265(a)(1), since the taxation of such income is ordinarily postponed rather than permanently exempted from tax.[10] It has also been held that legal expenses incurred in recovering compensation for a war loss are not disallowed by §265(a)(1) because such recoveries are includable in income if previously deducted with tax benefit; even though the taxpayer was entitled to exclude his recovery because the prior deductions were of no tax benefit, the court concluded that his recovery belonged in a "class of income" that is not "wholly exempt."[11]

Deductions allocable to both exempt and taxable income must be apportioned between the two categories, since only the former portion is subject to disallowance under §265(a)(1).[12]

2. *Section 212 deductions allocable to tax-exempt interest.* Deductions allocable to tax-exempt interest are disallowed by §265(a)(1) only if they arise under §212. Thus, amortization deductible under §167(a)(2) is not adversely affected by §265(a)(1).[13] Neither are state income taxes on interest exempt from federal but not state taxes because the deduction for these

---

[10] Cotton States Fertilizer Co. v. CIR, 28 TC 1169 (1957) (acq.) (involuntary conversion under statutory predecessor of §1033). See also Rev. Rul. 63-233, 1963-2 CB 113 (IRS follows cases holding that gain realized by corporation on sale of property pursuant to plan of complete liquidation but not recognized by virtue of pre-1987 versions of §§332 and 337 is not wholly exempt from income taxes for purposes of §265(a)(1); therefore, state income taxes paid on the gain are deductible).

For the rationale of the cases acquiesced in by Rev. Rul. 63-233, involving amounts that are permanently shielded from tax at corporate level, see CIR v. McDonald, 320 F2d 109 (5th Cir. 1963); CIR v. Universal Leaf Tobacco Co., 318 F2d 658 (4th Cir. 1963).

[11] Petschek v. US, 335 F2d 734 (2d Cir. 1964). See also California & Hawaiian Sugar Ref. Corp. v. US, 311 F2d 235 (Ct. Cl. 1962) (§265(a)(1) inapplicable to expenses of recovering invalidly imposed excise taxes paid when taxpayer was exempt organization).

[12] Reg. §1.265-1(c). See Fabens v. CIR, 519 F2d 1310 (1st Cir. 1975) (allocation of trust termination commissions in proportion to ratio of exempt income to total income during life of trust rejected since it did not reflect unrealized appreciation in trust assets; similar allocation valid as to annual commissions); Whittemore v. US, 383 F2d 824 (8th Cir. 1967) (similar result; extensive discussion); Rev. Rul. 77-466, 1977-2 CB 83.

[13] Manufacturers Hanover Trust Co. v. CIR, 431 F2d 664 (2d Cir. 1970); Early v. CIR, 52 TC 560 (1969), rev'd on other grounds, 445 F2d 166 (5th Cir.), cert. denied, 404 US 855 (1971). See also Rev. Rul. 61-86, 1962-1 CB 35 (state income

taxes is allowed under §164.[14] The principal expenses disallowed by this part of §265(a)(1) are charges for safe-deposit boxes, investment advice, and custodial services incurred by investors in state and local bonds.[15] Interest on debt incurred or continued to purchase or carry exempt obligations is also nondeductible by virtue of §265(a)(2), discussed elsewhere in this work.[16]

¶22.8 TAX SHELTER EXPENDITURES

In a pair of rulings involving expenditures of funds borrowed on a nonrecourse basis by participants in tax shelters, the IRS has ruled that the purported borrower made the expenditures on behalf of a party who guaranteed payment of the loan.[1] On this theory, the expenditure is an investment by the nominal payor, rather than a deductible business expense. Wholly novel so far as business expenses are concerned, the rationale of the rulings is analogous to a line of cases holding that funds borrowed on a nonrecourse basis to make capital outlays cannot be included in the basis of the property if repayment by the purported borrower is only a remote possibility.[2]

¶22.9 TAXABLE SOCIAL CLUBS AND OTHER MEMBERSHIP ORGANIZATIONS

Section 277 provides that deductions otherwise allowed to nonexempt social clubs and other membership organizations in furnishing services, insurance, goods, or other items to their members shall be allowed only to the extent of income derived during the same taxable year from transactions with members. The function of this restriction, which applies only if the organization is operated primarily to furnish goods or services to its mem-

---

taxes allocable to tax-exempt interest deductible under §164; state income taxes allocable to other exempt income not deductible).

[14] States commonly tax interest on bonds issued by other states and their agencies and political subdivisions, even though the interest is exempt from federal tax under §103.

[15] See, e.g., Mallinckrodt v. CIR, 2 TC 1128 (1943) (acq.), aff'd on other issues, 146 F2d 1 (8th Cir.), cert. denied, 324 US 871 (1945) (fees for investment advice, custodian and collection services, financial secretary, etc., disallowed to extent allocable to exempt income, including interest).

[16] See infra ¶31.2.1.

[1] Rev. Rul. 78-30, 1978-1 CB 133 (expenses incurred by an investor to dredge real estate developer's property, financed partly with nonrecourse debt guaranteed by developer); Rev. Rul. 77-125, 1977-1 CB 130 (film production).

[2] See infra ¶41.2.2.

bers,[1] is to prevent income from investments and transactions with outsiders from being offset by losses incurred in serving members for less than cost.[2] In this respect, therefore, §277 resembles §183, allowing deductions attributable to hobbies and other activities not engaged in for profit to be deducted only from income from the same activities.[3] Deductions disallowed by §277 can be carried forward indefinitely and applied against income from membership activities until exhausted, but they do not create net operating losses.[4]

The organization's membership income includes income from institutes and trade shows conducted primarily for the education of members and interest paid by members for the privilege of paying their dues in installments.[5]

Section 277 does not apply to tax-exempt social clubs or other membership organizations, certain financial institutions, stock or commodities exchanges, or membership organizations that made an election under §456(c) (relating to prepaid dues) before October 9, 1969.[6]

---

[1] See Armour-Dial Men's Club, Inc. v. CIR, 77 TC 1 (1981), aff'd, 708 F2d 1287 (7th Cir. 1983) (employees' club offering parties, tournaments, and outings to members at reduced or no cost was operated primarily for their benefit, not to benefit members' employer by promoting better employee relationships; §277 applicable).

[2] See generally S. Rep. No. 552, 91st Cong., 1st Sess., reprinted in 1969-3 CB 423, 471; Associated Master Barbers & Beauticians of Am., Inc. v. CIR, 69 TC 53, 70–74 (1977). For prior law, see Anaheim Union Water Co. v. CIR, 321 F2d 253 (9th Cir. 1963) (deductions applicable against outside income) and cases therein cited; see also supra ¶6.2 (re cost companies).

[3] For IRC §183, see supra ¶22.5.

[4] Associated Master Barbers & Beauticians of Am., Inc. v. CIR, supra note 2.

[5] See Prop. Reg. §1.277-1(d)(2). On whether amounts paid for stock by members with limited privileges generate income, see Oakland Hills Country Club v. CIR, 74 TC 35 (1980).

[6] IRC §277(b). For IRC §456(c), see infra ¶105.3.4; for tax-exempt social clubs, trade associations, and other membership organizations, see infra Ch. 102.

CHAPTER

23

Depreciation and Amortization

¶23.1 DEPRECIATION AND AMORTIZATION — INTRODUCTORY

¶23.1.1 Generally

In language that has hardly changed since the Revenue Act of 1913, §167(a) authorizes taxpayers to deduct "a reasonable allowance for the exhaustion, wear and tear (including a reasonable allowance for obsolescence) of property used in the trade or business or held for the production of income."[1] The constancy of this language, however, masks a sea of change over the years. The depreciation allowance is unique in the sense that while its importance to businesses (particularly manufacturing businesses) is obvious, the means by which it should be determined is not at all obvious. The lack of consensus on the treatment of such an important item invites repeated pleas for change, and Congress has responded often to these pleas; seldom is a major tax bill enacted without effecting some change in depreciation deductions.

The history of the tax rules on depreciation is too complex to recall fully here.[2] A brief summary of the developments since 1954 is appropriate, however, because most of the rules that have existed under the 1954 Code continue to apply to some property presently in use.

Originally, depreciation was determined by (1) ascertaining the period of time depreciable property was expected to be used in the taxpayer's business or income-producing activities (the useful life), (2) estimating what the property would be worth at the end of that period (the salvage value), and (3) allocating the excess of original cost over salvage value among the taxable years in the period of expected use.

In the beginning, the third of these steps was very simple; the only permitted method of allocation was the straight line method under which the excess of cost over salvage was spread in equal amounts over the years of the property's useful life. The Treasury adopted regulations in 1946 permitting certain accelerated methods, however, and Congress ratified this

---

[1] See Revenue Act of 1913, ch. 16, §IIB, 38 Stat. 167; see also Revenue Act of 1909, ch. 6, §38, 36 Stat. 113 (1909 corporate income tax) ("reasonable allowance for depreciation").

Until 1942, only trade or business property qualified for the depreciation deduction; for the enactment in 1942 of what is now §167(a)(2) (property held for the production of income), see infra ¶23.2.1 note 8.

[2] For a historical review of tax depreciation, see Lischer, Depreciation Policy: Whither Thou Goest, 32 Sw. LJ 545 (1978). For policy analysis of depreciation, see Auerbach, The New Economics of Accelerated Depreciation, 23 BCL Rev. 1327 (1982); McMahon, Reforming Cost Recovery Allowances for Debt Financed Depreciable Property, 29 St. Louis ULJ 1029 (1985); Steines, Income Tax Allowances for Cost Recovery, 40 Tax L. Rev. 483 (1985).

development in 1954 by statutorily authorizing several such methods, including the 200 percent declining method for new tangible property. Although there are substantial differences in detail, the common feature of all accelerated methods is that they provide allowances that are relatively large when the property is first placed in service and steadily decline in succeeding periods.[3]

The first two elements of the depreciation equation, useful life and salvage value, were based on estimates, and therefore were frequent points of contention between taxpayers and the IRS.[4] The IRS provided guideline lives for hundreds of categories of tangible personal property. A taxpayer was free to show, however, that the useful life of depreciable property in its business was shorter than the guideline life for the property, and the guidelines thus did not end the litigation over this issue. Salvage value was never the subject of IRS guidelines, but was less frequently litigated because it generally involves fewer dollars of tax liability and because in 1962 Congress enacted a provision allowing salvage to be reduced by 10 percent of original cost, expecting that this rule would often reduce salvage to zero and allow it to be ignored.

In 1972, the Treasury invented an ingenious solution to the useful life problem, an elective set of rules called the asset depreciation range (ADR) system. This system is also based on guideline lives, but offers several incentives for taxpayers to accept the guidelines. First, a taxpayer using the ADR system may elect any useful life within the range of 80 percent to 120 percent of the guideline life for the property. For the typical taxpayer that wants its depreciation deductions as quickly as possible, this means a 20 percent reduction of the guideline lives. Also, ADR allows salvage to be ignored in a greater range of cases. Finally, to reduce another point of frequent contention,[5] a taxpayer electing ADR may treat as repair costs an arbitrarily determined amount of its annual expenditures with respect to the property.

In 1981, Congress superseded ADR with comprehensive depreciation rules that depart so radically from their antecedents that a new name—accelerated cost recovery system (ACRS)—was thought necessary. The concept of useful life as an estimate of the period the property will be used in the taxpayer's business disappears under ACRS. In its place are statutorily prescribed recovery periods. The ACRS recovery periods are not meant to approximate actual useful life. Although they are related to useful life in the sense that longer-lived property generally has longer recovery periods than shorter-lived property, the recovery period for most depreciable property is

---

[3] See infra ¶23.6.
[4] See infra ¶23.4.
[5] See supra ¶20.4.8.

shorter than the property's economic life. The concept of salvage value is wholly alien to ACRS; salvage is ignored in all cases. Under the 1981 rules, further, depreciation is not computed by the use of depreciation methods, but by looking up the appropriate amount in a table given in the statutes or regulations. The tables were based upon familiar accelerated methods, but did not follow them strictly. The short recovery periods, the rule on salvage, and the tables were all meant to accelerate depreciation allowances as an incentive to increased investment in depreciable property.

The 1981 rules were buffeted by frequent amendments. In 1986, they were replaced with another comprehensive set of rules, also called ACRS. The principal difference between the 1981 and 1986 rules is that the latter generally provide longer recovery periods. Numerous more technical differences exist. The 1986 rules, for example, return to the technique of using depreciation methods rather than tables in determining the allowance. The substitution of prescribed recovery periods for actual useful life, however, persists in the 1986 rules, as does the rule that salvage is always ignored.

Old depreciation rules, more obviously than old soldiers, never die but merely fade away. The 1986 version of ACRS applies to property placed in service after 1986. The 1981 version applies to property placed in service during the period 1981 through 1986; this version must still be used in computing post-1986 deductions with respect to property acquired during the 1981–1986 period. The ADR system could be elected for any year during the period 1971 through 1980; the election for any year applies in that and all subsequent years, but only for the purpose of determining depreciation on property placed in service during the year of the election. The pre-ACRS rules apart from ADR apply to property placed in service for any year before 1981 in which ADR was not elected. Four systems can therefore apply in determining a taxpayer's depreciation deduction for any taxable year after 1986.

Since §167(a) is concerned not only with physical wear and tear but also with exhaustion and obsolescence, the allowance embraces intangible property with a limited useful life (e.g., patents, copyrights, contract rights, and franchises) as well as tangible property. The term "depreciation" is often reserved for tangible assets, with the term "amortization" being applied to the write-off of intangibles.[6] As employed by §167, however, "depreciation" ordinarily embraces both tangibles and intangibles, while "amorti-

---

[6] See, e.g., Accountants' Handbook 17-1 (Wixon, Kell & Bedford, eds.; Ronald Press, 5th ed. 1970) ("Amortization usually is related to bond premiums, leaseholds, patents, and other investments and intangibles"); compare Reg. §1.167(a)-3 ("depreciation" of intangibles).

Some statutory provisions refer solely to property that is depreciable under §167 (e.g., §§1221(2) and 1231(b)(1)), while others refer to both depreciation and amortization (e.g., §48(a)(1) ("property with respect to which depreciation (or amor-

zation" is customarily used in statutory provisions that either authorize write-offs for particular categories of property that are faster than the deductions allowed by §167 or permit the write-off of expenditures that do not qualify for any deductions under §167.[7] To avoid confusion, therefore, "depreciation" is used here to refer to deductions under §167 and "amortization" is employed as a generic label for allowances under provisions using that term, without regard in either case to whether the asset is tangible or intangible.

¶23.1.2 Function of Depreciation

In *United States v. Ludey,* decided in 1927, the Supreme Court gave the following much-quoted explanation for the depreciation deduction:

> The depreciation charge permitted as a deduction from the gross income in determining the taxable income of a business for any year represents the reduction, during the year, of the capital assets through wear and tear of the plant used. The amount of the allowance for depreciation is the sum which should be set aside for the taxable year, in order that, at the end of the useful life of the plant in the business, the aggregate of the sums set aside will (with the salvage value) suffice to provide an amount equal to the original cost. The theory underlying this allowance for depreciation is that by using up the plant, a gradual sale is made of it. The depreciation charged is the measure of the cost of the part that has been sold. When the plant is disposed of after years of use, the thing then sold is not the whole thing originally acquired. The amount of the depreciation must be deducted from the original cost of the whole in order to determine the cost of that disposed of in the final sale of properties.[8]

---

tization in lieu of depreciation) is allowable") and §1016(a)(2) (adjustment for "exhaustion, wear and tear, obsolescence, amortization, and depletion")).

[7] See, e.g., IRC §169 (amortization of pollution-control facilities over 60-month period), §248 (amortization of corporate organizational expenditures), discussed infra ¶¶26.6.3, 90.2.4. But see IRC §167(k) ("depreciation" used to describe five-year write-off of expenditures to rehabilitate certain low-income housing), discussed infra ¶26.6.5.

[8] US v. Ludey, 274 US 295, 300–01 (1927). In speaking of "capital assets," the Court is using the term not in its technical tax sense (for which see ¶51.1), but rather as a synonym for business plant and equipment. Other frequently quoted judicial explanations of the deduction:

> The end and purpose of [depreciation] is to approximate and reflect the financial consequences to the taxpayer of the subtle effects of time and use on the value of his capital assets. For this purpose it is sound accounting practice annually to accrue as to each classification of depreciable property an amount which at the time it is retired will with its salvage value replace the original

A definition of depreciation promulgated by the American Institute of Certified Public Accountants (AICPA) is very similar:

> Depreciation accounting is a system of accounting which aims to distribute the cost or other basic value of tangible capital assets, less salvage (if any), over the estimated useful life of the unit (which may be a group of assets) in a systematic and rational manner. It is a process of allocation, not of valuation. Depreciation for the year is the portion of the total charge under such a system that is allocated to the year.[9]

Section 167 permits the taxpayer to recover tax-free the cost (or other basis) of property that is exhausted in the process of generating business income. Thus, depreciation serves essentially the same function as the deduction for such business expenses as wages, rent, interest, and property taxes except that the allowance is not deducted in a single year but is spread over the asset's useful life. Depreciation is similar in this respect to depletion, which reflects the gradual exhaustion of mineral deposits as they are extracted and sold, and to the cost of goods sold, which is deducted by merchants and manufacturers as they dispose of their merchandise.

Although the Supreme Court's reference in *Ludey* to "the reduction, during the year, of the capital assets through wear and tear" might be taken to imply that a deduction is allowed each year for the asset's actual decline in value, the AICPA definition of depreciation as "a process of allocation, not of valuation" is a more accurate description of depreciation practices. Under the pre-ACRS rules, valuation plays a threshold role when anticipated salvage value is taken into account; the amount to be depreciated over the asset's useful life is restricted to the excess of the property's cost basis over salvage value, and the anticipated decline in value over the period of expected use is estimated when the property is placed in service. Once

---

investment therein. Or as a layman might put it, the machine in its life time must pay for itself before it can be said to pay anything to its owner.

Detroit Edison Co. v. CIR, 319 US 98, 101 (1943). [I]t is the primary purpose of depreciation accounting to further the integrity of periodic income statements by making a meaningful allocation of the cost entailed in the use (excluding maintenance expense) of the asset to the periods to which it contributes.

Massey Motors, Inc. v. US, 364 US 92, 104 (1960).

> The purpose of the statute allowing deductions for depreciation is to permit the taxpayer currently to receive income tax-free to the extent that wear and tear and time decrease the value of his investment, or what is treated as his investment, in the property.

Reisinger v. CIR, 144 F2d 475, 477–78 (2d Cir. 1944).

[9] See AICPA, Accounting Terminology Bull. No. 1 (1953), which discusses depreciation at some length and sets out numerous definitions of the term, along with its own formulation.

determined, however, this amount is allocated to the years of service by a method that does not purport to measure the actual decline in the asset's value from year to year.

Fluctuations in the cost of replacing the taxpayer's property are also disregarded. Laymen often think of accumulated depreciation as a reserve with which new machines can be purchased to replace worn-out equipment. This is an illusion because depreciation is computed with reference to an asset's cost (or other basis), and in a dynamic economy this almost never corresponds to the cost of replacing the asset, which reflects changes in the purchasing power of the dollar, technological improvements, and other factors. Moreover, since the deduction is a bookkeeping entry rather than a bank deposit, it does not build up a replacement fund.

¶23.1.3 Importance of Timing

The depreciation allowance is a corollary of the basic principle forbidding taxpayers to deduct the cost of acquiring, rehabilitating, or improving a long-lived asset.[10] Once capitalized, such an outlay can be recovered only by deductions over the asset's useful life or ACRS recovery period, as a loss on its abandonment, or as an offset against the proceeds in computing gain or loss on a sale or other disposition. Computed in the aggregate over the entire life of an enterprise, taxable income would be the same whether capital investments were deducted when made, depreciated, or deducted when the asset is disposed of. These alternatives also produce the same result in a particular year if the enterprise reaches a level of complete equilibrium during a period of price stability by purchasing and retiring the same number of assets, with the same per-unit cost, every year.

These lifetime and steady-state results are illustrated by Example 23-1, in which it is assumed that a taxpayer (1) engages in business for a period of six years, (2) buys a machine costing $3,000 with a useful life of three years at the beginning of each of the first four years, and (3) uses each machine for its entire life and then abandons it. Example 23-1 demonstrates the results under three alternatives: (1) deduct each outlay when made, (2) depreciate by the straight line method of deducting the cost of each machine in equal annual installments over its useful life, or (3) deduct the entire cost of each machine when it is abandoned. (These alternatives are given to illustrate the effects of two extremes and a simple middle ground; the first and third are not usually permitted, and the second is not the standard method under the ACRS rules.) The aggregate amount to be deducted over the six-year period is the same under all of the alternatives—$12,000, the cost of four machines costing $3,000 each. Moreover, in the third and fourth years of

---

[10] See supra ¶20.4.

operation, when the enterprise has reached a steady state, the deductions are the same, regardless of the charge-off method.

Example 23-1

Alternative Methods of Accounting for
Exhaustion of Business Asset

	Number of Machines			Charge Off Method*		
Year	Purchased on Jan. 1	In Use During Year	Retired on Dec. 31	Expensed	Straight Line Depreciation	Retirement
1	1	1	0	$3,000	$1,000	$-0-
2	1	2	0	3,000	2,000	-0-
3	1	3	1	3,000	3,000	3,000
4	1	3	1	3,000	3,000	3,000
5	0	2	1	-0-	2,000	3,000
6	0	1	1	-0-	1,000	3,000
Totals				$12,000	$12,000	$12,000

*Explanation of charge-off method:
Expensed: $3,000 deducted on acquisition of each machine.
Straight line depreciation: $3,000 × (1/3) = $1,000 per year for each machine in use.
Retirement: $3,000 deducted on retirement of each machine.

Example 23-1 also illustrates the differential impact of the three charge-off methods during the first, second, fifth, and sixth years of operation, when the enterprise is not in a steady state. The disparities, which are especially pronounced in the first and sixth years of operation, would be accentuated if the company grew and declined in a steeper fashion or if the cost of its machines fluctuated. In a dynamic economy, when the steady-state conditions postulated in the example rarely prevail, taxpayers almost always benefit from charging off capital outlays as rapidly as possible since the resulting reduction in tax liabilities makes cash available for investment in the business or distribution to investors. More depreciation now means less depreciation in the future. The offsetting tax liabilities, however, may be far in the future, and in the meantime the taxpayer can enjoy the equivalent of an interest-free loan. This opportunity to borrow from the future by accelerating current depreciation deductions is especially attractive for businesses in a period of expansion. Moreover, even steady-state taxpayers are likely to remember the happy years when accelerated depreciation was helpful, and on surveying the future, they will frequently be sufficiently optimistic about another golden age of expansion to prefer accelerated depreciation over more conservative practices.

The situation most frequently militating against accelerating depreciation deductions is an oversupply of deductions attributable to current losses or the carryforward of losses from prior years. Even in these circumstances, however, a taxpayer might depreciate as rapidly as possible because net operating losses can be carried forward for 15 years, and few taxpayers are so pessimistic as to devote much thought to the possibility of more than 15 years of unprofitability.

ACRS, in all of its guises since first adopted in 1981, accommodates taxpayers' usual preference for accelerated depreciation in several ways. ACRS recovery periods are generally shorter than the economic lives of the property. Salvage value is always ignored. Presently, the 200 percent declining balance method is available for most tangible personal property. Under this method, the deduction for the year depreciable property is placed in service is twice what it would be under the straight line method, but declines steadily in all subsequent years of the property's recovery period. Straight line depreciation is required for real property and some personal property, and may be elected for any property. Even when the straight line method is used, however, depreciation is often accelerated by shortened recovery periods and the rule allowing salvage to be ignored.

¶23.1.4 Economic Depreciation

An economist reading the AICPA definition of depreciation quoted above[11] would probably be struck by the sentence, "It is a process of allocation, not of valuation." The economist might respond, "True enough, it is a process of allocation, but how is the allocation to be made if not by value?" Under the most widely accepted definition, income is defined as the sum of the value of what the taxpayer consumes during the year and the change in the value of his wealth.[12] The only depreciation allowance permitted by this definition is a charge for the decline in an asset's value over the taxable year. What of the realization principle that gains and losses are not recognized for tax purposes until realized, usually by sale of the property? Our economist might concede that the principle should apply to depreciable property as well as to other property, and that changes in value due to the vagaries of the market can be ignored. Even under a realization system, however, economic depreciation should be an estimate, made when the property is placed in service, of the property's decline in value, year by

---

[11] Supra note 9.
[12] See supra ¶3.1.1.

year.[13]

In making this estimate, it is helpful to think of the value of a business or investment asset as the present value of the net cash flows expected to be generated by the asset over its productive life. When an asset is held solely for a business or investment use, it has no value apart from its potential to produce income for the owner. Its value is thus the price that would be paid for this income stream; because the income will not be received all at once, it must be reduced to present value.

If an asset has a limited life, the present value of future net cash flows declines as the asset's exhaustion approaches. The decline in any year equals (1) the present value at the beginning of the year of the net cash flows expected during that year and future years, over (2) the present value at the end of the year of the net cash flows expected in future years. Assume a piece of equipment is purchased to be held for rental; the equipment's useful life is five years, and $1,000 in net rents (after payment of all expenses other than depreciation and interest) will be received in each of those years. When the asset is purchased its value equals the present value of the right to receive $1,000 per year for five years. One year later, its value will be the present value of the right to four annual payments of $1,000 each. The excess of the first of these present value figures over the second is the decline in value over the year. By carrying this technique forward, the expected decline in value during each of the five years of useful life can be determined.

One concession is made to the realization principle:[14] The discount (interest) rate used in computing present values is the rate in effect when the asset is placed in service, and the net cash flows from the asset are projected at that time. Changes in value as a consequence of fluctuations in interest rates and the rental or use value of the particular property are ignored until the property is sold, just as they are for stocks, bonds, and other capital assets. As the Supreme Court has said, depreciation "is a process of estimated allocation which does not take account of fluctuations in valuation through market appreciation."[15]

---

[13] See Chirelstein, Federal Income Taxation 135 (Foundation Press, 5th ed. 1988); Kurtz, Real Estate Tax Shelter—A Postscript, 26 Nat'l Tax J. 341 (1973).

[14] For an argument that the very premise of economic depreciation is inconsistent with the realization principle, see Kahn, Accelerated Depreciation—Tax Expenditure or Proper Allowance for Measuring Net Income? 78 Mich. L. Rev. 1 (1980); Blum, Accelerated Depreciation: A Proper Allowance for Measuring Net Income?!! 78 Mich. L. Rev. 1172 (1980); Kahn, Accelerated Depreciation Revisited—A Reply to Professor Blum, 78 Mich. L. Rev. 1185 (1980).

[15] Fribourg Navigation Co. v. CIR, 383 US 272, 277 (1966). Although the Court refers only to market appreciation, the subject with which it was immediately concerned, the observation is equally applicable to declines in the market value of depreciable assets.

Example 23-2 shows economic depreciation in the example given above (five-year life, annual net cash flow of $1,000) assuming a discount rate of 10 percent. The price paid for the equipment is $3,791, the present value at 10 percent of five annual payments of $1,000 each. Economic depreciation consists of this price allocated among five annual allowances in ascending amounts.

Example 23-2

Economic Depreciation
Where Net Cash Flows Are Constant

| Year | Present value of future cash flows determined as of: | | Depreciation |
	Beginning of year	End of year	
1	$3,791	$3,170	$621
2	3,170	2,487	683
3	2,478	1,736	751
4	1,736	909	826
5	909	0	909

That depreciation should be smaller in earlier years than in later years runs against the common assumption that straight line depreciation is the least generous method worthy of consideration. The reasonableness of the ascending pattern of economic depreciation, however, is shown in Example 23-3, where the taxpayer's income from the investment is shown, in dollar amounts and as a percentage of the taxpayer's investment from time to time. Although the income declines in dollar amount as the years pass, the rate of return remains constant at 10 percent because the taxpayer's investment also declines, reflecting that some part of each $1,000 receipt is a recovery of a portion of the amount paid for the property.

Compare Example 23-3 with Example 23-4, where the same computations are made assuming depreciation is allowed in five annual installments of $758 each (straight line depreciation). In Example 23-4, income is constant at $242 per year, but the rate of return varies wildly from 6.3 percent to 31.9 percent. Aggregate income over the five-year period is the same under both methods ($5,000 less cost of $3,791, or $1,209), and the problem might be seen as one of allocating this income over the property's useful life. Straight line depreciation allocates the income in equal amounts among the five years, thereby ignoring that the taxpayer's investment declines year by year. Economic depreciation causes annual income to fall to reflect the declining investment, thereby keeping the rate of return on investment constant. Although an allocation scheme is, by definition, based on assumption rather than fact, it is certainly more reasonable to assume that the rate of return on each dollar invested remains constant than it is to assume that income remains constant in dollar amount, regardless of the amount invested.

Example 23-3

Income Computed With Economic Depreciation

Year	Rents Received	Depreciation	Net income	Unrecovered investment	Income as percentage of unrecovered investment
1	$1,000	$621	$379	$3,791	10%
2	1,000	683	317	3,170	10
3	1,000	751	249	2,487	10
4	1,000	826	174	1,736	10
5	1,000	909	91	909	10

Example 23-4

Income Computed With Straight Line Depreciation

Year	Rents Received	Depreciation	Net income	Unrecovered investment	Income as percentage of unrecovered investment
1	$1,000	$758	$242	$3,791	6.3%
2	1,000	758	242	3,033	8.0
3	1,000	758	242	2,274	10.6
4	1,000	758	242	1,516	15.9
5	1,000	758	242	758	31.9

The foregoing examples are based on a highly restrictive assumption, that net cash flow remains constant throughout the asset's useful life and then plummets to zero. It might be that a machine might decline in productivity gradually over time rather than dying suddenly at the height of its usefulness. As time passes, the machine might require repair with increasing frequency, with the consequence that gross income might fall as down time increases and net cash flow might be further eroded by rising repair costs. If this is so, economic depreciation would not follow the ascending pattern shown in Example 23-2, but would be more level or might even exhibit the descending pattern associated with accelerated depreciation. Example 23-5, illustrates this assuming that net cash flow from a depreciable asset is

$1,000 for the first year, but declines thereafter to $800, $600, $400, and $200 in the second through the fifth years. At a 10 percent rate of return, the cost of the equipment is $2,418.

Example 23-5

Economic Depreciation With Declining Net Cash Flows

| | Present value of future cash flows determined as of: | | |
Year	Beginning of year	End of year	Depreciation
1	$2,418	$1,660	$758
2	1,660	1,026	634
3	1,026	528	498
4	528	181	347
5	181	0	181

¶23.1.5 Expensing as Tax Exemption

When tax depreciation is more rapid than economic depreciation, most taxpayers benefit because the consequence of the acceleration is to defer tax liabilities. It is only a matter of timing; since the sum of all depreciation deductions is limited to the property's cost, large deductions in early years mean smaller deductions later on. A liability payable later, however, is less burdensome than one payable sooner. The present value of a person's tax liabilities, in other words, is reduced when the taxes are deferred.

This raises a further question, "Is it possible to accelerate depreciation deductions to such an extent that the acceleration reduces the present value of the tax liabilities to zero?" The answer is Yes; allowing the full cost of depreciable property to be deducted when the property is purchased has the same effect as exempting income from the property permanently from tax. Expensing, in other words, is equivalent to tax exemption.

The point is most easily illustrated by an example involving nondepreciable property. (This is so because with depreciable property there is a partial disinvestment each year, which complicates things but does not change the basic phenomenon.) Assume two individuals (A and B) each devote $1,000 of current salary to investment. A puts her money into an account (an IRA) that is subject to rules allowing a deduction for contributions to the account and exempting income on investments held in the account, but treating as taxable income 100 percent of any distribution from the account. B buys a municipal bond. If the tax rate is 28 percent, B has only $720 to invest because $280 of his $1,000 salary is taken in tax. A, in contrast, has $1,000 to invest, her $1,000 of salary income being offset by the deduction for the IRA contribution. Both investors liquidate their investments and spend the proceeds on consumption at the end of three years. Investment results, assuming both get an annual return of 10 percent, are shown in Example 23-6.

Example 23-6

Expensing vs. Exemption

	A	B
1. Amount invested	$1,000	$720
2. Income accumulations		
a. Year 1 (10 percent of line 1)	100	72
b. Year 2 (10 percent of sum of lines 1 and 2a.)	110	79
c. Year 3	121	87
3. Sum of amount invested and income accumulations	$1,331	$958
4. Tax on withdrawal from investment	373	–0–
5. Amount available for consumption	$ 958	$958

A expenses her investment, but is later taxed on all cash flows from the investment. She is in the same position as a purchaser of depreciable property who is allowed to deduct the full cost immediately, but as a consequence is taxed on the net cash flow from the property, unreduced by depreciation. *B*, in contrast, makes a straightforward tax-exempt investment. As Example 23-6 shows, the two investors have the same amount in the end. As Example 23-7 shows, both of them fare much better than a third investor, *C*, who makes a fully taxable investment. *C* is in the same position as an investor in depreciable property who is allowed economic depreciation.

Example 23-7

Fully Taxable Investment

1. Amount invested	$720
2. Income accumulations	
a. Year 1 (10 percent of line 1, less 28 percent thereof)	52
b. Year 2 (10 percent of sum of lines 1 and 2a, less 28 percent thereof)	77
c. Year 3	85
3. Sum of amount invested and income accumulations	$933
4. Tax on withdrawal from investment	–0–
5. Amount available for consumption	$933

Present law allows expensing within narrow limits. Section 179 allows the full cost of depreciable personal property to be deducted in the year the property is placed in service, but restricts each taxpayer to electing this treatment for no more than $10,000 of property purchased in any taxable year.[16]

Before 1986, the law went even further. As the Staff of the Joint Committee on Taxation reported, under the rules in effect during the period 1981 through 1986, "the tax benefits of the combination of the investment tax credit and accelerated depreciation were more generous for some equipment than if the full cost of the investment were deducted immediately—a result more generous than exempting all earnings on the investment from taxation."[17] This generosity has especially deleterious effects because it encourages taxpayers to make investments that would be losing ventures in a world without taxes, but are made profitable by the tax law.

Consider a hypothetical system in which taxpayers can claim a deduction for 120 percent of the cost of an asset and there is a 50-percent tax rate. A taxpayer purchases an asset for $100 which earns only $98 in the subsequent year, after which it is scrapped. This investment would clearly be unprofitable in a tax-free world because the $98 return would not be enough even to recoup the $100 paid for the asset, much less any return on the investment. However, in this hypothetical tax system, the $60 tax benefit that the taxpayer receives from the $120 tax deduction reduces his net cost of the asset to $40. Thus, the $49 after tax cash flow in year two is enough to yield a 22.5 percent return after taxes on the investment—enough to make the investment attractive to the taxpayer. The incentive for uneconomic investment would be eliminated if the taxpayer were allowed to expense his $100 investment in the year he made the investment.[18]

¶23.1.6 Effects of Inflation

Under present law, depreciation deductions are understated in periods of inflation. Inflation distorts the measurement of income whenever costs incurred in one period enter into income computations for another year. Assume a share of stock acquired two years ago for $100 is sold for $120. Under current law, there is a gain of $20. Economically, this is only true if

---

[16] See infra ¶23.8 for §179.

[17] Staff of Joint Comm. on Tax'n, 99th Cong., 2d Sess., General Explanation of the Tax Reform Act of 1986, at 98 (Comm. Print 1987).

[18] Staff of Joint Comm. on Tax'n, 97th Cong., 2d Sess., General Explanation of the Revenue Provisions of the Tax Equity and Fiscal Responsibility Act of 1982, at 35–36 (Comm. Print 1982).

the purchasing power of the dollar is the same today as it was two years ago. If today it costs $120 to buy goods that cost $100 two years ago (i.e., if 20 percent inflation has occurred), there is no economic gain because the value of the price received (120 of today's dollars) is equal to the value of the price paid (100 of the more valuable dollars of two years ago).

The problem in the example is that the subtraction for the cost basis of the property is understated because it is given in the dearer dollars of an earlier time but is subtracted from a receipt stated in cheaper current dollars. The same phenomenon occurs with respect to depreciation. As the Supreme Court said in *United States v. Ludley*,[19] depreciation is allowed because the use of an exhausting asset in business is like a sale of a portion of the asset each year. As in the example in the preceding paragraph, gain on this notional sale is overstated during a period of inflation if the subtraction for the property's cost basis is stated in dearer dollars of an earlier time.

The most direct solution to the inflation problem is to index depreciation allowances for inflation. Assume a machine is purchased for $1,000 and depreciation is allowed at the rate of $200 per year for five years. If inflation occurs at a compounded rate of 5 percent over this period, indexed depreciation allowances are as given in Example 23-8.

Example 23-8

Indexed Depreciation Allowances

Year	Unindexed allowance	Inflation factor*	Indexed allowance
1	$200	1.025	$205
2	200	1.076	215
3	200	1.130	226
4	200	1.187	237
5	200	1.246	249

*The inflation factor for the first year is 1.025 because, at an annual inflation rate or 5 percent, prices throughout the year are 2 1/2 percent higher on average than at the beginning of the year. The inflation factor for each subsequent year is 5 percent higher than for the preceding year.

An alternative to indexation is to substitute for annual depreciation allowances a single deduction for the year property is placed in service equal to the present value of the annual deductions that would otherwise be allowed. If the interest rate is 10 percent, for example, five annual deduc-

---

[19] See supra note 8.

tions of $200 each would be superseded by a deduction at the outset of $758 (the present value of an annual annuity of $200 for five years). This solution avoids the inflation problem by allowing the deduction when the cost is incurred. It is highly distortive of income because it greatly understates income in the year of purchase when the large deduction is allowed and overstates income in later years when the property produces income but no depreciation is available to shield it from tax. Over the long run, however, the distortion benefits neither the taxpayer nor the IRS. The tax reduction from big deduction in the year of purchase is like a loan from the government that the taxpayer repays in higher taxes in later years. Because the big deduction is less than the cost of the property ($758 deduction for cost of $1,000 in the example), the loan effectively bears interest.

Neither of the foregoing solutions, however, should be adopted except as part of rules comprehensively dealing with the effects of inflation on the measurement of income. In particular, depreciation cannot rationally be corrected for inflation without simultaneously providing for the effects of inflation on interest income and deductions. Comprehensive indexation systems are discussed elsewhere in this work.[20]

Acceleration in depreciation deductions, either by shortened recovery periods or by accelerated methods, is sometimes suggested as a solution for the inflation problem. It is a poor solution. Acceleration proposals are rarely calibrated to compensate accurately for any particular rate of inflation; if they were, they would not usually do the job because inflation varies from year to year.

¶23.1.7 Role of Basis in Depreciation

Section 167(g) provides that the basis for computing depreciation is the adjusted basis prescribed by §1011 for determining gain on a sale or other disposition of the property.[21] In computing basis, the taxpayer ordinarily starts with the property's cost. When money is borrowed to pay the purchase price or where portions of the purchase price are to be paid to the seller in deferred installments, the buyer's cost normally includes the portion of the price paid with borrowed money or to be paid in the future. In some circumstances, however, debt is not included in cost basis, particularly where it is without recourse and the circumstances suggest the property will not generate sufficient cash to ensure that the debt will be paid.[22] Also, the starting point is sometimes a transferred basis (e.g., the basis of property

---

[20] Supra ¶3.5.4.

[21] If the basis for determining gain differs from the basis used in computing loss, as is sometimes the case with property acquired by gift, the former is controlling. For the basis of property transferred by gift, see §1015(a), discussed infra ¶41.3.1.

[22] See infra ¶42.2.2.

in the hands of the donor if it was acquired by gift) or an exchanged basis (e.g., the basis of other property if it was exchanged for the current asset in a tax-free transaction), as is explained elsewhere in this work.[23] Once the original basis of the property is determined, it might have to be adjusted upward or downward to reflect capitalized improvements, casualty losses, and other amounts chargeable to capital account.[24]

Basis, however originally determined, is reduced by allowable depreciation (whether actually deducted or not) under the method selected by the taxpayer. If an excessive amount of depreciation is deducted, basis is reduced by the excess as well, unless it was of no tax benefit.[25] Thus, on a later sale or other disposition of the property, gain or loss will reflect the amount of depreciation charged against the property's basis.

¶23.1.8 Depreciable Interest

Since the depreciation deduction is computed on the adjusted basis of property and serves to compensate for the economic burden of exhaustion, wear and tear, and obsolescence, the person entitled to depreciate property is ordinarily its owner, whether or not the purchase price for the property has been fully paid.[26] The person considered owner of the property is not necessarily the title holder, however. If title is vested in an agent or dummy as a matter of convenience, for example, the principal or beneficial owner is entitled to the depreciation.[27] Sale-leaseback transactions often raise an issue of whether a person other than the titleholder owns the property in substance and therefore is entitled to the depreciation.[28] Similarly, mortgagees, vendors under conditional sales agreements, and others interested in property as security for a debt are not entitled to depreciation, even if they are indirectly adversely affected by wear and tear, exhaustion, and obsoles-

---

[23] Infra ¶41.6.

[24] See infra ¶42.1.

[25] See infra ¶42.3.

[26] For the basis of property acquired subject to mortgages or other encumbrances, see infra ¶41.2.2. See also Wagner v. CIR, 518 F2d 655 (10th Cir. 1975) (purchaser of property subject to lease is subject to benefits and burdens of ownership and entitled to depreciate property, despite postponed possession).

[27] See CIR v. Bollinger, 108 S. Ct. 1173 (1988) (corporation held title to real property as nominee of several partnerships in order to avoid usury law that would have applied if partnerships were title holders; held, partnerships considered owners for federal tax purposes because corporation held as agent, both in form and in substance); Rev. Proc. 88-3, 1988-1 IRB 29, at §4.0110 (IRS ordinarily will not rule on whether a taxpayer is entitled to depreciation "where the formal ownership of property is in a party other than the taxpayer, except when title is held merely as security"). See also infra ¶90.1.8 (corporations as nominees).

[28] See supra ¶4.4.2.

cence of the property because the owner might fail to pay the debt at maturity.

In some circumstances, a person other than the owner is the one whose economic enjoyment of particular property is adversely affected by its deterioration or obsolescence. As pointed out in an early decision by the Board of Tax Appeals:

> "Depreciation" is an allowance for the recovery of a capital investment. . . . It is not predicted upon ownership of the property, but rather upon an investment in property which is thereafter used. The important question is not, in whom vests the fee or when it vested, but who made the investment of the capital which is to be recovered over the period of the exhaustion of the property. The one who made the investment is entitled to its return.[29]

Thus, a lessee who constructs a building on leased land is entitled to depreciate it.[30] Similarly, a taxpayer who installs equipment or pays for improvements on someone else's property is permitted to depreciate the outlay, despite a loss of title, if the expenditure provides benefits over an extended period and, hence, does not qualify for deduction in the year it is paid or incurred.[31] Cases of this type can usually be viewed as permitting the taxpayer to depreciate an intangible (the exclusive right to use the property) with a useful life that is coextensive with the property's physical life, rather than

---

[29] Gladding Dry Goods Co. v. CIR, 2 BTA 336, 338 (1925). See also Hunter v. CIR, 46 TC 477, 489–90 (1966):

> It is axiomatic that to be entitled to depreciation under Section 167 the taxpayer must have an investment in the property sought to be depreciated . . . and that the investment must be of such a character as to give the taxpayer a depreciable interest in the property. Ownership of the property is usually required, but the existence of bare legal title in another does not always deprive the taxpayer of a depreciation deduction if it is shown that the taxpayer in fact is the one who suffers the economic loss of his investment by virtue of the wear and tear or exhaustion of the property. But the loss to the taxpayer must be a present one, not just a possibility, and it must relate to taxpayer's investment in the property. . . . Consequently, a stockholder is not usually entitled to a depreciation deduction for property owned by his corporation because he has no direct economic interest or investment in the property.

[30] See infra ¶23.1.5.

[31] D. Loveman & Son Export Corp. v. CIR, 34 TC 776, 806–07 (1960) (acq.), aff'd per curiam, 296 F2d 732 (6th Cir. 1961), cert. denied, 369 US 860 (1962) (cost of paving dead-end street leading to taxpayer's premises). See also Fall River Gas Appliance Co. v. CIR, 349 F2d 515 (1st Cir. 1965) (water heaters), and cases therein cited; Rev. Rul. 71-469, 1971-2 CB 120 (payments by public utility to customers to defray expense of converting equipment from steam heat to gas).

entailing depreciation of the property itself, ownership of which has been surrendered.

Property held by a life tenant is depreciable by the holder, as though he were the absolute owner, over the property's useful life or ACRS recovery period rather than over the expected term of the tenancy, and any unrecovered investment is depreciable by the remainderman when his interest becomes possessory.[32] A taxpayer who purchases a life estate, however, is entitled to depreciate the investment over the expectancy of the measuring life.[33]

When depreciable property is held in trust, the allowable deduction is apportioned between the income beneficiaries and the trustee in accordance with the trust instrument; if the instrument does not apportion the allowance, it is allocated in proportion to the trust income. Depreciation allowable on property held by an estate is allocated among the estate, heirs, legatees, and devisees in proportion to their pro rata shares of the estate's income.[34]

¶23.1.9 Leased Property and Leaseholds

Lessors are entitled to depreciate leased buildings, equipment, and other depreciable property over the asset's useful life (regardless of the term of the lease) because, as owners, they bear the burden of exhaustion, wear and tear, and obsolescence.[35] This general rule is subject to exceptions where a lessee agrees to return property of equivalent value at the end of the rental term[36] or where the purported lessor-owner is found, on the facts, to be the

---

[32] IRC §167(h); Reg. §1.167(h)-1(a). See generally Litwin, Apportionment of Date of Death Basis; Analyzing the Anomalies of Uniform Basis, 27 Tax L. Rev. 303, 312 (1972); infra ¶41.4.6.

[33] Bell v. Harrison, 212 F2d 253 (7th Cir. 1954).

[34] IRC §167(h). See infra ¶81.2.5.

[35] Reg. §1.167(a)-4 (last sentence). The courts have twice entertained the theory that property built to suit the special needs of a lessee can be depreciated by the lessor over the lease term if that is shorter than the property's normal recovery period, but in both cases the lessor lost on the facts. Ames v. CIR, 626 F2d 693 (9th Cir. 1980) (special-purpose property, but no proof that lessee would not renew lease); Potter v. CIR, 28 TCM (CCH) 1190 (1969) (taxpayer failed to prove that another lessee able to use the property could not be found). The argument is foreclosed for property placed in service after 1980 because the ACRS rules, which require that depreciation be taken over prescribed recovery periods rather than the useful life of the property in the taxpayer's business, provide no special rule for property built for a lessee.

[36] See Kem v. CIR, 432 F2d 961 (9th Cir. 1970) (lessee of cattle herd obligated to return herd of same or better quality and age composition; held, lessor suffered no depreciation); Royal St. Louis, Inc. v. US, 578 F2d 1017 (5th Cir. 1978) (same as to lessor of hotel furniture); Hibernia Nat'l Bank v. US, 569 F. Supp. 5 (ED La. 1983)

equivalent of a mortgagee.[37] The lessor may also write off expenses incurred to negotiate and arrange a lease (including brokerage commissions, legal fees, and the adjusted basis of demolished buildings) ratably over the life of the lease.[38]

When property is purchased subject to a favorable lease, the argument is sometimes made that a portion of the cost should be allocated to the lease, to be amortized over the lease term rather than depreciated over the recovery period for the property. A premium price might be paid for the property if the lease provides for higher rents or more favorable terms for the lessor than those obtainable in the market when the purchase occurs. The premium, the argument runs, is a cost of the lessor's rights under the lease, not of the leased property. One court has accepted the argument,[39] but

---

(allowing depreciation to taxpayer in *Royal St. Louis* for later years after lease amended to state that lessor's right to return hotel furniture was subject to usual exception for reasonable wear and tear). Cf. North Carolina Midland Ry. v. US, 163 F. Supp. 610 (Ct. Cl. 1958) (where lessee required to return leased railroad property "in at least as good a condition as at the beginning of the term," depreciation allowed to lessor because lessee's obligation did not protect against obsolescence); Rev. Rul. 62-8, 1962-1 CB 31 (obligation to replace, renew, and maintain property does not protect lessor against obsolescence).

A lessee who guarantees the lessor against depreciation can deduct actual maintenance expenses but cannot depreciate the property even if he has the equivalent of ownership under local law. Weiss v. Wiener, 279 US 333 (1929) (99-year lease renewable forever). If the issue were approached de novo, much could be said for allowing depreciation to such a lessee, but *Weiss v. Wiener* has probably been sanctified by long administrative and legislative acquiescence.

[37] See supra ¶4.4.2.

[38] Reg. §1.165-3(b)(2); Young v. CIR, 59 F2d 691 (9th Cir.), cert. denied, 287 US 652 (1932) (real estate commissions, legal fees, and title changes). See Handlery Hotels, Inc. v. US, 663 F2d 892 (9th Cir. 1981) (payment made to old tenant to cancel lease so that taxpayer could make new lease with new tenant; held, payment amortized over remaining term of old lease); Rev. Rul. 67-410, 1967-2 CB 93 (adjusted basis of building demolished by lessee is lease acquisition cost to be amortized by lessor over term of lease).

For expenses incurred by a lessor to terminate a lease, see Houston Chronicle Publishing Co. v. US, 481 F2d 1240 (5th Cir. 1973), cert. denied, 414 US 1129 (1974); Montgomery Co. v. CIR, 54 TC 986 (1970); Note, The Tax Treatment of the Cost of Terminating a Lease, 30 Stan. L. Rev. 241 (1977).

[39] CIR v. Moore, 207 F2d 265 (9th Cir. 1953), cert. denied, 347 US 942 (1954), where the issue was whether a portion of an heir's basis for land under §1014 could be allocated to an allegedly favorable lease on the land. The court said: "If the lease was one whose favorable rentals are subject to ultimate exhaustion, that portion of the [basis] attributable to . . . its 'premium' value, should be amortized through annual deductions allowable to the lessor." Id. at 276. See also Sullivan v. US, 618 F2d 1001 (3d Cir. 1980) (agreement allocating selling price between land and lease agreements held binding in characterizing seller's gain).

others have rejected it.[40]

If a lessee makes improvements that enhance the value of the lessor's interest and if this added value constitutes rent to the lessor, the lessor must include it in gross income and, hence, acquires a basis in the improvements that may be depreciated. Such an improvement might be considered rent where, for example, the lessee is required to erect a building meeting standards prescribed by the lease, with an expected useful life in excess of the term of the lease.[41] If the improvements do not constitute rent, however, they are excluded from the lessor's gross income by §109 even when the lease terminates; since the lessor acquires no basis in the improvements, he may not depreciate them.[42] If the property is sold, however, the new owner may allocate a portion of the purchase price to the tenant-constructed improvement equal to the value of the owner's interest in the improvement, regardless of whether the making of the improvement was rent to the original landlord.[43]

A lessee's expenditures in obtaining a lease may be deducted ratably over the lease term as business expenses if the lease is acquired for business purposes.[44] Under §178(a), the lease term is deemed to include any period covered by a renewal option held by the lessee if less than 75 percent of the lease acquisition cost is "attributable to the period of the term of the lease remaining on the date of its acquisition."[45] Subject to the same 75 percent

---

[40] E.g., American Controlled Indus., Inc. v. US, 55 AFTR2d 947 (SD Ohio 1984) (not officially reported) (purchaser not allowed to allocate between property and leases); Schubert v. CIR, 33 TC 1048 (1960), aff'd, 286 F2d 573 (4th Cir.), cert denied, 366 US 960 (1961) (heir not allowed to allocate §1014 basis between property and favorable lease on property). See also Michaelis v. CIR, 54 TC 1175, 1176 (1970) (taxpayer who inherited landlord's interest under lease, separate from feehold, not allowed to depreciate §1014 basis for lease "absent any showing that this was a *premium* lease, calling for rent in excess of fair market value"). For discussion of the panoply of issues raised by purchases and sales of property subject to leases, see Morris & Glicklich, Some Incongruities in the Taxation of Leased Real Property, 40 Tax Lawyer 85 (1986).

[41] See supra ¶16.1.

[42] Id. See also Reisinger v. CIR, 144 F2d 475 (2d Cir. 1944) (lessor denied depreciation although jointly liable for funds borrowed to finance lessee's improvements); Buzzell v. US, 326 F2d 825 (1st Cir. 1964) (same where lessor advanced funds for improvements to lessee, who was entitled to discharge liability by surrender of premises).

[43] World Publishing Co. v. CIR, 299 F2d 614 (8th Cir. 1962). See Feldman, Depreciation of Tenant Erected Improvements by Purchaser-Lessor, 1963 Wis. L. Rev. 484 (1963).

[44] Reg. §1.162-11(a) (aliquot part of costs deductible each year during term of lease). But see Minneapolis Sec. Bldg. Corp. v. CIR, 38 BTA 1220 (1938) (term of leasehold controlling despite shorter useful life of improvements).

[45] There is a technical glitch in §178. It refers to a lessee's deduction "for amortization under section 167" and various other provisions (not including §162);

limitation, the lease term also includes "any other period for which the parties reasonably expect the lease to be renewed." These rules are most obviously applicable to a payment made to acquire the lessee's rights under an existing lease or to a lump-sum bonus or premium paid to the lessor when a lease is made. They might also apply to legal fees and other costs incurred by a lessee in arranging a lease.

In applying the 75 percent limitation under §178, the phrase "term of the lease remaining on the date of its acquisition" refers to the original lease term, exclusive of periods for which the lease might be extended at the lessee's option. If a lease is acquired with an original term of 21 years and the lessee has options to renew for two successive terms of 21 years each, for example, the issue under the 75 percent rule is whether less than 75 percent of the acquisition cost is attributable to the original 21-year term. The answer depends on "the facts and circumstances of each case," but a method based on the present value of annuities is suggested in the regulations.[46]

A lessee may also write off costs of improvements he makes to the property, even though ownership vests in the lessor on construction or installation.[47] For improvements placed in service after 1986, the lessee's depreciation deduction is determined under the ACRS rules using the recovery period applicable to property of the class that includes the improvement, even if that period exceeds the remaining term of the lease.[48] If the lessee surrenders possession of the property before the end of the recovery period, a loss deduction is allowed for the improvement's remaining basis.[49]

For pre-1987 improvements, the lessee's investment is recoverable through allowances for depreciation over the useful life of the improvements, if that is equal to or shorter than the remaining life of the lease, or through ratable deductions "in lieu of allowances for depreciation" other-

---

the regulation allowing the amortization deduction, however, was promulgated under a regulation under §162, implying that the deduction is allowed under §162 rather than §167. If this implication is followed, however, §178 applies to nothing.

Section 178 was enacted in 1958, and applied until 1987 to improvement costs as well as to leasehold acquisition costs. For the pre-1987 version of §178, see infra text accompanying notes 48–53. For pre-1958 law, which is still controlling when §178 does not apply, see Alamo Broadcasting Co. v. CIR, 15 TC 534 (1950) (acq.) (renewal period ordinarily included).

[46] Reg. §1.178-1(b)(5).

[47] Reg. §1.167(a)-4. See generally Bartlett, Tax Treatment of Replacements of Leased Property and of Leasehold Improvements Made by a Lessee, 30 Tax Lawyer 105 (1976) (improvements on leasehold by lessee).

[48] IRC §168(i)(8).

[49] Staff of Joint Comm. on Tax'n, 99th Cong., 2d Sess., General Explanation of Tax Reform Act of 1986, at 108 (Comm. Print 1987) [hereinafter 1986 Bluebook].

wise.[50] In addition to the differing lengths of the recovery periods, the principal consequence of this distinction is that in the former situation an accelerated method of depreciation is usually available, while in the latter case the outlay is recovered by equal annual deductions over the remaining life of the lease.

An earlier version of §178 applies in determining the term of a lease under the rules for pre-1987 improvements. Under §178(a), as applied in this context, the term of a lease must include any period for which the lease may be renewed, extended, or continued pursuant to an option exercisable by the lessee if the remaining life of the lease (exclusive of renewals) on completion of the lessee-financed improvement is less than 60 percent of the improvement's useful life.[51] Even when this benchmark is exceeded, however, the lessee may ignore renewal options if nonrenewal is more probable than renewal.

The specified percentage is, in effect, a rule of thumb for determining when the lessee's expenditures are probably allocable in large part to renewal periods rather than to the lease's unexpired term. If, for example, a lessee spends $100,000 to erect a building with a useful life of 40 years when the remaining life of the lease is only 10 years, subject to renewal at his option for another 20 years, it is probably more realistic to amortize his expenditure over 30 years than over 10 years. The 1986 amendments take this analysis one step further in requiring that the lease term be ignored in determining the improvement's recovery period: Even in the absence of a legal right to renew, lessees rarely make substantial improvements without some assurance that the property will be available for their use throughout the economic useful life of the improvement; the most realistic assumption is therefore that the period of the lessee's use of the improvement will not be limited by the lease term.

Even under pre-1987 §178, depreciation is effectively required over the property's useful life or recovery period, determined without regard to the lease term or any renewal options, if lessor and lessee are related persons.[52] Under pre-1987 §178(c), however, renewal periods may be disregarded

---

[50] Reg. §1.167(a)-4. The regulation has not been amended since the introduction of the ACRS rules. Presumably, if 1981 ACRS rules apply, the ACRS recovery period is substituted for the property's useful life. See 1986 Bluebook, supra note 49, at 93. See Buddy Schoellkopf Prods., Inc. v. CIR, 65 TC 640 (1975) (nonacq. on other issues) (where lease term is indefinite, improvement must be depreciated over its recovery period, without regard to lease term).

[51] In determining the amortization period for pre-1987 lease acquisition costs, a renewal period is included if less than 75 percent of the costs are attributable to the lease term, exclusive of renewal periods.

[52] IRC §178(b) (before amendment in 1986). The related-person rule of pre-1987 §178(b) does not apply to expenditures to acquire a lease, but the regulations state that a tainted relationship "will be a significant factor" in determining the

when §§178(a) and (b) are inapplicable, unless the lease has been, or the facts show with reasonable certainty that it will be, renewed.[53]

¶23.1.10 Ancillary Problems

Depreciation deductions have numerous ancillary effects, which are discussed elsewhere in this work, including the following:

1. Recapture of certain depreciation deductions as ordinary income under §§1245 and 1250, even if the property is sold in a transaction that normally generates capital gain.[54]
2. Recognition of ordinary income rather than capital gain on certain transfers of depreciable property between related persons.[55]
3. Limits on the deduction of depreciation and other business expenses incurred in certain tax shelter and other passive activities.[56]

¶23.2 ELIGIBLE PROPERTY

¶23.2.1 Property Used in Business or Held for Production of Income

Section 167(a) restricts the depreciation deduction to (1) "property used in the trade or business" and (2) "property held for the production of income."[1]

The first category embraces the overwhelming bulk of depreciable assets—plant, machinery, and equipment used in business—along with most

---

proper amortization period. Reg. §1.178-1(d)(1)(ii). This caveat implies that related parties will find it difficult to establish that renewal options will not be exercised.

[53] See Uecker v. CIR, 81 TC 983 (1983) (under either "more probable" test of pre-1987 §178(a) or "reasonable certainty" test of pre-1987 §178(c), taxpayer's five-year lease of grazing rights on state lands considered renewable indefinitely).

[54] See infra ¶¶55.2, 55.3.

[55] See IRC §1239, discussed infra ¶54.11.

[56] See infra ¶25.10 (loss deductions limited to amount at risk in activities generating the losses), Ch. 28 (passive activity losses only deductible against income from passive activities).

[1] Rental property held by an investor is "used in a trade or business" if the property requires more than inconsequential management and maintenance activities. Under this expansive standard, single-family dwellings and property subject to net leases are about the only assets excluded from the first category but embraced by the second. See infra ¶51.3.

Revenue Ruling 74-528, 1974-2 CB 64, permits equipment of an unlawful gambling business to be depreciated, despite the fact that it was subject to confiscation for nonpayment of a tax on gaming machines. Query whether a burglar's tools are depreciable.

rental property.[2] The phrase "used in the trade or business" also appears in §§1221(2) and 1231(a), where its function is to remove such property from the "capital asset" classification and make it eligible for the special "hotch-pot" treatment mandated by §1231.[3] It is also closely linked with §162, allowing the taxpayer to deduct the ordinary and necessary expenses of "carrying on any trade or business," and §165(c)(1), relating to losses sustained in an individual's trade or business.[4] There is no statutory requirement that the term "trade or business" be given the same meaning in applying all these sections, but in the absence of a legislative direction or sound rationale justifying divergent interpretations, the courts and the IRS quite properly use the precedents interchangeably.[5]

A business taxpayer's stock in trade, being held for sale rather than "use," does not qualify for depreciation. If the taxpayer expects to sell merchandise at a loss, the inventory value may sometimes be written down under a lower-of-cost-or-market rule that recognizes the current decline in value as part of each year's cost of goods sold.[6] Also, depreciation on equipment used to construct long-lived property to be used in the taxpayer's business may not be deducted currently, but must be capitalized as part of the cost of the property, to be written off over its recovery period.[7]

The second category of depreciable property, "property held for the production of income," was made eligible for the depreciation allowance in 1942 by the enactment of the predecessor of §167(a)(2). Its primary function is to permit investors to depreciate rental property entailing so little management or maintenance activity that it does not constitute property

---

[2] See Rev. Proc. 79-44, 1979-2 CB 508 (depreciation on returnable bottles).

[3] For IRC §1231, see infra ¶54.1.1.

[4] For IRC §162, see supra ¶20.1; for IRC §165(c)(1), see infra ¶25.3.

[5] See Simonson v. US, 752 F2d 341 (8th Cir. 1985) (where taxpayers purchased truck with intention of entering grain hauling business, but change in business conditions prevented them from starting this activity, truck not depreciable because no trade or business).

[6] See Luhring Motor Co. v. CIR, 42 TC 732 (1964) (acq. on other issues) (automobile dealer denied depreciation on "company cars" used for less than year and then sold); Rev. Rul. 75-538, 1975-2 CB 34 (automobile dealer presumed to hold all cars, including company cars and demonstrators, for sale; presumption overcome only by clear showing "that the dealer looks to consumption through use of the vehicle in the ordinary course of business operation" to recover its cost). Compare Transwestern Pipeline Co. v. US, 639 F2d 679 (Ct. Cl. 1980) ("line pack," quantity of gas required to be kept in pipeline to maintain proper pressure, held depreciable); Nash v. CIR, 60 TC 503, 519 (1973) (acq.) (taxpayer, engaged in building and selling apartment houses, allowed to depreciate particular building held for investment).

For the lower-of-cost-or-market rule, see infra ¶105.4.

[7] See infra ¶105.4.

held in a trade or business.[8]

In conjunction, §§167(a)(1) and (2) allow depreciation deductions for all profit-oriented property but not for property devoted to personal use (e.g., the taxpayer's residence, family automobile, and clothing),[9] in keeping with the basic legislative policy of permitting the cost of making a living, but not the cost of living, to be deducted.

Property serving personal uses may be converted to business purposes, however, in which event the amount eligible for depreciation is the asset's adjusted basis or fair market value at the date of conversion, whichever is lower.[10] In the common situation of a personal residence vacated by the taxpayer and placed on the rental market, it has been held that the requisite conversion occurs when the property is listed for rental, even though some time elapses before a tenant is found.[11] If a personal residence is listed for sale rather than rental, however, depreciation is not allowable in the absence of a showing, which can seldom be made, that the taxpayer anticipated a post-conversion profit.[12] Similar skepticism is warranted with regard to

---

[8] See supra note 1. The predecessor of §167(a)(2) was enacted at the same time as the predecessor of §212, discussed in ¶20.5, which permits taxpayers other than corporations to deduct expenses paid or incurred for the production of income or for the maintenance of property held for the production of income.

[9] Reg. §1.167(a)-2. The disqualification of property held for personal use could apply to a corporation if it, for example, holds property as an accommodation for shareholders. See, e.g., Joell Co. v. CIR, 41 BTA 825 (1940) (acq.).

[10] See Reg. §1.167(g)-1 (depreciation), §1.165-9(b) (basis for determining loss on sale of converted property). See also infra ¶42.5.

[11] Robinson v. CIR, 2 TC 305 (1943) (acq.); Odom v. CIR, 38 TCM (CCH) 217 (1979) (property occupied rent-free by tenant not held for production of income). For restrictions on the deduction of expenses (including depreciation) attributable to dwelling units used for both personal and business (including rental) purposes during the same taxable year, see supra ¶22.6.

[12] Newcombe v. CIR, 54 TC 1298 (1970) (property offered for sale not "held for production of income" in absence of anticipated increase in value after listing; earlier cases summarized); Riss v. CIR, 56 TC 388, 415 (1971), aff'd on other issues, 478 F2d 1160 (8th Cir. 1973) (same principle applied to corporate property formerly held for shareholder's use); May v. CIR, 299 F2d 725, 728 (4th Cir. 1962) (abandonment of personal use did not convert palatial yacht's status "from fun-making to money-making"). See generally Byrne, Conversion of a Personal Residence to a Business or Investment Use for Tax Purposes, 8 Rut.-Cam. LJ 393 (1977); Fasan, Maintenance and Depreciation Deductions for a Personal Residence Offered for Sale, 25 Tax L. Rev. 269 (1970); Note, Depreciation of Improved Real Property Held Solely for Later Sale, 27 Stan. L. Rev. 177 (1974) (arguing that §167(a)(2) should allow depreciation of property held solely for investment). For the deductibility of losses on the sale of property of this type, see infra ¶25.3 (re §165(c)(2)).

For other attempts to establish that a personal residence is used for business purposes, see Industrial Research Prods., Inc. v. CIR, 40 TC 578, 588 (1963) (insufficient evidence that taxpayer used home for business purposes as inventor and consulting engineer); Cole v. CIR, 36 TCM (CCH) 1014 (1977) (builder's improvements

claims that part of a residence is "held for the production of income" as soon as the owner-occupant lists a room for rental, unless actual rental transactions or other activity affirmatively demonstrate that the room is no longer dedicated primarily to personal purposes.[13]

Property is often devoted to both personal and business or income-producing purposes, either simultaneously (e.g., a physician's personal residence with a wing used exclusively to receive patients) or successively (e.g., a building contractor's station wagon, used to haul tools and materials to job sites, as well as for family transportation).[14] The business portion of such dual-purpose property qualifies for depreciation, the amount allocable thereto being ordinarily estimated on a mileage, square-footage, or other reasonable basis.[15] Sporadic uses of a residence or other personal property for business activities, such as entertaining customers or typing business reports, however, do not give rise to depreciation deductions for the space temporarily devoted to these uses, even if the business connection is clear enough to permit the taxpayer's out-of-pocket expenses to be deducted.

¶23.2.2 Home Offices, Vacation Homes, and Property Used in Hobbies and Entertainment Facilities

The special rules, which are discussed elsewhere in this work, apply to four categories of assets where depreciation and other deductions were found susceptible to abuse: (1) dwelling units used for both personal and profit-oriented purposes (including rental); (2) property used in activities not engaged in for profit; (3) facilities used for entertainment, amusement, or recreation; and (4) expensive automobiles and personal computers.[16] The principal effect of these restrictions is to disallow deductions for depreciation and certain other expenses. If the activity produces income, however, depreciation is allowable in some situations, even if it would not otherwise be permissible, subject to limits based on the amounts of income and other expenses of the activity.

---

to residence not depreciable, despite claim they were used as model for inspection by customers).

[13] See Casey v. CIR, 24 TCM (CCH) 1558 (1965).

[14] Commuting to and from work is not a business use under either §162 or §167. See supra ¶21.1.3.

[15] For an unusually extensive discussion of the allocation problem, see International Artists, Ltd. v. CIR, 55 TC 94 (1970) (acq.), involving Liberace's home, used as a personal residence, movie studio, and home office; and see supra ¶22.6.

For mileage allowances for business use of automobiles, see supra ¶21.4.4.

[16] See IRC §280A (home offices, vacation homes, etc.), discussed supra ¶22.6; §183 (hobbies and other activities not engaged in for profit), discussed supra ¶22.5; §274(a)(1)(B) (entertainment, amusement, and recreation facilities), discussed supra ¶21.2.3; §280F (expensive cars and personal computers), discussed infra ¶23.10.

¶23.2.3 Commencement and Termination of Business Use of Depreciable Property; "Placed in Service," "Retired From Service," and First and Last Year Conventions

Depreciation is allowed from the time depreciable property is "placed in service" until it is "retired from service."[17] An asset is considered as "placed in service" when acquired and available for business use, even though testing is required or actual use is delayed.[18] The deduction for the first year is limited to a portion of a full year's depreciation appropriate for the period during which the asset is in service during the year. Both ACRS and the ADR system that preceded it do this with conventions that are described below in the discussions of these systems.[19] For property subject to neither of these systems, an allocation must usually be made on the basis of the period the property is actually in service during the year;[20] if numerous assets are acquired or disposed of during the taxable year, multiple-asset accounts can be maintained to simplify the taxpayer's accounting, with depreciation determined by use of an averaging convention based on an

---

[17] Reg. §1.167(a)-10(b). For the treatment of depreciable property on retirement from service, see infra ¶23.9.

[18] See Sears Oil Co. v. CIR, 359 F2d 191 (2d Cir. 1966) (barge ready for service in 1957 but not put to actual use until spring of 1958 due to ice in canal; depreciation for proportionate part of 1957 allowed); Rev. Rul. 79-98, 1979-1 CB 103 (utility plant placed in service when operational, although subsequently tested and not accepted from contractor until later date); Rev. Rul. 76-238, 1976-1 CB 55 (building placed in service on completion of construction when available for installation of equipment; machinery installed over a period of months not in service until production line available for production of product, with later testing to eliminate defects ignored). But see Consumers Power Co. v. CIR, 89 TC 710 (1987) (electric power generating plant not in service during year, even though it produced electricity sold to customers, because taxpayer had not "successfully . . . completed all phases of preoperational testing [needed to demonstrate] that it was available for service on a regular basis"); Cooper v. CIR, 34 TCM (CCH) 1396 (1975), aff'd per curiam, 542 F2d 599 (2d Cir. 1976) (equipment not in taxpayer's possession during taxable year, hence not available for service; depreciation denied); Biggs v. CIR, 27 TCM (CCH) 1177 (1968), aff'd on other issues, 440 F2d 1 (6th Cir. 1971) (depreciation denied; checks indicating payment insufficient evidence of when equipment put to use). For the time when property is considered placed in service when an ADR election is in effect, see infra ¶23.7.3 note 7.

[19] Infra ¶23.3 (ACRS), ¶23.7 (ADR).

[20] Reg. §1.167(a)-10(b). See Clairmont v. CIR, 64 TC 1130 (1975), aff'd by unpublished order (8th Cir. 1976) (improper to calculate first-year depreciation on basis of portion of construction season during which assets used; depreciation must be allocated over 12-month period, with deduction for proportionate part thereof); Hardin v. CIR, 32 TCM (CCH) 892 (1973), aff'd per curiam, 507 F2d 903 (4th Cir. 1974) (racehorse acquired December 4; depreciation allowable for remainder of that year only, notwithstanding race-eligibility rule that horse would age one year as of January 1).

assumed timing of additions and retirements.[21] For example, a "half year" convention may be adopted, based on the assumption that all additions and retirements occur at midyear, regardless of the actual dates, with the result that a half-year's depreciation is allowed on each item. Under the pre-ACRS rules, an averaging convention must be consistently followed, and may not be used in computing depreciation for large or unusual acquisitions that would distort the allowance for the year.[22]

Once an asset is placed in service, it is "used" in the taxpayer's business or income-producing activity, and may be depreciated until retired, sold, or abandoned, despite interruptions in actual use as a result of business exigencies.[23]

¶23.2.4 Wasting Investment Requirement

Property may not be depreciated unless the taxpayer's investment will be consumed, in part or whole, by the effects of exhaustion, wear and tear, or obsolescence. This requirement, which is inherent in the function of the deduction to permit a tax-free recovery of investment in depreciable property, is partially expressed in §167(g), providing that the property's adjusted basis for determining gain is to be used in computing depreciation. A taxpayer may not depreciate property whose basis has been reduced to zero by capital recoveries, prior depreciation, and similar charges,[24] even if it is still used in the business and has a residual fair market value that will be exhausted over time. The same is true of assets whose cost was properly deducted when created, such as mailing lists, contract rights, industrial know-how, and similar property entailing no capitalized outlay.[25] If the cost of acquiring depreciable property is erroneously deducted, it may not be subsequently depreciated unless the deduction is disallowed, in which event

---

[21] Reg. §1.167(a)-10(b).

[22] Id. (conventions include half-year assumption, uniform additions and retirements during taxable year, and full-year convention, under which all additions and retirements in first half of year are deemed made on first day of year and all additions and retirements in second half are deemed made on first day of following year); Rev. Rul. 73-202, 1973-1 CB 81 (convention unavailable for large and unusual purchases, which must be depreciated separately).

[23] P. Dougherty Co. v. CIR, 159 F2d 269 (4th Cir. 1946), cert. denied, 331 US 838 (1947) (barges available for use, although idle for protracted periods); Kittredge v. CIR, 88 F2d 632 (2d Cir. 1937) (winery depreciable although not in production for nine years). But see Thriftimart, Inc. v. CIR, 59 TC 598 (1973) (acq.), remanded by unpublished order (9th Cir. 1975) (property made available rent-free to charitable organization is no longer used in business for depreciation purposes, although taxpayer entitled to charitable contribution deduction).

[24] See infra ¶42.3 (adjustments to basis); see also IRC §362(c)(1) (zero basis for certain contributions to corporate capital), discussed infra ¶91.9.2.

[25] For advertising expenditures, see supra ¶20.4.5.

the taxpayer is entitled to depreciation for all open years.[26]

In addition to having an unrecovered investment in the property, the taxpayer must be able to show that the property is subject to exhaustion, wear and tear, or obsolescence during a period whose duration can be estimated with reasonable accuracy. Depreciation is denied to assets that are not adversely affected by the passage of time or by use in the taxpayer's business, such as works of art, antiques, and raw land, since the value on retirement from use is likely to equal or exceed the taxpayer's original cost or other basis.[27]

In theory, property that will become worthless if public taste or fashions change is depreciable, but in practice it is virtually impossible to estimate the useful life of assets dependent on the fickle wheel of fortune. Thus, investments in goodwill, secret formulas, and similar assets rarely qualify for depreciation and must be held in abeyance until the property is sold or abandoned. The taxpayer's basis is then offset against the sales proceeds or deducted as a loss.[28] In recent years, however, Congress has enacted a series of special provisions allowing taxpayers to deduct or amortize the cost of intangibles that would not ordinarily qualify for depreciation because their life-span is unpredictable, such as trademarks and trade names, newspaper subscriptions, and research and experimental expenditures.[29]

Real property and intangibles, discussed below,[30] are the areas that most frequently generate questions regarding the wasting character of particular assets.

---

[26] See Firemen's Ins. Co. v. CIR, 30 BTA 1004, 1012 (1934) (no depreciation for erroneously deducted capital outlays); Regs. §1.167(a)-10(a) (contra if erroneous deduction disallowed).

[27] See Rev. Rul. 68-232, 1968-1 CB 79 (works of art generally not depreciable); Hawkins v. CIR, 713 F2d 347 (8th Cir. 1983) (no investment credit for art works displayed in law office because property not depreciable; even if useful life in taxpayer's business could be established, no evidence that salvage would be less than cost); Harrah's Club v. US, 661 F2d 203 (Ct. Cl. 1981) (costs of restoring antique cars and preparing them for showing in museum not depreciable in absence of proof that cars deteriorate or lose value over time); Gudmundsson v. CIR, 37 TCM (CCH) 1249 (1978) (no evidence of probable remaining useful life of antique furniture); Judge v. CIR, 35 TCM (CCH) 1264 (1976) (cheap paintings used to decorate physician's office might be distinguished from works of art, but limited useful life not established). For the possibility of depreciating land in unusual circumstances, see infra ¶23.2.5.

[28] See infra ¶23.2.6.

[29] See infra ¶¶26.5, 26.6.

[30] Infra ¶23.2.5 (real property), ¶23.2.6 (intangibles).

¶23.2.5 Real Property

The regulations provide that "land apart from the improvements or physical development added to it" may not be depreciated,[31] and the IRS has applied this rule to agricultural land even where there is evidence that it will subside and be abandoned within a foreseeable period because of an anticipated drop in the water table.[32] The severe view adopted by the regulations avoids troublesome disputes regarding the impact of traffic patterns, demographic changes, and other socioeconomic factors on the useful economic life of urban land, and can be defended as a reasonable administrative interpretation of the statutory language. It is more dubious, however, as applied to land whose physical characteristics will be changed in the reasonably foreseeable future by erosion, loss of underground water, or similar causes.[33]

Attempts by taxpayers to unbundle their rights in land and allocate part of the cost to the right to lease it, in order to get a depreciable basis for this portion of the investment, have been unsuccessful. In an early case, the Board of Tax Appeals observed:

> A fee simple title is the highest estate in land contemplated by the law. In such a title all lesser estates, rights, titles, and interests merge. When all such interests so merge there is a complete solidification of title and the various interests going to constitute that title lose their identity and are no longer distinguishable. . . . The record discloses that the $1 per acre, which the taxpayer seeks to allocate as cost of the rights granted by him in his lease, was his valuation of his *right to grant an estate subordinate to his freehold*, i.e., his right to carve out of his freehold a base or an inferior estate. This we hold he cannot do. A freehold, like a lump of gold, may be partitioned and the fragments apportioned in severalty, but it is not divisible into elements so as to permit a valuation of its elements, because the gold is the element and

---

[31] Reg. §1.167(a)-2.

[32] Rev. Rul. 55-730, 1955-2 CB 53. See A. Duda & Sons v. US, 560 F2d 669 (5th Cir. 1977) (subsidence of peat soil; no deduction for depreciation or depletion); infra ¶24.1.1.

The restriction on depreciating land does not apply to an easement for a limited period, which is treated as an intangible that may be depreciated over its own useful life. See infra ¶23.2.6.

[33] In an unusual case, a taxpayer was allowed to depreciate a hole in the ground. Sexton v. CIR, 42 TC 1094 (1964) (acq. in result only) (taxpayer in rubbish business could depreciate difference between cost of land with large pits and estimated lower value of land when filled in). See also Sanders v. CIR, 75 TC 157 (1980) (*Sexton* followed where site had no physical characteristics specially suitable for landfill use, i.e., no holes); Rev. Rul. 74-282, 1974-1 CB 150 (pits purchased by strip miner as dumping area held subject to depreciation).

itself contains all of value there is in it.[34]

Man-made improvements to land qualify for depreciation.[35] If the improvement is not a building or other structure but a change in the physical nature of the land (e.g., by planting, excavating, or grading the property), the taxpayer might have difficulty in establishing its useful life. This burden can be sustained by demonstrating that the improvement is subject to physical deterioration over a reasonably foreseeable period (e.g., a dam or canal), is so closely associated with a particular building that it lacks an independent value (e.g., an access road to a lumber camp that will be abandoned when an existing stand of timber is harvested), or will be destroyed when a building is replaced (e.g., trees and shrubbery immediately adjacent to an apartment building).[36] Expenditures to clear and grade a building site that will continue to be useful when the existing building is replaced, however, are no more subject to depreciation than the cost of the raw land itself; according to the IRS, trees and shrubbery not adjacent to a building also fall under this ban.[37]

Under special provisions applicable to farmers, a miscellany of expenditures for man-made improvements to land, with useful lives that are difficult to estimate or of indefinite duration, may either be deducted when made or be amortized over a specified period. These provisions include §175 (soil and water conservation expenditures), §180 (fertilizer, etc.), and §182 (costs incurred before 1986 in clearing land for farming).[38] Also, §185

---

[34] Farmer v. CIR, 1 BTA 711, 713–14, 715 (1925).

[35] When improved real estate is purchased for a lump sum, the purchase price must be allocated between the nondepreciable land and the depreciable improvements. Reg. §1.167(a)-5. See infra ¶41.7.1.

[36] Rev. Rul. 75-137, 1975-1 CB 74 (depreciation allowed for cost of excavating canals and dredging channels in harbors, on showing that exhaustion is susceptible to measurement); Rev. Rul. 74-265, 1974-1 CB 56 (shrubbery and trees adjacent to garden apartments depreciable because they will be destroyed on replacement of building; contra for cost of clearing, grading, adding topsoil to the site, and planting around perimeter); Rev. Rul. 73-488, 1973-2 CB 207 (mining road); Rev. Rul. 68-281, 1968-1 CB 22 (logging roads). See Tunnell v. US, 512 F2d 1192 (3d Cir.), cert. denied, 423 US 893 (1975) (lagoons for waterfront mobile park); Wolfsen Land & Cattle Co. v. CIR, 72 TC 1 (1979) (periodic extensive maintenance of irrigation system); Trailmont Park, Inc. v. CIR, 30 TCM (CCH) 871 (1971) (grading and landscaping mobile home park); Rudolph Inv. Corp. v. CIR, 31 TCM (CCH) 573 (1972) (earthen water tanks and dams on ranch); Rev. Rul. 72-96, 1972-1 CB 66 (reservoir and dam depreciable over life of related generating facilities).

[37] Rev. Rul. 74-265, supra note 36. It is not clear why expenditures to plant ornamental trees and shrubs to beautify a building site should not be depreciable, even if they will outlast the building itself. See Johnson v. Westover, 55-1 USTC ¶9423 (SD Cal. 1955) (not officially reported) (taxpayer allowed to depreciate value of pasturage that was not natural growth but required replanting every 10 years).

[38] See infra ¶105.5.6.

once gave railroads an election to amortize costs of railroad grading and tunnel bores; the provision, however, has been repealed for costs incurred after 1986, and the status of such costs under general principles is unclear.[39]

¶23.2.6 Intangible Property

Section 167(a) does not distinguish between tangible and intangible assets. Section 168, however, limits the ACRS system to tangible property, and therefore leaves depreciation on intangibles subject to the pre-1981 law under §167. The regulations under §167, further, deal separately with intangibles, stating:

> If an intangible asset is known from experience or other factors to be of use in the business or in the production of income for only a limited period, the length of which can be estimated with reasonable accuracy, such an intangible asset may be the subject of a depreciation allowance. Examples are patents and copyrights. An intangible asset, the useful life of which is not limited, is not subject to the allowance for depreciation. No allowance will be permitted merely because, in the unsupported opinion of the taxpayer, the intangible asset has a limited useful life. No deduction for depreciation is allowable with respect to goodwill.[40]

The requirement that an intangible asset's useful life be subject to a reasonably accurate estimate and the regulations' disdain for the taxpayer's "unsupported opinion" are not repeated when the regulations deal with the depreciation of tangible assets.[41] This difference in tone seems to induce

---

[39] Compare Kansas City S. Ry. v. CIR, 76 TC 1067 (1981) (grading of rail roadways held depreciable because useful life adequately established by statistical methods taking both obsolescence and physical deterioration into account) with Burlington N., Inc. v. US, 676 F2d 566 (Ct. Cl. 1982) (depreciation denied for railroad grading and tunnel bores; taxpayer's statistical method (called "pompous pseudoscience" by concurring judge) was inadequate to establish reasonably ascertainable useful life).

[40] Reg. §1.167(a)-3. See generally Broenen & Reed, Amortizing Intangible Assets: Setting a Cost Basis and Determinable Life, 44 J. Tax'n 130 (1976); Broenen & Reed, Amortizing Intangible Assets: Effect of Going Concern Value and Abandonment, 44 J. Tax'n 331 (1976); Dubin, Allocation of Costs to, and Amortization of, Intangibles in Business Acquisitions, 57 Taxes 930 (1979); McDonald, Goodwill and the Federal Income Tax, 45 Va. L. Rev. 645 (1959); Schenk, Depreciation of Intangible Assets: The Uncertainty of Death and Taxes, 13 Wayne L. Rev. 501 (1967); Note, Depreciability of Going Concern Value, 122 U. Pa. L. Rev. 484 (1973); Note, Amortization of Intangibles: An Examination of the Tax Treatment of Purchased Goodwill, 81 Harv. L. Rev. 859 (1968).

[41] Reg. §1.167(a)-2.

greater severity at the audit level in examining deductions for the depreciation of intangibles than when tangible property is involved, despite the absence of explicit statutory support for distinguishing between them. These obstacles are probably attributable to certain facts of life, discussed below, rather than to the language of the regulations or the perversity of revenue agents.

1. *Immunity of intangibles to physical decay.* Although the physical life of virtually every tangible asset is adversely affected by the passage of time and by wear and tear in the taxpayer's business, intangibles are immune to physical forces. Unless limited in duration by statute or contract or so closely linked to a physical asset as to be rendered worthless by its retirement from service,[42] they might be unaffected by the mere passage of time. Because intangibles lack a built-in guarantee of physical deterioration, the taxpayer must establish that public taste or similar socioeconomic forces—which are more debatable and less susceptible to proof than physical forces—will cause the intangible to be retired from service and, what is even more difficult, establish a reasonable date for this event.[43]

Intangible assets whose legal life is limited by statute (e.g., patents and copyrights) or contract (e.g., contracts not to compete, leaseholds, and life estates) constitute major exceptions to these generalizations.[44] The legal limit on the life of such assets establishes an outer limit on the property's economic life. This does not preclude proof of a shorter useful life, attributable to foreseeable economic forces that will result in retirement of the intangible before its legal death. If the taxpayer is content to depreciate the asset over its legal life, however, the statute or contract is ordinarily the only evidence required to establish the asset's wasting character.[45] Although a

---

[42] See Panhandle E. Pipe Line Co. v. US, 408 F2d 690 (Ct. Cl. 1969) (easements depreciable over useful life of related pipeline); Chesapeake & Ohio Ry. v. CIR, 64 TC 352 (1975) (tunnel bores depreciable).

[43] See Liquid Paper Corp. v. US, 2 Cl. Ct. 284, 83-1 USTC ¶9305 (1983) (limited useful life established for secret formula for typewriter correction fluid; technological advances were eroding formula's value); Pennsylvania Power & Light Co. v. US, 411 F2d 1300 (Ct. Cl. 1969) (limited useful life established for easements even though they were valid under local law until abandoned). In unusual circumstances, a taxpayer may be able to establish that an intangible has become embodied in a tangible asset with a demonstrably limited life. See Texas Instruments, Inc. v. US, 551 F2d 599 (5th Cir. 1977) (cost of seismic information includable in cost of tangible personal property for investment credit purposes); Walt Disney Prods. v. US, 549 F2d 576 (9th Cir. 1976) (master film negatives).

[44] See infra notes 65–69 for special problems in depreciating life estates.

[45] See Reg. §1.162-11(a) (payment for leasehold); Reg. §1.167(a)-3 (patents and copyrights); Bell v. Harrison, 212 F2d 253 (7th Cir. 1954) (purchased life estate); Rev. Rul. 68-636, 1968-2 CB 92 (covenant not to compete). See also Securities-Intermountain, Inc. v. US, 460 F2d 261 (9th Cir. 1972) (amount paid for right to

covenant not to compete or other intangible of limited duration sometimes enables the protected business to entrench itself as securely as though the protection had a perpetual life, the IRS has evidently not attempted to deny depreciation on this ground.

An intangible's limited legal life is an inappropriate measure of its useful life, however, if it can be renewed repeatedly at the taxpayer's option or if experience indicates that renewal applications will be granted more or less as a matter of course. In *Nachman v. CIR*, for example, a taxpayer who paid $8,000 for a one-year city liquor license that had cost the original licensee $750 was denied the right to depreciate the premium because new licenses were not available and an existing license "carried with it by established custom, if not by law, a valuable renewal privilege."[46] Thus, the

---

service mortgage loans depreciable over average life of loan portfolio); Western Mortgage Corp. v. US, 308 F. Supp. 333 (CD Cal. 1969) (right to service existing mortgages held depreciable; investment divided between this depreciable right and nondepreciable right to service future loans, the useful life of which could not be estimated with reasonable accuracy); Lemmen v. CIR, 77 TC 1326 (1981) (acq.) (where purchaser of cattle made lump-sum payment to person who contracted to care for cattle, payment amortized over life of contract, plus renewal periods).

For problems in determining the amount to be allocated to a covenant not to compete or other depreciable intangible on the purchase of a going business, see supra ¶4.4.4 and infra ¶51.9.3; Winchell Co. v. CIR, 51 TC 657 (1969) (covenant not to compete not separable from purchased goodwill; depreciation denied).

When a taxpayer pays to be relieved of a contractual burden, the payment is ordinarily depreciable over the period that the rescinded agreement would have been in effect. See Rodeway Inns of Am. v. CIR, 63 TC 414 (1974) (acq.) (payment by grantor of franchise to compensate franchisee for terminating agreement depreciable over 5-year period, where evidence indicated that agreement, with 2- to 25-year life, would have remained in force not more than 5 years); Trustee Corp. v. CIR, 42 TC 482 (1964) (payment by lessor to lessee for cancellation of lease depreciable over unexpired period of lease). Compare Handlery Hotels, Inc. v. US, 663 F2d 892 (9th Cir. 1981) (payment made to old tenant to cancel lease so that taxpayer could make new lease with new tenant; held, payment amortized over remaining term of old lease), with Montgomery Co. v. CIR, 54 TC 986 (1970) (acq.) (similar payment held depreciable over life of new lease).

[46] Nachman v. CIR, 191 F2d 934, 935 (5th Cir. 1951). See also Richmond Television Corp. v. US, 354 F2d 410 (4th Cir. 1965) (costs incurred in anticipation of FCC license not depreciable, despite three-year legal life, because of high probability of renewal); Dobson v. US, 551 F. Supp. 1152 (Cl. Ct. (1982) (franchise agreements had no ascertainable useful life because they were renewable and "possessed strong prospects of continuity beyond the terms provided for in them"); Uecker v. CIR, 81 TC 983 (1983), aff'd per curiam, 766 F2d 909 (5th Cir. 1985) (grazing privileges on federal land not depreciable because regulations and policies gave taxpayers preferential rights to renew grazing privileges); Rev. Rul. 64-124, 1964-1 (part 1) CB 105 (same as to costs of obtaining FCC license). But see Chronicle Publishing Co. v. CIR, 67 TC 964 (1977) (acq.) (cable TV franchises depreciable despite potential renewal; see id. at 984–85 for possibility that renewals would create new assets rather than perpetuate old ones).

taxpayer's outlay "bought not only the operating right for the current year but also renewal privileges for future years."[47]

In a similar case the taxpayer was denied the right to depreciate its investment in a two-year affiliation contract with a national television network, which was subject to an unlimited number of automatic renewals in the absence of an affirmative act of termination by either party, despite expert testimony that the average life expectancy of any given contract could be determined by applying statistical theory to the industry's actual experience.[48] Reversing the Tax Court, which had held that this evidence justified an estimated 20-year life, the court of appeals concluded that "each contract is more unique than generic, which makes it questionable whether any meaningful general experience could ever be shown."[49] On the other hand, the IRS has ruled that renewable one-year professional football player contracts may be depreciated over their useful lives, which presupposes acceptance by the IRS of a method of estimating their duration notwithstanding the many variables that enter into the annual renegotiation process.[50] These two situations might be distinguished on the ground that whereas all football players are mortal, statistical evidence on industry experience with network affiliation contracts does not negate the possibility that a particular contractual relationship may continue indefinitely.

---

[47] A renewal provision can be disregarded, however, if it is unlikely to be exercised. See Birmingham News Co. v. Patterson, 224 F. Supp. 670 (ND Ala. 1963), aff'd per curiam, 345 F2d 531 (5th Cir. 1965) (automatic renewal unless either party gave notice of termination); Aiken Drive-In Theatre Corp. v. CIR, 15 TCM (CCH) 684 (1956) (same); Rodeway Inns of Am. v. CIR, supra note 45. For renewal options in leases, see supra ¶23.1.9.

[48] CIR v. Indiana Broadcasting Corp., 350 F2d 580 (7th Cir. 1965), cert. denied, 382 US 1027 (1966). See McCarthy v. US, 807 F2d 1306 (6th Cir. 1986) (baseball team's rights under broadcasting contracts not depreciable, even though contracts were for fixed terms, because "the current broadcasting contracts . . . are merely links in a perpetual chain of broadcasting contracts"); Roy H. Park Broadcasting, Inc. v. CIR, 78 TC 1093 (1982) (no depreciation on network affiliation contracts because taxpayer failed to establish estimated useful lives with reasonable accuracy). But see Super Food Servs., Inc. v. US, 416 F2d 1236 (7th Cir. 1969) (depreciation allowed on grocery store franchise contracts on basis of taxpayer's statistical evidence of duration).

[49] CIR v. Indiana Broadcasting Corp., supra note 48, at 583.

[50] Rev. Rul. 71-137, 1971-1 CB 104. See Laird v. US, 556 F2d 1224 (5th Cir. 1977), cert. denied, 434 US 1014 (1978) (useful life of 5.25 years held reasonable for particular team); KFOX, Inc. v. US, 510 F2d 1365 (Ct. Cl. 1975) (disc jockey contracts depreciable); First Northwest Indus. of Am., Inc. v. CIR, 70 TC 817 (1978), rev'd on other issues, 649 F2d 707 (9th Cir. 1981) (professional football players); Rev. Rul. 67-379, 1967-2 CB 127 (baseball player contracts depreciable). See also IRC §1056 (limiting amount of purchase price of team that can be allocated to player contracts); Selig v. US, 565 F. Supp. 524 (ED Wis. 1983) (extensive discussion of allocation problem apart from §1056).

2. *Absence of IRS guidelines for life of intangible assets.* When seeking to prove that an intangible asset's useful life is limited by anticipated obsolescence or other economic forces, the taxpayer faces an obstacle not encountered when depreciation is claimed for machinery, equipment, and similar tangible assets—the absence of IRS guidelines for establishing the asset's useful life.[51]

3. *Goodwill.* The difficulty of establishing a limited useful life for goodwill is elevated in the regulations to a rule of law that "no deduction for depreciation is allowable with respect to goodwill."[52] Were it not for this discouraging announcement, taxpayers would undoubtedly flood the IRS and the courts with claims that could not stand up under scrutiny; thus, the regulations serve to nip these foredoomed hopes in the bud. Satisfactory proof that goodwill has a limited useful life is feasible, however, in unusual circumstances—for example, goodwill associated with a physical asset, such as a highly advertised source of mineral water or a cave open to tourists that is subject to exhaustion or collapse in the foreseeable future. It is not clear, however, that the regulations would be interpreted to permit a deduction even on facts like these.[53]

4. *Customers' lists, etc.—the "mass asset" theory.* For the ordinary taxpayer, the status of goodwill in the rare situation permitting a reasonably accurate estimate of its useful life is of less importance than the uncertain scope of the term "goodwill"—in particular, its impact on the right to depreciate lists of customers and other records, acquired when a going business is purchased, that would be costly to create from scratch. If the price paid to acquire an enterprise exceeds the value of its physical assets, it is clear that an appropriate portion of the excess may be allocated to pat-

---

[51] See ABA Tax Section Recommendation No. 1975-1, 28 Tax Lawyer 1027 (1975), recommending legislation to permit amortization of the cost of intangibles failing to qualify for depreciation or amortization solely because the asset's useful life cannot be estimated with reasonable accuracy. The proposal applied to goodwill, going concern value, covenants not to compete without a specified term, secret processes and formulas, contract rights, customer lists, franchises with indefinite lives, and reorganization, recapitalization, and stock issue expenses.

[52] Reg. §1.167(a)-3. In Williams v. McGowan, 152 F2d 570 (2d Cir. 1945), Judge Learned Hand described goodwill as "a depreciable intangible," but this conclusion has not gained acceptance. For problems in the valuation of goodwill and other intangibles, see Forward Communications Corp. v. US, 608 F2d 485 (Ct. Cl. 1979).

[53] The regulations have denied depreciation to goodwill since 1927 (see TD 4055, VI-2 CB 63), following Red Wing Malting Co. v. Willcuts, 15 F2d 626 (8th Cir. 1926), cert. denied, 273 US 763 (1927) (depreciation deduction denied for goodwill of distillery forced out of business by national prohibition); Haberle Crystal Springs Brewing Co. v. Clarke, 280 US 384, 386 (1930) (same result, but on ground that Congress did not intend "partial compensation in the form of an abatement of taxes otherwise due" for a business whose continuation was regarded as "noxious").

ents, copyrights, leaseholds, covenants not to compete, and similar identifiable assets that can be separated from the newly acquired goodwill. Can anything, however, be allocated to lists of customers, subscription lists, insurance expirations, patient's records, and similar materials serving to preserve the clientele of the business?

The difficulty is that these assets are the documentary evidence of the "customer structure" that is usually regarded as the very core of goodwill.[54] Indeed, an important early development in the tax law was a series of cases assimilating such assets to goodwill for several purposes,[55] and treating them as unitary assets that retained their character even though the individual names constantly changed as old customers were lost and new ones were added.[56] Emphasizing this close link (if not actual overlap) between goodwill and lists of customers and similar intangibles, the IRS has customarily rejected attempts to depreciate such "mass assets," on the ground that they have a value of indefinite duration even if all the original customers drop out. Since taxpayers ordinarily deduct advertising and other expenditures incurred in adding names to customer lists, it is not surprising that the IRS views them as continuing entities.

After an extended review of the cases, however, the Court of Appeals for the Fifth Circuit concluded in *Houston Chronicle Publishing Co. v. United States*:

> [T]he "mass asset" rule does not prevent taking an amortization deduction if the taxpayer properly carries his dual burden of proving that the intangible asset involved (1) has an ascertainable value separate and distinct from goodwill, and (2) has a limited useful life, the duration of which can be ascertained with reasonable accuracy.[57]

---

[54] Accountants' Handbook 19-14 et seq. (Wixon, Kell & Bedford, eds.; Ronald Press, 5th ed. 1970); Note, Amortization of Intangibles: An Examination of the Tax Treatment of Purchased Goodwill, supra note 40, at 866.

[55] See Pevely Dairy Co. v. CIR, 1 BTA 385, 390 (1925) (acq.) (payment for retail milk routes, measured by number of customers obtained and retained for specified period, "resulted in the acquisition of a capital asset the principal element of which was goodwill"; hence a nondeductible capital outlay); Herald-Despatch Co. v. CIR, 4 BTA 1096, 1105 (1926) (acq.) (newspaper's circulation "possesses many of the attributes of good will, and yet comprises other elements not common to the latter"; cost includable in invested capital in computing excess profits tax); Commercial Nat'l Ins. Co. v. CIR, 12 BTA 655 (1928) (March 1, 1913 value of industrial insurance agent's "weekly debits" recognized in computing gain on sale of business).

[56] See, e.g., Commercial Nat'l Ins. Co. v. CIR, supra note 55. On selling a list of customers, taxpayers claiming long-term capital gains treatment can more easily establish that the asset was held for the requisite holding period if it is viewed as a single property than if the cost and holding period must be proved name by name.

[57] Houston Chronicle Publishing Co. v. US, 481 F2d 1240, 1250 (5th Cir. 1973), cert. denied, 414 US 1129 (1974). See Laird v. US, 556 F2d 1224 (5th Cir. 1977),

Although the opinion does not say so explicitly, the "limited useful life" standard can presumably be met by showing that the old customers will be lost within a predictable period of time, even if the taxpayer succeeds in getting new customers to replace them. Otherwise, depreciation would be restricted to businesses in a state of decline.

Following *Houston Chronicle Publishing Co.*, the IRS modified its posture by ruling that customer and subscription lists, location contracts, insurance expirations, and similar items are not indistinguishable from goodwill as a matter of law, thus clearing the way to a depreciation deduction if, as a factual matter, the taxpayer can satisfy the standards set out in that decision.[58] The ruling, however, goes on to dampen the taxpayer's optimism by announcing that "generally" these assets "are in the nature of goodwill" because they "represent the customer structure of a business, their value lasting until an indeterminate time in the future." This seems to imply continued adherence by the IRS to the theory that customer lists and similar assets are "self-regenerating" if the company is able to attract new customers to replace old ones.

The courts, however, have been applying more liberal principles, allowing taxpayers to depreciate customer lists, business records, and similar intangibles if a limited useful life can be plausibly established.[59] If the

---

cert. denied, 434 US 1014 (1978) (rejecting mass-asset theory as to football players' contracts); First Northwest Indus. of Am., Inc. v. CIR, 70 TC 817, 846–47 (1978) (same).

[58] Rev. Rul. 74-456, 1974-2 CB 65.

[59] See Richard S. Miller & Sons v. US, 537 F2d 446 (Ct. Cl. 1976) (insurance expirations separable from goodwill; limited useful life established); Los Angeles Cent. Animal Hosp., Inc. v. CIR, 68 TC 269 (1977) (acq.) (medical records of veterinary hospital distinguished from goodwill embodied in location, trade name, and continued patronage of neighborhood customers; amount allocable to records depreciable over seven-year period); Computing & Software, Inc. v. CIR, 64 TC 223 (1975) (acq.) (credit information files separable from goodwill since they had no relationship to preexisting business relationships and same information was sold to both old and new customers; six-year useful life); Holden Fuel Oil Co. v. CIR, 31 TCM (CCH) 184 (1972), aff'd per curiam, 479 F2d 613 (6th Cir. 1973) (75 percent of cost of list of retail customers allocated to wasting asset, depreciable over 15 years, and 25 percent to nondepreciable goodwill); Manhattan Co. of Va., Inc. v. CIR, 50 TC 78 (1968) (acq.) (similar 75-25 allocation of cost of laundry list; five-year life). See also Smith v. CIR, 36 TCM (CCH) 932 (1977) (IRS allowed amount paid by pathologist for professional practice to be depreciated over 15 years; dictum that proper period is purchaser's life expectancy). For recent cases disallowing depreciation deductions for intangibles in the nature of goodwill, see Ralph W. Fullerton Co. v. US, 550 F2d 548 (9th Cir. 1977) (no showing that assets in question were separable from goodwill); AmSouth Bancorporation v. US, 681 F. Supp. 698 (ND Ala. 1988) (bank's "customer deposit base" not depreciable because taxpayer failed to show value separate from goodwill); General Television, Inc. v. US, 449 F. Supp. 609, 612 (D. Minn. 1978), aff'd per curiam, 598 F2d 1148 (9th Cir. 1979) (subscriber

business also possesses assets of indefinite duration that command customer loyalty, such as a distinctive trade name and favorable location, part of the purchase price must be assigned to these items, and only the portion properly allocable to the wasting items may be depreciated.

Although customers' names are usually recorded in some tangible form, the asset is customarily described as "intangible." If the tangible evidence of the names is itself perishable, however, an appropriate part of the taxpayer's investment could be depreciated under the rules applicable to the physical asset. This is usually a de minimis amount.[60]

5. *Going concern value.* The courts have frequently recognized that the purchaser of a going business obtains more than "a congeries of uncoordinated physical assets" and that a premium is ordinarily paid for "assurance that the plant and equipment would all work together without need of costly and time-consuming adjustments and coordination."[61] Although sometimes categorized as goodwill, going concern value is actually an independent intangible. For example, an operating plant may be worth more than the sum of its parts, even if the business has been unprofitable in the past or is so new that it has not yet generated any goodwill. On purchasing a going business for a lump sum, taxpayers have customarily sought to establish the existence of a going concern value in order to increase the basis of the depreciable assets at the expense of nondepreciable goodwill and other intangibles. Several recent cases have held that the going concern value does not inhere in the tangible assets but is independent of and will outlive them, that its duration is indefinite, and that it may not be depreciated.[62]

---

contracts of purchased cable TV companies were "customer structures which included the expectancy of continued patronage," not distinguishable from goodwill); Robins & Weill, Inc. v. US, 382 F. Supp. 1207 (MDNC 1974) (insurance expirations had limited useful life, but cost not adequately separated from goodwill); Imperial News Co. v. US, 576 F. Supp. 865 (EDNY 1983) (purchaser of local magazine distribution business not allowed to depreciate distribution contracts because they were terminable at will and thus were nothing more than an expectation that publishers and national distributors would continue dealing with taxpayer). See also Sunset Fuel Co. v. US, 519 F2d 781 (9th Cir. 1975) (loss deduction under §165 denied for amounts allocated by taxpayer to individual accounts of customers who discontinued patronage); Rev. Proc. 75-39, 1975-2 CB 569 (method of allocating lump sum purchase price for radio and TV broadcasting stations between depreciable assets and nondepreciable goodwill, FCC license, and network affiliation contracts).

[60] But see Texas Instruments, Inc. v. US, 551 F2d 599 (5th Cir. 1977), and Walt Disney Prods. v. US, 549 F2d 576 (9th Cir. 1976), discussed supra note 43.

[61] Miami Valley Broadcasting Corp. v. US, 499 F2d 677, 680 (Ct. Cl. 1974).

[62] Id.; Concord Control, Inc. v. CIR, 78 TC 742 (1982) (acq.). See also Solitron Devices, Inc. v. CIR, 80 TC 1 (1983) (extensive analysis of nature of goodwill and its relation to going concern value). See generally Grigsby & Cotter, Amortization of Certain Intangibles, 1978 S. Cal. Tax Inst. 543, 555-70; Wiener, Going Concern Value: Goodwill by Another Name? 53 Tax Lawyer 183 (1979).

6. *Allocation of lump-sum purchase price.* When property is acquired for a lump sum, the buyer must allocate the purchase price among the acquired assets in proportion to their respective market values in order to compute depreciation and gain or loss on subsequent sales and other dispositions. Because market quotations are rarely available, especially for the components of a going business, controversy with the IRS regarding the validity of the taxpayer's allocation is almost inevitable. Although a lump-sum payment must be allocated whether the acquired assets are tangible or intangible, the problem arises more frequently when intangibles are involved, for two reasons. First, intangibles created by the taxpayer's own activities usually have an adjusted basis of zero because the asset came into being without a direct outlay of funds or as a result of deductible expenditures.[63] Thus, there is ordinarily no basis to be depreciated unless the asset was purchased, usually as part of a going business, the cost being a debatable portion of a lump-sum purchase price. Second, the allocation of large amounts to customer lists and other intangibles whose depreciability is debatable often stimulates the IRS to contend that most if not all of the amount so allocated represents the nondepreciable cost of goodwill.

7. *Franchises, trademarks, and trade names.* Section 1253, enacted in 1969, denies capital gains treatment to amounts received on the transfer of franchises, trademarks, and trade names, subject to qualifications discussed elsewhere in this work.[64] As explained therein, a corollary of the adverse treatment of the transferor is that the transferee may deduct periodic payments for the transferred item and may amortize lump-sum payments over a period of years.

8. *Life estates and terms of years.* A purchaser of a term interest, including a life estate, may usually amortize his basis ratably over the expected life of the interest.[65] Taxpayers have occasionally tried to exploit this rule to make depreciation effectively allowable with respect to nondepreciable property. Assume a parent purchases a life estate in a tract of land, and his children simultaneously purchase the remainder from the seller. The general rule would allow the parent to amortize the amount paid for the life estate over his life expectancy. If the parent had followed the more common practice of purchasing the land and leaving it to his children at death, in contrast, no depreciation or amortization would be allowable. The life-estate/remainder example comes especially close to the more common

---

[63] For the practice of deducting advertising expenses even if they generate long-lived goodwill, see supra ¶20.4.5. But see Durovic v. CIR, 542 F2d 1328 (7th Cir. 1976) (cost of free samples capitalized; amortization denied in absence of proof of useful life of benefits).

[64] Infra ¶52.5.1.

[65] E.g., Early v. CIR, 445 F2d 166 (5th Cir. 1971).

practice if, shortly before the purchase, the parent makes a gift to the children of money the children then use to buy the remainder.

The Tax Court has limited the depreciation of term interests in two recent cases. In *Lomas Santa Fe, Inc. v. CIR*, an owner of land conveyed the land, subject to a retained term of years for 40 years, to a wholly owned corporation.[66] The owner allocated his basis for the land between the retained term of years and the transferred remainder, and amortized the former over the 40-year period. The amortization deduction, however, was denied. In the court's view, a term interest may not be depreciated when the underlying property is nondepreciable and has been split by its owner into two interests without any new investment. This principle would apply, for example, if a landowner conveyed a remainder interest to her children, retaining an estate for her life; whether she had held the land for many years or purchased it just prior to the conveyance to the children would not affect the result.

The second case, *Gordon v. CIR*, is even closer to the example first assumed.[67] On several occasions, the taxpayer purchased life interests in tax-exempt bonds, while the remainder interests were simultaneously purchased by trusts he had created. The taxpayer claimed amortization deductions for the amounts he paid for his life interests. One hurdle—that the deductions were seemingly attributable to tax-exempt income, thus falling into the clutches of §265(a)(1), disallowing deductions for expenses allocable to tax-exempt income—was cleared by earlier decisions holding that §265(a)(1) does not apply to deductions for depreciation and amortization.[68] The Tax Court nevertheless denied the deductions because it found the substance of the transactions was that Gordon had purchased the bonds outright and had then transferred the remainder interests to the trusts. Under *Lomas Santa Fe*, such a splitting of interests in nondepreciable property does not make the amortization deduction available.

The *Gordon* opinion suggests that the step transaction doctrine may have a broad application in this context:

> In the context of a simultaneous, joint acquisition from a third party, it is appropriate to take into account the fact that the participation of the acquirer of the remainder interest is an essential element in affording the acquirer of the income interest the opportunity to obtain the tax benefit of an amortization deduction. This is particularly significant where the acquirer of the income interest and the acquirer of the

---

[66] Lomas Santa Fe, Inc. v. CIR, 74 TC 662 (1980), aff'd, 693 F2d 71 (9th Cir. 1982), cert. denied, 460 US 1083 (1983).

[67] Gordon v. CIR, 85 TC 309 (1985).

[68] E.g., Early v. CIR, supra note 65. See supra ¶22.7 for §265(a)(1).

remainder interest are related persons.[69]

9. *Vocational training.* As explained elsewhere in this work, the cost of vocational training could in theory be allocated over the taxpayer's business career, to be amortized during his productive years and deducted on retirement or death to the extent not previously written off. In practice, however, the IRS and the courts have not allowed taxpayers to write off their investments in human capital.[70]

¶23.3 ACCELERATED COST RECOVERY SYSTEM FOR PROPERTY PLACED IN SERVICE AFTER 1981

¶23.3.1 Introductory

Section 168, which establishes the accelerated cost recovery system, was enacted in 1981 and, after being repeatedly amended in various particulars, was extensively revised and restated in 1986.[1] Most tangible property, real and personal, placed in service after 1981 is only depreciable under ACRS. Intangibles, in contrast, cannot be depreciated under ACRS, and remain subject to the pre-ACRS rules under §167.

Congress' objective in enacting ACRS in 1981 was to provide more rapid write offs and to simplify the depreciation system. Prior law, it was concluded, did not "provide the investment stimulus that is essential for economic expansion."[2] In part, this was due to the effects of inflation:

> The real value of depreciation deductions allowed under [the pre-ACRS] rules has declined for several years due to successively higher rates of inflation. Reductions in the real value of depreciation deductions diminish the profitability of investment and discourage businesses from replacing old equipment and structures with more modern assets that reflect recent technology.[3]

---

[69] Gordon v. CIR, supra note 67, at 325.

[70] See supra ¶22.1.1.

[1] The version of §168 described in the text is that enacted in 1986, which generally applies to property placed in service after 1986; taxpayers, however, may elect to have it apply to property placed in service during the last six months of 1986. Pub. L. No. 99-514, §203(a)(1), 100 Stat. 2085 (1986). The effective date rules are modified by general transition rules for property in the pipeline on March 1, 1986, and by numerous "additional transitional rules." Pub. L. No. 99-514, supra, §§203(b), 204. See Staff of Joint Comm. on Tax'n, 99th Cong., 2d Sess., General Explanation of Tax Reform Act of 1986, at 110–26 (Comm. Print 1987) [hereinafter 1986 Bluebook].

[2] S. Rep. No. 144, 97th Cong., 1st Sess. 47 (1981).

[3] Id.

Also, there was a desire to tilt the economic balance in favor of savings: "[A] substantial restructuring of depreciation deductions," Congress thought, would be "an effective way of stimulating capital formation, increasing productivity and improving the nation's competitiveness in international trade."[4]

Prior law was "unnecessarily complicated," Congress concluded, because it required "determinations on matters, such as useful life and salvage value, which are inherently uncertain and, thus, too frequently result in unproductive disagreements between taxpayers and the Internal Revenue Service."[5] Also, prior law provided numerous elections between systems and methods, which could not be intelligently evaluated without substantial knowledge and skill. The capital cost recovery system avoids these complexities if it "de-emphasizes the concept of useful life, minimizes the number of elections and exceptions, and so is easier to comply with and to administer.[6]

Congress' principal technique for achieving these goals was to group most depreciable property into a small number of classes and allow property within each class to be depreciated over a recovery period usually much shorter than the economic useful life of the property. Under the 1981 legislation, most depreciable tangible personal property is placed into two classes, three-year property and five-year property, with recovery periods of three and five years, respectively. The division of various assets between these two classes is based on the useful life guidelines promulgated by the IRS under prior law; the class lives provided by these guidelines, however, were made mandatory for purposes of the ACRS classifications, leaving no room for argument over the issue of useful life, and the recovery period for each ACRS category was made shorter than the class lives of most of the property included in the category. Most real property was placed in a single class that was depreciable over 15 years; in this context also, the concept of useful life disappeared. Tables were provided that allow depreciation for a particular year to be computed as a prescribed percentage of the property's original cost. The percentages for all years always add up to 100 percent; salvage value thus is always ignored.

The 1981 rules were amended in 1982, 1984, and 1985, most significantly to increase the recovery period for real property to 18 years and then to 19 years.[7]

---

[4] Id.

[5] Id.

[6] Id.

[7] The real property recovery period was increased to 18 years because the 15-year recovery period was believed to be excessively fueling real estate tax shelters. Staff of Joint Comm. on Tax'n, 98th Cong., 2d Sess., General Explanation of the Revenue Provisions of the Deficit Reduction Act of 1984, at 326–27 (Comm. Print 1984). The increase to 19 years was made to raise revenue to pay for unrelated

The rules were restated in 1986, to apply to property placed in service after that year. Under the 1986 version of ACRS, personal property is divided among 6 classes with recovery periods ranging from 3 to 20 years. Real property is grouped into two classes, residential rental property and nonresidential real property, with recovery periods of 27.5 and 31.5 years. Generally, the 1986 recovery periods are intended to more closely approximate economic useful life, although some acceleration was retained, particularly for personal property. The tables of 1981–1986 law are replaced with rules requiring the use of depreciation methods. Real property, which is most severely treated by the 1986 amendments, must be depreciated by the straight line method, but the 200 percent declining method is used for most personal property. As under the 1981 rules, salvage value is always ignored.

The 1986 amendments reflect the general approach of the Tax Reform Act of 1986 to make taxes a more neutral presence in the economy. "Congress believed ACRS could be made more neutral by increasing the recovery period for certain long-lived equipment, and by extending the recovery period of real property."[8] The neutrality premise of the 1986 Act thus represents a complete turnabout from the philosophy of the 1981 legislation —that economic growth could be promoted by targeting particular types of investment for favorable tax treatment.

¶23.3.2 Property Subject to ACRS; Antichurning Rules

Section 168 applies to most tangible property. It applies to no intangible property, which continues to be depreciable, if at all, under the rules existing before the enactment of ACRS.

Section 168(f), further, excludes a few items of tangible property from ACRS. To preserve pre-ACRS rules authorizing some methods of depreciation that are not expressed in terms of years, §168 is inapplicable to property depreciated by such a method.[9] The units-of-production method is the most common method covered by this rule.[10] Other excepted property includes certain public utility property, motion picture films, video tapes, and sound recordings.[11] Motion picture films and video tapes are depreciable under §167(a), usually by an income forecast method.

---

revenue-losing provisions enacted simultaneously. H.R. Rep. No. 87, 99th Cong., 1st Sess. 12 (1985).

[8] 1986 Bluebook, supra note 1, at 98.

[9] IRC §168(f)(1). See infra ¶23.6.6 for these methods.

[10] "For example, depreciation is allowable with respect to landfills on a unit basis (without regard to whether the space for dumping waste was excavated by the taxpayer), to the extent capital costs are properly allocable to the space to be filled with waste rather than to the underlying land." 1986 Bluebook, supra note 1, at 100.

[11] IRC §§168(f)(2), (3), (4).

Also, property is sometimes excluded from ACRS (or shifted from post-1986 ACRS to 1981–1986 ACRS) by antichurning rules that are intended to frustrate schemes for shuffling property among taxpayers in order to bring it within a more favorable depreciation regime. In the absence of these rules, a taxpayer owning property acquired before the ACRS rules were enacted might sell it to a family member or related corporation during a year covered by ACRS in order to allow the new owner to take depreciation under the more liberal ACRS rules. Or, the property might be sold to a friendly buyer subject to an understanding that it would be sold back to the taxpayer sometime later. In such cases, the antichurning rules generally make ACRS inapplicable to the property, thus forcing it back to the pre-ACRS rules. The antichurning rules also sometimes apply to property changing hands after 1986 where the property is more favorably treated under the post-1986 rules than under the 1981–1986 version of ACRS.

The antichurning rules make ACRS inapplicable to personal property where (1) the property is acquired by the taxpayer in a post-1980 transaction, but was owned or used by the taxpayer at some time during 1980 or was owned or used during 1980 by a person related to the taxpayer,[12] (2) the property is purchased from the 1980 owner in a post-1980 transaction in which the user does not change (typically, property held as lessee in 1980 but later purchased from the lessor), and (3) the property is leased by the taxpayer to a person who owned the property in 1980 (typically, property purchased after 1980 from the 1980 owner in a sale-leaseback transaction).[13]

For real property, the second of the foregoing transactions is not disqualifying, but another disqualification is added: If real property is acquired in a nonrecognition exchange under §1031, 1033, 1038, or 1039, ACRS is inapplicable to any portion of the basis of the property that traces back to property held by the taxpayer or a related person in 1980.[14] If a taxpayer exchanges a building held in 1980 for another building in a post-1980 like-kind exchange qualifying for nonrecognition under §1031, for example, ACRS is unavailable with respect to the portion of the basis of the property received in the exchange that is inherited from the property given in the exchange under the exchanged basis rule of §1031(d).

Also, for both personal and real property, the disqualification extends to the case where (1) the taxpayer is a corporation or partnership and (2) the property is received in an organization, reorganization, or liquidation transaction that is encompassed by a nonrecognition provision coupled with a transferred basis rule. In this case, the disqualification only applies to the

---

[12] The term "related person" includes family members and entities contolled by the taxpayer or vice versa. IRC §168(e)(4)(D) (before amendment in 1986).

[13] IRC §168(e)(4)(A) (before amendment in 1986).

[14] IRC §168(e)(4)(B) (before amendment in 1986).

portion of the taxpayer's basis that traces back to the basis of a prior owner as of the end of 1980.[15] If the 1980 owner of property transfers it after 1980 to a corporation solely in exchange for stock and if the transaction is covered by the nonrecognition rule of §351(a), for example, the corporation is not eligible for ACRS. If gain is partially recognized by the transferor because he receives money in addition to stock of the corporation, in contrast, the corporation can use ACRS with respect to the addition to its adjusted basis that is made under §362(a) to reflect the boot.

The foregoing rules, although designed to frustrate manipulation, apply without regard to purpose. If the 1980 owner of property sells it and later buys it back, for example, ACRS is unavailable whether the sale and later repurchase were made for the purpose of getting ACRS deductions or for a purpose wholly unrelated to taxes. Lest any possibility of evasion be missed, however, a purpose rule is also included; property not caught by any of the foregoing rules is disqualified if it was acquired after 1980 and one of the principal purposes of the transaction was to avoid the rule denying ACRS to property placed in service before 1981.[16]

When ACRS was revised in 1986, Congress anticipated that taxpayers might churn property in order to take it out of the jurisdiction of the 1981–1986 ACRS rules and bring it within the ambit of the post-1986 rules. The 1986 amendments therefore require that the antichurning rules be applied twice to property acquired after 1986—once as the rules are written and described above, and a second time substituting "1985" for "1980."[17] If any of the tests is failed with the 1985 date, but not with the 1980 date, depreciation is determined under the 1981–1986 version of ACRS. Thus, if property acquired after 1986 was owned by the taxpayer in 1980, depreciation is determined under the pre-ACRS rules, whereas if the property was owned by the taxpayer in 1985 but not in 1980, depreciation is allowable under the 1981–1986 rules.

Because the 1986 revisions generally make ACRS allowances less generous, the application of the rules with reference to 1985 would often give taxpayers more rapid depreciation. This not being intended, a further provision states that the reference to 1985 is not made when it would increase the taxpayer's ACRS allowance for the first post-1986 year the property is in service.[18] Since depreciation for real property is universally slowed down by the 1986 amendments, the reference to 1985 is never made for residential rental property or nonresidential real property.

---

[15] IRC §168(e)(4)(C) (before amendment in 1986).
[16] IRC §168(e)(4)(F).
[17] IRC §168(f)(5)(A).
[18] IRC §168(f)(5)(B).

¶23.3.3   Applicable Recovery Period Under 1986 Rules

Under present law, ACRS deductions are determined by allocating the cost of ACRS property over "the applicable recovery period," using "the applicable depreciation method," applied with "the applicable convention."[19] The terms "applicable depreciation method" and "applicable convention" are described in the next section. The term "applicable recovery period" is discussed here.

An item is typically assigned a recovery period according to its "class life."[20] Class lives are prescribed for most items of tangible personal property under revenue procedures issued by the IRS whose history traces back to the guideline lives prescribed under earlier depreciation systems.[21] Property with a class life of four years or less, for example, is called three-year property, and is given a recovery period of three years. Nearly all personal property and a few items of real property are divided into the six classes shown in Table 23-1.

Table 23-1

ACRS Recovery Periods

Class Name	Class Life	Recovery Period
3-year property	4 years or less	3 years
5-year property	More than 4 but less than 10 years	5 years
7-year property	10 to 16 years	7 years
10-year property	16 to 20 years	10 years
15-year property	20 to 25 years	15 years
20-year property	25 years or more	20 years

---

[19] The IRS has prescribed tables for determining depreciation deductions that shortcut some of the procedures and computations described below. Rev. Proc. 87-57, 1987-2 CB 687, at §8. Many of the rules must be understood, however, in order to know which table applies in a particular case.

[20] IRC §§168(c), (e)(1), (i)(1).

[21] The class lives are given in Revenue Procedure 87-56, 1987-2 CB 4, modified by Rev. Proc. 88-22, 1988-18 IRB 38. See infra ¶23.4.4 for their history. The Treasury is directed to "monitor and analyze actual experience with respect to all depreciable assets," and, when appropriate, modify the class lives of property and prescribe class lives for property for which there presently are none. IRC §168(i)(1)(B). For the factors to be considered in evaluating class lives (including class lives prescribed by statute, described below), see 1986 Bluebook, supra note 1, at 103–04.

A few types of property are assigned by statute to particular categories, thereby superseding the IRS class lives for this property.[22] For example, automobiles and light general purpose trucks, which have a class life of three years and thus would otherwise be three-year property, are specially classified as five-year property. Computers, peripheral equipment, and high technology medical equipment are also placed in the five-year category.[23] Other special assignments include equipment used in research and experimentation (five-year property), race horses more than two years old and other horses more than twelve years old (three-year property), semiconductor manufacturing equipment (five-year property), single purpose agricultural or horticultural structures (seven-year property),[24] and a variety of less common items.

Most real property has never been given a class life, and is covered by two additional ACRS classes: residential rental property and nonresidential real property, with recovery periods of 27.5 years and 31.5 years.[25] The term "residential rental property" includes a building, at least 80 percent of the gross income from which consists of rents from the rental of nontransient living accommodations.[26] "Nonresidential real property" is all depreciable real property other than (1) residential rental property and (2) property that has a class life of less than 27.5 years.[27] Real property other than residential rental property that has a class life of less than 27.5 years is placed in one of the six classes described in Table 23-1.

---

[22] IRC §168(e)(3). These special assignments can be altered by the Treasury, based on its monitoring and analysis of "actual experience with respect to all depreciable assets," but no change can apply to property placed in service before 1992. IRC §168(i).

[23] IRC §§168(e)(3)(B)(iv), (i)(2). This property is referred to in the statute as "qualified technological equipment." Id. "High technology telephone station equipment installed on the customer's premises" is also qualified technological equipment. Id.

[24] The term "single purpose agricultural or horticultural structure" includes structures for housing and feeding livestock (including poultry), structures for housing equipment used in connection with livestock, greenhouses, and structures "specifically designed" for use in raising mushrooms. IRC §48(p). Structures for storing farm produce and equipment used in raising grain crops are not included.

[25] The make up of these two classes is frozen. Although the Treasury has the power to prescribe a class life for property that now has none and can also change most statutorily assigned class lives, this authority does not extend to residential rental property or nonresidential real property. IRC §168(i)(1)(B).

[26] IRC §§167(j)(2)(B), 168(e)(2)(A). A house or apartment is considered nontransient unless it is "a unit in a hotel, motel, inn, or other establishment more than one-half of the units in which are used on a transient basis." IRC §167(k)(3)(C). If the taxpayer occupies any portion of the building, the 80 percent test is applied as though the taxpayer paid himself rent equal to the fair rental value of this portion. IRC §167(j)(2)(B).

[27] IRC §§168(e)(2)(B), 1250(c).

Several types of property that might be considered real are specially classified as personal, and are therefore excluded from the categories "residential rental property" and "nonresidential real property." Fixtures other than buildings and their structural components, for example, are treated as personal property, regardless of their classification under local law, if they are used in manufacturing or any one of several other activities.[28] Single purpose agricultural structures and storage facilities (other than buildings) of distributors of certain petroleum products are also classified as personal.[29] An item within one of the foregoing categories falls into one of the ACRS classifications shown in Table 23-1. A single purpose agricultural structure, for example, is seven-year property. In addition, in order to give various special amortization rules exclusive jurisdiction within their bailiwicks, the real property classification excludes property subject to these rules, including pollution control facilities amortized under §169, child care facilities amortized under §188, costs of removing barriers to the handicapped and elderly amortized under §190, and reforestation expenditures amortized under §194.[30]

Property that has not been given a class life and is not residential rental property or nonresidential real property is seven-year property.

An addition or improvement to depreciable property is given a recovery period the same length as that of the underlying property, but the recovery period for the addition or improvement begins when it is placed in service, not when the underlying property was placed in service.[31] Assume residential rental property is placed service in 1987, but is improved in 1991. The original cost is recovered over 27.5 years beginning with 1987, and the improvement costs are recovered over 27.5 years beginning with 1991.

Prior to 1981, buildings were sometimes depreciated by a component method under which many elements of a building (e.g., heating and air conditioning systems, plumbing, wiring, interior walls) were depreciated separately from the structure itself, usually with shorter recovery periods than those typically required for buildings as a whole.[32] The 1981–1986 ACRS rules explicitly ban this method, requiring that a building be depreciated as a single property over the recovery period assigned to it;[33] although this provision is omitted from the 1986 version, no change was intended.[34]

---

[28] IRC §§1245(a)(3)(B), 1250(c).

[29] IRC §§1245(a)(3)(C), (E); 1250(c).

[30] IRC §§1245(a)(3)(D); 1250(c). See infra ¶26.4.3 for §169, ¶26.4.8 for §188, ¶26.4.4 for §190, and ¶26.4.5 for §194.

[31] IRC §168(i)(6).

[32] See infra ¶23.3.7.

[33] IRC §168(f)(1) (before amendment in 1986).

[34] 1986 Bluebook, supra note 1, at 109.

The ACRS rules make no distinction between new and used property. The same recovery period applies to both new and used property within a particular class. An automobile used in business is depreciable over five years, for example, whether it is a new Mercedes expected to give a decade or more of relatively trouble free service or an old junker on temporary reprieve from the auto graveyard.

¶23.3.4 Applicable Depreciation Method and Convention Under 1986 Rules

The depreciation deduction for a year is computed as a depreciation rate applied to either original or unrecovered cost of the property.[35] The methods for determining depreciation rates and the special rules for determining the deduction for the year property is placed in service or retired are described below, first with respect to tangible personal property and then for real property.

1. *Tangible personal property.* For tangible personal property, the applicable depreciation method is usually the 200 percent declining balance method; 15- and 20-year property, however, must be depreciated by a 150 percent declining balance method. Under a declining balance method, the depreciation rate is 200 or 150 percent, divided by the number of years in the recovery period.[36] For seven-year property, for example, the percentage is 28.57 percent (200 percent divided by seven). For each year, the percentage is applied to the excess of original cost over the sum of the deductions allowed for prior years. A switch is made to the straight line method, however, as soon as the switch increases the annual allowance.[37] The allowances are computed treating salvage value as zero.[38] The operation of these procedures is illustrated in Example 23-9.

A depreciation deduction is allowed for the year property is placed in service and for each succeeding year in the recovery period that the taxpayer holds the property. Property is placed in service when it "is first placed by the taxpayer in a condition or state of readiness and availability for a specifically assigned function."[39] The allowance for the year property is placed in service is determined by a convention under which the property is

---

[35] Computation of depreciation rates must be carried to at least hundredths of a percent. Rev. Proc. 87-57, 1987-2 CB 687, at §6.03.

[36] Rev. Proc. 87-57, supra note 35, at §6.04.

[37] IRC §168(b)(1). The 150 percent declining balance method is used for municipal wastewater treatment plants and sewers and for some telephone equipment. IRC §§168(b)(2), (e)(3)(D), (E).

[38] IRC §168(b)(4).

[39] Rev. Proc. 87-57, supra note 35, at §2.05. See also supra ¶23.2.3.

deemed placed in service at an arbitrarily designated time within the year, and a proportionate amount of a full year's allowance is permitted for the year.[40] The convention also determines how much of the recovery period falls in subsequent years.

Usually, a half-year convention is used under which all property is deemed placed in service at the midpoint of the year in which it is actually placed in service.[41] For a year consisting of 12 full months, the deduction under this convention for property placed in service during the year is one half of a full year's allowance, and the recovery period remaining in subsequent years is the recovery period for the property reduced by one half of a year.[42] For seven-year property, for example, the recovery period under the half-year convention consists of the year the property is placed in service, all of the next six years, and one half of the eighth year; a deduction, in other words, is allowed in each of eight taxable years.

A midquarter convention is substituted for the half-year convention if a taxpayer's acquisitions are lumped in the last three months of the taxable year.[43] This rule works as follows: The sum of the bases of depreciable tangible property placed in service during the last three months of the taxable year is compared with the aggregate basis of such property placed in service throughout the year. Residential rental property and nonresidential real property are excluded from both the three-month and the year-long figures. If the figure for the last three months exceeds 40 percent of the year-long figure, the midquarter convention must be used for all tangible property placed in service during the year other than residential rental property and nonresidential real property. The midquarter convention would apply, for example, if a taxpayer's acquisitions of depreciable tangible personal property for a year consisted of a $10,000 automobile placed in service on January 3 and a $100,000 dump truck placed in service on November 1; the ratio of last quarter purchases to the year's purchases is 91 percent ($100,000/$110,000), an amount well in excess of the 40 percent necessary to bring this convention into play.[44] "Where property is placed in service by a partnership, the 40-percent test generally will be applied at the partnership level, except in the case of partnerships that are formed or availed of to

---

[40] See id. at §5.01.

[41] IRC §§168(d)(1), (4)(A).

[42] If the taxable year consists of less than 12 months, the full year's allowance is doubly reduced, first to reflect the length of the taxable year and then under the convention. See Peters v. CIR, 89 TC 423 (1988) (limited partnership was organized on January 4, but had no assets or liabilities until, on December 29, it issued limited partnership interests and entered into equipment leasing deal; held, taxable year began on December 29 for purposes of ADR conventions discussed infra ¶23.7.4).

[43] IRC §168(d)(3).

[44] See Rev. Proc. 87-57, 1987-2 CB 687, at §5.01 Ex.

avoid the mid-quarter convention."[45]

Under the midquarter convention, each item is treated as though it were placed in service at the midpoint of the quarter in which it is actually placed in service.[46] In the example, the automobile is deemed placed in service at the midpoint of the first quarter, and the dump truck at the midpoint of the last quarter. Under this convention, the deduction for the year property is placed in service is the allowance for a full year multiplied by a fraction (1) whose numerator is the number of full quarters within the year the property is in service plus 0.5 and (2) whose denominator is four.[47] In the example, the deduction for the automobile is seven eighths of a full year's allowance (3.5/4), and one eighth (0.5/4) is allowed for the dump truck.

The system for tangible personal property is illustrated by Example 23-9, in which it is assumed that five-year property is purchased for $1,000. The applicable depreciation method is the 200 percent declining balance method, under which the annual allowance is a percentage of unrecovered cost equal to 200 percent, divided by the number of years in the recovery period. For five-year property, the percentage is 40 percent. If the half-year convention applies, the allowances are as given in Example 23-9. The cost of the property is allowed over six years, the first and last each accounting for half a year in the five year recovery period. The allowances for the fifth and sixth years are done by the straight line method because the resulting annual allowance of $115.2 for the fifth year (the unrecovered cost of $172.8 allocated two thirds to the fifth year and one third to the sixth year) exceeds the 200 percent declining balance allowance for the fourth year of $69.12 (40 percent of unrecovered cost of $172.8).

Example 23-9

ACRS for 5-Year Property
Using Midyear Convention

Year	Computation	Allowance
1	($1,000) (.4)/2	$200
2	($1,000 − $200)(.4)	320
3	($1,000 − $200 − $320)(.4)	192
4	($1,000 − $200 − $340 − $192)(.4)	115.2

---

[45] 1986 Bluebook, supra note 1, at 105. Also, an affiliated group of corporations is treated as one taxpayer in applying the test. Id.

[46] IRC §168(d)(4)(C).

[47] Rev. Proc. 87-57, supra note 44, at §5.05.

Year	Computation	Allowance
5	($172.8)(2/3)..	115.2
6	($172.8)(1/3)..	57.6
	Total..	$1,000

An election can be made to use the straight line method for tangible personal property.[48] When the election is made, the cost is recovered over the same recovery period and with the same first year convention as are used with the 200 percent declining balance method. For five-year property, the straight line allowance for a full 12 months is 20 percent of original cost, but, under the half-year convention, the year-by-year allowances are 10 percent of cost in the first year, 20 percent in each of the second through the fifth years, and 10 percent in the sixth year. For seven-year property, the allowances are 7.14 percent in the first year, 14.29 percent for the second through the seventh years, and 7.14 percent for the eighth year. The election is made year by year and class by class.[49] If the election is made for 1988 for seven-year property, for example, all seven-year property placed in service during 1988 must be depreciated by the straight line method in all years of its recovery period, but the 200 percent declining balance method may be used for other property placed in service during 1988 or for seven-year property placed in service during other years.

2. *Residential rental property and nonresidential real property.* The straight line method is mandatory for all residential rental property and nonresidential real property.[50] The allowances are computed treating salvage value as zero.[51] The first and last years' allowances are determined with a midmonth convention under which the property is deemed placed in service halfway through the month in which it is actually placed in service.[52]

These rules are most easily applied by determining a monthly depreciation rate. For residential rental property (which has a recovery period of 27.5 years or 330 months), the monthly allowance is 0.3030 percent of original cost (100 percent divided by 330). The allowance is 0.1515 percent of cost (one half of 0.3030) for the month the property is placed in service, 0.3030 of cost for each of the next 329 months, and 0.1515 for the 331st and final month. For nonresidential real property (whose recovery period is 31.5 years or 378 months), the allowances are 0.1323 percent of original

---

[48] IRC §168(b)(3)(C).
[49] IRC §168(b)(5).
[50] IRC §§168(b)(3)(A), (B).
[51] IRC §168(b)(4).
[52] IRC §168(d)(2), (4)(B).

cost for the first and last months, and 0.2646 percent for the intervening 377 months.

3. *Dispositions.* For the year property is sold or otherwise disposed of, depreciation is allowed according to the same convention used in determining the allowance for the year the property was placed in service. For example, under the half-year convention, which usually applies to personal property, all dispositions are deemed to occur at midyear, thus permitting one half of the normal allowance to be taken for the year of sale, regardless of when the sale occurs within the year.[53] However, "no depreciation is allowed in the case of property acquired and disposed of in the same year."[54]

4. *General asset accounts.* The Treasury is authorized to provide regulations permitting assets to be grouped in "general asset accounts."[55] Under regulations proposed under the 1981–1986 ACRS rules, such an account must consist of assets that although "not necessarily homogeneous," have the same class life and are placed in service in the same year.[56] Also, the assets in the account must be "numerous in quantity," and the cost of each item in relation to the cost of all items in the account must be sufficiently small that "separate identification is impracticable." The use of such accounts is elective, and the establishment of an account in one year does not bind the taxpayer to use such accounts for other property placed in service during that or other years.[57]

Under the proposed regulations, ACRS deductions with respect to a general asset account are determined as though the account were a single asset.[58] When items in the account are sold, the proceeds of sale are ordinary income until the aggregate reaches the original cost (or other unadjusted basis) of all assets in the account. Once this point is passed, sales proceeds are capital gain. ACRS deductions continue until the normal end of the account's recovery period, undiminished by reason of dispositions.[59]

---

[53] IRC §168(d)(4)(B). If, under the rule described above in the text accompanying note 46, a midquarter convention was applied for the year an item was placed in service, this convention also applies to a disposition of the item, and the disposition is treated as occurring at the midpoint in the quarter in which it actually occurs. IRC §§168(d)(3)(A), (4)(C). If the midquarter convention applies to an item sold by a calendar year taxpayer on June 17, for example, the allowance for the year is 3/8 of the normal allowance (all of the allowance for the first quarter of the year and one half for the second quarter).

[54] 1986 Bluebook, supra note 1, at 104.

[55] IRC §168(i)(4).

[56] Prop. Reg. §1.168-2(h)(2).

[57] Prop. Reg. §1.168-2(h)(3).

[58] Prop. Reg. §1.168-2(h)(1).

[59] For an account established in a year before 1986, dispositions sometimes cause the basis of the account to be increased to reflect recapture of the investment credit. Prop. Reg. §§1.168-2(h)(4), (5).

¶23.3.5 Alternative Depreciation System

An alternative depreciation system is provided under which depreciation is allowed on the straight line method over recovery periods intended to approximate the economic lives of the property—recovery periods, in other words, that are significantly longer than the usual ACRS periods.[60] This system is mandatory for some types of property and may be elected for other property.

Even when regular ACRS is used for regular tax purposes, alternative depreciation must be used in determining alternative minimum taxable income for purposes of the alternative minimum tax.[61] Also, a corporation must use the alternative system in determining its earnings and profits, regardless of what depreciation system is used in computing taxable income.[62]

1. *Mandatory use of alternative system.* Property that must be depreciated under the alternative depreciation system includes (1) property used "predominantly outside the United States,"[63] (2) property leased to a unit of government, a tax-exempt organization, or a foreign person, and (3) property financed directly or indirectly with borrowings the interest on which is exempt from tax under §103(a).[64] Also, the President has the power to require that the system be used for property imported from countries following restrictive or discriminatory trade policies.[65]

The property subject to the rule for property leased to governments, charities, and foreign persons is referred to as "tax-exempt use property."[66] Property is tax-exempt use property if the taxpayer-owner leases it to another person and the lessee is a "tax-exempt entity."[67] The latter term includes (1) the federal, state, and local governments and their agencies, (2) organizations that are exempt from tax, (3) nonresident alien individuals, (4) foreign corporations, trusts, and estates, and (5) international organizations.[68] Under this definition, a "tax-exempt entity" need not be either tax exempt or an entity.

---

[60] IRC §168(g)(1).

[61] See infra ¶111.3 for the alternative minimum tax.

[62] See infra ¶92.1.3 for earnings and profits.

[63] IRC §168(g)(1)(A). Section 48(a)(2) provides a definition of "used predominantly outside the United States" that is used for this purpose. IRC §168(g)(4).

[64] IRC §§168(g)(1)(C), (5). Some residential rental property described in §142(a)(7) is exempted from this rule. IRC §168(g)(5)(C).

[65] IRC §§168(g)(1)(D), (6).

[66] IRC §§168(g)(1)(B), (h).

[67] IRC §168(h)(1).

[68] IRC §168(h)(2).

The rule also applies if the property is leased to a partnership, S corporation, or other pass-thru entity that includes a tax-exempt entity as partner or shareholder. In this case, however, only a fraction of the property is tax-exempt use property, corresponding to the tax-exempt partner's or shareholder's proportionate interest in the lessee-entity.[69] If a lease is made to a partnership, 30 percent of the interests in which are held by a nonresident alien, for example, 30 percent of the property is tax-exempt use property and must be depreciated by the alternative system. If none of the other partners are tax-exempt, however, the remaining 70 percent of the property can be depreciated by the regular ACRS rules.

Further, property owned by a partnership can be tax-exempt use property, even though it is not leased, if (1) the partners include at least one tax-exempt entity and at least one person that is not tax exempt and (2) the tax-exempt partner's proportionate share of partnership income and deduction varies from item to item.[70] The purpose of this rule is to require that the slower depreciation for tax-exempt use property be used when partnership allocations shunt depreciation from tax-exempt to nonexempt partners. The tax-exempt use rule is subject to several exceptions. Property does not become tax-exempt use property, for example, by reason of a lease for a term that does not exceed the greater of three years or 30 percent of the property's class life.[71] A car rental company, for example, is not subject to the rule merely because it rents a car for a short term to a foreign visitor to the United States. Qualifed technological equipment is exempted if it is leased for no more than five years.[72] For purposes of both of these rules, however, the term of a lease generally includes any period covered by an option to renew, and the terms of successive leases made in one or a series of related transactions are aggregated.[73]

Also, nonresidential real property and residential rental property is not considered tax-exempt use property unless more than 35 percent of the property is leased by "disqualified leases."[74] Property leased to governmental, charitable, or foreign lessees is disqualified if (1) the property is financed by tax-exempt borrowing, (2) the lessee has an option to purchase the property at a fixed or determinable price, (3) the lease term exceeds 20 years, or (4) the taxpayer purchased or leased the property from the lessee or a related entity in a sale-leaseback or lease-leaseback transaction occurring

---

[69] IRC §168(h)(5).

[70] IRC §168(h)(6).

[71] IRC §168(h)(1)(C).

[72] IRC §168(h)(3)(A). See supra text accompanying note 23 for the definition of qualified technological equipment.

[73] IRC §168(i)(3).

[74] IRC §§168(h)(1)(B), (E).

more than 3 months after the lessee begins its use of the property.[75] An ordinary commercial or residential lease to a tax-exempt tenant thus does not usually force the property into the alternative depreciation system. Also, property leased to a domestic charity or other exempt organization is not tax-exempt use property if the lessee's predominant use of the property is in an unrelated trade or business.[76] Further, a lease to a foreign person does not taint property if (1) the lessee is subject to U.S. tax on more than one half of its income from the property, (2) the lessee is a controlled foreign corporation and more than 50 percent of its income from the property is currently included in the gross incomes of U.S. shareholders under subpart F, or (3) the property is a motion picture film or video tape intended as public entertainment or education or is a sound recording.[77]

2. *Elective use of alternative system.* Elections to use the alternative depreciation system can be made for any property that is not mandatorily subject to the system.[78] For nonresidential real property and residential rental property, the election is made property by property. For other property, the election is made class by class and year by year. If an election is made for seven-year property placed in service during 1988, for example, this property is subject to the system throughout its useful life,[79] but, in the absence of other elections, regular ACRS applies to property other than seven-year property placed in service in 1988 and to seven-year property placed in service in other years.

For property other than nonresidential real property and residential rental property, the alternative depreciation system is a third choice because the rules allow a choice between regular ACRS, which is accelerated depreciation, and straight-line depreciation over the ACRS recovery periods.[80] For nonresidential real property and residential rental property, there are only two choices: (1) regular ACRS, which is straight-line depreciation over 31.5 or 27.5 years, and (2) the alternative depreciation system, where the recovery period is 40 years.

3. *Application of alternative system.* Recovery periods under the alternative depreciation system are as follows:[81] The recovery period for nonresidential real property and residential rental property is 50 years.[82] For most

---

[75] IRC §168(h)(1)(B)(ii).

[76] IRC §168(h)(1)(D).

[77] IRC §168(h)(2)(B).

[78] IRC §168(h)(7)(A). The election is made property by property for nonresidential real property and residential rental property. Id.

[79] Once made, the election is irrevocable. IRC §168(h)(7)(B).

[80] See supra notes 48–49.

[81] IRC §168(h)(2)(C).

[82] The 40-year period also applies to section 1245 property that is real property (e.g., elevators and escalators) if no class life is prescribed for the property. IRC §168(g)(3)(E).

other property, the recovery period is usually the property's class life[83] or, if none is prescribed, 12 years. The recovery period for automobiles and light general purpose trucks, however, is five years in the alternative system, as in regular ACRS.[84] Qualified technological equipment also keeps the five-year recovery period it has under regular ACRS.[85] The statute, however, prescribes longer recovery periods in the alternative system than under ACRS for several types of property.[86] For example, single purpose agricultural and horticultural structures have a 15-year life under the alternative system. Regardless of the character of the property, further, the recovery period for tax-exempt use property that is leased may not be less than 125 percent of the lease term.[87]

Depreciation allowances under the alternative depreciation system are determined by the straight line method.[88] Salvage value, however, is deemed to be zero,[89] and the conventions that determine first and last year allowances are the same as under regular ACRS.[90]

¶23.3.6 Corporate and Partnership Nonrecognition Exchanges

Section 168(i)(7) provides special rules for property received by a corporation or partnership in an organization, reorganization, or liquidation transaction described in §332, 351, 361, 371(a), 374(a), 721, or 731.[91] The common feature of the transactions covered by these provisions is that the transferor's gain or loss qualifies for nonrecognition, in whole or in part, and the transferee (the taxpayer, in this context) takes the transferor's basis, sometimes adjusted for gain recognized by the transferor. Consistent with the transfer of basis from transferor to transferee, the transferee succeeds to the transferor's ACRS deductions. Assume seven-year property is acquired by an individual for use in his business in 1988, but is transferred at the beginning of 1990 to a controlled corporation in a transaction qualifying for nonrecognition of gain or loss under §351(a).[92] The corporation's ACRS allowances are those amounts that would have been allowed to the transferor for the period the corporation holds the property, determined as though the transferor had retained ownership.

---

[83] See supra note 21 for class lives.
[84] IRC §168(g)(3)(D).
[85] IRC §168(g)(3)(C); supra note 23 and accompanying text.
[86] IRC §168(g)(3)(B).
[87] IRC §168(h)(3)(A).
[88] IRC §168(g)(2)(A).
[89] Id.
[90] IRC §168(g)(2)(B).
[91] The same rules are found in §168(f)(10) of the 1981–1986 statute.
[92] See infra ¶91.1 for §351.

The situation is a bit more complex if the transferor recognizes all or a portion of its gain on the transfer and the transferee is given a basis step-up for this gain recognition. In this case, the rule described in the preceding paragraph applies to an amount of the transferee's basis equal to the transferor's basis, and the amount of the step-up is depreciated separately as though the transferee had purchased the property.[93] Assume the transferor in the example in the preceding paragraph receives boot in the exchange, and as a consequence recognizes gain of $20. If the property's basis to the transferor was $80, the corporation's basis is $100.[94] The corporation recovers $80 of its basis by succeeding to the transferor's allowances, and recovers $20 by separately depreciating the step-up for the boot under the ACRS rules.

A companion rule provides that "property which is disposed of and then reacquired by the taxpayer shall be treated . . . as if such property had not been disposed of."[95]

¶23.3.7 Property Placed in Service During the Years 1981 Through 1986

The rules for property placed in service during the years 1981 through 1986 differ significantly in both terminology and effect from those described above for property placed in service after 1986. Generally, the 1981–1986 rules group property into fewer classes and provide shorter recovery periods than the rules enacted in 1986.

1. *Personal property.* Under the 1981–1986 rules, personal property is grouped into four classes:[96] (1) 3-year property (property with a class life of four years or less and property used in research and experimentation), (2) 5-year property (personal property falling into no other class), (3) 10-year property (real property with a class life no longer than 12.5 years and certain property of public utilities), and (4) 15-year public utility property (other property of public utilities).[97] Because the latter two classes rarely applied to taxpayers other than public utilities, depreciable tangible person-

---

[93] IRC §168(i)(7)(A).

[94] IRC §362(a).

[95] IRC §168(i)(7)(C).

[96] IRC §168(c)(2) (before amendment in 1986).

[97] As under the post-1986 rules, the class lives are set by the IRS and published in revenue procedures. See supra note 21.

al property of most businesses was divided into two classes, three-year property and five-year property.

ACRS allowances for this property are determined by tables rather than through use of methods and conventions.[98] The tables are based on the 150 percent declining balance method and the half-year convention, but effectively lop half a year off each recovery period. For three-year property, for example, the table provides deductions of 25 percent, 38 percent, and 37 percent of original cost for the year the property was placed in service and the succeeding two years. Under the 150 percent method with a three-year recovery period and the half-year convention, 25 percent of cost is the appropriate allowance for the year the property is placed in service, and 38 percent is also the allowance for the next year;[99] the remainder of the property's cost, however, would be spread among the third and fourth years reflecting that the three-year recovery period consists of one half of the first year, all of the second and third years, and one half of the fourth year. The table, however, completes full recovery of cost in the third year, thus effectively providing a recovery year period of two and one-half years. The same phenomenon is seen in the tables for 5-year, 10-year, and 15-year public utility property. The percentages for five-year property, for example, are 15 percent of cost for the year the property is placed in service, 22 percent for the next year, and 21 percent for each of the succeeding three years, allowing full recovery over five taxable years, which amounts to four and one-half calendar years given that the first year's allowance is calculated as one half of a full year's allowance.

If property subject to the foregoing rules is sold or otherwise disposed of prior to the end of its recovery period, no depreciation is allowed for the year of the disposition.[100]

2. *Real property.* The rules for real property are more complex, both in their initial conception and because Congress tinkered with them often. All real property (other than low-income housing and items with class lives of 12.5 years or less) is placed in one class, initially called 15-year real property, then 18-year real property, and finally 19-year real property as Congress steadily receded from the generosity it exhibited in the original 1981 enactment of ACRS. The particulars are shown in Table 23-1.

---

[98] IRC §168(b)(1) (before amendment in 1986).

[99] The allowance for the year the property is placed in service is the rate for a full year (150 percent divided by the three-year length of the recovery period, or 50 percent), divided by two (one half of 50 percent is 25 percent). For the next year, the allowance is unrecovered cost (100 percent less the allowance of 25 percent for the prior year), multiplied by the rate for a full year (50 percent of 75 percent is 37.5 percent).

[100] IRC §168(d)(2)(B) (before amendment in 1986).

Table 23-1

Recovery Periods for Real Property
(Other Than Low-income Housing)
Placed in Service During 1981–1986

Date property placed in service	Recovery period
January 1, 1981 through March 15, 1984	15 years
March 16, 1984 through May 8, 1985	18 years
May 9, 1985 through December 31, 1986	19 years

ACRS allowances for 15-year, 18-year, and 19-year real property are determined under the 175 percent declining balance method. For 15-year real property, the allowances for the first and last years are determined with a whole-month convention under which the property is deemed to be in service for all of a month if it is actually in service during any portion of the month. For 18-year and 19-year real property, the midmonth convention is used; one half of the deduction for a full month is allowed for the month in which the property is placed in service or disposed of. The Treasury provided tables for determining the allowance for each year by simply applying a percentage given in the table to the property's original cost.[101]

Even more generous treatment was provided for low-income housing.[102] The recovery period for low-income housing stayed at 15 years after the period for other real property was raised to 18 and then 19 years. ACRS allowances for low-income housing, further, are determined by the 200 percent declining balance method, rather than the 175 percent method for other real property. Also, the whole-month convention continued to be used for low-income housing after the midmonth convention was mandated for other real property.

3. *Election of less acceleration.* An election was provided that allowed taxpayers to slow down the normal acceleration of ACRS allowances.[103] Depreciation on property covered by an election is computed on the straight line method. In addition, an electing taxpayer could choose to stay with the normal ACRS recovery period, to depreciate over a somewhat longer period, or to use a much longer period. The alternatives were 3, 5, and 12 years for three-year property, and 5, 12, and 25 years for five-year

---

[101] Rev. Proc. 1986-14, 1986-1 CB 542 (for 19-year real property); Notice 84-16, 1984-2 CB 475 (for 18-year real property); Notice 81-16, 1981-2 CB 545 (for 15-year real property).

[102] IRC §168(b)(4) (before amendment in 1986). For the definition of "low-income housing," see §§1250(a)(1)(B)(i), (ii), (iii), and (iv). See also IRC §168(c)(2)(F) (before amendment in 1986).

[103] IRC §168(b)(3) (before amendment in 1986).

property. For real property, the alternatives were the normal ACRS period (15, 18, or 19 years, depending on when the property was placed in service), 35 years, and 45 years.

For real property, the election was made property by property. For personal property, the election was made class by class and year by year. If the election was made for five-year property placed in service in 1984, for example, normal ACRS could be used for five-year property placed in service in any other year and for three-year property in all years. The same recovery period, however, is required for all property covered by an election for a particular class. If a 1984 election was made for five-year property, for example, it is not possible to depreciate some property covered by the election over five years, other property over 12 years, and still other property over 25 years.

When the election was made for personal property, allowances for the first and last years in the recovery period were determined with the half-year convention. If a 12-year recovery period was elected for five-year property placed in service in 1984, for example, the annual rate is 8 1/3 percent of original cost for a full year (100 percent divided by 12), and the allowances for each property are 4 1/6 percent of cost for the year the property is placed in service, 8 1/3 percent for each of the succeeding 11 taxable years, and 4 1/6 percent for the thirteenth year.

For real property, the same convention is used as under normal ACRS (the whole-month convention for 15-year property and the half-month convention for 18-year and 19-year real property). For a taxpayer who elected to depreciate 15-year real property over 35 years, for example, the allowance is 0.2381 percent of original cost for the month the property is placed in service and for each of the next 421 months.

¶23.4 USEFUL LIFE OF DEPRECIABLE PROPERTY NOT SUBJECT TO ACRS

¶23.4.1 Introductory

Depreciation on property not covered by ACRS is allowed over the useful life of the property. (Generally, ACRS applies to all depreciable property other than intangibles, tangible property placed in service before 1981, and a few tangible items placed in service after 1980.)[1] The principles and factors determining the length of "the relentless march . . . to the junk pile"[2] can be summarized as follows:

---

[1] See supra ¶23.3.2.
[2] Real Estate-Land Title & Trust Co. v. US, 309 US 13, 16 (1940).

For the purpose of section 167 the estimated useful life of an asset is not necessarily the useful life inherent in the asset but is the period over which the asset may reasonably be expected to be useful to the taxpayer in his trade or business or in the production of his income. This period shall be determined by reference to his experience with similar property taking into account present conditions and probable future developments. Some of the factors to be considered in determining this period are (1) wear and tear and decay or decline from natural causes, (2) the normal progress of the art, economic changes, inventions, and current developments within the industry and the taxpayer's trade or business, (3) the climatic and other local conditions peculiar to the taxpayer's trade or business, and (4) the taxpayer's policy as to repairs, renewals, and replacements. Salvage value is not a factor for the purpose of determining useful life. If the taxpayer's experience is inadequate, the general experience in the industry may be used until such time as the taxpayer's own experience forms an adequate basis for making the determination.[3]

The depreciation allowance includes an allowance for normal obsolescence which should be taken into account to the extent that the expected useful life of property will be shortened by reason thereof. Obsolescence may render an asset economically useless to the taxpayer regardless of its physical condition. Obsolescence is attributable to many causes, including technological improvements and reasonably foreseeable economic changes. Among these causes are normal progress of the arts and sciences, supersession or inadequacy brought about by developments in the industry, products, methods, markets, sources of supply, and other like changes, and legislative or regulatory action.[4]

Even before ACRS, this facts-and-circumstances standard was modified by (1) the ADR system adopted in 1971, permitting taxpayers to depreciate eligible assets on the basis of industry-wide class lives,[5] (2) §167(d), providing that an agreement between the taxpayer and the IRS on the useful life of particular property is binding in the absence of facts or circumstances not taken into account in adopting the agreement,[6] and (3) numerous statutory provisions permitting specified expenditures to be depreciated or amortized over prescribed periods, which are almost always shorter than the asset's useful life as otherwise determined.[7]

---

[3] Reg. §1.167(a)-1(b).

[4] Reg. §1.167(a)-9. For more on obsolescence, see infra ¶23.4.6.

[5] Infra ¶23.7.

[6] Infra ¶23.4.7.

[7] For the additional first-year depreciation allowance and the investment credit, see infra ¶¶23.8 and 27.1.

The useful life adopted for an asset in computing depreciation under §167 was also required to be used in determining the asset's eligibility for the additional first-year depreciation allowance under §179, which was restricted to property with a useful life of six years or more, and the investment credit under §38, which was limited to property with a useful life of three years or more.[8]

¶23.4.2 Facts-and-Circumstances Standard

Although the regulations permit use of the general experience of the industry in determining useful life, their primary emphasis is on "the period over which the asset may reasonably be expected to be useful to the taxpayer." The asset's physical life necessarily sets an outside limit to this period. Most assets, however, are withdrawn from service before they collapse, and some taxpayers regularly retire assets after a relatively short period of use. In *Massey Motors, Inc. v. United States*, the Supreme Court held that an automobile rental company, which ordinarily disposed of its rental cars after about 15 months of use because its customers demanded the most recent models, could not estimate salvage values and compute depreciation on the basis of the normal four-year useful life of similar vehicles in the hands of companies that did not have the same special need for late-model cars:

> [Depreciable] assets, employed from day to day in business, generally decrease in utility and value as they are used. It was the design of the Congress to permit the taxpayer to recover, tax free, the total cost to him of such capital assets; hence it recognized that this decrease in value—depreciation—was a legitimate tax deduction as business expense. It was the purpose of [§167(a)] and the regulations to make a meaningful allocation of this cost to the tax periods benefited by the use of the asset. In practical life, however, business concerns do not usually know how long an asset will be of profitable use to them or how long it may be utilized until no longer capable of functioning. But, for the most part, such assets are used for their entire economic life, and the depreciation base in such cases has long been recognized as the number of years the asset is expected to function profitably in use. The asset being of no further use at the end of such period, its salvage value, if anything, is only as scrap.

> Some assets, however, are not acquired with intent to be employed in the business for their full economic life. It is this type of asset, where

---

[8] IRC §46(c)(2) (investment credit); Reg. §1.179-3(a) (additional first-year depreciation); IRC §167(c) (minimum useful life for accelerated depreciation).

the experience of the taxpayers clearly indicates a utilization of the asset for a substantially shorter period than its full economic life, that we are concerned with in these cases. Admittedly, the automobiles are not retained by the taxpayers for their full economic life and, concededly, they do have substantial salvage, resale or second-hand value. Moreover, the application of the full-economic-life formula to taxpayers' businesses here results in the receipt of substantial "profits" from the resale or "salvage" of the automobiles, which contradicts the usual application of the full-economic-life concept. . . .

We therefore conclude that the Congress intended that the taxpayer should, under the allowance for depreciation, recover only the cost of the asset less the estimated salvage, resale or second-hand value. This requires that the useful life of the asset be related to the period for which it may reasonably be expected to be employed in the taxpayer's business. Likewise salvage value must include estimated resale or second-hand values.[9]

Under the regulations, so many factors are pertinent in determining a useful life that virtually no scrap of evidence is excluded, particularly since the regulations do not purport to provide an exhaustive catalogue.[10] For this reason it is impossible to offer useful generalizations, other than the observation that statements of opinion unbuttressed by facts are unlikely to overcome the presumption of correctness that attaches to the government's determination of a deficiency. On the other hand, recognizing that useful life is a prediction, courts are likely to respond more favorably to a taxpayer's well-supported case than to estimates by administrative officials whose knowledge is necessarily obtained from a distance.[11]

As for decisions at the administrative level, where the overwhelming number of useful life disputes are settled, the following exchange between the Commissioner of Internal Revenue and a tax practitioner concerning the use of expert testimony is instructive:

---

[9] Massey Motors, Inc., v. US, 364 US 92, 96–97, 107 (1960). Under *Massey Motors*, useful life is the period property is expected to be used in the taxpayer's business, not the period for which that use is expected to be most profitable. See Honodel v. CIR, 722 F2d 1462, 1469 (9th Cir. 1984) (rejecting taxpayer's argument that useful life of property held by tax shelter partnership should be "the period during which the asset would produce an acceptable rate of return, including tax benefits, to the investors").

For capital gains and depreciation recapture implications of *Massey Motors, Inc.*, see infra ¶55.2.1.

[10] Supra notes 3, 4.

[11] See, e.g., Hastings v. US, 279 F. Supp. 13, 15–18 (ND Cal. 1967); Casey v. CIR, 38 TC 357, 381–83 (1962) (acq.).

Commissioner Thrower: Mr. Richmond, where you refer to settlements . . . being reached between the scientific determination made by your client, and the scientific determination made by representatives of the Internal Revenue Service, is this figure arrived at through scientific determination, or is this more or less the result of a horse trade?

Mr. Richmond: I will say it is a scientific method called horse trading.[12]

Although useful life disputes ordinarily focus on the characteristics of the asset being depreciated, the depreciable life of an asset is sometimes determined by the useful life of another asset to which it is subservient. For example, a specially designed structure can be assigned the same useful life as the machinery it was built to house, on a showing that it will be replaced or abandoned when the latter is retired from service.[13] As pointed out previously, this "dominant asset" principle is ordinarily the only ground for depreciating expenditures to clear, grade, and landscape land, which otherwise are treated as increasing the taxpayer's nondepreciable investment in the land.[14]

¶23.4.3 Component and Composite Lives

Instead of computing depreciation asset by asset, taxpayers may aggregate their depreciable assets into categories of assets with similar useful lives or functions or in a single business-wide account. When assets with diverse useful lives are grouped together, an appropriate composite depreciation rate must be computed, usually on the basis of the weighted average of their separate useful lives, and this rate must be redetermined when additions, retirements, or replacements produce a substantial change in the relative

---

[12] Treasury Hearings on Asset Depreciation Range System 473 (1979), quoted in Griswold & Graetz, Federal Income Taxation: Principles and Policies 353 (Foundation Press 1976).

[13] Public Serv. Co. of NM v. US, 70-2 USTC ¶9721 (DNM 1969) (not officially reported) (conclusions of law no. 5), aff'd without discussion of this issue, 431 F2d 980 (10th Cir. 1970). But see Randolph's Est. v. CIR, 29 TCM (CCH) 1481 (1970) (steel construction, special electrical system, and railroad siding not enough to qualify taxpayer's building as structure that would be replaced contemporaneously with equipment that it housed, even though these features were incorporated to meet lessee's special needs). See also McWilliams v. CIR, 15 BTA 329, 339 (1929) (sawmill depreciable over estimated life of timber tract, for which it was built).

[14] See supra ¶23.2.5 note 36 and accompanying text.

proportion of long- and short-lived assets in the account.[15] When a composite rate is used by the taxpayer and the IRS assigns a longer useful life to the account, the taxpayer can prove the determination erroneous only by establishing the lives of all items included in the account.[16]

Under pre-ACRS law, an asset composed of separately replaceable components can sometimes be fragmented in computing depreciation, even though the components are interdependent parts of an integral whole. Instead of assigning a single useful life to a building, for example, the taxpayer can allocate its cost among such components as the shell, roof, plumbing and wiring, heating plant, air-conditioners, and elevators and depreciate each of these elements over its own useful life.[17] As Example 23-10 demonstrates, the use of component lives rather than the composite life of the building as a unit can accelerate the taxpayer's depreciation deductions. The annual deduction on the component method is $52,000 at the outset. At the end of five years, when the carpets are fully depreciated, the deduction will be $44,000 for the remaining original assets, and this amount will continue to drop as more components reach the end of their useful lives. With each decline, the cost of the replacement items will become depreciable. By contrast, a composite useful life of 28 years on the entire building would yield annual depreciation deductions of $30,000.

---

[15] Reg. §1.167(a)-7(d). See also Tribune Publishing Co. v. CIR, 52 TC 717 (1969), aff'd per curiam, 451 F2d 600 (9th Cir. 1971) (composite life for TV films rejected as inaccurate because it did not adequately reflect individual lives of separate items).

[16] Barron v. CIR, 22 TCM (CCH) 1655 (1963).

[17] See Merchants Nat'l Bank of Topeka v. CIR, 554 F2d 412 (10th Cir. 1977) (36 component accounts for office building); Fort Walton Square, Inc. v. CIR, 54 TC 653 (1970) (acq.); Rev. Rul. 73-410, 1973-2 CB 53 (component method of accounting for depreciation of used realty permitted if cost is properly allocated, useful lives are based on condition of components when acquired, and ADR system is not elected); Rev. Rul. 75-55, 1975-1 CB 74 (depreciation methods prescribed by §167(j)(4) or (5) applicable when component basis employed for used realty); but see Fieland v. CIR, 73 TC 743 (1980) (purchaser of building not entitled to component depreciation, except subject to Rev. Rul. 73-410, supra). See also Lesser v. CIR, 42 TC 688 (1964), aff'd per curiam, 352 F2d 789 (9th Cir. 1965), cert. denied, 384 US 927 (1966) (treatment of components that are deteriorated or slated for replacement when property is acquired); Reg. §1.165-3(a) (discussed infra ¶25.4.5) (lump sum paid for improved real estate must be allocated entirely to land if the building is to be demolished on acquisition in order to erect new structure).

For criticism of component depreciation and of such abuses as assigning the estimated composite life of the whole to the most durable element and unreasonably short lives to other components, see Joint Comm. on Tax'n, 95th Cong., 2d Sess., Tax Reduction and Reform Proposals (No. 3—Real Estate Depreciation) 13–19 (Comm. Print 1978). See Tidwell, Component Depreciation Can Be a "Cure" for Excess Depreciation, 55 Taxes 116 (1977).

Example 23-10

Depreciation of Apartment House—Component Lives

	Cost	Useful Life (Years)	Component Depreciation (Straight Line)
Carpet	$ 40,000	5	$ 8,000
Air conditioning equipment	80,000	8	10,000
Electrical fixtures	130,000	10	13,000
Roof	150,000	15	10,000
Building shell	440,000	40	11,000
Total	$840,000		$52,000

¶23.4.4 Standardized Useful Lives

In 1942, the IRS issued *Bulletin F*, containing estimated average useful lives and depreciation rates for several thousand classes of business assets, based "on the usual experience of property owners" following "a reasonable expense policy as to the cost of repairs and maintenance."[18] Use of these standardized lives was not compulsory, but they were widely employed by taxpayers to avoid controversy with revenue agents, who could insist that claims for shorter lives be substantiated by proof of the relevant facts and circumstances—a time consuming, expensive, and chancy procedure. In 1962, responding to claims that the prescribed useful lives had become outmoded by technological developments, the Treasury withdrew *Bulletin F* and issued Revenue Procedure 62-21, promulgating "guideline" lives for about 75 industry-wide categories of depreciable assets. The guideline lives, which were 30 to 40 percent shorter than the *Bulletin F* lives, were based on the experience of taxpayers whose depreciation claims fell in the thirtieth percentile, that is, whose useful lives were longer than 29 percent and shorter than 70 percent of the taxpayers in the same industry.[19]

Along with the 1962 guidelines, the IRS prescribed a reserve ratio test, designed to determine whether the taxpayer was actually using depreciable assets substantially longer than their guideline lives. The 1962 guideline lives were presumed acceptable unless subsequent events, as measured by the reserve ratio test, showed that they were not appropriate for the particu-

---

[18] For *Bulletin F*, see [1981] Index CCH Stand. Fed. Tax Rep. ¶310.

[19] Rev. Proc. 62-21, 1962-2 CB 418, revoked for post-1970 years by Rev. Proc. 72-10, 1972-1 CB 721, 731. See also summary in S. Rep. No. 437, 92d Cong., 2d Sess., reprinted in 1972-1 CB 559, 584; Mendenhall, New Depreciation Rate Guidelines, 40 Taxes 746 (1962).

lar taxpayer's circumstances.[20] Before the reserve ratio test came into effect, however, it had engendered so much controversy that it was substantially modified.[21] In 1971, it was eliminated for post-1970 taxable years when the guideline lives of Revenue Procedure 62-21 were supplanted by the ADR system.[22]

The guideline lives of Revenue Procedure 62-21 are inapplicable to assets placed in service after 1970. For property placed in service during the period 1971–1980, useful lives must be determined either under the elective ADR system[23] or under the facts-and-circumstances standard; both ADR and the facts-and-circumstances test are superseded by ACRS for property placed in service after 1980.[24] For the 1971–1980 period, however, Revenue Procedure 62-21 suggests benchmarks; an occasional revenue agent might even sneak a look as a rough-and-ready way to determine whether the useful life claimed by a taxpayer should be accepted without other substantiation.

¶23.4.5 Changes in Useful Life

An asset's useful life is determined by reference to the facts and circumstances known or reasonably anticipated at the end of the year for which the estimate is made.[25] If an estimate was erroneous when made, the allowances for all years not barred by the statute of limitations are corrected when the error is discovered. If the statute has run on one or more years for which erroneous deductions were taken, the impact of the error depends on whether the original estimate was too long or too short. If it was too long, the depreciation actually taken was less than the amount allowable, but the basis of the property must be reduced by the full amount allowable, even for years barred by the statute of limitations.[26] If the original life was too short,

---

[20] See Rev. Proc. 62-21, supra note 19, at question 3 and answer thereto. See also Matson Navigation Co. v. CIR, 67 TC 938 (1977) (application of Revenue Procedure 62-21 and reserve ratio test).

[21] See Rev. Proc. 65-13, 1965-1 CB 759; Pollock, Tax Depreciation and the Need for the Reserve Ratio Test (Treasury Tax Policy Research Study No. 2, 1968).

[22] TD 7128, 1971-2 CB 132 (withdrawing reserve ratio test for 1971 and future years); Rev. Proc. 72-10, supra note 19. For property placed in service before 1971, deductions for 1971 and subsequent years are governed by a class-life system, but deductions for pre-1971 taxable years are governed by Revenue Procedure 62-21 (including the reserve ratio test). See Reg. §§1.167(a)-12(a) through (e) (1971 and subsequent years), §1.167(a)-12(f) (pre-1971 years). See generally Scholler, Traller & Wagner, Treasury's Final Regulations for Depreciating Pre-1971 Property: How They Operate, 39 J. Tax'n 136 (1973).

[23] See infra ¶23.7.

[24] See supra ¶23.4.2.

[25] Casey v. CIR, 38 TC 357, 381 (1962) (acq.); CIR v. Mutual Fertilizer Co., 159 F2d 470 (5th Cir. 1947).

[26] IRC §1016(a)(2), discussed infra ¶42.3.

the taxpayer's basis is reduced by the deductions taken except to the extent that the excess over the proper amount was of no tax benefit.

If an asset's useful life is correctly estimated when the property is placed in service but is altered by subsequent events, future allowances may not be revised to reflect the change unless "the change in the useful life is significant and there is a clear and convincing basis for the redetermination."[27] Also, a shortened useful life is possible if obsolescence turns out to be greater than was assumed when the asset's useful life was estimated, but not "merely because in the unsupported opinion of the taxpayer the property may become obsolete."[28]

This resistance is discouraging to taxpayers who believe that a reduction in an asset's useful life is justified, but it also serves to protect them against IRS attempts to lengthen the period in the light of hindsight. They are also protected against IRS claims that the useful life of an asset should have been shortened in an earlier year because of a post-acquisition event and that the asset's basis must be charged with the additional allowable deduction even though it was in fact not taken when allegedly warranted. However, except as qualified by the requirement that the change in useful life be "significant" and be established by "clear and convincing" evidence, the process of revising an asset's useful life to conform to subsequent events ought to be governed by the same principles as the process of establishing its useful life when it is first placed in service.

¶23.4.6 Obsolescence

The regulations recognize that obsolescence may shorten the life of depreciable assets more rapidly than physical deterioration and that obsolescence can be "attributable to many causes, including technological improvements and reasonably foreseeable economic changes . . . normal progress of the arts and sciences, supersession or inadequacy brought about by developments in the industry, products, methods, markets, sources of supply, and other like changes, and legislative or regulatory action."[29] The Supreme Court has described obsolescence as follows: "Obsolescence may arise from changes in the art, shifting of business centers, loss of trade, inadequacy, supersession, prohibitory laws, and other things which, apart from physical deterioration, operate to cause plant elements or the plant as

---

[27] Reg. §1.167(a)-1(b). Compare Kansas City S. Ry. v. CIR, 76 TC 1067 (1981) (taxpayer initiated depreciation deductions for railroad grading it had previously treated as nondepreciable for lack of a determinable useful life; held, not a change in accounting method requiring prior IRS consent). See infra ¶105.6 for changes of accounting method.

[28] Reg. §1.167(a)-9.

[29] Id.

a whole to suffer diminution in value."[30]

Under pre-ACRS law, these factors, if anticipated when property is placed in service, justify an estimated useful life shorter than the asset's physical life. If obsolescence is more rapid than originally anticipated, the asset's useful life may be reduced to reflect the altered circumstances, provided the taxpayer proves that the asset will be retired sooner than expected. It is not enough to show that the taxpayer's facility is more costly to operate than newer models, that it is less profitable because competitors can produce a more advanced product, or that demand for the taxpayer's output has declined, since these disadvantages by themselves do not establish that the obsolete facility will be retired from service sooner than previously anticipated.[31] Obsolescence, in short, must diminish the asset's useful life; depreciation allowances may not be increased simply because economic or technological changes have put the taxpayer at a competitive disadvantage.[32]

In extreme cases, unforeseen extraordinary obsolescence can bring the asset's useful life to an abrupt end. If the asset is abandoned or permanently withdrawn from service and consigned to the scrap heap, the rules governing losses on retirement are applicable.[33]

---

[30] U.S. Cartridge Co. v. US, 284 US 511, 516 (1932), quoted with approval in Real Estate-Land Title & Trust Co. v. US, 309 US 13 (1940).

[31] See Zimmerman v. CIR, 67 TC 94 (1976) (construction of interstate highway, resulting in drastic change in traffic patterns; shorter life established for one motel but not for two others); American Valve Co. v. CIR, 4 BTA 1204 (1926) (acq.) (end of river freight service reduced remaining useful life of plant to 2.5 years). But see Real Estate-Land Title & Trust Co. v. US, 309 US 13 (1940) (obsolescence deduction denied for facility that was outmoded and duplicative but not permanently withdrawn from service); Coors Porcelain Co. v. CIR, 429 F2d 1 (10th Cir. 1970) (special-purpose building meeting AEC specifications; deduction denied despite cancellation of AEC contract, since taxpayer was exploring alternative uses); Dunn v. CIR, 42 TC 490 (1964) (effect of changing governmental farm policies insufficient to establish reduced useful life for surplus grain-storage facilities). See generally Note, Accounting for Extraordinary Obsolescence, 65 Harv. L. Rev. 1431 (1952).

[32] See Ames v. CIR, 626 F2d 693, 697 (9th Cir. 1980) (useful life cannot be revised to reflect "competitive failure of the venture in which the asset is used [because] the deduction is not intended to bail out business efforts that fail in the market place").

[33] Keller St. Dev. Co. v. CIR, 323 F2d 166 (9th Cir. 1963) (deduction for special-purpose equipment when plans for facility in which it would be housed were abandoned); Tanforan Co. v. US, 313 F. Supp. 796 (ND Cal. 1970), aff'd per curiam, 462 F2d 605 (9th Cir. 1972) (racetrack became useless as a result of legislation and public pressure).

For the deduction of obsolescent nondepreciable assets under §165(a) (relating to losses, discussed infra ¶25.4.4), see Reg. §1.165-2(a) (sudden termination of asset's usefulness, where business is discontinued or asset permanently discarded).

¶23.4.7   IRS Agreements re Useful Life

The fact that an asset's useful life as estimated by the taxpayer was accepted without change or was revised when the IRS audited an earlier year's return does not ordinarily preclude a reexamination of the same asset's useful life in a later year, even if there have been no significant changes in the interim.[34] Although a closing agreement under §7121 could be used to bind the IRS and the taxpayer to an agreed useful life,[35] a less cumbersome device to achieve this result was authorized in 1954 by the enactment of §167(d).[36] Under this provision, a written agreement specifying the useful life and rate of depreciation of an asset is binding on both the taxpayer and the IRS "in the absence of facts and circumstances not taken into consideration in the adoption of such agreement." The party initiating a change bears the burden of establishing the previously unconsidered facts and circumstances, and a change is prospective only.

The regulations provide that an agreement under §167(d) must set out "the facts and circumstances taken into consideration in adoption of the agreement."[37] Given the wide spectrum of facts that may be pertinent in establishing an asset's useful life, any narrative account or catalogue in an agreement is likely to be incomplete to some extent; if either the taxpayer or the IRS is determined to renounce an agreement, a pretext will probably be available in many cases. The tendency to let sleeping dogs lie, however, may result in the continued acceptance of most agreements, even if they could be undermined by a sufficiently aggressive search for facts and circumstances that were not considered when the agreements were executed.

¶23.5   SALVAGE VALUE OF PROPERTY NOT SUBJECT TO ACRS

¶23.5.1   In General

Under pre-ACRS law, the depreciation allowance is intended to permit taxpayers to deduct the cost of using depreciable property over its useful life. This cost is measured as the difference between the asset's cost (or other basis) and the estimated amount for which it can be disposed of on retirement from service. The latter amount, known as salvage value, is taken into account in one of two ways. Ordinarily, it is subtracted from the basis of the asset in fixing the amount to be depreciated. If, for example, an

---

[34] Wright Contracting Co. v. CIR, 36 TC 620, 636–37 (1961), aff'd on other issues, 316 F2d 249 (5th Cir.), cert. denied, 375 US 879 (1963).

[35] For closing agreements, see infra ¶112.1.5.

[36] See S. Rep. No. 1622, 83d Cong., 2d Sess. 26 (1954).

[37] Reg. §1.167(d)-1.

asset costing $100 has an estimated salvage value of $40 and is depreciated by the straight line method over a useful life of four years, the aggregate amount to be deducted is $60 ($100 less $40), and the annual deduction is $15 ($60/4).[1] Under other methods, the allowances are computed without reference to salvage value, but stop when the adjusted basis of the property (its cost or other basis, less depreciation already deducted) equals its salvage value. For example, under the 200 percent declining balance method, the depreciation rate is 200 percent divided by the asset's useful life, and this rate is applied each year to adjusted basis, reduced by depreciation for prior years but not salvage value. In the example, the rate under this method is 50 percent (200 percent divided by 4). The allowance for the first year of the property's useful life is $50 (50 percent of $100), but is limited for the second year to $10 since that amount plus the first year's deduction of $50 reduce unrecovered cost to $40, the asset's salvage value; no depreciation is allowable for the third or fourth year.[2] Whichever method of taking salvage value into account is used, the objective is to recognize that this amount is expected to survive the wear and tear, exhaustion, and obsolescence suffered by the asset during its use in the taxpayer's business.

Salvage value can be substantial if the taxpayer ordinarily disposes of assets when they are still in good operating condition, but can be no more than junk value if the asset is used until exhausted.[3] The impact of the taxpayer's business practice is dramatically illustrated by *Massey Motors, Inc. v. United States*, involving an automobile rental company that purchased cars for $1,650, expecting to sell them for about $1,380 after 15 months of use.[4] The taxpayer's effort to treat salvage value as zero, on the ground that the vehicles would have been worthless if used for their entire physical life (four years), was rejected by the Court, which held that the useful life and salvage value of a depreciable asset depend on the way it is used in the taxpayer's business, not on its inherent physical life or its economic life when used by other taxpayers for other purposes.

A taxpayer may use either gross salvage value (estimated gross receipts to be realized on disposition, less selling expenses if any) or net salvage value (gross salvage value less removal expenses), but the method chosen must be followed consistently.[5] If the taxpayer does not dispose of retired assets but instead relegates them to a scrap heap from which serviceable parts are rescued to maintain other assets, the asset's scrap value is its salvage value. The regulations do not mention "negative salvage," but one

---

[1] For another illustration, see infra Table 23-11, ¶23.6.
[2] See also infra ¶23.7.4 (salvage under ADR).
[3] Reg. §1.167(a)-1(c)(1).
[4] Massey Motors, Inc. v. US, 364 US 92 (1960), discussed supra ¶23.4.2.
[5] Reg. §1.167(a)-1(c)(1). See also Reg. §1.167(a)-11(d)(1)(i) (definition of "gross salvage").

court, in a decision that the IRS has announced it will not follow, allowed the use of negative salvage value by a taxpayer whose past experience established that the cost of removing retired assets (telephone poles) would exceed the amount to be received for them.[6] The IRS objects to negative salvage because its effect is to spread over the asset's useful life the costs to be incurred at the time of retirement in removing the asset, thereby allowing a future cost to be deducted years before it is incurred.[7]

Since an asset's salvage value, like its useful life, must be estimated on the basis of the relevant facts and circumstances as known at the time of acquisition, subsequent events can undermine its validity. The regulations state that salvage value may not be changed "merely because of changes in price levels," but that if the asset's useful life is redetermined, salvage value may be redetermined, "based upon facts known at the time of such redetermination of useful life."[8]

This provision seems to imply that an asset's salvage value may be changed only as a by-product of a change in its useful life, an event that is permissible only if there is "clear and convincing evidence" that a "significant" change is warranted.[9] Although post-acquisition facts warranting an increase or decrease in an asset's estimated useful life are probably the most common basis for changing its salvage value as well, it is also possible for salvage value to rise or fall as a result of causes other than changes in the price level, even though the asset's useful life is unchanged. Technological advances in a particular industry, for example, can depress the value of secondhand machines without reducing their useful life in the taxpayer's business. There is no sound reason for refusing to permit a change in salvage value in these circumstances, and the IRS, with support from the Tax Court, has ruled that the salvage value may be changed if the facts warrant, even if the asset's useful life is not changed at the same time.[10]

Although salvage value is the estimated amount to be realized on disposing of a retired asset and the regulations provide that an asset may not be depreciated below its reasonable salvage value, it has been held that depreciation may be taken in the year a depreciable asset is sold, even though the sales price exceeds the taxpayer's unrecovered basis at the begin-

---

[6] Portland Gen. Elec. Co. v. US, 223 F. Supp. 111 (D. Ore. 1963); Portland Gen. Elec. Co. v. US, 64-2 USTC ¶9636 (D. Ore. 1964) (not officially reported); Rev. Rul. 75-150, 1975-1 CB 73 (negative salvage not permissible).

[7] See IRC §461(h), discussed infra ¶105.3.

[8] Reg. §1.167(a)-1(c)(1).

[9] Reg. §1.167(a)-1(b), discussed supra ¶23.4.5.

[10] Rev. Rul. 62-92, 1962-1 CB 29, as modified by Rev. Rul. 67-272, 1967-2 CB 99; Durfee's, Inc. v. CIR, 25 TCM (CCH) 588 (1966). But see R.A. Heintz Constr. Co. v. US, 65-2 USTC ¶9455 (D. Ore. 1965) (not officially reported) (regulation precludes change in salvage value in absence of simultaneous change in useful life).

ning of the year. In *Fribourg Navigation Co. v. CIR*, the Supreme Court rejected the government's theory that the taxpayer sustained no depreciation in 1957 when a ship with an adjusted basis at the beginning of the year of about $327,000 and an estimated salvage value of $54,000 was sold during the year for $700,000.[11] Acknowledging that the sale of an asset for more than its depreciated basis might be evidence that its useful life or salvage value was miscalculated, the Court held that neither inference was warranted in the *Fribourg Navigation* case, where the sales price reflected a spectacular increase in the demand for cargo vessels following the 1956 blockage of the Suez Canal. On reviewing the legislative, administrative, and judicial history of the depreciation allowance, the Court concluded that Congress had in effect endorsed the taxpayer's right to depreciate assets in the circumstances presented by the case. Had the Court been writing on a clean slate, however, much could be said for the government's theory that the taxpayer's use of the asset in the year of sale cost it nothing and that a depreciation deduction was unwarranted, as three dissenting Justices argued.[12]

In *Fribourg Navigation*, the original salvage value estimate was admittedly reasonable when made. Indeed, it had been accepted by the IRS in a ruling issued to the taxpayer, and the disparity between the estimated amount and the sales price was attributable to a spectacular, unexpected, and short-lived change in the value of cargo ships. Thus, the decision does not prevent use of the asset's actual sale price as evidence that the salvage value was unreasonable when estimated. The Tax Court has held that under *Fribourg Navigation*, the taxpayer has the burden of proving that the estimate was reasonable and that the gain realized on the sale resulted from market appreciation.[13] For reasons explained elsewhere in this work, however, the subsequent enactment by Congress of §1245, requiring a recapture of depreciation when depreciable assets are sold, has substantially reduced the practical importance of the *Fribourg Navigation* principle.[14]

---

[11] Fribourg Navigation Co. v. CIR, 383 US 272 (1966).

[12] Id. at 288. The 1981–1986 version of ACRS allows no depreciation deduction in the year depreciable property is sold. IRC §168(d)(2)(B) (before amendment in 1986). The legislative history suggests no reason for eliminating the year of sale allowance, and the reason may be narrowly technical; unlike the pre-ACRS rules, the 1981–1986 rules contain no mechanism for allowing only part of a full year's deduction for the final year the taxpayer holds property. The post-1986 ACRS rules, which include such a mechanism, restore the year of sale allowance.

[13] Durfee's Inc. v. CIR, supra note 10. See also Macabe Co. v. CIR, 42 TC 1105 (1964) (holding, even before *Fribourg Navigation* was decided, that a sale for more than salvage value does not undermine the validity of the salvage estimate, where the sale occurred at an unexpectedly early point in the taxpayer's ownership).

[14] See infra ¶55.2.1.

¶23.5.2 Statutory Leeway in Estimating Salvage Value

Section 167(f), enacted in 1962, permits actual salvage value to be reduced by up to 10 percent of the asset's basis. For example, if the estimated salvage value of an asset costing $100 is $12, the taxpayer may use any amount between $2 and $12 as salvage value. The regulations provide that the 10 percent leeway is based on the asset's basis when salvage is originally estimated and that the dollar amount so determined does not have to be reduced when salvage is redetermined, even though the asset's basis at that time is its original cost less the depreciation already deducted.[15] Section 167(f) may eliminate some disputes between taxpayers and the IRS about the validity of estimates that in the last analysis rest on imponderables, but ordinarily the difference between the parties is too great to be eliminated by the 10 percent statutory leeway.

Section 167(f) only applies to depreciable personal property (other than livestock) with a useful life of three years or more. The disqualification of livestock and realty reflects the fact that depreciation deducted on these categories of depreciable asset was not subject to recapture when §167(f) was enacted. They were brought within the recapture mechanism in 1964 and 1969,[16] but Congress did not expand the coverage of §167(f) to reflect these changes.

¶23.6 DEPRECIATION METHODS AND RATES FOR PROPERTY NOT SUBJECT TO ACRS

¶23.6.1 Introductory

From 1913 to 1954, the federal revenue acts permitted taxpayers to deduct "a reasonable allowance" for exhaustion, wear and tear, and obsolescence of depreciable assets without describing or listing any specific depreciation methods,[1] and the regulations have long provided that the proper allowance is

> that amount which should be set aside for the taxable year in accordance with a reasonably consistent plan (not necessarily at a uniform rate), so that the aggregate of the amounts set aside, plus the salvage value, will, at the end of the estimated useful life of the depreciable

---

[15] Reg. §1.167(f)-1(c) Ex. 2.

[16] Section 1250, requiring recapture of depreciation on realty, was enacted in 1964. See infra ¶55.3. As to livestock, see IRC §1245(a)(2)(C) (added in 1969), discussed infra ¶55.2.2.

[1] See Revenue Act of 1913, ch. 16, §IIB, 38 Stat. 167; IRC §23(1) (1939) (as of 1954).

property, equal the cost or other basis of the property.[2]

During these formative years, the straight line method was almost universally used, except by public utilities, railroads, investors in rental real estate, and taxpayers in a few other industries.

The straight line method's popularity was due in large part to its simplicity: The asset's cost (or other basis), less the estimated salvage value (if any), is divided by its estimated useful life in years, and the resulting amount is the annual deduction. For example, if an asset costs $100, has an estimated salvage value of $20, and is expected to last for 10 years, the annual deduction is $8 ($80/10). Expressed as a rate of depreciation, the annual deduction is 10 percent of the amount to be depreciated. In addition to its simplicity, the straight line method has an aura of fairness because the same amount is deducted every year. For these reasons, it came to be regarded as the normal depreciation method, the reasonableness of which was self-evident. The propriety of other methods had to be established by reference to practices in the taxpayer's industry, expert testimony, or other evidence. In a 1955 text on depreciation, the authors wrote: "For income tax purposes other depreciation accounting methods are judged in terms of the closeness of their conformity to the straight line method."[3]

In 1954, Congress enacted §167(b), which explicitly endorsed the use of the straight line method and, more important, went on to authorize two accelerated depreciation methods—the "double declining balance" and "sum of the years-digits" methods—that quickly became attractive to tax-conscious businesses because they yield larger deductions in the early years of an asset's useful life than does the straight line method.

The importance of the statutory reference to the double declining balance and sum of the years-digits methods is that the taxpayer does not have to establish that they produce a "reasonable allowance" within the meaning of §167(a). That burden is eliminated by the introductory language of §167(b), which states that the term "reasonable allowance" as used in §167(a) "shall include" allowances computed under the methods listed in §167(b). For the announced purpose of "obtaining maximum incentive effect,"[4] §167(c) makes secondhand property ineligible for the double declining balance and sum of the years-digits methods.[5] The regulations, how-

---

[2] Reg. §1.167(a)-1(a), which is identical in this respect to Reg. 111, §29.23(1)-1 (1949). The 1949 regulations also provided that the amount to be depreciated "shall be charged off over the useful life of the property, either in equal annual installments or in accordance with any other recognized trade practice, such as an apportionment of the capital sum over units of production." Reg. 111, §29.23(1)-5 (1953).

[3] Grant & Norton, Depreciation 184 (Ronald Press 1955).

[4] S. Rep. No. 1622, 83d Cong., 2d Sess. 25 (1954).

[5] See infra ¶23.6.3.

ever, allow some used property to be depreciated under a somewhat less accelerated method, the 150 percent declining balance method.[6]

The 1954 changes were not intended to prohibit other methods that can be shown, by reference to the taxpayer's own circumstances or those prevailing in the industry, to produce a "reasonable allowance" within the meaning of §167(a). Preservation of this open-ended approach is reflected by the introductory clause of §167(b), which provides that the term "reasonable allowance" includes, "but shall not be limited to," the methods set out in that provision.

¶23.6.2 Straight Line Depreciation

The straight line method is authorized by §167(b)(1) for all types of depreciable property. It is the method employed by the IRS if the taxpayer neglects to take depreciation for a particular asset or fails to adopt an acceptable method.[7] It is also the point of reference for various rules making special provision for depreciation in excess of what might be considered normal, including §1250, under which the recapture of depreciation on real property is sometimes limited to the excess of the amount allowable over straight line depreciation;[8] §57(a)(7), treating deductions in excess of straight line depreciation on property placed in service before 1987 as "items of tax preference" in computing the alternative minimum tax;[9] and §312(k), requiring that straight line depreciation be used for non-ACRS property in computing corporate earnings and profits.[10]

These legislative references to the straight line method, coupled with the fact that no slower method is used in practice, lead many to assume that straight line is the true economic measure of depreciation, at least in an inflation-free environment. As shown elsewhere in this work, however, the straight line method is a highly accelerated method in many situations, where economic depreciation follows a pattern of allowances that begin small and increase year by year thereafter.[11]

---

[6] See infra ¶23.6.4.

[7] Reg. §§1.167(a)-10(a), 1.167(b)-1(a) (last sentence); see also infra ¶42.3. At one time the IRS took the position that the straight line method must be substituted if the taxpayer adopts an erroneous method, but the Tax Court held otherwise (Silver Queen Motel v. CIR, 55 TC 1101 (1971) (acq.)), and the IRS now follows the decision. Rev. Rul. 72-491, 1972-2 CB 104 (any proper method may be adopted to replace an erroneous method if the IRS disallows the improper method for the first year in which it is used or if the taxpayer files an amended return for that year before the following year's return is filed).

[8] For IRC §1250, see infra ¶55.3.1.

[9] For IRC §56, see infra ¶111.3.11.

[10] For IRC §312(k), see infra ¶92.1.3.

[11] Supra ¶23.1.4.

Further, it is not quite as simple as it appears at first. In its most uncomplicated application, it provides equal annual deductions over an asset's useful life. Changes in the asset's adjusted basis by reason of improvements or capital recoveries, however, produce corresponding changes in the amounts to be deducted thereafter, since the deduction for each year is determined by dividing the asset's adjusted basis at the beginning of the year, less its estimated salvage value, by its remaining useful life in years.[12] Changes in the asset's estimated useful life or salvage value also require a recomputation for subsequent years.

¶23.6.3 Double Declining Balance, Sum of the Years-Digits, and Other Methods

Section 167(b) allows the declining balance method, the sum of the years-digits method, and an amorphous third category of accelerated depreciation, but these methods are restricted to property meeting the standards of §167(c)—property constructed by the taxpayer or acquired and first used by him.[13] A complex set of additional restrictions was added in 1969 by the enactment of §167(j), which limits or forbids the use of these accelerated methods for most real property.[14] The statutory accelerated methods are described immediately following, and the limitations of §§167(c) and (j) are considered in the next section.

The accelerated methods of §167(b) only apply to property placed in service before 1981. For tangible property placed in service after 1980, depreciation is usually determined under ACRS, which is a self-contained system with its own provisions for acceleration.[15] Post-1980 tangible property may sometimes be taken out of ACRS, but only by the taxpayer electing a depreciation method other than one of the §167(b) accelerated methods. Intangibles, which are excluded from ACRS, are also excluded from §167(b).[16]

1. *The double declining balance method.* The declining balance method, first explicitly approved by a 1946 IRS ruling,[17] gained statutory

---

[12] Reg. §1.167(b)-1(a) (second sentence).

[13] See infra ¶23.6.4.

[14] Section 167(i), repealed for taxable years ending after December 31, 1978, also disqualified "suspension period" property—certain real property constructed or acquired between October 10, 1966 and March 9, 1967. See Zeitlin, Suspension of Investment Credit and Accelerated Depreciation—Application to Related Taxpayers, 25 NYU Inst. on Fed. Tax'n 1331 (1967).

[15] See supra ¶23.3.

[16] See infra §23.6.4.

[17] IT 3818, 1946-2 CB 42, modified by Rev. Rul. 59-389, 1959-2 CB 89. See also Reg. §1.167(b)-0(b) (use of 150 percent declining balance method after 1954); Rev.

recognition in 1954 with the enactment of §167(b)(2). When this method is used, the depreciation deduction is determined by multiplying the asset's adjusted basis at the beginning of the taxable year by a uniform rate, ordinarily expressed as a percentage (e.g., 125, 150, or 200 percent) of the straight line rate. Another way of expressing this is that the declining balance rate is a specified percentage (e.g., 125, 150, or 200 percent), divided by the property's useful life. Under the double declining balance method, for example, the annual rate for property with a useful life of 10 years is 20 percent (200 percent divided by 10). If the cost of the property is $100, the allowance for the first year is $20 (20 percent of $100) and the second year's allowance is $16 (20 percent of the excess of $100 over the first year's allowance of $20). The label "declining balance" refers to the fact that the asset's adjusted basis, to which the uniform rate is applied, declines from year to year.

The asset's salvage value is initially ignored under a declining balance method, but it serves as a floor below which the asset cannot be depreciated.[18] This is illustrated by Example 23-11, which compares depreciation under the double declining balance and straight line methods for an asset costing $1,000 whose salvage value is $300 and useful life is four years. The double declining balance rate of 50 percent (twice the straight line rate of 25 percent) produces a deduction for the first year of $500 (50 percent of cost). The allowance for the second year would be $250 if the rate were again applied to the asset's adjusted basis at the beginning of that year ($500), but the deduction is limited to $200 since that is sufficient to reduce the unrecovered cost to the asset's salvage value of $300.

Example 23-11

Double Declining Balance Depreciation— Effect of Salvage Value

Year		Straight Line	Declining Balance
1	....	$175	$500
2	....	175	200
3	....	175	–0–
4	....	175	–0–
	Total depreciation....................	$700	$700
	Unrecovered cost	$300	$300

Rul. 57-352, 1957-2 CB 150 (same), amplified by Rev. Rul. 59-389, 1959-2 CB 89, and clarified by Rev. Rul. 67-248, 1967-2 CB 98.

[18] Reg. §1.167(a)-1(a) (third sentence).

Because the annual deduction under a declining balance method is a percentage of the asset's adjusted basis at the beginning of each taxable year, the taxpayer's investment can never be depreciated down to zero. Indeed, the unrecovered "tail," the size of which depends on the depreciation rate and useful life of the asset, may exceed its salvage value. This phenomenon is illustrated by Example 23-12 for an asset with an eight year useful life that is purchased for $10,000 and has a salvage value of $400.

Example 23-12

Double Declining Balance Depreciation— Unrecovered Tail

Year	Straight Line	Declining Balance
1	$1,200	$2,500
2	1,200	1,875
3	1,200	1,406
4	1,200	1,055
5	1,200	791
6	1,200	593
7	1,200	445
8	1,200	334
Total depreciation	$9,600	$8,999
Unrecovered cost	$400	$1,001

Under the double declining balance method, the unrecovered tail for property with a three-year useful life is about 3.7 percent of the asset's cost or other basis; with an eight-year useful life, the tail is about 10 percent of cost. For useful lives between 10 and 100 years, this percentage rises gradually from 10.7 to 13.3 percent.[19] Section 167(e)(1) permits taxpayers using the declining balance method pursuant to §167(b)(2) to avoid the tail by switching to the straight line method at any time during the property's useful life.[20] On making the change, the taxpayer spreads the asset's unrecovered cost or other basis, less its salvage value, over its remaining useful life.[21] Typically, the switch is made as soon as the straight line method yields

---

[19] See Feinschreiber, The Impact of High Salvage Value on Double Declining Balance Depreciation, 20 SCL Rev. 47, 48–49 (1968).

[20] The IRS also allows a switch from the nonstatutory 150 percent declining balance method (supra note 17) to the straight line method. Rev. Rul. 74-324, 1974-2 CB 66.

[21] Reg. §1.167(e)-1(b).

a larger allowance than continued use of the declining balance method. The effect of such a switch on the facts of Example 23-12 is illustrated by Example 23-13.

Example 23-13

Switch From Double Declining Balance to Straight Line Depreciation

Year	Double Declining Balance	Straight Line
1	$2,500	
2	1,875	
3	1,406	
4	1,055	
5	791	
6		$ 658
7		658
8		657
Total	$7,627	$1,973

Cost	$10,000
Less: Depreciation in years 1–5	7,627
Adjusted basis at end of year 5	$ 2,373
Less: Salvage value	400
Balance to be depreciated on straight line basis in years 6–8	$ 1,973
Annual straight line allowance ($1,973/3)	$ 658
Recapitulation:	
Double declining balance depreciation	$ 7,627
Straight line depreciation	1,973
Salvage value	400
Cost	$10,000

If the estimated useful life of an asset being depreciated by the declining balance method changes in midstream,[22] the rate must be changed to the rate that would have prevailed if the revised useful life had been used when the original estimate was made.[23] For example, if an asset with an estimated

---

[22] For this possibility, see supra ¶23.4.5.
[23] Reg. §1.167(b)-2(c), held valid in Jones Bros. Bakery, Inc. v. US, 411 F2d 1282 (Ct. Cl. 1969).

20-year useful life (resulting in a double declining balance rate of 10 percent) is found at the end of the tenth year to have a remaining useful life of 15 rather than 10 years, the double declining balance rate falls to 8 percent (200 percent divided by revised estimated useful life of 25 years, measured from the time the property was placed in service), and this rate is thereafter applied to the asset's unrecovered cost or other basis.

2. *Sum of the years-digits method.* The sum of the years-digits method resembles the declining balance method in producing larger deductions in the early years of an asset's useful life than the straight line method. Unlike the declining balance method, however, it takes salvage value into account at the outset and, hence, does not leave an unrecovered tail. The annual allowance is a constantly declining fraction of the excess of original cost (or other basis) over salvage value, the numerator of the fraction being the number of remaining years in the asset's useful life and the denominator being the sum of the numbers making up its useful life (the "years-digits").

For property with a useful life of six years, the denominator is 21 (1 + 2 + 3 + 4 + 5 + 6). The deduction for the first year is 6/21 of the amount to be depreciated (cost or other basis, less estimated salvage value), and for the second year is 5/21 of the same amount.[24] The computations for the property's entire useful life are shown in Example 23-14, in which it is assumed that the property is purchased for $1,000 and has a salvage value of $160, producing a depreciable amount of $840.

When the useful life of an asset is changed, subsequent computations under the sum of the years-digits method are made as though a new asset had been acquired at the time of the change, with a useful life equal to the remaining useful life of the actual asset.[25] Thus, if the asset in Example 23-14 were found at the end of the fourth year to have a remaining useful life of three years, the denominator of the fractions to be used thereafter would be 6 (1 + 2 + 3), and the allowances for the remaining three years would be 3/6, 2/6, and 1/6, respectively, of the $120 remaining in the depreciable amount.

---

[24] Reg. §1.167(b)-3(a)(1). The method described in the text is the "whole life" plan. A variation (the "remaining life" plan) involves multiplying the asset's unrecovered cost or other basis as of the beginning of each taxable year, less its estimated salvage value, by a decimal given in a table. Reg. §1.167(a)-3(a)(2). Usually, the taxpayer may choose between these two variations, but the remaining life plan must be used in depreciating group, classified, and composite accounts. Reg. §1.167(b)-3(b)(1).

[25] Reg. §1.167(b)-3(a)(1)(ii). This mode of adjusting to a change in useful life presupposes use of the whole life plan (supra note 24). The decimals used under the remaining life plan adjust automatically to changes in the asset's estimated useful life.

Example 23-14

Sum of the Years-Digits Method

Year		Fraction of Depreciable Amount	Depreciation
1	....	6/21	$ 240
2	....	5/21	200
3	....	4/21	160
4	....	3/21	120
5	....	2/21	80
6	....	1/21	40
	Total depreciation........................		$ 840
	Salvage value...............................		160
	Cost.......................................		$1,000

3. Other statutory methods. Section 167(b)(4) authorizes the use of any other "consistent method," provided the accumulated deductions at the end of each year during the first two thirds of the asset's depreciable life do not exceed the aggregate amount that would have been deductible under the double declining balance method. The only method mentioned in the regulations as satisfying this provision is the sinking fund method.[26] The sinking fund method, however, almost always produces smaller deductions in the asset's earlier years than even the straight line method, and would ordinarily satisfy the "reasonable allowance" criterion of §167(a) without §167(b)(4). This fact, coupled with the absence of published rulings under §167(b)(4), suggests that it is not much utilized.

¶23.6.4 Property Eligible for Accelerated Depreciation

The accelerated depreciation methods authorized by §167(b), described in the preceding section, can only be used if the depreciable asset meets two sets of statutory conditions. The first set is imposed by §167(c), which was enacted in 1954 along with §167(b) itself; roughly speaking, it disqualifies short-lived, intangible, and used assets. The second is found in §167(j), enacted in 1969, which disqualifies certain categories of real property.[27]

---

[26] Reg. §1.167(b)-4(a). The sinking fund method is the same as economic depreciation as illustrated in Example 23-2 in ¶23.1.4.

[27] Also, §167(n), enacted in 1976 and repealed in 1981, requires the straight line method as a form of penalty where a certified historic structure was torn down or changed to make way for the property being depreciated. The rule applies if (1) a certified historic structure was demolished or substantially altered after June 30,

Some property excluded by §167(c) or (j) must be depreciated under the straight line method, but other such property qualifies for acceleration under methods falling somewhere between the straight line method and the most accelerated of the statutory methods.

1. *Restrictions of §167(c).* By virtue of §167(c), the §167(b) accelerated methods are only permissible for property that is tangible,[28] has a useful life of three years or more, and was either constructed, reconstructed, or erected by the taxpayer or was acquired and first used by him.[29] Secondhand property thus does not usually qualify whether the taxpayer is a purchaser, donee, or other transferee of a prior user. This disqualification, however, is lifted for certain transfers between parties to a corporate reorganization or to a consolidated tax return.[30]

The regulations allow the 150 percent declining balance method to be used for secondhand property disqualified by §167(c).[31] The 150 percent declining balance method is applied in the same way as the double declining balance method described earlier,[32] except that the annual rate is 150 percent of the straight line rate rather than 200 percent. The IRS denies even this version of the declining balance method to intangible assets and, except in rare circumstances, assets with a useful life of less than three years.[33]

1976 and (2) the expenditure being depreciated was incurred before 1982 in constructing a building or other structure on the site of the demolished historic structure or in reconstructing the substantially altered historic structure. For other provisions relating to historic structures, see infra ¶26.4.11.

[28] The statutory reference to intangibles is something less than a model of clarity, but the regulations exclude them, with clear support from the legislative history. Reg. §1.167(c)-1(a)(1) (second sentence); S. Rep. No. 1622, 83d Cong., 2d Sess. 202 (1954) (§167 "does not apply to intangible property such as patents, copyrights, and leases, etc."). See KIRO, Inc. v. CIR, 51 TC 155, 168 (1968) (acq. in result) (intangibles do not qualify for §167(b) accelerated methods).

For discussion of the relationship between intangibles and the tangible property resulting therefrom, see Texas Instruments, Inc. v. US, 551 F2d 599 (5th Cir. 1977) (cost of seismic information includable in cost of tangible personal property for investment credit purposes); Walt Disney Prods. v. US, 549 F2d 576 (9th Cir. 1976) (master film negatives).

[29] Also, the taxpayer's completion or acquisition of the property must have occurred after 1953. See Indian Creek Lumber Co. v. CIR, 43 TCM (CCH) 841 (1982) (reconditioned helicopters not new).

[30] Reg. §§1.167(c)-1a(4), (5), (6); Rev. Rul. 66-345, 1966-2 CB 67 (property acquired on complete liquidation of subsidiary).

[31] Reg. §1.167(b)-0(b). More generally, this regulation authorizes any method found acceptable before the enactment of §167(b) in 1954. For pre-1954 use of the 150 percent declining balance method, see supra note 17.

[32] Supra ¶23.6.3.

[33] Rev. Rul. 57-352, 1957-2 CB 150 (intangible property); Rev. Rul. 67-248, 1967-2 CB 98 (declining balance method does not result in reasonable allowance for

2. *Restrictions for section 1250 property.* Section 167(j) specially limits the right to use accelerated methods for "section 1250 property," which includes all depreciable real property except elevators, escalators, fixtures used in manufacturing and a few other activities, certain agricultural and storage facilities, and a few other items listed in §1245(a)(3).[34]

Section 167(j) classifies section 1250 property into five categories. Two categories (new residential rental property and pre-1969 property qualifying under a grandfather clause) are not limited at all, and can be depreciated under §167(b) as though §167(j) had not been enacted. A third category (new section 1250 property not within either of the first two categories) qualifies for 150 percent declining balance depreciation. The fourth category (used residential rental property with a useful life of 20 years or more) qualifies for a 125 percent declining balance rate, and the fifth category (other used property) may not use any version of the declining balance method. Used property was more strictly limited than new property in order to "to eliminate the repeated sale and resale of property for the purpose of tax minimization."[35]

Structurally, §167(j)(1) sets out the general rule that §167(b) does not apply to section 1250 property, which must instead be depreciated under (1) the straight line method, (2) the declining balance method, but at a rate not exceeding 150 percent of the straight line method, (3) any other consistent method producing an annual allowance during the first two thirds of the asset's useful life that does not exceed the amount computed under method 2, or (4) a method satisfying the "reasonable allowance" standard of §167(a). This general rule is subject to four exceptions:

a. *Residential rental property whose original use commenced with the taxpayer* qualifies for the methods listed in §167(b).[36] A building or structure is residential rental property if 80 percent or more of its gross rental income (including the rental value of any portion occupied by the taxpayer)

---

assets with useful life of less than three years except in rare and extraordinary circumstances).

[34] For §§1245 and 1250, see infra ¶¶55.2 and 55.3, respectively. To escape the restrictions of §167(j), elevators and similar items must be depreciated separately from the buildings in which they are located. See also supra ¶23.4.3 (re component accounts). Elevators and escalators placed in service after 1986 are section 1250 property, but §167(j) only applies to property placed in service before 1981.

See generally Guido, The Impact of the Tax Reform Act of 1969 on the Supply of Adequate Housing, 25 Vand. L. Rev. 289 (1972); Lane, Final Regs on Depreciation and Rehabilitation of Residential Property Clarify Many Areas, 37 J. Tax'n 18 (1972); Tucker, Analyzing the Impact of the 1976 Tax Reform Act on Real Estate Investments, 45 J. Tax'n 346 (1976).

[35] S. Rep. No. 552, 91st Cong., 1st Sess., reprinted in 1969-3 CB 423, 558.

[36] IRC §167(j)(2). Property located within a foreign country is subject to a special limitation related to that country's depreciation methods. IRC §167(j)(2)(A).

is from "dwelling units" (which excludes hotels, motels, and other establishments more than one half of whose units are used on a transient basis).[37] Since this test is applied year by year, a building may qualify for §167(b) depreciation in some years but not in others.

b. *Property constructed before July 25, 1969 or under contract for construction or permanent financing at that time* is also exempted from the restrictions of §167(j)(1), qualifying it for all of the §167(b) methods.[38] If property covered by this grandfather rule is destroyed or damaged by fire or other casualty, the rule applies to replacement property similar or related in service or use to the original property, up to the amount of the old property's adjusted basis at the time of the casualty.[39]

c. *Used residential rental property acquired after July 24, 1969 with a useful life of 20 years or more when acquired by the taxpayer,* qualifies for the 125 percent declining balance method or a method consistent with it as well as for the straight line method.

d. *Used section 1250 property that is not within the foregoing category and is acquired after July 24, 1969* is excluded from both the §167(b) accelerated methods and the less generous 150 percent declining balance method authorized by §167(j)(1) for other section 1250 property. The only depreciation methods that may be used for this property are the straight line method and any other method that the IRS determines will produce a reasonable allowance under §167(a), excluding declining balance methods, the sum of the years-digits method, and any other method whose use depends on §167(b)(4) or §167(j)(1)(C).

¶23.6.5 Nonstatutory Methods

Section 167(b), which explicitly authorizes use of the straight line, double declining balance, sum of the years-digits, and other accelerated methods meeting specific standards, provides that the statutory endorsement of these methods shall not "be construed to limit or reduce an allowance otherwise allowable under [the general rule of §167(a)]." Use of a nonstatutory method, however, is conditioned on proof that it produces a

---

[37] For computation of the property's gross rental income, see Reg. §1.167(j)-3(b)(2). See also Glenview Constr. Co. v. CIR, 77 TC 422 (1981), aff'd without opinion (3d Cir. 1981) (concrete slabs in mobile home park not residential because owner's income not rents from "dwelling units").

[38] IRC §167(j)(3). For the elaborate rules determining whether property qualifies under this exception, see Reg. §1.167(j)-4. See also Reg. §1.167(j)-7(a)(3) for the extent to which a transferee of depreciable property can qualify under the grandfather clause.

[39] Reg. §1.167(j)-7(a)(5). For the term "similar or related in service or use," see infra ¶44.3.3.

"reasonable allowance" within the meaning of §167(a). Thus, §167(b) preserves the qualified status of methods that were acceptable before 1954, when §167(b) was enacted. It also leaves room for new methods, although the IRS might react to innovations as do university faculties, whose watchword is "Nothing can be done for the first time."

The principal nonstatutory methods are:

1. *Depreciation based on production or use.* Under the unit-of-production method, the cost or other basis of the depreciable asset, less estimated salvage value, is divided by the number of units expected to be produced during its useful life, and the resulting unit cost is multiplied by the actual production in each taxable year to yield that year's deduction. If the asset's productive capacity is accurately estimated, the unit-of-production method matches depreciation to actual operations, increasing or decreasing the deduction to take account of multiple shifts, work stoppages, and other variations in the asset's use. This has the advantage of increasing deductions when income rises and reducing them in poor years. Approved by the regulations for use "under appropriate circumstances,"[40] the unit-of-production method is especially suitable for transportation equipment whose life can be estimated in terms of miles and for extractive industries, where the volume of ore, timber, or other material processed by equipment may be a more important determinant of useful life than the mere passage of time.

Similar in concept to the unit-of-production method are the operating-day and machine-hour methods, which are also suitable for assets that are affected primarily by actual use rather than by obsolescence or the mere passage of time. The cost of the depreciable asset, less its estimated salvage value, is spread over its estimated productive life in days or hours, and the per-day or per-hour amount is multiplied by the number of days or hours of actual use in the taxable year.[41]

These methods may be used in lieu of ACRS for tangible property placed in service after 1980.[42]

2. *Depreciation based on completed contracts.* For taxable years beginning before 1983, taxpayers using the completed contract method in computing income from long-term construction and similar contracts do not depreciate the property used in performing the contract in annual installments, but instead deduct in the year of completion the difference between

---

[40] Reg. §1.167(b)-0(b). See Cumberland Portland Cement Co. v. CIR, 29 TC 1185 (1958) (acq.) (change in unit cost under unit-of-production method); see also Reg. §§1.611-5(a), (b)(2) (unit-of-production method in extractive industries).

[41] Rev. Rul. 56-652, 1956-2 CB 125 (oil-drilling rigs and similar equipment); Western Mont. Lumber Co. v. CIR, 20 TCM (CCH) 1687 (1961) (machine-hour method for sawmill equipment).

[42] IRC §168(f)(1).

the asset's cost or other basis and its salvage value at that time.[43] This procedure is similar to treating the contract as a single unit of production to which the entire decline in the asset's value is allocable. For taxable years beginning after 1982, depreciation on assets used in performing long-term contracts is determined under the same rules as depreciation on property used in ordinary manufacturing.[44]

3. *Depreciation based on predicted income.* The IRS has ruled that motion picture and TV films may be depreciated by an "income forecast" method entailing an estimate of the total income to be derived from the asset during its useful life.[45] The deduction in any given year is then computed by multiplying the total production costs by a fraction, of which the numerator is that year's income and the denominator is the anticipated total income.[46] The estimate must be adjusted from time to time to reflect changes in the film's popularity. The acceptability of this method resulted from evidence that the useful life of films is dependent not on the mere passage of time but on the income they produce.

A variation on this method, sanctioned by the Tax Court, is an allocation of a TV film's cost to its various "runs," under which a proportionately higher amount is assigned to early runs, on evidence that they are more productive because they occur during prime time and attract the most viewers.[47] However, the Tax Court has upheld the IRS' rejection of a cost recovery method under which the taxpayer wrote off the film's cost against the first revenues received; the taxpayer asserted to no avail that the aggregate amount of income to be received could not be accurately predicted and

---

[43] Reg. §1.451-3(d)(5) (before amendment in 1985); see Lane v. CIR, 37 TC 188 (1961).

[44] See infra ¶106.3.3.

[45] Rev. Rul. 64-273, 1964-2 CB 62 (motion-picture films); Rev. Rul. 60-358, 1960-2 CB 68 (leased or rented TV films, taped shows for reproduction, and similar property). See Rev. Rul. 78-28, 1978-1 CB 51 (use of income forecast method by limited partnership tax shelter); Rev. Proc. 71-29, 1971-2 CB 568 (effect of syndication and TV exhibition of motion-picture films). See also S. Rep. No. 938, 94th Cong., 2d Sess., reprinted in 1976-3 CB (Vol. 3) 49, 110 (assumes income forecast method is normal method for films, etc., in recommending enactment of §280). See generally Levin & Adess, The Income Forecast Depreciation Method: Its Current Usage: Problems and Outlook, 40 J. Tax'n 70 (1974).

[46] See Gordon v. CIR, 766 F2d 293 (7th Cir. 1985) (numerator consists of income recognized under taxpayer's method of accounting; where taxpayer uses cash method, only amounts actually and constructively received are included); Greene v. CIR, 81 TC 132 (1983) (same; numerator is gross income less expenses of distribution).

[47] KIRO, Inc. v. CIR, 51 TC 155 (1968) (acq. in result). See Rev. Rul. 74-358, 1974-2 CB 43; see also Rev. Rul. 79-285, 1979-2 CB 91 (sliding scale method disallowed in absence of proof that deductions will correspond to flow of income).

that use of the straight line method would be artificial.[48]

4. *Interest methods.* Under the sinking-fund and other interest methods, used primarily by public utilities, deductions are computed on the assumption that interest is earned on the depreciation reserve. Allowances are lower in the earlier years of the asset's useful life and gradually rise, so that the depreciation reserve resembles a savings account to which equal deposits plus increasing amounts of interest are credited each year.[49]

5. *Retirement and replacement accounting.* Railroads and public utilities sometimes use a retirement or replacement method of depreciating certain assets. In a sense, these methods are the antithesis of depreciation because, instead of writing off the cost of an asset over its useful life, the taxpayer holds the cost in abeyance until the asset is retired, at which time it is written off in its entirety (retirement accounting) or the replacement asset's cost is deducted (replacement accounting).[50] It is doubtful that these methods would be approved by the IRS or the courts for industries where they are not already customary; they are barred by statute for all industries for years to which ACRS applies.[51] The issue is largely academic, however, because few if any taxpayers are attracted by methods that postpone deductions until the assets are retired.

6. *Depreciation of property whose cost depends on future revenues.* When the cost of property depends on future revenues from the property (as often happens with patents purchased for a percentage of future license fees), the straight line and other conventional methods can distort income because the aggregate amount to be depreciated is not yet known and these methods may only be applied to the payments already made. In these circumstances, the Tax Court has held that deducting the payments made during each taxable year produces a "reasonable allowance" within the meaning of §167(a).[52]

---

[48] Inter-City Television Film Corp. v. CIR, 43 TC 270 (1964).

[49] See Reg. §1.167(b)-4 (sinking-fund method). Sinking fund depreciation is the same as economic depreciation when the latter is calculated as shown in Example 23-2 in ¶23.1.4.

[50] See Baltimore & Ohio R.R. v. US, 603 F2d 165 (Ct. Cl. 1979); Chicago, Baltimore & Q.R.R. v. US, 455 F2d 993 (Ct. Cl. 1972), rev'd on another issue, 412 US 401 (1973); Boston & Maine R.R. v. CIR, 206 F2d 617 (1st Cir. 1953).

[51] IRC §168(f)(1). See also IRC §168(f)(3) (before amendment in 1986).

[52] Associated Patentees, Inc. v. CIR, 4 TC 979 (1945); Nat'l Util. Prods. Co. v. CIR, 37 TCM (CCH) 1851-18 (1978), and cases therein cited; Rev. Rul. 67-136, 1967-1 CB 58.

¶23.6.6 Intangible Property

Intangibles must usually be depreciated by the straight line method. ACRS never applies to intangible property.[53] The accelerated methods permitted by §167(b) may not be used for intangibles and the IRS even rules out the use of accelerated methods that are sometimes allowed apart from §167(b).[54] Intangible property may sometimes be depreciated by the income forecast method.[55] If the purchase price for an intangible is computed as a percentage of the taxpayer's revenues over the property's life, payments of these installments might be deductible as depreciation.[56] Otherwise, the straight line method is mandatory.

¶23.6.7 Election and Change of Depreciation Method

Under pre-ACRS law, a taxpayer may elect any permissible method of depreciation for a separate-asset or multiple-asset account by computing depreciation on that basis for the first taxable year in which depreciation is allowable. No formal application is required, and different methods may be elected for different assets. If no depreciation is claimed, however, use of the straight line method is ordinarily mandatory.[57]

Once elected, a depreciation method may not ordinarily be changed without permission from the IRS pursuant to §446(e).[58] Permission is not required, however, to change from the declining balance method to the straight line method or for changes in a few other special circumstances.[59]

---

[53] See supra ¶23.3.2.

[54] See supra ¶23.6.4 note 33 and accompanying text.

[55] See supra ¶23.6.5 notes 45–48 and accompanying text.

[56] See supra ¶23.6.5 note 52 and accompanying text.

[57] Reg. §1.167(b)-1(a) (use of straight line method if taxpayer has not adopted a different acceptable method). But see Reg. §1.167(a)-10(a) (exception if taxpayer failed to claim depreciation because item was erroneously treated as deductible expense); Rev. Rul. 67-49, 1967-1 CB 59 (straight line method not mandatory where taxpayer erroneously claimed amortization rather than depreciation in prior year). For the adoption of a proper method after an improper method is used, see Rev. Rul. 72-491, 1972-2 CB 104.

[58] Reg. §1.167(e)-1; Rev. Proc. 74-11, 1974-1 CB 420. For cases applying this rule, see Greene v. CIR, 81 TC 132 (1983); Wildman v. CIR, 78 TC 943 (1982); Standard Oil Co. (Ind.) v. CIR, 77 TC 349 (1981). For changes in accounting methods, see infra ¶105.6. A change in the asset's useful life does not carry with it a right to change the depreciation method. Casey v. CIR, 38 TC 357 (1962) (acq.); Rev. Rul. 74-154, 1974-1 CB 59.

[59] IRC §167(e)(1) (change to avoid unrecovered tail resulting from declining balance method; see supra ¶23.6.3); §167(e)(3) (change to straight line method for section 1250 assets; see infra ¶55.3); §167(j)(2)(C) (change required by change in status of section 1250 property); Rev. Rul. 74-324, 1974-2 CB 66 (change from 150 percent declining balance to straight line method does not require IRS consent).

¶23.7 ASSET DEPRECIATION RANGE SYSTEM

¶23.7.1 In General

In 1971, the Treasury promulgated the asset depreciation range system for the announced purpose of minimizing disputes between taxpayers and the IRS "as to the useful life of property, and as to salvage value, repairs, and other matters," and in the hope of stimulating investment and strengthening the competitive position of American industry in world markets.[1] The heart of the ADR system, which is elective, is a set of industry-wide class lives for depreciable assets. It is, however, a self-contained charter governing salvage values, retirements, repair deductions, and other matters, and a taxpayer making an ADR election is subject to all these interdependent rules. ADR may only be elected with respect to property placed in service before 1981; for subsequently acquired property it is superseded by ACRS.[2]

Because the ADR rules are elaborately intertwined with complex accounting principles and because the importance of the rules fades year by year as property subject to ADR elections is retired from service, only a summary of the main features of ADR is given here.[3]

¶23.7.2 Eligible Property

"Eligible property" for ADR purposes consists of all tangible depreciable property subject to §1245 or §1250 that is placed in service by the taxpayer during the period 1971 through 1980 and for which an asset guideline class and period are in effect for the taxable year of the election.[4]

---

[1] Reg. §1.167(a)-11(a)(1). ADR was initially promulgated without explicit statutory authorization. Section 167(m) was enacted a few months later, largely confirming the Treasury's authority but requiring a bit of fine tuning. See Bittker, Treasury Authority to Issue the Proposed "Asset Depreciation Range System" Regulations, 49 Taxes 265 (1971).

[2] IRC §167(m)(4). See supra ¶23.3 for ACRS.

[3] See generally Levine, An Analysis of the Planning Possibilities Existing Under the Current ADR System, 48 J. Tax'n 130 (1978); Scholler, Traller & Wagner, The ADR System: An Analysis of the Final Regs and How Practitioners Should Use Them, 39 J. Tax'n 16 (1973). See also Sunley, The 1971 Depreciation Revision: Measures of Effectiveness, 24 Nat'l Tax J. 19 (1971).

[4] Reg. §1.167(a)-11(b)(2). The guideline classes were periodically revised. The last listing during the ADR years is Revenue Proc. 77-10, 1977-1 CB 548, superseded by Rev. Proc. 83-35, 1983-1 CB 745, declared obsolete by Rev. Proc. 87-56, 1987-2 CB 674. Property first placed in service after 1970 by a transferee is not eligible if it was placed in service before 1971 by the transferor and acquired by the transferee through a "mere change in the form of conducting a trade or business." Reg. §1.167(a)-11(b)(7). For §§1245 and 1250, see infra ¶¶55.2 and 55.3.

Capitalized additions and improvements made during this period to existing assets are subject to the ADR rules if an election is in effect for the year they are first placed in service. The principal depreciable assets that are not eligible for ADR treatment are intangibles and, with certain exceptions, real property.[5]

¶23.7.3 Election

The ADR system is elective annually for eligible assets first placed in service in the year of the election, which are grouped in one or more "vintage" accounts that remain subject to the ADR rules until all assets in the account are retired from service. All eligible property first placed in service during the year of an election is subject to ADR, except (1) at the taxpayer's option, a limited amount of used property, (2) property not depreciated by the straight line, declining balance, or sum of the years-digits method, (3) property subject to statutory amortization (e.g., pollution control facilities under §169) or other special depreciation methods (e.g., expenditures to rehabilitate low-income rental housing under §167(k)), and (4) a few other items.[6]

Since an ADR election embraces only the eligible property first placed in service by the taxpayer during an election year, taxpayers could straddle the ADR and non-ADR rules by accelerating or postponing the date property is acquired or placed in service[7] and by segregating particular assets in a subsidiary or affiliate, at least if these gambits do not run afoul of the substance over form doctrine.

¶23.7.4 ADR Useful Lives; Salvage Value; First Year
Conventions

The ADR system provides a series of asset guideline periods, corresponding to useful lives, that either are industry-wide (agriculture, manufac-

---

[5] Buildings and other section 1250 property were not covered by an ADR election unless the IRS prescribed a class life for them, something that was never done. See Pub. L. No. 93-625, §5, 88 Stat. 2112 (1975), explained by S. Rep. No. 1357, 93d Cong., 1st Sess., reprinted in 1975-1 CB 517, 523; see also Rev. Proc. 77-10, 1977-1 CB 548 (re land improvements such as sidewalks, landscaping, docks, and canals).

[6] See Reg. §§1.167(a)-11(b)(5)(iv), (vi), (vii); Tennessee Natural Gas Lines, Inc. v. CIR, 71 TC 74 (1978).

[7] See Reg. §1.167(a)-11(b)(5). Property is placed in service when it is "in a condition or state of readiness and is available for a specifically assigned function" in the taxpayer's business or income-producing activity. Reg. §1.167(a)-11(e)(1). See also supra ¶23.2.3. For accounting conventions applied to additions and retirements, see Reg. §1.167(a)-11(c)(2).

ture of rubber and plastics products, wholesale and retail trade) or relate to functions without regard to the particular industry (office furniture and equipment, transportation equipment, land improvements, etc.). These categories are usually subdivided into more specialized classifications (e.g., "transportation equipment" distinguishes among automobiles, buses, light and heavy trucks, railroad cars, etc.).[8] For each such class, the ADR system specifies a guideline period, similar to the guidelines formerly applied by Revenue Procedure 62-21.[9] Most guidelines specify lower and upper limits (80 percent and 120 percent, respectively, of the norm), thus establishing a range within which the taxpayer may select a useful life for the particular vintage account.

Since the life adopted under ADR must also be used in computing the special first-year depreciation allowance, eligibility for accelerated depreciation under §§167(b) and 167(c), and the investment credit, use of the shortest life sanctioned by ADR sometimes had offsetting disadvantages.[10]

The salvage value of the assets in each vintage account was estimated when the account was created. Instead of directly reducing the aggregate amount to be depreciated, as under ordinary depreciation rules,[11] ADR salvage values serve only to limit the taxpayer's depreciation allowances during a vintage account's terminal years. Depreciation is computed without regard to salvage, but deductions stop once unrecovered basis for the assets in the account reaches salvage value.[12]

Depreciation for the year property is placed in service is determined under a half-year or modified half-year convention, at the taxpayer's election.[13] Under the half-year convention, all property placed in service during the year is deemed placed in service on the first day of the second half of the year. Under the modified half-year convention, property placed in service during the first half of the year is deemed placed in service on the first day of the year, whereas property placed in service during the last half of the year is deemed placed in service at midyear. If the taxable year consists of 12 months, the first-year allowance under either convention is at least one half of the allowance for a full year, regardless of how late in the year property is acquired. For short taxable years, in contrast, the allowance must be reduced to reflect the length of the taxable year before the applica-

---

[8] See Rev. Proc. 77-10, supra note 4.

[9] Supra ¶23.4.4 note 19.

[10] See Reg. §1.167(a)-11(g)(1). Once the shortest allowable period is elected for a particular class for a particular year, the IRS will not permit the taxpayer to change to a longer period when it is later discovered that the election puts the taxpayer into the clutches of one of these disadvantages. Rev. Rul. 82-22, 1982-1 CB 33.

[11] Supra ¶23.5.1.

[12] Reg. §1.167(a)-11(d)(1)(iv).

[13] Reg. §1.167(a)-11(c)(2).

ble convention is applied. If a partnership accounting on the calendar year is organized and acquires property on December 29, for example, the first-year allowance under the modified half-year convention is 3/365 of a full year's allowance.[14]

¶23.7.5 Retirements

Retirements of ADR assets are subject to complex rules, which distinguish between "extraordinary" retirements (all section 1250 property, section 1245 property retired by reason of casualty, and some other items) and "ordinary" retirements (all other retirements).[15] Gain or loss usually is not recognized on an ordinary retirement. Instead, the proceeds are added to the depreciation reserve, thus reducing the aggregate amount to be depreciated over the life of the vintage account and, in the case of declining balance depreciation, the annual allowance.[16] On an extraordinary retirement, however, the asset's unadjusted basis is removed from the vintage account along with its share of the depreciation reserve, and gain or loss is subject to the usual rules, including §§1231, 1245, and 1250 and the nonrecognition rules.

¶23.7.6 ADR Repair Allowances

Most ADR asset guidelines specify a repair allowance (as a percentage of the unadjusted basis of qualified property), designed to minimize disputes regarding the classification of expenditures that the taxpayer would like to deduct but that the IRS might classify as improvements subject to capitalization.[17] At the taxpayer's option, exercisable from year to year separately for each guideline class, expenditures up to the specified percentage may be deducted without question (the balance being capitalized) unless the expenditure is for an "excluded addition." This term is designed to disqualify substantial improvements (e.g., an expenditure over $100 that increases the productivity or capacity of an identifiable unit of property by more than

---

[14] See Peters v. CIR, 89 TC 423 (1988) (limited partnership was organized on January 4, but had no assets or liabilities until, on December 29, it issued limited partnership interests and entered into equipment leasing deal; held, taxable year began on December 29 for purposes of ADR convention).

[15] Reg. §1.167(a)-11(d)(3)(ii). See Lake Superior Dist. Power Co. v. CIR, 701 F2d 695 (7th Cir. 1983) (sale of transmission line to another power company was extraordinary retirement even though sale contract gave taxpayer-seller right to use line as though it continued to own it).

[16] Rev. Proc. 81-24, 1981-1 CB 693 (method of reducing salvage value attributable to ordinary retirements).

[17] For the normal distinction between deductible repairs and nondeductible capital outlays, see supra ¶20.4.8.

25 percent, that adds additional space to an existing building, etc.).[18]

¶23.8 ELECTION TO EXPENSE

Under §179, a taxpayer can elect to deduct 100 percent of the cost of "section 179 property" placed in service during the taxable year, up to a maximum of $10,000.[1] The term "section 179 property" includes most depreciable personal property.[2] To restrict the allowance to the small businesses it is intended to benefit, however, a taxpayer is excluded if he acquires $210,000 or more of otherwise eligible property during the taxable year.[3]

1. *Election.* Subject to these limitations, all taxpayers except estates and trusts are eligible for the election.[4] A partnership or S corporation, not its partners or shareholders, must make the election with respect to property purchased by the partnership or S corporation.[5] The election is made year by year, and must usually be made on the taxpayer's original return for the year. An election may be made by amended return only if it is filed before the due date (including extensions) of the return. Once made, an election cannot be revoked, except with IRS consent.[6]

2. *Section 179 property.* The deduction is allowed with respect to "section 179 property," which is defined as "section 38 property" that is acquired by "purchase" for use in the "active conduct" of a trade or business.[7] "Section 38 property" includes most tangible personal property with a

---

[18] Reg. §1.167(a)-11(d)(2). See IRC §263(e) (before repeal in 1981); Reg. §1.263(f)-1. See also Armco, Inc. v. CIR, 88 TC 946 (1987) (repair allowance for ferrous metals industry held invalid because unreasonably low).

[1] The $10,000 cap applies to property placed in service after 1986. The dollar limitation was $5,000 for the taxable years 1982 through 1986, and was zero for 1981. IRC §179(b)(1) (before amendment in 1986). For years before 1981, the dollar limitation was $10,000, but the §179 allowance was only 20 percent of the cost of eligible property; the maximum deduction was therefore $2,000. IRC §§179(a), (b)(1) (before amendment in 1981).

[2] See infra notes 7–14 and accompanying text.

[3] See infra text accompanying note 15. Ironically, the pre-1981 statute, which did not contain this limitation and was restricted to smaller taxpayers by only the relative disinterest large businesses have in such small dollar amounts, was entitled "Additional First-Year Depreciation Allowance for Small Business," whereas the term "small business" is nowhere to be found in the present statute.

[4] IRC §§179(d)(4), (5).

[5] Reg. §1.179-1(h). Also, the determination of whether the property is section 179 property is made at the entity level. Id.

[6] Reg. §1.179-4.

[7] IRC §179(d)(1). The words "active conduct" were added in 1986, but neither the statute nor the legislative history indicates how an actively conducted trade or

useful life of three years or more and a few other kinds of property.[8] An acquisition of property is a "purchase" unless the transferor is a related person or the taxpayer's basis is determined with reference to the adjusted basis of the transferor.[9] Property received by a corporation from a shareholder in exchange for stock is not section 179 property if the shareholder qualifies for nonrecognition under §351(a), for example, because a corporation succeeds to the shareholder's basis for such property under §362(a). The deduction is only allowed for the year property is placed in service,[10] and is thus unavailable if, during that year, the property is not section 38 property or is not used in a trade or business.

For taxpayers other than corporations, property leased to other persons is usually ineligible, even if it is section 179 property. This bar is lifted, however, if (1) the taxpayer manufactured or produced the property or (2) the lease term is less than 50 percent of the property's useful life and expenses other than interest, taxes, and depreciation exceed 15 percent of rental income for the first 12 months the property is leased.[11] Even when this disqualification is avoided, however, leased property does not qualify as section 179 property unless the taxpayer can show his leasing activities amount to "the active conduct of a trade or business."[12]

Subject to the dollar limitation, the taxpayer's entire basis for section 179 property may usually be expensed. A special rule, however, applies to

---

business differs from other trades and businesses. The statute also requires that the property be "recovery property," but a definition of the term "recovery property" is only found in the version of §168 that was repealed in 1986. IRC §168(c)(1) (before amendment in 1986).

The definition described in the text applies with respect to property placed in service after 1980. Previously, the term "section 179 property" was defined as depreciable tangible personal property with a useful life of six years or more that was purchased either for use in business or for the production of income. IRC §179(d)(1) (before amendment in 1981).

[8] IRC §48(a). See infra ¶27.2.

[9] IRC §179(d)(2); Reg. §1.179-3(d).

[10] IRC §179(a). Property is placed in service when it "is first placed by the taxpayer in a condition or state of readiness and availability for a specifically assigned function." Reg. §1.179-3(f). See supra ¶23.2.3.

[11] IRC §§46(e)(3), 179(d)(4). The application of this provision to property placed in service after 1986 is not entirely clear. The statute denies §179 expensing to a noncorporate lessor "unless the [investment] credit under section 38 is allowable with respect to such person for such property." IRC §179(d)(4). For years prior to 1986, satisfaction of the criteria described in the text was sufficient to qualify a noncorporate lessor for the credit. The credit, however, was repealed as of the end of 1985, and the language quoted above can no longer be literally satisfied. Congress, however, probably did not intend to disqualify all noncorporate lessors, and the quoted words should probably be read to allow §179 expensing if, but for its repeal, the taxpayer would be eligible for the credit.

[12] See supra text accompanying note 7.

property that is acquired in a nonrecognition exchange if the taxpayer's basis for the property is determined with reference to his basis for the property given in the exchange. A common case subject to the special rule is property received in a like-kind exchange, where gain is generally not recognized in the exchange, but the basis of the property received derives from the basis for the property exchanged.[13] When the special rule applies, the portion of the property's basis that transfers over from the property exchanged cannot be expensed under §179.[14] Any additional basis arising in the exchange (reflecting, for example, boot given by the taxpayer) can qualify under §179. Assume a new machine is acquired in a trade-in; for the new machine, the taxpayer gives an old machine (of like kind) with a basis of $120 plus cash boot of $800. The adjusted basis of the new machine is $920 (the sum of the old machine's basis and the boot), but only $800 (the boot) can be expensed under §179.

3. *Dollar limitation.* The $10,000 limitation is phased down, dollar for dollar, if the taxpayer's purchases of section 179 property for the year exceed $200,000.[15] The §179 deduction thus is denied if the aggregate cost of section 179 property placed in service during the taxable year is greater than $210,000.

Also, the deduction for any year may not exceed the taxable income "derived from the active conduct by the taxpayer of any trade or business."[16] Taxable income is determined for this purpose without any cost recovery allowance for section 179 property placed in service for the year.[17] The effect of the rule thus is that while the §179 allowance can reduce active business income to zero, it cannot produce a loss in the business.

When spouses file separate returns, the limitation is first determined as though they were one taxpayer, and the resulting amount ($10,000 or some lesser amount) is split between the spouses as they agree or, in the absence of agreement, 50-50.[18] A controlled group of corporations must also apportion a single $10,000 among themselves.[19] When a partnership or S corporation makes the election, the dollar limitation is applied both to the entity

---

[13] IRC §1031, discussed infra ¶44.2.

[14] Reg. §1.179-3(e).

[15] IRC §179(b)(2). This rule only applies in taxable years beginning after 1986.

[16] IRC §179(b)(3)(A). This limitation only applies for taxable years after 1986.

If a taxpayer subject to this limitation makes the §179 election, the disallowed amount is carried to the following year and added to the §179 deduction for that year, subject again to the taxable income limitation. IRC §179(b)(3)(B).

[17] IRC §179(b)(3)(B).

[18] IRC §§179(b)(4); Reg. §1.179-2(g), (f). For years prior to 1981, the cap was doubled when a joint return was filed, and a spouse filing separately was entitled to the same deduction as an unmarried person. IRC §179(b) (before amendment in 1980).

[19] IRC §§179(d)(5), (6); Reg. §1.179-2(b).

and to each partner or shareholder.[20]

If the cost of section 179 property placed in service during a year exceeds the dollar limitation, the election must designate the costs to be deducted under §179.[21] The deducted amount may consist of the entire cost of one or more items of section 179 property or a designated portion of the cost of one or more items.[22] Special limitations apply, however, if the designated property is an automobile or property used for both business and nonbusiness purposes.[23]

The benefit of §179 is recaptured if a taxpayer converts property expensed under §179 to a nonbusiness use.[24] A conversion to nonbusiness use is deemed to occur if 50 percent or more of the property's use in any taxable year is either personal use or a use in an activity for profit that is not a trade or business.[25] Unless the taxpayer is in business as a lessor, for example, a conversion to nonbusiness use occurs when property originally used in the taxpayer's trade or business is leased to someone else.

When the recapture rule applies, the recaptured amount is the excess of the §179 deduction over the portions of the deducted cost that would, in the absence of the §179 election, have been allowed as cost recovery under §168 for all years through the year of the conversion.[26] Assume property is purchased for use in an individual's trade or business, and $10,000 of its cost is expensed under §179; the next year, however, taxpayer's business use of the property ceases, and the property is leased. If ACRS deductions would have been 20 percent of cost for the year the property is placed in service and 32 percent for the next year, the recapture amount is $4,800 (the $10,000 deducted under §179, reduced by depreciation of $2,000 and $3,200 that

---

[20] IRC §179(d)(8); Reg. §§1.179-2(c), (d). The property's adjusted basis in the hands of the partnership or S corporation is reduced by the §179 deduction taken by the entity, even if one or more of the partners or shareholders is barred by the dollar limitation, as applied to him, from taking all of his share of the entity's deduction. Reg. §1.179-1(f)(2).

[21] Procedures for doing this are given in §1.179-4(a) of the regulations. See also Rev. Proc. 86-48, 1986-2 CB 745 (procedures for changing choices made under §179).

[22] Reg. §1.179-1(b). The length of time the taxpayer held the property during the year is not relevant. A deduction equal to the dollar limitation may, for example, consist of the cost of property purchased near the end of the year. Reg. §1.179-1(c).

[23] These limitations derive from §280F, which is described in ¶23.11.

[24] IRC §179(d)(10). The recapture rule was enacted in 1981. For property placed in service during the period 1981 through 1986, the rule only applies if the conversion to nonbusiness use occurs during the year of acquisition or one of the succeeding two years. IRC §179(d)(10) (before amendment in 1986). The two-year limitation was dropped for property placed in service after 1986.

[25] Reg. §1.179-1(e)(2).

[26] Reg. §1.179-1(e)(1).

would have been allowed for the two years but for the §179 election).[27] The recaptured amount is reported as ordinary income in the year of the conversion.[28]

¶23.9 WITHDRAWAL OF DEPRECIABLE ASSETS FROM SERVICE

When a depreciable asset is permanently withdrawn from use in the taxpayer's business or income-producing activity, the resulting tax treatment depends on whether the asset is sold, exchanged, or abandoned by the taxpayer or is retained and transferred to a scrap account (e.g., so that serviceable parts can be detached to repair other assets).[1] Property retained for standby use in the event that replacement equipment breaks down is not "permanently withdrawn" from service and remains subject to depreciation.[2]

If a depreciable asset is sold or exchanged, the taxpayer's gain (or loss) —the difference between the amount realized and the adjusted basis of the property—is recognized in accordance with the usual rules governing gain or loss on the disposition of property.[3] Gains and losses from sales or exchanges ordinarily go into the "hotchpot" described by §1231, except to the extent of depreciation recaptured by §§1245 and 1250.[4] On an abandonment, the taxpayer's unrecovered basis in the asset, if any, is ordinarily deductible under §165.[5]

---

[27] The hypothetical depreciation for the year of the conversion must be determined in light of the conversion. Assume depreciation for the second year is $3,200 if the property is held for business or investment use all year, but the taxpayer's use for the year is 60 percent personal and 40 percent business. The hypothetical depreciation for the second year is $1,280 (40 percent of $3,200), and the recapture is $6,720 (the excess of $10,000 over the sum of $2,000 and $1,280). See Reg. §1.179-1(e)(4) Ex. 2.

[28] Reg. §1.179-1(e)(1). For subsequent years, §168 depreciation is determined as though §179 had not been elected. Id. The recaptured amount is restored to the taxpayer's adjusted basis for the property. Reg. §1.179-1(e)(3).

[1] Reg. §1.167(a)-8. For the concept of retirement from service, see supra ¶23.2.3; for retirements from ADR vintage accounts, see supra ¶23.7.5.

[2] Calcasieu Paper Co. v. CIR, 12 TCM (CCH) 74 (1953) (standby power plant).

[3] See Prop. Reg. §1.168-6(a)(1).

[4] For IRC §1231, see infra ¶54.1.1; for IRC §§1245 and 1250, see infra ¶¶55.2 and 55.3.

[5] See infra ¶25.4.3 (abandonment losses); Prop. Reg. §1.168-6(a)(2) (this rule only applies if taxpayer "intend[s] to discard the asset irrevocably so that he will neither use the asset again, nor retrieve it for sale, exchange, or other disposition"). For the possibility of an extraordinary obsolescence deduction for property that is no longer useful but has not been physically discarded, see Reg. §1.167(a)-9 (retirement rules govern where usefulness of depreciable property suddenly terminates); Coors

Under pre-ACRS law, on the withdrawal from service of a depreciable asset that is included in a multiple-asset account rather than depreciated as a separate unit of property, its adjusted basis must be determined or reconstructed under rules set out in the regulations.[6] Taxpayers with multiple-asset accounts involving numerous acquisitions and retirements (e.g., a trucking company or automobile rental agency with a large fleet of vehicles) may short-cut the usual rules either by reporting all receipts from salvage as ordinary income or by charging the depreciation reserve with the full cost or other basis of retired assets and crediting it with all receipts from salvage, provided the practice is followed consistently and, in the opinion of the IRS, clearly reflects income.[7] Under ACRS, all receipts on disposition of assets in such accounts (referred to as general asset accounts) must be reported as income.[8]

If the withdrawn asset is retained for scrap or similar uses rather than disposed of or physically abandoned, gain is not recognized, but loss is recognized to the extent the asset's unrecovered basis exceeds its value.[9] Under ACRS, however, loss is never recognized on the scrapping of an asset held in a general asset account.[10] Under pre-ACRS law, loss can be recognized on the scrapping of property in a multiple-asset account if the retirement was "abnormal" or the account's depreciation rate was based on the maximum expected life of the longest-lived asset therein.[11] When the foregoing limitations bar a loss deduction, the loss is treated as unrealized or inchoate because the asset is still retained by the taxpayer, despite its permanent withdrawal from use in the business. The unrecognized loss, however, is taken into account either indirectly by a reduction in the depreciation reserve or directly by amortization over a period of years following the retirement.[12]

Porcelain Co. v. CIR, 429 F2d 1 (10th Cir. 1970) (no deduction allowed before "permanent withdrawal of depreciable property from use").

[6] Reg. §§1.167(a)-8(c)(1), (d).

[7] Reg. §1.167(a)-8(e)(2).

[8] See supra ¶23.3.4.

[9] Prop. Reg. §1.168-6(a)(3). Loss is not recognized, however, on a conversion to personal use. Id.

[10] See supra ¶23.3.4.

[11] Reg. §1.167(a)-8(a)(3). For the distinction between "normal" and "abnormal" retirements, see Reg. §1.167(a)-8(b).

[12] Reg. §1.167(a)-8(e)(1).

¶23.10 LUXURY AUTOMOBILES, ENTERTAINMENT FACILITIES, AND PROPERTY USED PARTIALLY FOR NONBUSINESS PURPOSES

Section 280F limits ACRS deductions, deductions for rent, and investment credits pertaining to automobiles, entertainment facilities, and computers. If any of these items is used for both business and nonbusiness purposes, ACRS deductions are determined on a straight line basis and the investment credit is denied unless the business use is more than one half of total use. Also, ACRS deductions and investment credits on a passenger automobile are subject to strict dollar limits, even if the car is used exclusively in business.

These limits were enacted in 1984 when ACRS deductions were highly accelerated under the 1981–1986 rules and the investment credit was in effect. The rule slowing down ACRS and denying the investment credit when nonbusiness use predominates over business use was enacted because Congress believed that "the incentives of the investment credit and ACRS were designed to encourage investment in new plant and equipment rather than to subsidize the purchase of personal property that is used incidentally or occasionally in the taxpayer's business."[1] As to the dollar limits on ACRS and investment credits for automobiles:

> Congress believed that [these] investment incentives . . . should be directed to encourage capital formation, rather than to subsidize the element of personal consumption associated with the use of very expensive automobiles. . . . To the extent [of the value of an automobile sufficient to provide] necessary transportation, the generally allowable tax benefits should be available. Beyond that point, however, the extra expense of a luxury automobile provides, in effect, a tax-free personal emolument which Congress believed should not qualify for tax credits or acceleration of depreciation deductions because such expenditures do not add significantly to the productivity which these incentives were designed to encourage.[2]

Although investment incentives were reduced in 1986 by the repeal of the investment credit and the lengthening of ACRS recovery periods, the strictures of §280F remain.

1. *Limits on ACRS on "listed property."* Under §280F(b), if a taxpayer owns "listed property" that is used for both business and other purposes,

---

[1] Staff of Joint Comm. on Tax'n, 98th Cong., 2d Sess., General Explanation of Revenue Provisions of Deficit Reduction Act of 1984, at 560 (Comm. Print 1984) [hereinafter 1984 Bluebook].

[2] Id. at 559.

ACRS deductions are sharply slowed down unless the business use predominates.[3] The term "listed property" includes most cars, trucks, entertainment facilities, and home computers.[4]

Business use is considered predominant for any year in which the ratio of business use to total use exceeds one half.[5] The numerator generally includes all use in the taxpayer's trade or business.[6] Personal use and use in profit-oriented activities not constituting a business are included in the denominator, but not the numerator. Use of an automobile in commuting to work is personal even if business calls are made from a carphone or business is discussed with associates.[7] Personal use by an employee of the taxpayer is considered a use in the taxpayer's business if (1) the value of this use is included in the employee's gross income as compensation and all applicable withholding requirements are complied with and (2) the employee is neither related to the taxpayer nor a greater than 5 percent shareholder or partner of the taxpayer.[8] If the taxpayer is in the business of leasing property to others, leased property is considered used in the business unless the lessee is a family member or other related person or is a person who owns more than 5 percent of the taxpayer's stock or is a greater than 5 percent partner in a taxpayer-partnership.[9] If a taxpayer's activities in connection with leased property are not a business, in contrast, the use is nonbusiness, regardless of who the lessee is.

When the predominant-use test is not satisfied with respect to an item of listed property, ACRS is determined by the alternative depreciation system, under which depreciation is computed by the straight line method over recovery periods intended to match economic useful life more closely than the usual ACRS recovery periods.[10] The lengthening of recovery peri-

---

[3] IRC §280F(b)(2). For periods prior to the repeal of the investment credit as of the beginning of 1986, failure to meet this predominant-use test also resulted in loss of the credit. IRC §280F(b)(1).

[4] See infra text accompanying notes 30–34.

[5] IRC §280F(b)(4).

[6] IRC §280F(d)(6)(B).

[7] 1984 Bluebook, supra note 1, at 566. Also, commuting is not made a business use by the fact that the taxpayer's car bears a sign advertising his business. Id. at 566–67.

[8] IRC §280F(d)(6)(C). The same rule applies to a personal use by any other person providing services to the taxpayer.

[9] IRC §280F(d)(6)(C). Relatedness is determined under the rules of §267(b), which are discussed in ¶78.3. IRC §280F(d)(6)(D).

[10] IRC §280F(b)(2). See supra ¶23.3.5 for the alternative depreciation system. The rule described in the text applies to property placed in service after 1986. For property placed in service previously, a taxpayer failing the predominantly business test must compute depreciation on the straight line method over the periods used in determining corporate earnings and profits under the pre-1986 rules. IRC §§280F(b)(2), (4)(B).

ods is often not significant in this context. Automobiles and computers, for example, have five-year recovery periods under both regular ACRS and the alternative depreciation system. For most listed property, however, regular ACRS is computed by the 200 percent declining balance method, which is considerably more accelerated than the straight line method required under the alternative system. In the year a $10,000 automobile is placed in service, for example, the regular ACRS allowance is $2,000 (one half of 40 percent of cost), whereas the alternative allowance is only $1,000 (one half of 20 percent of cost).

The predominant-use test is applied each year; if it is failed for any year, ACRS is determined under the alternative depreciation system for that year and all subsequent years. Further, if the test is met in the year property is placed in service, but is failed in a subsequent year, a recapture rule applies in the year of the failure.[11] Under this rule, the excess of ACRS actually allowed over what would have been allowed under the alternative system is computed for each prior year; for the year the test is failed, the taxpayer has gross income equal to the sum of these excesses for all prior years. The recapture rule was adopted because

> Congress was . . . concerned that some taxpayers acquired automobiles and other property very late in the taxable year and claimed a very high percentage of business use for that portion of the year. Business use in subsequent years would often be minimal. Taxpayers could nonetheless claim full ACRS deductions for that first year and not be subject to recapture by reason of greatly diminished business use in the subsequent years.[12]

To illustrate the recapture rule, assume the predominant-use test is met for the year a $10,000 automobile is placed in service, but is failed for the next year. Regular ACRS of $2,000 (one half of 40 percent of cost) is allowed for the first year. For the second year, however, the taxpayer must (1) determine depreciation for the year under the alternative depreciation system rather than regular ACRS and (2) report gross income of $1,000 (the excess of the $2,000 allowed for the prior year over the $1,000 that would have been allowed under the alternative system).

Expensing under §179 is also restricted.[13] Section 179 generally allows the cost of up to $10,000 of depreciable personal property acquired during the taxable year to be fully deducted immediately. If listed property is used for both business and nonbusiness purposes, however, none of its cost can be deducted under §179 unless the predominant-use test is met for the year

---

[11] IRC §280F(b)(3).
[12] 1984 Bluebook, supra note 1, at 560.
[13] IRC §280F(d)(1); Reg. §1.179-1(d). See supra ¶23.8 for §179.

the property is placed in service. If the test is met, a portion of the property's cost, proportionate to the business use during the year, can be expensed under §179. Assume a computer is purchased for $10,000, and 80 percent of its use in the year placed in service is in a trade or business. Subject to the dollar limitation of §179, up to $8,000 of the computer's cost can be expensed.

The predominant-use test does not apply when the standard mileage allowance is taken for business use of an automobile in lieu of itemizing depreciation and other expenses relating to this use.[14]

2. *Special rule for employees.* For purposes of the predominant-use test described in the preceding paragraphs, an employee's use of his own property "in connection with the performance of services as an employee" is not considered a business use unless it is "for the convenience of the employer and required as a condition of employment."[15] "To satisfy the condition of employment requirement, the use of the property by the employee must be a necessary prerequisite for the employee to properly perform the duties of his employment."[16]

Assume a professor does most of her writing on a personal computer provided by her university, but buys a second computer with her own funds so that she can do some of her work at home. Unless she can show that the second computer is used for the convenience of the university and is required as a condition of her employment, the second computer is deemed devoted solely to nonbusiness use, and the predominant-use rule is failed. The computer is nevertheless depreciable if actually used for business, but depreciation must be determined under the alternative depreciation system.

3. *Limits on ACRS for passenger automobiles.* Section 280F(a)(2) limits ACRS deductions for passenger automobiles used in business.[17] The term "passenger automobile" has a detailed statutory definition, described be-

---

[14] 1984 Bluebook, supra note 1, at 567. See supra ¶21.4.5 note 61 and accompanying text for the standard mileage allowance.

[15] IRC §280F(d)(3). "Congress intended the terms 'convenience of the employer' and 'condition of employment' to have the same meaning with respect to this provision as they do with respect to the exclusion from gross income for lodging furnished to an employee (see sec. 119)." 1984 Bluebook, supra note 1, at 568. See supra ¶14.5 for §119. See Rev. Rul. 86-129, 1986-2 CB 48 (on facts given, employee's home use of a computer found not to be for the convenience of the employer).

[16] 1984 Bluebook, supra note 1, at 568.

[17] Section 280F(a)(1) also limits the investment credit for a passenger automobile to $675. When credit is otherwise allowable at the normal pre-1986 rate of 10 percent, this rule disallows credit with respect to any excess of the purchase price over $6,750. The investment credit, however, is generally repealed for taxable years beginning in 1986 and thereafter. See infra ¶27.1.

low,[18] which includes most vehicles commonly thought of as automobiles and a few others.

Although the provision's title indicates its intended target is "luxury automobiles," the limits have been tightened to the point where they catch many cars not usually thought of as luxury items. For automobiles placed in service after 1986, the limits are $2,560 for the year an automobile is placed in service, $4,100 for the next year, $2,450 for the third year in the recovery period, and $1,475 for each succeeding year until cost is fully recovered.[19] Depreciation for a particular year is the lesser of the §280F(a)(2) cap or the ACRS deduction for the year (determined by either the regular rules or the alternative depreciation system under the predominant-use test previously described). The limits affect depreciation on any automobile costing more than $12,800.[20]

Assume a corporation pays $30,000 for an automobile it uses exclusively in its business. Under the ACRS rules, the automobile is five-year property, and ACRS allowances are $6,000, $9,600, $5,760, $3,456, $3,456, and $1,728 for the year the car is placed in service and the succeeding five years.[21] All of these allowances, however, exceed the §280F(a)(2) limits. Depreciation is thus $2,560, $4,100, and $2,450 for the year the car is placed in service and the succeeding two years, $1,475 for each of the fourth through seventeeth years, and $240 for the eighteenth year. If the car is junked before its nineteenth birthday, a loss deduction is allowed under §165 for the as-yet unrecovered cost.

If a passenger automobile is used for both business and pleasure, a complex ordering scheme applies.[22] The predominant-use test is applied first, but only for the purpose of determining whether ACRS is computed under the regular or alternative system. Next, the year's allowance is computed under whichever system is applicable as though the car were used exclusively for business, and the dollar limits of §280F(a)(2) are applied to

---

[18] Infra text accompanying note 31.

[19] IRC §280F(a)(2)(A). All passenger automobiles acquired in a nonrecognition transaction are treated as a single asset placed in service in the year the transaction occurs. IRC §280F(d)(10). If 100 executive automobiles are received by the acquiring corporation in a tax-free reorganization, for example, the ACRS deduction for all 100 cars is capped at $2,560 for the year of the reorganization and $4,100 the next year!

[20] For the year an automobile is placed in service, for example, the ACRS allowance is normally 20 percent of the car's cost. See infra note 21. For a car costing $12,800, this 20 percent allowance is $2,560, the maximum first-year deduction permitted by §280F(a).

[21] ACRS deductions for 5-year property are computed under the 200 percent declining balance method, usually with a half-year convention. The depreciation rate is 40 percent (200 percent divided by five) of unrecovered cost for each year except the first, where the rate is 20 percent of original cost. See supra ¶23.3.4.

[22] 1984 Bluebook, supra note 1, at 560–61.

the amount so determined. Finally, the amount remaining after §280F(a)(2) is apportioned between business and personal use.

Assume the car in the previous example is used 80 percent for business and 20 percent for personal purposes. Because the predominant-use test is met, regular ACRS applies. The regular ACRS allowance of $6,000 for the year the property is placed in service is cut down to $2,560 by §280F(a)(2). Of this amount, a deduction is allowed for 80 percent ($2,048), and the remaining $512 is a nondeductible personal expense.

The limits described in the preceding paragraphs apply to property placed in service after 1986. The limits have been repeatedly revised (three times by statutory amendment and once by automatic inflation adjustment) since they first became effective for automobiles placed in service after June 18, 1984.[23] Further revision will occur under a provision requiring inflation adjustments for 1989 and succeeding years.[24] The limits applicable for various periods are shown in Table 23-2.

If the taxpayer makes the expensing election under §179,[25] the foregoing limitations apply to both the §179 deduction and ACRS. No more than $2,560 of a passenger automobile's cost may be deducted under §179, and the §179 deduction reduces the normal ACRS deduction for the year, dollar for dollar.[26] Under current law, if $2,560 is deducted under §179, for example, no ACRS deduction is allowable for the year the property is placed in service.

Table 23-2

ACRS Ceilings for Automobiles Under §280F(a)(2)

Date Placed in Service	Ceilings Year-by-Year			
	1	2	3	Thereafter
January 1, 1987—December 31, 1988	$2,560	$4,100	$2,450	$1,475
April 3, 1985—December 31, 1986	$3,200	$4,800	$4,800	$4,800
January 1, 1985—April 2, 1985	$4,100	$6,200	$6,200	$6,200
June 19, 1984—December 31, 1984	$4,000	$6,000	$6,000	$6,000
Before June 19, 1984	None	None	None	None

4. *Treatment of leased property.* When property is leased, §280F is generally inapplicable to the lessor if he is "regularly engaged in the business

---

[23] See Rev. Rul. 86-107, 1986-2 CB 45 for the inflation adjustment.
[24] IRC §280F(d)(7).
[25] See supra ¶23.8.
[26] IRC §280F(d)(1); Reg. §1.179-1(d).

of leasing such property."[27] A modified version of the provision, however, applies to a lessee under a lease of 30 days or more.[28] The usual consequence of §280F, a reduction of ACRS deductions, cannot apply to a lessee because such deductions belong to the lessor. Instead, the lessee's deductions for rent are limited in a way intended to mirror the ACRS restrictions that would apply if the lessee owned the property. The statutes do not prescribe these limits, but direct that the Treasury do so, a job that has been done for earlier versions of the statute but not the present one.[29]

5. *Definitions of "passenger automobile" and "listed property".* The term "listed property" includes passenger automobiles and other transportation equipment; property used for entertainment, recreation, or amusement; and computers and peripheral equipment.[30]

The term "passenger automobile" has dual significance because this property is both "listed property" and subject to the §280F(a)(2) ceilings. The term has a detailed technical definition that is not necessarily restricted to vehicles used primarily for carrying people.[31] Under this definition, a "passenger automobile" (1) has four wheels, (2) is manufactured primarily for use on public streets and highways, and (3) has a gross vehicle weight of no greater than 6,000 pounds. If the taxpayer is in the business of "transporting persons or property for compensation or hire," a taxi, truck, or other vehicle used "directly" in the business is not a "passenger automobile." An ambulance or hearse used "directly" in the taxpayer's business is also excluded. The Treasury has power to exclude other trucks and vans.

Trucks and other vehicles not within the definition of "passenger automobile" are "other transportation equipment," and hence "listed property," unless they are unsuitable for personal use.[32] A cement truck or forklift, for example, is not listed property because the Treasury thought it unlikely that such a vehicle would be used to take the family on a Sunday jaunt. Also, a vehicle is not "other transportation equipment" if "substantially all of [its] use . . . is in a trade or business of providing to unrelated persons services

---

[27] IRC §280F(c)(1). The predominant-use test, however, apparently applies to a lessor if the lessee is a related person or a greater than 5 percent owner of the taxpayer. See supra text accompanying note 9.

A taxpayer is "regularly engaged in the business of leasing . . . only if contracts to lease such property are entered into with some frequency over a continuous period of time." Reg. §1.280F-5T(c). An employer allowing employees to use property is not regularly engaged in the business of leasing to the employees, even if rent is charged. Id.

[28] IRC §§280F(c)(2), (3).

[29] Reg. §§1.280F-5T(d), (e), (f); Rev. Rul. 86-87, 1986-2 CB 45.

[30] IRC §280F(d)(4)(A). The Treasury has power to add other types of property to the list. Id.

[31] IRC §280F(d)(5).

[32] Reg. §1.280F-6T(b)(2).

consisting of the transportation of persons or property for compensation or hire."[33] This exclusion might apply, for example, to a bus company's buses or a trucking company's trucks.

A computer or item of peripheral equipment is not "listed property" if it is "used exclusively at a regular business establishment and owned or leased by the person operating such establishment."[34] The rules for computers, in other words, are largely restricted to home computers. A computer in the taxpayer's home, however, is within the exception just quoted if it is used exclusively in an area of the home that is used exclusively as the principal place of the taxpayer's trade or business.

---

[33] IRC §280F(d)(4)(C).
[34] IRC §280F(d)(4)(B).

CHAPTER

24

Depletion

¶24.1 DEPLETION—IN GENERAL

¶24.1.1 Introductory

Section 611(a) permits holders of economic interests in mines, oil and gas wells, other natural deposits, and timber to deduct "a reasonable allowance for depletion and for depreciation of improvements, according to the peculiar conditions in each case."[1] Unlike land,[2] mineral deposits are wasting assets, whose owners must be allowed to deduct their investments over the life of the property if they are to be taxed on net income rather than on gross income or gross receipts.[3] Commenting on the depletion allowance's function, the Supreme Court said in *Paragon Jewel Coal Co. v. CIR*: "[T]he purpose of the allowance for depletion is to compensate the owner of wasting mineral assets for the part exhausted in production, so that when the minerals are gone, the owner's capital and his capital assets remain unimpaired."[4]

This statement, however, is only partially reflective of present law on depletion. Depletion allowances are computed by whichever of two methods—cost depletion or percentage depletion—produces the larger deduction for the current taxable year.[5] Cost depletion is allowed by §612 for virtually all exhaustible natural resources. As the name implies, cost depletion is based on the taxpayer's adjusted basis (ordinarily cost) for the mineral property. Since the taxpayer is allowed to deduct an appropriate portion of the property's adjusted basis for each unit that is extracted and sold, cost

---

[1] Although §611(a) authorizes an allowance for "depreciation of improvements," the regulations refer the taxpayer to the general rules for depreciation under §167, which are discussed in Chapter 23. Reg. §1.611-5(a). For use of the unit-of-production method to depreciate mine improvements, see supra ¶23.6.6.

For the depletion of timber, see infra ¶24.2.2.

See Maxfield, The Income Taxation of Mining Operations (Rocky Mt. Mineral Law Foundation 1975); McMahon, Fundmentals of Federal Income Taxation of Natural Resources, 3 J. Min. L. & Pol'y 225 (1988). Schmid, Mineral Properties Other Than Oil and Gas—Operation, BNA Tax Mgm't Portfolio No. 90-5th (1974); Chapoton, Income Tax on Transactions Commonly Handled by Natural Resource Practitioners, 27 Oil & Gas Tax Q. 209 (1978); McMahon, The Coal Depletion Allowance Deduction, 85 W. Va. L. Rev. 581 (1983). For a useful glossary, see Williams & Meyers, Manual of Oil and Gas Terms (Matthew Bender, 4th ed. 1976).

[2] Because land is not subject to exhaustion, wear and tear, or obsolescence, the owner's investment does not qualify for depreciation deductions under §167 except in rare circumstances. See infra note 13; supra ¶23.2.5.

[3] For the constitutional status of the depletion allowance, see Stanton v. Baltic Mining Co., 240 US 103 (1916), discussed supra ¶5.4.

[4] Paragon Jewel Coal Co. v. CIR, 380 US 624, 631 (1965).

[5] Cost depletion must be used in computing corporate earnings and profits, however, even if percentage depletion is used in computing taxable income. See Reg. §1.312-6(c)(1).

depletion is analogous to a manufacturer's deduction for depreciation on plant and equipment and a merchant's subtraction of the cost of goods sold in computing gross income. It is, in the Supreme Court's words in *Paragon Jewel Coal*, compensation to "the owner of wasting mineral assets for the part exhausted in production."

Percentage depletion, in contrast, cannot be explained as merely a cost recovery mechanism. It is allowed for almost all hard minerals and, in limited circumstances, for oil and gas. Under this method, depletion is a prescribed percentage of the taxpayer's gross income (but not more than 50 percent of the taxable income) from the mineral property. Percentage depletion is not restricted to the taxpayer's adjusted basis for the deposit, but continues as long as production holds up, even after prior deductions exceed the taxpayer's entire investment. Unlike the generalized allowance of cost depletion, percentage depletion is denied for some minerals. Soil, sod, dirt, turf, water, or mosses, for example, are disqualified from percentage depletion, but can qualify for cost depletion if extracted from an exhaustible source. The depletion rate varies from mineral to mineral, from 5 to 22 percent.

As the Supreme Court pointed out in *US v. Swank*:

> Because [percentage depletion] is computed as a percentage of his gross income from the mining operation and is not computed with reference to the operator's investment, it provides a special incentive for engaging in this line of business that goes well beyond a purpose of merely allowing the owner of a wasting asset to recoup the capital invested in that asset.[6]

For this reason, it has been a subject of intense controversy.[7] If percentage depletion, like cost depletion, were restricted to the taxpayer's adjusted basis, it probably would not be a lightning rod for tax reformers because, so

---

[6] US v. Swank, 451 US 571, 576 (1981).

[7] For discussion of the policy issues, see Baker & Griswold, Percentage Depletion—A Correspondence, 64 Harv. L. Rev. 361 (1951); Blum, How to Get All (but All) the Tax Advantages of Dabbling in Oil, 31 Taxes 343 (1953); Freeman, Percentage Depletion for Oil—A Policy Issue, 30 Ind. LJ 399 (1955); Galvin, The "Ought" and "Is" of Oil and Gas Taxation, 73 Harv. L. Rev. 1441 (1960); CONSAD Research Corp., The Economic Factors Affecting the Level of Domestic Petroleum Reserves (Dec. 27, 1968), in House Ways and Means Comm. & Senate Finance Comm., 91st Cong., 1st Sess., Treasury Department, Tax Reform Studies and Proposals, Pt. 9 (Comm. Print 1969); Mid-Continent Oil and Gas Association, Analysis and Comment Relating to the CONSAD Report on the Influence of U.S. Petroleum Taxation on the Level of Reserves, Hearings Before the Senate Finance Comm., 91st Cong., 1st Sess. 4627–47 (1969); 2 House Ways and Means Comm., Tax Revision Compendium, 86th Cong., 1st Sess. 933–1059 (1958); Brannon, Energy Taxes and Subsidies (Ballinger 1974).

limited, it could be a useful way of recognizing the erosion of wasting assets and would avoid the need for debatable estimates of the number of recoverable units in the deposit, as is required by cost depletion.

Controversy about percentage depletion was abated somewhat by the enactment in 1975 of strict limitations, examined below,[8] on the use of percentage depletion for oil and gas. More recently, percentage depletion for iron ore and coal (including lignite) has been cut back for corporations by a rule reducing the allowance by 20 percent in this context once the taxpayer's adjusted basis falls to zero.[9] For coal, for example, the normal rate of 10 percent of gross income only applies until the allowances fully recover the taxpayer's investment, at which point the rate falls to 8 percent. The benefits of percentage depletion are also partially offset by a rule treating depletion in excess of cost for all minerals as a tax preference item for purposes of the alternative minimum tax.[10] For a taxpayer who is subject to the alternative minimum tax, the inclusion of depletion in excess of cost in alternative minimum taxable income has the effect of imposing tax at 20 or 21 percent (depending on whether the taxpayer is a corporation or an individual) on the income that is offset by this depletion for regular tax purposes.

A third method, discovery value depletion, was allowed for certain mineral deposits from 1918 to 1954. Under this method, mineral deposits were valued within 30 days of discovery, and the discovery value rather than the taxpayer's cost was used as the basis for computing depletion deductions. The effect of discovery depletion was to exempt from tax income equal to the increase in the property's value due to the mineral discovery. It proved difficult to administer because of the necessity of valuing mineral properties within a short time of discovery and was supplemented in 1926 by percentage depletion. Initially allowed only for oil and gas properties and at the rate of 27.5 percent of gross income, percentage depletion was apparently intended to yield on average about the same deductions as discovery depletion. Percentage depletion for other minerals gradually replaced discovery depletion, which was finally eliminated in 1954.[11]

---

[8] Infra ¶24.3.3.

[9] IRC §291(a)(2). The 20 percent reduction applies for taxable years beginning after 1986. For a taxable year beginning in 1984 or 1985, the reduction is 15 percent of the excess of the §613 allowance over basis. The reduction rule is inapplicable for taxable years beginning before 1984.

[10] See infra ¶111.3 for the alternative minimum tax.

[11] For the main features of discovery value depletion, see H.M. Halloway, Inc. v. CIR, 21 TC 40 (1953) (acq.). See also Revenue Act of 1918, Pub. L. No. 254, §§214(a)(10), 234(a)(9), 40 Stat. 1057 (1919) (discovery value depletion); Report of Conference Comm., H.R. Rep. No. 356, 69th Cong., 1st Sess. (1926), reprinted in 1939-1 (Part 2) CB 361, 362–63; 67 Cong. Rec. 3018–19, 3761–78 (1926) (remarks of Senator Reed).

Neither cost nor percentage depletion is allowed unless the taxpayer owns an economic interest in a mineral property that is subject to exhaustion. A taxpayer who devised a method of sucking pollutants out of the air and processing them for sale would not be entitled to a depletion allowance, both for want of an economic interest in the air and because the extracted materials are constantly replenished by his fellow citizens. The Code does not define "economic interest" or mark out a boundary between exhaustible and inexhaustible minerals; these issues have instead been left for administrative and judicial development.[12] ,In the long run, all natural resources are exhaustible, but exhaustion for tax purposes is judged not sub specie aeternitatis but for the life span of mortals. In application, the distinction between exhaustible and inexhaustible sources has led to depletion allowances for sand and gravel deposited in a riverbed by glacial action or similar nonrecurring cause and for the exhaustion in underground reservoirs of water used for irrigation, but to the denial of allowances for saline minerals extracted from the Great Salt Lake (which are replenished by inflowing streams) and for land used for farming or grazing.[13] Also, "minerals from sea water, the air, or similar inexhaustible sources" are ineligible for depletion.[14]

On a disposition of property with respect to which depletion has been taken, under a recapture rule found in §1254, gain is treated as ordinary income to the extent of the sum of the depletion deductions previously taken (exclusive of percentage taken after the taxpayer's adjusted basis has

---

[12] For the term "economic interest," see infra ¶24.1.2.

[13] For riverbed sand, see Victory Sand and Concrete, Inc. v. CIR, 61 TC 407 (1974) (acq.) (taxpayer engaged in extracting and selling sand and gravel from river on a tract of land owned by it; deposit was partly replenished by flow of river, but quantity and quality were reduced by upstream flood-control facilities; held, taxpayer had economic interest in wasting asset); for IRS view, see Rev. Rul. 76-484, 1976-2 CB 185. For underground water, see US v. Shurbet, 347 F2d 103 (5th Cir. 1965) (underground water reservoirs not inexhaustible). For depletion of land, see A. Duda & Sons v. US, 560 F2d 669 (5th Cir. 1977) (depletion allowance denied to farmer raising vegetables on peat soil subsiding as result of agricultural processes; no "extraction"; extensive legislative history of depletion allowance); Meyers v. CIR, 66 TC 235 (1976) (acq.) (farmer engaged in producing and selling sod allowed depletion deduction for topsoil removed and sold with sod); Rev. Rul. 79-267, 1979-2 CB 243 (sod farmer denied cost depletion because amount of exhausted soil could not be established); Rev. Rul. 77-12, 1977-1 CB 161 (sod farmers must establish basis for topsoil to claim depletion). For depreciation of man-made improvements to land, see supra ¶23.2.5. See also Rev. Rul. 65-7, 1965-1 CB 254 (saline minerals in Great Salt Lake, being replenished by inflow from streams, "are virtually inexhaustible" and hence are not subject to depletion). After Revenue Ruling 65-7 was issued, §613(b)(7) was amended to authorize percentage depletion for minerals (other than sodium chloride) extracted from brines from a saline perennial lake.

[14] IRC §613(b)(7) (percentage); Reg. §1.611-1(d)(5) (cost).

been reduced to zero).[15] If mining exploration or development expenses or intangible drilling and development costs were written off as incurred, the recapture amount also includes these costs.[16]

¶24.1.2 Economic Interest in Minerals

In addition to showing that a mineral deposit is diminished by extraction, a taxpayer claiming depletion must establish his ownership of an economic interest in the deposit. It is not enough to be adversely affected by the exhaustion of a deposit. Depletion is not allowed, for example, to a processor whose plant will have to be abandoned when nearby mines owned by the suppliers of necessary raw materials are mined out. Depletion is also denied with respect to a deposit in which no private person has an economic interest (e.g., state property, with only contract rights in private persons).

Disputes concerning the economic interest concept most often arise when the right to extract minerals has been transferred from an acknowledged owner of the minerals to another person. Assume *A*, who owns Blackacre, makes a contract with *B* that entitles *B* to mine certain minerals from the property in exchange for one or more cash payments. Has *A* sold the minerals in place, thereby losing his right to depletion, but possibly qualifying the payments to be treated as capital gains? Or, has *A* retained an economic interest in the minerals, thereby preserving the right to depletion but characterizing the payments as ordinary income?[17] *A*'s interest in the tax treatment depends on the circumstances. If the transaction occurs in a year for which a preferential rate is provided for long-term capital gains, for example, *A* might prefer sale treatment, particularly if his basis for cost depletion is low and percentage depletion is not allowable or is at a low rate. In other circumstances, *A* might fight for the depletion allowance.[18]

---

[15] The recapture rule generally applies to depletion deductions, however, only if the property was placed in service by the taxpayer after 1986. Pub. L. No. 99-514, §413(c), 100 Stat. 2085 (1986).

[16] See infra ¶26.1.5.

[17] See infra ¶40.2 (taxable event), ¶52.1.1 (sale or exchange).

The economic interest concept is also a criterion determining whether a taxpayer may deduct intangible drilling and development costs under IRC §263(c), discussed infra ¶26.1.

[18] See, e.g., O'Connor v. CIR, 78 TC 1 (1982) (transfer of right to extract clay held to be lease, not sale as taxpayer-transferor contended, because economic interest retained; initial guaranteed payment and requirement that transferee obtain from property specified percentage of clay needed in transferee's brickmaking business did not support argument that lessee was buyer who agreed to extract definite quantity of clay; extensive analysis); Lesher v. CIR, 73 TC 340 (1979) (transfer of right to extract sand and gravel not sale because economic interest retained); Piper & Pond, Sale of Land by the Cubic Yard, 26 Tax Lawyer 463 (1973).

The concept of an "economic interest" in a mineral deposit does not appear in the statutes, but owes its origin and most of its development to the courts. The concept can be discerned in embryo in *Lynch v. Alworth-Stephens Co.*, a 1925 decision in which the Supreme Court rejected the government's claim that only the fee owner suffers a loss from exhaustion of an ore body and held that a lessee could also deplete its interest:

> While respondent does not own the ore deposits, its right to mine and remove the ore and reduce it to possession and ownership is property within the meaning of the general provision. Obviously, as the process goes on, this property interest of the lessee in the mines is lessened from year to year, as the owner's property interest in the same mines is likewise lessened. There is an exhaustion of property in the one case as in the other; and the extent of it, with the consequent deduction to be made, in each case is to be arrived at in the same way, namely, by determining the aggregate amount of the depletion of the mines in which the several interests inhere, based upon the market value of the product, and allocating that amount in proportion to the interest of each severally considered.[19]

The economic interest concept was more explicitly enunciated by the Supreme Court in *Palmer v. Bender*, decided in 1933, involving the lessees of certain oil and gas properties who engaged in drilling and then transferred their rights to other parties in return for a cash bonus, a payment from the first oil produced thereafter, and a continuing royalty of one eighth of the oil. The lessees were held entitled to depletion without regard to whether they owned the mineral deposit under local law.[20] It was enough, according to the Court, that they acquired an "economic interest" in the oil in place by virtue of the original leases and retained such an interest when granting the subleases:

> When the [taxpayers] transferred their operating rights to the two oil companies, whether they became technical sublessors or not, they retained, by their stipulations for royalties, an economic interest in the oil, in place, identical with that of a lessor. . . . Thus, throughout their

---

For the economic interest concept under §§631(b) and (c), relating to dispositions involving a retained "economic interest" in timber, coal, or domestic iron ore, see infra ¶¶54.3.1, 54.3.2, and 54.3.3. For discussion of problems created by contingent deferred payments, see infra note 67.

[19] Lynch v. Alworth-Stephens Co., 267 US 364, 370–71 (1925). The holding in *Alworth-Stephens*, embodied in §611(b)(1), is now so firm a cornerstone of depletion law that it is surprising to learn that the issue was ever contested.

[20] Palmer v. Bender, 287 US 551 (1933). For later changes in the status of lease bonuses, see infra ¶24.1.3.

changing relationships with respect to the properties, the oil in the ground was a reservoir of capital investment of the several parties, all of whom, the original lessors, the [taxpayers]and their transferees, were entitled to share in the oil produced. Production and sale of the oil would result in its depletion and also in a return of capital investment to the parties according to their respective interests. The loss or destruction of the oil at any time from the date of the leases until complete extraction would have resulted in loss to the [taxpayers].[21]

In a later case, *Helvering v. Bankline Oil Co.*, the Supreme Court denied depletion deductions to the operator of a refining plant that extracted gasoline from natural gas under contract with the producers.[22] Since the producers were obligated by contract to supply their natural gas to the taxpayer, it "obtained an economic advantage from the production of the gas," but, the Court held, "the controlling fact is that [the taxpayer] had no interest in the gas in place [and hence] no capital investment in the mineral deposit which suffered depletion" as the gas was extracted.[23]

Drawing primarily on the opinions in *Palmer v. Bender* and *Bankline Oil*, the regulations summarize the economic interest concept as follows:

> Annual depletion deductions are allowed only to the owner of an economic interest in mineral deposits or standing timber. An economic interest is possessed in every case in which the taxpayer has acquired by investment any interest in mineral in place or standing timber and secures, by any form of legal relationship, income derived from the extraction of the mineral or severance of the timber, to which he must look for a return of his capital. . . . A person who has no capital investment in the mineral deposit or standing timber does not possess an economic interest merely because through a contractual relation he possesses a mere economic or pecuniary advantage derived from production. For example, an agreement between the owner of an economic interest and another entitling the latter to purchase or process the product upon production or entitling the latter to compensation for extraction or cutting does not convey a depletable economic interest. Further, depletion deductions with respect to an economic interest of a corporation are allowed to the corporation and not to its shareholders.[24]

---

[21] Palmer v. Bender, supra note 20, at 558.

[22] Helvering v. Bankline Oil Co., 303 US 362 (1938).

[23] Id. at 368.

[24] Reg. §1.611-1(b)(1). See also Helvering v. O'Donnell, 303 US 370 (1938) (shareholder traded corporate shares for share of income from wells leased by the corporation; not entitled to depletion). For the status of shareholders of captive mining corporations ("cost companies") who are entitled to pro rata shares of the mineral produced and must pay their allocable portions of expenses, see Rev. Rul.

As used in the above extract from the regulations, the term "capital investment" does not require an investment of cash or property by the taxpayer, but can consist of an economic interest acquired by gift, inheritance, personal effort, governmental permits, or other circumstances. Moreover, while cost depletion is only permitted if the taxpayer has an adjusted basis in the mineral property, percentage depletion can be taken even if the adjusted basis in the taxpayer's hands is zero. A lessee with an economic interest, for example, can take percentage depletion even if it incurred no cost in obtaining the lease.

In numerous subsequent cases, the courts have wrestled with the economic interest concept, and the Supreme Court has contributed more than its normal share of decisions to this area. In *Kirby Petroleum Co. v. CIR*, for example, the Court held that a landowner who leased oil properties for a cash bonus, a conventional royalty, and a share of the lessee's net profits possessed an economic interest in the oil with respect to all three of these receipts: "Economic interest does not mean title to the oil in place but the possibility of profit from the economic interest dependent solely upon the extraction and sale of the oil."[25]

By requiring that the asserted economic interest be "dependent solely" on extraction and sale of minerals, the Court precluded a depletion deduction if the taxpayer can look to a source other than the mineral deposit for payment. The leading case on this point is *Anderson v. Helvering*, holding

---

56-542, 1956-2 CB 327 (rights and obligations create economic interests in shareholders), revoked without explanation by Rev. Rul. 77-1, 1977-1 CB 161.

Although the regulations, like *Palmer v. Bender*, reject local property labels as controlling, the taxpayer's legal rights under local law are not immaterial. See, e.g., Harrington v. CIR, 404 F2d 237 (5th Cir. 1968) (depletion denied as to oil pumped unlawfully from adjacent property); Cottingham v. CIR, 63 TC 695 (1975) (investors in bankrupt oil-drilling program acquired no economic interest in property in absence of proof that their funds were actually used for specific drilling activities; deduction for intangible drilling and development costs denied; same principle would no doubt apply to depletion).

The classic analysis of the economic interest concept is Sneed, The Economic Interest—An Expanding Concept, 35 Tex. L. Rev. 307 (1957); see also Sneed, Another Look at the Economic Interest Concept, 10 Inst. on Oil & Gas L. & Tax'n 353 (1959); Casey, The Economic Interest—Play It Again, Sam, 24 Tax Lawyer 129 (1970); Maxfield, Economic Interest—Some Further Thoughts, 51 NDL Rev. 457 (1974) (discussing, at 459, the status of persons with contract rights exterior to the chain of title to the mineral deposit).

[25] Kirby Petroleum Co. v. CIR, 326 US 599, 604 (1946). The taxpayer in *Kirby Petroleum* was entitled to a bonus and royalty as well as to a share of the operator's net profits. In Burton-Sutton Oil Co. v. CIR, 328 US 25 (1946), the Court held that the bonus and royalty were not necessary and that a retained share of net profits was sufficient to establish an economic interest. For carved-out interests in net profits, see Weinert's Est. v. CIR, 294 F2d 750 (5th Cir. 1961), and cases therein cited. For the status of lease bonuses since 1975, see infra ¶24.1.3.

that a taxpayer could not deplete amounts payable from the proceeds of oil produced by certain leases because the obligation was secured by the fee interest in the leased properties and hence could be satisfied by selling the nonmineral interests in the properties if necessary.[26]

A lessee, however, can have an economic interest even if his lease is subject to termination by the lessor on short notice. In *US v. Swank*, the Supreme Court held that a lessee of coal property was entitled to depletion even though the lessor reserved the right to terminate the lease on 30-days' notice.[27] In response to the government's contention that the taxpayer's interest was too fleeting to make any cost recovery mechanism appropriate, the Court noted that percentage depletion, the method utilized by the taxpayer, is allowed as a tax incentive, not merely for cost recovery. The Court could conceive of no reason for denying this tax incentive to taxpayers with short-term interests: "If the authorization of a special tax benefit for mining a seam of coal to exhaustion is sound policy, that policy would seem equally sound whether the entire operation is conducted by one taxpayer over a prolonged period or by a series of taxpayers operating for successive shorter periods."[28]

Two Supreme Court cases illustrate the difficulties in applying the concept of economic interest to less conventional mining operations. In *CIR v. Southwest Exploration Co.*, the Court held that the owners of coastal properties were entitled to depletion deductions with respect to royalties received under grants of drilling rights to an operator, who used their land for slant drilling in order to extract offshore oil from deposits below the adjacent ocean.[29] To bid for a state lease permitting extraction of the off-

---

[26] Anderson v. Helvering, 310 US 404 (1940). See also Standard Oil Co. (Indiana) v. CIR, 465 F2d 246 (7th Cir. 1972) (additional security not fatal to retention of economic interest where "too remote to be considered significant or substantial" relative to value of taxpayer's interest in oil and gas); CIR v. Donnell's Est., 417 F2d 106 (5th Cir. 1969) (taxpayer acquired economic interest in oil necessary to pay off production payment by promising to pay holder of production payment if lease failed to produce in sufficient quantities).

[27] US v. Swank, 451 US 571 (1981). For the prior history of the issue, see Bakertown Coal Co. v. US, 485 F2d 633 (Ct. Cl. 1973) (short lease-termination clauses do not negate presence of economic interest when taxpayer is a lessee); Rev. Rul. 77-481, 1977-2 CB 205 (IRS will not follow *Bakertown*). See also Rev. Rul. 83-160, 1983-2 CB 99 (revoking Rev. Rul. 77-481 to reflect decision in *Swank*).

[28] US v. Swank, supra note 27, at 585.

[29] CIR v. Southwest Exploration Co., 350 US 308 (1956). See Victory Sand and Concrete, Inc. v. CIR, 61 TC 407 (1974) (acq.) (riparian landowner had economic interest in sand and gravel in adjacent riverbed); Winters Coal Co. v. CIR, 496 F2d 995 (5th Cir. 1974) (lessee obligated to acquire surface rights to undertake strip mining; depletion allowed). But see CBN Corp. v. US, 364 F2d 393 (Ct. Cl. 1966), cert. denied, 386 US 981 (1967) (purchaser of produced gas, or an agent in sale of gas, had no economic interest); Scofield v. La Gloria Oil & Gas Co., 268 F2d 699

shore oil, the operator needed the permission of the riparian landowners. The Court held that this requirement of state law, coupled with the landowners' proximity to the shore, gave them an economic interest in the oil, even though none of it lay beneath their property. As a result, depletion deductions were allowed to both the landowners and the operator who held the requisite state permits, in proportion to their respective interests, rather than solely to the operator.

In *Parsons v. Smith*, however, the Supreme Court held that two companies engaged in strip mining coal under contracts requiring them to deliver the coal to the landowners for a specified amount per ton were not entitled to depletion.[30] The companies claimed that their contractual right to mine the coal and the use of their equipment and skill was a capital investment giving them an economic interest in the coal in place. This theory, however, was described by the Court as a legal fiction, negated by the following facts:

> (1) that petitioners' investments were in their equipment, all of which was movable—not in the coal in place; (2) that their investments in equipment were recoverable through depreciation—not depletion; (3) that the contracts were completely terminable without cause on short notice; (4) that the landowners did not agree to surrender and did not actually surrender to petitioners any capital interest in the coal in place; (5) that the coal at all times, even after it was mined, belonged entirely to the landowners, and that petitioners could not sell or keep any of it but were required to deliver all that they mined to the landowners; (6) that petitioners were not to have any part of the proceeds of the sale of the coal, but, on the contrary, they were to be paid a fixed sum for each ton mined and delivered, which was . . . agreed to be in "full compensation for the full performance of all work and for

---

(5th Cir. 1959), cert. denied, 361 US 933 (1960) (taxpayer extracting hydrocarbons from wet gas produced from several properties had no economic interest).

[30] Parsons v. Smith, 359 US 215 (1959). See Paragon Jewel Coal Co. v. CIR, 380 US 624 (1965) (same result for contract miners of coal under leases requiring them to mine substantially all recoverable coal for per ton fee; two Justices dissenting); C.J. Langenfelder & Son v. CIR, 69 TC 378 (1977) (acq.) (dredger did not acquire economic interest in dead oyster shells harvested under contract with state); Rev. Rul. 76-485, 1976-2 CB 187 (permit to dredge navigable river does not create economic interest in riverbed deposits). But see Mullins v. CIR, 48 TC 571 (1967) (depletion allowed where taxpayer entitled to sell mined coal to anyone and had absolute right to mine coal for fixed period or to exhaustion); Douglas Coal Co. v. US, 429 F. Supp. 322 (ND W. Va. 1977) (strip miner assumed entrepreneurial risks and thereby acquired economic interest, not merely economic advantage; depletion allowed); Weaver v. CIR, 72 TC 594 (1979) (exclusive contract to extract rock, sand, and gravel until exhaustion, requiring extensive investment in roads, etc., created economic interest despite 120-day cancellation privilege in owner; contra as to nonexclusive contract terminable at will; extended analysis).

the furnishing of all [labor] and equipment required for the work"; and (7) that petitioners, thus, agreed to look only to the landowners for all sums to become due them under their contracts.[31]

A fitting postscript to this discussion of the economic interest concept is the observation of Mr. Justice Frankfurter, no less true today than when written in 1946, that the field is rife with "gossamer lines [that] hardly can be held in the mind longer than it takes to state them."[32]

¶24.1.3 Allocation of Depletion Among Separate Owners

When the economic interests in a mineral deposit are split among two or more taxpayers, each of whose interest will be exhausted by extraction, the depletion allowance is allocated among them. Section 611(b) prescribes allocation rules for four situations: (1) In the case of a lease, the deduction is "equitably apportioned" between lessor and lessee;[33] (2) if property is held by a life tenant with remainder to another person, the life tenant is entitled to deplete the property as though he were the sole owner; (3) the deduction for trust property is allocated among the income beneficiaries and the trustee as the instrument provides or, in the absence of a provision, in proportion to the allocation of income; and (4) in the case of an estate, depletion is allocated to the parties in proportion to the allocation of income.[34]

These statutory rules are obviously incomplete. They fail, for example, to provide a method of allocating depletion deductions among tenants in common of mineral properties, who undoubtedly are entitled to deduct depletion in proportion to their fractional interests. Nor does the Code provide explicit standards for allocating the deduction among the multiplicity of other interests that have been developed in the extractive industries to marshal capital and technical skills and to spread the risk of failure in the exploitation of mineral deposits. Section 611(b)(1), which provides that the deduction shall be "equitably apportioned" between lessors and lessees, does not encompass all contractual arrangements, and in any event the concept of equitable apportionment is amorphous. As a result, the problem of allocating depletion among rival claimants has produced a vast body of litigation, especially in the petroleum industry, whose denizens, when they

---

[31] Parsons v. Smith, supra note 30, at 225.

[32] Burton-Sutton Oil Co. v. CIR, 328 US 25, 38 (1946).

[33] See Palmer v. Bender, 287 US 551 (1933).

[34] Although the statutory language is not explicit, the regulations provide that when depletion on the property of trusts and estates is allocated on the basis of income, the relevant standard is the income from the depletable property, not the commingled income from all trust assets. See Reg. §§1.611-1(c)(4), (5).

are not drilling for oil, devote their energies and ingenuity to dividing the ownership of both prospective and producing deposits in ways that Coke and Blackstone could not have foreseen. The IRS used the following example in a 1941 ruling:

> A, as a fee owner of oil lands, leased the lands to B in consideration of a cash payment of $100,000, an additional $100,000 payable out of one-sixteenth of the oil and gas if, as, and when produced, and a one-eighth royalty interest. B then assigned his leasehold interest to C in consideration of a cash payment of $200,000, and an additional $100,000, payable only out of one-sixteenth of the oil and gas if, as, and when produced. C assigned one-half of the lessee interest to D, who agreed to develop and operate the property, to advance C's share of the funds necessary for development costs and operating expenses, to sell all the oil produced and saved and credit C with one-half of the proceeds until all advances were fully recouped, and thereafter to operate the property and pay one-half of the proceeds from the sale of all oil produced, less one-half of the operating expenses, to C, who was not personally liable for any costs or expenses incurred or advances made. E drilled an oil well under an agreement with D entitling E to have delivered to his credit one-eighth of all the first oil and/or gas if, as, and only when the same is produced, saved, and marketed from the land until he received the sum of $25,000. Also, F paid D the sum of $15,000, which D covenanted to use in developing the property, and D agreed to pay F the sum of $25,000, payable out of one-eighth of the oil and/or gas if, as, and only when the same is produced, saved, and marketed from the leased land.[35]

When confronted by rival claimants for the depletion deduction, the courts often observe that two or more persons cannot deplete the same income.[36] While this principle is true, it may convey the erroneous implication that the extraction and sale of minerals always generate a fixed amount of depletion, to be allocated among the various interests in the mineral property. There are such cases, in which the IRS is a kind of stakeholder—

[35] GCM 22730, 1941-1 CB 214. This ruling is quoted to illustrate the multiplicity of interests encountered in this area, not for its legal conclusions, for which see American Bar Association, Tax Section, Report on Proposed Revision of G.C.M. 22730, 22 Tax Lawyer 263 (1969). See generally Linden, Income Realization in Mineral Sharing Transactions: The Pool of Capital Doctrine, 33 Tax Lawyer 115 (1979).

[36] See Parsons v. Smith, 359 US 215, 220 (1959); CIR v. Southwest Exploration Co., 350 US 308, 309 (1956); Helvering v. Twin Bell Oil Syndicate, 293 US 312 (1935); Quintana Petroleum Co. v. CIR, 143 F2d 588 (5th Cir. 1944) (so-called bonus exhaustion rule).

although not necessarily an indifferent one, since the tax rates of the competing claimants may differ.[37] There are also many situations in which assigning depletion to one taxpayer rather than another determines the aggregate amount of depletion as well as the taxpayers who can claim it. The contestants may, for example, have purchased their interests for different amounts, in which event their per unit allowances, computed on a cost basis, differ. Similarly, if one taxpayer uses cost depletion while the other uses percentage depletion, the aggregate amount to be deducted may be drastically affected by a determination that one claimant rather than the other is entitled to the allowance. Moreover, lessors can frequently take larger deductions for percentage depletion than their lessees, whose expenses in producing oil and gas reduce their taxable income and may trigger the rule limiting percentage depletion to 50 percent of taxable income.

The major arrangements for the division of ownership, and their effects on the rights of the parties to deplete their interests, are summarized briefly below. Each of these arrangements is subject to variations, however, since the parties to an agreement may insert terms of their own to meet special business or financial needs. These departures from the norm can alter the tax results described below.

1. *Bonuses.* When the owner of a mineral deposit (other than oil and gas) leases the property for a royalty and a bonus, both are subject to cost or percentage depletion; the payor treats the bonus as a capital investment that is recoverable by depletion.[38] If, however, the lease terminates or is abandoned before income is derived from production, the lessor's deduction with respect to the bonus is recaptured by requiring that gross income be recognized equal to the deduction and that the property's basis be increased in like amount.[39] Depletion of bonuses has been characterized as "synthetic

---

[37] When confronted by rival claims to depletion, the IRS may take inconsistent administrative positions, denying the depletion deduction to both. This tactic may backfire where the claimants go to different forums to hear their cases, creating the possibility of a double allowance of depletion. In *Southwest Exploration*, the government was forced to appeal the two separate cases to the Supreme Court to prevent a double depletion allowance. See Brief for Petitioner at 13-14, CIR v. Southwest Exploration Co., supra note 36.

[38] See Reg. §1.612-3(a)(1) (cost depletion), §1.612-3(d) (percentage depletion); Burnet v. Harmel, 287 US 103 (1932) (bonus subject to depletion); Shamrock Oil & Gas Corp. v. CIR, 346 F2d 377 (5th Cir.), cert. denied, 382 US 882 (1965) (lessee must report its share of production, unreduced by bonuses paid by it). In practice, landowners may find it virtually impossible to employ cost depletion because of difficulties in establishing the proper cost basis for the mineral deposit and in estimating future production or revenues.

[39] Reg. §1.612-3(a)(2); Douglas v. CIR, 322 US 275 (1944) (restoration of depletion even if deduction produced no tax benefit). But see Sloan v. US, 69-1 USTC ¶9355 (ND Tex. 1969) (not officially reported) (restoration not required where there

depletion" because the payments are not dependent on production.[40] The Supreme Court, however, upheld the allowance in *Herring v. CIR*,[41] and it might be justified on the theory that bonuses necessarily diminish the royalty rate the lessee is willing to pay, thus reducing the amount the lessor will receive over the property's life.

As explained later in this chapter, §613A(c) conditions the use of percentage depletion for oil and gas properties on actual production,[42] and Congress decided this restriction required that the allowance be denied with respect to "any lease bonus, advance royalty, or other amount payable without regard to production."[43]

2. *Advanced royalties.* Unlike bonuses, advanced royalties are deducted from the royalties that would otherwise be payable to the lessor when production occurs. The payee is entitled to depletion with respect to the advanced royalty, but the income from production that is retained by the payor to recoup the advance does not enter into the payee's depletion computations. If the prepayment is not fully recouped by the payor, further, the payee must include the excess depletion in income, since the prior deductions presupposed a level of production that was not attained.[44]

---

was some production, even though not in commercially profitable quantity); Rev. Rul. 73-537, 1973-2 CB 197 (restoration not required where taxpayer reported bonus as income but deducted no depletion).

[40] Driscoll v. CIR, 147 F2d 493, 495 (5th Cir. 1945).

[41] Herring v. CIR, 293 US 322 (1934). For extended analysis of this issue, see Shamrock Oil & Gas Corp. v. CIR, 35 TC 979, 1040–59 (1961), aff'd, 346 F2d 377 (5th Cir. 1965) (concluding at 1059 that "illogical the tax treatment of bonus payments may well be; perplexing it certainly is"). For depletion of "selection bonuses," see White Castle Lumber & Shingle Co. v. US, 481 F2d 1274 (5th Cir. 1973); Houston Farms Dev. Co. v. US, 131 F2d 577 (5th Cir. 1942).

[42] Infra ¶24.3.3.

[43] IRC §613A(d)(5). This provision applies to amounts received or accrued after August 16, 1986. The Treasury included a similar limitation in regulations proposed in 1977. Prop. Reg. §1.613A-7(f)(1); see Prop. Reg. §1.613A-3(a)(4) Ex. 4. The Supreme Court, however, rejected this position and held §613A(c) depletion allowable on lease bonuses and advanced royalties, even when such payments are made without regard to actual production. CIR v. Engle, 464 US 206 (1984). The Court stated that the 1975 addition of §613A merely restricted the classes of taxpayers eligible for percentage depletion with respect to oil and gas, but did not change, for those still entitled to it, the scheme established by *Herring v. CIR*. Congress, in turn, rejected this interpretation of its intentions: "In retaining percentage depletion for oil and gas properties, Congress wished to provide an incentive only with respect to actual production." Staff of Joint Comm. on Tax'n, 99th Cong., 2d Sess., General Explanation of Tax Reform Act of 1986, at 200 (Comm. Print 1987).

[44] See Reg. §1.612-3(b) (cost depletion), §1.612-3(d) (percentage depletion); Adams v. CIR, 58 TC 41, 68 (1972) (recipient of advanced royalties must restore depletion deductions on sale of property before advances earned by extraction); Aven v. US, 78-2 USTC ¶9729 (WD Okla. 1978) (not officially reported) (payments

For years, the regulations allowed payors of advanced royalties to deduct them either when paid or as the royalties are earned by the production and sale of minerals. A 1977 amendment to the regulations, however, generally eliminated the right to elect an immediate deduction.[45] The amendment was adopted in response to widespread use of advanced royalties in mining ventures packaged as tax shelters, many of which were based on nonrecourse financing of huge advanced royalties.[46] The right to elect an immediate deduction was preserved, however, for minimum royalties payable in "substantially uniform" amounts over the lease's term or, if less, 20 years.[47] Tax shelter offerings have been devised to exploit this rule also, but without much success.[48]

3. *Delay rentals.* A delay rental is a payment from lessee to lessor made to compensate the lessor when production is delayed beyond the date contemplated by the lease agreement. Since the lessee can avoid payment of delay rentals by developing the property promptly or abandoning the lease, they are rent in the hands of the payee, rather than compensation for diminution of the mineral deposit, and depletion is not allowed.[49]

4. *Net profits interest.* A net profits interest is a right to receive a share of gross production from a mineral property, measured by the net operating profits, which is either carved out of the working interest or retained when the working interest is transferred. Since 1946, when the Supreme Court held in *Kirby Petroleum Co. v. CIR* that a net profits interest is an economic interest in the mineral deposit, amounts received by the holder of such an

---

on overriding royalties treated as advanced royalties, not installment bonuses; recoupment need not be from same tract).

[45] Reg. §1.612-3(b)(3). See Rev. Rul. 80-70, 1980-1 CB 104; Rev. Rul. 80-73, 1980-1 CB 128. See also McCoy v. US, 802 F2d 762 (4th Cir. 1986) (rejecting argument that amendment invalid because Congress had adopted old rule by repeatedly reenacting relevant statutes); Wing v. CIR, 81 TC 17 (1983) (rejecting argument that amendment invalid because Administrative Procedure Act not complied with).

[46] In order to staunch the revenue losses caused by these shelter schemes, the amendment was made effective as of the day the Treasury proposed it, more than a year before it was finally adopted. See Redhouse v. CIR, 728 F2d 1249 (9th Cir. 1984) (retractive application of amendment upheld); US v. Flomenhoft, 714 F2d 708 (7th Cir. 1983) (criminal conviction for backdating to avoid effective date of amendment).

[47] Reg. §1.612-3(b)(3).

[48] Most of the unsuccessful tax shelter uses of the minimum royalty rule have involved royalties payable by the delivery of nonrecourse notes. Maddrix v. CIR, 708 F2d 946 (11th Cir. 1986); Ward v. CIR, 784 F2d 1424 (9th Cir. 1986); Capek v. CIR, 86 TC 14 (1986). See also Wing v. CIR, 81 TC 17 (1983).

[49] Reg. §1.612-3(c). For problems in distinguishing between delay rentals and lease bonuses, see also White Castle Lumber & Shingle Co. v. US, 481 F2d 1274 (5th Cir. 1973) ("selection bonuses" treated as delay rentals rather than lease bonuses; extended discussion by Judge Goldberg, rejecting taxpayer effort "to introduce yet another leprechaun into the mounting mythology of oil and gas taxation").

interest have been subject to depletion.[50]

5. *Production payments.* A production payment is a right to receive (in kind or in money) a share of the production from a mineral deposit, the aggregate amount being limited to a specified sum of money, quantity of the mineral, or period of time. The tax treatment of production payments is complicated by a turbulent history and is discussed below.[51]

6. *Carried interests.* A carried interest is an arrangement, employed especially in the oil and gas industry, by which one party (the "carrying party" or "carrier") defrays the cost of drilling and other activities on a mineral lease in return for a portion of the working interest of the lessee, usually consisting of a fraction of the interest plus a right to receive the production from the remaining part of the interest until his costs are recovered. At payout, the latter fraction of the working interest reverts to the owner of the working interest (the "carried party"), who is often a geologist or packager of an oil venture.

After extensive litigation involving carried interests that differed in certain details, the prevailing view of the courts as of 1969 was that the production applied to repay the carrier's outlay was taxable to (and depletable by) him, rather than includable in the carried party's income.[52] As a corollary, the carried party had no depletable interest in the property, and could not deduct intangible drilling and developments costs, which were instead allocable to the carrying party.

With the enactment in 1969 of §636, however, the status of carried interests became clouded again since the carrier's right to receive the production from part of the lease until recovery of his outlay might be viewed as a carved-out "production payment" to be treated as a mortgage loan to the carried party under §636(a). The IRS ruled in 1975, however, that the carrier is the owner of the entire working interest during the payout period, a status that is inconsistent with treating the arrangement as a production payment.[53] In keeping with this view, the proposed regulations under §613A provide that the carried party is entitled to percentage depletion under the independent producer exemption only when the carrying party has reached

---

[50] Kirby Petroleum Co. v. CIR, 326 US 599 (1946). See also Prop. Reg. §1.613A-7(f)(3) (in computing average daily production of oil and gas for purposes of §613A restrictions on percentage depletion, basis is "proportion of producing which produced the same fraction of the property's gross income as the fractional interest of the taxpayer in the net profits from the property").

[51] Infra ¶24.4.

[52] See, e.g., US v. Cocke, 399 F2d 433 (5th Cir. 1968), cert. denied, 394 US 922 (1969) (extended discussion of principles and earlier cases); Husky Oil Co. v. CIR, 83 TC 717 (1984) (following *Cocke*); Starcher, Unanswered Questions in Marathon Oil Case Leave Planning Opportunities, 38 Tax Notes 206 (1987).

[53] Rev. Rul. 75-446, 1975-2 CB 95. See Casey, Oil and Gas Joint Ventures and Partnerships: A Side Effect of Section 636, 27 Tax Lawyer 417 (1974).

payout and the carried party is receiving a share of the production.[54]

7. *Farm-outs.* The owner of a gas or oil lease who does not wish to bear the expense of drilling often farms out this burden to another operator under an agreement entitling the latter to an assignment of the lease or a fraction thereof on fulfilling the drilling obligation. Frequently the assignment covers the entire working interest in the drill site (possibly subject to an overriding royalty or production payment), plus a fractional working interest in the remainder of the leased acreage.

Under general tax principles, the interest received by the driller under a farm-out arrangement would be considered compensation for his services, taxed as ordinary income when received; similarly, the lessee would be treated as making a taxable disposition of this interest—a sale, in essence, in exchange for the driller's services. Under a long-standing doctrine unique to the natural resources area, however, a farm-out arrangement is viewed as a pooling of the capital of the lessee and driller and does not result in the realization of income by either party.[55] In 1977, the IRS limited this doctrine to a grant of rights to the drill site, ruling that the value of any rights assigned to the driller in the rest of the acreage was compensation for his capital and services.[56] Under the ruling, the compensatory segment is a taxable disposition by the lessee and causes the driller to have compensation income; the fair market value of the assigned rights when transferred is the measure of both the amount realized by the lessee and the driller's income. Although the point is not made explicit by the ruling, if the property is "proven," the transfer rationale evidently precludes the driller from taking percentage depletion on his share of the production from the nondrill site under a rule denying percentage depletion to transferred interests in proven properties.[57] On the other hand, since the driller's rights to the drill site production are attributable to the hypothesized pooling of capital rather than acquired by a taxable transfer, the production from this property could qualify for percentage depletion under the small producer exemption of §613A(c).[58]

Because "farm-out" is a generic label for a wide range of agreements, including leases by landowners who retain an overriding royalty, carried interests, and other arrangements shifting the costs of drilling and develop-

---

[54] Prop. Reg. §1.613A-7(f)(3).

[55] See generally Linden, supra note 35. For the status of contributed services under the pool of capital doctrine, see US v. Frazell, 335 F2d 487 (5th Cir. 1964), cert. denied, 380 US 960 (1965), discussed infra ¶85.3.4.

[56] Rev. Rul. 77-176, 1977-1 CB 77. See Burke v. Miller, 639 F2d 306 (5th Cir. 1981) (declining to enjoin enforcement of Rev. Rul. 77-176). See generally Russell, Tax Sharing Arrangements, 27 Oil & Gas Tax Q. 1 (1978).

[57] See IRC §613A(c)(9), discussed infra ¶24.3.3.

[58] For IRC §613A(c), see infra ¶24.3.3.

ment from one party to another, their tax consequences vary with the nature of the agreement, the most common varieties of which are described above.[59]

8. *Sales.* Finally, a sale of mineral properties does not generate depletable income for the seller, but instead causes him to recognize gain or loss on the sale. The sales price represents the present value of receipts that would otherwise be ordinary income subject to depletion, but this does not affect the taxation of the sale; just as a capital asset produces capital gain on a sale even though its sales price equals the discounted value of the ordinary income that the asset will produce in the future,[60] so the sale of a mineral property generates gain or loss, not depletable income.[61]

In determining whether a transaction is a sale, in which case the transferor is a seller realizing gain or loss, or a lease, in which case the transferor is a lessor realizing depletable income, the controlling factor is whether the transferor retained an economic interest in the mineral deposit. The cases and rulings developing this concept for depletion purposes therefore do double duty.[62] Thus, the IRS has ruled that a lump-sum payment received by a landowner for purportedly transferring fee simple title to all minerals under his land, subject to a reserved royalty interest, was ordinary income rather than the proceeds of a sale of a capital asset.[63] Citing *Palmer v. Bender*[64] and other economic interest cases, the ruling explained this result as follows:

> The cases cited show that the ordinary income character of such a cash payment is not dependent upon the retention by the grantor of ownership or any other form of legal interest in the mineral content of the land, and that it is not affected by the fact that the transaction may be cast in the form of a sale or that under local law title to the mineral in place passes immediately to the grantee upon execution of the instrument. In addition, the ordinary income character of such a cash

---

[59] See generally Bowden, Federal Income Tax Consequences Under Typical Farm Out Agreements, 3 Nat. Res. J. 470 (1964) (tax results changed by later law, but useful summary of varieties of farm-out agreements).

[60] See infra ¶51.10.5.

[61] See West v. CIR, 150 F2d 723 (5th Cir. 1945), cert. denied, 326 US 795 (1946) (sale versus lease). See generally Gregory, Tax Consequences and Distinctions Involved in the Sale or Lease of Oil and Gas Interests, 14 Nat. Res. J. 257 (1974).

[62] See supra ¶24.1.2. This application of the economic interest concept, however, does not go both ways; that the transferor retained an economic interest, and therefore made no sale, does not mean that the transferee acquired no economic interest. An economic interest, in other words, can be acquired other than by purchase.

[63] Rev. Rul. 69-352, 1969-1 CB 34.

[64] Palmer v. Bender, 287 US 551 (1933).

payment is not dependent on the presence or absence of any dominating purpose of the parties to secure development and operation of the property. In this respect, there need not be any existing production of mineral, nor any practical assurance thereof in the future; nor is it necessary that the grantor have the right to compel the drilling of wells. In such transactions, the grantor merely extends to the grantee exclusive exploitation privileges, retaining as his (grantor's) share of the whole reservoir of mineral, a right, upon production, to a portion of such mineral with all burdens of development and the operating costs to be borne by the grantee. So considered, the view that a grantor parts with no capital interest in the mineral, though the grantee acquires one, presents no logical difficulties since, though it may be a potentially highly valuable mineral interest, the grantee's interest ordinarily achieves such value as the result of the investment incident to exploitation, or by reason of discovery.[65]

Payments dependent on production are the principal characteristic of a mineral lease. A lease, however, is not transmuted into a sale by the payment of an additional amount that is independent of production, just as the character of a lease of commercial real estate is not altered by a prepayment of rent.[66]

On the other hand, if all of the payments to the grantor are fixed in amount and payable in all events, without regard to extraction or sale of the mineral, the transaction is a sale, on which the grantor realizes nondepletable gain or loss.[67] The sale-lease distinction usually requires a transaction to be assigned to one category or the other, but sometimes a single contract may be fragmented. For example, if a landowner sells the surface rights and buildings but leases the subsurface mineral rights, the disposition of the land is a sale, generating gain or loss, while the transfer of the mineral rights produces ordinary income subject to depletion.[68]

---

[65] Rev. Rul. 69-352, supra note 63.

[66] See Jahn v. CIR, 58 TC 456 (1972), aff'd per curiam, 475 F2d 1140 (6th Cir. 1973), and cases therein cited.

[67] Compare Ima Mines Corp. v. CIR, 32 TC 1360 (1959) (acq.) (fixed sum payable at minimum rate annually, with additional payments from net profits to be credited against purchase price; sale, despite buyer's limited power to abandon agreement by surrendering possession of property) with US v. White, 401 F2d 610 (10th Cir. 1968) (no fixed price; transaction held a lease; extended analysis). See generally Contingent Deferred Payments: A Study in Contradiction, 10 Oil & Gas Tax Q. 117 (1961). For the capital gain aspects of dispositions of mineral properties and timber, see infra ¶54.3. See also supra ¶4.4.2 (sale versus lease).

[68] See West v. CIR, 150 F2d 723 (5th Cir. 1945), cert. denied, 326 US 795 (1946) (Tax Court allocation of lump sum between capital gain on sale of land and depletable ordinary income affirmed). See also Rev. Rul. 82-221, 1982-2 CB 113 (fixed payment for 65 percent of estimated total mineral deposit, payable without

¶24.1.4 Separate vs. Combined or Aggregated Properties

Under §614, both cost and percentage depletion are computed property by property, rather than by lumping together all of the taxpayer's mineral properties, unless one or more operating oil and gas properties are "combined" or other interests are "aggregated." Moreover, by defining the term "property" to mean "each separate interest owned by the taxpayer in each mineral deposit in each separate tract or parcel of land," §614(a) leans heavily toward the multiplication of units.[69] In harmony with this theme, the regulations view each of the following situations as giving rise to two properties rather than one:

1. Ownership of a tract of land above a single mineral deposit, part of which is mined by the owner while the remainder is leased by him to another operator on a royalty basis (two "separate interests").
2. Ownership of a single tract of land above two distinct seams of coal (two "mineral deposits").
3. Acquisition, from different owners, of two tracts of contiguous land, which are operated as a single mining unit (two "separate tracts").
4. Acquisition, from the same owner in a single transaction, of two noncontiguous tracts, below which lies a single mineral deposit (two "separate tracts").[70]

As a modest offset to this propensity for fission, the regulations provide that two or more separate properties sometimes can be fused into a single property by transfer. For example, if a person acquires from separate owners two contiguous tracts, beneath which lies a single mineral deposit, but later transfers them to one transferee in a single transaction, the tracts are one property in the hands of the transferee.[71] The transfer of two leases to

---

regard to production, combined with option to mine remainder of deposit at set price per unit mined; held, sale of 65 percent, not subject to depletion; tax consequences of option not ruled upon); Rev. Rul. 68-361, 1968-2 CB 264 (on lease of mining equipment with mineral deposit for payments based solely on mineral production, taxpayer may depreciate amounts allocable to equipment).

[69] Section 614(a) defines property "for the purpose of computing the depletion allowance," but the regulations apply §614 "for purposes of subtitle A of the Code." Reg. §1.614-1(a)(1). See, e.g., Rev. Rul. 77-188, 1977-1 CB 76 (§614 definition applicable in determining extent of loss from abandonment of mineral tracts); for a contrary view, see Larsen v. CIR, 66 TC 478 (1976) (acq.) (no purpose served by "borrowing the technical aggregation rules governing the depletion allowance" in determining if costs associated with specific acreage have been abandoned).

[70] Reg. §§1.614-1(a)(3), -1(a)(5) Exs. 1, 3-5.

[71] Reg. §1.614-1(a)(5) Ex. 7. The tracts continue to be two properties, however, if they have a carryover basis in the hands of the transferee (e.g., in the case of a gift). Id. See also Reg. §1.614-1(a)(4).

one transferee, however, does not effect a fusion, presumably because the obligations to separate lessors are independent.[72]

Section 614 goes on to provide for the aggregation of two or more separate properties into a single property in three situations:

1. *Operating mineral interests in oil and gas wells.* All operating oil and gas mineral interests in one tract or parcel of land (but not interests in different tracts or parcels) are treated as a single property unless the taxpayer elects to treat them as separate.[73]

2. *Operating mineral interests in other deposits.* Two or more separate operating mineral interests (other than oil and gas wells) constituting part or all of an operating unit may either be aggregated or treated as separate properties, provided all operating interests in a single mine are treated consistently.[74] If a single tract or parcel of land contains a mineral deposit that is or will be extracted by two or more mines for which development or operating expenditures have been made, the taxpayer may elect to treat each mine, with the land and mineral deposit allocable to it, as a separate property.

3. *Nonoperating mineral interests.* Two or more separate nonoperating mineral interests in a single tract or parcel of land or in adjacent tracts or parcels may be aggregated with the permission of the IRS on a showing that tax avoidance is not a principal purpose of the combination.[75] The regulations give no examples of combinations that serve purposes other than tax avoidance. For tax years before 1958, when aggregations of nonoperating mineral interests were permissible if "undue hardship" would otherwise result, separate properties could be aggregated if it was impossible for the taxpayer to determine their boundaries, source, or costs or if a single royalty interest involved payments from several mineral deposits that could not be

---

The requirement of a single conveyance "contemplates simultaneous acts that are mutually or reciprocally dependent upon one another." See Rev. Rul. 68-566, 1968-2 CB 281 (oil leases awarded at same time not part of single conveyance because each award acted upon independently by federal government).

[72] Reg. §1.614-1(a)(5) Exs. 8, 9; Rev. Rul. 68-566, supra note 71 (conveyance of two contiguous leaseholds on government land results in two interests, not one).

[73] IRC §§614(b)(1), (2). For definitions of "tract or parcel of land" and "operating mineral interest," see Reg. §§1.614-1(a)(3), -3(c). For the effect of unitization or pooling agreements, see IRC §614(b)(3).

[74] IRC §614(c). For definitions of the terms "operating unit" and "mine," see Reg. §§1.614-3(d), (e).

[75] IRC §614(e). For the definition of "adjacent" and "nonoperating mineral interest," see Reg. §§1.614-5(d), (g).

[76] Reg. §1.614-5(a). See S. Rep. No. 1983, 85th Cong., 2d Sess., reprinted in 1958-3 CB 922, 1108 (aggregation resulting in "substantial reduction of tax" indicative of purpose to avoid tax); Miller v. US, 69-2 USTC ¶9578 (ED Okla. 1969) (not

separately identified.[76] Presumably these reasons for aggregating separate properties remain valid.

The tax effect of aggregating properties can be illustrated by assuming that a taxpayer owns Blackacre (adjusted basis, $1,000; 1,000 estimated recoverable units of minerals) and Whiteacre (adjusted basis, $1,000; 500 estimated recoverable units). Viewing the properties separately, the taxpayer's cost depletion allowance is $1 for each unit from Blackacre ($1,000/ 1,000 units) and $2 for each unit from Whiteacre ($1,000/500 units). If the properties are aggregated under §614, however, the per unit allowance is $1.34 ($2,000/1,500 units), without regard to the source of the units extracted and sold.

Aggregating two or more separate properties can also affect the percentage depletion deduction. If the gross income from Blackacre and Whiteacre is $10,000 each but, because of differences in operating expenses, they produce taxable income of $3,000 and $1,000, respectively, a taxpayer whose minerals qualify for a 10 percent depletion rate will be entitled to deduct $1,000 of percentage depletion on Blackacre's production but only $500 on Whiteacre's, if they are treated as separate, because percentage depletion may not exceed 50 percent of the taxable income from the property.[77] If the properties are combined, the allowance for percentage depletion rises to $2,000.

¶24.2 COST DEPLETION

¶24.2.1 Minerals

Cost depletion, authorized by §612, entails a spreading of the taxpayer's adjusted basis for depletable property over the number of units expected to be recovered, resulting in a deduction for each year of the cost attributable to the units sold during the year. The deduction must be computed individually for each separate "property," unless two or more properties are aggregated pursuant to §614.[1]

The basis used in computing cost depletion is the adjusted basis prescribed by §1011 for computing gain on a sale of the property.[2] When mineral properties include land and depreciable equipment, the adjusted basis allocable to the mineral deposit itself is the only portion subject to

---

officially reported) (aggregation of nonoperating interests approved, but purpose not stated in opinion).

[77] Infra ¶24.3.5.

[1] For the concept of a separate "property" and the aggregation of properties under §614, see supra ¶24.1.4.

[2] IRC §612. For IRC §1011, see infra ¶41.1.

depletion.[3] In the case of oil and gas wells, the taxpayer's basis includes intangible drilling and development costs unless, as usually occurs, the taxpayer elects to deduct the costs currently.[4] In the case of hard minerals, mine exploration and development expenditures are not usually included in the taxpayer's adjusted basis because, under provisions discussed in a later chapter of this work, the expenditures are generally deducted either as incurred or ratably as the minerals are produced and sold.[5]

Adjusted basis is reduced annually by the amount allowed or allowable as a depletion deduction, whichever is greater. Section 1016(a)(2) requires the taxpayer's basis to be reduced by depletion to the extent "allowable," even if the allowable deductions were not claimed or resulted in no tax benefit. Under §613(a), if both cost and percentage depletion apply to a particular natural resource, the larger deduction for the particular year is "allowable," and the taxpayer's basis is reduced accordingly. Once basis has been reduced to zero, cost depletion terminates, but percentage depletion continues to be permissible; percentage depletion in excess of cost usually has no effect on basis because the concept of negative basis is unknown.[6]

Once the aggregate amount to be depleted is determined, the cost depletion allowance per unit is computed by dividing this aggregate by the number of recoverable units, estimated "according to the method current in the industry and in the light of the most accurate and reliable information obtainable."[7] If a material change in the estimate is warranted as a result of

---

[3] Reg. §1.612-1(b). For the allocation of the cost of a larger property among its components, see Reg. §1.611-1(d)(4); Rev. Rul. 69-539, 1969-2 CB 141 (allocation based on proportion of fair market value of the mineral property to fair market value of all acquired assets). For factors used in ascertaining the value of a mineral interest, see Reg. §§1.611-2(d), (e); for application of these factors, see Hunt v. CIR, 37 TCM (CCH) 646 (1978) (allocation of basis for land to sand deposit). See generally infra ¶41.7.

[4] For this option, see infra ¶26.1.4.

[5] See infra ¶26.2. The ratable deduction for deferred mine development expenses is similar in concept to cost depletion, but can be taken even if depletion is computed by the percentage method. Currently deducted exploration expenses, in contrast, are subject to recapture through the disallowance of deductions for depletion when production from the mine begins.

[6] Rev. Rul. 75-451, 1975-2 CB 330 (after reducing property's basis to zero, percentage depletion must be applied to reduce basis of subsequent capital expenditures). For the effect on basis of excessive deductions, if they are not challenged by the IRS and disallowed, see infra ¶42.3.

[7] Reg. §1.611-2(c)(1). Section 1.611-2(a) deals with several problems in determining the number of recoverable units. When a taxpayer's interest consists of a right to a bonus or other payment expressed in dollars rather than in number of units of production, cost depletion cannot be computed on a per unit basis and some other method must be used. See Reg. §1.612-3(a) (basis allocable to production payment is fraction, of which numerator is amount received in current year and denominator is total amount to be received); see also Collums v. US, 480 F. Supp. 864 (D. Wyo.

subsequent development work or other events, the revised estimate is used for the year of the change and thereafter, unless and until another revision is warranted.[8] Cost depletion is based on the number of recoverable units and not on their market value, so changes in market prices do not affect the calculation directly. The concept of recoverable units, however, looks not merely to the physical size of the deposit, but also to the economic feasibility of extraction. The number of recoverable units thus can be revised to reflect a shift in economic feasibility resulting from a price change if the revision is well grounded on facts rather than on speculation.[9]

If the taxpayer's minerals qualify for percentage depletion and this method produces a larger deduction than cost depletion in some years but not in others, a return to cost depletion is complicated by the year-to-year change in the property's adjusted basis, which affects the per unit cost depletion allowance. Assume a taxpayer pays $100,000 for a mineral deposit with one million recoverable units. Cost depletion is 10 cents for each unit mined and sold during the first year. If depletion for this year is computed by the cost method, the cost depletion rate remains at 10 cents per unit for the second year. Assume 100,000 units are removed and sold in the first year, and depletion of $20,000 is allowed for the year under the percentage method. Cost depletion for the second year is approximately 8.89 cents per unit (the remaining basis of $80,000 divided by the estimated 900,000 remaining recoverable units).

Assume a revised estimate of reserves made at the beginning of the third year indicates that 1.2 million recoverable units remain. Cost depletion for the third and subsequent years is computed on the basis of the revised figure. If the taxpayer's adjusted basis in the deposit is $60,000 at the beginning of the third year, cost depletion for the year is 5 cents per unit (the remaining basis of $60,000 divided by the estimated 1.2 million remaining recoverable units). Cost depletion taken in either of the prior years

---

1979) (on transfer of wildcat leases subject to retained overriding royalty interest, taxpayer entitled to deduct entire cost of leases as cost depletion on showing that there was no reasonable expectation of production during terms of leases).

[8] IRC §611(a) (last sentence); Reg. §1.611-2(c)(2). For a retroactive change required by the IRS, effective to the date when the taxpayer should have changed an estimate, see Beck v. CIR, 15 TC 642, 658 (1950), aff'd per curiam, 194 F2d 537 (2d Cir.), cert. denied, 344 US 821 (1952).

[9] Cf. Black Gold Petroleum Co. v. CIR, 3 TCM (CCH) 241 (1944) (taxpayer's upward revision of number of recoverable units rejected; additional units recoverable only by installation of extra equipment, which government's expert witnesses testified was impractical from business standpoint). See also Rev. Rul. 67-157, 1967-1 CB 154 (speculation that increases in production costs will exceed estimated future selling price of coal does not support revision of recoverable units).

is not disturbed.[10]

¶24.2.2 Timber

Taxpayers with an economic interest in timber are allowed by §611(a) to deduct "a reasonable allowance for depletion." The depletion of timber is governed by substantially the same legal principles that apply to the depletion of mineral deposits, but there are a few important differences. First, timber qualifies only for cost depletion, not for percentage depletion. Second, because trees grow and reproduce themselves, changes in the quantity of depletable timber must be taken into account annually; otherwise, the taxpayer's original investment in timber could be spread over the amount of timber available when the tract was acquired and written off in full when that amount was cut, even though a substantial amount of standing timber remained on hand at the end of the period. Third, in contrast to the rich diversity of royalty and other divided interests spawned by the petroleum oil and gas industry, "cutting contracts" of one variety or another are the principal legal devices used by landowners to divide their interest in standing timber with lumbermen. Foresters are evidently better at splitting logs than economic interests.

The amount qualifying for depletion is the taxpayer's adjusted basis for the timber property, excluding amounts allocable to the land, depreciable equipment or other property, and immature timber until it becomes merchantable.[11] The depletable amount is increased by amounts paid or incurred for the preparation of timber sites for planting, for seedlings, and for planting, since these amounts are nondeductible capital outlays.[12] In applying these principles, it is necessary to distinguish among (1) expenditures for land and nondepreciable land improvements, which are not subject to either depreciation or depletion and can only be offset against the sales proceeds of the land when sold; (2) expenditures for depreciable equipment and improvements to the land, which qualify for depreciation rather than depletion; (3) amounts subject to depletion, such as reforestation costs, and (4) current silvicultural expenses, paid or incurred for normal maintenance,

---

[10] S. Rep. No. 665, 72d Cong., 1st Sess. (1932), reprinted in 1939-1 (Part 2) CB 496, 507–08; Wylie v. US, 281 F. Supp. 180 (ND Tex. 1968). For the retroactive application of a revised estimate if the taxpayer fails to act on it of his own motion, see Beck v. CIR, supra note 8.

[11] IRC §612; Reg. §§1.612-1(a), (b)(1); 1.611-3(d)(3). See also Bratton v. Rountree, 76-1 USTC ¶9198 (MD Tenn. 1976) (not officially reported) (on facts, IRS allocation of part of purchase price to immature timber not warranted).

[12] Reg. §1.611-3(a).

which are deductible under §162.[13] If the taxpayer's economic interest in the standing timber arises from a cutting contract, the depletable amount is the adjusted basis of the contract.[14]

The deduction for depletion on timber is determined on a per unit basis (e.g., board feet, cords) under a formula prescribed by the regulations:

$$D = \frac{AB \times UC}{UC + UOH}$$

> where
>
> $D =$ depletion
>
> $AB =$ adjusted basis of timber at end of year, before adjustment for the year's depletion allowance
>
> $UC =$ units cut during taxable year
>
> $UOH =$ units on hand at end of year.[15]

The number of units on hand at the end of the year may be determined by a timber cruise of the entire tract or representative samples or by applying a reasonable growth factor (e.g., 5 percent per year).[16]

A taxpayer depleting timber must maintain one or more timber accounts, stating the number of units that would have been determined by a "careful estimate" of the amount of merchantable timber that could have been cut and utilized in accordance with the standards prevailing in the region when the tract was acquired.[17] This estimate must be revised when necessary to reflect growth of the timber, changes in the standards of utiliza-

---

[13] See Rev. Rul. 75-467, 1975-2 CB 93 (reforestation expenditures are depletable outlays); Rev. Rul. 76-290, 1976-2 CB 188 (reforestation includes control of unwanted species); Rev. Rul. 66-18, 1966-1 CB 59 (brush removal a year or two after planting Christmas tree seedlings includable in planting expenditures, to be capitalized and recovered by depletion), modified by Rev. Rul. 71-228, 1971-CB 53 (expenses of shearing and pruning trees planted and grown for Christmas tree market deductible as business expense); Rev. Rul. 71-354, 1971-2 CB 246 (expenditures to build roads on federal forest area incurred by successful bidder for cutting contract are depreciable if necessary for taxpayer's logging operations; otherwise, includable in depletable basis of timber; federal "purchase credit" for building roads excluded from amount in either case); Drey v. US, 61-1 USTC ¶9116 (ED Mo. 1960) (not officially reported) (wages of foresters and timber cruisers deductible business expenses).

[14] For the cost of a cutting contract, see Bratton v. Rountree, supra note 11; Rev. Rul. 71-354, supra note 13.

[15] Reg. §1.611-3(b)(2).

[16] See Bratton v. Rountree, 76-1 USTC ¶9198 (MD Tenn. 1976).

[17] Reg. §§1.611-3(d)(1), (e).

tion, unaccounted-for losses, abandonments, and development work.[18] The regulations specify in detail how the fair market value of timber is determined when relevant to the computation of depletion, as in the case of inherited timber or when a lump-sum purchase price must be allocated between timber and land or between various types of timber.[19]

Under §631(a), taxpayers who own timber or have a contract to cut timber can treat the cutting of the timber, either for sale or for use in the taxpayer's business, as a sale or exchange of the timber. The disposal of timber under a contract by which an economic interest is retained by the owner or a person having cutting rights is similarly treated as a sale or exchange of the timber under §631(b). When these provisions apply, the taxpayer is entitled to §1231 treatment, but not to cost depletion.[20]

¶24.3 PERCENTAGE DEPLETION

¶24.3.1 Introductory

Unlike cost depletion, percentage depletion is based on the taxpayer's income from the mineral property rather than on its adjusted basis, and the allowance continues for the property's entire economic life, even after its basis has been recovered many times over. For minerals qualifying for percentage depletion, this method applies in any year in which it produces a larger allowance than cost depletion.[1]

There are three basic steps in the computation of percentage depletion, discussed in more detail below: (1) determination of whether the taxpayer's mineral qualifies for percentage depletion and, if so, the appropriate percentage, which varies from 5 to 22 percent depending on the mineral;[2] (2) application of the percentage rate to the taxpayer's "gross income from the property";[3] and (3) imposition of a limit of 50 percent of the taxpayer's "taxable income from the property."[4] Section 613A imposes an additional

---

[18] Reg. §1.611-3(e).

[19] Reg. §1.611-3(f). See Reg. §1.611-3(g) (once determined and approved, value is changed only for misrepresentation, fraud, or gross error); Ah Pah Redwood Co. v. CIR, 251 F2d 163 (9th Cir. 1957) (retroactive adjustments to reflect erroneous estimates not required); Rust-Owen Lumber Co. v. CIR, 74 F2d 18 (7th Cir. 1934) (gross error established).

[20] See Reg. §§1.611-1(b)(2), -3(b)(3). For IRC §§631(a) and (b), see infra ¶54.3.1.

[1] IRC §613(a). For the requirement that cost depletion rather than percentage depletion be used in computing corporate earnings and profits, see supra ¶24.1.1 note 5. See also supra ¶24.1.1 note 10 and accompanying text (percentage depletion as a tax preference if in excess of basis).

[2] Infra ¶24.3.2.

[3] Infra ¶24.3.4.

[4] Infra ¶24.3.5.

threshold step for oil and gas—whether the taxpayer is eligibile for percentage depletion—as well as other limits.[5]

Because the computation of percentage depletion is tied to the gross and taxable income "from the property,"it is necessary to determine whether the taxpayer has an economic interest in one property or in several. In the latter case, deductions must be computed separately for each property unless they are aggregated pursuant to §614.[6]

¶24.3.2 Qualifying Minerals

When first authorized in 1926, percentage depletion was only allowed for oil and gas, and the rate was 27.5 percent of gross income, a rate that seemed sacrosanct until it was lowered to 22 percent in 1969. Starting in 1932, when percentage depletion was authorized in lieu of discovery value depletion for coal, metal mines, and sulphur, Congress gradually enlarged the circle of qualifying minerals.[7] Presently, varying depletion rates, ranging from 5 to 22 percent, are specified for scores of minerals by §613(b).[8] For some minerals, the rate depends on the use to which the minerals are put in order "to prevent discrimination in percentage depletion rates between materials which are used competitively for the same purposes."[9] The applicable rate in these cases is determined by the "end use" of the mineral, and not by intermediate uses that produce a product for further utilization.[10]

---

[5] Infra ¶24.3.3.

[6] See supra ¶24.1.4.

[7] For discovery value depletion, see supra ¶24.1.1 note 11 and accompanying text.

[8] For technical problems in determining the category into which certain minerals fall, see, e.g., California Portland Cement Co. v. US, 67-1 USTC ¶9458 (CD Cal. 1967) (not officially reported), rev'd on other grounds, 413 F2d 161 (9th Cir. 1969) (chemical analysis of rock extracted from taxpayer's quarry showed average carbonates content of 80 percent; "common understanding" regarded it as limestone or calcium carbonates, not marble).

[9] S. Rep. No. 1622, 83d Cong., 2d Sess. 77 (1954).

[10] See G. & W.H. Corson, Inc. v. CIR, 453 F2d 578 (3d Cir. 1971). The most troublesome aspect of the "end use" test is the statutory phrase "similar purposes," which was interpreted in Corson to mean "uses reasonably commercially competitive with uses specifically enumerated," but by another court to mean purposes similar in a "conventional sense" to enumerated uses. See W.R. Bonsal Co. v. US, 72-1 USTC ¶9175 (WDNC 1971) (not officially reported). See also Maryland Green Marble Corp. v. US, 528 F2d 51 (4th Cir. 1975) (product could be used for road construction but was too costly to be commercially useful for that purpose; hence not subject to rate applicable to road construction materials); C.J. Langenfelder & Son v. CIR, 69 TC 378 (1977) (acq.) (shells used for oyster cultch entitled to 15 percent rate, not lower rate applicable to minerals with similar chemical attributes that are not reasonably commercially competitive).

Section 613(b)(7) prescribes a catchall rate of 14 percent for "all other minerals," with three groups of exceptions:

1. Soil, sod, dirt, turf, water, or mosses, which do not qualify for percentage depletion but may, if exhaustible, qualify for cost depletion.[11]
2. Minerals from seawater, the air, or "similar inexhaustible sources," which qualify for neither cost nor percentage depletion.
3. Oil and gas wells, which were removed from the general depletion provisions of §613 in 1975 in order to be given special treatment under §613A.[12]

Some minerals qualify for a higher rate under §613(b) if the deposit is located in the United States. Section 638, enacted in 1969, provides that the term "United States" includes, for this purpose, continental shelf areas over which the United States has exclusive rights under international law to the exploration and exploitation of natural resources.

¶24.3.3 Oil and Gas

Section 613A restricts the use of percentage depletion for oil and gas wells. The general rule of §613A(a) is that only cost depletion is allowed for oil and gas, but §§613A(b) and (c) set out two complex exceptions, which are briefly summarized below.[13]

1. *Independent producers and royalty owners.* Section 613A(c) allows percentage depletion for oil and gas at 15 percent,[14] subject to severe restric-

---

[11] For the "exhaustible source"requirement, see supra ¶24.1.1 note 13 and accompanying text. For distinctions between similar natural resources where one qualifies for percentage depletion and another does not, see Rev. Rul. 76-246, 1976-1 CB 176 (sand versus soil mixture); Rev. Rul. 57-336, 1957-2 CB 325 (peat versus moss). See also Rev. Rul. 79-411, 1979-2 CB 246 (soil and loam are natural deposits qualifying for cost but not percentage depletion).

[12] Infra ¶24.3.3; see also IRC §613(d) (§613A controlling).

[13] For detailed analysis of the 1975 legislation, see McMahon, Fundamentals of Federal Income Taxation of Natural Resources, 3 J. Min. L. & Pol'y 225 (1988); Englebrecht & Hutchins, Section 613A: A Decision Tree Analysis of Percentage Depletion Deductions for Oil and Gas, 26 Oil & Gas Tax Q. 54 (1977); Linden, Oil and Gas Depletion Regulations: Complexity Compounded, 24 Oil & Gas Tax Q. 351 (1976); Williams, Percentage Depletion Regulations: Let's Try It Again One *More* Time! 26 Oil & Gas Tax Q. 114 (1977).

[14] The rate was 22 percent for the calendar years 1975 through 1980, but was phased down to 20 percent for 1981, 18 percent for 1982, 16 percent for 1983, and 15 percent for 1984 and thereafter. IRC §613A(c)(5). Also, the rate was kept at 22 percent through 1983 for oil and gas extracted by certain secondary and tertiary

tions. Only domestic crude oil and natural gas qualify.[15] The allowance is only permitted for up to 1,000 barrels of oil per day or 6 million cubic feet of natural gas per day.[16] Because the allowance is tied to production quantities, a "lease bonus, advance royalty, or other amount payable without regard to production from property"cannot be depleted under this rule.[17] Also, §613A(c) is generally unavailable to taxpayers who have significant refining or retailing operations or are related to persons having such operations, a limitation that gives rise to the provision's title, "Exemption for Independent Producers and Royalty Owners."[18] Further, to discourage transfers calculated to avoid the foregoing limitations, the allowance is denied to taxpayers who acquire oil and gas properties after they are "proven."[19]

a. *Volume cap.* The 1,000-barrel or 6-million-cubic-feet cap is applied to the taxpayer's "average daily production," defined as aggregate production for the year divided by the number of days in the year.[20] For a 365-day year, for example, a taxpayer's production is wholly within the limitation if production for the year does not exceed 365,000 barrels.

When oil or gas is produced by a partnership or S corporation, the cap is applied to the partners or shareholders, not the partnership or corporation.[21] In the case of a trust or estate, the cap is applied at the entity level

---

processes. IRC §§613A(c)(6)(A)(ii), (C). The term "weaning" is not unique to the business of farming.

[15] For the meaning of "domestic," see IRC §613A(e)(3); see also IRC §638 ("United States" as a geographical term includes continental shelf areas).

[16] IRC §613A(c)(3). The 1,000-barrel cap applies for 1980 and subsequent years; it was 2,000 barrels for 1975 and was phased down in stages over the years 1976 through 1979. Id. For all years, the barrel limitation is converted for natural gas at the rate of 6,000 cubic feet of gas for each barrel of oil. IRC §613A(c)(4). If the taxpayer produces both oil and gas, the cap can be allocated between them, using the 6,000-to-one conversion ratio, by any proportions the taxpayer chooses. Id. Under the current limit, for example, percentage depletion could be claimed under §613A(c) with respect to 500 barrels of oil and 3 million cubic feet of natural gas.

If the taxpayer qualified under a more liberal set of rules provided by §613A(c)(6) for oil and gas produced before 1984 by secondary or tertiary processes, the 1,000-barrel or 6-million-cubic-feet cap for other oil and gas was reduced by the amount qualifying under the rules for secondary and tertiary production. IRC §613A(c)(3)(A)(ii).

[17] IRC §613A(d)(5).

[18] See infra text accompanying notes 32, 33.

[19] See infra text accompanying notes 34–36.

[20] IRC §613A(c)(2)(A).

[21] IRC §§613A(c)(7)(D), (13). The partnership's or corporation's basis for the property is allocated among the partners or shareholders, and each partner or shareholder computes his depletion separately. One partner or shareholder, for example, might take percentage depletion under §613A(c) while another uses cost depletion. A partner's or shareholder's share of partnership or corporate basis is adjusted for

and again, for percentage depletion allocated to beneficiaries, at their level.[22] For taxpayers with partial interests in the production from any property (including partners), total production is allocated among the interest holders according to their fractional share of revenues.[23]

A single 1,000-barrel or 6-million-cubic-feet cap must be shared by two or more taxpayers if they are (1) a controlled group of corporations, (2) businesses under common control, defined in terms of a 50 percent beneficial interest, or (3) a family, defined to include only spouses and their minor children.[24] Also, when individuals transfer oil and gas property to a corporation in exchange for stock, the cap applied to each transferor is reduced by some portion of the corporation's cap.[25]

Although §613A(c) is called "the small producer exemption" in the legislative committee reports,[26] oil and gas producers of any size qualify for percentage depletion on the limited amount of production covered by the provision. If a taxpayer has several oil and gas wells and average daily production from all of them exceeds the cap, the cap is prorated among the wells in proportion to average daily production.[27]

b. *Taxable income limitation.* Under §613A(d)(1), percentage depletion otherwise allowable under the foregoing rules is limited to 65 percent of the taxpayer's taxable income, computed without regard to percentage depletion under §613A(c) and the deductions for net operating loss and capital loss carrybacks.[28] Trusts compute the limitation without regard to deductions for distributions to beneficiaries.[29] Amounts disallowed by the 65

---

depletion deductions, and this adjusted basis is used in determining his distributive share of gain or loss on a sale of the property. See generally Lemons, Blau & Rohman, Depletion Problems for S Corporations and Partnerships, 68 J. Tax'n 176 (1988).

[22] Prop. Reg. §1.613A-3(f).

[23] IRC §613A(c)(2)(B).

[24] IRC §613A(c)(8); Prop. Reg. §1.613A-3(g) (business under common control). For periods before 1984, oil and gas extracted by certain secondary and tertiary processes was exempted from this rule. Prop. Reg. §1.613A-3(h)(2) Ex. 4.

[25] IRC §613A(c)(10). See S. Rep. No. 1039, 96th Cong., 2d Sess., reprinted in 1980-2 CB 691.

[26] Conf. Rep. No. 120, 94th Cong., 1st Sess. 630, reprinted in 1975-1 CB 624 (1975).

[27] IRC §§613A(c)(7)(A), (B).

[28] See Lastarmco, Inc. v. CIR, 79 TC 810 (1982), aff'd, 737 F2d 1440 (5th Cir. 1984) (taxable income determined for this purpose without deduction for dividends received allowed by §243(a)(1)).

[29] IRC §613A(d)(1)(D). This provision is inapplicable to a trust whose settlor died within the last six days of May 1970, a disqualification enacted at Senator Long's insistence to dispel rumors that the provision was designed to benefit members of his family. See 122 Cong. Rec. S24564-69 (daily ed., July 29, 1976).

percent limit may be carried forward to the following taxable years.[30]

This limitation looks to the taxpayer's taxable income from all sources and is imposed only after the depletion deduction has been filtered through §613(a), which, among other things, limits percentage depletion to 50 percent of the taxable income from the property.[31]

c.*Retailers.* Percentage depletion under §613A(c) is denied to retailers, defined by §613A(d)(2) as taxpayers who directly or through a related person (as defined) sell oil, natural gas, or products derived from oil or natural gas either through retail outlets operated by the taxpayer or a related person or to any person using the taxpayer's trademarks or distinguishing symbols or occupying premises owned or controlled by the taxpayer.[32] Bulk sales of oil or natural gas to commercial or industrial users and bulk sales of aviation fuel to the Department of Defense are not considered retail sales. Also, taxpayers with gross receipts from all retail outlets of not more than $5 million for the year are exempted from this disqualification.[33]

d.*Refiners.* Section 613A(d)(4) imposes a further disqualification if the taxpayer or a related person engages in the refining of crude oil and the refinery runs exceed 50,000 barrels on any day during the taxable year.

e.*Transfers of "proven" oil and gas property.* If a "proven" oil or gas property is transferred or subleased after 1974, the transferee or sublessee is ineligible for percentage depletion under §613A(c).[34] A property is "proven" if its principal value has been demonstrated at the time of the transfer by prospecting, exploration, or discovery work. Other properties can be freely

---

[30] The proposed regulations would allow a perpetual carryover for any amounts disallowed by the 65 percent limit. Prop. Reg. §1.613A-4(a)(2) Ex. 2.

[31] See infra ¶24.3.5. For the application of the 50 percent limitation where both oil and gas are extracted from one property, see IRC §613A(c)(7)(D). See generally Steinmann & Willis, Solving the Complexities Involved in the Computation of Percentage Depletion, 55 Taxes 674 (1977).

[32] See Witco Chem. Corp. v. US, 742 F2d 615, 620, 624 (Fed. Cir. 1984) (retail means "sales made in small quantities to ultimate consumers to meet personal needs, rather than for commercial or industrial uses of the articles sold"; trademark rule includes only sales under contracts "that *explicitly* require the use of the taxpayer's mark in marketing or distribution").

[33] See Witco Chem. Corp. v. US, supra note 32 (where taxpayer leases premises to retailer, taxpayer's sales to retailer, not retailer's sales, included in applying $5 million ceiling).

[34] IRC §613A (c)(9)(A). An election by an existing corporation to become an S corporation is treated as a transfer of all of its assets for this purpose. IRC §613A(c)(13)(C)(ii). See Rev. Rul. 84-14, 1984-1 CB 147 (neither transfer to grantor trust nor reconveyance to grantor on termination of trust is a disqualifying transfer if trustee must maintain reserve for depletion and income on investments of reserve are taxable to grantor).

Property transferred before 1984 is exempted from this disqualification if oil or gas is extracted from it by a secondary or tertiary process. Prop. Reg. §1.613A-3(h)(2) Ex. 4.

transferred, however, presumably on the theory that the loss of percentage depletion on transfers of wildcat properties would inhibit exploration activities.

The disqualification of proven properties is aimed at tax-avoidance transfers that move oil and gas properties from taxpayers who cannot use percentage depletion (e.g., retailers, refiners, and independent producers with production in excess of their depletable quantities) to taxpayers who qualify for percentage depletion. The disqualification, however, is not so restricted and applies with equal force to transfers between two taxpayers who are otherwise fully qualified to use percentage depletion, even if the aggregate amount of percentage depletion would not be swollen by the transfer.

The disqualification of transferred interests is mitigated by exempting certain transfers between related persons. Subject to a variety of detailed conditions, this exemption covers (1) transfers at death, (2) certain §351 transfers to controlled corporations,[35] (3) changes of trust beneficiaries as a result of death, birth, or adoption, (4) transfers within a controlled group of corporations, (5) transfers between business entities under common control or between members of the same family, and (6) transfers between trusts and related persons in the same family.[36]

2. *Regulated gas and gas sold under fixed contracts.* Section 613A(b)(1) allows percentage depletion for regulated natural gas and natural gas sold under fixed contracts and prescribes a rate of 22 percent.[37] This rule is largely obsolete because "regulated natural gas" disappeared with deregulation of natural gas production, and "natural gas sold under a fixed contract" only includes gas sold under a contract that was in force on February 1, 1975 and at all times thereafter until the time of sale and that precludes any adjustment to the price to compensate for the loss of percentage depletion.

3. *Natural gas from geopressured brine.* Section 613A(b)(2) allows percentage depletion at 10 percent for natural gas from geopressured brine, but only if the gas is taken from a well the drilling of which began during the period September 30, 1978 through December 31, 1983.[38]

---

[35] For §351 transfers by individuals, see IRC §613A(c)(10), discussed supra text accompanying note 25.

[36] IRC §613A(c)(9)(B). See Prop. Reg. §1.613A-3(h) (transfer rules), §1.613A-7(n) through (p) (definitions); Rev. Rul. 80-43, 1980-1 CB 133 (S election not a transfer). Transfers do not adversely affect the exemption of secondary and tertiary production. Prop. Reg. §1.613A-3(h)(1). See generally Linden, An Analysis of the "Transfer Rule" of the Proposed Regs. on Oil and Gas Depletion, 45 J. Tax'n 112 (1976).

[37] IRC §613A(b); Prop. Reg. §§1.613A-7(b), (c), (d).

[38] See S. Rep. No. 1324, 95th Cong., 1st Sess., reprinted in 1977-3 CB (Vol. 2) 309, 344 (1977).

4. *Geothermal steam.* Section 613(e) allows percentage depletion at the rate of 15 percent on geothermal deposits located in the United States or a possession thereof.[39]

¶24.3.4 Gross Income From the Property

Percentage depletion is computed by applying the percentage specified by §613(b) to "the gross income from the property," after excluding rents or royalties paid or incurred by the taxpayer in respect of the property.[40] Since rents and royalties are subject to either cost or percentage depletion in the hands of the recipient, their exclusion in computing the payor's gross income from the property prevents double deductions for the same income.[41] Bonus payments in the current year or prior years are treated as excludable royalties to the extent allocable to the current year's sales, and advanced royalties are excludable when they are deducted by the payor.[42] Ad valorem and gross production taxes paid by lessees or operators on behalf of lessors or owners of working interest are includable in the lessor's or owner's gross income and qualify as "gross income from the property" when paid out of income from production.[43]

Determination of the "gross income from the property" is ordinarily simple in the case of oil or gas, since it is the amount for which the taxpayer sells the product "in the immediate vicinity of the well" or, if the taxpayer transports or refines the oil or gas before sale, the "representative market or

---

[39] The 15 percent rate applies in taxable years beginning after 1983. The rate is 16 percent for taxable years beginning in 1983, 18 percent for 1982, 20 percent for 1981, and 22 percent for 1978, 1979, and 1980. IRC §613(e)(1)(2). The rule is inapplicable for taxable years ending before October 1, 1978.

Geothermal deposits were originally classified as a gas for depletion purposes. Reich v. CIR, 454 F2d 1157 (9th Cir. 1972). The enactment of §613(e) separated these deposits from the rules applicable to natural gas. IRC §613(e)(3); S. Rep. No. 1324, supra note 38, at 342–43.

[40] For separate versus aggregated properties, see IRC §614, discussed supra ¶24.1.4.

[41] But see Rev. Rul. 81-266, 1981-2 CB 139 (royalties excluded from lessee-payor's gross income from property even though lessor-payee denied percentage depletion under restrictive rules for oil and gas, described supra ¶24.3.3).

[42] Reg. §1.613-2(c)(5)(ii) (bonuses), §1.613-2(c)(5)(iii) (advanced royalties).

[43] Rev. Rul. 72-165, 1972-1 CB 177 (to extent there is insufficient income from production, tax payments treated as delay rentals, deductible by the payor and taxable to the payee as ordinary income not subject to depletion). See also Rev. Rul. 79-27, 1979-1 CB 217 (excise taxes under Black Lung Benefits Act); Rev. Rul. 75-182, 1975-1 CB 176. See generally Fiske, Gross Income From Mining Property, 36 J. Tax'n 114 (1972).

field price" before transportation or conversion into a refined product.[44] By basing depletion on a constructive price determined by reference to the wellhead market price, the regulations avoid giving an advantage to integrated producers, whose gross income from the sale of refined products is much greater than the wellhead price received by nonintegrated producers for their crude.

For minerals other than oil and gas, the computation of "gross income from the property" is more complicated because the extracted substances are often sold only after processing, rather than in their crude state on emerging from the mine. Building on this technical fact of life, mineral producers have persistently sought to base the depletion allowance on the value of the refined product—the more refined, the better—since any given percentage rate produces a larger deduction if applied to the value of a highly processed product than to the value of the mineral in its crudest form. Salt, for example, might be worth $10 a ton if valued early in the extractive process, but $2,000 a ton after being purified and packed in tiny containers for use by airline passengers.[45]

Since 1944, §613(c)(1) has provided that "gross income from the property" means, for properties other than oil and gas wells, "gross income from mining." From 1944 until 1961, "mining" was defined to include not merely the extraction of the minerals from the ground,[46] but also "the ordinary treatment processes normally applied by mine owners or operators in order to obtain the commercially marketable mineral product," plus certain transportation expenses.[47] As interpreted by the Supreme Court in *United States v. Cannelton Sewer Pipe Co.*, this vague language referred to the first point at which a commercially marketable product was obtained, even if its sale in that form would not generate a profit.[48]

Congress decided in 1961 that greater specificity was needed. The general definition of mining was displaced by an amended §613(c)(2), which provides that a treatment process is considered mining only if it is specified

---

[44] Reg. §1.613-3(a). For problems in determining the representative market or field price, see Warner Co. v. US, 504 F2d 689 (3d Cir. 1974), cert. denied, 421 US 930 (1975); Panhandle E. Pipe Line Co. v. US, 408 F2d 690 (Ct. Cl. 1969); Petroleum Exploration v. US, 404 F. Supp. 93 (ND W. Va. 1975), aff'd, 551 F2d 308 (4th Cir. 1977).

[45] See generally White & Brainerd, Percentage Depletion of Minerals—A Costly Study in Definitions, 34 Taxes 97 (1956).

[46] For the extent to which processing minerals from the waste or residue of prior mining operations constitutes "the extraction of the ores or minerals from the ground" under §613(c)(3), see Reg. §1.613-4(i).

[47] IRC §114(b)(4)(B) (1939); IRC §613(c)(2) (1954) (until amended in 1961).

[48] US v. Cannelton Sewer Pipe Co., 364 US 76 (1960); see Fernald, Gross Income From Mining: A Critique of *Cannelton*, 23 NYU Inst. on Fed. Tax'n 1379 (1965).

in §613(c)(4), is necessary or incidental to a process so specified, or is brought within the depletion base by regulations.[49] The term "mining" also includes transportation of the minerals from the point of extraction to processing plants up to 50 miles away, or more if the IRS finds that "physical and other requirements" necessitate transportation for a greater distance.[50]

The fascinating, if bewildering, list of industrial techniques in §613(c)(4) bears witness to the success of one industry after another in persuading Congress that its depletable base should be determined after one or more steps in the processing of the raw mineral.[51] If a latter-day Michelangelo purchased a marble quarry to ensure a source of suitable stone, he would no doubt seek to apply the 14 percent depletion rate for marble to the value of the stone after "treatment" by his mallet and chisel rather than to its value at the quarry.

If the taxpayer sells the minerals immediately after applying the processes specified by §613(c)(4), gross income from mining ordinarily equals the sales proceeds.[52] If the taxpayer goes on to refine the product further,

---

[49] For the authority to add to the list by regulations, see IRC §613(c)(4)(I); Reg. §1.613-4(f)(5) (crushing, grinding, classification by size, drying to remove free water, and washing are includable incidental additional processes, subject to certain qualifications); but see Reg. §1.613-4(g)(2) (disqualifying processes applied after a nonmining process). See also §613(c)(5), which lists processes that are not considered as mining unless otherwise provided.

For a detailed examination of a taxpayer's technical processes in determining the location of the cutoff point, with a discussion of whether the pre-1961 "commercially marketable"standard has any continued force, see Barton Mines Corp. v. CIR, 446 F2d 981 (2d Cir. 1971); Carborundum Co. v. CIR, 70 TC 59 (1978).

See Rev. Rul. 86-81, 1986-1 CB 249 (where owner of coal property leases it to another in exchange for a royalty, buys substantially all of the lessee's output from the property, and performs on the purchased coal only operations described in §613(c)(4), none of the income on resale of the coal is from mining because it is not derived from mining operations).

[50] IRC §613(c)(2); see Reg. §1.613-4(h) (requests for inclusion of cost of transporting minerals more than 50 miles). See Rowe v. US, 655 F2d 1065 (Ct. Cl. 1981) (transportation included in mining only when minerals transported to taxpayer/mine-operator's processing facility, not when transported to facility operated by person purchasing minerals from taxpayer); Nicewonder v. US, 81-2 USTC ¶9723 (WD Va. 1981) (same).

[51] The addition of the decarbonation of trona to §613(c)(4)(E) in 1974 was memorialized by the senior author of this work as follows:

A mining tycoon from Verona
Said: "I wanna get rich, and I'm gonna.
"If you let me deplete,
"I won't have to cheat,
"Just watch me decarbonate trona."

[52] For the effect of discounts and other price reductions, see Reg. §1.613-4(e).

using processes that are not mining within the meaning of §613(c)(2), gross income from mining is a constructive price at the cutoff point between the qualified and nonqualified processes. The regulations provide for use of a "representative market or field price" for the mineral prior to the application of nonmining processes if such a price can be determined for minerals of like kind and grade.[53] As explained by the regulations:

> The objective in computing gross income from mining by the representative market or field price method is to ascertain, on the basis of an analysis of actual competitive sales by the taxpayer or others, the dollar figure or amount which most nearly represents the approximate price at which the taxpayer, in light of market conditions, could have sold his ores or minerals if, prior to the application of nonmining processes, the taxpayer had sold the quantities and types of ores and minerals to which he applied nonmining processes. . . . The taxpayer's own actual sales prices for ores or minerals of like kind and grade shall be taken into account when establishing market or field prices, provided that those sales are determined to be representative.[54]

In the absence of a representative market or field price, the regulations ordinarily require use of a "proportionate profits" method, under which gross income is reconstructed by multiplying the taxpayer's gross sales by a fraction whose numerator is mining costs and whose denominator is total costs.[55] The gross sales figure used in this computation is gross sales from the "first marketable product" in the taxpayer's operations.[56]

¶24.3.5 Taxable Income Ceiling

Percentage depletion may not exceed 50 percent of the taxpayer's taxable income from the property, computed before deducting depletion. Because of this restriction, set out in §613(a) (second sentence), percentage depletion is curtailed for economically marginal operations, and is denied if the taxpayer incurs a loss; the taxpayer can, however, shift to cost depletion if that produces a larger allowance.

---

[53] Reg. §1.613-4(c).

[54] Id.

[55] Reg. §1.613-4(d)(4)(ii). Other methods can be used if approved by the IRS. For the proportionate profits method, see Southwestern Portland Cement Co. v. US, 435 F2d 504 (9th Cir. 1970) (allocation of transportation and warehousing expenses); Standard Lime & Cement Co. v. US, 329 F2d 939 (Ct. Cl. 1964) (operating costs and profits); Monsanto Co. v. CIR, 86 TC 1232 (1986) (fuel costs); Carborundum Co. v. CIR, 70 TC 59, 63–64 (1978) (effect of treatment processes).

[56] Reg. §1.613-4(d)(4). For the meaning of "first marketable product" in the cement business, see CIR v. Portland Cement Co., 450 US 156 (1981).

Although §613(a) does not explicitly say so, "taxable income" for purposes of the 50 percent ceiling is computed consistently with "gross income from the property"—that is, by taking account of mining processes listed in §613(c)(4), and using the representative-market-price or proportionate-profits method of computing income from mining if nonmining processes are applied before the minerals are sold.[57] To compute "taxable income from the property,"therefore, the taxpayer starts with "gross income from the property" and then subtracts all allowable deductions (except depletion) attributable to mining processes, including operating expenses, selling expenses, administrative overhead, depreciation, deductible taxes, and losses.[58] Expenditures that are attributable both to the depletable mineral property and to other activities are allocated between them. These principles are elaborated and illustrated by the regulations.[59]

The third sentence of §613(a) permits the taxpayer to reduce the deductions allocated to income from the property by the amount of a gain on the sale of depreciable assets if the gain is taxed as ordinary income by §1245 and is allocable to the mining property. By increasing taxable income from the property, this increases the 50 percent ceiling on percentage depletion, offsetting to some extent the reduction in taxable income and the ceiling that resulted in earlier years from the depreciation subsequently recaptured by §1245.[60]

¶24.4 PRODUCTION PAYMENTS

¶24.4.1 Introductory

Production payments are used for various financial and tax purposes in the oil and gas industry and, less commonly, in other extractive industries.

---

[57] Supra ¶24.3.4.

[58] Reg. §1.613-5(a). Net operating losses carried forward from prior years are not deducted in determining taxable income from the property, even if the losses arose, in whole or in part, from the same property. Rev. Rul. 60-164, 1960-1 CB 254. Currently deducted intangible drilling and development expenses, however, reduce taxable income from the property. Helvering v. Wilshire Oil Co., 308 US 90, rehearing denied, 308 US 638 (1939); Rev. Rul. 77-136, 1977-1 CB 167 (IDC of nonproductive wells). For the effect of bonus payments on computation of the lessee's taxable income, see Rev. Rul. 79-73, 1979-1 CB 218; Price & Cassell, Revenue Ruling 79-73 Ignores Tax Reduction Act of 1975, 28 Oil & Gas Tax Q. 76 (1979).

[59] Reg. §§1.613-5(a), (c). In allocating indirect expenses to be "properly apportioned,"the regulations presumably reflect the Tax Court's refusal to hold that overhead costs must be allocated among activities and properties in proportion to direct costs. See Tennessee Consol. Coal Co. v. CIR, 15 TC 424 (1950) (acq.).

[60] See Reg. §1.613-5(b); S. Rep. No. 1881, 87th Cong., 2d Sess., reprinted in 1962-3 CB 703, 806.

A production payment (sometimes called an "in oil payment," "gas payment," or "mineral payment") is a right to receive a share (in kind or in money, usually free of operating expenses) of the production from a mineral deposit when, as, and if produced, up to an aggregate amount specified in terms of money, quantity of mineral, or period of time. An example is a right to receive the gross income from production until $100, plus interest at the rate of 6 percent per year, has been received. A production payment may be a charge against all production from the burdened property, or it may be limited to income from a specified portion (e.g., 50 percent of production). It can be "carved out" of an existing mineral interest and transferred by the creator, or it can be retained on a disposition of the underlying interest. A retained production payment can either be held by the creator as an independent asset until it pays out or be transferred by sale, gift, or other disposition.

By virtue of §636,[1] enacted in 1969, a carved-out production payment is ordinarily treated as a mortgage loan by the transferee to the holder of the underlying interest. Assume B pays $100 to A in exchange for the right to receive 50 percent of the production of A's oil well until the value received equals $100 plus interest at 6 percent. Under §636(a), the parties are treated as though B had lent $100 to A on the security of the oil well. A retained production payment, in contrast, is treated by §636 as a purchase money mortgage to the seller if retained on a sale of mineral properties or as a bonus to the lessor if retained in a leasing transaction. If A sells his oil well to B for $400, retaining the right to 50 percent of future production until $600 plus interest at 6 percent has been received, the parties are treated as though the property had been sold for $1,000, payable $400 down and $600 in future installments.

---

[1] For the effective dates of §636, including certain transitional rules for production payments created before January 1, 1971 and for taxable years ending before August 7, 1969, see Reg. §1.636-4.

For a detailed explanation of the legislation, see S. Rep. No. 552, 91st Cong., 1st Sess., reprinted in 1969-3 CB 423, 538. See generally Berry, Production Payments—Vagueness in the Regulations, 22 Oil & Gas Tax Q. 51 (1973); Casey, Oil and Gas Joint Ventures and Partnerships: A Side Effect of Section 636, 27 Tax Lawyer 417 (1974); French, Recent Developments in Oil and Gas Operations, 23 Tul. Tax Inst. 136–47 (1974); Joyce & Del Cotto, The AB (ABC) and BA Transactions: An Economic and Tax Analysis of Reversed and Carved Out Income Interests, 31 Tax L. Rev. 121 (1976).

In Carr Staley, Inc. v. US, 496 F2d 1366 (5th Cir. 1974), cert. denied, 420 US 963 (1975), it was held that §636(b) does not deny due process to the purchaser of mineral property subject to a retained production payment by taxing him on the seller's income, since in the court's view the retained production payment was properly analogized by Congress to a purchase money mortgage given to secure the unpaid balance of the purchase price of the property.

While production payments can serve a variety of business purposes, their use before 1969 for three tax-avoidance purposes generated controversy, led to litigation, and finally elicited the enactment of §636.

1. *Transformation of ordinary income into capital gain.* One tax-avoidance plan involving carved-out production payments was the sale of a production payment that was virtually certain to pay out within a few years in the hope of reporting the selling price as long-term capital gain. In *CIR v. P.G. Lake, Inc.*, however, the Supreme Court held that such a transaction generated ordinary income subject to depletion.[2] The Court summarized the facts of one of the five cases consolidated for argument as follows:

> Lake is a corporation engaged in the business of producing oil and gas. It has a seven-eighths working interest in two commercial oil and gas leases. In 1950 it was indebted to its president in the sum of $600,000 and in consideration of his cancellation of the debt assigned him an oil payment right in the amount of $600,000, plus an amount equal to interest at 3 percent a year on the unpaid balance remaining from month to month, payable out of 25 percent of the oil attributable to the taxpayer's working interest in the two leases. At the time of the assignment it could have been estimated with reasonable accuracy that the assigned oil payment right would pay out in three or more years. It did in fact pay out in a little over three years.[3]

Rejecting the taxpayer's claim that the transaction was the sale of a capital asset, the Court said:

> We do not see here any conversion of a capital investment. The lump sum consideration seems essentially a substitute for what would otherwise be received at a future time as ordinary income. The pay-out of these particular assigned oil payment rights could be ascertained with considerable accuracy. . . . The substance of what was assigned was the right to receive future income. The substance of what was received was the present value of income which the recipient would otherwise obtain in the future. In short, consideration was paid for the

---

[2] CIR v. P.G. Lake, Inc., 356 US 260 (1958). The *Lake* case involved five cases from the Court of Appeals for the Fifth Circuit, which were consolidated for argument. The Court did not attribute its grant of certiorari to a conflict among the circuits but to "the public importance of the question." Id. at 261. In four of the cases the taxpayer transferred a production payment for cash. In the fifth, the consideration was an interest in a ranch. The court of appeals held that the transfer was a tax-free exchange of real property held for investment for other property of a like kind under §1031, discussed infra ¶44.2, but the Supreme Court held that the exchange was a taxable event generating ordinary income.

[3] Id. at 261–62.

right to receive future income, not for an increase in the value of the income-producing property.[4]

2. *Acceleration of income.* Although the government won the *Lake* case, the Court's opinion tended to support taxpayers in the use of carved-out production payments as a method of accelerating income where the taxpayer preferred to report the amount received currently rather than in later years. For example, a taxpayer with an expiring net operating loss carryover might sell a production payment, report the proceeds currently, and use the carryover to eliminate tax liability.

Another example was a taxpayer whose current taxable income from a mineral property was so low that his depletion deduction was curtailed by the rule limiting percentage depletion to 50 percent of taxable income.[5] By selling a production payment, current taxable income (and hence the 50 percent ceiling) could be lifted and full advantage taken of percentage depletion. Assume a taxpayer anticipated receiving $100 of gross income from an oil or gas property in a given year, qualifying for a percentage depletion at the pre-1969 rate of 27.5 percent, but expected that because of heavy operating expenses, taxable income would be only $10. On these facts, the percentage depletion deduction was limited to $5 (the lower of 27.5 percent of $100 or 50 percent of $10). By selling a production payment for $100, however, gross income could be increased to $200, taxable income to $110, and depletion to $55. Of the $50 increase in the depletion deduction, $27.5 is attributable to the production payment; as to this amount, the sale simply accelerates a deduction that would otherwise be available in later years if the 50 percent limit did not interfere. The other $22.5 of the increased deduction, however, is attributable to the current year's production of $100.

Although the Supreme Court did not address itself in *Lake* to arrangements of this type, it virtually validated them by seemingly holding that the consideration for a production payment is ordinary income (subject to depletion) when received. This implication was strengthened by the Court's failure to mention an alternative rationale for denying capital gain treatment in the *Lake* case—that the transfers were methods of borrowing funds, equivalent to nonrecourse mortgages secured by production from the property. Viewed in this light, the transferor would realize no income on "selling" the payment, but would report the production when it occurred and was used to discharge the nonrecourse debt. Had this theory been accepted in *Lake*, the taxpayers would have realized ordinary income (subject to depletion) when the production payment paid out, not when they sold the payment. Since the loan theory of production payments had been

---

[4] Id. at 265–66.
[5] For the 50 percent limit, see supra ¶24.3.5.

accepted and applied by the Court of Appeals for the Seventh Circuit in 1956,[6] the Court's failure to mention it when deciding *Lake* in 1958 was especially pointed.

3. *ABC transactions. Lake* also tended, by indirection, to validate a third tax-avoidance technique, the so-called ABC transaction, which worked as follows: *A*, the owner of an interest in mineral property worth $1,000, sold it to *B* for $400, retaining a production payment of $600 (plus interest on the deferred payments), and then sold the production payment to *C* for $600. Since the two sales terminated *A*'s interest in the property, they qualified for capital gain treatment. As the production payment paid out, *C* recovered his $600 investment plus interest. *B* acquired a $1,000 property for $400 plus deferred payments of $600, but the production used to pay the latter amounts was not included in his income when generated by the property, since *C* rather than *B* was considered to be the owner of the production.

The ABC transaction was, in effect, a do-it-yourself cost recovery scheme. If *B* had purchased the mineral property by paying $400 down and giving *A* or *C* a nonrecourse mortgage on the property of $600, his $1,000 investment (including the $600) would have been written off under the depletion rules. The effect of the ABC transaction was to exclude $600 from *B*'s income as it was paid to *C*, leaving only $400 to be recovered through depletion. The timing of the tax allowance for the $600, in other words, was determined by the terms of the arrangement with *C*, not the cost recovery rules provided by the Code.[7]

---

[6] CIR v. Slagter, 238 F2d 901 (7th Cir. 1956).

[7] The legislative history of §636 states that the problem in the ABC transaction was that it allowed *B* to pay for the property with "pre-tax"dollars because the $600 going to *C* was essentially part of the purchase price for the property but was wholly excluded from *B*'s income. H.R. Rep. No. 413 (part 1), 91st Cong., 1st Sess. 140 (1969). The purchase price for property, however, can be paid from pretax funds whenever the purchaser can arrange to pay the price in installments matching the cost recovery rules applied to the property. Assume a purchaser of an apartment building pays for it with money borrowed under a mortgage whose principal is payable in 28 equal annual installments. If the building is depreciable on a straight line basis over 28 years, the mortgage is effectively paid with pretax dollars because the portion of the rents used to pay mortgage principal is insulated from tax by the depreciation deductions. The problem with the ABC transaction was that the production payment was paid from pretax dollars even if the payout was more rapid than the cost recovery rules that would otherwise apply to the property. That is, the ABC transaction effectively allowed the buyer to cook up his own cost recovery scheme.

For attempts to adapt the ABC technique to other industries, see infra ¶40.6.4. For a detailed examination of the ABC transaction, concluding that the tax advantages were overstated and that a change in tax treatment would be "hazardous in the

¶24.4.2 Carved-Out Production Payments

Section 636 treats most production payments as debt rather than as economic interests in the property from which they are paid. Carved-out production payments are treated by §636(a) as mortgage loans. As a consequence, the amount received by the transferor is not currently includable in income, but the production used to pay off the transferor is included in the transferee's income, and subject to depletion, when generated by the property.[8] If the property is sold or otherwise transferred before the production payment pays out, the unpaid balance is part of the amount realized by the transferor on the disposition.[9] The transferee, like a mortgage lender, is taxed on the interest component,[10] but, having no economic interest in the property, is not eligible for depletion.

Where a production payment is carved out for the exploration or development of mineral properties, the payment is treated as a loan only to the extent that the amount received by the creator would be gross income in the absence of §636(a).[11] This obtuse exception refers to a rule developed before the enactment of §636(a) under which the sale of a production payment to finance exploration or development was viewed as a contribution by the transferee to the pool of capital required to develop the property.[12] Since this contribution (unlike the amounts usually received by the creator of a carved-out payment) was not included in the recipient's gross income, the transaction did not lend itself to the income acceleration devices that were the target of §636(a). The prior law treatment of transactions of this type as

---

extreme . . . to the economy and strength of the nation at large," see Wilkinson, ABC Transactions and Related Income Tax Plans, 40 Tex. L. Rev. 18 (1961).

[8] If a production payment is not sold by its creator but is used to pay a preexisting debt, make a gift, contribute to the capital of a controlled corporation, the transfer of the payment is given the same effect as though the transferor had issued a promissory note to the transferee. Reg. §1.636-1(a)(1)(i).

[9] Reg. §1.636-1(c)(1)(i). In the case of a retained production payment created upon disposition of a mineral property, however, the amount to be included by the transferor is its fair market value rather than the principal amount. Reg. §1.636-1(c)(1)(ii) Ex. 2.

[10] Reg. §1.636-1(a)(1)(ii). If interest is not expressed, it may be imputed under the original issue discount rules, discussed infra ¶54.4.

[11] IRC §636(a) (second sentence).

[12] GCM 22730, 1941-1 CB 214, 221–22. See also US v. Frazell, 335 F2d 487 (5th Cir. 1964), cert. denied, 380 US 961 (1965); Linden, Income Realization in Mineral Sharing Transactions: The Pool of Capital Doctrine, 33 Tax Lawyer 115 (1979).

If a production payment is burdened by drilling and development expenses, it may be a working interest allowing the assignee to claim intangible drilling and development expenses. See Rev. Rul. 75-446, 1975-2 CB 95; infra ¶26.1.

joint ventures or partnerships is thus preserved. In keeping with this treatment, the transferee is permitted to deplete the payments as received.

If a carved-out production payment is transferred to finance operations rather than exploration or development, the joint venture analogy is not used, and the transaction is considered a mortgage loan under the general rule of §636(a). It is therefore necessary to distinguish exploratory and developmental activities (defined by the regulations as "necessary for ascertaining the existence, location, extent, or quality of any deposit of mineral or . . . incident to and necessary for the preparation of a deposit for the production of mineral") from operations related "primarily to the production of mineral."[13]

¶24.4.3 Retained Production Payments

When a production payment is retained on the sale of a mineral property, §636(b) treats the payment as a purchase money mortgage given by the buyer to the seller, which does not qualify as an economic interest in the property. This rule, designed to cope with ABC transactions, means that the seller of the underlying property must include the production payment in determining the amount realized (and hence the gain or loss) on the sale, and cannot deplete the production income received by him as the payment pays out.[14] Conversely, the buyer includes the production payment in his basis for the property, reports the production income applied to pay off the production payment, and is entitled to cost or percentage depletion thereon.[15]

Assume A sells her oil well to B for $400, retaining the right to 50 percent of future production until $600 plus interest at 6 percent has been received. The parties are treated as though the property had been sold for $1,000, payable $400 down and $600 in future installments. The selling price in A's sale is $1,000, and, apart from gain on the sale, A is only taxed on the interest element in the subsequent payments. All revenues from the property, including the amounts paid to A, are part of B's gross income, subject to depletion.

---

[13] Reg. §1.636-1(b). See Rev. Rul. 74-549, 1974-2 CB 186 (carved-out production payments sold by strip miner to finance removal of overburden and purchase earth-moving equipment for same purpose; held, mortgage loans under §636(a)). See also James A. Lewis f.c. Eng'g, Inc. v. CIR, 339 F2d 706 (5th Cir. 1964) (§61(a) case; held, expenses relating to production are outside pool-of-capital concept; question whether pool of capital can include mineral interests received for services).

[14] For the effect of a disposition of a retained production payment by sale or its use to make a gift, pay a debt, etc., see supra note 8.

[15] Reg. §1.636-1(a)(1)(ii). See Reg. §1.636-1(a)(3) Ex. 3.

Production payments retained by the lessor in a leasing transaction are subject to §636(c), which requires the lessee to treat the payment as a bonus payable by him to the lessor in installments. This means that the amounts used to pay off the production payment are included in the lessee's gross income.[16] Section 636(c) does not affect the treatment of the lessor, with the consequence that the production payment is an economic interest of the lessor in the mineral property and the receipts as it pays out are ordinary income to the lessor, subject to depletion.[17]

¶24.4.4 Scope of Term "Production Payment"

Although the term "production payment" is a bit hazy around the edges, §636 does not define it. The regulations fill the gap with the following definition:

> The term "production payment" means, in general, a right to a specified share of the production from mineral in place (if, as, and when produced), or the proceeds from such production. Such right must be an economic interest in such mineral in place. It may burden more than one mineral property, and the burdened mineral property need not be an operating mineral interest. Such right must have an expected economic life (at the time of its creation) of shorter duration than the economic life of one or more of the mineral properties burdened thereby. A right to mineral in place which can be required to be satisfied by other than the production of mineral from the burdened mineral property is not an economic interest in mineral in place. A production payment may be limited by a dollar amount, a quantum of mineral, or a period of time. A right to mineral in place has an economic life of shorter duration than the economic life of a mineral property burdened thereby only if such right may not reasonably be expected to extend in substantial amounts over the entire productive life of such mineral property.[18]

---

[16] Reg. §§1.636-2(a), (c). See Reg. §1.612-3(a) (cost depletion of bonuses); §1.613-2(c)(5)(ii) Ex. 2 (pre-1975 bonuses).

[17] Reg. §§1.636-2(b), (c).

[18] Reg. §1.636-3(a)(1). See also Freede v. CIR, 86 TC 340 (1986) (holders of working interests in gas well (sellers) made "take or pay" contract under which they agreed to sell all output of well for 20 years to other party to contract (purchaser) and purchaser agreed to pay for at least 80 percent of deliverable capacity of well; if it took delivery of less, it had to pay currently for 80 percent, but was entitled to future delivery of shortfall; held, payments for amounts in excess of current deliveries were production payments, and thus were loans, not gross income, to sellers; three dissents); Rev. Rul. 76-34, 1976-1 CB 177 (royalty percentages fluctuating with production; held, not equivalent to production payment because economic life runs for

The regulations go on to include in the term "production payment" any right that is "in substance economically equivalent to a production payment . . . regardless of the language used to describe such right, the method of creation of such right, or the form in which such right is cast (even though such form is that of an operating mineral interest)."[19] The breadth of this definition raised a question about the status of carried interests, but the IRS does not treat such interests as production payments.[20]

In defining the term "production payment" to exclude rights that are not wholly dependent on the extraction of minerals from the burdened property, the regulations echo the pre-1969 case law, under which royalties guaranteed by the lessee do not give the lessor an economic interest in the property, so that income used to satisfy the obligation is taxable to the lessee, subject to depletion.[21] Since payments on such obligations must come from the lessee's after-tax dollars, there was no need to subject them to the rules laid down by §636.

As for rights whose expected life is not shorter than the economic life of the underlying property, their exclusion from the definition of "production payments" seems to acknowledge that long-lived production payments are hardly distinguishable from the underlying property with which they are coextensive and hence are not suitable vehicles for the tax-avoidance plans against which §636 is aimed. Even before the enactment of §636, the IRS had recognized that production payments are not ordinarily instruments of tax avoidance if the payment constitutes the assignor's entire depletable interest in the property or a fraction extending over its entire life.[22]

---

duration of mineral property). See generally Singhal, Identifying a Production Payment, 27 Oil & Gas Tax Q. 377 (1979).

[19] Reg. §1.636-3(a)(2).

[20] See Casey, Oil and Gas Joint Ventures and Partnerships: A Side Effect of Section 636, 27 Tax Lawyer 417 (1974).

[21] See Anderson v. Helvering, 310 US 404 (1940); Gibson Prods. Co. v. US, 637 F2d 1041 (5th Cir. 1981); CIR v. Donnell's Est., 417 F2d 106 (5th Cir. 1969). The courts are split over whether this rule applies when the payment is secured by something other than production, but the other security is economically insignificant. Compare Christie v. US, 436 F2d 1216 (5th Cir. 1971) (any nonproduction security disqualifies) with Standard Oil Co. v. CIR, 465 F2d 246 (7th Cir. 1972) (only economically significant nonproduction security disqualifies).

[22] IT 4003, 1950-1 CB 10, declared obsolete by Rev. Rul. 70-277, 1970-1 CB 280. See Rev. Rul. 86-119, 1986-2 CB 82 (owner of nonproducing oil and gas lease sold a right to a stipulated percentage of net monthly proceeds from the property until the aggregate reached twice the price paid; held, transaction a sale of a royalty interest, not a production payment; because of uncertainty that there would be any net monthly proceeds, the right, when created, was not "reasonably expected to have an economic life of shorter duration than the economic life of the burdened mineral property"); Rev. Rul. 76-34, 1976-1 CB 177.

¶24.4.5 Collateral Consequences of §636 Characterizations

In a series of recent cases involving oil and gas deals structured as tax shelters, taxpayers have picked up the sword of §636 and tried to use it against the Treasury.[23] A typical fact pattern is as follows: *A* sells unproven oil and gas property to *B* for $250, payable $100 down and $150 by *B*'s promissory note. Simultaneously, *A* agrees to drill a well on the property for $750, payable $300 in cash and $450 by *B*'s note. In total, *B* pays $400 in cash and $600 by notes. The notes are without recourse and are payable solely from the production from the property.[24] *B* argues: (1) Because the notes are payable only from production, they constitute a $600 production payment retained by *A* on the sale; (2) under §636(b), a retained production payment is treated as a purchase money mortgage; (3) under general tax principles, the cost basis of property includes any portion of the purchase price payable by a purchase money mortgage, and *B*'s basis for the property is thus $1,000 (the sum of the $400 cash down payment and the $600 in notes); and (4) because a purchase money mortgage is a liability, all of the $750 to be paid *A* for the drilling of the well, including the portion paid by note, accrues immediately and can be deducted as an intangible drilling and development cost.[25]

B's argument prevailed in the Tax Court, which noted that §636(b) characterizes a production payment as a purchase money mortgage "for purposes of this subtitle," including all substantive income tax provisions of the Code.[26] The three Courts of Appeal that have addressed the issue, however, have denied *B*'s claim, holding that §636(b) does not supersede the principles denying effect to a liability, for purposes of both the basis and accrual rules, if the debt is contingent or speculative. The Court of Appeals for the First Circuit summarized these principles in *Brountas v. CIR* as follows:

> The liabilities that investors typically are allowed to include in basis are relatively definite liabilities such as those upon which a lender

---

[23] CRC Corp. v. CIR, 693 F2d 281 (3d Cir. 1982), cert. denied, 462 US 1106 (1983); Brountas v. CIR, 692 F2d 152 (1st Cir. 1982); Gibson Prods. Co. v. US, 637 F2d 1041 (5th Cir. 1981). *CRC Corp.* and *Brountas* were appeals from a single Tax Court decision. See also Dillingham v. US, 81-2 USTC ¶9601 (WD Okla. 1981) (not officially reported).

[24] In each of the cases, the notes were also secured by operating equipment on the property, which was held in one of the decisions to violate the rule described above in ¶24.4.4 (note 21 and accompanying text) that a production payment must be secured exclusively by production. Gibson Prods. Co. v. US, supra note 23.

[25] For intangible drilling and development costs, see infra ¶26.1.

[26] Brountas v. CIR, 73 TC 491 (1979), rev'd, CRC Corp. v. CIR, supra note 23; Brountas v. CIR, supra note 23.

might rely when he advances money to a borrower. [It is] proper to include nonrecourse debt in basis only insofar as the value of property securing the debt is equal to or greater than the face amount of the debt. [Further,] highly contingent or speculative obligations are not includible in basis before the uncertainty surrounding them is resolved.[27]

Similarly, a contingent obligation does not accrue as a deduction until the contingency is resolved because, before then, "'all the events' necessary to determine the fact and amount of liability [have] not yet occurred."[28] This is not to label the obligation a sham: "A note may have economic substance yet be so contingent as not to warrant its accrual as a present expense."[29]

The court concluded that these principles applied to production payments. Section 636, the court noted, was meant to place a purchaser of oil and gas property in a transaction including a production payment in a position equivalent to that of a buyer of nonmineral property, such as an apartment building. The Tax Court's reading of the provision did just the opposite, giving a preference to purchasers in transactions including production payments. Neither does the language of §636 require the Tax Court's construction. The common law principles excluding some liabilities from basis, for example, are not inconsistent with the §636(b) characterization of some production payments as liabilities.[30] The Court of Appeals for the Fifth Circuit responded more curtly to the Tax Court's holding: "We do not interpret §636 to produce such an absurd result."[31]

---

[27] Brountas v. CIR, supra note 23, at 157. For more on these principles, see ¶41.2.2.

[28] Brountas v. CIR, 692 F2d 161 (1st Cir. 1982).

[29] Id.

[30] The opinion in one of the other cases states: "The essential flaw in the Tax Court's reasoning . . . is that section 636 does not by its terms make any change in the rule that speculative or contingent liabilities may not be accrued and deducted." CRC Corp. v. CIR, 693 F2d 283 (3d Cir. 1982).

[31] Gibson Prod. Co. v. US, 637 F2d 1041 (5th Cir. 1981).

CHAPTER

25

Losses

¶25.1 INTRODUCTORY

Section 165(a) allows taxpayers to deduct "any loss sustained during the taxable year and not compensated for by insurance or otherwise." In its simple phraseology, this fundamental provision resembles §61(a), defining gross income, and §162(a), allowing deductions for business expenses. Like these other basic provisions, §165 covers a vast miscellany of events and transactions and is subject to numerous statutory and administrative qualifications that belie its simple language.

Among the many issues raised by claims under §165(a), the following, discussed in more detail later in this chapter, bear special note:

1. Identifying the person who sustained the loss and hence is the proper taxpayer to claim the deduction.[1]
2. Determining whether the alleged loss arises from a closed transaction or instead reflects only a temporary fluctuation in the value of property or a financial setback that might be reversed by future events.[2]
3. Ascertaining whether the loss is compensated for by insurance or otherwise.[3]
4. Computing the deductible amount.[4]
5. Applying various rules disallowing deductions for certain losses.[5]
6. Distinguishing between capital and ordinary losses.[6]

---

[1] Infra ¶25.2.
[2] Infra ¶25.4.
[3] Infra ¶25.5.
[4] Infra ¶25.6.
[5] Infra ¶25.7.
[6] Infra ¶25.8.2.

7. Properly treating recoveries of amounts deducted as losses in an earlier year.[7]
8. Distinguishing between losses, expenses, and bad debts.[8]
9. Applying the at risk rules of §465 relating to losses incurred in activities financed in part with nonrecourse financing.[9]
10. Applying the rules barring losses from passive activities from being deducted against any income other than income from other passive activities.[10]
10. Carrying net operating losses to earlier and later taxable years.[11]

Section 165(j), added in 1982, bars any deduction for loss sustained on the disposition or worthlessness of a registration-required obligation (as defined) issued after December 31, 1982 unless the obligation is registered or the issuer paid a penalty tax on the obligation's issuance. The provision has nothing to do with the determination of whether or in what amount loss has been realized, but is one of a package of provisions attacking the tax enforcement problems caused by bearer bonds.[12]

¶25.2 PROPER CLAIMANT

The deduction for losses under §165(a) must be claimed by the real party in interest—the taxpayer who sustained the loss for which the deduction is claimed. The principal sources of ambiguity and confusion in applying this pervasive principle are:

1. *Nominal versus beneficial ownership.* In the overwhelming bulk of cases, nominal and beneficial ownership of property coincide, and losses are properly claimed by the person having title to property giving rise to the loss. If the property is held by a nominee, however, the beneficial owner is ordinarily entitled to the deductions even if the arrangement is designed to avoid the claims of creditors.[1] If the nominee or owner of record is held out to a government agency as the true owner, the parties may be held to their

---

[7] Infra ¶25.8.4.
[8] Infra ¶25.8.5.
[9] Infra ¶25.11.
[10] Infra Ch. 28.
[11] Infra ¶25.11. For carryovers of capital losses, see infra ¶50.2.5 (individuals), ¶50.3.2 (corporations).
[12] See infra ¶111.1.9.
[1] Interstate Realty Co. v. CIR, 25 BTA 728 (1932) (acq.) (corporation entitled to deduct losses of business conducted in name of its shareholders because of restrictions in corporate charter); Bloch v. CIR, 6 BTA 563 (1927) (acq.) (husband filing separate return entitled to deduct loss on sale of stock held in wife's name to avoid creditors' claims). See Juniper Inv. Co. v. US, 338 F2d 356 (Ct. Cl. 1964) (loss

representations, either by way of estoppel or because the documentation is considered more reliable than their oral disclaimers.[2]

2. *Financial assistance to relatives and friends.* Taxpayers extending financial assistance to relatives and friends may not deduct losses incurred in a business or investment financed with the funds if the advance is a gift or loan; the deductions belong instead to the transferee.[3] Holding in a case of this type that a father who advanced funds to his son for an investment could not deduct the loss when the enterprise failed, the Court of Appeals for the First Circuit observed tartly: "Had the company prospered, one may readily imagine that the father would not have been the one to report the income."[4] If the assistance is effected by guaranteeing payment of the beneficiary's debts, however, losses sustained on making good on the guaranty are properly claimed by the guarantor, although the absence of any opportunity for profit on the transaction may cause problems.[5] Moreover, a beneficiary who is guaranteed against losses is not entitled to deductions under §165(a) because the loss is "compensated for" within the meaning of §165(a).[6]

---

attributable to payment serving solely shareholder interests; held, loss sustained by shareholders, not by corporation).

[2] See, e.g., Sangers Home for Chronic Patients, Inc. v. CIR, 72 TC 105 (1979) (filing corporate returns for many years creates equitable estoppel against reporting on individual or partnership basis); Moyer v. CIR, 9 TCM (CCH) 1043 (1950), aff'd per curiam, 193 F2d 876 (3d Cir. 1952) (taxpayer's father treated as true owner of strip mining business; records of representations to government lending agency were "contemporaneous, more specific, and more reliably reflecting the true intention of the parties"). But see Tillapaugh v. CIR, 31 TCM (CCH) 10 (1972) (on facts, undertaking business did not belong to taxpayer, although she worked in business and was described as "manager" in state license).

[3] Kamborian's Est. v. CIR, 469 F2d 219 (1st Cir. 1972) (1971) (claim that transferee of funds was transferor's agent in making losing investment rejected on facts); Loewenstein v. CIR, 27 TCM (CCH) 1112 (1968) (husband filing separate return denied deduction for casualty loss of jewelry given to wife). See Campbell v. CIR, 39 TCM (CCH) 287 (1979) (parents entitled to deduction for worthless securities, although registered in names of children, where gift was not complete and parents had reported income from securities on their returns).

[4] Kamborian's Est. v. CIR, supra note 3.

[5] If a guarantor's payment of the guaranteed debt subrogates the guarantor to the creditor's claim against the primary obligor, the guarantor's loss stems from the worthlessness of this claim, and therefore is classified as a bad debt subject to the rules of §166, which usually allow a deduction whether or not the loss is incurred in business or a profit-seeking activity. In the absence of such a subrogation, §165(a) denies the guarantor's loss unless it is incurred in business or a transaction entered into for profit. See infra ¶25.8.5.

[6] Dunne v. CIR, 75 F2d 255 (2d Cir. 1935) (taxpayer indemnified against loss by friend who recommended investments not entitled to deduction). See Paddock v. US, 58-1 USTC ¶9138 (SD Cal. 1957) (not officially reported) (under agreement between divorced couple, former husband recommended investments, from which

3. *Closely held corporations.* The business affairs of closely held corporations are often conducted in disregard of formalities, and controlling shareholders often refer to the enterprise as "my" or "our" business. The possessive pronoun may accord with the economic realities, but the corporation is nevertheless a separate entity. Shareholders are rarely entitled to deduct corporate losses on their own returns.[7] Even if a shareholder makes a corporate expenditure with his personal funds, the outlay is not a personal loss because the payment is usually characterized as a contribution to the corporation's capital or as a loan.[8] In either case, any loss resulting from the expenditure belongs to the corporation, and the shareholder sustains no deductible loss unless and until the stock becomes worthless or the debt becomes uncollectible.

Occasionally, however, a court is persuaded that the parties did not intend to create a corporation, that the corporation was only a nominee or title-holding entity, that a corporate business was transferred to the shareholders before the disputed loss occurred, or that the shareholders and corporation engaged in a joint venture or conducted businesses that were separable although affiliated. In these situations, which must be regarded as exceptional, the losses are deductible by the ostensible shareholders.[9]

¶25.3 RELATION TO BUSINESS AND PROFIT-ORIENTED TRANSACTIONS

By itself, the general rule of §165(a) allows losses to be deducted whether or not they are incurred in a business or a profit-oriented transaction.

---

he was to receive half the profits in return for defraying any net loss; held, he can deduct payment to wife to defray losses).

[7] See, e.g., Weigman v. CIR, 47 TC 596 (1967), aff'd per curiam, 400 F2d 584 (9th Cir. 1968) (business losses belong to corporation, despite frequent disregard of separate status), and cases therein cited; Evans v. CIR, 557 F2d 1095 (5th Cir. 1977) (same); Rink v. CIR, 51 TC 746 (1969) (acq.). See also Interstate Realty Co. v. CIR, 25 BTA 728 (1932) (acq.); infra ¶90.1.1 (corporations as separate entities).

[8] E.g., Cooper v. CIR, 61 TC 599 (1974) (shareholders paid corporation's operating loss each year in proportion to stock holdings; held, contributions to capital). See also infra ¶91.9.3 (contributions to capital), ¶91.10.1 (shareholder loans to corporations).

[9] See, e.g., Blue Flame Gas Co. v. CIR, 54 TC 584, 598–600 (1970) (no stock issued and no assets transferred to corporation); Czvizler v. CIR, 12 TCM (CCH) 386 (1953) (corporate form used to facilitate transfer of liquor license; all other assets of business held in individual transferee's name); Halprin v. CIR, 4 TCM (CCH) 789 (1945), aff'd per curiam, 154 F2d 112 (2d Cir. 1946) (corporation held legal title only until shareholder could arrange permanent financing). But see Haas v. CIR, 18 TCM (CCH) 401 (1959) (on facts, joint venture composed of individual and controlled corporation disregarded for want of business purpose and economic reality), and cases therein cited. See also infra ¶90.1.8 (nominee and dummy corporations).

Under §165(c), however, losses incurred by individuals, trusts, estates, and partnerships,[1] may only be deducted if they are incurred in a trade or business (§165(c)(1)), are incurred in a transaction entered into for profit (§165(c)(2)), or are caused by fire, storm, shipwreck, other casualty, or theft (§165(c)(3)). If property damaged by casualty is used in the taxpayer's business or profit-oriented activities, the loss is deductible in full. If the deduction rests solely on §165(c)(3), however, the loss is only allowable to the extent it exceeds a prescribed floor. Casualty losses are examined later in this work[2] and are discussed only incidentally in this chapter.

The principal issues raised by the "business" and "transaction entered into for profit" requirements of §§165(c)(1) and (2) can be categorized as follows:

1. *Business losses.* The standards determining whether an individual's loss was "incurred in a trade or business" within the meaning of §165(c)(1) are substantially identical with those determining whether expenses qualify for deduction under §162(a). Both provisions require that the item be paid or incurred "in carrying on any trade or business," a requirement discussed in detail elsewhere in this work.[3] The term "business" implies not only an activity conducted for profit rather than pleasure, but also a degree of regularity and continuity, as distinguished from a few isolated profit-oriented transactions.[4] An additional gloss on the term was enunciated by the Supreme Court in *Higgins v. CIR*, holding that the management of the taxpayer's own investment securities is not a trade or business even if it entails substantial expenses for clerical services and office space.[5]

2. *Losses in transactions entered into for profit.* Losses from activities lacking the regularity and continuity required to qualify as a "trade or business" may be deducted under §165(c)(2) if incurred "in any transaction entered into for profit."[6] Since the disposition of depreciated property can-

---

[1] For application of §165(c) to estates, trusts, and partnerships, see IRC §§641(b), 703(a).

[2] Infra ¶34.1.

[3] Supra ¶¶20.1.2, 20.2. See also infra ¶33.6 ("business" versus "nonbusiness" bad debts); US v. Generes, 405 US 93, 103 (1972) (implying uniformity of standards under §§162(a), 165(c)(1), and 166(d)(2)).

[4] See, e.g., McDowell v. Ribicoff, 292 F2d 174 (3d Cir. 1961) (nonprofessional executrix' part-time management of relative's estate not a business).

[5] Higgins v. CIR, 312 US 212 (1941), discussed supra ¶20.5.1.

[6] See, e.g., Imel v. CIR, 61 TC 318, 327 (1973) (acq.) (loss incurred on guaranteeing obligation of taxpayer's corporation). But see McGlothlin's Est. v. CIR, 44 TC 611, 621–22 (1965), aff'd on other grounds, 370 F2d 729 (5th Cir. 1967) (transaction for benefit of corporation provided only "indirect" benefit to shareholder, hence was not entered into for profit).

For the deductibility of costs of unsuccessful searches for business and profit-oriented transactions, see Todd v. CIR, 77 TC 246 (1981), aff'd per curiam, 682 F2d

not produce a profit, the "transaction" to which §165(c)(2) refers is not the sale itself. Rather, the requirement is that the investment or activity must be undertaken with the expectation of profit. This point is illustrated by a 1965 ruling, showing that the IRS can be nice to almost anyone, which held that an embezzler may deduct amounts repaid to his victim as losses under §165(c)(2) because the embezzlement was a transaction entered into for profit.[7] Profit-oriented investments that go sour are transactions entered into for profit, even if the taxpayer's only objective in taking the final step is to forestall a greater loss or to register the abandonment of his original high hopes and even if the taxpayer sells at a particular time in order to establish a tax loss.[8]

It has been held that a transaction is not entered into "for profit," in contrast, if the sole potential benefit is a tax savings.[9] Also, a purported loss fails the for-profit requirement if the transaction from which it arises is a sham lacking in economic reality. An extensive body of cases has applied these principles to straddle transactions structured to allow investors to take losses in one year that are matched by built-in gains expected to be recognized in the next year.[10] If there is also a reasonable prospect of economic

---

207 (9th Cir. 1982) (physician's loss on abandoning plans to construct apartment building not incurred in trade or business but only in transaction entered into for profit; taxpayer had not broken ground or rented any apartments and thus was not in trade or business of renting apartments); Rev. Rul. 79-346, 1979-2 CB 84 (transaction for profit only if taxpayer goes beyond general search for or prelimary investigation of business or investment and focuses "on a specific acquisition"); supra ¶20.4.4. See also infra ¶26.4.2 (amortization of start-up expenses).

[7] Rev. Rul. 65-254, 1965-2 CB 50. See Rev. Rul. 82-74, 1982-1 CB 110 (where taxpayer had his building burned down to collect insurance proceeds, ordinary income recognized on receipt of proceeds to extent they exceeded building's basis, but deduction in equal amount allowed under §165(a) when taxpayer required to repay proceeds on discovery of arson).

[8] See Terry v. US, 10 F. Supp. 183 (D. Conn. 1934).

[9] Knetsch v. US, 348 F2d 932 (Ct. Cl.), cert. denied, 383 US 957 (1965) (§165(c)(2) not satisfied by investment on which sole anticipated gain was tax reduction); Ginsburg v. CIR, 35 TCM (CCH) 860 (1976) (same for tax shelter investment in cattle venture).

[10] Sochin v. CIR, 843 F2d 351, 354 (9th Cir. 1988) (deductions denied for losses in straddles and forward contracts in mortgage-backed securities; transactions found to be shams because lacking in "economic effects other than the creation of income tax losses"); Freytag v. CIR, 89 TC 849 (1987) (losses allegedly sustained under forward contracts in mortgage-backed securities not deductible because transactions not bona fide or, if they were, not engaged in for profit); Price v. CIR, 88 TC 860 (1987) (Treasury bill straddles disregarded as shams); Glass v. CIR, 87 TC 1087, 1177 (1986) (losses on straddle transactions on London Metal Exchange denied because each transaction "lacked economic substance and was a sham"); Fox v. CIR, 82 TC 1001 (1984) (losses incurred in offsetting options transactions nondeductible because transactions not entered into for profit); Smith v. CIR, 78 TC 350 (1982) (straddle transaction in silver futures was not a sham and was a closed transaction,

gain, however, the transaction qualifies even though the taxpayer was motivated in part by knowledge that a loss, if incurred, would be deductible from income otherwise subject to high marginal tax rates.[11]

It is sometimes said that a loss on a sale is not deductible unless the taxpayer gets "the highest and best price" for the property.[12] Although a sale for less than the property's fair market value undoubtedly calls for a searching inquiry, the standard of "the highest and best price" is not a shibboleth. For example, the sale of property for less than its fair market value to achieve a business or profit-oriented objective should ordinarily be viewed as a combination of (1) a sale of the property for its fair market value, justifying a deduction under §165(c)(2) if the imputed sales price is less than the property's adjusted basis and (2) a transfer of part of the imputed sale price to the transferee.

Losses incurred on a disposition of investment property acquired by gift or inheritance point out an awkward aspect of the statutory language, since the property is not acquired by the taxpayer in a transaction entered

---

but deduction for loss disallowed because transaction not entered into for profit). See also US v. Winograd, 656 F2d 279 (7th Cir. 1981), cert. denied, 455 US 989 (1982) (upholding criminal conviction based on theory that losses in commodity straddle transactions were unreal because sales were rigged); US v. Baskes, 687 F2d 165 (7th Cir. 1982) (similar to *Winograd*).

Section 1256, enacted in 1981, eliminates the gimmick attempted in most of the foregoing cases by requiring that regulated futures contracts, foreign currency contracts, and many options be "marked to market" as of the last day of each taxable year, thus requiring accrued gains as well as losses to be recognized annually, regardless of when positions are closed out. See infra ¶40.8 for §1256. Section 108 of the Tax Reform Act of 1984 (Pub. L. No. 98-369, 98 Stat. 494) provides amnesty for straddle losses on positions entered into before 1982, but only if the straddle transactions were entered into for profit. See Miller v. CIR, 836 F2d 1274 (10th Cir. 1988) (TRA 1984 §108 amnesty for straddles "entered into for profit" is only available if taxpayer's primary motivation was profit, not tax savings; statement in legislative history that "a reasonable prospect of any profit from the transaction" is sufficient found inconsistent with plain meaning of statute); Wehrly v. US, 808 F2d 1311 (9th Cir. 1986) ("entered into for profit" requirement of TRA 1984 §108 satisfied "if there is a reasonable prospect of any profit from the transaction"); Forseth v. CIR, 85 TC 127 (1985) (TRA 1984 §108 only applies to genuine straddle transactions, not to shams); Perlin v. CIR, 86 TC 388 (1986) (applying rule of TRA 1984 §108 that presumes straddles entered into for profit where taxpayer is a dealer or is otherwise "regularly engaged in investing in regulated futures contracts").

[11] In re King, 545 F2d 700 (10th Cir. 1976) (speculative oil and gas transactions entered into for profit, notwithstanding potential tax write-offs).

[12] See Feine v. McGowan, 188 F2d 738, 740 (2d Cir. 1951); Evans v. Rothensies, 114 F2d 958, 962 (3d Cir. 1940) (loss on sale for less than fair market value disallowed; "the disposition of property as well as its acquisition is material to the question whether the transaction was entered into for profit"); Miller's Est. v. CIR, 27 TCM (CCH) 1140 (1968), aff'd per curiam, 421 F2d 1405 (4th Cir. 1970) (property sold for half its market value to taxpayer's child; loss disallowed).

into for profit in the ordinary meaning of these words. Yet, taxpayers are regularly allowed to deduct losses on selling such property. Section 1015(a) even provides a special basis for determining a donee's loss on disposition of property acquired by gift. In effect, the prior owner's profit objective runs with the property, enabling the transferee to satisfy the requirements of §165(c)(2) by proxy.

On the other hand, if inherited property was used by the decedent for personal purposes (e.g., as a residence), the courts have treated the fact that the property was acquired by inheritance as a neutral circumstance and have focused on the use to which it was put by the heir after acquiring it.[13] On the rationale that the heir's actions can constitute the requisite transaction entered into for profit, the courts have allowed losses to be deducted if attributable to a post-acquisition decline in value while the heir is endeavoring to rent or sell the property.[14]

Although they differ in phraseology, §165(c)(2) is complementary to §212(2); if expenses are deductible under §212(2) because paid or incurred for the management, conservation, or maintenance of property "held for the production of income," a loss on a sale or other disposition of the property is ordinarily deductible under §165(c)(2).[15] Conversely, if property is acquired in a transaction entered into for profit within the meaning of §165(c)(2), expenses incurred in managing, conserving, or maintaining the property are ordinarily deductible under §212(2). Section 167(a)(2), allowing depreciation deductions for property "held for the production of income" similarly has much in common with §165(c)(2), as does §183, which distinguishes between activities engaged in for profit and activities not engaged in for profit.[16]

3. *Overlapping jurisdiction.* Since losses incurred by individuals may qualify for deduction by passing either the trade-or-business test of §165(c)(1) or the transaction-entered-into-for-profit test of §165(c)(2), these provisions are often asserted by taxpayers as alternative grounds. In allowing a deduction, it is not usually necessary for the courts to choose between them; losses of both types are equally "adverse in financial conse-

---

[13] Marx v. CIR, 5 TC 173, 174 (1945) (acq.) (loss on inherited yacht, never used by decedent's widow, allowed; that it was acquired by inheritance "is, by itself, neutral"); Campbell v. CIR, 5 TC 272, 274 (1945) (loss on inherited residence allowed; "the important inquiry is: To what use was the property put after it was acquired by inheritance?").

[14] Waterman's Est. v. CIR, 195 F2d 244 (2d Cir. 1952) (divided court) (sale by executor); Williams v. CIR, 1 BTA 1101 (1925) (acq.) (sale by heir); Reynolds v. CIR, 4 TCM (CCH) 837 (1945), aff'd, 155 F2d 620 (1st Cir. 1946) (inherited jewelry).

[15] For §212(2), see supra ¶20.5.

[16] For §§167(a)(2) and 183, see supra ¶¶23.2.1 and 22.5.

quences to the taxpayer."[17] The two categories of allowable deductions, however, must sometimes be segregated. For example, business losses are ordinarily deductible from gross income in computing adjusted gross income (AGI), but losses on transactions entered into for profit must be itemized and deducted from AGI unless attributable to the sale or exchange of property.[18] A similar preference for business losses is found in §172, relating to net operating loss deductions.[19]

4. *Mixed profit-personal objectives.* Neither §165(c)(1) (business losses) nor §165(c)(2) (losses on transactions entered into for profit) is satisfied by losses incurred on a sale or other disposition of property used solely for personal purposes, like the taxpayer's residence or vacation home. However, losses on sales of property regularly devoted to business or profit-oriented uses as well as personal uses, such as a physician's automobile or a family farm, can be bifurcated, thus permitting a deduction under §165(c)(1) or (2) for any loss attributable to the business or profit-oriented activities.[20]

If the taxpayer entertains simultaneous mixed motives with respect to the entire property, however, the primary motive controls whether the loss is deductible.[21] In the case of a residence, further, the IRS and courts are understandably skeptical of claims that the property was acquired primarily as an investment, rather than for personal occupancy.[22] Also, where financial transactions enhance the taxpayer's personal reputation or benefit his relatives or friends, losses are often disallowed because the transaction cannot be shown to have been entered into primarily for profit rather than for nonmaterial benefits.[23]

---

[17] US v. Generes, 405 US 93, 103 (1972).

[18] Compare IRC §62(a)(1) (all trade or business deductions deductible in determining AGI unless incurred by employee) with IRC §62(a)(3) (losses from sale or exchange of property). See also §62(a)(9) (bank depositor's §165 deduction for penalty on premature withdrawal of time deposit deductible in determining AGI); Rev. Rul. 82-27, 1982-1 CB 32 (applying IRC §62(a)(9) to forfeiture of principal where penalty exceeds accrued and unpaid interest). For AGI, see supra ¶2.1.3.

[19] See IRC §§172(c), (d), discussed infra ¶25.11.2.

[20] Rev. Rul. 72-111, 1972-1 CB 56 (dual-use automobile). See also supra ¶¶23.2.1, 23.2.2 (depreciation on dual-use property).

[21] Helvering v. National Grocery Co., 304 US 282, 289 n.5 (1938), and cases therein cited.

[22] See McAuley v. CIR, 35 TCM (CCH) 1236 (1976). See generally Epstein, The Consumption and Loss of Personal Property Under the Internal Revenue Code, 23 Stan. L. Rev. 454 (1971).

[23] E.g., Arata v. CIR, 277 F2d 576 (2d Cir. 1960) (voluntary payments by controlling shareholder to former owner of business acquired by corporation at nominal price not made for profit, but out of "feeling of obligation"); Lewis v. CIR, 253 F2d 821 (2d Cir. 1958) (amounts spent by author to defend suits to have him declared insane nondeductible; suits directed "at the totality that is the individual,"

5. *Converted property.* Property acquired for personal reasons can be converted by the taxpayer to business or profit-oriented purposes. In the latter case, the "transaction entered into for profit" is the taxpayer's change of mind, as evidenced by such facts as termination of personal use, physical alterations, and renting the property. In the case of a personal residence, the regulations specify that a loss on a sale is allowable if, "prior to the sale, [the property is] rented or otherwise appropriated to income producing purposes and is used for such purposes up to the time of the sale."[24]

To prevent deductions for declines in value accruing while property is held for personal use, the adjusted basis of converted property for determining loss is the lower of the property's adjusted basis or fair market value when converted, plus or minus adjustments for improvements, depreciation, or other items chargeable to capital account subsequent to the conversion.[25] This method of computing the taxpayer's loss is illustrated by an example in a later chapter of this work.[26]

Conversely, if property acquired and used for business or profit-oriented purposes is converted to personal use, a loss on a sale or other disposition may not be deducted under §165(c)(1) or (2), even if the decline in the property's value occurred while it was used in the taxpayer's business and would have been deductible had the property been sold at the time it was converted. A foresighted taxpayer could take the loss deduction by selling the property rather than converting it, even if similar property were then purchased for personal use. A sale coupled with a prearranged repurchase of the same property, however, would no doubt be viewed as a conversion in substance, resulting in disallowance of the loss.

6. *Corporations.* Section 165(c), which limits individuals' loss deductions to losses incurred in business or a transaction entered into for profit or sustained in a casualty, does not apply to corporations, which are only subject to the general rule of §165(a), stating flatly that "any loss sustained during the taxable year" is deductible if not compensated for by insurance

---

not at occupational activities); Goldsborough v. Burnet, 46 F2d 432 (4th Cir. 1931) (expense of reimbursing mother-in-law for losses on stock whose purchase taxpayer had recommended); De Pinto v. US, 407 F. Supp. 1 (D. Ariz. 1975), aff'd, 585 F2d 405 (9th Cir. 1978) (deduction denied for expense of settling shareholder derivative suit incurred by director serving because of friendship with majority shareholder; activity not primarily undertaken to advertise taxpayer's medical practice); Stein v. US, 240 F. Supp. 818 (SD Iowa 1964), aff'd per curiam, 346 F2d 569 (8th Cir. 1965) (civic pride and belief in deceased father's ideals negate profit motive); Rev. Rul. 72-193, 1972-1 CB 58 (estate cannot deduct loss on decedent's annuity policy; primary purpose was lifetime security). See also supra ¶20.2.11.

[24] Reg. §1.165-9(b)(1).

[25] Reg. §1.165-9(b)(2). For the requirements of a conversion, see Gevirtz v. CIR, 123 F2d 707 (2d Cir. 1941). See also supra ¶23.2.1 notes 10–12.

[26] Infra ¶42.5. See also Reg. §1.165-9(c) Exs. 1, 2.

or otherwise. This unqualified language does not permit loss deductions for payments properly chargeable to capital account.[27] It might, however, permit family corporations to deduct losses on country estates and similar assets even if they are used by the controlling shareholders for personal purposes and offer no prospect of corporate profit.[28] This possibility, however, was substantially undermined by a 1977 decision of the Court of Claims, holding that a family corporation's loss on the sale of a vacation home occupied by its shareholders—even though covered by the general rule of §165(a)—was disallowed by §274(a), because it was used for "entertainment, amusement, or recreation" within the meaning of §274(a).[29] Moreover, under a 1978 amendment to §274(a), losses attributable to such facilities are nondeductible regardless of their contribution to the taxpayer's business.[30]

¶25.4 CLOSED TRANSACTION REQUIREMENT

¶25.4.1 Introductory

Section 165(a) only allows losses "sustained during the taxable year." The regulations expand on this terse language by requiring losses to be "evidenced by closed and completed transactions, fixed by identifiable events," and by stating that "only a bona fide loss is allowable" and that "substance and not mere form shall govern in determining a deductible loss."[1] The objective of these requirements is to restrict deductions to "economically genuine realizations of loss."[2]

---

[27] See Nalco Chem. Co. v. US, 561 F. Supp. 1274 (ND Ill. 1983) (disallowing deduction for payment to foreign subsidiary pursuant to agreement to hold subsidiary harmless for foreign exchange loss on loan to another corporation in which taxpayer had an interest; payment arose from taxpayer's status as shareholder and thus was contribution to capital, not deductible loss).

[28] Compare International Trading Co. v. CIR, 484 F2d 707 (7th Cir. 1973) (family corporation may deduct loss on sale of lakefront property used exclusively for shareholders' personal activities) with Juniper Inv. Co. v. US, 338 F2d 356 (Ct. Cl. 1964) (corporate veil pierced to allocate loss to shareholders and disallow deduction at corporate level). For a similar problem in the relationship between §§162(a) and 212, see supra ¶20.5.1 note 18.

For treatment of the rental value of the property as a taxable dividend to the shareholders, see infra ¶92.2.

[29] W.L. Schautz Co. v. US, 567 F2d 373 (Ct. Cl. 1978).

[30] See supra ¶21.2.3. For additional restrictions on deductions by S corporations, see IRC §183 (activities not engaged in for profit) and §280A (residential property), discussed supra ¶¶22.6 and 22.5.

[1] Reg. §§1.165-1(b), (d)(1).

[2] McWilliams v. CIR, 331 US 694, 699 (1947) (disallowing loss on sale of stock where taxpayer's spouse simultaneously purchased same number of shares of identi-

Litigation most often arises in this context when the IRS asserts that (1) the taxpayer sustained a loss, but in an earlier or later year ("wrong year") or (2) the taxpayer has not yet sustained a loss, although one may be sustained in a later year ("too early to tell"). The "wrong year" objection is illustrated by a taxpayer's claim that his stock in Consolidated Boondoggles, Inc. became worthless in 1988, when CBI lost its largest customer and closed its only plant, to which the IRS responds by asserting either that CBI was already hopelessly insolvent at the beginning of 1988 or that it was a viable enterprise at the end of 1988 and that its prospects for improvement did not evaporate until it was adjudicated bankrupt in 1989. The "too early to tell" objection is illustrated by a taxpayer's claim of a loss deduction on the abandonment of some of the items acquired in the purchase of a going business, to which the IRS responds that the amount paid for the business should be allocated wholly to the items not abandoned and that until the later items are sold or abandoned in some future year, it will not be known whether the taxpayer sustained a loss.[3]

These objections often overlap. Since the taxpayer has the burden of proving that a loss was sustained in the year for which it was claimed, the IRS response often takes the form: "If a loss was sustained, which we do not concede, it did not occur in the year claimed."

¶25.4.2 Sales

The overwhelming bulk of losses arises on the sale of listed securities in arm's length transactions with anonymous outsiders on organized stock exchanges. Such a sale is a quintessential "closed transaction," betokening a bona fide loss. Sales of depreciated property, however, can also be devices "for realizing tax losses on investments which, for most practical purposes, are continued uninterrupted."[4] For example, a sale followed immediately by a repurchase of the same or similar property preserves the taxpayer's investment without significant interruption. A sale to a member of the taxpayer's family can also perpetuate the taxpayer's investment in substance although terminating it in form. Recognizing these facts of life, the Code disallows losses on so-called wash sales where stock or securities are sold but substantially identical property is purchased within 30 days before or after the sale (§1091) and on sales between related persons (§267(a)), even if the sale is made at the market price and therefore registers a genuine decline in the value of the property between the date of acquisition and the date of

---

cal stock). See Rev. Rul. 81-2, 1981-1 CB 78 (where timber producer's seedlings died other than by casualty, cost of replacement seedlings may not be deducted under §165(a), but must be capitalized).

[3] See infra ¶25.4.5.

[4] McWilliams v. CIR, supra note 2, at 700.

disposition.[5]

These statutory safeguards against the premature deduction of losses are neither comprehensive nor preemptive, however, and they leave room for administrative and judicial determinations that a particular sale is only a provisional step, rather than a "closed transaction." The principal targets for disallowance are (1) sales subject to agreements or options to repurchase, which in appropriate circumstances may be disregarded as sham transactions or, in less pejorative language, as preserving the substance of ownership,[6] (2) matched transactions that are not technical wash sales because they involve property other than stock or securities or a longer interval than the 30 days prescribed by §1091,[7] and (3) sales to related persons who are not within the tainted circle described by §267 but who ensure perpetuation of the taxpayer's financial interest in the property because of the "subtle tie of affectionate interest found among families and friends, business or otherwise."[8] In *Scully v. US*, for example, loss on a sale between two trusts was disallowed because the transaction did not "vary control or change the flow of economic benefits."[9] The trusts were created by different persons (a husband and wife) and at different times (the husband's inter vivos and the wife's by will on her subsequent death). The trustees and beneficiaries, however, were the same, and the terms of the two trusts were substantially identical. The assets of the trusts consisted of land that was managed as a unit. It was not relevant, the court found, that the sale was made for a business purpose, not to generate a loss deduction.[10] Because the transaction did not change control over the property or affect the beneficial interests in it, the loss was nondeductible, regardless of underlying motivations. Also, the IRS and the courts are always on the alert for more complicated devices creating the semblance but not the reality of a loss, especially if accompanied by egregious departures from economic reality, such as

---

[5] For §§1091 and 267(a), see infra ¶¶44.7 and 78.1.

[6] See Du Pont v. CIR, 118 F2d 544 (3d Cir.), cert. denied, 314 US 623 (1941) (losses disallowed where friends sold stock to each other at the end of one year and by prearrangement repurchased the stock early in the following year).

[7] See Rev. Rul. 77-185, 1977-1 CB 48 (matched transactions in silver futures), and cases therein cited; Rev. Rul. 78-414, 1978-2 CB 213 (same as to Treasury bills). See generally Henze, Transactions in Options: Some New Wrinkles and Old Risks, 4 Rev. Tax'n Individuals 70 (1980).

[8] Du Pont v. CIR, supra note 6, at 545. See Fender Trust No. 1 v. US, 577 F2d 934 (5th Cir. 1969) (sales of bonds followed by repurchases from bank by taxpayers owning 70.7 percent of bank's stock).

[9] Scully v. US, 840 F2d 478, 485 (7th Cir. 1988).

[10] The sale was made by the wife's testamentary trust to raise funds to pay estate taxes. The selling price equaled the value placed on the land in the estate tax return and the sale was initially reported as producing no gain or loss. The loss arose because the estate tax value of the land, and hence its basis under §1014, was raised on audit.

artificial prices."

By an irony of legislative policy, taxpayers falling afoul of the nonstatutory common law that has developed under §165(a) can be worse off in the end than those whose losses are subject to automatic disallowance under §1091 or §267(a), since the rigors of the latter provisions are softened by rules taking the disallowed loss into account at a later time.[12] By contrast, the courts have not developed a body of ancillary law to ensure that taxpayers failing in an attempt to recognize losses prematurely will be able to recognize them when their economic interest in the property is finally terminated. The outcome over the long haul, therefore, is problematic and may depend more on the form of the failed transaction than on its financial impact.

¶25.4.3 Abandonment

Another method of closing out a losing investment, especially business or income-producing physical property that is devoid of value, is abandonment. Because an abandonment is not a "sale or exchange" of the property within the meaning of §1222 or §1231(a), the taxpayer's loss is not a capital loss, and it may therefore be deducted from ordinary income. This important distinction between abandonment losses and losses on sales and exchanges occasionally creates a dispute over whether an asset withdrawn from business use has been abandoned or sold.[13]

The most common bone of contention in abandonment cases is whether the property was discarded or only shelved temporarily in the hope that it would become useful again in the future. The possibility of residual or potential value can be eliminated by consigning outworn assets to the city dump, but the regulations do not require taxpayers to go this far to abandon property for tax purposes. If nondepreciable property "is permanently discarded from use," the regulations allow a resulting loss to be deducted, even without an "overt act of abandonment" or loss of title to the property.[14] Under the verbal formula adopted by the regulations for depreciable property, a loss from "physical abandonment" is recognized if "the intent of the

---

[11] See Decon Corp. v. CIR, 65 TC 829 (1976); Investors Diversified Servs., Inc. v. CIR, 325 F2d 341 (8th Cir. 1963) (failure to prove sales to subsidiaries at fair market value).

[12] For these relief measures, see §1091(d) (basis of property purchased increased by disallowed loss) and §267(d) (disallowed loss reduces transferee's gain on subsequent sale), discussed infra ¶¶44.7.1 and 78.1.3.

[13] See Bloomington Coca-Cola Bottling Co. v. CIR, 189 F2d 14 (7th Cir. 1951) (on facts, outmoded plant sold rather than abandoned). If property passes to a creditor on foreclosure of a mortgage or by a conveyance in lieu of foreclosure, it is treated as sold to the creditor, not abandoned. See infra ¶52.1.3.

[14] Reg. §1.165-2(a).

taxpayer [is] irrevocably to discard the asset so that it will neither be used again by him nor retrieved by him for sale, exchange, or other disposition."[15] The regulations also permit losses on depreciable assets to be deducted when the assets are "retired" by being permanently withdrawn from use in the business or income-producing activity—an action that falls short of a physical abandonment because it can be accomplished by transferring the property to a supplies or scrap account, even though the property might later be cannibalized for spare parts or other salvageable items.[16]

An abandonment (including a retirement of depreciable property) must be contrasted with mere nonuse. Even if the asset has lost most of its value, the decline in its value may not be deducted until the taxpayer's investment is closed; halfway measures are not enough. Athletic coaches might announce that quitters never win, but taxpayers who keep trying to salvage something from their failing investments are likely to be told that they may not deduct the loss until they unequivocally abandon the property or external events render it worthless. The applicable principles were summarized by the Court of Appeals for the Fourth Circuit:

> The scheme of our tax laws does not . . . contemplate . . . a series of adjustments to reflect the vicissitudes of the market, or the wavering values occasioned by a succession of adverse or favorable developments. . . . Normally, the loss involved in impaired usefulness is recognized on sale or other disposition. It may also be recognized as deductible when an event has definitely set at rest the possibility of future use. . . . But where . . . the possibility is not remote that the owner will alter its decision not to use a portion of the property for a particular purpose, no deduction is allowable.[17]

In the words of the Tax Court, "abandonment constitutes not merely shrinkage in value but the complete elimination of all value in an asset and the recognition by the owner that the asset no longer possesses any utility."[18]

---

[15] Reg. §1.167(a)-8(a)(4). See Daily v. CIR, 81 TC 161 (1983) (taxpayer, who had interest in building as purchaser under land sale contract, could not recognize loss on attempted abandonment; because seller had right to specific performance, taxpayer could not irrevocably discard property as regulations require).

[16] Reg. §1.167(a)-8(a)(3) (loss based on difference between property's adjusted basis and its estimated salvage value or fair market value at retirement, subject to qualifications). See also Aetna-Standard Eng'r Co. v. CIR, 15 TC 284, 297–98 (1950) (rationale for distinguishing between abnormal and normal retirements from multiple-asset accounts); supra ¶23.9 (withdrawal of depreciable assets from service).

[17] Citizens Bank of Weston v. CIR, 252 F2d 425 (4th Cir. 1958) (basement of building not abandoned despite discontinuance of use for storage following flood).

[18] Louisville & Nashville R.R. v. CIR, 66 TC 962 (1976) (railroad grading and ballast not abandoned despite removal of track).

In the final analysis, a determination that the taxpayer abandoned an asset rests on an analysis of all the facts, including the taxpayer's intent, and this makes it impossible to extract much guidance from the welter of litigated cases. "Abandonment of [the property] in a practical sense" is enough,[19] but the retention of possession and title to property invites a dispute no matter how clearly a decline in value is established, unless the taxpayer takes such drastic steps as junking the property, going out of business unequivocally, or, in the case of a building, boarding it up and letting it go to wrack and ruin.[20] Lest it be thought that the reluctance of courts to find that property has been abandoned is always unfavorable to the taxpayer, it should be noted that a relaxed judicial attitude would encourage the IRS to argue that property was abandoned earlier than claimed by the taxpayer, especially if the statute of limitations bars a refund for the earlier year.[21]

Abandonment claims involving intangible business assets, such as goodwill, customer lists, and trade names, raise special problems, since these assets cannot be physically abandoned and mere nonuse does not

---

[19] O'Connor's Est. v. CIR, 7 TCM (CCH) 43 (1948).

[20] See, e.g., Talache Mines v. US, 218 F2d 491 (9th Cir. 1954), cert. denied, 350 US 824 (1955) (no abandonment of mining claims by taxpayer retaining legal rights of exploitation); Shoolman v. CIR, 108 F2d 987 (1st Cir.), cert. denied, 310 US 637 (1940) (decision to invest no more money in real estate parcel and instructions authorizing secretary to release interest therein; held, insufficient to establish loss); United Cal. Bank v. CIR, 41 TC 437 (1964), aff'd per curiam, 340 F2d 320 (9th Cir. 1965) (building not abandoned despite nonuse and later demolition); Offshore Operations Trust v. CIR, 32 TCM (CCH) 985 (1973) (unused building not abandoned because later "retrieved" by sale); Jones Beach Theatre Co. v. CIR, 25 TCM (CCH) 527 (1966) (cost of acquired enterprise not deductible while corporate taxpayer remained in existence; "mere nonuse" not tantamount to abandonment). For successful abandonment claims, on facts not always clearly distinguishable from the foregoing cases, see Tanforan Co. v. US, 313 F. Supp. 796 (ND Cal. 1970), aff'd per curiam, 462 F2d 605 (9th Cir. 1972) (abandonment of racetrack occurred when racing operations were discontinued and all personalty was assigned; subsequent sale of property was "fortuitous"); Ford v. US, 67-2 USTC ¶9546 (WD Ky. 1967) (not officially reported), aff'd per curiam, 402 F2d 791 (6th Cir. 1968) (abandonment of leasehold improvements established when company offices were moved, despite later efforts to sublet); Hummel v. US, 227 F. Supp. 30 (ND Cal. 1963) (deduction allowed despite later use of "abandoned" property in "build to suit" lease of property by taxpayer); Hanover v. CIR, 38 TCM (CCH) 1281 (1979) (building locked, boarded, and barricaded; utilities, insurance, maintenance, and heat discontinued; held, sufficient physical acts).

[21] For example, in Sansberry v. US, 70-1 USTC ¶9216 (SD Ind. 1970) (not officially reported), the IRS disallowed an abandonment loss claimed for 1962 on the ground that the property became worthless in 1946, 1959, or 1961. The court held for the taxpayer because the IRS was unable "to fix on a definite date of abandonment" and the taxpayer "was a frugal and farsighted man, slow to abandon any property of the slightest profit-making potential." For the effect of the statute of limitations, see infra ¶25.8.3.

preclude a revival of the intangible's value and usefulness. If the enterprise remains in business, the loss must be evidenced by alterations in its operations that clearly eliminate the intangible asset as an income-producing factor in the continuing activities. The cost of a customer list or a prime location, for example, can be rendered worthless if the company moves to a new territory, but its trademarks and trade names might continue to have some value even if they are less familiar to new customers than to the old ones.[22] Two threshold hurdles in this area, which can be insurmountable even if the taxpayer permanently abandons an operating division or product line, are (1) proof that the taxpayer's goodwill or other intangibles can be divided between the abandoned activities and the continuing ones[23] and (2) determination of the adjusted basis of the abandoned intangibles, partic-

---

[22] For cases involving business intangibles, see Parmelee Transp. Co. v. US, 351 F2d 619 (Ct. Cl. 1965) (transfer service had goodwill in unwritten arrangements with customer railroads, which was abandoned when business terminated following customer defection to competitor); Joffre v. US, 331 F. Supp. 1177 (ND Ga. 1971) (liquor store's goodwill was in its location); Metropolitan Laundry Co. v. US, 100 F. Supp. 803 (ND Cal. 1951) (old plant condemned, causing move to new community; abandoned laundry routes had "distinct transferable value"); Massey-Ferguson, Inc. v. CIR, 59 TC 220 (1972) (acq.) (move to new location; held, distributorship system, going concern value, and one trade name abandoned, but another trade name and product line not abandoned); Solar Nitrogen Chems., Inc. v. CIR, 37 TCM (CCH) 1849-71 (1978) (business discontinued and assets leased following decline in wholesale market; wholesale goodwill abandoned, but retail goodwill retained); Rev. Rul. 57-503, 1957-2 CB 139 (book club allowed loss for goodwill abandoned on going out of business). See generally Broenen & Reed, Amortizing Intangible Assets, 44 J. Tax'n 130, 331 (1976) (two-part series, including abandonment issues).

[23] See Sunset Fuel Co. v. US, 519 F2d 781 (9th Cir. 1975) (no deduction on loss of individual customers from purchased fuel oil route); Gulf Oil Corp. v. CIR, 86 TC 135, 163 (1986) (rejecting deduction for loss on purported abandonment of portion of mineral lease; taxpayer continued to make all payments under lease because lessor would not accept partial termination; deduction "must be supported by an act of abandonment"); Rudd v. CIR, 79 TC 225 (1982) (dividing goodwill between firm name, which was abandoned, and other aspects of goodwill, which were not); Nicolazzi v. CIR, 79 TC 109 (1982) (where taxpayer made 600 applications for mineral leases from federal government and obtained one, entire program is one transaction, designed to maximize chance of obtaining at least one lease, and costs of 599 unsuccessful applications not deductible); Beatty v. CIR, 46 TC 835 (1966) (no loss on change in liquor license law; mere diminution in value of single asset, not complete abandonment or worthlessness of distinct rights); Half Moon Fruit & Produce Co. v. CIR, 40 TCM (CCH) 96 (1980) (taxpayer's acreage allotment did not become worthless when Department of Agriculture allowed rice crops to be marketed without allotment; rights continued to have value); Rev. Rul. 83-137, 1983-2 CB 41 (no deduction for fee paid for expert advice on land available for lease from federal government and for filing applications on taxpayer's behalf because no closed transaction until conclusion of five-year period during which applications might be filed); Rev. Rul. 74-306, 1974-2 CB 58 (no loss on suspension of single feature of government price-support and conservation program; no way to sever this feature from

ularly if they were acquired by the taxpayer on purchasing a going concern for an unallocated lump-sum amount.[24]

A related issue arises when a taxpayer purchases a going business or other collection of assets with a preformed intent to discard or abandon some of the items. An abandonment in these circumstances might merely establish that the entire purchase price was paid for the rest of the property and that no loss was sustained on the abandonment.[25] Similarly, where a going business is sold and the seller abandons assets of the business not wanted by the buyer, the adjusted basis of the unwanted items might have to be taken into account in computing the gain on the sale of the wanted items, rather than being deducted separately as an abandonment loss.[26] Under similar principles, taxpayers acquiring or purchasing partially or wholly worthless debts who later write them off as uncollectible may not deduct more than the debt's value when acquired.[27]

Capital outlays that do not create assets in a conventional sense may be deducted if incurred in a business or profit-oriented transaction that is discontinued because the taxpayer's plan cannot be achieved. An example is the cost of preparing for a public offering of stock, which, although normally capitalized, may be deducted as a loss under §165(a) if the plan is abandoned because of adverse market conditions.[28]

¶25.4.4 Worthlessness

Securities usually cannot be abandoned in any meaningful sense. Even if the taxpayer papers a recreation room with the certificates or burns them in the presence of a skeptical revenue agent, the taxpayer's legal rights often

---

value of entire program). See also supra ¶23.2.6 (depreciation of "mass asset" intangibles).

[24] See supra ¶4.4.4 and infra ¶51.9.2 (allocation of lump-sum sales price).

[25] See Dane County Title Co. v. CIR, 29 TC 625 (1957) (no abandonment loss for title plant acquired on purchase of competitor; predominant purpose was not to acquire records but to eliminate competition, which would have been achieved even if records were destroyed); Wood County Tel. Co. v. CIR, 51 TC 72 (1968) (acquisition of telephone company with intent to scrap outmoded manual equipment on conversion to dial phones). But see J.B.N. Tel. Co. v. US, 638 F2d 227 (10th Cir. 1981) (abandonment of obsolete phone systems shortly after acquisition qualifies for loss deduction because no initial intention to abandon). The issue, and the resolution of it in *J.B.N. Tel.*, is reminiscent of the pre-1984 law on the demolition of buildings, described below in ¶5.4.5.

[26] See Southern Pac. Transp. Co. v. CIR, 75 TC 497 (1980) (no loss deduction where depot retired as part of sales transaction).

[27] See American Credit Corp. v. CIR, 32 TCM (CCH) 122 (1973), and cases therein cited.

[28] Rev. Rul. 79-2, 1979-1 CB 98.

persist.[29] For this reason, the "closed transaction" evidencing loss on the worthlessness of securities is the event or concatenation of events resulting in worthlessness, rather than an explicit action by the taxpayer. Moreover, even in the case of property that can be abandoned in the traditional sense, proof of worthlessness entitles the taxpayer to deduct the loss even if the property is not abandoned until a later year.[30]

The loss-from-worthlessness area has been blessed, or perhaps plagued, by two rhetorical flourishes that describe polar extremes: The taxpayer does not have to be "an incorrigible optimist"[31] and wait until the last possible minute to write off an investment as worthless. On the other hand, he may not be "a Stygian pessimist"[32] and write it off as soon as trouble looms on the horizon. Alas, most cases fall between these two extremes, in a murky interval that may span several years. The applicable standards were summarized by the Board of Tax Appeals in the following frequently quoted passage in *Morton v. CIR*, decided in 1938:

> From an examination of [the] cases it is apparent that a loss by reason of the worthlessness of stock must be deducted in the year in which the stock becomes worthless and the loss is sustained, that stock may not be considered as worthless even when having no liquidating value if there is a reasonable hope and expectation that it will become

[29] But see Arkin v. CIR, 76 TC 1048 (1981) (investor in land trust entitled to deduct loss on notifying trustee and other beneficiaries that he was abandoning his interest).

[30] See, e.g., Gordon v. CIR, 134 F2d 685 (4th Cir. 1943) (realty subject to liens exceeding value held worthless, despite retention of title); Rev. Rul. 54-581, 1954-2 CB 112 (loss on worthlessness deductible despite postponement of sale, abandonment, and loss of title until later years). For losses of intangibles claimed to result from changes in government regulations, see Rev. Rul. 84-145, 1984-2 CB 47 (no deductible loss when deregulation sharply reduced value of airline's route authorities; mere diminution in value not deductible); Rev. Rul. 82-67, 1982-1 CB 32 (deductible loss occurred when "rice history acreage" abolished as criterion for federal benefits to rice growers); Turner, Income Tax Deduction for Losses Caused by Government Deregulation, 60 Taxes 314 (1982). But see Proesel v. CIR, 77 TC 992 (1981) (motion picture not worthless after rejection by major studios and independent distributors; negotiations continued for several years thereafter). Compare A.J. Indus., Inc. v. US, 503 F2d 660 (9th Cir. 1974) (rejecting claim of preabandonment worthlessness on ground that management's judgment of continuing value is entitled to great weight) with Superior Coal Co. v. CIR, 145 F2d 597 (7th Cir. 1944), cert. denied, 324 US 864 (1945) (worthlessness determined by objective, not subjective, test).

[31] US v. S.S. White Dental Mfg. Co., 274 US 398, 403 (1927) (assets of business became worthless when seized as enemy property).

[32] Ruppert v. US, 22 F. Supp. 428, 431 (Ct. Cl.), cert. denied, 305 US 630 (1938) (debt not worthless where taxpayer continued to extend credit to debtor and later collected).

valuable at some future time, and that such hope and expectation may be foreclosed by the happening of certain events such as the bankruptcy, cessation from doing business, or liquidation of the corporation, or the appointment of a receiver for it. . . .

The ultimate value of stock, and conversely its worthlessness, will depend not only on its current liquidating value, but also on what value it may acquire in the future through the foreseeable operations of the corporation. Both factors of value must be wiped out before we can definitely fix the loss. If the assets of the corporation exceed its liabilities, the stock has a liquidating value. If its assets are less than its liabilities, but there is a reasonable hope and expectation that the assets will exceed the liabilities of the corporation in the future, its stock, while having no liquidating value, has a potential value and cannot be said to be worthless. The loss of potential value, if it exists, can be established ordinarily with satisfaction only by some "identifiable event" in the corporation's life which puts an end to such hope and expectation.

There are, however, exceptional cases where the liabilities of a corporation are so greatly in excess of its assets and the nature of its assets and business is such that there is no reasonable hope and expectation that a continuation of the business will result in any profit to its stockholders. In such cases the stock, obviously, has no liquidating value, and since the limits of the corporation's future are fixed, the stock, likewise, can presently be said to have no potential value. Where both these factors are established, the occurrence in a later year of an "identifiable event" in the corporation's life, such as liquidation or receivership, will not, therefore, determine the worthlessness of the stock, for already "its value had become finally extinct." . . . In cases where the stock has concededly lost any liquidating value in a certain year, but an event occurs in a subsequent year which the taxpayer claims is "identifiable," and where the Commissioner of Internal Revenue has determined that stock became worthless in the year in which it lost its liquidating value, then the taxpayer, in order to be entitled to the loss deduction in the latter year, has the burden of proving that, although the stock lost its liquidating value in the prior year, it continued to have a potential value until the occurrence of the event.[33]

---

[33] Morton v. CIR, 38 BTA 1270, 1278–79 (1928) (nonacq.), aff'd, 112 F2d 320 (7th Cir. 1940). See also infra ¶33.3 (criteria determining when debts are worthless). For the disallowance of losses for stock in corporations having residual liquidating value, see, e.g., Richards v. CIR, 35 TCM (CCH) 1709 (1976) (stock not worthless because fair market value of assets exceeded balance sheet liabilities); Rev. Rul. 77-17, 1977-1 CB 44 (stock not worthless as result of corporate bankruptcy proceeding where corporation had two sound subsidiaries and shareholders had prospect of

Since the decision in *Morton*, the regulations have been amended to require that securities must be "wholly worthless" before a deduction is allowable.[34] The adverb "wholly," however, seems to be a meaningless intensifier, as in "wholly unique." At any rate, if there is a difference between "worthless"— the verbal formula used by the regulations in force for the taxable year in the *Morton* case—and "wholly worthless," the current language, it has not perceptibly altered judicial attitudes.[35]

Whether the potential value of an enterprise has been wiped out by an identifiable event is a question of fact, requiring all relevant circumstances to be examined.[36] In this case-by-case process, the occurrences that are most likely to qualify are cessation of business, receivership, foreclosure, sale of all assets, liquidation, and bankruptcy.[37] Default on a major obligation is also significant.[38] On the other hand, no single event is necessarily sufficient. Even the cessation of operations and sale of all assets might not be a "closed transaction" if there is a possibility of recovering something by litigation.[39]

---

receiving stock in reorganized entity). But see Textron, Inc. v. US, 561 F2d 1023 (1st Cir. 1977) (potential future tax advantages through use of corporate shell did not give value to otherwise worthless securities).

For a special rule applicable to banks and other institutions subject to federal and state regulations, see Reg. §1.165-4(b) (write-down required by authorities to reflect worthlessness is prima facie evidence, but not conclusive, of worthlessness).

[34] Reg. §1.165-5(b) (noncapital assets), §1.165-5(c) (capital assets). For §166(a)(2), permitting partially worthless debts to be deducted, see infra ¶33.4.

[35] See, e.g., Post v. CIR, 39 TCM (CCH) 311 (1979), quoting the *Morton* opinion at length and disallowing a $13 million deduction after extensive analysis of the company's financial data and business prospects.

[36] See Boehm v. CIR, 326 US 287, 292–93 (1945) (deduction denied where numerous identifiable events occurred prior to year of claimed worthlessness).

[37] See, e.g., Austin Co. v. CIR, 71 TC 955 (1979) (vote to sell assets of foreign subsidiary and liquidate it); Scifo v. CIR, 68 TC 714 (1977) (acq.) (strike, bankruptcy petition, and shutdown of plant); Malmstedt v. CIR, 35 TCM (CCH) 199 (1976), remanded on other grounds, 578 F2d 520 (4th Cir. 1978) (foreclosure sale of principal asset); Goldberg v. CIR, 29 TCM (CCH) 74 (1970) (cessation of operations and filing petition in bankruptcy); Rev. Rul. 72-470, 1972-2 CB 100 (corporation's equity of redemption did not negate finality of foreclosure sale).

[38] See Jessup v. CIR, 36 TCM (CCH) 1145 (1977) (call of loan by corporation's bank).

[39] See Ramsay Scarlett & Co. v. CIR, 521 F2d 786 (4th Cir. 1975) (taxpayers had prospect of recovery from banks that cashed checks drawn by embezzlers); Scofield's Est. v. CIR, 266 F2d 154 (6th Cir. 1959) (trustee had reasonable grounds to believe he could recover from manager of corpus for diversion of trust assets); Bail Fund of Civil Rights Congress v. CIR, 26 TC 482 (1956) (acq.) (indemnity agreements); Anderegg v. CIR, 37 TCM (CCH) 1851 (1978) (liquidation not controlling); Rev. Rul. 77-18, 1977-1 CB 46 (shareholder lawsuit to rescind merger negates worthlessness of stock); Rev. Rul. 76-41, 1976-1 CB 52 (no loss on foreign government's seizure if taxpayer can expect to regain ownership through U.S. court proceeding). For cases finding insufficient prospect of recovery to bar deduction, see Poe v. US,

These potential-recovery cases can be described as denying deductions because no loss has yet been sustained[40] or because, if sustained, the loss is compensated for by insurance or otherwise.[41] If the taxpayer's reimbursement claim covers only part of the loss, however, the balance may be deducted as worthless.[42]

¶25.4.5 Demolition of Buildings

A common method of closing out an investment in a building is demolition. Section 280B(a), enacted in 1984, provides, however, that no deduction may be taken for loss sustained on the demolition of a structure or for the costs of the demolition.[43] Instead, the adjusted basis of the demolished structure and the demolition costs are added to the adjusted basis of the land on which the structure was located.

A demolition predating the enactment of §280B(a) is usually considered an identifiable event establishing a loss equal to the taxpayer's remaining adjusted basis in the building, increased by the cost of demolition or decreased by any net proceeds, such as amounts received for salvageable items.[44] This principle is subject to a major exception: If the property was purchased with the intent to demolish the building, whether immediately or at a later time, the taxpayer's entire basis must be allocated to the land,

---

194 F. Supp. 93 (D. Colo. 1961) (taxpayers reasonably gave up hope of recovery from bank for its failure to insure; deduction allowed despite later recovery); Coastal Terminals, Inc. v. CIR, 25 TC 1053 (1956) (collapse caused by failure of soil foundation, clearly not covered by insurance); Fiscella v. CIR, 35 TCM (CCH) 548 (1976) (abandonment loss allowed for cost of franchise; taxpayer's counterclaim when sued by franchiser was merely "a defensive measure" with "no hope of recovery"); Anderson v. CIR, 18 TCM (CCH) 549 (1959) (taxpayer knew defendants in lawsuit were insolvent).

[40] See Reg. §§1.165-1(d)(2)(i), (ii); 1.165-1(d)(3).

[41] See Rev. Rul. 78-388, 1978-2 CB 110.

[42] Reg. §1.165-1(d)(2)(ii); Gale v. CIR, 41 TC 269 (1963) (difference between damage and maximum insurance coverage deductible in year of fire). But see Hudock v. CIR, 65 TC 351, 358–61 (1975) (no deduction in year of fire when amount to be received on insurance policy was uncertain; estimate of proceeds rejected).

[43] In its present form, §280B applies for taxable years beginning after 1983. For prior years, the provision only applies to demolitions of certified historic structures. IRC §280B (before amendment in 1984).

[44] Reg. §1.165-3(b)(1). But see Reg. §1.165-3(b)(2) (no deduction for demolition pursuant to lease; basis of building transferred to lease and subject to amortization); Levinson v. CIR, 59 TC 676 (1973) (same); Wilson v. US, 588 F2d 1168 (6th Cir. 1978) ("pursuant to lease" includes permissive as well as mandatory demolition; review of cases); Grossman v. CIR, 74 TC 1147, 1158 (1980) (regulation only applicable if there is "a definite link between the demolition and the lease").

leaving nothing to be deducted when the building is destroyed.[45] In the same vein, no part of the cost of the property may be allocated to the old building and then transferred to the structures constructed to replace it.[46] The regulations set out a long list of factors to be weighed in determining whether the crucial intent to demolish the building existed when the property was acquired or arose subsequently.[47]

In disallowing any deduction for the demolition of buildings acquired with intent to demolish them, the regulations view the taxpayer as buying the land and getting the unwanted and useless structures for nothing;[48] they are not "improvements," but burdens. It could be said, therefore, that assignment of the entire purchase price to the land is required by basis allocation principles rather than by the loss determination rules of §165. Indeed, if destruction of the existing buildings is required to put the land to its highest and best use, it is arguable that no one would pay anything for the buildings, except by error, whether he intended to demolish the buildings or not; but in determining the taxpayer's right to a deduction, the regulations are content to distinguish among purchasers by reference to the individual's state of mind.

At the other end of the spectrum, a pre-1984 demolition of a building does not yield a deductible loss if it is incidental to a sale of the property; the loss is then treated as a selling expense, which reduces the taxpayer's capital gain (or increases the capital loss) on the disposition.[49]

Congress rejected the regulations in favor of the flat deduction ban of §280B(a) because the intention-based rules of the regulation were found to have presented "significant enforcement problems," and to have allowed taxpayers passing the intent test to deduct costs that are "in the nature of

---

[45] Reg. §1.165-3(a)(1). For the provisional allocation of basis to the building for the purpose of computing depreciation between acquisition and demolition, see Reg. §1.165-3(a)(2).

[46] Reg. §1.165-3(a)(3). Phipps v. CIR, 5 TC 964 (1945), holding to the contrary, was superseded by the current regulations, which were promulgated in 1966 and have been accepted by the courts.

[47] Reg. §1.165-3(c)(2). See also Pappas v. CIR, 78 TC 1078 (1982) (on facts, building not acquired with intent to demolish); Canelo v. CIR, 53 TC 217, 227–29 (1969) (nonacq.), aff'd per curiam, 447 F2d 484 (9th Cir. 1971) (intent to demolish formed after acquisition).

[48] See Wood County Tel. Co. v. CIR, 51 TC 72, 78–79 (1968) (purchaser who intends to demolish improvements "obviously is interested in acquiring only the land"; allocation of entire price to land reflects "actual intention of the purchaser").

[49] See Storz v. CIR, 68 TC 84, 97–98 (1977), rev'd on another issue, 583 F2d 972 (8th Cir. 1978) (on facts, demolition not integrally related to sale; ordinary loss allowed), and cases therein cited.

capital costs [rather] than current expenses."[50]

¶25.5 INSURANCE OR OTHER COMPENSATION

Losses may only be deducted under §165(a) if "not compensated for by insurance or otherwise." For a deduction to be allowable under §165(a), there must have been "a financial detriment actually suffered by the taxpayer," resulting from a "transaction which when fully consummated left the taxpayer poorer in a material sense."[1] The compensation restriction is most frequently encountered as a barrier to deductions when insured property is damaged by fire or other casualty, but it also prevents the deduction of other types of losses covered by insurance, such as a business enterprise's liability for injuries caused by defective products or negligence by its employees. The restriction applies equally to a reimbursement from a source other than insurance.

There is some authority for the proposition that a loss may not be deducted if the taxpayer fails to pursue an insurance claim or other right to reimbursement.[2] If the taxpayer waives a right to collect from a relative or friend, this theory is valid because the waiver is an indirect gift, but a waiver based on a hardheaded business or financial judgment is another matter. Employers held liable for the negligence of their employees under the doctrine of respondeat superior, for example, rarely sue the negligent employees for reimbursement. Yet, it would fly in the face of economic reality to hold that the employer's payments to the injured parties may not be deducted under §165(a) because the employer has a theoretically valid claim to be reimbursed by the employee who is primarily responsible for the loss. The statute denies losses "compensated" by insurance or other reimbursement arrangement, not losses "covered" by such an arrangement. The likely purpose of the "compensated for" limitation, further, is to make sure

---

[50] Staff of Joint Comm. on Tax'n, 98th Cong., 2d Sess., General Explanation of the Revenue Provisions of the Deficit Reduction Act of 1984, at 1178 (Comm. Print 1984).

[1] Horne v. CIR, 5 TC 250, 250–54 (1945) (wash sale of membership on commodity exchange; loss nondeductible).

[2] Kentucky Utils. Co. v. Glenn, 394 F2d 631 (6th Cir. 1968) (less than full compensation for loss to equipment accepted from insurer in settlement by which insurer acceded to taxpayer's wish that insurer not pursue subrogation rights against manufacturer of equipment; held, portion of loss borne by taxpayer, to extent in excess of policy deductible, was "compensated for by insurance" and cannot be deducted); H.D. Lee Mercantile Co. v. CIR, 79 F2d 391 (10th Cir. 1935) (failure to make claim against supplier of defective goods bars deduction); Rev. Rul. 78-141, 1978-1 CB 58 (same where lawyer paid client to rectify erroneous advice but failed to seek reimbursement under malpractice insurance policy). See also ¶20.1.4 (failure to claim reimbursement for business expenses).

that the taxpayer bears the burden of losses deducted under §165(a), a policy that is as fully satisfied when an insurance claim is forgone as when there is no insurance at all. For these reasons, the more recent decisions have allowed loss deductions where an insurance claim is waived "for sound and practical reasons not primarily motivated by tax considerations."[3] The policy of the IRS, however, still seems to be to deny these deductions.[4]

Where insurance claims are pursued, the principal problem in applying §165(a) is one of timing. Under the regulations, taxpayers having "a reasonable prospect of recovery" may not deduct the loss unless and until "it can be ascertained with reasonable certainty whether or not such reimbursement will be recovered," an issue that can be resolved by settlement, adjudication, or abandonment of the claims.[5] If the claim for reimbursement covers only part of the loss, however, the uninsured portion may be deducted when the casualty or other event generating the loss occurs.[6]

If the taxpayer is later reimbursed for a loss that was properly deducted when sustained (e.g., because the prospect of recovery was insubstantial at that time or the amount of coverage was underestimated), the tax for the year of the loss is not recomputed. Instead, the recovery must be included in gross income when received, subject to the tax benefit exclusion allowed by §111, discussed earlier in this work.[7]

In disallowing any deduction for losses compensated for by insurance "or otherwise," §165(a) encompasses reimbursement of the taxpayer's loss by a tort-feasor, supplier, or other person liable under tort or contract law. Reimbursement can bar a deduction even if it is not in cash. For example, if a defective machine purchased by the taxpayer is replaced by the supplier or accepted as part payment on another item, the taxpayer's loss is eliminated or reduced pro tanto. The same result should be reached even if the adjustment is more circuitous, such as the grant of a royalty-free license to use a patent as compensation for the defective product.[8]

---

[3] Miller v. CIR, 733 F2d 399, 404 (6th Cir. 1984) (insurance claim not filed for fear insurer would cancel policy; *Kentucky Utils.*, supra note 2, overruled). See Hills v. CIR, 691 F2d 997 (11th Cir. 1982) (same result on similar facts).

[4] See Rev. Rul. 78-141, supra note 2.

[5] Reg. §1.165-1(d)(2)(i) (existence of reasonable prospect of recovery "is a question of fact to be determined upon an examination of all facts and circumstances"). See also infra ¶34.4 (casualty losses).

[6] Reg. §1.165-1(d)(2)(ii).

[7] Reg. §1.165-1(d)(2)(iii); for §111, see supra ¶5.7.3.

[8] See Holder v. US, 444 F2d 1297 (5th Cir. 1971) (owner-lessor suffered no deductible loss when lessee demolished building under lease requiring replacement with other buildings meeting specified standards). See also Rev. Rul. 77-17, 1977-1 CB 44 (victim of stock fraud not entitled to worthless stock or theft deduction where issuer was being reorganized in bankruptcy and taxpayer would receive stock in reorganized corporation); Rev. Rul. 77-18, 1977-1 CB 46 (same where taxpayer had

In some cases, an offsetting benefit is so closely intertwined with the alleged loss that it is not clear whether a deduction is barred because the taxpayer suffered no loss or because a sustained loss was redressed by compensation. For example, if the parties to a business agreement get into a controversy about its meaning and settle their dispute by rescinding the old agreement in favor of a new one, the transaction might generate a deductible loss for one of the parties. The novation, however, is more likely to be viewed either as producing no loss or as compensating for any loss that would otherwise have been sustained.

The reaches of the offsetting-benefit concept, however, are uncertain, as is illustrated by a series of cases involving deductions claimed by television stations on termination of network affiliation contracts. In *Forward Communications Corp. v. US*, a station that had been affiliated with two networks was held to have sustained a deductible loss when it voluntarily terminated one of the affiliations in anticipation of a reshuffling of local affiliations when a new station entered the market.[9] The court rejected the trial judge's conclusion that the loss had been compensated for because revenues increased after the dual affiliation ended, saying: "The statute does not bar a deduction for a loss actually incurred merely because the taxpayer is able to effect an offsetting gain on a different although contemporaneous transaction."[10] In *Hearst Corp. v. US*, in contrast, a station was allowed no loss deduction when its sole network affiliation was terminated because its favorable position as channel 2 in a market served by only two VHF stations assured that another network would affiliate with the station; the relevant asset thus was the right to affiliate, not a particular affiliation, and this asset was not lost.[11]

Similar tension is seen in other contexts. In *George Freitas Dairy, Inc. v. US*, for example, the Court of Appeals for the Ninth Circuit allowed a deduction for loss of the taxpayer's milk production quotas even though the taxpayer received certain offsetting benefits under a new legislative quota system (which could be withdrawn by a public agency at will) because the legislation "was not primarily compensatory in purpose or effect."[12] On the

---

reasonable prospect of recovery through action for rescission and participation in bankruptcy reorganization).

[9] Forward Communications Corp. v. US, 608 F2d 485 (Ct. Cl. 1979).

[10] Id. at 501.

[11] Hearst Corp. v. US, 13 Cl. Ct. 178, 87-2 USTC ¶9491 (1987). See also Meredith Broadcasting Co. v. US, 405 F2d 1214 (Ct. Cl. 1968) (deduction allowed when station lost affiliation with all four networks); Roy H. Park Broadcasting, Inc. v. CIR, 56 TC 784 (1971) (deduction allowed on loss of one of two affiliations); Bernstein, Disallowance of Loss Deductions in Shifts of Network Affiliations, 57 Taxes 199 (1979).

[12] George Freitas Dairy, Inc. v. US, 582 F2d 500 (9th Cir. 1978). See also Boston Elevated Ry. v. CIR, 16 TC 1084, 1111–12 (1951) (nonacq.), aff'd on another

other hand, benefits under a federal disaster relief act have been held to be "compensation" within the meaning of §165(a), rather than gifts, with the result that they reduced pro tanto the taxpayers' deductible loss for earthquake damage to their home.[13]

It is tempting to distinguish between recoveries by reference to whether the amount would be includable in gross income if received in a later year; if so, disallowing the deduction is tantamount to taxing the recovery. On the other hand, if the recovery would be excludable from income (e.g., under §102, relating to gifts), then allowing the deduction despite the recovery is an indirect way of excluding the recovery from income. For borderline receipts, however, this advice puts the cart before the horse because, under the tax benefit doctrine, the taxability of the receipt in a later year may depend on whether it is viewed as a recovery of an amount previously deducted.[14]

Although they do not involve "compensation" in a technical sense, situations in which no loss results from the termination of an investment if the taxpayer got what he paid for are analogous to the no-deduction-for-a-compensated-loss principle. For example, the premium paid for a policy of fire insurance is not lost if the insured gets through the year without sustaining any fire damage and hence receives no cash from the insurer.

¶25.6 AMOUNT DEDUCTIBLE

Section 165(b) limits the amount that may be deducted under §165(a) to the adjusted basis of the property as fixed by §1011 for determining loss on a sale or other disposition. For example, if property costing $1,000 increases in value to $1,500 and then becomes worthless, the loss is $1,000, not $1,500; the taxpayer's paper profit of $500, not having been realized

---

issue, 196 F2d 923 (1st Cir. 1952) (deduction allowed where state guaranty of specified level of income "did not undertake to compensate petitioner for any particular loss" and would generate taxable income in future); Rev. Rul. 87-117, 1987-2 CB 61 (electric company allowed deduction for costs of nuclear plant abandoned when partially completed, even though company given rate increase to cover these costs).

[13] Shanahan v. CIR, 63 TC 21 (1974); Rev. Rul. 76-144, 1976-1 CB 17. See also Dunne v. CIR, 75 F2d 255 (2d Cir. 1935) (deduction denied to taxpayer investing in securities at instance of friend who agreed to indemnify taxpayer against loss and made good on promise); Bryan's Est. v. CIR, 74 TC 725 (1980) (no deduction for loss covered by recovery from trust fund compensating clients for losses incurred because of attorneys' unethical behavior); Johnson v. CIR, 66 TC 897 (1976) (loss on termination of partnership when taxpayer's partner died disallowed because proceeds of keyman insurance were intended to compensate for loss of taxpayer's investment).

[14] For the tax benefit doctrine, see supra ¶5.7.1.

and included in income, may not be deducted when it evaporates. In the same vein, if business property costing $1,000 is depreciated down to $50 and then becomes worthless, the loss under §165(a) is $50, no matter how valuable the property might have been. If the basis for determining gain is different from the basis for determining loss, as in the case of property received by gift,[1] the latter amount is controlling in computing the deduction under §165.

Indirect proof of the taxpayer's adjusted basis is acceptable if persuasive, but in the last analysis taxpayers have the burden of proving adjusted basis when deducting losses under §165(a). Under a 1931 Supreme Court decision, taxpayers encountering practical difficulties in carrying their burden of proof because of the passage of time or loss of records get sympathy, but nothing more:

> The impossibility of proving a material fact upon which the right to relief depends simply leaves the claimant upon whom the burden rests with an unenforceable claim, a misfortune to be borne by him, as it must be borne in other cases, as the result of a failure of proof.[2]

The *Cohan* principle, permitting estimates in appropriate cases, applies only if the taxpayer first shows that he is entitled to a deduction in some amount and that uncertainty exists only as to the exact amount.[3] It is of no avail, therefore, if the taxpayer is unable to make a threshold showing that the property's adjusted basis was more than zero. This may be an insurmountable obstacle in the absence of records if the property's original basis could have been reduced to zero by prior deductions for depreciation or other charges.[4]

Taxpayers frequently sustain losses on discharging liabilities incurred in transactions entered into for profit. Although money is not ordinarily viewed as having a "basis" for tax purposes, these out-of-pocket expenditures are clearly deductible.[5] Section 165(b) applies when a loss is attributa-

---

[1] See IRC §1015(a), discussed infra ¶41.3.1.

[2] Burnet v. Houston, 283 US 223, 228 (1931).

[3] Cohan v. CIR, 39 F2d 540 (2d Cir. 1930), discussed supra ¶20.1.9.

[4] See, e.g., Oates v. CIR, 316 F2d 56 (8th Cir. 1963) (failure to establish proper adjustments for prior sales and other dispositions when claiming loss on cattle-raising venture; *Cohan* inapplicable); Mueller v. CIR, 60 TC 36, 40–41 (1973), aff'd on this issue, 496 F2d 899 (5th Cir. 1974) (no proof of adjusted basis). For a special rule shifting the burden of proof to the government in certain situations involving the basis of property acquired by gift, see IRC §1015(a) (last sentence), discussed infra ¶41.3.4.

[5] E.g., Stamos v. CIR, 22 TC 885, 892 (1954) (legal expenses incurred in connection with guaranty given in a transaction entered into for profit), and cases therein cited; Rev. Rul. 65-254, 1965-2 CB 50 (embezzler can deduct repayment of ill-gotten gains as loss from transaction entered into for profit).

ble to property, but it is not otherwise a barrier to deductions under §165(a).

On the other hand, deductions may not be bottomed on the taxpayer's failure to collect an amount that would be taxable if received, unless it was includable in gross income in an earlier year when the taxpayer's rights accrued. Despite a leading Supreme Court case holding that uncollected and unreported income may not be deducted,[6] untutored taxpayers, and some who should know better, regularly petition the courts to allow them to deduct wages earned but not collected, rent owed to them by unreliable tenants, the sales price of goods sold on credit to defaulting buyers, and anticipated profits that did not materialize.[7] A right to receive income has no adjusted basis until the item is reported as gross income.[8] Since a taxpayer using the cash method of accounting reports the receipt of income, not the right to receive it, the right's basis is zero for such a taxpayer, as is the deduction under §165(a) if the right becomes worthless.[9]

Although the taxpayer's financial detriment in these situations is real, it is adequately, and automatically, reflected by excluding the lost amount from gross income. The adjustment can be illustrated by comparing A, who earns and collects wages of $1,000, with B, who earns the same amount but fails to collect it because the employer disappears. The financial spread between A and B is $1,000, and A reports $1,000 more than B on his tax return. Were B allowed to deduct $1,000, the spread between their reported incomes would be $2,000—twice the financial difference separating them. If B had other income against which this deduction could be taken and if his

---

[6] Hort v. CIR, 313 US 28 (1941).

[7] See, e.g., US v. Fitzsimmons, 712 F2d 1196 (7th Cir. 1983) (dentist convicted of filing false return where deductions taken for hypothetical value of time spent in providing free services to special patients and waiting time when patients failed to keep appointments); Escofil v. CIR, 464 F2d 358 (3d Cir. 1972) (anticipated earnings); Marks v. CIR, 390 F2d 598 (9th Cir.), cert. denied, 393 US 883 (1968) (loss of income following revocation of teacher's credentials); Alsop v. CIR, 290 F2d 726 (2d Cir. 1961) (royalties embezzled by author's agent); Holman v. CIR, 66 TC 809 (1976), aff'd on other grounds, 564 F2d 283 (9th Cir. 1977) (lost income of lawyers expelled from law partnership); Crossland v. CIR, 33 TCM (CCH) 1278 (1974), aff'd without opinion, 76-1 USTC ¶9188 (wages lost through unemployment); Hendricks v. CIR, 26 TCM (CCH) 636 (1967), aff'd per curiam, 406 F2d 269 (5th Cir. 1969) (difference between agreed fee and amount received); Rev. Rul. 55-405, 1955-1 CB 26 (loss of interest when bonds were inadvertently held beyond maturity dates). See also Gertz v. CIR, 64 TC 598 (1975) (no bad-debt deduction on failure of employer to pay income earned); Rev. Rul. 80-17, 1980-1 CB 45 (alien not allowed to deduct loss on confiscation of property by country of which he was a citizen, where income from property would not have been subject to U.S. taxation).

[8] For the cash method of accounting, see ¶105.1.5.

[9] For the failure of a cash-basis taxpayer to collect amounts that were improperly accrued in prior years, compare Smith v. Fahs, 50-2 USTC ¶9433 (SD Fla. 1950) (not officially reported) (deduction allowed) with Redcay v. CIR, 12 TC 806 (1949) (contra).

tax rate were 28 percent, he would be $280 better off than if no wages had been earned.

A related, but less clear-cut, issue arises when an embezzler records false purchases equal to his thefts, thereby increasing the cost of goods sold and decreasing gross income. The IRS holds that the victim of the embezzlement may not deduct the embezzlement loss because the embezzled funds were not reported as gross income.[10] The Tax Court disagrees, finding the understatement of gross income to be an accounting error that the IRS should correct directly (if caught in time), rather than indirectly by disallowing an out-of-pocket loss admittedly sustained.[11]

¶25.7 DISALLOWED LOSSES

Because losses can easily be exaggerated and are sometimes fictitious, the Code restricts or disallows deductions for many categories of losses thought by Congress to be particularly susceptible to abuse. Some of these limitations apply only to losses in the technical sense of the term—amounts otherwise deductible under §165(a). Others apply to losses in a broader sense—the excess of business or profit-oriented deductions over the taxpayer's income.

The principal restrictions, which are discussed elsewhere in this work, are:

1. Section 165(d), allowing losses from wagering transactions to be deducted only to the extent of wagering gains.[1]
2. Section 183 (applicable to individuals and S corporations), restricting deductions incurred in hobbies and other activities not engaged in for profit to an amount determined by reference to the taxpayer's gross income from the activities.[2]
3. Section 267(a), disallowing losses from sales or exchanges of property between related persons (as defined).[3]
4. Section 271, disallowing deductions for worthless securities and bad debts if the debtor is a political party.[4]
5. Section 274(a), disallowing deductions attributable to facilities used for entertainment, amusement, or recreation.[5]

---

[10] Rev. Rul. 81-207, 1981-2 CB 57.
[11] B.C. Cook & Sons v. CIR, 59 TC 516 (1972).
[1] Infra ¶25.9.
[2] Supra ¶22.5.
[3] Infra ¶78.1
[4] Infra ¶102.5.
[5] Supra ¶21.2.3.

6. Section 280A (applicable to individuals and S corporations), restricting deductions for dwelling units used by the taxpayer or certain other persons as a residence during the taxable year.[6]
7. Section 465 (applicable to individuals and certain closely held corporations), permitting the excess of the taxpayer's deductions from each business or profit-oriented activity over the gross income from the activity to be deducted from other income only up to the amount that the taxpayer has at risk (as defined) in the loss activity.[7]
8. Section 469 (applicable to individuals, estates, trusts, personal service corporations, and certain other closely held corporations), which forbids the deduction of losses from passive activities against any income other than income from other passive activities.[8]
9. Section 1091, disallowing deductions for losses in wash sales of stock or securities.[9]

In addition to these statutory restrictions, the deduction of losses under §165(a) is subject to disallowance under the judge-made frustration-of-public-policy doctrine, examined earlier in the context of business expenses.[10] This judicial restriction has been superseded by more precise statutory rules so far as business expenses are concerned, but the IRS contends that the judicial principles continue to apply to the deduction of losses under §165(a), and its contention has been upheld by the courts.[11]

¶25.8 ANCILLARY MATTERS

¶25.8.1 Accounting Method

By allowing a deduction for losses "sustained" during the taxable year, §165(a) seems oblivious to the taxpayer's accounting method. This initial impression is fortified by the regulations, which require losses to be evidenced "by closed and completed transactions, fixed by identifiable events."[1] Although these requirements ordinarily prevent accrual basis tax-

---

[6] Supra ¶22.6.
[7] Infra ¶25.10.
[8] Infra Ch. 28.
[9] Infra ¶44.7.
[10] Supra ¶20.3.3.
[11] Rev. Rul. 77-126, 1977-1 CB 47 (deduction of loss from forfeiture of unlawful gambling devices would frustrate public policy); Holt v. CIR, 69 TC 75 (1977), aff'd per curiam, 611 F2d 1160 (5th Cir. 1980) (same as to confiscated truck used to transport marijuana). For other cases in this area, see supra ¶20.3.3 note 39.
[1] Reg. §1.165-1(b), discussed supra ¶25.4.1.

payers from deducting unrealized declines in value,[2] they do not put cash basis and accrual basis taxpayers on a plane of complete equality. The principal differences between them are:

1. *Inventory losses.* A lower-of-cost-or-market rule allows depreciated inventory items to be written down to market value under some methods of inventory accounting.[3] Since inventory accounting can only be used by accrual basis taxpayers, the lower-of-cost-or-market rule is never available to a taxpayer on the cash method.

2. *Accrued liabilities.* If a business loss entails an out-of-pocket expenditure, such as a liability under a guaranty or an obligation to pay damages to the victim of the taxpayer's negligence, the loss is deductible by an accrual basis taxpayer when all events fixing the liability and amount occur.[4] By contrast, a cash basis taxpayer may not deduct the loss until the liability is paid.

This distinction between cash basis and accrual basis taxpayers evidently accounts for a puzzling IRS ruling, holding that a cash basis taxpayer who made a purchase on credit of stock that became worthless could deduct the loss only when he later made payments on a promissory note evidencing his obligation for the purchase price.[5] The original basis of property purchased on credit, however, includes the entire price, including amounts to be paid in future installments, and under §165(b), adjusted basis is the measure of a loss on worthlessness. The ruling's rationale for delaying the deduction for the unpaid portion of the purchase price is unclear.

3. *Uncollected income.* As explained earlier, losses resulting from the taxpayer's failure to collect wages, rent, or any similar item may not be deducted unless the item was previously includable in gross income.[6] Accrual basis taxpayers, who must usually accrue income of this type in advance of receipt, are entitled to a deduction when accrued income proves to be uncollectible, but cash method taxpayers get no such deduction.

---

[2] See C.F. Mueller Co. v. CIR, 40 BTA 195, 202–04 (1939) (accrual basis taxpayer may not deduct unrealized losses on securities held for investment).

[3] See, e.g., Reg. §1.165-4(c) (securities dealers); for the valuation of inventories, see generally infra ¶105.4.4.

[4] For the all-events rule, see infra ¶105.3.5. For a special rule applicable to contested liabilities, which covers both accrual basis and cash basis taxpayers, see IRC §461(f), discussed infra ¶105.3.5.

[5] Rev. Rul. 74-80, 1974-1 CB 117, purporting to restate IT 1167, I-1 CB 149 (1922), which apparently involved a loss resulting from giving a negotiable note to a thief who falsely represented that stock would be issued therefor, rather than a loss from stock that was validly issued and thereafter became worthless.

[6] Supra ¶25.6.

¶25.8.2 Ordinary vs. Capital Losses

Section 165(a) permits losses to be deducted, but by itself does not determine whether the deductible amount is an ordinary loss or a capital loss. The proper characterization of losses depends on other provisions, the most important of which are:

1. *Sale or exchange of capital asset.* Section 165(f) provides that a loss on a sale or exchange of a capital asset is deductible only to the extent permitted by §1211 (limitation on deduction of capital losses) and §1212 (capital loss carrybacks and carryovers). In effect, §165(f) incorporates by reference the immense body of law, of both statutory and judicial origin, determining whether property is a "capital asset," whether its disposition is a "sale or exchange," and whether these technical requirements are waived because of special circumstances.[7]

To avoid §165(f), taxpayers often argue that an ambiguous or complex transaction created a loss from abandonment or worthlessness, since these events give rise to ordinary losses even if the property is a capital asset.[8] For its part, the IRS endeavors whenever possible to characterize these border-line events as sales or exchanges of capital assets. Occasionally, taxpayers succeed in establishing that property was abandoned or became worthless, generating an ordinary loss, despite a later sale of salvageable components for nominal amounts.[9] On the other hand, the IRS has been upheld in its contention that the conveyance of mortgaged property to the creditor is a sale, subject to §165(f), even if the mortgagor is not personally liable and hence gets nothing in return, not even a release from liability.[10] Moreover, a loss occurring after the sale of a capital asset (e.g., payment of a liability attributable to the sale) might be related back and characterized as a capital

---

[7] See infra Chs. 51 ("capital asset"), 52 ("sale or exchange").

[8] For worthless securities, however, see IRC §165(g), discussed below. In taxable years beginning before 1984, losses on demolitions of buildings also are sometimes deductible as ordinary losses. See supra ¶25.4.5.

[9] See Rhodes v. CIR, 100 F2d 966 (6th Cir. 1939) (Florida coastal real estate rendered worthless by hurricane; ordinary loss despite sale for nominal amount in later year); Tanforan Co. v. US, 313 F. Supp. 796 (ND Cal. 1970), aff'd per curiam, 462 F2d 605 (9th Cir. 1972) (racetrack abandoned despite later sale of some personalty); Industrial Cotton Mills Co. v. CIR, 43 BTA 107 (1940) (acq.) (ordinary loss on discarding equipment, despite sale to secondhand dealer for salvage value). But see Terminal Co. v. US, 296 F. Supp. 1084 (D. Del. 1969) (goodwill sold rather than abandoned); Fancher v. US, 62-2 USTC ¶9819 (DSD 1962) (not officially reported) (liquor license sold, not abandoned, although city would have to approve reissuance to transferee); Collin v. US, 57 F. Supp. 217 (ND Ohio 1944) (quitclaim of partner's interest to another partner for discharge of liability on note; held, sale, not abandonment).

[10] Rev. Rul. 78-164, 1978-1 CB 264; see infra ¶43.5.2.

loss, even though, viewed in isolation, it does not entail a sale or exchange.[11]

2. *Worthless securities.* Under 165(g), if a security (as defined) is a capital asset and becomes worthless during the taxable year, the resulting loss is treated as a loss from the sale or exchange of a capital asset on the last day of the taxable year. This provision not only confers "sale or exchange" status on the event of worthlessness, but also affects the holding period of the worthless security.[12]

¶25.8.3 Extended Statute of Limitations

Because financially troubled transactions can drag on for many years, it is often difficult to pinpoint the taxable year in which a loss is sustained. As explained earlier, the proper year falls somewhere during the period that it takes for a "Stygian pessimist" to become an "incorrigible optimist,"[13] and this conversion might take many years. Moreover, in findin g that a loss was not sustained in the taxable year under examination, neither the IRS nor the courts have any obligation to designate the correct year. In short, the taxpayer must pick the shell that conceals the pea—and must find the right one before the statute of limitations runs.[14]

If a loss claimed on a return is disallowed by the IRS on audit on the theory that the claim is premature, the taxpayer ordinarily can file timely protective claims for all plausible later taxable years. However, if the statute of limitations for the year under audit has been extended,[15] the statute on later years might run before any adjustment is proposed for the audit year. In this situation, however, §§1311(b)(2)(B) and 1312(4) usually mitigate the effect of the statute of limitations, thus enabling the taxpayer to claim a refund for the proper later year if the IRS succeeds in disallowing the deduction for the audit year.[16]

---

[11] See, e.g., Brown v. CIR, 529 F2d 609 (10th Cir. 1976) (liability of taxpayer under insider trading laws was capital loss because directly related to purchase and sale of stock) and cases therein cited; see also infra ¶51.10.6. Compare Michtom v. CIR, 626 F2d 815 (Ct. Cl. 1980) (taxpayer sought bad-debt treatment on sale of stock received in liquidation of claim against broker under subordination agreement; held, loss from sale of capital asset, not related back to subordination agreement) with Meisels v. US, 732 F2d 132 (Fed. Cir. 1984) (taxpayer, whose payment to brokerage firm under subordination agreement gave her claims against firm's securities, later received a much smaller payment in consideration of her release of these claims; held, capital loss because taxpayer in effect purchased right to securities by prior payment and sold this right for later payment).

[12] See infra ¶52.3.

[13] Supra ¶25.4.4 notes 31, 32.

[14] For the statute of limitations, see generally infra ¶113.1.

[15] See infra ¶113.4 (extension of time if more than 25 percent is omitted from gross income), ¶113.5 (consents to extend statute of limitations).

[16] For these mitigation provisions, see infra ¶113.9.

On the other hand, if a deduction is disallowed on the theory that the loss occurred in an earlier year, a protective claim for refund for the proper year may already be barred when the audit occurs. In this situation, the mitigation rules of §§1311 and 1312 do not open up the earlier year, and the deduction may be permanently lost. A partial remedy is provided by §6511(d)(1), which extends the normal three-year period of limitations on refund claims to seven years in the case of losses from worthless securities and bad debts.[17] In addition, taxpayers fearing a one-sided shell game can engage in self-help by claiming deductions in the alternative for all plausible taxable years before the statute of limitations runs on any of them.

¶25.8.4 Recoveries of Deducted Amounts

For many reasons, taxpayers claiming losses under §165(a) may subsequently recover part or all of the amount deducted. An unexpected event might restore value to property that was discarded or abandoned but to which the taxpayer retained title, a claim for fraud or misrepresentation might be brought against a vendor or vendee as a result of after-discovered evidence, or an insurance claim viewed as hopelessly feeble might shower the taxpayer with gold.

If the loss was properly deducted on the facts as reasonably known at the time, tax liability for the deduction year may not be recomputed to reflect the recovery. The recovery is instead a classic example of a tax benefit item—an amount that must be included in gross income when received or accrued (depending on the taxpayer's accounting method) unless the earlier deduction (or some part of it) produced no tax benefit.[18]

¶25.8.5 Losses vs. Expenses and Bad Debts

It is sometimes necessary to determine whether a transaction produced (1) a "loss" within the meaning of §165(a), (2) an "expense" under §162 or §212, or (3) a "worthless debt" under §166. All three financial detriments are "losses" in the layman's sense of the term and the taxpayer is usually entitled to a deduction in all three cases. There are, however, important differences among them, including:

1. Expenses are almost always deductible from ordinary income, while losses and worthless debts frequently generate capital rather than ordinary losses.[19]

---

[17] See infra ¶113.8.
[18] For the tax benefit doctrine, see generally supra ¶5.7.
[19] For losses, see supra ¶25.8.2; for nonbusiness bad debts, see infra ¶33.6.

2. Section 267(a) disallows deductions for losses on sales and exchanges of property between related persons (as defined), but it does not apply to payments to a related person that can be characterized as "expenses," nor to worthless debts where creditor and debtor are related.[20]

3. Bad debts are deductible whether attributable to the taxpayer's business, a profit-oriented transaction, or personal motives. By contrast, losses sustained by individuals are deductible only if they arise from the taxpayer's business, a transaction entered into for profit, or casualty,[21] while expenses may be deducted only if related to the taxpayer's business or income-producing activities.

4. The frustration-of-public-policy restriction on deductions is codified by §162 for expenses, but not for losses or bad debts.[22]

5. Deductions for expenses are determined by the amount paid or incurred; losses of property and deductions for bad debts are limited to the taxpayer's basis for the worthless item.[23]

In the overwhelming bulk of cases, it is not difficult to determine whether a transaction or payment resulted in a loss, expense, or bad debt, but sometimes the borderline is blurred because the event exhibits characteristics belonging to possibly two or all three categories.

The criteria determining whether an advance of funds creates a "debt" have been extensively developed by the courts,[24] and the distinction between bad debts and losses is best drawn by applying the "debt" criteria: If they are met, an uncollectible advance belongs in the "bad debt" category and is not a "loss" within the meaning of §165(a).[25] The most litigated aspect of the distinction between bad debts and losses is encountered in cases involving guaranties by taxpayers of the debts of other persons, usually a family corporation or business affiliate. In *Putnam v. CIR*, the fountainhead of learning on this subject, the Supreme Court pointed out that a guarantor

---

[20] For §267(a), see infra ¶78.1.

[21] See supra ¶25.3.

[22] See supra ¶20.3.3; supra ¶25.7 note 11.

[23] See IRC §§165(b), 166(b), discussed supra ¶25.6, infra ¶33.2; R.R. Hensler, Inc. v. CIR, 73 TC 168 (1979) (acq.) (repairs to business property damaged by casualty deductible as expenses under §162, without regard to property's adjusted basis or taxpayer's claim against insurance company).

[24] See infra ¶33.2.

[25] See Spring City Foundry Co. v. CIR, 292 US 182, 189 (1934) (statutory predecessors of §§165 and 166 are "mutually exclusive"); Proesel v. CIR, 77 TC 992, 1001 (1981) ("loss cannot be both a business loss and a bad debt"; taxpayer's loss not a bad debt because no enforceable right to receive fixed sum, only unliquidated claim for breach of contract); Perrotto v. CIR, 36 TCM (CCH) 464 (1977) (§166 takes precedence in case of overlap with §165); Smith v. CIR, 38 TCM (CCH) 322 (1979) (deposit in bankrupt credit union created debt subject to §166, not §165 loss).

who makes payment under his guarantee becomes subrogated to the creditor's claim against the debtor, so that "the loss sustained by the guarantor unable to recover from the debtor is by its very nature a loss from the worthlessness of a debt."[26] As a result, the guarantor's claim for deduction is governed by §166, relating to bad debts, not by §165, relating to losses. When applied to a noncorporate guarantor acting in the capacity of an investor, *Putnam* results in a capital loss under §166(d), relating to nonbusiness bad debts.[27]

The Tax Court has held that *Putnam* does not apply if the guarantor pays the debtor's debt in circumstances creating no right of subrogation under the law of suretyship (e.g., if the guarantor pays only part of the underlying debt) and that a nonsubrogated guarantor sustains an ordinary loss under §165(a).[28] Several other courts, however, have held that *Putnam* subjects the guarantor's loss to §§166(a) and (d) even in the absence of subrogation.[29]

As for the distinction between "losses" and "expenses," it was described—a trifle blithely, perhaps—as "self-evident" by the Tax Court in a 1977 case contrasting the unlawful use of liquor to entertain clients (an "expense," deductible only if permitted by §162) with the confiscation of unlawful liquor by law-enforcement officials (a "loss," deductible only if permitted by §165).[30] The distinction can also be illustrated by contrasting damage to business property by fire (a loss subject to §165) with the cost of keeping the property in good repair (an expense subject to §162).[31] Another illustration is supplied by a 1979 ruling, in which the IRS held that financial losses suffered by a brokerage firm as a result of mistakes in executing

---

[26] Putnam v. CIR, 352 US 82, 85 (1956).

[27] For §166(d), see infra ¶33.6.

[28] Rietzke v. CIR, 40 TC 443, 450–53 (1963); Stoody v. CIR, 66 TC 710, 714–16 (1976) (reaffirming *Rietzke* principle, but not applying it because case subject to review by court of appeals rejecting *Rietzke*).

[29] In re Vaughan, 719 F2d 196 (6th Cir. 1983); US v. Hoffman, 423 F2d 1217 (9th Cir. 1970); Stratmore v. US, 420 F2d 461 (3d Cir.), cert. denied, 398 US 951 (1970). See Celanese Corp. v. US, 8 Cl. Ct. 456, 85-2 USTC ¶9517 (1985) (*Putnam* applied where guarantor of debt of subsidiary waived its right to subrogation in connection with disposition of subsidiary's stock). See also Stahl v. US, 441 F2d 999 (DC Cir. 1970) (for compensation, taxpayer allowed securities firm to use her securities as capital to satisfy SEC requirements; held, transaction created bailment, not loan to firm or guaranty of its debts; when securities not returned, loss deductible under §165).

[30] Holt v. CIR, 69 TC 75 (1977) (forfeiture of truck used to transport marijuana generated loss, not expense; held, nondeductible under frustration-of-public-policy doctrine).

[31] See R.R. Hensler, Inc. v. CIR, 73 TC 168 (1979) (acq.).

customer orders are business expenses deductible under §162(a) if the error does not result in the acquisition of securities for the firm's own account, but if the firm acquires securities for its own account as a result of the error, the expenditure is a capital outlay, which generates a loss only when the securities are sold.[32]

¶25.9 GAMBLING LOSSES

Section §165(d) provides that losses from "wagering transactions shall be allowed only to the extent of the gains from such transactions." The regulations state flatly that losses "shall be allowed as a deduction" up to the statutory limit, thus allowing losses to be taken against winnings even if sustained by a tourist or addict who plays for excitement and knows that losses will exceed gains over the long haul.[1] In effect, this places gambling in the same boat as hobbies—gains are taxed only if and to the extent that they exceed losses.[2] Moreover, like hobby losses, disallowed gambling losses die at the end of the taxable year in which they are sustained; they do not create net operating losses that can be carried over to other years, even if the taxpayer is luckier in the other years.[3]

Although §165(d) applies to both professional and amateur gamblers, individual taxpayers who are not engaged in the business of gambling may not deduct gambling losses in computing adjusted gross income, and therefore can take the §165(d) deduction only by electing to itemize deductions.[4] Gains and losses, however, can probably be netted to some extent in determining gross income (e.g., on a per-game or per-session basis); otherwise, nonitemizing taxpayers would have to keep records of every roll of the dice in a craps game and every bet in poker in order to compute adjusted gross income.[5]

---

[32] Rev. Rul. 79-80, 1979-1 CB 86.

[1] Reg. §1.165-10. See Presley v. CIR, 38 TCM (CCH) 1301 (1979) (§165(d) covers all gambling, whether in business, recreation, or sport; gains and losses from all types of gambling netted).

[2] For §183, relating to hobbies and other activities not engaged in for profit, see supra ¶22.5.

[3] Offutt v. CIR, 16 TC 1214 (1951) (net operating loss denied to professional as well as amateur gamblers).

[4] IRC §62(a); Heidelberg v. CIR, 36 TCM (CCH) 566 (1977). For the election to itemize deductions, see infra ¶¶30.4, 30.5.1.

[5] See Winkler v. US, 230 F2d 766 (1st Cir. 1956) (professional gambler's gains and losses netted on per-race basis in determining whether gross income exceeded $600 and hence created duty to file return; extensive analysis); Szkiresak v. CIR, 40 TCM (CCH) 208 (1980) ("impractical to record every roll of the dice or spin of the [roulette] wheel").

The term "wagering transactions" in §165(d) has spawned a small body of interpretative authority. For example, the IRS has ruled that the purchase of a ticket in a raffle sponsored by a charitable organization is a wagering transaction; the amount paid for the ticket is not a charitable contribution because each purchaser obtains a chance to win and hence receives full consideration for the amount paid.[6] Also, a casino that hired shills to round out gambling tables when there were insufficient genuine patrons was required to take the shills' losses (which it defrayed) into account in netting gambling gains and losses under §165(d), on the ground that it was engaged in wagering transactions through agents.[7] On the other hand, it has been held that payments received by a gambler for protecting other gamblers from arrest are not gambling gains that may be offset by gambling losses.[8] In addition, an ingenious effort to construe "wagering transactions" to include speculation in high-risk securities was summarily dismissed by the Tax Court with the observation that "investing in capital assets is not a wagering transaction" within the meaning of §165(d).[9] Thus, a gambler who consistently wins at the racetrack and loses on the stock market gets the worst of both tax worlds—ordinary income and capital losses.

For proof of gambling gains and losses, see Mack v. CIR, 429 F2d 182 (6th Cir. 1970) (checks cashed at racetrack plus additional amount); Stein v. CIR, 322 F2d 78 (5th Cir. 1963) (records inadequate); Showell v. CIR, 286 F2d 245 (9th Cir.), cert. denied, 366 US 929 (1961) (same); Delgozzo v. CIR, 46 TCM (CCH) 1590 (1983) (that losing track tickets were sequentially numbered tended to corroborate taxpayer's claim that he purchased them); Salem v. CIR, 37 TCM (CCH) 614 (1978) (demeanor; losing track tickets); Rev. Proc. 77-29, 1977-2 CB 538 (proper records). See also infra ¶114.4 (fraud prosecutions). See generally Dooher, Losses—Theft, Wagering, War and Confiscation, BNA Tax Mgm't Portfolio No. 278-2d, pt. II-A (1979).

[6] Rev. Rul. 83-130, 1983-2 CB 148.

[7] Nitzberg v. CIR, 580 F2d 357 (9th Cir. 1978). See Miller v. Quinn, 792 F2d 392 (3d Cir. 1986) (dealer in lottery tickets subject to §165(d) limit with respect to cost of unsold tickets, even though sponsor of lottery required dealers to bear this cost; because dealer could have disposed of tickets by selling at discount or giving them to charity, failure to do so suggests dealer intended to play lottery); Boyd v. US, 762 F2d 1369 (9th Cir. 1985) (manager of poker room at casino received part of house take from poker games; held, not gambling winnings; net losses incurred by manager in playing with own money during working hours were gambling losses even though this play undertaken to attract customers).

[8] Cohen v. CIR, 176 F2d 394 (10th Cir. 1949). See Williams v. CIR, 41 TCM (CCH) 312 (1980) ("toke" income received by dealer in casino not gambling winnings, and may not be offset by personal gambling losses).

[9] Jasinski v. CIR, 37 TCM (CCH) 1 (1978).

¶25.10 LIMITATION OF DEDUCTIONS TO AMOUNTS AT RISK

¶25.10.1 Introductory

To combat a dramatic increase in the use of tax shelters, Congress enacted §465 in 1976 to limit the deduction of otherwise allowable losses to the amount the taxpayer has "at risk." Originally, the limitation only applied to four activities: farming, oil and gas exploration and exploitation, motion-picture films and video tapes, and equipment leasing.[1] The at risk rules were expanded in 1978 to cover losses from all business and profit-oriented activities except the holding of real property (other than mineral property) and equipment leasing by certain closely held corporations.[2] Another exemption for active businesses of closely held corporations was added in 1984, but the exemption for real property was eliminated in 1986.

Section 465 is a limitation on deductions for "losses," defined by §465(d) as the excess of the deductions allocable to a covered activity over the gross income from the activity. A loss in this sense is fundamentally different from the type of losses deductible under §165(a). Losses of the latter type must be aggregated with business expenses, depreciation, and all other relevant deductions allocable to the activity in determining whether the taxpayer suffered a loss within the meaning of §465(d); they have no independent relevance as far as the at risk rules are concerned. The at risk limitation is applied annually. Losses in excess of the limitation are carried forward for use in later years in which the activity generates a profit or the taxpayer's amount at risk is increased.

The targets of the at risk rules and their impact are best understood in their historical context. The tax shelters that Congress sought to curb in 1976 and 1978 took many forms but ordinarily had two features in common: Investors put up relatively little cash and hence had little to lose if the venture failed, but the venture borrowed heavily on a nonrecourse or other basis entailing no personal liability for the investor, so that the investor's deductions for depreciation, amortization, intangible drilling and develop-

---

[1] For the 1976 provisions, see Joint Comm. on Tax'n, 94th Cong., 2d Sess., General Explanation of the Tax Reform Act of 1976, reprinted in 1976-3 CB (Vol. 2) 411, 428–29; Weisner, Tax Shelters — A Survey of the Impact of the Tax Reform Act of 1976, 33 Tax L. Rev. 5, 7–39 (1977).

[2] For the 1978 provisions, see Joint Comm. on Tax'n, 95th Cong., 2d Sess., General Explanation of the Revenue Act of 1978, at 129–37 (Comm. Print 1979); H.R. Rep. No. 1445, 95th Cong., 2d Sess., reprinted in 1978-3 CB (Vol. 1) 181, 241–47. The 1978 expansion of §465 rendered unnecessary a portion of §704(d), enacted in 1976, that disqualified some nonrecourse financing in determining partners' deductions for partnership losses, and this restriction was accordingly repealed for taxable years subject to the expanded version of §465.

ment costs, business expenses, interest, or other items greatly exceeded the cash outlay. This leveraging aspect of virtually all classical tax shelters was based on the long-established right to deduct interest, business expenses, and other out-of-pocket items when paid or incurred, even if they are defrayed with borrowed funds, and on the fact that depreciation and amortization are computed on the full adjusted basis of property, even if it is purchased with funds borrowed on a nonrecourse basis. In effect, the tax law gives taxpayers "advance credit" for the debt.[3]

In addition to producing large deductions for minimal cash outlays, tax shelters took advantage of a basic structural feature of the federal income tax system, so pervasive that it is virtually taken for granted: Generally, all income and all deductions are amalgamated in computing taxable income. This global concept of taxable income allowed tax shelter deductions to be taken against salaries, professional fees, dividends, interest, and business income of all types, resulting in dramatic reductions in the investor's current tax liabilities and correspondingly large increases in spendable funds.[4] The term "tax shelter" refers to the use of deductions and credits from an investment to shelter unrelated income from tax.

The most popular investments for tax shelters were real estate, cattle, and oil and gas ventures. Promoters and investors, however, were not fussy when searching for prospects. Railroad boxcars, secondhand computers, lithographs, video tapes, Mexican vegetables, and virtually anything else could serve as an investment vehicle, provided it crammed an abnormal amount of deductions into the first year or two of the taxpayer's participation, usually by taking advantage of statutory provisions for the write-off or rapid depreciation or amortization of capital outlays.

The nonrecourse borrowings that provided the leverage sometimes reflected nothing more than an inflated purchase cost of an investment whose seller was adequately compensated by the down payment. If the inflated balance of the alleged price was actually paid, so much the better from the seller's perspective. Even if nothing more was paid, however, the alleged debt served to promote sales of the shelter by promising inflated deductions to investors.

In theory, leveraged tax shelters only defer tax liabilities, not eliminate them. If the investment is successful, it in time generates net income equaling or exceeding the expenditures deducted in the shelter's early years, and the inclusion of this income on the investor's return increases taxable income by at least as much as the taxable income of the earlier years was

---

[3] Mayerson v. CIR, 47 TC 340, 352 (1966) (acq.) ("advance credit" for debt equalizes all owners of property, whether they pay cash or borrow with or without personal liability). See infra ¶¶41.2.2, 43.5.2.

[4] For a detailed illustration, see McKee, The Real Estate Tax Shelter: A Computerized Expose, 57 Va. L. Rev. 521 (1971).

reduced by the deductions. Since much of the cash reflecting this income must be used to pay off debt financing the investment, the investor often must draw on other funds to pay the deferred taxes.

On the other hand, if the investment fails before the borrowed funds are repaid, a foreclosure of the mortgage securing the debt is treated as a sale to the creditor for unpaid balance of the indebtedness, producing phantom income because the taxpayer's basis was reduced by the early deductions to either zero or a nominal amount.[5] A transfer of the property to the creditor in lieu of foreclosure or an abandonment of the investment with the creditor's concurrence has the same consequence. Just as in the case of the successful shelter, therefore, the taxpayer eventually has taxable income equal to the prior deductions, but no new cash to pay the resulting tax liability.[6]

Whether the shelter succeeds or fails, however, the taxpayer has an opportunity in the interim to invest the amount of taxes saved or to savor the pleasures of spending it. Assume a capital outlay of $100 is deducted in year 1, but this deduction is offset by income of $100 that must be reported in year 10. If the tax rate is 50 percent in all years, the deduction saves $50 of tax in year 1, and the income increases tax by $50 in year 10. If the savings in year 1 are invested at 10 percent interest (5 percent after taxes), it grows to $81 by year 10, leaving the investor with $31 after paying the year 10 tax of $50. Assume the taxpayer borrowed $90 of the investment's purchase price, and pretax cash flows from the investment are just sufficient to pay interest and principal on the loan and return to the taxpayer his $10 equity investment. Before taxes, the investment breaks even for the taxpayer. After taxes, taking into account the $31 profit from the tax deferral, the taxpayer more than triples his investment (getting back $41 on an investment of $10), realizing an after tax rate of return of more than 15 percent per annum. Given the assumed tax rate of 50 percent, a 15 percent rate of return after taxes is equivalent to a bank account producing taxable interest at an annual rate of 30 percent—all from an investment that, apart from taxes, is completely barren of profit.

Further, by entering into a new shelter when the original one reached the fatal crossover point, an investor could avert the evil day. If the deferral is prolonged until the investor dies, §1014, which gives a fresh fair market value basis to property received from a decedent, often makes the deferral permanent. In the example, if the investor dies before year 10 and if his heir receives the remaining cash flows from the investment but is excused from

---

[5] See Bittker, Tax Shelters, Nonrecourse Debt, and the *Crane* Case, 33 Tax L. Rev. 277 (1978), and articles therein cited.

[6] For an examination of proposed escapes from this painful dilemma, see Ginsburg, The Leaky Tax Shelter, 53 Taxes 719 (1975); Kanter, Existing Tax Shelters: Is It Possible to Cope? 56 Taxes 822 (1978).

paying the $50 tax in year 10, the rate of return on the investment rises to the equivalent of a pretax annual yield of nearly 47 percent on a fully taxable investment. Even if the day of reckoning cannot be put off until death, the taxpayer might be in lower tax brackets (e.g., as a result of retirement) when deferral ends.

Finally, in the case of failed shelters—and there are many because the area became a happy hunting ground for shady promoters—some investors never fully comprehend their obligation to include the borrowed funds in gross income when the shelter terminates, and others manage to forget this unpleasant fact of life.[7] After all, the notion that a business failure can produce income is counterintuitive, and so is the idea that investors derive a benefit from being relieved of nonrecourse debt—even if it was the sole reason why they were able to deduct more than they invested in the shelter. By hook or by crook, therefore, deferral often turns into permanent elimination of the tax liabilities.

Section 465 modifies the two structural features of the federal income tax system on which tax shelters depend: (1) the aggregation of all ordinary income and deductions, regardless of source, in computing taxable income on a global basis and (2) the taxpayer's right to deduct expenditures even if financed with funds borrowed on a nonrecourse basis. Section 465 modifies the global feature of prior law by segregating all income and deductions for each of certain specified activities. Within each segregated channel, deductions may be applied up to the full amount of the income produced by the same activity. If the result is a net loss for the activity, however, §465's second modification comes into force: The net loss may be dumped into the channels reserved for other activities only to the extent the taxpayer is at risk in the activity producing the loss. To be at risk in an investment requires either the commitment of the taxpayer's funds and property or the assumption of personal liability for borrowed funds; nonrecourse financing does not qualify.[8]

Underlying these rules are two value judgments. First, within each covered activity, the taxpayer should be allowed to deduct all expenses against all income, a policy that is adopted even for hobbies and other activities not engaged in for profit.[9] Second, if the taxpayer incurs a net loss in a covered activity, it should be deductible against income from other activities only if and to the extent that the taxpayer is or might someday be out-of-pocket for the loss.

---

[7] For special procedures for auditing the returns of partnerships and their partners, enacted in 1982 to facilitate audits where members of tax shelter partnerships are numerous and scattered throughout the country, see infra ¶111.1.5.

[8] See infra ¶25.10.4.

[9] See IRC §183, discussed supra ¶22.5.

Neither of these changes, however, is applied generally throughout the tax law. Channelization is an exception to the basic principle that taxable income is computed on a global basis. For example, taxpayers who finance all business and profit-oriented activities with their own funds or with debt entailing personal liability continue to compute taxable income on a global rather than channelized basis. Second, §465's at risk principle does not supplant or repeal the basic rule that expenditures are deductible even if financed with nonrecourse debt. For example, taxpayers whose business or profit-oriented activities fall into a single channel may apply all deductions, regardless of how the expenditures are financed, against their income, and they may carry a net loss over to other taxable years under the rules for net operating losses. Indeed, nonrecourse-financed expenditures are fully taken into account even by taxpayers investing in tax shelters, up to the income produced by the segregated activity; and excess deductions are carried forward for application in the same manner in later years. Finally, neither of §465's qualifications of prior law affects publicly held corporations, which fall outside its jurisdiction.[10]

The significance of the at risk rules is substantially diminished for taxable years after 1986 by the enactment of the passive activity loss rules of §469, discussed in another chapter.[11] Section 469 is based on a channelization approach similar to, but much broader than, that of §465. Under §469, losses from passive activities may only be deducted from income from other passive activities. Subject to many modifications and exceptions, the term "passive activity" is defined as a trade or business in which the taxpayer does not materially participate. Section 469 effectively creates a channel consisting of all business and profit-oriented activities of the taxpayer, exclusive of (1) businesses in which the taxpayer materially participates (e.g., a professional practice) and (2) portfolio investments (e.g., stocks and bonds). The §469 channel includes substantially all tax shelter investments, but also includes much more. An investment as silent partner in the pizza parlor operated by the taxpayer's brother-in-law, for example, goes into the §469 channel even if the taxpayer is seeking shelter from domestic acrimony, not taxes.

The at risk rules, however, remain in the law, and must be applied before a loss from an investment is tested under the passive activity provisions. Most losses that are denied by §465 would be caught by §469 if the at risk rules did not exist. Section 465, however, has independent significance in some cases. Investments in oil and gas, for example, are generally exempted from §469, but are subject to §465. Also, §469 creates a single channel for all passive activities, whereas, under §465, each investment is

---

[10] See infra ¶25.10.2.
[11] Infra Ch. 28.

placed in a separate channel. Section 469, for example, allows a loss from one passive activity to be deducted against income from all other passive activities. If the loss exceeds the taxpayer's amount at risk in the loss activity, however, §465 bars the deduction of the loss against any other income, thus preventing it from coming into the §469 hotchpot.

¶25.10.2 Covered Taxpayers and Activities

Although aimed primarily at tax shelters, §465 does not use this term, and its application does not depend on the taxpayer's income level or intent or on whether the activity produces an abnormal amount of deductions by taking advantage of any particular statutory provisions or tax accounting methods.[12] Like many legislative responses to tax abuse, therefore, §465 casts a shadow on transactions and activities far removed from the targeted area. It is therefore especially important to delineate the taxpayers and activities that it covers and, conversely, those exempted from its jurisdiction.

1. *Covered taxpayers.* The loss limitation rule of §465(a)(1) applies to losses incurred by individuals, trusts, estates and certain closely held corporations, but only if the losses arise from activities covered by §465.[13] These taxpayers are subject to §465(a)(1) whether the covered activities are carried on directly by them or indirectly as partners or shareholders of a partnership or S corporation. In the latter case, the limitation applies to their shares of the losses of the partnership or S corporation.

In subjecting individuals to its restrictions, §465(a)(1) resembles §183 (relating to hobbies and other activities not engaged in for profit) and §280A (disallowing certain expenses allocable to dwelling units used by the taxpayer or other specified persons as a residence during the same taxable year).[14] The application of the at risk rules to closely held corporations, however, is an innovation in the jurisdictional reach of provisions designed to curb tax avoidance. A corporation is subject to §465(a)(1) if it is a C corporation (a corporation that has not elected to be an S corporation) and satisfies the personal holding company stock ownership rules of §542(a)(2), which encompass any corporation more than 50 percent of whose stock (by value) is owned at any time during the last half of the taxable year by not

---

[12] See Peters v. CIR, 77 TC 1158 (1981) (at risk rules apply to covered activities whether or not carried on as tax shelters).

[13] For the inclusion of trusts and estates, see IRC §641(b). Originally, S corporations were also subject to §465(a)(1). A 1982 amendment deleted S corporations from the list of covered taxpayers. If an S corporation shareholder is a covered taxpayer, however, §456(a)(1) applies to his shares of the corporation's losses.

[14] For IRC §§183 and 280A, see supra ¶¶22.5 and 22.6.

more than five individuals. Although a provision of the personal holding company rules is incorporated by reference in this definition, a corporation satisfying the ownership test is subject to the at risk rules whether or not it is a personal holding company.

Since direct, indirect, and constructive ownership are taken into account in determining the number of individual shareholders owning the requisite amount of stock,[15] virtually all family corporations satisfy the stock ownership test and are therefore subject to §465 if they engage in a covered activity. It is entirely possible for a corporation to become subject to §465 without realizing it because there is no formal mechanism by which a corporation can determine whether stock owned by a dozen ostensibly unrelated shareholders is imputed to one or two individuals.[16]

If a corporation's outstanding stock is owned by fewer than ten individuals, the stock ownership test is necessarily satisfied, since more than 50 percent of the stock must be owned by five or fewer of them. If the stock is more widely dispersed or is owned in whole or in part by trusts, estates, partnerships, or other corporations, a closer examination of the facts is required to determine whether §465 applies. For convenience, the terms "closely held" and "publicly held" are used in the discussion that follows to distinguish corporations subject to §465 from those that are exempt.

2. *Covered activities.* Section 465(a)(1) imposes its limitations on any covered taxpayer "engaged in an activity to which this section applies," and §465(c) lists the covered activities. The list begins with five particular activities: (1) holding, producing, or distributing motion-picture films or video tapes; (2) farming, within the broad definition of §464(e); (3) leasing section 1245 property, as defined by §1245(a)(3) (primarily business equipment, but also some items of tangible realty other than buildings and their structural components); (4) exploring for or exploiting oil and gas resources; and (5) exploring for or exploiting geothermal deposits.[17] In each case, the activity is covered only if engaged in by the taxpayer as a trade or business or for the production of income. This excludes hobbies, but since the focus of

---

[15] For use of the attribution rules of §544 (modified to eliminate attribution from one partner to another in determining the ownership of stock), see S. Rep. No. 498, 96th Cong., 2d Sess. 42 (1980).

[16] See Coshocton Sec. Co. v. CIR, 26 TC 935 (1956) (taxpayer was a personal holding company, even though some of its stock was owned by another corporation that would not have disclosed beneficial ownership, so taxpayer could not have ascertained its status).

For attempts by covered corporations to avoid the at risk rules by (1) organizing a nominally capitalized subsidiary that ostensibly accepts full liability for the risk and (2) filing a consolidated return with the subsidiary, see Reg. §5.1502-45.

[17] The first four of these categories were covered by the 1976 version of §465; the fifth was added in 1978. See supra note 2.

§465 is on business deductions, the business and production-of-income requirements are virtually always satisfied.

Section 465(c)(3), enacted in 1978, expands the coverage to embrace any other activity engaged in by the taxpayer as a business or for the production of income. This dragnet proviso, applicable to taxable years beginning after December 31, 1978, is the major innovation of the 1978 revision of §465. The 1978 expansion covers virtually all profit-oriented activities, including such diverse fields as manufacturing, wholesale and retail trade, rendition of personal and professional services, and investing in marketable securities—no matter how remote from the rash of tax shelters evoking the enactment of §465 in 1976. The dragnet proviso has diverse and sometimes surprising consequences. For example, a taxpayer who has reached the income-recognition phase of a tax shelter investment may not apply losses from his regular occupation against the tax shelter income, except to the extent he is at risk from his investment in the regular business.

3. *Separation and aggregation of covered activities.* The impact of §465 often depends on whether a group of transactions constitutes one activity or more than one. For example, if two oil wells are a single activity, the losses from one may be freely applied against income from the other, and the taxpayer may have no net loss from the activity to be limited by §465(a)(1). If each well is a separate activity, in contrast, the losses from an unprofitable well may be applied against the income from a profitable one only to the extent the taxpayer is at risk in the loss well.

Under §465(c)(2), each film or video tape, each leased item of section 1245 property, each farm, each oil and gas property, and each geothermal property constitutes a separate activity. Thus, in the case of oil and gas, all wells on the same "property" constitute a single activity, but a taxpayer with wells on two or more properties is engaged in two or more separate activities for purposes of §465.[18]

Originally, activities of a partnership or S corporation within each of five specified categories of activities could be aggregated.[19] For example, all of a partnership's films and video tapes could be aggregated, as could all of the partnership's leased section 1245 property, but leased section 1245 property could not be aggregated with films and video tapes or vice versa. This rule was eliminated in 1984 and a much narrower rule was substituted, allowing a partnership or S corporation to aggregate all leased section 1245 property placed in service within a particular year.[20] In other situations, the

---

[18] For the aggregation of mineral properties in computing percentage depletion, see supra ¶24.1.4. For an analogous distinction between separate and aggregated activities in applying §183, relating to hobbies and other activities not conducted for profit, see supra ¶22.5.3.

[19] IRC §465(c)(2) (before amendment in 1984).

[20] IRC §456(c)(2)(B)(i).

statute no longer allows partnerships and S corporations to aggregate their activities, but the Treasury has found the disaggregation of these entities difficult to implement and has granted a series of one-year reprieves from the repeal of the pre-1984 rule.[21]

When the new dragnet proviso was added in 1978 to cover all other business and income-producing activities, Congress did not undertake to divide the multifarious activities covered by it into separate activities. Instead, the Treasury was authorized to prescibe regulations for the segregation or aggregation of these newly covered activities[22] and to take "tax shelter characteristics" into account in presciibing the necessary rules:

> Tax shelter characteristics which may be taken into account in the regulations include the presence of accelerated deductions, mismatching of income and deductions, substantial nonrecourse financing, novel financing techniques which do not conform to standard commercial practices, property whose value is subject to substantial uncertainty, and the marketing of the activity to prospective investors as a tax shelter. In the absence of the regulations permitting or requiring aggregation, it is anticipated that each investment which is not part of a trade or business will be treated as a separate activity, and separate investments will not be aggregated.[23]

The 1978 legislation contains two safe harbors, both found in §465(c)(3)(B). First, all activities covered by the dragnet proviso that constitute a trade or business are treated as a single activity if the taxpayer actively participates in the management of the business. Second, activities of a partnership or S corporation, if reached only by the dragnet proviso, must be similarly aggregated if 65 percent or more of the losses is allocable to persons actively participating in the management of the business. Among the hallmarks of "active participation" in management are participation in operation or management decisions, performance of services, and hiring and discharging employees; conversely, noninvolvement in management and operations, authority to discharge only the manager of the enterprise, and use of an independent contractor as the manager tend to establish a lack of active participation.[24] Since the aggregation rules embrace activities only if they constitute "a" trade or business, they do not allow the amalgamation of two or more separate businesses, even if the taxpayer actively manages

---

[21] Reg. §1.465-1T (pre-1984 rule applies for 1984); Ann. 87-26, 1987-15 IRB 39 (same for 1985 and 1986). The Treasury's action flatly contradicts the statute, but will presumably be given effect for lack of anyone with standing to complain.

[22] IRC §465(c)(3)(C).

[23] H.R. Rep. No. 1445, supra note 2, at 244.

[24] Id. at 243.

them both.[25]

4. *Excluded activities.* Sections 465(c)(4) and (7) exclude closely held corporations from the application of the at risk limitation with respect to many active businesses. Also, for all taxpayers, the limitation is inapplicable to real property (other than mineral property) placed in service by the taxpayer before 1987.

The §465(c)(4) exemption applies to active equipment leasing operations of some corporations. To qualify, a corporation must be a C corporation and must be "actively engaged in equipment leasing." The latter requirement is met only if at least 50 percent of the corporation's gross receipts for the taxable year come from the leasing of equipment and the purchasing, servicing, and selling of equipment held for lease. The equipment must be section 1245 property, and may not be a sound recording or other "tangible or intangible assets associated with literary, artistic, or musical properties."

The 50 percent test of §465(c)(4) is usually applied to a controlled group of corporations by aggregating the gross receipts of all members of the group, and therefore cannot usually be satisfied by a leasing subsidiary of a controlled group engaged primarily in other activities. The §465(c)(4) exemption, however, is allowed for a "qualified leasing group," defined as one or more members of a controlled group of corporations which members, in the aggregate, (1) have gross receipts from leasing during the taxable year that amount to at least $1 million and make up at least 80 percent of their gross receipts, (2) have at least three employees engaged substantially full-time in activities of the leasing business, and (3) engage in at least five leasing transactions during the year.

The idea of exempting active businesses from the at risk limitation was expanded in 1984 with the enactment of §465(c)(7), which makes the limitation inapplicable to many active businesses of C corporations other than equipment leasing. It exempts any loss of a "qualifying business," defined as an "active business" that meets the following three tests. First, at least one management employee must be employed full-time in the business during all of the taxable year (or if the taxable year consists of less than 12 months, during all of the 12-month period ending with the taxable year). Second, continuously throughout this period, at least three employees (exclusive of any employee who owns more than 5 percent of the corporation's stock) must work full-time in the business. Third, business deductions (not including interest, taxes, and depreciation) must exceed 15 percent of gross income for the taxable year. An equipment leasing business may not benefit

---

[25] For the concept of a separate business, see §355(b) (discussed infra ¶94.1.4), which is relevant although not necessarily controlling in the application of §465(c)(3)(B).

from this rule, even if all of the three tests are met. Personal service corporations and personal holding companies are also ineligible. If a corporation is a partner of a partnership, however, the rule may apply to the corporation's distributive share of the active business income of the partnership.

When the dragnet proviso of §465(c)(3) was enacted in 1978, Congress excepted the holding of real property (other than mineral property) from its reach. This exemption has been repealed for losses from property placed in service after 1986,[26] but the application of the at risk rules to this property is still softened by rules, described below, defining the amount at risk in a real property investment to include some nonrecourse debt.[27] When the exemption applies, personal property and services incidental to living accommodations (but not meals or nursing care)[28] are treated as part of the activity of holding the underlying real property. The ownership and operation of a hotel, for example, can be covered by the exemption. However, the exemption does not apply to real property used in the five activities listed in §465(c)(1) (farming, leasing section 1245 property, etc.); such property is instead treated as part of the specified activity subject to the at risk limitation.

The real property exemption is a one-way street. Exempted real property losses may be applied freely against the taxpayer's income from other activities, but losses from activities covered by §465 may be applied against real property income only to the extent the taxpayer is at risk in the loss activity.

¶25.10.3 Losses Subject to At Risk Limitation

Section 465 permits deductions incurred in an activity to be applied freely against the income generated by that activity, and intervenes only when a loss incurred in a covered activity would otherwise reduce income from other sources. The term "loss" is defined for this purpose by §465(d) as the excess of (1) the deductions allowable for the taxable year that are allocable to a covered activity over (2) the income received or accrued by the taxpayer from the activity during the same taxable year. In other words, the "section 465(d) loss," to use the terminology of the proposed regula-

---

[26] If an interest in an S corporation, partnership, or other pass-thru entity is acquired after 1986, the repeal applies to the taxpayer's share of the entity's real property losses even if the entity was organized before 1987 or holds real property that it placed in service before 1987. Pub. L. No. 99-514, §503(c)(2), 100 Stat. 2085 (1986).

[27] See infra ¶25.10.4.

[28] For the allocation of income and deductions if separable services are supplied, such as meals and health care, see H.R. Rep. No. 1445, supra note 2, at 244.

tions,[29] is the net loss from the covered activity.

If part or all of a taxpayer's loss from a covered activity is disallowed because of the at risk limitation, the unallowable amount is carried forward under §465(a)(2) to the next taxable year for application against the income (if any) from the loss activity and, if the taxpayer's at risk investment increases, against income from other activities. Section 465(a)(2) only allows a loss to be used only in the immediately succeeding year, but it then melds together with current deductions, which might create another carryover to the following year. The disallowed amount, in other words, carries forward indefinitely until it is allowed or the activity terminates.[30]

The income and deductions allocable to an activity may consist of a mixture of specially treated items, such as tax preference items and long-term and short-term capital losses. The proposed regulations prescribe ordering rules that allocate these items between the loss year and the later years to which disallowed losses are carried and that determine the order in which items carried forward from two or more loss years are to be applied.[31]

¶25.10.4 Computation of At Risk Amount

The heart of §465 — or, from the taxpayer's perspective, its fist — is §465(b), prescribing the amount that taxpayers have "at risk" in covered activities, since this limits the amount of loss allocable to a covered activity that may offset income from other sources. Section 465(b) is meant to provide a measure of the taxpayer's economic exposure to losses of an activity subject to §465. The amount at risk in an activity can only be computed after a threshold determination has been made of the boundaries of the "activity" in question.[32] In a particular case, the amount at risk consists of one or more of the following:

1. *Contributions of money and property.* Under §465(b)(1)(A), the taxpayer is at risk to the extent of the money and property contributed to the activity, including the cost of acquiring an interest therein.[33] Property is taken into account in the amount of its adjusted basis, regardless of its market value. Any excess of the property's fair market value over its basis is disregarded because it is not part of the taxpayer's investment in the property, and has not been taken into income. On the other hand, because high-

---

[29] Prop. Reg. §1.465-11(a).

[30] Prop. Reg. §1.465-2(b); see also H.R. Rep. No. 1445, supra note 2, at 241.

[31] Prop. Reg. §1.465-38.

[32] See supra ¶25.10.2.

[33] See Prop. Reg. §1.465-22(d) (purchase price of interest in activity treated as contribution). For contributions of encumbered property, see Prop. Reg. §1.465-23(a)(2).

basis property with a low market value is taken into account at the higher figure, the unrealized loss can serve as a foundation for deductions from ordinary income, even if a sale of the property would produce a capital loss.

2. *Borrowed amounts.* Usually, the taxpayer is at risk for amounts borrowed "for use in the activity" in two situations.[34] First, such a borrowing is included to the extent of the taxpayer's personal liability for repayment. Second, in the absence of personal liability, a debt is included in the at risk amount to the extent of the value of property that secures it if the property is neither used in this activity nor "directly or indirectly financed by indebtedness which is secured by property" used in the activity. A nonrecourse loan whose proceeds are used to buy property for a §465 activity might be included in the at risk amount, for example, if the loan is secured by the taxpayer's personal residence, but not if it is secured by the property purchased with the loan proceeds or other property used in the activity. Further, giving the mortgage on the residence does not bring the debt into the at risk amount if, for example, property of the §465 activity is used as security for a second loan whose proceeds are used to pay off the previous mortgage indebtedness on the residence.

The foregoing rules have been the subject of several recent cases involving the issue of when a limited partner is at risk on borrowings of his partnership. In one of these cases, the Tax Court stated:

> The relevant question is who, if anyone, will ultimately be obligated to pay the partnership's . . . obligations if the partnership is unable to do so. It is not relevant that the partnership may be able to do so. The scenario that controls is the worst-case scenario, not the best case. . . . The critical inquiry should be who is the obligor of last resort, and in determining who has the ultimate economic responsibility for the loan, the substance of the transaction controls.[35]

Under this test, the court has held that a limited partner's guarantee of partnership debt usually does not put the partner at risk because he has a right to be indemnified by the primary obligor, the partnership, for any amounts paid under the guarantee.[36] The court acknowledged that "a guarantor's right of subrogation against the primary obligor is a mere formalism" where the primary obligor (partnership) has no substantial assets apart from the property securing the guaranteed liability.[37] If the obligation is well secured, however, "the likelihood of [the guarantors'] having to make good

---

[34] For rules treating an investor in real property as being at risk on some nonrecourse indebtedness, see infra text accompanying notes 46–55.

[35] Melvin v. CIR, 88 TC 63, 75 (1987).

[36] Peters v. CIR, 89 TC 423 (1988); Brand v. CIR, 81 TC 821 (1983).

[37] Peters v. CIR, supra note 36, at 443.

under their personal guarantees is remote."[38] If the guarantee is a mere formalism, in other words, the right of subrogation prevents the guarantor from being at risk even if this right is also a mere formalism. If a guarantee is a meaningful assumption of liability, in contrast, the guaranteeing partner is at risk unless the right of subrogation is a realistic shield against ultimate liability.[39]

Also, if a limited partner is obligated to contribute to the partnership in the future, he is at risk to the extent this obligation makes the partner the person ultimately liable for partnership debt. Such ultimate liability might be established, for example, by a pledge of the partner's obligation to a lender as security.[40] In Pritchett v. CIR, limited partners were held to be at risk on a partnership obligation where, although in form only the general partner was personally liable, the general partner had an unconditional right to require additional contributions from limited partners to cover their shares.[41] The limited partners were found to be presently at risk although the obligation was payable first from income generated by the property securing it and payment from other sources (including additional contributions from the partners) could only be required when the obligation matured after 15 years.

The ultimate-liability test also applies to investors other than limited partners.[42] Within or outside the partnership context, however, a taxpayer is

---

[38] Id.

[39] Melvin v. CIR, supra note 35; Abramson v. CIR, 86 TC 360 (1986) (where each partner guaranteed ratable share of partnership's nonrecourse debt, each was at risk for amount guaranteed because his "liability . . . ran directly to the 'obligee' and . . . was personal").

[40] Melvin v. CIR, supra note 35, at 75 (declining to follow provision of proposed regulations that partner's obligation to contribute does not increase amount at risk until obligation becomes payable).

[41] Pritchett v. CIR, 827 F2d 644 (9th Cir. 1987).

[42] See Larsen v. CIR, 89 TC 1229 (1987) (taxpayer, buyer-lessor in sale-lease-back transaction, purportedly "assumed" debt incurred by seller-lessee in its purchase of the property, but assumed amount not treated as part of taxpayer's purchase price; held, purported assumption is in essence a guarantee, not included in taxpayer's amount at risk); Bennion v. CIR, 88 TC 684 (1987) (joint venture assumed debt on purchase of property from person who had assumed debt under similar circumstances; held, joint venture at risk because assumption made it ultimately liable on default); Baldwin v. US, 88-1 USTC ¶9151 (SD Cal. 1987) (not officially reported) (in sale-leaseback transaction, rents to be paid by seller-lessee coincided in amount and time with payments by buyer-lessor on recourse note given in payment of purchase price; held, buyer-lessor at risk because payments on note would continue to be payable even if seller-lessee were discharged of rental obligation in bankruptcy; "relevant question . . . is who will ultimately be obligated to pay the debt in the worst-case scenario, . . . the inquiry is not the degree of risk . . . but rather the extent to which [taxpayers] were at risk under any circumstance").

not at risk, notwithstanding an unambiguous statement of personal liability in the loan documents, if the "alleged loan transactions [have] no economic substance and [are] entered into solely in an attempt to avoid the at risk rules."[43]

When the ultimate-liability test is met, the taxpayer is at risk in the dollar amount he could be required to pay. No reduction to present value is required, even if the liability is payable in the future and the taxpayer assumes responsibility for principal, but not interest, on the debt.[44]

Additional therapeutic limits on the amount of borrowed funds taken into account are imposed by §465(b)(3), disqualifying amounts borrowed from anyone with an interest in the activity (other than as a creditor) or from anyone who is related to a person (other than the taxpayer) who has such an interest.[45] For example, amounts borrowed by a limited partner from the general partner in the same partnership are excluded from the at risk computation by virtue of these limitations, even if the taxpayer is personally liable on the indebtedness.

3. *Nonrecourse debt on real property.* Under §465(b)(6), owners of real property are treated as being at risk with respect to some nonrecourse debt.[46] This treatment applies to debt "with respect to which no person is personally liable for repayment" if the liability is not "convertible debt,"[47] and the following three requirements are met:

---

[43] Capek v. CIR, 86 TC 14 (1986).

[44] Follender v. CIR, 89 TC 943 (1987).

[45] This restriction applies to all activities listed in §465(c)(1), but applies to activities covered by the 1978 dragnet proviso of §465(c)(3) only to the extent prescribed by regulations. IRC §465(c)(3)(D). See H.R. Rep. No. 1445, supra note 2, at 245 (regulations may apply restrictions to debts with tax shelter characteristics, such as loans on terms not applicable to loans from unrelated lenders and arrangements to shift from recourse to nonrecourse status in later years). See also Waddell v. CIR, 86 TC 848 (1986), aff'd, 841 F2d 264 (9th Cir. 1988) (where payments under note are contingent on profits, holder of note has an interest in the activity other than as creditor); Rev. Rul. 80-327, 1980-2 CB 23 (limited partner not at risk as to portion of price paid for partnership interest that was borrowed from general partner). But see Larsen v. CIR, supra note 42 (taxpayer, buyer-lessor in sale-leaseback transaction, made agreement with seller-lessee (who subleased to user of property) under which seller-lessee would sell or release property as taxpayer's agent on expiration of sublease and would receive a portion of the profits from this transaction; held, seller-lessee did not have interest other than as creditor).

For taxable years beginning before 1984, this restriction also applies to amounts borrowed from persons related to the taxpayer.

[46] See generally NY State Bar Association Section of Taxation, Report on Qualified Nonrecourse Financing, 39 Tax Notes 1111 (1988).

[47] IRC §465(b)(6)(B)(iv).

First, the debt must be a borrowing "with respect to the activity of holding real property," and must be secured by "real property used in such activity."[48] The activity of holding real property includes "the holding of personal property and the providing of services which are incidental to making real property available as living accommodations."[49] If money is borrowed to finance the purchase or construction of an apartment building and incidental personal property and to provide working capital for the management of the building, for example, the rule may apply to all of the liability, not just the portion incurred in the purchase of the building. Borrowings to finance personal property and working capital with respect to nonresidential real property, in contrast, are apparently not covered by the rule. The rule never applies, further, to debt relating to "mineral property."[50]

Second, the lender must be an unrelated person or a government agency, or the borrowing must be governmentally guaranteed.[51] If the borrowing is neither made nor guaranteed by a government, the lender must usually be a person who is "actively and regularly engaged in the business of lending money." Also, this lender may not be related to the taxpayer, and may not be (1) a person from whom the taxpayer acquired his interest in the property, (2) a person who received a fee in connection with the taxpayer's acquisition of his interest, or (3) a person related to a person who sold the taxpayer his interest or received a fee in that sale.[52] Loans from a promoter of a real estate tax shelter or from an entity related to the promoter, for example, cannot qualify. Where a loan would qualify, but for the fact that the lender is related to the taxpayer, the related-lender prohibition is waived if "the financing from the related person is commercially reasonable and on substantially the same terms as loans involving unrelated persons."[53]

When these requirements are met, a taxpayer is at risk "with respect to the taxpayer's share" of the debt.[54] If the taxpayer directly owns the property or an undivided interest in it, his share is 100 percent of the debt or a fraction of the debt corresponding to the taxpayer's fractional interest in the property. If the property is held by an S corporation in which the taxpayer is a shareholder, the taxpayer has no share of the liability because corporate debt is not reflected in the adjusted basis or other tax characteristic of the

---

[48] IRC §§465(b)(6)(A), (B)(i).
[49] IRC §465(b)(6)(E)(i).
[50] IRC §465(b)(6)(E)(ii).
[51] IRC §465(b)(6)(B)(ii).
[52] IRC §§46(c)(8)(D)(iv); 465(b)(6)(B)(ii), (D)(i).
[53] IRC §465(b)(6)(D)(ii).
[54] IRC §465(b)(6)(A).

shareholder's stock. If the taxpayer is a partner in a partnership that holds real property financed by qualifying nonrecourse debt, the taxpayer's share of the debt for this purpose equals the share assigned to him under §752.[55]

4. *Protection against loss.* Even if an amount otherwise qualifies for inclusion in the taxpayer's at risk investment, it is disqualified by §465(b)(4) if the taxpayer is protected against loss by nonrecourse financing, guaranties, stop loss agreements, or similar arrangements. Although this overriding disqualification is aimed primarily at funds borrowed on a nonrecourse basis, it applies equally to cash and property contributed by the taxpayer to the activity if the taxpayer is protected against loss by a repurchase agreement or other arrangement. Under the proposed regulations, protection against loss includes a partner's right to contributions from other partners, and personal liabilities dependent on the occurrence of a contingency create a risk only if the contingency is so likely to occur that the taxpayer is not "effectively protected against loss." However, insurance against casualties or tort liabilities does not ordinarily constitute protection against loss within the meaning of §465(b)(4).[56] Under the proposed regulations, personal liabilities that will become nonrecourse obligations on the occurrence of a specified event or on the lapse of time may be included in the amount at risk if they are motivated primarily by business rather than tax considerations and are consistent with normal commercial practice.[57] Such arrangements, however, are closely scrutinized, and temporary liability is often found to be lacking in substance.[58]

---

[55] IRC §465(b)(6)(C). See infra ¶85.3.5 for §752.

[56] Prop. Reg. §§1.465-6(b), (c). For examples of stop loss arrangements, see Cooper v. CIR, 88 TC 84 (1987) (right to resell equipment to promoter of equipment deal for amount equal to balance due on debt); Capek v. CIR, 86 TC 14 (1986) (minimum entitlements under investment arrangement equal to debt payments); Rev. Rul. 83-133, 1983-2 CB 15 (provision allowing investor to be relieved of all liability on recourse note by withdrawing from project and transferring property securing note to third party); Rev. Rul. 78-413, 1978-2 CB 167 (cross-indemnification by investors in movie film tax shelter). But see Gefen v. CIR, 87 TC 1471, 1503 (1986) (limited partner who assumed pro rata share of partnership's recourse debt was not protected against loss by lease of partnership property to "a strong credit risk" or by insurance policy that guaranteed a minimum resale price on conclusion of lease). See generally Weisner, supra note 1, at 20–25.

[57] Prop. Reg. §1.465-5.

[58] Porreca v. CIR, 86 TC 821 (1986) (taxpayer protected against loss where notes were purportedly with recourse during specified period, but no substantial payments required during that period and notes could be made nonrecourse by small payment at end of period); Rev. Rul. 82-225, 1982-2 CB 100 (recourse obligation that could be converted to nonrecourse under certain conditions treated as nonre-

Nonrecourse financing is disqualified by §465(b)(4) even if it is so amply covered by the value of the pledged property that there is little or no likelihood of default. On the other hand, if the taxpayer is personally obligated to repay borrowed funds, they can probably be included in the at risk amount even if the taxpayer is head over heels in debt and spends his income as fast as it is earned (or faster), so that the creditor, for practical purposes, must look solely to the encumbered property for repayment. It is possible, however, that vague warnings in the proposed regulations against attempts to avoid the limitations of §465 presage an attempt by the IRS to disregard ostensible personal liabilities that are grossly excessive in amount.[59]

5. *Changes in at risk amount.* Section 465(b)(5) provides that losses incurred in a covered activity and deducted from another activity's income reduce the taxpayer's at risk amount for later years. This provision is obviously required to prevent the same at risk amount from being used year after year, but it is only one element in a running account required to make the at risk concept work properly. The proposed regulations fill in the aching gap left by the statutory language with a network of accounting rules, including provisions for increasing the at risk amount by the net income from the activity and for decreasing the amount by cash withdrawals.[60]

The increases and decreases in the at risk amount required by these and other transactions are comparable to adjustments in the basis of a partner's interest in a partnership, which, like the at risk amount, imposes a limit on the deduction of the partner's share of the partnership's losses.[61] Another point of resemblance is that a running account of the taxpayer's at risk amount is required for each covered activity, just as a separately computed basis is necessary for each partnership interest if a taxpayer is a member of two or more firms.

---

course because conditions had no substantial economic relationship to activity); Rev. Rul. 82-123, 1982-1 CB 82 (note not included in amount at risk where borrower could elect to change from recourse to nonrecourse if IRS Appellate Division should determine that any tax benefit set out in prospectus was unavailable); Rev. Rul. 81-283, 1981-2 CB 115 (recourse loan that debtor could change to nonrecourse at end of secured property's useful life by making specified payment only included in at risk investment to extent of payment required to convert to nonrecourse).

[59] See Prop. Reg. §1.465-1 (substance prevails over form), §1.465-4(a) (pattern of conduct to avoid §465).

[60] See, e.g., Prop. Reg. §1.465-22(b) (withdrawal of money), §1.465-22(c) (income and loss), §1.465-23(a)(2)(ii) (reduction of encumbrances on property contributed to activity), §1.465-24(b) (repayment of debt for which taxpayer personally liable), §1.465-25(a)(2) (repayment of nonrecourse debt).

[61] See infra ¶86.4.

¶25.10.5 Recapture of Losses if At Risk Amount Drops Below Zero

Although the taxpayer's at risk amount limits the extent to which losses incurred in a covered activity may be applied against income from other activities, it is possible for the amount to drop below zero. For example, if a taxpayer purchases an interest in an activity with $1,000 of borrowed funds for which he is personally liable and deducts $250 of depreciation with respect to the activity, his at risk amount is $750 ($1,000 minus $250). If, in the following year, he receives a distribution of $900 from the activity or if $900 of the debt is converted to a nonrecourse obligation or protected against loss by a guaranty, his at risk amount is minus $150 ($750 minus $900).

Under §465(e), a taxpayer whose at risk amount falls below zero must recognize gross income equal to the deficit for the year in which it arises. It is then treated as a deduction allocable to the activity, deductible in subsequent years subject to the at risk limitations applicable to those years. Negative at risk amounts are subject to this treatment only to the extent of the excess of (1) losses from the activity allowed as deductions in prior taxable years beginning after December 31, 1978 over (2) amounts includable in gross income with respect to the activity. When these rules apply, the effect is that losses deducted in a prior year are recaptured by including an equal amount in gross income for the current year, but the recaptured loss is then added to the disallowed losses being carried forward for eventual deduction when the activity produces income or the at risk amount is increased. The application of the rules to the example given in the preceding paragraph is shown in Example 25-1.

Example 25-1

Recapture of Losses When at Risk Amount Is Less Than Zero

1. Initial at risk amount (funds borrowed with personal liability)	$1,000
2. Less: Cash received (or reduction in personal liability)	900
3. Net at risk amount	$ 100
4. Loss allowed (year 1)	$ 250
5. Less: Amount recaptured (year 2)	150
6. Net loss allowed (two-year period)	$ 100
7. Net amount disallowed (carried forward to later years)	$ 150

¶25.11 NET OPERATING LOSS CARRYBACKS AND CARRYOVERS

¶25.11.1 Introductory

Under §172, net operating losses are ordinarily carried back to the three taxable years before the loss year and forward to the 15 succeeding years, allowing the expenses of earning income to be taken into account over a 19-year cycle.[1] When carried back, a net operating loss (NOL) reduces the taxable income of the carryback year, resulting in a recomputation of the tax liability and a refund or credit of the excess amount paid. Carryovers produce a similar reduction in the taxable income of later years, but they directly reduce the tax due when the return is filed, so that a refund or credit is not usually necessary.

The statutory predecessor of §172 entered the tax law in 1918, primarily to permit losses incurred in converting from war production to peacetime activities to be applied against the profits realized in either the first preceding or the first succeeding year.[2] With modifications, this innovation was retained until 1933, when it was repealed to protect the Treasury against a loss of revenues from unprecedented business losses during the Depression.[3] In 1939, however, the carryover device was restored,[4] and with revisions it seems to have become a permanent structural feature of the tax law.

In 1976, the Supreme Court, expanding on an earlier statement, summarized the objectives of the NOL deduction as follows:

---

[1] For different carryback and carryover periods prescribed for special classes of taxpayers and losses, see infra ¶25.11.3. For a summary of the legislative history of the net operating loss deduction, see US v. Foster Lumber Co., 429 US 32 (1976). For economic and policy issues, see U.S. Dep't of Treasury & Joint Comm. on Internal Revenue Tax'n, 80th Cong., 1st Sess., Business Loss Offsets (1947); Barlev & Levy, Loss Carryback and Carryover Provisions: Effectiveness and Economic Implications, 28 Nat'l Tax J. 173 (1975); Capisano & Romano, Recouping Losses: The Case for Full Loss Offsets, 76 Nw. U.L. Rev. 709 (1981) (suggesting replacement of carrybacks and carryovers of NOLs with refundable credit in amount of tax that would have been payable on earnings equal to NOL).

[2] Revenue Act of 1918, Pub. L. No. 254, §204, 40 Stat. 1057, 1060 (1919); S. Rep. No. 617, 65th Cong., 3d Sess. (1918), reprinted in 1939-1 (Part 2) CB 117, 121–22 (without carryover provisions, law "does not adequately recognize the exigencies of business and, under our present [wartime] high rates of taxation, may often result in grave injustice").

[3] National Industrial Recovery Act of 1933, Pub. L. No. 67, §218(a), 48 Stat. 195, 209.

[4] Revenue Act of 1938, Pub. L. No. 554, §26(c), 52 Stat. 447, 467. The NOL rules were broadened the next year. Revenue Act of 1939, Pub. L. No. 155, §211(b), 53 Stat. 862, 867.

In [Libson Shops v. Koehler, 353 US 382, 386 (1957),] the Court said that the net operating loss carryover and carryback provisions "were enacted to ameliorate the unduly drastic consequences of taxing income strictly on an annual basis. They were designed to permit a taxpayer to set off its lean years against its lush years, and to strike something like an average taxable income computed over a period longer than one year."

There were, in fact, several policy considerations behind the decision to allow averaging of income over a number of years. Ameliorating the timing consequences of the annual accounting period makes it possible for shareholders in companies with fluctuating as opposed to stable incomes to receive more nearly equal tax treatment. Without loss offsets, a firm experiencing losses in some periods would not be able to deduct all the expenses of earning income. The consequence would be a tax on capital, borne by shareholders who would pay higher taxes on net income than owners of businesses with stable income. Congress also sought through allowance of loss carryovers to stimulate enterprise and investment, particularly in new businesses or risky ventures where early losses can be carried forward to future more prosperous years.[5]

Three aspects of §172 are worthy of preliminary note. First, in the case of individuals, §172 applies primarily to losses incurred in business, as distinguished from losses attributable to investments and to unused itemized deductions and personal and dependency exemptions.[6] Second, §172 oscillates between a "taxable income" and an "economic income" approach in computing losses. For example, a business loss qualifies for carryover even though the taxpayer received tax-exempt income in the loss year exceeding the business loss; in this respect, the standards that apply in determining taxable income are also used in computing NOLs. On the other hand, net capital gains are taken into account in full, without regard to the deduction formerly allowed by §1202, in determining whether the taxpayer sustained a loss; in this respect, §172 adopts an economic income approach.[7] Third, net capital losses are not subject to §172, but are instead governed by a separate carryover scheme prescribed by §1212.[8]

---

[5] US v. Foster Lumber Co., supra note 1, at 42.

[6] IRC §172(d)(4), discussed infra ¶25.11.2.

[7] Three other adjustments reflecting an economic income approach—for tax-exempt interest, the excess of percentage over cost depletion, and the untaxed portion of dividends received by corporations—were eliminated in 1954. See S. Rep. No. 1622, 83d Cong., 2d Sess. 31–32 (1954).

[8] For IRC §1212, see infra ¶50.2.5 (individuals), ¶50.3.2 (corporations).

The major steps in the computation of a NOL deduction, described in detail below, are:

1. Computation of the amount of the NOL incurred in the loss year.[9]
2. Determination of the carryback and carryover years to which the NOL is carried.[10]
3. Recomputation of the tax liability for the earliest year to which the NOL is carried.[11]
4. If the NOL is not fully used in the earliest year to which it is carried, computation of the amount remaining for use in the next year.[12]
5. Allocation of the NOL to the proper person in the case of such events as marriage, divorce, death, and corporate reorganizations and to such entities as trusts, estates, partnerships, and S corporations.[13]

¶25.11.2   Computation of Net Operating Loss

Section 172(c) defines net operating loss as the excess of the deductions allowed by the income tax provisions of the Code over the taxpayer's gross income, subject to the modifications prescribed by §172(d). Because §172(d) distinguishes corporations from other taxpayers in several respects, these two groups are discussed separately below.

All taxpayers, however, are subject to §172(d)(1), providing that, in computing the NOL for a given year, no NOL from another year shall be allowed. This is an essential technical principle, whose function can be illustrated by assuming that a corporation organized in 1988 sustains business losses of $100,000 each in 1988 and 1989. If its NOL for 1989 included both the current loss and the loss carried forward from 1988, the 1988 loss would expire not in 2003, its normal expiration date, but in 2004, the last year to which 1989's losses may be carried. If 1990 were also a loss year, the 1988 and 1989 losses would both get another year's lease on life. To ensure that each year's losses are carried forward for the prescribed period and no longer, §172(d)(1) provides that NOLs carried over from other years are disregarded in determining whether the taxpayer has a NOL for the current year.

1. *Corporate taxpayers.* For corporations, the only other significant modification is prescribed by §172(d)(5), providing that the deduction for

---

[9] Infra ¶25.11.2.
[10] Infra ¶25.11.3.
[11] Infra ¶25.11.4.
[12] Infra ¶25.11.5.
[13] Infra ¶25.11.6.

dividends received shall be computed without regard to §246(b), which limits a corporation's deductions for dividends received to 80 or 70 percent (depending on whether the taxpayer owns 20 percent or more of the payor's stock) of taxable income, determined before the deductions for dividends received and NOLs.[14] The removal of this limit means that a corporation can sustain a NOL even if it reports taxable income, provided there would have been a NOL if the dividends-received deduction had not been limited by §246(b). This phenomenon is illustrated by Example 25-2, which assumes (1) gross income of $400,000 in the loss year, $100,000 of which consists of dividends from corporations in which the taxpayer's interest is less than 20 percent, and (2) business deductions of $375,000.

Example 25-2

Computation of Corporate Taxpayer's NOL

	Before Modification	*After Modification*
1. Business deductions	$375,000	$375,000
2. Plus: Deduction for dividends received	17,500*	70,000**
3. Total deductions	$392,500	$445,000
4. Less: Gross income	400,000	400,000
5. Excess of deductions over gross income (NOL)	–0–	$ 45,000

---

*Under §246(b), 70 percent of the lower of dividends received ($100,000) or taxable income before deduction for dividends received ($25,000).

**Under §§172(d)(5) and 243(a), 70 percent of dividends received.

Until repealed for taxable years beginning after December 31, 1979, modifications were also made for partially tax-exempt interest and for Western Hemisphere Trade Corporations, both of which are now extinct creatures.[15]

2. *Other taxpayers.* In determining whether individuals and other noncorporate taxpayers sustained a net operating loss, §172(d) prescribes more elaborate rules than for corporations, primarily to prevent investment expenses, itemized personal deductions, and personal and dependency exemptions from being carried from one year to another.

---

[14] For the dividends received deduction, see infra ¶90.2.3.

[15] IRC §172(d)(5) (before amendment in 1980). For partially tax-exempt interest, see supra ¶15.1; for Western Hemisphere Trade Corporations, see infra ¶68.1.

First, personal and dependency exemptions are disregarded in determining whether noncorporate taxpayers have an excess of deductions over gross income.[16] Second, for taxable years before 1987, when §1202 allows a deduction for 60 percent of net capital gain, this deduction is disregarded in computing the NOL.[17]

Third, deductions not attributable to the taxpayer's trade or business are allowed only to the extent of nonbusiness gross income.[18] If these items exceed the taxpayer's nonbusiness gross income, the excess may not create or increase a NOL and, hence, may not be used to reduce taxable income in other years.

In drawing the line between trade or business deductions and other deductions, the term "trade or business" has its conventional meaning,[19] except that (1) casualty losses in excess of the nondeductible floor are treated as business deductions, even when involving property devoted to personal use, such as the taxpayer's residence or pleasure car;[20] (2) gains and losses from the sale or other disposition of real property and depreciable property are treated as business gains and losses if the property is used in the taxpayer's trade or business;[21] (3) wages and salaries are treated as business income, so deductions allocable thereto constitute business deductions;[22] and (4) the deduction allowed to a partner or sole proprietor for contributions on his own behalf to a qualified pension or profit sharing plan is treated as a nonbusiness deduction.[23]

Also, the standard deduction (for taxable years after 1986) or the zero bracket amount (ZBA) (for taxable years before 1987) is also treated as a nonbusiness deduction if the taxpayer does not elect to itemize deductions.[24] This permits nonitemizers to reduce nonbusiness income by the standard

---

[16] IRC §172(d)(3). This modification also covers the analogous exemptions allowed to trusts and estates by §642(b).

[17] IRC §172(d)(2)(B) (before amendment in 1986). For §1202, see infra ¶50.2.2.

[18] IRC §172(d)(4). For the constitutionality of this restriction, see Mannette v. CIR, 69 TC 990 (1978), and cases therein cited.

[19] See supra ¶¶20.1.2, 20.5.1. See also infra ¶33.6 (nonbusiness debts).

[20] IRC §172(d)(4)(C). For casualty losses, see infra ¶34.1.

[21] IRC §172(d)(4)(A). Before the enactment of this provision in 1954, the courts were divided on whether losses on the sale of business assets, such as a farm or factory, were business losses if the taxpayer did not sell property of this type on a regular basis. See Goble v. CIR, 23 TC 593 (1954) (extensive discussion, with citations).

[22] See Reg. §1.172-3(a)(3).

[23] IRC §172(d)(4)(D). For this deduction, see infra ¶62.2.6.

[24] Because the ZBA was not a deduction for other purposes, its treatment as such under §172 was made explicit in the statutes. IRC §172(d)(8) (before repeal in 1986). The standard deduction is not mentioned in §172, but falls under §172(d)(4) because it is a deduction and is not attributable to the taxpayer's trade or business. For the standard deduction and ZBA, see infra ¶30.5.

deduction or ZBA, in the same way that itemizers can reduce nonbusiness income by their itemized deductions. For both classes of taxpayers, this method of marshaling nonbusiness deductions against nonbusiness income conserves business deductions for the NOL.

The limit imposed by §172(d)(4) requires distinctions to be drawn between some items that are treated alike for most other tax purposes. For example, income items and capital gains are ordinarily includable in gross income whether derived from the taxpayer's business, investments, or hobbies, but those attributable to the taxpayer's business must be segregated in applying §172(d)(4). Similarly, expenses generated by the taxpayer's profit-oriented activities are ordinarily deductible under either §162 (business expenses) or §212 (expenses of property held for the production of income), but §172(d)(4) differentiates between expenses allowed by §162 and those allowed by §212.

In applying §172(d)(4), it can be advantageous for a taxpayer to assign a borderline activity, such as a weekend farm, to the nonbusiness side of the boundary line if it generates a profit, since the income may then be reduced by nonbusiness deductions (including itemized personal deductions), thus increasing the likelihood that the taxpayer's business deductions will create a NOL. On the other hand, if the activity operates at a loss, business status is preferable, since the deductions may then create or increase a NOL.[25] For this reason, if the profitability of an activity of this type fluctuates widely,

---

[25] For unsuccessful attempts to classify receipts as nonbusiness income, see Roberts v. CIR, 258 F2d 634 (5th Cir. 1958) (salaries and director's fees); Batzell v. CIR, 266 F2d 371 (4th Cir. 1959) (salary received by lawyer for temporary government service during Korean War). But see Rev. Rul. 66-327, 1966-2 CB 357 (shareholder-employee's pro rata share of S corporation's income; held, not business income where services were compensated by reasonable salary).

For the status of various expenses and losses, see Payte v. US, 626 F2d 400 (5th Cir. 1980), cert. denied, 450 US 995 (1981) (deduction for interest on debt incurred to purchase interest of deceased business partner not attributable to taxpayer's trade or business); Purvis v. CIR, 530 F2d 1332 (9th Cir. 1976) (taxpayer held investor rather than trader; losses subject to §172(d)(4) limitation); Alvarez v. US, 431 F2d 1261 (5th Cir. 1970), cert. denied, 401 US 913 (1971) (loss on Cuban expropriation of right to receive indemnification payments for rental property; held, nonbusiness deduction); Todd v. CIR, 77 TC 246 (1981), aff'd per curiam, 682 F2d 207 (9th Cir. 1982) (physician's loss on abandoning plans to construct apartment building not incurred in trade or business because taxpayer had not broken ground or rented any apartments and thus was not in trade or business of renting apartments); Mannette v. CIR, 69 TC 990 (1978) (embezzler's deduction for repayment of embezzled funds to victim is nonbusiness deduction); Mohr v. CIR, 45 TC 600 (1966) (loss relating to franchised automobile dealerships promoted by taxpayer; held, nonbusiness because taxpayer was an investor rather than dealer in franchises). But see Rev. Rul. 72-195, 1972-1 CB 95 (deductible moving expenses are business deductions); Rev. Rul. 70-40, 1970-1 CB 50 (state income taxes, interest on federal income taxes, and litigating expenses are business expenses where allocable to business income).

success in a litigated case for a particular year, whether achieved by the taxpayer or the IRS, can prove to be a Pyrrhic victory.

Capital gains and losses are another complicating factor in applying §172(d)(4) because nonbusiness capital losses may only be applied against nonbusiness capital gains, while business capital losses may be applied against both business and nonbusiness capital gains.[26] Net capital losses are excluded from NOLs by §172(d)(2), however, whether attributable to business or nonbusiness activities. This is not surprising, since §1212(b) permits noncorporate taxpayers to carry unused capital losses forward indefinitely.[27] It is less obvious, however, why investment expenses, such as interest, advisory fees, clerical expenses, and legal and accounting fees, may not create a NOL even if they exceed investment income.[28]

¶25.11.3 Years to Which Net Operating Losses Are Carried

Having computed the NOL for a loss year, the taxpayer must determine the year or years to which it may be carried. The basic principle, prescribed by §172(b)(1), is that an NOL is a "net operating loss carryback" to the three taxable years immediately preceding the year of the loss and a "net operating loss carryover" to the 15 immediately succeeding years. Because they require old returns to be exhumed and refunds to be claimed, carrybacks are more cumbersome than carryovers.

The standard 19-year cycle is modified by §172(b) for a few classes of taxpayers and losses. A bank, for example, is allowed a 10-year carryback and a 5-year carryover for NOLs attributable to bad debt losses incurred during a taxable year beginning during the period 1987 though 1993.[29] Also, any taxpayer is allowed a 10-year carryback (and the usual 15-year carryover) for an NOL attributable to product liability or "deferred statutory or tort liability."[30] Several other modifications have either expired or have very narrow applications.[31]

---

[26] Reg. §1.172-3(a)(2); Erfurth v. CIR, 77 TC 570 (1981) (regulation valid). See Crow v. CIR, 79 TC 541 (1982) (acq.) (determining loss on sales of two blocks of stock to be business and nonbusiness capital losses, respectively).

[27] For §1212(b), see infra ¶50.2.5.

[28] For §163(d), limiting the deduction of excess investment interest, see infra Ch. 48.

[29] IRC §172(b)(1)(L).

[30] IRC §§172(b)(1)(I), (J); 172(j), (k). For an explanation of the product liability rule, which covers losses that are likely to be large and sporadic, see Joint Comm. on Tax'n, 95th Cong., 2d Sess., General Explanation of the Revenue Act of 1978, at 232–34 (Comm. Print 1979).

[31] See IRC §172(b)(1)(D) (no carryback, 10 years forward for foreign expropriation losses or, in the case of Cuban expropriation losses, 20 years forward); §172(b)(1)(E) (no carryback and 15 years forward for real estate investment trusts

Taxpayers entitled to carry losses back may elect under §172(b)(3)(C) to relinquish the entire carryback period for an NOL sustained in any post-1975 taxable year, in which event the NOL is used only prospectively. This election, which must be made by the due date (including extensions) for filing the taxpayer's return for the year of the loss, is irrevocable for the year made, but does not affect NOLs sustained in other years.[32] The election was authorized by Congress in 1976 for the benefit of taxpayers with NOLs that would normally be carried back to years in which their tax liability was offset by investment and foreign tax credits.[33] In these circumstances, the carryback reduced or eliminated precredit tax, and hence the credits, but produced no actual tax savings. Although the retroactively unemployed credits could be carried forward under their own rules,[34] the applicable carryover period might well be shorter than the carryover period for the NOL. By electing to relinquish the NOL carryback period, therefore, the taxpayer keeps the previously claimed credits in force for the carryback years, while preserving the longer-lived NOL for use prospectively. The election might also appeal to taxpayers who want to avoid exhuming skeletons in their carryback years. In this situation, however, an election entails offsetting costs and risks by postponing the day when the NOL will produce a cash benefit and increasing the likelihood that it will expire before it can be used.

Whichever period is applicable, §172(b)(2) requires an NOL be carried first to the earliest permissible year, and any unabsorbed amount is then carried forward year by year in chronological order until the NOL is fully absorbed or expires. In general, any period for which a tax return is required counts as one of the years in the carryback or carryover period. For example, a short taxable year resulting from a change of the taxpayer's account-

---

(REITs)); §172(b)(1)(F) (10 years back, 5 years forward for banks and certain other financial institutions for the years 1976 through 1986); §172(b)(1)(G) (10 years back, 5 years forward for the years 1970 through 1986 for Banks for Cooperatives organized under the Farm Credit Act of 1933); §172(b)(1)(H) (10 years back, 5 years forward for the years 1981 through 1986 for the Federal National Mortgage Association and for the years 1985 and 1986 for the Federal Home Loan Mortgage Corporation—but only for losses other than mortgage disposition losses); §172(b)(1)(I) (before repeal in 1986) (no carryback, 10 years forward for General Stock Ownership Corporations); §172(b)(1)(M) (10 years back, 8 years forward for losses of thrift institutions for the years 1982 through 1985).

[32] The election must be exercised by an affirmative statement of intention to accept both the benefits and burdens of the election. The filing of a return that only carries forward an NOL is not an effective election. Young v. CIR, 783 F2d 1201 (5th Cir. 1986).

[33] Joint Comm. on Tax'n, 94th Cong., 2d Sess., General Explanation of the Tax Reform Act of 1976, reprinted in 1976-3 CB (Vol. 2) 200–02.

[34] For the carryover of investment credits and foreign tax credits, see infra ¶¶27.1.2 and 69.1.4.

ing period is a year in determining the number of years to which an NOL may be carried.[35] If a taxpayer sustains NOLs in two or more years, the oldest loss is used first—a first–in, first–out (FIFO) priority principle that ordinarily increases the likelihood that NOLs will be used before they expire.[36] In the unusual case where the carryback period for an earlier NOL is longer than that for an NOL from a later year, however, the FIFO principle is disadvantageous because it requires long-lived NOLs to be used before short-lived NOLs.

To avoid giving with one hand and taking away with the other, §6511(d)(2) extends the statute of limitations for claiming credits and refunds for NOL carryback years from the normal three-year period to the period ending three years after the due date (including extensions) of the return for the loss year.[37] The extended statute of limitations, however, helps only those who help themselves. If a taxpayer neglects to carry an NOL back to the earliest proper year, it is nevertheless treated as though it had been used in that year to the extent allowable, even if the taxpayer discovers the error after the extended statute of limitations has run on a claim for refund or credit.[38]

¶25.11.4 Computation of NOL Deduction

After the amount of an NOL and the years to which it must be carried are determined, the NOL is converted into a "net operating loss carryback" or "net operating loss carryover" by §172(b)(1)(A) or (B) and then into a "net operating loss deduction" by §172(a). The conversion is simplicity itself if the taxpayer has only one NOL. In this situation, it is carried back to the third year preceding the taxable year (or to the first succeeding year if the carryback is waived), and is an NOL deduction for that year. If the NOL carryback exceeds the taxable income of the first year to which it is carried, it is reduced in the manner described below in determining the amount, if any, that may be carried to the second year in the carryback-carryover cycle, and this adjustment process is repeated for each succeeding year until the NOL is fully used or expires unused.

---

[35] See Reg. §1.172-4(a)(2). For short taxable years resulting from a change of accounting periods, see infra ¶105.1.3.

[36] See Reg. §1.172-4(a)(3) (second sentence).

[37] For §6511(d)(2), see infra ¶113.1.

[38] See, e.g., Byron Weston Co. v. US, 87 F. Supp. 955 (Ct. Cl. 1950) (taxpayer erroneously carried NOL forward instead of back; held, refund for earlier year to which it should have been carried barred by statute of limitations). But see Rev. Rul 81-88, 1981-1 CB 585 (where adjustments for carryback year are barred by statute of limitations, §172 applied as though return for carryback year were correct).

If there is at no time more than one NOL, the NOL deduction for each of the years in the cycle is the amount of the NOL carryback or carryover for that year. If the taxpayer has two or more NOL carrybacks and/or carryovers to the same year by virtue of sustaining NOL losses in two or more years, the NOL deduction for the year to which they are carried is the sum of these amounts.

In recomputing an individual taxpayer's tax liability for a carryback year, all deductions dependent on adjusted gross income (AGI) and taxable income are recomputed, with the exception of the charitable deduction, and credits are also recomputed if they are related to the amount of the tax liability.[39] The charitable contribution is probably left intact, despite the reduced AGI resulting from the NOL deduction, on the theory that the taxpayer might have relied on the amount of AGI as originally computed in making the contributions and that a retroactive reduction in AGI should not result in a disallowance of contributions made in good faith on the basis of the facts then known. The NOL deduction, however, is taken into account in computing the ceiling on the charitable deduction for a carryover year because the NOL deduction can be as readily computed as any other deduction before the close of the carryover year.

The use of an NOL deduction in a carryback year is illustrated by Example 25-3, which assumes (1) the taxpayer incurs an NOL of $13,400 in 1991, and carries it back to 1988, and (2) the 1988 return reports (a) gross income of $50,000, (b) a long-term capital loss of $1,000, (c) charitable contributions of $15,000 to so-called 30 percent charities,[40] $3,000, and (e) personal and dependency exemptions of $5,700. The taxpayer files a joint return in both 1988 and 1991. On these assumptions, the NOL carryback from 1991 generates a refund or credit of $2,059, as shown by Example 25-3.

The only changes taken into account by Example 25-3 result from the NOL deduction. If the normal three-year statute of limitations has not run on a carryback year, both the IRS and the taxpayer may correct any errors, such as the omission of taxable income or the failure to claim allowable deductions. In contrast, if the normal statutory period on adjustments has

---

[39] IRS Pub. No. 535, Business Expenses and Operating Losses 36 (rev. Nov. 1979). The same principles are applied by §1.172-5(a)(3)(ii) of the regulations to determine the carryover to the following year, except for the charitable contribution. The preservation of the charitable contribution as originally claimed is mandated by §170(b)(1)(F). See also A&A Distribs., Inc. v. US, 81-1 USTC ¶9136 (D. Mass. 1981) (not officially reported) (compromise under §7122(a) did not bar refund based on NOL carryback from later year).

[40] So called because the deduction for such charitable contributions is limited to 30 percent of the taxpayer's contribution base — defined by §170(b)(1)(F) as adjusted gross income computed without NOL carrybacks. See infra ¶35.3.2.

Example 25-3

Computation of Tax Liability for NOL Carryback Year

	1988 Tax Liability As Reported	As Recomputed
1. Gross income	$50,000	$ 50,000
2. Capital loss	(1,000)	(1,000)
3. NOL deduction (from 1991)	–0–	(13,400)
4. Adjusted gross income	$49,000	$ 35,600
5. Charitable contribution deduction—lesser of gifts ($15,000) or 30 percent of AGI as reported	(14,700)	(14,700)
6. Medical expenses—$3,000 spent, less 7.5 percent of AGI	–0–	(330)
7. Personal and dependency exemptions	(5,700)	(5,700)
8. Taxable income	$28,600	$ 14,870
9. Tax liability	$ 4,290	$ 2,231
10. Less: Recomputed tax liability	2,231	
11. Refund or credit	$ 2,059	

run,[41] §6511(d)(2) reopens the carryback year to allow credit or refund, but only "to the extent of the amount of the overpayment attributable to such carryback." In the latter case, tax for the carryback year is only altered by the carryback and any arithmetical recomputations resulting from applying the NOL deduction to the return as filed, precluding the correction of extraneous errors. The IRS, however, might assert otherwise barred errors by way of equitable recoupment.[42] At most, this would result in a partial or complete disallowance of the claim for refund or credit, since §6511(d)(2) does not permit the assessment of an otherwise barred tax deficiency for the carryback year.

¶25.11.5 Effect of Intervening Years on Unused Net Operating Losses

Example 25-3 hypothesized a 1991 NOL of $13,400, which is used in its entirety in 1988, the earliest carryback year. To illustrate the adjustments required when the NOL is not fully used in the earliest year to which

---

[41] For the normal three-year period and its extension in cases of large omissions from gross income, waivers of the statutory period, and fraud, see infra ¶113.1.

[42] For equitable recoupment, see infra ¶113.10.

it is carried, Example 25-4 assumes that the NOL carryback from 1991 to 1988 is $40,000 rather than $13,400. On this revised hypothesis, recomputed taxable income for 1988 is zero, and the tax paid for that year is refunded in its entirety, which might suggest that the NOL carryback to 1989, the next carryback year, is $25,130—the 1991 NOL ($40,000) less the taxable income reported for 1988 ($14,870) that was eliminated when the 1991 NOL was carried back to 1988. This intuitive conclusion, however, would be wrong.

NOL carrybacks and carryovers are adjusted under §172(b)(2) as they are carried through one or more intervening years to the next relevant year. The carryback or carryover is reduced in rotation by the taxable income of each intervening year, modified by some of the adjustments that were employed when the NOL was originally computed.[43] Moreover, modified taxable income must be computed for an intervening year even if the intervening year showed a loss before the modifications were made, since it might reduce the amount that may be carried to the following year by "absorbing," in the language of the regulations, part or all of the net operating loss.[44] In making the necessary computations, the tax law applicable to the intervening year is applied, rather than the law of the loss year or of the year to which the loss is being carried.[45] If the statute of limitations has run for any intervening year, however, errors on the return for that year are not corrected.[46]

The modifications for individuals are: (1) The deduction for capital losses from sales and exchanges of capital assets is limited to the includable gains from such transactions; (2) the deduction of 60 percent of net capital gain allowed by §1202 for years before 1987 is denied; and (3) personal and dependency exemptions are not allowed.[47] Having made these modifications, the taxpayer must recompute any deductions related to taxable income or adjusted gross income to reflect the resulting increases or decreases in these amounts.[48]

---

[43] See supra ¶25.11.2.

[44] See Reg. §1.172-4(a)(3) (use of term "absorb"); Rubin v. CIR, 26 TC 1076 (1956), rev'd on procedural grounds, 252 F2d 243 (5th Cir. 1958) (loss of about $11,000 turned into modified taxable income of about $67,000 by modifications under prior law).

[45] IRC §172(e); Reg. §1.172-1(e).

[46] Rev. Rul 81-88, 1981-1 CB 585. See Brandon v. US, 204 F. Supp. 912 (ND Ga. 1962) (taxpayer with 1952 NOL failed to carry it forward to 1953; held, error does not preclude carrying 1954 NOL back to 1953).

[47] IRC §172(b)(2)(A). See also §172(b)(2)(B), under which the taxable income for the intervening year is modified to reflect NOLs from years prior to the loss year, but not those from subsequent years.

[48] Reg. §1.172-5(a)(3)(ii).

Like the modifications that were originally made in the loss year to determine the amount of the NOL, these modifications in the taxable income of the intervening years are made because the deductions for net capital gains and the personal and dependency exemptions do not reflect economic losses and, hence, can be viewed as partially redressing the taxpayer's original loss. Elimination of the deduction for capital losses reflects the fact that they may be carried independently under §1212(b).

The effect of these modifications is illustrated by Example 25-4, which is based on the facts of Example 25-3, except that it assumes (1) the NOL carryback from 1991 to 1988 was $40,000 rather than $13,400, (2) in the course of computing the NOL carryback to 1989, the taxpayer discovered that a deductible casualty loss of $500 (after reduction by the nondeductible floor) was overlooked when the 1988 tax return was prepared, and (3) the statute of limitations for 1988 has not run. On these assumptions, the NOL carryback to 1978 is $2,000 (Example 25-4, line 9).

Example 25-4

Computation of NOL to Reflect Modified
Taxable Income of Intervening Year

	1988 Taxable Income	
	As Reported	As Modified
1. Gross income	$50,000	$50,000
2. Capital loss	(1,000)	–0–
3. Adjusted gross income	$49,000	$50,000
4. Casualty loss	–0–	(500)
5. Charitable contributions—Lesser of gifts ($15,000) or 30 percent of AGI as reported or as modified	(14,700)	(15,000)
6. Medical expenses—$3,000 spent less 7.5 percent of AGI as reported or as modified	–0–	–0–
7. Personal and dependency exemptions	(5,700)	–0–
8. Taxable income	$28,600	$34,500
9. Portion of 1991 NOL carried to 1989—$40,000 less 1988 modified taxable income	$ 5,500	

For corporations, the only important modification of the intervening year's taxable income required by §172(b)(2) is a recomputation of the dividends-received deduction without regard to the taxable-income limit of

§246(b).[49] When applicable, this modification is advantageous to the taxpayer, since the NOL carryback or carryover is reduced by less than the taxable income of the intervening year.

¶25.11.6 Changes of Taxpayer Status, Identity, and Ownership

During the 19-year carryback-carryover cycle, taxpayers sustaining NOLs can experience many changes of status, identity, and ownership. For example, individuals might marry, get divorced, or die, and corporations might be sold to new shareholders, merge, liquidate, or split up. The principal events of this type and their effects on the NOL deduction are described below.

1. *Joint/separate returns of married couples.* If a married couple files joint returns for every year in the 19-year cycle, they compute joint NOL carrybacks or carryovers in the same manner as an unmarried individual, but on the basis of their combined NOLs and combined taxable income.[50] If they file a joint return for a year for which the NOL deduction is claimed but separate returns for all other years in the cycle, their separate carrybacks and carryovers are combined into a joint carryback or carryover for the deduction year.[51] Other patterns of joint/separate returns require their joint returns to be unbundled under elaborate rules prescribed by the regulations and illustrated with examples.[52]

2. *Bankruptcy.* In *Segal v. Rochelle*, the Supreme Court held that a claim for refund based on an NOL carryback constitutes property passing to the trustee in bankruptcy for the benefit of the taxpayer's creditors.[53] In *Davis v. CIR*, in contrast, the Tax Court held that an individual's NOLs (as distinguished from a claim for refund based on an application of them in prebankruptcy years) are not transferable, even to his bankruptcy estate.[54]

---

[49] For the effect on corporate NOLs of the alternative capital gain computation during intervening years, see US v. Foster Lumber Co., 429 US 32 (1976).

[50] Reg. §1.172-7(c).

[51] Reg. §1.172-7(b).

[52] Reg. §§1.172-7(d) through (g). See also Calvin v. US, 354 F2d 202 (10th Cir. 1965) (NOL sustained prior to marriage may be applied only against portion of joint income attributable to spouse sustaining the loss); Campbell v. US, 581 F. Supp. 1274 (ND Tex. 1984) (in community property state, one half of net operating loss on joint return may be carried back to separate return of each spouse for carryback year prior to taxpayers' marriage); Rev. Rul. 86-58, 1986-1 CB 365 (procedure for computing each spouse's share of overpayment resulting when postdivorce NOL of one spouse is carried back to predivorce joint return year); Rev. Rul. 75-368, 1975-2 CB 480 (NOL sustained after divorce may be applied only against taxpayer's share of taxable income reported on joint returns filed during marriage).

[53] Segal v. Rochelle, 382 US 375 (1966).

[54] Davis v. CIR, 69 TC 814 (1978).

The *Davis* decision was overturned in 1980 with the enactment of §1398(g), providing that the bankruptcy estate of a noncorporate bankrupt succeeds to the debtor's NOLs.[55] Also, under §1398(i), the debtor succeeds to the estate's NOLs on termination of the proceeding, whether these NOLs arose during the bankruptcy administration or were inherited from the debtor under §1398(g). Section 1399 requires that a corporation and its bankruptcy estate must be treated as the same taxpayer, thus ensuring continuity in the use of NOLs in this context as well.

3. *Death.* Because decedents and their estates are different taxpayers, NOLs may not be carried forward from a deceased individual's returns to the estate's returns or back from the estate's returns to the deceased's returns.[56] This principle, however, does not preclude carrybacks and carryovers as between the decedent and the decedent's surviving spouse if joint returns were filed for some or all of the pre-death years.[57]

4. *Trusts and estates.* Trusts and estates, like other taxpayers, are entitled to carry NOLs from one year to another under §172, subject to regulations prescribed pursuant to §642(d), which are mainly concerned with the effect of charitable contributions.[58] In addition, on the termination of a trust or estate, unexpired carryovers are inherited by the beneficiaries succeeding to its property.[59] Excess deductions incurred by the trust or estate in its final taxable year similarly pass to the beneficiaries, who may take these deductions into account in determining whether they incurred an NOL for the year in which the excess deductions arise.

5. *Partnerships.* Because they are treated as conduits rather than taxable entities, partnerships are excluded from the NOL mechanism. Instead, their income and deductions are allocated among the partners, each of whom makes a separate NOL computation after aggregating the allocated partnership items with all other income and deductions reported on his or her own return.[60]

6. *S corporations.* Net operating losses incurred by S corporations are passed through to their shareholders, in accordance with principles summa-

---

[55] See IRC §1398(j)(2) (carrybacks allowed from estate to debtor and from debtor's postbankruptcy year to prebankruptcy year).

[56] Rev. Rul. 74-175, 1974-1 CB 52 (NOL reported on decedent's final tax return may not be deducted by the decedent's estate or carried over to subsequent years).

[57] See Ferguson, Freeland & Stephens, Federal Income Taxation of Estates and Beneficiaries 118–21 (Little, Brown 1970).

[58] See Reg. §1.642(d)-1; Ferguson, Freeland & Stephens, supra note 57, at 306–10.

[59] IRC §642(h), discussed infra ¶81.6. See also Ferguson, Freeland & Stephens, supra note 57, at 632–53.

[60] For the allocation of partnership items, see infra ¶86.2.

rized elsewhere in this work.[61] As a corollary, NOLs incurred in election years are disregarded in computing the corporation's NOL deduction for nonelection years, while NOLs incurred in nonelection years are not taken into account in determining the corporation's taxable income for election years.[62]

7. *Corporations—changes of ownership, mergers, etc.* Corporate NOLs are not ordinarily affected by changes in stock ownership, since the corporation is a separate taxable entity from its shareholders. In order to curb the acquisition of shell corporations whose only significant assets are NOLs, however, §382 prescribes elaborate rules for the reduction or elimination of NOLs on a significant change of ownership of a corporation.[63]

By itself, §172 provides for the carryback and carryover of NOLs from the loss year to the same taxpayer's returns for other taxable years. The same-taxpayer principle creates difficulties when two or more corporations are merged or undergo other changes from which only one entity emerges. Section 381 prescribes rules for the survival and transfer of tax attributes, including NOL carrybacks and carryovers, in the case of mergers and other tax-free corporate acquisitions.[64]

¶25.11.7 Ancillary Matters

1. *Accelerated NOL procedures.* In keeping with the remedial function of §172, taxpayers sustaining an NOL may apply under §6411 for a tentative carryback adjustment of the earlier year's tax liability. Under this provision, the IRS must, within 90 days, (1) make a limited examination of the application for omissions and computational errors, (2) apply the resulting decrease in tax liability for the carryback year against the taxpayer's unpaid taxes, and (3) refund any balance. The application can be denied if it contains material omissions or computational errors, however, unless the IRS determines that the errors can be corrected within the 90-day period.[65] Section 6411 applies not only to adjustments based on NOL carrybacks but also to claims for the carryback of net capital losses, unused investment credits, unused WIN credits, and unused new-job credits.

---

[61] See infra ¶95.6. See also Bittker & Eustice, Federal Income Taxation of Corporations and Shareholders ¶6.07 (Warren, Gorham & Lamont, Inc., 5th ed. 1987).

[62] IRC §1371(b).

[63] See infra ¶95.5.4.

[64] See infra ¶95.5.2.

[65] See Reg. §1.6411-2(c) (disallowance of tentative adjustment conclusive, but taxpayer may file normal claim for refund). See also Rev. Rul. 78-369, 1978-2 CB 324 (claim under §6411 in proper form must be allowed, even if deficiency has been proposed exceeding tax paid plus loss); Rev. Rul. 60-215, 1960-1 CB 642 (50 percent fraud penalty where refund was induced by fraud).

   The refund procedure has sometimes been abused by tax shelter investors using it to turn large questionable deductions into quick cash, and this has provoked the IRS to restrict the procedure. Section 6213(b)(3) allows the IRS to make an offsetting assessment without sending a notice of deficiency if it determines that the adjustment under §6411 is excessive. The IRS applied this offset in a 1984 ruling involving an abusive tax shelter.[66] The taxpayer in the ruling filed a timely application for tentative refund of 1981 taxes, based on a reported NOL for 1984. The NOL consisted of a tax shelter loss that the IRS determined was based on a gross valuation overstatement. Within 90 days after receiving the application, the IRS allowed the tentative adjustment as required by §6411(b), but made an identical assessment for the same year under §6213(b)(3); the taxpayer got no refund. Temporary regulations have been promulgated to allow this two-step where the reported NOL derives from a partnership loss that ordinarily could only be adjusted under the partnership audit rules.[67]

   Section 6411 provides only provisional relief, since the allowance of an application does not preclude the IRS from proceeding with its normal audit adjustments, including correction of the NOL deduction.[68] Conversely, IRS action on an application for a tentative carryback adjustment does not prevent the taxpayer from filing a claim for refund or credit in the normal manner.

   A companion measure is §6164, permitting corporations anticipating an NOL carryback to extend the time for payment of taxes for the immediately preceding taxable year (subject to interest) by filing a statement setting out the estimated amount of the expected NOL and other relevant information. The extension is automatic, but it may be terminated by the IRS if it concludes that the application is clearly erroneous or unreasonable in a material respect or that collection of the postponed amount is in jeopardy. The IRS is also authorized to require a bond to insure ultimate payment of the postponed amount.

   2. *Interest.* If taxes for a carryback year were underpaid, the taxpayer is charged interest on the underpayment until the filing date for the loss year,

---

[66] Revenue Ruling 84-175, 1984-2 CB 296.

[67] Reg. §301.6231(c)-1T. See infra ¶111.1.5 for the partnership audit rules.

[68] See Crismon v. US, 550 F2d 1205 (9th Cir. 1977) (application for tentative carryback adjustment does not constitute claim for refund or toll statute of limitations); Thrif-Tee, Inc. v. US, 492 F. Supp. 530 (WDNC 1979) (applicaton for tentative carryback adjustment is not claim for credit or refund; no penalty prescribed for IRS failure to act within 90-day period); Zarnow v. CIR, 48 TC 213 (1967) (IRS' failure to act on application for tentative adjustment within prescribed 90-day period does not prevent later determination of deficiency); Pesch v. CIR, 78 TC 100 (1982) (refund made more than 90 days after application for tentative adjustment may be recovered through deficiency procedures; IRS not limited to suit to recover erroneous refund; *Zarnow* followed).

even if the underpayment is wholly eliminated by the carryback, since the Treasury was entitled to hold the deficiency until the end of the loss year, when the carryback came into existence.[69] For the same reason, penalties for negligence or fraud that are valid on the facts known when a return is due or filed are not eliminated by later net operating losses that, when carried back, wipe out the taxpayer's income or tax liability for the earlier year.[70] In the same vein, in computing interest in the taxpayer's favor on a refund attributable to an NOL carryback, the computational period does not start with the carryback year but only when the right to the refund arises at the end of the loss year.[71]

3. *Alternative minimum tax.* An NOL deduction may not offset more than 90 percent of a taxpayer's alternative minimum taxable income, computed without the NOL. One effect of this rule is that a taxpayer with NOL deductions that eliminate all regular tax liability usually owes some alternative minimum tax.[72]

---

[69] IRC §6601(d)(1); Reg. §301.6601-1(e)(1). See US v. Koppers Co., 348 US 254 (1958); Manning v. Seeley Tube & Box Co., 338 US 561 (1950); Rev. Rul. 82-48, 1982-1 CB 211 (interest on tax, period for payment of which was extended by §6164, runs from due date as determined by §6152, which allows corporation to pay tax in two installments, until last day of loss year); infra ¶114.1.

[70] See US v. Keltner, 675 F2d 602 (4th Cir.), cert. denied, 459 US 832 (1982) (criminal conviction for tax evasion under §7201 sustained despite subsequent NOL that eliminated tax liability when carried back because, at time return and correct tax were due, deficiency existed; "lucky loser" defense rejected); Auerbach v. CIR, 216 F2d 693 (1st Cir. 1954); Nick v. Dunlap, 185 F2d 674 (5th Cir. 1950), cert. denied, 341 US 926 (1951).

[71] IRC §§6611(b), (f)(1).

[72] For the alternative minimum tax, see infra 111.3.12.

CHAPTER
26

Other Business Deductions

¶26.1 INTANGIBLE DRILLING AND DEVELOPMENT COSTS —OIL AND GAS

¶26.1.1 Introductory

As an exception to §263(a)'s prohibition of the deduction of capital expenditures, §263(c) permits taxpayers to elect to deduct intangible drilling and development costs (IDC) relating to oil, gas, and geothermal wells located in the United States.[1] Section 263(c) does not authorize this election directly, but instead directs the Treasury to prescribe regulations granting an election "corresponding to the regulations . . . which were recognized and approved by the Congress in House Concurrent Resolution 50, Seventy-ninth Congress." This curious statutory language requires an introductory historical note, particularly since it seems to preclude IRS modification of the rules prevailing in 1945, when the Seventy-ninth Congress approved House Concurrent Resolution 50.

The Treasury first permitted taxpayers to deduct IDC for oil and gas wells in 1916. This election was continued in subsequent years, despite the absence of any statutory authority for the deduction of capital expenditures, except for cryptic references in the Revenue Acts of 1918 and 1921 to the depletion of "cost including cost of development not otherwise deducted."[2] In *F.H.E. Oil Co. v. CIR*, decided in 1945, the Court of Appeals for the Fifth Circuit held that the regulations permitting the IDC election were invalid because the statutory predecessor of §263(a) prohibited any deduction for the cost of "permanent improvements or betterments made to increase the

---

[1] See generally Fielder, The Option to Deduct Intangible Drilling and Development Costs, 33 Tex. L. Rev. 825 (1955); McMahon, Fundamentals of Federal Income Taxation of Natural Resources, 3 J. Min. L. & Pol'y 225, 287–298 (1988).

[2] Reg. 33, art. 170 (1916); Revenue Act of 1918, Pub. L. No. 254, §234(a)(9), 40 Stat. 1057 (1919); Revenue Act of 1921, Pub. L. No. 98, §234(a)(9), 42 Stat. 227. See generally Harper Oil Co. v. US, 425 F2d 1335 (10th Cir. 1970) (extensive account of regulation's "curious history"); Exxon Corp. v. US, 547 F2d 548, 554 n.9 (Ct. Cl. 1976) (principal articles cited).

value of any property or estate."[3] Within a few weeks after this decision, Congress shored up the regulations by enacting House Concurrent Resolution 50, declaring (on thin evidence) that Congress "has recognized and approved" the disputed regulations.[4] Although the resolution lacked the authority of a statute, it was not challenged by the Treasury.

In 1954, the regulations gained formal statutory approval with the enactment of §263(c). In 1978, Congress directed the Treasury to expand the regulations to include IDC in connection with geothermal deposits.[5]

Usually, if a taxpayer does not elect to deduct IDC, the costs increase the basis of the affected property and are recovered by depreciation deductions if they relate to physical properties and by depletion otherwise.[6] Section 59(e), however, provides a third option—amortizing IDC ratably over 10 years. The latter option is typically adopted to avoid the alternative minimum tax, and is discussed below in that context.[7] Whether capitalized IDC are recovered by depreciation and depletion or by 10-year amortization, costs not recovered prior to a disposition or abandonment of the property serve to reduce the taxpayer's gain or increase loss on the sale or abandonment.

Since percentage depletion is unaffected by the adjusted basis of the property, taxpayers entitled to use this method of depleting oil and gas properties almost always benefit from electing to deduct IDC under §263(c). An election, however, carries with it a few offsetting disadvantages, which are discussed below.[8]

The contention has been made that the §263(c) election entitles a cash basis taxpayer to an immediate deduction for amounts paid for intangible drilling and development services to be performed for the taxpayer in a

---

[3] F.H.E. Oil Co. v. CIR, 147 F2d 1002 (5th Cir.) (regulations held invalid), reh'g denied, 149 F2d 238 (revised opinion, following briefs asserting that invalidity of regulations could result in a billion dollars of tax deficiencies, holding regulation inapplicable but adhering in dictum to view that regulations were invalid when issued, even if sanctioned by subsequent congressional acquiescence), second reh'g denied, 150 F2d 857 (1945) (House Concurrent Resolution entitled "to most respectful consideration by the courts [but it] does not make law, or change the law made by a previous Congress and President," since not approved by President or passed over his veto).

[4] H.R. Cong. Rec. No. 50, 59 Stat. (Part 2) 844 (1945).

[5] See S. Rep. No. 529, 95th Cong., 2d Sess., reprinted in 1978-3 CB (Vol. 2) 199, 281. The term "geothermal deposits" is defined in §613(e)(3). For the status of geothermal IDC before 1978, see Reich v. CIR, 454 F2d 1157 (9th Cir. 1972) (certain geothermal wells qualify as "gas" wells; IDC deductible); Miller v. US, 78-1 USTC ¶9127 (CD Cal. 1977) (not officially reported) (contra as to certain exploratory drilling relating to water and steam).

[6] See infra ¶26.1.4.

[7] Infra ¶26.1.6.

[8] See infra ¶26.1.6.

future year. The IRS has allowed the deduction where a payment was made in one year for work to be done early in the next and there was a business purpose for the prepayment. In a case where a prepayment was made for drilling and development work to be done at an unspecified future date and the payee, rather than doing the work himself, was to contract with others to have the work done, the IRS required the prepayment to be capitalized and written off under §263(c) when the work was done.[9] The courts, which have generally supported the IRS in this context, have framed the issue as being whether the prepayment is an immediate payment of IDC (currently deductible) or is a deposit that might be applied in the future in payment of IDC (deductible when so applied).[10]

The right to expense IDC is limited to costs of drilling and developing wells within the United States; costs of foreign wells must be recovered over a period of time under rules described below.[11] Also, corporations that have retail or refining operations can expense only 70 percent of their IDC.[12]

¶26.1.2 Qualified Operators

The regulations grant the election to deduct IDC to "operators," a term that embraces "one who holds a working or operating interest in any tract or parcel of land either as a fee owner or under a lease or any other form of contract granting working or operating rights."[13] This requirement invokes the "economic interest" concept used in determining the taxpayer's right to deductions for depletion, leading two courts of appeals to observe that the privilege of expensing intangible drilling and development costs is inextricably tied to the same economic interest consideration required for the depletion deduction.[14]

Qualified expenses undertaken directly or through contract are deductible at the operator's election, whether incurred prior or subsequent to the formal grant or assignment of operating rights,[15] but only to the extent

---

[9] Rev. Rul. 80-71, 1980-1 CB 106.

[10] Keller v. CIR, 725 F2d 1173 (8th Cir. 1984); Schiavenza v. US, 720 F2d 1117 (9th Cir. 1983).

[11] Infra text accompanying notes 47–50.

[12] Infra text accompanying notes 51–52.

[13] Reg. §1.612-4(a) (first sentence). For the disallowance of IDC attributable to deviated wells, bottomed outside the operator's leasehold, see CIR v. Donnell's Est., 417 F2d 106 (5th Cir. 1969); Rev. Rul. 69-262, 1969-1 CB 166.

[14] Schiavenza v. US, 720 F2d 1117 (9th Cir. 1983); CIR v. Donnell's Est., supra note 13, at 111. For the economic interest concept, see supra ¶24.1.2.

[15] Reg. §1.612-4(a) (last two sentences). See also Bernuth v. CIR, 470 F2d 710 (2d Cir. 1972) (artificial allocation of IDC must be recast to reflect basis of taxpayer's working interest); Rev. Rul. 73-211, 1973-1 CB 303 (same).

allocable to the operator's fractional interest.[16] The balance of the expenses, which in effect are costs of acquiring the assigned rights, must be capitalized and recovered through depletion.[17] On the other hand, operators can qualify for the IDC election even if their ownership of the working interest is temporary. For example, the IRS ruled that the assignee of the working interest in an oil and gas lease who agreed to drill and complete a well under an agreement allowing him to recover 200 percent of the drilling and development expenses plus the equipment and operating costs necessary to produce that amount could deduct the IDC, even though the working interest reverted to the assignor at the end of the payout period.[18] If the assignee of a working interest pays the estimated cost of drilling to the assignor under an agreement requiring the transferred funds to be used solely for drilling, there is some authority for disallowing the §263(c) deduction to the assignee on the ground that the drilling and development are not "undertaken" by him within the meaning of the regulations.[19] On the other hand, the expenses can be deducted even if fixed in amount and incurred under a turnkey contract by which the drilling contractor agrees to drill and equip the well; the contract price, however, must be allocated between IDC and the depreciable equipment. Moreover, if the contractor is also the promoter of the project or is related to the promoter, amounts paid by the investors to acquire shares of the working interest must not be deducted in the guise of IDC.[20]

---

[16] See Burns v. CIR, 78 TC 185 (1982) (determining portion allocable to investor in debt-financed tax shelter deal).

[17] For the effect of various carried-interest arrangements, see Rev. Rul. 71-207, 1971-1 CB 160 (on facts, carrying party owns entire working interest until payout and can deduct all IDC); Rev. Rul. 69-332, 1969-1 CB 87 (same); Rev. Rul. 71-206, 1971-1 CB 105 (on facts, carrying party can deduct one fourth of IDC); Rev. Rul. 70-336, 1970-1 CB 145, modified by Rev. Rul. 80-109, 1980-1 CB 129 (carrying party can deduct fraction of IDC attributable to permanent fractional share of working interest). On Rev. Rul. 70-336, see Singhal, Limitations on Deduction of Intangible Drilling Costs Should Not Be Applicable to Development Costs, 25 Oil & Gas Tax Q. 42 (1977). For the meaning of the term "carried interest" and the treatment of such interests under the depletion deduction, see supra ¶24.1.3.

[18] Rev. Rul. 75-446, 1975-2 CB 95.

[19] See Platt v. US, 207 F2d 697 (7th Cir. 1953); Phillips v. US, 233 F. Supp. 59 (ED Tex. 1964), aff'd per curiam, 66-1 USTC ¶9157 (5th Cir. 1965) (not officially reported) (operator status not attained until after IDC incurred); Rev. Rul. 75-304, 1975-2 CB 94 (same).

[20] Bernuth v. CIR, 470 F2d 710 (2d Cir. 1972), and cases therein cited; Rev. Rul. 73-211, 1973-1 CB 303. See Stanton v. CIR, 26 TCM (CCH) 191 (1967) (drilling expenses reasonable).

¶26.1.3 Qualified Expenses

Section 263(c) directs the Treasury to issue regulations permitting taxpayers to elect to deduct "intangible drilling and development costs," without describing or defining the costs affected by the election, except to say that the regulations must correspond to those approved by Congress in 1945.[21] The regulations provide that IDC can be either capitalized or expensed, at the taxpayer's election, implying that the election covers items that would otherwise be nondeductible capital expenditures.[22] The regulations go on to provide that the option applies to an operator's expenditures for wages, fuel, repairs, hauling, supplies, and other costs, but only to the extent they are incident to and necessary for the drilling of wells and the preparation of wells for the production of oil or gas.[23] Examples are costs incurred in:

1. Drilling, shooting, and cleaning wells.
2. Clearing ground, draining, road making, surveying, and geological work necessary in preparation for the drilling of wells.
3. Constructing derricks, tanks, pipelines, and other physical structures necessary for the drilling of wells and the preparation of wells for the production of oil or gas.[24]

The regulations provide that "in general" the option only applies to items without salvage value, but that labor, fuel, repairs, hauling, and supplies are considered as not having salvage values, even if incurred in installing physical property that does have salvage value.[25] These items must be distinguished from expenditures for tangible property that ordinarily has a salvage value, such as materials used in structures in the wells and on the property, drilling tools, pipe, casing, tanks, engines, and other equipment, which must be capitalized and recovered by depreciation deductions over their useful lives.[26]

---

[21] See H.R. Cong. Rec. No. 50, supra note 4.

[22] Reg. §1.612-4(a).

[23] Id.

[24] Id.

[25] Id. See Exxon Corp. v. US, 547 F2d 548 (Ct. Cl. 1976) (expenses for labor, fuel, etc., incident to building offshore platforms for drilling wells deductible, even though incurred in land-phase construction of platforms that could be moved if no successful wells were drilled); Standard Oil Co. (Ind.) v. CIR, 77 TC 349 (1981) (expenses for labor, fuel, etc., incident to preparation of offshore drilling platforms deductible; theory of *Exxon* rejected, but platforms in question were not of type ordinarily having salvage value); Gulf Oil Corp. v. CIR, 87 TC 324 (1986) (*Standard Oil* followed on similar facts); Rev. Rul. 70-596, 1970-2 CB 68.

[26] Reg. §1.612-4(c)(1). See also Harper Oil Co. v. US, 425 F2d 1335 (10th Cir. 1970) (casings installed to prevent contamination must be depreciated rather than

The most notable costs falling outside §263(c)'s jurisdiction are geological and geophysical exploration expenditures incurred to obtain and accumulate data for decisions about the acquisition or retention of mining properties. These costs of determining the existence, location, and extent of oil and gas are added to the basis of the property acquired or retained, and are recovered by depletion or offset against the proceeds on sale of the property.[27] If no areas of interest are located and identified by the taxpayer, the geological and geophysical expenditures are deductible as a loss under §165 when the project area is abandoned as a potential source of mineral production.[28] This possibility is a fertile source of dispute because it is not easy to determine the scope of the taxpayer's areas of interest in order to fix the time when hope of production was abandoned.

Geological and geophysical expenditures are not excluded from an election under §263(c), however, unless they are "exploratory" since the regulations permit the cost of geological work required to prepare for the drilling of wells to be deducted.[29] As described by the Tax Court, these deductible items are "the costs of preparations for the drilling of particular wells after the drilling has been at least tentatively decided upon"; the

---

expensed, even though practical impediments and state law precluded salvage); Rev. Rul. 70-414, 1970-2 CB 132 (list of items whose costs do not qualify as IDC, including pumping equipment, flow lines, storage tanks, treating equipment, and salt water disposal equipment).

[27] Rev. Rul. 77-188, 1977-1 CB 76, and cases therein cited. See Louisiana Land & Exploration Co. v. CIR, 7 TC 507, 516 (1946), aff'd on other issues, 161 F2d 842 (5th Cir. 1947) (geophysical survey to determine whether land should be explored by drilling was "the first step in the overall development of oil of these tracts," generating benefits allocable to entire useful life of areas being developed; expenditures must be capitalized); Rev. Rul. 83-105, 1983-2 CB 51 (giving several examples illustrating allocation of geological and geophysical expenditures to various tracts of land and areas of interest and clarifying proper timing of abandonment loss); Rev. Rul. 80-342, 1980-2 CB 99 (oil companies formed consortium to drill test well and share resulting information in bidding on oil and gas leases; held, not deductible as intangible drilling and development expenditures, but treated as capital outlays allocable to leases obtained as result of information); Rev. Rul. 80-153, 1980-1 CB 10 (payor of bottom hole contribution must capitalize amount as cost of obtaining exploratory information; payment includable in recipient's gross income). See also supra ¶20.4.4 (capitalization of business preoperating expenses).

[28] Rev. Rul. 77-188, supra note 27. Compare American Smelting & Ref. Co. v. US, 423 F2d 277 (Ct. Cl. 1970) (losses deductible when each separately acquired lease option relinquished) with Rev. Rul. 77-187, 1977-1 CB 50 (IRS will not follow American Smelting & Refining Co.; loss deductible when "area of interest" abandoned as potential source of mineral production). See also Rev. Rul. 61-206, 1961-2 CB 57 (no deductible loss on abandonment of test hole drilled to ascertain existence of water if drilling is integral part of development of water well in same area).

[29] Reg. §1.612-4(a). See also Reg. §1.612-4(b)(1).

dividing line "is the point at which the preparations for drilling begin."[30]

Application of this distinction is most contentious in the context of exploratory wells. The Tax Court has rejected the IRS view that §263(c) should be limited to "the intangible costs of drilling only those shafts drilled after a taxpayer has decided to commence preparing to produce a reservoir."[31] Restricting the expensing option, the court noted, "would deny, in offshore wells, the IDC deduction to the very entrepreneurs for whom it was enacted—those investors who take the enormous risks entailed in drilling the wildcat wells—and would allow the IDC deduction only for those low-risk wells drilled after the wildcatters had found the oil or gas."[32] Instead, the court held, the deduction must be allowed for IDC relating to any well "drilled in search of hydrocarbons [that is] designed and drilled in such a manner that [it] would have been capable, upon encountering hydrocarbons and upon appropriate completion of such shafts by the operator, of conducting or aiding in the conduction of hydrocarbons to the surface."[33]

Just as there is a dividing line between exploration and development, so there is a line between development and operations. Once the latter line is crossed, the taxpayer's expenditures no longer qualify as IDC. Instead, they are either capitalized (and recovered through depletion or, if allocable to property with a limited useful life, through depreciation) or deducted as business expenses under §162, depending on their status under the rules for distinguishing capital expenditures for currently deductible costs.[34] Al-

---

[30] Standard Oil Co. (Ind.) v. CIR, 68 TC 325, 348 (1977) (acq.) (extensive analysis). See Central Oil Co. v. US, 71-1 USTC ¶9257 (SD Miss. 1970) (not officially reported), rev'd on another issue sub nom. Green v. US, 460 F2d 412 (5th Cir. 1972) (jury instructions re distinction between exploration and development). See also Reg. §1.612-4(a) ("cleaning of wells" within §263(c) option); Producers Chem. Co. v. CIR, 50 TC 940, 961–62 (1968) (acq.) (fracturing to open new producing zone for old wells qualifies as IDC); Monrovia Oil Co. v. CIR, 28 BTA 335 (1933), aff'd on another issue, 83 F2d 417 (9th Cir. 1936) (deepening well). See generally Linden, Review of Offshore Drilling—What Are Intangibles? 26 Inst. on Oil & Gas L. & Tax'n 441 (1975). See also Sun Co. v. CIR, 677 F2d 294 (3d Cir. 1982) (taxpayer allowed to deduct cost of drilling exploratory offshore oil wells from mobile rigs); Gates Rubber Co v. CIR, 74 TC 1456 (1980), aff'd per curiam, 694 F2d 648 (10th Cir. 1982) (same; *Standard Oil* followed); Rev. Rul. 88-10, 1988-6 IRB 5 (same).

[31] Gates Rubber Co. v. CIR, 74 TC 1456, 1476 (1980) (acq.), aff'd per curiam, 694 F2d 648 (10th Cir. 1982). See Sun Co. v. CIR, 677 F2d 294 (3d Cir. 1982) ("Obviously, such a construction would have the effect of turning the Congressional objective of rewarding risk-taking on its head.").

[32] Gates Rubber Co. v. CIR, supra note 31, at 1477.

[33] Id. at 1480.

[34] See Reg. §1.612-4(c). See Burnet v. P-M-K Petroleum Co., 24 BTA 360 (1931) (acq. on this issue), rev'd by stipulation, 66 F2d 1009 (8th Cir. 1933) (workover costs deductible as operating expenses); Rev. Rul. 70-414, 1970-2 CB 132 (producing well completed when casing, including so-called Christmas tree (valves and pipes controlling flow of oil and gas), is installed).

though currently deductible operating expenses and IDC are both deductible, they must be segregated, even if the taxpayer elects to expense IDC under §263(c). This is because expensed IDC are subject to recapture under §1254 and are sometimes preference items that cause the taxpayer to be subject to the alternative minimum tax, while expenses deductible under §162 entail neither of these consequences.[35]

¶26.1.4 Exercise of Option

The regulations provide that the option to deduct IDC may be exercised by claiming the costs as a deduction on the return for the first year in which they are paid or incurred and that no formal statement is necessary.[36] The courts may bail out a taxpayer who fails to deduct IDC on the first relevant return, but shows an intent to make a timely election, on the ground that the regulations are directory rather than mandatory.[37] "[A]n after-the-fact choice in the light of actual and apparent tax consequences," however, is likely to be rejected.[38] An election to deduct or capitalize IDC is binding for all IDC paid or incurred by the taxpayer during the year the election is made and all subsequent years.[39] In the case of partnerships, however, the election is made at the partnership level, and this enables taxpayers who wish to escape an earlier, ostensibly permanent election to do so by conducting later operations in partnership form.[40]

A failure to deduct IDC is tantamount to an election to capitalize the costs and recover them through depreciation or depletion.[41] Taxpayers elect-

---

[35] See infra ¶26.1.6.

[36] Reg. §1.612-4(d). If the taxpayer has capitalized IDC for any prior year, an election to expense them under §263(c) might be a change in accounting method that can only be made with IRS consent. See Standard Oil Co. (Ind.) v. CIR, 77 TC 349 (1981) (leaving basic issue undecided, but holding IRS consent unnecessary where taxpayer that historically expensed IDC seeks to redefine borderline between qualifying and nonqualifying costs).

[37] See Goodall's Est. v. CIR, 391 F2d 775, 803–05 (8th Cir. 1968), cert. denied, 393 US 829 (1969) (evidence established intent to deduct IDC), and cases therein cited; CIR v. Sklar Oil Corp., 134 F2d 221 (5th Cir. 1943) (deduction of some IDC on first return constituted election notwithstanding capitalization of other qualified IDC).

[38] Goodall's Est. v. CIR, supra note 37, at 805; CIR v. Titus Oil & Inv. Co., 132 F2d 969 (10th Cir. 1943) (election cannot be made on untimely amended return). See also Haggar Co. v. Helvering, 308 US 389 (1940) (effect of tentative return for similar purpose); Degnan v. CIR, 136 F2d 891 (9th Cir.), cert. denied, 320 US 778 (1943) (delinquent original return not "first return" for analogous purpose). See also infra ¶¶111.1.7, 111.1.8 (re amended, tentative, and defective returns).

[39] Reg. §1.612-4(e).

[40] Bentex Oil Corp. v. CIR, 20 TC 565 (1953).

[41] Reg. §1.612-4(d).

ing to capitalize IDC are granted a rarely exercised second election by the regulations for IDC in drilling nonproductive wells. Dry hole costs can be deducted as ordinary losses if the taxpayer clearly elects to do so on the return filed for the first year in which a nonproductive well is completed.[42] This election is also binding for all dry hole costs for later years. In the absence of this secondary election, dry hole costs must be recovered through depreciation to the extent represented by physical property and by depletion otherwise.[43]

Although an election to deduct IDC under §263(c) affects all oil and gas properties owned by the taxpayer, owners of fractional interests are entitled to elect individually, unaffected by the actions of their co-owners, unless they constitute an association taxable as a corporation.[44] A partnership election is binding as to all partnership properties, but each partner elects individually as to his nonpartnership interests.[45] In the same vein, a trust's election does not affect the right of the trustee or beneficiaries to make separate elections as to their individually owned properties.[46]

¶26.1.5 Limitations for Foreign Wells and Wells Owned by Integrated Oil Companies

Section 263(c) does not apply to IDC associated with productive wells located outside the United States, and an integrated oil company can expense only 70 percent of its otherwise qualifying IDC. The rules for foreign wells and wells owned by integrated oil companies are described below.

1. *Foreign wells.* Section 263(i) generally makes the expensing election of §263(c) inapplicable to IDC relating to an oil, gas, or geothermal well located outside the United States. Instead, a taxpayer can add these IDC to the well's basis for purposes of computing cost depletion. Alternatively, the taxpayer can elect to deduct them in 10 equal annual installments, beginning with the year in which they are paid or accrued. The term "United States" includes the states and the District of Columbia,[47] plus continental

---

[42] Reg. §1.612-4(b)(4). See Burke & Cole, Establishing Deductions for Worthless Oil and Gas Properties, 26 Oil & Gas Tax Q. 391 (1978).

[43] Reg. §1.612-4(b)(4).

[44] See Reg. §1.612-4(a); Wheelock v. CIR, 28 BTA 611 (1933) (acq.), aff'd without discussion of this point, 77 F2d 474 (5th Cir. 1935). For separate elections by corporations filing consolidated returns, see Rev. Rul. 69-590, 1969-2 CB 170.

[45] See Reg. §1.703-1(b); Rev. Rul. 54-42, 1954-1 CB 64. See also Bentex Oil Corp. v. CIR, 20 TC 565 (1953) (on facts, taxpayer was member of partnership or joint venture, which was entitled to exercise option to deduct IDC).

[46] See Dye v. CIR, ¶42,563 P-H Memo TC (1942) (trust election not binding on trustee's individually owned properties).

[47] IRC §7701(a)(9).

shelf areas adjacent to U.S. territorial waters "over which the United States has exclusive rights, in accordance with international law, with respect to the exploration and exploitation of natural resources."[48] The denial of the §263(c) election with respect to foreign wells was a response to the fact that in 1986, "domestic production of oil, gas, and other minerals [was] depressed and subject to serious international competition."[49]

Section 263(i) contains an exception that allows the expensing option of §263(c) for IDC relating to a foreign well that is "nonproductive." Also, §263(i) was enacted in 1986 and generally applies to costs paid or incurred after 1986.[50] For costs paid or incurred before 1987, §263(c) applies equally to foreign and domestic wells.

2. *Partial disallowance for integrated oil companies.* By reason of §291(b), an integrated oil company can expense only 70 percent of its IDC otherwise qualified under §263(c).[51] The other 30 percent is deducted in 60 equal monthly installments, commencing with the month in which the costs are paid or incurred. The term "integrated oil company" refers to a corporation that has economic interests in crude oil deposits and also carries on substantial retailing or refining operations.[52]

¶26.1.6 Ancillary Effects of Election to Deduct IDC

Although electing to deduct IDC is ordinarily advantageous to taxpayers, the benefits are subject to the following limitations and offsetting adverse consequences:

1. *Alternative minimum tax.* Under §57(a)(2), IDC are often treated as items of tax preference for purposes of the alternative minimum tax.[53] The amount of the preference is computed as follows: The taxpayer's IDC from

---

[48] IRC §638(1).

[49] Staff of Joint Comm. on Tax'n, 99th Cong., 2d Sess., General Explanation of the Tax Reform Act of 1986, at 197 (Comm. Print 1987).

[50] Pub. L. No. 99-514, §411(c), 100 Stat. 2085 (1986). A transition rule allows prior law to continue to apply to costs relating to wells in the North Sea if the taxpayer's interest in the well (1) is a minority interest under a license granted by the Netherlands or the United Kingdom and (2) was acquired before 1986. Id.

[51] This rule applies in taxable years beginning after 1982. The percentage remaining eligible for expensing was 85 percent for taxable years beginning in 1983 and 1984, and was lowered to 80 percent for taxable years beginning in 1985 and thereafter. The present percentage (70) applies to costs paid or incurred after 1986. P.L. No. 99-514, supra note 50.

[52] IRC §291(b)(4). An oil producer is deemed to be a substantial retailer or refiner if it is subject to the rules disqualifying retailers and refiners from taking percentage depletion. IRC §§613A(d)(2), (3); 4992(b); 4996(a)(1). See supra ¶24.3.3 for the percentage depletion rules for oil and gas.

[53] See infra ¶111.3.12 for the alternative minimum tax.

all oil and gas properties are aggregated, including only IDC deducted under §263(c) and excluding costs of nonproductive wells. From this aggregate are subtracted the deductions for IDC that would have been allowed for the year if IDC for all years had been capitalized and recovered ratably over 120 months. From the amount remaining is subtracted 65 percent of the taxpayer's net income from oil and gas properties.[54] The amount remaining after this second subtraction is the item of tax preference. The preference rule applies in like manner if IDC for geothermal deposits are deducted under §263(c); if the taxpayer has both oil and gas wells and geothermal wells, the preferences for these two types of properties are computed separately.

The charaterization of IDC as a preference item can be avoided by electing to amortize the costs over a 10-year period in lieu of expensing them under §263(c).[55] If this option is elected, 10 percent of IDC are deducted in the year the expenditures are made, and an additional 10 percent is allowed for each of the succeeding nine years. Although the principal reason for making the election is usually to avoid or reduce the alternative minimum tax, the 10-year write-off rule applies to an electing taxpayer in computing regular taxable income, as well as in determining the alternative minimum tax. The election can be made with respect to all or any portion of the taxpayer's IDC for a particular year. When IDC are incurred by a partnership or S corporation, the election is made at the partner or shareholder level.

2. Recapture. If gain is recognized on a disposition of an interest in oil, gas, or geothermal property, a recapture rule found in §1254 requires that all or a portion of the gain (the recapture amount) be treated as ordinary income. The recapture amount is the lesser of the gain or the sum of (1) the IDC deducted under §263(c) by the taxpayer or any other person that would otherwise have been reflected in the adjusted basis of the property[56] and (2) all depletion taken with respect to the property (excluding percentage depletion in excess of cost).[57] The recapture amount must be recognized even if

---

[54] The subtraction is 100 percent of this net income for taxable years before 1987. IRC §57(a)(11) (before amendment in 1986).

[55] IRC §59(e).

[56] IDC that have been deducted under the 10-year amortization rule of §59(e) or the 60-month amortization rule of §291(b) are included in the recapture amount as though they had been expensed under §263(c). IRC §§59(e)(5)(A); 291(b)(2). See supra ¶16.1.5 for §291(b).

For property placed in service before 1987, expensed IDC are included in the recapture amount only to the extent they exceed the amounts by which cost depletion deductions would have been increased if the IDC had been capitalized. IRC §1254(a)(4) (before amendment in 1986).

[57] Depletion is only included in the recapture amount with respect to property placed in service after 1986.

the taxpayer disposes of the interest in a transaction on which gain is not ordinarily recognized unless the transfer is exempted pursuant to §1254(b) by regulations similar to those issued under §§617(g), 1245(b) and (c), and 751.[58] In general, these rules exempt gifts, transfers at death, like-kind exchanges, partnership contributions, and transfers to controlled corporations.

3. *Ceiling on percentage depletion.* In applying a rule limiting percentage depletion to 50 percent of taxable income from the property, IDC deducted under §263(c) with respect to a property reduce taxable income from the property.[59]

4. *At risk rules.* If deducted under §263(c) rather than capitalized, IDC enter into the computation of losses subject to the at risk rules of §465, discussed elsewhere in this work.[60]

¶26.2 MINING EXPLORATION AND DEVELOPMENT EXPENDITURES

¶26.2.1 Introductory

Section 617(a) permits taxpayers to elect to deduct mining exploration expenditures paid or incurred before the mine's development stage, instead of capitalizing them.[1] Section 616(a) similarly allows an expensing of expenditures for the development of mines and other natural deposits, if paid or incurred after the existence of minerals in commercially marketable quantities has been established.[2] Neither provision applies to oil or gas wells or to expenditures for the acquisition or improvement of depreciable property. The technology of the particular industry determines whether an expenditure relates to exploration (subject to §617), to development (subject to §616), or to operations (subject to neither provision). Generalizations about their application therefore are either vague or, if specific, perilous.

---

[58] Such regulations have been proposed, but they have not yet been made final. Prop. Reg. §1.1254-2. See Joint Comm. on Tax'n, 94th Cong., 2d Sess., General Explanation of the Tax Reform Act of 1976, reprinted in 1976-3 CB (Vol. 2) 1, 67 n.4 (typical farmout arrangement not a disposition if shift in interests occurs under agreement made before IDC paid or incurred). See generally Crichton, Recapture of Intangibles Under Section 1254, 30 Inst. on Oil & Gas L. & Tax'n 509 (1979); Klein, The Oil and Gas Fund After Tax Reform, 27 Oil & Gas Tax Q. 38 (1978).

[59] Reg. §1.613-5(a); Helvering v. Wilshire Oil Co., 308 US 90, rehearing denied, 308 US 638 (1939). For the 50-percent-of-taxable-income limitation, see supra ¶24.3.5.

[60] Supra ¶25.11.

[1] See infra ¶26.2.2.

[2] See infra ¶26.2.3.

A third provision relating to mineral exploration and development, §621, excludes from gross income both payments and the forgiveness of loans by federal agencies to encourage exploration, development, or mining of critical and strategic minerals and metals under a program requiring the taxpayer to render an accounting to the appropriate agency. Excluded amounts cannot be deducted or taken into account in computing depletion, depreciation, or gain or loss on a disposition of the property unless repaid by the taxpayer, in which event the amount is either deductible or includable in the basis of the property at the time of the repayment.

¶26.2.2 Exploration Expenditures

Section 617(a)(1) grants taxpayers an election to deduct expenditures paid or incurred during the taxable year "for the purpose of ascertaining the existence, location, extent, or quality of any deposit of ore or other mineral," provided the expenditure (1) is paid or incurred before the beginning of the development stage of the mine and (2) is not otherwise allowable as a deduction.[3] The election does not apply to expenditures incurred in exploring for oil or gas.[4] It is also inapplicable to expenditures for the acquisition or improvement of depreciable property, but depreciation on such property, if allocable to exploration, is treated as an exploration expenditure. Further, if mineral property is located outside the United States, the §617(a) deduction is denied, and exploration expenditures relating to the property must either be added to the property's basis for cost depletion or be written off ratably over 10 years.[5] An additional restriction, relating to minerals that do not qualify for percentage depletion, is a virtual dead letter because all minerals now qualify for percentage depletion unless they come from an inexhaustible source like the air or seawater.[6]

---

[3] But see Snyder v. CIR, 86 TC 567 (1986) (§617 deduction denied for amount paid for filing of unpatented mining claim where payment was made pursuant to a promotion in which tax benefits were stressed and taxpayer was aware that value of claim was "totally speculative"; negligence penalty imposed); Kilroy v. CIR, 32 TCM (CCH) 27 (1973) (alternative holding — §617 not applicable to expenditures attributable to hobbies).

For the treatment of production payments carved out to finance exploration or development of mineral properties, see IRC §636(a); Rev. Rul. 74-549, 1974-2 CB 186; supra ¶24.4.1.

[4] For the deduction of intangible drilling and development expenditures incurred in exploring for oil, gas, and geothermal deposits, see supra ¶26.1.

[5] IRC §617(h). This rule only applies to costs paid or incurred after 1986. Exploration costs paid or incurred during the period 1970 through 1986 and allocable to foreign properties are deductible under §617(a) up to a lifetime limit of $400,000. IRC §617(h) (before amendment in 1986); Reg. §1.617-2(b).

[6] See supra ¶24.3.2.

An election under §617(a) applies not only to exploration expenditures in the year for which the election is made, but also to similar expenditures in later years, unless it is revoked with IRS consent.[7] When permitted, a revocation operates retroactively, requiring the taxpayer's tax liability for all prior years covered by the election to be recomputed; §617(a)(2)(C) extends the statutory period for the assessment of deficiencies accordingly.

The regulations provide that the exploration stage of the taxpayer's activities terminates and the development stage begins when, in consideration of all facts and circumstances, including the taxpayer's actions, deposits are disclosed in sufficient quantity and quality so that commercial exploitation by the taxpayer is reasonably justified.[8] Core drilling to ascertain the existence of commercially marketable ore is an exploration activity, for example, as is exploratory drilling from within an existing mine to ascertain the existence of what reasonably appears to be a different ore deposit. In contrast, core drilling "to further delineate the existence and location of an existing commercially marketable deposit to facilitate its development" is a development activity subject to §616 rather than to §617.[9]

Although §617 applies to some expenditures that would otherwise be nondeductible capital outlays, it does not encompass amounts paid to acquire a working or operating interest. For example, if a taxpayer agrees to pay all exploratory expenditures in return for an undivided three-fourths interest in a mineral lease, three fourths of the expenditures can be deducted under §616, but the remaining one fourth is the cost of the taxpayer's interest in the lease, which is recoverable through depletion or deductible as a loss if the lease proves to be worthless.[10]

---

[7] See Reg. §1.617-1(c)(1) (elections), §1.617-1(c)(3) (revocations). An election can be made at any time prior to the expiration of the statute of limitations on claims for refund for the year of election. IRC §617(a)(2)(B). If an election is made during the last two years of this limitations period, however, the statute of limitations on assessments of deficiencies is extended for two years from the date of the election. IRC §617(a)(2)(C).

[8] Reg. §1.617-1(a). See generally Grossman & Johnson, The Distinction Between Exploration and Development Expenditures in the Hard Minerals Industry, 27 Tax Lawyer 119 (1973).

[9] Grossman & Johnson, supra note 8. See also Santa Fe Pac. Ry. v. US, 378 F2d 72 (7th Cir. 1967) (exploration expenditures treated as such rather than as development expenditures, even though incurred after existence of mineral in commercially marketable quantity was disclosed); DeBie's Est. v. CIR, 56 TC 876 (1971) (extensive analysis of distinction between exploration and development); Kilroy v. CIR, 32 TCM (CCH) 27 (1973) (expenditure to find new mining techniques rather than to find new mines did not qualify; taxpayer's telephone, auto, and home office expenses too remote from exploration); Rev. Rul. 75-122, 1975-1 CB 87 (distinction between exploration expenditures and research and development expenditures subject to §174).

[10] See Reg. §1.617-1(b)(3).

If a taxpayer deducting exploration expenditures under §617(a) receives a bonus or royalty before the property reaches the producing stage, depletion is denied with respect to the bonus or royalty, except to the extent the depletion deduction, computed under the usual rules for depletion, exceeds the §617(a) deductions with respect to the property.[11] Assume a taxpayer receives a $100 bonus that would otherwise qualify her for percentage depletion at 22 percent; the taxpayer has deducted $15 under §617(a) for the current and prior years. The rule described here limits the percentage depletion deduction to $7.

Once the property reaches the producing stage, expenditures deducted under §617(a) must be recaptured by one of two alternative methods of recapture. At the taxpayer's election, the "adjusted exploration expenditures" are includable in gross income when the mine reaches "the producing stage."[12] The term "adjusted exploration expenditures" refers to the sum of the §617 deductions taken with respect to the property, both by the taxpayer and by any other person whose expenditures, if not so deducted, would be reflected in the taxpayer's basis for the property.[13] If the taxpayer received a bonus or royalty before the property reached the producing stage, adjusted exploration expenditures are reduced by the amount of percentage depletion lost under the rule described in the preceding paragraph. Amounts included in gross income under this option are treated as paid or incurred when the mine reaches the producing stage and as properly chargeable to capital account,[14] which entitles the taxpayer to include them in the depletable basis of the minerals and to offset any unrecovered amount against the amount realized on a sale or other disposition of the property.

If the taxpayer does not elect the foregoing method of recapturing the deducted expenditures, the depletion deductions otherwise allowable with respect to the property (not merely those allocable to the particular mine) are disallowed until the expenditures have been fully recaptured.[15] Because this method of recapturing §617 expenditures spreads them out over a period of time, it is ordinarily preferable, but taxpayers with net operating loss carryovers that are about to expire may find it preferable to include the exploration expenditures in gross income as soon as the mine reaches the producing stage. Accelerated recapture may also be elected in preference to deferred recapture in order to increase taxable income in a year in which the rule restricting percentage depletion to 50 percent of taxable income would

---

[11] IRC §617(c).

[12] The election must be made no later than the due date of the return (taking extensions into account) for the year the property reaches the producing stage. For the term "producing stage," see Reg. §1.616-2(b).

[13] IRC §617(f)(1).

[14] IRC §617(b)(1)(A); Reg. §1.617-3(a)(2).

[15] IRC §617(b)(1)(B); Reg. §1.617-3(a)(1)(i).

disallow part of the taxpayer's otherwise deductible depletion.[16] Whichever recapture method applies, §617 expenditures must be allocated to specific mines, since both methods apply to particular mines as they reach the producing stage.[17]

¶26.2.3 Development Expenditures

Section 616(a) allows the deduction of all expenditures paid or incurred during the taxable year for the development of a mine or other natural deposit, if paid or incurred after the existence of ores or minerals in commercially marketable quantities has been disclosed.[18] Section 616(a) does not apply to oil and gas wells or to expenditures for the acquisition or improvement of depreciable property, but depreciation itself can be a development expenditure. Further, if mineral property is located outside the United States, §616(a) does not apply, and development expenditures must either be added to the property's basis for cost depletion or be written off ratably over 10 years.[19] Under §616(b), taxpayers eligible for the §616(a) deduction can elect to forgo it and to instead treat development expenditures as deferred expenses to be included in the basis of the property and deducted on a ratable basis as the minerals are sold.

Development expenditures occupy a middle ground between exploration expenditures and operating expenses. Although all three can be deducted as paid or incurred, they differ in three important respects: (1) Exploration expenditures are deductible only if the taxpayer so elects, development expenditures are deductible unless the taxpayer elects otherwise, and operating expenses must be deducted; (2) exploration expenditures, if deducted, are subject to recapture when the mine reaches the producing stage,[20] while neither development nor operating expenditures are subject to recapture; and (3) exploration and development expenditures, if not deducted, are included in the basis of the property, but capitalized exploration expenditures are recovered through depletion while deferred development expenditures are deducted separately from depletion.

Because each of the three categories of expenditures has its own tax consequences, they must be distinguished—an especially difficult task if, as is possible, all three activities proceed at the same time. Under the regula-

---

[16] For the 50-percent-of-taxable-income limitation, see ¶24.3.5.

[17] Reg. §1.617-3(d)(3). See Rev. Rul. 77-188, 1977-1 CB 76.

[18] For the treatment of production payments carved out for the exploration or development of mineral properties, see IRC §636(a); Rev. Rul. 74-549, 1974-2 CB 186; supra ¶24.4.1.

[19] IRC §616(d). This rule only applies to costs paid or incurred after 1986, and §616 applies equally to foreign and domestic costs paid or incurred previously.

[20] Supra ¶26.2.2.

tions, the development stage of a mine is reached when, taking into account all facts and circumstances, including the taxpayer's actions, deposits of the mineral are shown to exist in sufficient quality and quantity reasonably to justify commercial exploitation by the taxpayer.[21] To qualify as development expenditures, however, costs not only must be paid or incurred after the existence of minerals in commercially marketable quantities is established, but also must be paid or incurred for the development of the mine or other natural deposit.[22] Thus, if the purchase price of a mine includes an amount intended to reimburse the seller for his development expenditures, the expenditures are not deductible by the buyer.[23] Similarly, if a taxpayer agrees to pay all expenditures required to develop a deposit in return for a three-fourths interest in a mineral lease, only three fourths of the expenditure can be deducted because the remaining onefourth is the cost of acquiring the taxpayer's interest in the lease.[24]

In two important Court of Claims cases, this acquisition-cost analysis was qualified by an emphasis on the taxpayer's primary purpose, under which the incidental acquisition of property rights does not preclude a deduction under §616 if the taxpayer's primary purpose in making the expenditure is to gain access to areas in which to conduct development activities.[25] With support from other courts, however, the IRS rejects this interpretation, arguing that the acquisition of property rights makes the expenditure a capital outlay to be recovered through depletion and that §616(a) is limited to expenditures "resulting directly from such physical mining processes or activities as the driving of shafts, tunnels, galleries, and similar operations undertaken to make the ore or mineral in place accessible for production operations."[26] The IRS distinguishes development expenditures from operating expenses, in contrast, by describing the former as

---

[21] Reg. §1.616-1(a); Grossman & Johnson, supra note 8.

[22] Santa Fe Pac. Ry. v. US, 378 F2d 72 (7th Cir. 1967). See Cushing Stone Co. v. US, 535 F2d 27 (Ct. Cl. 1976) (expenditures to relocate utility transmission lines constituted development expenditures); Rev. Rul. 66-170, 1966-1 CB 159 (contra); New Quincy Mining Co. v. CIR, 36 BTA 376 (1937) (embezzlement loss during development stage not incurred for development of mine).

[23] Reg. §1.616-1(b)(4). But see IRC §381(c)(10) (carryover of §616 deferred expenses in certain corporate acquisitions); Philadelphia & Reading Corp. v. US, 602 F2d 338 (Ct. Cl. 1979) (transferee under §351 not barred).

[24] Reg. §1.616-1(b)(3).

[25] Cushing Stone Co. v. US, supra note 22; Kennecott Copper Corp. v. US, 347 F2d 275 (Ct. Cl. 1965). See also Amherst Coal Co. v. US, 295 F. Supp. 421 (SD W. Va. 1969), aff'd per curiam, 71-1 USTC ¶9223 (4th Cir. 1971) (not officially reported) (cost of access roads deductible as development expenditure, although roads would also benefit mine in production stage).

[26] Rev. Rul. 67-35, 1967-1 CB 159 (IRS will not follow Kennecott). See also Geoghegan & Mathis, Inc. v. CIR, 453 F2d 1324 (6th Cir. 1972); H.G. Fenton Material Co. v. CIR, 74 TC 584 (1980) (cost of obtaining permits must be capital-

"expenditures that benefit an entire mineral deposit or large areas of a mineral deposit" by providing "benefits that extend over relatively long periods of extraction of the valuable ore or mineral," as contrasted with day-to-day operating expenses that are "integrally related to extraction of a limited area of the [mineral] to be mined."[27]

If the taxpayer elects under §616(b) to defer rather than deduct development expenditures, they are not recovered through depletion, but instead are deductible on a ratable basis as the minerals are sold.[28] This method of amortizing the deferred expenditures is similar to cost depletion, but it produces an additional deduction if percentage depletion is applicable. Elections can be made mine by mine and year by year. An election, however, must cover all development expenditures for the taxable year for each mine covered by the election, and elections cannot be revoked.[29]

If an election to defer development expenditures is made while the mine is still in the development stage, it covers only the excess of the expenditures over the net receipts, if any, from sales. This limitation, however, does not apply to development expenditures made when the mine is in a producing state—defined by the regulations as the time "when the major portion of the mineral production is obtained from workings other than those opened for the purpose of development, or when the principal activity of the mine or other natural deposit is the production of developed ores or minerals rather than the development of additional ores or minerals for mining."[30]

¶26.2.4 Limitations Applicable to Both Exploration and Development Expenditures

1. *Thirty percent reduction for corporations.* Section 291(b) scales back a corporation's deductions under §§616 and 617. Under this provision, §§616(a) and 617(a) can apply to only 70 percent of a corporation's mining exploration and development expenditures. The other 30 percent is amortized ratably over 60 months, beginning with the month in which the expen-

---

ized, but cost of removing sand from mining site was deductible despite incidental benefit to taxpayer's other property).

[27] Rev. Rul. 77-308, 1977-2 CB 208.

[28] IRC §616(b). For the allocation of deferred expenses among the mineral units sold, see Reg. §1.616-2(f). See also Philadelphia & Reading Corp. v. US, 602 F2d 338 (Ct. Cl. 1979) (successor in §351 transaction entitled to amortize transferor's deferred expenses).

[29] For the method of electing, see Reg. §1.616-2(e). See also Reg. §1.616-2(c) (transfer of mineral interest after election).

[30] Reg. §1.616-2(b).

ditures are paid or incurred.[31]

2. *Alternative minimum tax.* Deductions for mining exploration and development expenditures are slowed down in the computation of alternative minimum taxable income, the base on which the alternative minimum tax is imposed.[32] Specifically, the deductions allowed by §§616 and 617 are not permitted for this purpose; the alternative minimum tax allowance for mining exploration and development expenditures (including any portion subject to 60-month amortization under §291(b) for regular tax purposes) is determined by capitalizing all such expenditures made after 1986 and amortizing them ratably over 10 years, beginning with the year in which they are made. If the property is abandoned before the end of the amortization period, the unrecovered portion of the expenses is allowed as a loss for alternative minimum tax purposes.

Under §59(e), a taxpayer can elect 10-year amortization for regular tax purposes, in which case mining exploration and development expenditures are treated identically in determining regular taxable income and alternative minimum taxable income.[33] This election can be made year by year with respect to all or any portion of the costs that would otherwise be deductible under §616 or §617 for the year. When mining exploration and development expenditures are made by a partnership or S corporation, the election is made at the partner or shareholder level.

The foregoing rules do not apply to expenditures relating to oil, gas, and geothermal wells, which are treated similarly but not identically under the alternative minimum tax.[34]

---

[31] These percentages apply to costs paid or incurred after 1986. When §291(b) was first enacted, effective for taxable years beginning after 1982, the percentages were 85 percent currently deductible and 15 percent amortized. The percentages were thereafter revised to 80 and 20 for taxable years beginning after 1984. Also, for costs paid or incurred before 1987, the amortized portion is recovered in five annual installments computed as 15 percent of the capitalized amount for the year the costs are paid or incurred, 22 percent for the next year, and 21 percent for each of the next three years. IRC §291(b)(3) (before amendment in 1986).

[32] IRC §56(a)(2). For the alternative minimum tax, see infra ¶111.3.12.

[33] IRC §59(e). If the statute is read literally, costs subject to 60-month amortization under §291(b) do not qualify for 10-year amortization under §59(e). The latter provision only applies to amounts that in the absence of the §59(e) election, "would have been allowable as a deduction for the taxable year in which paid or incurred under . . . section 616(a) . . . or section 617(a)," and §291(b) describes an amount subject to 60-month amortization as a reduction of "the amount allowable as a deduction . . . under section 616(a) or 617(a)." The literal application of the statute, however, is inconsistent with its intent because amounts amortized over 60 months for regular tax purposes are subject to 10-year amortization for alternative minimum tax purposes and the objective of §59(e) is to allow the same method to apply for both purposes.

[34] See supra ¶26.1.6.

3. *Recapture on disposition.* If gain is realized on a disposition of property as to which mining exploration or development expenditures have been deducted under §617(a) or §616(a), §1254 usually requires that at least part of the gain be reported as ordinary income. The ordinary income amount is the lesser of the gain or the sum of (1) any amounts deducted under §§617 and 616 by the taxpayer or a prior owner of the property if, in the absence of these deductions, the amounts would have been included in the taxpayer's adjusted basis for the property and (2) depletion taken with respect to the property (exclusive of percentage depletion in excess of basis). If the taxpayer has elected to amortize mining exploration or development expenditures over 10 years under §59(e), amortization deductions are treated for this purpose as though they had been taken under §617 or §616.[35] Also, for a corporation, all previously deducted exploration and development expenditures are included in the recapture amount, including both the 70 percent deductible under §§617(a) and 616(a) and the 30 percent written off over 60 months under §291(b).[36] The ordinary income amount must usually be recognized even if the disposition is a nonrecognition transaction, but this rule is subject to a few exceptions that are described elsewhere in this Chapter in connection with the application of §1254 to oil and gas.[37]

Section 1254 applies to a disposition of mining property (other than oil, gas, and geothermal wells) only if the property was placed in service after 1986. For property placed in service before 1987, mining exploration expenditures (but not development expenditures) are recaptured on disposition under §617(d), which requires that gain be recognized as ordinary income up to the amount of the adjusted exploration expenditures for the property. "Adjusted exploration expenditures" consists of the sum of the amounts deducted under §617(a), reduced by the otherwise allowable depletion deductions that were lost under the various predisposition recapture rules within §617.[38] Section 617(d) differs from §1254 principally in that (1) it encompasses neither development expenditures nor depletion and (2) the recapture potential under §617(d) disappears once the taxpayer reaches the point where exploration expenditures would have been fully recovered by depletion in the absence of the §617(a) deduction.

Section 617(d) applies to a sale, exchange, involuntary conversion, or other disposition, and often requires that the ordinary income amount be recognized even though the disposition is one in which gain is not usually recognized. As with other recapture provisions, however, §617(d) exempts gifts, transfers at death, and certain other tax-free dispositions by adopting

---

[35] IRC §59(e)(5)(A).
[36] IRC §291(b)(3).
[37] Supra ¶26.1.6.
[38] IRC §617(f)(1). See supra ¶26.2.2 text accompanying notes 12–17 for the predisposition recapture rules.

the exceptions and limitations applicable to the recapture of depreciation under §1245.[39]

¶26.3 RESEARCH AND EXPERIMENTAL EXPENDITURES

¶26.3.1 Introductory

At the taxpayer's election, §174 allows research and experimental expenditures in connection with a trade or business to be deducted as paid or incurred or to be deferred and amortized over at least 60 months.[1] The regulations provide that expenditures of this type that are neither deducted nor deferred and amortized are chargeable to capital account,[2] in which event they are (1) deducted through depreciation over the estimated useful life of the asset generated by the expenditures, (2) held in abeyance and offset against the sales price of the asset if it does not have a limited useful life, or (3) deducted as a loss if the asset is abandoned or the research project is a failure.

Section 174 was enacted in 1954 "to eliminate uncertainty and to encourage taxpayers to carry on research and experimentation."[3] It was also asserted that §174 would be "particularly valuable to small and growing businesses" because under pre-1954 law small companies had more difficulties than large ones in sustaining deductions for research expenses.[4] The uncertainty that §174 was designed to eliminate arose because the only statutory authority under prior law for deducting research and experimental expenditures was §162, relating to ordinary and necessary business expenses, which only allows expenses incurred in carrying on an existing business and permits no deduction for costs with a sufficiently long-range impact to constitute capital outlays.[5] In the latter situation, the capitalized amount can be deducted through depreciation only if a limited useful life can be ascribed to the results of the research. It is also often difficult to determine when a line of research has ended in a blind alley, justifying an

---

[39] For §1245, see infra ¶55.2.3.

[1] See generally Alexander, Research and Experimental Expenditures Under the 1954 Code, 10 Tax L. Rev. 549 (1955); Blake, Research & Experimental Costs, 16 NYU Inst. on Fed. Tax'n 831 (1958); Horwood & Hindin, Supreme Court Adopts Liberal Definition of R&D Deductibility Under Section 174, 41 J. Tax'n 2 (1974).

Section 41 allows a credit against tax for some research expenses. See infra ¶27.4.2.

[2] Reg. §1.174-1.

[3] S. Rep. No. 1622, 83d Cong., 2d Sess. 33 (1954).

[4] Snow v. CIR, 416 US 500, 503 (1974) (quoting Congressman Reed, chairman of the House Ways and Means Comm.).

[5] See generally supra ¶20.4.1.

abandonment loss, and when it is only temporarily stymied or has yielded benefits to other lines of research. By electing either to deduct research and experimental expenditures under §174(a) or to defer and amortize them under §174(b), the taxpayer can avoid these impalpable distinctions.[6]

Section 174 only applies to expenditures paid or incurred "in connection with [the taxpayer's] trade or business." The Supreme Court observed in *Snow v. CIR* that this phrase is broader than the language of §162, which allows expenses paid or incurred "in carrying on" the taxpayer's trade or business, and that §174 can be used by companies "that are upcoming and about to reach the market" as well as by existing businesses.[7] The looseness of the trade-or-business requirement as so construed has made the expensing option of §174(a) a favorite of tax shelter promoters. In *Green v. CIR*, however, the Tax Court warned that *Snow* did not issue a carte blanche for the expensing of any cost that can fit within the description "research or experimental":

> Although the Supreme Court established in *Snow* that the taxpayer need not currently be producing or selling any product in order to obtain a deduction for research expenses, it did not eliminate the "trade or business" requirement of section 174 altogether. For section 174 to apply, the taxpayer must still be engaged in a trade or business *at some time*, and we must still determine, through an examination of the facts of each case, whether the taxpayer's activities in connection with a product are sufficiently substantial and regular to constitute a trade or business for purposes of such section.[8]

In *Green*, a partnership that contracted for research work to be done for it by someone else was held ineligible under §174 because the partnership's activities never went beyond investment.[9] More broadly, the *Snow* rule allowing §174 to apply to embryo business enterprises probably does not extend to irregular and sporadic profit-oriented activities in the absence of evidence that they will develop into a business if the research is successful.

---

[6] For these problems under pre-1954 law, which continue to arise if the taxpayer does not elect to deduct or defer and amortize research expenditures under §174, see Alexander, supra note 1, at 549–52.

[7] Snow v. CIR, supra note 4, at 504. See also Rev. Rul. 71-162, 1971-1 CB 97 (§174 encompasses expenditures to develop new products or processes, even if unrelated to taxpayer's current product lines or manufacturing processes). For investigative and preoperating expenses, see supra ¶20.4.4. See also Lee, Pre-Operating Expenses and Section 174: Will *Snow* Fall? 27 Tax Lawyer 381 (1974).

[8] Green v. CIR, 83 TC 667, 686–87 (1984).

[9] Section 174 was held inapplicable on similar facts in Spellman v. CIR, 845 F2d 148 (7th Cir. 1988) (summary judgment for government affirmed); Levin v. CIR, 832 F2d 403, 406 (7th Cir. 1987) ("The concept of 'trade or business' is plastic, . . . but it hardly follows that anything goes.").

A fortiori, §174 does not embrace research conducted as a hobby or any other project not engaged in for profit.[10]

¶26.3.2 Scope of Research and Experimental Expenditures

The regulations define "research and experimental expenditures" as research and development costs "in the experimental or laboratory sense," including costs incident to the development of pilot models, processes, products, formulas, inventions, and similar property; costs incurred in improving any of these items; and legal and other expenses incurred in obtaining a patent.[11] The principal borderline expenditures raising issues under §174 are:

1. *Operating expenditures.* The regulations provide that the term "research and experimental expenditures" does not include the cost of testing products or materials for quality control or of efficiency surveys, management studies, consumer surveys, advertising, or promotional activities.[12] Whether these expenditures are deductible or not depends on whether they qualify under §162 as ordinary and necessary business expenses.[13]

---

[10] Gyro Eng'r Corp. v. CIR, 33 TCM (CCH) 1343 (1974) (expenses of research conducted as hobby nondeductible, distinguishing *Snow*, which involved "a partnership that was actively developing an incinerator for the purpose of profitably marketing it even though the partnership was not yet producing any products"). See Mayrath v. CIR, 357 F2d 209 (5th Cir. 1966) (pre-*Snow* hobby case); Asta v. CIR, 35 TCM (CCH) 492 (1976) (teacher's research not related to any trade or business). For hobby expenses, see generally supra ¶22.5; see also supra ¶20.5.1 (difference between sporadic profit-oriented activities and a business in applying §§162 and 212).

For a zany effort to deduct living expenses under §174, on the theory that they were part of gross national product and hence related to the taxpayer's economic research, see Johnson v. CIR, 37 TCM (CCH) 1231 (1978) (deduction disallowed; taxpayer's good faith questioned).

[11] Reg. §1.174-2(a)(1).

[12] Id. See also Mayrath v. CIR, 41 TC 582, 590 (1964), aff'd on other grounds, 357 F2d 209 (5th Cir. 1966) (deductions were not for "expenditures of an investigative nature expended in developing the *concept* of a model or product"); Rev. Rul. 80-245, 1980-2 CB 72 (public utility's expenditures for environmental impact studies relating to proposed nuclear power plant are not research or experimental expenditures); Rev. Rul. 71-363, 1971-2 CB 156 (advertising agency's expenses for sales promotion materials not deductible under §174); Rev. Rul. 67-401, 1967-2 CB 123 (legal and accounting expenses relating to tax and rate-regulation aspects of public utility's research project not research expenditures "in the experimental or laboratory sense"). But see Rev. Rul. 73-275, 1973-1 CB 134 (engineering expenses incurred to develop machine system to suit customer's special needs deductible, even though each design results in production of only one system).

[13] For §162, see generally supra Ch. 20.

The distinction drawn by the regulations is consistent with the National Science Foundation's distinction between "basic and applied research in the sciences and engineering and the design and development of prototypes and processes" and "quality control, routine product testing, market research, sales promotion, sales service, research in the social sciences or psychology, and other nontechnological activities or technical services."[14] The Financial Accounting Standards Board similarly distinguishes research ("planned search or critical investigation" to develop a new product, service, or process or to significantly improve an existing one) and development ("conceptual formulation, design, and testing of product alternatives, construction of prototypes, and operation of pilot plants") from "routine or periodic alterations to existing products, production lines, manufacturing processes, and other on-going operations," as well as market research and testing.[15]

2. *Land and depreciable assets.* Section 174(c) explicitly disqualifies expenditures to acquire or improve land or depreciable or depletable property, even though it is to be used in connection with research or experimentation. For example, expenditures to construct and equip a research laboratory cannot be deducted or amortized under §174, but are instead subject to the normal rules requiring them to be capitalized and depreciated. Depreciation allowances on the facility, however, are research and experimental expenditures under §174.[16]

If research and experimental expenditures result in a depreciable end product to be used in the taxpayer's trade or business, such as a patent, any amounts that have not been deducted or amortized when the end product comes into being become the basis of the product and can be depreciated over its estimated useful life.[17]

3. *Mineral exploration expenditures.* By virtue of §174(d), expenditures to ascertain the existence, location, extent, or quality of oil, gas, or other minerals cannot be deducted or amortized under §174. These expenditures, however, do qualify for generous treatment under other statutory provisions.[18]

---

[14] National Science Foundation, Research and Development in Industry 1973 (Government Printing Office 1974).

[15] FASB, Statement of Financial Accountancy Standards No. 2—Accounting for Research and Development, reprinted in 138(6) J. Acct. 81, 82 (Dec. 1974).

[16] See Reg. §1.174-2(b)(1).

[17] Reg. §§1.174-2(b)(2), -4(a)(4).

[18] See supra ¶26.1 (intangible drilling and development expenses incurred in oil and gas activities), ¶26.2 (expenses for development of mines and natural deposits other than oil and gas wells). See also Rev. Rul. 75-122, 1975-1 CB 87 (line between research and experimental expenditures and mine development expenditures).

4. *Literary projects.* The regulations exclude expenditures for literary, historical, and similar research projects, presumably on the ground that they are not the type of activities contemplated by Congress in enacting §174.[19] The IRS has announced that the costs of developing computer programs, including ancillary descriptive documents, are so similar to research and experimental expenditures as to warrant similar accounting treatment and that the software expenses can be either deducted or deferred and amortized under rules analogous to those of §174, whether or not the software is patented or copyrighted.[20]

5. *Commissioned research.* Section 174 covers not only in-house research and experimental expenditures, but also amounts paid for work performed by others for the taxpayer's benefit.[21] The cost of land or depreciable property to which the taxpayer acquires ownership rights and the costs of purchasing patents, models, products, or processes from other persons, however, do not qualify.[22] Payments by members of trade associations to foster research have been held deductible under §174 in several IRS rulings, even though the taxpayers were evidently not the sole beneficiaries of the activities financed by them.[23]

¶26.3.3 Election to Deduct or Amortize

Under §174(a), qualified expenditures can be deducted in the year paid or incurred, rather than charged to capital account. If this method of accounting for qualifying expenditures is adopted, it must be used for all qualifying expenditures in the taxable year of adoption and all subsequent years, unless the IRS consents to a different method for part or all of the

---

[19] Reg. §1.174-1(a)(1). See Quinn v. CIR, 33 TCM (CCH) 310 (1974) (travel expenses incurred in seeking suitable locale to film *Zorba the Greek* not allowable under §174 because encompassed by reference to "literary, historical and similar projects"). Section 263A and the regulations thereunder require that prepublication expenditures of authors and publishers and the production expenses of producers of motion pictures, videotapes, and sound recordings must be capitalized as the basis of their works. See infra ¶105.4.

[20] Rev. Proc. 69-21, 1969-2 CB 303.

[21] If the taxpayer's only substantial activity is the commissioning of research, however, §174 might be unavailable for the lack of a trade or business. See supra text accompanying notes 6–10.

[22] Reg. §1.174-2(a)(1), (2). See also Reg. §1.174-2(b)(3) (machine purchased subject to performance guaranty, turnkey contract with guaranty of productive capacity, etc.); but see Rev. Rul. 66-30, 1966-1 CB 55 (payments to holders of U.S. patents and patent applications for foreign rights to the inventions are not expenses of research conducted by others on taxpayer's behalf).

[23] Rev. Rul. 73-324, 1973-2 CB 72 (payments to association's research fund); Rev. Rul. 73-20, 1973-1 CB 133 (same).

expenditures.[24] The expensing method can be elected without IRS consent by claiming a deduction on the return for the first taxable year in which qualifying expenditures are paid or incurred.[25] If it is not adopted for the first permissible year, IRS consent is required to adopt the method for a later year.

Instead of being expensed, qualified expenditures can be deferred and amortized under §174(b)(1) at the taxpayer's election, provided they are chargeable to capital account but not to depreciable or depletable property. Thus, expenditures cannot be amortized but must instead be depreciated if they culminate in property with a determinable useful life.[26]

When an amortization election is properly made, the expenditures are amortized ratably over a period of not less than 60 months, as selected by the taxpayer, beginning with the first month in which the taxpayer realizes benefits from the expenditures—which, in the absence of a showing to the contrary, is the month in which the taxpayer first puts the process, invention, or other property created by the expenditures to an income-producing use.[27] The basis of the property produced by the expenditures must be reduced by the larger of (1) the amortization allowed, except to the extent the deduction produces no tax benefit or (2) the amount allowable.[28] Should the results of the research project be abandoned before the expenditures have been fully amortized, the unrecovered balance can be deducted as a loss under §165.[29]

The amortization election is unavailable if the taxpayer has elected the expensing option under 174(a).[30] In other words, the statutes do not allow the expensing of some expenditures and the amortization of others. When available, however, the amortization election can be limited to one or more research projects, and different amortization periods can be assigned to

---

[24] IRC §174(a)(3); Reg. §1.174-3(a). See also Rev. Rul. 58-78, 1958-1 CB 148 (election permitted regardless of method of accounting in reporting research expenditures on taxpayer's books of account and financial statements); Rev. Rul. 58-74, 1958-1 CB 148 (taxpayer electing expensing method who failed to deduct all qualified expenditures should file amended return, since election is binding and allowable amounts cannot be deducted in later years).

[25] IRC §174(a)(2); Reg. §1.174-3(b)(1); Rev. Rul. 70-637, 1970-2 CB 64 (taxpayer failing to elect by due date of return cannot elect thereafter by amended return or claim for refund); Rev. Rul. 58-356, 1958-2 CB 104 (expensing election effective although research expenses were included in expense accounts for salaries, supplies, etc., rather than shown on return as separate item).

[26] Reg. §1.174-4(a)(2).

[27] Reg. §1.174-4(a)(3).

[28] IRC §1016(a)(14); Reg. §1.1016-5(j). See infra ¶42.3 (similar basis adjustments for depreciation).

[29] Reg. §1.174-4(a)(3). For §165 (abandonment losses), see supra ¶25.4.3.

[30] Reg. §1.174-4(a)(1).

each project.[31] The election must be made not later than the due date (including extensions) of the return for the taxable year to which the method is to apply.[32] Once made, however, the election and the chosen amortization periods are controlling for subsequent taxable years unless the IRS allows the taxpayer to shift to a different method or period.[33]

The alternative minimum tax rules contain a second amortization election, described more fully below,[34] whose availability is not affected by elections previously made under §174.

¶26.3.4 Treatment Under Alternative Minimum Tax

In determining alternative minimum taxable income (the base on which the alternative minimum tax is imposed), research and experimental expenditures of a taxpayer other than a corporation must be capitalized and amortized over 10 years, beginning with the year in which the expenditures are made.[35] Neither expensing under §174(a) nor 60-month amortization under §174(b), in other words, can be used by such a taxpayer for purposes of the alternative minimum tax, regardless of the method used in determining regular taxable income. Corporations, in contrast, can use both of the §174 options for alternative minimum tax as well as regular tax purposes.

Buried within the alternative minimum tax rules is an election, available to any taxpayer, to amortize research or experimental expenditures over 10 years for regular tax purposes.[36] This election can be made for all or any portion of these expenditures incurred during any year, even if an expensing or amortization election under §174 applies to other expenditures made in the same or other years. Although the purpose of the election is to allow the same method to be used for both regular and alternative minimum tax purposes, it is not so limited; it can be made by a corporation that is not otherwise affected by the alternative minimum tax rules for research and experimental expenditures or by an individual who is not subject to the alternative minimum tax, even without the election.

---

[31] Reg. §1.174-4(a)(5) (election can be made for all expenditures or only those for particular project); §1.174-4(a)(3) (amortization period can vary from project to project).

[32] For the method of making the election, see Reg. §1.174-4(b); Rev. Rul. 76-324, 1976-2 CB 77 (claim on return without written election not sufficient).

[33] IRC §174(b)(2); Reg. §1.174-4(b).

[34] Infra ¶26.3.4.

[35] IRC §56(b)(2). See infra ¶111.3.12 for the alternative minimum tax.

[36] IRC §59(e).

¶26.4 DEDUCTION AND AMORTIZATION OF CERTAIN CAPITAL OUTLAYS

¶26.4.1 Introductory

The general depreciation and amortization rules[1] are supplemented by several special provisions allowing capital outlays to be deducted currently, amortized over periods shorter than the property's useful life, or amortized over arbitrarily designated periods where depreciation would normally be denied for lack of an ascertainable useful life. In the latter situation, were it not for the special provision, the taxpayer's investment would be held in abeyance, to be offset against the sales proceeds if the asset is sold or to be deducted as a loss if it becomes worthless and is abandoned. The function of most of these provisions is to provide incentives for investments that Congress views as socially desirable but not sufficiently profitable to be made without a subsidy, to alleviate inequalities among taxpayers, or to eliminate uncertainty by establishing a permissible period for the amortization of assets whose useful life is inordinately difficult to determine. Many of the provisions have expired or been repealed in recent years as tax incentives have generally fallen out of favor.

¶26.4.2 Business Start-Up Expenditures

Section 195 allows an election whereby the costs of starting up a business can be amortized ratably over a period of 60 months or more.[2] The provision was enacted in 1980 in order to "encourage formation of new businesses and decrease controversy and litigation arising under [prior] law with respect to the proper income tax classification of startup expenditures."[3]

The election applies to "start-up expenditures," defined as costs paid or incurred in (1) investigating the creation or acquisition of an active trade or business, (2) creating such a trade or business, or (3) carrying on a profit-oriented activity in anticipation of the activity becoming an active trade or business.[4] Such a cost, however, only qualifies to the extent it would be

---

[1] For depreciation and amortization, see generally supra Ch. 23.

[2] See generally Seago, The Treatment of Start-up Costs Under Section 195, 66 J. Tax'n 362 (1987); Shapiro & Shaw, Start-Up Expenditures—Section 195: Clarification or More Confusion? 1982 S. Cal. Tax Inst. ¶1100; Solomon & Weintraub, Business Start-Up Expenses and Section 195: Some Unresolved Problems, 60 Taxes 27 (1982).

[3] H.R. Rep. No. 1278, 96th Cong., 2d Sess. 10, reprinted in 1980-2 CB 709. For the prior law, see supra ¶20.4.4.

[4] IRC §195(c)(1). Congress intended that "start-up expenditures" include costs of the types involved in Blitzer v. US, 684 F2d 874 (Ct. Cl. 1982) (management fee

deductible if incurred in operating an existing business of the same type. "Thus, amounts paid or incurred in connection with the sale of stock, securities, or partnership interests . . . e.g., securities registration expenses, underwriters' commissions, etc., are not startup expenditures."[5] Also, interest, taxes, and research or experimental expenditures that qualify for immediate deduction under §§163, 164, and 174 are not start-up expenditures. The costs of inventory and depreciable property (including "expenses incident to a lease and leasehold improvements") are not covered by §195, but are instead subject to the cost recovery rules generally applicable to such property.[6] Further, the purchase price of a business (as distinguished from costs incurred in investigating the purchase opportunity) do not qualify under §195.

Examples of start-up expenditures are

> investigatory costs incurred in reviewing a prospective business prior to reaching a final decision to acquire or to enter that business. These costs include expenses incurred for the analysis or survey of potential markets, products, labor supply, transportation facilities, etc. Eligible expenses also include startup costs which are incurred subsequent to a decision to establish a particular business and prior to the time when the business begins. For example, startup costs include advertising salaries and wages paid to employees who are being trained and their instructors, travel and other expenses incurred in lining up prospective distributors, suppliers or customers, and salaries or fees paid or incurred for executives, consultants, and for similar professional services.[7]

Expenses incurred in expanding an existing business, in contrast, are not start-up expenditures, but instead are deductible as paid or incurred.[8]

Section 195 does not apply to costs incurred in investigating a passive investment, and the distinction between business and other profit-oriented

---

paid by partnership organized to build and operate housing complex before first rents received); Brotherman v. US, 6 Cl. Ct. 407, 84-2 USTC ¶9846 (1984) (costs incurred by cable television operator before first revenues received from subscribers); Hoopengarner v. CIR, 80 TC 538 (1983) (rent paid under ground lease where taxpayer acquired lease in order to build and operate office building on the land and rent in question paid before building completed); Johnsen v. CIR, 83 TC 103 (1984) (management fee and loan costs of partnership organized to develop apartment project, paid before first rental income received). See Staff of Joint Comm. on Tax'n, 98th Cong., 2d Sess., General Explanation of the Revenue Provisions of the Tax Reform Act of 1984, at 296 (1984) [hereinafter 1984 Bluebook].

[5] H.R. Rep. No. 1278, supra note 3, at 11.
[6] IRC §195(c)(1). H.R. Rep. No. 1278, supra note 3, at 11.
[7] Id. at 10–11.
[8] Id. at 11.

activities is thus crucial to its application. Generally, an activity is a business if its expenses are deductible under §162, but not if §212 is the basis for the taxpayer's deductions.[9] "Further, in the case of rental activites, there must be significant furnishing of services incident to the rentals to constitute an active business."[10] Costs incurred in investigating the purchase of an apartment or office building, for example, are not eligible under §195 unless that taxpayer's activities in the operation of the building will go beyond routine maintenance and management.

Also, where costs relate to the acquisition of an existing business, the taxpayer qualifies under §195 only if he acquires "an equity interest in, and actively participates in the management of, the trade or business," a requirement that is always met by the purchase of a sole proprietorship but cannot be met by the purchase of "a bond or other debt instrument (even if convertible), preferred stock, or a limited partnership interest."[11] A common stock acquisition is a nonqualifying investment, rather than a business purchase, unless "in substance, [it] is the acquisition of the assets of a trade or business," as in the case of "the acquisition of a corporation which is then liquidated" or where the acquired corporation becomes a member of an affiliated group (including the taxpayer) that files consolidated returns.[12] A general partnership interest is a business purchase rather than an investment "if the taxpayer actively participates in the management of the trade or business."[13]

When the election is made, the taxpayer must also select an amortization period, which can be of any length so long as it is not shorter than 60 months. The amortization period begins with the month "in which the active business begins."[14] An acquired business is deemed to commence when the taxpayer acquires it; the Treasury is authorized to provide rules for determining when a business created by the taxpayer is deemed to begin, but has not yet done so.[15] Implicit in the starting date rule is that §195 is inapplicable where the taxpayer incurs otherwise qualifying costs in investigating or starting up a venture that never gets off the ground.[16] If the trade or business is "completely disposed of" by the taxpayer before the end of the amortization period, the unamortized portion of the costs can be deducted as a loss under §165.[17]

---

[9] Id.
[10] Id.
[11] Id. at 11–12.
[12] Id. at 12.
[13] Id.
[14] IRC §195(b)(1).
[15] IRC §195(c)(2).
[16] H.R. Rep. No. 1278, supra note 3, at 12–13.
[17] IRC §195(b)(2).

The election must be made by the due date (including extensions) of the return for the year in which business operations begin.[18] When made, the election and the amortization period chosen apply for that year and all subsequent years. When start-up expenditures are incurred by a partnership, the election is made by the partnership, not the partners individually.[19] If the election is not made, start-up expenditures must be capitalized, and can only be deducted when the business is abandoned or sold.[20]

¶26.4.3 Pollution Control Facilities

To encourage private industry to invest in antipollution facilities that "generally do not result in any increase in the profitability of a plant," Congress in 1969 enacted §169, permitting certified pollution control facilities to be amortized, at the taxpayer's election, over 60 months, beginning with the month following completion or acquisition of the facility or with the following taxable year.[21]

Section 169(d) imposes several restrictions that a facility must meet to qualify. The facility must be "a new identifiable treatment facility which is used in connection with a plant or other property in operation before January 1, 1976." Only tangible property can qualify, and buildings and structural components are excluded, except for buildings used exclusively as treatment facilities. Also, the function of the facility must be "to abate or control water or atmospheric pollution or contamination by removing, altering, disposing, storing, or preventing the creation or emission of pollutants, contaminants, wastes, or heat." Further, the facility must be certified by federal and state authorities as conforming to prescribed standards for the prevention, abatement, or control of water or air pollution, and it must

---

[18] IRC §195(d).

[19] H.R. Rep. No. 1278, supra note 3, at 13.

[20] The statute says "no deduction" is permitted for start-up expenditures in the absence of an amortization election. IRC §195(a). The title of §195(a) and the legislative history indicate, however, that only a current deduction is barred and that start-up expenditures not covered by an election are capitalized, not permanently banished from the ken of the taxman. See 1984 Bluebook, supra note 4, at 296.

[21] S. Rep. No. 552, 91st Cong., 1st Sess., reprinted in 1969-3 CB 423, 580. For later amendments, see Joint Comm. on Tax'n, 95th Cong., 2d Sess., General Explanation of the Revenue Act of 1978, at 149 (1979) [hereinafter 1978 Bluebook]; Joint Comm. on Tax'n, 94th Cong., 2d Sess., General Explanation of the Tax Reform Act of 1976, reprinted in 1976-3 CB (Vol. 2) 1, 631 [hereinafter 1976 Bluebook]. See generally Givelber & Schaffer, Section 169 of the Internal Revenue Code: An Income Tax Subsidy for the Control of Pollution, 14 Ariz. L. Rev. 65 (1972); McDaniel & Kaplinsky, The Use of the Federal Income Tax System to Combat Air and Water Pollution: A Case Study in Tax Expenditures, 12 BC Indus. & Com. L. Rev. 351 (1971).

not significantly increase the output, capacity, or useful life of the taxpayer's plant or reduce its operating costs.

In the same vein, §169(e) forbids the certification of facilities whose costs will be met over the facility's useful life by the recovery of wastes or otherwise. If the facility has a useful life in excess of 15 years, the amortization rule only applies to a portion of its basis (equal to the entire cost multiplied by a fraction whose numerator is 15 and whose denominator is the facility's useful life).[22] The basis of dual-purpose facilities must also be split, since only the pollution control portion of the cost qualifies under §169.[23]

Amortization under §169 displaces otherwise allowable depreciation deductions, except for any part of the facility's basis that does not qualify for amortization. At the taxpayer's election, however, amortization under §169 can be terminated at any time, in which event depreciation deductions are thereafter allowable, based on the facility's estimated remaining useful life as of the termination of amortization.

¶26.4.4 Removal of Barriers to Handicapped and Elderly

Section 190 was enacted in 1976 to promote more rapid modification of business facilities and vehicles for use by the handicapped and elderly so that they might "increase their involvement in economic, social and cultural activities."[24] Under §190, taxpayers can deduct expenditures, otherwise chargeable to capital account, to remove architectural and transportation barriers in order to make facilities or public transportation vehicles owned or leased in connection with the taxpayer's business more accessible to handicapped and elderly persons, subject to Treasury certification that removal of the barrier conforms to prescribed standards. The deduction cannot exceed $35,000 for any taxable year ($25,000 for taxable years beginning before 1984).

¶26.4.5 Reforestation Expenditures

Section 194, enacted in 1980, allows an election to amortize a limited amount of reforestation expenditures over 84 months. The term "reforestation expenditures" refers to "direct costs incurred in connection with forest-

---

[22] IRC §169(f)(2).

[23] Reg. §1.169-2(a)(3).

[24] 1976 Bluebook, supra note 21, at 652. As first enacted, the provision expired at the end of 1982. It was rejuvenated, however, for the years 1984 and 1985, and was made permanent in 1986. The provision therefore applies to expenditures made in taxable years beginning after 1976, except for taxable years beginning during 1983. IRC §190(d).

ation or reforestation by planting or artificial or natural seeding," including the costs of seeds or seedlings, labor, tools, and depreciation on equipment used in planting or seeding.[25] The costs of preparing the site are also included. If the taxpayer is reimbursed for any of these costs under a governmental cost-sharing program, however, the reimbursed costs are not reforestation expenditures unless the reimbursement is included in gross income. Only costs required to be capitalized under the general capitalization rules, further, are reforestation expenditures; costs that could be deducted as paid or incurred in the absence of §194 are not required to be amortized under that provision.[26]

No more than $10,000 of reforestation expenditures made by the taxpayer during any year can qualify for amortization under §194.[27] This ceiling is reduced to $5,000 if the taxpayer is a married person filing a separate return. Moreover, all members of a controlled group of corporations must share a single $10,000 cap.[28] When reforestation expenditures are incurred by a partnership or S corporation, the ceiling is applied first to the entity and then to each partner or shareholder with respect to his share of the qualifying expenditures of the entity.[29] The ceiling is zero for a trust. An estate's ceiling is $10,000, but it is apportioned between the estate and its beneficiaries.

Reforestation expenditures are amortizable under §194 only if they are included in the basis of "qualified timber property," defined as land located in the United States, "which will contain trees in significant commercial quantities and which is held by the taxpayer for the planting, cultivating, caring for, and cutting of trees for sale or use in the commercial production of timber products."[30] The taxpayer can be either owner or lessee of the land, but must own the trees. A tract on which less than one acre is planted with seedlings cannot qualify, apparently because of the "significant commercial quantities" limitation.[31] Property planted with "ornamental trees, such a Christmas trees" cannot qualify, apparently because such trees are not considered timber.[32] If the taxpayer's otherwise qualifying reforestation expenditures exceed the ceiling described in the preceding paragraph and are incurred with respect to two or more qualified timber properties, the

---

[25] IRC §194(c)(3).

[26] Conf. Rep. No. 1320, 96th Cong., 2d Sess. 18, reprinted in 1980-2 CB 487; Reg. §§1.194-1(a), -3(c)(1).

[27] IRC §194(b).

[28] See Reg. §1.194-2(b)(4).

[29] See Reg. §§1.194-2(b)(5), (6).

[30] IRC §194(c)(2).

[31] Conf. Rep. No. 1320, supra note 26, at 19; Reg. §1.194-3(a).

[32] Reg. §1.194-3(a). This limitation derives from the legislative history, which ties it to the word "timber." Conf. Rep. No. 1320, supra note 26, at 17.

ceiling is allocated among the properties in any way the taxpayer chooses.[33]

Reforestation expenditures qualifying for amortization under §194 are deducted in 84 equal monthly installments, beginning with the sixth month of the taxable year during which the costs are paid or incurred.[34] The amortization period thus usually consists of six months of the year in which the costs are paid or incurred, all of the next six years, and six months of the eighth year.

Amortization under §194 is elective. The election is made by claiming an amortization deduction on a timely filed return for the year in which reforestation expenditures are incurred and including with the return a statement describing the nature and amounts of the costs, the dates on which they were incurred, the type of timber, and the taxpayer's purpose for growing the timber.[35] "The election is to be made annually on a property-by-property basis."[36] Once made for a particular year with respect to particular property, it applies to all reforestation expenditures made during the year on the property (subject to the $10,000 ceiling), and it can only be revoked with IRS consent, which will not be given if "the only reason for the desired change is to obtain a tax advantage."[37]

If gain is recognized on a disposition of property with respect to which a §194 election has been made, the gain is ordinary income under §1245 up to the amount of the amortization deductions taken prior to the disposition.[38]

¶26.4.6 Newspaper and Magazine Circulation Expenditures

Section 173, originally enacted in 1950, allows a deduction for costs incurred by a newspaper, magazine, or other periodical "to establish, maintain, or increase [its] circulation."[39] The provision eliminates the need to

---

[33] IRC §194(c)(4); Reg. §1.194-2(b)(2).

[34] IRC §194(a). If the taxable year consists of less than 12 months, the amortization period begins with the first month of the second half of the year. Id.

[35] Reg. §1.194-4(a).

[36] Conf. Rep. No. 1320, supra note 26, at 17.

[37] Reg. §1.1944(c).

[38] IRC §1245(a)(3)(C). See infra ¶52.2 for §1245.

[39] See Washington Post Co. v. US, 405 F2d 1279 (Ct. Cl. 1969) (newspaper publisher's contributions to profit sharing plan for benefit of affiliated dealers deductible under §173; no need to determine whether amounts were reasonable compensation for services under §162); Rev. Rul. 67-201, 1967-1 CB 66 (sales commissions paid to solicitors are circulation expenditures, but expenses for supplies used in printing and shipping periodicals do not qualify); Rev. Rul. 54-3, 1954-1 CB 67 (publisher promising to give a stated percentage of subscription price paid by new subscribers to charitable organization can deduct cost of campaign, including contributions).

distinguish between expenditures deductible currently as costs of renewing or maintaining circulation and capital expenditures incurred to create or build a circulation base.[40] Amounts paid to acquire any part of the business of another publisher cannot be deducted under §173, however, even if the purpose of the acquisition is to remove a competitive threat to the taxpayer's existing subscription list rather than to acquire new customers.[41] Section 173 is also inapplicable to expenditures for land or depreciable property, although depreciation deductions can presumably be circulation expenditures.

A taxpayer can choose to capitalize circulation expenditures that would be capitalized in the absence of §173. This election, which perpetuates the distinction between expenses to renew or maintain the periodical's existing circulation and outlays to establish or enlarge its readership, applies to all amounts that are properly capitalizable, and it is binding for all subsequent years unless the IRS consents to a revocation. Whether amounts charged to capital account under this election can be depreciated or deducted thereafter (e.g., as worthless) depends on the general rules of §§162, 163, and 461.[42]

¶26.4.7 Farming Expenditures

Taxpayers engaged in the business of farming are allowed to treat certain expenditures for soil and water conservation, fertilizer, and the clearing of land, which otherwise would be chargeable to capital account, as currently deductible expenses. The provisions that authorize these deductions, §§175, 180, and (until its repeal in 1986) 182, are discussed elsewhere in this work.[43]

¶26.4.8 Child Care Facilities

Citing "a great need for making child care facilities available if we are to provide an opportunity to work to mothers who desire to do so," Con-

---

[40] For the legislative history of §173, see Florida Publishing Co. v. CIR, 64 TC 269, 276–77 (1975), aff'd by unpublished opinion (5th Cir., Apr. 26, 1977).

[41] Florida Publishing Co. v. CIR, supra note 40 (purchase of entire business to eliminate competition). Compare Rev. Rul. 74-103, 1974-1 CB 62 (purchase of another publisher's circulation list is nondeductible expenditure to acquire part of its business) with Zimmerman & Sons v. US, 72-2 USTC ¶9585 (ED Wis. 1971) (not officially reported) (contra). See also Triangle Publications, Inc. v. CIR, 54 TC 138, 151–52 (1970) (acq. on another issue) (on purchase of stock of taxpayer's franchisee, amount allocable to subscription list qualified under §173; franchisee not a "publisher" within meaning of §173).

[42] Reg. §1.173-1(c)(1) (last sentence). For the depreciation of customer lists and other intangibles, see supra ¶23.2.6.

[43] See infra ¶105.5.6.

gress in 1971 enacted §188, allowing an employer's expenditures for qualified child care facilities to be amortized, at the taxpayer's election, ratably over a period of 60 months, beginning with the month in which the property is placed in service.[44] To qualify, the expenditure must be made before January 1, 1982, and must be a cost of acquiring, constructing, reconstructing, or rehabilitating facilities primarily for children of the taxpayer's employees.[45] The expenditure, further, must be chargeable to capital account. Property not subject to depreciation, such as land, does not qualify, nor does property located outside the United States.[46] Amortization under §188 is in lieu of depreciation deductions otherwise allowable for the same expenditure.

An election under §188 is irrevocable as to the expenditure to which it relates, but taxpayers can elect to amortize some eligible expenditures while depreciating others, even if they are for items relating to the same facility and are incurred in the same taxable year.[47] If the taxpayer ceases to use a facility for child care purposes, the election is terminated, and depreciation deductions are thereafter allowed, based on the property's estimated remaining useful life and salvage value, determined as of the termination date.[48]

¶26.4.9 Expenditures to Rehabilitate Low-Income Rental Housing

Section 167(k), which was enacted in 1969 to encourage the rehabilitation of existing structures but was allowed to expire at the end of 1986, permits expenditures incurred to rehabilitate low-income rental housing to be depreciated on a straight line basis over 60 months, without taking salvage value into account.[49] The provision applies to qualified rehabilita-

---

[44] S. Rep. No. 437, 92d Cong., 2d Sess., reprinted in 1972-1 CB 595. See generally Roth, Amortization of Expenditures for Child Care Facilities, 57 Taxes 133 (1979). Before 1977, §188 also allowed expenditures for certain on-the-job training facilities to be amortized.

[45] See Reg. §1.188-1(d)(4) (definition of qualified child care facility; general-purpose recreation room and screened-off areas do not qualify).

[46] IRC §188(b).

[47] Reg. §1.188-1(a)(2).

[48] Reg. §1.188-1(a)(4). This rule requires some modification for property placed in service after 1980 because such property is subject to ACRS, under which neither useful life nor salvage value is an element of the depreciation calculus. See supra ¶23.3. Probably, depreciation is allowed over the remainder of the property's ACRS recovery period, using the same method of depreciation that would have applied in the absence of §188 but applying it to the basis remaining when care use terminates.

[49] The regulations require that the election be made by the filing of a rather detailed statement with the taxpayer's return. Reg. §1.167(k)-4. See Rev. Rul. 82-103, 1982-1 CB 34 (election not valid unless it is possible to determine solely from

tion expenditures incurred during the period July 24, 1969 through December 31, 1986.[50]

Rehabilitation expenditures, if otherwise qualified, are subject to a floor and a ceiling, both computed on a per-unit basis: Section 167(k) does not apply to expenditures for a dwelling unit paid or incurred during a particular year unless the expenditures for the unit during the current year and the prior or subsequent year exceeds $3,000.[51] This limitation is presumably intended to ensure that the rehabilitation is substantial enough to warrant the benefit of rapid depreciation. Second, the aggregate amount depreciated under §167(k) for any unit usually may not exceed $20,000.[52] This ceiling, however, is raised to $40,000 if the rehabilitation is done

---

return and attachments thereto that election is intended and what property is to be covered); but see Tipps v. CIR, 74 TC 458 (1980) (acq.) (statment with return stating that per-unit data were available in taxpayer's office for field audit sufficient, notwithstanding lack of full compliance with regulations).

[50] As enacted, §167(k) was set to expire at the end of 1974, but the terminal date was put off several times. The original expiration date was specified to "provide time for the Congress to evaluate the effectiveness and the cost of this new incentive." S. Rep. No. 552, supra note 21, at 559. A three-year extension was made in 1978 "to avoid discouraging this rehabilitation." S. Rep. No. 1263, 95th Cong., 2d Sess., reprinted in 1978-3 CB (Vol. 1) 315, 486. The final extension in 1984 was made because "special tax incentives continue to be needed to ensure that affordable housing is available to individuals of limited means"; it was not made permanent because of a felt need for "ongoing review as economic conditions change." Staff of Joint Comm. on Tax'n, 98th Cong., 2d Sess., General Explanation of Revenue Provisions of Deficit Reduction Act of 1984, at 1180 (Comm. Print 1984).

The provision was allowed to expire at the end of 1986 because a low-income housing credit (see infra ¶27.5) was then substituted for a variety of low-income housing allowances, in the belief that the credit would be "a more efficient mechanism for encouraging the production of low-income rental housing." Staff of Joint Comm. on Tax'n, 99th Cong., 2d Sess., General Explanation of the Tax Reform Act of 1986, at 152 (Comm. Print 1986).

See generally Belin, Real Estate Rehabilitation: A New Tax Incentive; The Tax Rules, 29 NYU Inst. on Fed. Tax'n 1055 (1971); Rehabilitation Projects and Middle and Low Income Housing: A Panel Discussion, NYU Inst. on Fed. Tax'n 1159 (1971); Meir, Tax Shelters and Real Estate: The Rehabilitation of Low Income Housing, 7 Suffolk UL Rev. 1 (1972); Note, Accelerated Depreciation for Housing Rehabilitation, 79 Yale LJ 961 (1970).

[51] IRC §167(k)(2)(C). The $3,000 floor is an all-or-nothing condition; thus, if the expenditures in the taxable year are $2,000 and those in the prior or subsequent year are $1,000, none of the current year's expenditures qualify; but if the expenditures in the current year were $2,100 rather than $2,000, they would all qualify.

If the taxpayer does not know when filing his return whether expenditures for the year will qualify, the §167(k) election can be made either by filing a statement with the return indicating an intent to satisfy the $3,000 limitation in the following taxable year or by filing an amended return within a specified time period. Reg. §1.167(k)-4(a)(2).

[52] IRC §167(k)(2)(A).

under a federal or state housing program, financially responsible tenants are allowed to purchase their units, and the taxpayer's ability to profit from the lease or sale of the units is sharply limited.[53] There is no dollar limit on the aggregate amount to be deducted under §167(k). Thus, if the taxpayer incurs $20,000 of qualified expenditures for each of 100 units, $2 million may be deducted over the 60-month period specified by §167(k)(1).

The term "rehabilitation expenditures" is defined by §167(k)(3)(A) to mean that amounts are chargeable to capital account, incurred for property or additions or improvements to property with a useful life of five years or more, and incurred in connection with the rehabilitation of an existing building (which need not have been used for residential purposes before the rehabilitation); it does not, however, include the cost of acquiring the building itself. The concept of "rehabilitation" includes provision of related facilities, such as a parking lot for tenants and the conversion of unused space (e.g., an attic) to dwelling units, but it does not embrace new construction (e.g., new outer walls) or an enlargement of the building's area (e.g., a new wing).[54]

The effect of nonrehabilitation activity on the status of other expenditures depends on what is done. Thus, if the old structure, including the outer walls, is demolished, the taxpayer's expenditures fall wholly outside of §167(k) because there is no "rehabilitation" of an existing structure. If, however, the existing structure is preserved but enlarged, the expenditures to rehabilitate the old area qualify under §167(k), even though the cost of enlarging the building's area is not a "rehabilitation expenditure" and hence must be depreciated under the normal rules of §167 or §168. Similarly, expenditures to rehabilitate or construct commercial units in an existing structure do not qualify for rapid depreciation under §167(k), but this activity does not disqualify expenditures to rehabilitate dwelling units in the same structure.

The term "dwelling unit" is defined by §167(k)(3)(C) to mean a house or apartment in a building or structure, excluding units in a hotel, motel, and other establishments in which more than one half of the units are used on a transient basis.[55]

The legislative objective of increasing the supply of low-income rental housing is fostered by §167(k)(3)(B), which requires the rehabilitated dwelling units to be held for rental to individuals and families of low or moderate

---

[53] IRC §167(k)(2)(B); Reg. §1.167(k)-2(f).

[54] Reg. §1.167(k)-3(a). Expenditures benefiting two or more dwelling units (e.g., parking facilities, entrance-ways, heating systems) are allocated among the units or between the dwelling units and any commercial units. Reg. §1.167(k)-2(d).

[55] "[T]ransient basis" refers to occupancy for more than one half of a unit's rental days during the taxable year by tenants who occupy it for less than 30 days each. Reg. §1.167(k)-3(c)(2).

income, as determined by the IRS in a manner consistent with the Leased Housing Program under section 8 of the United States Housing Act of 1937. Pursuant to this authority, the regulations prescribe in great detail the rental policies that must be followed by the rehabilitated project.[56]

When elected, the 60-month write-off of rehabilitation expenditures displaces any otherwise allowable depreciation or amortization for the same expenditures, including the expensing election of §179.[57] The cost of the building itself, however, as well as expenditures to enlarge its area, rehabilitate commercial space, or accomplish other purposes that do not qualify under §167(k) or that exceed the $20,000 per-unit limit, can be depreciated under the general ACRS or depreciation rules. As a partial offset to the generous terms of §167(k), the excess of the taxpayer's deductions over straight line depreciation is an item of tax preference in computing the alternative minimum tax or its predecessor, the minimum tax on tax preferences.[58] If the property is disposed of during the 200-month period after it was placed in service, the taxpayer is subjected by §1250 to a stricter than normal depreciation recapture rule.[59]

¶26.4.10 Railroad Grading, Tunnel Bores, and Rolling Stock

Section 185, repealed in 1986, permits qualified railroad grading and tunnel bores to be amortized over 50 years, at the taxpayer's option. The provision applies to costs paid or incurred before 1987.[60] If amortization is elected under §185, no deduction is allowed for retirement or abandonment unless attributable to fire, storm, or other casualty; the amortization deductions, however, continue. Also, under §185(h), the investment credit (before its repeal in 1986) was denied to property qualifying for amortization under §185, whether or not the amortization election was made.

Apart from §185, a railroad's costs for grading and tunnel bores are depreciable if a reasonably ascertainable useful life can be shown.[61] If such a useful life cannot be shown, the costs can usually be written off only when

---

[56] Reg. §1.167(k)-3(b).

[57] For IRC §179, see supra ¶23.8.

[58] IRC §57(a)(2) (before amendment in 1986), §57(a)(7) (after amendment in 1986). For the minimum and alternative minimum taxes, see infra ¶¶111.3.11, 111.3.12.

[59] For IRC §1250, see infra ¶55.3.1.

[60] Pub. L. No. 99-514, §242(a), 100 Stat. 2085 (1986). The provision only applies in taxable years beginning after 1968, but, for these years, covers property placed in service before as well as after the effective date. See 1976 Bluebook, supra note 21, at 475.

[61] Compare Burlington N., Inc. v. US, 676 F2d 566 (Ct. Cl. 1982) (actuarial method based on statistical data failed to establish reasonably ascertainable useful life for gradings and tunnel bores) with Kansas City S. Ry. v. CIR, 76 TC 1067

the property is retired from service or abandoned. The difficulty of establishing useful life, and the lack of any meaningful write-off when this burden could not be met were the principal reasons for the enactment of §185 in 1969.[62]

Section 184, also enacted in 1969, permits the amortization of qualified railroad rolling stock over 60 months.[63] The provision, however, only applies to rolling stock placed in service during the years 1969 through 1975. It was enacted in 1969 to provide an incentive for the continued modernization of railroad equipment after the repeal in that year of the investment credit.[64] The terminal date reflects the fact that the investment credit, after being reinstated, was amended in 1976 to permit railroads to apply unused investment credits against a higher percentage of tax liability than is normally allowed.[65] Section 184 was not revived when this special dispensation expired in 1982.

¶26.4.11 Rehabilitation of Certified Historic Structures

Section 191, enacted in 1976 and repealed in 1981, provided a fast write-off for costs incurred in rehabilitating certain historic structures. The provision was adopted in recognition that "the rehabilitation and preservation of historic structures and neighborhoods is an important national goal" that could be advanced by enlisting private funds in the preservation movement through a tax incentive.[66] It was replaced in 1981 with a credit for historic rehabilitation expenditures.[67]

During its brief lifespan, §191 allowed qualified expenditures for the rehabilitation of certified historic structures (as defined) to be amortized over 60 months.[68] Alternatively, if the structure was substantially rehabilitated (as defined), the taxpayer could elect under §167(o) to be treated as the original owner of the property, which allowed it to be depreciated by the declining balance method rather than on a straight line basis. Although

---

(1981) (useful life for grading of rail roadways adequately established by statistical methods, obsolescence as well as physical deterioration being taken into account).

[62] See S. Rep. No. 552, supra note 21, at 582–84.

[63] See also Greenville Steel Car Co. v. US, 615 F2d 911 (Ct. Cl. 1980) (§184 not applicable to manufacturer leasing railroad cars to nonrailroad companies).

[64] See S. Rep. No. 552, supra note 21.

[65] See IRC §46(a)(8); 1976 Bluebook, supra note 21, at 473; 1978 Bluebook, supra note 21, at 147–48.

[66] 1976 Bluebook, supra note 21, at 655.

[67] See infra ¶27.2.2.

[68] See generally Hessel, Tax Incentives for Preservation and Rehabilitation of Historic Properties, 5 J. Real Est. Tax'n 5 (1977); Tucker & Shull, Tax Advantages and Problems Connected With "Certified Historic Structures," 48 J. Tax'n 40 (1978).

depreciation is normally not allowed for property devoted to personal uses, §191 was not restricted to property used in the taxpayer's trade or business or held for the production of income, and apparently permitted amortization deductions for expenditures to rehabilitate a historic structure used as the taxpayer's residence.

¶26.4.12 Trademark and Trade Name Expenditures

Until its repeal in 1986, §177 permitted an election to amortize trademark and trade name expenditures ratably over a period of 60 months or more.[69] By reason of the repeal, §177 only applies to expenditures paid or incurred before 1987.[70] For periods after 1986 (and for prior periods in the absence of an election under §177), these expenditures ordinarily are not deductible as current expenses, but must instead be capitalized. Further, they cannot usually be depreciated because the useful lives of most trademarks and trade names are not ascertainable.[71] Thus, the taxpayer must hold the capitalized amount in abeyance, either to be offset against the proceeds of any sale of the trademark or trade name or to be deducted as a loss if it is abandoned.

The announced reason for enacting §177 was to give small companies, which ordinarily hire outside attorneys to register and protect their trademarks and trade names, the benefits enjoyed by large companies, which frequently use in-house counsel for these purposes and deduct their salaries without separating out the portion that should be capitalized.[72] In repealing the provision, Congress decided that "the possibility that some taxpayers may fail accurately to compute nondeductible expenses [is not adequate] justification for permitting rapid amortization. Furthermore, to the extent such mischaracterization occurs, a five-year amortization provision only partially alleviates any unfairness."[73] The amortization rule of §177 is not a satisfactory cost recovery rule because "there is no basis for a presumption that a trademark or trade name will decline in value," and a tax incentive is not appropriate because there is no evidence that "investment in trade-

---

[69] See generally Cohan, Income Tax Considerations in Trademarks and Unfair Competition, 39 Taxes 528 (1961); Kragen, New Section 177 Aids Trademark Owners, But Buyers Don't Get Any Help, 6 J. Tax'n 279 (1957); Mann, Tax Treatment of Trademark Litigation Expenses, 55 Trademark Rep. 39 (1965).

[70] Pub. L. No. 99-514, §241, 100 Stat. 2085 (1986).

[71] See Medco Prods. Co. v. CIR, 523 F2d 137 (10th Cir. 1975) (legal fees incurred in suit to compel competitor to terminate use of taxpayer's trademark must be capitalized and cannot be amortized under §177 in absence of timely election). See also supra ¶23.2.6 (goodwill not ordinarily depreciable).

[72] S. Rep. No. 1941, 84th Cong., 2d Sess., reprinted in 1956-2 CB 1227, 1232.

[73] Staff of Joint Comm. on Tax'n, 99th Cong., 2d Sess., General Explanation of the Tax Reform Act of 1986, at 143 (Comm. Print 1987).

marks and trade names produces special social benefits that market forces might inadequately reflect."[74]

To qualify for amortization under §177, pre-1987 expenditures must be (1) directly connected with the acquisition, protection, expansion, registration, or defense of a trademark or trade name, (2) chargeable to capital account, and (3) not part of the consideration paid for an existing trademark, trade name, or business. Expenses satisfying the first of these requirements virtually always satisfy the second as well, except for expenses attributable to the recovery of damages in an infringement action. The third requirement precludes the amortization of the cost of acquiring an existing trademark or trade name, even if the taxpayer's purpose is to eliminate competition with the taxpayer's own trademark or trade name rather than to use the acquired item. Typical qualifying expenses are legal fees paid to register a trademark, artists' fees and similar design expenses, and litigation expenses incurred in infringement proceedings.[75]

On making an election, the taxpayer can select any amortization period of 60 months or more, beginning with the first month of the taxable year in which the expenditure is paid or incurred, determined in accordance with the method of accounting used by the taxpayer in computing taxable income. The capitalized amount must be reduced by the amortization allowed or allowable.[76] Although the regulations do not say so explicitly, presumably unamortized expenditures can be deducted as a loss under §165 if the trademark or trade name becomes worthless and is abandoned before the end of the amortization period.

If two or more qualifying expenditures are made in the same year, a taxpayer can elect as to none, some, or all of the expenditures, and can designate different amortization periods for different expenditures, even if they relate to the same trademark or trade name. Once an election is made, however, the designated amortization period cannot be changed, even if the trademark or trade name turns out to be depreciable under §167 because its useful life can be ascertained.[77]

---

[74] Id.

[75] Reg. §1.177-1(b)(1). See also Medco Prods. Co. v. CIR, supra note 71.

[76] IRC §1016(a)(16) (before amendment in 1986); Reg. §1.1016-5(m) (reduction in basis for amortization allowed unless of no tax benefit, but not less than amount allowable). See also infra ¶42.3.

[77] See Reg. §1.177-1(a)(2), (3). See also Reg. §1.177-1(c) (time and manner of making election); Rev. Rul. 79-333, 1979-2 CB 110 (taxpayer electing to amortize certain legal expenses incurred in trademark infringement litigation cannot later elect to amortize other expenses of the same litigation incurred in the same year that were originally deducted as current expenses but disallowed on audit as capital outlays).

CHAPTER

27

Business Credits

¶27.1 BUSINESS CREDITS—IN GENERAL

¶27.1.1 Introductory

A variety of credits are allowed to business and profit-seeking taxpayers.[1] The most durable of these credits, the credit for foreign income taxes, is generally regarded as part of the normative structure of the income tax, as a necessary device for alleviating international double taxation of income. It is discussed elsewhere in this work.[2] Most of the other credits were enacted to provide tax incentives, and many of them have been repealed or allowed to expire in recent years as tax incentives have fallen out of favor. Most of the credits discussed in this chapter fall into the latter category, including the investment credit (repealed in most applications as of the end of 1985),[3] the targeted jobs credits (applicable to wages paid before 1989),[4] the research credit (expiring at the end of 1988),[5] the credit for clinical testing expenses relating to drugs for rare diseases and conditions (applicable to expenses incurred before 1991),[6] and the low-income housing credit (for rental housing placed in service during the years 1987, 1988, and 1989).[7]

¶27.1.2 General Business Credit

Sections 38 and 39, enacted in 1984, provide a uniform set of rules for the allowance, limitation, and carryover of four business-related credits, the investment credit, the targeted jobs credit, the credit under §40(a) for users and sellers of fuels including alcohol, the research credit, and the low-income housing credit. Prior to its repeal in 1986, the employee stock ownership credit of former §41(a) was also subject to these rules.

In the aggregate, the credits subsumed into the general business credit cannot exceed the sum of 100 percent of the first $25,000 of the taxpayer's net tax liability and 75 percent of net tax liability in excess of $25,000.[8] "[N]et tax liability" is the taxpayer's tax liability after reduction by all other

---

[1] See Hoff, The Appropriate Role for Tax Credits in an Income Tax System, 35 Tax Lawyer 339 (1982) (criticizing use of credits other than for prepaid tax and foreign income taxes).

[2] Infra Ch. 69.

[3] See infra ¶27.2.

[4] See infra ¶27.3.

[5] See infra ¶27.4.2.

[6] See infra ¶27.4.3.

[7] See infra ¶27.5.

[8] IRC §38(c)(1). The allowable percentage for taxable years beginning in 1984 and 1985 is 85 percent of the excess over $25,000. IRC §38(c)(1) (before amendment in 1986).

credits except the refundable credits.[9] The refundable credits are the credits for tax withheld on wages (§31), the earned income credit (§32), the credit for tax withheld on income of nonresident aliens and foreign corporations (§33), the credit for exempt uses of gasoline (§34), and the credit for over-payments of tax (§35).

Assume a taxpayer's tax before credits is $100,000, and the taxpayer has a credit for foreign income taxes of $25,000 and an investment credit of $70,000. Since the foreign tax credit is neither a business credit subject to these rules nor a refundable credit, the taxpayer's net tax liability is $75,000, the excess of the tax before credits ($100,000) over the foreign tax credit ($25,000). The limitation on the investment credit (the only credit included in the general business credit) is $62,500, as shown in Example 27-1.

Example 27-1

Limitation on General Business Credit

1. Computation of net tax liability
   a. Tax liability before credits $100,000
   b. Less: Nonrefundable credits not included in general
      business credit (foreign tax credit) 25,000
   c. Net tax liability .... $ 75,000
2. Computation of limitation on general business credit
   (investment credit)
   a. 100 percent of $25,000 of net tax liability .... $ 25,000
   b. Plus: 75 percent of remaining net tax liability (75 percent
      of $50,000) 37,500
   c. Maximum general business credit .... $ 62,500

If the sum of the business credits for a taxable year exceeds this limitation, the excess is carried back to the preceding 3 years and forward to the succeeding 15 years.[10] A carryback or carryover is allowed as a credit in a year to which it is carried to the extent of the unused limitation for the carryback or carryover year. If carrybacks or carryovers from more than one year are carried to a single taxable year, the carried amounts are used in chronological order, starting with the oldest carried amount and proceeding in chronological order until the limitation is reached.[11] Any part of a carried

---

[9] IRC §38(c)(2).
[10] IRC §39(a)(1).
[11] IRC §§39(b), (c).

amount that is not used in this way and does not expire is carried to the next year. This ordering of the carried amounts maximizes the potential for benefit from carrybacks and carryovers because it uses first those amounts that are nearest to their expiration dates.

If a carryover expires unused, or if a taxpayer dies or ceases to exist before a carryover can be used, the unused amount is allowed as a deduction in the last taxable year to which it is carried.[12] An unused investment credit is not deductible unless the basis of the property for which the credit is being allowed has been reduced under §48(q).[13]

In conjunction with the repeal of the general investment credit in 1986, Congress required that credit carryovers be reduced as of July 1, 1987 by 35 percent of the amount attributable to the investment credit (excluding any investment credit allowed under the energy percentage or the rehabilitation percentage).[14] If a taxable year of the taxpayer begins on July 1, 1987, the reduction is made to all carryovers to that year, and applies to the use of the carryovers in that and all subsequent years. In other cases, a partial reduction is made in the carryovers to the year that includes July 1, 1987, and the full 35 percent reduction is made in the carryovers to the following year.[15]

¶27.2 INVESTMENT CREDIT

¶27.2.1 Introductory

During most of the period 1962 through 1985, an investment credit was allowed for taxpayers purchasing tangible personal property and a few other types of property for use in their businesses and profit-seeking activities. The credit was initially 7 percent of the basis or cost of qualifying property, but was later raised to 10 percent.

The credit was enacted in 1962 "to encourage modernization and expansion of the Nation's productive facilities."[1] The expansion rationale is reminiscent of President Kennedy's promise "to get this country moving

---

[12] IRC §§196(a), (b). This deduction is not allowed for the ESOP credit (even before its repeal in 1986), but a similar deduction was provided for this credit by §404(i).

[13] For §48(q), see infra ¶27.2.4.

[14] IRC §49(c)(2). See infra ¶27.2.2 for the energy and rehabilitation percentages.

[15] IRC §§49(c)(3), (5)(A).

[1] S. Rep. No. 1881, 87th Cong., 2d Sess., reprinted in 1962-3 CB 707, 717. For economic analysis of the credit, see A Review of Selected Tax Expenditures, Hearings Before the Subcomm. on Oversight of the House Ways and Means Comm., 96th Cong., 1st Sess., Ser. 96-28 (Mar. 22-28, 1979); Bradley & Oliver, Investment Tax Credit—The Illusory Incentive, 2 Va. Tax Rev. 267 (1983); Sunley, Towards a More Neutral Investment Tax Credit, 26 Nat'l Tax J. 209 (1973).

again."[2] The investment credit was largely repealed in 1986 and continues in effect only for certain reforestation and rehabilitation expenditures. The policy underlying the repeal stands in stark contrast to that expressed in 1962:

> The Congress concluded that the surest way of encouraging the efficient allocation of all resources and the greatest possible economic growth was by reducing statutory tax rates. A large reduction in the top corporate tax rate was achieved by repealing the investment tax credit without reducing the corporate tax revenues collected. One distorting tax provision was replaced by lower tax rates that provide benefits to all investment. A neutral tax system allows the economy to most quickly adapt to changing economic needs.[3]

Because of the credit's avowed function of encouraging investment, it was frequently amended as fashions in thinking about the nation's economic health shifted. It was "suspended" from October 10, 1966 to January 1, 1968 and "terminated" as of April 18, 1969 for a period that, as it turned out, only lasted until August 15, 1971.[4] Only time will tell whether the policy underlying the repeal in 1986 is a passing fad or a permanent shift away from the use of tax incentives.

Because the allowance is a credit rather than a deduction, its value does not depend on the taxpayer's tax bracket. It reduces tax liability, dollar for dollar, in the year qualifying property is placed in service or, if the credit exceeds certain limitations in that year, in specified preceding and subsequent carryover years.[5] For this reason, at the pre-1986 rate of 10 percent, the credit has substantially the same effect as a 10 percent reduction in the cost of the qualified property. Further, the basis of property qualifying for the credit is usually reduced by only one half of the credit, which places the taxpayer in a better position than if the property had been purchased for 90

---

[2] The Treasury's original proposal would have restricted the credit to investments above the taxpayer's historic level. This effort to confine the allowance to "investment which would not have been undertaken without this inducement" was abandoned as the bill moved through Congress, and the credit as enacted encompasses all qualifying investment, whether the taxpayer is expanding or retrenching. Hearings on the President's 1961 Tax Recommendations Before the House Ways and Means Comm., 87th Cong., 1st Sess., Vol. 1, at 26 (1961) (statement of Secretary of the Treasury C. Douglas Dillon).

[3] Staff of Joint Comm. on Tax'n, 99th Cong., 2d Sess., General Explanation of the Tax Reform Act of 1986, at 98–99 (Comm. Print 1987).

[4] Statutory provisions reflecting the treatment of "suspension" and "termination" property (formerly §§49 and 50) were repealed as obsolete in 1978. See Lazisky v. CIR, 72 TC 495 (1979) (construction of repealed §50); Erving Paper Mills Corp. v. CIR, 72 TC 319 (1979) (construction of repealed §49).

[5] For the carryback and carryover rules, see supra ¶27.1.2.

percent of its cost.[6]

In general outline, the credit is a simple and straightforward allowance, but it is encumbered by a maze of qualifications, which are discussed below. Roughly speaking, property placed in service before 1986 qualifies for the credit if it (1) is used in the taxpayer's business or profit-oriented activities, (2) is depreciable, (3) (for property placed in service before 1981) has an estimated useful life when placed in service of three years or more, and (4) is either tangible personal property or other tangible property (excluding buildings and their structural components) used for manufacturing, production, extraction, or certain other activities. These threshold requirements are subject to numerous exceptions, which distinguish between new and used property and take into account the property's type, location, physical character, industrial use, and other features.[7] Because of this profusion of categories, the credit rules are sometimes analogized to a laundry list; the comparison, however, is unfair to the neighborhood laundry, which charges the same price for a shirt whether the customer wears it at home or in the office, is married or single, drives to work or goes by bus, or exhibits other specialized characteristics that do not affect the prices of hot water, soap, or labor.

In an unusual intervention into the way tax allowances are reflected for financial accounting purposes, the Revenue Act of 1971 provides that taxpayers shall not be required by any federal agency to use any particular method of accounting for the investment credit, but that they must disclose the method used in any report to a federal agency and must use the same method in all such reports unless a change is permitted by the IRS.[8]

¶27.2.2 Investment Credit Property

The investment credit is allowed with respect to "section 38 property," a term that is defined in great detail, but includes principally (1) qualified rehabilitation expenditures, (2) certain reforestation expenditures, (3) energy property, and (4) tangible personal property.[9] Property in the first three of these categories continues to qualify for the credit, at least for some property in some years. Property in the fourth category is ineligible for the

---

[6] See infra ¶27.2.4.

[7] See generally Note, The Great Section 38 Property Muddle, 28 Vand. L. Rev. 1025 (1975).

[8] Revenue Act of 1971, Pub. L. No. 92-178, §101(c), 85 Stat. 497, 499. See also S. Rep. No. 437, 92d Cong., 1st Sess. (1971), reprinted in 1972-1 CB 559, 568; infra ¶105.4.3 (use of LIFO inventory method in financial reports if elected for federal income tax purposes).

[9] IRC §§46(a), 49(a).

credit after 1986, but continues to be "section 38 property," a term that is utilized in several statutory provisions not repealed in 1986.

1. *Qualified rehabilitation expenditures.* A "qualified rehabilitation expenditure" is a capital expenditure incurred in rehabilitating nonresidential real property or residential rental property that is a "qualifed rehabilitated building."[10] Neither the cost of the building nor of any "enlargement" of it can qualify. Also, costs of rehabilitating a certified historic structure or a building in a registered historic district do not qualify unless the rehabilitation is certified by the Interior Department to be consistent with the historic character of the building or the district in which it is located. Rehabilitation expenditures made by a lessee can qualify if the term of the lease (not including renewal periods) is at least as long as the ACRS recovery period for the improvements.

A building (including its structural components) is a "qualified rehabilitated building" if (1) the building is "substantially rehabilitated," (2) in the rehabilitation, at least 50 percent of the external walls remain as external walls, at least 75 percent of the external walls remain as external or internal walls, and at least 75 percent of the "internal structural framework . . . is retained in place," (3) the building was placed in service by the taxpayer before rehabilitation work began, and (4) the building's first use occurred before 1936.[11] A building is "substantially rehabilitated" if, over a 24-month period designated by the taxpayer, qualified rehabilitation expenditures exceed the taxpayer's adjusted basis for the building and its structural components as of the beginning of the 24-month period. If the taxpayer's basis is $5,000 or less, the qualified rehabilitation expenditures during the 24-month period must also exceed $5,000. The 24-month period can be lengthened to 60 months if the taxpayer has architectural plans and specifications showing how the work is to be done in phases, but the period must in any event end with or within the taxable year for which the credit is claimed.

A "certified historic structure" is relieved of several of the foregoing requirements, including the requirements concerning the retention of exter-

---

[10] IRC §48(g)(2)(A). For the terms "nonresidential real property" and "residential rental property," see supra ¶23.3.2. The rules for qualified rehabilitation expenditures were first enacted in 1978, but have undergone repeated amendment since then. The rules described in the text generally apply to property placed in service after 1986. For the original enactment, see Conf. Rep. No. 1800, 95th Cong., 2d Sess., reprinted in 1978-3 CB (Vol. 1) 521, 560.

During the period November 1, 1978 through December 31, 1981, some rehabilitation expenditures could be amortized over 60 months under a rule applicable only when the investment credit was forgone. IRC §191 (before repeal in 1981). See Rev. Rul. 82-142, 1982-2 CB 73.

[11] IRC §48(g)(1).

nal walls and internal structural framework and the requirement that the building have been used before 1936. The term "certified historic structure" includes any building listed in the National Register and also includes a building located in a registered historic district that is certified by the Interior Department "as being of historic significance to the district."[12]

2. *Reforestation expenditures.* Under §48(a)(1)(F), reforestation expenditures that qualify under a special amortization rule found in §194 are section 38 property.[13] The amortization rule applies to no more than $10,000 of expenditures by the taxpayer in any particular year. The companion credit rule is noteworthy principally because it survived the general repeal of the credit in 1986.

3. *Energy property.* The term "energy property" includes a grab bag of items Congress chose to favor at various times. Most of them are equipment using fuels other than oil and gas or equipment used in producing energy from sources other than oil and gas.[14] The credit rules for energy property were introduced in 1978, and expired at various times during the period 1982 through 1988.[15]

4. *Items not qualifying for credit after 1985.* Although no longer qualifying for the investment credit, the following categories are also "section 38 property": (1) tangible personal property (other than air conditioning and heating units); (2) other tangible property (not including buildings and their structural components) used in manufacturing, research, and a few other activities; (3) elevators and escalators constructed by the taxpayer or acquired new; (4) single purpose agricultural or horticultural structures,[16] and storage facilities of distributors of petroleum and petroleum products. Property is included within these categories, however, only if it qualifies for depreciation,[17] is used in business or held for the production of in-

---

[12] IRC §48(g)(3).

[13] See supra ¶26.4.5 for §194.

[14] IRC §48(l).

[15] See infra text accompanying note 58.

[16] For these structures, see IRC §48(p); see also infra note 32 and accompanying text.

[17] Examples of property disqualified for being nondepreciable are property used for personal purposes, land and other property deemed inexhaustible, and property for which a reasonably ascertainable useful life cannot be shown. See supra ¶23.2. See Rev. Rul. 83-109, 1983-2 CB 16 (leased property can be section 38 property to lessor if he is entitled to depreciation, whether or not lessee uses property in trade or business or profit-oriented activity).

If property is used for both business and personal purposes, the depreciable portion qualifies for the investment credit under §48(a)(1). Reg. §1.48-1(b)(2). If, however, depreciation is disallowed under §274, relating to entertainment facilities, the property does not qualify. Also, §48(a)(8) disqualifies property subject to amortization elections under §§167(k), 184, 188, and 191, relating to rehabilitated low-income rental housing, railroad rolling stock, child care facilities, and certified his-

come,[18] and (for property placed in service before 1981) has a useful life when placed in service of three years or more. These basic categories, further, are subject to a long list of exceptions, which are summarized below.[19] Intangible property does not qualify, but motion picture films and videotapes, which have both tangible and intangible aspects, qualify if they meet requirements stated in §48(k).

a. *Tangible personal property.* The regulations define "tangible personal property" to mean "any tangible property except land and improvements thereto," which disqualifies buildings and other inherently permanent structures and their structural components, such as swimming pools, paved parking areas, docks, bridges, and fences.[20] The term includes "all property (other than structural components) which is contained in or attached to a building," such as production machinery, transportation and office equipment, display racks, shelves, and signs, as well as property "in the nature of machinery" outside the structure, even if affixed to the ground, such as gasoline pumps, car lifts, and automatic vending machines.[21] In classifying property for this purpose, local law is not controlling. Thus, fixtures can be "tangible personal property" even if they are real property under local law.[22]

These interpretations create no problems for the vast bulk of business equipment, which is clearly on the qualified side of the boundary, or for buildings, which are on the wrong side. They have also spawned a flood of rulings and judicial decisions classifying borderline assets. Because these determinations inevitably turn on the physical and functional characteristics of particular assets and are unaccompanied by photographs to enlighten those unacquainted with the relevant technology, they are of limited precedential value. A 1975 Tax Court decision, however, summarized the principal questions as follows:

1. Is the property capable of being moved, and has it in fact been moved?

---

toric structures. See also Coca-Cola Bottling Co. of Baltimore v. US, 487 F2d 528 (Ct. Cl. 1973) (taxpayer having a choice between expensing and depreciating property must depreciate to qualify for investment credit); Reg. §1.48-1(b)(3) (property improperly expensed qualifies for credit if IRS disallows deduction and requires property to be depreciated).

[18] See Pike v. CIR, 78 TC 822 (1982) (credit denied to tax shelter investor because property not used in trade or business or for production of income; promotional brochure stated "we intend to generate losses").

[19] See generally Note, The Great Section 38 Property Muddle, 28 Vand. L. Rev. 1025 (1975).

[20] Reg. §1.48-1(c). But see IRC §48(a)(9) (materials used to replace railroad tracks qualify in specified circumstances).

[21] Reg. §1.48-1(c).

[22] Id.

2. Is the property designed or constructed to remain permanently in place?
3. Are there circumstances tending to show that the property may or will have to be moved?
4. How substantial a job is removal of the property and how time consuming is it? Is the property "readily removable"?
5. How much damage will the property sustain upon its removal?
6. How is the property fixed to the land?[23]

At one time, the IRS interpreted the regulation's disqualification of "inherently permanent structures" to encompass movable property serving the same functions as inherently permanent structures (e.g., movable floating docks functioning in the same manner as docks moored to the land). After several defeats in court, the IRS abandoned this position and ruled that the distinction between "personal" and "inherently permanent" property "should be made on the basis of the manner of attachment to land or the structure and how permanently the property is designed to remain in place."[24] A related point, conceded by the IRS at the same time, is that the same principles apply in determining whether a removable part of a building is a "structural component" of the building.

Another important change of position by the IRS concerns the status of property that is both "in the nature of machinery" and an "inherently permanent structure." Having argued at one time that machinery is not tangible personal property if inherently permanent, in 1974 the IRS conceded in *Weirick v. CIR* that the terminal towers of a commercial ski lift, containing machinery to operate the tow cables, qualified as "tangible per-

---

[23] Whiteco Indus., Inc. v. CIR, 65 TC 664, 672–73 (1975) (acq.) (citations omitted) (outdoor advertising signs are tangible personal property). For other items held to qualify, see Southland Corp. v. US, 611 F2d 348 (Ct. Cl. 1979) (outdoor advertising signs); Standard Oil Co. (Ind.) v. CIR, 77 TC 349 (1981) (outdoor advertising signs, lighting systems, and supporting poles bolted to concrete foundations, but not concrete foundations embedded in soil); Scott Paper Co. v. CIR, 74 TC 137 (1980) (portions of electrical distribution system of paper and pulp mills); Rev. Rul. 80-151, 1980-1 CB 7 (outdoor advertising displays); Rev. Rul. 77-8, 1977-1 CB 3 (house trailer used as contractor's office on construction sites); Rev. Rul. 69-170, 1969-1 CB 28 (seats and scoreboard equipment in sports stadium); Rev. Rul. 67-349, 1967-2 CB 48 (wall-to-wall carpeting); Rev. Rul. 66-329, 1966-2 CB 16, modified by Rev. Rul. 79-343, 1979-2 CB 18 (automatic feeding, watering, and ventilating equipment in hog raising facility); Rev. Rul. 65-79, 1965-1 CB 26 (bank vault doors, night depository facilities, and drive-up teller windows, but not drive-up teller booths).

[24] Rev. Rul. 75-178, 1975-1 CB 9. But see Dixie Manor, Inc. v. US, 79-2 USTC ¶9469 (WD Ky. 1979) (not officially reported), aff'd by order, 81-1 USTC ¶9332 (6th Cir. 1981) (Rev. Rul. 75-178 does not allow credit for air conditioning units and partitions installed by lessee of shopping center); Consolidated Freightways, Inc. v. US, 620 F2d 862 (Ct. Cl. 1980) (truck docking facilities not qualified).

sonal property" although sunk in foundations containing between 50 and 100 cubic yards of concrete.[25] On the basis of this acknowledgment that "machinery" status prevails over "permanence," the Tax Court went on to hold that the taxpayer's intermediate line towers supporting the lift cables, also permanently attached to the land, were "in the nature of machinery" because they were "so closely related in design, construction and function [to the terminal towers] that they cannot be treated realistically as two separate groups of assets."[26] Illustrating the possibility of different results for separable components of an integrated installation, however, the court then held that earthen ramps constructed to enable skiers to reach the ski lift were not "in the nature of machinery" because the ski lift machinery would operate in exactly the same way—but without skiers—if the ramps had not been constructed.

b. *Other tangible property.* Tangible property that is not "personal" can qualify under §48(a)(1)(B) if it meets both a negative and a positive test: (1) It must not be a building or structural component thereof; and (2) it must be used as an integral part of manufacturing or other specified activity or as a research or storage facility in connection with one of the specified activities.

The negative rule is elaborated at some length by the regulations, which contrast apartment houses, factory and office buildings, warehouses, stores, and other "buildings" (disqualified) with structures that are essentially items of machinery or equipment and their closely related housing structures, such as oil tanks, silos, blast furnaces, and brick kilns (qualified).[27] To illustrate the disqualification of structural components of a building, the regulations distinguish between walls, windows, central air conditioning and heating systems, plumbing and plumbing fixtures, and sprinkler systems (disqualified) and machinery installed solely to meet temperature or humidity requirements essential to operate other machinery or to process materials or foodstuffs (qualified).[28] While a separate facility serving the needs of the machinery qualifies, facilities serving "the overall needs . . . of the building system" are nonqualifying structural components of the building even though larger in capacity because they also service the machinery.[29]

---

[25] Weirick v. CIR, 62 TC 446, 452–53 (1974).

[26] Id. at 453.

[27] Reg. §1.48-1(e)(1).

[28] Reg. §1.48-1(e)(2).

[29] See Ponderosa Mouldings, Inc. v. CIR, 53 TC 92 (1969) (sprinkler system in woodworking factory not qualified); Rev. Rul. 70-160, 1970-1 CB 7 (boilers supplying steam for furniture factory qualified, but not electrical system serving needs of both building and machinery); Rev. Rul. 68-405, 1968-2 CB 35 (heavy duty insulation in refrigerated building not qualified).

The regulations provide that the term "building" "generally means any structure or edifice enclosing a space within its walls, and usually covered by a roof, the purpose of which is, for example, to provide shelter or housing, or to provide working, office, parking, display or sales space." Some courts have tended to carve out, and qualify for the investment credit, "specialized structures whose utility is principally and primarily a significantly contributive factor in the actual manufacturing or production of the product itself," even if they provide work space and shelter for the taxpayer's employees.[30] Other courts confine the "specialized structure" exemption to structures that either function as machines or are so closely related to machinery housed therein that they will be replaced contemporaneously with the machinery.[31] To sidestep this controversy in one context, Congress enacted §48(a)(1)(D) in 1978, providing that "single purpose agricultural or horticultural structures" qualify as section 38 property even if they provide shelter and work space.[32] The single-purpose test rules out structures with space for functions not essential for their agricultural or horticultural uses (e.g., a check-out counter for customers).

Property not disqualified by the negative test (property that is not a building or structural component thereof) must also meet the positive test, which requires that it be used for one of three classes of activities

Manufacturing, etc. The first class of qualifying activities consists of manufacturing, production, and extraction, and of the furnishing of transportation, communications, electrical energy, gas, water, and sewage dispos-

---

[30] Thirup v. CIR, 508 F2d 915, 919 (9th Cir. 1974) (extensive flower greenhouses, where half of taxpayer's workers spent most of their working days, qualified; working space was merely incidental to principal function of structure). See Rev. Rul. 77-363, 1977-2 CB 10, modified by Rev. Rul. 79-343, 1979-2 CB 18 (IRS will not follow *Thirup* because "function of providing work space is no less important than the function of providing an environment conducive to plant growth"); Rev. Rul. 79-343, 1979-2 CB 18 (Rev. Rul. 77-363 modified to take account of 1978 legislation, for which see infra text accompanying note 32).

[31] A.C. Monk & Co. v. US, 686 F2d 1058 (4th Cir. 1982) (primary criterion whether structure could feasibly be adapted if factory used to produce other things); Yellow Freight Sys., Inc. v. US, 538 F2d 790 (8th Cir. 1976) (trailer truck loading docks and inspection lanes in freight terminal resembling building in both "appearance" and "function"); Valmont Indus., Inc. v. CIR, 73 TC 1059 (1980) (galvanizing facilities); Rev. Rul. 79-406, 1979-2 CB 18 (self-service car wash structure not qualified). See generally Maples, When Will a Building Qualify for the Investment Credit: An Analysis, 51 J. Tax'n 358 (1979).

[32] See IRC §48(p) (definition of "single purpose agricultural or horticultural structure"). For further explanation, see S. Rep. No. 1263, 95th Cong., 2d Sess., reprinted in 1978-3 CB (Vol. 1) 315, 414–15; Conf. Rep. No. 1800, supra note 10, at 560–62.

al services.[33] To qualify, property must be used "as an integral part" of one of these activities, a standard that is satisfied if the property "is used directly in the activity and is essential to the completeness of the activity," but not if the relationship is more remote.[34] The regulations contrast property used to acquire or transport raw materials or supplies to the point of manufacturing (e.g., docks, railroad tracks, and bridges) with pavements, parking areas, advertising displays, and other property whose relationship to the manufacturing activity is too attenuated.[35] As interpreted by the regulations, the statutory reference to "furnishing . . . services" embraces only taxpayers engaged in the trade or business of supplying these services.[36] Thus, the operators of a mobile home park were held not entitled to an investment credit on installing water, electrical, and gas distribution systems, even though they billed tenants for these services, because their activities were insufficient to constitute a business of furnishing utility services.[37]

Research facilities. The second class of qualifying property consists of research facilities used in connection with any of the foregoing activities. The "in connection with" relationship of this rule is less exacting than the "integral part" standard of the rule described in the preceding paragraph.[38]

Storage facilities. The third class of qualifying property consists of facilities for the bulk storage of fungible commodities (including liquids and gases) used in connection with—but not necessarily as an integral part of—any of the foregoing activities. This rule was enacted in 1971 to clear up an ambiguity in prior law, where storage facilities could qualify only if constituting "an integral part" of manufacturing, production, or other specified

---

[33] See Reg. §1.48-1(d)(2); Rev. Rul 81-66, 1981-1 CB 19 (operation of cafeterias is retailing, not manufacturing, despite preparation of food and drink by cafeteria employees); Rev. Rul. 80-341, 1980-2 CB 24 (raising of fish, as distinguished from merely catching them, is production; concrete raceways and concrete-lined water diversion canals qualify); Rev. Rul. 68-279, 1968-1 CB 18 (contra for lobster pounds constructed by wholesaler to hold lobsters until marketable). For an unsuccessful argument deserving a prize for ingenuity, see Mt. Mansfield Co. v. CIR, 50 TC 798 (1968), aff'd per curiam, 409 F2d 845 (2d Cir. 1969) (ski slopes and trails do not furnish "transportation services").

[34] Reg. §1.48-1(d)(4). See Rev. Rul. 81-120, 1981-1 CB 20 (water piping system, waste-water collection tank, and deep well for waste removal and disposal held to be "integral part" of chemical manufacturing activity).

[35] Id. See also Rev. Rul. 66-89, 1966-1 CB 7, modified by Rev. Rul. 79-343, 1979-2 CB 18 (illustrations of farm property satisfying "integral" standard—fences, wells, paved barnyards, etc.).

[36] Reg. §1.48-1(a).

[37] Evans v. CIR, 48 TC 704 (1967), aff'd per curiam, 413 F2d 1047 (9th Cir. 1969). But see Westroads, Inc. v. CIR, 69 TC 682 (1978) (shopping center engaged in business of generating and distributing electricity to tenants).

[38] Reg. §1.48-1(d)(5).

activities.[39] Although the facility must be used in connection with manufacturing or other specified activities, the taxpayer need not itself be engaged in the qualifying activity.[40] To qualify, however, the facility must be used principally for "bulk storage," construed by the regulations to refer to the storage of a large mass of commodities before consumption, utilization, sorting, or packaging.[41]

c. *Intangible property.* Intangible property generally is not section 38 property. Thus, the costs of producing and obtaining patents, copyrights, subscription lists, and other intangible assets have never qualified for the investment credit.[42] If depreciable tangible property (e.g., a typewriter) is acquired in order to produce an intangible asset, however, the tangible property qualifies as section 38 property even if depreciation thereon cannot be deducted but must instead be added to the basis of the unqualified intangible asset.[43] Moreover, the Court of Appeals for the Fifth Circuit has held that the investment credit can be claimed for the cost of collecting seismic data recorded on tapes and films sold to the taxpayer's customers, since these items are tangible property.[44] Also, special legislation enacted in

---

[39] See S. Rep. No. 437, 92d Cong., 1st Sess. (1971), reprinted in 1972-1 CB 559, 574. Cases decided under prior law are cited in Rev. Rul. 71-359, 1971-2 CB 61, modified by Rev. Rul. 84-60, 1984-1 CB 13 (taxpayer's activities of drying, cleaning, bagging, and shelling peanuts constitute "manufacturing or production"; storage facilities used in connection therewith qualify).

[40] Reg. §1.48-1(d)(5)(i).

[41] Reg. §1.48-1(d)(5)(ii). See Brown-Forman Distillers Corp. v. US, 499 F2d 1263 (Ct. Cl. 1974) (facilities holding barrels of aging bourbon whiskey qualified as storage facilities, citing other cases); Merchants Refrigerating Co. v. US, 79-1 USTC ¶9270 (WD Cal. 1979) (not officially reported), aff'd per curiam, 659 F2d 116 (9th Cir. 1981), cert. denied, 456 US 973 (1982) (meaning of "bulk storage" and "fungible commodities"); Lesher v. CIR, 73 TC 340 (1979) (building to store hay and feed livestock qualified; extensive analysis); Catron v. CIR, 50 TC 306 (1968) (acq.) (portion of structure used as storage facility qualified; IRS theory that allocation is not permissible rejected); Rev. Rul. 80-195, 1980-2 CB 20 (structure to store different grades and forms of aluminum scrap that are not intermingled held not qualified because not used to store "fungible" commodities).

[42] Reg. §1.48-1(f).

[43] Id. (last sentence); Reg. §1.48-1(b)(4). See also United Telecommunications, Inc. v. CIR, 589 F2d 1383 (10th Cir.), cert. denied, 442 US 917 (1979).

[44] Texas Instruments, Inc. v. US, 551 F2d 599 (5th Cir. 1977). See Mapco, Inc. v. US, 556 F2d 1107 (Ct. Cl. 1977) (damage payments to landowners includable in cost of constructing qualified pipelines, rather than attributable to nonqualified perpetual right-of-way easements). But see Bank of Vt. v. US, 88-1 USTC ¶9169 (D. Vt. 1988) (not officially reported) (computer software recorded on magnetic tape not tangible because software could have been transmitted electronically and thus was "not dependent on the magnetic tape for its existence"); Ronnen v. CIR, 90 TC 74 (1988) (same); Rev. Rul. 80-327, 1980-2 CB 23 (of amount paid for engraved plates and right to publish books printed from plates, only amount allocable to plates qualifies for credit because right to publish is intangible). Compare Rev. Rul. 81-239,

1976 explicitly permits expenses for motion picture and television videotapes to qualify, subject to a percentage limitation and other qualifications.[45]

d. *Ineligible property.* The eligibility criteria described above disqualify
several categories of property, of which the principal ones are (1) property
not subject to depreciation or amortization (e.g., property devoted exclusively to personal purposes and land), (2) property placed in service before
1981 with a useful life when placed in service of less than three years, (3)
most buildings and structural components, and (4) intangible property.
Even if property avoids disqualification at the threshold by satisfying the
standards of §48(a)(1), it is not section 38 property if it falls within any of
the following categories of assets:

Foreign use or origin. Property used predominantly outside the United
States is disqualified by §48(a)(2), with the exception of aircraft, ships, and
a few other items. A companion disqualification is imposed by §48(a)(7) on
property "completed outside the United States" or having a basis less than
50 percent of which is attributable to value added within the United States,
subject to exemption by executive order.[46]

Tax-exempt organizations. Property used by a tax-exempt organization
cannot qualify unless used predominantly in an unrelated trade or business

---

1981-2 CB 10 (publisher's payments to author and costs of evaluating and revising
manuscript are costs of intangible property; costs of preparing manuscript for compositor and compositor's costs are costs of tangible property—the film from which
printing plates are made).

[45] IRC §48(k). The 1976 legislation is explained at length in Joint Comm. on
Tax'n, 94th Cong., 2d Sess., General Explanation of the Tax Reform Act of 1976,
reprinted in 1976-3 CB (Vol. 2) 1, 188–98. See Goodson-Todman Enters., Ltd. v.
CIR, 784 F2d 66 (2d Cir. 1986) (provision of statute denying credit for films or tapes
"the market for which is primarily topical or is otherwise essentially transitory in
nature" held inapplicable to tapes for television game show; regulation construing
this provision to deny credit for all game shows held invalid); Cosby v. US, 8 Cl. Ct.
428, 85-2 USTC ¶9502 (1985), aff'd, 795 F2d 999 (Fed. Cir. 1986) (same for variety
and game show video tapes); Apis Prods., Inc. v. CIR, 86 TC 1192 (1986) (same for
variety show); Encyclopedia Britannica Educ. Corp. v. US, 84-2 USTC ¶9538 (ND
Ill. 1984) (not officially reported) (no credit for educational filmstrips).

For litigation under prior law, see Bing Crosby Prods., Inc. v. US, 588 F2d 1293
(9th Cir. 1979) (master negatives qualified for credit), and cases therein cited. For
taxable years beginning before January 1, 1975, taxpayers may elect to compute the
investment credit for films and videotapes under §804(c) of the Tax Reform Act of
1976, which was not incorporated into the Code. See generally Bennett & Forester,
The Investment Tax Credit for Motion Pictures and Television Films and Tapes—
The Unique and New Rules Under the Tax Reform Act of 1976, 1979 S. Cal. Tax
Inst. 295; Williams, The Investment Tax Credit in Connection With Record Masters
and Motion Pictures—The Only Game in Town, 52 S. Cal. L. Rev. 1121 (1979).

[46] See Reg. §1.48-1(g) (foreign use), §1.48-1(o) (foreign origin); Roux Laboratories, Inc. v. US, 76-2 USTC ¶9751 (MD Fla. 1976) (not officially reported) (application of rule to domestically made components installed in foreign-made machinery).

whose income is subject to tax under §511.[47] Property used by the United States, a state or political subdivision, or an international organization (which are not subject to the tax on unrelated business income) is also disqualified.[48] The latter rule also applies to property leased to a foreign person unless the property is used in an activity generating income taxable by the United States.[49] The primary application of these rules is where a private, taxable U.S. resident leases property to a tax-exempt entity, government, or foreign person.[50] Rehabilitation expenditures are exempted from both rules.

Lodging. Property used predominantly for lodging is disqualified by §48(a)(3).[51] This disqualification, however, does not apply to nonlodging commercial facilities open to outsiders on the same basis as lodgers, to hotels and motels whose accommodations are used predominantly by transients, or to coin-operated vending machines, washers, and dryers.[52]

Livestock. Horses are disqualified by §48(a)(6), but other livestock (including poultry) can qualify unless substantially identical livestock is sold or disposed of within a prescribed period in a transaction not subject to §47(a). Although §48(a)(6) states flatly that livestock other than horses "shall be treated as section 38 property," this blanket statement was clearly not intended to exempt livestock from the basic rules of §48(a)(1). Livestock acquired for personal use, for example, should not qualify.

Boilers. As an antipollution measure, §48(a)(10), enacted in 1978, disqualifies boilers fueled primarily by oil or gas unless (1) the use of coal is precluded by federal or certain state air pollution regulations or (2) the

---

[47] IRC §48(a)(4); Reg. §1.48-1(j). See Kleinsasser v. US, 707 F2d 1024 (9th Cir. 1983) (§48(a)(4) applies to property used by religious or apostolic organization exempt under §501(d) even though such an organization cannot have unrelated business income). For §511, see infra ¶103.3.

[48] IRC §48(a)(5). Property used by the International Telecommunications Satellite Consortium or any successor is exempted from this rule. Id.; Reg. §1.48-1(k). See Xerox Corp. v. US, 656 F2d 659 (Ct. Cl. 1981) (copying machines placed by taxpayer with exempt organizations and government agencies qualified for credit because machines used by taxpayer to provide copying services to organizations and agencies, not used by organizations and agencies themselves); Note, *Xerox Corp. v. United States* and the Investment Credit: When Is Property Used by the Government? 1 Va. Tax Rev. 173 (1981).

[49] This disqualification applies only if the property is placed in service by the taxpayer after May 23, 1983.

[50] See Rev. Rul. 83-109, 1983-2 CB 16.

[51] See Aaron Rents, Inc. v. US, 462 F. Supp. 65 (ND Ga. 1978) (credit allowed to lessor for furniture leased to occupants of apartments, but denied as to furniture leased to persons providing lodging facilities to tenants; extensive analysis); Rev. Rul. 81-133, 1981-1 CB 21 (same).

[52] For illustrations of these distinctions, see Reg. §1.48-1(h).

boiler is to be used for a residential facility, office building, or certain other exempt uses.

¶27.2.3 Amount of Investment Credit

For property placed in service before 1986, the credit is usually 10 percent of the cost of qualified property. The computation, however, is complicated by numerous details. The credit is made up of three elements, each of which is affected by various factors, including the useful life of the property, whether it is new or used when placed in service, and the taxpayer's tax liability. Some of these factors determine not only the amount of the credit, but also who is entitled to claim it.

1. *Tripartite credit.* The credit consists of three components; "the regular percentage," "the energy percentage," and "the rehabilitation percentage."[53]

For property placed in service before 1986, the regular percentage is 10 percent of the qualified investment. For property placed in service after 1985, the regular percentage usually does not apply.[54] Transition rules allow the regular percentage to apply to property that was placed in service after 1985 if the taxpayer was substantially committed to the purchase or construction of the property at the end of 1985.[55] For taxable years beginning after July 1, 1987, the regular percentage is effectively reduced from 10 percent to 6.5 percent for property covered by the transition rules.[56] Reforestation expenditures treated as section 38 property, however, qualify indefinitely for the regular percentage at the full 10 percent rate.[57]

---

[53] IRC §§46(a), (b). The rehabilitation percentage applies for taxable years beginning after 1983. For prior years, the third element of the computation was "the ESOP percentage," which applied to corporations with employee stock ownership plans (ESOPs) qualifying under §409. For ESOPs and §409, see infra ¶62.1. See also IRC §48(n) (before repeal in 1984) (qualification for ESOP percentage).

[54] IRC §49(a).

[55] The principal transition rules apply in three cases: where (1) the taxpayer had a binding contract to purchase or construct the property on December 31, 1985, (2) on that date the taxpayer had begun construction of the property and had incurred or committed to 5 percent of the property's cost (or if less to $1 million of the cost), or (3) the property consists of an equipped building or plant whose construction had begun by December 31, 1985 and more than 50 percent of whose cost had been incurred or committed by that date. IRC §§49(b)(1), (e); Pub. L. No. 99-514, §203(b), 100 Stat. 2085 (1986). Also, certain progress expenditures made before 1986 qualify for the regular percentage even if the property is placed in service after 1985. IRC §49(b)(2).

[56] IRC §49(c)(1). A proportionate reduction occurs for a taxable year that begins before and ends after July 1, 1987. IRC §49(c)(3).

[57] IRC §49(b)(3).

Generally, the energy percentage only applies to energy property placed in service before 1983, although this aspect of the credit was phased out more slowly for a few types of property. The instances in which credit is allowed for energy property placed in service after 1985, and the credit rates for this property, are shown in Table 27-1.[58]

Table 27-1

Investment Credit for Energy
Property Placed in Service After 1985

Type of property	Description	Credit rate
Solar energy	Equipment using solar energy to heat or cool a structure or to generate electricity	15% (1986) 12% (1987) 10% (1988)
Geothermal	Equipment used to produce energy from a geothermal deposit	15% (1986) 10% (1987–88)
Ocean thermal	Equipment used in two designated locations to convert ocean thermal energy to usable energy	15% (1986–88)
Biomass	Boilers and burners using fuels other than oil, gas, or coal and equipment for converting such fuels	15% (1986) 10% (1987)

The rehabilitation percentage is generally 10 percent of the qualified rehabilitation expenditures with respect to a qualified rehabilitated building, but is increased to 20 percent if the building is a certified historic structure.[59]

2. *Qualified investment.* Each of the three percentages described above apply to the taxpayer's "qualified investment" in property eligible for that

---

[58] Also, under a transition rule, the credit is allowed at 10 percent for a broad range of energy property constructed under long-term contracts if (1) the property is placed in service no later than the end of 1990, (2) planning for the project was completed by the end of 1982, and (3) substantial contracts were let by the end of 1985. IRC §46(b)(2)(C).

[59] For property placed in service before 1986, the credit rates were (1) 25 percent for certified historic structures, (2) 20 percent for buildings at least 40 years old when rehabilitation begins, and (3) 15 percent in other cases. IRC §46(b)(4) (before amendment in 1986). The pre-1986 percentages also apply to property placed in service as late as the end of 1993 if it qualifies under various transition rules. Pub. L. No. 99-514, §251(d), 100 Stat. 2085 (1986). See supra text accompanying notes 10–12 for the terms "qualified rehabilitation expenditures," "qualified rehabilitated building," and "certified historic structure."

percentage. For new section 38 property placed in service after 1981 (including qualified rehabilitation expenditures), "qualified investment" is defined by §46(c)(7) as 100 percent of the property's basis unless the property is three-year property under the pre-1987 ACRS rules, in which case qualified investment is limited to 60 percent of basis.[60] For new section 38 property placed in service before 1981, qualified investment is defined by §46(c)(1) as 100 percent of the property's basis if it has a useful life when placed in service[61] of seven years or more, 66⅔ percent if its useful life is five years or more but less than seven years, and 33⅓ percent if its useful life is three years or more but less than five years.[62] The principal point of contention in the application of the foregoing rules is the composition of the "basis" against which the percentages are applied.[63] The same percentages apply to used section 38 property, but the base is the property's cost rather than its basis, reflecting the requirement of §48(c) that used property must

---

[60] See supra ¶23.3.7 for the pre-1987 ACRS rules.

[61] For the meaning of the statutory term "placed in service," see Reg. §1.46-3(d); see also Rev. Rul. 65-104, 1965-1 CB 28 (citrus trees placed in service when they reach an income-producing stage); Rev. Rul. 78-433, 1978-2 CB 121 (aircraft requiring testing by manufacturer not placed in service by purchaser by testing activities); supra ¶23.2.3 (when property is placed in service for depreciation purposes).

[62] The applicable percentage is increased to 100 percent for certain pollution control facilities and commuter highway vehicles with useful lives of at least five or three years, respectively, by IRC §§46(c)(5) and (c)(6); see also IRC §46(c)(3) (increase in amount of qualified investment for certain public utility property).

For the relation between the estimated useful life of property for investment credit purposes and its life for depreciation or amortization purposes, see Reg. §1.46-3(e); Note, Lives for Investment Credit and Depreciation Can Differ, 30 J. Tax'n 120 (1969).

[63] The IRS once contended that where a taxpayer constructs section 38 property for its own use, depreciation on equipment used in the construction project, although required to be capitalized into the property's basis for other tax purposes, could not be included in basis for purposes of determining the investment credit. The IRS theory was that including depreciation in basis would allow the taxpayer to take two credits, one for the construction equipment and another for the constructed asset, for a single cost. The theory won judicial acceptance, but the Tax Court held that basis for credit purposes includes depreciation if no credit was allowed on purchase of the construction equipment. United Telecommunications, Inc. v. CIR, 65 TC 278 (1975), supplemented by 67 TC 760 (1977), aff'd, 589 F2d 1383 (10th Cir. 1978), cert. denied, 442 US 917 (1979). The IRS accepted this modification. Rev. Rul. 81-1, 1981-1 CB 18.

Also, if the taxpayer pays an inflated price, the credit is calculated on the true cost of the property. See Lemmen v. CIR, 77 TC 1326 (1981) (acq.) (cost of cattle in tax shelter in excess of fair market value allocated to maintenance contract; basis of cattle limited to fair market value). See also Oglebay Norton Co. v. US, 610 F2d 715 (Ct. Cl. 1979) (basis includes amounts paid with tax-deferred Merchant Marine Act capital construction funds); Zuanich v. CIR, 77 TC 428 (1981) (contra); Hudson v. CIR, 77 TC 468 (1981) (basis does not include currently deductible sales tax).

be acquired "by purchase" to qualify for the investment credit.[64]

3. *Used versus new property.* Sections 48(b) and (c) distinguish between "new section 38 property" and "used section 38 property." The former consists of property (1) whose construction, reconstruction, or erection is completed by the taxpayer after December 31, 1961 or (2) that is acquired thereafter if the original use commences with the taxpayer after December 31, 1961.[65] Taxpayers who purchase and reconstruct used equipment may escape the "used property" limitation so far as their reconstruction expenses are concerned, but if similarly reconditioned property is purchased, it must be treated as used property.[66] Also, qualified rehabilitation expenditures are treated as "new section 38 property."[67]

To prevent shuttling property back and forth between related taxpayers in order to manufacture investment credits without contributing to the economy as a whole, §48(c) allows the credit with respect to used property only if it is (1) acquired by the taxpayer by purchase and (2) not used after the acquisition by a person who either used the property previously or is related to such a person.[68]

In addition, the cost of used section 38 property to be taken into account in computing the taxpayer's qualified investment is limited to $125,000 per taxable year.[69] A single $125,000 cap is allocated among all

---

[64] For the meaning of "cost" as applied to used property, see IRC §48(c)(3)(B); Reg. §1.48-3(b).

[65] These requirements are elaborated by Reg. §1.48-2. See Rev. Rul. 81-305, 1981-2 CB 12 (cost of removing and reconstructing roof in order to install used equipment added to cost of used equipment).

[66] See Reg. §1.48-2(b)(7) (use of reconditioned property does not commence with purchaser; but use of parts constituting not more than 20 percent of total cost in property reconstructed by taxpayer does not render reconditioned property "used"); Rev. Rul. 79-331, 1979-2 CB 19 (railroad cars altered for somewhat different function remained used property); Rev. Rul. 70-135, 1970-1 CB 10; Rev. Rul. 68-111, 1968-1 CB 29.

[67] IRC §48(g)(4).

[68] The term "purchase" is defined by §48(c)(3)(A) by reference to §179(d)(2), and the tainted relationships are listed in §§179(d)(2)(A) and (B). For §179, relating to the additional first-year depreciation allowance, see supra ¶23.8. See Sherar v. US, 413 F2d 986 (9th Cir. 1969) (sale-leaseback; property by prior use in unprofitable business); Crawford v. CIR, 70 TC 46 (1978) (used property disqualified because previously owned by corporation of which taxpayer and father owned 90 percent of stock; although bank foreclosed mortgage and taxpayer bought property from bank, its intervention did not purify property); Moradian v. CIR, 53 TC 207 (1969) (acq.) (taxpayer entitled to credit on purchasing half interest in property used before acquisition by partnership of taxpayer's vendor and her husband and after purchase by partnership of taxpayer and her husband).

[69] The ceiling is $100,000 for taxable years beginning before 1981. IRC §48(c)(2)(A) (before amendment in 1981). It rose to $150,000 for taxable years

members of a controlled group of corporations.[70] In the case of partnerships, the dollar limit applies to the firm itself as well as to each partner. The $125,000 limit is reduced to $62,500 for married persons filing separate returns unless the taxpayer's spouse has no qualifying used section 38 property for the taxable year.

If the cost of qualified used property placed in service during any credit year exceeds the dollar limitation, the taxpayer must designate the items to be taken into account.[71] The used property that is not selected, however, cannot be carried over for use in a later year in which the used property placed in service is less than the applicable dollar limit.

4. *Leased property.* Although the investment credit is ordinarily allowed only to the owner of qualified property,[72] §48(d) allows lessors of new section 38 property to elect to shift the credit to the lessee by treating the lessee as having purchased the property for its fair market value, subject to various qualifications.[73] This election makes it possible for the credit to be shifted to a lessee who can use it to better advantage than the lessor. An example is where the lessor's tax liability is too low to absorb the credit in the year of acquisition or in the years to which unused credits can be carried. Also, because §46(e)(3), described in the following paragraph, denies the credit to the lessor in certain net lease arrangements, the only way to prevent a loss of the credit where §46(e)(3) applies is an election under §48(d) to treat the lessee as the owner of the property.

---

beginning after 1987, but because of the repeal of the general credit, the $150,000 limitation seldom, if ever, applies.

[70] For the term "controlled group," see IRC §48(c)(3)(C).

[71] Reg. §1.48-3(c)(4).

[72] See, e.g., Swift Dodge v. CIR, 692 F2d 651 (9th Cir. 1982) (open-end leases of motor vehicles by car dealer were conditional sales contracts, and dealer not entitled to investment credit).

[73] For details, see Reg. §1.48-4, but note subsequent changes in §48(d). See Comdisco, Inc. v. US, 756 F2d 569 (7th Cir. 1985) (lessee-sublessor allowed credit even though (1) agreements with owner-lessor ambiguous, (2) ultimate user of property (alleged to be taxpayer's sublessee) contracted with owner only, and (3) evidence suggested that taxpayer's interest was as agent in transaction by which owner purchased property and that investment credit was intended as taxpayer's commission; court inferred from legislative history an intention that §48(d) be applied liberally); Faulkner v. CIR, 88 TC 623 (1987) (where lessor qualifies for credit but elects to pass it to lessee under §48(d), lessee gets credit even if he could not qualify if he were owner); Rev. Rul. 84-4, 1984-1 CB 19 (where lessor granted "lessee" nonexclusive license to use property, lessee not qualified for pass through because lease must be "conveyance of exclusive possession of specific property"). See also Haddock v. CIR, 70 TC 511 (1978) (lessee acquired property by exercising option to purchase; held, since no election was made to treat lessee as owner, property is neither "new" nor "used" section 38 property in hands of lessee-purchaser; credit denied); Illinois Valley Paving Co. v. CIR, 687 F2d 1043 (7th Cir. 1982) (same).

Section 46(e)(3), a provision designed to limit the availability of the credit to tax shelter investors, provides that a lessor who is not a corporation usually cannot qualify for the credit. The credit is allowed to a noncorporate lessor, however, if the lessor manufactured or produced the leased property.[74] Also, a noncorporate lessor that did not manufacture the property is allowed the credit if two requirements are met: (1) the lease term must be less than 50 percent of the class life used to classify the property in determining ACRS deductions[75] and (2) the lessor's deductions under §162(a) (exclusive of interest, taxes, and depreciation) must exceed 15 percent of rental income during the first 12 months of the lease term.[76] Although §46(e)(3) does not usually apply to corporations, it is applicable to a lessor that is an S corporation. When property is held by a partnership, the provision applies in determining the credit available to any partner other than a corporate partner that has not elected under subchapter S. Qualified rehabilitation expenditures, in contrast, are exempted from the provision.

5. *S corporations, trusts, estates, and partnerships.* Section 1366(a) allows each shareholder of an S corporation to take his ratable share of the corporation's investment credits. Similar apportionment rules are prescribed for trusts, estates, and partnerships.[77]

Section 48(q), described below,[78] usually requires that the basis of section 38 property be reduced by 50 percent of the investment credit. When

---

[74] IRC §46(e)(3)(A). See Carlson v. CIR, 712 F2d 1314 (9th Cir. 1983) (lessor not a manufacturer where property assembled on lessee's premises by lessee's workmen selected by lessee's general manager; although lessor paid cost of assembly, he failed to show that he controlled operations).

[75] IRC §46(e)(3)(B). For property placed in service before 1981, the property's useful life, rather than its class life, is used for this purpose. See Hoisington v. CIR, 833 F2d 1398 (10th Cir. 1987) (this requirement not met where fixed term of lease exceeds 50 percent of useful life even if lease allows lessee to cancel on 30 days notice and more than one half of lessees exercise this option); Bloomberg v. CIR, 74 TC 1368 (1980) (where term of lease exceeded 50 percent of estimated useful life of equipment, credit denied notwithstanding early cancellation of lease). Compare McNamara v. CIR, 827 F2d 168, 171 (7th Cir. 1987) (if stated term of lease is less than 50 percent of useful life and if lease is not sham, 50 percent requirement met even if parties "realistically contemplate continuous renewal" throughout useful life) with Connor v. CIR, 847 F2d 985 (1st Cir. 1988) (rejecting *McNamara*; "the taxpayer must show that the parties, when they made the lease, realistically contemplated that the lease would cover less than 50 percent of the property's useful life").

[76] IRC §46(e)(3)(B). See Nelson v. CIR, 793 F2d 179 (8th Cir. 1986) (when lease made, lessor made payment to lessee as compensation for lessee's agreement to assume responsibility for repairs to leased property; held, payment does not count as §162 deduction because it is capital expenditure); Miller v. CIR, 85 TC 1064 (1985) (requirement can be met even if taxpayer not in trade or business of leasing property, notwithstanding reference to §162(a)).

[77] See Reg. §1.48-6 (trusts and estates), §1.46-3(f) (partnerships).

[78] Infra ¶27.2.4.

the §48(q) reduction is required with respect to property held by a partnership or S corporation, a corresponding reduction must be made in each partner's or shareholder's basis for his partnership interest or stock.[79] Presumably, the basis of each partner or shareholder is reduced by 50 percent of the credit allowable to him with respect to the partnership's or corporation's investment.

6. *At risk rules.* Section 46(c)(8), enacted in 1981 and substantially revised in 1984, denies the investment credit with respect to the portions of the cost of section 38 property that are financed by certain nonrecourse borrowings. The rule is a companion to §465, which denies loss deductions in excess of the amounts the taxpayer has at risk, and §46(c)(8) only applies to taxpayers that are also subject to §465.[80] When §46(c)(8) applies, the basis or cost of the property is reduced by the amount of any nonrecourse debt securing the property unless the debt is "qualified commercial financing." The latter term is defined as a borrowing from an unrelated person who (1) is in the business of lending money, (2) lends to the taxpayer no more than 80 percent of the property's basis or cost, (3) neither sold the property to the taxpayer nor received a fee in connection with the taxpayer's purchase, and (4) is not related to a person who made the sale or received such a fee. The last two of these requirements are waived if the loan is made or guaranteed by a government agency.

Credit denied under §46(c)(8) is allowed in subsequent years as the taxpayer pays down the disqualifying nonrecourse debt.[81] Conversely, if the amount of nonqualified nonrecourse financing is increased after the year credit is allowed, credit is recaptured by adding to the taxpayer's tax for the year of the increase an amount equal to the excess of (1) the credit allowed over (2) the credit that would have been allowed if the higher amount of nonrecourse financing had been obtained at the outset.[82] Also, if property financed with nonqualifed nonrecourse financing is leased and the lessor elects to pass the credit on to the lessee, the lessee's credit is usually limited to the same extent as the lessor's would have been in the absence of the pass through.[83]

7. *Regulated utility companies.* Section 46(f) denies the investment credit to certain regulated utility companies if the credit will flow through to its customers by virtue of a reduction in rates or in the base to which the allowable rate of return is applied.[84] The objective of this restriction is to ensure that the investment credit subsidizes the utility's investments, rather

---

[79] IRC §48(q)(6).
[80] For §465, see supra ¶25.10.
[81] IRC §46(c)(9).
[82] IRC §47(d).
[83] IRC §48(d)(6).
[84] See Temp. Reg. §9.1; Prop. Reg. §1.46-5; Rev. Rul. 78-193, 1978-1 CB 12.

than lower rates for customers.[85]

8. *Safe harbor and finance leases.* Section 168(f)(8), as in effect in the period 1981 through 1986, gave tax effect to certain leasing transactions that had little or no nontax significance to the parties, but were structured to enable loss companies and other taxpayers with a surfeit of investment credits and depreciation deductions to sell these allowances to profitable companies that could use them to reduce their income tax bills. In the 1981 version of the provision, these leases were known as safe harbor leases.[86] The safe harbor rules were restricted in 1982 and were replaced for 1984 through 1986 by a still more limited vehicle called finance leases. The rules on safe harbor and finance leases do not apply for property placed in service after 1986.

¶27.2.4 Basis Reduction

Section 48(q) requires that the basis of section 38 property be reduced by 50 or 100 percent of any investment credit allowed with respect to the property.[87] A basis reduction for 100 percent of the credit might be justified on the ground that the taxpayer should have no basis for the portion of the property's purchase price that is effectively paid for by the government through the credit. The policy underlying §48(q), however, is much narrower. Congress discovered in 1982 that amendments enacted in 1981 had made the combination of the investment credit and depreciation deductions more advantageous than an immediate write-off of the cost of depreciable property. Since an immediate write-off is mathematically equivalent to an exemption of income from the property from tax,[88] the 1981 rules effectively provided a negative rate of tax on income from depreciable property. Section 48(q) was one of several provisions enacted in 1982 to "make the combination of ACRS cost recovery deductions and the regular investment credit no more generous than expensing at a 10 percent after-tax

---

[85] See Hearings on Tax Legislation Before the House Ways and Means Comm., 96th Cong., 2d Sess. (Apr. 15, 1980) (statement of Daniel I. Halperin, Deputy Assistant Secretary of the Treasury).

[86] See Greene v. CIR, 88 TC 376 (1987) (role of business purpose, economic substance, and profit motive in transactions involving safe harbor leases). See generally Odell & Fritch, New Concepts in Equipment Leasing (Law and Business 1981); Koffey, Safe Harbor Leasing, 1982 S. Cal. Tax Inst. ¶200; Warren & Auerbach, Tax Policy and Equipment Leasing After TEFRA, 96 Harv. L. Rev. 1579 (1983).

[87] Section 48(q) applies to property placed in service after 1982. Basis was required to be reduced by 100 percent of the credit when the credit rules were first enacted in 1962, but this rule was repealed, effective for property placed in service after 1963. IRC §48(g)(1) (before repeal in 1964). See Reg. §1.48-7. No basis reduction is required for property placed in service during the period 1964 through 1982.

[88] See supra ¶23.1.5.

discount rate."[89]

The amount of the basis adjustment is 50 percent of the credit for all property placed in service after 1982, except in three cases. First, the reduction is 100 percent of the credit for qualified rehabilitation expenditures.[90] Second, the reduction is also 100 percent where credit is allowed at the regular percentage after 1985 under transition rules accompanying the repeal of the general credit.[91] Third, except in cases covered by the foregoing 100 percent rules, a taxpayer can avoid the basis reduction altogether for credit allowed under the regular percentage by electing instead to reduce that percentage.[92] For an electing taxpayer, the regular percentage is reduced to 4 percent of basis for property that is three-year property under the ACRS rules and to 8 percent for all other property. The election thus allows a taxpayer to keep all of his basis by agreeing to a one-third reduction in the credit for three-year property or a 20 percent reduction for other property. The election is made property by property, but once made for a particular item is revocable only with IRS consent.[93]

A basis reduction under §48(q) is treated as depreciation in applying the recapture rules of §§1245 and 1250, with the consequence that the taxpayer's ordinary income on a disposition of the property might be increased by the amount of the §48(q) reduction.[94]

¶27.2.5 Recapture of Investment Credit

Section 47 requires that the credit be recaptured in whole or in part if the property is disposed of before the end of the time periods prescribed in the statutes. Recapture is also required if, before the expiration of the applicable recapture period, the property ceases to satisfy the definition of section 38 property. Recapture is effected by increasing the taxpayer's tax for the year of recapture by the portion of the credit required to be recaptured.

---

[89] Staff of Joint Comm. on Tax'n, 97th Cong., 2d Sess., General Explanation of the Revenue Provisions of the Tax Equity and Fiscal Responsibility Act of 1982, at 36 (Comm. Print 1982) [hereinafter 1982 Bluebook].

[90] IRC §§48(q)(1), (3). The reduction is 50 percent rather than 100 percent if the rehabilitated building is a certified historic structure and is placed in service before 1987. IRC §48(q)(3) (before amendment in 1986).

A special rule is also provided for films. IRC §48(q)(7).

[91] IRC §49(d).

[92] IRC §48(q)(4).

[93] For property held by a partnership, the election is made at the partnership level even though the credit passes through to the shareholders. 1982 Bluebook, supra note 89, at 36.

[94] IRC §48(q)(5). For §§1245 and 1250, see infra ¶¶55.2, 55.3.

For property depreciable under the ACRS rules for property placed in service during the period 1981 through 1986, recapture occurs by a schedule.[95] For property that is three-year property under the 1981–1986 ACRS rules, 100 percent of the credit is recaptured if the property is disposed of or otherwise ceases to be section 38 property within one year after it is placed in service; the recapture percentage is 66 percent during the second year after the property is placed in service, 33 percent during the third year, and zero thereafter. For other property, recapture is required if the disposition or other disqualifying event occurs within five years after the property is placed in service, and the recapture percentages are 100, 80, 60, 40, and 20 for these five years. Given the credit rates of 6 percent for three-year property and 10 percent for other property, the foregoing rules have the effect of allowing credit, after recapture, of 2 percent of basis or cost for each year the property is held.

For property not subject to the 1981–1986 ACRS rules, recapture is required only if the disposition or other disqualifying event occurs before the end of the useful life used in computing the credit. When the recapture rule applies to such property, the recapture amount is determined by recomputing the credit substituting (1) the period from the date it was placed in service until the date of the disposition or other disqualifying event for (2) the useful life as estimated in the credit year.[96] For example, if property with an estimated useful life of six years when placed in service is sold during the fourth year, the credit previously allowed is recomputed by substituting 33⅓ percent (the percentage applicable to property with an estimated useful life of three to five years) in computing the taxpayer's qualified investment under §46(c) for 66⅔ percent (the applicable percentage for property with an estimated useful life of five to seven years). If the property is disposed of during the sixth year, however, no adjustment is required because the applicable percentage is the same whether the estimated useful life is five or six years.[97] At the other extreme, if the property is sold during the second year, the entire amount of the credit would be recaptured, because property with

---

[95] IRC §47(a)(5). See supra ¶23.3.7 for the 1981–1986 ACRS rules. See generally Dorr, Working With the Investment Credit Recapture Rules: A Blend of the Old and the New, 56 J. Tax'n 354 (1982).

[96] Special computations are prescribed by: (1) §47(a)(2) for property becoming public utility property subject to the limitation provided by §46(c)(3); (2) §47(a)(3) for termination of "progress expenditure property" status; (3) §46(a)(4) for a change in the use of commuter highway vehicles as defined by §46(c)(6)(B); (4) §47(a)(6) for aircraft used outside the United States; and (5) §46(a)(7) for motion picture films and videotapes.

For the interplay between the recapture rule and the pre-1986 add-on minimum tax, see Segal v. CIR, 89 TC 816 (1987).

[97] See Reg. §1.47-1(a)(2)(i).

an estimated useful life of less than three years does not qualify for the credit.

Since any increase in tax liability occurs in the recapture year, there is no need to extend the statute of limitations for the credit year. Taxpayers cannot avoid recapture when applicable by filing amended returns for the credit year and eliminating the credit.[98] If the credit being recaptured has not yet been fully allowed but resides in a carryover, the recapture amount is first applied in reduction of the carryover, and only the excess of the recapture amount over the unused carryover is added to the tax for the recapture year.[99]

Section 47 covers not only sales, exchanges, gifts, abandonments, and other "dispositions,"[100] but also events by which the property "ceases to be section 38 property with respect to the taxpayer," such as the conversion of property from business to personal use or, in the case of dual-use property, an increase in the proportion of personal use.[101] In addition, the regulations provide that a reduction in the basis of section 38 property by virtue of a refund of part of the purchase price is a pro tanto cessation of its qualified status.[102] Thus, there is no rest for the weary: Until the period of potential recapture has passed, the taxpayer must determine every year whether it would qualify as section 38 property if currently placed in service.[103] Moreover, since investment credits are passed through when earned by S corporations, trusts, and estates, and partnerships to their shareholders, beneficiaries, and partners, these individuals are also subject to the recapture rules when the property is disposed of by the entity or ceases to be section 38 property in its hands.[104]

---

[98] Goldstone v. CIR, 65 TC 113 (1975).

[99] IRC §47(a)(5)(D). For property placed in service before 1981, any unused but still viable carryover from the credit year is reduced; next, any unused carryover from other years that could have been used in the credit year is reduced; finally, if these adjustments do not absorb the disparity between the credit actually earned and the amount claimed, the remaining amount increases the taxpayer's tax liability for the recapture year. Reg. §§1.47-1(a)(1), (b), (d).

[100] Reg. §§1.47-2(a)(1), (d). No disposition is deemed to occur if the basis of property is reduced on account of a cancellation of indebtedness of the taxpayer. IRC §1017(c)(2) (effective for taxable years after 1980); Panhandle E. Pipe Line Co. v. US, 654 F2d 35 (Ct. Cl. 1981) (same result for prior years); Rev. Rul. 84-134, 1984-2 CB 6 (accepting decision in *Panhandle*). See supra ¶6.4 for the discharge of indebtedness rules.

[101] Reg. §1.47-2(e).

[102] Reg. §1.47-2(c).

[103] Reg. §1.47-2(a)(2).

[104] See Reg. §1.47-4 (S corporations), §1.47-5 (trusts and estates), §1.47-6 (partnerships); Galant, Partners, Subchapter S Shareholders and Beneficiaries—Beware: Investment Credit Recapture, 52 Taxes 417 (1974). Also, a shareholder of an S corporation must recapture credit on a sale of his stock; the amount of the recapture

Sections 47(b) and (e), and the regulations thereunder, contain six dispensations from these recapture principles: (1) If the taxpayer dies, the resulting transfer is not a disposition;[105] (2) transfers between spouses, whether made during the marriage or incident to divorce, are exempt; (3) transfers by corporations are exempt if subject to §381(a), relating to corporate acquisitions in which the transferor's tax attributes are inherited by the acquiring corporation;[106] (4) a "mere change" in the form of conducting the taxpayer's trade or business is exempt if the property is retained in the business as section 38 property and the taxpayer retains a substantial interest in the business;[107] (5) sale-leaseback transactions do not ordinarily trigger recapture;[108] and (6) on a disposition of used property, a taxpayer who acquired other qualified used property in the credit year that was not selected for credit purposes can substitute property not originally selected for the

---

is computed as though the corporation then sold the ratable share of its section 38 property that is allocable to the stock sold. Charbonnet v. US, 455 F2d 1195 (5th Cir. 1972); Ranier v. US, 88-1 USTC ¶9286 (ED Ky. 1988) (not officially reported).

[105] IRC §47(b)(1); see Reg. §1.47-3(b).

[106] IRC §47(b)(2). For IRC §381(a), see infra ¶95.5.2.

[107] IRC §47(b); Reg. §1.47-3(f). See Loewen v. CIR, 76 TC 90 (1981) (acq.) (mere change in form where transfer of investment credit property to newly formed wholly owned corporation, coupled with year-to-year lease of real property and fixtures, encompassed substantially all business assets); Rev. Rul. 83-65, 1983-1 CB 10 (explaining acquiescence in *Loewen*); Soares v. CIR, 50 TC 909 (1968) (on facts, more than mere change); Rev. Rul. 86-116, 1986-2 CB 9 (recapture excused where lessee of property used in its business (which had been allowed credit by reason of a pass through election by the lessor) transferred leasehold to partnership in exchange for 50 percent partnership interest; lessor simultaneously transferred ownership of the property to the partnership). See also Borgic v. CIR, 86 TC 643 (1986) (taxpayer transferred to wholly owned farming corporation equipment that he had formerly leased to corporation for use in its business; held, transfer satisfies requirement of regulations that property be used in same trade or business because taxpayer was a farmer and was not engaged in a leasing business). But see Siller Bros., v. CIR, 89 TC 256 (1988) (recapture required when property distributed to partner in liquidation of partnership because, under §732(b), partner's basis is determined without reference to partnership's basis); Blevins v. CIR, 61 TC 547 (1974) (gift of 53 percent of taxpayer's stock following conversion of partnership into corporation triggered recapture).

For S corporations, see Reg. §1.47-4(b) (S election constitutes disposition of corporation's property unless corporation and shareholders consent to joint and several liability for recapture on later dispositions); Tri-City Dr. Pepper Bottling Co. v. CIR, 61 TC 508 (1974) (regulation valid); Long v. US, 652 F2d 675 (6th Cir. 1981) (regulations valid in requiring recapture on liquidation of one-man S corporation whose business was continued); Ramm v. CIR, 72 TC 671 (1979) (use after liquidation of S corporation did not qualify); Rev. Rul. 69-168, 1969-1 CB 24 (reorganization of S corporation).

[108] Reg. §1.47-3(g). But see Rev. Rul. 87-73, 1987-2 CB 28 (recapture usually required on a sale-leaseback where buyer-lessor is a tax-exempt organization).

property disposed of.[109]

If the basis of the property was reduced under §48(q) when the credit was taken, basis is increased by 50 percent of the recaptured credit.[110] The basis increase occurs immediately before the event causing the recapture.

¶27.3 TARGETED JOBS AND WIN CREDITS

For years prior to 1989, §51 provides a credit, called the targeted jobs credit, for portions of the wages of employees found by Congress to require special aid because they experience high unemployment rates even when the national overall rate is low or because of other special employment circumstances.[1] For years prior to 1982, a similar credit was also allowed for expenditures under work incentive programs. These credits are described below.

1. *Targeted jobs credit.* The targeted jobs credit equals 40 percent of "qualified first-year wages," which consists of the first $6,000 of the wages paid during the first year of employment to any employee who belongs to a "targeted group."[2] The maximum credit for each targeted employee is thus $2,400 (40 percent of $6,000). The credit is in lieu of the usual deduction for this portion of the wages.[3] It is elective, but is allowed unless the employer affirmatively elects not to take it.[4]

The targeted groups include (1) individuals who are physically or mentally disabled and are referred to the employer upon completion of a vocational rehabilitation program, (2) recipients of supplemental security income benefits under the Social Security Act, and (3) welfare recipients.[5] Also, an individual from an economically disadvantaged family (as defined) is a targeted group member if he also possesses one of the following characteristics: (1) is between the ages of 18 and 25; (2) is a Vietnam veteran; (3) was convicted of a felony or released from prison during the preceding five years; (4) is between the ages of 16 and 20 and enrolled in a vocational

---

[109] Reg. §1.47-3(d). For the original selection of used property for credit purposes, see Reg. §1.48-3(c)(4).

[110] For §48(q), see supra ¶27.2.4.

[1] See Joint Comm. on Tax'n, 95th Cong., 2d Sess., General Explanation of the Revenue Act of 1978, at 163 (Comm. Print 1979).

[2] IRC §51(a), (b). The term "wages" has the same meaning here as under the federal unemployment tax (FUTA) rules, and generally includes all "remuneration for employment." IRC §§51(c)(1), 3306(b). See also Rev. Rul. 82-43, 1982-1 CB 10 ("wages" for this purpose do not include meals and lodging excludable under §119 [supra ¶14.5]).

[3] IRC §280C(a).

[4] IRC §51(j).

[5] IRC §51(d).

education program that combines work and study; or (5) is between the ages of 16 and 18 and hired for summer work.[6]

For such an employee's wages to qualify for credit, the employment must last for at least 90 days or the employee must complete at least 120 hours of service.[7] Also, the credit is denied for wages paid to an employee who is related to or a dependent of the employer or of a person owning more than 50 percent of the employer's stock.[8] At least one half of the employee's work must be in the employer's trade or business, a limitation that usually denies the credit for household help.[9] No credit is given for wages for a period during which the employer gets payments for the employee under a federally financed on-the-job training program.[10] If the employer receives work supplementation payments under the Social Security Act with respect to an employee, a portion of the employee's wages equal to these payments is not qualified.[11] If there is a strike or lockout, wages paid to an employee who does the same work as the striking or locked out employees do not qualify.[12] Further, if an employer ever employed the employee while he was not a member of a targeted group, wages paid after a subsequent rehiring while the individual belongs to such a group are not qualified.[13]

In applying the $6,000 ceiling and the other limitations on the credit, all members of a controlled group of corporations are treated as a single employer, and trades and businesses under other forms of common control are also aggregated.[14] Other limitations apply to tax-exempt organizations, trusts, and estates, and a few other types of employers.[15]

The targeted jobs credit was adopted in 1977 as a temporary expedient,[16] but its life was extended several times before it finally expired at the end of 1988.[17]

2. *Work incentive program expenditures.* During the period 1971 through 1981, a credit was allowed to employers for wages paid to eligible employees—primarily welfare recipients—up to specified percentages of

---

[6] For summer workers in this last category, the credit is only allowed with respect to the first $3,000 of the employee's wages. IRC §51(d)(12)(B)(iii).

[7] IRC §51(i)(3). This requirement is reduced to 14 days or 20 hours for a summer worker hired under §51(d)(12).

[8] IRC §51(i)(1).

[9] IRC §51(f).

[10] IRC §51(c)(2)(A).

[11] IRC §51(c)(2)(B).

[12] IRC §51(c)(3). This rule only applies after 1986.

[13] IRC §51(i)(2).

[14] IRC §§52(a), (b).

[15] IRC §§52(c), (d), (e).

[16] For the 1977–1978 new jobs credit, see S. Rep. No. 66, 95th Cong., 1st Sess., reprinted in 1977-1 CB 469, 486; Hjorth, New Jobs Tax Credit, 55 Taxes 707 (1977).

[17] IRC §51(c)(4).

their compensation during the first two years of employment.[18] This credit was enacted in the hope of remedying the failure of the 1967 Work Incentive Program to place welfare recipients in jobs, a deficiency attributed by Congress to the prior emphasis on classroom instruction rather than employment-based training.[19] The credit was allowed for 50 percent of the first $6,000 of wages paid to each eligible employee during the first year of employment and 25 percent of the first $6,000 paid during the second year.[20] Wages paid to nonbusiness employees, such as domestic servants, qualified for the credit, but the rate was reduced to 35 percent for the first year, second-year wages did not qualify, the maximum amount taken into account was $12,000, and the dependent care credit was inapplicable.[21]

The credit could not exceed the employer's tax liability for the year, reduced by the sum of the foreign tax credit, the credit for the elderly, the investment credit, and the credit for political contributions.[22] Unused credits could be carried back and applied against tax liability incurred in the three taxable years preceding the excess credit year, and any balance could be carried forward to the seven succeeding taxable years.[23] The deduction for wages was reduced by the credit allowable for the taxable year, determined without regard to the amount of tax liability, so that the employer can deduct only the net cost of a WIN employee's services.[24]

An employee's wages qualified for the credit only if the employee was certified by the Department of Labor or a comparable state or local agency as either (1) being eligible for federal financial assistance to families with dependent children and having received such assistance during the 90-day period immediately preceding the date of hiring by the employer or (2) placed in employment under a work incentive program established pursuant to the Social Security Act.[25] Also, he had to be employed by the employer on a substantially full-time basis for more than 30 consecutive days. The employee, further, could not displace any other person employed by the employer, and could not be a migrant worker. The taxpayer's relatives and

---

[18] IRC §§40, 50A, 50B (before repeal in 1984). The credit was terminated by the enactment in 1981 of §50B(a)(5), providing that the credit cannot apply to amounts paid or incurred after 1981, but the statutory provisions were not repealed until 1984.

[19] S. Rep. No. 437, 92d Cong., 1st Sess. (1971), reprinted in 1972-1 CB 559, 631; Joint Comm. on Tax'n, 95th Cong., 2d Sess., General Explanation of the Revenue Act of 1978, at 171 (Comm. Print 1979).

[20] IRC §50A(a)(1) (before repeal in 1984).

[21] IRC §50A(a)(4) (before repeal in 1984).

[22] IRC §50A(a)(3) (before repeal in 1984).

[23] IRC §50A(b).

[24] For IRC §280C(a) (before amendment in 1984). See S. Rep. No. 66, supra note 16, at 489.

[25] IRC §50B(h) (before repeal in 1984).

dependents were ineligible; if the taxpayer was a corporation, trust, or estate, this disqualification extended to the relatives and dependents of the controlling shareholders and to the grantors, beneficiaries, and fiduciaries of trusts and estates and their relatives and dependents.[26] Expenses paid or incurred for employment outside the United States were also disqualified.[27]

To prevent subversion of the $6,000 limit and the two-year employment limit on eligibility by shuttling employees back and forth between related employers, the employees of all members of a group of corporations under common control were treated as though they were employed by the same employer, apportioning the credit among the actual employers.[28] Similar principles were prescribed for the employees of partnerships, proprietorships, and other trades and businesses that are under common control.[29]

¶27.4 RESEARCH CREDITS

¶27.4.1 Introductory

Two credits are allowed for research expenses. Section 41 allows a broad-based credit for expenses incurred in research activities, but usually limits the credit to 20 percent of the amount by which current research costs exceed the average of such costs over the preceding three years. For taxable years after 1985, this credit is part of the general business credit, and thus is subject to the various restrictions on the general business credit.[1] The §41 credit, however, expires as of the end of 1988.

Section 28, in contrast, provides a narrowly focused credit for costs incurred in testing drugs for rare diseases and conditions, but allows credit for 50 percent of these expenses, without any threshold. Section 28 applies to expenditures paid or incurred after 1982 and before 1991.

¶27.4.2 Research Credit

The research credit was enacted in 1981 because Congress believed that "a substantial tax credit for incremental research and experimental expenditures [would] overcome the resistance of many businesses to bear the significant costs of staffing, supplies and certain computer charges which must be incurred in initiating or expanding research programs."[2] The

---

[26] IRC §50B(c)(3) (before repeal in 1984).
[27] IRC §50B(c)(2) (before repeal in 1984).
[28] IRC §50B(g)(1) (before repeal in 1984).
[29] IRC §50B(h)(2) (before repeal in 1984).
[1] See supra ¶27.1.2 for the general business credit. For similar limitations under prior law, see IRC §30(g) (before amendment in 1986).
[2] H.R. Rep. No. 201, 97th Cong., 2d Sess. 111, reprinted in 1981-2 CB 352.

credit was one of several provisions enacted in 1981 that were "designed to stimulate a higher rate of capital formation and to increase productivity."[3]

Normally, the credit is 20 percent of the excess of the "qualifed research expenses" for the year over the "base period research expenses."[4] Basically, this amounts to 20 percent of the amount by which current research expenses exceed the average of such expenses over the preceding three years. If the taxpayer makes "basic research payments," however, credit is also allowed for 20 percent of these payments.[5] The credit applies to expenses paid or incurred and payments made before 1989. The meanings of the several terms of art in the preceding sentences are described below.

1. *Credit for qualified research expenses.* "[Q]ualifed research expenses" are costs of engaging in "qualified research," defined as research "undertaken for the purpose of discovering information which is technological in nature, and the application of which is intended to be useful in the development of a new or improved business component of the taxpayer."[6] This definition is applied separately to activities and costs relating to each "business component," defined as a "product, process, computer software, technique, formula, or invention" that is intended to be held for sale or license or for use in the taxpayer's trade or business.[7] Also, "any plant process, machinery, or technique for commercial production of a business component" is considered a separate business component, as to which the definition of qualified research must be separately satisfied.

Further, to be qualified research, the activities relating to a business component must pass unscathed through a mine field of disqualifying rules.[8] Substantially all of the activities must be "elements of a process of experimentation" relating to "new or improved function, performance, or reliability or quality," not to "style, taste, cosmetic, or seasonal design

---

[3] Id.

[4] IRC §41(a). The credit rate is 25 percent for taxable years beginning before 1986. IRC §30(a) (before amendment in 1986). Regulations were proposed under the research credit rules as they existed in 1983, but have not been finalized. See Prop. Reg. §1.44F-1 et seq. The research credit is a peripatetic provision, beginning life in 1981 as §44F and moving to §30 in 1984 and to §41 in 1986.

[5] This rule applies only for taxable years beginning after 1985. For the prior treatment of basic research payments, see IRC §30(e) (before amendment in 1986).

[6] IRC §41(d)(1)(B). The present definition of "qualified research" applies only to taxable years beginning after 1985. Previously, "qualified research" was defined as any activity the costs of which qualified for deduction under §174, excluding only research carried on outside the United States, research in the social sciences and humanities, and research funded by a grant or contract. IRC §30(d) (before repeal in 1986).

[7] IRC §41(d)(2).

[8] IRC §41(d).

factors."⁹ Further, research does not qualify if it (1) occurs "after the beginning of commercial production of the business component," (2) relates to "the adaptation of an existing business component to a particular customer's requirement or need," (3) consists of reverse engineering of an existing component, or (4) is funded by a grant from or contract with a government agency or private entity.¹⁰ Costs of developing computer software primarily for the taxpayer's own use cannot qualify unless the taxpayer's use of the software will be in qualified research. Also disqualified are "routine data collection," "routine or ordinary testing or inspection for quality control," research in "the social sciences, arts, or humanities," efficiency surveys, research on management functions or techniques, and advertising, promotions, and other forms of market research, testing, and development. Qualifying research can only be conducted in the United States.

Finally, the expenses must be of a type that can be deducted currently under §174(a) and must be paid or incurred in carrying on a trade or business.¹¹ Section 174(a) applies to research and experimental costs paid or incurred "in connection with a trade or business," a standard that is less rigorous than the carrying-on requirement of the credit rules.¹² Also, expenditures of "a hobby or a financing arrangement" fail to meet the trade or business requirement.¹³

If a particular set of activities is "qualifed research," costs of the research are "qualified research expenses" and thus potentially eligible for the credit, if they are "in-house research expenses" or "contract research expenses."¹⁴ "[I]n-house research expenses" include (1) wages of employees engaged in qualified research and employees who provide "direct supervison or direct support" of qualifed research,¹⁵ (2) costs of supplies consumed in qualified research, and (3) costs of renting computers and computer time for use in the research.¹⁶ The term "supplies" is defined to

----

⁹ IRC §§41(d)(1)(C), (3).

¹⁰ IRC §41(d)(4).

¹¹ IRC §41(b)(1)(A). See supra ¶26.3 for §174.

¹² H.R. Rep. No. 201, supra note 2, at 112.

¹³ Id.

¹⁴ IRC §41(b)(1).

¹⁵ The term "wages" generally includes all compensation subject to wage withholding. IRC §§41(b)(2)(D), 3401(a). The earned income of a partner or sole proprietor, however, is considered wages for this purpose, while wages qualifying the taxpayer for the targeted jobs credit do not. If "substantially all" of an employee's work during the taxable year consists of qualified research or direct supervision or support, his entire wage is a research expense even if some nonqualifying work is done; in other cases, an apportionment is needed for employees engaged only partly in qualifying work. IRC §41(b)(2)(B).

¹⁶ IRC §41(b)(2). For taxable years beginning before 1986, rents for all personal property used in research qualify. IRC §30(b)(2)(A)(iii).

exclude land and depreciable property, and depreciation on such property does not qualify, even if the property is used exclusively in qualified research.[17]

The other branch of qualified research expenses, "contract research expenses," consists of 65 percent of amounts paid or incurred pursuant to contracts under which persons other than the taxpayer's employees perform qualified research for the taxpayer.[18] The disallowance of 35 percent of the costs under such contracts is probably meant to produce a rough equivalence with the disallowance of depreciation allocable to in-house activities. If the contract price for research work is paid or accrued before the services are performed, the price is taken into account in computing contract research expenses for the year in which the work is done.

The credit for "qualified research expenses" is 20 percent of the excess of these expenses for the year over "base period research expenses." The latter term is usually the average of the taxpayer's qualified research expenses for the three taxable years preceding the current year.[19] At a minimum, however, base period research expenses are 50 percent of qualified research expenses for the current year. The maximum credit is thus 10 percent of qualified research expenses (20 percent of the excess of qualified research expenses over 50 percent thereof).

2. *Credit for basic research payments.* Credit is also allowed for portions of a taxpayer's "basic research payments." A basic research payment can be made to (1) a college or university, (2) a tax-exempt organization whose primary function is to conduct scientific research, and (3) a tax-exempt organization that promotes scientific research through grants to and contracts with colleges and universities.[20] Such a payment must be for "basic research," defined as an "original investigation for the advancement of scientific knowledge not having a specific commercial objective."[21] Basic research, further, cannot be done in "the social sciences, arts, or humanities," and must be done within the United States. A basic research payment must be made in cash and is taken into the account for the year in which the cash payment is made.

The amount of the credit is 20 percent of the excess of (1) the basic research payments made during the taxable year over (2) "the qualified

---

[17] To curb evasion of the noncreditability of depreciation expense, an amount paid for computer time is disqualified where the payee and the taxpayer are essentially swapping the use of "substantially identical" computers. IRC §41(b)(2).

[18] IRC §41(b)(3).

[19] IRC §41(c). The three-year averaging period is shortened for the first taxable year ending after June 30, 1981 and the succeeding year.

[20] IRC §41(e)(6). A private foundation cannot qualify under either of the latter two descriptions.

[21] IRC §41(e)(7).

organization base period amount."[22] The latter term refers to the sum of the "minimum basic research amount" and the "maintenance-of-effort amount."[23] The minimum basic research amount is usually 1 percent of the average of the taxpayer's in-house research expenses and contract research expenses during a base period. For corporations accounting by the calendar year, the base period is 1981 through 1983; for other corporations, the period consists of the taxable year ending in 1984 and the preceding two years. If the taxpayer did not exist during the base period, the minimum basic research amount is 50 percent of the basic research payments made during the taxable year. The maintenance-of-effort amount is included in the qualified organization base period amount to prevent taxpayers from redesignating deductible charitable contributions as creditable basic research payments; it is defined as the excess of the taxpayer's average contributions to colleges and universities over the 1981–1983 period (adjusted for inflation), over the amount of such contributions for the taxable year.[24]

The portion of the basic research payments that is excluded by the base period threshold is treated as a contract research expense for purposes of the rules on qualified research expense, where it is subject to the rules generally applied to qualified research expenses, except that the payments are exempted from the requirement that the costs be paid or incurred in carrying on the taxpayer's business.[25]

The credit for basic research payments is allowed only to corporations and is denied to S corporations, personal holding companies, and corporations "the principal business of which is the performance of services."[26]

¶27.4.3 Clinical Testing Expenses for Drugs for Rare Diseases or Conditions

Section 28 allows a credit, at the election of the taxpayer, for certain expenses incurred in human clinical testing related to the use of a drug for a rare disease or condition. A rare disease or condition is one that occurs so infrequently that there is no reasonable expectation of recovering from sales of the drug the costs of its development. The credit is 50 percent of the current year's qualified clinical testing expenses (defined in general by the same criteria as are used in defining qualified research expenses under §41, except that 100 percent rather than 65 percent of contract research expenses qualify). Expenses of testing done outside the United States are disqualified unless the "testing population" in the United States is insufficient and

---

[22] IRC §41(e)(1)(A).
[23] IRC §41(e)(3).
[24] IRC §41(e)(5).
[25] IRC §41(e)(1)(B).
[26] IRC §§41(e)(7)(E), 414(m)(3).

certain other requirements are met.[27]

The credit, further, is restricted to the excess of (1) the regular tax for the year (after subtraction of the credit for foreign income taxes) over (2) the tentative minimum tax computed for purposes of the alternative minimum tax.[28] This limitation denies the credit for a year when the alternative minimum tax applies (e.g., when the tentative minimum tax exceeds the regular tax). For a corporation that has no items of tax preference or other alternative minimum tax adjustments, the limitation restricts the credit to 14 percent of taxable income (regular tax of 34 percent of taxable income less the tentative minimum tax of 20 percent of alternative taxable income, which in this case equals taxable income).

If the credit is elected, no expense qualifying for the credit may be taken into account in determining the credit under §41, and no deduction may be made for qualified clinical testing expenses up to the amount of the credit (determined without regard to the limitation of the credit by the tax otherwise due).[29]

The credit applies to expenditures paid or incurred after 1982 and before 1991.

¶27.5 LOW-INCOME HOUSING CREDIT

Section 42 provides a credit to the owners of some low-income housing.[1] The credit, which is available only for housing placed in service during the calendar years 1987, 1988, and 1989, is allowed over a 10-year period, beginning with the year the property is placed in service or, if the taxpayer so elects, the following year. The annual installments of credit are calculated to have a present value equal to 30 percent of cost if the building is federally subsidized or is acquired used, or 70 percent of cost if it suffers from neither of these disabilities.

The credit was enacted in 1986 in hopes that it would be an "efficient mechanism for encouraging the production of low-income rental housing," and replaced several low-income housing allowances that Congress thought "operated in an uncoordinated manner, resulted in subsidies unrelated to

---

[27] IRC §28(d)(3).

[28] IRC §28(d)(2). This limitation applies for taxable years beginning after 1986. For previous years, the credit is allowed up to the full amount of the tax due after the foreign tax credit.

[29] IRC §280C(c).

[1] See generally Staff of Joint Comm. on Tax'n, 99th Cong., 2d Sess., General Explanation of the Tax Reform Act of 1986, at 152–73 (Comm. Print 1987) [hereinafter 1986 Bluebook]; Callison, New Tax Credit for Low-Income Housing Provides Investment Incentive, 66 J. Tax'n 100 (1987); Strobel & Childs, Recent Regulations and the Blue Book Clarify Low-Income Housing Rules, 67 J. Tax'n 400 (1987).

the number of low-income individuals served, and failed to guarantee that affordable housing would be provided to the most needy low-income individuals."[2]

1. *Buildings qualifying for credit.* Generally, a building qualifies for the credit if it (1) is residential rental property and (2) constitutes or is part of a project that meets a 20-50 test or a 40-60 test.[3] The 20-50 test is satisfied if, during a 15-year period beginning with the year the credit is first allowed, (1) at least 20 percent of the rental units are occupied by individuals whose incomes are no greater than 50 percent of the area median gross income and (2) the gross rent charged for each of these units is restricted to 15 percent of area median gross income. The term "gross rent" means the amounts received by the landlord, including federal rent subsidies. The 40-60 test is the same, except that 40, 60, and 18 are substituted for 20, 50, and 15. That is, the 40-60 test allows higher income tenants to be taken into account (60 percent of area median gross income rather than 50 percent) and allows rents for low-income apartments to be a higher percentage of area median gross income (18 percent rather than 15 percent), but requires that a higher percentage of the tenants meet the income test (40 percent rather than 20 percent). The compliance period is 15 years under both tests. The taxpayer must choose between the 20-50 and 40-60 tests for the first year in which credit is allowed, and must meet the same test in each year of the 15-year compliance period.

Additional qualifications must be met when the credit is sought for a used building.[4] The building must be acquired by purchase from an unrelated person. It cannot be acquired in a nonrecognition transaction in which the taxpayer takes its basis for the building from the transferor (e.g., a tax-free transfer to a corporation or partnership in exchange for stock or a partnership interest). An antichurning rule denies the credit if the building was placed in service by a prior owner during the 10 years preceding the taxpayer's acquisition of it. Also, a prior owner's rehabilitation of the building during the preceding 10 years disqualifies the building if (1) rehabilitation expenditures were 25 percent or more of the building's basis immediately before the rehabilitation began and (2) these expenditures were written off over 60 months under §167(k).[5]

---

[2] 1986 Bluebook, supra note 1, at 152.

[3] IRC §§42(a)(1), (c)(2), (g), (i)(1). See supra ¶23.3.3 for the meaning of "residential rental property." See Notice 88-80, 1988-30 IRB 28 for requirements relating to tenants' income.

[4] IRC §42(d)(2).

[5] See supra ¶26.4.9 for §167(k). A waiver of one or both of the 10-year rules can sometimes be obtained for federally assisted buildings. IRC §42(d)(6); Reg. §1.42-2T. Also, if the prior owner claimed credit under §42 but disposed of the property before the end of the 10-year period over which credit is allowed, the taxpayer can step into

2. *Computation of the credit.* The credit is allowed annually for 10 years, beginning with the year the property is placed in service or, if the taxpayer elects, with the following year.[6] The annual credit is the product of the credit percentage and the "qualified basis."[7]

The credit percentage for property placed in service in 1987 is (1) 9 percent if the property is a new building that is not federally subsidized or (2) 4 percent if the building is either federally subsidized or not new.[8] A building is considered federally subsidized if the building or its operation is financed by a tax-exempt bond issue of a state or local government or by a loan from the federal government at a below-market interest rate.[9] For property placed in service after 1987, the percentages are pegged so that the 10 annual installments of credit have a present value at the beginning of the credit period equal to 70 percent of cost for new nonsubsidized housing and 30 percent of cost for other housing.[10]

The applicable credit percentage is applied to the building's "qualified basis," which generally is the portion of the building's cost that is allocable to units set aside for low-income tenants. More technically, "qualified basis" is a prescribed fraction of the "eligible basis" of the building.[11] The eligible basis is the adjusted basis of the building when acquired if it is purchased new or is the sum of acquisition cost and depreciable improvements made during the first year if the building is used.[12] Only the adjusted basis or cost attributable to residential units and appurtenant common areas is eligible, however. Also, eligible basis is reduced if units other than low-income units "are above the average quality standard of the low-income units in the building" or if a grant is received from federal funds.

The fraction applied to eligible basis to determine qualified basis varies from year to year. It is the lower of (1) the ratio of the number of low-

---

the prior owner's shoes, taking the credits that would have been allowed to the prior owner if he had retained the building. IRC §42(d)(7).

[6] IRC §§42(a), (f)(1).

[7] IRC §§42(a), (c), (d).

[8] IRC §42(b)(1). For the definitions of "new" and "used," see IRC §§42(i)(4), (5).

[9] IRC §42(i)(2). The owner of a federally subsidized building, however, can use the higher percentage for nonsubsidized buildings if he elects to exclude an amount equal to the federally subsidized financing from the adjusted basis figure used in computing the credit.

[10] IRC §42(b)(2). The present value computations are based on the applicable Federal rates determined under §1274(d) for the month in which the building is placed in service. For the procedures for determining the percentages, see Rev. Rul. 88-6, 1988-4 IRB 5.

[11] IRC §42(c)(1).

[12] IRC §42(d). If, however, a building is acquired in a nonrecognition exchange in which the property received takes the basis of the property exchanged (e.g., a like-kind exchange under §1031), eligible basis is limited to any new basis arising from boot given by the taxpayer.

income units in the building to all units or (2) the ratio of the floor space of the low-income units to the floor space of all units in the building.[13] A "low-income unit" is one that (1) is occupied by a tenant whose income does not exceed 50 or 60 percent of area median gross income (depending on whether the building qualifies under the 20-50 or 40-60 test) and (2) is rented for no more than 15 or 18 percent of area median gross income (depending again on which of these tests is used).[14] A unit meeting these tests does not qualify as a "low-income unit," however, if it is not "suitable for occupancy" or is used "on a transient basis." Apartments set aside for rent to low-income tenants at restricted rents, however, are counted as low-income units even if they happen to be vacant when these tests are applied for a particular year. The fraction is usually computed annually. For the first year of the credit period, however, the fraction is the average of fractions determined as of the close of each month in the year (the fractions being zero for the months before the building is placed in service).[15]

The aggregate of the 10 installments of credit, finally, is subject to a dollar limitation, determined as follows:[16] Each state is annually allocated credit equal to $1.25 multiplied by the number of people residing in the state. The state reallocates this credit among the owners of low-income housing.[17] The ceiling on the credits for a particular building is the amount allocated to it by this procedure.[18]

Assume a new building is constructed without federal subsidy at a cost of $10 million, and is placed in service in 1987. The credit percentage is nine. Assume the state in which the building is located assigns $1 million of its 1987 allocation to the building. If 20 percent of the building is low-income housing during 1987, the credit for the year is $180,000 (9 percent of 20 percent of $10 million). If the low-income portion of the building rises to 23 percent in 1988, the credit for that year is $207,000 (9 percent of 23 percent of $10 million). The credit is computed in the same way for the years 1989 through 1996 until the $1 million ceiling is reached.

The credit is part of the general business credit, and therefore is subject to the general business credit limitations.[19]

3. *At risk rules.* If a building is financed by a nonrecourse loan, its adjusted basis is usually reduced by the amount of the loan for purposes of figuring the credit.[20] The reduction is not made, however, if (1) the taxpayer

---

[13] IRC §§42(c)(1), (i)(3).
[14] IRC §42(i)(3).
[15] IRC §42(f)(2).
[16] IRC §42(h).
[17] For the allocation of a state's allotment, see Reg. §§1.42-1T(c), (d).
[18] See Reg. §1.42-1T(e).
[19] See supra ¶27.1.2 for the general business credit.
[20] IRC §42(k).

acquires the building from an unrelated person and (2) the loan either is made or guaranteed by a government agency or is made by a "qualified person." There are two types of qualified persons: (1) a lender who is actively and regularly engaged in the business of lending money and who is not, except as lender, involved in the transaction by which the taxpayer acquires the building and (2) an exempt organization whose exempt purposes include the promotion of low-income housing and who lend no more than 60 percent of the building's cost.

4. *Recapture rule.* As described above, the low-income housing credit is a percentage of the portion of a building's cost that is allocable to low-income units.[21] Because the credit is allowed over 10 years, whereas the credit is given as compensation for setting aside units for low-income tenants for 15 years, portions of prior credits are recaptured if the low-income set-aside is reduced before these 15 years pass.

The recapture rule applies if the building's "qualified basis" for any year during the 15-year compliance period is less than the qualified basis for the preceding year.[22] "[Q]ualified basis" is the figure to which the credit percentage is applied in determining the credit, and generally is the building's acquisition cost multiplied by the ratio of low-income apartments to all apartments.[23] Recapture thus occurs if the number or size of the apartments set aside for low-income tenants decreases at any time during the compliance period. Recapture also occurs on a sale of the building unless the taxpayer furnishes a bond to secure any recapture on a subsequent reduction of the low-income set-aside and it is reasonable to expect that the 20-50 or 40-60 test will be satisfied throughout the remainder of the compliance period.

When the recapture rule applies, the taxpayer's tax for the year is increased by the excess of (1) the portion of the §42 credits for all prior years that is allocable to the reduction in qualified basis over (2) the portion of those credits that would have been allowed if the credit period under §42 were 15 years rather than 10. Also, a further addition to tax is made for interest at the rate on overpayments of tax. The interest is nondeductible.

¶27.6 EXEMPT USES OF GASOLINE, ETC.

Section 34 provides a credit equal to the federal taxes on gasoline and petroleum products that would otherwise be refundable to the taxpayer under §§6420, 6421, and 6427 because the taxable items were used for exempt activities, such as farming, off-highway purposes, and public trans-

---

[21] See supra text accompanying notes 11–15.
[22] IRC §42(j).
[23] See supra text accompanying notes 11, 12.

portation. The credit was enacted in 1965 for administrative convenience to "relieve the Internal Revenue Service of the burden of processing some 1.4 million separate gasoline tax refund claims" and also to "encourage the more than half of the 3.5 million farmers who presently file income tax returns but do not file for gasoline tax refunds to claim the refunds for which they are eligible."[1] In keeping with its remedial function, the credit is not limited to the taxpayer's otherwise computed tax liability, but is instead refundable to the extent of any excess over the taxpayer's liability.[2]

---

[1] S. Rep. No. 324, 89th Cong., 1st Sess., reprinted in 1965-2 CB 676, 718.
[2] IRC §6401(b)(1).

CHAPTER

28

Limitation on Losses and Credits From Passive Activities

¶28.1 INTRODUCTORY

Section 469, enacted in 1986, is the capstone of Congress' nearly 20-year long struggle against tax shelters.[1] Very generally, it prevents losses and credits attributable to passive activities from being applied in reduction of tax on other income. The term "passive activity" refers to an investment in a trade or business in which the investor is not an active participant. A

---

[1] See generally ABA Section of Taxation, Special Task Force on Passive Losses, Preamble to the Comments on PAL Proposed Regulations, 39 Tax Notes 1325 (1988); Rubin, Sticking PIGS: Real Estate Under the Passive Loss Regulations, 39 Tax Notes 867 (1988); Rock & Shaviro, Passive Losses and the Improvement of Net Income Measurement, 7 Va. Tax Rev. 1 (1987).

limited partnership interest in a partnership engaged in an equipment leasing business is a typical example of a passive activity. The §469 limitation applies to individuals, estates, trusts, and personal service corporations. Also, closely held C corporations that are not personal service corporations are subject to a more limited rule that allows passive activity losses and credits to reduce tax on active business income but not on dividends, interest, and other portfolio income.

The reasons for §469 were explained as follows:

> In recent years, it has become increasingly clear that taxpayers are losing faith in the Federal income tax system. This loss of confidence has resulted in large part from the interaction of two of the system's principal features: its high marginal rates . . . and the opportunities it provides for taxpayers to offset income from one source with tax shelter deductions and credits from another. . . .
>
> Extensive shelter activity contributes to public concerns that the tax system is unfair, and to the belief that tax is paid only by the naive and the unsophisticated. This, in turn, not only undermines compliance, but encourages further expansion of the tax shelter market, in many cases diverting investment capital from productive activities to those principally or exclusively serving tax avoidance goals.
>
> The . . . most important sources of support for the Federal income tax system are the average citizens who simply report their income (typically consisting predominantly of items such as salaries, wages, pensions, interest, and dividends) and pay tax under the general rules. To the extent that these citizens feel that they are bearing a disproportionate burden with regard to the costs of government because of their unwillingness or inability to engage in tax-oriented investment activity, the tax system itself is threatened.
>
> Under these circumstances, . . . decisive action is needed to curb the expansion of tax sheltering and to restore to the tax system the degree of equity that is a necessary preconditon to a beneficial and widely desired reduction in rates.[2]

The obvious solution to the tax shelter problem is the elimination of all of the tax preferences exploited by tax shelter investments. This solution was rejected for several reasons. First, the elimination of all preferences is much more difficult than might at first seem to be the case. The system would not be preference free unless all economic income were taxed, and many aspects of the determination of economic income (e.g., measuring unrealized appreciation and computing economic depreciation) are not fea-

---

[2] S. Rep. No. 313, 99th Cong., 2d Sess. 713–14 (1986).

sible in practice.[3] Second, although many preferences were eliminated or cut back simultaneously with the enactment of §469 in 1986, Congress found that many of the remaining preferences are "socially or economically beneficial . . . when . . . used primarily to advance the purposes upon which Congress relied in enacting them, rather than to avoid taxation of income from sources unrelated to the preferred activity."[4] Most of the remaining preferences are intended "to benefit and provide incentives to taxpayers active in the businesses to which the preferences were directed."[5]

Section 469 was therefore enacted to direct the benefits of tax preferences "primarily to taxpayers with a substantial and *bona fide* involvement in the activities to which the preferences relate."[6] The provision does not deny all benefit from preferences to nonparticipating investors, but rather restricts them to "the use of preferences to reduce the rate of tax on income from those activities."[7]

Although the limitation is intended as a restraint on tax shelters, it has a much broader application. The term "passive activity" is not limited to tax shelter investments, but includes, for example, a taxpayer's investment as silent partner in her brother-in-law's plumbing business. The losses limited by §469 include not only the artificial accounting losses historically associated with tax shelters, but also real economic losses.

Section 469 essentially creates a basket containing all of a taxpayer's investments from passive activities, and isolates losses and credits within the basket from other income. Losses from one passive activity can be deducted against income from other passive activities. Section 469, in other words, only prevents a net loss from all passive activities from being deducted against other income. Special care was taken to keep salary income and income from portfolio investments out of the passive activity basket because the sheltering of these two types of income from tax was the primary objective of the tax shelter movement.

The usual effect of §469 is to suspend rather than to permanently disallow the losses and credits caught in its web. A loss or credit made nondeductible by §469 is carried forward to succeeding years until it is allowed. Normally, loss carryovers are allowed only against income from passive activities, and credit carryovers can only offset tax on income from passive activities. Suspended losses, however, are potentially allowable against unrelated income when the taxpayer's interest in the passive activity is sold or exchanged. The policy of §469 is to limit artificial accounting losses, but not to deny real economic losses. A net loss from passive activi-

---

[3] See supra ¶3.1 for economic income and ¶23.1.4 for economic depreciation.
[4] S. Rep. No. 313, supra note 2, at 715.
[5] Id.
[6] Id. at 716.
[7] Id.

ties thus is generally suspended until the taxpayer, by closing out his investment, establishes the amount of economic loss, if any.

¶28.2 TAXPAYERS SUBJECT TO LIMITATIONS

The passive loss and credit limitations of §469 apply to individuals, estates, trusts, closely held C corporations, and personal service corporations.[1] They do not apply to partnerships or S corporations because these entities are treated as conduits for federal tax purposes, and the limitations thus apply to partners and shareholders subject to §469 when passive activity losses and credits are allocated to them. If a passive activity is carried on by a partnership comprised of individuals, for example, the partnership's return is prepared without regard to the §469 limitations, but §469 restricts the partners' right to take their distributive shares of passive activity loss or credit of the partnership.

A corporation is subject to §469 only if it is a closely held C corporation or a personal service corporation. Individual taxpayers are the primary target of §469, and corporations are covered only to the extent considered necessary to protect the integrity of the provision's application to individuals.[2] A personal service corporation is subject to §469 in order to prevent passive activity losses from being deducted against an individual's personal services income, whether this income is earned directly or through a personal service corporation. If personal services corporations were not covered, a lawyer, for example, could shelter income from her law practice by incorporating the practice and causing the corporation to make tax shelter investments. Closely held C corporations are subject to a limited version of §469 in order to prevent individuals from transferring portfolio investments to such corporations as a device for avoiding the rule forbidding the deduction of passive activity losses against portfolio income.

A corporation is a "closely held C corporation" if (1) it has not elected to be an S corporation and (2) more than 50 percent of its stock is held, at some time during the last half of the taxable year, by five or fewer individuals.[3] Stock attribution rules are used in applying the five-or-fewer-individuals test.[4]

A corporation is a "personal service corporation" if (1) its "principal activity is the performance of personal services," (2) these services are "substantially performed" by employees who own stock in the corporation,

---

[1] IRC §469(a)(2).
[2] S. Rep. No. 313, 99th Cong., 2d Sess. 721–22 (1986).
[3] IRC §§465(a)(1)(B), 469(j)(1), 542(a)(2), 1361(a)(2).
[4] IRC §544(a).

and (3) the corporation's employees own more than 10 percent of its stock.[5] The attribution rules of §318(a) are applied in determining stock ownership for this purpose,[6] except that stock owned by a corporation is attributed ratably to all of its shareholders, not just those holding 50 percent or more of the shareholder-corporation's stock, as is usual under §318(a).[7] Thus, if personal services are performed by a corporation whose shareholders include other corporations (the shareholder corporations) and if these services are substantially performed by employees who are shareholders of the shareholder corporations, the services-performing corporation can be a personal services corporation.[8]

¶28.3 ACTIVITIES COVERED

¶28.3.1 Introductory

The §469 limitations apply to losses and credits attributable to a "passive activity."[1] Generally, a passive activity is "any activity (A) which involves the conduct of any trade or business, and (B) in which the taxpayer does not materially participate."[2] Property held for rental is a passive activity, however, regardless of the extent of the owner's involvement in the management or operation of the property.[3] In contrast, a working interest in an oil or gas well is not a passive activity, whether or not the taxpayer participates materially, if the interest is held directly or through a pass through entity that does not limit the taxpayer's liability for development or operating costs.[4] These and other rules defining the term "passive activity" are discussed in more detail below.

¶28.3.2 Definition of "Trade or Business"

The term "trade or business" is not comprehensively defined, but generally includes any activity constituting a trade or business for purposes of §162, which allows deductions for the ordinary and necessary expenses of a

---

[5] IRC §§269A(b), 469(j)(2). See Lipton & Serling, Passive Activity Loss Limitations Can Have Unexpected Impact on Corporations, 68 J. Tax'n 20 (1988).

[6] IRC §§269A(b)(2), 469(j)(2). See infra ¶93.1.7 for §318(a).

[7] IRC §§318(a)(2)(C), 469(j)(2)(B).

[8] H.R. Rep. No. 841, 99th Cong., 2d Sess. II-140 (Conf. Rep. 1986).

[1] IRC §469(a)(1).

[2] IRC §469(c)(1).

[3] See infra ¶28.3.7.

[4] See infra ¶28.3.8.

trade or business.[5] Also, a research or experimental activity is considered a trade or business for this purpose if expenses of the activity are deductible under §174, whether or not the activity is a trade or business for other purposes.[6]

By contrast, the activity of trading in personal property for one's own account is never a trade or business for this purpose, regardless of how it is characterized for other purposes.[7] For example, if a partnership is organized to trade in stocks and bonds for its own account, the partnership's activity is not passive with respect to any partner, and its dividends, interest, and securities gains and losses are thus excluded from each partner's passive activity hotchpot. The purpose of this rule seems to be to prevent portfolio income from being considered passive, and it might be limited to trading in securities and commodities traded on organized markets.

The Treasury has the power by regulation to treat as businesses for purposes of §469 investments and activities that are not otherwise considered businesses and for which deductions are allowable under §212.[8] This authority is meant to be exercised to include "activities that give rise to passive losses intended to be limited under the provision, but that may not rise to the level of a trade or business."[9] The "production of portfolio income," however, can never be passive.[10] To date, this regulatory power has not been exercised.[11]

¶28.3.3 Material Participation by Individuals

An investment in a trade or business is a passive activity only if the taxpayer does not "materially participate" in the business. An individual participates materially in a trade or business if he "is involved in the operations of the activity on a basis which is regular, continuous, and substantial."[12] This test must be met by the individual's personal work in the activity whether the activity is owned directly as a sole proprietorship or an indirect interest is held as a partner or an S corporation shareholder.[13]

---

[5] Reg. §1.469-1T(e)(2)(i)(A). See supra ¶20.1.2 for the meaning of "trade or business" under §162.
[6] IRC §469(c)(5); Reg. §1.469-1T(e)(2)(i)(A)(2). See infra ¶26.4 for §174.
[7] Reg. §1.469-1T(e)(6).
[8] IRC §469(c)(6). Section 212 allows deductions for ordinary and necessary expenses of investments and other profit-seeking activities that are not trades or businesses. See supra ¶20.5 for §212.
[9] H.R. Rep. No. 841, 99th Cong., 2d Sess. II-138 (Conf. Rep. 1986).
[10] H.R. Rep. No. 841, supra note 9.
[11] Reg. §1.469-1T(e)(2)(ii).
[12] IRC §469(h)(1).
[13] S. Rep. No. 313, 99th Cong., 2d Sess. 720 (1986).

An example of a taxpayer "likely" to meet this requirement is "an individual who works full-time in a line of business consisting of one or more business activities" or an individual whose "involvement in [an] activity is [his] principal business."[14] "For example, an individual who spends thirty-five hours per week operating a grocery store, and who does not devote a comparable amount of time to any other business, clearly is materially participating in the business of the grocery store."[15] On the other hand, an individual may participate materially in more than one activity. For example, "a farmer who lives and works on his farm and 'moonlights' by operating a gas station" might be a material participant in both activities.[16]

In an effort to make the material participation test as objective as possible, the regulations identify seven situations in which an individual's participation in a trade or business is material:

1. *500-hour test.* An individual is a material participant in an activity for a taxable year if he participates in it for more than 500 hours during the year.[17] With a few exceptions noted below, all hours of work in connection with the activity are counted as participation.[18]

The capacity in which the work is done is irrelevant, but the taxpayer must have an interest in the activity, either directly or as partner or S corporation shareholder, when the work is done. Assume a restaurant business is carried on by a limited partnership that has one general partner (*X* Corporation) and one limited partner (*A*, an individual). The partnership agreement requires that *X* manage the business, and *X* does this by hiring *A* (who is not a shareholder) to work in the restaurant as manager for 30 hours per week. Because *A* satisfies the 500-hour test, she is a material participant in the business even though her work in the business has no direct connection with her interest as limited partner.[19]

The work of spouses is aggregated in computing hours of participation, and both spouses are considered material participants if the sum of their hours of work for the year exceeds 500.[20] This rule applies even if only one of the spouses owns an interest in the activity and applies whether or not the spouses file a joint return.

---

[14] H.R. Rep. No. 841, supra note 9, at II-147; S. Rep. No. 313, supra note 13, at 732.

[15] Id. at 732–33.

[16] Staff of Joint Comm. on Tax'n, 99th Cong., 2d Sess., General Explanation of the Tax Reform Act of 1986, at 238 (Comm. Print 1987) [hereinafter 1986 Bluebook].

[17] Reg. §1.469-5T(a)(1).

[18] Reg. §1.469-5T(f).

[19] Reg. §1.469-5T(k) Exs. 1, 2.

[20] IRC §469(h)(5); S. Rep. No. 313, supra note 13, at 730 n.16; Reg. §1.469-5T(f)(3).

Work is not counted, however, if it is not "of a type that is customarily done by an owner of such an activity" and one of the taxpayer's principal purposes for doing the work is to satisfy the material participation test.[21] Assume a lawyer owns a football team; she works full-time in her law practice and spends no substantial time working in the football business. In order to avoid §469, she hires her husband to work 15 hours per week as receptionist in the team's business office. Although a spouse's work is normally counted in determining the taxpayer's participation, whether or not the spouse has an interest in the business, the husband's work is ignored in this case because receptionist work is not customarily done by owners of football teams and is done here in order to sidestep the §469 limitations.[22]

Work done in the taxpayer's capacity as investor is also excluded from the tally unless the taxpayer is "directly involved in the day-to-day management or operations of the activity."[23] Work done in an investor capacity includes reviewing financial statements and other reports on the activity, preparing analyses of these reports for the taxpayer's personal use, and monitoring the activity "in a nonmanagerial capacity."

Hours of work may be proven by "any reasonable means."[24] Contemporaneous daily records are not required. Adequate proof might be given, for example, by measuring hours of work during a representative period and extrapolating a figure for the year as a whole from this sample. The hours spent during the sample period could be established by such evidence as "appointment books, calendars, or narrative summaries."

The definition of "participation" described in the preceding paragraphs is also used in applying the other tests of the regulations described below.

2. *Substantially all work required in activity.* The legislative history of §469 says that when an individual "does everything that is required to be done to conduct [an]activity," he is a material participant "even though the actual amount of work to be done to conduct the activity is low in comparison to other activities."[25] The regulations pick up this rule, providing that an individual is a material participant in an activity for a taxable year if his work in the activity during the year "constitutes substantially all of the participation in such activity of all individuals (including individuals who are not owners of interests in the activity).[26]

3. *Major-participant test.* One hundred hours of qualifying work is sufficient to constitute material participation if this work is no less than the participation of any other person in the activity for the year, including the

---

[21] Reg. §1.469-5T(f)(2)(i).
[22] Reg. §1.469-5T(k) Ex. 7.
[23] Reg. §1.469-5T(f)(2)(ii).
[24] Reg. §1.469-5T(f)(4).
[25] H.R. Rep. No. 841, supra note 9, at II-148.
[26] Reg. §1.469-5T(a)(2).

participation of employees and others who own no interest in the activity. Assume two workers in an automobile assembly plant carry on a weekend carpentry business as partners; they work eight hours each Saturday in the business. Although neither of the partners works 500 hours per year in the business, each puts in more than 100 hours and works as much as any other person in the business. Both are material participants.[27]

4. *Significant participation rule.* An individual is a material participant in a trade or business qualifying as a "significant participation activity" if the taxpayer's participation in all significant participation activities exceeds 500 hours for the year. A "significant participation activity" is a trade or business in which the taxpayer performs more than 100 hours of qualifying work during the year but, apart from this rule, does not do enough work to satisfy the material participation requirement.[28] A business in which the taxpayer's work falls in the range of 101 to 500 hours annually, for example, is usually a significant participation activity.

Assume an accountant owns two businesses on the side, a restaurant and a shoe store; most of the work in the two businesses is done by employees, but the owner works 400 hours during the taxable year in the restaurant and 150 hours in the shoe store. The restaurant and shoe store are significant participation activities because the taxpayer works more than 100 hours in each. Because her work in the significant participation activities exceeds 500 hours during the year, she is a material participant in both of them.[29]

5. *Prior material participation.* Even in the absence of any personal involvement in the activity for the current year, an individual is a material participant if he was a material participant under one or more of the other rules of the regulations for at least 5 of the preceding 10 taxable years.[30] These five years need not be consecutive. Assume an individual completely retires after many years of full-time employment by an S corporation of which he is a shareholder. Under this rule, the individual continues to be a material participant in the business for five years after her retirement because she satisfied the 500-hour rule during at least 5 of the 10 years

---

[27] Reg. §1.469-5T(k) Ex. 3. The example evidences a willingness to apply the rule with some flexibility. Over a year's time, one of the partners would surely put in a few more hours (or at least a few more minutes) than the other since it would not be feasible to precisely coordinate the first fall of the hammers in the morning and the last in the evening. This lack of equality in effort would disqualify one of the partners under a strict application of the rule. The example can be read to say that as long as the participants in a venture intend that their labor contributions be equal and generally stick with that intention, none will be deemed to work less than the others.

[28] Reg. §1.469-5T(c).

[29] Reg. §1.469-5T(k) Ex. 4.

[30] Reg. §1.469-5T(a)(5).

preceding each of the first 5 post-retirement years.[31]

A similar but even more liberal rule is provided for a "personal service activity," defined as (1) a business of performing personal services in "the fields of health, law, engineering, architecture, accounting, actuarial science, performing arts, or consulting" or (2) any other business of performing personal services if "capital is not a material income-producing factor" in the business.[32] An individual is a material participant in a personal service activity if he was a material participant for at least three prior years, which need not be consecutive and are not restricted to any particular time period before the taxable year.[33]

In applying prior-participation rules, it is sometimes necessary to determine whether an individual materially participated in an activity for a year before 1987, the first year to which §469 applies. The materiality of a taxpayer's participation for a pre-1987 year is determined by applying only the 500-hour rule described above.[34]

6. *Facts and circumstances test.* An individual who fails to satisfy any of the foregoing tests is nevertheless a material participant if a review of the facts and circumstances shows his participation in the activity during the taxable year to be regular, continuous, and substantial.[35] The regulations preclude some taxpayers from satisfying the facts and circumstances test. An individual who puts in no more than 100 hours of work on an activity during the taxable year, for example, is not a material participant under any circumstance.[36] The regulations do not list the facts and circumstances considered relevant in the application of the test, but the legislative history fills this gap, at least partially, as follows:

Presence at site of activity. A relevant factor is "whether, and how regularly, the taxpayer is present at the place or places where the principal operations of the activity are conducted."[37] For example, an individual who raises horses on land on which her principal residence is located is more likely to be a material participant than an individual owning a horse raising operation that is located hundreds of miles from where she lives and works as an employee or professional practitioner.

---

[31] Reg. §1.469-5T(k) Ex. 5. If the individual acquired her stock in the employer during the five years preceding her retirement, in contrast, she would not be a material participant after her retirement because only work done while the taxpayer holds an interest in the business counts. Reg. §1.469-5T(k) Ex. 6.

[32] Reg. §1.469-5T(d).

[33] Reg. §1.469-5T(a)(6).

[34] Reg. §1.469-5T(j).

[35] Reg. §1.469-5T(a)(7).

[36] Reg. §1.469-5T(b)(2)(iii).

[37] 1986 Bluebook, supra note 16, at 238.

Physical proximity, however, is not sufficient by itself. Even if the owner of a horse farm lives on the farm, regular, continuous, and substantial involvement in the operation must be shown. This might consist, for example, of "hiring and from time to time supervising those responsible for taking care of the horses on a daily basis, along with making decisions (i.e., not merely ratifying decisions) regarding the purchase, sale, and breeding of horses."[38]

Conversely, not being present at the location of the principal operations of an activity is not fatal. An owner of an interest in a barge transporting grain along the Mississippi River, for example, might materially participate by working "on a regular basis at finding new customers for the barge service, and [negotiating] with customers regarding the terms on which the service is provided," even if none of these activities occur on or near the barge.[39]

Professional services as independent contractor. Providing legal, tax, or accounting services as an independent contractor or as an employee of an independent contractor is not usually material participation in the business purchasing the services.[40] For example, if a member of a law firm provides legal services for a partnership and also invests in the partnership, her work as lawyer for the partnership does not make her a material participant in the partnership's business. This is so whether the lawyer acts in her usual independent-contractor role in representing the partnership or performs these services under any other form of arrangement.

Management. Work in either management or operations can qualify as material participation. Management activities, however, are viewed skeptically because experience has shown "that a test based on participation in management is subject to manipulation and creates frequent factual disputes between taxpayers and the Internal Revenue Service."[41] The "genuineness and substantiality [of management activities] are difficult to verify."[42]

In particular, "a merely formal and nominal participation in management, in the absence of a genuine exercise of independent discretion and judgment, does not constitute material participation."[43] An example of formal and nominal participation in management is where the "taxpayer has little or no knowledge or experience" in the business and makes decisions that are "unimportant to the business."[44] The taxpayer's decisions are unim-

---

[38] Id.
[39] Id.
[40] S. Rep. No. 313, supra note 13, at 735.
[41] H.R. Rep. No. 841, supra note 9, at II-148; S. Rep. No. 313, supra note 13, at 734 n.20.
[42] 1986 Bluebook, supra note 16, at 240.
[43] S. Rep. No. 313, supra note 13, at 734.
[44] Id.

portant if the economic risks they entail are outweighed by the tax benefits flowing from classifying the activity as nonpassive.[45] Also, management is not material if "the management decisions being made by the taxpayer are illusory (e.g., whether to feed the cattle or let them starve)."[46]

Even when management activities go beyond the formal and nominal, they are not material participation unless they are continous and substantial. An "intermittent role in management" is not sufficient.[47]

Moreover, the regulations exclude management activities from consideration in two situations. First, a taxpayer's management work in connection with an activity is ignored if any other person receives compensation for management services performed for the activity. This exclusion applies where the "taxpayer has little or no knowledge or experience" in the business and "merely approves management decisions recommended by a paid advisor,"[48] but goes well beyond such obvious cases. Second, a taxpayer's management work is ignored if some other unpaid manager (e.g., fellow partner or S corporation shareholder) spends more time than the taxpayer on managing the activity.[49]

Employees and agents. Only the taxpayer's own activities are taken into account; activities of employees and agents are not attributed to the taxpayer. If the taxpayer's own activities are sufficient, however, the "fact that [he] utilizes employees or contract services to perform daily functions in running the business does not prevent [him] from qualifying as materially participating."[50]

Other participation tests. That the taxpayer satisfies a participation test found in a provision other than §469 is irrelevant to the application of the facts and circumstances test.[51] Participation tests are found, for example, in §1402 (relating to the social security tax on self-employment income) and §2032A (providing a special estate tax valuation for certain farmland), but satisfaction of either or both of these tests is not helpful in establishing material participation under §469.

Test applied annually. The facts and circumstances test, like the more objective tests of the regulations, is applied annually.[52] A taxpayer can thus be a material participant with respect to a particular investment in some years but not in others. To satisfy the test for a particular year, the taxpayer

---

[45] Id.
[46] 1986 Bluebook, supra note 16, at 239.
[47] S. Rep. No. 313, supra note 13, at 734.
[48] Id. See Reg. §1.469-5T(k) Ex. 8.
[49] Reg. §1.469-5T(b)(2)(ii)(B).
[50] S. Rep. No. 313, supra note 13, at 735.
[51] Reg. §1.469-5T(b)(2)(i).
[52] S. Rep. No. 313, supra note 13, at 731.

must participate materially throughout the year.[53] Participation on each day of the year, however, is not required. A taxpayer's principal business activity does not become passive, for example, merely because she takes a vacation. All that is required is that the taxpayer's involvement be regular, continuous, and substantial for the year as a whole.

7. *Interests in partnerships and S corporations.* The material participation test is applied to a partner or shareholder of an S corporation by looking to the personal participation by the partner or shareholder in the entity's trades or businesses.[54] If a particular partner does not participate materially in a particular business of the partnership, for example, the partner's interest in the business is a passive activity even though the business might not be passive with respect to other partners and other businesses of the partnership might not be passive with respect to the taxpayer.

Because regular, continuous, and substantial involvement in the business is inconsistent with the status of limited partner, the holder of a limited partnership interest usually is not considered a material participant in any partnership business.[55] This rule applies whether a limited partnership interest is held directly or indirectly. It applies, for example, where "the taxpayer owns a general partnership interest, or stock in an S corporation, and the partnership or corporation in which the taxpayer owns such interest itself owns a limited partnership interest in another entity."[56]

A partnership interest is a limited partnership interest for this purpose if it is designated as such in the partnership agreement or if the holder's liability for partnership debts is limited to a "determinable fixed amount," which might be either the amount of the partner's capital contribution or the sum of this contribution and additional amounts the partner can be required to contribute.[57] If the taxpayer holds both general and limited partnership interests in one partnership, however, both interests are treated as general for this purpose, and both are therefore nonpassive if the taxpayer's activities as general partner satisfy the material participation test.[58]

The regulations provide a few exceptions. First, an interest in a business as limited partner is active rather than passive if the limited partner works more than 500 hours in the business during the taxable year in any

---

[53] 1986 Bluebook, supra note 16, at 235.

[54] Reg. §1.469-2T(e)(1).

[55] IRC §469(h)(2). The Treasury has the power to relax this rule by regulation. Id.; S. Rep. No. 313, supra note 13, at 731–32.

[56] Id. at 731.

[57] Reg. §1.469-5T(e)(3)(i).

[58] Reg. §1.469-5T(e)(3)(ii). A contrary rule is suggested in the legislative history. S. Rep. No. 313, supra note 13, at 731.

capacity.[59] Assume a restaurant business is carried on by a limited partnership whose general partner is a corporation; an individual, *A*, is both the sole shareholder of the corporation and the limited partner of the partnership. The partnership agreement requires that the corporation manage the business, and the corporation does so by hiring *A* as an employee to work in the business for 30 hours per week. Because *A* satisfies the 500-hour test, her limited partnership interest is active, not passive.[60]

Second, under rules described earlier,[61] an individual who does no work in an activity during the current year is a material participant if (1) he was a material participant for at least five of the preceding ten years or (2) the activity is a personal service business and the taxpayer was a material participant for at least three prior years. Since these rules require no present involvement in the activity, the regulations allow them to apply to a limited partner.[62]

¶28.3.4 Material Participation by Corporations

A closely held C corporation or personal service corporation materially participates in a business it carries on if shareholders holding more than one half of its stock by value are material participants in the business.[63] A professional corporation engaged in the practice of law materially participates in its law business, for example, if more than 50 percent of its stock is held by lawyers who are regularly, continuously, and substantially involved in the practice. If a corporation is a member of an affiliated group filing a consolidated return, it is deemed a material participant in its business if persons holding more than 50 percent of the stock of any member of the group materially participate in the business.[64] If a more than 50 percent shareholder of a parent corporation materially participates in a business of a subsidiary, for example, the subsidiary is a material participant in that business.

Also, a closely held C corporation that is not a personal service corporation is a material participant in a business if (1) at least one full-time employee of the corporation is active in the management of the business throughout the taxable year, (2) at least three employees, each of whom owns no more than 5 percent of the corporation's stock, work full-time in

---

[59] Reg. §1.469-5T(g)(3)(i). See supra text accompanying notes 17–24 for the 500-hour test.

[60] Reg. §1.469-5T(k) Exs. 1, 2.

[61] Supra text accompanying notes 30–34.

[62] Reg. §1.469-5T(e)(2).

[63] IRC §469(h)(4). See Lipton & Serling, Passive Activity Loss Limitations Can Have Unexpected Impact on Corporations, 68 J. Tax'n 20 (1988).

[64] H.R. Rep. No. 841, supra note 9, at II-140; Reg. §1.469-1T(h)(4).

the business throughout the year, and (3) deductible expenses of the business (other than depreciation, interest, and taxes) amount to more than 15 percent of gross income.[65]

¶28.3.5 Material Participation by Estates and Trusts

A decedent's estate or a trust (other than a grantor trust) is a material participant in a trade or business it carries on if "an executor or fiduciary, in his capacity as such, is so participating."[66] An entity organized as a trust is classified as an association taxable as a corporation, however, if it is a joint enterprise for the conduct of a business for profit. A trustee's conduct of activities sufficient to satisfy the material participation test, in other words, often causes the trust to be treated as a corporation. An entity treated as a trust for tax purposes, in other words, is unlikely to be a material participant in any activity.[67]

Whether a grantor trust is a material participant, in contrast, depends on the activities of the grantor, not those of the trustee, consistent with the rules that tax such a grantor on trust income as though he were owner of the trust assets.[68] The material participation test can therefore be satisfied with respect to an activity of a grantor trust without the trust being classified as something other than a trust.

¶28.3.6 Farming

In two situations, an owner of an interest in a farming business is deemed a material participant even if he is not involved in the business regularly, continuously, and substantially.[69] The first is where the taxpayer is retired or disabled and was regularly, continuously, and substantially involved in the business when he retired or became disabled. The second is where the taxpayer is a surviving spouse of a person who was regularly, continuously, and substantially involved in the business and the taxpayer's interest in the farm was received from the spouse.

Also, according to the Staff of the Joint Committee on Taxation, a farm owner who does no physical work on the farm is considered a material participant in the farming activity if farm income is treated as self-employ-

---

[65] IRC §§465(c)(7)(C), 469(h)(4)(B).
[66] S. Rep. No. 313, supra note 13, at 735.
[67] 1986 Bluebook, supra note 16, at 242 n.33.
[68] See infra Ch. 80 for grantor trusts.
[69] IRC §469(h)(3); Reg. §1.469-5T(h)(2).

ment income for purposes of the social security tax on such income.[70] Moreover, mere decision making by a farm owner is considered material if it is "*bona fide* and undertaken on a regular, continous, and substantial basis."[71] This decision making might, for example, pertain to

(1) crop rotation, selection, and pricing, (2) the incursion of embryo transplant, or breeding expenses, (3) the purchase, sale, and leasing of capital items, such as cropland, animals, machinery, and equipment, (4) breeding and mating decisions, and (5) the selection of herd or crop managers who then act at the behest of the taxpayer, rather than as paid advisors directing the conduct of the taxpayer.[72]

¶28.3.7 Rental Activities

A "rental activity" is passive even if the taxpayer in fact participates actively in the management of the rental property or even if operation and management of the property requires so little activity as not to be a trade or business.[73] If an individual's principal activity is management of rental buildings he owns, for example, the ownership and management of the buildings is nevertheless a passive activity. Conversely, an owner who leases property under a net lease requiring the tenant to maintain the property and pay all expenses is engaged in a passive activity even if the owner's activities with regard to the property are so minimal as not to qualify as a trade or business.

Congress explained the reasons for this rule as follows:

Rental activities generally require less ongoing management activity, in proportion to capital invested, than business activities involving the production or sale of goods and services. Thus, for example, an individual who is employed full-time as a professional could more easily provide all necessary management in his spare time with respect to a rental activity than he could with respect to another type of business activity involving the same capital investment. The extensive use of rental activities for tax shelter purposes under present law, combined with the reduced level of personal involvement necessary to conduct such activities, make clear that the effectiveness of the basic passive loss provision could be seriously compromised if material par-

---

[70] 1986 Bluebook, supra note 16, at 238–39. According to the regulations, satisfying the participation test of the self-employment tax rules is generally not sufficient to show material participation under §469. See supra text accompanying note 51.

[71] 1986 Bluebook, supra note 16, at 241.

[72] Id.

[73] IRC §§469(c)(2), (4).

ticipation were sufficient to avoid the limitations in the case of rental activities.[74]

The term "rental activity" includes "any activity where payments are principally for the use of tangible property."[75] The providing of tangible property for use by a customer is a rental activity whether it takes the form of a lease or "a service contract or other arrangement that is not denominated a lease."[76] In other words, the substance of an arrangement, not its form, determines whether it is a rental. Examples of rental activities are "a bare boat charter, or a plane under a dry lease (i.e., without pilot, fuel or oil)," a "net lease of property,"[77] and most "long-term rentals or leases of property (e.g., apartments, leased office equipment, or leased cars)."[78]

Several types of transactions in which the use of tangible property is provided to customers are not rental activities, however, including transactions that are primarily sales of services,[79] uses of taxpayer's property that are incidental to nonrental activities of the taxpayer,[80] and contributions of property or its use to partnerships, S corporations, and joint ventures.[81] These transactions are described more fully below.

1. *Rental versus services activities.* Providing the use of property to customers is not a rental activity if services rendered to the customers predominate the relationship. More specifically, where services are provided, the activity is not a rental unless the gross income from the activity "represents . . . amounts paid or to be paid principally for the use of such tangible property."[82] For example, "operating a hotel or other similar transient lodging . . . is not a rental activity" because "substantial services are provided" and income from the facility thus does not consist primarily of payments for the use of tangible property.[83] More generally, the "use of tangible property for short periods, with heavy turnover among the users of the property, may cause an activity not to be a rental activity, especially if significant services are performed in connection with each new user of the property."[84] A car rental business, for example, is not a rental activity if rentals are for short periods and "the lessor furnishes services including

---

[74] S. Rep. No. 313, 99th Cong., supra note 13, at 718.
[75] IRC §469(j)(8).
[76] Reg. §1.469-1T(e)(3)(i).
[77] H.R. Rep. No. 841, supra note 9.
[78] S. Rep. No. 313, supra note 13, at 720; 1986 Bluebook, supra note 16, at 249.
[79] See infra text accompanying notes 82–98.
[80] See infra text accompanying notes 99–105.
[81] See infra text accompanying notes 108–109.
[82] Reg. §1.469-1T(e)(3)(i).
[83] S. Rep. No. 313, supra note 13, at 720; 1986 Bluebook, supra note 16, at 217.
[84] Id. at 248.

maintenance of gas and oil, tire repair and changing, cleaning and polishing, oil changing and lubrication and engine and body repair."[85] In these and other cases where "expenses of day-to-day operations are not insignificant in relation to rents produced by the property" the activity is not considered a rental activity.[86]

The regulations provide three rules for applying the services versus rental distinction. The first is the most clear-cut and is essentially a safe harbor. Under this rule, an activity is not a rental activity if "the average period of customer use for [the] property is seven days or less."[87] This rule, for example, probably covers most car rental businesses. In determining the average period of use, however, a customer is deemed to use property during all of any period during which he "has a continuous or recurring right to use [the] property," whether this right arises under a single contract or a series of renewals.[88] For example, if a golf course sells monthly passes, purchasers of the passes are deemed to use the property for one month.[89]

The second rule provides that an activity is not a rental activity if the average period of customer use is no longer than 30 days and "significant personal services" are provided.[90] The average period of use is computed in the same way as under the seven-day rule described in the preceding paragraph. Whether personal services are significant depends on such factors as "the frequency with which such services are provided, the type and amount of labor required to perform such services, and the value of such services relative to the amount charged for the use of the property."[91]

This test has both a qualitative and a quantitative aspect. Qualitatively, services are not considered significant if the customer could not lawfully use the property without them or if they consist of repairs that extend the life of the property beyond the period of the customer's use. Also, services to real property tenants are not significant if they consist of "cleaning and maintenance of common areas, routine repairs, trash collection, elevator service, . . . security at entrances or perimeters, [or other services] commonly provided in connection with long-term rentals of high-grade commercial or residential real property." Services not within any of these excluded classes are significant if they are supplied in substantial quantity. Maid and linen services provided by an apartment hotel, for example, are not significant if

---

[85] Id. at 249.

[86] Id.

[87] Reg. §1.469-1T(e)(3)(ii)(A).

[88] Reg. §1.469-1T(e)(3)(iii).

[89] Reg. §1.469-1T(e)(3)(viii) Ex. 10. The golf course, however, escapes classification as a rental activity under another rule of the regulations described below in the text accompanying note 107.

[90] Reg. §1.469-1T(e)(3)(ii)(B).

[91] Reg. §1.469-1T(e)(3)(iv).

the cost of these services is less than 10 percent of the amounts charged to tenants. Maintenance and repair sometimes satisfy both the qualitative and quantitative requirements, at least if the property is personal. The regulations give an example of a lessor of copying machines whose maintenance and repair services to customers have a value in excess of 50 percent of rents received; the services are said to be significant.[92]

Under the third of the regulation rules, an activity is not a rental activity if "extraordinary personal services" are provided to the customer, regardless of the average period of customer use.[93] A service is extraordinary if the customer's use of the taxpayer's property is incidental to the service.[94] For example, a hospital renders extraordinary services to its patients because a patient's occupancy of a hospital room is incidental to the services provided by doctors, nurses, and other hospital staff. Also, a school's provision of dormitory rooms for students is incidental to the services provided by the school's teaching staff. Although a trucking company's customers use its equipment in a certain sense, this use is incidental to the provision of transportation services if the company operates the trucks.[95]

By contrast, assume a lessor of copying equipment agrees to maintain and repair the equipment for customers; maintenance is required so often and is so labor intensive that the value of the maintenance and repair services exceeds 50 percent of the amounts paid by customers. A customer's use of a copying machine is not incidental to the maintenance and repair services, and the lessor is therefore engaged in a rental activity unless it can qualify under the 30-day rule described earlier.[96]

If an operation is considered a rental activity, notwithstanding the presence of services, either of two treatments is possible.[97] If the services "are incidental to the activity (e.g., a laundry room in a rental apartment building)," they are considered part of the rental activity. If the services are not incidental, but instead "rise to the level of a separate activity," the rental activity and the services are treated as two activities. In the latter case, the rental activity is passive, and the material participation test is applied to determine whether the service activity is passive.[98]

2. *Use of property provided incidentally to another activity.* An activity is not a rental activity if renting is incidental to a nonrental activity of the taxpayer.[99] This rule applies only in the four situations described below.

---

[92] Reg. §1.469-1T(e)(3)(viii) Ex. 2.
[93] Reg. §1.469-1T(e)(3)(ii)(C).
[94] Reg. §1.469-1T(e)(3)(v).
[95] Reg. §1.469-1T(e)(3)(viii) Ex. 3.
[96] Reg. §1.469-1T(e)(3)(viii) Ex. 1.
[97] H.R. Rep. No. 841, supra note 9, at II-148.
[98] See supra ¶28.3.3 for the material participation test.
[99] Reg. §1.469-1T(e)(3)(ii)(D).

Incidental to investment purpose. A taxpayer's rental of property is incidental to an investment purpose, and hence not a rental activity, if (1) the principal purpose for holding the property is to realize gain through appreciation in value and (2) gross rents for the year are no greater than 2 percent of the lesser of the property's cost or value. For example, a taxpayer who holds land for appreciation, but leases it to a rancher for grazing in order to cover some of the costs of carrying the land, is not engaged in a rental activity for a year in which the rents are less than 2 percent of the property's cost or value.[100] Property is held for "appreciation," however, only if the owner seeks gain through a rise in value because of market changes, not the addition of improvements. For example, if land is purchased with the intention of building a shopping center on it but is leased pending the start of contruction, the land is not considered to be held for appreciation.[101]

Incidental to business use. Rentals are not a rental activity if they are incidental to a business use, i.e., if the property is normally used by the taxpayer in a business other than rental but is rented to others when not needed in the business. More specifically, (1) the property must be used "predominantly" in a nonrental business either during the taxable year or during two of the five preceding years and (2) gross rents for the taxable year cannot exceed 2 percent of the property's cost (or, if less, its value). Assume a farmer leases out a portion of the land historically used in his farming business (but continues the business on the remainder of the land). If annual rents do not exceed 2 percent of the property's cost or value, the farmer is not engaged in a rental activity during the first three years of the lease because, during each of these years, the predominant-use requirement is met for at least two of the preceding five years.[102]

In contrast, property leased out pending a future use in a trade or business cannot qualify under this rule. For example, if land is purchased with the intention of building a shopping center on it, but is leased to another business until construction begins, the owner is engaged in a rental activity during the lease period.[103]

Incidental to purpose to hold for sale to customers. Rental is considered incidental to a holding for sale and is not a rental activity, if (1) the property is sold or exchanged in a taxable transaction during the year and (2) the taxpayer is a dealer in such property at the time of the sale.[104]

Employee's use for employer's convenience. An employer's rental of lodging to an employee is incidental to the activity in which the employee is

---

[100] Reg. §1.469-1T(e)(3)(viii) Ex. 5.
[101] Reg. §1.469-1T(e)(3)(viii) Ex. 7.
[102] Reg. §1.469-1T(e)(3)(viii) Ex. 6.
[103] Reg. §1.469-1T(e)(3)(viii) Ex. 7.
[104] S. Rep. No. 313, supra note 13, at 720.

employed if the lodging is furnished for the employer's convenience.[105]

3. *Nonexclusive use.* Customers' use of property is not a rental activity if the property is "customarily" made available "during defined business hours for nonexclusive use by various customers."[106] A golf course is an example covered by this rule.[107]

4. *Contributed property.* A taxpayer does not engage in a rental activity by providing property to a partnership, S corporation, or joint venture if (1) the taxpayer owns an interest in the entity, (2) the entity is not engaged in a rental activity, and (3) the property is provided in the taxpayer's capacity as owner of an interest in the entity.[108] A partner's interest in a nonrental partnership, for example, is not a rental activity merely because the partner's contribution for his interest consists of property that is used by the partnership in its business. This is so whether the partner's contribution is reflected in his proportionate interest in partnership income or through a guaranteed payment under §707(c). The partner apparently is engaged in a rental activity, in contrast, if the property is not contributed to the partnership's capital but the partner instead leases it to the partnership in a transaction made in a capacity other than as partner.

An example of the application of the contributed-property rule to a joint venture is where a landowner enters into a crop-share lease with a tenant under which the tenant agrees to farm the land and the landowner and tenant agree they will each bear one half of the tenant's expenses and receive one half of the crops harvested from the land. According to the regulations, the use of the land is the landowner's contribution to a joint venture that is not itself a rental activity, and the landowner is thus not engaged in a rental activity.[109]

5. *Relationship to §280A.* Rental of a dwelling unit is not a passive activity if the taxpayer also uses the property for personal purposes and this personal use is sufficient to make §280A applicable to the property.[110] Section 280A sharply limits the deduction of losses with respect to property used for both personal and business or rental purposes (e.g., a business office in the taxpayer's residence or a rental of a vacation home during periods the taxpayer does not use it).[111] This property is exempted from §469 in order to give the §280A limitations exclusive jurisdiction.

---

[105] For the convenience-of-the-employer test, see §119, discussed supra ¶14.5.
[106] Reg. §1.469-1T(e)(3)(ii)(E).
[107] Reg. §1.469-1T(e)(3)(viii) Ex. 10.
[108] Reg. §§1.469-1T(e)(3)(ii)(F), (vii).
[109] Reg. §1.469-1T(e)(3)(viii) Ex. 8.
[110] Reg. §1.469-1T(e)(5).
[111] See supra ¶22.6 for §280A.

¶28.3.8 Working Interests in Oil and Gas Properties

A working interest in oil or gas property is not considered passive, even if the taxpayer is wholly inactive in the management of the property, if the taxpayer's ownership interest is direct or through an entity in which his liability is not limited.[112] An interest as a general partner in a partnership holding a working interest, for example, is not passive, but an interest as limited partner is.[113]

Congress included the exception for working interests because, when §469 was enacted in 1986, "the oil and gas industry [was] suffering severe hardship due to the worldwide collapse of oil prices," and "relief for this industry require[d] that tax benefits be provided to attract outside investors . . . willing to accept an unlimited and unprotected financial risk proportionate to their ownership interests in the oil and gas activities."[114]

1. *Definition of "working interest."* This exemption only applies to a "working interest," defined as "an interest with respect to an oil and gas property that is burdened with the cost of development and operation of the property."[115] The characteristics of a working interest usually include

> responsibility for signing authorizations for expenditures with respect to the activity, receiving periodic drilling and completion reports, receiving periodic reports regarding the amount of oil extracted, possession of voting rights proportionate to the percentage of the working interest possessed by the taxpayer, the right to continue activities if the present operator decides to discontinue operations, a proportionate share of tort liability with respect to the property (e.g., if a well catches fire), and some responsibility to share in further costs with respect to the property in the event that a decision is made to spend more than amounts already contributed.[116]

---

[112] IRC §§469(c)(3)(A), (4). See White, Impact of Passive Loss Rules on Owners of Oil and Gas Interests, 68 J. Tax'n 342 (1988); White, How the Passive Loss Limitation Rules Will Affect Working Interests, 67 J. Tax'n 138 (1987).

[113] An indirect interest in a working interest probably qualifies as not passive under this rule if the taxpayer holds a limited liability interest (e.g., a limited partnership interest or shares in an S corporation), but has given guarantees or made other agreements that make him liable on all debt relating to the working interest. The statute, however, is not clear on the point.

[114] S. Rep. No. 313, supra note 13, at 717–18 (1986).

[115] S. Rep. No. 313, supra note 13, at 744. This definition is borrowed from the definition of "operating interest" found in §614(d) and the regulations thereunder. Reg. §1.469-1T(e)(4)(iv).

[116] S. Rep. No. 313, supra note 13, at 744.

A right to decline to make further contributions under a buyout or nonparticipation agreement, however, is not inconsistent with the holding of a working interest; neither is insurance against tort liabilities. Examples of interests not qualifying as working interests are "rights to overriding royalties, production payments, [and] contract rights to extract or share in oil and gas, or in profits from extraction, without liability to share in the costs of production."[117]

2. *Requirement of unlimited liability.* A working interest is not exempted from §469 unless it is held directly or indirectly through an entity that does not limit the taxpayer's liability. Liability must be unlimited with respect to both drilling and operations.[118]

Most obviously, an interest as limited partner in a partnership or shareholder in an S corporation never qualifies for the exemption even if the entity owns otherwise qualifying working interests. Where the working interest is held by a lower-tier entity, the exemption is lost if personal liability is cut off at any tier. "For example, a general partner in a partnership that owns a limited partnership interest in [another]partnership that owns a working interest is not treated as owning a working interest."[119]

The exemption is also denied to an interest held in a "form of ownership that is substantially equivalent in its effect on liability to a limited partnership interest or interest in an S corporation, even if different in form."[120] In other words, an interest held indirectly through an entity other than a limited partnership or S corporation cannot qualify if "under applicable State law, . . . the potential liability of a holder of such an interest for all obligations of the entity [is limited] to a determinable fixed amount (for example, the sum of the taxpayer's capital contributions)."[121] This standard, however, is not inconsistent with all liability limitations. The holder of an interest in an entity can qualify even if state law limits the holder's liability for debts of the entity to an amount proportionate to his interest in the entity (e.g., a 10 percent owner cannot be held liable for more than 10 percent of any debt of the entity).[122]

Also, limitations on liability not deriving from form of organization are ignored. The exemption can apply even if the taxpayer's liability is limited by an indemnification or stop loss agreement or by insurance.[123] A general partner who is jointly and severally liable for all partnership debts, for example, can qualify even if his fellow general partners agree to indemnify

---

[117] Id.
[118] Reg. §1.469-1T(e)(4)(i)(B).
[119] S. Rep. No. 313, supra note 13, at 745.
[120] 1986 Bluebook, supra note 16, at 251.
[121] Reg. §1.469-1T(e)(4)(v)(A)(3).
[122] Reg. §1.469-1T(e)(4)(v)(C) Ex. 2.
[123] Reg. §1.469-1T(e)(4)(v)(B).

him against any loss beyond his capital contribution.[124]

3. *Economic performance rule.* To prevent evasion of the unlimited-liability rule, the regulations sometimes partially disqualify a working interest from the exemption if a deduction is allowed for the cost of a service when the taxpayer has unlimited liability, but the service is not performed until after the unlimited liability has been eliminated.[125] The partial disqualification occurs in this circumstance if the working interest would be a passive activity of the taxpayer in the absence of the working-interest exemption and the taxpayer reports a loss from the interest for the year.

Assume a partnership makes payment in 1987 for drilling work to be done during 1987 and 1988. Under the economic performance rule of §461(h), an advance payment for a service is normally not deductible until the service is performed.[126] An exception, however, allows an immediate deduction for an advance payment for the drilling of an oil or gas well if drilling commences no later than the ninetieth day of the next year.[127] The partnership in the example thus can deduct all of the drilling payment in 1987 even though some of the drilling work is done in 1988. Assume that one of the partnership's general partners has the right to convert her interest to a limited partnership interest at any time and that she exercises this right at the end of 1987. Assume further that the working interest would be passive with respect to this partner in the absence of the working-interest exemption and that loss from the interest is reported for 1987. The rule described here applies to the partner because (1) the deduction for the cost of the drilling is allowed for a year when she has unlimited liability, but (2) economic performance with respect to a portion of the deducted cost does not occur until unlimited liability disappears.

When the rule applies, the working interest is treated in part as a passive activity for the year of the deduction (referred to as a "disqualifed deduction") even though the working-interest and unlimited-liability requirements are fully satisfied for the year. The taxpayer's share of the disqualified deduction is allocated to the passive portion of the interest. Also, the taxpayer's share of gross income from the interest is prorated between the passive and nonpassive portions according to the ratio of the disqualified deduction to all deductions from the interest for the year. Assume the converting partner's distributive share partnership deductions in the example is $150 for 1987 and $50 of this share consists of the disqualified deduction. The $50 and one third of the partner's share of partnership income for the year are allocated to the passive portion of the

---

[124] Reg. §1.469-1T(e)(4)(v)(C) Ex. 1.
[125] Reg. §1.469-1T(e)(4)(ii).
[126] See infra ¶105.3 for §461(h).
[127] IRC §461(i)(2).

interest. The excess of the $50 over the gross income allocated to the passive portion is passive activity loss.

4. *Effect of exemption.* When a working oil or gas interest is considered not passive under this rule, losses and credits from the interest are allowed to reduce tax on all types of income, including salary and portfolio income. Under a rule discussed elsewhere, if an interest ever qualifies for the exception, net income from interest in subsequent years is treated as nonpassive, whether or not the interest continues to qualify for the exception.[128]

¶28.4 LOSSES SUBJECT TO LIMITATION

¶28.4.1 Introductory

Section 469(a)(1) bars any deduction for a "passive activity loss." A passive activity loss is an excess of (1) the sum of all losses for the taxable year incurred in passive activities over (2) the sum of all income from these activities.[1] The income or loss from a passive activity is the excess of gross income from the activity over otherwise allowable deductions allocable to it or vice versa.[2] The deductions taken into account include ordinary and necessary expenses of the trade or business that comprises the activity, and interest, taxes, and losses attributable to the activity.[3] Passive activity income and losses are sharply distinguished from services and portfolio income, the two types of income Congress was most anxious to insulate from passive activity losses.

The rules for identifying the gross income and deductions of a passive activity are discussed first below. Various elaborations on and exceptions from these rules are discussed thereafter, including the meanings of the terms "personal service income"[4] and "portfolio income,"[5] rules that reclassify some passive income as nonpassive,[6] and the classification of the distributive share of a partner of a publicly traded partnership.[7] The final portions of this section describe the more liberal version of the passive

---

[128] Infra ¶28.4.2 text accompanying notes 41–44.

[1] IRC §469(d)(1). Net income from a passive activity, in other words, is first offset by losses from other passive activities, and nonpassive losses (including net operating loss deductions) are deducted against passive income only if there is net income from all passive activities for the year.

[2] Reg. §1.469-2T(b)(1).

[3] H.R. Rep. No. 841, 99th Cong., 2d Sess. II-139 (1986). See infra Ch. 48 for the allocation of interest expense among various categories, including passive activities.

[4] Infra ¶28.4.3.

[5] Infra ¶28.4.4.

[6] Infra ¶28.4.5.

[7] Infra ¶28.4.6.

limitations for closely held C corporations that are not personal service corporations[8] and the relationships between the rules for computing passive activity losses and credits and other limitations, including the at risk rules and the limitations on deductions of capital losses.[9]

¶28.4.2 Gross Income and Deductions of a Passive Activity

Neither the statute nor the regulations provide a comprehensive rule for identifying the gross income of a passive activity. Presumably, this gross income includes all income from the property and dealings that comprise the activity. The regulations elaborate in detail on when gain or loss on a sale or exchange of property is passive activity income or loss; they also provide extensive guidance on what deductions are allocable to passive activities. These regulations and a few other specialized rules are described below.

1. *Gain or loss on disposition of passive activity or asset thereof.* Gain or loss on a sale or exchange of a passive activity or an asset used in a passive activity is included in computing income or loss from the activity.[10] Whether the property is a passive activity or an asset of a passive activity is determined at the time of the disposition. Gain or loss on a sale of a trade or business is not passive activity gain or loss, for example, if the business was formerly a passive activity but no longer is passive at the time of sale (because, for example, the taxpayer has become a material participant). Also, when a passive activity or an asset thereof is sold in an installment sale, all installments of the gain are passive activity income even if the sale terminates the taxpayer's participation in the activity.[11] A contract or option to acquire a passive activity is not itself a passive activity, and gain or loss on a disposition of the contract or option thus is not passive activity gain or loss.[12]

If a discrete portion of an item of property is used in a passive activity and the remainder of the property is used in another activity, gain or loss on a sale of the property must be apportioned "in a reasonable manner," and only the portion allocated to the passive use is passive activity gain or loss.[13] Assume a taxpayer owns a 10-story office building, 7 floors of which are used in a business in which the taxpayer materially participates and 3 of which are leased to tenants and thus constitute a passive activity. If the

---

8 Infra ¶28.4.7.
9 Infra ¶28.4.8.
10 Reg. §§1.469-2T(c)(2)(i), (d)(5)(i).
11 Reg. §1.469-2T(c)(2)(i)(D) Ex. 2.
12 Reg. §1.469-2T(c)(2)(i)(D) Ex. 3.
13 Reg. §§1.469-2T(c)(2)(i)(C), (d)(5)(iii)(A).

floors are of equal value, 30 percent of any gain or loss on the sale is passive.[14]

An apportionment is also required if, during the 12 months preceding the sale, the property is used some of the time in a passive activity and the remainder of the time in other activities.[15] Assume a building historically used in a passive activity is converted to use in a business in which the taxpayer materially participates, but the taxpayer sells the building five months later. Five twelfths of the gain or loss on the sale is apportioned to the active business and seven twelfths to the passive activity.

An exception to the foregoing rule allows all of the gain or loss to be assigned to the activity in which the property was predominantly used during the 12 months preceding the sale if the property's value exceeds neither $10,000 nor 10 percent of the value of all assets used in the activity. Assume the owner-operator of an apartment building (a passive activity) uses a personal computer 70 percent of the time for work relating to the building during the 12 months preceding the taxpayer's sale of the computer. All of the gain or loss on the sale may be treated as passive activity gain or loss if the value of the computer is no greater than the larger of $10,000 or 10 percent of the value of the assets of the apartment activity (including the computer).

An antiavoidance rule knocks a gain out of the passive category altogether if the property is "substantially appreciated" when it is sold or exchanged and its use was switched from another use to a passive activity shortly before the sale.[16] Property is substantially appreciated for this purpose if its value exceeds 120 percent of its adjusted basis. The term "substantially appreciated" might be misleading because it includes property that has not appreciated over its original cost and has a value in excess of basis solely because of accelerated depreciation. Gain on a sale of substantially appreciated property is reclassified as nonpassive under the antiavoidance rule unless the property was used in a passive activity for either (1) 20 percent or more of the time the taxpayer held the property or (2) all of the 24 months preceding the sale. The date of sale, further, is accelerated for this purpose to the time when the taxpayer makes an oral or written agreement to sell the property or acquires the right to put the property at a specified price to another person.

---

[14] Reg. §1.469-2T(c)(2)(i)(D) Ex. 4.

[15] Reg. §§1.469-2T(c)(2)(ii), (d)(5)(ii).

[16] Reg. §1.469-2T(c)(2)(iii). A taxpayer caught by this rule qualifies for a consolation prize if the property was held for an investment purpose (other than use in a passive activity) for more than 50 percent of the time the taxpayer owned it. In this case, the gain is treated as investment income that can be offset by investment interest expense under §163(d). See infra Ch. 48 for §163(d).

Assume a taxpayer sells a building held for 13 years; the building is held for rental (a passive activity) at the time of sale, but for the first 11 years and 3 months of the taxpayer's holding period, the building was used in a business in which the taxpayer actively participated. Even though the building is used in a passive activity when the sale occurs, the gain is entirely nonpassive because the passive use (21 months) is less than both 24 months and 10 percent of the taxpayer's holding period.[17]

2. *Gain or loss on disposition of interest in partnership or S corporation.* Gain or loss on a sale or exchange of an interest in a partnership or of stock in an S corporation is passive if the entity (1) is engaged in a business that is passive with respect to the partner or shareholder and (2) holds no assets apart from the assets of this business.[18] If the entity has more than one activity (including at least one passive activity), the gain or loss must be apportioned among the activities, even if all of them are passive. The apportionment is needed to show the gain or loss allocable to the taxpayer's interest in each passive activity and the gain or loss allocable to his interest in all nonpassive activities, including active businesses and investment activities. For this purpose, all of the entity's portfolio assets are lumped together as a single investment activity.[19]

If gain is recognized on the disposition of the partnership interest or S stock, a fraction of the gain is allocated to each passive activity of the entity.[20] The numerator of the fraction is the net gain that would have been allocated to the partner or shareholder if the entity had sold all assets of the passive activity for an amount equal to their fair market value. The denominator is the net gain that would have been allocated to the partner or shareholder if the entity had sold the assets of all its "appreciated" activities for their fair market values. An activity of the entity is appreciated for this purpose if, on a sale of all assets of the activity, net gain would have been allocated to the partner or shareholder.[21]

Conversely, if loss is realized on the disposition of the partnership interest or S stock, a fraction of the loss is allocated to each of the entity's passive activities.[22] The numerator of the fraction is the net loss that would have been allocated to the partner or shareholder if the entity had sold all assets of the activity. The denominator is the partner's or shareholder's share of the net loss on a hypothetical sale of all of the entity's "depreciated" activities, defined as those activities that would have generated net loss for

---

[17] Reg. §1.469-2T(c)(2)(iii)(F) Ex.
[18] Reg. §1.469-2T(e)(3).
[19] Reg. §1.469-2T(e)(3)(v). A "portfolio asset" is property of a type that produces portfolio income. See infra ¶28.4.4 for portfolio income.
[20] Reg. §1.469-2T(e)(3)(ii)(B)(1).
[21] Reg. §1.469-2T(e)(3)(ii)(E)(1).
[22] Reg. §1.469-2T(e)(3)(ii)(B)(2).

the partner or shareholder if the entity had sold the assets of the activity for their fair market value.[23]

The hypothetical gains and losses referred to in the two preceding paragraphs are determined, at the entity's choice, as of (1) the date of the partner's or shareholder's disposition or (2) the first day of the taxable year of the entity in which that disposition occurs.[24] The latter alternative, however, is lost if, between the beginning of the year and the date of the disposition, (1) the entity disposes of more than 10 percent of the assets of any of its activities or (2) the selling partner or shareholder contributes to the entity substantially appreciated or depreciated property having a value exceeding 10 percent of the value of his partnership interest or S stock at the beginning of the year. If the entity is a partnership that has made an election under §754, all basis adjustments available to the selling partner as a consequence of the election are taken into account in computing the hypothetical gains or losses.[25]

To illustrate these rules, assume an individual recognizes gain of $200 on a sale of a 25 percent interest in a partnership that has four activities: business X, in which the individual materially participates; business Y, in which she also materially participates; business Z, in which the partner does not materially participate; and a portfolio of investments in marketable securities. The values, adjusted bases, and potential gains and losses of the partnership's assets used in these activities are given in Example 28-1. Because loss is inherent in the partnership's assets used in activity X, none of the partner's gain is allocated to this activity. The gain is instead allocated among businesses Y and Z and the investment securities, in proportion to the partner's share of the potential gains inherent in partnership assets used in these activities. The allocation of the $200 is thus $64 to business Y (active business income), $120 to business Z (passive activity income), and $16 to the marketable securities (portfolio income).

The foregoing rules cannot be applied without full information about the values and adjusted bases of the entity's assets. If the data on adjusted basis is unobtainable, the gain or loss must be allocated among activities in proportion to the fair market values of the assets of the entity used in the activities.[26] No rule is provided for cases where information on the fair market values of the assets is unavailable.

Under an antiavoidance rule described above,[27] gain on a sale or exchange of an asset of a passive activity is reclassified as nonpassive income

---

[23] Reg. §1.469-2T(e)(3)(ii)(E)(2).
[24] Reg. §1.469-2T(e)(3)(ii)(D)(1).
[25] Reg. §1.469-2T(e)(3)(ii)(D)(2).
[26] Reg. §1.469-2T(e)(3)(ii)(C).
[27] Supra text accompanying notes 16–17.

Example 28-1

Apportionment of Gain on
Disposition of Partnership Interest

1. Gains inherent in partnership assets:

	Fair market value	Adjusted basis	Potential gain	Allocable to interest sold
Business X	$480	$680		
Business Y	620	300	$320	$ 80
Business Z	800	200	600	150
Marketable securities	100	20	80	20
Total				$250

2. Gain on sale allocated to partner's interest in:

Business X ($200 × 0/$250)	–0–
Business Y ($200 × $80/$250)	$ 64
Business Z ($200 × $150/$250)	120
Investment securities ($200 × $20/$250)	16
Total	$200

if the property is substantially appreciated and was recently converted from a nonpassive to a passive use. This rule is adapted to apply also to the case where the rule would have applied on a sale of an asset by a partnership or S corporation, but the partner or shareholder sells, not the entity.[28]

3. *Passive activity deductions.* A deduction is taken into account in determining passive income or loss if it "arises . . . in connection with the conduct of an activity that is a passive activity for the taxable year."[29] Such a deduction is included in the calculation for the year in which it would be allowed in the absence of §469 and the capital loss limitations of §1211.[30] For individuals, these deductions are taken into account whether they are allowable in determining adjusted gross income (so-called above-the-line deductions) or are itemized deductions.[31]

---

[28] Reg. §1.469-2T(e)(3)(iii). For an illustration of the application of the rule, see Reg. §1.469-2T(e)(3)(vii) Ex. 2.

[29] Reg. §1.469-2T(d)(1)(i).

[30] Reg. §1.469-2T(d)(8).

[31] Staff of Joint Comm. on Tax'n, 99th Cong., 2d Sess., General Explanation of the Tax Reform Act of 1987, at 218 (Comm. Print 1987) [hereinafter 1986 Bluebook].

Under rules discussed elsewhere in this work,[32] interest expense is allocated among various categories subject to differing limitations, including the passive loss limitations. Interest expense allocated under these rules to a passive activity is taken into account in computing income or loss from the activity.[33]

Net operating loss carrybacks and carryovers are never passive deductions.[34] Deductions arising in a passive activity enter into the computation of a net operating loss only when §469 allows the deduction. Since the deductions must run the gauntlet of the passive loss limitation on the way to becoming a net operating loss, it would not be appropriate to subject them to the limitation a second time in a carryback or carryover year. Capital loss carrybacks and carryovers are exempted from the limitation for the same reason.

A state, local, or foreign income tax is not a passive deduction even if the income subject to the tax is passive income.[35] Conversely, a refund of such a tax, if included in gross income, is not passive income.[36] Also, the charitable deduction allowed by §170 is never a passive deduction.[37]

4. *Spouses filing jointly.* Spouses filing a joint return are treated as one taxpayer in applying §469.[38] Gross income and deductions from the passive activities of both spouses are thus combined in a single aggregate, which allows loss from a passive activity of one spouse to be deducted against income from a passive activity of the other spouse.

5. *Adjustments relating to changes of accounting method.* When a taxpayer changes his method of accounting, §481 requires that gross income or a deduction be reported to account for any items that would otherwise be omitted or counted twice because of the change. This gross income or deduction (the §481 adjustment) must usually be reported in installments over a period of years beginning with the year of the change.[39] Each installment is passive activity income or deduction if the accounting change pertains to an activity that was passive when the change was made.[40] The status of the activity when each installment is reported is irrelevant. If the accounting change pertains to two or more activities, at least one of which is passive, the §481 adjustment is traced to the activities by applying the

---

[32] Infra Ch. 48.

[33] Reg. §1.469-2T(d)(3).

[34] Reg. §1.469-2T(d)(2)(ix). A net operating loss deduction is nonpassive even if it represents a loss incurred before 1987 in an activity that became a passive activity with the enactment of §469. 1986 Bluebook, supra note 31, at 222–23.

[35] Reg. §1.469-2T(d)(2)(vi).

[36] Reg. §1.469-2T(c)(7)(iii).

[37] Reg. §1.469-2T(d)(2)(viii). See infra Ch. 35 for the charitable deduction.

[38] Reg. §1.469-1T(j)(1).

[39] See infra ¶105.6.

[40] Reg. §§1.469-2T(c)(5), (d)(7).

adjustment rules to them separately, and each installment of the adjustment is prorated among the activities in the same proportions as the total adjustment.

6. *Net income from working interests in oil and gas wells.* An interest in an oil and gas well is exempted from the passive activity limitations if the interest is a working interest and is held by the taxpayer directly or through an entity that does not limit the taxpayer's liability for drilling or operating costs.[41] Generally, this exception is applied year by year. For example, if a taxpayer acquires a general partnership interest in a partnership owning a working interest in an oil and gas well, but later exercises an option to convert the general partnership interest into a limited partnership interest, the exception is available to the partner before the conversion but not after. For any year covered by the exception, gross income and deductions from the interest are excluded from the computation of passive activity loss.

There is, however, one lingering effect of the exception in years after an interest has ceased to qualify. Once loss from a working interest has been allowed under the exception, any subsequent net income from the interest is treated as income that is not passive, with the consequence that losses and credits from other passive activities cannot be used to reduce tax on the income.[42] This rule applies even if the interest does not satisfy the working-interest or personal-liability requirement for the income year and net loss from the interest would be subject to the §469 limitation. The rule is apparently meant to prevent taxpayers from having the best of both worlds by qualifying for the exemption in loss years (thus allowing the losses to be taken against unrelated income) and disqualifying the interest for years in which net income is realized (thus allowing losses from other passive activities to be taken against this income).

The rule also applies to net income from property received in exchange for a qualifying working interest in a nonrecognition exchange. Assume losses are taken when a working interest in an oil well is held directly, but the interest is subsequently transferred to a partnership in exchange for a limited partnership interest. If the partner's distributive share of partnership items ever includes net income from the working interest, this income is considered nonpassive, notwithstanding the rule that limited partnership interests are always passive.

---

[41] See supra ¶28.3.8.

[42] IRC §469(c)(3)(B); Reg. §1.469-2T(c)(6). Only net income from the property is affected by this rule. If the working-interest exception is inapplicable for the income year and the interest is then passive, all deductions from the activity and gross income equal to the deductions are included in computing passive activity loss for the year. Since these two amounts offset each other, their inclusion is usually inconsequential.

Moreover, for purposes of this rule, the working interest is deemed to include any property whose value "is directly enhanced by any drilling, logging, seismic testing, or other activities any part of the costs of which were borne by the taxpayer as a result of holding the working interest."[43] For example, if the results obtained by drilling on one tract indicate the presence of oil and gas on another tract, the two tracts are treated as one for this purpose, whether or not they are considered one for other purposes.[44] As a consequence, if the taxpayer's interest in the former tract is, for example, a general partnership interest qualifying for the working interest exception, but her interest in the latter tract is a nonqualifying limited partnership interest, the taxpayer's shares of gross income and deductions from the two tracts are aggregated in applying the net income rule, even though the two interests are considered separate for other purposes.

¶28.4.3 Personal Service Income

Salaries, professional fees, and other compensation for personal services can never be passive income. This exclusion encompasses all "earned income (within the meaning of section 911(d)(2)(A)),"[45] gross income recognized under §83 when property is received in connection with the performance of services,[46] taxable distributions under qualified pension, profit sharing, stock bonus, and annuity plans,[47] gross income under nonqualified deferred compensation plans,[48] and the taxable portion of social security benefits.[49]

Another example of compensation income is "a guaranteed payment to a partner (including a limited partner) attributable to the performance of personal services."[50] Assume a real estate developer receives a fee for services performed for a rental real-property partnership in which he holds a partnership interest. The developer's distributive share of partnership income or loss is passive under the rule that all rental activities are passive,[51]

---

[43] Reg. §1.469-2T(c)(6)(iii).

[44] Reg. §1.469-2T(c)(6)(iv) Ex. 1.

[45] IRC §469(e)(3). See infra ¶65.4.5 for the definition of earned income.

[46] Reg. §1.469-2T(c)(4)(i)(B). See ¶60.4 for §83.

[47] Reg. §1.469-2T(c)(4)(i)(D). See ¶61.5 for the taxation of participants in such plans.

[48] Reg. §1.469-2T(c)(4)(i)(D). See infra ¶60.2 for nonqualified deferred compensation plans.

[49] Reg. §1.469-2T(c)(4)(i)(E). See supra ¶16.5 for the taxation of social security benefits.

[50] S. Rep. No. 313, 99th Cong., 2d Sess. 720 (1986). The result is the same whether the compensation is for current, past, or future services. 1986 Bluebook, supra note 31, at 218.

[51] See supra ¶28.3.7.

but the fee, being compensation for personal services, is not. The fee thus might be taxed while partnership losses are nondeductible. Similarly, if a shareholder of an S corporation receives a salary as an employee of the corporation, the salary is not passive income even if the corporation's only activity is a rental activity or some other activity that is passive with respect to a shareholder. A partner's distributive share of partnership income under §704(b) and an S corporation shareholder's pro rata share of the corporate income, however, is not personal services income, but is characterized according to the nature of the income at the entity level.[52]

Also, if an individual's "personal efforts significantly contributed to the creation of [intangible] property," gross income from the property cannot be passive.[53] This rule applies, for example, to income from a "patent, copyright, or literary, musical, or artistic composition." Most commonly, the rule applies to royalty income, but any other form of gross income from the property is also covered.

Moreover, an amount received by an individual under a covenant not to compete is nonpassive, regardless of any connection the covenant may have to any present or former passive activity of the individual.[54]

¶28.4.4 Portfolio Income

The gross income of a passive activity usually does not include interest, dividends, annuities, or royalties.[55] Moreover, gain or loss on a disposition of property usually cannot be passive if (1) the property is "held for investment" but is not an interest in or asset of a passive activity or (2) it is property "of a type" that produces interest, dividends, annuities, or royalties.[56] This income, gain, and loss is collectively known as "portfolio income." Portfolio income is excluded from passive activity income and loss because "portfolio investments ordinarily give rise to positive income, and are not likely to generate losses which could be applied to shelter other income."[57] Also, "to permit portfolio income to be offset by passive losses or credits would create the inequitable result of restricting sheltering by individuals dependent for support on wages or active business income, while permitting sheltering by those whose income is derived from an investment

---

[52] Reg. §1.469-2T(c)(4)(i)(F).

[53] Reg. §1.469-2T(c)(7)(i).

[54] Reg. §1.469-2T(c)(7)(iv).

[55] IRC §469(e)(1)(A)(ii).

[56] IRC §469(e)(1)(A)(ii). If a mineral production payment is treated as a loan under §636, the amount of the payment considered to be interest is interest for purposes of the portfolio income rules; if the payment is not treated as a loan, it is considered a royalty. Reg. §1.469-2T(c)(3)(iii)(C). See supra ¶24.4 for §636.

[57] S. Rep. No. 313, supra note 50, at 728.

portfolio."[58]

Examples of portfolio income are "dividends on C corporation stock, REIT and RIC dividends, interest on debt obligations, and royalties from the licensing of property."[59] Dividends from an S corporation are also portfolio income if the S corporation was formerly a C corporation and the dividends are paid from earnings and profits accumulated before the S election.[60]

Portfolio income of a pass through entity (partnership, S corporation, or trust) retains its character as such in the hands of its owners. For example, if a rental real estate partnership invests its cash flow in securities pending distribution to partners, dividends and interest on the securities are portfolio income. If the partnership's rental business is a passive activity with respect to a particular partner, his distributive shares of rental losses thus cannot be deducted against his share of the dividends and interest income. When an interest in a pass through entity is sold, gain or loss on the sale must be apportioned if the entity carries on a business that is passive with respect to the seller, but that also has portfolio or other nonpassive assets. "For example, if a general partnership owns a portfolio of appreciated stocks and bonds and also conducts a business activity, a part of the gain on sale of a partnership interest would be attributable to portfolio income and would, consequently, be treated as portfolio income."[61]

Exceptions from the portfolio rule are made for dividends, interest, and other income earned in the ordinary course of a trade or business and for interest on loans to a pass through entity in which the lender has an interest. Also, rules are provided identifying the deductions allocable to portfolio income. These exceptions and rules are described below.

1. *Ordinary business income.* Income that would otherwise be portfolio income is excluded from that category if it is "derived in the ordinary course of [a] trade or business."[62] An example is interest income of a bank received in the ordinary course of its business of lending money. Other examples are (1) dividends, interest, and gains on a broker/dealer's inventory of securities (excluding securities held for investment), (2) a retailer's interest income on charge accounts and installment contracts, and (3) a patronage dividend to a patron of a cooperative to the extent the dividend

---

[58] Id.

[59] S. Rep. No. 313, supra note 50, at 728. Another example is subpart F income taxable to a U.S. shareholder under §951(a). 1986 Bluebook, supra note 31, at 231 n.24. See infra ¶68.3 for subpart F.

[60] 1986 Bluebook, supra note 31, at 231 n.24.

[61] S. Rep. No. 313, supra note 50, at 729. See supra text accompanying notes 20–26 for the apportionment rules.

[62] IRC §469(e)(1)(B); Reg. §1.469-2T(c)(3)(ii).

is based on patronage in the course of the patron's business.[63] This income is instead treated as income of the primary activity (e.g., banking, dealing in securities, or retailing); whether it is passive or not depends on whether the person reporting it participates materially in the business.

Interest on an installment obligation received in a sale of a business asset is not ordinary business income for purposes of the foregoing rule unless the sale is to a customer in the ordinary course of business. For example, if a farmer makes an installment sale of a portion of his farmland, interest on the installment obligation is not covered by this rule and is therefore portfolio income.[64]

Royalties qualify for the active business exception only if the taxpayer created the licensed property or "performed substantial services or incurred substantial costs with respect to the development or marketing of [the]property."[65] The substantial-services-or-costs test is satisfied for a taxable year if (1) development and marketing costs incurred during the year exceed 50 percent of gross royalties from the property for the year or (2) cumulative development and marketing costs for all years up through the taxable year exceed 25 percent of the sum of the price paid for the property and all other capital expenditures with respect to it.[66] Also, if development and marketing costs fall short of both the 50 percent and the 25 percent levels, the substantial-services-or-costs test is met if the facts and circumstances show that development and marketing services or costs are substantial.

An item is not considered derived in the ordinary course of business, however, merely because it is income from an investment of working capital or other amounts set aside for business needs.[67] Assume a partnership that owns and operates rental real property invests cash held as working capital in its rental business or to finance future capital improvements to its property. Interest or dividends on the temporary investments are not included in the partners' passive activity income or losses. As a consequence, the part-

[63] S. Rep. No. 313, supra note 50, at 729; Reg. §1.469-2T(c)(3)(ii)(F). Interest on accounts receivable of a seller of goods or services, however, qualifies only if "credit is customarily offered to customers of the business." Reg. §1.469-2T(c)(3)(ii)(B).

[64] Reg. §1.469-2T(c)(3)(iv) Ex. 1.

[65] Reg. §1.469-2T(c)(3)(iii)(B). If the property is held by a partnership, S corporation, estate, or trust, this rule is applied by looking to the activities and costs of the entity, not its owners.

[66] For an example of the application of this rule, see §1.469-2T(c)(3)(iv) Ex. 5 of the regulations. The rule is applied at the entity level where licensed property is held by a pass through entity, and a disproportionate allocation of development and marketing costs to a particular partner of a partnership holding such property is therefore of no help in qualifying the partner under the rule. Reg. §1.469-2T(c)(3)(iv) Ex. 6.

[67] IRC §469(e)(1)(B).

ners might be taxed on the interest or dividends, but be denied deductions for losses incurred in the rental business. Neither is income from investments of business reserves within the rule's protection. Assume a limited partnership that owns and operates a low-income housing project is required by the laws governing such housing to maintain a reserve for repair and maintenance. Interest and dividends on investments made of the reserve fund are portfolio income.[68] "Although setting aside such amounts may be necessary to the trade or business, earning portfolio income with respect to such amounts is investment-related and not a part of the trade or business itself."[69]

2. *Interest on installment sale of passive activity.* While gain or loss on a sale of an interest in a passive activity (or property used in the activity) is itself passive, interest on an installment obligation received in the sale is portfolio income unless the sale is made in the ordinary course of the taxpayer's business.[70]

3. *Self-charged interest.* The legislative history suggests that regulations might be issued allowing portfolio interest income to be offset, at least in part, by passive activity loss where the income is essentially a return on the taxpayer's interest in the passive activity. Such interest income is sometimes referred to as "self-charged interest."

Assume a partnership borrows money from a partner with respect to whom the partnership's business is a passive activity. The partner reports on his return (1) interest income on the loan and (2) his distributive share of the corresponding interest expense of the partnership. If the rules were strictly applied, (1) the partner's interest income would be taxable as portfolio income and (2) his share of the partnership's interest deduction might be part of a nondeductible passive activity loss. The resulting net tax liability is not appropriate to the extent that "in economic substance the taxpayer has paid the interest to himself "; it should be avoided by allowing the taxpayer's distributive share of the partnership's interest deduction to be taken against the interest income.[71] The same solution is suggested for a case where a shareholder of an S corporation makes a loan to the corporation.

In the partnership case, however, if the lender-partner's distributive share of the partnership's interest deduction is increased by a special allocation, the partner's deduction against the interest income is limited to an amount equal to the share of the partnership deduction he would have taken in the absence of the special allocation.[72] Assume a partner receives $100 of interest on a loan to the partnership; although the partner has only a

---

[68] Reg. §1.469-2T(c)(3)(iv) Ex. 2.
[69] S. Rep. No. 313, supra note 50, at 729–30.
[70] 1986 Bluebook, supra note 31, at 232–33.
[71] H.R. Rep. No. 841, 99th Cong., 2d Sess. II-146, II-147 (1986).
[72] 1986 Bluebook, supra note 31, at 234.

40 percent interest in the partnership, the partnership agreement allocates to her 100 percent of the partnership's deduction for the interest. The partner can offset against the interest income only $40 of the interest deduction; the remaining $60 enters into the computation of the partner's share of income or loss from another partnership activity, which may be a passive activity.

4. *Deductions allocable to portfolio income.* Expenses relating to portfolio income cannot be taken in determining passive income or loss. Specifically, expenses (other than interest) are excluded if they are "clearly and directly allocable to" portfolio income, and interest expense is excluded if it is "properly allocable" to this income.[73] The phrase "clearly and directly allocable" encompasses expenses "incurred as a result of, or incident to, an activity in which such gross income is derived or in connection with property from which such gross income is derived."[74] General and administrative expenses and salaries of officers seldom meet this standard.

¶28.4.5 Passive Activity Income Reclassified as Nonpassive

The Treasury is authorized to provide by regulation that some "net income or gain from a . . . passive activity [is] to be treated as not from a passive activity."[75] It is intended that this authority be exercised with respect to income from investments that technically fall within the definition of passive activity, but in substance are more like portfolio investments. Inclusion of income from these investments in the netting of income and losses from passive activities could undermine the "purpose of the passive loss provision [to] prevent . . . the sheltering of positive income sources through the use of tax losses derived from passive business activities."[76] In the vernacular of the profession, the reclassification rules are meant to curb passive income generators (PIGs).

The regulations identify six such investments, which are described below:[77]

1. *Activities in which taxpayer significantly participates.* Net income (but not net loss) from a taxpayer's "significant participation passive activities" is reclassified as nonpassive.[78] A "significant participation passive ac-

---

[73] IRC §469(e)(1)(A)(ii). For the allocation of interest deductions, see infra ¶31.4.

[74] Reg. §1.469-2T(d)(4).

[75] IRC §469(*l*)(3).

[76] H.R. Rep. No. 841, supra note 3, at II-147.

[77] If an activity or investment falls within two or more of these rules, it is governed by the rule that reclassifies the largest amount of income as nonpassive. Reg. §1.469-2T(f)(8).

[78] Reg. §1.469-2T(f)(2).

tivity" is a trade or business in which the taxpayer participates for at least 100 hours during the taxable year, but which is nevertheless passive because the taxpayer's participation is not sufficiently regular, continuous, and substantial to meet the material participation test.[79]

The first step in the application of the rule for significant participation passive activities is to aggregate together all gross income and deductions from these activities. If the aggregate is a loss, the rule does not apply, and the gross income and deductions from the activities are lumped with the income and deductions of all other passive activities in determining passive activity income or loss for the year. If the aggregate is net income, in contrast, gross income equal to the net amount is nonpassive, but the deductions from the activity and an equal amount of gross income remain passive.

If the taxpayer has more than one significant participation passive activity, the nonpassive amount is allocated among them as follows: The excess of gross income over deductions (or vice versa) is computed for each significant participation passive activity. If all activities show net income, the nonpassive amount for each activity equals the net income from the activity. If some significant participation passive activities have net income but others have losses, all gross income and deductions of the loss activities remain passive, and the nonpassive amount for each profitable activity is the net income from the activity multiplied by a fraction. The numerator of the fraction is the nonpassive amount and the denominator is the sum of the net income from all significant participation passive activities that have net income.[80]

The rule for significant participation passive activities seems to be a hedging of the Treasury's bets. The regulations give a restrictive definition of "material participation" in order to subject to §469 all of the activities generating the artificial accounting losses Congress meant to limit. By casting a broad net, however, the regulations make it possible for taxpayers to bring within the passive hotchpot activities generating a fairly predictable stream of income that can soak up the truly passive losses that are the principal target of §469. To limit this possibility, significant participation passive activities are subjected to the worst of both worlds: Net losses from the activities are passive, but net income is nonpassive.

2. *Ground leases and similar property.* Another example of income subject to reclassification is rent under a ground lease. In this situation, the leased land is passive under the rule that all rental activities are passive.[81] The ground lease, however, assures a return with little expense and there-

---

[79] Reg. §1.469-5T(c). See supra ¶28.3.3 for the material participation test.
[80] For an illustration of this procedure, see Reg. §1.469-2T(f)(2)(iii) Ex.
[81] See supra ¶28.3.7.

fore resembles an investment in a bond. Ground rents, Congress concluded, should be insulated from offset by losses from other passive activities in the same way that passive activity loss is prevented from reducing tax on interest from a bond.[82]

The regulations generalize from this case and require that income from a rental activity be reclassified as nonpassive if less than 30 percent of the cost of property used in the activity is depreciable.[83] The reclassified income might be rents or gain on a sale of the activity or property used in it. Assume a partnership buys vacant land for $300, makes $100 of improvements, and leases the property. Although the activity (being a rental activity) is passive, both rents from the tenant and any gain recognized on a sale of the property are reclassified as nonpassive.

If the taxpayer has deductions allocable to an activity generating income subject to reclassification under this rule, the reclassification only applies to net income from the activity. Net loss remains passive. Also, for a year in which there is net income, all deductions allocable to the activity (including loss on a sale of the property) and an equal amount of gross income stay in the passive hotchpot. Income recharacterized by this rule is considered portfolio income for purposes of §163(d), which limits deductions for investment interest expense to the amount of the taxpayer's portfolio income for the year.[84]

3. *Passive lending businesses.* The regulations contain an elaborate rule recharacterizing as nonpassive portions of the interest income earned in an active lending business in which the taxpayer does not participate materially.[85] The rule could apply, for example, to a limited partner in a partnership whose sole activity is to carry on the business of lending money. The rule, however, is restricted to cases where the owners of the business have equity investments that are substantial in relation to the loan portfolio; when applicable, the rule only recharacterizes the portion of the interest income from the activity that is attributable to the taxpayer's equity investment.

More specifically, the rule applies to a passive activity that is an "equity-financed lending activity," defined as a trade or business of lending money in which liabilities do not exceed 80 percent of the business's "interest-bearing assets."[86] The liability and asset figures are averages of the busi-

---

[82] H.R. Rep. No. 841, supra note 3, at II-147.
[83] Reg. §1.469-2T(f)(3). This rule applies in taxable years beginning after 1987. Reg. §1.469-11T(a)(2)(i).
[84] Reg. §1.469-2T(f)(10). See infra Ch. 48 for §163(d).
[85] Reg. §1.469-2T(f)(4). This rule applies in taxable years beginning after 1987. Reg. §1.469-11T(a)(2)(i).
[86] Reg. §1.469-2T(f)(4)(ii).

ness's indebtedness and interest-bearing assets during the taxable year.[87] The term "interest-bearing assets" encompasses all assets of the business that produce interest income, including customer loans, deposits in banks, government obligations, and corporate bonds. All liabilities of the business are included in the liability average, except liabilities secured by tangible property, liabilities that do not bear interest, and liabilities incurred for the purpose of pushing the relevant percentage above 80.[88] If the business is carried on by an entity, only debts of the entity are included.

If a passive activity is an equity-financed lending activity, the rule recharacterizes as nonpassive a portion of the taxpayer's gross income from the activity equal to the lesser of the "equity-financed interest income" or the "net passive income" from the activity for the year.[89] The equity-financed interest income is a fraction of the taxpayer's share of net interest income from the activity.[90] The numerator of the fraction is the excess of (1) the average balance during the year of the business's interest-bearing assets, over (2) the business's average indebtedness for the year. The denominator of the fraction is the average of the interest-bearing assets.

Assume a limited partnership engaged in a lending business has average interest-bearing assets for 1988 of $20 million; average indebtedness of the business for the year is $11 million. The business is an equity-financed lending activity because average indebtedness is less than 80 percent of average interest-bearing assets. The fraction described in the preceding paragraph is 9/20 (the excess of $20 million over $11 million divided by $20 million) or 45 percent. Each partner's equity-financed interest income thus consists of 45 percent of his distributive share of the partnership's net interest income.

"Net interest income" is defined as the excess of the gross interest income of the business over expenses "reasonably allocable" to this gross income, exclusive of interest expense on indebtedness included in the business's average liabilities.[91] The expenses deducted in determining net interest income might include depreciation, interest on debt secured by tangible property used in the business, and costs of advertising, loan processing and servicing, and insurance. Assume the partnership in the example has $2.2 million of gross interest income for 1988 and $300,000 of expenses other than interest for the year. Net interest income is $1.9 million, and 45 percent of it, or $855,000, is equity-financed. For a limited partner with a 1

---

[87] The averages may be computed daily, monthly, or quarterly, at the taxpayer's option. Reg. §1.469-2T(f)(4)(vii).

[88] Reg. §1.469-2T(f)(4)(vi). A liability issued with original issue discount is considered to be interest-bearing for this purpose. Id.

[89] Reg. §1.469-2T(f)(4)(i).

[90] Reg. §1.469-2T(f)(4)(iii).

[91] Reg. §1.469-2T(f)(4)(iv).

percent interest in the partnership, equity-financed interest income is $8,550.

The amount recharacterized as nonpassive income is the lesser of equity-financed interest income or net passive income from the activity. Assume the partnership in the example has $990,000 of interest expense, so that its taxable income is $910,000 ($2.2 million of interest income, less $990,000 of interest expense, less $300,000 of other expenses). Assume a 1 percent limited partner of the partnership borrowed money to purchase her interest and incurred interest expense on the loan of $4,000 for 1988. Net passive income from the interest is $5,100 ($9,100 distributive share of partnership taxable income, less $4,000 of interest expense). All of the net passive income is recharacterized as nonpassive because it is less than the partner's equity-financed interest income.

Income recharacterized as nonpassive by this rule is considered portfolio income for purposes of §163(d), which limits deductions for investment interest expense to the amount of the taxpayer's portfolio income for the year.[92]

4. *Rental incidental to development.* When property is developed or improved and then held for rental, the development or improvement activities are deemed separate from the rental activity, thus allowing the possibility that the former might not be passive while the latter is.[93] The drafters of the regulations decided that this bifurcation could lead to inappropriate results in cases where the property is sold soon after the rental activity commences. Gain on the sale is income of the rental (passive) activity, even though it arises in large part from the development or improvement activity, which might not be passive. This offers a possibility of artificially generating passive income to soak up passive losses from unrelated activities.

The regulations therefore recharacterize net income from a rental activity as nonpassive if all of the following three facts are present:[94] First, the taxpayer must recognize gain from a disposition of the property for the taxable year. Although rents might also be caught up in the recharacterization, gain on sale is the source of potential abuse, and the rule therefore does not apply in the absence of such gain. Second, rental use of the property must have commenced during the 24 months preceding the date on which a contract for the sale or exchange was made. Once rental use exceeds 24 months, the regulation drafters apparently concluded, gain on disposition might consist in large part of appreciation occuring during the rental period, and therefore should not be related back to the development or

---

[92] Reg. §1.469-2T(f)(10). See infra ¶31.3.5 for §163(d).

[93] For the rules defining the scope of an "activity," see infra ¶28.11.

[94] Reg. §1.469-2T(f)(5). This rule applies in taxable years beginning after 1987. Reg. §1.469-11T(a)(2)(i).

improvement. Rental use commences when "substantially all of the property is first held out for rent and is in a state of readiness for rental."[95] Third, the taxpayer must have participated either materially or significantly in an activity whose purpose was "enhancing the value of [the] property."[96] Examples of value-enhancing activities are construction, renovation, and the leasing-up of a building with substantial vacant portions, but other activities can also qualify. The value-enhancing activity and the taxpayer's participation in it can occur at any time prior to the property's disposition.

When all three of these facts are present, gross income from the rental activity is recharacterized as nonpassive in an amount equal to the net rental activity income for the year from the property whose disposition triggers the rule's application. This net income consists of the excess of gross income from the property for the year (including rents and gain on the disposition) over deductions reasonably allocated to it.[97] The deductions allocated to the property include prior years' losses from the property that were barred by §469 when incurred and have been carried over to the year of sale under §469's carryover rule.[98] If there is no such excess (i.e., if the activity shows a loss for the year), the rule does not apply.

5. *Rental to nonpassive activity.* If a taxpayer leases property to a trade or business in which he materially participates, the rental activity is passive under the rule categorizing all rental activities as passive,[99] but net income from the property is reclassified as nonpassive income.[100] This rule applies, for example, if an individual leases a building to an S corporation and the individual both owns stock of the corporation and participates materially in the corporate business in which the building is used. In the absence of reclassification under this rule, the rents would be passive income to the individual, and thus could be offset by unrelated passive losses, while the corporation's deduction for the rents would reduce the individual's share of

---

[95] Reg. §1.469-2T(f)(5)(ii).

[96] Reg. §1.469-2T(f)(5)(i)(C). An individual significantly participates in an activity if he spends at least 100 hours on the activity during the year but does not satisfy the material participation test. See supra ¶28.3.3 for the material participation test.

The rule also applies if the value-enhancing activity related to other property and the adjusted basis of the property sold derives in any part from that of the other property. Id. The rule applies, for example, if a partnership constructs building *A*, exchanges that building for building *B* in a transaction in which gain or loss is not recognized, leases up building *B*, and sells the building within 24 months thereafter.

[97] Reg. §§1.469-2T(f)(9)(iii), (iv).

[98] See infra ¶28.8 for the carryover rule.

[99] See supra ¶28.3.7.

[100] Reg. §1.469-2T(f)(6). This rule applies in taxable years beginning after 1987. Reg. §1.469-11T(a)(2)(i). Rents under a "written binding contract" made before February 19, 1988, moreover, are permanently exempted from the rule's application. Reg. §1.469-11T(a)(2)(ii).

the corporation's active income. Without the reclassification, in other words, the rental arrangement would have the effect of converting active income into passive income.

6. *Interests in licensing entities.* Although royalties are generally portfolio income (and hence nonpassive), a rule described above allows royalties to be treated as ordinary business income (and hence potentially passive) if recognized in a trade or business that either created the licensed property or incurred significant costs in developing or marketing the property.[101] The authors of the regulations feared that the latter rule might be exploited as a means of artificially generating passive income. The abuse case in this situation is where an interest in a partnership or S corporation carrying on a licensing business is acquired after the entity has created the licensed property or incurred significant development or marketing costs and is largely assured of a steady stream of income. Royalties classified as ordinary business income thus are reclassified as nonpassive income for a taxpayer who makes such a late-in-the-day acquisition.[102]

¶28.4.6 Income From Publicly Traded Partnerships (Master Limited Partnerships)

If interests in a partnership are traded on an established securities market or if there is some other form of secondary market for the interests, the partnership might be treated as a corporation under legislation enacted in 1987.[103] Such a partnership is referred to in the statutes as a publicly traded partnership, but is commonly known as a master limited partnership. When a publicly traded partnership is classified as a corporation, partnership income and loss does not pass through to the partners, thus eliminating the question of the classification of passed through items under the passive activity rules. Distributions from such partnerships are dividends, treated as portfolio income under the passive activity rules.

The regular pass through regime for partnerships, however, continues to apply to some publicly traded partnerships, principally partnerships holding passive investment assets, partnerships engaged in activities pertaining to real estate, oil and gas, or other natural resources, and partnerships organized before enactment of the 1987 legislation, which are general-

---

[101] Supra text accompanying notes 65–66.

[102] Reg. §1.469-2T(f)(7). This rule applies in taxable years beginning after 1987. Reg. §1.469-11T(a)(2)(i).

Income recharacterized by this rule is considered portfolio income for purposes of §163(d), which limits deductions for investment interest expense to the amount of the taxpayer's portfolio income for the year. Reg. §1.469-2T(f)(10). See infra ¶31.3.5 for §163(d).

[103] See infra ¶90.1.4.

ly allowed to retain partnership status until 1996. Section 469 is separately applied to a partner's distributive share of such a partnership's income and loss.[104] A distributive share of a loss of the partnership cannot be deducted against any other type of income, including income from other publicly traded partnerships, until the partnership interest is disposed of. Instead, each partner's share of the loss is carried forward as a deduction against the partner's share of income from the partnership in subsequent years.

Also, if such a partnership has both portfolio income and loss from a business activity in the same year, a partner's share of these two items must be kept separate.[105] The former retains its character in the partner's return as portfolio income. The latter is a passive activity loss because "partners in publicly traded partnerships [are] treated as passive with respect to their interests in the partnership."[106] The loss thus cannot be deducted currently because, under the rule described in the preceding paragraph, it cannot be combined with income and loss from other passive activities.

¶28.4.7 Special Rule for Closely Held C Corporations

The bite of §469 is sharply reduced for closely held C corporations that are not personal service corporations.[107] A passive activity loss of such a corporation is deductible against all other income of the corporation except portfolio income.[108] The income against which passive losses can be taken is referred to as "net active income."[109] Such a corporation's passive activity loss, in other words, is nondeductible only to the extent it exceeds net active income. Similarly, passive activity credits are allowed to offset tax on net active income, but not tax on portfolio income.

Net active income is computed excluding all gross income and deductions of passive activities, gross income constituting portfolio income, and all deductions (including interest deductions) allocable to portfolio income. Also excluded (and effectively treated as portfolio income) are (1) income from working interests in oil and gas that qualify for exemption from §469[110] and (2) income from trading in securities for the corporation's account where the corporation does not materially participate in the trading

---

[104] IRC §469(k). See generally Lipton, Section 469 and PTPs: Impact of the Omnibus Reconciliation Act of 1987, 38 Tax Notes 183 (1988).

[105] H.R. Rep. No. 391, 100th Cong., 2d Sess. 1073 (1987).

[106] Id.

[107] See supra ¶28.2, text accompanying notes 3–8, for definitions of "closely held C corporation" and "personal service corporation." See Lipton & Serling, Passive Activity Loss Limitations Can Have Unexpected Impact on Corporations, 68 J. Tax'n 20 (1988).

[108] IRC §469(e)(2). See supra ¶28.4.4 for portfolio income.

[109] IRC §469(e)(2)(B).

[110] See supra ¶28.3.8.

activity.[111]

The passive activity rules have two primary effects on these corporations. First, a passive loss cannot be deducted against interest, dividends, securities gains, and other portfolio income. Second, when passive losses exceed net active income, the excess cannot be carried back as a net operating loss, but can be carried forward indefinitely under the carryover rule of §469.[112]

Assume a closely held C corporation has (1) passive activity loss of $550, (2) net active income of $400, and (3) portfolio income of $100. The corporation's taxable income is $100 because the passive activity loss can be taken against the net active income but not the portfolio income. The undeducted $150 of passive activity loss is carried forward under the §469 carryover rule and is not a net operating loss for purposes of §172.[113]

If a closely held C corporation (other than a personal service corporation) has credits from passive activities, these credits are allowed to the extent of the tax on the corporation's net active income.[114] If the corporation has both losses and credits from passive activities, the losses are allowed first, and the credits are allowable only to the extent of the tax on the excess of the net active income over the passive activity loss for the year. Nonpassive credits are also allowed before passive credits. The ceiling on allowable passive credits is thus the tax on the excess of net active income over passive loss, reduced by nonpassive credits.

If a closely held C corporation is a member of an affiliated group that files a consolidated return, §469 is applied on a consolidated basis, so that passive activity loss computed for the group is allowed to the extent of net active income of the group.[115] The scope of a passive activity of a consolidated group is defined without reference to corporate boundaries; one member of the group can be engaged in several activities, and a single activity can be carried on by two or more members of the group.[116]

---

[111] Reg. §1.469-1T(g)(4). See supra ¶28.3.2 for additional rules on securities trading.

[112] Infra ¶28.8.

[113] For the effect of a NOL carryback on the application of these rules see §1.469-1T(g)(4)(iii) Ex. 2 of the regulations.

[114] Reg. §1.469-1T(g)(5).

[115] H.R. Rep. No. 841, supra note 3, at II-140; Reg. §1.469-1T(h)(3).

[116] 1986 Bluebook, supra note 31, at 221. See infra ¶28.11 for more on the definition of "activity."

¶28.4.8 Interaction With At Risk Rules, Rules on Capital Gains and Losses, and Other Principles

1. *At risk rules.* Whether loss sustained in a passive activity is determined after application of the at risk rules of §465.[117] That is, if a passive activity is financed by nonrecourse borrowing or other arrangements that limit the taxpayer's amount at risk, §469 only applies to losses not made nondeductible by the at risk rules.

The at risk rules, like §469, merely suspend loss deductions caught in their web and usually do not have the effect of permanently disallowing them. If loss from a passive activity is suspended under the at risk rules when sustained, but is allowable for a later year under the carryover provision of the at risk rules, the loss enters into the computation of passive activity income or loss for the latter year.[118] Generally, a loss suspended by the at risk rules is passive when released from suspension under those rules if the activity is passive for the year in which the at risk suspension ends. A loss suspended under the at risk rules for a year beginning before 1987 is not passive, however, regardless of when the at risk suspension ends.[119]

Conversely, the at risk rules are applied as though §469 did not exist.[120] For example, a taxpayer's amount at risk is reduced by losses until it reaches zero, at which point the at risk rules bar further losses. This reduction is made for a particular loss even if §469 suspends the loss.

2. *Loss limitations for partners and S shareholders.* Under §1366(d), a shareholder of an S corporation is barred from deducting his share of corporate losses once the basis of his stock has fallen to zero, but the disallowed losses carry forward indefinitely and are allowed to the extent of any basis for the stock in a subsequent year. Section 704(d) imposes essentially the same limitation on a partner's deductions for partnership losses. A loss that is barred by §1366(d) or §704(d) for a particular year is ignored in determining passive activity income or loss for the year; instead, the loss is taken into account in applying the §469 limitation when the loss is allowed by §1366(d) or §704(d).[121]

When §1366(d) or §704(d) applies, the barred loss is deemed to consist of a ratable portion of the shareholder's or partner's share of each item of deduction or loss of the entity.[122] This proration need not be done, however, unless some aspect of the §469 rules turns on the character of items includ-

---

[117] S. Rep. No. 313, supra note 50, at 723. See supra ¶25.10 for §465.
[118] S. Rep. No. 313, supra note 50, at 723.
[119] Reg. §1.469-2T(d)(2)(x).
[120] S. Rep. No. 313, supra note 50, at 723.
[121] Reg. §1.469-2T(d)(6).
[122] Reg. §1.469-2T(d)(6)(ii).

ed in the barred and allowed portions of the loss.[123]

3. *Capital gains and losses.* In the determination of income or loss from a passive activity, capital gains and losses are commingled indiscriminately with ordinary income or losses. Except to the extent that a capital loss is made nondeductible by §469, however, capital gains and losses from passive activities are amalgamated with other capital gains and losses in applying the rules for such gains and losses.[124]

Assume an individual has an interest in a passive activity that generates $10,000 of capital gain and $12,000 of ordinary loss for a particular year. There is passive loss of $2,000, which is suspended by §469. The $10,000 capital gain, however, is included in gross income as capital gain. If the individual has nonpassive capital loss of $10,000 for the year, it is netted against the passive gain in applying the limitation imposed by §1211(b) on the deduction of capital losses.

Assume another individual's passive activity generates $10,000 of ordinary income and $12,000 of capital loss. Passive loss is again $2,000, but the suspended deduction is capital in this instance and therefore will be a capital loss deduction when §469 allows it to be deducted. The remaining $10,000 of the $12,000 capital loss enters into the computation of taxable income for the current year. If the individual has no other capital gains or losses for the year, §1211(b) allows $3,000 of this $10,000 to be deducted immediately against ordinary income, and the remaining $7,000 carries forward under the capital loss carryover rules of §1212(b). Since the §1212(b) carryover consists of an amount that has already run the §469 gauntlet, §469 has no application when it is used in later years.

¶28.5 CREDITS SUBJECT TO LIMITATION

Section 469(a)(1) denies any "passive activity credit." A passive activity credit is an excess of (1) the sum of the credits otherwise allowable for the taxable year that are attributable to passive activities over (2) the regular tax liability allocable to these activities.[1] In other words, credits attributable to passive activities are only allowed to the extent of the regular tax allocable to the activities. The disallowed credits carry over to subsequent years under a rule described later in this chapter.[2]

1. *Credits subject to §469.* The credits subject to §469 are: (1) the general business credit (which subsumes the investment, targeted jobs, re-

---

[123] Reg. §1.469-2T(d)(6)(v).
[124] Reg. §1.469-1T(d).
[1] IRC §469(d)(2); Reg. §1.469-3T(a).
[2] Infra ¶28.8.

search, and low-income housing credits); (2) the credit allowed by §936 for corporations operating primarily in Puerto Rico or a possession of the United States; (3) the credit allowed by §28 for costs incurred in testing drugs for rare diseases; and (4) the credit allowed by §29 for producing fuel from nonconventional sources.[3] The foreign tax credit is exempt from the §469 limitation because it is subject to its own limitation.[4]

A credit of one of the types covered by §469 is attributable to a passive activity if it "arises in connection with the conduct of an activity that is a passive activity for [the] taxable year" or if it arose in connection with a passive activity during a prior year and is carried over to the current year under the carryover rule of §469.[5] A credit that arose in a taxable year beginning before 1987 (i.e., before §469 came into the law) is not subject to §469, however, even if it is carried to a post-1986 year under a carryover rule in the provisions allowing the credit.[6]

Most of the credits covered by §469 are also subject to limitations found in the credit-granting provisions that restrict the credits to specified portions of the taxpayer's precredit tax. The general business credit, for example, is restricted to 100 percent of the first $25,000 of the taxpayer's precredit tax plus 75 percent of the excess; amounts exceeding this limitation are carried to other years.[7] A credit attributable to a passive activity is first subjected to §469, and the tax-liability based restrictions of the credit-granting provisions are not applied until §469 allows the credit to be taken.[8] Section 469 therefore applies in the year in which the credit would be allowed in the absence of §469 and the limitations of the credit-granting provisions. The investment credit, for example, is generally allowed for the year property is placed in service, and that year is therefore the year in which the credit becomes subject to §469.[9]

If the limitations on the general business credit prevent the credit from being taken for the year in which it escapes the bonds of §469, it is thereafter treated as a nonpassive credit in applying the carryover rules for the

---

[3] Reg. §1.469-3T(b)(1)(i). See supra ¶27.1.2 (general business credit), ¶27.4.3 (credit for testing rare drugs), infra ¶67.2 (possessions corporation credit).

[4] S. Rep. No. 313, 99th Cong., 2d Sess. 723 n.10 (1986). See infra Ch. 69 for the foreign tax credit.

[5] Reg. §1.469-3T(b)(1). If an investment credit is allowed for progress expenditures on property not yet placed in service, the credit is passive if "it is reasonable to believe that [the] property will be used in a passive activity of the taxpayer when it is placed in service." Reg. §1.469-3T(b)(2). See Reg. §1.469-3T(f) Ex. 2.

[6] Reg. §1.469-3T(b)(4).

[7] IRC §§38(c), 39. See also IRC §28(d)(2) (credit for testing drugs for rare diseases limited to excess of regular tax over tentative minimum tax), §29(b)(5) (similar limitation for credit for producing fuels from nonconventional source).

[8] S. Rep. No. 313, supra note 4, at 723; Reg. §1.469-3T(c).

[9] Reg. §1.469-3T(f) Ex. 1.

general business credit and is never again restrained by §469. Under the general business credit rules, unlike §469, carryovers expire if not used within a designated period. If a credit is first suspended under §469, but is later allowed under §469's carryover rule, only to enter into a second carryover under the general business credit rules, the aging of the latter carryover begins when the credit is released from the hold of §469 and becomes part of the general business credit.[10]

2. *Regular tax attributable to passive activities.* Credits from passive activities are allowed to the extent of the regular tax on income from these activities. The regular tax attributable to passive activities is zero unless the taxpayer has net income from these activities for the year. Losses from passive activities thus are first offset against income from other passive activities, and credits can be used only if net income remains after this offset.

If there is net passive income, the regular tax attributable to it is the excess of the tax actually imposed for the year over the tax that would have been imposed if the net passive income were omitted from the tax base.[11] For example, if the regular tax for a particular year is $80, but would be $50 if net passive income were excluded, $30 of the tax is allocable to net passive income, and as much as $30 of credits from passive activities can be used.[12] The tax attributable to net passive income is necessarily zero, notwithstanding the presence of net passive income, if the actual regular tax for the year is zero (e.g., because of losses in a business in which the taxpayer materially participates).[13]

For individuals, estates, and trusts, the term "regular tax" usually refers to total federal income tax.[14] A corporation's regular tax liability does not include the accumulated earnings tax, the personal holding company tax, and a few other special income taxes.[15] The regular tax includes the alternative minimum tax as well as the tax imposed by §1 (for individuals and other noncorporate taxpayers) or §11 (for corporations).

---

[10] Staff of Joint Comm. on Tax'n, 99th Cong., 2d Sess., General Explanation of the Tax Reform Act of 1986, at 224 (Comm. Print 1987) [hereinafter 1986 Bluebook]; Reg. §1.469-3T(e).

[11] S. Rep. No. 313, supra note 4, at 723–24; Reg. §1.469-3T(d)(1).

[12] For another example, see Reg. §1.469-3T(f) Ex. 3.

[13] Reg. §1.469-3T(f) Ex. 4.

[14] IRC §§26(b), 469(j)(3). A few penalty taxes on premature distributions from retirement savings plans are excluded. Id.

[15] Id.

¶28.6 EFFECTIVE DATES AND PHASE-IN FOR INTERESTS HELD ON OCTOBER 22, 1986

¶28.6.1 Effective Dates

Subject to the phase-in rule described below, §469 applies in taxable years beginning after 1986 to losses and credits from passive activities acquired before as well as after the provision's effective date.[1] Assume an individual, whose taxable year is the calendar year, is a partner in a partnership using a taxable year ending January 31. Section 469 applies to the partner's distributive share of partnership items for the partnership year February 1, 1986 through January 31, 1987 because this share is reported on the partner's return for the calendar year 1987, which begins after 1986.[2] The effective date is put off for as long as six years for investors in some low-income housing projects.[3]

Only losses incurred and credits arising in post-1986 years are subject to §469; amounts carried from a prior year are not affected.[4] A net operating loss carried from prior years to a taxpayer's first taxable year beginning after 1986, for example, is not limited by §469, even if the loss was incurred in an activity that is treated as passive for post-1986 years. Similarly, an investment credit carried from a pre-1987 year is not limited in the year in which it is allowable under the investment credit carryover rules.

¶28.6.2 Phase-In Rule

Section 469 applies to passive activity losses and credits recognized in taxable years beginning after 1986, generally without regard to whether the taxpayer's interest in a passive activity was acquired before or after the provision came into the law. The disallowance rule of §469(a), however, is phased in for interests held on the date of the provision's enactment, October 22, 1986. The disallowance of a passive activity loss or credit from such an interest is 35 percent for taxable years beginning in 1987, 60 percent for 1988, 80 percent for 1989, 90 percent for 1990, and 100 percent for 1991 and succeeding years.[5] In other words, the holder of such an interest is allowed, free of the §469 limitation, 65 percent of the loss or credit from the

---

[1] Pub. L. No. 99-514, §501(c)(1), 100 Stat 2085 (1986); Reg. §1.469-11T(a)(1).

[2] Reg. §1.469-11T(a)(5) Ex. 1. Under §706(a), a partner's distributive share of partnership items is includable in the partner's return for the taxable year of the partner that includes the last day of the partnership's taxable year.

[3] Pub. L. No. 99-514, supra note 1, at §502.

[4] Id. at §501(c)(2).

[5] IRC §§469(m)(1), (2).

activity for a taxable year beginning in 1987, 40 percent for 1988, 20 percent for 1989, 10 percent for 1990, and zero for later years.

This phase-in rule applies only for the year in which the loss is incurred or the credit is first allowed.[6] It works as follows: Passive activity loss and credit are first computed by the usual rule—aggregating income, losses, and credits from preenactment interests with those from other passive activities. At this stage, losses from all passive activities, whether acquired before or after the date of enactment, are allowed against net income from all interests; credits are allowed to the extent of the regular tax on any net income from all passive interests combined. If losses from all passive activities exceed income from these activities or if credits from the activities exceed regular tax on income from the activities, the excess is a passive activity loss or credit that would normally be barred by §469(a).

For a taxable year beginning before 1991, however, the phase-in rule allows the applicable percentage of the portion of the passive activity loss or credit that is attributable to preenactment interests. For losses, the portion attributable to preenactment interests is the lesser of (1) the passive activity loss or (2) the amount that would be the passive activity loss if only current losses from preenactment interests were considered in the calculation.[7] The effect of this procedure is that losses from preenactment interests are first taken against income from all passive activities, and only the applicable percentage of net loss for the year from all preenactment interests (or if less, from all passive interests, whenever acquired) is allowable without regard to §469.

Assume an individual owns interests in two passive activities during 1987: activity X, which is a preenactment interest that generates loss of $1,000 for 1987, and activity Y, which was acquired during 1987 and has income of $900 for the year. The loss from preenactment interests is $100, that amount being the lesser of the passive activity loss ($100) or the amount that would be the passive activity loss if only preenactment interests were taken into account ($1,000). The deduction for the loss from preenactment interests is $65 (65 percent of $100).[8]

---

[6] IRC §469(m)(1)(B).

[7] IRC §469(m)(3)(A). In other words, the preenactment loss is the excess of (1) the passive activity loss over (2) the amount that would be the passive activity loss if carryovers from other years and losses from interests that are not preenactment interests were ignored. Reg. §1.469-11T(b)(3).

[8] Reg. §1.469-11T(b)(5) Ex. 1. For an example where the taxpayer has more than one preenactment interest, see Reg. §1.469-11T(b)(5) Ex. 3. For the interaction between the rules for preenactment interests and the rule allowing up to $25,000 of losses from rental real estate activities against nonpassive income, see Reg. §1.469-11T(b)(5) Ex. 4. See infra ¶28.7 for the $25,000 allowance.

Similarly, the preenactment credit is the lesser of (1) the passive activity credit for the year or (2) the amount that would be the passive activity credit if credit carryovers from prior years and current credits from interests other than preenactment interests were ignored.[9] This procedure has the effect of allowing credits first against the regular tax on any net income from passive activities and of permitting the phase-in rule to apply only to any amount remaining after this use of the credits.

The passive activity loss or credit that is not allowed by the phase-in rule is carried to the following year, where it is subject to the full rigor of §469 and cannot benefit from a second application of the phase-in rule. Assume an individual owns an interest in only one passive activity for 1987 and 1988, and this interest is a preenactment interest; current losses are $300 for 1987 and $200 for 1988.[10] The portions of these losses that are allowable in 1987 and 1988 are shown in Example 28-2.

Example 28-2

Use of Carryovers Under Phase-In Rule

1. For 1987:
   a. Passive activity loss.. $300
   b. Portion allowed under phase-in rule (65 percent of passive activity loss)... $195
   c. Carryover to 1988 .... $105
2. For 1988:
   a. Passive activity loss:
      Current loss from passive activity............................... $200
      Plus: Carryover from 1987.. 105　$305
   b. Lesser of:
      Passive activity loss.. $305
      Passive activity loss including only current loss from preenactment interests .... 200　$200
   c. Portion allowed under phase-in rule (40 percent of line 2b)..... $ 80
   d. Carryover to 1989 (line 2a less line 2c)................................... $225

---

[9] Reg. §1.469-11T(b)(4). See Reg. §1.469-11T(b)(5) Ex. 5.
[10] Reg. §1.469-11T(b)(5) Ex. 2.

An interest in a passive activity qualifies as a preenactment interest if the three requirements described below are satisfied:[11] First, the taxpayer must own the interest on October 22, 1986 or must acquire it pursuant to a "written binding contract" made on or before that date.[12] For this purpose, stock in a C corporation is not considered to be an interest in any activity of the corporation.[13] Assume that on October 22, 1986, an individual owns stock of a C corporation engaged in a trade or business in which the shareholder does not participate materially. If the corporation subsequently elects to be an S corporation or distributes the business to the shareholder in liquidation, the phase-in rule will not apply to losses from the business reported on the shareholder's return because the shareholder did not have a qualifying interest on October 22, 1986. Similarly, if the holder of a preenactment interest dies after October 22, 1986, neither the decedent's estate nor his heirs qualify.[14]

Also, this requirement is not met unless, on October 22, 1986, the taxpayer's interest was an interest in an "activity"; it is not enough that the taxpayer then held an interest in property. Assume an individual owns a house that was used as her personal residence for several years before 1987 but was converted to rental use during 1987. The phase-in rule does not apply because the house was not used in an activity on October 22, 1986.[15]

The second requirement of the definition of preenactment interest is that the activity must be conducted on October 22, 1986. This requirement is waived, however, if at least 50 percent of the property used in the activity (1) existed or was under construction on August 16, 1986 or (2) was acquired or constructed pursuant to a contract in effect on that date.[16] Also, there is no requirement that the activity would have been a passive activity on October 22, 1986 or any other date before 1987 if §469 had then been in effect.

The third requirement is that the taxpayer's ownership of the interest must continue uninterrupted from October 22, 1986 to the end of the year for which loss or credit is claimed. If the extent of the taxpayer's interest changes after October 22, 1986, this requirement has the effect of limiting the preenactment interest to the smallest interest held at any time after that date.[17] For example, if an individual holds a 10 percent interest in a partnership on October 22, 1986, but acquires an additional 5 percent interest

---

[11] IRC §469(m)(3)(B).
[12] For the meaning of "binding written contract," see Reg. §1.469-11T(c)(7).
[13] Reg. §1.469-11T(c)(2)(ii). A "C corporation" is any corporation that has not made an election under subchapter S to be an S corporation. IRC §1361(a)(2).
[14] Reg. §1.469-11T(c)(4) Ex. 4.
[15] Reg. §1.469-11T(c)(4) Ex. 1.
[16] IRC §469(m)(3)(B)(iii); Reg. §1.469-11T(c)(3).
[17] Reg. §1.469-11T(c)(5)(i).

thereafter, only the 10 percent interest qualifies.[18]

¶28.7 EXCEPTION FOR RENTAL REAL ESTATE

¶28.7.1 Introductory

A limited exception is provided for "natural persons" who "actively participate" in rental real estate activities. For such a taxpayer, passive activity losses from these activities and the deduction equivalent of passive activity credits[1] from the activities are allowed up to $25,000 each taxable year,[2] and the bar of §469(a) only applies to the excess over $25,000. The excess, further, is carried to the next year under the carryover rule described below;[3] the carryover, together with current losses credits from rental real estate activities, is allowed in the carryover year to the extent of $25,000.[4] The benefit of the rule, however, is phased out for taxpayers with adjusted gross income exceeding $100,000 and is denied altogether when adjusted gross income exceeds $150,000.[5]

The rule is intended to provide "a limited measure of relief . . . in the case of certain moderate-income investors in rental real estate, who otherwise might experience cash flow difficulties with respect to investments that in many cases are designed to provide financial security, rather than to shelter a substantial amount of other income."[6] Various aspects of its application are described more fully below.

¶28.7.2 Meaning of "Rental Real Estate Activities"

The $25,000 rule only applies to "rental real estate activities," defined as "rental activities" involving real property. The definition of "rental activities" under the rule treating all such activities as passive applies here as well.[7] For example, under this definition, a hotel is not a rental activity and

---

[18] Reg. §1.469-11T(c)(5)(iii) Ex. 1.

[1] See infra ¶28.7.7 for the deduction equivalent of a credit.

[2] IRC §§469(i)(1), (2).

[3] See infra ¶28.8.

[4] H.R. Rep. No. 841, 99th Cong., 2d Sess. II-141 (Conf. Rep. 1986). The $25,000 rule applies to a carryover, however, only if the taxpayer is an active participant in the activity in both the year in which the loss was incurred and the carryover year. It is inapplicable where loss in excess of $25,000 in an active year is carried to a year after the taxpayer's active participation ceases. Id. at n.2. Also, if an individual is not an active participant in some years, but later becomes an active participant, the rule does not apply to carryovers from nonactive to active years. Id.

[5] See infra ¶28.7.6.

[6] S. Rep. No. 313, 99th Cong., 2d Sess. 718 (1986).

[7] S. Rep. No. 313, supra note 6, at 737. See supra ¶28.3.7 for this definition.

thus cannot qualify for the $25,000 allowance. If a hotel is a passive activity under the general definition of that term, in other words, losses incurred in the hotel business are subject to the full rigor of §469, unmitigated by the $25,000 allowance.

¶28.7.3 Definition of "Active Participant"

The $25,000 allowance is only available to taxpayers who actively participate in rental real estate activities. To be an active participant, an individual must have some personal involvement in the activity and must own at least 10 percent by value of all of the interests in the activity.[8] A general partner who is substantially involved in a partnership's business of owning and operating apartment buildings, for example, actively participates in the business if she has at least a 10 percent interest in partnership profits and capital.

1. *Requisite personal involvement.* The quantity of personal involvement required by the active participation test is less than that required to meet the material participation test.[9] If it were not, no one could qualify for the $25,000 allowance because a taxpayer who satisfies the material participation test is not subject to the §469 limitations and thus has no need for the $25,000 allowance.

In particular, an individual is an active participant in a rental real estate activity even if his involvement is not regular, continuous, and substantial "so long as [he] participates . . . in a significant and *bona fide* sense."[10] This significant participation can consist of "the making of management decisions or arranging for others to provide services (such as repairs)."[11] These management decisions can consist of "approving new tenants, deciding on rental terms, approving capital or repair expenditures, and other similar decisions."[12] The active participation requirement can be met by an individual who rents out a house formerly used as her principal residence or who rents out a vacation home for periods she is not using it, even if a rental agent is retained and repairs and other services in connection with the property are performed by contractors.[13]

This minimal level of involvement, however, must be shown by the taxpayer's activities alone because the activities of agents and employees are

---

[8] IRC §469(i)(6)(A).
[9] S. Rep. No. 313, supra note 6, at 737. See supra ¶28.3.3 for the material participation test.
[10] S. Rep. No. 313, supra note 6, at 737.
[11] Id.
[12] Id. at 738.
[13] Id.

not attributed to the taxpayer. Further, "a merely formal and nominal participation in management, in the absence of a genuine exercise of independent discretion and judgment, is insufficient."[14] The active participation requirement is not met by an investor who purchases real property through a tax shelter promotion that includes an elaborate system for presenting management decisions to the investor, who "ratifies such judgments without independently exercising judgment."[15]

Moreover, a limited partner can never be an active participant.[16] The lessor under a net lease is "unlikely" to be sufficiently involved.[17]

2. *Requirement of 10 percent ownership.* Even if an individual's personal involvement in a rental real estate activity is sufficient to meet the standard described in the preceding paragraphs, the individual is not an active participant unless he has an interest of at least 10 percent in the activity. The purpose of the 10 percent rule is to deny the $25,000 allowance to interests in syndicated real estate shelters; "active participation by a less than 10 percent owner typically represents services performed predominantly with regard to ownership interests of co-owners," rather than the sort of self-management of the taxpayer's own assets that is meant to qualify for the allowance.[18]

The 10 percent rule is not met if (1) the taxpayer's interest is less than 10 percent at any time during the taxable year and (2) he holds some interest in the activity when this occurs.[19] The $25,000 allowance is denied, for example, if one half of a 15 percent interest is sold during the year, but not if the entire interest is sold.

3. *Spouses as active participants.* The involvement and interests of spouses are aggregated in applying the active participation test.[20] An individual whose involvement is less than active or whose interest is less than 10 percent thus satisfies the test if his spouse meets the requirement or if the involvement and interests of the spouses, when aggregated, rise to the required levels.

---

[14] Id.

[15] Id.

[16] IRC §469(i)(6)(C). If an individual holds both general and limited partnership interests in a limited partnership, however, he probably could be an active participant with respect to both interests. The $25,000 allowance is never available for an interest in a publicly traded partnership. IRC §469(k). See infra ¶90.1.4 for the definition of publicly traded partnership.

[17] S. Rep. No. 313, supra note 6, at 738.

[18] Id. at 737.

[19] H.R. Rep. No. 841, supra note 4.

[20] IRC §469(i)(6)(D).

¶28.7.4 Special Rules for Low-Income Housing and Rehabilitation Investment Credits

The active participation requirement (including the usual requirement that the taxpayer have a 10 percent or greater interest) is waived for the low-income housing credit if (1) the property qualifying for the credit is placed in service by December 31, 1989 or (2) at least 10 percent of the costs of the property are incurred by that date and the property is placed in service by December 31, 1990.[21] Also, the active participation requirement is waived for the rehabilitation investment credit regardless of when the property is placed in service.[22] In these circumstances, for example, a limited partner is allowed to take a low-income housing or rehabilitation investment credit having a deduction equivalent of up to $25,000, even if her interest in the partnership is less than 10 percent.

¶28.7.5 Taxpayers Eligible for $25,000 Allowance

The $25,000 allowance is usually restricted to taxpayers who are "natural persons." The term "natural persons" is used instead of "individuals" to make it clear that the exception does not apply to trusts.[23] Trusts were excluded because it was feared that taxpayers would otherwise transfer their rental real estate into several trusts, thereby getting multiple $25,000 allowances.[24]

Some estates, however, qualify for the exception for a limited period of time. If a decedent was an active participant in a rental real estate activity when he died, his estate may take up to $25,000 in passive activity loss or credit from the activity in each of its first two taxable years.[25] This rule is provided "to facilitate the administration of the estate without requiring the executor or fiduciary to reach decisions with respect to the appropriate disposition of the rental real property within a short period following the taxpayer's death."[26] Since the reason for the rule pertains to estate administration, the rule does not apply to a nonindividual distributee of the estate.

If a decedent's surviving spouse is an active participant in a rental real estate activity in which the decedent participated actively, the $25,000 cap is effectively shared by the estate and the surviving spouse. The sharing is

---

[21] IRC §469(i)(6)(B); Pub. L. No. 99-514, §501(c)(3), 100 Stat. 2085 (1986). See infra ¶27.5 for the low-income credit.

[22] IRC §469(i)(6)(B). See infra ¶27.2 for the rehabilitation investment credit.

[23] H.R. Rep. No. 841, supra note 4, at II-142.

[24] Staff of Joint Comm. on Tax'n, 99th Cong., 2d Sess., General Explanation of the Tax Reform Act of 1986, at 218 n.12 (Comm. Print 1987) [hereinafter 1986 Bluebook].

[25] IRC §469(i)(4)(A).

[26] H.R. Rep. No. 841, supra note 4, at II-142.

accomplished by reducing the estate's allowance by the amount of passive activity loss or credit allowed to the spouse under the $25,000 rule for any taxable year ending with or within that of the estate.[27] If the spouse's adjusted gross income exceeds $100,000, further, the amount allowed to the estate is reduced by the losses and credits that would have been allowed to the spouse in the absence of the phase-out rule for taxpayers with adjusted gross income exceeding $100,000.[28]

¶28.7.6 Computation and Application of $25,000 Amount

If an individual is an active participant in more than one rental real estate activity, a single $25,000 cap applies to the losses and credits from all of them. If there is net income from some rental real estate activities and losses from others, the income and losses are aggregated, and up to $25,000 of net loss from all of them is allowed.[29] For example, if a $30,000 loss is sustained in one rental real estate activity and $20,000 of net profit is earned in another, there is net loss of $10,000, all of which can be allowed under the $25,000 rule. If there is net loss in all rental real estate activities but net income from other passive activities, however, the rental real estate losses are first deducted against the passive income and only the remainder, if any, is deductible against nonpassive income, subject to the $25,000 ceiling.[30]

Moreover, if the taxpayer's adjusted gross income exceeds $100,000, the cap is phased down at the rate of 50 cents for each dollar of excess.[31] An individual whose adjusted gross income is $150,000 or more thus gets no benefit from this rule. Adjusted gross income is computed for this purpose without any deduction for passive activity losses.[32] If an individual's adjusted gross income consists of $130,000 of salary income and $50,000 of losses from rental real estate activities, for example, adjusted gross income is $130,000 for this purpose, and the $25,000 cap is reduced by $15,000 (one half of $30,000) to $10,000. Also, adjusted gross income is determined without the inclusion of social security benefits required by §86 or the deduction for IRA contributions allowed by §219.[33] For purposes of the low-income housing credit and the rehabilitation credit, the phase out begins when adjusted gross income exceeds $200,000, rather than $100,000.[34]

---

[27] IRC §469(i)(4)(B).
[28] See infra ¶28.7.6 for the phase-out rule.
[29] H.R. Rep. No. 841, supra note 4.
[30] 1986 Bluebook, supra note 24, at 219.
[31] IRC §469(i)(3)(A).
[32] IRC §469(i)(3)(D).
[33] IRC §469(i)(3)(D). See supra ¶16.5 for §89 and infra ¶62.5 for §219.
[34] IRC §§469(i)(3)(B), (C).

If losses from rental real estate activities in which the taxpayer actively participates exceed $25,000 (or the lesser amount remaining after application of the phase-down rule), all passive activity losses from the activities are prorated between the allowed and disallowed amounts.[35] For example, if a taxpayer has losses of $20,000 and $30,000 in a particular year from two rental real estate activities and is allowed $25,000 of this loss, the allowed amount consists of loss from the first activity of $10,000 ($25,000 multiplied by $20,000/$50,000) and $15,000 of loss from the second. If losses from these activities are less than $25,000, but the $25,000 cap is exceeded when the deduction equivalent of credits is added in, the losses are deemed fully allowed, and the portion of each credit deemed allowed is determined by an allocation procedure similar to the one for losses.[36] These allocations are important in applying the rules for dispositions of interests in passive activities.[37]

The amount allowable under the $25,000 rule sometimes exceeds the taxpayer's income from other sources. In such a case, the amount allowable under the rule enters into the net operating loss for the year and may be carried back and forward under the net operating loss rules.[38]

A single $25,000 allowance is permitted on a joint return even if both spouses have qualifying interests in real estate rental activities. A married individual who files a separate return is denied the $25,000 allowance unless he lives apart from his spouse at all times during the taxable year.[39] "Absent such a rule, married taxpayers where one spouse would be eligible for a portion of the $25,000 amount if they filed separately would have an incentive so to file; Congress concluded that rules that encourage filing separate returns give rise to unnecessary complexity and place an unwarranted burden on the administration of the tax system."[40] For separately filing spouses who live apart, the $25,000 ceiling (and the $100,000 and $200,000 figures used in the phase-out rule described above) are sliced in half.[41]

---

[35] IRC §469(j)(4).

[36] S. Rep. No. 313, supra note 6, at 721, 724. "Losses are allowed before credits because credits are considered in the nature of incentives which may not bear a relation to accurate measurement of income or loss from an activity." 1986 Bluebook, supra note 24, at 219.

[37] Infra ¶28.10.

[38] S. Rep. No. 313, supra note 6, at 722. See infra ¶25.11 for the NOL rules.

[39] IRC §469(i)(5)(B).

[40] 1986 Bluebook, supra note 24, at 220.

[41] IRC §469(i)(5)(A).

¶28.7.7 Deduction Equivalents of Credits

If the taxpayer has credits from a rental real estate activity in which he actively participates, the credits are restated as a deduction equivalent in applying the foregoing rules. The deduction equivalent of a credit is the amount of deduction that would reduce the taxpayer's regular tax by an amount equal to the credit.[42] Assume a taxpayer is within the income range where the benefits of the 15 percent rate and personal exemptions are being phased out.[43] A dollar of additional deduction reduces the taxpayer's tax by 33 cents, and a deduction of $3.03 reduces tax by $1. The deduction equivalent of a credit is thus 3.03 times the amount of the credit. The computation is more complex if the deduction equivalent would reduce taxable income below a break-point in the rate brackets. If the deduction equivalent in the example would reduce taxable income below the point where the phase-out of the 15 percent bracket and personal exemptions begins, some portion of the credit would reduce tax at the 28 percent rate, and the multiplication factor for determining the deduction equivalent of that portion would be 3.57 (that is, 1 divided by .28). The deduction equivalent in this case would be (1) the excess of taxable income over the starting point of the phase-out plus (2) 3.57 times an amount equal to the excess of the credit over 33 percent of the amount determined in (1).

For purposes of the $25,000 allowance, this can be done somewhat more simply as follows: Credits from rental real estate activities are allowed in an amount equal to (1) the taxpayer's tax computed with actual losses from rental real estate activities being taken up to the $25,000 ceiling, but with all credits ignored, over (2) the tax computed (again without credits) as though losses from these activites were large enough to use up the entire $25,000 allowance.[44] If the losses consume the entire allowance, (1) and (2) are equal, and no credits are allowed. If the allowance is not fully used by losses, on the other hand, the combination of the losses and credits equal to the excess of (1) over (2) is just sufficient so that tax on $25,000 of unrelated income is eliminated.

¶28.8 CARRYOVERS OF SUSPENDED LOSSES AND CREDITS

A passive activity loss or credit disallowed by §469 for any year is carried forward and treated as a deduction or credit of the activity for the

---

[42] IRC §469(j)(5).
[43] See IRC §1(g), discussed supra ¶2.2.1.
[44] 1986 Bluebook, supra note 24, at 224.

next taxable year.[1] If the carryover becomes part of a nonallowable passive activity loss or credit for the carryover year, it is carried forward to the succeeding year by another application of the carryover rule. The rule thus carries disallowed losses and credits forward indefinitely until they are used.

If a §469 carryover is carried to a year in which the taxpayer has net income from passive activities, the net passive income for the current year is first reduced by the carryover. Nonpassive losses (including NOLs) are applied against passive income only if (and to the extent) net passive income remains after application of the §469 carryover.[2]

Some specialized problems in the application of the carryover rule are discussed below, including the rules applied when it is necessary to trace carryovers to particular activities, the situation where an activity is no longer passive in a carryover year, and the application of the carryover rules to spouses.

1. *Allocating losses from passive activities between amounts currently allowed and amounts carried forward.* Under rules described below,[3] suspended losses from a passive activity are allowed when the taxpayer's entire interest in the activity is sold or exchanged in a taxable transaction. For purposes of these rules, it is necessary to identify the portion of a carryover that derives from each passive activity if the taxpayer has more than one. This is done as follows: Losses from passive activities (including both current losses and carryovers from prior years) are first applied against current income from passive activities, and a net loss carries forward. The carryover is allocated among separate passive activities in proportion to the losses from activities that generate losses.[4] In other words, the carryover includes loss from each passive activity equal to the carryover multiplied by a fraction whose numerator is the loss from the activity for the year (including carryovers from prior years) and whose denominator is the losses (so computed) for all passive activities.

Assume an individual owns interests in three passive activities: *A*, *B*, and *C*. The gross income and deductions from the activities, the computation of the passive activity loss for the year and the carryover to the next year, and the allocation of the carryover among the loss activities are shown in Example 28-3.[5]

---

[1] IRC §469(b).
[2] S. Rep. No. 313, 99th Cong., 2d Sess. 722–23 (1986).
[3] See infra ¶28.9.
[4] S. Rep. No. 313, supra note 2, at 722.
[5] The example is taken from §1.469-1T(f)(2)(i)(D) Ex. 1 of the regulations.

Example 28-3

Allocation of Suspended Losses Among Passive Activities

	Activities			
	A	B	C	Total
1. Gross income	$70	$40	$120	$230
Less: Deductions	160	200	80	440
Net income or (loss)	($90)	($160)	$ 40	($210)

2. Passive activity loss for year and carryover $210

3. Sum of losses from passive activities (denominator of apportionment fraction)... $250

4. Portion of carryover allocable to:

   a. Activity A

     ($210 × $90/$250)....................... $75.6

   b. Activity B

     ($210 × ($160/$250)................................. $134.4

2. *Allocating particular deductions.* It is sometimes necessary to know not only how much of the loss from an activity has been allowed and how much carries forward, but also how much of each deduction has been allowed and how much is included in the carryover. For example, a capital loss from a passive activity is subject to the limitations on capital loss deductions for the year in which it successfully runs the §469 gauntlet. Whether this year is the year in which the loss is realized, or some subsequent year, depends on whether the loss is matched against current passive income or finds its way into a carryover.

This allocation is usually accomplished by prorating the carryover from the activity among all deductions from the activity.[6] In Example 28-3, there are deductions attributable to activity *A* of $160, of which $75.6 are not currently allowed but enter into the carryover. Of each deduction, 47.25 percent (75.6/160) is deemed to be part of the carryover, and 52.75 percent is deemed allowed currently.[7]

---

[6] Reg. §1.469-1T(f)(2)(ii).

[7] This methodology becomes quite complex in subsequent years. In the following year in Example 28-3, the $75.6 carryover, allocated among all the otherwise deductible items for the first year, is part of the deductions taken in determining whether the activity shows a loss for the second year. If there is loss, the deductions (including the carryover) are apportioned under the rule described in the text. This apportionment is a second application of the apportionment procedure to the deduc-

3. *Spouses filing jointly.* Spouses filing a joint return are generally treated as one taxpayer in applying §469. If both spouses own interests in one passive activity, however, the allocation rules described above must be applied separately with respect to the interest of each spouse.[8] If joint returns are filed for all years until both spouses have disposed of their interests and all carryovers have been used or eliminated, the separate allocations have no effect. If a passive activity loss is carried from a year for which a joint return is filed to a year in which separate returns are filed, however, the apportionment of the carryovers is essential to the preparation of the separate returns.[9] Also, if either spouse dies or makes a gift of his or her interest, the apportionment is needed in the application of the rules for carryovers attributable to interests transferred at death or by gift.[10]

4. *Carryovers from former passive activities.* An activity generating a carryover might no longer be a passive activity in the carryover year. For example, a taxpayer who did not participate materially in an activity during the year in which loss is sustained might be a material participant in the year to which the loss is carried under the carryover rule.

In this case, the carryover is first applied against any net income from the activity for the current year.[11] (Losses from other passive activities, however, are not deductible against this income.) If the carryover attributable to the former passive activity exceeds the activity's current net income, the excess is treated as passive activity loss that is deducted against net income from other passive activities; any portion that remains after this offset is carried to the following year. Because the activity is no longer passive, current losses and credits are not limited by §469.

Similar treatment applies to a corporation that is a closely held C corporation or a personal service corporation when a passive activity loss is incurred, but that loses this status before the carryover is used.[12] Similar

---

tions for the first year included in the carryover. The same thing happens in succeeding years, with the consequence that so long as there is a carryover, every deduction for the activity's entire history enters into the allocation for each year. The unused portions of the deductions for earlier years get smaller and smaller, but never disappear. It would be simpler to allocate current deductions first against current income and include the carryover in the allocation only if there is net income before the carryover is taken into account.

[8] Reg. §1.469-1T(j)(2)(i).

[9] Reg. §1.469-1T(j)(3).

[10] See infra ¶¶28.9.5 and 28.9.6 for the rules on transfers at death and gifts.

[11] IRC §469(f)(1); S. Rep. No. 313, supra note 2, at 727. The taxpayer, however, must have convincing proof that the nonpassive activity carried on currently is the same activity as the passive activity that generated the carryover. S. Rep. No. 313, supra.

[12] IRC §469(f)(2). See H.R. Rep. No. 841, 99th Cong., 2d Sess. II-139, II-140 (Conf. Rep. 1986).

procedures are also used to identify the source of credit carryovers.[13]

¶28.9 ALLOWANCE OF LOSSES WHEN INTERESTS IN PASSIVE ACTIVITIES ARE DISPOSED OF

¶28.9.1 Introductory

Passive activity losses made nondeductible by §469 are generally allowed in the year in which the taxpayer disposes of his entire interest in the activity.[1] Section 469 is meant to curb artificial tax losses, not the ultimate deductibility of economic losses. When an investment in a passive activity is sold and the cumulative result of the investment (including gain or loss on sale) is a loss, the loss is an economic loss, not an artificial tax loss, and ought to be allowed. As Congress explained:

> [P]rior to a disposition of the taxpayer's interest, it is difficult to determine whether there has actually been gain or loss with respect to the activity. For example, allowable deductions may exceed actual economic costs, or may be exceeded by untaxed appreciation. Upon a taxable disposition, net appreciation or depreciation with respect to the activity can be finally ascertained.[2]

The rules provide separately for several types of dispositions, which are described below.

¶28.9.2 Sales, Taxable Exchanges, and Abandonments of Entire Interests

If a taxpayer's entire interest in a passive activity is sold or exchanged in a transaction in which all gain or loss is recognized, losses from the activity not allowed in any previous year are deductible in the year of the sale or exchange.[3] An abandonment also triggers recognition of accumulated undeducted losses if the abandonment is "a fully taxable event" that entitles the taxpayer to deduct the basis of his interest as a loss under §165(a).[4]

The foregoing rules apply when "a taxpayer" disposes of or abandons his interest in a passive activity.[5] The legislative history, however, says they

---

[13] Reg. §1.469-1T(f)(3).
[1] See generally Banoff, Sales and Redemptions of Partnership Interests Under the Passive Loss Regulations, 68 J. Tax'n 332 (1988).
[2] S. Rep. No. 313, 99th Cong., 2d Sess. 725 (1986).
[3] IRC §469(g)(1)(A).
[4] H.R. Rep. No. 841, 99th Cong., 2d Sess. II-143 (Conf. Rep. 1986).
[5] IRC §469(g)(1).

also allow suspended losses to a partner or S corporation shareholder when the partnership or corporation disposes of its entire interest in a passive activity, even though the "taxpayer" disposes of nothing in this situation.[6] If a partnership or S corporation carries on more than one activity, the entity's sale or exchange of all assets of a passive activity is sufficient to make the rule applicable, even if other assets are retained.[7] "Similarly, if a grantor trust conducts two separate activities, and sells all the assets used or created in one activity, the grantor is considered as disposing of his entire interest in that activity."[8]

If the parties to a sale or exchange are related in a way described in §267(b) or §707(b)(1), the losses are further deferred until the interest is again sold or exchanged in a taxable transaction to a person not related to the taxpayer.[9] Assume an individual sells an interest in a passive activity to his sister, a person related to him in a way described in §267(b). For the year of the sale and each succeeding year so long as the sister holds the interest, the taxpayer's losses from the activity are deductible only against his income and gain from this and other passive activities of the taxpayer. Deferred losses, for example, are deductible against any gain on the sale to the sister. If the sister subsequently sells the interest in a taxable transaction to a person not related to the taxpayer under §267(b), the taxpayer can then deduct any losses from the activity that have not previously been allowed.

Also, a purported sale of a taxpayer's entire interest in a passive activity does not trigger the allowance of suspended losses unless the sale is genuine. "For example, sham transactions, wash sales, and transfers not properly treated as sales due to the existence of a put, call, or similar right relating to repurchase, do not give rise to the allowance of suspended losses."[10]

When applicable, the rule allows a deduction for (1) passive activity losses from the activity for prior years that have been carried forward to the year of the sale, exchange, or abandonment, (2) loss from the activity for the current year, and (3) loss on the sale, exchange, or abandonment.[11] This

---

[6] H.R. Rep. No. 841, supra note 4, at II-145.

[7] S. Rep. No. 313, supra note 2, at 725.

[8] Staff of Joint Comm. on Tax'n, 99th Cong., 2d Sess., General Explanation of the Tax Reform Act of 1986, at 226 (Comm. Print 1987) [hereinafter 1986 Bluebook].

[9] IRC §469(g)(1)(B).

[10] 1986 Bluebook, supra note 8, at 227. See also H.R. Rep. No. 841, supra note 4, at II-143.

[11] Loss on the sale or exchange is taken into account for this purpose only to the extent it is allowable under §1211, which limits deductions for capital losses to the amount of the taxpayer's capital gains for the year plus (if the taxpayer is not a corporation) $3,000. IRC §469(g)(1)(C). Any portion of the loss on the sale or exchange that is made nondeductible by §1211 is carried forward to other years

aggregate is allowed first against any net income or gain from the activity for the current year (including any gain on the sale or exchange of the taxpayer's interest in the activity), second against net income or gain for the year from all other passive activities, and third against other income or gain. The income other than passive activity income thus can be offset by loss from the passive activity disposed of only to the extent that passive activities (including the activity disposed of) show an aggregate loss for the year, taking carryovers into account.

To the extent that suspended losses have reduced the basis of property, gain on the disposition is effectively a recapture of these losses. Typically, the gain on sale equals the excess of accumulated tax losses over any economic loss from the investment. The losses allowed against other income under this rule thus are usually economic losses, not artificial accounting losses.

¶28.9.3   Installment Sales of Entire Interests

If a taxpayer's entire interest in a passive activity is sold in an installment sale and gain on the sale is reported by the installment method, the rules described above are also applied by the installment method.[12] Previously undeducted losses from the activity are cumulated to the date of sale. A portion of this aggregate is deductible in each year that gain on the sale is recognized. The deductible portion for a particular year is the aggregate loss multiplied by a fraction whose numerator is the gain on the sale recognized for that year and whose denominator is the gross profit on the sale.[13] The deductible amount for each year is taken first against the gain on the sale, second against other passive activity income for the year, and third against other income.

Assume an interest in a passive activity (basis $20) is sold for $100; passive activity losses of $200 have accumulated undeducted while the seller held the interest. Gross profit on the sale is $80 ($100 selling price less $20 basis). If the gross profit includes no recapture gain required to be immediately recognized under §453(i), the gross profit percentage is 80, and, on a receipt of a payment of, say, $40, (1) the gain recognized by the seller for this year is $32 (80 percent of $40), and (2) the deductible portion of the $200 of accumulated loss is $80 ($200 multiplied by $32/$80).

---

under the capital loss carryover rules of §1212. See H.R. Rep. No. 841, supra note 4, at II-144.

    [12] IRC §469(g)(3).

    [13] The gross profit is the excess of the total contract price (including the face amount of all deferred payments) over the adjusted basis of the property sold in the sale. Reg. §15a.453-1(b)(2)(v).

¶28.9.4 Dispositions of Less Than All of Taxpayer's Interest and Nonrecognition Transactions

No special rules are provided for cases where a taxpayer makes a taxable sale or exchange of less than all of his interest in a passive activity or where such an interest is disposed of in a nonrecognition transaction. The rule for complete dispositions is inapplicable to partial dispositions because "the issue of ultimate economic gain or loss on [the taxpayer's] investment in the activity remains unresolved" after a partial disposition.[14] Similarly, following most nonrecognition transactions, "the taxpayer retains an interest in the activity, and hence has not realized the ultimate economic gain or loss on his investment in it."[15]

Because gain or loss on a disposition of a passive activity interest is itself passive,[16] recognized gain (including boot in what would otherwise be a nonrecognition transaction) can be offset by suspended and current losses from this and other passive activities, and recognized loss adds to passive activity loss.[17] Accumulated and current loss from the activity that is not allowed in the year of the disposition carries forward under the carryover rule. When less than all of an interest is disposed of, all losses from the activity, including the portions allocable to the interest disposed of, presumably adhere to the retained interest, and thus can be taken in full if the retained interest is later sold or exchanged in a taxable transaction. Also, when an interest in a passive activity is exchanged in a nonrecognition transaction for another interest in a passive activity, the suspended losses from the old interest adhere to the new interest.[18]

¶28.9.5 Transfers at Death

When an individual dies owning an interest in a passive activity, a portion of the losses from the activity are rendered permanently nondeductible if the decedent's estate or other successor takes a basis for the interest that is greater than the decedent's basis just before his death.[19] Generally, under §1014(a), the adjusted basis of property acquired from a decedent is the fair market value of the property on the date of death or alternate valuation date for estate tax purposes.

This rule applies to a passive activity loss for the decedent's final taxable year and to losses from the activity that were disallowed by §469 in

---

[14] S. Rep. No. 313, supra note 2, at 726..
[15] Id. at 726–27.
[16] See supra ¶28.4.2.
[17] S. Rep. No. 313, supra note 2, at 719 n.7, 727.
[18] Id. at 726–27.
[19] IRC §469(g)(2).

prior years and carried to the final taxable year. The permanently disallowed portion of this aggregate is an amount equal to the excess of the adjusted basis of the interest to the decedent's estate or other successor over the decedent's adjusted basis immediately before he died. The portion that is not disallowed is deductible on the decedent's final return, first against income from the activity for the taxable year, second against other passive activity income for the taxable year, and finally against nonpassive income.[20]

The rationale for this rule is as follows: a §1014(a) step up in the basis of an interest in a passive activity permanently exempts gain accrued in the activity from tax. The policy of §469 that passive loss deductions should never exceed economic loss would be violated by rules that allowed full deductibility of loss when gain is partially exempt. This policy thus requires that loss must be made permanently nondeductible in an amount equal to the gain exempted by the basis step up.

¶28.9.6 Gifts

If an interest in a passive activity is transferred by inter vivos gift, all accumulated undeducted losses allocable to the interest become permanently nondeductible. In lieu of the deduction for these losses, the donee's adjusted basis for the interest is increased by the sum of the losses.[21] This rule applies to a gift of a portion of the donor's interest in a passive activity, as well as to a gift of the entire interest. On a gift of less than all of a donor's interest, accumulated losses are prorated between the portions transferred and retained.[22]

The rule applies to "passive activity losses allocable to" the transferred interest. These losses are identified as follows: Losses from prior years are carried to the year of the gift under the usual rules, and these losses, together with any loss from the activity for the year, are included in the computation of the passive activity loss for the year. Both accumulated and current losses from the activity can thus be deducted against income for the year from this and other passive activities. The portion of the accumulated and current losses that is not allowed in this way is added to the donee's basis.

The policy underlying this treatment seems to be as follows: A gift is not an appropriate occasion for reckoning up the economic results of an investment in a passive activity. Because the donor no longer owns the interest, accumulated losses attributable to the interest should not be carried forward further to be potentially deductible against income from other

---

[20] IRC §§469(g)(1)(A), (2)(A).
[21] IRC §469(j)(6).
[22] IRC §469(j)(4).

passive activities. Neither should the accumulated losses be carried to the donee's returns because the donee did not hold the interest when the losses were incurred. A basis increase is thus provided in lieu of the potential deduction to give the donee something resembling a fresh start.

The added basis is tacked on to the donor's basis, which transfers to the donee under §1015(a).[23] If the sum of the donor's basis and the suspended losses exceeds the fair market value of the property at the time of the gift, however, loss on a subsequent sale or exchange of the property is restricted by §1015(a) to the amount by which the date-of-gift fair market value exceeds the amount realized in the disposition. Losses realized after the gift are subject to §469 if the property is a passive activity in the donor's hands.

¶28.10 ALLOWANCE OF CREDITS WHEN INTERESTS IN PASSIVE ACTIVITIES ARE DISPOSED OF

If a taxpayer's basis for an interest in a passive activity or for property used in the activity was reduced by a credit barred by §469, the taxpayer can elect to restore this basis reduction in determining gain or loss on a disposition of the interest or property.[1] The election, however, is not available unless the disposition is a sale, taxable exchange, or abandonment of the taxpayer's entire interest in the activity from which the credit arose. Moreover, if the election is made, credit equal to the restoration is permanently lost. This election could apply, for example, in conjunction with a rule under the investment credit provisions that require a reduction of the basis of property qualifying for that credit equal to 50 percent or 100 percent of the credit.[2]

Assume an investor in a passive activity qualifies for a $50 rehabilitation credit under the investment credit rules and thus is required to reduce the adjusted basis of the rehabilitated property by $50. If the $50 credit is

---

[23] S. Rep. No. 313, supra note 2, at 726 n.12.

[1] IRC §469(j)(9). "The purpose for providing this election is to permit the taxpayer to recognize economic gain or loss, taking account of the full cost of property for which no credit was allowed." H.R. Rep. No. 841, 99th Cong., 2d Sess. II-144 (1986).

Under the statute, the restoration rule seemingly applies to unused credit carried forward under the rules allowing the credit. If elected, it would, for example, restore basis lost on account of a credit that has not yet been used because of the tax-liability limitation on the general business credit. The legislative history, however, says the restoration rule applies only to credit barred by §469. H.R. Rep. No. 841, supra, at II-144.

[2] IRC §48(q). Although the investment credit is largely repealed, it continues for a few types of investments, including certain rehabilitations of older buildings. See infra ¶27.2.1. The application of the restoration rule to the rehabilitation credit is illustrated in the legislative history. H.R. Rep. No. 841, supra note 1, at 144–45.

suspended by §469 and the suspended credit is not allowed by the time the investor sells her entire interest in the passive activity, she can elect to restore the $50 to the property's basis immediately before the sale, thus reducing gain or increasing loss on the sale by that amount. The election, however, cancels the credit.[3]

Apart from this basis restoration rule, no special provision is made for passive activity credits carried to the year in which an interest in a passive activity is disposed of. The term "passive activity credit" refers to an excess of credits from passive activities over the regular tax allocable to income from these activities.[4] Gain on the disposition is income from a passive activity, and regular tax on this gain thus can be offset by credits from passive activities, including credits carried from prior years. Any credit not allowed in this way is carried forward to succeeding years even though the taxpayer no longer has an interest in the passive activity that generated the credit.

Under a rule described above, losses are allowed in full when a taxpayer's entire interest in a passive activity is sold or exchanged in a taxable transaction. This rule does not apply to credits because "the purpose of the . . . rule is to allow real economic losses of the taxpayer to be deducted, [and] credits . . . are not related to the measurement of such loss."[5]

¶28.11 DEFINITION OF "ACTIVITY"

The term "activity" is not defined by §469, but occupies a central role in the provision's application. For example, if an investment constitutes one activity, the taxpayer escapes §469 by showing that he materially participates in the activity as a whole; if two or more segments of the investment are considered separate activities, the material participation test is applied separately for each segment, and any segment in which the taxpayer is not a material participant is subject to §469.[1] Another example is where an interest in a passive activity is sold or exchanged in a taxable transaction: Suspended losses attributable to the activity are fully deductible if the interest disposed of is the taxpayer's entire interest in the activity, but the losses continue to be restricted to offsetting income from passive activities if the interest is merely part of the taxpayer's investment in a larger activity.[2] Also, the boundaries of a rental real estate activity must be

---

[3] Staff of Joint Comm. on Tax'n, 99th Cong., 2d Sess., General Explanation of the Tax Reform Act of 1986, at 228 (Comm. Print 1987).

[4] See supra ¶28.5.

[5] S. Rep. No. 313, 99th Cong., 2d Sess. 725 (1986).

[1] See supra ¶28.3.3 for the material participation test.

[2] See supra ¶28.9 for dispositions of interests in passive activities.

defined in order to apply the rule limiting the $25,000 allowance for losses in such an activity to individuals having a 10 percent or greater interest in the activity.[3] Moreover, the basic purpose of the §469 limitation requires a definition of "activity" that includes within a taxpayer's passive activities all investments generating losses of the kind intended to be limited, while excluding investments yielding the active business income, personal service income, and portfolio income intended to be isolated from passive losses.

Whether a taxpayer prefers a narrow or broad definition of the term depends on the context. A taxpayer seeking to offset particular deductions against particular income wants a definition broad enough to bring the deductions and income within the same activity. On the other hand, a taxpayer who has sold an interest in a passive activity wants a definition that is narrow enough to qualify the sale as a disposition of her entire interest in the activity. Overall, both taxpayers and the Treasury are probably best served by an evenhanded definition.

According to the legislative history, an activity is a group of "undertakings [comprising] an integrated and interrelated economic unit, conducted in coordination with or [in] reliance upon each other, and constituting an appropriate unit for the measurement of gain or loss."[4] This definition should be applied in "a realistic economic"way.[5] "In general, normal commercial practices are highly probative in determining whether two or more undertakings are or may be parts of a single activity."[6]

Among the relevant factors are "the degree of organizational and economic interrelationship in various undertakings, the business purpose which is (or might be) served by carrying on the various undertakings separately or together . . . and the similarity of the various undertakings."[7] The economic-integration test is not satisfied, in contrast, merely because the taxpayer has "ultimate management responsibilities with respect to different undertakings" or "the undertakings have access to common sources of financing"or share a common name.[8]

---

[3] See supra ¶28.7 for the $25,000 allowance.

[4] S. Rep. No. 313, 99th Cong., 2d Sess. 739 (1986).

[5] Id.

[6] Id. at 740.

[7] Id. (quoting from Reg. §1.183-1(d)(1)). The §469 definition of "activity" is intended to be the same as that used under §183 (relating to losses in activities not carried on for profit), with one difference. The §183 regulations state that the taxpayer's grouping of undertakings into activities will be followed unless it is artificial, but this rule does not apply under §469. Id. at 739 n.29. Also, the term "activity" has a narrower meaning under the at risk rules of §465 because the purposes of those rules require a focus on the relationship between particular debt and particular assets. Id. at 739 n.28. See supra ¶¶22.5 and 25.10 for §§183 and 465.

[8] S. Rep. No. 313, supra note 4, at 740.

Generally, the providing of a product or service is an activity separate from the providing of a "substantially different" product or service.[9] Operating a restaurant, for example, is usually a separate activity from carrying on research and development. The providing of dissimilar products or services is a single activity, however, if the products or services are "customarily or for business reasons provided together."[10] A department store, for example, constitutes one activity even though it sells disparate products.

Conversely, a taxpayer can have two or more activities involving the same product. For example, "different stages in the production and sale of a particular product" usually are not a single activity unless they are "carried on in an integrated fashion"; operating a gas station and drilling for oil are separate activities.[11] Moreover, a taxpayer can have two or more activities providing the same product or service at the same stage of production. Two real estate rental projects, for example, are separate activities if they are "built and managed in different locations."[12] Also, a farm is generally considered a separate activity from any other farm owned by the same taxpayer.[13]

Two or more research and development projects are treated as one activity if the economic-integration test is satisfied by interrelationships among the projects "with regard to personnel, facilities used, or the common use of knowhow" developed in the projects.[14]

> For example, if a particular research project is terminated, but knowhow developed from the project contributes to a subsequent project, it may be inaccurate to view the termination as establishing a loss [because] any economic success realized by the second project may be attributable in part to amounts spent on the first project.[15]

The undertakings of a partnership or S corporation do not necessarily comprise one activity. Such an entity may be engaged in two or more activities, or a single activity may be carried on by two or more entities. If a partnership has two or more activities, for example, a partner's distributive share of losses from one of the activities may not be deducted against his share of income from another partnership activity unless both or neither of

---

[9] Id. at 739.

[10] Id.

[11] Id. at 740.

[12] Id.

[13] To say that one farm is a separate activity from another farm often merely shifts the definitional problem to a different term: "Are the taxpayer's agricultural pursuits one farm or two?"

[14] Id.

[15] Id.

the activities are passive. Thus, passive activity losses cannot be made deductible against portfolio income by simply causing a partnership to invest in both a passive activity and portfolio assets. Where one activity is carried on by two or more entities, a sale of the taxpayer's interest in one of the entities, for example, is not sufficient to bring the rules for complete dispositions into play.

Any undertaking that is specially classified under §469 is considered an activity separate from all other undertakings, regardless of actual integration, if this separation is necessary to fulfill the function of the special classification.[16] The performance of services as an employee or professional practitioner, for example, is considered inherently active, and therefore cannot be aggregated with any other undertaking, regardless of how closely the two undertakings are related. Similarly, a working interest in oil and gas is a separate activity if it qualifies as nonpassive under the exception for such interests.[17] A nonworking interest, for example, cannot be brought within this exception by showing that it is integrally connected with a qualifying working interest. Also, a rental real estate activity is separate from all other undertakings of the taxpayer, regardless of actual integration, if the taxpayer is eligible to deduct up to $25,000 of losses from the activity against nonpassive income.[18]

Moreover, because rental activities are always passive, regardless of the extent of the taxpayer's personal involvement in them, such an activity is deemed separate from any other activity.[19] For example, if a partnership constructs an apartment building and thereafter operates it as a rental facility, the construction and operation phases are separate activities; a general partner who materially participates in the business thus may deduct construction period losses free of the §469 limitation even though the limitation applies to losses incurred during the operations phase. Similarly, if a partnership engaged in business as a travel agency owns the building in which the agency is located and rents out portions of the building not needed in the business, it is deemed engaged in two activities, the travel agency business and a rental activity; a partner who materially participates in the agency business thus cannot deduct his share of rental losses against his share of the agency's income.

---

[16] S. Rep. No. 313, supra note 4, at 741.

[17] See supra ¶28.3.8 for this exception.

[18] See supra ¶28.7 for the $25,000 allowance for rental real estate losses.

[19] Staff of Joint Comm. on Tax'n, 99th Cong., 2d Sess., General Explanation of the Tax Reform Act of 1986, at 249 (Comm. Print 1987). See supra ¶28.3.7 for the rule classifying all rental activities as passive.

free, the benefit might be wholly or partially excluded as a no-additional-cost service, qualified employee discount, or de minimis fringe.[53]

When the foregoing requirements are satisfied, "the exclusion applies whether the qualified employee discount is provided through a direct reduction in price or through a cash rebate from the employer or a third party."[54]

For goods, the exclusion is limited to an amount equal to the price normally charged to customers multiplied by the employer's usual mark-up.[55] The amount of a discount is the excess of the regular price to customers over the price to the employee.[56] The usual mark-up is referred to as the "gross profit percentage," and is defined as the ratio of (1) the excess of the employer's sales revenues over its cost of goods sold to (2) the sales revenues.[57] Assume an employer's sales for a year are $1 million and its cost of goods sold is $600,000. The gross profit percentage is 40 percent (excess of $1 million over $600,000, divided by $1 million), and a discount on a good normally selling for, say, $50 is fully excludable if it does not exceed $20. If the discount exceeds the cap, the excess is gross income. In the example, the employee would have $5 of gross income if the $50 good were discounted to $25 for him.

For services, the maximum exclusion under the employee discount rule is 20 percent of the regular price.[58] On a service for which the employer charges nonemployee customers $50, for example, a discount of up to $10 to an employee is fully excludable, but any excess of the discount over $10 is gross income unless the discount is embraced by the exclusion for no-additional-cost services or the de minimis exclusion.

---

[53] Id. at 850.

[54] Id. at 849.

[55] IRC §§132(c)(1)(A), (2).

[56] The regular price might itself be a discounted price. If, for example, "a discount is regularly provided by the employer in the ordinary course of business through arrangements negotiated with large groups of consumers (e.g., to all members of professional associations)," the discounted price to these consumers is the regular price from which employee discounts are computed. 1984 Bluebook, supra note 4, at 854.

[57] The gross profit percentage can be determined by aggregating all sales revenues and costs of goods sold in the line of business in which the employee works. Id.; Reg. §1.132-3T(c). Alternatively, separate percentages can be computed for various segments of the line. "For example, a retail department store business may compute a gross profit percentage for the store business as a whole, or may compute different gross profit percentages for different departments or types of merchandise (high markup items versus low markup items), provided such classifications are made on a reasonable basis." 1984 Bluebook, supra note 4, at 854. The percentages, whether done on an aggregate or segmented basis, must be based on sales and costs for "a representative period, such as the prior year." Id.

[58] IRC §132(c)(1)(B).